INN SPOTS

By Nancy and Richard Woodworth

& SPECIAL PLACES

IN NEW ENGLAND

A guide to where to go, stay, eat and enjoy in 35 of the region's choicest areas.

Wood Pond Press
West Hartford, Conn.

The authors value their reputation for credibility and have visited the places included in this book. They have seen them all, which gives them a rare perspective in the field. Unlike others, they do not ask the owners to fill out information forms or to approve the final copy. Nor do they rely on researchers or field inspectors who come and go with varying perspectives and loyalties to do their leg work. They make their recommendations based on their experiences and findings. No fees are charged for inclusion.

Prices, hours and menu offerings at inns and restaurants change seasonally and with business conditions. Readers should call ahead to avoid disappointment. The prices and hours reported in this book were correct at presstime and are subject, of course, to change. They are offered as a relative guide to what to expect. Rates quoted are for bed and breakfast, unless otherwise specified (MAP, Modified American Plan, breakfast and dinner; EP, European Plan, no meals).

For updates between editions, check out the Wood Pond Press web site at www.getawayguides.com. Favorite inns, B&Bs, restaurants and attractions from this book and from others by the authors are detailed under Getaway Guides On Line.

The authors welcome readers' reactions and suggestions.

Cover Photo: Guest room with balcony at Mayflower Inn, Washington, Conn.

Library of Congress Catalog No. 86-50203.

ISBN No. 0-934260-95-8

Published in the United States of America.

Seventh Edition

Contents

Introduction

This is yet another inn guide. But it's far more, too.

We enjoy reading other books and browsing Internet guides, but rarely do they tell us what we *really* want to know – which inns and B&Bs are especially good and what they are like, where to get a good meal and what are the don't-miss sights and activities in the area. Nor do they convey a real sense of the place.

These insights are what we share with you. We start not with the inn but with the area (of course, the existence of inns or lack thereof help determine the 35 special destination areas to be included). Then we tour each area, with the eyes and ears of the first-time visitor as well as the perspective of seasoned travelers and journalists. We visit the inns, the restaurants and the attractions. We *work* these areas as roving journalists, always seeking out the best and most interesting. We also *live* them – staying in, eating in, and experiencing as many places as time and budget allow.

The result is this book, a fully updated seventh edition at a time when few other independent inn guidebooks are still being published. It's a selective compendium of what we New Englanders think are the best and most interesting places to stay, eat and enjoy in 35 favorite destinations in our special part of the world.

The book reflects our tastes. We like creature comforts such as modern bathrooms and comfortable reading areas in our rooms. We expect to find welcoming innkeepers and like to meet other inn guests, but we also value our privacy. We seek interesting and creative food and pleasant settings for meals. We enjoy unusual, enlightening things to do and places to experience. We want to receive value for our time and money.

While making our rounds, we no longer are surprised by how many innkeepers say we are among the few guidebook writers who actually visit their facility and do not expect them merely to fill out a questionnaire and forward it with a considerable fee. Because our names and credibility are on the line, we visit in person rather than send stand-ins or freelancers who come and go with the seasons.

We also are not surprised by how many inns report getting bookings from the Internet. The prospective guest wants the immediacy, the ability to see pictures and get detailed descriptions, the instant gratification of a quick, visual reservation. We do, too. And yet, the realists among both innkeepers and inn-goers worry that Internet travelers find only what the website wants them to know. They miss the perspective offered by well traveled observers who have been there.

The inn experience is highly personal, both for the innkeeper and the inn-goer. The listing services, the advertising and the website fluff do not have an objective perspective. Nor can they convey the personality or the nuances of the place.

That's the role of experienced guidebook writers who make the rounds year after year and report things as they find them. Yes, the schedule is hectic and we do keep busy on these, our working trips that everyone thinks must be nothing but fun. Nonetheless, it's rewarding both to experience a great inn and to discover a promising B&B. We also enjoy savoring a good meal, touring a choice museum, poking through an unusual store and meeting so many interesting people along the way.

So that's what this book is about. We hope that you enjoy its findings as much as we did the finding.

Nancy and Richard Woodworth

About the Authors

Nancy Webster Woodworth began her travel and dining experiences in her native Montreal and as a waitress in summer resorts across Canada during her McGill University years. She worked in London and hitchhiked through Europe on \$3 a day before her marriage to Richard Woodworth, whom she met while skiing at Mont Tremblant. She started writing her "Roaming the Restaurants" column for the West Hartford (Conn.) News in 1972. That led to half of the book, *Daytripping & Dining in Southern New England,* in 1978. She since has co-authored Inn Spots & Special Places / Mid-Atlantic, Inn Spots & Special Places in the Southeast, Getaways for Gourmets in the Northeast, Waterside Escapes in the Northeast, New England's Best and *Best Restaurants of New England.* She and her husband have two grown sons and live in West Hartford.

Richard Woodworth has been an inveterate traveler since his youth in suburban Syracuse, N.Y., where his birthday outings often involved adventures by train with friends for the day to nearby Utica or Rochester. After graduation from Middlebury College, he was a reporter for newspapers in Syracuse, Jamestown, Geneva and Rochester before moving to Connecticut to become editor of the West Hartford News and eventually executive editor of Imprint Newspapers. With his wife and sons, he has traveled to the four corners of this country, Canada and portions of Europe, writing their findings for newspapers and magazines. With his wife, he has co-authored *Inn Spots & Special Places / Mid-Atlantic, Inn Spots & Special Places in the Southeast, Getaways for Gourmets in the Northeast, Best Restaurants of New England, Waterside Escapes in the Northeast* and their newest book, *New England's Best.* He also was co-author and editor of *Celebrate! West Hartford, An Illustrated History* for the town's Sesquicentennial. Between travels and duties as proprietor of Wood Pond Press, he tries to find time to ski or head south in the winter and weed the garden or head north in the summer.

Excerpts from the authors' books are on line at www.getawayguides.com. The authors may be reached by e-mail at woodpond@ntplx.net.

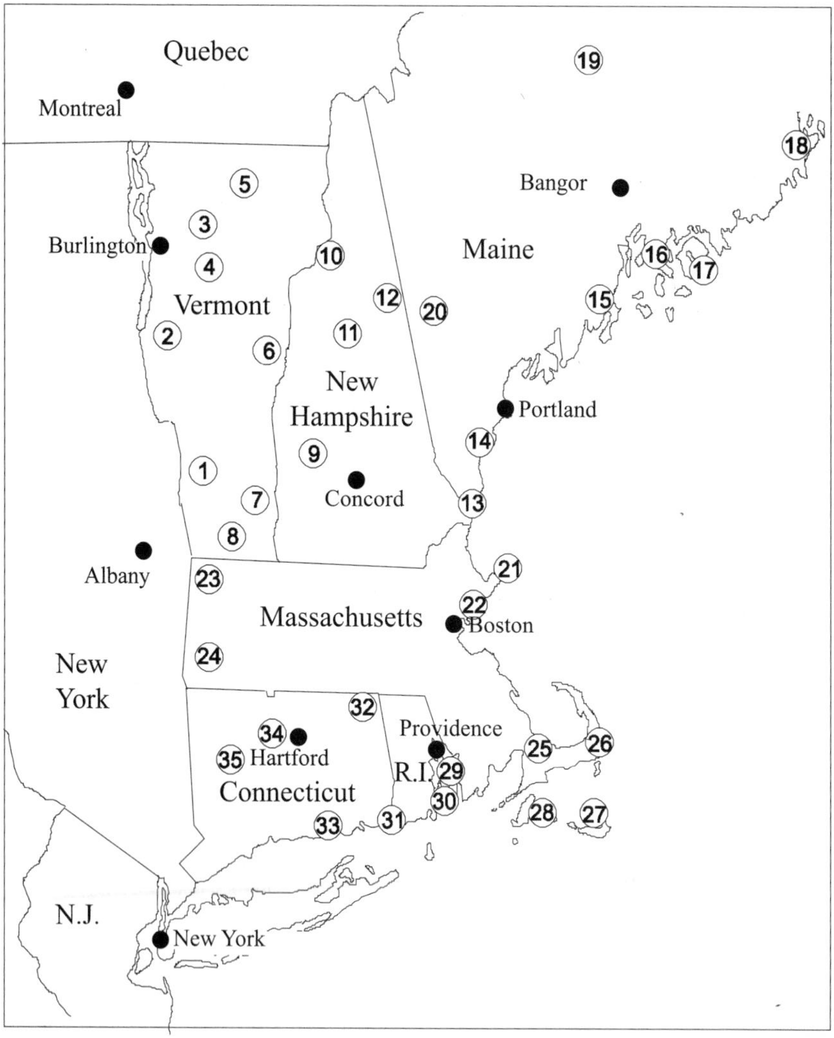

INN SPOTS AND SPECIAL PLACES IN NEW ENGLAND

1. Dorset
2. Middlebury
3. Stowe
4. Waitsfield/Warren
5. Craftsbury/Burke
6. Woodstock/Quechee
7. Newfane/Grafton
8. West Dover
9. Sunapee
10. Franconia/Sugar Hill
11. Squam Lakes
12. Jackson
13. Portsmouth
14. Kennebunkport
15. Camden
16. Blue Hill/Deer Isle
17. Mt. Desert Island
18. Eastport/St. Andrews
19. Greenville/Moosehead
20. Oxford Hills and Lakes
21. Rockport
22. Marblehead
23. Williamstown
24. Lenox
25. Sandwich
26. Chatham
27. Nantucket
28. Edgartown
29. Bristol
30. Newport
31. Watch Hill/Stonington
32. Northeast Connecticut
33. Essex/Old Lyme
34. Farmington Valley
35. Litchfield

Historical marker outside Dovetail Inn tells about Dorset.

Dorset, Vt.

The Town that Marble Built

There is marble almost everywhere in Dorset, a town that marble helped build and upon which it has long prospered.

You see it on the sidewalks all around the picturesque green, on the porch at the historic Dorset Inn and on the terrace at the newer Barrows House, on the side of the turreted United Church of Christ and on the pillars of the Marble West Inn. The sight of an entire mansion built of marble stuns passersby along Dorset West Road.

It seems as if all Dorset has been paved with marble – and with good intentions. Here is what residents and writers alike have called the perfect village. Merchant Jay Hathaway phrased it well in a Dorset Historical Society lecture: What could be better than running "a small country store nestled in the mountains of Vermont in a town that is as close to perfect as Dorset?"

A village of perhaps 1,800 (about two-thirds of its population during the height of its marble-producing days a century ago), it's a mix of charm and culture in perfect proportion.

Dorset is unspoiled, from its rustic Dorset Playhouse (the oldest summer playhouse in the state) to its handsomely restored inn (the oldest in the state) to its Dorset Field Club (the oldest nine-hole golf course in the state) to its lovely white, green-shuttered homes (many among the oldest in the state) to its two general stores, both of them curiously different relics of 19th-century life. Here is a peaceful place in which to cherish the past.

Barely six miles away is Manchester, one of the more sophisticated tourist destinations around. Some of its visitors, who come to shop until they drop, don't know about nor are they particularly interested in Dorset. But people in Dorset can take advantage of all Manchester's urbane attractions as desired.

So the Dorset visitor has the best of both worlds – a tranquil respite amid a myriad of activities and attractions. What could be more copasetic?

Inn Spots

Cornucopia of Dorset, 3228 Route 30, Box 307, Dorset 05251.

One of the more inviting and elegant B&Bs anywhere is offered by Donna Butman, a Connecticut native who returned to her family's roots in 2000. "I was B&B shopping and Vermont clicked," said Donna, who left Colorado and a twenty-year career in sales and marketing for the town in which her grandmother was born.

She took over a winning B&B and kept everything basically the same. Having prepared for her career change with three months of "inn-sitting" at a friend's B&B in Sedona, Ariz., she pledged that Cornucopia's traditional culinary forte would continue. "We're using many of the same menus and recipes," she said.

Cornucopia lives up to its name, offering an abundance of warmth, comfort and personality. It has only four guest rooms and a cottage suite, but what accommodations they are! All air-conditioned and with large, modern baths, they contain king or queensize poster or canopy beds, all afluff with down comforters or colorful quilts and pillows and merino wool mattress pads. All have fireplaces. Upholstered chairs flank three-way reading lamps. Terrycloth robes, bowls of fruit, freshly baked cookies, telephones, CD players and Crabtree & Evelyn toiletries are the norm. Check out the walls in the rear Dorset Hill Room; they are painted in two kinds of white stripes that look like wallpaper. We found the Mother Myrick Room particularly comfortable with a kingsize bed against a wall of shelves containing books and photos.

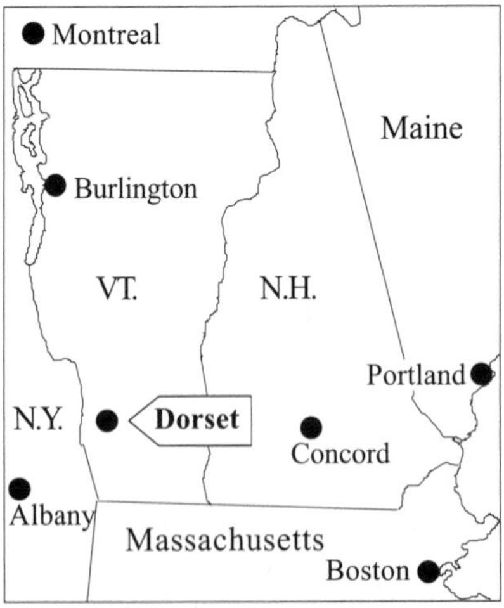

The rear Owl's Head Cottage with a cathedral-ceilinged living room, fireplace, eat-in kitchen and a queensize loft bedroom has a stereo and a private sun deck.

The common rooms are more than an adjunct – they are the focal point of Cornucopia. Off a small, cozy library is an inviting living room with overstuffed sofas. Both have fireplaces. Beyond is an enormous dining room opening into a sunroom, a contemporary area that's cool and shaded in the summer, warm and bright in winter. It is here that we gravitate to study the leather scrapbooks of restaurant menus and area attractions, browse through a cornucopia of

Side sunroom opens onto marble patio at back of Cornucopia of Dorset.

magazines or pore through a hardbound book called "At the Movies," listing all the video tapes for the VCR.

Outside are a marble patio and a covered porch. Enough bird feeders are attached to the sunroom windows to accommodate a flock.

Breakfast is served by candlelight at a pair of formal tables in the airy dining room. One repast started with fresh orange juice and a colorful dish of honeydew melon, nicely pre-sliced into bite-size pieces and topped with raspberries, strawberries, kiwi and banana slices, and vanilla yogurt. The pièce de résistance was a baked croissant à l'orange with crème fraîche. Colombian coffee and Twining's English tea accompanied. The baked raspberry pancake served on another occasion was so good that we asked for the recipe. Other specialties include baked ham and egg cup with cheddar cheese, maple swirl french toast soufflé and breakfast enchiladas.

The goodies don't end there. Complimentary champagne or sparkling cider are served at check-in, and help-yourself coffee, tea and hot chocolate are at hand 24 hours a day. Upon returning from dinner, you'll find your bedroom lights dimmed and candy – perhaps a slice of buttercrunch from our favorite Mother Myrick's confectionery store in Manchester – on the pillow of a bed turned down ever so artistically.

In the room are stationery and stamped envelopes and postcards upon which we'd spread the word, "great place – you ought to be here."

(802) 867-5751 or (800) 566-5751. Fax (802) 867-5753. www.cornucopiaofdorset.com. Four rooms and one cottage with private baths. Doubles, $180, foliage and holidays $200. Cottage, $270, foliage and holidays $300. Two-night minimum weekends and foliage. Children over 16.

Squire House, 3395 Dorset West Road, Box 798, Dorset 05251.

When he was preparing to retire from Citibank, Roger Squire and his wife Gay looked for a new home in which to operate a B&B. They initially had their sights set on Montana, but soon settled on Dorset. "We'd never been here before," said Gay. "But when we saw this house, we knew this was it."

The Squires purchased the 1918 country estate on eleven acres and set about renovating a house that once was the largest in Dorset but had fallen into disrepair. They moved from New York's Westchester County and settled into the maid's wing, sharing the rest of their home with overnight guests.

"We want people to feel like they're visiting friends at their country estate," said Gay. Guests enjoy the run of a large and beautiful house, superior accommodations and the warmth of hospitable hosts.

Furnished with antiques and oriental rugs, the house unfolds off both sides of a long, wide foyer. First comes a library/TV room with one of the structure's five fireplaces. Next is a music room – Roger plays the flute and Gay the piano – set up for impromptu recitals (practicing musicians get a ten percent discount). Beyond is a large and elegant living room with windows on three sides. Across the hallway is a stunning dining room, paneled in rich wood original to the house. Off it is a huge, dream of a kitchen for people who like to cook.

Upstairs are two large carpeted bedrooms and a suite with antique queensize beds. The bedrooms are handsomely decorated and outfitted with all the comforts of a well endowed country home. The room and the suite come with tiled, wood-burning fireplaces. The other room has a small TV and a collection of antique needlework. The suite's sitting room has oriental rugs, a plasma TV and a daybed that converts into twin beds.

The Squires emerge from the servants' wing to welcome guests with afternoon tea. The next morning, they share cooking duties to present a three-course breakfast amid English china and family silver at a table for six in the dining room. It starts with fresh fruit and homemade granola. The main course could be a mushroom omelet or vegetarian frittata, crème brûlée french toast or light, feathery buttermilk pancakes.

Like good servants, the Squires do everything themselves. Roger wields a mean vacuum cleaner, Gay says. And both enjoy hosting friends in the country. For passing travelers, better hosts would be hard to find.

(802) 867-0281. Fax (802) 867-2565. www.squirehouse.com. Two rooms and one suite with private baths. June-October and December-February: doubles $185, suite $250. Rest of year: doubles $165, suite $225. Children over 16.

Dovetail Inn, Main Street, Box 976, Dorset 05251.

Nicely located facing the green in the heart of town just across from the Dorset Inn (in fact it was once an inn annex and housed chauffeurs and staff in the posh days) is the two-building Dovetail. Jim and Jean Kingston, he a marine engineer and now a local property manager, moved from Connecticut in 1984 and, as they say, picked a thriving area.

They have refurbished the nine guest rooms and a two-room suite in one Federal-style structure, and added a sitting room with a TV and butler's pantry stocked with hot and cold beverages. The other building houses their quarters and a cheery "keeping room" for guests' use. On the second floor landing is a nook with a window seat and many books for borrowing.

Rooms vary in size and all have air conditioning. All but one come with queensize or king/twin beds. Each has a sitting area with a couple of easy chairs (ours had a sofa) and pretty new wallpaper and curtains. The Village Suite in front can

Squire House was once the largest country estate in Dorset.

accommodate four, what with a queensize bed with a hand-painted headboard in the bedroom, an adjoining sitting room with queen sofabed, new corner gas fireplace and TV, and two bathrooms. The prized Hearthside room in back offers a fireplace and kitchenette-wet bar, a queensize poster bed, loveseat, TV, a private deck and easy access to the gardens.

Jim, a woodworker of note, built the pencil-post queen bed in one room, and refers to the "magic headboards" in another – "I move them to make the beds twins or king-size," he quips.

In the back yard, the Kingstons tired of the upkeep of the 20-by-40-foot swimming pool they inherited from the Dorset Inn and filled it in with a terrace and gardens "so we finally have a back yard," Jean said. They also have a front porch with rocking chairs for viewing the Dorset green. Friendly hosts, they welcome guests with tea and cookies in the afternoon.

The continental buffet breakfast consists of juice, fresh fruits or compotes, muffins (the orange ones were delicious), breads and coffeecakes. You may have it brought to your room in a basket, if you wish.

Why the name Dovetail? "I like quality building and furniture," says Jim, "and a cutesy name didn't fit Dorset." Stability does, and with all these years of innkeeping, the Kingstons provide it.

(802) 867-5747 or (888) 867-5747. Fax (802) 867-0246. www.dovetailinn.com. Ten rooms and one suite with private baths. Doubles, $80 to $165 weekends, $65 to $150 midweek; $85 to $195 foliage. Suite, $240 weekends and foliage, $155 midweek.

Marble West Inn, Dorset West Road, Dorset 05251.

The historic Holley-West house, a stately Greek Revival built in the 1840s by the owner of a marble quarry, is graced with seven marble columns in front.

Since becoming a B&B in 1985, three successive sets of owners have redecorated and furnished with great style and taste. They retained the extraordinary stenciling (done by Honey West, one of the quarry owner's daughters) in the front entry and upstairs hall, and several other unusual decorative and architectural features, such as the low stairway banisters installed for a woman in the West family who was less than five feet tall. Swagged draperies, fine oriental rugs, antique musical instruments and furniture upholstered in Waverly fabrics and chintz welcome guests into the main parlor. It's open to the dining room, where ten Queen Anne chairs flank a solid

Marble columns grace Greek Revival facade of Marble West Inn.

mahogany table. The adjacent library has a marble fireplace, comfortable furniture, a nifty window seat and a help-yourself wine bar.

The main floor also contains the West Suite with a working fireplace, a queensize bed topped with a down comforter, a sitting room with sofa and wing chairs, and a small sunroom just big enough for two. Off the library at the other end of the house is the Birch Suite with a kingsize bed, sitting area, a shower tucked into the small, ingenious bathroom space and a private patio.

Upstairs off two stairways are six other attractive guest rooms. Each is amply furnished with Laura Ashley or Ralph Lauren fabrics, oriental rugs and CD players, and chocolates await on the nightstands. We're partial to the rear-corner Dorset Room with a canopied kingsize Shaker bed, gas stove, lots of floral chintzes and windows on three sides. The windows were opened wide on a warm autumn evening for cross-ventilation, and we didn't hear a sound all night.

Breakfast is by candlelight in a serene dining room with gray walls, floral swags, colorful oriental rugs on a polished dark wood floor and a ficus tree in one corner. Innkeeper Paul Quinn, whose family lives in a separate building behind the house, serves a three-course meal. Ours started with orange juice, a half grapefruit enhanced by just enough maple syrup and coconut to sweeten the tartness, and piping-hot morning glory muffins. The main course was walnut pancakes, half a dozen "medallions" garnished with cranberries and served with delicious mild sausages imported from Pennsylvania. Other possibilities include eggs benedict, cheese and chive omelets and french toast stuffed with bananas.

In the afternoon, Paul puts out tea or sherry and baked goods. He does the cooking, but his wife Pamela, who works in real estate, helps with the five-course gourmet dinners he offers guests on off-peak weekends.

Fed by a passing creek, a two-tiered pond out back provides a home for 27-inch rainbow trout. Around the grounds, Adirondack chairs face the pond as well as a croquet lawn.

(802) 867-4155 or (800) 453-7629. www.marblewestinn.com. Six rooms and two suites with private baths. Doubles, $109 to $149, off-season $79 to $139. Suites, $139 to $189, off-season $119 to $159. Children over 12.

Barrows House, Route 30, Dorset 05251.

We don't know what is more appealing about the Barrows House: the comfortable rooms and cottages amid eleven acres of park-like grounds with a swimming pool, two tennis courts and an intricate gazebo, or the meals in the greenhouse addition that extends the dining room to the outdoors.

Black wicker rockers are at the ready behind the columns that front the 200-year-old main house, which has a pleasant fireplaced living room, the expansive rear dining rooms (see Dining Spots), upstairs guest rooms and, beside a canopied outdoor patio, a charming tavern notable for its trompe-l'oeil walls of books so realistic you feel you're in a library.

There are eight rooms upstairs in the main inn. Most popular, however, are twenty scattered in eight outbuildings converted into sophisticated lodging. Each house has its own sitting room, porch or terrace. Five suites have fireplaces and sitting rooms. Wallpapers, draperies and quilts are coordinated, and all are filled with nice touches like ruffled pillows and patchcraft hangings.

Since their arrival in 1993, innkeepers Jim and Linda McGinnis have sponsored the annual "Littlest Music Festival," a series of four benefit Sunday afternoon concerts on the inn's lawn in June and early July. Attendees contribute food items and cash for the Manchester Area Food Cupboard.

The inn also has found a niche in welcoming children and pets. Dogs can stay in one of two separate accommodations for families with dogs for $20 a day.

(802) 867-4455 or (800) 639-1620. Fax (802) 867-0132. www.barrowshouse.com. Eighteen rooms and ten suites with private baths. Doubles, $140 to $245 June-October, winter weekends and holidays; $125 to $210 rest of year. Add $60 for MAP. Two-night minimum weekends. Children and pets welcome.

The Dorset Inn, 8 Church St., Dorset 05251.

Vermont's oldest continuously operated country inn, with a history dating back to 1796, was nicely renovated in 1984 and 1985 by what chef-owner Sissy Hicks bills as "the inspired revival of an historic site." It hasn't changed much since, as befits such an historic inn.

Overnight guests are greeted by a stunning collection of blue glass displayed in lighted cases at the top of the stairway on the second floor. Rooms on the two upper floors have been redone with carpeting, modern baths with wood washstands, print wallpapers and antique furnishings. Two of the nicest are the third-floor front corner rooms, one with twin sleigh beds, two rockers, Audubon prints and floral wallpaper, and the other with a canopy bed, marble table and wallpaper of exotic animals and birds. A second-floor corner suite overlooking the green includes a sitting room with TV, telephone and refrigerator and a bedroom with kingsize bed. A second corner suite with queen bed and a pull-out couch also has a TV, as do four rooms at the rear of the ground floor. Beds are about equally split between queens, doubles and two twins.

On the ground floor, stuffed bears in little chairs welcome guests in the newly refurbished reception area, graced with oriental rugs on wide-plank floors. The main sitting room appeals with comfortable furniture around a fireplace, a collection of blue and white china on the mantel, scrubbed wide-plank floors and a small television set. Beyond is a cheery, porch-like breakfast room with Vermont-woven mats atop wood tables and green floral curtains against small-paned windows that extend to the floor.

The inn serves a hearty breakfast (sourdough or fruit pancakes, all kinds of eggs, bacon, ham and sausage). In the rear section are an attractive, country-style dining room (see Dining Spots) and a pleasant taproom with a big oak bar.

In 2003, the inn added The Studio, a petite day spa open by appointment, and added spa cuisine to the dinner fare.

(802) 867-5500 or (877) 367-7389. Fax (802) 867-5542. www.dorsetinn.com. Twenty-nine rooms and two suites with private baths. Rates, B&B. Doubles, $200 weekends, $175 midweek in summer; $175 weekends, $145 midweek in winter; $220 in foliage, $145 weekends, $125 midweek in spring. Two-night minimum peak weekends. Children over 5.

Inn at West View Farm, 2928 Route 30, Dorset 05251.

The accommodations have been upgraded, the bar and waiting area expanded, and a comfy parlor and sun porch added in a reincarnation of the old Village Auberge. It was given new life in 2000 by New Yorkers Christal Siewertsen, the innkeeper, and her husband Raymond Chen, the chef. They closed the dining room for redecorating and reopened for the summer season to good reviews.

The couple, since joined by a newborn son, took over an inn with a side entry and reception area and a welcoming common area that was lacking earlier. No longer must arriving overnight guests share a small parlor with waiting dining patrons. Everyone can enjoy the expanded lounge, a large sitting room with a fireplace and two sofas, and an exceptionally nice enclosed side porch full of white wicker sofas and chairs.

The four original guest rooms upstairs have been redecorated, and six tidy rooms with full baths have been added. All but two have queensize beds, and one is a suite with a sitting room.. They are nicely furnished with country antiques.

Breakfast is served to inn guests in the cheery, plant-filled bay-window end of the dining room. Eggs any style, pancakes, croissants and pain perdu with various fillings are among the offerings.

(802) 867-5715 or (800) 769-4903. Fax (802) 867-0468. wwwinnatwestviewfarm.com. Nine rooms and one suite with private baths. Memorial Day to Labor Day: doubles, $125 to $170. Foliage, $150 to $200. Rest of year: $110 to $155. Two-night minimum weekends. Children over 12.

Dining Spots

Chantecleer, Route 7A, East Dorset.

As far as local residents are concerned, there's near unanimity about the Chantecleer in East Dorset. The food is consistent, the service professional and the atmosphere rustically elegant. It's also considered rather pricey.

Swiss chef Michel Baumann acquired the contemporary-style restaurant fashioned from an old dairy barn in 1981. His menu features Swiss and French provincial cuisine, from whole dover sole filleted tableside to roasted Long Island duckling with plum-ginger sauce.

Our party of four sampled a number of the autumn offerings, starting with a classic baked onion soup, penne with smoked salmon, potato pancakes with sautéed crabmeat and a heavenly lime butter sauce, and bundnerfleisch fanned out in little coronets with pearl onions, cornichons and melba rounds. For main courses, we savored the rack of lamb, veal sweetbreads morel, sautéed quail stuffed with mushrooms duxelles and the night's special of boneless pheasant from a local farm, served with smoked bacon and grapes, among other things. Fabulous roesti

Dorset Inn is Vermont's oldest continuously operated inn.

potatoes upstaged the other accompaniments, puree of winter squash, snow peas and strands of celery.

Bananas foster, grand marnier layer cake, crème brûlée and trifle were worthy endings for a rich, expensive meal. A number of Swiss wines are included on the reasonably priced wine list, and Swiss yodeling music may be heard on tape as background music.

(802) 362-1616. Entrées, $28 to $35. Dinner by reservation, nightly except Tuesday from 6.

Inn at West View Farm, 2928 Route 30, Dorset.

Ex-Manhattan chef Raymond Chen has elevated the dining experience at this inn previously known as the Village Auberge. Upon taking over the inn with his wife Christal, he redecorated and set the white-clothed tables in the European style, with heavy silver cutlery face down. He reinstated a regular dinner schedule and invited patrons to "rediscover a tradition of excellence in fine dining."

The dining room with its striking built-in china cabinets and a large bay window at the far end is about the only vestige of its long life as the Village Auberge. An addition houses Clancy's Tavern, an attractive room with dark green wainscoting and beams, where the polished wooden tables are topped with English placemats.

Chef Ray cooks in the new American style with international flourishes. His dish of mushroom and mascarpone raviolis with spinach and white truffle oil is a signature starter. Others could be Thai curry-crusted shrimp with tamarind sauce, hoisin-glazed quail with crispy rice noodles and roasted sweetbreads with fried spinach and sauce gribiche.

The wine-braised beef short ribs is so popular that Ray cannot take it off the menu. Another favorite is pan-roasted free-range chicken with roasted garlic jus, rosemary potato gratin and haricots verts. Other entrées include phyllo-wrapped halibut with champagne beurre blanc, hanger steak with balsamic-onion marmalade and lamb shanks with rosemary-olive sauce.

Save room for the signature warm Valrhona chocolate cake with vanilla ice cream, Vermont maple cheesecake with pecan cookies or the refreshing trio of strawberry, citrus and mango sorbets. Gourmet magazine requested the recipe for the buttermilk panna cotta with caramelized bananas and blackberries.

(802) 867-5715 or (800) 769-4903. Entrées, $26 to $29. Dinner, Thursday-Monday from 6. Closed two weeks in April and November.

The Dorset Inn, On the Green, Dorset.

Interesting, creative food has been emanating from the kitchen of this venerable inn since owner Sissy Hicks took over the chef's chores in 1984.

The main dining room is handsome in hunter green with white trim and wainscoting. A focal point is a spotlit glass cabinet displaying cups and horse figurines along one wall. Out back are a tavern with dining tables and a large oak bar, and in front, a garden dining porch that's especially pleasant for lunch.

Known for her home-style American cuisine, Sissy Hicks changes her menu seasonally. She also has changed the previously separate tavern and dining room menus into one that serves both areas. Now you'll find a hefty burger (for a hefty price) on the same menu as grilled lamb chops with garlic-shallot confit. Not to mention sautéed chicken tenders alongside a grilled angus steak served with "James Beard's sauce." At least five vegetarian items – including baked eggplant crêpes and grilled polenta with sautéed mushrooms – are usually offered.

Among appetizers, we found the crabmeat mousse with a cucumber-mustard dill sauce and a few slices of melba toast enough for two to share. Having been advised that the calves liver was the best anywhere, we had to try it. Served rare as requested with crisp bacon and slightly underdone slices of onion, it was superb. The fresh trout, deboned but served with its skin still on, was laden with sautéed leeks and mushrooms. Each came with a different vegetable; other side dishes listed on the menu carry a surcharge. A Wente chardonnay, golden and oaky, was a good choice from the reasonably priced wine list.

Pies, bread pudding with whiskey sauce and crème brûlée are on the dessert menu. We chose a kiwi sorbet, wonderfully deep flavored, accompanied by a big sugar cookie. One of the favorite fall desserts is Sissy's cider sorbet with spiced wine sauce.

(802) 867-5500. Entrées, $12.50 to $23. Lunch daily in summer and fall, 11:30 to 2. Dinner nightly, 5 to 9. Closed Monday and Tuesday in winter.

Barrows House, Route 30, Dorset.

Innkeepers Jim and Linda McGinnis preside over a dining operation that's long been known for good food in pleasant surroundings. The focal point for many is the sunken greenhouse on the side, where you almost feel you're dining under the stars. The main dining room has been redecorated with nicely spaced tables dressed in white and sage green, to coordinate with the colors in the hand-painted murals of Dorset on the walls. The adjacent cozy tavern, with its trompe-l'oeil walls of books, also is a pleasant spot for dining.

The menu features contemporary New England cuisine, each item paired with a suggested wine. At one visit, we started with smoked tuna with caper and red onion crème fraîche and a tartlet of smoked scallops and mussels with scallions and

Norcross-West marble quarry (1785) at southern entrance to Dorset is nation's oldest.

red peppers, both excellent. Main courses were grilled chicken with fresh berries, mint and grand marnier and pan-roasted veal tenderloin with pancetta, tomatoes and shiitake mushrooms. They were accompanied by a platter of vegetables served family style, on this night spaghetti squash creole, lemon-scented broccoli, carrot puree with maple syrup, and risotto with fennel and red peppers. Vegetables have always been a Barrows House strong point; one summer dinner brought carrots glazed with raisins and ginger, asparagus with hollandaise, squash and spinach with dill, and warm potato salad. Recent entrées ranged from hazelnut-encrusted arctic char with a sundried tomato-dill sauce to tournedos rossini. The Chesapeake-style crab cakes are a fixture among both the appetizer and entrée selections.

A huckleberry tart, crème caramel and cappuccino ice cream are temptations from the dessert list.

(802) 867-4455 or (800) 639-1620. Entrées, $17.95 to $29.95. Dinner nightly, 6 to 9.

Diversions

Marble. It's everywhere, and hard to miss around Dorset. Take a gander at the large marble mansion on Dorset West Road, set back in the trees south of Marble West Inn. Although none of the six quarries that once made Dorset the most extensive quarrying center in Vermont still operates, people swim in an abandoned marble quarry that's most picturesque on the east side of Route 30 just south of the village. Recently identified by huge slabs of marble placed haphazardly beside the road, the Norcross-West Quarry (1785) is the oldest in the United States. Look for the oldest marble house in the U.S. next to the quarry.

Back Roads. They're all around, but a few are special. Dorset West Road and adjacent West Road in Manchester take you past some interesting and impressive country homes. Dorset Hollow Road makes a gorgeous circle that takes about ten minutes by car. The Danby Mountain Road winds through secluded forests and, if you keep bearing right at every intersection, you eventually come to a dead end with a spectacular wide-open view across the hillsides toward mountain peaks 50 miles away. The sight at fall foliage's height actually produced a few "wows" out of us and lived up to Dovetail innkeeper Jim Kingston's promise of one of the best foliage trips in Vermont.

Local Lore. During Vermont's Bicentennial, the **Dorset Historical Society and Museum** moved to the Bley House, donated as its headquarters. It's open Wednesday, Friday and Saturday from April-October. Take a recorded village walking tour, learn about the local marble and cheese-making industries or trace the genealogy of a Vermont ancestor here. Another local gem is the **Dorset Village Public Library** with its McIntyre Art Gallery, located in the restored Gray's Tavern building at Church and Main Streets, open daily except Sunday.

Dorset Playhouse, Cheney Road, Dorset.

Tucked away in the trees just off Church Street, the rustic, all-wood barn with the red and white awning on the side was the first summer theater in Vermont. Since 1976, it has been home to the Dorset Theater Festival, a non-profit professional theater company importing casts from New York and Los Angeles. Its rediscovery of Cole Porter's 1938 musical "You Never Know" went on national tour. Other new plays have gone on to New York and Washington.

(802) 867-5777. Performances nightly except Monday, June-September. Tickets, $23 to $36.

Merck Forest & Farmland Center, (802) 394-7836. These days it's rare to find so large and unspoiled an area so available for public use as this 2,820-acre preserve northwest of Dorset off Route 315 in Rupert. Twenty-seven miles of roads and trails are accessible for hiking and cross-country skiing in the forests, meadows and mountains. Established by George Merck of chemical-company fame, it is a non-profit outdoor education center open to the public year-round. Scholars study the organic garden, the maple sugaring and forest management. Hikers, campers and cross-country skiers enjoy the trails to Birch and Beebe ponds and the vista of the Adirondacks from the Viewpoint. The forest is a New England treasure.

Shopping. Peltier's General Store has been the center of Dorset life since 1816, the more so since it was acquired in 1976 by Jay Hathaway and his wife Terri, who augmented its everyday goods with exotica like balsamic vinegars, cheddar cheese from Shelburne Farms, aromatic coffee beans and fine wines. Just back from New York with an array of new items, Jay said his store "is ever-changing because we don't want to be routine." Peltier's celebrated its 175th anniversary during Vermont's Bicentennial and abounds with every need from newspapers to champagne.

Equally historic but thoroughly unchanging through six generations of a single family is the **H.M. Williams General Store,** two attached barns identified by a small sign at the southern edge of town and an incredible jumble of merchandise placed helter-skelter (foodstuffs amidst the hardware, boxes of ladies' shoes identified with a cardboard sign: "With this quality and these prices, let the big boys compete"). Prices are marked by crayon and the cash register is a pouch worn around his waist by proprietor Dennis Brownlee. While we waited for 50 pounds of sunflower birdseed for a bargain $13.10, the woman ahead of us bought 50 pounds of rabbit pellets and was told where she could find a bale of hay.

A few other Dorset stores like the **Flower Brook Pottery** and **The Old Cow's Tail** and **Judd Gregory Antiques** are of interest. The **Dorset Gallery** on the Green represents many artists, while the **Gallery on the Marsh** features the fine art of John Pitcher and Sue Weston. More than 200 heirloom quilts are offered by **Marie Miller American Quilts**. South of town is the **J.K. Adams Co.** factory store, which stocks a large assortment of woodware and housewares made from native hardwoods for the likes of L.L. Bean and Williams Sonoma. Butcher blocks, knife racks, bowls, cutlery and homespun tablecloths are for sale at substantial savings. Its great new kitchen store stocks cooking accessories and housewares you might not find elsewhere.

Adjacent Manchester offers fine shopping opportunities, especially in its ever-growing array of fashionable outlet stores.

Southern Vermont Arts Center, West Road, Manchester.

High up a mountainside along the back road between Manchester and Dorset is this special place not to be missed. The oldest cultural institution in Vermont, it was started in 1929 when five local artists banded together to display their works at the Dorset Town Hall. Inside a 28-room Georgian Colonial mansion known as Yester House are galleries with changing exhibits, an expanded performing arts hall seating 400, and a café for lunch. The new Elizabeth de C. Wilson Museum is described as the center's crown jewel. Designed by architect Hugh Newell Jacobsen, it is a stunning contemporary facility with soaring, skylit spaces in which to display the center's 800-piece permanent collection and traveling exhibitions. The Manchester Garden Club restored and maintains the Boswell Botany Trail, a three-quarter-mile walk past hundreds of wildflowers and 67 varieties of Vermont ferns, all identified by club members. An hour's hike through the woods is another attraction, and the sculpture garden featuring a 285-year-old sugar maple is bordered by amazing vistas.

(802) 362-1405. www.svac.org. Open Tuesday-Saturday 10 to 5, Sunday noon to 5. Closed two weeks in late April and early May. Adults, $6.

Extra-Special

Mother Myrick's Confectionery & Ice Cream Parlor, Route 7A, Manchester Center.

We can't ever seem to get through this area without stopping at Mother Myrick's, the ultimate ice-cream parlor and confectionery shop. One of the things that lures us is the fudge sauce – so good that a friend to whom we give it hides her jar in a cupboard and eats it with a spoon. Here you can buy the most extraordinary homemade chocolates, get a croissant and cappuccino in the morning, tea and a slice of Vermont maple cheesecake in the afternoon, or a piece of grand marnier truffle cake and espresso at night. Ice-cream sodas, milkshakes, floats, sundaes and pastries are served in a fantastic art-deco setting with etched-glass panels, bentwood cases, light columns and the like done by gifted Vermont craftsmen.

(802) 362-1560 or (888) 669-7425. www.mothermyricks.com. Open daily 10 to 6, summer and peak periods, 10 to 10.

Middlebury College campus overlooks town and mountains, as viewed from Mead Chapel.

Middlebury, Vt.

Robert Frost Country

The poet Robert Frost spent the last 23 summers of his life in the mountains outside Middlebury. Little wonder. This rather rugged area enlivened by a college town is mountain country, Frost country, an area of rambling white houses, red barns and green fields – the essence of Vermont, if you will.

The poet who adopted New England and made it his own also adopted the Middlebury area. The small cabin where he slept is not open to the public, but there's a nearby interpretive trail where you can get a taste of his enduring poetry and the sights that inspired him. The Middlebury College library houses many of his first editions. The founder of the town's Vermont Book Shop knew the poet well and the store stocks many of his works. And the college's Bread Loaf mountain campus carries on his tradition with its annual summer writers' conference.

Middlebury is, for us, the epitome of the New England college town. The campus of the "college on the hill" on the west side of town is unusually picturesque, its newer gray limestone buildings complementing the older ones dating back to the college's founding in 1800. One of us first saw the campus on a snowy April day in the 1950s and decided then and there that this was to be the college for him. In summer, when the regular college is not in session, its famed Summer Language Schools turn the area into a rural United Nations as graduate students chat in almost every language.

The college gives the town its solid heritage and vibrant character. ("The strength of the hills is His also" are the words etched above the portals of the striking college chapel in which Robert Frost lectured to turn-away student audiences every few years.) And a returning alumnus is struck by a new dynamic – an array of restaurants and shops that is remarkable for a town its size (8,000). Except for annoying new traffic lights along main Route 7, Middlebury somehow remains a tranquil college town.

To the east are East Middlebury and Ripton, quiet mountain hamlets, Middlebury's bucolic Bread Loaf campus and the college's impressive Snow Bowl ski area. To the west lies the Champlain Valley, a surprisingly vast and undeveloped expanse sidling up to Lake Champlain. To the north are Vergennes, which claims to be the nation's smallest city, the mountain community of Bristol and sylvan Charlotte, where mountains and lake meld in a wondrous panorama. The vistas of water and mountains are stunning, thanks to the Green Mountains on the east, the Adirondacks to the west and Lake Champlain shimmering in the middle.

This is an area of charming contrasts, one where lake and mountains, simplicity and sophistication, co-exist to near perfection.

Inn Spots

Swift House Inn, 25 Stewart Lane, Middlebury 05753.

A rambling white clapboard manse, built in 1814 and once the home of a Vermont governor, is the focal point of this elegant inn and restaurant acquired in 2003 by James and Katrina Kappel.

Shedding pharmaceutical careers in Indianapolis to become innkeepers, the Kappels took over an exceptional place founded by John Nelson and his late wife Andy. The Nelsons had started with ten rooms in the main house, added five more in the modest Gatehouse Annex and restored the side 1886 carriage house as the crowning touch: six deluxe rooms with fireplaces, double jacuzzis, kingsize beds, TVs and telephones. Rooms are handsomely outfitted with poster beds and handmade quilts, and the bathrooms are knockouts. One in the Gatehouse, done up with white wicker and purple walls, has bath pillows "so you can lie in the whirlpool tub with a good book," our guide explained.

Rooms come with amenities like oversize beds, telephones and terrycloth robes that help give the inn its four-diamond AAA rating. We first enjoyed the Governor's Room, upstairs in the front corner of the main house, elegantly traditional in blue florals, with a kingsize bed, antique armoire, fireplace, two wing chairs, TV and a writing desk. Bedside chocolates accompanied a note of welcome from the innkeepers.

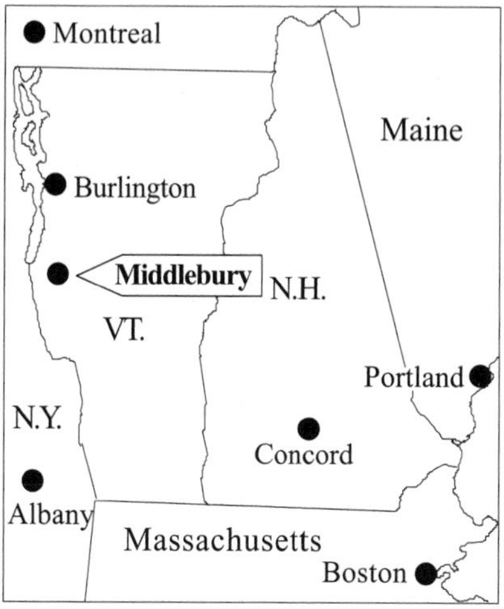

A subsequent stay was in the prized Mansfield Room on the lower level of the carriage house. It is large, light and airy in bleached pine with an abundance of windows screened by Indian shutters. We sipped cocktails on our own patio beside a rose garden, watched the TV news from a sofa and wing chair (each flanked by good reading lamps) in the ample sitting area, and stepped up into a kingsize bed. The front foyer had a closet with an ironing board, the dressing area

Swift House Inn is known for fine lodging and dining.

was equipped with a coffeemaker, and the lavish bathroom with double jacuzzi positively shone with solid brass fixtures.

Public rooms in the inn include a wide hall used as a parlor with one of the inn's many fireplaces, the restaurant and a comfortable little cocktail lounge with five seats at the bar. A steam room and sauna are available in the carriage house. The expansive grounds are dotted with Adirondack chairs and private hideaways for two.

Dinner service in the inn's gracious dining rooms was restored in 2003 after a three-year hiatus. A continental breakfast with fresh fruit, cereal, muffins and fabulous popovers is included in the rates; more elaborate fare can be ordered for a surcharge. After breakfast, settle on the front porch for a look down the wide lawns toward the Adirondack mountains in the distance.

(802) 388-9925. Fax (802) 388-9927. www.swifthouseinn.com. Twenty-one rooms with private baths. Doubles, $90 to $180. Carriage house, $225 to $245.

Whitford House, 912 Grandey Road, Addison 05491.

Their daughter attended Middlebury College and they fell in love with the area, so Midwesterners Bruce and Barbara Carson decided to retire here after 30 years in California. "We wanted an old house, off the beaten path, with a mountain vista," Barbara said. They got their wish in spades.

They restored a 1790s house located along a gravel road on 37 acres in the back of beyond, with a panoramic view of the Adirondack Mountains across nearby Lake Champlain. Near a wild bird preserve, they lie under a snow geese flyway. Eight sheep share the back yard with a stunning sculpture of a horse, made by a friend from vines and sticks found on the property.

The prize accommodation here is a guest cottage. It harbors a large bedroom with twin beds that are usually joined as a king, a full bath with a radiant-heated floor, a comfortable sitting room, a kitchenette and windows all around to take in the views.

The pale yellow house is no slouch. Guests enter through the rear into a great room with slate floor, fieldstone fireplace, baby grand piano and tall windows onto the mountains. You'd never guess it once was the buggy barn, occupied by swallows and hornets when the Carsons arrived in 1992. Next comes a pantry as big as some kitchens. Here is where the Carsons offer wine, beer and hors d'oeuvres for guests in the late afternoon. The pantry adjoins an open kitchen, which obviously is the heart of the house. Orange juice and coffee are put out in the morning in the side library, which opens onto a rear deck. Another favorite spot for lounging is a front porch furnished with rockers. In the front of the house is a corner dining room, where the table is set for a candlelit breakfast for eight.

Across the hall is a guest bedroom with a four-poster double bed and a private bath with an old five-seater (which they found cantilevered off the back of the house) incorporated into the top of the barnwood wall for decorative – and conversational – purposes.

Upstairs are two more guest rooms with king/twin beds, each with private bath, plus the owners' kingsize suite, which they have been known to vacate for guests.

The entire place is furnished with family heirlooms, antiques and unexpected finds, including an old milk chest from a dairy barn that was converted into a corner china cabinet in the dining room. The room is lit entirely by candles for breakfast, a hearty affair that brings fresh fruit, zucchini bread, croissants and perhaps vegetable frittata, baked eggs florentine or belgian waffles. "I love to cook," says Barbara in an understatement.

Lately she has offered candlelight dinners to guests by reservation with a week's advance notice.

Many guests find the Carsons' welcome so warm and the surroundings so relaxing that they scarcely leave the property.

(802) 758-2704 or (800) 746-2704. Fax (802) 758-2089. www..whitfordhouseinn.com. Three rooms and one cottage with private baths. Doubles, $110 to $125. Cottage, $225. Add $25 each for foliage and special weekends. Children and pets accepted.

Cornwall Orchards Bed & Breakfast, 1364 Route 30, Cornwall 05753.

Sturdy Adirondack-style chairs on the idyllic rear deck here overlook what remains of Cornwall Orchards, once the town's biggest employer, and the distant Adirondacks. Some of the apple trees still dot the property, but the original 1783 farmhouse on fourteen rural acres just south of Middlebury has been turned into a stylish B&B by Robert and Juliet Gerlin.

Former Connecticut residents where he was a lawyer, they were smitten with the area when their children attended Middlebury College. They spent a year renovating, adding dormers and six bathrooms before opening in 1995. The rambling, pale yellow structure lent itself to the purpose, what with a comfortable living room with fireplace, a dining room and a substantial country kitchen, which opens onto that great rear deck.

Three guest rooms with full baths occupy wings on the ends of the main floor. The largest is typical with a down duvet on the queensize bed, shiny hardwood floors and navaho white walls. Two upstairs bedrooms have bathrooms with tiled showers. One has a queen bed and the other twins. Decor is crisp and simple.

Juliet prepares a full breakfast incorporating ingredients from nearby farms. Expect fresh fruit, homemade granola and perhaps organic blueberry pancakes with bacon from Pork Chop Farm or scrambled eggs from eggs supplied by the free-range chickens next door.

Juliet grew up in England and worked many years as assistant to a well-known musician and composer. Here she is a part-time assistant to a professor at Middlebury.

(802) 462-2272. www.cornwallorchards.com. Five rooms with private baths. Doubles, $100. Children welcome. No credit cards.

Middlebury Inn, Court House Square, Middlebury 05753.

Since 1827, this mellow red-brick inn of the old school has dominated the village square. The obligatory (but seemingly seldom used) rockers are lined up on the marble floor of the side porch near the entry.

The 45 rooms in the rambling main building have been renovated, upgraded and redecorated under innkeepers Frank and Jane Emanuel. So have ten more in the adjacent Porter House Mansion. Varying in shape and size, all have high ceilings, brass fixtures and intricate moldings as well as TV and two telephones. Four have whirlpool tubs and five are two-bedroom suites.

Twenty rooms in a rear motel annex are large and modern. Each contains two double beds or a double and twin bed plus a queensize sofabed for family use. They also have hair dryers and coffeemakers.

The inn's spacious lobby, where complimentary afternoon tea is served, has nooks for reading or playing checkers and lots to look at. The Country Peddler gift shop offers everything from books to maple syrup. You can order cocktails and sandwiches on the screened porch in summer, or a full range of luncheon entrées in the Rose Room.

More formal is the pillared, blue and white Founders Room. Traditional New England cuisine takes on contemporary accents in a dinner menu ranging from potato-crusted salmon fillet to venison with bourbon-chutney glaze. Light fare and desserts like baked Vermont apple crisp and maple-marble cheesecake are among the evening offerings in the pleasant Morgan Tavern.

Continental breakfast is included in the rates.

(802) 388-4961 or (800) 842-4666. Fax (802) 388-4563. www.middleburyinn.com. Seventy-five rooms and suites with private baths. Doubles, $98 to $270. Suites, $145 to $375.

Entrées, $16.75 to $24.95. Lunch, 11:30 to 2. Dinner, 5:30 to 8:30.

The Inn on the Green, 19 South Pleasant St., Middlebury 05753.

The Middlebury green gained a new hostelry with the opening of this 1803 landmark listed on the National Register. Steve and Micki Paddock, longtime owners of the Blue Spruce Motel south of town, fulfilled a dream from the days when they managed a coastal inn.

The stately house, painted gray-blue with white trim, has been restored with great care and with guests' privacy in mind. The main floor holds a small common room that doubles as a reception area/office, and two suites. The rear Bristol has two bedrooms, one with queen bed and one with twins, plus a sitting room. The Addison in front has an antique day bed in the sitting room, a queen bed topped with a quilt and nine pillows in the bedroom, and two chairs in a bay window. As is the case throughout, the walls are painted interesting colors (the sitting room dark blue, the bedroom pale yellow) and are decorated with quilts, plates and paintings for sale.

Other guest rooms, all with queen beds and private baths, are located upstairs in the house and on two floors of a carriage house to the side and rear, next to a Baptist church. Those on the upper level of the carriage house are cozy with slanted ceilings.

All of the rooms, true to their period, are curtain-less. Instead, the windows may be screened with louvered blinds. The TV set rests atop a table on wheels. Amenities are a monogrammed robe in the bathroom, a basket of Haversham and Holt toiletries, and bottles of Poland Spring water.

Zinnias brighten side yard of restored Inn on the Green.

There being no appropriate common space, the staff delivers continental breakfast to the guest rooms. Orange juice, fruit and pastries are the fare.

(802) 388-7512 or (888) 244-7512. www.innonthegreen.com. Nine rooms and two suites with private baths. Doubles, $140 to $195, foliage $175 to $225, midweek in winter $98. Two-night minimum peak weekends. Children welcome.

Waybury Inn, 457 East Main St. (Route 125), Box 27, East Middlebury 05740.

"The Bob Newhart Show made us famous," advertises this establishment, whose facade served as the fictional New England inn on the TV sitcom. But the inn has been attracting travelers since 1810, lately under the auspices of owner Joe Sutton, a Burlington hotelier.

Away from the mainstream, the Waybury is quiet and peaceful, with a wide, shaded front porch and a side deck upon which to while away the hours. You can swim in a river gorge almost across the street, or stroll up the road into the mountains.

The fourteen guest rooms have been redecorated and upgraded, many with king poster and queen sleigh beds. They are simply furnished in homey Vermont style. Our large room had comfy twin beds, a red velvet rocking chair, a sofa and fresh white curtains. Top of the line are the Breadloaf, a roomy space with king bed and sitting area, and the refurbished Robert Frost, the "honeymoon suite" with a kingsize poster bed and an antique desk in which couples leave notes in a secret drawer.

The recently spiffed-up parlor and reception area on the main floor harbors books, games and a small TV.

Meals are served in the Coach Room and porch (see Dining Spots) or in the rear pub, which sports some of the signs and props that were used when the Newhart show was filmed here. A full country breakfast is included in the rates.

(802) 388-4015 or (800) 348-1810. Fax (802) 388-1248. www.wayburyinn.com. Fourteen rooms with private baths. Doubles, $125 to $215 in summer and fall, $90 to $165 in winter and spring.

By the Way B&B, 407 East Main St. (Route 125), East Middlebury 05740.

Her artworks and those of her late husband adorn the walls of this homey B&B run with TLC by artist Nancy Simoes. The art, the country antiques, the colorful garden in front of the wide wraparound veranda and the spacious rear lawn with a swimming pool set this place apart.

Guests enjoy a comfortable, book-filled living room with TV and a dining room with a pine harvest table in the middle and a schoolmaster's desk in a bay window. Upstairs are a front bedroom with a double bed, game table, small TV and built-in desk, and a larger rear bedroom with twin beds and some of the five generations of family antiques with which the house abounds. A private guesthouse with kitchen, living room, porch and a deck off the upstairs bedroom also is available.

A hammock and lounge chairs await beside the swimming pool in the long back yard hedged for privacy. An ancient maple shades Adirondack chairs.

Nancy serves a continental breakfast in summer and more substantial fare, such as eggs or french toast, the rest of the year.

(802) 388-6291 or (800) 769-6145. Two rooms and a guest house with private baths. Doubles, $85 to $105. Guesthouse, $195. Children over 8. No credit cards.

The Chipman Inn, Route 125, Ripton 05766.

In a real country hamlet in the heart of Robert Frost country, this small, informal inn dating from 1828 is operated by Bill Pierce and his wife, Joyce Henderson. There's lots of space to spread out – in the comfy parlor with a big fireplace by the little bar, in a lounge full of hooked rugs, in a sitting area with magazines in the upstairs hall, and in the stenciled dining room where prix-fixe dinners are served occasionally by reservation at 7:30 for $25.

The day's menu is posted with appropriate wine suggestions. The meal begins with hors d'oeuvres at 7 in the lounge; salmon mousse, marinated mushrooms and prosciutto could be the fare. Lentil or asparagus soup and salad precede the single-entrée main course, perhaps loin of pork roast with rosemary and garlic or wiener schnitzel with vegetables of the day. Maple-walnut pie or chocolate pâté with raspberry sauce could be the dessert.

All eight homey guest rooms are pleasantly furnished with antiques. One has a sitting room and another a skylight. They generally have a double or queen bed and a twin bed, or combination thereof. Two have a double bed and one has a double and two twins. One with twin poster beds has a private bath in the hall. There's no television, Joyce is quick to point out, but there are plenty of books for amusement. And there's no pool, "but mountain lakes and streams abound."

Bill makes granola for the hearty breakfast, which includes a choice of egg dishes.

(802) 388-2390 or (800) 890-2390. www.chipmaninn.com. Eight rooms with private baths. Doubles, $95 to $135; foliage, $115 to $150. Children over 12.

Strong House Inn, 94 West Main St., Vergennes 05491.

The vitality and enthusiasm of its owners pervades this 1834 Federal-style B&B, listed on the National Register of Historic Places and nicely located on six acres on the crest of a hill at the western edge of town.

Mary and Hugh Bargiel, transplants from Florida where both were with the Burger King headquarters, have upgraded the property and marketed their offerings with a flair that won Mary the Vermont Lodging and Restaurant Association's B&B operator of the year award in 1997.

Strong House Inn is based in rural Federal-style building.

The substantial residence, built by the local bank president for whom it is named, offers six rooms and a simple Victorian suite with queen poster bed up against the wall and a sitting room with a sloping ceiling and a tapestry sofabed.

Rooms vary widely in size and style, from the queen-canopied Empire Room with two leather chairs facing a fireplace to the new Vermont Room, a hideaway with beamed ceiling, sturdy queen country pine bed and french doors opening onto a small balcony. The English Garden Room is barely big enough for a double bed against one wall, and has a private bath down the hall. All have TVs and telephones.

Six deluxe rooms have been added in the new Rabbit Ridge Annex. Two on the second floor with beamed cathedral ceilings offer kingsize poster beds, fireplaces and french doors onto private balconies. The ultimate is the Adirondack Room, done in the style of the great Adirondack camps with a canopied kingsize bed, a floor-to-ceiling stone fireplace, wet bar, double jacuzzi tub and private deck.

Mary, a stickler for detail, stenciled the ivy in one room, made the bed quilts and offers quilting seminars. She also offers afternoon snacks and a breakfast to remember in the large and fancy dining room. The fare at our visit included yogurt with blueberries and bananas, and fruit crêpes with strawberry topping. Other treats are a four-cheese and herb quiche, frittatas and eggs in puff pastry. Mary says that french toast made with real french bread is her claim to fame.

On summer evenings, guests can enjoy a bottle of wine taken from the inn's little tavern to the back-yard gazebo as the sun sets over the Adirondacks. The grounds also contain a goldfish pond, skating pond, snowshoeing and walking trails, and two sled runs.

(802) 877-3337. Fax (802) 877-2599. www.stronghouseinn.com. Thirteen rooms and one suite with private baths. Doubles, $80 to $275. Suite, $125. Add $30 for foliage and special-event weekends.

The Inn at Baldwin Creek, 1868 Route 116 North, Bristol 05443.

After a dozen years in its small and quirky location in downtown Bristol, the ever-popular Mary's Restaurant moved to a truly rural location three miles north of town. The move allowed it to enlarge its dining operation and to morph into a cozy bed-and-breakfast inn as well.

Linda Harmon and her husband, Doug Mack, the chef, turned the main floor of a 1796 Vermont farmhouse into a restaurant with a new commercial kitchen (see Dining Spots).

The couple share the upstairs of the sprawling house with overnight guests in four country-charming rooms. Three rooms come with queen beds. The Maple is a two-room suite with king bed and a trundle day bed that converts to two twins.

The 25-acre property includes a heated swimming pool, perennial gardens and paths down to Baldwin Creek.

Rates include afternoon tea and a three-course gourmet breakfast. The choice for main course might be pumpkin pancakes or omelets, and folks rave about Doug's oatmeal with maple syrup and spiced nuts.

Mary's is a founding member of the Vermont Fresh Network, a statewide farm-chef cooperative that promotes Vermont farming by connecting farms to restaurants. The inn's summer package plans include cooking lessons and tours of participating farms.

(802) 453-2432 or (888) 424-2432. Fax (802) 4533-2432. www.innatbaldwincreek.com. Three rooms and one suite with private baths. May-October: doubles, $125 to $185. November-April: doubles, $95 to $140.

Where to Eat

The Storm Café, 3 Mill St., Middlebury.

Two Culinary Institute of America grads took over this successor to the late Otter Creek Café, which had provided one of our best dinners ever. Karen and John Goettelmann share cooking duties and have settled into a dinner routine after going with lunch only while they started a family.

The setting in the Frog Hollow Mill is perfect, inside in the lower level of an 1840 mill building or outside on a deck overlooking the churning Middlebury Falls of Otter Creek, the longest waterway in the state.

The Goettelmanns' changing dinner menu is nothing if not eclectic. At a winter visit, you could make a meal of paneer masala or "stormy gumbo," a warming and moderately spicy creole stew of shrimp, scallops, chicken, chorizo sausage, tomatoes, vegetables and okra. Or you could opt for grilled salmon fillet over wilted greens tossed with shiitake mushrooms, sundried tomatoes, bacon and red onions; paella "with a stormy twist" (apparently the variety of toppings), and braised lamb shanks in red wine sauce. The New York strip steak was peppered, grilled and topped with brie and a rich port wine demi-glace.

Appetizers included the signature roasted garlic and potato soup, sautéed shrimp tossed with a zesty concoction of bloody mary ingredients (including vodka), smoked salmon napoleon, spicy steamed mussels and – something of an oddity for a preliminary – smashed potatoes: pan-fried red bliss spuds topped with caramelized onions, roasted garlic and bacon with a chèvre and sour cream spread.

Worthy endings include warm apple crêpes, espresso profiteroles, crème brûlée and frozen apricot soufflé.

Multi-level dining areas at Tully & Marie's look out onto Otter Creek.

The café's modest list of wines and beers is overshadowed by its repertoire of teas and coffees.

(802) 388-1063. www.stormcafe.com. Entrées, $15.95 to $21.95. Dinner, Tuesday-Saturday 5 to 9.

Tully & Marie's, 5 Bakery Lane, Middlebury.

This is the worthy successor to the long-running Woody's, a California-style eatery lovingly tended by Woody Danforth, who retired far too early. He sold to chef Laurie Tully Reed and his wife, Carolyn Dundon. They changed the name to incorporate each of their middle names and kept things much the same, and regulars say the food is better than ever.

The contemporary, four-level restaurant with enormous windows overlooking Otter Creek looks like a cross between a sleek diner and an ocean liner. Eating outside on the curved wraparound deck, right above the creek, is like being on a ship – an illusion heightened by mirrors in the interior dining areas.

Laurie changed the menu to emphasize ethnic and American fusion cooking and vegetarian dishes. We sampled several at an autumn lunch: a fiery sweet potato and jalapeño soup, an ample Thai chicken salad and a hefty avocado, tomato and bacon melt on focaccia with sweet potato fries, all delicious.

The treats continue at dinner. Typical starters are smoked salmon and wasabi aioli rolls, a boldly seasoned casserole of marinated artichoke hearts, and pan-blackened tuna with wasabi and pickled ginger. Main dishes range from spicy salmon veracruz and sautéed crab cakes with a roasted red pepper and lemon coulis to chicken saltimbocca, roasted duck burrito and honey-mustard crusted rack of lamb with rosemary jus. Vegetarians praise the tofu curry, pad Thai and grilled portobello mushrooms, which Laurie calls a "vegetarian london broil."

Desserts include pear-mascarpone trifle, midnight espresso mousse and crème caramel.

(802) 388-4182. www.tullyandmaries.com. Entrées, $16 to $22. Lunch, Monday-Saturday 11:30 to 3. Dinner nightly, 5 to 9 or 10. Sunday brunch, 10:30 to 3.

Swift House Inn, 25 Stewart Lane, Middlebury.

One of the legacies of the inn's late co-founder, chef Andrea Nelson, is the restaurant that was her pride and joy. New owners James and Katrina resumed dinner service after a three-year hiatus upon acquiring the inn in 2003. Award-winning chef Marty Holzberg, who worked his culinary magic in the Swift House kitchen in its heyday, returned to his former haunt after a stint at the Jackson House in Woodstock.

Dining is by candlelight in three small and serene dining rooms – one a library – appointed in hunter green. The Mediterranean-inspired fare ranges from grilled yellowfin tuna with veal marrow jus and Hudson Valley foie gras to stuffed boneless quail and locally raised pork osso buco.

A complimentary amuse-bouche – goat cheese and mango salsa on crostini, garnished with an edible flower – and superior crusty sliced breads got our dinner off to a good start. One of us enjoyed an appetizer of foraged mushroom cassoulet and a sensational duck confit napoleon with local chèvre and field greens. The other loved the signature rustic Tuscan bean soup with pancetta cracklings and the panko-crusted lamb chop laced with parmigiano-reggiano.

Dessert was a house specialty, Andy Nelson's original coffee-toffee pecan torte, a dessert that any chocoholic would love.

(802) 388-9925. Entrées, $16 to $26. Dinner Thursday-Monday, 6 to 9.

Christophe's on the Green, 5 North Green St., Vergennes.

Taking over the small restaurant in the landmark 1793 Stevens House facing the village green, French chef Christophe Lissarrague quickly gained a reputation for offering the most exciting dining in the area. Tables are on two levels in a sleek, pale yellow room with dark brown trim. Christophe is in the kitchen and his wife Alice, a native of nearby Shelburne, is out front.

The with-it menu is available à la carte (with all choices for each course the same price) or prix-fixe, $41 for three courses. It starts with such exotica as pheasant consommé with red pepper puree and foie gras raviolis, boursiche of sweetbreads and snails with tarragon sauce and baby greens, and salad of frisée, baked goat cheese and leg of rabbit with smoked hazelnuts and carrot vinaigrette.

The half-dozen main courses range from pan-seared grouper with clams, squid ink vermicelli, black capers and baby bok choy to roasted piglet with fried prosciutto and bacon sauce. A lasagna of jonah crab, tomato confit and spinach might include parsley and hazelnut sauce. Oven-roasted free-range poussin comes with foie gras sauce and wild mushroom flan. Filet mignon might be served en croûte with perigord sauce and chanterelles. A cheese tray is offered following the entrée.

Masterful desserts are frozen whisky mousse with stewed plums, cocoa soufflé with frozen hazelnut ganache, coconut and rum savarin with caramelized pineapple and a trio of sorbets (banana, blood orange and muscat wine) or ice creams (coconut, honey-rosemary and cappuccino), served with petits fours.

(802) 877-3413. Prix-fixe, $41; entrées, $25.50. Dinner, Tuesday-Saturday 5:30 to 9:30. Closed November and January.

Fire & Ice, 26 Seymour St., Middlebury.

Opened by Middlebury graduates in 1974 and greatly expanded over the years, this is a sight to behold. A 1997 renovation doubled the footprint and expanded the kitchen, salad bar and lobby. The result is a ramble of rooms highlighted by Tiffany or fringed lamps, brass chandeliers, boating and sport fishing memorabilia. One room has a copper-dome ceiling and an upside-down canoe hangs from the ceiling of the lounge.

Co-owner Dale Goddard's restored 22-foot Philippine mahogany runabout is moored majestically in a lobby surrounded by salad bars. "I had fun with this," says Dale, who bills it as Middlebury's "museum dinner house." He calls the decor eclectic but notes recurring themes of college, fishing, skiing, family, dungeon and bordello. More than 200 people can be seated at booths and tables, in nooks and crannies – some off by themselves in lofts for two and others in the midst of the action around the massive copper bar.

The food is consistently first-rate and the staff obliging. The stir-fries are famous, as is the shrimp bar, which includes all the shrimp you can eat. The Sunday salad bar adds soup and crab legs, and the event is billed as "just like Sunday dinner at grandma's."

Prime rib and steaks are featured, anything from blackened rib to châteaubriand and steak au poivre. Roast duckling, chicken boursin and cashew chicken stir-fry are specialties. A light fare menu also includes the 55-item salad and bread bars.

The restaurant's name comes from the title of a Robert Frost poem. The fire reflects the cooking and the ice the drink mixing that goes on here.

(802) 388-7166 or (800) 367-7166. www.fireandicerestaurant.com. Entrées, $15.95 to $24.95. Lunch, Friday-Saturday noon to 5. Dinner nightly from 5, Sunday from 1.

Mary's at Baldwin Creek, 1868 Route 116 North, Bristol.

Marking its 20th anniversary in 2003, this pioneering restaurant launched a weekly farmhouse dinner series that featured chef-owner Doug Mack's favorite local purveyors and the foods they produce. The summer-long series was a natural for Doug, a founding member of the Vermont Fresh Network, a statewide cooperative connecting farmers and chefs. Besides hosting the dinner series, he sponsored a Feast of Our Farms harvest celebration in September, a tasting buffet in the inn's Red Barn, guided farm tours and hands-on cooking classes.

Promoting farm purveyors comes naturally to Doug and his wife, Linda Harmon, who founded Mary's in a small and wonderfully quirky Bristol storefront in 1983. They moved a decade later to a 1796 Vermont farmhouse, where they converted the main floor into a restaurant with a new commercial kitchen and began taking in overnight guests upstairs.

Dining in the restaurant's three charming dining rooms is much the same as always – "same menu, same food," in Linda's typical understatement. Mary's has always had one of the more interesting menus and wine lists around. At various occasions, we've enjoyed the tomato-dill bisque, the black bean soup with ham chunks and avocado cream, seafood crêpes and a pasta dish with chicken, asparagus and sundried tomatoes. The house salad is enhanced with crunchy almonds and a garlic-maple vinaigrette, The signature cream of garlic soup is a garlic lover's delight, available by the cup, bowl or by the quart to take home. Other starters might be sweet corn and garlic flan, crab cakes with key lime-coconut sauce, the house-smoked brook trout with salmon roe and fireworks shrimp (which really is fiery).

Dinner entrées range from cornmeal-coated catfish with lemon-thyme cream to chicken breast baked with 40 cloves of garlic. Bay scallops and shrimp might be tossed with vegetables and pasta in a light spinach-pesto-clam broth. The cedar-planked duck breast arrives with a black pepper butter and amaretto-flamed peaches. The "East Meets West" grilled Montana angus beef tenderloin is served with onion-tomato relish and topped with blue cheese-tarragon butter.

Desserts include bananas foster, raspberry-chambord mousse crêpe and Savannah peanut pie.

(802) 453-2432 or (888) 424-2432. www.innatbaldwincreek.com. Entrées, $18.75 to $28. Dinner, Wednesday-Sunday 5:30 to 9:30. Closed first week of April and first week of November.

Dog Team Tavern, Dog Team Road, Middlebury.

Generations of starving Middlebury College students have filled their tummies here, including one of us who used to O.D. on the sticky buns when his visiting parents treated him to a meal out. Built in the early 1920s by Sir Wilfred and Lady Grenfell, the rambling, atmospheric structure was operated by the Grenfell Mission as a teahouse and outlet for handicrafts from Labrador. New ownership has maintained the tradition of the Joy family, who turned it into a restaurant in the 1940s.

You order from the traditional blackboard menu as you enter and wait for your table, either in the delightfully old-fashioned living room filled with nostalgia like a collection of old campaign buttons, or in the large and airy lounge, where chips and dips are served with drinks. Off the bar is a pleasant, two-level deck overlooking Otter Creek.

When you're called into the charming dining room with a view of the birches and the rippling stream, you eat (and eat and eat). We've been doing so here for more than 40 years, and are always amazed how they can still serve such huge amounts of food for the price, from the poor man's ham or fried chicken with fritters to the big spender's seafood combo, prime rib or boneless sirloin. The price of the entrée includes soup, an assortment of goodies from brass buckets on the spinning relish wheel that's brought to your table, salad, bread sticks, the Dog Team's famous sweet sticky buns, and a multitude of vegetables like your mother used to make, served family style. For dessert, if you can face it, there might be homemade pies, chocolate delight or a Bartlett pear with crème de menthe.

One of us feels that far too much food is served, but the other generally is up to the challenge.

(802) 388-7651 or (800) 472-7651. Entrées, $12.95 to $25.95. Dinner nightly, Monday-Saturday 5 to 9, Sunday noon to 9.

Waybury Inn, Route 125, East Middlebury.

Dinner and Sunday brunch are served in the cranberry and white Coach Room or on the enclosed side porch of the inn pictured on the Bob Newhart Show. An interesting pub menu is offered in the Pub and Club Room out back, dark and cozy as can be.

We went here for years just for the London broil with the best mushroom sauce ever, but that specialty has been missing from the recent repertoire. The extensive menu focuses instead on such entrées as the new specialty scallops (a different presentation every night), shrimp yucatan in a crispy tortilla shell, and black and

Exterior of Waybury Inn served as fictional inn portrayed on Bob Newhart show.

tan roast duck with orange-sesame sauce. Kentucky bourbon steak and rack of lamb with rosemary brown sauce are entrée fixtures.

Dinners begin, as they have for years, with a kidney-bean relish for which so many people asked for the recipe that it has been printed on a postcard. Typical appetizers are mushrooms and goat cheese in puff pastry, wild boar sausage and pecan-fried calamari with a ginger-soy sauce.

Chocolate bombe, frangelico crunch cake and crème brûlée are popular desserts.

(802) 388-4015. Entrées, $18.50 to $29.50. Pub, $8.95 to $12.50. Dinner nightly, 5 to 9. Sunday brunch, 11 to 2.

The Otter Creek Bakery, 14 College St., Middlebury.

Ben and Sarah Wood patterned their original cafe and bakery in Frog Hollow Mill on the models they know in San Francisco. Problem was that Sarah's bakery became the tail that wagged the dog and Ben closed the cafe (the space since taken over by the Storm Café) to concentrate on the growing bakery business up the street.

Here the baked goods are sensational as ever, and the Woods have garnered quite a following for their mail-order cookies and dough (chunky peanut butter, maple-oatmeal-raisin and lemon-pecan among them). Not to mention their delectable raspberry almond crunch cheesecake, praline almond tort and other sweets that defy categorization. Now they're doing a land-office takeout business with sandwiches (we liked the Otter Creek pâté and the Norwegian smoked salmon) in the $4.50 to $4.95 range. They also have soups, salads and pizzettes to go. And, of course, the requisite fancy coffees.

(802) 388-3371. Open Monday-Saturday 7 to 6 (to 8 in summer), Sunday 7 to 3.

Diversions

Middlebury College, Route 125, occupies a 1,200-acre campus on the southwest edge of Middlebury. It is notable for the consistent use of gray limestone in its buildings as well as for its summer foreign language schools. Founded in 1800, the college has evolved from the lower Old Chapel-Painter Hall row to the hillside beside Le Chateau. Now more than 2,000 undergraduates are enrolled at one of the top-ranked liberal-arts colleges in the country. Hundreds of graduate students flock to the eight Summer Language Schools and the Bread Loaf School of English, where 250 writers attend the annual Bread Loaf Writers Conference, the oldest and largest in the country (Robert Frost is remembered as "the godfather of Bread Loaf"). The college library has excellent collections in its Robert Frost Room. Middlebury's $16 million Center for the Arts is a state-of-the-art showplace for the performing arts, five galleries housing the Middlebury College Museum of Art, the college's top-flight concert series and even a café called Rehearsals.

Vermont State Craft Center/Frog Hollow, 1 Mill St., Middlebury.

Just off Main Street in the center of Middlebury, this is one of our favorite crafty places anywhere, and 150,000 visitors a year agree. With windows onto the Otter Creek falls, it's a fine showplace for sculpture and pottery. Inside the renovated mill is a 3,000-square-foot treasure trove of pottery, stained glass, pewter, quilts, pillows, wall hangings, jewelry and stuffed and wooden toys, all by Vermont artists. We managed to resist some great sculptures of dogs and bunnies ($450 to $675). We could not resist a woodcut print by artist Sabra Field, a Middlebury grad with a wonderful sense of design, and for years now her "Apple Tree Winter" with chickadee perched on a branch has been ensconced in our dining room. The nation's first state craft center has expanded to locations in Burlington and Manchester.

(802) 388-3177. www.froghollow.org. Open Monday-Saturday 9:30 to 5, also Sundays 11 to 4, spring through fall. Free.

Henry Sheldon Museum of Vermont History, 1 Park St., Middlebury

Bachelor Henry Sheldon bought the brick 1829 Judd-Harris House opposite Cannon Park and opened it as a museum in 1884, advertising it with a twenty-foot sign that read "Sheldon's Art and Archeological Museum." It was the first village museum in the country, our guide said.

The place is a find, filled with all sorts of odd but interesting items like a mousetrap that kills a rodent by drowning it in a cylinder of water, a pair of shoes worn by Calvin Coolidge as a child, newspapers from the 1800s and a collection of old dentist's tools, including a primitive ether bottle. There's even a stuffed cat – it seems that Sheldon, the town clerk, saved everything.

The highlights of one of the most exemplary museum collections in Vermont are exhibited in room settings in the elegant Federal house built by local marble merchants. Middlebury's garden clubs have created an early Victorian garden next door. Changing history and art exhibits are shown in the Cerf Gallery. The Fletcher Community History Center, a wing connecting the museum and the Stewart-Swift Research Center, replaced the old summer kitchen and woodshed.

(802) 388-2117. www.henrysheldonmuseum.org. Open Monday-Saturday 10 to 5. Adults, $4.

UVM Morgan Horse Farm, 74 Battell Drive, Weybridge.

Col. Joseph Battell of Middlebury, whose name graces three college dormitories, established this farm, just northwest of Middlebury past the covered bridge. It is now managed by the University of Vermont. The Morgan, America's first breed of horse, is Vermont's state animal. Most of the Morgan horses alive today can be traced to this site, where they are bred, trained and sold. You can tour the stables on the hour, watch a twenty-minute video show and observe the horses as they are trained. At the right time of day, you can even hear the horses neighing and see them waiting for their hay, which slides down a trough into their stalls three times a day. The lush lawns include a picnic area. The 1878 barn is on the National Register of Historic Places.

(802) 388-2011. Tours daily on the hour, 9 to 4, May-October. Adults, $4.50.

Mountain Tours. A favorite mountain loop starts in East Middlebury and follows Route 116 to Bristol, a town perched on a shelf and notable for its Lord's Prayer Rock (the prayer is chiseled on the rock along the New Haven River just east of town). Head east on Route 17 past the entry to the Lincoln Gap (itself worth a detour) onto what's locally called the McCullogh Turnpike to the top of the Appalachian Gap. Continue down the east slope past Mad River Glen and Sugarbush North ski areas to Route 100 in Waitsfield. Head south through Warren to Hancock, where you turn west on Route 125 past Texas Falls, a beautiful little series of cascades in a chasm where Middlebury students cooled off in the old days before guard rails were added and swimming was prohibited. At the top of the Hancock Gap is the Middlebury College Snow Bowl and, starting down the west slope, the Bread Loaf mountain campus with its old yellow wood dormitories and green Adirondack chairs scattered about the lawns. The Middlebury River alongside Route 125 below Ripton is another favorite cooling-off or picnicking spot in season. For a more spectacular option (in terms of mountain panoramas), head west through the Brandon Gap (Route 73) rather than Route 125.

Robert Frost Interpretive Trail, off Route 125 between Ripton and Middlebury's Breadloaf campus. "Please take your time and leave nothing but your footprints," urges the sign at the start of this easy-to-walk, three-quarter-mile trail blazed in 1976 by the U.S. Youth Conservation Corps. Several benches are strategically placed for creative contemplation. This is a thoroughly delightful way to spend an hour or two, reading some of Frost's poems mounted on plaques en route. Meadows, woods, groves of birches and streams are traversed and identified. Frost lived and worked within a mile of here; the fields and forests were the inspiration for his poems and mentioned in many. Nearby is the Robert Frost Wayside Area with picnic tables and grills in a grove of red pines that Frost pruned himself. Up a dirt road is the Homer Noble Farm, site of the log cabin where Frost spent his last 23 summers.

Lakeshore Tours. For glimpses of Lake Champlain to the north and west of Middlebury, follow the rural lakeshore road, variously called Lake Road and Lake Street from Shoreham north through Bridport, Addison and Panton to Basin Harbor. You'll be surprised to discover how undeveloped such a large lake can be. About the only commercial enterprises we encountered were the Bridge Family Restaurant near Chimney Point, the Yankee Kingdom Farm Stand and Vermont's Own Products. A couple of waterfowl areas, the D.A.R. and Button Bay state parks, and the fascinating Mount Independence State Historic Site are worthwhile stops along the way.

Shopping. The compact center of Middlebury is still a downtown, claiming a Ben Franklin variety store and a movie theater. The biggest store in town, appropriately, is the **Alpine Shop,** corner of Main and Merchants Row. Inside in a ramble of rooms on two floors you'll find summer and winter clothes, Austrian boiled wool jackets, cuddly Lanz nightgowns, boots for all reasons, jewelry, gifts and skiwear. They even have Lederhosen. The shop's predecessor was the first and biggest single customer of Geiger of Austria, a partnership that prompted the location of the Geiger factory off Route 7 on Exchange Street just north of town (it sells overstock at its **Geiger Collections** store at 38 Pond Lane).

One of our favorite bookstores anywhere is the neatly jumbled **Vermont Book Store,** whose former owner knew Robert Frost. It has one of the country's largest collections of Robert Frost works, including out-of-print collector's items. Also along Main Street you'll find funky women's clothes at **Wild Mountain Thyme**, antique jewelry and vintage apparel at **Bejewelled,** and kitchenware and housewares at **Dada. Greenfields Mercantile** is a showcase for the clothing, bags and accessories of American designers working in hemp and other sustainable and recycled fibers. **Sweet Cecily,** billed as "a country store for today," stocks great cow pottery, cow placemats and painted cabinets among its folk art and fine crafts. **Forth 'n Goal** is a sporting goods store that features the Middlebury Collection of college clothing and accessories.

Other shops are found in restored mill buildings around Frog Hollow, site of the Vermont State Craft Center. Fun gifts and accessories are among the eclectic stock at **4 Dogs & a Wish,** "a store for eccentric people and their pets." The **Otter Creek Craft Gallery** is located in the old Star Mill. **Middlebury Mountaineer** carries outdoor sporting gear and apparel. **Great Falls Collection** (up a staircase beside the Otter Creek falls) has unusual jewelry, home accessories and nature and garden items. From Frog Hollow a 276-foot pedestrian bridge across Otter Creek yields a view of the falls and connects with the **Marble Works,** a collection of businesses, offices and specialty stores in old white marble factory buildings. Local producers back up their trucks and tailgates to the parking lot for the small farmer's market (where we bought some delicious bread, corn and salsa) beside the falls on Wednesday and Saturday mornings. Here also is the showroom for **Danforth Pewterers,** where we ogled all the pewter products from thousands of buttons for $1 to dinner plates for $72. A dolphin on a corded necklace for $12 caught our eye. The new **American Flatbread Restaurant** sells gourmet pizzas to go and is open for dinner Friday and Saturday evenings. Restaurant seating is in the oven room where diners can see the fire as bakers and cooks prepare each flatbread to order.

Stop for a beer at the **Otter Creek Brewery,** 85 Exchange St., where tours are given daily at 1, 3 and 5 and you can sip free samples and browse through the brewhouse gift store. Open daily 10 to 6.

Extra-Special

Woody Jackson's Holy Cow Store, 44 Main St., Middlebury.

The cows and colors of Vermont, as depicted by local artist Woody Jackson, are on display in this whimsical shop. The Middlebury graduate's trademark cows are the motif on everything from golf balls to light switch plates, pocket knives to tablecloths. Here are many of the items available on his clever "cowtalogue" website and then some. The gift shop has relocated into the center of town from the main floor of his production facility at 52 Seymour St.

(802) 388-6739. Open Monday-Saturday 9 to 5, Sunday noon to 5. weekends to 4.

Village of Stowe nestles in valley beneath Mount Mansfield.

Stowe, Vt.

A Resort for All Seasons

When former Olympic skier Phil Mahre first saw Stowe clad in summer's green rather than winter's white, he was struck by its beauty. So were many in the Eastern Ski Writers audience he addressed that August day.

Most downhill skiers haven't been to Stowe in what for them is the off-season. But the undisputed Ski Capital of the East is a year-round destination resort, more than its newer, less endowed competitors can hope to be.

For one thing, Stowe *is* Stowe, a legendary village unto itself about eight miles from Mount Mansfield, a legendary ski area unto itself. The twain meets all along the Mountain Road, which links village and mountain. Such a marriage between town and ski area is unrivaled in New England and rich in history – a history unequaled by any other ski town in the country, according to Stowe Mountain Resort officials.

The ski resort was led for years by Sepp Ruschp, who left Austria in 1936 to be ski instructor for the fledgling Mount Mansfield Ski Club. The alpine mystique of the area was enhanced by Baroness Maria von Trapp and her family, whose story was immortalized by "The Sound of Music," when they founded the Trapp Family Lodge.

The rolling valley between broad Mount Mansfield on the west and the Worcester Mountains on the east creates an open feeling that is unusual for northern New England mountain regions. In Stowe's exhilarating air, recreation and cultural endeavors thrive.

Cross-country skiing complements downhill in winter. Other seasons bring golf, tennis, polo, horseback riding, hiking, performing arts, art exhibits and enough sights to see and things to do to make credible the area's claim to being a world-class resort.

Foremost a ski center, Stowe is somewhat lacking in inns and B&Bs of the classic New England variety. Instead, it has resorts, motels, ski dorms, condominiums and more Alpine/Bavarian chalets and lodges than you'll find just about anywhere this side of the Atlantic.

Still, Stowe is Stowe, a storybook New England ski town dominated by Vermont's highest peak. It's a place to be treasured, by skier and non-skier alike.

Inn Spots

Edson Hill Manor, 1500 Edson Hill Road, Stowe 05672.

A French Provincial-style manor with old English charm, built in 1940 as a gentleman's estate, became a country inn in 1954. It obtained a new role in life after its purchase by Eric and Jane Lande, well-traveled ex-Montrealers of the fabled Bronfman family, who had set up a thriving maple-syrup business at their Vermont farm in nearby Johnson. They lured veteran local hotelier Billy O'Neil to be their fulltime manager and later acquired Ten Acres Lodge, another of Stowe's best-known small inns. In 2000, they sold Edson Hill to Billy and Juliet O'Neil, who embarked on further enhancements.

A mile-long country lane leads from the white post gates to the manor, which a loyal following considers one of the few true country inns in the Stowe area. It retains its original private-home flavor except in the four newer carriage houses with modern accommodations.

Set high amidst 225 secluded acres, it has a spectacular terrace beside a spring-fed, kidney-shaped swimming pool, a pond stocked for trout fishing, an upgraded cross-country ski center and stables for horseback riding.

The manor was a prime location in 1980 for the filming of winter scenes for Alan Alda's movie, "The Four Seasons." The famous Mercedes scene took place on the pond.

Inside the manor are nine guest rooms, a pine-paneled parlor with oriental rugs and Delft tiles around the fireplace, a library with more books and magazines than anyone could possibly read, a refurbished downstairs lounge, plus a redecorated dining room where meals are available to the public (see Dining Spots). The beams in the large parlor are said to have come from Ethan Allen's barn. Many of the striking artworks are by Canadian artist Lillian Freeman.

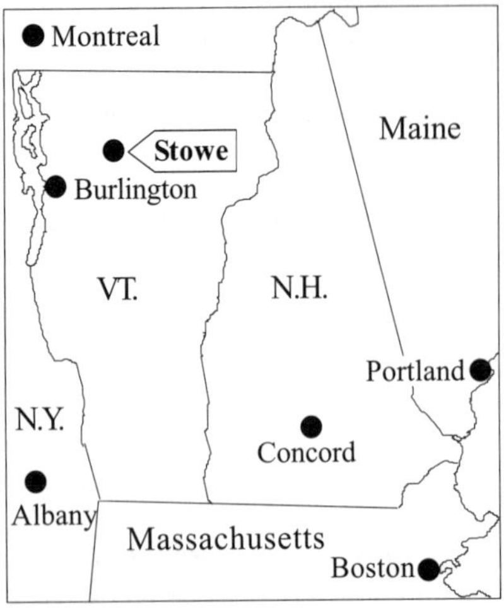

Each of four carriage houses, up a hill beyond the inn, has four spacious guest rooms done in the decor of the original manor with beamed ceilings, pine-paneled walls, brick fireplaces and private baths. Billed as the inn's luxury units with one kingsize or two queen beds, they accommodate two to four people.

All told, five rooms in the manor plus

Edson Hill Manor occupies 225-acre hillside property high above village of Stowe.

those in the carriage houses contain working fireplaces – a great attraction for winter visitors. We'd happily settle any time in the manor's large Studio, which has queensize bed, fireplace, skylight (this was formerly an artist's studio) and an exceptionally nice sitting area with picture windows overlooking the pool, pond and gardens.

Breakfasts are a treat. The buffet table contains several hot entrées – on one winter morning, scrambled eggs with spinach and goat cheese, blackberry waffles and polenta. Fresh juices, fruit platters, and homemade breads and muffins accompany.

Now as owner of the inn he had managed for nearly a decade, Billy O'Neil set out to further enhance the Edson Hill experience. He redecorated the dining room and bar area and gave a facelift to rooms in the Carriage House, upgrading decor, redoing baths and removing carpeting to expose antique pine flooring.

(802) 253-7371 or (800) 621-0284. Fax (802) 635-2694. www.stowevt.com. Twenty-five rooms and suites with private baths. Doubles, $139 to $199; $139 weekends and $99 midweek in April, May and November. Two-night minimum weekends.

Stone Hill Inn, 89 Houston Farm Road, Stowe 05672.

The young owners of this sprawling hilltop contemporary inn knew exactly what they wanted: an upscale place for couples seeking romantic getaways with all the comforts of home.

Hap and Amy Jordan, who met when he became chef at her family's restaurant in Virginia Beach, bought ten acres of woods, one of the last parcels available along Mountain Road. They proceeded to build a nine-bedroom, gray clapboard structure that looks like a house and provides the amenities of a small hotel.

Why Stowe? "We wanted a B&B – not an inn – with a lot of good restaurants nearby," said Amy. "And there was a void. No place in Stowe had what we offer. We're a small and private retreat, a destination unto ourselves."

Guest rooms at Stone Hill Inn open onto lawn and gardens.

A retreat bathed in luxuries, we should add. The Jordans were able to build what they wanted from scratch, providing central common areas and large guest quarters spaced apart on the ground floor in two wings. Rooms have extra-thick walls for privacy, individual thermostats, and windows or french doors opening to rear lawns and gardens.

Though decorated differently, guest rooms are basically identical. "We built the inn around the bathrooms," said Hap. Each has a large, see-through gas fireplace open to bedroom and bath, a gleaming space with a whirlpool tub for two, candles, thick terry bath sheets, double vanities and separate shower.

In terms of decor, Amy said, "we started with the fabrics and the rooms just evolved." The Cotton Brook is "regal and elegant" in beiges and earth tones and a black iron fabric-canopy bed, while the neighboring White Birch is colorful in cranberry and country florals. Each room has a kingsize bed with a small stuffed moose at rest on top of the down comforter, plush seating and a TV/VCR.

The open common room has a massive stone fireplace in the center, separating a game room with a billiards table on one side from a sumptuous sitting area on the other. Tall windows look out onto showy gardens, stone walls and a man-made waterfall. A large reading room offers another fireplace.

The Jordans welcome guests with substantial hors d'oeuvres – perhaps shrimp rémoulade or pan-seared duck with port wine demi-glace. These are put out in a round-the-clock guest pantry with a microwave and a refrigerator stocked with complimentary soft drinks, snacks and fruit.

An elaborate breakfast is provided at nine tables for two in a sunny, high-ceilinged breakfast wing with windows on three sides and an improbably high shelf holding country collectibles overhead. Hap cooks and Amy serves, with fresh fruit and baked goods to start. There's a choice of three entrées. The day of our visit it involved eggs any style (the apple and brie omelet was especially recommended), gingerbread pancakes, and Canadian bacon and leek quiche.

The property includes an outdoor hot tub, hammocks and wooded walking trails meandering down to a pond.

(802) 253-6282. Fax (802) 253-7415. www.stonehillinn.com. Nine rooms with private baths. Doubles, $295 to $325, $350 to $375 foliage and Christmas, $250 to $295 spring and fall. Two-night minimum weekends and foliage. Closed in April and three weeks in late November.

Green Mountain Inn, 18 Main St., Box 60, Stowe 05672.

Its deep red facade a National Historic Register landmark in the center of the village since 1833, Stowe's oldest inn has been carefully upgraded and expanded in recent years by Marvin Gameroff and sons Simon and David, formerly of Montreal.

The complex includes the formal **Main Street Dining Room** for breakfast and the legendary **Whip Bar & Grill** downstairs (see Dining Spots). The latter is where the action is, in the cozy bar as well as in the cafeteria-style grill and on the outdoor deck by the pool, which is heated for use year-round. A couple of small parlors in front convey the New England inn charm.

The inn now totals 100 guest accommodations in a patchwork of buildings that culminate in the luxurious new Mansfield House. Forty rooms and three jacuzzi suites are in the rambling main inn, which has been updated, albeit with an antique look. The modern baths, color TVs and phones are combined with twin or queensize canopy beds, floral quilts, custom-designed reproduction furniture manufactured specially for the inn, period wallpapers and stenciling. Fifteen rooms are in the three-story Annex, a former motel building behind the inn; many have balconies overlooking the outdoor pool, brook and gardens. The clubhouse/health center includes eight fireplace rooms and two suites, all with queen canopy beds, fireplaces and jacuzzis. The suites add a kitchen, living room and dining area.

Recent additions include eight luxury rooms in the new Mill House, adjacent to the clubhouse building on the site of a former lumber mill. Each has a queen canopy bed, fireplace, sitting area, VCR and a large bathroom with oversize jacuzzi opening into the bedroom.

The Mansfield House, opened in 2000 behind the inn, offers the 22 most luxurious accommodations. Among them are twelve suites and two "grand rooms" with down-duvet-covered king or queen canopy beds, handsome living rooms with marble fireplaces, fireside double jacuzzis, marble bathrooms, mini-bars and coffeemakers, DVD/CD players and surround-sound stereo, handcrafted furnishings and original artworks. Guests here enjoy afternoon tea and cookies in the living room and a "petite breakfast" delivered with the morning newspaper to bedroom or living room.

In 2002, the inn opened the first of several Depot Street townhouses, fully equipped suites of two or three bedrooms.

The health center in the clubhouse offers a spa program. An enclosed walkway connects the main inn to the Depot Building shopping complex next door.

(802) 253-7301 or (800) 253-7302. Fax (802) 253-5096. www.greenmountaininn.com. Eighty-one rooms and 24 suites with private baths. Rates, EP. Summer and winter: doubles $125 to $255, suites $215 to $405. Foliage: doubles $165 to $275, suites $295 to $325. Rest of year: doubles $125 to $195, suites $245 to $285. Children and pets welcome.

Stowehof Inn, 434 Edson Hill Road, Box 1139, Stowe 05672.

"Slow – Deer Crossing," warns the sign as you drive up the steep road to the Stowehof, whose soaring Alpine exterior is a hilltop landmark hereabouts. "No

Tree trunks support porte cochere at entrance of Stowehof Inn.

parking – sleigh only," reads the sign at the door. Such touches reflect the character of this unusual, thoroughly charming place that grew from a private ski house into one of Stowe's larger inns.

At the front entrance, the trunks of two maple trees support the enormous porte cochere above the small purple door. More tree trunks are inside the huge living room, nicely broken up into intimate nooks and crannies, the two-level dining room, the downstairs game room and the Tyrolean Tap Room. The bell tower, the sod roof laced with field flowers and the architecture are reminiscent of the Tyrolean Alps. The upstairs library and game room is a replica of the interior of an old Vermont covered bridge. Little white lights twinkle all around.

Owners Chris and Susan Grimes offer 46 guest rooms, some of them unusually large and sumptuous. They totally refurbished the inn, adding antiques and replacing dated furniture and equipment – a total of 30 dumpsters' worth in four months, according to Chris.

All rooms have balconies or patios with views in summer of lovely clumps of birches, a swimming pool, a trout pond, lawns and the mountains. Terrycloth robes, duvet covers and Godiva chocolates are among the amenities.

The Grimeses opened an indoor pool called Poolhof, a sauna and a workout room, and added massage therapy and concierge services.

The well-appointed **Emily's** dining room comes with beamed ceiling, fireplaces and windows looking onto outdoor pool and mountains. There's also dining in summer on the terrace. The regional American dinner menu changes several times weekly. The traditional specialties of wiener schnitzel and beef wellington have been augmented by the likes of pan-seared diver scallops, grilled bison sirloin and steak diane. Lighter fare is available in the **Coslin's Pub,** which opens onto the poolside patio and hot tub.

Locals advise going to Stowehof just to see it or to take the romantic sleigh ride for two. We think it's an equally appealing place in which to stay.

(802) 253-9722 or (800) 932-7136. Fax (802) 253-7513. www.stowehofinn.com. Forty-six rooms with private baths. Rates, B&B. Summer and winter: doubles $113 to $248. Foliage: $150 to $305. Spring and late fall: $83 to $180.

Entrées, $22 to $30. Dinner nightly, 6 to 9:30, Tap Room from 4.

Ye Olde England Inn, 433 Mountain Road, Stowe 05672.

Stowe seems an unlikely spot for an English coaching inn, but this restored and expanded inn is British all the way from the bright red phone booth out front to the menu in the pub and the "Anglo" and "Saxon" on the license plates of the owners' cars.

Transplanted Brits Chris and Lyn Francis, skiers both, are more in evidence at their inn than are many innkeepers in the area. Chris and two friends formed the Stowe Polo Club and have gotten the community involved. He also spearheaded Stowe's annual British Invasion in mid-September, a four-day celebration of classic cars and "all manner of other things British."

All seventeen of the inn's original guest rooms have private baths and seven have jacuzzis. They are spacious, decorated in Laura Ashley style, contain Gilchrist & Soames amenities and, on the third floor, are notable for interesting shapes and views of the mountains. Three luxury two-bedroom English "cottages" in a building out back beside the swimming pool each contain a fireplace, jacuzzi, cable TV, lounge-dining area and kitchen facilities. The newest are ten "super-luxurious suites" in the Bluff House, perched atop a granite bluff with spectacular views of the Worcester Mountain range. Each has a queensize four-poster in the bedroom, a bath with jacuzzi and separate shower, a private deck and a "lounge" with fireplace, sofabed, wet bar, refrigerator and microwave.

English-style tea is offered in the afternoon. An English breakfast is served in the beamed Copperfields dining room in season.

Dinner is served and a pub-type menu is available all day in **Mr. Pickwick's Pub & Restaurant** with a hearthstone fireplace or on canopied decks, lined with umbrellas advertising British ale and presenting a scene straight from the English countryside. The extensive menu offers quite a range from bangers and mash and braised rabbit to breast of pheasant and beef Wellington. The mixed grill here teams buffalo medallions, poussin and venison sausage. A six-course tasting menu is available on weekends.

We enjoyed a lunch of spinach salad in a tostada shell and a good steak and kidney pie served inexplicably with a side bowl of gravy (could it have been for dipping the french fries in?), all washed down with pints of Whitbread and Watneys ales, presented in proper pub glasses. The list of more than 150 foreign beers and ales is extraordinary, and one can even get ale by the yard. In the evening, live entertainment is enjoyed by the laid-back crowd.

(802) 253-7558 or (800) 477-3771. Fax (802) 253-8944. www.englandinn.com. Seventeen rooms, ten suites and three cottages, all with private baths. Rates, B&B. Doubles, $129 to $199; cottages, $219 to $309; suites, $159 to $325. Foliage: doubles, $199 to $209; cottages, $289 to $299; suites, $229 to $365. Two-night minimum weekends.

Entrées, $17.95 to $25.95. Lunch daily, 11:30 to 4. Dinner, 4 to 10.

Trapp Family Lodge, 700 Trapp Hill Road, Box 1428, Stowe 05672.

The Trapp family whose saga inspired "The Sound of Music" bought this sprawling property overlooking the Worcester Mountain Range four years after fleeing the Nazi takeover of Austria. They started taking in guests in a rustic 27-

room lodge in 1950. After the original was destroyed in a disastrous fire, an exotic 93-room resort opened in 1983, replicating some of the original's charm in a Disneyesque kind of way.

Now it's an expanding, 2,700-acre resort with panoramic mountain views, a major cross-country ski center and a multitude of family activities, all overseen by Johannes von Trapp, who lives nearby.

Hand-carved balustrades, steeply pitched gables and a cedar shake roof with an Austrian bell tower accent the Tyrolean architecture of the main lodge, where guest rooms come with kingsize or two queen beds. They are appointed with European-style furnishings, telephones and TVs, and most have flower-bedecked balconies or patios for taking in the views. A favorite accommodation is the kingsize von Trapp Suite, once the residence of the Baroness.

A lodge addition in 2000 produced 23 luxury rooms, including nine junior suites with whirlpool tubs and three executive suites with fireplaces, double whirlpool tubs and wet bars. The Berg Haus, located just below the lodge, contains twenty motel-style rooms.

The first of 100 planned time-share villas opened in 2003.

Modern European cuisine is served to the accompaniment of live harp music in the lodge's dining room, where dinner is prix-fixe in three or five courses ($36 or $42). Casual fare is available in the lounge. All is overseen – and said to be improved – by new executive chef Juergen Spagolla from Austria. For a more traditional alpine lunch experience, tourists in particular are attracted to the famed Austrian Tea Room (see Dining Spots) across the road.

(802) 253-8511 or (800) 826-7000. www.trappfamily.com. One hundred seven rooms and nine suites with private baths. Rates, EP. Doubles $260 to $305, suites $340 to $600. Holiday periods, doubles $374 to $530, suites $474 to $960.

Dinner nightly, 5:30 to 9. Prix-fixe, $36 to $42.

The Gables Inn, 1457 Mountain Road, Stowe 05672.

What many consider to be the best breakfast in town is served at the Gables, either under yellow umbrellas on the front lawn (facing a spectacular view of Mount Mansfield), on the front porch or on tables inside. Owners Annette Monachelli and Randy Stern are keeping up a tradition of fine food and lodging that has been The Gables' trademark for the past 25 years.

Twelve guest rooms in the main inn and four in a renovated carriage house sport country furniture, antiques and homemade wreaths. All have private baths, most gleaming white and modern. The inn's prized Gables Suite offers a lace-canopy queensize bed, fireplace, sofa, TV and a double jacuzzi in a corner of the room.

Much in demand are four spacious rooms in the air-conditioned Carriage House, which shows no trace of its motel-annex heritage. These come with cathedral ceilings, wood-burning fireplaces, whirlpool jets in the bathtubs, queensize beds and television, and more room than we could possibly put to use between a swim in the pool, reading on the lawn and a sensational breakfast the next morning. The occupants before us on a cool summer night had obviously used the fireplace; the inn goes through at least ten cords of wood a year.

Top of the line are two Riverview Suites converted from a neighboring homestead. Each has a kingsize bed made of cedar fence posts with a split-rail fence for a headboard, a dual wood-burning fireplace shared by bedroom and living room, a convenience center with refrigerator and microwave, and a double jacuzzi tub. The

Breakfast on the lawn is a summer tradition at The Gables Inn.

upstairs suite with cathedral ceiling has a balcony off the bedroom and a deck off the living room. The wraparound porch off the main-floor suite faces the inn's pool area.

A swimming pool and hot tub, and a large, comfortably furnished den and living room with TV are other attractions in this homey place. In winter the downstairs den becomes a cozy après-ski bar with a selection of beers and wines. Complimentary hot hors d'oeuvres accompany the beverages.

As for that breakfast, it's open to the public, and some days the kitchen serves as many as 300. Aside from all the old standbys, one can feast on eggs benedict, kippers or chicken livers with onions and scrambled eggs, matzoh brei, or "Two on a Raft," poached eggs on an English muffin garnished with tomato and herbs served beneath a blanket of molten Vermont cheddar.

In the summer a chef grills chicken and burgers on the front lawn for a garden barbecue lunch – a popular break for strollers and cyclists on the Stowe Recreation Path across the street.

(802) 253-7730 or (800) 422-5371. Fax (802) 253-8989. www.gablesinn.com. Fifteen rooms and three suites with private baths. Summer and winter: doubles $83 to $190, suites $158 to $235. Foliage: doubles $110 to $190, suites $225 to $235. Spring and fall: doubles $78 to $115, suites $150 to $165.

Breakfast daily, 8 to 10:30, weekends to 12:30. Lunch in summer, noon to 2.

Brass Lantern Inn, 717 Maple St. (Route 100), Stowe 05672.

This 1800 farmhouse and carriage barn that housed the old Charda restaurant was in sad shape when it was acquired in 1988 by Andy Aldrich, a home builder. "I could look at the property and see the potential," he said. Doing most of the work himself and with his son Dustin, he undertook a total restoration, "doing all the things people think about doing when they're upgrading."

The result is a comfortable, air-conditioned B&B with a pleasant mix of old and new and an award from the Vermont Builders Association for restoration. The walls are stenciled and baskets hang from the beamed ceiling in the dining room. Modern baths, six with whirlpool tubs, adjoin the nine soundproofed bedrooms. Six have fireplaces and queensize beds. Each has stenciled walls, wide-planked floors, exposed beams, brass or canopy beds with handmade quilts, and two wing chairs. The honeymoon room has a heart-shaped headboard and footboard on the queensize iron bed and a couple of "frolic pillows" on the floor near the fireplace.

Guests gather around the fireplace in the spiffy, L-shaped living room or on a back porch and gravel terrace overlooking the mountains. A native Vermonter who grew up on a dairy farm, Andy features Vermont Fresh Network products on his breakfast menu, which changes daily. The guest book is full of raves about the apple crêpes and the waffles with rhubarb and strawberry sauce, and his breakfasts won three consecutive awards annually from the Gourmet Dining Society of North America. Sourdough french toast was the entrée at our visit. Broccoli-mushroom quiche, vegetable omelets, blueberry pancakes or scrambled eggs with Cabot cheese and bacon are other possibilities. Tea and baked goods are offered in the afternoon.

Andy's hospitality and commitment to the industry earned him the title of Vermont B&B Innkeeper of the Year in 2001, as voted by his peers in the Vermont Restaurant and Lodging Association.

(802) 253-2229 or (800) 729-2980. Fax (802) 253-7425. www.brasslanterinn.com. Nine rooms with private baths. Doubles, $90 to $175, foliage and Christmas week $110 to $225.

Dining Spots

Blue Moon Café, 35 School St., Stowe.

Well-known local chef Jack Pickett, who first made his name at Ten Acres Lodge, established his own fine restaurant along a side street in Stowe. It's amazingly small, a main room with a dining bar and five tables plus two enclosed front porches, each with three tables for two. A side patio nearly doubles the size in summer – one record night the café served 95 dinners.

Jack sold lately to his longtime manager, Jim Barton and his wife Donna, but continued in the kitchen, which continues to offer exciting food in a simple bistro atmosphere. The meal could begin with creamy carrot-ginger soup with cilantro, tequila-cured salmon with blue corn cake, chipotle-mango crème fraîche and tomatillo sauce, venison carpaccio, or a winter salad of grilled sweet potatoes, frisée, clementines and pecans.

For the main course, how about grilled yellowfin tuna with tomatillo salsa fresca and smoked yellow pepper coulis, banana leaf-steamed halibut with Thai coconut curry, basil-infused rock cornish game hen, sweet and sour braised local rabbit, and grilled New York strip steak with cognac cream?

Among desserts are an acclaimed crème brûlée, white chocolate mousse with caramelized banana, and a chocolate terrine with crème anglaise.

(802) 253-7006. www.bluemoonstowe.com. Entrées, $18.50 to $26. Dinner nightly, 6 to 9:30.

The Old Vienna Tea Room & Restaurant, 2038 Mountain Road, Stowe.

What a delectable anomaly is this! Occupying a portion of a restored farmhouse turned into a chic European clothing and furniture store, it started in 2000 with breakfast service, then added lunch. Now it serves lunch, afternoon tea and dinner daily – to a small but growing clientele that consider it among the top dining experiences in Stowe.

Refined continental cuisine with an emphasis on Austrian specialties is offered by idiosyncratic owner André Noel, who oversees and staffs the small restaurant at the side of his wife Romy's fashionable store, Romy's Alpenhaus. He's the chief server and head honcho, which allows him to open and close the very personal establishment somewhat at whim.

The food is prepared by young chef Roland Schupfer, also from Austria. His is a changing panoply of Austrian and domestic treats: one night a couple of exceptional wiener schnitzel dishes, chicken cordon bleu, Viennese veal goulash with homemade spaetzle, pan-seared arctic char with tarragon crème fraîche, roasted trout with citrus beurre blanc and rack of lamb with roasted garlic-mustard sauce.

You might start with one of the Austrian soups, roasted rabbit loin with lentils and cherry tomatoes over mesclun greens or the signature potato blinis topped with sour cream and sturgeon and salmon caviars. Finish with a trio of ice creams or a selection of Viennese cakes and pastries from the pastry shop.

Dining is by candlelight at cushioned curved banquettes in the open main room behind the pastry shop and in more intimate alcoves in a side room. The stone well that furnished water for the original farmhouse is a focal point of the main room. A small bar occupies a portion of the clothing shop.

(802) 253-9500. Entrées, $18.50 to $28.50. Lunch, 11:30 to 3. Tea, 3 to 5. Dinner nightly by reservation, 6 to 9.

Michael's On the Hill, 4182 Route 100 North, Waterbury Center.

The old Villa Tragara, long a favorite of Stowe area diners, gave way in 2002 to this highly acclaimed establishment. Swiss chef-owner Michael Kloeti, a veteran of New York restaurants and the Three Clock Inn in South Londonderry, took over the 1820 farmhouse and wowed the locals with his innovative European cuisine. Michael is happiest in the kitchen, turning over front-of-the-house duties to his wife Laura, a Culinary Institute of America-schooled chef and manager.

The couple seat 80 diners in the enclosed wraparound porch, where every table gets a view of the mountains and countryside, and in a renovated barn room. A pianist entertains on weekends in the lounge.

Expect such entrées as roasted monkfish with shellfish stew and lemon-mascarpone risotto, roasted pork loin with pancetta, roasted veal chop with chanterelles and roasted garlic, and herb-crusted rack of lamb. Typical starters are grilled shrimp with a beet and pear salad with kaffir-lime vinaigrette, Maine crab salad with avocado, and seared foie gras with cherries and homemade brioche.

Laura's love for cooking is reflected in the desserts, perhaps chocolate truffle torte with passionfruit sauce, pecan tart with bourbon-vanilla sauce and maple crème brûlée.

(802) 244-7476. www.michaelsonthehill.com. Entrées, $15.95 to $29.95. Dinner nightly except Tuesday, 5:30 to 9. Sunday brunch, 10 to 1:30.

Mes Amis Restaurant-Bistrot, 311 Mountain Road, Stowe.

A classically trained French chef presents affordable French and continental fare at this restaurant in a converted house perched on a hilltop. Chef-owner Carole Fisher, a Californian who grew up in Montreal, worked with chef-owner Jean Lavina at the late, great Isle de France up the road before opening her own restaurant. She and her husband Peter offer a short menu that would be at home in Provence.

They seat 55 diners in several rooms, one lit by twined lights overhead and another with a display of antique glass on high shelves. There are a timbered pub, and a patio for outdoor dining in season.

Look for starters like a classic onion soup au gratin, oysters bourguignonne, baked stuffed clams angelique, escargots en phyllo and polenta provençale with a white wine-tomato-garlic sauce. Typical entrées are sweet potato-crusted salmon with a maple-balsamic glaze, panko-crusted swordfish with the house peppercorn-brandy cream sauce, roasted duck with a "Lavina hot and sweet sauce," chicken marsala, beef stroganoff and filet mignon. Dessert could be profiteroles, meringue glacée, chocolate-amaretto mousse or bananas royale flambé.

The establishment does not take reservations, so expect a wait at peak periods.

(802) 253-8669. Entrées, $16.95 to $21.95. Dinner, Tuesday-Sunday 5:30 to 10.

Edson Hill Manor, 1500 Edson Hill Road, Stowe.

New owners Billy and Juliet O'Neil continue the fine-dining tradition at this hilltop French Provincial-style manor with old English charm. The inn's pleasant dining room, a destination for the public, and the walkout lounge area have been redecorated with a more traditional, Victorian feeling.

Their chef presents regional American cuisine with international accents. The dinner menu might start with house-cured gravlax with a brie turnover and vodka rémoulade, cajun paella, Thai steamed mussels or an intriguing dish called smoked duck french toast, with truffled mascarpone and thyme gravy. Among main courses are seared rare tuna loin with panang-mussel sauce and nishaki rice, pan-broiled duck breast with a sour cherry-sake reduction and filet mignon with roasted onion sauce and grilled tomato salsa.

Desserts could be sour cream apple pie with coconut-raisin sauce, sweet port crème brûlée with ginger-blueberry sauce or pumpkin-chocolate bread pudding with cinnamon crème anglaise.

(802) 253-7371 or (800) 621-0284. Entrées, $17.50 to $23.50. Dinner nightly, 6 to 9.

The Whip Bar & Grill, Green Mountain Inn, Main Street, Stowe.

The Whip is the casual and creative culinary focal point of the Green Mountain Inn. Downstairs, it's smartly decorated and striking for the antique buggy whips in the wall divider separating bar from dining room and over the fireplace. Just outside is a most attractive deck, where the garden furniture is navy and white and tables are shaded by white umbrellas.

The day's specials are chalked on blackboards above cases where the food is displayed. Some of the dishes are calorie-counted for those who are there for the inn's spa facilities. Country pâté with cornichons on toast points, smoked salmon with capers, Mexican vegetable soup, salads with dressings devised by the Canyon Ranch in Arizona, crabmeat on a croissant with melted cheddar, open-face veggie melt (184 calories) – this is perfect grazing fare.

At lunchtime, you might find a smoked turkey sandwich with cranberry mayo, black pepper fettuccine alfredo, lobster ravioli on greens with mint vinaigrette or a flatbread pizza. Or try an overstuffed sandwich on thick slices of homemade oatmeal-honey bread, a trademark as well known as the Whip's riding paraphernalia.

Main dishes like coconut-crusted red snapper with pineapple salsa, cilantro-seared tilapia fillet with mango relish, roast Quebec duckling with blackberry gastrique, maple-marinated pork chops and roasted pheasant with lingonberries are posted starting at 6 at night.

Coffee-almond crunch tart, raspberry bash, lemon cream carrot cake and a sac de bon bon for two are some of the ever-changing desserts.

(802) 253-7301. www.thewhip.com. Entrées, $14.50 to $21.95. Lunch daily, 11:30 to 5:30. Dinner, 5:30 to 9:30 or 10.

The Shed, Mountain Road, Stowe.

An institution among skiers for years, the Shed has grown from its original shed to include a wraparound solarium filled with Caribbean-style furnishings, trees and plants, plus a menu offering something for everyone. Following a disastrous 1994 fire, owners Ken and Kathy Strong rebuilt it bigger and better than ever, and added a microbrewery and pub featuring European-style ales brewed on the premises.

Rebuilt to look old, the expansive main dining room has bright red walls, a beamed ceiling, a stone fireplace in the center and green woven mats on wood tables flanked by high-back chairs. Also popular is the outdoor deck brightened by planters full of petunias in summer.

The food is with-it, from nachos to bruschetta to onion blossoms to chalupa taco salad to Asian stir-fry noodles. You can get shrimp mediterraneo, herb-crusted tuna with roasted fennel cream sauce, chicken marsala, hoisin pork tenderloin, filet mignon, prime rib and goodness knows what else from the extensive menu.

Desserts run to cheesecake, apple pie and brownie à la mode.

The omelet and belgian waffle buffet had people lined up outside for Sunday brunch on the holiday weekend we tried to get in. Sundays at the Shed now feature eggs benedict for $9.95.

(802) 253-4364. Entrées, $14.95 to $18.95. Lunch daily, 11:30 to 4:30. Dinner, 5 to 10, late menu to midnight. Sunday brunch, 10 to 2.

Olives Bistro, 1056 Mountain Road, Stowe.

Creative Mediterranean cuisine is featured in this bistro, the latest incarnation of a series of restaurants in the Stowe Center Shops. Hand-painted murals impart the look of a walled, wisteria-laden courtyard in the mountains of Italy, and there's a flower-bedecked patio for dining in summer.

Chef-owner Jeff Brynn from Shelburne and his wife Charlotte from New Zealand moved here after running a pastry shop Down Under. The restaurant had been known for its Mediterranean flavor, including such dishes as Greek lasagna, shrimp Mediterranée and chicken Portuguese. Jeff, who trained at the New England Culinary Institute, kept those on the menu and added his own dishes, among them a dynamite whisky steak with whisky demi-glace, pan-seared pork tenderloin with an artichoke-tomato-red wine sauce, and arctic char. Sangria mussels, Maine crab cakes with dill-dijon mustard and baked mussels over mesclun greens are typical appetizers. For dessert, look for espresso cheesecake, apple crisp and banana chocolate torte.

(802) 253-2033. Entrées, $14.95 to $18.50. Dinner nightly from 5.

Restaurant Swisspot, 128 Main St., Stowe.

Skiers have always been partial to fondues. They're the specialty at this small and enduring place, brought to Stowe in 1968 after its incarnation as the restaurant in the Swiss Pavilion at Expo 67 in Montreal.

The menu doesn't change much, nor do the prices. The classic Swiss cheese fondue with a dash of kirsch, $24.95 for two, made a fun meal for our skiing family. Also good is the beef fondue oriental, served with four sauces. There are eight made-to-order quiches and a dozen entrées like bratwurst, chicken and dumplings, wiener schnitzel and sirloin steak.

The dessert accent is on Swiss chocolate, including a chocolate fondue with marshmallows and fruits for dunking.

(802) 253-4622. Entrées, $11.95 to $16.95. Lunch on weekends and holidays from 11:30. Dinner nightly, 5 to 10. Closed spring and late fall.

Austrian Tea Room, Trapp Family Lodge, Luce Hill Road, Stowe.

In summer or foliage season, we know of no more charming place for lunch or a snack than the rear deck of the Austrian Tea Room, with planters of geraniums and petunias enhancing the view across the countryside and horses grazing nearby. Surely you can feel the spirit of the late Maria von Trapp (who lived at the lodge until her death in 1987) and the Trapp Family Singers. It's a majestic setting where you feel on top of the world.

The broccoli, ham and swiss quiche and the grilled shrimp caesar salad looked great, as did the curried chicken and rice salad in a pineapple shell. We opted for a bratwurst with German potato salad and sauerkraut (the latter two surprisingly mild – better for tourist tastes?) and the cold pineapple-walnut soup with a smoked salmon plate. There are open-face sandwiches, entrées like Hungarian beef goulash with noodles, fancy drinks, cafe Viennoise and Austrian wines by the glass or liter.

Those Austrian desserts we all know and love – sacher torte, linzer torte, apfelstrudel and the like – are in the $4 range. With a cup of cafe mocha, they make a delightful afternoon pick-me-up.

(802) 253-8511. Entrées, $5.50 to $10.50. Open daily in summer and foliage, 10:30 to 5:30. Dinner, Friday and Saturday 6 to 8 in July and August.

Diversions

Mount Mansfield. Skiing is what made Stowe famous, legions of skiers having been attracted to New England's most storied mountain since the East's first chairlift was installed in 1940. Today, Mount Mansfield has sleek eight-passenger gondola cars among its eight lifts and vastly expanded snowmaking. Nearly one-third of its slopes are for expert skiers, including the awesome "Front Four" – the precipitous National, Goat, Starr and Liftline trails, so steep that on the Starr you cannot see the bottom from the ledge on top. They almost make the fabled Nosedive seem tame. There's easier terrain, including the 3.7-mile-long Toll Road, and the related Spruce Peak area across the way is an entire mountain with gentle trails, a sunny southeast exposure and a special section for new skiers. Combined with accommodations and nightlife, the total skiing experience ranks Stowe among the top ski resorts in the world. And it's getting even better. Stowe Mountain Resort's ten-year expansion plan through 2010 calls for more lifts and snowmaking, a 35-acre ski village at the base of Spruce Peak, a 200-room slopeside hotel, 335 condos, a 60-unit private lodging facility and an eighteen-hole golf course.

Summer at Mount Mansfield. The **Stowe Gondola** takes visitors 7,700 feet up to the Cliff House, just below Vermont's highest summit (adults $9, Memorial Day to late October). Cars can drive up the 4.5-mile **Stowe Auto Road,** known to skiers who ease down it in winter as the Toll Road (cars $15, daily late May to mid-October). The **Alpine Slide at Spruce Peak** appeals especially to children; you take a chairlift up and slide down (single rides, $9; daily in summer, weekends in spring and fall).

Horse-drawn sleigh carries passengers across snow-covered fields at Stowe.

Smugglers' Notch. Up the Mountain Road past the ski area you enter the Mount Mansfield State Park, passing picnic areas and the Long Trail. A couple of hairpin turns take you into Smugglers' Notch, a narrow pass with rock outcroppings jutting into the road in places and 1,000-foot cliffs looming on either side. It's a quiet, awe-inspiring place to pause and gawk at such rock formations as Elephant Head, King Rock and the Hunter and His Dog. Stop at Smugglers' Cave and, farther on, hike into Bingham Falls. The road is not for the faint-hearted (it's closed in winter, for good reason). We drove back from Jeffersonville after a summer thunderstorm and found waterfalls that had been trickles on the way over suddenly gushing down the rocks beside the lonely road.

The fledgling **Vermont Ski Museum** at 1 South Main St. in the restored 1813 Old Town Hall in the center of Stowe traces the evolution of skiing, ski facilities and ski equipment in Vermont. You will see the lifts that took the first skiers up Vermont mountains and the skis that brought them down. You'll learn how the ski resorts developed and discover the more than 85 Vermont ski areas that disappeared along the way. Open daily except Tuesday, 10 to 6; donation.

The Arts. The hills are alive with the sound of music as the Stowe Performing Arts series offers Sunday evening concerts in summer in the concert meadow near the Trapp Family Lodge. The Vermont Mozart Festival also presents concerts there. More concerts are staged at the Stowe Mountain Performing Arts Center, a 12,000-seat amphitheater at the base of Spruce Peak. The **Stowe Theatre Guild** presents its summer season at the Town Hall Theater. The **Helen Day Art Center** hosts rotating exhibits in a restored 1863 Greek Revival structure that once was the high school on School Street.

The **Stowe Recreation Path** is the pride of the community. Opened in 1984 with an extension in 1989, the much-used, nationally recognized 5.3-mile walking and biking greenway starts in the village behind the Community Church and roughly parallels the Mountain Road up to Brook Road. It meanders through meadows and glades, criss-crossing the West Branch River eleven times over wooden bridges..

The **Cold Hollow Cider Mill,** south of town along Route 100, consists of a pair of large and intriguing red barns where you can watch cider being made (and drink the delicious free samples). For more than 25 years the Chittenden family also have sold tart cider jelly, cider donuts and other apple products as well as cookbooks, wooden toys, gourmet foods and every kind of Vermont jam or preserve imaginable.

Nearby, all kinds of cheeses and dips may be sampled (and purchased) at the large **Cabot Annex Store.** Also part of the complex are branches of Burlington's **Lake Champlain Chocolates,** which caters to Stowe's sweet tooth, **Vermont Teddy Bear Company** and **Snow Farm Vineyard.**

Shopping. Shops and galleries are concentrated along Main Street in Stowe and scattered in ever-increasing numbers along Route 100 South and the Mountain Road. Along Main Street in the village, **Shaw's General Store** considers itself 108 years young and carries almost everything, especially sporting goods, sportswear, gifts and oddities. Nearby are the **Old Depot Shops,** an open, meandering mall of a place containing **Vermont Furniture Works, Stowe Mercantile** and **Bear Pond Books.** Tread the creaky floorboards of **Val's Country Store** for T-shirts, maple syrup, candy and such. **Gracie's Gourmutt Sho**p features dog-emblazoned clothes and gifts as well as specialty foods from Gracie's restaurant.

Up the Mountain Road at the Straw Corner Shops are the **Stowe Craft Gallery** and the **Stowe Coffee House.** Farther along at 108 West are **Stowe Kitchen, Bath & Linens,** with everything for the home. The gourmet-to-go **Harvest Market** is the place for specialty foods, wine and espresso. **Wendy's Closet** at the Gale Farm Center carries women's clothing and accessories. Local artists are among those showing at the **Robert Paul Galleries** in the Baggy Knees Shopping Center. At the Red Barn Shops, **Mountain Cheese and Wine** carries an impressive selection, **Samara** features works of Vermont craftsmen and **The Yellow Turtle** offers "classy clothes for classy kids," the kind that well-heeled grandparents like to buy.

Extra-Special

Ben & Jerry's Ice Cream Factory, Route 100, Waterbury.

Just south of Stowe, this factory producing 130,000 pints daily of the ice cream that transplanted Vermont characters Ben Cohen and Jerry Greenfield made famous is one of Vermont's busiest tourist attractions. And with good reason. During half-hour guided tours, you see a humorous multimedia show, watch the ice cream being made, learn some of the history of this intriguing outfit that donates one percent of its profits to peace and, of course, savor a tiny sample, obtained by lowering a bucket on a rope to the production area below. At busy times, the place is a madhouse – with live music outside, lineups of people waiting to buy cones, a gift shop filled with Vermont cow-related items, and every bit of publicity Ben and Jerry ever got decorating the walls. If you can't get inside, at least buy a dish or cone of ice cream from the outdoor windows.

(802) 244-8687 or (866) 258-6877. Tours daily 9 to 8 in summer, to 6 in fall, 10 to 5 rest of year. Adults $2, under 12 free.

Skiers enjoy fresh powder conditions on a sunny day at Sugarbush.

Waitsfield and Warren, Vt.

The Spirit of the Valley

More than most Vermont areas known for skiing, the Mad River Valley is a year-round paradise for sports enthusiasts.

The focus, of course, is on skiing – at the venerable and spartan Mad River Glen, a challenging area for hardy, serious skiers, and at Sugarbush, the tony resort spawned by and for jet setters. Both are very much "in" with skiers, for vastly differing reasons.

In the off-season, which extends from May into November, there are the conventional athletic pursuits associated with other destination ski resorts, such as golf and tennis. There also are the more unusual: mountaineering, polo, rugby, cricket, Icelandic horse trekking and soaring.

Off-mountain, activity centers along Vermont Route 100, which links the villages of Waitsfield and Warren. Curiously, Waitsfield (the home of Mad River Glen) is busier and more hip in the Sugarbush style. Warren (the address for Sugarbush) is in the Mad River Glen tradition, remote and seemingly bypassed by the times.

The skiing spirit extends to the entrepreneurial. An uncommon number of craft ventures thrive here, as do unusual businesses. An unassuming enterprise that ships frozen pizzas to connoisseurs around the East has turned Waitsfield into the pizza capital of northern New England.

The spirit of the valley – considered unique by its adherents – emerges from its rugged terrain as well as from the contrasting mix attracted by its two skiing faces.

Unlike other ski resorts where one big mountain crowns a plateau, here mountains crowd the valley on all sides, forging several narrow valleys that leave some visitors feeling hemmed in. To understand, you have only to stay in summer in a remote chalet at Mad River Glen, the mountains rising in silence all around, or descend the back road from Roxbury Gap, one of Vermont's more heart-stopping drives, which rewards the persevering with awesome close-ups of some of the state's highest peaks.

The chic of Sugarbush joins with the rusticity of Mad River to present choices from racquetball to backpacking, from boutiques to country stores, from nightclubbing to roadhouses. For fine dining, the valley is in the vanguard among Eastern ski resorts.

Although the valley is at its best and busiest in the winter, its spirit spans all seasons.

Inn Spots

The Pitcher Inn, 275 Main St., Box 347, Warren 05674.

The old Pitcher Inn, which burned to the ground in 1993, has been rebuilt in grand style. The loggers who frequented the rustic place in the 1800s wouldn't recognize its reincarnation, nor would any of the folks who might have breakfasted here over the years, including innkeeper Heather Carino, who occasionally started the day here with her parents on ski trips from their home in Greenwich, Conn.

Winthrop Smith of the founding Merrill Lynch family financed the rebuilding and installed newlywed daughter Heather and her husband John as innkeepers. Reborn like a phoenix, the three-story, pristine white building is a beauty with upstairs balconies overlooking the village and rear porches looking onto the rushing Mad River.

Call the Pitcher spectacular, deluxe, whimsical, sumptuous – superlatives hardly do it justice. A better guidepost may be its quickly won affiliation with the Relais & Chateaux international hotel group.

The eleven stunning guest accommodations contain all the creature comforts, and all but two have wood-burning fireplaces. Some have steam showers. Jacuzzi tubs, telephones, stereo systems, computer-fax hookups and hidden TV/VCRs are standard. Each incorporates a Vermont theme in its decor and furnishings. The least expensive School Room comes with a kingsize bed, private porch, and old slate chalkboards on the walls and a school desk reminiscent of a one-room schoolhouse. The Mallard adds a bed shaped like a duck, a sofabed, antique duck decoys and antique guns in a display case; its ceiling is domed to give the illusion of a duck blind.

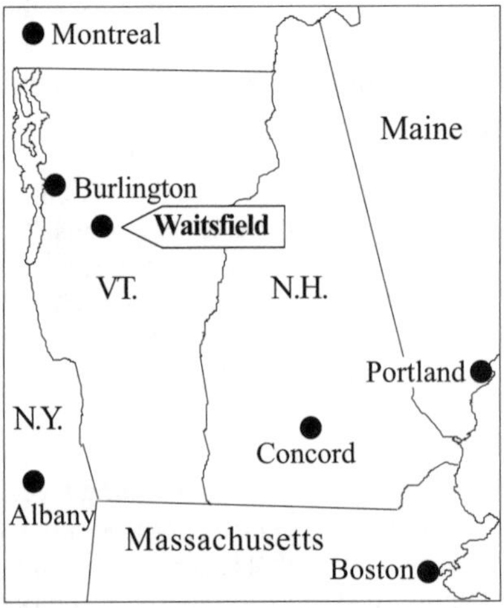

The much photographed Trout room, with a separate seating area and private curving porch, is a sight to behold. Bedposts and columns are cut trees, looking as if they're growing out of the floor, with real red stones at their base. In the bathroom, fish are painted around the jacuzzi tub, the vanity drawers are fronted by logs and birch bark surrounds the mirrors. Oars adorn a wall in the

Trees and trout are themes of Trout room at Pitcher Inn.

leather sitting area, where an antique outboard motor is attached to the end of a rustic desk made of a slab of wood. The desk doubles as a fly-tying station for fishermen who can fish off the back porch if they choose. We never did find the TV, which pops out by remote control from a counter beneath a flying trout sculpture separating the sitting area from the plump kingsize bed.

The Trout is the most popular first-time room because it can be pictured and described. The huge Lodge room cannot. It's supposed to be a Masonic temple, but some liken it to an Egyptian harem (Cleopatra, we couldn't find you). They rave in the guest diary about the "creativity" and "perfection," but how to describe the sum total of the space with a reclining couch and a freestanding bed in the center, gold stars on the ceiling and a TV that rises out of a lectern?

Repeat guests like to sleep around, as it were. After trying the Trout and the Lodge, they inevitably go for the third-floor Ski Room, which lives up to its billing as lavishly rustic. Old skis and bamboo poles are everywhere, the kitchenette is called a snack bar with a real picnic table, three upright toboggans form part of the kingsize headboard between two birch trees and the incredibly colorful patchwork quilt is made of discarded ski jackets. Across the mural-adorned foyer is the Mountain, a dark replica of a fire tower with a mountain mural on the walls and snowshoes on the ceiling. The king bed is in an open cabin enclosure with a ribbed tin roof.

After the Disneyesque approach, tasteful though it is, more traditional rooms like the Calvin Coolidge may come as a relief. Although it has many of the same amenities, it is supposed to be more like the bedroom in which the Vermonter was born – minus the new wall mural of Warren in the 1920s and the wide columned front porch. Not to mention the bathroom with deep jacuzzi, marble steam shower and silver star wallpaper with presidential ribbon bunting.

The adjacent barn holds a couple of two-bedroom suites, each with a fireplaced living room. The saddles in the main-floor suite carry out a stables theme, while the Hayloft is outfitted with antique barn supplies and may well be the most extravagant hayloft ever built.

Two large common rooms in the main inn offer comfy seating around fireplaces. There also are a library and a downstairs billiards/game room, which opens onto a porch, terrace and a colorful garden retreat beside the river. Incidentally, check out the tracks of animal footprints in the colorcast cement floor of the Tracks lounge. You'll find moose, bear, deer, what have you – all identified by artworks on the walls

The inn's elegant and airy dining room is open to the public for breakfast as well as dinner. Overnight guests have their choice of the full breakfast menu, which is offered in a sunny area off the dining room overlooking the river. Afternoon tea also is included.

(802) 496-6350 or (888) 867-4824. Fax (802) 496-6354. www.pitcherinn.com. Nine rooms and two suites with private baths. Doubles, $330 to $600. Suites, $660. Two-night minimum weekends, five-night minimum at Christmas.

The Inn at the Round Barn Farm, 1661 East Warren Road, Waitsfield 05673.

The Joslin Round Barn – a National Historic Landmark and one of the last remaining of its kind in Vermont – is a focal point of this deluxe and animated B&B. Its three vast floors have been renovated into a cultural center, a theater, a space for meetings and weddings, and the headquarters of the Round Barn Farm Cross-Country Ski Center. There's even a 60-foot-long lap pool on the lower level.

The inn is not in the Round Barn as one might think, however. Rather, it occupies a gracious farmhouse and connecting carriage house next door, has six comfortable bedrooms and five extravagant suites, luxurious common rooms and a terraced, 85-acre back yard that rolls down a hill to a couple of ponds and meanders uphill past cows grazing in the distance. It's an idyllic setting, and an exciting B&B.

Jack and Doreen Simko, longtime skiers in the valley, retired from the family floral business in New Jersey to open the inn with daughter AnneMarie in 1987. So expect to see flowers and greenery throughout the house, pots of flowering hibiscus on the terrace, and flowers sprouting from piles of rocks beneath a giant apple tree. Relaxing on the back terraces is a treat, what with animals grazing, a few barns scattered up the hill, whimsical things like a cow made out of iron and, at our first visit, a pen with Jack's three pet pigs – gifts for his 50th birthday. There's only one pig now, and a newer attraction is an undulating, fourteen-foot-deep spring-fed pond for swimming, canoeing and fishing.

Our original stay coming at the end of one of the hottest summers ever, we passed up the two largest rooms with jacuzzi tubs in the main house in favor of the breezy Palmer Room at the rear corner. It had a high-back Victorian queen bed sporting a crazy quilt made in 1915, lovely lace curtains and a framed fan on the wall.

Raspberry-cranberry walls enhance the Joslin Room, with its kingsize canopy bed, fireplace and a huge bathroom complete with wing chair, oriental rug, steam shower and corner jacuzzi tub for two. Three people can sleep comfortably in the spacious, ground-level Terrace Room, which has a queensize bed and sitting area with sofabed.

Joslin Round Barn and landscaped lawns are focal points of Inn at the Round Barn Farm.

Other than the Joslin, the prime accommodations have been in four mini-suites with queen or kingsize beds, steam showers, gas fireplaces and separate sitting areas beneath twenty-foot beamed ceilings in the rear loft area of the original carriage house. The top-of-the-line Richardson suite contains a sunken bathroom with an oversize jacuzzi (you can watch the farm animals outside the window as you soak), a separate shower, and his and her vanities. Relax on the chintz loveseat or chaise lounge beside the marble fireplace and you may never leave.

Striking fabrics on canopies and window treatments provide colorful accents against the barnwood walls in each mini-suite; even the custom-designed Kleenex boxes match the decor. Although not as splashy as some, the pristinely white Dana Room at the end is favored by honeymooners for its Schumacher wall coverings and its crown-canopied black iron queensize bed draped in chiffon.

The new Abbott is a true suite, with a kingsize four-poster bed and a TV concealed in an antique armoire and an adjoining living room with gas fireplace and oversize whirlpool tub in the corner. The bath has a double vanity and glass-enclosed steam shower.

Besides fine oriental and Claire Murray rugs, terrycloth robes, stenciling and other interesting decorative touches, the inn has nightly turndown service with chocolate chip cookies as well as toiletries like Neutrogena conditioners and moisturizers.

The main floor offers a large, elegant library with walls of books, a fireplace and a fancy stereo system issuing forth perhaps Mozart or Vivaldi. A less formal game room downstairs contains a pool table, TV and VCR, and a refrigerator stocked with sodas, spring water and cheese.

At cocktail time, AnneMarie, now the innkeeper, gets creative with canapés, usually putting out something like guacamole or a hot shrimp dip. In winter, the inn offers candlelight dinners every other Friday night for guests, $35 prix-fixe.

Breakfast is served in an expansive dining area fashioned from the original milking barn. Vines trail around the beams and the colorful tables are set with fresh flowers and striking ceramic napkin rings. We feasted on raspberries and bananas in cream, followed by a fantastic omelet blending bacon, cottage cheese, onions, red peppers and basil from the garden. AnneMarie's cinnamon-raisin belgian waffles with maple cream is another favorite, and her pumpkin soufflés are a hit during foliage season.

Based on requests of guests, the Simkos began bottling the raspberry sauce they serve with their cottage-cheese pancakes. Said a California friend who was enjoying a reunion with the Simkos and joined us all at the breakfast table: "These are high-energy people with 85 irons in the fire. Staying with them is like being part of the family." The Simkos have retired to their nearby ski house, but AnneMarie, now married and the mother of two, continues the family tradition.

(802) 496-2276. Fax (802) 496-8832. www.innattheroundbarn.com. Eleven rooms and one suite with private baths. Doubles, $130 to $240, $155 to $265 foliage and holidays. Suite, $260, $295 foliage and holidays. Children over 15. Two-night minimum weekends.

West Hill House, 1496 West Hill Road, Warren 05674.

A wonderfully secluded setting on fifteen acres next to the Sugarbush Golf Course and Ski Touring Center, a quaint Vermont farmhouse dating to 1862 and welcoming hosts commend this seven-room B&B. Not to be overlooked are luxury amenities, gourmet breakfasts, occasional dinners and charming common rooms.

The place reflects the talents of owners Dotty Kyle and Eric Brattstrom, originally from Maplewood, N.J. Dotty, an artist and accomplished cook, painted the beautiful border of flowers that winds around the living room, stairway and cathedral ceiling. She also painted the floral borders that match the prized wildflower quilt on the queen bed in the upstairs Wildflower Room, and was about to paint "a tropical mural or something" in the new Four Poster Suite.

Her husband, a construction project manager, built the wall of shelves in the living room to house part of their huge book collection. He added a rear wing to provide a skiers' entry, powder room and a huge great room with a stone fireplace and a large sunroom with a vaulted ceiling and a wood stove. The sunroom opens through french doors onto a side deck overlooking rock gardens. Look there for the birdbath that Eric carved with a shallow end for chickadees and a deep end for blue jays.

His latest ingenious project was to raise a sloping roof on the second floor and build outward to provide another deck and space for larger baths – two with double jacuzzis – for four guest quarters and a fireplace for the only bedroom that lacked one.

The dormer windows and sloping ceilings in the main house yield nooks and crannies, which the artist in Dotty has turned to good advantage. She sponge-painted the walls light green in one bedroom and added a queen bed in the main-floor Stetson Suite, where we enjoyed the extra space of a sitting room with a TV. Eric has since redone its bathroom, adding a jacuzzi tub, pedestal sink and two-person steam bath/shower. Other premier accommodations are main-floor Allen Room with a king/twin bed configuration and the Wildflower with a double jacuzzi tub and fireplace. Tops now is the beamed Four Poster Suite, up its own spiral staircase above the great room with a queen four-poster featherbed and a fireplace. The new addition gives it a sitting/bedroom, deck, spa room, double jacuzzi and a second fireplace.

All rooms have queen or king/twin beds and fireplaces. Thick towels, down pillows and comforters, attractive quilts and assorted toiletries are the norm.

Front veranda of West Hill House overlooks gardens and valley.

Arrangements of fresh or dried flowers and bowls of seasonal candies are placed about.

Guests relax on the wicker-filled front porch or the large side deck facing bird feeders, tiny red squirrels, a gazebo, new ponds and prolific gardens. Another haunt is the cozy barnwood-paneled living room with its treasury of books, vaulted ceiling, wide-board floors and a large recessed fireplace at one end, Best of all is the rear great room which, Dotty thinks, sounds pretentious "but everybody says 'what a great room!'" A pantry holds a refrigerator and wet bar, where guests help themselves to cookies, soft drinks, cider and wine.

Breakfast in the beamed English antique dining room begins with a fresh fruit bowl ("we have a blueberry patch that won't quit," Dotty advised) or, in our case, bananas West Hill (like bananas foster, spiked with rum) and scones. An herbed cheese omelet and bacon followed. Other treats include "the best sticky buns in the world – I've always loved them and worked very hard to get them the way I want them." Among main courses are baked apple pancakes, banana-nut waffles and vegetable soufflés.

On Saturday nights or by reservation, Dotty prepares optional candlelight dinners with soup, salad, entrée and dessert. Favorites include roast chicken basted with maple syrup over roasted vegetables, braised pork chops with onions and apples, and steak diane.

Her renovated kitchen includes a wood-burning bake oven in which Dotty bakes flatbreads and other treats for guests. West Hill also has a liquor license as a convenience for guests.

The architect who helped design the renovations was so impressed with Eric's work at the inn that he brought a group of his students here to meet "a builder who makes his new work look as if it has always been here."

(802) 496-7162 or (800) 898-1427. Fax (802) 496-6443. www.westhillhouse.com.. Six rooms and two suites with private baths. Doubles, $135 to $180 weekends, $125 to $170 midweek. Two-night minimum weekends, three-night minimum foliage and holidays. Children over 12.

Rear deck is favorite gathering spot for guests at Beaver Pond Farm B&B.

Beaver Pond Farm Bed & Breakfast, 1225 Golf Course Road, Warren 05674.

A farmhouse this may be, but an elegant one it is indeed. Located off a quiet country road, the light green house with green roof overlooks a beaver pond, the Sugarbush Golf Club and rolling hillsides.

Longtime owners Betty and Bob Hansen sold to Nancy and Bob Baron from Chicago, who reopened the B&B in December 2003 after renovating the attached barn for living quarters for their young family and redecorating the guest rooms that had been closed for a few years.

Moving here for a lifestyle change, the Barons share their gorgeous property and home with guests, who enjoy a stylish living room with fireplace, a beamed dining room with a long harvest table on an oriental rug and a small library. A small bar allows guests to help themselves to complimentary coffees and teas, as well as soft drinks, beer and wine for an additional charge. Best of all, perhaps, is a fabulous rear deck that runs the length of the house, where guests like to watch the beaver in the pond.

Upstairs, reached by two separate staircases, are four guest rooms with king or queen beds dressed with fine linens and down comforters. Two rooms that formerly shared a bath in the older section have been turned into one large and cheery yellow room with kingsize four-poster bed and a daybed with a trundle bed beneath. A fifth room with queensize bed, adjoining the rear deck on the main floor, was being readied for occupancy in mid-2004.

All rooms are furnished with period antiques, reproduction furniture and oriental rugs. They come with comfy spa robes (for use in the new hot tub on the outdoor deck), hair dryers and clock radio/CD players. Each is equipped for internet access, TV/VCR and DVD players.

Nancy, who attended culinary school in Chicago, was following in the footsteps of her predecessor, whom fellow innkeepers considered the best cook in the valley. Guests find breakfast to be a highlight of the day. It begins with seasonal fruits, homemade granola with local yogurt, and fresh sweet breads, muffins or scones.

The main course could be quiche, a goat cheese and prosciutto frittata or upside-down apricot french toast and apple-maple syrup.

The Barons welcome guests in the afternoon with homemade cookies, Vermont cheese and crackers, finger sandwiches or hot chili and a specially prepared beverage.

(802) 583-2861 or (800) 685-8285. Fax (802) 583-2860. www.beaverpondfarminn.com. Five rooms with private baths. Doubles, $125 to $145.

The Sugartree, 2440 Sugarbush Access Road, Warren 05674.

Energetic owners are leaving their mark on the Sugartree, an inviting inn transformed from what essentially had been a ski chalet for 30 years. Frank and Kathy Partsch traded corporate life in Boston for new roles as jack-of-all-trades innkeepers. Besides their hospitality roles, Frank has put his handyman/carpentry talents to good use and Kathy has taken up sewing. Her job description lists cook, decorator, work as an insurance adjuster and volunteer stints at the local Chamber of Commerce.

Guests arriving at the homey, nine-bedroom inn see evidence of Frank's talents immediately. He renovated the office/reception area at the entry to make it seem less like an office. It opens into a fireplaced suite he created with a small wicker sitting room, a queensize bedroom and a renovated bath with a vanity he made himself in a workshop rapidly taking over the garage. He also built a ski room with an intriguing contraption to blow-dry and warm wet ski boots.

More of Frank's handiwork is evident in the spacious living room. He built the tall clock as well as the wood-carved folk art Santa Clauses lined up along the fireplace mantel. The figures often reflect local activities, from skiing Santas to one with a tennis racquet. Kathy has made quilts for the guest rooms. "I couldn't sew before I got here," she confessed. Now she has dressed up several bedrooms with quilts, one made of 800 pieces. She made curtains for the sitting room in the suite, and found an antique pump organ for the living room. The bedrooms are furnished in country style with puffy curtains, shams, dust ruffles, crocheted bed canopies, samplers, needlework wall hangings and wreaths on the doors. All but two have queensize beds, and two were completely renovated with new carpeting, furniture and paint jobs in peach and teal. The modernized bathrooms have glycerin soaps, herbal bath grains and built-in hair dryers.

The rooms are named for birds that frequent the inn's feeders. Each has the appropriate painting by a local artist on the door and on the key chain.

The Partsches serve a full country breakfast in the dining room. The menu, posted on a blackboard, included juices, apple crisp, bacon and french toast with orange sauce or maple syrup at a recent visit. Baked eggs with three cheeses, sour cream coffeecake and assorted berry pancakes are other specialties, nicely detailed in a cookbook sold at the inn. Cookies and perhaps chocolate fondue are put out in the afternoon.

Outside, summer's trees, incredible gardens and window boxes envelop the inn in its own delightful island of color and greenery. There's a gazebo, and Frank has put in a rock garden and an herb garden. In winter, when the trees are bare, the landscape opens onto the mountains and guests can see skiers at Sugarbush across the way.

(802) 583-3211 or (800) 666-8907. Fax (802) 583-3203. www.sugartree.com. Eight rooms and one suite with private baths. Doubles, $99 to $125, $99 to $150 in winter, $135 to $175 foliage and holidays. Two-night minimum peak weekends. Children over 7.

The Featherbed Inn, 5864 Main St. (Route 100), Waitsfield 05673.

There are plump featherbeds on the beds, naturally, and featherbed eggs are the breakfast specialty at this historic and stylish B&B opened by New Jersey transplants Clive and Tracey Coutts.

After three years of painstaking renovations, the place bears faint resemblance to its background as the area's first B&B/ski lodge in the 1950s. The result is the more remarkable in that the couple did most of the work themselves. He handled the construction, even putting 3,000 of the original bricks into the foundation and the living-room fireplace. She did the decorating, window treatments and some spectacular stenciling.

Two pleasant guest rooms are at one end of the main floor and share a den with television. Upstairs are three more bedrooms and two suites, all with private baths. The Ilse Room at the north end has a skylit, beamed cathedral ceiling with a loveseat in the corner, a hooked rug on the original softwood flooring and an antique quilt on the queensize sleigh bed. The prized Beatrice Suite in the middle of the house holds a queensize bed whose quilt coordinates with the floral swags draped across three windows and the fabric on the rare spindle bench beneath. The suite is also notable for fancy stenciling along the chair rails, a wet bar with refrigerator, and a small bedroom equipped with a day bed and trundle bed. The Alexandra Room at the south end has a queensize iron bed and two wing chairs. The sprinkling of antiques and period memorabilia produces a simple but cheery look, one in keeping with the early 19th-century origin of the house.

A rear cottage offers two garden-level rooms and an upstairs room with the original beams. All have queensize featherbeds and country furnishings.

Tracey's stenciling, evident in most rooms, reaches its zenith in the informal, main-floor lodge room. Here, beneath a beamed ceiling, stenciled geese and ducks fly up and around the windows and french doors in random procession. The room is sunny in wicker, the doors open onto an outdoor deck and an open fireplace is ablaze in winter. Guests also enjoy a handsome living room, where Clive may play for singalongs around the grand piano. Teal wainscoting and a lace-covered table enhance the formal dining room.

Tracey often serves featherbed eggs in individual ramekins, eirkuchen (German pancakes stuffed with apples or peaches), or french toast stuffed with creamed cottage cheese sweetened with maple syrup and fruit. These treats follow a fancy fruit course (perhaps baked pineapple or a pear compote with cider and spices) and homemade apricot or strawberry breads. Fruit and cheese, cookies, tea and hot cider are put out in the afternoon.

(802) 496-7151. Fax (802) 496-7933. www.featherbedinn.com. Seven rooms and three suites with private baths. Doubles, $95 to $140. Suites, $130 to $150. Add $15 for foliage and holidays. Two-night minimum weekends. Children over 10.

The Lareau Farm Country Inn, 46 Lareau Road, Box 563, Waitsfield 05673.

This really is a farm with gardens, two dogs, four cats, seven horses and occasionally chickens and pigs, the whole menagerie dubbed the Lareau Zoo and the name delightfully emblazoned on sweatshirts, aprons, T-shirts and the like. The 1852 farmhouse with a barn, woodshed and appropriate 67-acre country setting along Route 100 flatlands that were farmed until a few years ago by the Lareau family was converted into an inn in 1984 by Pennsylvanian Sue Easley, who has been expanding and upgrading ever since.

Back porch at Lareau Farm Country Inn overlooks fields and mountains.

In the Mad River on the property, a ten-foot-deep swimming hole is flanked by rocks. "The water is so clear you can see the brown trout," according to Sue. Actually, there are three swimming holes: one for the public and families, one for house guests and one for skinny-dipping ("we send one couple at a time," advises Sue). The flora and fauna on the property are so interesting that Sue has published a detailed walking trail guide for guests.

Since she pieced together the squares for ten bed quilts in her first summer, she has added bathrooms and expanded to thirteen guest rooms. In the former woodshed, the dirt floors have given way to carpeting, but the four rooms retain some of the original posts and beams amid such conveniences as modern baths. Brass bedsteads and rockers are mixed with a profusion of hanging plants.

An addition to the rear of the main house holds four guest rooms, all with full baths and queensize beds, a much-enlarged dining room and a sitting room around the fireplace in the former kitchen.

A queensize room with a two-person jacuzzi in the oversize bath is among the other five rooms in the oldest part of the house, built in the 1700s. The framed antique lace wedding collars and cuffs that decorate the room prompt the designation Bridal Suite.

The main structure, a later addition to the original, has a parlor full of Victorian furniture and stuffed animals. Guests like to laze on the assortment of porches that wrap all the way around the house.

The main gathering place has turned out to be the huge rear dining room and back porch with six columns obtained at auction. Pretty in beige and blue, the dining room has four big tables, oriental rugs and windows on three sides. "It's changed our orientation," says Sue, "bringing the focus out back." Adirondack chairs are gathered on the back lawn for gazing across the farmlands up against the mountains.

For breakfast, Sue whips up homemade muffins or breads and perhaps an egg soufflé casserole and blueberry or banana-oat bran pancakes. She has a beer and wine license, and provides hors d'oeuvres and setups for guests in the winter.

The farm's old slaughterhouse has been turned into the home of the locally famous American Flatbread business and restaurant (see Dining Spots).

Lareau Farm offers sleigh rides and cider parties. It donates food leftovers to Meals on Wheels and gives a percentage of the room rates to the Nature Conservancy ("our way of trying to protect Vermont's future," says Sue). One year every guest received a cookie cutter in the shape of a maple leaf for use as a napkin ring. It symbolized her theme to be "a cut above."

(802) 496-4949 or (800) 833-0766. Fax (802) 496-7979. www.lareaufarminn.com. Eleven rooms with private baths and two with shared bath. Doubles, $80 to $135 weekends, $70 to $110 midweek. Two-night minimum weekends.

1824 House Inn, 2150 Main St. (Route 100), Waitsfield 05673.

New owners John Lumbra and Karl Klein came well prepared for innkeeping when they took over the 1824 House. John had served as a personal chef after culinary training at Johnson & Wales University and Karl had worked at a five-star hotel before pursuing a career as a residential contractor.

John served meals of such distinction they drew outside guests for dinner. Karl started restoring the 150-year-old post and beam barn in back to serve as a reception area for weddings and functions. Together they spiffed up the guest rooms, imparting a simple yet elegant look in keeping with the house's designation on the National Register of Historic Places.

Enter the ten-gabled farmhouse through a foyer/parlor, where the fireplace is stoked on cool days and guests listen to the extensive selection of CDs. Off one side is the dining room open to a small enclosed porch, where memorable breakfasts as well as dinners are served. Off another side is the Windham room with a queen bed and full bath.

Altogether, the inn offers four large kingsize rooms and four smaller queensize rooms on two floors. All have down featherbeds, and the king beds are convertible to twins. The second-floor Bennington, off a stairwell from the dining room, has a king bed and a sitting area filled with antiques. It's considered the most romantic room, while the recently renovated main-floor Franklin Room with queen bed at the rear of the inn is the most private. It is near the television room, which occupants may use as a semi-private sitting room.

Food is a feature, starting with John's extravagant three-course breakfasts that might feature a vegetable frittata or an herbed egg tart with gruyère cheese. Afternoon refreshments include cookies and selections from the inn's beer and wine inventory.

In the evening, he offers four-course dinners to inn guests and outsiders who manage to book a table in the 24-seat dining area.

The meal is prix-fixe, with several choices for each course. Everything is made from scratch in house. An autumn menu began with a choice of mussels in wine and garlic sauce, linguini with puttanesca sauce, or lobster ravioli with chive oil and cream sauce. Butternut squash and apple soup or a salad of mixed greens, toasted pine nuts and shepherd's cheeses followed. For the main course, there was a choice of fish of the day, chicken marsala, bacon-wrapped filet mignon stuffed with blue cheese or rack of lamb with thyme oil. Desserts were crème brûlée, cheesecake with raspberry sauce or vanilla bean ice cream with orange fennel brittle.

Accents of greenery enhance pristine dining room at Pitcher Inn.

The tranquil, fifteen-acre property includes trails, gardens and a swimming hole in the Mad River.

(802) 496-7555 or (800) 426-3986. Fax (802) 496-7559. www.1824house.com. Eight rooms with private baths. Doubles, $125 to $138, $138 to $148 foliage, $80 to $90 midweek in summer.

Dinner by reservation, Wednesday-Sunday 5:30 to 8. Prix-fixe, $40.

Dining Spots

The Pitcher Inn, 275 Main St., Warren.

Reborn after a disastrous fire, this glamorous hostelry is "committed to filling not only the footprint of the old Pitcher Inn but its boots as well," according to innkeeper Heather Carino. And it's doing that quite successfully.

With tall windows and parquet floors, the 40-seat restaurant is traditional with well spaced white-linened tables flanked by fine windsor chairs, white tapers in silver candlesticks, a large raised fireplace, a grand piano and accents of greenery. The Brook Room overlooking the Mad River to the side is used for overflow, and a table for two in the corner, with windows onto the flood-lit stream, is the best in the house.

Chef Susan Schickler's fare is contemporary American and the menu is printed nightly. A recent October evening opened with such exotic dishes as a roasted beet and oxtail borscht with sour cream, twice-baked cheese soufflé with parmesan cream and roasted pepper salad, escalope of veal over a smoky bacon flageolet ragoût, and seared foie gras with apples, grapes and moscato d'asti.

Main courses included wild striped bass with preserved lemon gnocchi, sautéed duck breast with roasted shallot jus, pan-roasted pork tenderloin with apple-gewürztraminer sauce and roast venison loin with apple-brown butter vinaigrette. Grilled wahoo with crab and corn salsa and a lemon beurre blanc, grilled yellowtail snapper with corn and fava bean succotash, and grilled veal chop with lemon herb butter were other selections.

Exotic dessert choices are warm gianduja-filled chocolate cake with toffee sauce and caramelized bananas, plum clafoutis with crème anglaise and plum sorbet, and a trio of banana, strawberry and cantaloupe sorbets with almond shortbread.

The 6,500-bottle wine cellar is distinguished, specializing in American boutique wineries at affordable prices.

Be advised that you can eat down in the handsome wine cellar at a table for six. The $100 per-person tab yields a five-course dinner with wines tailored to your wishes.

(802) 496-6350 or (888) 867-4824. Entrées, $24 to $34. Dinner nightly except Tuesday, 6 to 9.

The Common Man, 3209 German Flats Road, Warren.

Here is the ultimate incongruity: a soaring, century-old timbered barn with floral carpets on the walls to cut down the noise and keep out wintry drafts. Crystal chandeliers hang from beamed ceilings over bare wood tables set simply with red napkins and pewter candlesticks. A table headed by a regal Henry VIII chair occupies a prime position in front of a massive, open fieldstone fireplace.

The whole mix works, and thrivingly so since its establishment in 1972 in the site we first knew as Orsini's. Destroyed by fire in 1987, it was replaced by a barn dismantled in Moretown and rebuilt here by English proprietor Mike Ware. He operates one of the more popular places in the valley, with an air of elegance but without pretension.

The extensive wine list comes in two picture frames, hinged together to open like a book, and contains good values. Ingenious, custom-made brackets hold wine buckets at the edge of the tables.

The escargots maison "served with our famous (and secret) garlic butter sauce" leads off the French/continental menu. Other appetizers include a daily charcuterie, gravlax and Vermont goat cheese baked in puff pastry. We can vouch for the Vietnamese shrimp with chilled oriental noodles and a peanut sesame sauce, and a classic caesar salad.

Main courses like monkfish grenobloise, roast duck with a sauce of Belgian cherries and cherry herring liqueur, and sautéed Vermont veal with local mushrooms represent uncommon fare – not to mention value – for common folk. At one visit, the fresh Vermont rabbit braised with marjoram and rosemary was distinctive, and the Vermont sweetbreads normande with apples and apple brandy were some of the best we've tasted. Our latest dinner produced a stellar special of penne with smoked chicken and asparagus and a plump cornish game hen glazed with mustard and honey.

Desserts include kirschen strudel, marquise au chocolat and meringue glacé. The mandarin orange sherbet bearing slivers of rind and a kirsch parfait were refreshing endings to an uncommon meal.

(802) 583-2800. www.commonmanrestaurant.com. Entrées, $16 to $26. Dinner nightly from 6 or 6:30 (from 5:30 or 6 in winter). Closed Monday, mid-April to mid-December.

The Spotted Cow, Bridge Street Marketplace, Waitsfield.

Courtly ex-Bermudian Jay Young sold his old Jay's luncheonette nearby to open a fine-dining restaurant a week before the Mad River lived up to its name and flooded downtown Waitsfield in June 1998. Although he arrived on the scene to find a refrigerator afloat in his dining room, he and his wife, Renate, decided to repair the damage to their 1850 building and open his now-acclaimed eatery. He and the owner of the nearby Artisans' Gallery are credited with sparking the revival of the center of Waitsfield. "We were the first to come back and others followed," said Jay.

The small restaurant is a charmer, with 30 seats at tables and two booths, a changing display of potted flowers, fine artworks and a wall of windows onto an alleyway that cuts through the center of the arty marketplace beside the covered bridge.

Chef Eric Bauer, who joined the Youngs from Chez Henri, cooks "classical French with regional overtones." That translates to dinner entrées like baked ginger-lime cod finished with an avocado mousse, pan-fried coho salmon finished with smoked salmon-dill butter and two caviars, sautéed veal sweetbreads with a tomato-caper vinaigrette, pan-roasted squab with dried cherries and port, and grilled venison loin glazed with Vermont chèvre.

But that's getting ahead of ourselves. You must try the specialty Bermuda fish chowder, a family recipe that Jay brought from his father's restaurant in Bermuda. Two "secret" ingredients – a dollop of sherry infused with peppers and a hefty splash of Gosling's black rum – are added at the table. The chowder is to die for, at lunch or dinner. You might also try the grilled duck and shiitake salad for lunch or the ragoût of lobster and salmon redolent with black truffles and oyster mushrooms for dinner. Bermuda fish fillet, Bermuda conch fritters and Bermuda codfish cakes are other specialties.

The restaurant is a labor of love for Jay, who greets guests, tends bar and washes all glasses and silverware by hand because he doesn't want detergent to spoil the taste of his food or wine. That's part of why he chose the name for his restaurant. Like the spotted owl, the spotted cow and the Vermont dairy farm are an endangered species. So, he feels, is the art of fine dining. Both should be preserved, come hell or – in his case – high water.

(802) 496-5151. Entrées, $19.95 to $25.95. Lunch in season, Tuesday-Sunday 11 to 3. Dinner, Tuesday-Sunday from 5.

Millbrook Inn & Restaurant, 533 Millbrook Road (Route 17), Waitsfield.

Everyone considers this small inn with an unexpected emphasis on fine Indian cooking one of the better places to eat in the Mad River Valley. It's been lovingly run since 1979 by chef Thom Gorman, innkeeper with his wife Joan.

The restaurant seats 30 in a fireplaced dining room at candlelit tables covered with paisley cloths. Anadama bread, Joan's specialty, is made in house, as are pastas and acclaimed desserts, from scratch. Start with mushrooms à la Millbrook, stuffed with a secret blend of ground veal and herbs, if it's offered. Entrées include a daily roast, shrimp scampi, five-peppercorn beef, vegetable pasta roulade, cheese cannelloni made with Vermont cheddar and fresh basil, and three-cheese fettuccine tossed with Cabot cheddar, parmesan, Vermont mascarpone and sundried tomatoes. There are also four dishes from the Bombay region, where Thom lived for two years while in the Peace Corps. The badami rogan josh, local lamb simmered in all kinds of spices and yogurt and served with homemade tomato chutney, is a longtime favorite. Another is the seafood mélange of mussels, scallops and shrimp spiced with Thai-style green curry and served over rice.

Millbrook has a wine and beer license, with well-chosen selections tailored to go with assertive Indian food. As for those famous desserts, ice creams like chocolate chip and brickle candy are made here – "we're the only place in Vermont that doesn't serve Ben & Jerry's," says Thom – as are a signature apple brown betty and white chocolate mousse pie with a chocolate cookie crumb crust. In summer, open berry pies (maybe a raspberry and blackberry combination) are gobbled up.

Upstairs are seven guest rooms with private baths, decorated with stenciling and interesting handmade quilts and comforters. A full breakfast with choice of menu is served. Doubles are exceptionally good value at $150, MAP.

(802) 496-2405 or (800) 477-2809. www.millbrookinn.com. Entrées, $11.50 to $17.95, Dinner nightly, 6 to 9. Closed Tuesday in summer, April to mid-June and mid-October to mid-December.

Chez Henri, Sugarbush Village, Warren.

The longest-running of the valley's long runners, Chez Henri is starting its fifth decade as a French bistro, wine bar and after-dinner disco. Almost as old as Sugarbush itself, it's tiny, intimate and very French, as you might expect from a former food executive for Air France.

Henri Borel offers lunch, brunch, après-ski, early dinner, dinner and dancing – inside in winter by a warming stone fireplace and a marble bar and occasionally outside on summer weekends on a small terrace bordered by a babbling mountain brook.

The dinner menu, served from 4 p.m., starts with changing soups and pâtés "as made in a French country kitchen," a classic French onion soup or fish broth, and perhaps mussels marinière, a trio of smoked seafood with greens or steak tartare "knived to order."

Entrées, served with good French bread and seasonal vegetables, often include bouillabaisse, coq au vin, calves liver with onion-turnip puree, roasted duck with fruit or green peppercorn sauce, veal normande, filet au poivre and rack of lamb. Some come in petite portions, and a shorter bistro menu is available as well at peak periods.

Crème caramel, coupe marron and chocolate mousse are among the dessert standbys. The wines are all French.

(802) 583-2600. Entrées, $14.50 to $24.50. Open daily from 11:30 in ski season. Weekends in summer, hours vary.

The Warren House Restaurant & Rupert's Bar, 2585 Sugarbush Access Road, Warren.

Skiers heading for Sugarbush once stopped at the Sugarbush Sugarhouse for pancakes and homemade syrup. Today, they stop at a vastly expanded dining establishment with a smashing greenhouse room for good food offered by new owners Chris Jones and Joel Adams, who took over the highly rated Sam Rupert's restaurant after it closed.

They offer a comfortable, welcoming bar and casual fine dining in the atmosphere of an old Vermont sugarhouse. The menu features modern American cuisine by a Culinary Institute of America-trained chef, Kurt Hekeler.

Founder George Schenk bakes pizzas in earthen oven at Flatbread Kitchen.

Expect to start with appetizers like seared sea scallops in an Asian garlic black sauce or slow-roasted St. Louis pork ribs with house-made whisky barbecue sauce. Typical entrées are bouillabaisse, pan-roasted arctic char with key lime-cilantro vinaigrette over green herbed risotto, wild striped bass over quinoa salad, merlot-braised duckling with sausage, braised lamb shank with rosemary, and grilled New York strip steak with gorgonzola-roasted garlic butter.

Dessert could be strawberry napoleon with maple pastry cream, bittersweet chocolate torte with bourbon-caramel sauce and chocolate pots de crème in toasted wonton cups.

(802) 583-2421 or (800) 817-2055. www.thewarrenhouse.com. Entrées, $12.95 to $18.95. Dinner nightly, from 5:30.

Flatbread Kitchen, 46 Lareau Road, Waitsfield.

The American Flatbread pizzas that got their start in the outdoor wood-burning oven at Tucker Hill Lodge are now produced for the gourmet trade in the old slaughterhouse at Lareau Farm. Here, in an 800-degree wood-fired earthen oven with a clay dome, founder George Schenk and staff create the remarkable pizzas that are frozen and sold at the rate of more than 2,000 a week to grocery stores as far south as Florida in a "responsible food" phenomenon that is making Waitsfield the pizza capital of northern New England.

We were among their first on-site customers the first time we stopped by for a tour and a snack. They since have opened a wildly popular weekend restaurant, serving flatbreads, great little salads dressed with homemade ginger-tamari vinaigrette, wine and beer to upwards of 250 people a night at tables set up around the production facility's oven room and kitchens and outside on the inn's west lawn. The delicious flatbreads with asiago and mozzarella cheeses and sundried tomatoes have made many a convert of pizza skeptics. How could they not, when the night's flatbread specials might pair roasted chicken with white beans, sage, braised kale and organic red onions, or bay scallops with lemon vinaigrette, fennel, leeks and red peppers. The bakers use organically grown flour with restored wheat germ, "good Vermont mountain water" and as many Vermont products as they can.

Lately, George expanded the dining room and renovated part of the horse barn into a waiting room and "museum." He also opened a second American Flatbread Restaurant over the mountain in Middlebury.

Each night's dinner menu is dedicated to an employee, a friend, "our animal neighbors" or maybe the people of Afganistan or Iraq. George's heart-felt "dedications," posted around the facility, make for mighty interesting reading.

(802) 496-8856. www.americanflatbread.com. Flatbreads for two, $9.75 to $14.50. Dinner, Friday and Saturday 5:30 to 9:30.

The Warren Store Deli, Warren.

At the rear of the Warren Store is a delightful place for breakfast or lunch. You can get a three-egg omelet or breakfast burrito for $2 to $3. For lunch, how about turkey à la king on buttered linguini with tossed salad and French bread, or any number of possibilities from the gorgeous array of gourmet salads and sandwiches in the $4 to $6 range? Finish with a huge chocolate-chip cookie or one of the treats from the ice-cream stand. Take it all outside to tables on a deck under a green striped canopy beside the roaring falls of the Mad River, where our tomato-dill soup and a pesto-provolone sandwich tasted extra good on a summer day. The store also has a fine selection of rare wines.

(802) 496-3864. Open daily, 8 to 7, Sunday to 6.

Diversions

Downhill skiing reigns supreme and gives the valley its character.

Mad River Glen, Route 17, Waitsfield. Billed as a serious place for serious skiers, Mad River has been challenging hardy types since 1948 ("ski it if you can," is its motto). There are no frills here: little snowmaking, a few lifts including the original, diesel-powered single chairlift (with blanket wraps provided to ward off the chill) to the summit, hair-raising trails like Paradise and the Fall Line, plenty of moguls and not much grooming, and a "Practice Slope" steep enough to scare the daylights out of beginners (the Birdland area is fine for intermediates). And, blessedly for skiers, snowboards have been banned here. There's a Mad River mystique (blue jeans and milk runs) that you sense immediately and attracts you back. Former Owner Betsey Pratt, who bought the area in 1972 with her late husband, still skis it every day, but the place is now owned by a cooperative of loyal skiers – the only such skier-owned mountain in the country.

Sugarbush, 2405 Sugarbush Access Road, Warren. Founded in 1958 and among the first of Vermont's destination ski resorts, Sugarbush with its own "village" at its base appealed immediately to the jet set and fashion models and became known as "Mascara Mountain." From its original gondola lift to its expert Castle Rock area, from its clusters of condos and boutiques to its indoor Sports Center, Sugarbush draws those who appreciate their creature comforts – and good skiing as well (the Glades offer the best glade skiing in the East). Recently the fastest-growing destination ski resort in New England, Sugarbush was acquired in 2001 by Summit Ventures, three local skier/investors led by Winthrop Smith, owner of the Pitcher Inn. The home of famed extreme skiing brothers John and Dan Egan, Sugarbush offers the first guided backcountry skiing in the East. The Slide Brook Express connects Sugarbush and neighboring Mount Ellen/Sugarbush North (which has the valley's greatest vertical drop, 2,600 feet). Local innkeepers were instrumental in 2001 in getting Sugarbush and Mad River to offer an interchangeable lift ticket for lodging guests.

Other sports. This is a four-season sports area with a difference. Yes, there is golf, at the Robert Trent Jones-designed **Sugarbush Golf Club** par-72 course with water hazards (pond or brook) affecting eight consecutive holes. Yes, the **Sugarbush Health & Racquet Club** has indoor and outdoor tennis courts, racquetball and squash courts, indoor and outdoor pools, whirlpools and an exercise facility.

But there's much more: this is something of an equestrian center with a number of stables offering trail rides. Among them are the **Vermont Icelandic Horse Farm,** which specializes in horse trekking on one of the oldest and purest breeds in the world – anything from half-day rides to four-day inn-to-inn rides to six-day mountain expeditions. The **Sugarbush Polo Club,** started in 1962 by skiers using ski poles and a volleyball, now has three polo fields for games and tournaments, staged Thursday, Saturday and Sunday afternoons June through September.

Soaring via gliders and sailplanes is at its best from the Warren-Sugarbush Airport, where instruction and rentals are available. Biplane rides for one or two persons also go from the airport, which hosts an annual air show early in late June.

For hiking and backpacking, the Long Trail is just overhead; innumerable mountain peaks and guided tours beckon. Sugarbush has a mountain biking center at Lincoln Peak. The Mad River and Blueberry Lake are ready for swimming, canoeing and fishing. The Mad River rugby team plays throughout the summer and fall at the Waitsfield Recreation Field. The Mad River Valley Cricket Club stages charity events. Finally, a round-robin English croquet tournament is staged in mid-summer.

Clearwater Sports, Route 100, Waitsfield, offers canoes, kayaks, mountain bikes, snowboards and such for rent, and leads day trips for canoeing, biking and hiking.

Scenic drives. The Lincoln Gap Road, the McCullogh Turnpike (Route 17) beyond Mad River Glen and the steep Roxbury Gap Road each have their rewards. For the most open vistas and overall feeling for the area, traverse Brook Road and Waitsfield Common Road out of Warren, past the landmark Joslin Round Barn and Blueberry Lake, Sugarloaf Airport and come the back way into Waitsfield.

Shopping. Waitsfield has three shopping complexes, each worthy of exploration: the Mad River Green and the Village Square along Route 100 and the Bridge Street Marketplace beside Vermont's second oldest covered bridge, newly revitalized following a disastrous 1998 flood. Check out the new **Artisans' Gallery,** other art and craft galleries, antiques shops and the fine **Bridge Street Bakery.** It offers great Portuguese breads, baked goods and snacks (cranberry buns with orange crème, gorgeous fresh fruit Danish pastries, ham and Vermont cheddar croissants, and maybe even a hearty sausage stew with French bread).

Our first stop at every visit is **The Store** in the red 1834 Methodist Meeting House along Route 100. Owner Jackie Rose, dean of the area's merchants (hers was the first store at Sugarbush Village), has an exceptional and vast array of Vermont foods, books, accessories, gifts, Christmas things, and a lovely collection of handmade quilts and pillows. A rear children's room resembles a giant toy box, while the second floor is stocked with antique furniture.

The well-known Green Mountain Coffee Roasters was founded in the Mad River

Green, and the **Three Mountain Café** here continues to feature its coffees. **The Collection,** "three stores in one," offers high-quality American arts and crafts, antiques and accessories as well as gifts and toys. **A Schoolhouse Garden** shows dried floral designs, Vermont-made furniture and accents for home and garden. A farmers' market with produce and crafts is a highlight Saturday mornings from May into October.

In Village Square, the **Blue Toad** flower shop also offers particularly nice, inexpensive baskets from twenty countries and good greeting cards, as well as English tin boxes and jelly beans. **Tulip Tree** shows Vermont crafts and art, including lots of cows and many of the prints by Sabra Field, our favorite Vermont artist.

Along Route 100 are **Luminosity** stained glass and **Cabin Fever Quilts,** stocking a wondrous array of handmade quilts in the Old Church. **Waitsfield Pottery** sells nice lamps and vases, mostly in greens and blues, produced in the basement of an 1845 house. You can watch glass blowers in action at **Mad River Glass,** a studio and gallery.

In tiny Warren, everything you need and a lot you don't expect is found at the **Warren Store,** a lively old-fashioned general store with provisions, fine wines and a deli, plus upstairs, the **More Store,** with handicrafts from around the world, kitchenware, jewelry, apparel and cards. Lots of the things here are from India. Owner Carol Lippincott's criterion is "products with integrity." Up the street, blue and white stoneware made on the premises is displayed on the lawn in front of the **Warren Village Pottery. The Bradley House** shows some whimsical crafts and furnishings among its sophisticated stock. We were struck by the unusual candles, bowls painted with Vermont scenes, and "Memories of Skiing," a box of old skis for a cool $500. Next door, **Parade Gallery** offers fine art and photography. Down the street is **Barn-It-All!** for antiques and collectibles.

The **von Trapp Greenhouse,** run by Maria von Trapp's grandson Tobi, off a dirt road east of Waitsfield Common, is worth a visit (open May-July, limited hours). Beautiful display gardens surround the family's alpine-style house. There's a retail shop in front of one of the two greenhouses, which furnish lavish floral arrangements and produce for the valley's inns and restaurants.

Extra-Special

All Things Bright and Beautiful, 27 Bridge St., Waitsfield.

In two houses next to the covered bridge is the ultimate collection of stuffed animals – mainly bears, outfitted in everything from a London bobby's uniform or a wedding dress to ski vests that proclaim "Save the Bear." Twin sisters Bonnie and Gaelic McTigue preside over an enterprise that "started with Christmas and teddies" and just keeps expanding. A cheery "hello" emanated from Gael hidden behind a Christmas tree at a desk painting Christmas ornaments one summer day when we entered the **Tree Top Christmas Shop.** In the **Teddy Bear Shop** in the other house, Bonnie was assisted by Bridget the cat atop the cash register and Megan the dog on a wicker loveseat in front of one of twelve rooms chock full of character. We picked up a few of Gael's remarkable hand-painted birds for Christmas presents. It's a bit overwhelming, but the twins are both characters and their shops are not to be missed.

(802) 496-3997. www.allthingsbright.com. Open daily, 9 to 6.

United Church is on view from gazebo on Craftsbury Common.

Craftsbury/Burke, Vt.

The Look and Lifestyle of a Century Ago

Picture the picture-perfect Vermont town: a white-spired church and public buildings facing the village green, pristine clapboard houses on shady lawns, cows grazing against a hilly landscape, youngsters picking wildflowers along the road.

The town is Craftsbury, population 1,000. And the picture is of Craftsbury Common, a hilltop village of perhaps 200 souls in the middle of nowhere – the west-central section of Vermont's most remote region, the Northeast Kingdom.

Craftsbury Common indeed has a common, which is nearly as big as the rest of the village. It's a serene two acres or so flanked by a few houses (one turns out to be an annex of an inn) and institutional buildings. Among them are the nation's smallest accredited college, the state's smallest public high school, a rickety post office, a wonderful little library and a funeral home, the village's only commercial enterprise other than the inn. North of the village is a sports/education center believed to be unique in the world.

A few miles downhill from Craftsbury Common's perch astride a ridge is the village of Craftsbury, site of the town hall, the Catholic church, two general stores and another inn. From here an unnumbered road leads to East Craftsbury, home of a Presbyterian church and a nursery.

That's about it for Craftsbury, the most prosperous part of a Northeast Kingdom that reflects the Vermont of old, uncondoed and uncutesied. Nearby is Greensboro, a lakeside summer colony of academics and the "metropolis" of the immediate area, the place where the flatlanders go to pick up the New York Times. Beyond are the Burkes – East Burke, Burke Hollow et al – at the foot of Burke Mountain, a ski area and a center of sophistication in the Northeast Kingdom.

A bit farther afield but worth the trip is Lake Willoughby, the "Lucerne of America." It's a sight to behold from an inn on its sharply rising shores.

Vermont's most rural region is an area of tranquility, scenic beauty, little-traveled byways, country stores and, rather unexpectedly, considerable summer music and exotic garden enterprises. Time spent here celebrates the look, the landscape and the lifestyle of a century ago.

Inn Spots

The Inn on the Common, 1165 North Craftsbury Road, Box 75, Craftsbury Common 05827.

This uncommon inn in postcard-perfect Craftsbury Common took on a new lease in life in 2003. Jim and Judi Lamberti left the large Inn at Essex outside Burlington, the 120-room country hotel and restaurant they helped found in 1989, to run a smaller inn of their own. Their choice: a distinctive inn that ex-New Yorkers Penny and Michael Schmitt had built over three decades from a four-bedroom B&B with shared baths into a sixteen-room inn and restaurant full of character.

The high-powered Lambertis, who had been voted Vermont innkeepers of the year in 1994, moved onto the premises. They planned to launch a full-scale revitalization of the inn's buildings, grounds and guest services, and eventual room upgrades.

First they put their stamp on the inn's traditionally guests-only dining room, which overlooks a spectacular specimen rose garden. They renamed it Trellis (see Dining Spots) and broadened its appeal both to inn guests and the community.

Jim, who was president-elect of the New England Innkeepers Association, took a liking to hosting the innkeepers' traditional cocktail hour, mixing drinks for guests at a small bar in a corner of the original inn's front library. He and Judi also preside through the extended dinner hour in the innkeeping tradition of times past.

Meanwhile, the Lambertis pledged to enhance an inn that always had been a class act. The sixteen guest rooms are spread out in three restored Federal houses. All have sitting areas made for relaxing instead of show and are stylishly furnished with vivid, color-coordinated prints and fine wallpapers, good artworks and antiques.

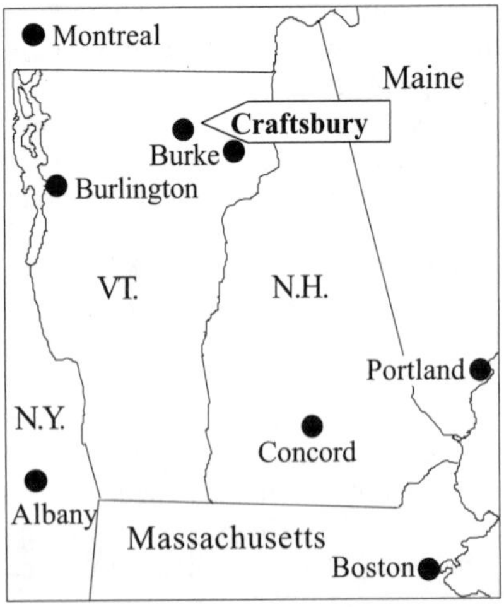

We're partial to the South Annex across from the main inn. Here, besides the office and a lounge with TV/VCR, is our favorite Room 12, main floor rear. It contains a kingsize bed, a sofa, a reclining chair custom-designed for a frequent guest, an enormous bathroom that doubles as a dressing area and plenty of room to spread out. Others like the upstairs Room 10 with its wood stove, a queensize canopy bed covered with a hand-stitched quilt, a sofa and two side chairs, and an old butter churn in the bathroom.

Upstairs in the main inn with a great view of the gardens and mountains to the rear is Room 3, The Porch. For what

Picket fence surrounds main building at The Inn on the Common.

once was a porch it has what the innkeepers call serious furniture (meaning antiques), plus two leather chairs that are so soft you think you'll never get up.

Another guest favorite is glamorous Room 5 in the main inn, decorated in red wisteria.

These are among the eight deluxe rooms, which cost $20 more than the others but are worth it. Every room is a treasury of caring touches, however. The Schmitts favored those in the North Annex, their last acquisition, where they were able to do everything they wanted to. It's a couple of blocks removed from the main inn and the only one actually facing the serene, expansive common.

Besides the dining room and a library, the main inn has a parlor on the main floor. Its five guest rooms are up a steep, tightly curved staircase.

Breakfast is almost as much a culinary treat as dinner, especially for those on the MAP plan (continental breakfast is complimentary for B&B guests). The menu offers several choices. Juice, a platter of fresh fruit and cranberry-lemon muffins came first at our visit. The herbed-cheddar quiche with Canadian bacon was a succulent special. Shirred eggs and Vermont-made sausage were accompanied by thick toasted bread.

Enjoy the rose and perennial gardens. Play tennis on a clay court. Swim in the natural-looking, free-form gunite pool sequestered behind the South Annex. Read a book in your room or relax over afternoon tea or hot chocolate in the lounge. Almost every creature comfort you could want is at the uncommon Inn on the Common, and all the area's rural pleasures are close at hand.

(802) 586-9619 or (800) 521-2233. Fax (802) 586-2249. www.innonthecommon.com. Sixteen rooms with private baths. Rates, MAP. Doubles, $240 to $340 in summer, $270 to $370 in foliage, $210 to $310 in winter. Children and pets accepted. Closed in April.

The Craftsbury Inn, 107 South Craftsbury Road, Craftsbury 05826.

A white-columned building across from the general store houses ten guest rooms and a restaurant of note (see Dining Spots). Bill Maire and his wife Kathy moved from the mountains of Arizona to take over the inn and restaurant in 2000 and embarked on significant upgrading.

They refurnished the long front parlor, which offers a small fireplace (from the original post office in Montpelier) and a piano beneath an embossed pressed-tin ceiling. Adjacent are a game room with library and video cassettes, and a sitting room with an antique cast-iron stove and TV. A pubby bar was added in the Flight Deck lounge, filled with aviation memorabilia reflecting the innkeepers' long association with civil and military aviation. Guests also enjoy wraparound verandas on two floors.

The Maires refurbished all of the upstairs guest rooms "from the walls out," putting up new wallpaper and getting rid of what Bill referred to as the 1950s maple. In its stead are antiques and reproduction furnishings. Two rooms have queen beds and the rest one or two doubles or twins. Four rooms in the oldest section of the house share a large hall bath.

A full breakfast is served guests in the sunny Atrium dining room overlooking English gardens and a rear yard bordered by the Black River, which winds around the property. The choice might be eggs any style, a mushroom or cheese omelet, or french toast.

(802) 586-2848 or (800) 336-2848. Fax (802) 586-8060. www.craftsburyin.com. Six rooms with private baths and four rooms with shared bath. Doubles, $115 to $125 with private bath, $90 shared. Children and pets accepted.

Lakeview Inn, Main Street (or Breezy Avenue, Box 180), Greensboro 05841.

This 1872 structure began as a boarding house and later served as an inn, to which guests arrived by horse and carriage from the railroad stop at Greensboro Bend. Listed on the National Register, the property was acquired and restored by John Hunt, and reopened in 1998 as an inn run by his wife, Kathy Unser. John also bought the Vermont Daylilies enterprise and moved it to the rear of the property, where the display gardens feature more than 500 varieties (and put on a better show than does Caspian Lake, which is no longer readily evident from the front porch of the inn).

The interior retains the original wide-board floors, but otherwise the renovations took away the patina of age. The hallway floors are polished (and accented with stylish carpet runners), the new bathrooms are modern and the walls have been painted light colors. Kathy decorated all nine guest rooms on the second floor in about the same spiffy yet spare style with fishnet canopy beds, small rugs, an antique desk and a single chair. Beds are queensize except for two with twins. The third-floor suite is one of the oddest we've encountered, though quite suitable for families. The stairway leads to an open living room, off which are three bedrooms (two with a queen bed each and one with twin beds). The extra-large bathroom has a shower. The living room has nothing to keep the kids amused.

The inn contains two small common rooms, one on the main floor with a TV set. Another on the second floor is called the "quiet room" (no TV), with little to distract from the gorgeous view out the back.

The biggest common area is actually a dining area, a quite large and nondescript space called the **Constant Bliss Café and Bakery.** Constant Bliss, it seems, was a Revolutionary War hero whose legacy here is a pastry display case and counter in a rear corner beside the kitchen. Inn guests enjoy a breakfast of breads and muffins from the bakery, plus a specialty entrée each morning.

Side porch at WilloughVale Inn yiel0ds full-length view of Lake Willoughby.

At our October visit, the dining area was filling fast with leaf-peepers and locals seeking lunch from a selection of deli-type soups, sandwiches and salads, plus a few entrées. In summer, the café serves dinner. The choices change daily, but favorites include fresh sesame and garlic fillet of salmon, roasted pork tenderloin with apple chutney and filet mignon with bourbon and molasses glaze, available here or to go. Constant Bliss, we think, would choose to eat on the screened porch overlooking the lily gardens and mountains.

(802) 533-2291. www.lakeviewinnbb.com. Nine rooms and one three-bedroom suite with private baths. Doubles, $135 to $165. Suite, $350. Children welcome.

WilloughVale Inn, 793 Vermont Route 5A, Westmore 05860.

Overlooking the length of beautiful Lake Willoughby from its more built-up, less picturesque north end, this has been a restaurant, an inn with lodging facilities and – the prize, we think – four cottages across the road and right on the lake. David Gameroff, whose family owns the Green Mountain Inn in Stowe, acquired the inn in 1996 and breathed new life into an establishment that had grown tired.

Room sizes and bed configurations vary, but all come with Vermont hand-crafted furnishings, sprightly decor and televisions. Best of the older rooms is the deluxe Lupine Room with queen canopy bed, sofa and upholstered chair, and a bathroom with a jacuzzi tub for two, a separate shower and a double vanity. Part of the large main-floor dining room was renovated in 2001 to produce two deluxe rooms, the Governor Aiken and the Gazebo. Each has a king bed, fireplace, double jacuzzi and TV/VCR, plus big windows and a private porch with sweeping views of the lake. Amenities here include microwaves, refrigerators and coffeemakers, features also available in the newly renovated Harter Suite, which has a living room with fireplace and jacuzzi bath.

Our favorite among the cottages is the Angler with a queen bed, a sunken living room, kitchen, a screened porch and a deck with lounge chairs, right at lake's edge.

Each of the other cottages has two bedrooms and either a dining area or eat-in kitchen. There are gathering spots on the front porches and in the inn's library, which has antique books and games. A continental breakfast is served.

A small dining room and the taproom remain open for limited dining for guests and the public, by reservation. The menu is simple but serviceable, starting with such appetizers as chicken wings and artichoke dip. Typical entrées are shrimp scampi parmesan, baked haddock and shrimp, herb-crusted chicken, grilled pork chops and filet mignon oscar. Desserts include chocolate truffles and cheesecake.

(802) 525-4123 or (800) 594-9102. www.willoughvale.com. Ten rooms, one suite and four cottages with private baths. Doubles $129 to $234 in summer, $79 to $199 rest of year. Cottages, $219 to $249 in summer, $149 to $209 rest of year. One-week minimum in cottages in July and August; two-night minimum in June, September and winter. Children and pets accepted. Closed in April.

Entrées, $15.95 to $21.95. Dinner by reservation, 5:30 to 9, nightly except Tuesday in summer, Thursday-Saturday in off-season.

Highland Lodge, 1608 Craftsbury Road, Greensboro 05841.

On a hillside across the East Craftsbury Road from Caspian Lake is a country inn of the old school. "A real refuge from the busyness of modern life" is how its brochure describes it. Families comprise the bulk of the devoted clientele. Built in the 1860s as a farmhouse, it was converted into an inn in the 1920s. It's now run by David and Wilhelmina Smith, the second generation of an innkeeping family.

Accommodations are basic in eleven guest rooms, reached by three separate staircases from the main floor. Each has an assortment of queensize or twin beds (sometimes both) with white Bates spreads, Ethan Allen furniture and sheer white curtains. Amenities in the bath consist of a small bar of Ivory soap and a box of Kleenex. The rooms are spotless, but not the kind in which to linger.

That's fine, because much of the downstairs is given over to three side-by-side common rooms. One is a cozy library with a corner fireplace, another has a TV and a wood stove, and one in the middle contains a grand piano with a sign regulating the hours of play.

Out back, behind the gift shop and office, is a children's library and game room where the ping-pong table was getting a good workout the rainy day we visited. On summer mornings, youngsters aged 4 to 9 link up with the "Play Lady," who devises crafts programs and nature hikes.

Across the street are a clay tennis court and, down a path, the lodge's private beach and "bathhouse," which looked to us like a boathouse. Rowboats, paddleboats and canoes may be borrowed to explore Caspian Lake, which the Smiths say is Vermont's cleanest. Along its shores are Victorian cottages favored by academics and writers.

Three meals a day are served in the restaurant, which is open to the public (see Dining Spots), except on summer Mondays when lunch is a picnic at the beach.

Just behind the lodge is a lineup of ten white cottages, each with one to three bedrooms. Four are winterized and some have kitchenettes.

In winter, the lodge's cross-country ski center has 50 kilometers of trails linked to the network at the Craftsbury Outdoor Center.

(802) 533-2647. Fax (802) 533-7494. www.highlandlodge.com. Eleven rooms and eleven cottages with private baths. Rates, MAP: doubles $202.50 to $260, cottages $270 to $290. Closed mid-October to Christmas and mid-March to Memorial Day.

Terrace tables outside Wildflower Inn provide panoramic view.

The Wildflower Inn, Darling Hill Road, Lyndonville 05851.

If you're among those inn-goers who feel the children should go with you, here's the place. Mary and Jim O'Reilly have eight of their own – the number used to change annually, a staffer advised as she counted up on her fingers – and think families should vacation together.

And what a place they have for family vacations: Twenty-one rooms and suites (some with bunk beds), a full-service restaurant and lunch snack bar, a swimming pool, a petting barn with farm animals, horse-drawn hay and sleigh rides, indoor and outdoor play areas, a skating pond, tennis court, batting cage, soccer field, hiking and nature trails, flower gardens, an indoor sauna and hot tub, and a supervised children's program. Little wonder the place is generally booked far ahead when school's out in summer.

And what a location: Atop a ridge with a view that won't quit, revealing undulating mountains and valleys to the west. The place is paradise on earth for families of young children, who were everywhere in evidence at our latest visit. Some were cavorting in the pool as their mother camcorded the event for posterity and their father relaxed in an Adirondack chair to enjoy the vista with the day's newspaper. Others were climbing aboard the horse-drawn wagon for a hay ride. Still others were snacking on afternoon lemonade and cookies in the inn's living room.

Accommodations are two suites upstairs in the main house, nine rooms and three suites in the rambling carriage house across the way, and six more rooms and suites in the Meadows complex (the first of the O'Reillys' homes here, long since outgrown – they moved to a new hilltop house nearby in 1997). Down the road is a School House Cottage with queen bed, double jacuzzi, kitchenette, sitting area and french doors onto a deck. It's a bit removed from the hubbub and billed as the honeymoon suite.

Rooms come with varying bed configurations, from a few with queen or king beds to the more common double beds and doubles with bunks. The Grand Meadow Suite in the O'Reillys' former quarters includes a queen bedroom with jacuzzi tub, living/dining area, TV/VCR, full kitchen and a second bedroom with double bed and bath. Four more rooms and suites in the Meadows Complex have kitchenettes and patios or decks sharing the awesome view. All are comfortably furnished and appointed with stenciling, hooked rugs, quilted comforters and country effects – no antiques to be broken and no television. Supervised morning activities and nightly movies keep the children occupied.

When he's not cooking some mighty good meals, chef Tom Barth leads backwoods trail rides. "Most of the staff are multi-faceted," Mary O'Reilly advised. "They have to be when they're dealing with families."

A full country breakfast is included in the rates. Dinner is available to guests and the public in a pleasant, 40-seat dining room open onto an enclosed sun porch overlooking the mountains. In addition to a children's menu and early serving hours, a more sophisticated menu allows parents to eat well and in peace while youngsters are entertained. About ten entrées, including one or two for vegetarians, are offered nightly. Typical are spicy grilled yellowfin tuna with tomato compote, ginger-glazed chicken with mango chutney and sirloin steak sautéed with mushrooms.

A deck off the game room is the setting for snacks and lunch from an outdoor snack bar near the pool area.

(802) 626-8310 or (800) 627-8310. Fax (802) 626-3039. www.wildflowerinn.com. Thirteen rooms and eight suites with private baths. Summer: doubles $149 to $169, suites $199 to $289. Winter: doubles $99 to $129, suites $149 to $259. Two-night minimum weekends. Children welcome. Closed April and first three weeks of November.

Entrées, $15.95 to $18.95. Dinner nightly in summer, 5:30 to 9; Thursday-Sunday in winter.

The Inn at Mountain View Farm, Darling Hill Road, Box 355, East Burke 05832.

Set on 440 pastoral acres with views of the Willoughby Gap and Burke Mountain, the only intact turn-of-the-century stock farm in Vermont is now home to a small inn and gourmet restaurant.

Marilyn Pastore operates an inn in the former creamery, which still holds the boiler and engine that powered the churns in the architecturally grand creamery, and a farmhouse. Local philanthropist Elmer Darling raised prize-winning Jersey cattle on the farm, which is notable for the farmhouse, monumental barns, outbuildings, perennial gardens and a sylvan landscape that constitute the last gentleman's farm remaining in the Northeast Kingdom.

The classic red-brick, Georgian-style creamery with a butter churn cupola has been refurbished as the centerpiece of the inn. Across the courtyard is the main farmhouse, with several larger and more deluxe units for overnight guests. The periphery of the courtyard is framed with striking red barns that hold farm animals and invite exploration. The perennial gardens behind the barns and afternoon horse-drawn wagon rides are attractions.

Upstairs in the creamery are eight bedrooms and a two-bedroom family suite named for Vermont towns. Four rooms have queen beds, three have doubles and one has twins, while the Creamery Suite has a queen and two twin beds. Each is furnished with handmade quilts, botanical prints, antiques and coordinated fabrics.

The newest quarters are in two wings of the farmhouse. Three are colorful and spacious one-room "suites" with queensize beds, one with a fireplace and the other two with jacuzzi tubs. The Westmore Wing here is billed as a vacation rental for families or groups. The main floor has a kitchen, dining area and a common living

Inn at Mountain View Farm is part of attractive farm complex.

room with a fireplace. Upstairs is a luxury suite with queensize bed and bath with jacuzzi tub, plus a loft with a sofabed. A second guest room offers twin cannonball beds and a full bath.

Back in the creamery, the spacious downstairs common room with fireplace is dressed in traditional and contemporary furnishings in what Marilyn calls an English country manor style. Here is where watermelon slices and cranberry spritzers were set out the afternoon of our visit. Tea and sweets are offered in cooler months.

A black iron stove serves as a buffet table in the dining room. The day starts with a hearty breakfast of fresh fruit from the farm, cereals, yogurt, homemade sweet breads and a main dish, perhaps vegetable frittata, apple or blueberry pancakes, or french toast.

Most evenings, the dining room turns into **Darling's,** featuring elegant country cuisine. An inventive menu offers the likes of pan-seared red snapper with citrus beurre blanc, Tuscan chicken stew and filet mignon with wild mushroom demi-glace. The meal could start with mussels zuppa or spicy calamari over spinach. Worthy endings include chocolate raspberry soufflé and ginger ice cream in a pizzelle cup.

(802) 626-9924 or (800) 572-4509. www.innmtnview.com. Twelve rooms and two suites with private baths. Doubles, $150 to $235. Westmore Wing, $385.

Entrées, $17 to $24. Dinner by reservation, nightly except Tuesday 5 to 9. Restaurant closed November and April.

Craftsbury Outdoor Center, Lost Nation Road, Box 31, Craftsbury Common 05827.

Tucked away off a dirt road past Little Hosmer Pond not far from Great Hosmer Lake, this is unlike any eating and lodging establishment we have known. It's a full-fledged sports and education center, the only one that its director knows of in the world. And the public is cordially invited.

Think of a summer camp for adults and you have an idea of the Craftsbury Center, which the original owners of the Inn on the Common were instrumental in founding in 1978 on the site of the old Cutler School for boys. Here, up to 100 folks gather for lodging, meals and a variety of recreation and education options, from informal to formal.

The 170 acres lend themselves to cross-country skiing. In summer, the center runs adult programs for walking, mountain biking, sculling, elder hostels and more.

Most guests are involved in one or more of the ongoing programs, but the transient public is welcome for meals and overnight stays. Lodging is in facilities that are a cross between summer camp and boarding school: "your typical square, unadorned dormitory room sharing baths with three to ten other rooms," says a spokesman. They include 31 small rooms, nine larger rooms, seven rooms with private baths, two apartments and four housekeeping cabins.

Healthful, all-you-can-eat meals are served buffet style in a dining hall furnished with picnic tables, an old piano and oars hanging on the walls. The food is so popular that it spawned a cookbook, now in its second printing.

(802) 586-7767 or (800) 729-7751. Fax (802 586-7768. www.craftsbury.com. Thirty-three rooms with shared bath, seven with private bath, two apartments and four housekeeping cabins. Rates AP. Doubles, $128 to $162 shared bath, $188 to $198 private bath, $215 to $235 apartment or cottage.

Breakfast at 8, lunch at 12:30, dinner at 6. Dinner, $13.50.

Dining Spots

Trellis, 1165 North Craftsbury Road, Craftsbury Common.

Dinner at the sophisticated Inn on the Common is available to the public as well as inn guests, as new owners Jim and Judi Lamberti have sought to reach out to the community. They hired as chef German-born Christoph Wingensiefen, a Craftsbury resident who had been executive sous chef at Stowe's Top Notch Resort.

The redecorated dining room is elegant as can be, with big windows onto an outdoor deck beside the rose garden. Twenty-five diners can be accommodated at two seatings. Dining is by candlelight, with candles flickering in hurricane chimneys on the tables and in reflective wall sconces.

The short menu changes seasonally and is available à la carte, a change from the prix-fixe format of the past. It's served at individual tables, as opposed to the large communal tables that made for the convivial dinner parties we enjoyed here in days gone by.

Following cocktails and hors d'oeuvres in the library and parlor, diners adjourn to a candlelit dining room dignified by fine linens, china and crystal. At our latest autumn visit, the starters were butternut squash soup, curry-seared mahi mahi with ratatouille and a frisée and spinach salad with blue cheese, apples and dried cranberries.

Entrées, which come with a garden salad and fresh bread, included crispy duck breast with apricot-brandy sauce, seared filet mignon with truffle-bordelaise sauce, and venison loin with walnut demi-glace. Desserts were apple-cranberry crisp with ice cream or frozen chocolate mocha terrine with raspberry coulis.

The inn's carefully chosen wine list is pricey, but a low markup produces great values. Coffee and chocolates are served after dinner in the library, where guests like to linger over cordials.

(802) 586-9619 or (800) 521-2233. Entrées, $18.50 to $21.50. Dinner nightly, seatings 5:30 to 7:30. Closed in April.

The Craftsbury Inn, 107 South Craftsbury Road, Craftsbury.

A handsome Atrium dining room overlooking spotlit gardens and upscale food commend this restaurant that's open to the public by reservation. Dining is at round tables set with linens, candles and fresh flowers in an elegant room with wainscoting and big windows onto the back yard.

Dinner is à la carte, and chef-owner Bill Maire changes his French/American menu seasonally. You might start with Canadian pea soup, warm beef tenderloin and wild mushroom salad, curried scallops in puff pastry, risotto with porcini mushrooms and goat cheese, or escargots bourguignonne. Main courses range from four-cheese tortellini to grilled rack of spring lamb. Choices include Maryland crab cakes, prosciutto-wrapped baked fillet of salmon, chicken vol-au-vent with mango sauce and beef tenderloin with wild mushroom ragu. Dessert could be Quebec apple cake, chocolate-raspberry tuxedo pie, New York cheesecake with amaretto or chambord, or maple waffle with ice cream and chocolate sauce.

Bill, who was wine and spirits manager for the Arizona Biltmore Resort & Spa, is naturally proud of his wine list. It reflects his preference for good wines at reasonable prices, especially those of undiscovered and underrated vineyards.

(802) 586-2848 or (800) 336-2848. Entrées, $16 to $22. Lunch in season, Tuesday-Saturday 11:30 to 2. Dinner by reservation, Tuesday-Saturday 5 to 9. Sunday brunch, 10 to 1. Afternoon tea, Saturday and Sunday 1 to 4. Closed April and first two weeks of November.

Highland Lodge, Caspian Lake Road, Greensboro.

Lunch on the front porch with a distant view of Caspian Lake is a summertime treat here, and we were surprised how many were enjoying it on a raw, dank day. The menu covers the basics, but the daily specials can get interesting: a warm spinach salad with grilled duck breast and a rabbit and ham stew with buttermilk biscuits and rainbow coleslaw at our visit. The problem was they'd run out of the spinach-duck salad and one special was sort of lacking: the borscht with Ma Smith's beets didn't seem like the real thing and its accompaniment, half a beer cheese and tomato sandwich on wheat bread, was rather strange-tasting. The sautéed sea scallops with snow peas on rice was much more successful.

The chefs create a new dinner menu each night, but the format stays the same. It features homemade soups and appetizers; salads with local greens and homemade dressings; and occasionally imaginative entrées and specials. Grilled black angus sirloin steak is a staple, but other entrées could be striped bass fillet spiced with pepper and lemon, grilled mustard-glazed chicken breast and maple-cured Vermont ham with apple chutney. Starters could be celery-apple soup with blue cheese mousse, fresh fruit cup or herbed goat cheese with provençal olives. For dessert, try the blueberry-lemon cream cake or chocolate cream pie.

Some people come here just for the lodge's special dessert hour, starting nightly at 7:30. In addition to the specials, they go for things like chocolate mousse parfait, ishkabibble (brownie à la mode with hot fudge sauce) and something called forgotten dessert, a meringue with ice cream and strawberries. The lodge also has a short menu of lighter dinner fare. The L-shaped dining room with a wood stove is rustic and pretty in pink, but we'd choose the porch overlooking lake and sunset any time we could.

(802) 533-2647. Entrées, $20 to $23. Lunch in season, Tuesday-Sunday noon to 2. Dinner nightly by reservation, 6 to 8. Sunday brunch, 11 to 2. Closed mid-October to Christmas and mid-March to Memorial Day.

River Garden Café, 427 Main St. (Route 114), East Burke.

Robert Baker, who owned a restaurant called Sofi in New York City, had been coming to the Northeast Kingdom on vacations for more than twenty years. New York got to be too much and he and David Thomas headed to East Burke in 1992 to open this café with gardens leading to the East Branch of the Sutton River in back. With the staff (including the owners) often in green striped shirts, a window seat full of pillows in the cozy front bar, a long screened back porch, a collection of kitschy salt and pepper shakers, and "jadeite" tables from the '30s, it's quite offbeat and charming.

Chef Steven Hartwell's "new culinary age" menu is fairly sophisticated for the area and the prices are right. You can snack on anything from bruschetta or artichoke dip to grilled shrimp caesar salad or a Jamaican jerk chicken salad with a spicy lime vinaigrette. Or go for filet mignon with a merlot sauce or grilled lamb loin with a sundried tomato-basil vinaigrette, the most expensive entrées on the menu that ranges from Mediterranean salmon and chicken Santa Fe to fajitas and pork medallions madeira. Salads, burgers, pizzas, vegetarian dishes and specials like warm duck salad with apricot-curry dressing and mango chutney often have the place full shortly after 5 o'clock.

Crème brûlée is a dessert specialty. Or you might find triple chocolate torte, seasonal fruit cobblers or a chipwich, two cookies centered with ice cream and topped with chocolate sauce and whipped cream.

(802) 626-3514. www.rivergardencafe.com. Entrées, $15.95 to $21.95. Lunch, Wednesday-Saturday 11:30 to 2. Dinner, Wednesday-Sunday 5 to 9. Sunday brunch, 11 to 2. Closed November and April.

The Pub Outback, 482 Route 114, East Burke.

Housed in a barn "outback of Bailey's & Burke" country store, this is a lively, casual place beloved by skiers. Focal points on the main floor are a long, rectangular bar in the center and two solariums used as non-smoking dining areas. Above the bar is a free-standing dining loft, open on all sides with beams overhead and barn artifacts here and there. Tables are custom-inlaid with local memorabilia, and it's all unexpectedly airy and contemporary.

Bowls of homemade popcorn stave off hunger as diners select from an all-day international menu of appetizers, salads, sandwiches and vegetarian dishes. West Indian roti (curried chicken and potato in a pastry with mango chutney), black bean cakes with cilantro salsa and sour cream, bruschetta, wontons, oriental chicken salad and a chef's salad topped with grilled chicken, steak and ham are among the possibilities. Main courses include garlic-sesame stir-fries, seafood-stuffed sole, chicken cordon bleu, old-fashioned pot roast and three versions of steak.

(802) 626-1188. www.thepuboutback.com. Entrées, $9.95 to $16.95. Dinner nightly, 4 to 9 or 10.

Diversions

There's a lot to see and do – or nothing to see and do – in the Northeast Kingdom, depending on your point of view. The scenery varies from low-key to spectacular. This remains an essentially rural, old-fashioned area where folks meet at the general stores or at the farmer's market (Saturday mornings in season on Craftsbury Common). Church suppers and band concerts are the social gatherings of importance.

All kinds of sports and educational pursuits are offered on the property and under the auspices of the **Craftsbury Outdoor Center**. Walking, running, hiking, bicycling, sculling, cross-country skiing, horseback riding – you name it, they've got it.

Craftsbury Common is a wonderful hilltop town with a serene common and an institutional presence lent by Craftsbury Academy, the state's smallest public high school and one of the town's drawing cards for newcomers, and Sterling College, the nation's smallest degree-granting, accredited college with about 70 students involved in environmental studies.

Another must-see spot is scenic **Darling Hill Road** in Lyndonville and East Burke. The ridge is lined with stately farms and manicured estates, with views of Burke Mountain on one side and Willoughby Gap on the other. Elmer Darling's former mansion once served as a men's dormitory for Lyndon State College. He was a benefactor of the college on Vail Hill, along with friend Theodore N. Vail, first president of AT&T.

Music. The **Craftsbury Chamber Players** are in such demand that they cross the state on a pre-season tour and share their talents with audiences in Burlington and Burke Mountain each summer. They're in residence at the Town House in Hardwick from mid-July to mid-August, playing Thursday evenings at 8. They also give free afternoon mini-concerts "for children and their friends" in Hardwick, at the East Craftsbury Presbyterian Church and the Greensboro Fellowship Hall. The annual **Summer Music from Greensboro** series takes place in the Church of Christ sanctuary and the Greensboro Fellowship Hall. The Greensboro Association has sponsored concerts on a dock at Caspian Lake every summer Sunday at 7:30 for nearly 50 years. The signature scene in Craftsbury Common is the summer band concerts in the bandshell on the common Sunday nights at 7 in July and August. Those who remain in their vehicles honk their horns if they like what they hear.

Gardens. Gardeners in the know flock to **Perennial Pleasures Nursery** in East Hardwick, where two acres of perennial and herb gardens are on display and English cream tea is served by reservation on the lawns outside the Brick House, a one-time Victorian B&B, Tuesday-Sunday from noon to 4. Old-fashioned, hardy perennial flowers and herbs from the 17th to 19th centuries are the specialties. Gardeners also seek out places like **Stone's Throw Gardens** in Craftsbury for hardy perennials, including heritage roses and lilies, displayed on several levels around a restored 1795 farmhouse, against stone walls and in fields strewn with flowers. Other favorites for rare varieties are **Vermont Daylilies** and **Dooryard Lilacs** in Greensboro.

Shopping. There's not much of it, but what there is is interesting. **Willey's** in the center of Greensboro is a general store to end all general stores. Celebrating its 100th birthday in 2000, this local institution is a ramble of rooms, with three levels of hardware and housewares, a rear meat market and grocery and an upstairs for clothing. It's the kind of place where you'll find an open box of dog biscuits sandwiched between a display case of Timex watches and a crate of peaches. Across the aisle are shelves of chewing tobacco. Bulletin boards on either side of the entry dispense fascinating information. One poster announced a public forum on the future of Greensboro, "Condos or Cupolas?" Across the street is **The Miller's Thumb,** two levels of gifts built around a chute opening onto the basement mill and waterfall. The selection of colorful Italian pottery, antique pine furniture and specialty foods here is exceptional.

The center of East Burke has several shops of interest. Penny candy, Vermont specialty foods, country clothing, crafts and more are offered at the with-it **Bailey's & Burke Country Store.** Across the street, mountain bikes, canoes, kayaks, clothing and sports accessories are available at **East Burke Sports.** Eclectic crafts, gifts and collectibles are the forte of **Lasso the Moon.** Three styles of beers and tours are offered at the **Trout River Brewing Company** in Lyndonville.

Circus Smirkus, 1 Circus Road, Greensboro.

Circus Smirkus, an incredible youth acrobatic and clown circus that tours New England each summer, is based in a farm meadow and barn in Greensboro. Rob Mermin, who ran off to Europe to apprentice himself to circus life and eventually became director of the Ringling Bros. and Barnum & Bailey Clown College, founded the summer camp and touring troupe in 1987 to give youngsters aged 10 to 18 a chance to run away to their own, well disciplined circus. The camp is held on the Sterling College campus in Craftsbury. The touring troupe presents its season opening and closing shows in a 700-seat, one-ring big top in Greensboro between twice-weekly jaunts for seven weeks in July and August across New England.

(802) 533-7443. www.smirkus.org. Tour and show schedule varies annually.

Cabot Creamery, 2870 Main St., Cabot.

If this area has a real, live tourist attraction, this is it. Upwards of 350 people on busy days visit the Cabot Farmers' Cooperative Creamery, begun in 1919 when 94 dairy farmers founded the original creamery plant to churn butter. Today, nearly 500 Vermont farmers sell milk to the creamery, which produces twenty to thirty tons of cheese daily. Its sharp Vermont cheddar won top honors in the U.S. Championship Cheese Contest in Wisconsin, which considers itself the home of American cheddar, and it is sold at Harrods in London. Following a video presentation, visitors leave on guided tours of the manufacturing plant. Through windows into the production areas you can watch many of the 250 employees as they separate the curds from the whey, mold the cheese into 42-pound blocks and package it for aging in the huge uphill warehouse. The half-hour tour tells you all you might want to know about cheese. At tour's end, you get to sample low-fat, jalapeño, sharp and extra-sharp varieties to spur sales in the gift shop. The visitor center is dedicated to the unheralded role of farm women everywhere.

(802) 563-2231 or (800) 837-4261. Tours daily every half hour, 9 to 5, June-October, Monday-Saturday 9 to 4, February-May and November-December. No cheese production on Sunday and one day at midweek. Adults, $1.

Extra-Special

Old Stone House Museum, 28 Old Stone House Road, Brownington.

This charming place is part of the out-of-the-way Brownington Village Historic District, a time warp listed on the National Register. The impressive structure lives up to its billing as "the rarest kind of museum: a building as fascinating as the collection it houses." The four-story structure was built stone by stone in the 1830s by the Rev. Alexander Twilight, who is believed to have been America's first black college graduate (Middlebury) and its first black legislator, and his neighbors. The school in which he taught the region's school children for two decades is history, but the 30-room monument still instructs and inspires. It's filled with antiques and memorabilia displayed by the Orleans County Historical Society. You can see Alexander Twilight's desk and Bible there.

(802) 754-2022. Open Wednesday-Sunday 11 to 5, mid-May through mid-October. Adults, $5.

Glass blower Simon Pearce set up shop in this restored mill beside Ottaquechee River.

Woodstock-Quechee, Vt.

Chic Blend of Old and New

Picture the perfect Vermont place and you're likely to picture Woodstock, the historic shire town portrayed by the media as the picture-perfect New England village.

Picture an old river town with handsome 19th-century houses, red brick mill, waterfall and covered bridge and you have Quechee, the hamlet being restored to reflect Vermont as it used to be.

Join them with Rockefellers, Billingses, Pearces and other old names and new entrepreneurs, and you have an unusual combination for a chic, changing dynamic.

Carefully preserved and protected, Woodstock has such an impressive concentration of architecture from the late 17th and 18th centuries that National Geographic magazine termed it one of the most beautiful villages in America. That it is, thanks to its role as a prosperous county seat following its settlement in 1765 and to early popularity as both a summer and winter resort. Vermont's first golf course was established south of town around the turn of the last century and the nation's first ski tow was installed on a cow pasture north of town in 1934.

That also was the year when Laurance S. Rockefeller married local resident Mary Billings French, granddaughter of railroad magnate Frederick Billings. The Rockefeller interests now are Woodstock's largest landowner and employer. They buried the utility poles underground, provided a home and much of the stimulus for the Woodstock Historical Society, bought and rebuilt the Woodstock Inn, acquired and redesigned the golf course, bought and upgraded the Suicide Six ski area, built a multi-million-dollar indoor sports and fitness center and opened the Billings Farm & Museum. The Rockefeller home and 550 acres of surrounding gardens and woodlands now form the Marsh-Billings-Rockefeller National Historic Park, Vermont's first and the first anywhere to focus on conservation history.

Entrepreneur Simon Pearce, the Irish glass blower, has provided some of the same impetus for neighboring Quechee. He purchased an abandoned mill as a site for his glass-blowing enterprise, powered it with a 50-year-old turbine using water from the river outside, added more craftspeople and a restaurant, and sparked a crafts and business revival that has enlivened a sleepy hamlet heretofore known mainly for its scenic gorge.

In this inspirational setting of old and new, entrepreneurs are supported, and arts and crafts are appreciated.

Inn Spots

Twin Farms, Box 115, Barnard 05031.

A dozen miles north of Woodstock at the edge of the unlikely hamlet of Barnard lies the ultimate in small, luxury country resorts, one attracting jet-setters from across the world. The secluded farm once owned by writers Sinclair Lewis and Dorothy Thompson was converted to the tune of $11 million into the East's most sumptuous inn in 1993. One of a kind, it offers six suites and nine cottages, superb dining and a full-time staff of 30 to pamper up to 30 guests. The rates – $950 to $2,600 a night for two – includes meals, drinks and recreational activities.

Twin Farms is deluxe, of course, but understated and not at all ostentatious – not nearly as drop-dead showy as one might expect from its Zagat Survey rating as the top inn in the country. "The idea is you're a guest at somebody's country estate for the weekend," says Beverley Matthews, managing director with her husband Shaun, both of whom are British and who come with impeccable resort-management credentials. "For our guests, money is not an object. Time is."

The idea evolved after the Twigg-Smith family of Honolulu acquired the estate's main Sonnenberg Haus and ski area as a vacation home in 1974 when chef Sepp Schenker left to open his nearby Barnard Inn. In 1989, Laila and Thurston Twigg-Smith acquired the other half of Twin Farms from Sinclair Lewis's grandchildren, returning the estate to its original 235 acres. Son Thurston (Koke) Twigg-Smith Jr. and his wife Andrea, twenty-year residents of Barnard, managed the development phase of Twin Farms.

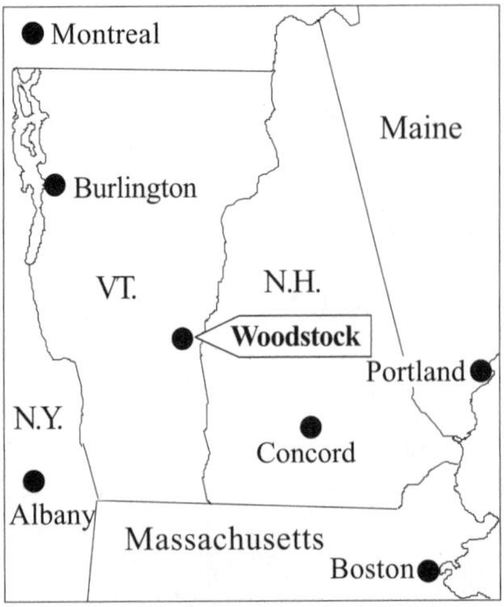

Their resources and taste show throughout the property, from the electronically operated gates at the entrance to the fitness center with spa treatment rooms and separate Japanese furo soaking tubs beneath a creekside pub reached by a covered bridge.

In the main house, three living rooms, each bigger than the last, unfold as the innkeeper Michael Beardsley welcomes guests. One with a vaulted ceiling opens onto a library loft and soaring windows gazing onto a 30-mile view toward Mount Ascutney.

Extravagant Studio with its soaring living room ceiling is biggest cottage at Twin Farms.

Upstairs are four bedrooms bearing some of the Twin Farms trademarks: plump kingsize feather beds, tiled fireplaces, comfortable sitting areas, fabulous folk art and contemporary paintings, TV/VCR/stereos, tea trays with a coffee press and Kona coffees from the family-owned corporation, twin sinks in the bathrooms, baskets of all-natural toiletries, terrycloth robes, and unbleached and undyed cotton towels. They impart a feeling of elegant rusticity, but come with every convenience of the ultimate home away from home.

Less antiquity and even more convenience are found in the newly built stone and wood guest cottages, each with at least one fireplace, a screened porch or terrace, an incredible twig-sided carport and its own private place in the landscape. The Perch, for instance, is situated above a small stream and beaver pond. It harbors luxuriant seating around the fireplace, a desk, a dining area, a refrigerator with ice maker, a bed recessed in an alcove and shielded by a hand-carved arch of wooden roping, a wicker-filled porch where a wood sculpture of a shark hangs overhead, and a bathroom with a copper tub the size of a small pool and a separate shower stall, both with windows to the outdoors.

The newest cottage is the largest. The 3,000-square-foot Chalet, on the edge of the ski slope, has a two-story-high living room with birch tree rafters, floor-to-ceiling stone fireplace and windows, bedroom with second fireplace, and his and hers bathrooms, one with a circular mosaic deluge shower and the other with skirted soaking tub beside the window. An enclosed porch adds a hot tub.

The second largest cottage – the contemporary Studio with a two-story window and loft bedroom – fulfills an artist's dream. The soaring Treehouse is furnished in Adirondack twig. The Japanese-style contemporary motif of the Orchard Cottage is striking, from its split-ash herringbone woven ceiling and white ash floors to the bamboo-framed marquetry breakfast table. Even more stunning is the Moroccan theme in the Meadow Cottage, likened to a desert king's traveling palace. The bedchamber is beneath a tented ceiling holding a chandelier of colored glass, and an inglenook fireplace of intricate mosaic tiles is framed by multi-colored banquettes and terra cotta floors. After these, the Log Cabin offers a Vermont-like respite.

Good food and drink (from help-yourself bars) are among Twin Farms strong points. Guests meet at 7 o'clock for cocktails in a changing venue – perhaps the wine cellar, one of the living rooms or, the night before our visit, in the Studio. A set, four-course dinner is served at 8 at tables for two in a baronial dining hall with chandeliers hanging from the vaulted ceiling and fieldstone fireplaces at either end.

Talented chef Neil Wigglesworth came here from The Point on Saranac Lake in the Adirondacks, a smaller but similarly grand inn that has been somewhat upstaged by Twin Farms. A typical dinner might start with medallions of lobster with avocado relish and angel-hair pasta, followed by warm red-cabbage salad with slices of smoked chicken. The main course could be veal mignon with timbales of wild rice and xeres sauce or five-spiced duck with nut-brown cabbage and golden beets. For dessert? Perhaps fresh figs with beummes de venese ice cream and peach-caramel sauce. Coffee, cheeses and a glass of aged port might round out the evening.

Breakfast is continental if taken in the guest rooms and cooked to order in the dining room from a small menu – raspberry pancakes or eggs benedict with lobster the day we visited.

Lunch is a movable feast, depending on the day and guests' inclinations. It could be a sit-down meal in the dining room, a picnic anywhere, or a barbecue beside the inn's seven-acre Copper Pond or at its own ski area, where there's never a lineup for the pomalift. Afternoon tea is a presentation worthy of the Ritz, complete, perhaps, with little gold leaves on one of the five kinds of tea pastries.

The creekside pub, incidentally, is nearly a museum piece with its collection of beer bottles from around the world. Beer-bottle caps cover the light shades over the billiards table, outline the mirror and sconces above the fireplace, and cover the candlesticks on the mantel. Even a pub chair is dressed in beer caps – a dramatic piece of pop art from the Twigg-Smiths' renowned art collection. Such are some of the delights and surprises encountered by guests at Twin Farms.

(802) 234-9999 or (800) 894-6327. Fax (802) 234-9990. www.twinfarms.com. Six suites and nine cottages with private baths. Suites, $950 and $1,100. Cottages, $1,500. Studio, $1,900. Chalet, $2,600. All-inclusive, except for 15 percent service charge and 9 percent state tax. Two-night minimum weekends, three nights on holidays. Children over 18.

The Jackson House Inn, 114-3 Senior Lane, Woodstock 05091.

Recently expanded, this three-story Victorian house on four acres of beautiful grounds west of the village offers sumptuous accommodations and a superior restaurant (see Dining Spots). All is overseen by new owner Carl Delnegro, who had his own consulting business in New York, and his wife Linda, who moved into the innkeepers' quarters from their home in nearby Plymouth.

Luxury starts in the main house, where some of the nine guest rooms and two suites are worthy of coverage in antiques and decorator magazines. Each is different

New addition (right) blends well with old at Jackson House Inn.

and eclectically furnished with such things as antique brass lamps on either side of the bathroom mirror, a marble-topped bedside table, an 1860 sleigh bed, an 1840 English mahogany pedestal desk, a prized Casablanca ceiling fan, Chinese carved rugs, hand-woven throws coordinated to each room's colors, an antique three-drawer sideboard with its faded original green paint and much more.

The third floor has been converted into two large one-room "suites" with queensize cherry sleigh beds, Italian marble baths and french doors onto a rear deck overlooking a spectacular English garden. We found plenty of room in the Francesca suite to spread out on an upholstered sofa, a wing chair and, on the deck beyond, two lounge chairs. The mirrored bathroom was so sparkling it looked as if we were the first ever to use it. Upon our return from dinner, a couple of Godiva chocolates were on our pillows.

The latest in creature comforts are evident in four large one-room "suites" in a new wing off the east side of the inn. These have sitting areas, gas fireplaces and modern bathrooms with cherry floors, whirlpool or massage therapy jetted tubs, separate showers and towel warmers.

During our latest stay in Clara's Corner, the queensize Sheraton poster bed was topped with red and gold Anichini fabrics and a sheeted duvet. Antique pots and vases graced the shelves, and an array of antique pillboxes topped a lace doily on a side table. There were fresh flowers, assorted fruits for nibbling and replacement towels at turndown. The staff even produced a new toothbrush for the one that had been forgotten.

Guests gather in the elegant parlor and intimate library for complimentary champagne or wine and an elaborate buffet of hors d'oeuvres before dinner. And we mean elaborate. One occasion produced California rolls, curried grilled chicken with diced green apple on a chickpea flour crisp and prosciutto-wrapped black mission figs.

The treats continue in the morning. The buffet might be laden with homemade granola, spiced pear yogurt, fruit compote with peach schnapps, and an array of sliced fruit, from pineapple to kiwi to cantaloupe. Juices, scones, croissants and muffins come next. The main course in one case was a scrambled egg and country sausage tart with goat cheese. Others could be ricotta pancakes, brioche french toast or – one we'll never forget – poached eggs on dill biscuits with poached salmon and hollandaise sauce.

After all this, settle into a deep wing chair in the library or retire to a lounge chair around the pond in the remarkably landscaped back yard for a morning nap. Or work it off in a small spa located on the lower level. It includes exercise equipment and a steam room. Here also is the inn's only TV.

(802) 457-2065 or (800) 448-1890. Fax (802) 457-9290. www.jacksonhouse.com. Nine rooms and six suites with private baths. Doubles, $195 to $260. Suites, $290 to $390. Two-night minimum weekends. Children over 14.

Woodstock Inn and Resort, 14 The Green, Woodstock 05091.

The biggest institution in town, the Woodstock Inn is solid. Solid, as in the 1823 Paul Revere bell weighing 1,463 pounds standing guard outside its newish 18th-century-style wing or the expanses of rich hardwoods comprising floor, walls and ceiling of the elegant Richardson's Tavern.

The inn sits majestically back from the green, its front facing a covered bridge and mountains, the rear looking across the pool and putting green and down the valley toward its golf course and ski touring center. The resort's other leisure facilities include the Suicide Six ski area, ten tennis courts and two lighted paddle tennis courts, an indoor sports and fitness center, and such activities as sleigh rides, dogsledding and horseback riding.

The interior of the inn is impressive as well. Built by Rockresorts in 1969 after Laurance Rockefeller found the original Woodstock Inn beyond salvation, it contains a lobby warmed by a ten-foot-high stone fireplace around which people always seem to be gathered, a large and glamorous dining room, a café, a wicker sunroom and lounge where afternoon tea is served, an always-busy gift shop and a smashing barnwood library outfitted with books and the day's Boston and New York newspapers.

The main inn has three stories in front and four in the rear, the lowest downstairs from the lobby. The 144 guest accommodations are among the more comfortable in which we've stayed: spacious rooms with handmade quilts on the beds, upholstered chairs, three-way reading lights, television, telephones, and large bathrooms and closets. Walls are hung with paintings and photographs of local scenes.

The most prized rooms seem to be 34 in the newer rear brick tavern wing, 23 with fireplaces and three with sitting-room porches overlooking the putting green. They are notable for graceful reading alcoves, dark blue and burgundy bed coverings matching the carpets, TVs on wheels hidden in cupboards, mini-refrigerators, and double marble vanities in the bathrooms. Interestingly, except for four suites, they seem smaller and more intimate than many of the rooms in the main inn. Covered parking is provided in a garage below.

The long main dining room, lately doubled in size, has large windows onto a spacious outdoor terrace overlooking the pool, putting green and gardens. Dinner is served nightly, the contemporary fare ranging from potato-crusted Atlantic salmon or shrimp and sweetbreads to veal medallions with dill beurre blanc or pine nut-

Maple Leaf Inn is new, built-to-look old Victorian structure set back in the woods.

crusted rack of lamb with toasted cumin jus. The elaborate Sunday buffet brunch is enormously popular.

The stylish **Eagle Café** offers a more casual lunch or dinner. We've enjoyed interesting salads and, most recently, smoked chicken and green onion quesadillas and a grilled chicken sandwich with melted jack, roasted peppers and herbed mayonnaise on toasted focaccia.

Stop for a drink or light fare in the sophisticated **Richardson's Tavern,** as urbane a nightspot as you'll find in Vermont.

(802) 457-1100 or (800) 448-7900. Fax (802) 457-6699. www.woodstockinn.com. One hundred thirty-three rooms and nine suites with private baths. Rates, EP. Doubles $199 to $389. Suites $499 to $609. Value season (March-April and November to mid-December): doubles $129 to $248, suites $350 to $450.

Entrées, $21.95 to $31.95. Lunch, 11:30 to 2. Dinner, 6 to 9. Sunday brunch, 10 to 1.

The Maple Leaf Inn, Route 12, Box 273, Barnard 05031.

The would-be innkeepers from Texas could not find the perfect old New England inn in their search among existing buildings. So they built it – a brand new, meant-to-look-old Victorian structure with the requisite gingerbread and gazebo – in a clearing amid sixteen acres of maples and birches at the end of a long driveway in tiny Barnard.

For their opening, Gary and Janet Robison from Houston engraved their names and the 1994 date – as they would for a cornerstone – at the beginning of the sidewalk leading to their impressive Victorian manse. "We couldn't resist," said Gary. "It's the child in all of us."

Up the long sidewalk, guests head to the wraparound front porch with its corner gazebo and authentic Tennessee oak rockers. Enter the front door, its window engraved with a maple leaf. On the right is an intimate library, full of foreign travel books and artifacts from the days when the Robisons lived abroad. On the left is a parlor with a corner fireplace, one of seven wood-burning fireplaces in the house and all topped with different antique mantelpieces. The traditional furniture here blends nicely with the occasional antique. Beyond and still farther out in this undulating house that seems to have a surfeit of windows everywhere is a fireplaced dining room, its five tables for two set for breakfasts by candlelight. "We cater to the getaway couples market," explains Gary.

Couples get away in seven comfortable bedrooms, most positioned to have windows on three sides. Five have fireplaces and all are air-conditioned. All have modern baths (four with whirlpool tubs), kingsize beds, sitting areas, TV/VCRs secreted in the armoires, ceiling fans and closets. An unusual picket fence affair replaces the usual headboard behind the kingsize bed in the main-floor Country Garden Room because the Robisons preferred not to block the window against which the bed rests. The pickets also continue the theme of the fences and gardens just outside. This room is typical with its swivel club chair/rockers, colorful bed quilt, gray carpeting and walls, and sheer lace curtains. Each mantelpiece holds what Gary calls an antique doodad. The four upstairs corner rooms are named and decorated for each season. Janet spent a week in each room creating the remarkable stenciling. She stenciled an elaborate winter village over the fireplace and around the doors and windows in the Winter Haven Room in which we stayed.

The Robisons have added two more rooms on the third floor, each with king bed, sitting area and two-person soaking tubs. They are value-priced so those on tighter budgets may enjoy the hosts' hospitality and amenities that merit AAA's four-diamond award.

The candlelight breakfast is a highlight of one's stay. Ours began with buttermilk scones garnished with flowers. The accompanying orange and cranberry-apple butters were shaped like maple leaves, and the preserves were presented in leaf dishes. Next came a fruit course of sautéed bananas with Ben & Jerry's ice cream. The main course was stuffed french toast with peach preserves and cream cheese, garnished with nasturtiums.

In the afternoon, the Robisons serve tea and wine with crackers and cheese. They also have a beer and wine license for room service.

Two chocolates are placed at bedside at nightly turndown. You may find a jar of maple syrup wrapped in a ribbon or a personalized wood Christmas ornament in the shape of a maple leaf hung on the doorknob. Hospitable Janet could send you home with a farewell package of pumpkin bread or muffins.

(802) 234-5342 or (800) 516-2753. www.mapleleafinn.com. Seven rooms with private baths. Doubles, $160 to $230, foliage and holidays $190 to $260. Deduct $30 midweek except peak periods. Two-night minimum weekends, holidays and foliage season. No children.

Ardmore Inn, 23 Pleasant St., Woodstock 05091.

A structure that looks like a covered bridge stands beside this restored white Georgian Greek Revival house that for years was the home of the well-known F.H. Gillingham family. The look was created by opening the rear of what had been a garage – it seems it was the only way for cars to get through to park in the back yard of the inn.

Charlotte and Cary Hollingsworth, flatlanders transplanted from Southern California, took over the vintage 1850 inn in 2003 virtually sight unseen. The couple had always wanted to see New England in foliage season. Although a bit late, they took a four-day vacation over New Year's 2003, fell in love with Vermont and put in a bid for the Ardmore Inn, next door to the B&B where they had been staying. "When we got home, we made an offer without having seen the inside," Cary said.

Ardmore Inn wears its Christmas finery.

The couple drove across the country with their possessions and took over the Ardmore in July 2003, opening to a full house. And, yes, they were as pleased with the inside – once they saw it – as they were with Vermont's changing seasons and the spectacular foliage that followed.

The impressive house with distinguished palladian windows was previously run by a priest from Our Lady of Snows church across the street. He named it Ardmore, which means "Great House" in the Irish tradition.

The Hollingsworths were taken by prized features of the house, such as the etched glass in the solid mahogany front door, the circular moldings around the original light fixtures on the ceilings and the recessed pocket windows screened with Irish lace curtains in the fireplaced living room.

The five guest rooms are painted in light pastel colors, furnished with antiques and oriental rugs, and outfitted with designer linens and towels. The mint-green Sheridan bedroom, main-floor front, has a queen bed and is accented with Waverly fabrics. The bathroom here has a walk-in Vermont marble shower and jacuzzi. The biggest bedroom is in the upstairs rear. Called Tarma, Irish for sanctuary, it lives up to its name with a kingsize bed, a fireplace, a loveseat facing a marble coffee table, and guardian angels as nightlights. The inn's own toiletries are placed in little white baskets.

A couple more fireplaces and a jacuzzi were added lately to the guest-room repertoire.

Breakfast is served for ten at an English mahogany banquet table inlaid with rosewood. Cary does the cooking, preparing a tropical fruit salad with sour cream-honey-mango sauce, lemon-poppyseed muffins and ham and cheese frittatas the morning of our visit. French toast stuffed with cranberry cream cheese was on tap the next day. There may be a breakfast "dessert," perhaps a piece of cheesecake or a scoop of ice cream or sorbet.

Afternoon refreshments are offered on the rear screened veranda in summer.

(802) 457-3887 or (800) 497-9652. Fax (802) 457-9006. www.ardmoreinn.com. Five rooms with private baths. Doubles, $110 to $175.

The Charleston House, 21 Pleasant St., Woodstock 05091.

When we first saw the Charleston House, it was festooned for Christmas, inside and out, and looked like a spread for House Beautiful.

But the red brick 1835 Greek revival townhouse is gorgeous at any time of year. Named for the hometown of the original innkeeper, it remains the epitome of Southern charm and hospitality under owners Dixi and Willa Nohl. They spent a weekend here in 1997, learned the place was for sale and started the purchase process on the spot. Dixi had been general manager of Burke Mountain ski area and Mad River Glen, and grew up in the lodging business in St. Anton in his native Austria. He and his wife wanted to stay in Vermont but distance themselves a bit from the skiing world.

Listed in the National Register of Historic Places, the house is elegantly furnished with period antiques and an extensive selection of art and oriental rugs.

A substantial recent addition – nicely secluded in back – contains three deluxe guest rooms with queen beds, jetted tubs, fireplaces, TVs and porches. Two on the ground floor are named for nearby Mount Peg and Mount Tom. The premium upstairs guest room was converted from the former innkeepers' quarters. The former kitchen became an extra-large bathroom and the sitting area has a sofa and fireplace. The porch, backing up to a wooded area, is "like being in a tree house," says Willa.

Another favorite room is the Summer Kitchen, downstairs between the original house and the new addition. It is cozy and romantic with four-poster queen bed, TV and two wing chairs angled beside the fireplace.

Five guest rooms upstairs in the main house have queen beds. One has twins.

Stunning floral arrangements and lovely needlepoint pillows adorn the dining room and the comfortable living room.

The breakfasts by candlelight here are such an attraction that the former owners put together a cookbook of recipes, called *Breakfast at Charleston House*. Willa continues to serve old favorites along with her own. Among specialties are puffed pancakes filled with peaches, a California omelet, macadamia-nut waffles with papaya and strawberries, and Charleston strata, an egg dish with sausage and apples.

At our latest visit, the main dish was pancakes – so "light and mouthwatering," according to a lady guest, "that where ordinarily I would have one I ended up having three." A tea aficionado, she was impressed with the Nohls' collection of teas – "some that I hadn't even heard of."

Such are the special touches hospitable innkeepers who have found their niche.

(802) 457-3843 or (888) 475-3800. www.charlestonhouse.com. Nine rooms with private baths. Doubles, $115 to $220; foliage, $125 to $235. Two-night minimum weekends and during foliage. Children over 10.

The Canterbury House, 43 Pleasant St., Woodstock 05091.

The British flag flies in front of this 1880 Victorian townhouse, which takes its theme from that hallmark of English literature, Chaucer's *Canterbury Tales.* New owners Sue and Bob Frost from New Jersey kept the theme of the former boarding house-turned-B&B, as imparted by earlier owners whose daughter was married to a

Kedron Valley Inn faces old tavern building (left) in South Woodstock.

Brit. The Frosts have made cosmetic improvements and imbued the place with energy and enthusiasm.

The bedrooms, while generally smaller than some in town, are cheerfully decorated with period antiques and reproductions. The Reeve's Tale, off the dining room on the main floor, has a queensize wicker bed covered with a country quilt. Six rooms upstairs vary from the Shipman's Tale, the smallest with double bed and a bath across the hall, to the redecorated Squire's Tale, with queen bed of country pine. Sue did the floral stenciling that graces this and other rooms. Up steep stairs is Chaucer's Garret, a third-floor mini-suite with a kingsize bed topped with a floral comforter and a sitting area with TV.

A favorite hideaway is the Monk's Tale, fashioned from an attached rear garage and reached by a separate entrance. Decorated in florals, it has an ornate carved oak queen bed, a gas fireplace, TV and a clawfoot tub.

Guests congregate in a comfortable, family-style living room with a fireplace. In the morning the action is at a communal breakfast for sixteen in the large dining room that is at the heart of this house. "Sue cooks and I serve," says Bob, who claims his kitchen role is limited to coffee service. French toast, egg casserole or quiche might be the entrée of the day

(802) 457-3077 or (800) 390-3077. Fax (802) 457-4630. www.thecanterburyhouse.com. Seven rooms with private baths. Doubles, $130 to $165, foliage $145 to $180. Two-night minimum peak weekends and in foliage. No children.

Kedron Valley Inn, Route 106, South Woodstock 05071.

This historic inn in the hamlet of South Woodstock, the heart of Vermont's horse country, has long been a favorite of the equestrian set as well as others seeking a rural setting. Innkeepers Jack and Nicole Maiden, who took over in 2002, redecorated the public rooms, installed a long bar in the tavern to make it more of a pub and started updating the guest rooms. "Our signature is service and attention to detail," said Jack, who picked up on the importance of such things while serving as chief operating officer for the Eileen Ford model agency in New York.

Accommodations include thirteen rooms in the three-story inn dating to the 1830s, seven in the old tavern building, and six out back in the motel-style log lodge rechristened the Country Cottages. Rooms vary in size. Most have canopy beds covered with antique quilts or down duvets. All have TV/VCRs and Bose radios.

Twenty have fireplaces or wood stoves, and five have whirlpool tubs. A collection of old bottles is over the mantel in the much-photographed corner Room 2, with a kingsize four-poster bed and a flat-screen TV with VCR/DVD. We liked even better our tavern room, twice as big as the norm with three closets, beamed ceiling, bentwood rockers, a large bathroom, and a four-poster canopied bed with frilly sheets. The largest rooms and suites generally are in the tavern building, where day beds or pullout sofas can accommodate families.

The Maidens converted a house on the property into a two-bedroom cottage with living room and kitchen, and planned to convert two rooms in the main building into suites in 2004.

Above the inn is a spring-fed pond for swimming. Lawn chairs are scattered about to take in the view of cows grazing on the hillside. Equestrians can rent horses in nearby stables, and the inn can arrange horse and buggy rides.

Overnight guests get a full country breakfast, from omelets to blueberry pancakes. It's served in the sunny terrace room.

(802) 457-1473 or (800) 836-1193. Fax (802) 457-4469. www.kedronvalleyinn.com. Twenty-three rooms, five suites and one cottage with private baths. Doubles, $131 to $221, suites, $248 to $297. Foliage and holidays: doubles $163 to $253, suites $279 to $327.

The Carriage House of Woodstock, 455 Woodstock Road (U.S. Route 4 West), Woodstock 05091.

The owners of this turreted B&B with a wraparound veranda up against the road knew they wanted to be innkeepers since they became engaged on a trip to Woodstock in 1989. The chance for Debbie and Mark Stanglin came in 2000. With their young daughter, they left corporate life in New York's Westchester County and acquired the recently renovated Carriage House of Woodstock.

The Stanglins offer seven carpeted bedrooms on three floors of the main house. All have queensize beds and are named after covered bridges in Vermont. They're furnished in a fresh, flouncy style that Mark called "relaxed Victorian." Two on the third floor command higher prices. The Taftsville has an extra twin bed and a TV/VCR, while the Moxley adds a whirlpool tub.

Two other premium rooms are in the walkout basement beneath the rear carriage house. Each comes with a whirlpool tub, TV and french doors to the outside. The largest, the Stowe Hollow Room, has a kingsize bed and a fireplace.

Victorian antique display items and family mementos are housed in custom-made glass cases separating the newly fireplaced living room and the dining room in the main structure. From the spectacular cathedral-ceilinged kitchen come breakfasts that start with a fruit plate and raspberry or pumpkin-chocolate chip muffins or perhaps a popover. The main course could be strawberry-oatmeal Belgian waffles, orange-coconut pancakes or breakfast burritos with sweet roasted jalapeño salsa. Guests gather in the kitchen for English shortbread cookies in the afternoon.

(802) 457-4322 or (800) 791-8045. www.carriagehousewoodstock.com. Nine rooms with private baths. Doubles, $110 to $150 June to late September, $125 to $180 in foliage, $95 to $140 rest of year. Two-night minimum in foliage season. Children over 10.

The Quechee Inn at Marshland Farm, Quechee Main Street, Quechee 05059.

This venerable establishment – a beautifully restored 1793 farmstead built by Vermont's first lieutenant governor – is every Hollywood set designer's idea of what a New England country inn should look like: a pure white rambling Vermont farmhouse, red barns out back against a backdrop of green mountains and, across the quiet road, the Ottauquechee River heading into Quechee Gorge.

The interior lives up to expectations as well: a welcoming beamed and barnwood living room, lately expanded and so carefully integrated with the older section that many don't notice the change. There's a rustic, stenciled restaurant and 25 comfortable guest rooms and suites. All come with brass and four-poster canopy beds, Queen Anne-style furnishings, wing chairs, braided and Chinese rugs on wide-plank floors and, a surprise for the purists, TV and telephones.

With fifteen rooms in the original farmhouse and ten more on the second floor of a wing that houses the expanded common rooms and restaurant, the inn is large enough to be a focal point for activity – a Christmas Eve open house for inn guests, cocktails before a crackling fire in the lounge, summer get-togethers on the canopied patio, the Wilderness Trails Nordic Ski School headquartered in a small barn. The Vermont Fly Fishing School is based here, and guests have golf, tennis, swimming and skiing privileges at the private Quechee Club.

A full breakfast buffet – from fruits and yogurts to scrambled eggs and sausages – is complimentary in the main dining room or on the canopied deck. Coffee, tea and fruit breads are offered in the afternoon.

Most people enjoy drinks by the fire in the living room/lounge before adjourning for dinner in the antiques-filled dining room. Beamed ceilings, wide-plank floors and lovely pink and blue stenciled borders on the walls provide the setting for some interesting cuisine. Recent choices included Mediterranean bouillabaisse, grilled pork tenderloin with roasted plum sauce, and rack of lamb with green peppercorn pesto. A light supper menu is available as well.

(802) 295-3133 or (800) 235-3133. Fax (802) 295-6587. www.quecheeinn.com. Twenty-three rooms and two suites with private baths. July to mid-October: doubles $140 to $215, suites $205 to $245. Rest of year: doubles $90 to $145, suites $135 to $175. Two-night minimum most weekends and throughout foliage.

Entrées, $20 to $29. Dinner nightly, 6 to 9.

Dining Spots

The Jackson House Inn & Restaurant, 114-3 Senior Lane, Woodstock.

The pride of the Jackson House Inn is its restaurant, housed in a stunning rear addition with a cathedral-ceilinged dining room harboring big windows onto four acres of gardens. Nicely spaced tables are flanked by chairs handcrafted by Charles Shackleton, a local furniture designer. The focal point is a soaring, see-through open-hearth fireplace of Pennsylvania granite. A stone mason laid it slab by slab, a laborious process that took three weeks and appears so natural one wonders how it's held together.

Executive chef Graham "Elliot" Bowles, who trained with some of the nation's leading chefs, prepares exotic and exciting new American cuisine. Dinner is prix-fixe ($55), with several choices for each of three courses. The chef also offers an eleven-course tasting menu that samples much of the night's menu plus an eleven-course vegetarian menu (both $95).

A typical autumn dinner might start with a truffled parsnip bisque, wild king salmon tartare with lemon crème fraîche or walnut-crusted foie gras over a roasted apple. Main courses range from sautéed snapper with blood orange essence and grilled yellowfin tuna with red wine froth to grilled beef tenderloin with elderberry jus.

Our tasting dinner in the candlelit dining room included appetizers of pan-seared diver scallops with house-cured bacon vinaigrette and pheasant confit and wild mushroom criminate with a young field green salad. The main course, designed to showcase a masterful 1996 echezeaux from Labouré-Roi in Burgundy, was slow-braised short ribs of beef with an oxtail croquette.

These riches were topped off by a warm liquid-center chocolate cake with white chocolate ice cream and cardamom-ginger crème brûlée.

Those with more willpower (and wherewithal) might opt for the vegetarian tasting menu ($95). It's an eleven-course fiesta from cheddar and gold potato blini with arugula salad to French lavender flan with creamy almond sauce.

(802) 457-2065 or (800) 448-1890. Prix-fixe, $55. Dinner by reservation, Wednesday-Sunday 6 to 9.

The Prince and the Pauper, 34 Elm St., Woodstock.

A cocktail lounge with the shiniest wood bar you ever saw is at the entry of what many consider to be Woodstock's best restaurant. Tables in the intimate, L-shaped dining room (many flanked by dark wood booths) are covered with linens, oil lamps and flowers in small carafes. The lamps cast flickering shadows on dark beamed ceilings, and old prints adorn the white walls, one of which has a shelf of old books.

Chef-owner Chris J. Balcer refers to his cuisine as "creative contemporary" with French, continental and international accents.

Meals are prix-fixe for appetizer, salad and main course. The soup of the day could be lobster and corn chowder or Moroccan lentil, the pasta perhaps basil fettuccine with a concasse of tomatoes and garnished with goat cheese, and the pâté Vermont pheasant teamed with orange chutney. There's a choice of six entrées, perhaps vegetable-wrapped striped bass with a chive-butter sauce, roast duckling with a sauce of kiwi and rum, and filet mignon au poivre. The specialty is boneless rack of New Zealand lamb royale, baked in puff pastry.

Homemade bread, house salad and seasonal vegetables accompany. The interesting wine list, honored by Wine Spectator, is strong on Californias.

Desserts might be a fabulous raspberry tart with white chocolate mousse served with raspberry cabernet wine sauce, strawberry sabayon with triple sec or homemade Jack Daniels chocolate-chip sorbet. Top them off with espresso, cappuccino or an international coffee.

A bistro menu is available in the elegant lounge. Hearth-baked pizzas, grilled rainbow trout, sautéed chicken with calvados and Indonesian lamb curry are typical offerings.

(802) 457-1818. www.princeandpauper.com. Prix-fixe, $41. Dinner nightly, 6 to 9 or 9:30; jackets requested. Bistro, entrées, $13.95 to $15.95, nightly 5 to 10 or 11.

Barnard Inn Restaurant, 5518 Route 12, Barnard.

This serene, sophisticated restaurant has long been considered one of the best in Vermont. Innovative new American cuisine is the hallmark of owners Will Dodson and Ruth Schimmelpfennig, Culinary Institute of America graduates who formerly operated two neighborhood restaurants in San Francisco. Tiring of the urban pace, they bought the landmark 1796 brick house with 60-seat restaurant on twelve secluded acres a dozen miles north of Woodstock. They moved in upstairs and not only transformed the restaurant but welcomed their first child in 2001.

The husband-and-wife team lightened up the decor in four cozy, elegantly Colonial dining rooms and added a tavern menu to the charming tavern in back. They also made the menu less daunting, while retaining continental overtones.

Fireside dining at Barnard Inn.

From the kitchen comes the inn's longtime specialty, roast duck. Their version on a winter menu was a medium-rare breast of muscovy duck and a duck leg confit, with a classic glace de volaille accented with maple syrup. Other entrées included wild striped bass with roasted bell pepper coulis, Maine lobster risotto, venison medallions with zinfandel-sour cherry sauce, and rack of lamb with porcini mushroom glace de veau.

You might start with roasted chicken and four-mushroom broth, scallop and rock shrimp cakes with green chile aioli, beef carpaccio and veal sweetbreads with a potato pancake. Finish with frozen grand marnier soufflé with blackberry sauce, lemon custard pie with chantilly crème fraîche, Ruth's signature vanilla bean crème brûlée or a trio of grapefruit-campari, lemon zest and mango sorbets.

The 200-choice wine selection is as well considered as the rest of the fare.

(802) 234-9961. Entrées, $23 to $27. Dinner, Tuesday-Sunday from 6; nightly in fall. Closed Monday and Tuesday in winter.

Simon Pearce Restaurant, The Mill, Quechee.

The restaurant beside the Ottauquechee River has as much integrity as the rest of Irish glass blower Simon Pearce's mill complex. The chefs train at Ballymaloe in Ireland, and they import flour from Ireland to make Irish soda and Ballymaloe brown breads.

You sit on sturdy ash chairs at bare wood tables (dressed with white linens at night). The heavy Simon Pearce glassware and the deep brown china are made at the mill. Irish or classical music plays in the background. Through large windows you have a view of the river, hills rising beyond. A large dining addition looks through a handsome arched window out onto the falls and, in season, an enclosed terrace with retractable full-length windows that can be opened to the outside is almost over the falls.

Several wines from the Wine Spectator award-winning list are available by the glass. At lunches we've tried both the house white and red as well as spicy bloody marys with a real kick, while nibbling the sensational Ballymaloe bread.

The menu changes frequently but there are always specialties like the delicious beef and Guinness stew, a generous lunch serving of fork-tender beef and vegetables, served with a small salad of julienned vegetables. Other midday entrées include lamb and rosemary pie, warm goat cheese salad, Maine crab and cod cakes with roasted red pepper coulis, and brochettes of beef tenderloin with crispy sweet potatoes. The pasta salad, a huge heap of spirals, featured many vegetables and a splendid dressing of oil, vinegar, basil and parmesan cheese. Hickory-smoked coho salmon with potato salad and a skewer of grilled chicken with a spicy peanut sauce and a green salad with vinaigrette also were extra-good.

The walnut meringue cake with strawberry sauce, a menu fixture, is crisp and crunchy and melts in the mouth. Cappuccino cheesecake, chocolate rum cake, Irish apple cake and pecan pie are other possibilities, but when we go back, which we seem to do often, nothing but the walnut meringue cake will do.

At night, a candlelight dinner might start with smoked salmon with a root vegetable pancake and lemon-chive crème fraîche or grilled portobello mushrooms with shaved parmesan, fennel and watercress. Main courses could be grilled swordfish with lime hollandaise, poached salmon with white wine sauce, crisp roast duck with mango chutney sauce, scallops of veal with sundried tomatoes, and spice-crusted venison loin with blackberry-peppercorn sauce.

Naturally, you can get beers and ales from the British Isles. You also can buy loaves of the restaurant's wonderful bread and flavored vinaigrettes.

Here's a restaurant that's so unpretentious but so appealing that we're not surprised that some of the traveling friends we've directed there for lunch liked it so much they returned for an encore the next day.

(802) 295-1470. Entrées, $20 to $28. Lunch daily, 11.30 to 2:45. Dinner nightly, 6 to 9.

Parker House Inn, 1792 Quechee Main St., Quechee.

After fourteen years in sales in Chicago, Walt Forrester decided to attend the Culinary Institute of America and team up with his wife Barbara, a sometime pastry chef, in the hospitality business. The Parker House Inn is the fortuitous result. Moving here with their teenagers, who sometimes helped in the dining room, they have changed the restaurant's focus from haute French to what Barbara calls "American comfort food," presented with style. One look at the choice wine list harboring five prized pinot noirs from Oregon hints of treats to come.

The atmosphere is elegant in two dining rooms and a rear cocktail lounge opening onto the river balcony. Dinner begins with an amuse-gueule, in our case roasted eggplant, red peppers and fennel pickled with garlic. A sampler of three appetizers produced a stellar grilled portobello mushroom with warm Vermont goat cheese on a spinach salad, a mushroom cap stuffed with an escargot and a country pâté. An extraordinary house salad of California mesclun with mustard vinaigrette and goat cheese followed.

Among main courses, the pork normandy sauced with apples, leeks, cider and applejack, and the pan-seared Long Island duck breast marinated with soy sauce, garlic and ginger lived up to advance billing. Other possibilities ranged from Maine crab cakes atop a roasted red pepper coulis to rack of lamb with rosemary-cabernet sauce. After a couple of Barbara's desserts, apple crisp with vanilla ice cream and chocolate-almond torte, we lingered over cappuccino and savored the memory of an unforgettable meal.

The inn also offers seven rooms for overnight guests for $125 to $150 a night.

(802) 295-6077. Entrées, $17 to $26. Dinner nightly except Tuesday, 5:30 to 9.

Kedron Valley Inn, Route 106, South Woodstock.

The dining experience at this inn has been upgraded by new owners Jack and Nicole Maiden.

They redecorated the main dining room in Polo/Ralph Lauren equestrian decor and created an inviting tavern/pub with a new bar and a tavern menu.

Guests relax on plush sofas and chairs beside a fireplace in the tavern before or after dinner, which is served at white-clothed tables lit by candles in hurricane lamps in the beamed dining and outside on a porch in season.

The inn's executive chef of eight years, Jim Allen, oversees a concise seasonal menu that ranges from sautéed shrimp and mushrooms tossed with fettuccine and reggiano-parmigiano to grilled filet mignon with a roasted garlic-wine demi-glace. The inn's signature Maine salmon stuffed with an herbed seafood mousse and wrapped in puff pastry with a beurre blanc sauce is superb. We also were impressed with a special of baked pheasant stuffed with local chèvre and topped with roasted macadamia nut butter. Roasted chicken ragoût and smoked duck salad with a brie crostini on greens were autumn favorites at our visit.

Seafood terrine, grilled local andouille sausage and a grilled portobello mushroom topped with mozzarella are typical appetizers. We liked the sea scallops sautéed with citrus-saffron butter and the country-style blend of venison, pork and veal pâté mixed with dried apples and calvados, served with French bread and homemade chutney.

The tavern menu offers five kinds of burgers and a handful of entrées.

(802) 457-1473 or (800) 836-1193. Entrées, $22 to $27. Dinner, Thursday-Monday 6 to 9, nightly in foliage. Tavern from 5, entrées $12.50 to $15.95.

Bentleys Restaurant, 3 Elm St., Woodstock.

Entrepreneurs David Creech and Bill Deckelbaum Jr. started with a greenhouse and plant store in 1974, installed a soda fountain, expanded with a restaurant catering to every taste at every hour, added a specialty-foods shop, and then developed the colorful Waterman Place with retail stores and a fun, casual restaurant called **FireStones** with a wood-fired oven in a 100-year-old house along Route 4 in Quechee.

The flagship of it all is the original Bentleys, a casual, engaging and often noisy spot at the prime corner in Woodstock. On several levels, close-together tables are set with small cane mats, Perrier bottles filled with flowers, and small lamps or tall candles in holders. Old floor lamps sport fringed shades, windows are framed by lace curtains, the plants are large potted palms, and walls are covered with English prints and an enormous bas-relief.

The menu is interesting as well. For lunch, we enjoyed the specialty French tart, a hot puff pastry filled with vegetables in an egg and cheese custard, and a fluffy quiche with turkey, mushrooms and snow peas, both accompanied by side salads. From the dessert tray came a delicate chocolate mousse cake with layers of meringue, like a torte, served with the good Green Mountain coffee in clear glass cups.

Appetizers, salads, sandwiches and light entrées such as sausage crespolini and cold sliced marinated flank steak make up half the dinner menu. The other side offers more hearty fare from maple-mustard chicken to filet mignon with béarnaise sauce. With options like these, it's little wonder that Bentleys is always crowded.

(802) 457-3232. www.bentleysrestaurant.com. Entrées, $15.95 to $19.95. Lunch. Monday-Saturday 11:30 to 3 (late lunch menu 3 to 5). Dinner nightly, 5 to 9:30 (late dinner to 11). Sunday brunch, 11 to 3.

Mangowood Restaurant, 530 Woodstock Road (Route 4 West), Woodstock.

The newly styled restaurant at the old Lincoln Inn at the Covered Bridge conveys a distinct Asian accent, thanks to co-owner Teresa Tan from Singapore and her executive chef, the locally well-known James "Shadow" Henahan.

Teresa is known for her dumplings, among them crispy pork and shrimp with three dipping sauces, but leaves most of the cooking to Shadow, who has imparted Asian flavors to his contemporary American fare. The house specialty is sirloin steak with a garlic marinade and sautéed Asian greens. You also might try Teresa's Singapore laska, chicken and prawns in a spicy coconut cream broth, or the tender rack of pork confit with lychee-mango sauce.

Expect starters like Asian lobster bisque and roast duck quesadilla with cilantro crème fraîche. Sweet endings are maple-ginger crème brûlée, bittersweet chocolate grand marnier pot de crème and a trio of sorbets, including lychee-ginger.

Dinner is served in two royal blue and white dining rooms, one bearing a wall of paintings of crazed chefs. Drinks and appetizers are available in a comfy living-room-style bar with a fireplace and on the Mango's Terrace bar outside.

Although the restaurant is the priority, Teresa and co-owner Amy Martsolf offer six guest rooms with private baths, $125 a night.

(802) 457-3312. www.lincolninn.com. Entrées, $23 to $26. Dinner, Tuesday-Saturday 6 to 9, nightly in foliage season.

Diversions

The sportsman and the sightseer have plenty to do in the Woodstock-Quechee area. You can ski at Suicide Six, not far from Gilbert's farm where Woodstockers installed the nation's first rope tow in 1934, or you can ski at nearby Killington, the East's largest ski area. You can golf at the historic Woodstock Country Club, site of Vermont's first golf course and home also of the fine Woodstock Ski Touring Center, or at a newer golf course in Quechee. You can hike through the Quechee Gorge area or the hundreds of acres of forests maintained by the Woodstock Inn. You can climb a switchback trail up Mount Tom for a bird's-eye view of the area. You can walk around the village green and center, marveling in the architectural variety and browsing through the Dana House Museum of the Woodstock Historical Society. But it is arts, crafts and shopping that make Woodstock so appealing for many.

Arts and Crafts. A sculpture of a man walking five dogs, taken out to the sidewalk every morning, attracts visitors into the spectacular **Stephen Huneck Gallery** at 49 Central St., where the sign says "dogs welcome" on the door. Animals (especially dogs and cats) are the theme of Vermont resident Huneck, one of America's hottest artists, who's known for playful hand-carved furniture, jewelry and sculpture. The smallest pins start at $10 but you could spend up to $30,000. You'll come out of here chuckling and feeling that the world isn't such a bad place, after all.

The Vermont Workshop, 73 Central St., is said to be the oldest gallery in Woodstock, having evolved from a summer workshop established in 1949. Everything from woven mats and interesting lamp shades to wall hangings and cookware is for sale in room after room of great appeal. **Gallery on the Green** shows the works of more than 40 New England artists in six galleries. Original oils and watercolors by Robert O. Caulfield are displayed at the **Caulfield Art Gallery.** Paintings, sculptures, pottery and handcrafted furniture are shown at **Polonaise Art Gallery. Southwest Accents** specializes in fine art and jewelry from Mexico and the American Southwest. **Russian Renaissance** claims one of the most extensive collections of Russian art and artifacts in this country. Handcrafted jewelry and pottery are the specialties of **Woodstock Artisans.**

Shopping. Check out the pottery depicting fish by Giovanni DeSimone, a student of Picasso, at **Aubergine,** a kitchenware shop, where you might find a thermos full of chocolate-raspberry coffee to sample and some dips to spread on crackers. **Unicorn** stocks handicrafts and jewelry by New England artisans and some clever games and toys.

The children dressed in flannel shirts sitting outside **The Vermont Flannel Co.** looked so real that we almost spoke to them. You can barely get through the aisles at **Primrose Garden,** there are so many silk flowers spilling from the shelves. One of us admired the jewelry and the mini-birch-bark canoes at **Arjuna,** an international store "bearing antiques and adornments from as far away as Sumatra and as near as the Adirondacks." **Morgan-Ballou** offers classic apparel for the well-dressed Woodstock woman. **Who Is Sylvia** stocks vintage and antique clothing.

F.H. Gillingham & Co. at 16 Elm St. is the most versatile store of all. Run by the Billings family for over 100 years, it's a general store, but a highly sophisticated one – offering everything from specialty foods and wines to Quimper pottery and hardware – and so popular that it does a land-office mail-order business. Here you'll probably find every Vermont-made dressing, candy, condiment and more. Owner Jireh Swift Billings's young son represents the ninth generation of the Swift family, dating to the 1600s.

Billings Farm & Museum, Route 12 and River Road, Woodstock.

This working dairy farm and living agricultural museum on the northern edge of Woodstock portrays the Vermont farm of yesteryear. It operates in partnership with the new Marsh-Billings-Rockefeller National Historic Park across the street. Artfully presented, life-like exhibits in 19th century barns depict the seasonal round of activities that shaped the lives and culture of rural Vermonters. The restored and furnished 1890 farmhouse – hub of the farm and forestry operation more than a century ago – shows the creamery where butter was produced, the farm office and family living quarters. Visitors wander through the kitchen garden, where heirloom vegetables and herb varieties grow. Down a path the modern farm is evident. Visitors can see the Jersey herd, calves, sheep, oxen and teams of Belgian horses, and the milking barn is open. "A Place in the Land," a 30-minute documentary film on the history of conservation stewardship in America, is shown hourly in the visitor center.

(802) 457-2355. www.billingsfarm.org. Open daily 10 to 5, May-October; also weekends at Thanksgiving, in December and winter holidays, 10 to 3. Adults, $8.

Marsh-Billings-Rockefeller National Historical Park, 54 Elm St., Woodstock.

Opened in 1998, Vermont's first national park is the only national park to focus on conservation history and the evolving nature of land stewardship in America. The park is named for George Perkins Marsh, one of the nation's first global environmental thinkers, who grew up on the property, and for Frederick Billings, an early conservationist who established a progressive dairy farm and managed forest on the former Marsh farm. The house was occupied until lately by Billings's granddaughter, Mary French Rockefeller, and her husband, conservationist Laurance S. Rockefeller. They established the Billings Farm & Museum to continue the farm's working dairy and left the estate's residential and forest lands to the people.

A variety of ranger-led walks and talks trace the history of conservation in the surrounding 550-acre forest, which harbors twenty miles of carriage roads and trails crisscrossing Mount Tom. Ninety-minute guided tours show rooms on the first and second floors of the 1805 mansion and formal grounds. The house is simple and elegant, not opulent, and looks as if the Rockefellers had just stepped out for morning coffee and were coming back any minute. The extensive collection of American landscape paintings is the most remarkable feature.

(802) 457-3368. Tours daily, Memorial Day through October, daily 10 to 4, reservations recommended, adults $6. Forest and trails open daily, free.

VINS Nature Center, Route 4 West, Quechee.

Raptor exhibits are the highlight of the new Vermont Institute of Natural Science nature center on 47 acres of rolling forestland just west of the famed Quechee Gorge. Bald eagles, hawks, owls, peregrine falcons and other birds of prey that have been injured in accidents are on display in a series of huge outdoor flight enclosures that make up the only living museum devoted to birds of prey in the Northeast. Naturalists lead walks and offer exciting flight programs. Among the more than 40 birds we saw was Vermont's tiniest avian predator, the three-ounce saw-whet owl. Moving from southwest Woodstock to a more accessible location in 2004, the center has outdoor interpretive exhibits, nature trails and a nature shop.

(802) 457-2779. www.vinsweb.org. Open daily, 10 to 4; hours vary. Adults, $8.

Extra-Special

Simon Pearce, The Mill at Quechee.

Every time we're in the area, we stop at Simon Pearce's magnificent mill, partly because it's all so fascinating and partly because there's always something new. Simon Pearce is the glass blower who left Ireland in 1981 to set up business in the abandoned flannel mill beside the Ottauquechee. The site is inspiring: thundering waterfalls, covered bridge, beautifully restored mill and classic white Vermont houses all around. The interior has a fine restaurant (see Dining Spots) and a handsome shop offering glass, pottery and Irish woolens, all beautifully displayed, plus a second floor with seconds at 30 to 40 percent off, although even then, everything is expensive. Downstairs is a glass-blowing area, a working pottery, the hydro station with enormous pipes from the river and a steam turbine that provides enough power to light the town of Quechee as well as serve the mill's energy needs (melting sand into glass, firing clay into porcelain and stoneware). "The whole idea was to become self-sufficient and provide an economic model for small business in Vermont," says Simon. The mill is zoned utility in the sub-basement, manufacturing in the basement, retail in the restaurant and shop, office-retail on the second floor and residential on the third, where Simon once lived with his family. The enterprise is growing all the time, opening retail shops around the Northeast and expanding its production capability with a custom-designed glass facility and a pottery in nearby Windsor. We defy anyone not to enjoy, learn – and probably buy.

(802) 295-2711. Open daily, 9 a.m. to 9 p.m.

The Old Tavern in Grafton is a classic inn of its genre.

Newfane/Grafton, Vt.

The Essence of Vermont

There's not much to do in Newfane, Grafton and Vermont's surrounding West River Valley. And that's the way the inhabitants like it.

The interstates, the ski areas, the tony four-season destination resorts are some distance away. This is the essence of old Vermont, unspoiled by tourism and contemporary commercial trappings.

The meandering West River creates a narrow valley between the mountains as it descends toward Brattleboro. Along the way are covered bridges (one is the longest in Vermont), country stores, flea markets and a couple of picture-book villages.

The heart of the valley is Newfane, the shire town of Windham County, until lately without so much as a brochure to publicize it. In 1824, Newfane "moved" to the valley from its original site two miles up Newfane hill and now has fewer residents than it had then. The Newfane green is said to be Vermont's most-photographed. Clustered around the green are the white-columned courthouse, the matching Congregational church, the town hall, two famed inns, two country stores and, nearby, some houses – and that's about it.

Upriver is Townshend ("Historic Townshend," one of the area's few tourist brochures calls it), with a larger green and more business activity, though that's relative. Beyond is Jamaica, an up-and-coming hamlet with some good art galleries and gift shops.

And out in the middle of nowhere to the north is Grafton. Preserved by the Windham Foundation, it's the quintessential 19th-century Vermont hamlet where the utility wires have been buried underground and the sophistication of better-known Vermont towns considered quintessential is noticeably absent. Here is a piece of yesteryear, preserved for posterity.

There are back roads and country stores to explore, but for many visitors this quiet area's chief blessing is its collection of fine inns and restaurants amidst a setting of Vermont as it used to be.

Inn Spots

The Four Columns Inn, 230 West St., Box 278, Newfane 05345.

Ever since famed French chef René Chardain left the Old Newfane Inn to open the Four Columns, this inn has been widely known for outstanding cuisine (see Dining Spots). Under the auspices of subsequent innkeepers, it has become known for comfortable, even luxurious overnight accommodations as well.

Sixteen guest quarters are located in the main restaurant building and in the four-columned inn in front, built in 1830 by General Pardon Kimball for his Southern-born wife as a replica of her girlhood home. Twelve have gas fireplaces, and half of those have double jacuzzis and/or decks.

Two of the more deluxe were created by recent innkeepers Pam and Gorty Baldwin from office space above the main inn's foyer and new stairway. With vaulted ceilings, they offer see-through fireplaces between bedroom and large tiled bath, complete with two-person whirlpool tubs and separate showers. The one in front, Suite 15, has an iron canopy bed, pale yellow walls accented with red-orange, club chairs in the bedroom and a chaise lounge in the bath. Even more dramatic is Suite 12 in back with skylit bath. It adds a sitting alcove and a rear balcony overlooking the trout pond.

Top of the line is now Suite 4, again with king bed and double-sided fireplace. Its bath has a two-person whirlpool and a waterfall shower, and a wall of arched windows beneath the cathedral ceiling looks across the tops of maple trees onto the town green.

With one exception, rooms have king or queensize beds. They are decorated colorfully with hooked rugs, handmade afghans and quilts. Suite 3, with a four-poster bed, comes with a jacuzzi for two in a marble bathroom that's larger than the bedroom. Suite 18 is newly equipped with a gas fireplace, kingsize sleigh bed and a freestanding soaking tub in a corner near the bathroom. Another favorite is the third-floor hideaway, with trim of old wood and Laura Ashley fabrics in shades of deep rusts. It has a canopied bed set into an alcove, plush beige carpeting and a sitting room with a private porch overlooking the Newfane green.

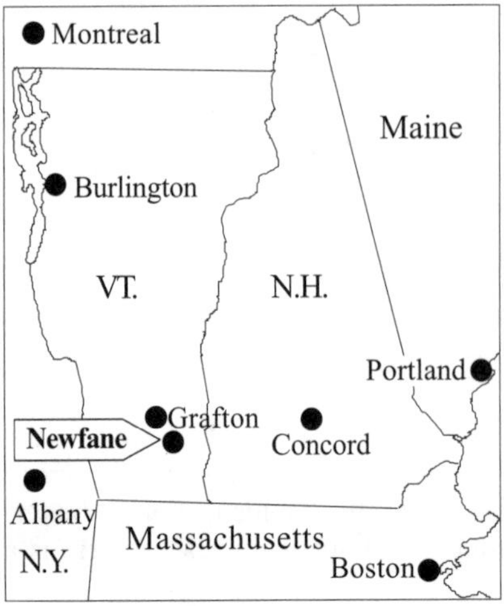

The longtime breakfast cook prepares a healthful country breakfast. The buffet table contains fresh orange juice, ample fruit, yogurt, homemade granola, hot oatmeal in winter and an assortment of homemade muffins, scones and croissants.

The 150-acre property also has a swimming pool, hiking trails, lovely gardens and spacious lawns on which to relax in country-auberge style.

Guest rooms are in front and restaurant at rear of Four Columns Inn.

(802) 365-7713 or (800) 787-6633. Fax (802) 365-0022. www.fourcolumnsinn.com. Ten rooms and six suites with private baths. Doubles, $150 to $175 weekends and foliage, $125 to $155 midweek. Suites, $250 to $340 weekends and foliage, $190 to $280 midweek. Two-night minimum weekends and in foliage. Children and pets welcome.

Windham Hill Inn, 311 Lawrence Drive, West Townshend 05359.

Up a steep hill so far off the main road that we had to stop to ask if we were on the right track is this gem of an inn, a speckled brick and white wood structure built in 1825 and distinguished by a suave oval sign and a commanding view of the West River Valley. Once here, you tend to stay here, which is why innkeepers Marina and Joe Coneeny, corporate dropouts from Connecticut, go out of their way to make their guests' stays so comfortable and satisfying.

The Coneenys took over a going concern, their predecessors having remodeled bathrooms, added fireplaces and upgraded beds so that all but one of the 21 rooms have king or queensize. Sixteen have fireplaces or Vermont Casting stoves. They're furnished with a panache that merited a six-page photo spread in Country Decorating magazine.

We stayed in the rear Tree House (so named because it gives the feeling of being up in the trees), which has a Vermont Castings stove and an idyllic deck from which to enjoy the view.

Other popular rooms are the five fashioned from nooks and alcoves in the White Barn annex, particularly the two sharing a large deck overlooking the mountains, and the renovated Taft Room with fireplace, bay window and floor-to-ceiling bookshelves. Even these have been upstaged by three deluxe rooms carved out of the former owners' quarters in the south wing. These come with kingsize beds, two armchairs in front of the fireplace, and jacuzzis or freestanding soaking tubs.

Top of the line are three extra-spacious rooms in the third-floor loft of the barn. Each has a king bed, fireplace and private deck facing the mountains. Two have double soaking tubs and the other a double jacuzzi. The one in the middle has a winding staircase up to the cupola with a window seat and a 360-degree view.

The staff offer pampering touches, from complimentary juices and Perrier in

Dining room at Windham Hill Inn looks onto lawns and pond.

baskets in each room to candy dishes at bedside and Mother Myrick's chocolates on the pillows at nightly turndown, when small votive candles are lit.

Food is taken seriously at Windham Hill. The inn's Frog Pond Dining Room has been enlarged to make more room for the public (see Dining Spots). Overnight guests enjoy a full breakfast served amid a background of taped chamber music, antique silver and crystal. Expect fresh orange juice in champagne flutes, breakfast breads and fresh fruits, and a main dish like waffles, eggs mornay or griddle cakes shaped like little doughnuts, made of winter wheat and cornmeal.

Other rooms at guests' disposal are the large and sunny Music Room with windows on three sides (with a restored 1911 Steinway grand piano and a collection of 400 CDs for guests' use), a couple of parlors with wood-burning fireplaces and a handsome bar room.

Outside are a heated gunite swimming pool and clay tennis court.

(802) 874-4080 or (800) 944-4080. Fax (802) 874-4702. www.windhamhillinn.com. Twenty-one rooms with private baths. Doubles, $195 to $345; $50 surcharge during foliage and Christmas week. Two-night minimum most weekends. Children over 12. Closed week before Christmas.

Three Mountain Inn, Route 30, Box 180, Jamaica 05343.

This venerable 1797 inn looks its age, but took on new life – in more ways than one – in mid-1999. David and Stacy Hiler celebrated the inn's purchase by Stacy giving birth to their first-born, a son. "It was a close race," she said. "We signed the papers at 4:30 and were at the hospital by midnight."

The inn is as much a tale about people as about an aging hostelry in need of new blood. The Hilers, who live on site, are joined in the venture by his mother, Heide Bredfeldt, and his stepfather, Bill Oates, well-known inn consultants, who were getting a first-hand taste of what they had been telling prospective innkeepers for years.

With Stacy tending to the children, David shared innkeeping duties with Heide, whose deft touch is apparent in recent refurbishing and upgrades. All but two of the inn's fifteen accommodations now have fireplaces, four have whirlpool tubs and all but one double have queen or kingsize beds.

It is the details that fulfill the inn's new motto, "We Give You Vermont," as orchestrated by Heide. In redoing the Robinson House annex next door, tall windows were installed in the rear guest rooms to yield views of the close-up mountains. The paintings in the rooms are Vermont originals, as are most of the period accessories. The seven rooms here were reconfigured, enlarged and decorated with style. The premier Jamaica Suite, main floor rear, has a queensize poster bed, a sitting room with a gas fireplace and a loveseat that opens into a twin bed, a private patio and a bath with double whirlpool tub and rainforest shower. The last two amenities also are found in the Weston and Wardsboro rooms in the upstairs rear, each with queen bed and soaring picture windows. All rooms are appointed with luxurious linens and bedding, plus the thickest bathrobes you ever saw.

The seven accommodations in the main house vary from a couple of simple, cozy rooms with a double or queen bed to a corner room in shades of green and rose with private balcony, kingsize four-poster bed and TV/VCR in the "Wing Up" above a stable. Architect Rodney Williams of the nearby Inn at Sawmill Farm designed the wing with his trademark barnwood and beamed-ceiling touches.

Similar attributes enhance the Sage Cottage in the rear, rebuilt to offer a cozy, cathedral-ceilinged space with a queensize sleigh bed beneath a skylight, a double whirlpool tub in one corner and two comfortable chairs beside a gas fireplace in the opposite corner. Wicker chairs on the front porch look onto the gardens, pool area and two life-size fiberglass cows grazing in the back yard.

The inn's common rooms include a large keeping room with an original Dutch oven fireplace, a spacious library that doubles as a conference room and three dining rooms (see Dining Spots). Before or after-dinner drinks are offered in an atmospheric pub with wide-planked pine walls and floors.

Executive chef Ronit Penso prepares a sumptuous breakfast buffet with a selection of hot entrées. Pecan waffles, baked orange french toast, cheddar and chive strata, homemade biscuits and blueberry muffins are typical fare.

(802) 874-4140 or (800) 532-9399. Fax (802) 874-4745. www.threemountaininn.com. Thirteen rooms, one suite and one cottage with private baths. Doubles, $145 to $235. Suite, $295. Cottage, $325. Foliage and holidays: doubles, $145 to $235; suite, $290; cottage, $295.

The Old Tavern, Grafton 05146.

Here is the epitome of an old Vermont inn in the epitome of an old Vermont hamlet. It's located at what passes for Grafton's main intersection, across from the small red brick town hall and down the hill from two white-spired churches. And it's been serving travelers since 1801, when it opened as a tavern on the old Boston to Montreal stage road.

This is no converted inn. It's the real thing – a living museum of the way things were, as preserved and restored starting in 1963 by the nonprofit Windham Foundation, which saved the inn and kept much of Grafton in a time warp. Staying in the inn's annexes or one of its five houses is "like staying in the beautiful old Vermont house you'd want to buy if you were moving here," in the words of innkeeper Kevin O'Donnell. But the historically accurate ambiance comes with some of today's comforts, at least as far as private baths, Gilbert & Soames toiletries and afternoon tea are concerned.

The guest rooms, authentic to the period (no phones or TV), range from cozy and a mite drab through a number of sizable, charming and quite comfortable quarters to the frankly elegant, amenity-laden hideaways demanded by today's boomers. None would qualify for a spread in a contemporary interiors magazine, let alone an AAA rating. Yet the special character of the place prompted travel connoisseur Andrew Harper to name it a hideaway of the year in 1995 in the same breath as The Point in New York's Adirondacks and Carmel Valley Ranch in California.

Accommodations consist of eleven rooms in the main building, twenty in the connected Windham and Homestead annexes across the street, and five guest houses that sleep from six to sixteen people.

No two rooms are alike, and nearly every one is a favorite with someone among the inn's loyal following, many of whom return year after year to the same quarters.

The most elegant quarters are four in White Gates, around the corner from the little White Church. Guests in four bedrooms here enjoy an enormous living room with fireplace and TV, plus a formal dining room and big kitchen. Eight original Spy prints (part of the inn's extensive collection by the Vanity Fair artist) line the curving staircase in the two-story-high hall. Upstairs is the bridal suite, the boomers' choice. It comes with queensize fabric canopy bed, a settee and two wing chairs, a writing desk in the window overlooking the stables, and a large and fancy new bathroom with double vanity, jacuzzi tub and separate shower.

Our favorites are in the Homestead and Windham annexes, perhaps the elegant rooms with plush chairs and twin canopy beds or twins and a sofabed in the rear overlooking the back lawn and a spring-fed swimming pond. We'd swim, amble about town, catch up on reading in a variety of comfy living rooms or the cozy den and do plenty of nothing, as Grafton addicts are prone to do.

Then we'd mosey across the street to one of the inn's three adjoining dining rooms – the Formal, the intimate and historic Pine Room or the casual skylit Garden Room – for a trendy dinner of caramelized sea scallops with saffron potatoes, wild mushroom salad, black truffle veal demi-glace, herb salad and golden caviar or grilled beef tenderloin with tomato eggplant relish, haricots vert, celeriac potato cake and balsamic veal sauce. Whew! (The menu does note "The Plain Deal." To quote: "Any entrée can be prepared minus the sauces. For example: plain grilled beef tenderloin with green beans and mashed potatoes"). The atmospheric Phelps Barn Pub, with live music on many weekends, would be just the place for a nightcap.

For breakfast the next morning, we'd spring for something like pancakes with real maple syrup to complete this retreat to the good old days. We might even try the new Daniels House Café for lunch or light supper.

For anyone with an ounce of nostalgia, the Old Tavern and Grafton deliver an aura of the past that one can truly feel. It is a total experience that exceeds the sum of its parts.

(802) 843-2231 or (800) 843-1801. Fax (802) 843-2245. www.old-tavern.com. Forty-six rooms and suites with private baths in main inn, two annexes and five houses. Doubles, $185 to $350 weekends, $135 to $280 midweek ($115 to $200, midweek in off-season). Foliage and holidays: doubles, $195 to $390. Closed late March through April.

Entrées, $26 to $33. Lunch daily, noon to 2, Memorial Day through October, weekends rest of year. Dinner nightly, 6 to 9. Café, entrées $7.95 to $13, open daily 11 to 6:30.

The Inn at Woodchuck Hill Farm, Middletown Road, Grafton 05146.

Without so much as a sign for identification purposes, this out-of-the-way farm complex astride a hill off unpaved Middletown Road has been housing guests since 1968. It was started by antique dealers who ran a shop on the property, but was taken over lately by their son and daughter-in-law, Mark and Marilyn Gabriel, both clinical social workers with an office in Grafton. Accommodations are varied and the feeling laid-back, reflecting the Grafton of old, without the meticulous refinements of the Windham Foundation.

The main floor of the rambling, unassuming white farmhouse holds an atmospheric country dining room with three tables set with woven mats, and a large beamed living room with a window seat, fireplace and well-worn oriental rugs. The living room opens onto a big square porch full of wicker furniture, including a glider swing, and hanging fuchsia plants that frame a mountain view into New Hampshire. Beer and wine are available in a lounge or on the porch, where Grafton cheddar cheese and crackers are complimentary.

The largest guest accommodations in the main house are in the west wing: a suite with kingsize bed downstairs and, upstairs, a carpeted studio suite with quilt-covered queen bed, small kitchen and a private deck shaded by birch trees. Upstairs in the main house are six more bedrooms. They range from two with twins or a short antique double tester bed sharing a bath to a couple on the third floor with a double or king and an extra bed each and a hall sitting room with a TV.

The prime accommodations are across the road in a small barn. The Barn Residence on the lower floor sleeps up to four in a king-bedded loft with half bath and a large main-floor room with queen sofabed, full kitchen and dining area, TV and wood stove. There's a neat little sitting room in a silo with windows on three sides. Upstairs in another section of the barn is a beamed bedroom with private bath, double cannonball bed and corner fireplace. It can be rented alone or as part of the barn suite, which has two bedrooms, full bath, kitchenette and corner fireplace.

The Spruce Cottage in which Mark's late parents ran an antiques shop was converted into a three-bedroom cottage sleeping seven.

The Gabriels serve a full breakfast of the cook's whim, he says. Those quarters with kitchenettes are stocked with the makings for breakfast.

Behind the barn is a small trout pond, complete with a canoe and a gazebo. Beyond in the woods is a wood-fired steam room and sauna.

The Gabriels sometimes close the main house in the winter for lack of use, but otherwise are open year-round.

(802) 843-2398. www.woodchuckhill.com. Four rooms and four suites with private baths; two rooms with shared bath; one three-bedroom cottage. Doubles, $89 to $135. Suites, $155 to $260. Cottage, $375. Children welcome.

The Old Newfane Inn, Route 30, Newfane 05345.

Built in 1787, this classic New England inn along the green proclaims itself "virtually unchanged for more than 200 years" and proud of it. Even the spectacular banks of vivid phlox outside the entrance have stood the test of time.

For more than twenty years, German chef Eric Weindl and his wife Gundy have run the place in the continental style, with an emphasis on their restaurant (see Dining Spots). Theirs is one of the few area inns we know of requiring a two-night minimum stay any time.

The ten old-fashioned (the Weindls call them quaint) guest rooms upstairs are meticulously clean. Most are furnished with twin beds, pretty floral wallpapers, samplers and wall hangings, wing chairs and rockers. Eight have private baths and one is a suite. Several rooms, which once were part of the ballroom, have gently curved ceilings and access to a side balcony looking onto the green.

Guests enter via a front porch with a lineup of rocking chairs into a lobby whose walls are hung with faded magazine articles touting the inn. Off the entry on one side is a parlor with fireplace, upholstered chairs and sofa. On the other side is a narrow and dark beamed dining room.

A continental breakfast is included in the rates.

(802) 365-4427. www.oldnewfaneinn.com. Eight rooms and one suite with private baths. Doubles, $125. Suite, $155. Two-night minimum. Children over 7. Closed November to mid-December and April to mid-May.

Dining Spots

The Four Columns Inn, 250 West St., Newfane.

Long known for some of southern Vermont's finest food, this inn's sophisticated dining room has a new look as well. It combines beamed ceilings and a huge fireplace with stylish window treatments, pristine white table linens, shaded oil lamps, strikingly modern Villeroy & Boch chargers and three pieces of new stemware at each setting. The expanded and refurbished lounge is decorated with a stunning impressionistic mural of 1850s Newfane progressing through the seasons. The lounge opens onto a side deck with umbrellaed tables overlooking gardens and a trout pond, a pleasant spot for a cocktail.

Pristine dining room at Four Columns Inn.

The cuisine offered by longtime chef Gregory Parks is as sophisticated as the setting.

Chef Greg's appetizers are some of Vermont's most exotic: perhaps salmon tartare with avocado, tobiko and miso tapenade; spicy quail with greens, goat cheese and smoked bacon, and seared foie gras with napa cabbage, poached pears and cranberries.

Entrées range from crispy free-range baby chicken with a porcini essence to veal T-bone with five-peppercorn sauce. Examples are grilled salmon and shrimp with a Thai lemongrass and coconut broth, pistachio-crusted swordfish fillet with a saffron-citrus sauce, and seared venison loin with a spiced zinfandel glaze and sundried cherries.

The dessert repertoire here has long been famous. It might include pumpkin cheesecake, chocolate pâté, raspberry torte, hazelnut layer cake with mocha cream, and homemade sorbets and ice creams. You can stop in the lounge to enjoy one from the cart, even if you haven't dined at the inn.

(802) 365-7713 or (800) 787-6633. Entrées, $25 to $34. Dinner nightly except Tuesday, 6 to 9.

Windham Hill Inn, West Townshend 05359.

Five-course dinners of distinction are served nightly to guests and, increasingly, the public in the inn's expanded restaurant. Patrons gather for drinks and hors d'oeuvres in a new bar area off the inn's parlor. Then they adjourn to an enlarged dining room dressed in pale pink, with oriental scatter rugs, upholstered chairs at well-spaced tables, and views onto lawns and Frog Pond.

Sous chef Kathleen King took over the kitchen in 2002, about the time the inn was purchased by Joe and Marina Coneeny, she with a special interest in food, having worked for Dean & DeLuca and later a catering business. Dinner is available prix-fixe ($45) or à la carte, with four to six choices for most courses on the changing menu.

Chef Kathleen's starters at a recent autumn visit included smoked boar sausage ragu with tagliatelle pasta and aged parmesan, grilled molasses-marinated shrimp with roasted pear chutney and a salad of black mission figs with herbed goat cheese, maple walnuts and honey-port glaze.

An orange sorbet over raspberry sauce refreshed the palate for the main course. Choices ranged from pan-seared black bass with wild mushroom beurre blanc to rack of lamb with port-balsamic reduction. The chef stuffed a roasted chicken with wild rice and dried fruit salad and marinated double-cut pork chops in hoisin and cilantro. Vegetarians were pleased with the honey-roasted acorn flan with carrots, celery root, squash, wilted greens and pomegranate molasses.

Desserts were individual lemon meringue tartlet, bittersweet chocolate mousse cake, caramelized banana and walnut napoleon and a trio of sorbets

(802) 874-4080 or (800) 944-4080. Entrées, $27 to $31. Prix-fixe, $45. Dinner nightly, 6 to 8:30. Closed week before Christmas.

Three Mountain Inn, Route 30, Jamaica.

The AAA accorded a four-diamond award to this venerable inn's upgraded restaurant with two cozy dining rooms, each warmed by a fireplace. Chef Ronit Penso, a New England Culinary Institute graduate, replaced founding chef William Hollinger in 2003 and imbued the contemporary American fare with a touch of flair from her Middle Eastern background.

Dinner is available prix-fixe or à la carte from the same menu, and begins with a complimentary amuse-bouche. The meal might start with an unusual celeriac, lemon and blue cheese soup (a product of the chef's heritage), grilled ahi tuna on cellophane noodles or pan-fried foie gras on a cranberry-shallot-ginger relish with red wine-maple glaze.

The night's five entrées, one of them vegetarian, could include grilled swordfish and roasted pork tenderloin with red curry, coconut milk and peanut sauce. Pan-fried venison medallions with cider-pecan cream sauce is a seasonal autumn favorite.

Desserts sound ordinary but take on added dimension, as in pumpkin cheesecake with raspberry coulis, candied ginger and whipped cream or key lime pie augmented with raspberry coulis and seasonal berries.

A fully stocked and atmospheric pub offers guests a spirited after-dinner retreat.

(802) 874-4140 or (800) 532-9399. Prix-fixe, $50 for four courses. Entrées, $32 to $34. Dinner, Wednesday-Sunday 6 to 8:30..

The Old Newfane Inn, Route 30, Newfane.

German-born chef-owner Eric Weindl, who trained in a Swiss hotel, cooks in what he calls the classic French and continental style at this classic New England inn dating to 1787. The food is as predictable as when we first went out of our way to eat here more than three decades ago during a ski trip to Mount Snow – that is to say good, if not exciting.

A few daily specials spark up the enormous printed menu, which remains virtually unchanged over the years and lists most of the standards, ranging from marinated herring and shrimp cocktail through cream of garlic soup and escargots bourguignonne. Shrimp scampi, frog's legs provençal, capon cordon bleu, duckling à l'orange, veal goulash, pepper steak flamed in brandy and venison medallions with green peppercorns are a few of the entrées, accompanied by seasonal vegetables and salad. Châteaubriand "served the proper way" and rack of lamb bouquetière are available for two. Featured desserts include peach melba, Bavarian chocolate cream pie, cherries jubilee and pear hélène.

The decor matches the vision of what tourists think an old New England inn dining room should look like. Narrow and beamed with a wall of windows onto the green, it has a timbered ceiling, white lace curtains, pewter plates on the tables, shiny dark wood floors and a massive brick fireplace.

(802) 365-4427. Entrées, $20 to $28. Dinner nightly from 6. Closed Monday in off-season and November to mid-December and April to mid-May.

Diversions

There aren't many diversions – at least of the traditional tourist variety. For those, head for Brattleboro, Wilmington, Weston or Manchester, all within less than an hour's drive. In the West River Valley, you simply relax, hike or drive scenic back roads, and browse through flea markets, antiques shops and country stores.

One of the best selections of custom-made quilts in New England is carried at **Newfane Country Store,** a store chock full of "country things for country folks." Some of the quilts, which represent a local cottage industry, hang outside and beckon passersby in for herbs, jams and jellies, penny candy, maple syrup, sweaters, Christmas ornaments and such.

Other general stores are the **Newfane General Store,** a family-operated grocery store and deli, the **Townshend Corner Store** with a 1949 vintage soda fountain and the **West Townshend Country Store,** a fixture since 1848 with foods, gifts, cookware, old pickle and cracker barrels (would you believe pickled limes?), spruce gum and two-cent penny candy. There's an entire wall of beer steins with family crests in the $10 range.

Newfane's off-the-beaten-path West Street also is home to a couple of unusual, part-time enterprises. New and used books with a New England theme are represented seasonally at **Olde and New England Books**, located in a barn behind the first frame house (1769) in Newfane. Just beyond, the British flag on the side door of a stark white house identifies **The British Clockmaker,** where antique clocks and music boxes are restored and sold.

Along Route 30 in Townshend, **Lawrence's Smoke Shop** carries maple products and corn-cob smoked bacon, ham and other meat products as well as jellies, honey and fudge, and they'll make up sandwiches. The **Taft Hill Collection** offers fine gifts, hand-painted glassware and chin, antiques and furnishings for the home. The **Big Black Bear Shop,** the company store at Mary Meyer stuffed toys on Route 30 in Townshend, is where doting grandmothers and the objects of their affections can go wild. The **Townshend Furniture Co.** factory has an outlet store with Colonial, country and contemporary pine furniture, plus English country antiques and used furniture in the Back Store.

Flea markets seem to pop up all along Route 30. The original Newfane flea market, Vermont's largest now in its fourth decade, operates every Sunday from May through October one mile north of the Newfane common. The Old Newfane Barn advertises an auction every Saturday at 6:30. The Townshend flea market, beginning at the ungodly hour of 6 a.m. every Sunday, is considered a bit schlocky.

Swimming is extra-special in the Rock River, just off Route 30 up the road to South Newfane. Cars and pickup trucks in a parking area identify the path, a long descent to a series of swimming holes called locally "Indian Love Call," with sections for skinny-dippers, the half-clothed and the clothed. More conventional swimming is available in the West River reservoir behind the Townshend Dam off Route 30 in West Townshend.

Jamaica State Park, off Route 30, Jamaica. This 772-acre park with three hiking trails is considered a godsend for visitors to the area. From the parking area at the park entrance just north of town, an old railroad bed meanders along the bank of the West River for several miles and provides easy walking, jogging or biking. Near the start of the trail is Salmon Hole, with a beach for swimming. Near trail's end, an old switch road branches off along Cobb Brook for another mile. It leads to Hamilton Falls, a 125-foot-long stretch of three pools cascading into each other, so perfect that you'd think it was manmade. Park admission, $1.50.

Extra-Special

Grafton. For some, this postcard-perfect hamlet just north of Windham Hill and the West River Valley is a destination in itself. Off the beaten path, it was put on the map by the Windham Foundation, which was launched in 1963 after the town had gone downhill. More than twenty buildings in town have been restored, including the foundation-owned Old Tavern, and Grafton is recognized today as one of New England's finest 19th-century villages. There are other attractions in this tiny town of 600, where hilly dirt roads pass stately homes, both old and new. We enjoyed watching cheese being made as we bought some Covered Bridge cheddar at the Grafton Village Cheese Co., the foundation-backed cheese factory. Shoppers enjoy the excellent Gallery North Star, the crafts at Grafton Handmade, the bronze sculptures at the seasonal Jud Hartmann Gallery, and the gifts at Tickle Your Fancy and the Daniels House. Also worth a look are the Grafton Village Store, a historical society museum showing area crafts and tools, a demonstration flock of sheep, and some of the marked nature trails at the year-round Grafton Ponds hiking and cross-country ski center. There are two covered bridges, a working blacksmith shop and two landmark churches. As Graftonites proclaim laconically, "there is always nothing to do, plenty of nothing."

West Dover Inn and Congregational Church are landmarks in center of town.

West Dover, Vt.

Fun Place in the Snow

If it weren't for the late ski pioneer Walter Schoenknecht and his vision for a showy ski resort called Mount Snow, West Dover might still be little more than a stagecoach stop on the back road from Wilmington to who-knows-where. It could have followed the path of Somerset, the sprawling township beyond Mount Snow's North Face, which has one of Vermont's largest lakes and nary a human resident – just the remnants of a ghost town vanished in the wilderness.

Flushed with success from his Mohawk Mountain ski area in northwest Connecticut, Walt Schoenknecht developed something of a skiing Disneyland on a 3,556-foot peak slumbering above West Dover in the 1950s. It had a glitzy gondola, enclosed bubble chairlifts, easy wide slopes and a heated outdoor swimming pool in which people frolicked all winter. Here was the closest major ski and fun resort to Eastern metropolitan areas, and the snow bunnies from the city turned out in droves.

Other ski areas, inns and lodges, restaurants and condos followed, and the boom was on all along the river that gives the Deerfield Valley its name. Mount Snow pioneered as a four-season resort with its own Snow Lake Lodge and an eighteen-hole golf course. It now bills itself as New England's mountain-biking capital, and recently opened the 203-room Grand Summit Resort Hotel & Conference Center.

Still, winter fun reigns around West Dover, and snowboarding and cross-country skiing are growing faster than the traditional downhill variety. High season is winter. Lodging rates generally are lower in summer, and vary widely depending on weekday or weekend, length of stay and holiday periods.

While Mount Snow has evolved under the ownership of Killington and the American Skiing Co., so has the Deerfield Valley. Inns and restaurants are proliferating as West Dover takes ever more advantage of its place in the sun and snow.

Inn Spots

The Inn at Sawmill Farm, Route 100, Box 367, West Dover 05356.

To hear Ione and Rod Williams tell it, they never planned to live in Vermont, much less run an inn. He was an architect and she an interior designer in New Jersey. On a ski trip to Mount Snow, a blizzardy day forced them off the slopes and into a real-estate office. The agent took them directly to the old Winston Farm they had been admiring for years. "We've never been sure who was more surprised that day when we bought the farm – we or the realtor," the Williamses recall.

That was in 1968. Their creative minds went to work and the idea for an inn evolved. They spent the next few years turning the 1799 columned farmhouse, a dilapidated barn, a wagon shed and other outbuildings on the site of an 18th-century sawmill into an inn that is a model of sophistication and distinction, one that recently was elevated to Relais & Chateaux status under second-generation innkeepers, son Brill Williams (the chef and now the owner) and daughter Bobbie Dee, the general manager.

In designing what became a pioneering model of today's urbane country inn, Rod Williams retained elements of the barn (hand-hewn beams. weathered posts, boards and doors) so guests would know they're not in the city. Dining rooms, the small bar, living room, loft room, entry, lobby and corridors to guest rooms all meld together rustic-fashionably and with unfolding fascination.

The most deluxe accommodations are eleven outlying rooms and suites with fireplaces. Six sport new whirlpool tubs and separate showers as the inn keeps up with the times. A new luxury suite in the carriage house does it up in spades with a cathedral-ceilinged living room with a stone wall including a fireplace and built-in TV and sound system, king bedroom with Federal mahogany headboard, bath with jacuzzi and glassed-in shower, and a wraparound deck overlooking the grounds.

Our mid-price master bedroom typified accommodations in the main inn. Extra-spacious, it had a kingsize bed, a desk-like table and chair, three upholstered chairs in a sitting area around a wood table with a good porcelain reading lamp, two sinks in a dressing area outside the bathroom, a dresser and a large plant in a wooden stand. Wallpaper, upholstery, bedspread and even the shower curtain were in the same country floral print, and the lush green towels matched the thick carpeting. Beyond was a small balcony overlooking the pool.

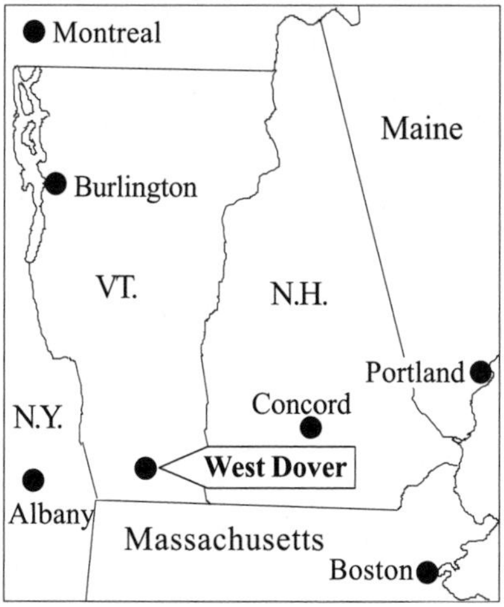

And then there are the extras: little gold packages of Lake Champlain chocolates in your room, afternoon tea with nut bread and ginger cookies in front of the large brick fireplace in the living room, superb dinners (see Dining Spots), hearty breakfasts, a sparkling swimming pool, two spring-fed trout ponds, a tennis court and the historic section of West Dover just below.

The large brick hearth of the inn's cathedral-ceilinged living room, festooned with copper pots and utensils, is the focal point for guests who luxuriate on comfortable sofas or wing chairs covered in chintz and read the magazines displayed on a beautiful copper table. Other groupings are near the huge windows that give a perfect view of Mount Snow. The loft room upstairs has more sofas, an entire wall of books and the inn's only television set, which is rarely in use.

Breakfasts are a delight in the sunny greenhouse dining room facing the pool in summer and a flock of chickadees at the bird feeders in winter. You get a choice of all kinds of fruits, oatmeal and fancy egg dishes. We especially liked the baked eggs Portuguese and the eggs Buckingham, the latter an intriguing mix of eggs, sautéed red and green peppers, onion and bacon seasoned with dijon mustard and worcestershire sauce, served atop an English muffin, covered with Vermont cheddar cheese and then baked. A great way to start the day.

(802) 464-8131 or (800) 493-1133. Fax (802) 464-1130. Fourteen rooms, four suites and three one-room cottages with private baths. Rates, MAP. Doubles, $400 to $450 weekends, $375 to $420 midweek. Suites and cottages, $475 to $850 weekends, $450 to $750 midweek. Add $50 for foliage and holidays. Closed April to late May.

Deerhill Inn, 14 Valley View Road, West Dover 05356.

High on a hill overlooking the valley and the Green Mountains, this rambling, multi-level inn is quiet and comfortable. And ever so eclectic, from the lavish garden decor in the restaurant (see Dining Spots) to the varied styles of the fifteen guest quarters, no two of which are at all alike.

The public rooms were originally decorated by Ione Williams of the Inn at Sawmill Farm, a former innkeeper's aunt. They now bear the imprint of subsequent owners Linda and Michael Anelli, who sold a turnkey operation in 2002 to Stan Gresens and Michael Allen.

Like their predecessors, Michael is in the kitchen, utilizing his background as a chef in Boston restaurants. Stan, a former industrial design consultant who owned and managed rental properties in Boston, handles the innkeeping duties.

The Deerhill reflects the flair of Linda Anelli, for whom art and flowers were a passion. A veritable gallery of local art – now called the Art on the Mountain Gallery – hangs on the walls of the large first-floor living room and is for sale. Guests often gather here for cocktails on overstuffed sofas and wing chairs facing a gleaming copper-topped coffee table in front of a massive fieldstone fireplace. More art graces the second-floor living room, which is reserved for inn guests. It has another large brick fireplace, conversation groupings and enormous pillows to sit on. A library alcove with shelves of books and a TV set is at the head of the stairs.

The guest quarters, located in various sections and on different levels, are notable for bright and cheery decor. On a summer visit, we enjoyed one of the front rooms with a long, full-length balcony equipped with wicker rockers for watching the sun set over the mountains. The queen canopy bed was outfitted with designer linens and pillows – flannel sheets are employed in winter. The bath was equipped with Turkish terrycloth robes and Aloe Vera toiletries by Crabtree & Evelyn. Two armchairs flanked the fireplace, a pastoral mural graced one wall, and bowls of fruit and candy were at hand. Behind was a 20-by-40-foot swimming pool, surrounded by cutting gardens that furnished the bouquets for guest rooms and restaurant tables.

The cozy and much-photographed Lilac Room won the old Country Inns magazine's Waverly Room of the Year award in 1996. It has a king bed with a picket-fence headboard, sponge-painted walls and a deck facing the pool. Two rear rooms

Lush plantings provide colorful welcome at entry to Deerhill Inn.

with vaulted ceilings and kingsize beds open onto private decks. A fan is displayed on the wall and the queen bed has a canopy of mosquito netting in a room with an oriental theme.

The new owners converted four of the six standard rooms from double beds to queen beds and added a double jacuzzi tub in the Garden Suite.

Breakfast, available from a full menu, is a culinary treat. Juice and strawberries with cantaloupe, garnished with a pansy, preceded our breakfast: a mushroom and cheese omelet with home fries in one case, a simple poached egg in the other.

Afternoon tea with delectable scones, apple crisp cake and assorted cookies welcomes guests at peak periods. A tiny taproom with three bar stools and three chairs is available for drinks.

(802) 464-3100 or (800) 993-3379. Fax (802) 464-5474. www.deerhill.com. Thirteen rooms and two suites with private baths. Weekends: doubles $130 to $200, suites $230 and $250. Midweek: doubles $115 to $180, suites $205 and $225. Foliage and holidays: doubles $165 to $240, suites $270 and $290. Add $80 for MAP. Children over 12.

West Dover Inn, 108 Route 100, Box 1208, West Dover 05356.

The area's original country inn began life as a stagecoach stop and tavern in 1846. Recently restored, the good-looking, pristine white structure with columns outlining front porches on both the first and second floors is a cheerful presence in the heart of West Dover's historic district.

It is run personally by Ed Riley, who returned to his native Vermont in 2003 after 24 years in management with corporate hotels around the world, including a stint as general manager of the famed Equinox in Manchester. He refurbished the public rooms and made cosmetic upgrades to the accommodations.

The inn harbors twelve rooms and suites, all with TVs hidden in cupboards or armoires. Eight have queen beds, six have fireplaces and four suites have whirlpool tubs. Expect period furnishings, antiques, light painted walls and floral wallpapers, and whimsical accents like a stuffed koala bear, made by a housekeeper and perched on the bed of the South Suite.

Most in demand are the four suites, which are located in rear sections away from the road. The Haystack and Mount Snow suites in a 1992 addition above the restaurant wing have thick carpeting, queensize brass or poster beds, and sitting rooms with gas fireplaces. They convey a feeling of contemporary luxury, as opposed to the North and South suites upstairs in the original structure, which retain their original wide-board floors and wood-burning fireplaces. Other rooms vary, from a small double with hooked rugs in the old house to an odd-looking family room that resembles a ski dorm, with a lineup of two twin beds and a double. A guest favorite is the light and airy front room with a double and a twin bed. It opens onto the second-story porch.

Ed refurbished the large main-floor living room, which is cheery and comfortable. He redecorated the main dining room, the cozy tavern and redid the sunny rear breakfast room in gray and white. The last is the site for an ample repast, from Belgian waffles to cheddar omelets.

(802) 464-5207. Fax (802) 464-2173. www.westdoverinn.com. Eight rooms and four suites with private baths. Summer: doubles $110 to $130, suites $155 and $175. Foliage: doubles $138 to $179, suites $218 and $241. Winter: doubles $155 to $189, suites $230 and $258. Children over 12. Closed mid-April to mid-May.

The Four Seasons Inn, 145 Route 100, Box 2540, West Dover 05356.

Expatriate Brits Ann and Barry Poulter had enjoyed renovating houses in their spare time, but this was something else: a rundown, 24-room ski lodge and restaurant that catered to the bus group trade. The couple spent three years and several million dollars renovating what a fellow innkeeper termed "a dump" into an almost all-new, fifteen room, generally upscale inn that aforementioned innkeeper calls "the best rooms in the valley."

Certainly the common rooms and eight of the guest rooms rank among the best in this stark white, two-level structure that looked quite unremarkable from the road upon opening in 2003. The interior is another story.

"We gutted it and started over – Ann designed and I constructed," said Barry, a former Manhattan ad agency art director who did much of the renovation work himself.

The main entry opens into a foyer with a wood-paneled bar that proved so inviting it doubles as the reception area. Across the way is a stunning living room with massive fieldstone fireplace, plush dark brown sofas and chairs in one section and lighter furnishings in the front section. Dividers topped by colorful teapots separate the two sections from each other and from the expansive rear breakfast room, sunny and elegant with individual tables draped in yellow and white. It opens onto a lovely back deck overlooking the North Branch of the Deerfield River and woods beyond.

Several more small common rooms are scattered here and there through the various wings of the inn. The most deluxe guest rooms are six above the main-floor common areas in the South Wing, plus two in North Wing. All have step-up king or queen canopy or poster beds, gas or wood-burning fireplaces and modern baths with jacuzzi tubs. Five have private balconies. Each is individually decorated by Ann, who is partial to subtle floral wallpapers, 300-count bed linens, down comforters, Molton Brown toiletries from England and TV/DVD players concealed in armoires. Five are "demi-suites" with substantial sitting areas or alcoves behind arched doorways. The cathedral-ceilinged honeymoon suite comes with surround sound, flat-screen TV and a jacuzzi for two in the bedroom.

Old ski lodge has been transformed into new Four Seasons Inn.

Seven standard rooms in the North Wing with queen beds, shower baths and table-top TVs are modest in comparison.

The Poulters serve a full breakfast, ordered off a menu. Choices include challah french toast, buttermilk pancakes with "blueberries we pick ourselves," eggs any style and the house specialty, baked eggs in ham crisps.

(802) 464-8303 or (877) 531-4500. Fax (802) 464-3323. www.thefourseasonsinn.com. Nine rooms and five demi-suites with private baths. Winter and foliage: doubles $165 to $250 weekends, $150 to $220 midweek; suites $275 to $325 weekends, $130 to $275 midweek. April to mid-September: doubles $130 to $180 weekends, $120 to $160 midweek; suites $195 to $235 weekends, $175 to $195 midweek. Two-night minimum weekends.

Snow Goose Inn, Route 100, Box 366, West Dover 05356.

A grand entry way supported with 150-year-old, hand-hewn beams salvaged from an old Vermont barn lead into this twelve-bedroom lodge screened from the road by evergreen trees.

Philip and Suzanne Waller took over the old Shield Inn in 1999. Changing the name of an inn with a good reputation is not to be taken lightly. But the new name is just one of the transformations that have turned the Shield into the Snow Goose. The inn has been torn apart and rebuilt. No detail was overlooked, from plush featherbeds and top-quality linens in every room to the addition of private decks, french doors, larger windows, Waverly wallpapers and period antiques throughout the building.

Five guest rooms are in the original section of the house, built as a lodge in 1959. Six rooms and two suites are in a three-story wing added in 1991 by previous owners. All have updated baths and television. Many have wood-burning fireplaces, two-person jacuzzi tubs and private decks. Queen or king beds, comfortable chairs and floral fabrics abound.

The inn's long living room is open to a smaller living room at one end and an area for dining at the other. Wine and hors d'oeuvres welcome guests in the late afternoon.

British-born Philip cooks the breakfasts. Juice, fresh fruit and muffins precede the entrée, chosen from a menu that changes daily. Main courses might be Swedish pancakes with blueberry sauce or french toast. The Wallers even import their favorite H&H bagels from New York City.

(802) 464-3984 or (888) 604-7964. Fax (802) 464-5322. www.snowgooseinn.com. Eleven rooms and two suites with private baths. Fall-winter: doubles $125 to $210 weekends, $105 to $160 midweek; suites, $250 to $360 weekends, $195 to $250 midweek. Spring-summer: doubles $140 to $250 weekends, $120 to $185 midweek; suites $195 to $230 weekends, $175 to $195 midweek. Children over 10.

Doveberry Inn, Route 100, West Dover 05356.

Glowingly described by a fellow innkeeper as "a diamond in the rough" in its early stages, the Doveberry has upgraded its accommodations and matured into what Condé Nast Traveler ranks as one of America's 25 top inns with super chefs.

Owners Michael and Christine Fayette, who are well known for their restaurant (see Dining Spots), live on the premises and offer overnight guests a variety of rooms with king, queen or two double beds. All have TV/VCRs, and some with skylights convey a contemporary air. Two rooms were enlarged and renovated and three deluxe newcomers emerged in 2002, thanks to a three-story addition to the south end of the building.

The three new rooms come with whirlpool tubs, fireplaces and balconies or decks – "anything and everything that anybody ever asked for in the past," in Michael's words. The renovated Blue Room with queen bed gained a whirlpool tub, and the Green Room became a suite with king bed and twin and a fireplace stove. Christine decorated all the new rooms with wallpaper above painted wainscoting, country accents and lots of pillows.

Overstuffed dark blue sofas and armchairs are grouped around the open brick hearth that warms the large common room. Tea and cookies are served here in the afternoon.

Guests order a complimentary breakfast from a full menu. Choices range from belgian waffles to eggs benedict with a crab cake.

(802) 464-5652 or (800) 722-3204. Fax (802) 464-6229. www.doveberryinn.com. Eleven rooms with private baths. Fall-spring: doubles, $125 to $215 weekends, $115 to $170 midweek. Summer: doubles, $115 to $135 weekends, $85 to $115 midweek. Two-night minimum weekends.

Trail's End, 5 Trail's End Lane, Wilmington 05363.

Tucked beneath towering pines off a quiet country road in neighboring Wilmington, Trail's End is an architecturally interesting blend of ski lodge and inn with thirteen guest rooms and two suites.

The centerpiece is the striking living room/dining room area, with soaring windows sloping up and outward, a cathedral ceiling, a gigantic stone fireplace, two stories of stone walls and an unusual wall of cistern wheels that must be seen to be believed. Against the windows is a lineup of built-in sofas, capable, no doubt, of seating half the house. Above is a ramp crossing to a corner loft television area overlooking the whole scene.

The low-ceilinged dining room has three large round tables, plus a smaller dining room for those who like privacy.

The heart of the house is the open kitchen, where new owner Kevin Stephens from Boston's North Shore and staff prepare a full breakfast of the guest's choice. "We just finished serving 30 people homemade granola, eggs any style, blueberry pancakes and french toast," Kevin said one winter weekend. Since it was his busy season, the avid skier had not yet found time to ski.

Scouring the East Coast to buy an inn in a year-round resort area, he took over what Kevin called "an incredibly solid business" from founding innkeepers Mary and Bill Kilburn, who moved to a smaller B&B in West Barnstable on Cape Cod. He planned few changes, other than adding an eight-foot Olhausen pool table in a large, rustic fieldstone-floored room with books and games.

Over the years, the accommodations have been upgraded to the point where the innkeeper called them "picture-perfect in sophisticated country style," each done in a different color scheme and furnished with antiques. Each has a queen bed or a double and twin bed. Four with fireplaces also have TV.

Occupants of the two skylit fireplace suites might seldom leave their quarters. Each has a queensize canopy bed, a bathroom with oversize whirlpool tub, a wet bar area with mini-refrigerator and microwave, a sitting area with small TV and a stone fireplace, and a sunken sitting room with a daybed. The one we admired most added a second bathroom and a private outdoor deck.

The ten acres of grounds are most appealing with a heated swimming pool, a stocked trout pond, a hidden clay tennis court and beautiful English gardens.

(802) 464-2727 or (800) 859-2585. Fax (802) 464-5532. www.trailsendvt.com. Thirteen rooms and two suites. Summer and fall: doubles $110 to $150, suites $160 to $180. Winter: doubles, $130 to $160, suites $190. Two-night minimum weekends. Children welcome.

Dining Spots

The Inn at Sawmill Farm, Route 100, West Dover.

The food served up by engineer-turned-chef Brill Williams, son of founding innkeepers Rodney and Ione Williams, is worthy of the magnificent setting they created.

The three attractive, candlelit dining rooms display the owners' collection of folk art. The main room has white beams, theorem and oil paintings, rose and ivory wallpaper (even on the ceiling), a lovely china cabinet and tables set with white linens, heavy silver and pretty floral china. We like best the adjacent Greenhouse Room, a colorful plant-filled oasis.

The menu is larger and appears more dated – shrimp in beer batter, lobster savannah, breast of pheasant forestière, Indonesian curried chicken breast with coconut and bananas – than one might expect, with many favorites remaining year after year.

But Brill Williams does not rest on reputation. For starters, we liked the thinly sliced raw prime sirloin with a shallot and mustard sauce, and the sauté of chicken livers with onion brioche and quail egg. Next came delicate green salads and a basket of good hot rolls and crisp, homemade melba toast. Entrées range from potato-encrusted black grouper with orzo and beurre blanc sauce to grilled venison served on a crouton with duxelle of wild mushroom. We found outstanding both the rabbit stew and the sweetbreads with white truffle butter sauce on a bed of french-fried spinach.

Desserts are grand. Fresh coconut cake, apple tart with hard sauce, chocolate whisky cake with grand marnier sauce and bananas Romanoff were among the choices at our visit. The espresso is strong, and better-than-usual decaffeinated coffee is served in a silver pot.

The inn's wine cellar, which Brill says he has developed "more as a hobby than a business," has been ranked among the top 82 in the world by Wine Spectator.

At our latest visit, the inn offered an additional four-course, prix-fixe menu with several choices among the day's selections. It represented unusual value at $42.

(802) 464-8131 or (800) 493-1133. Entrées, $29 to $38. Dinner nightly by reservation, 6 to 9. Jackets preferred. Closed April to late May.

Deerhill Inn & Restaurant, Valley View Road, West Dover.

This inn's restaurant generally ranks right up there with the better-known Inn at Sawmill Farm. Its reputation was established by longtime owner Michael and Linda Anelli, who earlier had launched the Two Tannery Road Restaurant nearby.

The tradition continues under new chef and co-owner Michael Allen, who had cooked in Boston restaurants and before that at the famed Whistling Oyster in Ogunquit, Me. He calls his fare "creative American," based on a foundation of "comfort food," and maintained many of the inn's specialties.

To the traditional â-la-carte format he added a four-course prix-fixe menu that rotates every two weeks. The latter might open with pan-braised sea scallops served with a "ravioli" of braised celery root stuffed with portobello mushrooms, or smoked duck breast with a salad of roasted beets. A spinach salad laden with mushrooms, blue cheese and pancetta could follow. The main course at our latest visit offered a choice of pan-seared red snapper with red onion marmalade, cumin-crusted pork tenderloin with orange sauce and sautéed sirloin of venison wrapped in smoked bacon and served in a white wine and juniper sauce. Dessert could be pineapple tarte tatin with burnt sugar ice cream, peanut butter pudding with roasted bananas or – the ultimate in comfort food – chocolate angelfood cake with hot fudge and bananas.

Our nicely paced dinner began with potato and leek soup and a portobello mushroom stuffed with lobster and crab. Among entrées, the sliced grilled leg of lamb with a wedge of saga blue cheese and the five-layer veal with roasted red pepper sauce proved exceptional.

A Forest Glen merlot accompanied from what the host called "our NAFTA wine list." A marked departure from the famous wine cellars of two nearby establishments, it was totally North and South American – from Chile to Virginia to Oregon – and pleasantly priced.

The inn's bent for art and flowers shows up in two colorful dining rooms in the country garden style. Well-spaced tables are dressed in white over provençal-style floral cloths. There's a lot to look at, from a garden mural and floral paintings to ivy and tiny white lights twined all around.

(802) 464-3100 or (800) 993-3379. Entrées, $24 to $30. Prix-fixe, $45. Dinner nightly except Wednesday, 6 to 9:30.

Two Tannery Road, 2 Tannery Road, West Dover.

The first frame house in the town of Dover has quite a history. Built in the late 1700s, it became the summer home in the early 1900s of President Theodore Roosevelt's son and daughter-in-law. In the early 1940s it was moved to its present location, the site of a former sawmill and tannery. It became the first lodge for nearby Mount Snow and finally a restaurant in 1982.

Along the way it has been transformed into a place of great attractiveness, especially the main Garden Room with its vaulted ceiling, a many-windowed space

Northern Italian food is hallmark of chef-owned Doveberry Inn.

so filled with plants and so open that you almost don't know where the inside ends and the outside begins. A pleasant lounge contains part of the original bar from the Waldorf-Astoria.

Longtime chef Brian Reynolds has spiced up the continental/American fare with starters like Acadian pepper shrimp, grilled cajun steak tips and spicy Thai turnovers with chili-garlic dipping sauce. We enjoyed the garlicky frog's legs as well as the duck livers with onions in a terrific sauce.

Nearly two dozen entrées plus nightly specials range from cioppino to grilled spice-rubbed lamb medallions with apple-currant sauce. "Tannery Two" might pair baked Acadian shrimp and grilled oriental salmon with a sesame-ginger sauce. Veal is a specialty, so we tried veal granonico in a basil sauce as well as grilled New Mexican chicken with chiles, herbs and special salsa, accompanied by a goodly array of vegetables – broccoli, carrots, parsley and boiled new potatoes in one case, rice pilaf in the other.

A four-layer grand marnier cake with strawberries – enough for two to share – testified to the kitchen's prowess with desserts.

(802) 464-2707. www.twotannery.com. Entrées, $23 to $30. Dinner, Tuesday-Sunday 6 to 9:30 or 10.

Doveberry Inn, Route 100, West Dover 05356.

Excellent northern Italian fare is offered here by chef-owner Michael Fayette, who trained at Paul Smith's College in New York and 21 Federal in Nantucket, and his wife Christine, the baker. They have added a wine bar in the common room, and attract the public for dessert and cappuccino as well as dinner in the evening.

Thirty diners can be seated in a two-part, beamed room at tables covered with handmade quilt overcloths that change with the seasons.

Michael's menu changes weekly. Typical starters include grilled shrimp over fennel risotto with a touch of armagnac, pan-seared scallops on a bed of braised leeks with port wine reduction, and grilled quail with sundried tomatoes, mushrooms and rosemary. A house salad is included with the meal.

Main courses vary from rare grilled tuna accented with white truffle oil and served over creamy risotto to rack of lamb with a black cherry demi-glace. A specialty is wood-grilled veal chop with wild mushrooms. Sautéed rabbit with apples, figs and dried cranberries and seared venison with a mustard seed demi-glace are seasonal treats.

Christine might prepare orange-cinnamon crème brûlée, zuccota cake, mascarpone cheesecake, a plum napoleon and cannolis for dessert.

(802) 464-5652 or (800) 722-3204. Entrées, $21 to $28. Dinner nightly except Tuesday, 6 to 9. Closed two weeks in early November and early May.

Le Petit Chef, Route 100, Wilmington.

The outside of this low white 1850 farmhouse smack up against the road to Mount Snow looks deceptively small. The inside houses three intimate dining rooms, a spacious lobby abloom with spring flowers in midwinter and a veritable gallery of art work, plus an inviting lounge.

Chef-owner Betty Hillman, whose mother Libby is the cookbook author, studied in France and her formerly classic French menu has become more contemporary of late, to considerable acclaim.

Starters include a signature tomato, basil and goat cheese tart, seared foie gras with caramelized apple and onion confit, fricassee of escargots and wild mushrooms, and a lobster and guacamole salad garnished with crisp wontons.

Typical main dishes are shrimp en brochette grilled on a rosemary branch and served on a tomato and feta risotto, Mediterranean bouillabaisse, sliced moulard duck with red onion marmalade, grilled veal chop with a balsamic reduction and beef tournedos on a crouton garnished with merlot sauce and a ragoût of wild mushrooms. A classic rack of lamb is available for two.

Homemade lemon sorbet and ice creams, fresh fruit tarts, apple cake, crunchy meringue and chocolate torte are among desserts.

(802) 464-8437. Entrées, $25.50 to $34. Dinner nightly except Tuesday, 6 to 9 or 10.

West Dover Inn, 108 Route 100, West Dover.

The restaurant at the West Dover Inn has been upgraded by new owner Ed Riley, a seasoned hotelier who proclaimed his among the best three in the valley not long after taking over in 2003. He retained Dawn Hastings as executive chef and gave her free rein in the kitchen.

The restaurant in the inn's north wing contains a timbered and paneled dining room with the requisite casual country look, white tablecloths topped by glass, flickering oil lamps and a fireplace along one side. At the far end with a separate entrance is a lounge with a long bar. The main room opens into a breakfast room that Ed redecorated in gray and white and uses for overflow on busy nights.

The short menu changes with the seasons. Appetizers vary from a classic shrimp cocktail to Asian spring rolls, from almond-crusted duck tenders with a sweet and sour dipping sauce to spinach and artichoke dip with grilled ciabata bread.

Typical main courses are grilled salmon fillet paired with lobster and shrimp tortellacci in a saffron-chardonnay sauce, herb-crusted porcini chicken with marsala wine glaze and grilled sirloin steak in a bourbon marinade with green peppercorns and roasted garlic. A house specialty is honey-hoisin glazed roast duck with a tangy plum sauce.

Homemade desserts include apple crisp, flourless chocolate torte and French vanilla crêpe.

(802) 464-7264. Entrées, $23 to $30. Dinner, Wednesday-Sunday 6 to 9 in season, Thursday-Saturday rest of year.

The Hermitage, Coldbrook Road, Wilmington.

The dinner menu at the Hermitage rarely changes. It doesn't have to. People flock to the venerable inn's restaurant much like the game birds that legendary innkeeper Jim McGovern used to raise on the 24-acre property. Jim, one of whose talents is cooking, specializes in game dishes and also is a connoisseur of wines.

In season, lunch and brunch are served outside on a marble patio or inside in a recently expanded front dining room lightened up with cream-colored walls and yellow-over-white tablecloths. Beyond the smoky, expanded bar is a large vast dining room often used for functions. Upholstered and wing chairs flank widely spaced tables set with white linens and blue overcloths, white china and heavy silver. Walls are covered with the "naif" prints of Michel Delacroix, and hand-carved decoys are everywhere.

The extensive dinner menu is basically variations on a shrimp, trout, veal and game theme. You can get baked trout stuffed with crabmeat, a duet of shrimp and Spanish sausage over arborio rice, chicken gorgonzola atop linguini, wiener schnitzel or sautéed venison with roasted garlic sauce. But who wouldn't opt for the nightly game bird specials – perhaps pheasant, quail, goose, wild turkey or, one time we visited, partridge?

The Wine Spectator grand award-winning cellar contains more than 2,000 labels. The weighty wine tome, one of the best in the world, covers 74 pages and has a table on contents and an index. Its contents are also available in a wine shop beneath the inn.

For Sunday brunch, we sampled the mushroom soup with a rich game pâté on toast triangles plus a house specialty, four mushroom caps stuffed with caviar and garnished with a pimento slice and chopped raw onion on a bed of ruby lettuce. The chicken salad was an ample plateful colorfully surrounded by sliced oranges, apples, green melon, strawberries, grapes and tomatoes on a bed of bibb lettuce. The portions were large enough that we could not be tempted by such desserts as a hot Indian pudding, a maple parfait made with Hermitage syrup or fresh strawberries on homemade shortcake.

(802) 464-3511. Entrées, $18 to $30. Dinner nightly, 5 to 11. Sunday brunch, 11 to 2.

Diversions

Skiing. Mount Snow virtually put West Dover on the map and remains the stellar attraction today. Long known as a great beginners' area and a lively place for après-ski (with the stress on après more than ski), it nonetheless has always appealed to us for its wide-open, almost effortless intermediate skiing. Since founder-showman Walter Schoenknecht sold to the business types from Killington (now the American Skiing Co. behemoth), Mount Snow has been upgraded in terms of snowmaking and lift capacity. Gone is the heated outdoor swimming pool, an icon of its era, in which teenyboppers shrieked in lieu of skiing. More emphasis is on the North Face, a challenging area for advanced skiers, blessedly away from the crowds. **Haystack,** a smaller mountain (1,400-foot vertical drop, compared with Mount Snow's 1,900), is connected with Mount Snow by a free shuttle. Since 1997, the new owners have poured millions into Mount Snow/Haystack and new lifts, including the world's longest "magic carpet," a 400-foot-long surface lift moving people in the base and hotel area around the Grand Summit Resort Hotel. Mount Snow now claims five mountain areas and the most lifts in the East.

Cross-Country Skiing. Where skiers gather, cross-country is usually available, too. So it is with the Deerfield Valley, which has three major touring centers. The **Hermitage Ski Touring Center,** run by the Hermitage inn, has 50 kilometers of groomed trails next to Haystack. It is part of the rugged Ridge Trail, a five-mile-long mountaintop touring trail that winds up and down four peaks between Haystack and Mount Snow. **Timber Creek Cross Country Ski Center** offers a meandering, groomed trail system across from Mount Snow. The **White House Cross Country Ski Center,** run by the White House Inn in Wilmington, has fourteen miles of trails through woods and hills east of Wilmington.

Other Seasons. Two of Vermont's largest lakes are close at hand for boating, fishing and swimming: Somerset Reservoir in the wilderness northwest of Mount Snow and Harriman Reservoir/Lake Whitingham south of Wilmington. Golf is available at the eighteen-hole Mount Snow Golf Club and the eighteen-hole Haystack Golf Club championship course.

Transportation. For those who want to get around without wheels, ride **the MOOver,** the Deerfield Valley's community-sponsored shuttle system. A free bus makes stops at more than 30 points along Route 100 between Mount Snow, West Dover and Wilmington. In the making is the ten-mile **Valley Trail,** a state-funded recreational pathway connecting the center of West Dover with Mount Snow and Wilmington. With an impressive **mountain biking center** and the country's first mountain bike school, Mount Snow claims to be the mountain bike capital of the East.

Shopping. West Dover is little more than a hamlet with some landmark structures that make up what one innkeeper calls an emerging "Historic Mile." Most of the shopping opportunities are down the valley in Wilmington, where there are fascinating shops. The usual ski clothing boutiques abound, of course, and more trendy little shopping clusters open along Route 100 almost every year.

Hayloft Gallery claims the most eclectic display of fine art in Vermont, including an outdoor gallery of architectural artifacts around gardens and a pool. **Swe Den Nor Ltd.** offers Scandinavian furniture, accessories and gifts. **The Cupola** and **Equipe Sport** are leading sports outfitters.

Taddingers is an expansive country store with seven unusual shops under one roof, including Orvis, a Christmas room and all kinds of antiques and accessories. We're partial to the Vermont specialty foods section, the Wilcox Ice Cream parlor and the Nature Room full of more kinds of birdhouses than we thought existed.

Extra-Special

The Marlboro Music Festival, Marlboro.

Popular with West Dover visitors is the summer tradition at Marlboro College in nearby Marlboro, where chamber music concerts are presented each weekend from early July to mid-August. The music school was founded in 1952 by pianist Rudolf Serkin. Considered the nation's best chamber music series, the concerts by 70 festival players are incidental to their studies. Tickets usually are sold out by spring, but seats may be available on the screened porch outside the 650-seat concert hall in Persons Auditorium. For advance tickets, contact Marlboro Music Festival, 135 South 18th St., Philadelphia, Pa. 19103, (215) 569-4690; after June 6, Marlboro Music Festival, Box K, Marlboro 05344, (802) 254-2394.

Lake Sunapee is quiet in early morning in this view from Scenic Three Mile Loop.

Sunapee Region, N.H.

The Lure of the Lakes

The fortuitous combination of lakes, mountains and meadows makes the Sunapee Region a choice year-round attraction, especially for the sportsman and those who are drawn to the water.

Lake Sunapee, New Hampshire's third largest, and its neighbors, Little Sunapee and Pleasant Lake, provide all kinds of water pleasures within view of Mount Kearsarge, central New Hampshire's highest peak, and Mount Sunapee, a state park and ski area. In between on the rolling flatlands are four golf courses and two tennis clubs.

So it comes as no surprise that historic New London, the largest village in the region (year-round population, 3,200, but swelled by second-home residents, tourists and students at Colby-Sawyer College), is a mecca for the affluent. Its hilltop setting with posh contemporary homes, country clubs and trendy shops casts an unmistakable aura of prosperity. Legend has it that the song made famous by Kate Smith, "When the Moon Comes Over the Mountain," was written by a Colby-Sawyer student as she watched it rise above Mount Kearsarge.

Little Sunapee and Pleasant lakes, hidden from the tourists' path, are happily unspoiled. Some of the Lake Sunapee shoreline is surprisingly undeveloped as well, and old Sunapee Harbor – the heart of the lake resort region – looks not unlike a cove transplanted from the coast of upper Maine.

The area's inns, most of which have been around a while, reflect the charm and variety of the region.

Inn Spots

The Inn at Pleasant Lake, 125 Pleasant St., New London 03257.

Young Mississippi guy meets Connecticut gal at ski resort in Colorado. He trains at Culinary Institute of America. He cooks and she learns front office at top-rated inn in Virginia. Together they purchase old country inn in the state where she had summered with her parents.

Brian and Linda MacKenzie turned up in 1997 at the area's oldest operating inn, built in 1790 as a Cape farmhouse and converted in 1878 into a summer resort. They changed the name (from Pleasant Lake Inn), added some high-end guest rooms, offered a formal afternoon tea and a dining experience like that they'd understudied at Clifton, a top-rated inn in Charlottesville, Va., and lent youthful enthusiasm to an inn in need of a new lease on life.

The setting is super, down a long hill north out of New London at the end of Pleasant Lake. From the front windows and from the beach across the road, you look down the lake toward Mount Kearsarge at the far end.

The MacKenzies upsized some of the beds in guest rooms on the second and third floors, all pleasantly furnished with country antiques and some with Laura Ashley accents. They saved the best for their newest suites and "junior suites" with sitting areas. The first was fashioned from the former innkeepers' quarters on the third floor. Here, with a fine lake view, are a queen bed and a sitting area with a sofabed, plus a jacuzzi tub. Other good lake views are offered from a pair of second-floor junior suites, one with a king poster bed and the other with a queen bed and jacuzzi tub. A recent addition is a renovated bath with a whirlpool tub and separate shower in a second-floor junior suite with queen bed and view of a pond. New in 2001 was a third-floor junior suite with queen bed, day bed in the sitting area and bath with whirlpool tub.

The couple also instituted afternoon tea in the style of Clifton. Served on the enclosed flagstone porch overlooking the lake, this is no ordinary tea. Besides the usual, you'll get juices, fruit, a sampling of sweets and fancy imported cheeses and crackers.

Come dinnertime, chef Brian emerges toward the end of the cocktail reception to describe the evening's dinner menu. Guests adjourn to the main dining room for a meal to remember (see Dining Spots).

Brian (or his pastry chef) is back in the kitchen in the morning to prepare a full country breakfast for guests. After the preliminaries, guests can expect a hot entrée, perhaps poached eggs with mushroom béchamel sauce and sausage, or pecan and blueberry-baked french toast with bacon.

The inn offers a gym with Nordic equipment to burn off any extra calories.

(603) 526-6271 or (800) 626-4907. Fax (603) 526-4111. www.innatpleasantlake.com. Five rooms, three junior suites and two suites with private baths. Doubles, $110 to $135. Suites, $175. Two-night minimum summer weekends.

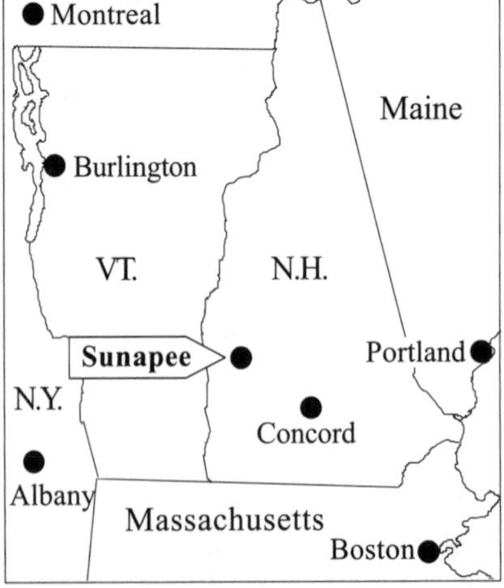

Dexter's Inn, 258 Stagecoach Road, Sunapee 03782.

Its facilities and location a mile or so up a country lane, high above Lake Sunapee, make this small resort a retreat for those seeking peace and quiet as well as sports enthusiasts.

Dexter's Inn occupies hilltop house dating to 1801.

Long known as Dexter's Inn and Tennis Club, its name was changed and its emphasis altered by Emily and John Augustine from New York City, who returned to her native New Hampshire and bought the property in 2002 from the Simpson/Durfor family. They turned it into a year-round, family-oriented B&B, staying open in winter to add skiing at Mount Sunapee to the inn's traditional sports offerings. (The inn was launched in 1948, the same year that the Mount Sunapee State Park ski area opened).

Located off a country lane high above Lake Sunapee, the twenty-acre property draws sports enthusiasts who enjoy three all-weather tennis courts plus a swimming pool, shuffleboard, croquet, volleyball and a horseshoe pit. The sports theme continues inside the large barn recreation room, with bumper pool and ping-pong tables. Youngsters have a new playroom of their own off the lounge in the main inn.

The Augustines offer ten comfortable guest rooms in a pale yellow residence dating to 1801 and seven more in an annex. Beds vary from kingsize and double to twins, and the Colonial decor lives up to guests' descriptions as cute and charming. The front rooms afford glimpses of the lake in the distance. Rooms in the annex and barn have high ceilings. Two have queensize canopy beds, and another has sliding doors onto a patio.

The Holly House Cottage is a two-bedroom, two-bath house with a living room, kitchen and porch. Claiming the best views on the property and quickest access to the tennis courts, it's available for up to eight people. The Augustines also offer a two-bedroom "efficiency condo": in the former innkeepers' house nestled between the Holly House Cottage and the inn.

Guests gather in the main inn's living room full of overstuffed furniture and walls of books, a pine-paneled tavern room with a fireplace and TV, and on a screened porch outfitted with wicker. The dining room yields a view of the lake as well as a buffet breakfast of fruit, pastries, egg dishes and pancakes or Belgian waffles.

(603) 763-5571 or (800) 232-5571. www.dextersnh.com. Seventeen rooms and two cottages with private baths. Doubles, $130 to $195. Cottages, $300 to $400 in summer, $225 to $300 in winter.

Abandoned summer resort has been transformed into Rosewood Country Inn.

The Rosewood Country Inn, 67 Pleasant View Road, Bradford 03221.

Electric candles are lighted in the windows of this expansive, rose-trimmed beige building that comes as a beacon for visitors arriving after a roundabout ride on back roads west of Bradford. The inviting facade is a sign of things to come. Inside this new B&B fashioned from an old summer resort is a stylish, comfortable place that's quite unexpected out here, seemingly in the middle of nowhere.

Rhode Island transplants Lesley and Dick Marquis opened in 1992 after a year's worth of renovations to the abandoned Pleasant View Farm, once a summer resort accommodating 100 guests, including the likes of Jack London, Mary Pickford, Charlie Chaplin and the Gish sisters. "This was a nightmare," recalled Lesley, showing photos of the neglected interior.

You'd never guess today. The Marquises and their contractor transformed the center section of the structure from head to toe, creating five spacious, handsomely appointed common rooms on the main floor and seven bedrooms with private baths upstairs. Lesley stenciled the intricate rose design that flows atop the walls from room to room, coordinating with changing fabrics and styles of window treatments along the way. The decor is handsome in rose colors in the formal living room and its arched annex. The side tavern room with TV and potbelly stove is bright and airy in the California style. In the center of the structure is an enormous dining room, big enough for a restaurant, with tables set for the inn's "candlelight and crystal" breakfast. Beyond the dining room is an open guest kitchen, family room and gift shop, all opening onto a broad deck overlooking the inn's twelve rolling acres of woods and fields.

Upstairs, the comfortable guest quarters are nicely decorated in a range of styles with painted walls, stenciling and coordinated fabrics. Roses and grapevines twine around the canopy above the queensize bed in the bridal suite, where a wicker loveseat is cosseted in a corner turret. Sturbridge and Williamsburg are the respective themes of two third-floor Colonial rooms. Whimsical accents abound, from a little white dress hanging in the bridal suite to gloves resting on a table in a Victorian suite to a bed warmer perched on the bed in the Williamsburg room.

In 1998, the Marquises added five deluxe rooms they call suites above their new function room. All have fireplaces and king or queensize beds. The bathrooms in two have double jacuzzis and the rest have five-foot-wide, double-headed showers for two. The third-floor Dreamcatcher Suite is billed as the best in the house. Furnished in what Lesley calls a Lake Placid motif, it has a kingsize Old Hickory bed, a rustic log corner fireplace, sofabed and wing chairs, TV/VCR in an armoire and large bath with double jacuzzi, twin pedestal sinks and corner shower. The corner Douglas Fairbanks Suite with most of the same attributes has six windows onto the mountains. Another corner suite, Mary Pickford, overlooks a gazebo and footbridge.

Breakfast is served in the dining room, on the porches or the rear deck. A fruit course (at our visit, peaches with raspberries and vanilla yogurt) and pastries (perhaps cinnamon swirl muffins) come first. The main event could be a breakfast quiche or french toast with strawberry maple syrup (made by a neighbor from maple trees on the inn's property). The signature dish is oven-baked cinnamon-apple pancakes with cider sauce.

(603) 938-5253 or (800) 938-5273. www.rosewoodcountryinn.com. Eleven rooms with private baths. Doubles, $139 to $279 May-December, $119 to $239 rest of year. Two-night minimum weekends. Children over 12.

Follansbee Inn on Kezar Lake, 2 Keyser St., North Sutton 03260.

"Welcome to the Follansbee Inn – a great place to relax and enjoy a slower pace of living," according to the sign at the porch entry to this rambling old inn fronting on Kezar Lake.

A big place with a hotel-style main floor and twenty guest accommodations, it seems smaller and is much more friendly than the country hotel that opened in 1840, thanks to innkeepers Cathy and Dave Beard of Colorado. And with a church beside, a cemetery behind and a lake in front, the setting is classic rural New England.

Off a second-floor hall full of antiques are eleven guest rooms with private baths. Furnished in cozy country style, all have been spruced up with Eisenhart Vintage wallpapers, new mattresses, carpeting, large towels and bayberry soap made especially for the inn. Beds are king, queen, double or twins and topped with quilts. Our corner room overlooking the lake had good cross-ventilation, a plus on a sultry night.

The Beards have made considerable improvements on the third floor, which formerly had twelve rooms with shared baths. A reconfiguration in 2001 resulted in five rooms with private baths and a couple of two-room suites with jacuzzi baths.

The homey main floor has a cozy sitting room paneled in barnwood and furnished with patchwork cushions, baskets and all kinds of games, and a large front parlor, a bit more formal but most comfortable. It opens onto a dining room, where breakfast usually starts with fresh fruit and homemade granola and features an entrée such as crème brûlée french toast, puffed apple pancake or eggs benedict.

Besides partaking of the innkeepers' hospitality, guests enjoy peaceful Kezar Lake, where swimming and boating beckon, and 500 wooded acres for hiking and cross-country skiing.

(603) 927-4221 or (800) 626-4221. www.follansbeeinn.com. Sixteen rooms and two suites with private baths. Doubles, $110 to $130. Suites, $175 and $195. Children over 10. Closed parts of April and November.

Colonial Farm Inn, Route 11, Box 1053, New London 03257.

Bob and Kathryn Joseph got their feet wet at a small B&B in Sutton Mills before deciding to open a larger, full-service country inn east of New London. They took over a handsome, 1836 center-chimney Colonial residence, of which they are only the fourth owners, and spent five months renovating prior to opening. They now offer six guest rooms, a choice little restaurant (see Dining Spots) and a growing antiques business.

Up a pulpit staircase and leading off rambling halls are the well-spaced bedrooms, handsomely decorated by Kathryn, who had been in the window design business. Everything in the rooms is carefully color-coordinated, from dust ruffles to pillows to balloon shades on the windows. She used picture framing to outline the head of the double bed in the Cabbage Patch Room. The rear Southport Room is decked out in white and blue Laura Ashley prints. The largest room is the Wauwinet, with a queensize poster bed – it's named after an area in Nantucket, "where we were married," Kathryn advises. It comes with a handsome leather reading chair and a wicker rocker, and a pedestal sink in the modern bath.

Guests enjoy a spacious common room with a vaulted ceiling on the second floor. Fashioned from an attic, it contains an antique pool table, games and a TV set. There's also a cozy front parlor shared with outside guests arriving for dinner.

A full breakfast includes fruit, muffins and a main dish, perhaps frittata, eggs or pancakes flavored with orange juice, blueberries or toasted walnuts.

In the carriage house beside the main house is Colonial Farm Antiques, where twelve dealers show their wares.

(603) 526-6121 or (800) 805-8504. Fax (603) 641-0314. www.colonialfarminn.com. Six rooms with private baths. Doubles, $105 to $145, $95 to $125 in winter. Two-night minimum peak weekends.

Hide-Away Inn, Twin Lake Villa Road, Box 1249, New London 03257.

This establishment gained a wide reputation as a restaurant under former owners Wolf and Lilli Heinberg. Their successors focused variously on either food or lodging end of the business. Current owners Michael and Lori Freeman were working on upgrading both lodging and dining.

The lodge-style structure, whose walls are paneled in Oregon fir, is outfitted with sturdy maple furniture and a few antiques. Upstairs are five guest rooms and a suite with private baths, one in the hallway. All have queensize beds, three of them canopies. One of two rooms with fireplaces is the Steven Anthony Suite, with a canopy bed, sitting room with sofabed, and two bathrooms. The other fireplace is in the Captain's Quarters, which has a built-in bookcase for a bed headboard and nautical decor. The Grace Litchfield Room with an iron bed, cedar armoire, wicker settee and windows on three sides also is popular. All the rooms are homey and retain their lodgey look and feeling.

Guests share the spacious entry parlor, which has a great stone fireplace, with waiting diners. A smaller common room is available on the side. The main gathering spot is the downstairs Pipedream Lounge, with a bar, game tables, a dartboard and plenty of sofas and chairs for lounging around a TV/VCR. The wine cellar off the lounge is used for wine tastings.

Guests eat breakfast in the library. Fresh fruit is followed by a choice of perhaps eggs benedict or blueberry pancakes one day, an "omelet roll" of spinach and parmesan cheese or french toast the next.

Linda and Brian MacKenzie promote the dining experience at The Inn at Pleasant Lake.

The inn has an autographed copy of *Collected Poems* by Grace Litchfield, which turned up in nearby Potter Place. Signed "Hide-Away, New London," it is one of the prized works of the poet-author for whom the lodge was built as a hideaway in the 1930s.

(603) 526-4861 or (800) 457-0589. Fax (603) 526-4258. www.hideawayinn.net. Six rooms with private baths. Doubles, $95 to $135. Suite, $160. Children over 10.

Dining Spots

The Inn at Pleasant Lake, 125 Pleasant St., New London.

Taking his cue from the Virginia country inn where he was sous chef, Brian MacKenzie has transplanted a successful upscale southern formula up north.

"I like Craig's style," Brian says, referring to his mentor, former chef-innkeeper Craig Hartman at Clifton, whose meals and inn experience have been among the highlights of our travels. The Clifton style is not unique, but it is delivered to perfection and with nuances rarely attempted, let along achieved, elsewhere.

Here, the style begins during the 6:15 cocktail reception. In chef's whites, Brian emerges from the kitchen to detail the evening's five-course, prix-fixe menu – which sounds simple but requires a bit of showmanship not to bore one's captives to tears. Dinner is served at 7 in a 40-seat dining room, where well-spaced tables are set with white linens and crystal.

The night of our visit, the meal began with potage lyonnaise with chive oil and romano croustades, a salad of organic baby greens with roasted pine nuts and a sherried mango vinaigrette, and Italian bread with whipped butter. A raspberry sorbet with fresh kiwi prepared the palate for the main course, a choice of pan-seared swordfish with a marchand du vin sauce or roasted angus tenderloin with a chasseur sauce and basil pesto. Dessert was a dark chocolate terrine with two sauces and fresh raspberries.

The next night produced a choice of grilled wahoo with a citrus vinaigrette and roasted eggplant relish or baron of bison roulade with bordelaise sauce and an exotic mushroom duxelles. Dessert was cheesecake with a raspberry coulis, one of Brian's few departures from a chocolate theme that won him top prize in the regional chocolate contest.

(603) 526-6271 or (800) 626-4907. Prix-fixe, $52. Dinner by reservation, Wednesday-Sunday at 7.

La Meridiana, Route 11 at Old Winslow Road, Wilmot.

You can tell there's a culinary master in the kitchen of this old, rambling farmhouse, its dining room entered via a long corridor running the length of the building. A collection of Italian cookbooks is on display in the hall, and the wine list bears many interesting Italian vintages at affordable prices. You may hear chef-owner Piero Canuto singing arias in the kitchen. When he makes his rounds after dinner, he'll show you pictures of his hometown in northern Italy.

Peter makes most of his own pastas and encourages sharing of dishes at no extra cost. "Our menu is designed for you to choose as much or as little as your appetite allows." Prices are so low as not to be believed.

Start with crostini with chicken livers, squid salad, hot or cold antipasto or carpaccio. Most entrées are in the $10 range, and veal chop baked with mushrooms and fontina cheese tops the price list at $15.95. When did you last see sautéed trout, calves liver, chicken cacciatore or pork cutlets for $9.95 or less in a top restaurant? Entrées come with fresh vegetable and potato of the day. The menu is supplemented by many specials, among them osso buco and lamb casserole. People come especially for the rack of lamb, we were advised.

Desserts might be pumpkin pudding with mascarpone cheese, chocolate mousse cake, frozen chocolate soufflé and tiramisu.

The candlelit dining room is country Italian with posts and hand-hewn beams, attractive hanging lights, handsome oak chairs with round backs at white linened tables, fresh flowers and a fieldstone fireplace.

(603) 526-2033. Entrées, $8.95 to $19.95. Lunch in season, Monday-Saturday 11:30 to 1:30. Dinner nightly, 5 to 9. Sunday, brunch 11:30 to 1:30, dinner 3 to 8.

Potter Place Inn & Restaurant, 88 Depot St., Andover.

Giovanni Leopardi cooked for leading hotel and restaurant chains across the world before settling in 2002 in the Potter Place section of Andover. He and his wife Melba bought the late 18th-century farmhouse known as Potter Place Inn & Restaurant and moved in upstairs. They closed the inn rooms, redid the main-floor restaurant and started advertising "inspired cuisine."

"Inspired" it certainly is, according to area gourmands who showed their receptivity to a contemporary global menu offering more than the prevailing meat and lasagna fare. Inspired as in one autumn night's specials such as roasted monkfish with tamarillos, poblano peppers and tequila, garnished with mizuna leaves; veal sweetbreads sautéed with mushrooms and sherry, and grilled wild boar chops with an apple-sage-rum compote. These are in addition to regular entrées from Alaskan salmon fillet and roasted Cornish hen to braised lamb shanks and rack of veal. "I do a lot of wild game," said the chef, citing upcoming specials of kangaroo and antelope.

Candlelight dinners as well as guest rooms are offered at Colonial Farm Inn.

Appetizers include carpaccio, escargots bourguignonne and baked stuffed clams. The pastas might be lobster ravioli, goat cheese tortellini and homemade spaghetti with baby clams. Desserts vary from mascarpone-maple syrup cheesecake and french apple tart to homemade ice creams and tiramisu.

Rather remarkably given the scope of the menu and the size of the restaurant (more than 100 seats), Giovanni does basically all the cooking himself and prepares his own breads, pastas, soups, sauces and desserts.

All this inspired fare is served in four simple but historic-looking dining rooms with beamed ceilings, draperies that match the burnt orange wainscoting and captain's chairs at well-spaced, white-clothed tables.

(603) 735-5141. www.potterplaceinn.com. Entrées, $18 to $26. Dinner, Tuesday-Saturday from 5:30. Closed two weeks in November and February.

Colonial Farm Inn, Route 11, New London.

Bob and Kathryn Joseph learned to cook at a small B&B in Sutton Mills before opening this small inn and restaurant. Their impressive center-chimney Colonial holds two fireplaced dining rooms seating a total of 30. The candlelit rooms have the requisite beamed ceilings and wide-plank floors, and are done in warm salmon and platinum colors, from the walls to the table linens to the china. Lately, Bob built a new screened dining porch in the rear. With five tables, it is quite elegant and graced, like the other rooms, with oriental rugs on the wide-board floors.

Bob, who does the lion's share of the cooking, offers four starters: on a typical night, a sampler of pâtés and terrines, wild mushroom soup, eggplant bruschetta and the signature house salad, a mix of red and green leaf lettuces tossed with dijon dressing and sprinkled with toasted walnuts and blue cheese. The house specialty is tenderloin of beef sautéed with burgundy-shallot sauce. Other main courses could be sautéed sea scallops with lemon butter on a bed of wilted belgian endive, venison loin served with a cranberry compote, and veal rib chop with a rosemary compound butter. Potatoes au gratin and carrots glazed with honey and brandy might accompany.

Desserts include apple-raspberry pie, homemade profiteroles with vanilla ice cream and bittersweet chocolate sauce, and chocolate pâté with ground almonds and strawberry puree. Port and stilton are available after dinner.

(603) 526-6121 or (800) 805-8504. Entrées, $16 to $26. Dinner by reservation, Wednesday-Saturday 6 to 8.

Millstone Restaurant, 14 Newport Road, New London.

A lofty cathedral ceiling with skylights lends an airy feel to this casually elegant American bistro and wine bar that is popular with the Colby-Sawyer College crowd. Owned by veteran restaurateur Tom Mills, it's the original and flagship of his now trio of restaurants. Inside are well-spaced tables covered with linens. There's a pleasant, canopied brick terrace for garden dining in the summer.

Main courses listed on the large and varied dinner menu run the gamut from quite a variety of pasta dishes to trout amandine, cedar-planked salmon with maple-currant glaze, shrimp satay, calves liver, duck marinated in tequila and lime, grilled lamb steak with ginger and hoisin, and filet mignon.

Among appetizers are escargots, crab quesadilla, Maine crab cakes with mango salsa and mushrooms gratinée. Desserts include profiteroles au chocolat, marble cheesecake, belgian chocolate mousse pie and maple crème caramel.

Owner Mills also operates the larger and more down-to-earth **Flying Goose Brew Pub & Grille** at the junctions of Routes 11 and 114 at the other end of town.

(603) 526-4201. www.millstonerestaurant.com. Entrées, $13.95 to $24.95. Lunch daily, 11:30 to 2:30. Dinner nightly, 5 to 9. Sunday brunch, 11 to 2:30.

The Anchorage, 71 Main St., Sunapee Harbor.

"Every summer – the world's most hectic restaurant." The menu's slogan is on the mark at least locally. But as run by owners Jeffrey and Rose Follansbee, who earlier made the New London Inn a mecca for gourmet dining, it's considered a consistent, casual and all-around eatery right beside the harbor.

Here the Follansbees have a total of 140 seats in a couple of dining rooms, the rear bar and outside on an expansive deck at water's edge. Besides sprucing up the long and narrow main room with deep green booths and yellow walls, they've upscaled the menu from its traditional beer and sandwich days. Jeff oversees the cooking, featuring soups, salads, specialty sandwiches, fresh seafood and steaks.

At a recent lunch, we were well pleased with an enormous cobb salad, nicely presented the traditional way with the unexpected fillip of corn salad, and the signature "paradise burger" with the works and a mountain of fries and a side salad with a choice of eight dressings. The ice water came with a wedge of lemon.

Dinner entrées are served with soup or salad and fresh breadsticks. They include the likes of grilled salmon with tamari-ginger sauce, grilled pork chops with Asian marinade and fire-roasted fuji apples, pasta fra diavolo and outback filet mignon. The signature dessert is a "peanut monster" designed for sharing. It's a chocolate peanut brownie topped with vanilla and chocolate ice cream, hot fudge and peanuts in a huge goblet for two.

On summer weekends, the Anchorage opens at 8 a.m. for breakfast and offers live entertainment and dancing from 9 to midnight.

Lately, the Follansbees have expanded their casual dining concept back to New London with the opening of the year-round **North End Pizzeria, Pub & Grill**.

(603) 763-3334. Entrées, $10.99 to $17.99. Lunch daily, 11:30 to 4. Dinner, 4 to 9 or 10. Closed Monday in off-season. Open May through Columbus Day.

Hide-Away Inn, Twin Lake Villa Road, New London.

"An old friend is back in town," advertised this old-timer. And so it is. After a lengthy hiatus, subsequent owners revived the restaurant that founding owners Wolf and Lilli Heinberg made famous.

The fare is not the world-class caliber that prompted us once to drive three hours from Hartford for dinner. But locals applaud the food, served in three small dining rooms and an enclosed wraparound dining porch at a recent visit.

Chef Lori Freeman, innkeeper with her husband Michael, trained in the culinary arts in Michigan. She turns out wide-ranging fare mixing traditional with international, augmenting a seasonal menu with nightly specials.

Dinner might begin with lobster bisque, vegetable spring rolls or a concoction called Thai money bags – shrimp, vegetables and ginger tied in a wonton and fried golden brown. Main courses include scampi-stuffed sole, rainbow trout, seared scallops in lime beurre blanc, chicken saltimbocca, duck à l'orange and grilled lamb chops. Desserts could be raspberry crème brûlée, maple walnut-praline cake or Bailey's Irish Cream and white chocolate cheesecake.

(603) 526-4861 or (800) 457-0589. Entrées, $10.95 to $22.95. Dinner nightly, 5:30 to 9. Closed Wednesday in winter.

Bellissima, 976 Route 103, Newbury.

Veteran area restaurateur Tom Mills created a triumvirate of restaurants in 2003 with the opening of this brick-oven trattoria in the Newbury Harbor Plaza across from Lake Sunapee. This occupies the prime spot at the lake end of the strip plaza, and tables on two levels take advantage of the water view. Beyond the view there is little in the way of decor: a mural of an Italian scene on one wall, and an open kitchen in the far corner.

The airy setting is geared for family dining, casual and affordable. But the northern Italian menu is a cut above and offers something for everyone. The brick oven turns out eight kinds of pizza, and diners are urged also to create their own pies. There are five kinds of pasta, including one with mussels fra diavolo for a bargain $12.95. Main courses range from grilled Idaho trout to Tuscan pork, veal marsala and steak milanese.

Start with bruschetta, fried calamari with the house marinara sauce or fried mozzarella. Finish with mascarpone cheesecake, spumoni or tiramisu.

(603) 763-3290. www.bellissima-trattoria.com. Entrées, $11.95 to $16.95. Lunch and dinner daily, 11:30 to 9 or 10.

The Flying Goose Brew Pub & Grille, 40 Andover Road (Route 11), New London.

Long known as the Gray House, a traditional restaurant and ice cream stand, this was refashioned for the 21st century by Tom Mills of the Millstone Restaurant. Starting with the Four Corners Grille, he opened the Flying Goose Brew Pub here and in 2003 again changed the name.

It's still a pub, featuring sixteen handcrafted ales and an old-fashioned root beer, all brewed in house. It's also a casual, affordable grill featuring basic steaks and chops plus authentic pit-style barbecue. The barbecue slow roasts and smokes baby back ribs, pulled pork, rotisserie chicken and Texas-style sausages. They're available individually or in combination platters.

Otherwise, look for five kinds of steak from teriyaki to sirloin grilled with Guinness stout, grilled snapper, jambalaya, fish and chips, and veal parmesan. Nachos, quesadillas, stuffed potato skins and chicken tenders are the appetizer favorites.

The rear windows of the main dining room and the artifact-filled pub look onto an endless mountain view. The canopied rear porch captures the best views of all.

(603) 526-6899. www.flyinggoose.com. Entrées, $11.95 to $19.95. Lunch and dinner daily, 11 to 9.

Jack's Coffee, 180 Main St., New London.

Jack Diemar wrote a business plan for a coffee shop as the final project for an entrepreneurship class at Skidmore College. The plan was put on hold while he and his bride-to-be Jody, both professional bicyclists, were training and visited New London, where his grandfather had owned a business called the Wicker Loft. The vast space occupied for a few years by Baynham's Country Store and Café was available, and the couple decided to put Jack's business plan to work. Or perhaps it was vice-versa.

At any rate, they opened a coffee bar in the former soda fountain, added an internet café and convenience-store beverages and newspapers, and started lunch service. Other Jack's followed in the Powerhouse Mall in West Lebanon and in downtown Newport.

It turned out, as their ads says, that coffee was just the beginning. In 2003, Jack's in New London spread its wings, opening for dinner as well as breakfast and lunch. Expect a short contemporary menu beginning with several appetizers and salads. Main courses could be grilled sweet and sour tuna steak, duck breast and leg, and beef tenderloin au poivre. It's fairly fancy stuff for what began as a coffee shop.

(603) 526-8003. www.jackscoffee.com. Entrées, $15.50 to $19.95. Breakfast and lunch daily, 7 to 5, Sunday to 2. Dinner, Wednesday-Saturday 5:30 to 9, Sunday 5 to 8.

Diversions

Sports. All the usual are available, plus some in abundance. Golfers have their choice of four semi-public country clubs and smaller courses: the venerable Lake Sunapee Country Club, the hilly and challenging Eastman Golf Links in Grantham, picturesque Twin Lake Village beside Little Sunapee, and the Country Club of New Hampshire, rated one of the nation's top 75 public courses by Golf Digest. Downhill skiers get their fill at Mount Sunapee, and cross-country skiers take over the fairways at the area's golf clubs in winter.

Cultural Offerings. Since 1933, the **New London Barn Players,** New Hampshire's longest operating summer theater, have presented matinee and nightly performances of six musicals and two dramas from mid-June to Labor Day at the Barn Playhouse, 84 Main St., (603) 526-4631 or 526-6710. **Summer Music Associates,** (603) 526-8234, presents a series of concerts in the Sawyer Center Auditorium at Colby-Sawyer College or in First Baptist Church. **Band concerts** are scheduled summer Wednesdays, Saturdays and Sundays in Sunapee Harbor and Fridays at the Mary D. Haddad Memorial Bandstand in New London.

Despite its generally low-key flavor, the area bustles during the League of New Hampshire Craftsmen's annual crafts fair, the nation's oldest, which attracts 1,500 craftsmen and 50,000 visitors for a week in early August to Mount Sunapee Resort.

Mount Sunapee State Park, Route 103, Sunapee. A 700-foot-long beach is great for swimming in the crystal-clear waters of Lake Sunapee. Across the road is the 2,700-foot high Mount Sunapee, crisscrossed with hiking, mountain biking and ski trails and its summit lodge accessible in summer and winter by a high-speed quadruple chairlift. Summit barbecues are offered in summer. The formerly state-run ski area has been leased to the owners of Okemo Mountain Co. in Vermont. Their renamed Mount Sunapee Resort has an in-line skate park and hosts such special events as a gem and mineral festival, a summer music festival and the New England championship Lake Sunapee Bike Race.

Mount Sunapee has been undergoing a renaissance, and so is **Sunapee Harbor,** which fell on hard times after being the center of resort activity early in the 20th century. By 1990, most of the buildings around Sunapee Harbor were boarded up. Today, thanks to the efforts of the improvement-minded Sunapee Harbor Riverway Corp., the harbor is blossoming once more. Flower beds brighten a waterfront park, and a large bandstand – on the site of the last of the grand local hotels – is the scene of summer concerts and performances. The most visible presence looming above the harbor is the newly restored Knowlton House, which is not a Victorian inn but rather a wedding and party facility.

The **Sunapee Historical Society,** housed in a former livery stable across from the harbor, operates a small seasonal museum Tuesday-Sunday 1 to 4 and Wednesday 7 to 9. It's filled with photos of the old hotels and memorabilia of the lake's steamboat era.

Lake Sunapee. Until the 1920s most visitors to Lake Sunapee arrived in the area by train and got around by boat, so no road was built around the shoreline and some of it remains undeveloped. Three lighthouses that once guided steamboats still flash their beacons along the nine-mile length of the lake. The best way to see the lake up close is to get out on the water. From Sunapee Harbor, the 150-passenger **M.V. Mt. Sunapee II** gives 90-minute narrated tours the length of Lake Sunapee at 2 p.m. daily July through Labor Day, and weekends from Memorial Day to Columbus Day. The steamer **M.V. Kearsarge** offers buffet-dinner cruises at 6:30 nightly except Monday in summer.

Another way to view the lake is to drive the Scenic Three-Mile Loop around Sunapee Harbor. You'll find striking new houses interspersed with older cottages.

Shopping. For a town its size, New London has more than its share of good shopping – spread out along much of the length of Main Street and clustered in shopping centers and a mall along Newport Road (Route 11) on the southwest edge of town. At 107 Newport Road, **In-gre'di-ents** is an exceptional specialty foods shop featuring wines, cheeses, flowers, vitamins, organic meats and a host of health foods. Along Main Street are the **Spring Ledge Farm** flower and produce stand, excellent crafts stores like **Artisan's Workshop**, and the kind of clothing stores one finds in college towns, including **The Lemon Twist Shop, Pick Up Sticks** and **LisAnn's. C.B. Coburn** has "unique gifts for home and palate." **Morgan Hill Bookstore** has a choice selection, plus cards and music. **Wildberry Bagel Co.** offers New York-style bagels, espresso, soups and sandwiches here and at a new branch in Sunapee Harbor.

The old-fashioned **Wild Goose Country Store,** advertising collectibles and penny candy, and the **Harborside Trading Co.,** with clothing and souvenirs, draw shoppers in Sunapee Harbor. **Deck Dock** is a fine home and garden store beside the harbor.

Nunsuch, Route 114, South Sutton.

Worth a side trip (call ahead) is the picturesque home and farm of Courtney

Haase, producer of Udderly Delicious goat cheese, voted the best in New Hampshire. Not your ordinary cheesemaker, Courtney is a former cloistered nun who founded the business with her proper New Orleans mother Rita, who has five offspring scattered around the world. Their 21 milking goats, all but one named for nuns Courtney has lived with (to the amusement and consternation of some), yield about 70 pounds of cheese a day, which she sells herbed or plain from her kitchen or by mail-order. We bought some of the herbed variety and another with sundried tomatoes and black olives to take home and they were delicious. At a recent visit, Courtney had acquired a smoker and was starting to smoke some of her cheese. She also sells pasteurizing equipment in an enterprise called 2nd 2 Nun. Hers is the demonstration farm for the Small Dairy Project, an area enterprise she heads that has helped get more than 200 cheese makers licensed across the country.

(603) 927-4176. www.nunsuch.org. Open daily by appointment.

Muster Field Farm Museum, Harvey Road, North Sutton.

Atop a hill off a dirt road out in the middle of nowhere is this working farm museum, a 250-acre National Trust property where knowing locals buy their farm produce. Twenty farm buildings have been saved from destruction and moved to the militia muster field across from the 1787 Matthew Harvey Homestead. They include barns, an icehouse, blacksmith shops, corncribs and an 1810 schoolhouse, spread out plantation style in clusters. Visitors can obtain produce and enjoy the setting – a quite idyllic spot – on self-guided tours during the week. A better time to visit and get a sense of the low-key evolving place is Sunday when the homestead is open for tours and guides help trace the evolution of early farming in New Hampshire. The best time is special weekends when coopers, quilters, a beekeeper, farrier and occasionally some of the militia demonstrate activities of days long gone.

(603) 927-4276. www.musterfieldfarm.org. Farm stand open seasonally, Wednesday-Sunday 10 to 6. House tours, Sunday 1 to 4. July-September. Grounds open daily, 10 to 5. Free.

Extra-Special

The Fells at the John Hay National Wildlife Refuge, Route 103-A, Newbury.

Three generations of diplomat John Hay's family have enjoyed the rugged landscape and cultivated gardens they developed along nearly 1,000 hillside acres above Lake Sunapee since 1891. Now the public also can enjoy a rare combination of nature preserve, botanical garden, library, historic house and landscape in a single location. The Fells Estate is maintained as a state historic site, and the gardens were replanted in 1994 by the national Garden Conservancy as a regional center for horticultural education. The property includes the 163-acre John Hay National Wildlife Refuge. Depending on the season, masses of mountain laurel, rhododendrons, azaleas, blueberries, perennial borders, a rose terrace, a rock garden, an old walled garden and more can be seen. Noted nature writer John Hay, son of the late horticulturist and archeologist Clarence Hay, and his sister Adele frequent a private cottage reserved for their use. Visitors park in a lot off Route 103-A and walk a quarter of a mile to the main house and gardens.

(603) 763-4789. www.thefells.org. House open weekends and holidays 10 to 5, Memorial Day through Columbus Day. Grounds open daily, dawn to dusk, adults $4.

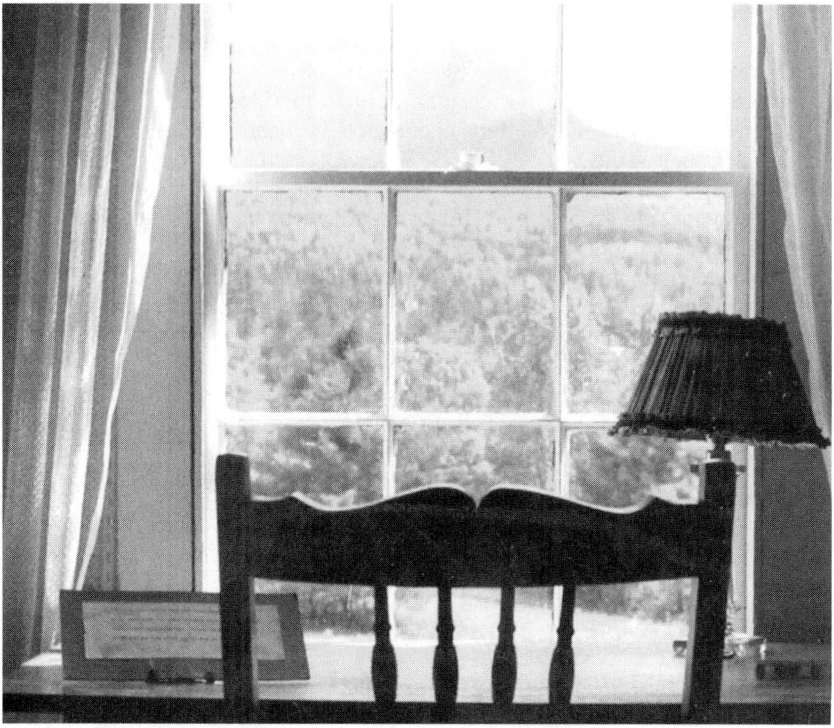

Robert Frost worked at this desk in Franconia with a view of Cannon Mountain.

Franconia/Sugar Hill, N.H.

The Road Less Traveled

The lines are from Robert Frost: "Two roads diverged in a wood, and I – I took the one less traveled by, and that has made all the difference."

They were written when the poet lived in Franconia beneath Cannon Mountain, and the road less traveled has made a difference historically in maintaining the Franconia area as an island of serenity just beyond the crowds.

Even the opening of the stunning Franconia Notch Parkway connecting completed portions of Interstate 93 on either side of the notch failed to bring in the hordes. Many people don't know about the area's history and beauty, said one innkeeper. "They think that beyond the Old Man of the Mountain, there are just woods and Canada."

Indeed, Franconia and its upcountry neighbor, Sugar Hill, are remote and relatively untouched by the usual trappings of tourism. They retain much of the look and the flavor of the late 19th century when they were noted mountain resort areas. In the 1930s, Austrian Sig Buchmayer established the country's first ski school at Peckett's-on-Sugar Hill (now designated by a primitive historic marker) and Cannon Mountain dedicated skiing's first aerial tramway.

But for the mystique of the name, one might not be aware of the area's storied past. Gone are the large hotels and, as ski areas go, Cannon keeps a low profile.

Today, the crowds and the condos halt below Franconia Notch to the south, leaving Cannon Mountain, Franconia, Sugar Hill, Bethlehem and even the "city" of Littleton for those who appreciate them as vestiges of the past.

For those who want action, the magnificent Franconia Notch State Park stretching eight miles through the notch offers outdoor activities and some of the Northeast's most spectacular sights.

But the road less traveled takes one beyond. There are few better places for fall foliage viewing than from Sunset Hill or the ridge leading up to Sugar Hill above Franconia. The heights afford sweeping vistas of the towering White Mountains on three sides and toward Vermont's Green Mountains on the fourth.

In winter, downhill skiers revel in the challenges of Cannon Mountain, the venerable World Cup area so full of skiing history that the New England Ski Museum is located at its base.

In spring and summer, the quiet pleasures of an area rich in history and character suffice. The Frost Place, the Sugar Hill Historical Museum and the Sugar Hill Sampler are classics of their genre.

Don't expect trendy inns, fancy restaurants or tony shops. Immerse yourself instead in the beauty and the tranquility of New England as it used to be.

Little wonder that long after he left, poet Frost wrote, "I am sitting here thinking of the view from our house in Franconia." It's unforgettable.

Inn Spots

Rabbit Hill Inn, Off Route 18, Lower Waterford, Vt. 05848

If you have an iota of romance in your soul, you'll love this white-columned "inn for romantics" in a tiny hillside hamlet just across the Connecticut River from New Hampshire. Where else would you find, upon retiring to your room after a candlelight dinner, the bed turned down, the radio playing soft music, the lights turned off, a candle flickering in a hurricane chimney, and a small stuffed and decorated heart on the bed to use as a "do not disturb" sign and yours to take home?

That's just a sample of the care and concern that innkeepers Leslie and Brian Mulcahy show for their guests. They served three years as assistants to innkeeper icons Maureen and John Magee before buying the highly revered establishment in 1997 when the Magees opted for a change of scenery. Taking their cues from their predecessors, who had a bent for the theatrical, the Mulcahys "set the stage, and our guests are the players."

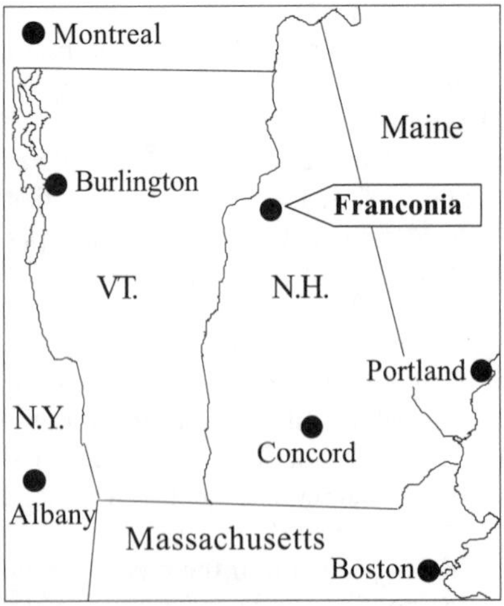

Upon arrival, Brian is apt to greet you with a "welcome to our home." In your room is a personal note of welcome from Leslie, who already has sent a postcard to say they are "looking forward to your upcoming visit." Depending on the season you'll find hot or iced tea, perhaps flavored with red clover, and delicious pastries in the afternoon in the cozy parlor. Next to it is a pub, the Snooty Fox,

Aptly named Canopy Chamber awaits guests at Rabbit Hill Inn.

with comfortable sofas and upholstered chairs in one section and a newer section with game tables, an authentic 18th-century barn decor and handcrafted Vermont furniture. Across the road are a small gazebo near a pond for swimming and fishing, a bridge, a tree swing and nature trails.

The nineteen guest accommodations, all with private baths and most with air-conditioning, are in the 1825 main inn, a carriage wing and the 1795 tavern building next door. Part of the tavern's basement has been converted into a video den with a TV and VCR.

Rabbit Hill has been decorated with loving care. Each room has a theme and twelve have working fireplaces with andirons in the shape of rabbits. Even in the ballroom wing, where the rooms go off an interior corridor like that of many a motor hotel, they are done in a most unmotel-like way. Three rooms on the lower floor here were gutted and turned into two deluxe rooms with corner fireplaces and sitting areas, and one has a soaking tub for two. Our room, Clara's Chamber, contained many mementos of its namesake as well as the standard room diary in which guests record their feelings and rave about the innkeepers.

Among the more prized accommodations is the Tavern's Secret, transformed from two existing rooms and a bath at the rear of the building next door. The secret? Pull forward what appears to be a floor-to-ceiling bookcase opposite the fireplace and you find a gleaming bathroom with brass fixtures and a double jacuzzi. Romantics can enjoy the fireplace from either the kingsize canopy bed or the jacuzzi.

No sooner was this completed than Rabbit Hill set about creating the Nest, converting an office and private quarters upstairs into a fireplaced bedroom with custom-made queen canopy bed, a European dressing room with a whirlpool tub for two and a private sun deck. The subsequent Loft and the Turnabout quickly followed.

The Mulcahys quickly turned four more rooms into luxury quarters. Their grandest suite is the Jonathan Cummings, a fireplaced bedroom with queen canopy bed and a spacious dressing/sitting room with another fireplace facing a 44-jet hydro-massage tub for two. A private screened porch yields a scenic mountain view. The renovated Samuel Hodby suite (named after the original owner in the late 18th century) has a canopy king bed covered with lacy pillows, a sofa sitting area and a luxury bath with 48-jet hydro-massage tub for two, all focusing on the glow of the Georgian fireplace. The Victorian Molly's Promise offers a hand-carved, mansion-style king bed and a sofa sitting area with a corner fireplace, plus a large bath with whirlpool tub for two and a separate double shower. Similar accoutrements adorn the renovated Carriage Corner, done in American country style, where Leslie says guests "enjoy the ultimate bubble bath by the fire."

Recently, two small rooms on the first floor of the ballroom wing were converted into the newest luxury room, making a total of nine. With a rustic Vermont cabin theme, the Cedar Glen features a handmade cedar-log kingsize bed and a whirlpool tub for two, both facing a fireplaced sitting area. Later, three smaller rooms down the hallway were converted into two larger rooms with fireplaces.

Two front porches, one on the second floor awash with wicker, are where guests like to sit and watch the distant mountains. Downstairs in the parlor, the innkeepers keep adding to a collection of books written by guests. Everywhere are rabbit items, many of them gifts sent by people who have stayed here.

Breakfast is an event at Rabbit Hill. It is served by candlelight in the dining room after 8:15 but you can find coffee in the pub earlier. To the accompaniment of the soundtrack from "The Sound of Music," we helped ourselves to a buffet spread of orange juice, a chilled fruit soup, a cup of melon pieces and tiny blueberries, homemade granola and assorted pastries. Two changing main dishes are prepared to order: at our visit, a poached egg on a croissant with cheese sauce, home fries and bacon as well as pancakes with bananas and strawberries. The granola is so good that guests buy packages to take home.

The inn's restaurant (see Dining Spots) is the finest in the area.

(802) 748-5168 or (800) 762-8669. Fax (802) 748-8342. www.rabbithillinn.com. Ten rooms and nine luxury rooms and suites with private baths. Rates, MAP. Doubles, $275 to $315. Luxury rooms and suites, $385 to $400. Add $35 for foliage. Two-night minimum weekends. Children over 12.

Adair, 80 Guider Lane, Bethlehem 03574.

A "welcome slate," bearing the names and hometowns of arriving guests, is posted in the wide entry hall of this rural inn of uncommon charm. It's the first of many thoughtful touches guests will find at Adair. The hilltop mansion was built in 1927 as a wedding gift for Dorothy Adair Hogan from her father, nationally famous Washington trial lawyer Frank Hogan. The early guest list included presidents, governors, senators, judges, sports figures and actors. Helen Hayes visited each summer for many years.

Today's guests enjoy an AAA four-diamond inn run by Judy and Bill Whitman, she a former caterer and he a former ad executive in Chicago. The Whitmans offer eight large bedrooms (six with fireplaces), a fireplaced suite and a recently converted,

Hilltop mansion built in 1927 welcomes guests today as Adair.

private fireplaced cottage with two bedrooms and a full bath. They lease their dining operation to Tim and Biruta Carr, owners of our favorite Tim-Bir Alley, who moved their restaurant lock, stock and barrel from an alley in Littleton to the main floor of Adair (see Dining Spots).

Adair's country-estate-style rooms on the second and third floors are named after nearby mountains, which is fitting given their scenic surroundings. Rooms are tastefully decorated and comfortable, and all have king or queen beds. We enjoyed the front Lafayette Room, a commodious affair including a queensize bed, a sitting area with a gas fireplace and a bath with a two-person soaking tub. A stash of thick towels was wrapped and tied with green string. Also notable were an assortment of the inn's own toiletries and a gift basket bearing an Adair bookmark and a crock of the inn's maple syrup.

Assorted hats found in the attic now rest atop a shelf on the landing of the main staircase, which is lined with a library's worth of books. Guests also enjoy a grand, fireplaced living room with several sitting areas and a remarkable, all-granite (from walls to ceiling) basement taproom with TV/VCR, an imposing old Oliver Briggs Boston pool table and a small bar with setups. Out back are a large flagstone patio, terraced gardens and a rear lawn sloping down to a tennis court and a water garden beside a gazebo. There's not a sign of civilization in sight.

The Whitmans serve an elegant breakfast in the dining room, a potpourri of stunning black oriental fabric walls, pale yellow curtains, large Chinese figurines and mirrored sconces. It might start with a variety of juices, fresh berries, yogurt, granola and popovers and end up with spinach and artichoke frittata or lemon chiffon pancakes. Fruit-filled french toast with Vermont cob-smoked bacon was the delicious fare at our latest visit. Homemade cakes and cookies accompany afternoon tea.

Some 130 of Judy's favorite recipes from her years as caterer and innkeeper have been compiled in the inn's new cookbook, "Scratch Made Easy at Adair" ($17.95).

(603) 444-2600 or (888) 444-2600. Fax (603) 444-4823. www.adairinn.com. Eight rooms, one suite and one cottage with private baths. Doubles, $175 to $250. Suite, $295. Cottage, $355. Add $50 during foliage. Deduct $35 midweek, November-May. Two-night minimum weekends and foliage season.

Sunset Hill House, 231 Sunset Hill Road, Sugar Hill 03585.

The landmark annex building that was all that was left of a famous hotel straddling the 1,700-foot-high ridge of Sugar Hill has been nicely transformed into an urbane country inn. Lon and Nancy Henderson bought the inn in 2000 and continued to make improvements to take the inn "to the next level," in Lon's words. Both he and his wife took early retirement from the military to raise their young family in what they consider a postcard setting atop a mountain ridge.

The restored hotel holds 21 guest accommodations containing king or queen beds covered by quilts or duvets. All have new baths (some with fiberglass showers, others with refurbished clawfoot tubs) with the inn's own toiletries. They also have a simple but stylish, uncluttered look with Waverly prints, coordinated colors and handmade draperies. Nancy is partial to yellows, florals, birds and bugs for decor, as evidenced from a guided tour of an assortment of rooms. Nearly half the rooms have a fireplace, whirlpool tub or both. At one visit, we could see the sun both rise and set from our second-floor north corner bedroom with windows on three sides. More recently, we luxuriated in one of two new master suites, each with a king bed, living room with TV, fireplace, two-person whirlpool tub and separate shower. Ours had an enormous four-poster bed with a hidden jewelry compartment, a wood stove, a wet bar/kitchenette and a private balcony overlooking the mountains.

The adjacent Hill House is more like a B&B. Six oversize rooms are decorated in spiffy country inn style, some with separate sitting area, two with porches and all with mountain views. The best room here comes with a kingsize bed, fireplace and a two-person whirlpool tub.

The public spaces are beauties. Along the front of the main inn is a succession of three open, airy living rooms with fireplaces and splashy floral arrangements. One holds the inn's TV. Strung along the rear are four elegant dining rooms with windows onto the mountain panorama and one of the best fall foliage views in New England. On the other side of the reception desk is a tavern, which is fun for drinks or light fare.

Rates include a full breakfast with juice, fresh fruit with yogurt and homemade granola, wonderful coffeecake and chocolate-chip scones and a choice of entrées, from a Cuban omelet to steak and eggs.

Evidence of the innkeepers' brand of hospitality is the most enlightening orientation book of any inn we know. Found in each guest room, the hefty volume offers page after page of suggestions from Nancy. Everything from driving tours to shopping tips reflects her self-styled status as "the world's happiest innkeeper."

Of course, you may not want to stray far from the inn. Outside in front is the ridge-top Sunset Hill Golf Course, a conservation-protected landmark that is New Hampshire's oldest nine-hole layout. It includes a pond (for ice skating in winter) and a network of cross-country ski trails, which the Henderson family enjoys as much as their guests.

Mountains provide scenic backdrop for Sunset Hill House and Hill House annex.

Behind the inn is a most attractive rock-rimmed swimming pool – an all-new heated pool within a pool because the old one was deemed beyond repair. Beyond is a wedding arbor framing Mount Lafayette and an awesome mountain vista.

(603) 823-5522 or (800) 786-4455. Fax (603) 823-5738. www.sunsethillhouse.com. Twenty-six rooms and two suites with private baths. Doubles $100 to $225, suites $275 and $325. Foliage: doubles $195 to $325, suites $375 to $495. Two-night minimum most weekends and throughout foliage season.

Lovett's Inn By Lafayette Brook, 1474 Profile Road (Route 18), Franconia 03580.

The guest book here is full of the usual accolades plus one: "There's no place like home except Lovetts." That sums up the allure of the rural inn and restaurant cast over the years since its founding in 1929 by Charlie Lovett Jr.,

Although the inn, a fixture for two generations, added a swimming pool a few years ago for its summer clientele, it seems at its best in the winter – and we'll always remember it that way. We were lucky enough to stumble onto one of its fireplaced cottages during a snowstorm more than 30 years ago and liked it so well we stayed for two nights.

Since acquiring the property in 1998, tireless innkeepers Jim and Janet Freitas have reconfigured the public rooms and upgraded the facilities and decor.

The main house, dating to 1794 and listed in the National Register of Historic Places, holds a candlelit dining room (see Dining Spots) and a pleasant lounge with a curved marble bar. Across the foyer are an old-fashioned Victorian parlor with beamed ceiling and a sunken TV room with a wood stove and an antique radio.

The Freitases have renovated the upstairs guest quarters. Two rooms that shared a bath were turned into the Nicholas Powers Suite with oriental carpets on the refinished hardwood floors, a queensize canopied poster bed, a sitting room and a bath with whirlpool tub. The Hitchcock Suite with queen bed and whirlpool tub also has a sitting room. The Sweet Serenade has a kingsize bed. Two smaller rooms have antique double beds.

Summer or winter, we'd choose one of the sixteen units in seven cottages scattered beside the pool and around the lawns. Each has a wood-burning fireplace and a small patio with chairs for gazing upon Cannon Mountain. Some have kingsize beds and three have whirlpool tubs. All come with sitting areas and small television sets. The elongated narrow bathrooms at the rear are ingenious as well as serviceable.

The three-bedroom Stonyhill Cottage has a central living room with a stone fireplace, a queensize bedroom with double jacuzzi tub, and two smaller bedrooms with double or twin beds.

A full breakfast could include a spinach and gorgonzola omelet or banana nut pancakes.

(603) 823-7761 or (800) 356-3802. www.lovettsinn.com. Three rooms, two suites and sixteen cottage units with private baths. Doubles, $125 to $235. Cottage, $435. Add $40 for foliage and holidays. Deduct $10 for winter. Closed in early November and April.

Sugar Hill Inn, Route 117, Franconia 03580.

Nestled into the side of Sugar Hill is this old white inn, built as a farmhouse in 1789, its wraparound porch sporting colorfully padded wicker furniture and flower boxes that enhance the mountain views.

New energy has been infused into the inn following its acquisition in 2002 by Judy and Orlo Coots, who took an innkeeping seminar eleven years earlier and finally found the Sugar Hill Inn as the perfect fit. He is a trained chef and she a massage therapist, and both went to work exercising their talents to take the inn "to the next level." Their young daughter Olivia adds her own brand of energy.

Straw hats decorate the doors of the main inn's lodgings. They exude country charm with four-poster and canopy beds, hand stenciling, delicate wall coverings, heirloom coverlets, and antiques. Among the pluses are sitting areas, brass bedside lamps and pillows that accent the muted decor. We found stenciling on the wood rim of the mirror in our bathroom. All rooms are different, with choice of twin, double, queen and king beds.

The newest are five luxury rooms and suites with whirlpool or two-person soaking tubs and gas fireplaces. Two have private decks. One has a fireplace made of antique bricks with century-old king's pine used above the mantel, which was salvaged from the original farmhouse. Robes, hair dryers, bottled water and coffeemakers are extra touches.

Six cottage rooms in back have been remodeled and winterized with new picture windows (for enjoying the mountain views), gas fireplaces and king or queen beds. Each has its own front porch with wicker chairs and flower boxes.

Two living rooms in the main inn are available for guests. One next to the dining room has a wood stove, TV and piano. The other contains a gas fireplace and the reception desk. A cozy pub contains a three-stool bar, fireplace and tables with games to play.

The Cootses recently produced a spa room where Judy offers facials and massage therapy.

Orlo, an eighteen-year chef who once worked with Russell Stannard of nearby Rabbit Hill Inn fame at a suburban Boston restaurant, does the inn's cooking. Dinner is offered by reservation in a country-pretty dining room. The mushroom-dill soup, a holdover on the menu, is renowned, as is the mustard-crusted rack of lamb. Other choices include cornbread-crusted cod, roast pork loin with spiked applesauce, and grilled brace of quail with peppery balsamic syrup. We remember fondly a dinner of sautéed veal with champagne sauce, followed by bread pudding with warm whisky sauce. Chocolate pâté is a new dessert favorite.

The breakfasts are treats as well. Ours started with orange juice laced with

Carriage on side lawn is trademark of Sugar Hill Inn.

strawberries, followed by blueberry muffins. Then came a choice of cinnamon french toast or swiss and cheddar cheese omelet, both excellent.

(603) 823-5621 or (800) 548-4748. Fax (603) 823-5639. www.sugarhillinn.com. Four rooms, five suites and six cottages with private baths. Rates, B&B: doubles $100 to $155, suites $175 to $225. Foliage, MAP: doubles $255 to $320, suites $345 to $380. Two-night minimum in foliage season and special weekends. Children welcome in cottage rooms.

Prix-fixe, $40. Dinner by reservation, Thursday-Sunday 6 to 8, nightly in foliage season.

Bungay Jar Bed & Breakfast, Easton Valley Road, Box 15, Franconia 03580.

The mountains of the Kinsman Range loom behind this exceptional B&B, hidden on eight acres without a neighbor in sight and named for the legendary wind that funnels from Mount Kinsman through the Easton Valley.

Longtime owner Kate Kerrigan and her lawyer-husband, Lee Strimbeck, built their place from a four-level, 18th-century barn that was dismantled and moved to the site in 1967. The hayloft became a two-story living room holding many sitting areas, a reading corner and a fireplace.

Each of the three upper floors contains two guest rooms – in general, the higher you go, the more remarkable the room and the more stunning the vista. The ultimate is the Stargazer Suite, where a telescope is aimed on the Kinsman Range or the tramway atop Cannon Mountain. It has a kingsize bed beneath four skylights, an antique gas fireplace, a clawfoot tub under antique leaded-glass windows, a toilet behind a cloister table, and a twig loveseat and armchairs.

On the lower level are the Saffron Room and the Garden Suite. The latter has a kingsize bed, gas fireplace, freestanding double jacuzzi, TV/VCR and a small kitchen area. It opens through french doors onto a private patio overlooking the rear gardens.

Bungay Jar has had its ups and downs since its purchase by Alvin Moss from Arizona for his California daughter and son-in-law. They didn't take to innkeeping and left him holding the bag, so to speak. In 2003, he hired Heidi Schell, who had worked with the original owner, to run the inn until he could sell it. She assured that everything was the same as it was, minus Kate, even down to her favorite breakfasts of oatmeal pancakes and cheddar strata.

(603) 823-7775 or (800) 421-0701. www.bungayjar.com. Two rooms and four suites with private baths. Doubles, $110 to $145, suites $130 to $195. Foliage: doubles $125 to $175, suites $155 to $230.

Foxglove, Route 117, Sugar Hill 03585.

A watercolor of foxgloves on the enclosed front porch welcomes guests to this inviting B&B, named for the former owner's favorite flower. Kathy and John "J.R." Riley, who were reunited at a high school reunion in Massachusetts, embarked on their marriage by deciding to buy the inn at the corner of Lovers Lane and spending more time together. "We liked the name Lovers Lane and want to share the romance of it all," said Kathy. "And we certainly do spend time together," added J.R.

An artist who teaches decorative arts classes, Kathy had a good eye for decorating the rambling, three-section country house dating to the turn of the last century. The original pantry is now a foyer and shop. The dining room opens onto a rear glassed-in porch and three acres of park-like gardens and woods, dotted with hideaway terraces, trickling fountains and quiet glades. The dainty living room, decorated to the max, is housed in a front turret.

Each of the six guest quarters has a king or queensize beds and each has its own personality. The elegant Cosmopolitan on the main floor has a queen poster bed amid dark blue striped walls and ceiling, with an oriental rug on the floor. Kathy painted a mural of lilacs in the bath of the upstairs Ashley Room, which has a clawfoot tub and English country decor. About half the second floor is given over to the new Agnes Muriel Suite with kingsize bed and a sitting room with TV/VCR. Kathy faux painted the walls and added gas fireplaces in two guest rooms in the rear carriage house. The kingsize Garden Room here opens onto a deck.

Breakfast in the dining room or porch turns out to be quite a feast. You might start with baked apple and homemade cheddar cheese muffins, followed by an egg casserole with roasted red peppers and home fries. Kathy's sausage meatloaf might be another morning's highlight.

The Rileys welcome guests with afternoon wine and cheese or a pot of tea.

(603) 823-8840 or (888) 343-2220. Fax (603) 823-5755. www.foxgloveinn.com. Six rooms with private baths. Doubles, $110 to $145, foliage $140 to $175.

The Franconia Inn, Easton Road, Franconia 03580.

Situated by a meadow with Cannon Mountain as a backdrop, this rambling white structure looks the way you think a country inn should look and is the area's largest and busiest. "We have a reputation for lots of activities," says Alec Morris, innkeeper with his brother Richard for their parents, who run a resort in the Ozarks.

Thirty-two rooms and suites on two floors have been gradually upgraded since the Morrises took over the vacant inn in 1980. Most of the changes were cosmetic, but every guest room now claims a private bath and carpeting.

Rooms vary in size and beds; some connect to become family suites. The Morrises have added matching window cornices and bedspreads and larger beds. We like pine-paneled Room 27 with a pencil-post, canopied queensize bed, a duck bedspread, matching curtains and a lamp base in the shape of a duck. A suite includes a bedroom with queen bed, a living room with fireplace and sofabed, a kitchenette, whirlpool tub and a balcony. The corner rooms are best in terms of size and view.

The newly renovated Kinsman Cottage next to the inn offers a loft apartment with queen bedroom and kitchen as well as a ground-floor suite with kingsize bed and jetted tub.

The inn's main floor has a living room and oak-paneled library with fireplaces, a pool room, a game room with pinball machines, and a screened porch with wicker furniture overlooking a large swimming pool. Downstairs is the spacious **Rathskeller Lounge** with entertainment at night and, beyond, a hot tub in a large room paneled in redwood.

The attractive dining room, open to the public, features a short contemporary menu. Typical entrées are Maine crab cakes with chipotle mayonnaise, seared duck breast with pear and ginger marmalade, and mozzarella-crusted lamb loin with a raspberry-horseradish sauce.

Outside there is swimming in a pool or in a secluded swimming hole in the Ham Branch River. Four clay tennis courts and a glider/biplane facility are across the street ("soaring lets you see the mountains from the ultimate vantage point – the sky," says Alec). The stables next door house horses for trail rides. In the winter, the barn turns into a cross-country ski center; sleigh rides and snowshoeing are other activities. Movies are shown at night.

(603) 823-5542 or (800) 473-5299. www.franconiainn.com. Twenty-nine rooms and three suites with private baths. Rates, B&B. Doubles $125 to $155. Suites, $180 to $205. Add $30 for foliage and Christmas. Closed April to mid-May.

Entrées, $16.95 to $25.95. Dinner, 6 to 8:30 or 9. Closed Monday-Thursday in off-season.

The Hilltop Inn, 1348 Main St. (Route 117), Sugar Hill 03585.

Prolific hanging baskets of fuchsias on the front porch greet summertime visitors to the Hilltop Inn, whose flower beds have been featured in a floral magazine. Baskets of dried flowers or wreaths on the doors welcome them to their rooms.

Mike and Meri Hern have upgraded their 1895 Victorian home, adding private baths for every room and considerable stenciling and hand-painted furniture. The homey guest rooms lack pretension. Handmade quilts, European cotton or English flannel sheets, a decorating motif of bunnies, and bedside mints are among special touches. One two-room suite includes a kingsize bed and a day bed, while two other rooms have a king bed and a twin bed. The fancy hand stenciling on the walls of the inn's Victorian living room matches the inn's china pattern of pink morning glories. Also striking is the Tiffany-era lamp against a backdrop of draped lace curtains.

A full country breakfast buffet is set out mornings from 8:30 to 9:30 in the large dining area, and may be taken in season to the side deck. Guests help themselves to baked goods, cob-smoked meats and perhaps cheese soufflé, quiche or golden raspberry and blueberry pancakes, made with berries picked by the innkeepers.

(603) 823-5695 or (800) 770-5695. Fax (603) 823-5518. Five rooms and one suite with private baths. Doubles, $90 to $120. Foliage: $125 to $195. Two-night minimum summer and holiday weekends and foliage season. Pets welcome.

Angel of the Mountains, 2007 Main St., Box 487, Bethlehem 03574.

Pink with white trim, this handsome gabled Victorian has a wraparound porch and common rooms full of rich wood paneling. Sally and Ben Gumm – he a former newspaper publisher of our acquaintance from Connecticut – took over the former Gables B&B in 1999 and gave it a new name.

Gables and wraparound porch enhance facade of Angel of the Mountains.

Hand-carved fireplaces and lavish woodwork in two sitting rooms and the dining room lend an elegant ambiance. Up a majestic center staircase are three bedrooms with queensize beds, private baths and panoramic views of Mount Washington and the Presidential Range. A side carriage house with queen bedroom, kitchen, living room, TV/VCR and full-length deck overlooks the pool installed by the original owner and the adjacent tennis courts on the site of what had been a hotel.

Wine and cheese are offered in the late afternoon. Breakfast the next morning includes an artfully presented fruit course, homemade muffins and an entrée like eggs florentine, frittata or french toast.

The Gumms lead "mystery lantern walks" around of historic Bethlehem on summer weekends. The 75-minute walking tour, lit by kerosene lanterns, illustrates the people and events that once made Bethlehem a premier tourist destination.

(603) 869-6473 or (888) 704-4004. www.angelofthemountains.com. Three rooms and a carriage house with private baths. Doubles, $98 to $110; foliage and holidays, $129 to $140. Carriage house, $159 for two, $199 for four; foliage and holidays, $199 for two, $239 for four.

The Beal House Inn, 2 West Main St., Littleton 03561.

Built in 1833, the Beal House Inn has been serving travelers since Mrs. Beal opened the doors of her Colonial home smack up against the main street to overnight lodgers in 1938. The inn has undergone countless changes and upgrades under a succession of owners (four in the last decade alone), so it reveals the patina as well as the quirks of age and different personalities.

It has been improved lately by Jose Luis and Catherine Pawelek, he an Argentine chef of some renown and she raised in the Netherlands. Both worked in the hospitality and travel fields for twenty years before opening the first of three restaurants in Florida in 1993 and then looking for a small New Hampshire inn in 2000.

They upgraded three rooms and five suites, the latter enhanced with queensize poster beds topped with down comforters, sitting rooms with porcelain gas stoves, satellite TVs and mini-refrigerators. One is the main-floor Mrs. Beal's Boudoir, "named for the woman who started it all and quite a character," according to Catherine. This has been upstaged by the Notchway, the former owners' quarters on the third floor of the original farmhouse section. The pine-paneled space is now a two-bedroom suite likened to having "your own private camp." It includes a sitting room with a wall of windows onto the back yard, bedrooms with queensize and double beds, a private deck, a refrigerator and coffeemaker, and a bath with clawfoot tub. Another favorite is the Garden Suite with a front living room and a rear bedroom with queen poster bed and a double jacuzzi tub – the last also a feature in the Flume Suite.

The rooms vary from the Rose Chamber, a large first-floor space with a queen sleigh bed with a lush fabric spread and matching swag draperies, a glowing antique rose chandelier and a bath with soaking tub, to the cozy Blue Room with a full-size pencil-post bed in an intimate nook at the top of the stairs.

Guests enjoy a couple of common rooms and a three-course gourmet breakfast.

(603) 444-2661 or (888) 616-2325. www.bealhouseinn.com. (603) 444-2661 or (888) 616-2325. Three rooms and five suites with private baths. May to mid-September: doubles $125 to $140, suites $165 to $205. Foliage, doubles $135 to $155, suites $175 to $245. Rest of year: doubles $115 to $125, suites $155 to $195. Closed first three weeks of November.

Dining Spots

Rabbit Hill Inn, Lower Waterford, Vt.

The doors to the Rabbit Hill dining room are kept closed until the dinner hour, so that first-time inn guests will appreciate the drama of a candlelit room, silver gleaming atop burgundy mats on polished wood tables and napkins folded into pewter rings shaped like rabbits. Even the electrified lanterns and chandeliers look like candles. Fresh flowers and porcelain bunnies on each table add to the charm, and a spinning wheel stands in the middle of the room. A second dining room has been added behind the original to accommodate a growing clientele attracted by the food and the magical atmosphere.

Chef Russell Stannard implements a changing, interesting prix-fixe menu in a style he calls "creative seasonal contemporary." It offers a choice of appetizer or soup, salad, entrée, dessert and beverage.

We feasted on cream of celery soup with pimento and chives and a great dish of scallops and three-pepper seviche with mint, papaya and toasted pine nuts, delicate salads with a creamy dressing, and a small loaf of piping-hot whole wheat bread served with the butter pat shaped like a bunny, with a sprig of parsley for its curly tail. Citrus sorbet drenched in champagne cleared the palate quite nicely. Main courses were a spicy red snapper dish and sautéed chicken with bananas, almonds and plums, served with an asparagus-leek tart and garnished with baby greens. Sautéed potatoes shaped like mushrooms were a novel touch. With desserts of homemade peanut-brittle ice cream in an edible cookie cup and double chocolate-almond pâté with crème anglaise came brewed decaf coffee with chocolate shells filled with whipped cream to dunk in – a great idea.

Other choices might be steamed lobster tail and grilled shrimp presented with mango, ginger butter and pumpkin ravioli and garnished with marinated sesame seaweed and pineapple relish; grilled cocoa-cinnamon spiced duck breast with a strawberry-balsamic vinaigrette, and grilled cumin-dusted beef tenderloin with a tomatillo-garlic ragoût.

A harpist or a pianist often plays during dinner on weekends. This is a serene dining room, in which no detail has been overlooked and solicitous service is well paced. Plan on at least two hours for a fulfilling meal and evening.

(802) 748-5168 or (800) 762-8669. Prix-fixe, $45. Dinner nightly by reservation, 6 to 9. Closed first two weeks of November.

Tim-Bir Alley, Old Littleton Road, Bethlehem.

For its first ten years, this little establishment named for its owners, Tim and Biruta Carr, was a culinary landmark in the basement of a building down an alley in downtown Littleton. It moved in 1994 from the alley to a 200-acre rural estate and two small and elegant dining rooms on the main floor of an inn called Adair, where the Carrs serve some of the area's most sophisticated and inventive food.

After optional cocktails with snacks served in the inn's basement Granite Tavern or outside on the flagstone terrace, patrons adjourn to the dining room for a meal to remember. The menu, which changes weekly, offers six entrée choices from garlic-basil tuna with roasted Mediterranean relish to ginger and soy-scented grilled quail with molasses barbecue sauce.

Our latest dinner here began with fabulous chicken-almond wontons with coconut-curry sauce and delicate salmon pancakes on a roasted red pepper coulis. For main courses, we enjoyed the breast of chicken with maple-balsamic glaze and plum-ginger puree and the pork tenderloin sauced with red wine, grilled leeks and smoked bacon.

Follow this assertive fare with, perhaps, peach ricotta strudel with caramel sauce, mango cheesecake with banana-coconut compote and honey-caramel sauce, and carrot-hazelnut cake with warm brandy sauce. The well-chosen wine list is affordably priced.

(603) 444-6142. Entrées, $18.95 to $24.95. Dinner by reservation, Wednesday-Sunday 5:30 to 9. Closed in November and April.

Beal House Inn Restaurant, 2 West Main St., Littleton.

The former carriage house at the side of the Beal House Inn has been converted into a winning café lovingly run by Jose Luis Pawelek, an Argentine chef of some renown, and his wife Catherine, who was raised in the Netherlands.

Oriental rugs dot the polished wood floors of the intimate dining room seating a total of 40. Musical instruments pose with artworks on the siena-colored walls above the original tin wainscoting in an elegant, white-tablecloth setting. A jazzy upstairs lounge decked out in white lights has a glistening wood floor and a copper-topped martini bar ranked as New Hampshire's best (252 martinis listed at last count).

Jose does the cooking, offering a fairly extensive menu of superior contemporary international fare, every item so tempting it makes choosing difficult.

Appetizers range from a medley of wild mushrooms in puff pastry to wood-grilled scallops and shrimp served on a buttermilk corn cake in a pool of smoky hot chipotle butter. Main courses include potato-crusted haddock with a roasted red-pepper sauce, duckling sauced with crème de cassis, and black angus tenderloin with a trio of sauces. The house specialty is cioppino in a spicy marinara sauce over linguini. Interesting sauces are the chef's forte: the snapper tropical is sautéed with mango,

Musical instruments enhance decor at Beal House Inn Restaurant.

banana, grapes and dark rum, and the salmon with strawberries, balsamic vinegar and a cabernet reduction.

The treats continue for dessert, perhaps the dream terrine (frozen white-chocolate mousse with chambord-infused raspberry mousse served with warm bittersweet chocolate sauce) and Catherine's tarte tatin, enhanced with peach or mango and served with French vanilla ice cream and a warm ginger-caramel sauce.

(603) 444-2661 or (888) 616-2325. www.bealhouseinn.com. Entrées, $16 to $25. Dinner, Wednesday-Saturday 5:30 to 9, Sunday 5:30 to 8.

Sunset Hill House, Sunset Hill Road, Sugar Hill.

Four elegant dining rooms seating a total of 100 are strung along the rear of this refurbished inn, their tall windows opening onto the Franconia, Kinsman and Presidential ranges. The rooms are handsome with yellow Schumacher bird-print wallpapers, oriental print carpets and well spaced tables set with white linens and china, candles in hurricane chimneys and vases of alstroemeria.

Veteran chef Joe Peterson's contemporary fare and the staff's flawless service are the match for a mountain view unsurpassed in the area. We were impressed by starters of grilled boar sausage, served sliced with a soothing maple crème fraîche, and the seared ahi tuna steak with spicy mango-habañero and sweet ruby grapefruit sauces. The unusual house salad was tossed with a tequila-jalapeño dressing.

Main courses included a superb filet mignon with a lemon-spinach peanut sauce, served with shiitake mushrooms and roasted new potatoes, and juniper-accented medallions of venison in a pinot noir reduction. Innkeeper Nancy Henderson's favorite baked chicken stuffed with goat cheese and a mixed grill of duck sausage, pork and lamb loin proved good choices at another visit. Broiled rainbow trout with horseradish-apple cream, cider-brined Iowa pork and duckling Bombay are other signatures.

White chocolate cheesecake, iced lemon soufflé cake and bananas foster were among sweet endings. The wine list is ranked among the best in the state.

(603) 823-5522 or (800) 786-4455. Entrées, $22 to $27. Dinner nightly except Monday, 5:30 to 9, Memorial Day to foliage; nightly in foliage and holiday weeks. Rest of year: Thursday-Sunday 5:30 to 9.

Lovett's Inn By Lafayette Brook, Profile Road, Franconia.

A little concrete fisherman sits with his pole at the end of the diving board over a pond formed by Lafayette Brook across the road. Illuminated at night, he attracts the curious to this inn's well-known restaurant, a fixture in the area since the days of Charlie Lovett.

Before dinner, people usually gather around the curved marble bar (obtained from a Newport mansion) in the renovated lounge for socializing. Dinner is served in a country elegant, beamed dining room, with oriental carpets on the refinished hardwood floors.

Chef-owner Janet Freitas, who formerly owned restaurants in northern Massachusetts, does the cooking – quite a feat inasmuch as she also handles innkeeping duties with her husband Jim as well. At our latest October visit, she was so whipsawed between giving us a tour, showing guests their rooms and taking phone calls that it was a wonder she could still prepare dinner that evening for a nearly full house.

But dinner she does, with considerable aplomb. She has it down to a routine, changing only the presentations and sauces occasionally on a menu that lists nine entrées. Typical are pan-seared Chilean sea bass with a red pepper coulis, chicken florentine, roast duck with a raspberry-vinaigrette sauce, veal genovese and herb-crusted rack of lamb with a red wine-dijon sauce.

Shrimp cocktail, goat cheese strudel and crab cakes with tomato salsa make good starters. Desserts are extravagant, from hot Indian pudding with ice cream to flourless chocolate torte and crème brûlée.

(603) 823-7761 or (800) 356-3802. Entrées, $18 to $22. Dinner, Wednesday-Sunday 6 to 8 or 8:30.

The Grand Depot Café, 25 Cottage St, Littleton.

For a leisurely dinner of refined contemporary continental cuisine, this handsome restaurant in the town's former railroad depot fills the bill. The high-ceilinged dining room in the old waiting room looks like a French salon, dressed with white-clothed tables, shaded oil lamps and fine paintings and framed French posters. Several more tables are available in the small lounge, which has an ornate gold mirror and quite a collection of hats around the bar.

Well-known local chef-owner Frederick Tilton, a Francophile through and through, has a loyal following. Main dishes range from potato-crusted Atlantic salmon with a lemon-mustard sauce and grilled yellowfin tuna with a sundried tomato and kalamata olive sauce to chicken cubano and grilled venison steak with a red currant sauce. Three of the dozen or so entrée choices are vegetarian. The big-spender's favorite is the filet mignon served on a potato pancake garnished with roasted mushroom caps and finished with a parslied garlic butter.

Appetizers could be the house chicken liver pâté, escargots bourguignonne or carpaccio of barbary duck marinated in armagnac and fennel. Desserts include key lime cheesecake, apple crisp and quite a choice of unusual sorbets and gelatos.

Chef Rick is especially proud of the extensive wine list and the roster of single-malt scotches. He's also known for an eclectic bar menu of global fare.

(603) 444-5303. Entrées, $14.95 to $32, bar menu $6.95 to $14.95. Dinner, Monday-Saturday 5 to 9.

Cold Mountain Café & Gallery, 2015 Main St., Bethlehem.

Some of the area's most interesting fare emanates from the kitchen of this quirky, 34-seat storefront. It's also served up at prices from yesteryear by chef-owners David Brown and Jack Foley. Imagine, rack of lamb for dinner for $15.95.

The entrée price includes a house salad as well as starch and vegetable. Expect the likes of baked salmon with tamari-ginger glaze, chicken breast with a Thai curry sauce and pork medallions with mango chutney.

Interesting salads, quesadillas, quiches and sandwiches are featured on the lunch menu. Cappuccino, beer and wines are the beverages of choice.

Dining takes place in a spare room with pale yellow walls hung with changing local art, halogen lights and votive candles on bare wood tables.

(603) 869-2500. Entrées, $10.95 to $15.95. Lunch, Monday-Saturday 11 to 3:30. Dinner, Monday-Saturday 5:30 to 9 or 9:30. No credit cards.

Dutch Treat Restaurant, Main Street, Franconia.

This sprawl of a place looks like a roadhouse, and sported a couple of makeshift signs –"downtown bar and grille" and "R.I.P., Old Man" – at our 2003 visit shortly after the collapse of the legendary Old Man of the Mountain.

So we were quite unprepared for the caliber of the food or the creativity of the kitchen, as orchestrated by the Opalinsky family since 1973. A quick lunch produced a turkey navy bean soup, a fine spinach and artichoke salad, and a croque monsieur. These were impressive enough to suggest a return for dinner, perhaps for seafood en papillote, Japanese-crusted porterhouse pork chops or top round of lamb with port wine and peppercorn gravy. Appetizers such as mussels marnière, fried calamari tossed with pineapple curry, crab-stuffed portobello mushroom and sesame pork dumplings with ponzu dipping sauce also tempted.

The family-style dining room and the large bar and lounge aren't anything to write home about, but the food is.

(603) 823-8851. Entrées, $7.95 to $15.95. Breakfast, lunch and dinner daily, 7 a.m. to 8 or 9 p.m.

Polly's Pancake Parlor, Hildex Maple Sugar Farm, Route 117, Sugar Hill.

Polly and Wilfred "Sugar Hill" Dexter opened their pancake parlor in 1938, when they charged 50 cents for all you could eat, mainly to have a way to use up their maple syrup. Their daughter, Nancy Dexter Aldrich, her husband Roger and their daughter Kathie and son-in-law, Dennis Cote, operate the farm and restaurant now. They charge considerably more than 50 cents, but it's still a bargain and a fun place to go for breakfast or lunch and a slice of local life.

Bare tables sport red mats shaped like maple leaves, topped with wooden plates hand-painted with maple leaves by Nancy Aldrich, who, in her red skirt and red bow, greets and seats diners, many of whom seem to be on a first-name basis. Red kitchen chairs and sheet music pasted to the ceiling add color to this 1830 building, once a carriage shed. Big louvered windows afford a stunning view of the Mount Lafayette range beyond.

You can watch the pancakes being made in the open kitchen. The batter is poured from a contraption that ensures they measure exactly three inches.

Pancakes are served with unlimited maple syrup, granulated maple sugar and maple spread; an order of six costs $5.40 for pancakes made with white flour, buckwheat, whole wheat or cornmeal. All are available with blueberries, walnuts or coconut for $6.70. The Aldriches grind their own organically grown grains and make their own breads, sausage and baked beans (with maple syrup, of course). Waffles, seven inches wide, are available in all the pancake versions.

If, like us, you don't really crave pancakes in the middle of the day, try the homemade soups (lentil is especially good), quiche of the day (our ham and cheddar melted in the mouth) or a super-good BLT made with cob-smoked bacon.

The homemade pies are outstanding. Hurricane sauce, made from apples, butter and maple syrup, is served over ice cream. The back of the menu lists, for extra-hearty eaters, all-you-can-eat prices.

The coffee, made with spring water, is great and a glass of the spring water really hits the spot (no liquor is served). The shop at the entry sells pancake packs, maple syrup and sugar, jams and jellies and even the maple-leaf painted plates.

(603) 823-5575. Open daily, 7 to 3, mid-May to mid-October. Open weekends, early spring and late fall. Closed December-March.

Diversions

Franconia Notch State Park, south of Franconia. The wonders of one of the nation's most spectacular parks are well known. Thousands visit the Flume, a 700-foot-long gorge with cascades and pools (adults, $8), and the Basin and gaze at the rock outcroppings, most notably what's left of the fallen Old Man of the Mountain, the Granite State's longtime icon, which collapsed in 2003. Echo Lake at the foot of Cannon Mountain is fine for swimming. Cannon Mountain has retired its original 1938 aerial tramway but a modern replacement carries tourists to the summit for the views that skiers cherish – and gets them back down without the challenges that hardy skiers take for granted. Summit barbecues are offered on summer Saturdays from 4:30 to 7 for $7 (plus $10 for the tram ride). In the large visitor center at the southern entrance to the park, a good fifteen-minute movie chronicles years of change in the area and advises, "when you see Franconia Notch today, remember it will never be quite the same again."

Cannon Mountain. In an era of plasticized, free-wheeling skiing and snowboarding, the serious ski areas with character are few and far between. One of the last and best is Cannon, which considers itself the first major ski mountain in the Northeast (1937). Operated as a state park, it remains virginal and free of commercialism. The setting is reminiscent of the Alps, when you view the sheer cliffs and avalanche country across Franconia Notch on Lafayette Mountain and the majestic peaks of the Presidential Range beyond. From the summit, much of the skiing varies from tough to frightening, as befits the site of America's first racing trail and the first World Cup competition. But there is plenty of intermediate and novice skiing as well.

New England Ski Museum, next to the tram station at Cannon Mountain, Franconia.

Skiers in particular enjoy this small museum that houses the most extensive collection of historic ski equipment, clothing, photography and literature in the

Northeast. The maroon parka belonging to the founder of the National Ski Patrol is shown, as is a photo of him taken at Peckett's-on-Sugar-Hill. One of the more fascinating exhibits traces the evolution of ski equipment. "Ski Tracks" is an informative and impressive thirteen-minute audio-visual show with 450 slides tracing the history of New England skiing.

(603) 823-7177 or (800) 639-4181. www.nesm.org. Open daily noon to 5, Memorial Day-Columbus Day and December-March. Free.

Sugar Hill Historical Museum, Main Street, Sugar Hill.

Sugar Hill people say not to miss this choice small place, and they're right. Established as a Bicentennial project by proud descendants of Sugar Hill founders, it displays an excellent collection in a modern, uncluttered setting and gives a feel for the uncommon history of this small hilltop town, named for the sugar maples that still produce maple syrup ("everyone who can, taps the trees," reports the museum director). The life of the community is thoroughly chronicled in photographs and artifacts. The Cobleigh Room recreates a stagecoach tavern kitchen from nearby Lisbon, and the Carriage Barn contains mountain wagons and horse-drawn sleighs, including one from the Butternut estate that used to belong to Bette Davis.

(603) 823-8142. Open July to mid-October, Thursday-Saturday 1 to 4. Free.

Sugar Hill Sampler, 71 Sunset Hill Road, Sugar Hill.

A horse was grazing out front on a recent visit to this store and museum behind the Homestead Inn, where commercialism gives way to personality and history. The large dairy barn, with nooks and crannies full of New England items for souvenir shoppers, is literally a working museum of Sugar Hill history. Owner Barbara Serafini is the sixth-generation descendant of one of Sugar Hill's founders and takes great pride in sharing her thoughts and possessions, even posting handwritten descriptions on the beams. In one rear section full of family memorabilia, she displays her grandmother's wedding gown, which she wore in a pageant written by her father and presented for President Eisenhower on the occasion of the Old Man of the Mountain's birthday in 1955. Amid all the memorabilia is an interesting selection of quaint and unusual merchandise, including maple syrup made by the Stewart family on Sugar Hill, and a special spiced tea mixture called Heavenly Tea. Regional foods are featured, and you can taste samples of several. Toys, collectibles, quilts and Christmas decorations are displayed in nooks off the main barn.

(603) 823-8478. www.sugarhillsampler.com. Open daily, 9:30 to 5, mid-May through October, 10 to 4 in November and December, weekends mid-April to mid-May.

Sunset Hill Golf Course, Sunset Hill Road, Sugar Hill.

Atop a ridge that lives up to its name, this 1,977-yard golf course put into play in 1897 is the oldest nine-hole layout in New Hampshire. The clubhouse is also the oldest extant clubhouse for any course in the state (built in 1899 for the 1900 season) and remains practically unchanged today. The owners of the Sunset Hill House across the street saved the property from condo development and had both the course and the clubhouse accepted for the state historic registry in 2002. By today's standards the course is short (six par 4s and three par 3s), but in the days of hickory clubs and leather balls, "it was a much different beast," according to innkeeper Lon Henderson. "Today our motto is family fun. It's just hard enough to give an expert golfer a challenge and forgiving enough to give a beginner a boost of confidence." The price is right – it's the least expensive golf course in the area – and the views are stupendous. Says Lon: "It's not unusual for the inn to empty out at sundown to applaud one of our absolutely spectacular sunsets."The price is right – it's the least expensive golf course in the area – and the views are stupendous.

Shopping. In Sugar Hill, **Harman's Cheese and Country Store,** a tiny place with a large mail-order business, proclaims "the world's greatest cheddar cheese." Many of its food and local items are one of a kind, according to owner Maxine Aldrich, who with daughter Brenda is carrying on the late Harman family tradition. **Sugar Hill Antiques** and **P.C. Anderson Handmade Furniture** appeal to special interests.

In Franconia, the **Garnet Hill** factory store stocks firsts and seconds of fine bedclothes (English flannel sheets, comforters and the like), as well as pricey children's clothing, all in natural fibers. Stop at the **Quality Bakery** (home of Grateful Bread) for a loaf of soy-sesame bread. Two dozen varieties of breads and rolls are made; "we mill our own flour and our sourdough starter came from Germany 50 years ago," said the owner. We liked the local handcrafts displayed by volunteers at **Noah's Ark,** a shop run by the Church of Christ.

A special place near Bethlehem is the **Bethlehem Flower Farm,** 4123 Main St. (on Route 302 east toward Twin Mountain), which specializes in daylilies. Owners Joan and Bob Schafer grow more than 100 varieties, with names like Precious One, Christmas Carol and Gentle Shepherd, which Joan will dig for purchasers straight out of the fields. Also on the premises are a woodland walk that takes about twenty minutes, The Gift Barn and Abigail's Country Collectibles, and Lily's Café where you may get a light lunch. Bob says "we have the world's best chili," served with a corn muffin. Open Memorial Day to Columbus Day, Thursday-Sunday 10 to 5.

Another seasonal outing that draws customers from near and far involves the **Christmas Tree Farm** at the 2,000-acre **Rocks Estate** at 4 Christmas Lane, Bethlehem. Named for the glacial boulders that were removed from the fields to make sweeping stone walls, The Rocks is a National Register working farm and forest with 55,000 Christmas trees in the ground. Six miles of trails are open to the public year-round for hiking and cross-country skiing.

Extra-Special

The Frost Place, Ridge Road off Route 116, Franconia.

The farmhouse in which the poet lived from 1915 to 1920 and in which he summered through 1938 is a low-key attraction not to be missed. It was here he wrote most of his best-known works, a spokesman said of the property opened by the town of Franconia as a Bicentennial project in 1976. The house remains essentially unchanged from the 1920s. Each summer a different visiting poet occupies most of it, but the front room and a rear barn are open with displays of Frost memorabilia, including his handwritten "Stopping by Woods on a Snowy Evening" and a rare, large photo of Frost at age 40 working at his desk in the room. Out back, a half-mile nature trail has plaques with Frost's poems appropriate to the site; in two cases, the poems are on the locations where he wrote them. As if the poetry and setting weren't enough, the stand of woods happens to contain every variety of wildflower indigenous to Northern New England.

(603) 823-5510. www.frostplace.com. Open daily except Tuesday 1 to 5, July to Columbus Day; also weekends, Memorial Day through June. Adults, $3.

Squam Lake is visible through porte cochere at The Manor on Golden Pond.

Squam Lakes, N.H.

Midas Touches Golden Pond

The movie "On Golden Pond" cast the largest private lake in the country quietly into the public eye.

"Before the movie, not that many people knew the lake was here," said Pierre Havre, who with his wife Jan restored a rundown resort into The Manor on Golden Pond, shortly after the movie debuted. Now retired, they started something of a boom in year-round innkeeping in an area that long has been a low-key haven for homeowner-members of the influential Squam Lakes Association, whose membership reads like a Yankee who's who.

Now, the Holderness area between Squam and Little Squam lakes has two inns and the surrounding area has at least half a dozen bed-and-breakfast establishments. Meredith, just east of the Squam Lakes at the closest section of better-known Lake Winnipesaukee, is the site of larger inns of more recent vintage.

Passersby see the striking sign in front of the Inn on Golden Pond and "stop just to ask if this is the place where the movie was filmed," notes innkeeper Bill Webb. It isn't, but like most of the Squams' entrepreneurs, he takes full advantage of the association.

Visitors board pontoon craft for cruises along the 50-mile shoreline of Squam Lake to see the sights that Katharine Hepburn and Henry Fonda made famous (the Thayer house, Purgatory Cove) and sample the changing moods of a very special lake. Its water is so pure that the 1,000 or so homeowners drink straight from the lake and its setting is so quiet that it's a nesting place for loons, which are the lake's trademark.

Beyond the lake, quaint downtown Holderness is undergoing something of a rebirth. Nearby, the historic town of Center Sandwich – a picturesque crafts colony that is everybody's idea of what an old New England village should be – and the upscale pleasures of Meredith also beckon visitors.

Thanks to the continuing emergence of some good inns, they have a home base from which to enjoy the charms of Golden Pond.

Inn Spots

The Manor on Golden Pond, Shepard Hill Road, Box T, Holderness 03245.

This is the largest and most luxurious of Squam Lake inns. It is also the only one with lake frontage and access, a major plus.

Built in 1903 by an Englishman who had made a fortune as a Florida land developer, the mansion with its leaded windows, gigantic fireplaces and oak and mahogany paneling is a gem. High on Shepard Hill, commanding a panoramic view of mountains and glimpses of Squam Lake, the honey-colored stucco structure has a porte cochere for an entrance and thirteen acres for a yard. A large swimming pool off to one side, a clay tennis court in the pines and a broad lawn set up for croquet enhance the picture. Down at the beach and boathouse, a raft, canoes and paddleboats are available.

The location and the setting attracted Brian and Mary Ellen Shields to move their family from suburban Toronto to acquire the inn in 1999 and launch some upgrades. The elegant look begins in the expansive living room, where a custom-made area rug on the restored original floors, comfortable new furnishings and fine English antiques show the taste and flair of Mary Ellen, an interior decorator. Beyond is a cozy library opening through french doors onto a walled front patio with dark green molded chairs at marble tables – a delightful spot to which we repaired after helping ourselves to the sumptuous afternoon tea spread set out in the library. An atmospheric piano bar called the Three Cocks Pub, paneled in rich woods and ever so elegant with copper tables and a copper bar, is a convivial setting for cocktails or after-dinner drinks.

Ten of the seventeen guest rooms upstairs in the main house have wood-burning fireplaces and six have whirlpool baths. Handsome in coordinated Laura Ashley fabrics and fancy window treatments, they are outfitted with both antiques and remote-control TVs. Top of the line, literally, is the new cathedral-ceilinged Avon Room on the third floor. Not your typical attic makeover, this Wedgwood blue and white beauty has a kingsize sleigh bed beneath a skylight in the center, a plush sitting area beside a raised-hearth fireplace nestled amid bookshelves, a mirrored circular whirlpool tub in an alcove and a writing desk in the dormer window. We were happily ensconced in the second-floor Windsor room, with a fireplace and big front windows facing the lake. It was pretty in salmon and sage green, with the comforter on the queensize poster bed matching the balloon curtains and the

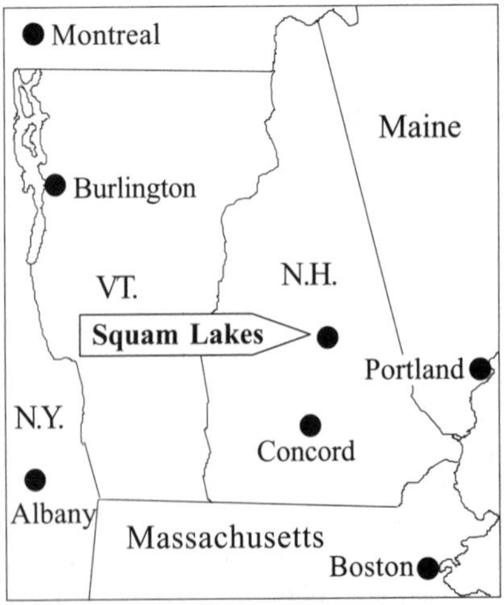

cover on the nightstand. A large antique armoire and a writing desk bearing an unusual desk lamp with a silver teapot as a base were other attributes. Another favorite is the ivory and black Buckingham, a huge corner room with a marble fireplace and kingsize tester bed upon which the ebony silk spread matches the window treatments. A small box of Godiva chocolates is presented on arrival, and gold-wrapped chocolate medallions are on your pillow in the evening.

Four colorful, kingsize bedrooms, one with a double jacuzzi, are available seasonally in the nearby Carriage House. Two formerly rustic cottages between the inn and the Carriage House have been greatly upgraded, each with two luxury rooms called Annex Chambers. Sumptuously furnished, they have canopied king beds, fireplaces and whirlpool tubs, and french doors open onto decks with lake views. The Cotswold Cottage has a living room, king bed and screened porch. Smack beside the lake is our favorite Dover Cottage, which has two bedrooms and a kitchen/living room with fireplace, available weekly for $2,500.

A full breakfast is served in the front dining room, the original billiards room. It proved an elegant spot for an ample breakfast of fresh fruits, lemon-poppyseed bread, unusually good coffee and a choice of main dishes, in our case shirred eggs and a quiche of tasso ham and shiitake mushrooms. Both came with potatoes sautéed with onions and peppers, and sausage or bacon. The seven entrées range from eggs benedict to belgian waffles.

The inn's elegant restaurant (see Dining Spots) is known locally for special-occasion dining. The former library has been converted into a massage room, where a team of masseuses is on call.

(603) 968-3348 or (800) 545-2141. Fax (603) 968-2116. www.manorongoldenpond.com. Twenty-five rooms and two cottages with private baths. Doubles, $225 to $375, mid-May through October; $180 to $375, rest of year. Cottages by the week, $300 and $425. Two-night minimum foliage and peak weekends. Children over 12. Closed week before Christmas.

The Inn on Golden Pond, Route 3, Box 680, Holderness 03245.

Franconia native Bonnie Webb and her Massachusetts-born husband Bill operate this bed-and-breakfast inn in a 110-year-old residence with a rear section dating back 200 years.

No, the inn is not on Golden Pond (it's across the road from Little Squam, which is hidden by trees in summer) and "other than the fact that Jane Fonda once used the upstairs bathroom, we have no connection with the movie," the inn's fact sheet tells guests.

The Webbs, who are among New Hampshire's longest serving innkeepers, have spruced up the place considerably since their start in 1984. All eight guest quarters are handsomely appointed with king, queen or twin beds, pretty curtains with matching cushions, hooked rugs and needlepoint handwork done by Bonnie. A recent addition enlarged the second-floor Rabbit's Hole room with a sitting area beside a picture window and a new bath, as well as giving a small sitting room to the kingsize Bear's Den suite on the third floor. The Porcupine Hollow suite has a larger sitting room and a king bedroom. Each room is named for an animal and has a needlepoint sign with the appropriate animal thereon. Bonnie also makes the mints that are put on the pillows when the beds are turned down at night.

The spacious, comfortably furnished living room, with a fireplace and numerous books and magazines, is particularly inviting for reading and quiet conversations. The large rear window looks onto a treed lawn with garden chairs and a hillside of

55 acres for cross-country skiing. A smaller room offers cable TV and, almost covering one wall, a fascinating map with colored pins locating "our guests' other homes" – a vivid example that Bill cites as "our version of urban sprawl." A 60-foot-long front porch is a relaxing spot in summer.

A full breakfast is served at individual tables in the attractive pine dining room, expanded when the Webbs added a second floor to the attached rear shed. Gratinéed eggs, blueberry muffins, homemade bread for toasting, cereal and fruit were the fare at our latest visit. Blueberry-stuffed french toast and stuffed apple pancakes are favorites. Bonnie sells a little cookbook of her breakfast specialties for $4. She also stocks New England foods and crafts in the inn's small gift shop.

(603) 968-7269. Fax (603) 968-9226. www.innongoldenpond.com. Six rooms and two suites with private baths. Mid-May through October: doubles $140, suites $175. Rest of year: doubles $115, suites $150. Two-night minimum weekends in season. Children over 10.

The Glynn House Inn, 59 Highland St., Ashland 03217.

The crown jewel on a residential side street in Ashland, this turreted, 1890 Queen Anne-style house blends Victoriana and romance. New owners Jim and Gay Dunlop, who took over in 2001 from the B&B's founders, offer thirteen plush accommodations and gourmet breakfasts.

The Dunlops have redecorated all the common rooms and hallways, including new wall coverings, oriental carpets and furnishings they brought with them from their home in North Carolina. Off the parlor is the front veranda, a fine spot for relaxing with iced tea and cookies.

Four bedrooms and four suites are located in the main house, while a rear carriage house adds two rooms and three suites. All rooms come with triple-sheeted beds, TV/VCR and telephone. Suites add fireplaces, whirlpool tubs, CD players, spa therapy bath products and decanters of sherry.

The guest room decor and furnishings have been updated and most are not nearly so Victorian as when we stayed. Our second-floor Harrison Room in front, quiet as could be since this is a street with little traffic, still has its fishnet canopy queen bed, a huge armoire, and a pedestal sink and a jacuzzi tub open to the room, but the Victorian loveseat at the foot of the bed has been replaced by a couple of traditional arm chairs. A doll was ensconced on the mahogany queen bed in the corner facing the fireplace in the Taft Room next door, quite frilly with floral curtains and a little lace-covered table between two side chairs.

Victoriana gives way to a more traditional look in the Monroe, the original honeymoon suite at the side of the main floor. Recently redecorated, it has a double jacuzzi beside the fireplace and a queen bed dressed in French country toile facing the fireplace. At the rear of the house is a newer honeymoon suite with a living room with TV, fireplace and queensize sofabed, and a kingsize bedroom and whirlpool bath upstairs. The Dunlops added two spacious suites on the third floor. One has a circular living room with five windows in the top of the turret. The other has a sitting room with a sofabed and a kingsize bedroom rich in burgundy and gold, with a fireplace and a whirlpool tub in the corner.

Three suites with rather contemporary decor are located in the rear carriage house. Its second floor also has two bedrooms, one of them quite small and simple.

Early risers can enjoy coffee before they sit down in a candlelit dining room at a lace-covered table expandable to seat sixteen. Classical music played as the innkeepers served a fresh fruit cup, orange juice and a delicate cheese strudel with raspberry jam. The main course involved a choice of french toast or eggs benedict, the latter really special, served with hash browns. Belgian waffles are a recent favorite.

(603) 968-3775 or (800) 637-9599. Fax (603) 968-9415. www.glynnhouse.com. Six rooms and seven suites with private baths. Doubles, $119 to $199. Suites, $195 to $239.

Meredith Inn, 2 Waukewan St., Meredith 03253.

This Victorian "Painted Lady" on a Meredith hilltop was refurbished from top to bottom in 1997 by the former owners of the Rangeley Inn in Maine. Janet Carpenter wanted a smaller inn when her parents retired, so they helped get her started in the handsome Hawkins-Deneault House, once the home of a doctor and then a dentist but lately an apartment house. Starting from scratch with a new furnace, new electrical system and new bathrooms, Ed and Fay Carpenter undertook ten months of renovations before they and Janet launched an eight-room B&B.

Turret enhances facade of Meredith Inn.

Coming from an inn background in a resort area, they knew exactly what they wanted: jacuzzi tubs, king or queen beds, a couple of fireplaces, TVs and telephones, lace curtains and a light Victorian feeling in a house full of 19th-century marvels.

Rooms are spacious and handsomely furnished. The premier Room 8 comes with a kingsize mahogany bed, gas fireplace and an enormous bathroom, with a two-person whirlpool tub, antique oak commode and a bidet. There are removable newel posts on several beds ("for hiding your jewels," Janet said as she pulled one open to show), etched brass doorknobs with matching plates, beautiful hardwood floors, shellacked southern yellow pine woodwork and turrets with window seats (and one in which Ed hoped to install a circular bed).

In a main-floor front room that was once the dentist's office, Janet found a dental pick when cleaning out the closet. She had it framed and furnished the bedroom with other dental memorabilia.

Ed's father made the grandfather's clock and much of the furniture that graces the living room. Some of the furnishings were the family's and "some we picked up antiquing," Janet said with a wink.

Janet serves a full breakfast in a small breakfast room. Expect fresh fruit and yogurt, juice and perhaps french toast, omelets or an apple-filled crêpe with ricotta cheese, a recipe from her sister Susan, who had been chef at the Rangeley Inn.

(603) 279-0000. www.meredithinn.com. Eight rooms with private baths. Doubles, $125 to $175.

Squam Lake Inn, Shepard Hill Road, Box 695, Holderness 03245.

New owners from California took over this century-old Victorian farmhouse B&B in 2003 and changed its name once again. Rae Andrews and Cindy Foster preferred a lake theme and name to the old Pressed Petals Inn. The former owner pressed flowers as a sideline and thought that name had a better ring to it than the original Curmudg-Inn, opened a few years earlier by a retired physician who billed himself as innkeeper and resident curmudgeon.

Rae and Cindy had vacationed for ten years at the home of Rae's parents on Lake Winnipesaukee and "fell in love with the area," according to Cindy. Her 13-year-old daughter and Rae's parents help with the inn, "so it's a real family affair."

Besides changing the name, the pair changed the room motif and decor from flowery to watery, with more of a "vintage, cottagey, lake feeling" in Cindy's words. The open living room and adjoining dining room are furnished in eclectic style.

Bedrooms on the first and second floors come in a variety of shapes and sizes, some with corner cupboards that you'd expect in a dining room. Five beds are queensize and three are kingsize. They bear damask linen sheets and are covered with white spreads and down pillows. The Squam and Chocorua rooms have sitting areas and gas fireplaces. All come with luxuriant towels, robes and Crabtree & Evelyn toiletries.

Complimentary beverages are served in the afternoon. Breakfast could be four-grain blueberry pancakes with maple sugar bacon, belgian waffles with strawberries and whipped cream, omelets or eggs benedict. The meal is taken in the dining room or in season on the spacious new mahogany side deck that looks to be straight out of California redwood country.

(603) 968-4417 or (800) 839-6205. Fax (603) 968-3661. www.squamlakeinn.com. Eight rooms with private baths. Doubles, $130 to $180 mid-May through October, $120 to $150 rest of year.

Strathaven, 576 North Sandwich Road (Route 113), North Sandwich 03259.

There is artistry as well as hospitality here. Betsy Leiper, an embroidery teacher from suburban Philadelphia, and her husband Tony bought this rural manse as a summer home for their family of seven in 1978; upon his retirement from Bell Telephone in 1981, they decided to live here year-round. When the Corner House asked if the Leipers would take their overflow, Strathaven became a low-key B&B. "We found it an inexpensive way to entertain," says Tony.

And entertain they do, in a grand, beamed living room beneath a cathedral ceiling, amid bookshelves, an upright piano and sectional seating facing picture windows overlooking rear gardens and pond. Or in a front solarium facing more gardens – just the spot for soup and a sandwich between cross-country expeditions in the winter. Or in the fireplaced dining room with a twelve-foot-long table and a wonderful glass cabinet full of china. The sideboard here was carved by Betsy's father, who also fashioned the mantelpiece displayed over a bay window and painted the watercolors that grace the house. Betsy's maternal grandfather did the oil portraits throughout.

Guest rooms and restaurant at Inn at Bay Point face Lake Winnipesaukee head-on.

Betsy's embroidery shows up here and there, perhaps as crewel work on the valances in a pretty blue downstairs bedroom with two double beds and a loveseat beneath the window in between. A second downstairs room in gold also has two double beds and a private bath. Upstairs in the older section of the house (1830 to 1840) are two more double rooms that share a hall bath with the host and hostess. The Quimby Room bears the maiden name and portrait of Betsy's mother, a musician who played with the Boston Conservatory. The Victorian Room contains a shelf of cottages and castles from England, acquired during her annual group tours for embroiderers.

Guests enter the house through the kitchen, which says something about the hospitality of the place. Tony prepares a full breakfast: juice, cereal, homemade breads, omelets, three pancakes and sausages and coffeecake – "any or all of the above." Between meals, he serves as town treasurer and conducts cross-country ski expeditions on trails he cut on the property, videotaping guests' exploits and recording their pratfalls. In summer he joins guests on the front or side porches where, he quips, it's so quiet that "we sit and count cars."

(603) 284-7785. www.strathaveninn.com. Two rooms with private bath and two rooms with shared bath. Doubles, $75 to $80. Children and well-behaved pets welcome. No credit cards.

Inn at Bay Point, Route 3 at Route 25, Meredith 03253.

This deluxe, full-service inn is right on Lake Winnipesaukee. Edward "Rusty" McLear, developer of the Inn at Mill Falls and Mill Falls Marketplace across the street, acquired a corner office structure that previously housed a bank and undertook a total rehab to turn it into this 24-room inn with a ground-floor restaurant first called The Boathouse Grille and now **Lago** (see Dining Spots).

Guest rooms are on the three upper floors and all face the lake. Nineteen come with private balconies. Thirteen of the balconied rooms have queensize beds with a queen sofabed in the sitting area. Three substitute leather wing chairs for the sofabeds and two premium rooms contain kingsize beds, jacuzzi tubs and fireplaces. The spacious, front-corner penthouse on the fourth floor has a king bed, a queen sofabed in the sitting area, jacuzzi, fireplace, wet bar and balcony.

Rooms vary in size and shape, making use of nooks and crannies with a loveseat here, a shelf of books there. Those that appear smaller compensate with large bathrooms.

Loveseats are in front of the fireplace in the lobby, which opens through french doors onto a waterside deck. The shoreline features a private dock, a beach and a whirlpool spa area.

Full breakfast is available in the restaurant. A complimentary continental breakfast is served in the lobby on weekdays in the off-season.

The inn's success spurred its owner to develop a larger inn and conference center nearby in 2004 (see below).

(603) 279-7006 or (800) 622-6455. Fax (603) 279-6797. www.millfalls-baypoint.com. Twenty-four rooms with private baths. May-October: doubles $199 to $269, penthouse $289. Rest of year: doubles $149 to $199, penthouse $249.

The Inns at Mill Falls, 312 Daniel Webster Hwy., Route 3, Meredith 03253.

The Inns at Mill Falls began with a restored nineteenth-century linen mill, a covered bridge, and a 40-foot waterfall. Where they end is anyone's guess.

With two Bostonians as partners, Edward "Rusty" McLear developed the first Inn at Mill Falls, a 54-room hotel, as the final phase of Mill Falls Marketplace, a shopping and restaurant complex fashioned from the old mill site at the western end of Lake Winnipesaukee. "We couldn't understand why a beautiful resort area like this had nothing more than a couple of cottages in which to stay," Rusty explained.

That was back in 1983, and now – three inns later under the name the Inns at Mill Falls – comes the crowning glory. The nearby Church Landing project is "by far the most exciting that we've undertaken since the initial Mill Falls renovation," says Rusty.

On target for opening in May 2004 was a large conference center, inn, restaurant and health club on a 3.5-acre peninsula jutting into the lake with two sandy beaches and water on three sides. Known as Church Landing, the development incorporates the former St. Charles Church as well as new construction in the shingled camp style of the 1880s. The project's linchpin is a 300-seat conference center. Visitors will be well housed at the **Inn at Church Point,** a three-story hostelry with 58 waterfront rooms and suites reflecting Adirondack style. All have gas fireplaces and private balconies, and some have jacuzzi tubs. The site also holds the Common Man chain's new 200-seat **Lakehouse r**estaurant and lounge, the reincarnation of the former Boathouse Grille, relocated from the Inn at Bay Point. A health club with massage area, jacuzzi and sauna area includes an indoor/outdoor pool.

The first **Inn at Mill Falls** is a white frame structure on five levels. The inn has rooms of varying size and color schemes, decorated in contemporary French country style with matching draperies and bedspreads, plush chairs, television sets and spacious baths, each with a basket of amenities. Old samplers on the walls, framed pictures of 19th-century Meredith, plants in an old sleigh and antique headboards lend a bit of history.

Original Inn at Mill Falls (left) and Marketplace flank waterfall in Meredith.

The inn connects with the marketplace, which has fifteen shops, the Waterfall Café and Giuseppe's Pizzeria & Ristorante.

After opening the Inn at Bay Point across the street in 1995 (see above), Rusty acquired property southeast of the inn facing Route 3, razed a restaurant and opened a third inn, **The Chase House at Mill Falls.** It has twenty rooms and three suites with fireplaces, some with in-room jacuzzis and balconies facing the lake across the street. **Camp,** a new restaurant in the Common Man chain, serves dinner nightly here.

(603) 279-7006 or (800) 622-6455. www.millfalls.com.

Inn at Mill Falls: Fifty-four rooms with private baths. Doubles, $119 to $239 May-October, $99 to $189 rest of year.

Chase House: Twenty rooms and three suites with private baths. Doubles $189 to $299 May-October, $139 to $259 rest of year.

Church Landing: Fifty-eight rooms and suites with private baths. Doubles, $209 to $359.

Dining Spots

The Manor on Golden Pond, Shepard Hill Road, Holderness.

The main dining room here is a picture of elegance, from its leaded windows and tiled double-sided fireplace to the crystal chandelier hanging from the beamed ceiling covered with rich floral wallpaper. Draperies and window treatments match the wallpaper. Exotic roses and napkins fanned in crystal wine glasses accent the candlelit tables dressed in cream and burgundy linens.

Dinner is à la carte, the contemporary American menu changing weekly. The fare ranges from cumin and molasses-charred salmon fillet with lemon beurre blanc to herb-encrusted venison leg with port wine demi-glace. Châteaubriand with three-

Windowed alcove offers view from small dining room at The Corner House Inn.

cheese potato gratin and sautéed snap peas is available for two. Also available is a six-course tasting menu for the entire table, $65 per person.

Our dinner began with a pan-seared scallop with white truffle emulsion, followed by a tempura soft-shell crab with soy and ginger sauce and seafood chowder with a roasted garlic crouton. Following a green salad with roasted vegetables and citrus vinaigrette, a champagne sorbet cleared the palate. Entrées were pistachio-crusted lamb loin with a dried cherry and juniper sauce with calvados, and maple-glazed beef tournedos with green tomato relish. A bottle of Conn Creek zinfandel accompanied from a choice but affordable wine list.

Dessert was an award-winning Remy-Martin chocolate torte and a raspberry crème brûlée, two of the more decadent choices from a selection that also included plum crisp with buttermilk ice cream and an iced Godiva chocolate liqueur latte.

New Age background music, flickering candlelight and exceptional food contributed to a memorable experience.

(603) 968-3348 or (800) 545-2141. Entrées, $30 to $38. Dinner by reservation, nightly 6:30 to 8:30 in summer and fall; Wednesday-Sunday 6 to 8, rest of year.

The Corner House Inn, 22 Main St., Center Sandwich.

Over the years, innkeeper Jane Brown and her chef-husband Don have created one of the area's more popular restaurants in this delightful Victorian house in the center of town. They also teamed up with fellow restaurateur Alex Ray of the Common Man to open a restaurant and catering service near Plymouth.

Dinner is by candlelight in a rustic, beamed dining room with blue and white tablecloths and red napkins, or in three smaller rooms off the other side of the entry. The striking quilted pieces on the walls are for sale by Anne Made; the same for the artworks from Surroundings gallery.

Lunches are bountiful and bargains; we saw some patrons sending half of theirs back for doggy bags. We, however, enjoyed every bite of the Downeaster, two halves of an English muffin laden with fresh lobster salad, sprouts and melted

Swiss cheese. We also tried a refreshing cold fruit soup (peach, melon and yogurt, sparked with citrus rinds) and the crêpe of the day, a Corner House tradition and this time filled with ground beef and veggies. Desserts included cappuccino cheesecake, frozen chocolate kahlua pie or piña colada sherbet.

Except for specials, the menu rarely changes, nor do the prices. For dinner, you might start with a cup of the inn's famous lobster and mushroom bisque, mushroom caps stuffed with spinach and cheese, crab cake with cajun tartar sauce or sesame chicken with honey dip. Entrées range from chicken piccata or cordon bleu or a single lamb chop "for those who like to clean their plate" to a pair of two-inch-thick lamb chops. One diner said the last, a house specialty, were the best she'd ever had. Shellfish sauté, seafood mixed grill, brandied peach duckling, pork zurich, five pasta dishes and filet mignon bordelaise are among the choices. Grilled swordfish, venison au poivre and New Zealand rack of lamb were specials at a recent visit.

The wine list is affordably priced. "Sandwich was a dry town when we came here and they finally granted us a beer and wine license," Jane said, "so they must think we're all right."

Lately, they closed their upstairs guest rooms and opened the casual **Corner House Pub,** with what Jane calls "a fun menu" of lobster rolls, fish and chips, chicken caesar salad and such.

(603) 284-6219. Entrées, $12.95 to $19.95. Lunch, Monday-Saturday 11:30 to 2, to 2:30 in season. Dinner nightly, 5:30 to 9, to 9:30 in season. Pub open daily from 4:30. Closed Monday, November-May.

The Common Man, Ashland Common, Ashland.

Founded in 1971 by Alex Ray and hailed for food that is the some of the most consistent in the area, the Common Man attracts enormous crowds – we faced a half-hour wait for a table at 8:30 one Wednesday evening. It also has spawned many other restaurateurs, Jane and Don Brown of the Corner House among them, as well as other restaurants around New Hampshire.

A jigsaw puzzle awaits on a table near the entrance. Inside, old records, sheet music and Saturday Evening Post covers are for sale. Upstairs is a vast bar and grill with buckets and lobster traps hanging from the ceiling, a long pine counter set for Chinese checkers and chess, plush sofas in intimate groupings and an umbrellaed outside deck overlooking the shops of Ashland Common. Pizzas, nachos, burgers and an uncommon number of snack foods are offered here nightly from 4 to 11.

The treats begin at the door, where you'll find an array of crackers, cheese spreads and dips to assuage hunger. The rustic, beamed main dining room, separated into sections by a divider topped with books, is crowded with tables sporting a variety of linens and mats, chairs and banquettes.

The dinner menu is straightforward and priced right, from several chicken dishes to rack of lamb. Planked "grate steak" serving "from one ridiculously hungry person to three very hungry people," complemented with a medley of vegetables, is one of the best bargains around for $26.95. We can vouch for the prime rib and the "uncommon steak," served with potatoes and excellent tossed romaine salads. A bottle of the house cabernet, specially blended by a California winery and something of a precedent among New Hampshire restaurants, was a fine accompaniment. Another innovation at our table was a box of menu recipes, marked "please don't steal" (they're meant to tempt the palate, rather than be specific).

Desserts vary from white chocolate bread pudding and a baked-to-order baked apple to a creamy cheesecake and white chocolate mousse. As you leave, a sign at the reception desk invites you to "take home a bar of our uncommon white chocolate."

(603) 968-7030. www.theCman.com. Entrées, $12.95 to $19.95. Lunch, Monday-Saturday 11:30 to 3 Dinner nightly, 5 to 9 or 9:30.

Walter's Basin Restaurant & Bar, 15 Main St. (Route 3), Holderness.

Finally, a good restaurant right on the lake – at the channel where Little Squam joins Big Squam and named for the elusive fish in the movie "On Golden Pond."

Fashioned from a bowling alley and a restaurant, it's a huge, unlikely sprawl of a place, from the plant-filled foyer with a fountain to the lounge in which you feel as if you're on a boat while imbibing at the stunning square copper bar in the center.

The two-level dining room in back has granite tables and a fish theme: quilted fabric fish on the walls, glass fish-shaped dishes, and salt and pepper shakers shaped like trout. With big windows onto the water, it's quite a stage for Andrew Cook, who started just out of college. He's a partner with friends of his parents, financial angels Charles and Dorothy Benson of Florida, all on hand at our initial visit.

Their chef delivers an extensive menu of American fare. Crab cakes with chipotle rémoulade, lobster pizza, mussel stew, roast duck quesadilla and slow-cooked pork ribs are among the appetizers.

Expect main courses like pan-seared rainbow trout amandine ("Sorry Walter!" exclaims the menu), grilled swordfish with rock shrimp, lobster raviolis, spice-rubbed pork tenderloin with cider demi-glace, and pepper-seared sirloin steak spiked with bourbon.

Burgers, tortilla wrap sandwiches, quesadillas and "square meals" are featured on the lunch menu and under light fare.

(603) 968-4412. Entrées, $16.95 to $23.95. Lunch daily, 11:30 to 2. Dinner, 5 to 9. Sunday brunch, 10 to 1. Closed Tuesday and Wednesday in winter, also all of November and December.

Italian Farmhouse, Route 3, Plymouth.

Country Italian cuisine and atmosphere galore are offered by Jane and Don Brown of the Corner House in partnership with Alex Ray of the Common Man in this sprawling farmhouse and barn they dubbed a "cucina povera" (country kitchen).

Done with great style, as in their other restaurants, the tables in the barn dining room and four smaller rooms in the main 1849 structure are covered with red and white checkered cloths and topped with chianti bottles holding melting candles. There's lots to look at, yet the ambiance remains sedate.

The hearty Italian menu is country-priced. Cioppino, fettuccine alfredo with lobster and New York sirloin command top dollar, but the homemade pizzas, pastas and most dishes are under $12. The assertive farmhouse chicken on bowtie pasta and accompanying garlic bread were more than we could eat. Those with bigger appetites could start with artichokes pomodoro, fried calamari or caesar salad and finish with tortoni, spumoni, citrus flan or pecan pie.

(603) 536-4536. Entrées, $10.95 to $15.95. Dinner nightly, 5 to 9.

Lago, Routes 3 and 25, Meredith.

Area restaurateur Alex Ray leased the main floor of the Inn at Bay Point to develop this waterfront prize, first known as the Boathouse Grille and converted in late 2003 into an Italian trattoria. Lago, Italian for lake, offers authentic Italian fare and "bella" lake views in a redesigned and refurbished space.

A bar in front opens to a dining area appointed in rustic cocoa and taupe colors with old farm-style pine tables, black and white photographs, hand-painted murals of Italian scenery on the walls, a partly open corner kitchen, and a long and idyllic dining deck beside Lake Winnipesaukee.

Lago's traditional Italian menu features simple eclectic fare from crusty ciabatta bread, polenta and gnocchi to house-made pastas like pappardelle and tortellini.

Fresh fish and hearty meats are offered as main courses. The strong Italian wine list features robust Tuscan wines.

(603) 279-2253. Entrees, $13.95 to $19.95. Lunch daily, 11:30 to 3. Dinner nightly, 5 to 9 or 9:30.

Mame's, 8 Plymouth St., Meredith.

Owner John Cook takes pride in the fine restoration of the brick house and barn once owned by a 19th-century physician. A meandering series of small dining rooms on the main floor is topped by a large lounge on the second.

The extensive menu is traditional steak and seafood with a continental flair, from seafood diane and lobster-scallop divan to prime rib and veal sautéed with crabmeat and scallops. Baked stuffed shrimp, Southwest chicken alfredo, veal marsala and steak au poivre are other favorites. The prices are reasonable, and the atmosphere intimate and romantic. Mud pie, bread pudding and black-bottom cheesecake are among desserts.

A tavern menu is available all day and evening.

(603) 279-4631. www.mamesrestaurant.com. Entrées, $11.95 to $21.95. Lunch daily, 11:30 to 3. Dinner, 5 to 9:30. Sunday brunch, 11 to 2.

Diversions

Squam Lake. The lake made famous in the movie "On Golden Pond" is so screened from public view that passersby get to see it only from a distance or up close at precious few points. But you can – and should – experience it by tour boat. Capt. Joe Nassar's **Squam Lakes Tour** gives two-hour excursions on a 32-foot pontoon boat daily at 10, 2 and 4 from his residence off Route 3 half a mile south of Holderness. Sunset cruises are offered weekends in summer.

We're partial to the original **Golden Pond Tour,** now run by Squam Lakes Natural Science Center. Former innkeeper Pierre Havre was our knowledgeable and talkative guide on a 90-minute tour of the lake, which leaves from the Route 3 bridge in Holderness two or three times daily from Memorial Day through foliage season. The center's naturalist tells the history, relates vignettes, stops to watch nesting loons and visits the places made famous in the movie. "That's the Thayer cottage," he says from a distant vantage point before discreetly passing the house loaned for the summer's filming and so remote that many locals have yet to find it. Purgatory Cove with Norman's famous rock was as foreboding the stormy day we visited as it was during the dramatic scene in the film. "Even on a sunny day," our guide related, "you'll generally see no more than a dozen boats on the second biggest lake in New Hampshire."

Chocorua Island, also called Church Island, is a favorite stop on both boat tours. The site of the first boys' camp in America, it has an inspiring outdoor chapel in which summer worship services, complete with crank organ, have been conducted continuously by area churches since 1903. On Sunday morning, the dock area is said to resemble the approach of the Spanish armada as upwards of 250 churchgoers arrive in a variety of boats.

Holderness. Huddled around the little Squam River channel that joins Big Squam and Little Squam lakes, the small downtown area of Holderness is on its way up. Town officials and merchants developed a meandering "reflection path" with benches upon which to sit and reflect along the waterfront. The **Loon's Nest Gift Shop,** situated in an 1812 farmhouse at Curry Place, purveys loon-related gifts, decorative accessories, jewelry, specialty foods and more. We liked the tote bag emblazoned: "It's Never Too Late to Love a Loon." Just north of town on Route 113 is **Longhaul Farm at Squam Lake,** a country store and garden center specializing in organic garden supplies and specialty gifts.

Center Sandwich, an historic district, still looks much as it did two generations ago when Mary Hill Coolidge and the Sandwich Historical Society organized a display of hooked and braided rugs that led to the opening of a crafts shop. Known as **Sandwich Home Industries,** the shop became the first home for the League of New Hampshire Craftsmen. It is open daily from mid-May through mid-October with myriad craft and gift items, from carved birds to cribbage boards, handmade clothes to silver jewelry. We could spend hours (and a small fortune) here. Free crafts demonstrations are given several days a week in summer, and an outdoor art exhibit is staged during Sandwich Old Home Week in mid-August. The Sandwich Fair, one of New England's outstanding country fairs, has been held annually in mid-October since 1910. Summer residents might go home after Labor Day, but they often return for the fair.

The main roads and byways of this picturesque village lead to any number of interesting crafts and antiques shops. Surroundings, long a favorite gallery in the center of town, occupies expanded quarters next to owner Jessie Barrett's home a mile south on Holderness Road. Now called **Surroundings at Red Gate,** its four rooms display fine and country art. We were intrigued by the handweaving (vests, pillows, jumpers and much more) at **The Designery,** a fascinating shop and studio in the former high school, open Tuesday-Saturday 10 to 5. We also admired the wonderful pillows, especially those with cat portraits, done by Anne Perkins of **Anne Made.** Her wall hangings, quilts and pillows decorate the walls of the nearby Corner House Inn and are snapped up by purchasers almost as fast as she puts them up.

Shopping. A mecca for shoppers is **The Common Man Company Store** across from the landmark restaurant of that name in Ashland. Its two floors are chock full of gifts, accessories and specialty foods, including the restaurant's own label wines. Across the courtyard from the restaurant is a showroom for the **New England Winter Fleece Co.**

The **Mills Falls Marketplace** in Meredith contains nearly twenty enterprises from **The Country Carriage** with country gifts and accessories to **Northern Air** for cottage fashions and accessories. We liked the birdhouses, garden benches and the cans labeled "Grow Your Own Forest" at **Upcountry Pastimes.** Absent are the souvenir shops indigenous to much of the Lakes Region. We overheard one customer ask if a shop had any T-shirts with "Meredith" printed on the front. No, was the reply – you have to go to Weirs Beach to find that kind of thing. Lamented the customer: "But then it won't say 'Meredith.'" Similarly, the loon items at the Squam Lakes Natural Science Center's Nature Store and Gift Shop in Holderness signify, but do not say, Squam Lakes.

Annalee Doll Museum and Gift Shop, 44 Reservoir Road, Meredith, is a gift shop, a museum, a Factory in the Woods and more, attracting sightseers by the carload. From humble beginnings, Annalee Thorndike has built quite an operation in her Meredith complex. Although we personally are not crazy about these dolls, we must be in the minority because the Annalee Doll Society has more than 23,000 members. There are dolls for all occasions and seasons, especially Christmas, with Santas and Mrs. Santas and elves galore. Mice are dressed as Pilgrims for Thanksgiving, bunnies for Easter and kids in costume for Halloween. Little frogs surround a pond in one corner of the shop. Although commercial, it's fun – especially for collectors and youngsters. Open daily 9:30 to 5, Memorial Day to Halloween. Free.

Extra-Special

Squam Lakes Natural Science Center, Junction of Routes 3 and 113, Holderness. Nature bursts forth in all its glory at this growing 200-acre wildlife sanctuary and nature center. The highlight is a nearly mile-long exhibit trail featuring more than 40 species of native New Hampshire animals – from white-tailed deer and bobcats to black bears and mountain lions – in natural enclosures. A bird exhibit includes an outdoor songbird aviary. Trailside buildings are full of hands-on exhibits, games and puzzles of particular appeal to the young and young at heart, and daily programs are offered in summer. A two-story exhibit building features a black bear exhibit, including a simulated bear den that allows visitors to climb inside and be part of a bear's habitat. Three other self-guided trail include one to the summit of Mount Fayal, which yields spectacular views of Squam Lake. Kirkwood Gardens is a three-acre garden at the western edge of the old Holderness Inn. It includes a fern garden, a butterfly garden and a garden of indigenous shrubs and flowers particularly attractive to birds. The garden adjoins the center's excellent Nature Gift Shop, relocated to the old inn grounds in downtown Holderness, which sells gifts, toys and books with a nature theme. We admired a tile-top table bearing loons for $195. Displayed outside at one visit was a Maine woodsman's weather stick, a rustic weather predictor. "They really work," said a sign, noting that when the stick bends down, it portends bad weather. It was bending down, and a hurricane brushed by the next day.

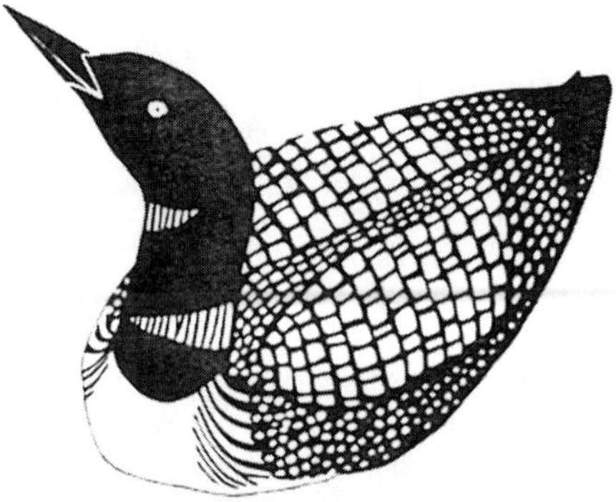

(603) 968-7194. www.nhnature.org. Trail and exhibits open daily 9:30 to 4:30, May-October. Adults, $9 in summer, $7 in spring and fall.

Sleigh rides and skating are featured on "Victorian Afternoon" at Nestlenook Farm.

Jackson, N.H.

A Rugged Mountain World

Drive through the old red covered bridge into Jackson and you enter another world.

It's a world isolated from the hubbub and congestion of the lower Mount Washington Valley. It's enveloped by mountains of the Presidential Range, tiptoeing toward the East's highest peak (6,288 feet). It's a highland valley of pristine air, scenic beauty, and peace and quiet. It's a European-style mountainside village of 600 residents and often a greater number of visitors.

Jackson is one of the nation's earliest year-round destination resorts, dating to pre-Civil War days and not much changed since its heyday around the turn of the last century when up to 40 trains a day delivered travelers to grand hotels in one of New England's most exclusive resort areas. It's a village of spirited tradition and pride, from the local book based on recipes used in Jackson's early lodges to the Jackson Resort Association's claim that "nowhere else in the world will you find a more concentrated area of diverse recreational opportunities."

Today, skiing is the big draw in Jackson and its sister hamlets of Glen, Intervale and Hart's Location. There are three downhill ski areas, Wildcat, Attitash and Black Mountain; a world-class cross-country center in the Jackson Ski Touring Foundation, and fabled Tuckerman Ravine, where the diehards climb to the headwall of Mount Washington for one last run in June.

The two worlds of skiing – alpine and nordic – co-exist in friendly tension. Explained the local leader who was staffing the village information center when we first stopped: "The foundation wanted to advertise 'Ski Tour Jackson' and Black Mountain wanted to stress alpine, so we ended up simply 'Ski Jackson.'"

There are modern-day amenities, two golf courses among them. But this is a rugged area, better epitomized by the Appalachian Mountain Club hiking camp at

Pinkham Notch than the Mount Washington Auto Road (its bumper stickers boasting "This Car Climbed Mount Washington"), better experienced from a secluded mountain inn than from one of the chock-a-block motels down the valley in North Conway.

Inn Spots

The Inn at Thorn Hill, Thorn Hill Road, Box A, Jackson 03846.

Probably Jackson's best view of the Presidential Range is from this handsome yellow hilltop structure, designed in 1895 by architect Stanford White and grandly rebuilt in 2003 following a major fire.

A broad sweep of the mountains, wide enough to encompass the weather station atop Mount Washington, opens from the wraparound veranda, the library and lounge as well as guest rooms on the second and third floors. The building's sixteen new guest quarters are the ultimate in luxury with all the latest amenities from fireplaces and whirlpool tubs to TVs with DVD players and private telephone lines with data ports.

Some of New Hampshire's best meals are served in the inn's enlarged restaurant and pub (see Dining Spots). Spa services have been added in the basement.

The disastrous fire in 2002 only temporarily halted the efforts of innkeepers Jim and Ibby Cooper to elevate Thorn Hill into one of New England's most deluxe inns. Jim, who had been in food and beverage management for the Four Seasons hotel chain in Florida, already had developed one of the country's finer wine cellars and his daughter and son-in-law, both chefs, had just taken over the kitchen.

The rebuilt inn gave the Coopers the chance to raise the bar to meet higher guest expectations, in Jim's words.

The inn has been reconfigured in an L-shape and enlarged to nearly double the size of the original. The main floor holds a library, a 60-seat dining room and a 40-seat lounge in a newly added turret. In the finished basement are a private dining room, an exercise room and spa in the turret area, and a 10,000-bottle wine cellar.

The second and third floors contain twelve large guest rooms and four suites, each with king or queen bed, sitting area, gas fireplace and TVs, which had been lacking before. Bathrooms gleam with white tile and marble vanities. Each has a two-person jacuzzi tub, and some have steam showers.

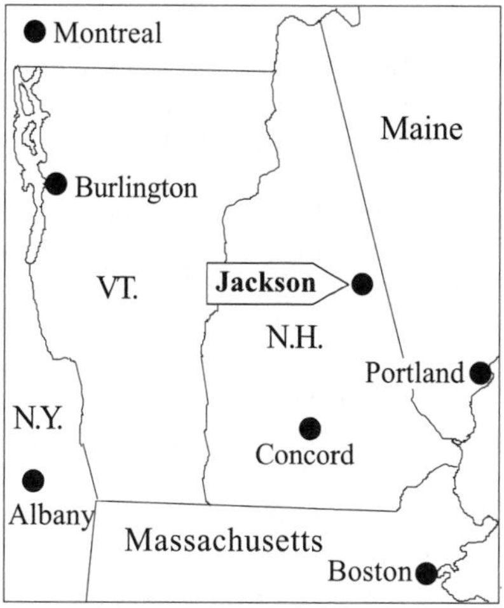

All are sumptuously furnished with antiques, colorful wallpapers and oriental rugs. Sachet pillows are scattered about the beds, and there are many special touches. Tuckerman's Suite is stunning with a kingsize bed and a two-way fireplace also visible in the living room, which has a window seat and a wet bar with mini-refrigerator. The bath, also with a window seat, has a two-person jacuzzi tub and a steam shower for two.

Before the fire, the Coopers had added a deck and an outdoor hot tub to the carriage house, which shed its ski-chalet appearance. Five rooms and a suite were redone in a North Country look with Adirondack furnishings and new baths (four with jacuzzis).

They also upgraded three outlying cottages with gas fireplaces and double jacuzzis. We enjoyed our stay in the Notch View Cottage, a two-room affair equipped with a queensize bed and a front porch that catches the evening breeze. Two other renovated cottages with decks are close by, and a pleasant swimming pool is screened from view by a hedge.

Breakfast, served formally on white china, lives up to the inn's culinary reputation. Ours started with five kinds of juices, homemade breads and muffins, and granola and cereals. The main course could be the inn's spicy chicken hash with poached eggs and peppered hollandaise sauce or grand marnier french toast with peach conserve, both excellent.

The inn's new spa facility has a steam and sauna room and three rooms for massage, hydro-massage, facials, rubs and wraps.

(603) 383-4242 or (800) 289-8990. Fax (603) 383-8062. www.innatthornhill.com. Seventeen rooms, five suites and three cottages with private baths. Doubles, $125 to $250, suites and cottages $190 to $290. Foliage and holidays: doubles $175 to $300, suites and cottages $240 to $350. Two- or three-night minimum most weekends and peak periods. Children over 8.

The Notchland Inn, Route 302, Hart's Location 03846.

This choice, small, self-contained inn with quite a history is spectacularly situated off by itself in the White Mountain National Forest, on the other side of Mount Crawford from Jackson. It's blessed with 400 acres of woods and gardens and a mile and a half of frontage on the Saco River, which has been dammed to create a nifty pond with two private swimming holes.

The many-gabled stone manor house, built in 1862 , has been an inn since the 1920s. It was put on the knowledgeable inngoer's map by ex-New Yorkers Les Schoof and Ed Butler, who took over the historic property in 1993 and made gradual upgrades. Still hands-on but now with assistants, the owners offer guests creature comforts and then some. The partners – who have raised personalized innkeeping to an art form – give tours of the public areas for guests upon arrival, chat with them at meals and take their photos upon departure.

The main inn holds an acclaimed dining room plus seven guest rooms and three premium suites, each with king or queen bed and wood-burning fireplace. Decor is a mix of Victorian and traditional. Understated Laura Ashley wallpapers and fabrics are among the stylish decorative accents.

A favorite among the premium suites is the kingsize Carter Suite with a large balcony and a whirlpool tub. The Kinsman Suite has a kingsize bed and an old-fashioned soaking tub and steam shower. It's full of Asian art collected by Les from his previous life as executive director of the American Ballet Theater, whose posters on the walls prompted him to name the corridor leading to the suites "the dance hall." The Evans Suite has a queensize bed beneath a skylight and a see-through fireplace serving a raised double jacuzzi tub overlooking a loveseat sitting area, which opens onto a rear balcony.

Two newly renovated suites are beside the inn in the Schoolhouse building, which served as a one-room school until the 1920s. We were happily ensconced in the upstairs suite with an extra-comfortable mattress on the queensize bed, a spacious

Notchland Inn occupies gabled stone manor house surrounded by mountains.

bath with corner tub and hand-held shower, and a large sitting area with a plump club chair and a loveseat, both with ottomans, facing the fireplace and an arched window looking onto Mount Hope.

The inn's wonderful front parlor with a huge fireplace was designed by Arts and Crafts pioneer Gustav Stickley, the noted furniture maker. Other common areas are a music and game room with piano and stereo, and a sun room with wicker furniture looking onto the property, where the owners raise llamas and miniature horses. A gazebo next to a small pond behind the inn houses a hot tub.

A full breakfast is served in a charming wing that was once the tavern in Abel Crawford's early White Mountain Hotel – the tavern was moved to this site in the 1920s. Beyond the fireplaced dining room with tables spaced well apart is a sunken dining room that served as a stage for the tavern as well as another sun room variously called garden room, plant room or conservatory.

Big windows in the dining room overlook the pond and gazebo on one side and prolific gardens and Mount Hope on the other. Excellent dinners are served to inn guests and the public at a single seating at 7.

The chef creates a new prix-fixe menu nightly, but there's always a choice of two appetizers and two soups, three entrées, salad and three desserts. You make your choices upon check-in, so each course of every meal can be served simultaneously.

Our leisurely, two-hour dinner began with a couple of masterful soups, two-color tomato and squash and a Creole fish chowder, whose delicacy masked assertive tastes – a phenomenon that held true throughout the meal. Appetizers were Mediterranean goat cheese wrapped in grape leaves and a suave corn custard served on a pool of red bell pepper coulis. Main courses were roast chicken breast topped with crispy prosciutto and grilled rib lamb chops with herbed mint sauce. The perfect mixed green salads that followed refreshed the palate for a couple of exceptional desserts, bread pudding with a spiced peach sauce and a cornmeal peach tart with ginger crème anglaise.

Breakfast the next morning proved exceptional as well. The usual preliminaries here were delivered with variety and in abundance. Main courses involve a choice of pancakes, french toast (the one with orange spiced sauce was super) and eggs any style. We heard one guest order "eggs any style," but we held out for an omelet with the works – everything but the kitchen sink. Delicious. As is the entire Notchland Inn experience.

(603) 374-6131 or (800) 866-6131. www.notchland.com. Seven rooms and five suites with private baths. Doubles, $190. Suites, $220 to $250. Add $50 for foliage and holidays. Two-night minimum weekends and holidays, three-night minimum in foliage.

Dinner by reservation, Tuesday-Sunday at 7. Prix-fixe, $35.

Nestlenook Farm Resort, Dinsmore Road, Box Q, Jackson 03846.

The plaque out front understates: "A new romance, Nov. 1, 1989, Robert and Nancy Cyr." Local condominium developer Robert Cyr invested big bucks and grand ideas into the transformation of a rustic B&B specializing in horseback riding into a deluxe fantasyland built around the oldest house in Jackson.

The Cyrs sought romance and a gingerbread look and ended up with an abundance of both. Such is their appeal to passersby along Route 16 that tours of the property are given daily at 2 p.m.

Behind the locked front doors of beveled glass lie a lovely living room with beamed ceiling and fireplace, a tin-ceilinged breakfast room, an intimate tap room and a bird cage full of finches in the lobby.

Upstairs are five bedrooms and two suites, each named for the Jackson artist whose paintings hang in the room. All have two-person therapy spa tubs and 19th-century parlor stoves or fireplaces and are decorated to the hilt. Everything is pink and mint green and ever-so-coordinated in the prized William Paskell Room, which has a hand-carved four-poster kingsize bed with a crocheted canopy, cherry and mahogany furnishings, fireplace and french doors opening onto a small balcony. The Horace Burdick Suite includes a queensize bed and a small sitting room with a ruffly day bed for a third guest. The penthouse master suite takes up the entire third floor and accommodates four guests in three rooms, including a separate jacuzzi room with wet bar.

A low-fat country breakfast is served in the dining room at seven tables set with high-back chairs and fine English china. It includes fresh oranges and grapefruit, cereals, homemade muffins and perhaps the house specialty, an omelet stuffed with fresh vegetables.

Gingerbread and romance continue outside onto landscaped grounds outfitted with statuary, gardens and even a big pond into which a waterfall trickles beneath a curving bridge. Music is piped into a huge gazebo, complete with a fireplace, park benches, a ceiling fan and a red sleigh in the middle. Horses, deer, sheep, llamas and donkeys from Nestlenook's petting farm graze in a nearby pasture.

A riverside chapel (for making or renewing marriage vows), a heated pool, sleigh or horse-drawn trolley rides and daily massages also help the resort live up to its billing as "fantasyland."

The expanding 65-acre Victorian Village now includes twelve villas containing deluxe rooms and suites plus more suites in hilltop chateaus.

(603) 383-9443 or (800) 659-9443. Fax (603) 383-4515. www.luxurymountaingetaways.com. Five rooms and two suites with private baths. Memorial Day to mid-September and mid-October to mid-December: doubles $140 to $250, suites $190 to $340. Foliage and mid-December through March: doubles, $185 to $330, suites $250 to $360. Two-night minimum stay. Children over 12. Closed April to Memorial Day.

Restored Wentworth Resort Hotel retains style of its Victorian beginnings.

The Wentworth, Route 16A, Jackson 03846.

Built in 1869, the Wentworth was the grand hotel of Jackson at the turn of the century when Jackson had 24 lodging establishments. Abandoned for a time, it was restored in 1983 into a luxury resort with modern conveniences but retaining much of the style and charm from its golden era. It really came into its own after its acquisition in 1991 by Fritz and Diana Koeppel, he a Swiss-born hotelier who had been with the Ritz and Four Seasons chains and was general manager of the Banff Springs Hotel in the Canadian Rockies.

Their move East was a homecoming of sorts for Diana, a native of East Conway. A wide search for a three-season resort of their own near skiing, golf and the ocean led the couple to The Wentworth.

The eighteen-hole golf course behind the hotel is part of the Jackson Ski Touring Center layout in the winter. Other facilities include condominiums, clay tennis courts, swimming pool, cocktail lounge and an elegant restaurant (see Dining Spots).

The turreted, yellow and green Victorian structure plus annexes and outbuildings (some with great views of the golf course) contain a total of 55 guest rooms with private baths and TV.

Plushly carpeted halls lead to twenty spacious rooms on the second and third floors of the main inn. All are beautifully restored in different shapes and sizes, with private baths (most have refinished, old-fashioned Victorian clawfoot tubs with showers), French Provincial furnishings and an upholstered chair under a reading lamp. Beige patterned draperies and bedspreads are coordinated with restful cream walls and rust carpeting. The Koeppels warmed up the rooms with inn touches like dried flowers and stenciling.

Lately, they have upgraded the outbuildings. There are three new suites in the Arden, each with kingsize sleigh bed, whirlpool tub and fireplace, and four in the

Sunnyside with similar amenities, except for one with a hot tub on its balcony. Other suites emerged around an inner courtyard with a hot tub in the Amster.

Back in the main building, Victorian antiques have been added to cozy seating areas near the fireplace in the large, formal lobby. A function room along a rear sun porch was converted into a pool room and library. Beyond is a dining deck with tables topped with Samuel Adams umbrellas. Antique couches and small tables grace the lounge.

Regional American cuisine is featured in the candlelit dining room (see Dining Spots).

(603) 383-9700 or (800) 637-0013. Fax (603) 383-4265. www.thewentworth.com. Fifty-five rooms and suites with private baths. Rates, MAP: doubles, $175 to $325; foliage and Christmas week, $215 to $355. Two-night minimum some weekends and peak periods.

Snowflake Inn, Main Street, Jackson 03846.

Quite a presence in the center of town is this inn that opened in 2003 on a prime piece of property that formerly housed the famed Jack Frost Shop and the Jackson Ski Touring Foundation. The shop went bankrupt, the foundation relocated and the six-acre parcel was eventually acquired by Sue and Gary Methot, who owned three motels in Hampton Beach before moving to the mountains for this venture. They built a long and handsome, two-story structure that includes a large lobby, indoor jetted spa that looks like a small swimming pool, large lobby and twenty hotel-style guest accommodations with gas fireplaces and two-person jacuzzis. The pale yellow structure also houses an art gallery, craft store and the new Jack Frost Shop, as well as the owners' quarters in the attic.

Their motel background may explain this venture's similarities to a motor inn, although hands-on innkeeper Sue would cringe at the suggestion. She calls it a romantic, upscale, adult-oriented hotel. The aforementioned indoor pool with walls of windows turns out to be a shallow, eighteen-jet whirlpool spa with a swim-against resistance current and waters kept at 92 to 94 degrees.

The two-story lobby includes a soaring stone fireplace and a second-floor billiards area ("no games for kids here," Sue stressed). The lobby also serves as the site for evening coffee and morning continental breakfast with fresh pastries from the Village Bistro.

The Snowflake is mainly about the latest in rooms – or suites, as they are called here. The typical one has a small, window-less sitting area inside the door, separated by a bathroom from the kingsize bedroom beyond. Each has a flick-on gas fireplace, flat-screen TV and DVD/VCR player, telephone, a two-person whirlpool tub in the bedroom and a shower with two heads and two seats in the bathroom. Spa services are available in the privacy of one's guest room as part of the inn's featured spa packages.

Three "deluxe" rooms are located on the street side, which get reduced rates because of traffic noise. Three "super suites" plus a meeting area are situated above the Jack Frost store. These have jacuzzi tubs in the bathrooms, with two-sided fireplaces opening onto tub and bedroom, and bigger bedrooms with sitting areas and 35-inch TV sets, plus front sitting rooms with 20-inch flat-screen TVs. Sue reports that guests named their favorite the Gazebo Suite for its windowed turret.

(603) 383-8250 or (888) 383-1020. www.snowflakeinnjackson.com. Twenty suites with private baths. Doubles, $175 to $350 July-October and winter, $165 to $325 rest of year.

Lush flowers greet summer guests at Christmas Farm Inn.

Christmas Farm Inn, Route 16B, Box CC, Jackson 03846.

A basket of bright red buttons proclaiming "We Make Memories" is beside an arrangement of garden flowers inside the entrance to this ever-expanding property where Christmas is reflected all year long. The buttons are part of the continuing promotion effort for the inn lately acquired by the Tolley family, who own motor inns in North Conway and Portland, Me. The flowers are from the well-landscaped grounds, which are frequent winners in the valley's annual garden competition.

Few inns have such a fragmented history: part jail, part church, part inn, part farmhouse, part sugarhouse. The property was given by a Philadelphian as a Christmas present in the 1940s to his daughter, who tried and failed at farming on the rocky hillside before the place was revived as an inn. Hence the name, and whence all nicely detailed on the back of the dinner menu.

A Christmas tree is decked out in white lights all year in a corner of the front living room of this inn, located off by itself above Jackson Village. Bingo, games and movies on the VCR are nightly features of the adjacent TV/game room. The rear barn has a huge game room with ping-pong, bumper pool, large-screen TV, an enormous fireplace and a sauna. Across the road are a swimming pool with a cabana where lunch is available, a putting green, shuffleboard and volleyball court. Everywhere you look are paths, brick walls and gardens with flowers.

Oh yes, about the guest accommodations, of which there are 41, all with private baths and telephones. Nine in the main inn have Christmasy names like Three Wise Men and those of Santa's reindeer, and are decorated in sprightly Laura Ashley style. The spacious Blitzen and Vixen have jacuzzis as well. The red and green 1777 Salt Box out back has nine deluxe rooms. More luxurious are the four suites in the barn, each with a sitting area with sofa and velvet chair, television, high sloped ceilings, large baths and loft bedrooms. Five recently redecorated cottages, each with two kingsize bedrooms with connecting living room, large sun decks, TV and fireplace, are first to be rented in the winter. Other accommodations are in the Log Cabin and an expanded honeymoon suite with living room and double jacuzzi in the Sugar House.

Newest is the Carriage House, set on a hillside above the main inn with a fireplaced great room, fitness center and massage room. It contains twelve luxury suites, each with king bed, whirlpool tub, fireplaced sitting room with TV, wet bar and a private deck. These were opened under the watchful eye of hotelier Michael Tolley, youngest son of George and Naomi Tolley, who live nearby.

The former Christmas theme has been toned down in the large, candlelit country dining room, pleasant in white and green. The year-round decor now sports fanned napkins on mint green cloths with white overlays, delicate stemware, cushioned wood chairs, pretty floral window treatments and plants all around. Little white lights twinkle and classical music plays as diners enjoy entrées ranging from roasted chicken breast with lemon-thyme jus to grilled New York sirloin with garlic-chive butter.

(603) 383-4313 or (800) 443-5837. Fax (603) 383-6495. www.christmasfarminn.com. Eighteen rooms, sixteen suites and seven cottages with private baths. Rates, MAP. Doubles $158 to $245, suites and cottages $178 to $450. Two-night minimum winter weekends.

Entrées, $17 to $28. Dinner nightly by reservation, 5:30 to 9.

Dana Place Inn, Pinkham Notch, Route 16, Jackson 03846.

Harris and Mary Lou Levine never expected to own an inn, but they went to lunch with a broker and somehow got talked into buying Dana Place in 1985. They've been busy upgrading the inn ever since, except for a brief hiatus when they sold to an absentee owner who doubled the inn's size within a couple of years and nearly ran it into the ground. "We felt we had left the job unfinished," said the Levines, who reacquired the inn and returned it to stability.

Following its expansion, the historic Dana Place is an unusual mix. It's at once a rural country inn with a few quaint rooms with shared baths rented as family suites, juxtaposed against luxury suites in three recent additions. Its elegant, high-ceilinged Lodge Room with a fireplace, a huge sectional, oriental rugs and quite a library is New England traditional; the airy new addition with an indoor free-form swimming pool and a jacuzzi is anything but. The lobby and entry have been expanded and the side patio enclosed to make a bar and cocktail lounge with a dance floor. An addition nearly doubled the size of the dining room (see Dining Spots). Two clay tennis courts were installed.

The out-of-the-way location of the inn, which still carries the name of the original owners of the Colonial farmhouse/inn from which all these additions have sprung, is special. It's up in the mountains some 1,000 feet above North Conway, just before you reach Pinkham Notch in the midst of the White Mountain National Forest, and right beside the Ellis River at the base of Mount Washington.

The Ellis River cross-country ski trail, one of the most skied trails in the country, ends at the inn, and skiers often come inside for lunches of hearty soups and chili in the lounge. In summer, inn guests cool off in a picturesque swimming hole in the rushing river.

The 35 guest quarters vary in size and decor from rustic to deluxe. All have been redone with pretty floral wallpapers, period furnishings and wreaths or straw flowers on the doors. The large room with sitting area in which we first stayed in the original inn has a view over the gardens toward Mount Washington, a kingsize platform bed and a large modern bathroom with tub and shower. At another visit, we enjoyed one of the ten large "porch rooms" in a rear addition, with decks or balconies overlooking the Ellis River and mountains. Our corner room had not one but two decks (on the rear and on the side), and the sound of the rippling river lulled us to sleep at night.

Six more rooms are available in two guest houses with contemporary cedar facades and more modern furnishings beside the river. One is called the Tree House for the tree growing through two of its porches. Its third floor contains a family suite for six, and the five bedrooms in the building can be private or inter-connected, making it good for groups.

A country breakfast is served (and available to the public from a menu). We liked the eggs benedict and the omelet of the day (onions, green peppers and cheese), the latter a huge plate bearing garlicky hash browns and whole wheat toast, more than one could finish. Afternoon tea produces a changing array of goodies, perhaps spice cake, peanut-butter squares and nut breads, served in the pleasant Pinkham Notch Pub. Aprés-ski nibbles are put out in winter.

(603) 383-6822 or (800) 537-9276. Fax (603) 383-6022. www.danaplace.com. Thirty-five rooms and suites with private baths. Doubles, $155 to $250, MAP. B&B when available, $135 to $185. Children and pets accepted in certain rooms.

The Crowe's Nest, Thorn Mountain Road, Box 427, Jackson 03846.

After twenty years of living and traveling around the world during his career with Coopers & Lybrand, innkeeping was a natural transition for Myles and Christine Crowe when they returned to the United States. Entertaining friends and visitors had become a weekly event. "I was already doing it," said Christine. "I just wasn't making a career of it."

The Crowes bought a private residence and three acres on a hillside just a stone's throw above Jackson Village and started a B&B with two guest rooms in 1998. Next they renovated the rear barn into the Lodge to add five more rooms, some with fireplaces, balconies and jacuzzi tubs. While Myles runs a financial-planning consulting business, Christine pampers B&B guests in an inn that exudes what she calls "refined country" charm.

The main house holds a living room full of prized possessions, books and magazines (plus a grand piano topped with family photos), a dining room and a sun porch upon which breakfast is served. Upstairs are a snug queensize bedroom and a larger, homey bedroom with a double and twin bed and a balcony from which, Christine claims, you can actually see the colors changing across the way on Iron Mountain during foliage season.

For their premier accommodations, the Crowes gutted the barn, which was built in 1922 entirely from wood cut on the property. They saved floors and rebuilt the interior from scratch. A two-story high foyer/common room with a gas fireplace leads to three rooms and two suites on two floors. The main floor holds a large premier room with kingsize bed and fireplace and two rooms with queen beds and sunporch sitting areas. The second floor consists of two premier suites with fireplaces, balconies and enclosed sun porches that double as sitting rooms or extra bedrooms for children. One with a kingsize bed has a double jacuzzi tub. The other with a queen bed has a single jacuzzi. Rooms are comfortably furnished with antiques from around the world – a horsehair rug from Argentina here, or a baby blanket chest from an obscure island in the Yellow Sea there. Original artworks from across Asia include a hand-calligraphed prayer written for Christine by a Bhuddist monk.

Breakfast is a three-course treat, as you'd expect from a woman who published a 270-page cookbook entitled *Friends and Family,* written for her career-bound daughters and distributed privately to those for whom the book was named. Specialties include florentine frittata and a baked apple pancake she calls a johnny jump-up. Pears in mascarpone custard, cheddar cheese and chive biscuits and specially blended chicory coffee might accompany.

(603) 383-8913 or (800) 511-8383. www.crowesnest.net. Seven rooms with private baths. Doubles, $105 to $175, foliage $135 to $225.

Carter Notch Inn, Carter Notch Road (Route 16B), Box 269, Jackson 03846.

During a varied career in retail and condominium management, Jim Dunwell always wanted to return to his roots as an innkeeper in Jackson. The opportunity arose in 1995 when the century-old owners' residence for the Eagle Mountain House hotel became available. Located apart from but in the shadow of the six-story resort hotel, "it had the cute cottage-style facade and size we wanted," said Jim. "But it was a mess inside."

Renaissance man Jim, a former Navy helicopter pilot with a hotel degree from Michigan, undertook six months of renovations and alterations, doing most of the work himself and losing 50 pounds in the process. Wife Lynda did the decorating and pitched in during time off from her retail store. They created a sparkling main floor with an oversize living room, a dream of a kitchen, and a dining room with a built-in sideboard and a table for eight overlooking the side porch. Jim added central air conditioning and retained the original elevator in a closet to lift construction materials for a rear deck with a hot tub off the second floor.

They added private baths for each for seven guest rooms on the second and third floors. A light and airy look prevails in comfortable rooms of various sizes and bed configurations, ranging from queensize to double with twin. A front room with bow window has a queen bed and day bed done in Laura Ashley floral prints, the comforters matching the window shams. Quilts, straw hats, dried flowers, oak and wicker are the norm. In 1999 Jim upgraded three rooms on the third floor. Two with fireplaces, double jacuzzi tubs and balconies are most in demand.

In the morning, he serves a full breakfast in the dining room or on the porch. Guests help themselves to the cold buffet set out on the built-in sideboard he made. Then he brings in "my choice" from a repertoire of twenty: grand marnier french toast one day, scrambled eggs with brie and mushrooms in puff pastry the next. "I do everything myself," he says matter-of-factly. "Even the chambermaiding, except on days when we have a total turnover."

Having overseen start-ups at the Village House and the Inn at Thorn Hill locally and the Eastman House in North Conway, he and Lynda knew what they wanted when they were ready for their own inn – "the best product at the lowest price in town." The location is quiet and the view from the wraparound front porch is of a golf course and mountains. "This is a perfect size for us to focus on our guests," says Jim.

(603) 383-9630 or (800) 794-9434. www.carternotchinn.com. Seven rooms with private baths. Doubles, $99 to $159 in summer, $129 to $199 in foliage. Two-night minimum on winter weekends. Closed two weeks in early November and month of April.

Carter Notch Inn is former owner's residence for Eagle Mountain House at right.

Eagle Mountain House, Carter Notch Road (Route 16B), Jackson 03846.

A picturesque row of high-backed rockers is lined up on the 380-foot-long veranda that's longer than a football field in front of this grand old hotel dating to 1879. The interior was restored in 1986 into a 92-room hotel and condominium center run by Colony Hotels & Resorts.

Although the establishment has an institutional-condo air, there's no denying the location – up in the mountains, facing a beautiful golf course and a colorful little pool and tennis court. Many rooms have sitting areas with sturdy mountain furniture, TVs hidden in the armoires and queensize beds. The rates are considered good value.

Off a rambling front lobby are the Eagle Landing Tavern (lunch is served here or poolside in busy seasons), a health club, the Veranda Cafe and a huge dining room. The fare ranges from baked haddock with lobster sauce and filet of ostrich to venison sauté and rack of lamb.

(603) 383-9111 or (800) 966-5779. Fax (603) 383-0854. www.eaglemt.com. Ninety-three rooms and suites with private baths. Rates, EP: doubles $89 to $159, suites $109 to $159. Foliage and holidays: doubles $129 to $169, suites $159 to $199. Two-night minimum peak periods and some weekends.

Entrées, $14.95 to $22.95. Dinner nightly from 6.

Dining Spots

The Inn at Thorn Hill, Thorn Hill Road, Jackson.

The acclaimed dining operation at Thorn Hill has been expanded following a fire that destroyed the inn and restaurant in 2002.

Rebuilt in 2003, the inn's main floor includes a dining room seating 60, a smaller private dining room, an expanded pub/lounge and a larger kitchen for chefs McKaella and Richard Schmitt, daughter and son-in-law of the owners. There also are a chef's table for eight in the kitchen for special culinary occasions, as well as a dining area in innkeeper Jim Cooper's new 2,500-bottle wine cellar.

Chef Richard offers three-course dinners for guests and the public, plus frequent wine dinners. His opening menu started with the likes of warm lobster vichysoisse, bacon-wrapped scallops on truffled polenta, Thai coconut-steamed mussels, and Nigerian prawn pad thai in sweet and sour sauce.

Main courses included lobster and scallop risotto in lobster cream with wasabi caviar, sake-marinated halibut on crispy soba noodles, braised pheasant with dried cherries, and lamb loin poached in olive oil with roasted garlic, harissa and port wine reduction. Richard's version of surf and turf – called "steak and potato two ways" – pairs Hawaiian tuna and New York sirloin.

Desserts are pastry chef McKaella's forte. Her repertoire is full of surprises: a honey-roasted pear with gorgonzola-dulce ice cream and a balsamic syrup, sautéed chioga beets with clotted cream, blood-orange gélee with a crème fraîche panna cotta, and frozen coconut mousse with a corn rum cake and grilled pineapple. Her "warm chocolate cake sundae" features root beer ice cream.

A tapas menu is offered in the lounge.

(603) 383-4242. Entrées, $22.95 to $29.95. Dinner nightly, 6 to 9. Lounge menu, 5 to 10.

Thompson House Eatery (T.H.E.), Route 16A at 16, Jackson.

An old red farmhouse dating from the early 1800s holds an expanded restaurant renowned for salads, sandwiches and original dishes, plus a gift gallery and recently T.H.E. Farm Stand.

At the heart of it all is chef-owner Larry Baima, lately joined by Hoke Wilson, the talented chef who had put the Inn at Thorn Hill's restaurant at the cutting edge of New Hampshire dining.

In the 27 years since it opened, T.H.E. has created many unusual dishes, some of them vegetarian. Sandwiches have flair: a crab cake BLT with herbed rémoulade sauce; turkey with asparagus spears, red onions, melted Swiss and Russian dressing; knockwurst marinated in beer and grilled with tomatoes, bacon, cheese and mustard. Ditto for salads: a spicy vegetable salsa piled on greens with kidney and garbanzo beans, shredded cheddar, sweet peppers, sprouts and more, garnished with taco chips, or cheese tortellini and rotini tossed with a sundried tomato and basil vinaigrette, served atop greens with artichoke hearts.

Dinner entrées often include "Baked Popeye," a notable spinach casserole with mushrooms, bacon and cheese, with an option of adding scallops. At one of our visits, the pork tenderloin piccata and a special of scallops with spinach, plum tomato sauce and ziti made a fine dinner by candlelight on one of the flower-bedecked rear patios flanked by huge pots of tomatoes and basil.

Swiss chocolate truffle, Dutch mocha ice cream and wild berry crumble are great desserts. Kona coffee and black raspberry are among the flavors of ice cream available at the soda fountain. There's a full liquor license as well.

Patrons eat in several small, rustic rooms and alcoves at tables covered with pastel floral cloths, in a glamorous skylit room (made by enclosing a former deck) with slate floors, chandeliers and hanging plants, or outside on canopied patios and a front deck.

(603) 383-9341. www.thompsonhouseeatery.com. Entrées, $18.95 to $24.95. Lunch, Wednesday-Sunday 11:30 to 3:30. Dinner nightly except Tuesday, 5:30 to 9 or 10. Closed in April and November.

Wildcat Inn and Tavern, Route 16A, Jackson.

Food is what the Wildcat Inn is known for. The old front porch had to be converted into dining space to handle the overflow from the original two dining rooms, as cozy and homey as can be. There's also outdoor dining at white wrought-iron tables scattered around the prize-winning gardens in back – as idyllic a setting for summer lunch as can be found in the area.

Sitting beneath a portrait of Abraham Lincoln, we savored an autumn lunch in a small, dark inner room with bare floors, windsor chairs, woven tablecloths and blue and white china. An exceptional cream of vegetable soup was chock full of fresh vegetables; that and half a reuben sandwich made a hearty meal. We also liked the delicate spinach and onion quiche, served with a garden salad dressed with creamy dill.

Dinner entrées range widely from lasagna to beef oscar. Wildcat chicken is served like cordon bleu but wrapped in puff pastry and topped with mustard sauce. Lobster lorenzo is the tavern's version of lobster fettuccine. You also can get mondo chicken with Italian sausage and apricot brandy, shrimp and scallop scampi and "the extravaganza" – shrimp, lobster and scallops sautéed with vegetables and served with linguini or rice pilaf.

The desserts slathered with whipped cream are memorable. Chocolate silk pie, mocha ice cream pie, frozen lemon pie and the Mount Washington brownie topped with vanilla ice cream, hot fudge sauce, whipped cream and crème de menthe are tempters.

Upstairs on the second and third floors, owners Marty and Pam Sweeney offer fourteen B&B guest rooms with private baths (doubles, $99 to $139).

(603) 383-4245 or (800) 228-4245. www.wildcattavern.com. Entrées, $16.95 to $23.95. Lunch, 11:30 to 3, daily in summer, weekends in winter. Dinner nightly, 6 to 9 or 10.

The Wentworth, Route 16A, Jackson.

Regional American cuisine is featured in this Victorian hotel's candlelit dining room, which boasts an AAA four-diamond award. The setting is elegant, enhanced with sponge-painted walls, upholstered French Provincial chairs and skirted tables with floral prints.

The concise dinner menu opens with appetizers like steamed vegetable wontons with Thai dipping sauce, New England fish cake with celeriac rémoulade, and "grilled and chilled" quail on baby greens. The mixed green salad with a cabernet vinaigrette is enlivened with haricots verts, kalamata olives and bermuda onion.

Typical entrées range from pan-seared halibut with tomato aioli to herb-crusted rack of lamb over roasted shallots and asparagus. The grilled salmon might come with bacon lardons and the pan-roasted chicken with mission fig jus and a cinnamon-roasted apple.

Dessert could be peaches and cream pie, Maine raspberry-chocolate cake and blueberry napoleons served on vanilla anglaise.

(603) 383-9700 or (800) 637-0013. Entrées, $21 to $27. Dinner nightly, 6 to 9 or 10. Closed in April and November.

The Rare Bear at The Bernerhof, Route 302, Glen.

The main floor of this turreted Victorian inn is a restaurant and pub leased to young chefs Scott and Teresa Stearns. They renamed the restaurant The Rare Bear, a bistro featuring contemporary American cuisine, and continue to direct the inn's A Taste of the Mountains cooking school on occasional weekends in late fall, winter and spring.

Dana Place Inn offers dining and lodging against a rural backdrop of river and mountains.

Formerly known for Swiss cuisine, the bistro still serves holdover specialties, such as wiener schnitzel and a wild mushroom and fontina cheese strudel. But the new chefs have broadened the horizons to appeal to a more adventurous clientele and offer a five-course tasting menu that changes nightly. Typical among their changing entrées are basil-crusted salmon with preserved lemon-tomato broth on a bed of couscous, cherry-glazed duck breast with a red wine-cherry chutney, and rosemary-crusted lamb with ratatouille sauce.

Appetizers include a sautéed crab cake with watermelon salsa, mussels steamed in a coconut-lemon grass broth, coriander-rubbed lamb skewers on a basmati rice salad and cucumber sauce, and a warm duck salad with a sherry-truffle vinaigrette. Among desserts are flourless chocolate cake with coconut sorbet and warm apple galette with caramel sauce and vanilla ice cream.

Meals are served in a warren of dining rooms amidst pine paneling, beamed ceilings, crisp white linens, a piano and a Swiss stove.

The casual, European-style Black Bear Pub has an oak-paneled bar and an appealing pub menu, with more than 90 beers from micro-breweries.

Upstairs, new Bernerhof owners George and June Phillips offer seven rooms and two suites for overnight guests for $79 to $175.

(603) 383-4414. www.bernerhofinn.com. Entrées, $22 to $29; pub, $11 to $18. Dinner nightly in season, from 6. Pub nightly, 5 to 9:30.

Dana Place Inn, Route 16, Jackson.

The three dining rooms here are country elegant with an accent of Danish contemporary. There's a cozy room with Scandinavian teak chairs. The skylit and airy lower level has large windows for viewing the spotlit gardens, crabapple trees and bird feeders outside, and a large addition offers round tables at bay windows with views of the river. White cloths, pink napkins and oil lamps provide a romantic atmosphere.

The continental/American dinner menu is quite extensive and, we've found over the years, consistently good. Among signature dishes are brandied apple chicken (featured in Bon Appétit magazine), lobster alfredo, and chicken and portobello mushrooms in puff pastry. We've enjoyed appetizers of Dungeness crab cakes, moist and succulent, a chock-full fish chowder and blackened carpaccio served over an extra-spicy mustard sauce. The house mimosa salads were so abundant they nearly spilled off their plates. Main dishes of beef tenderloin wrapped in applewood-smoked bacon, veal oscar and tournedos choron came with sugar snap peas and choice of creamy cheese potatoes or broccoli and pesto pilaf. Among desserts were a good strawberry tart, a refreshing lemon mousse with chambord sauce, cappuccino cheesecake and original sin chocolate cake, the last described by our server as "just fudge."

Wintertime lunches are popular. Up to 300 people a day come in for sustenance off the Ellis River Cross-Country Trail that ends here.

(603) 383-6822 or (800) 537-9276. Entrées, $15.95 to $22. Lunch in winter, 11 to 3. Dinner nightly, 6 to 9.

Red Parka Pub, Route 302, Glen.

This steakhouse is the perfect place for aprés-ski, from the "wild and crazy bar" with a wall of license plates from across the country (the more outrageous the better) to the "Skiboose," a 1914 flanger car that pushed snow off the railroad tracks and now is a cozy dining area for private parties. Somehow the rest of this vast place remains dark and intimate, done up in red and blue colors, red candles and ice cream-parlor chairs. A canopied patio provides outdoor dining in summer.

The menu, which comes inside the Red Parka Pub Tonight newspaper, features hearty steaks, barbecued ribs, teriyakis and combinations thereof, and homemade desserts like mud pie and Indian pudding. Start with nachos, Buffalo wings, spudskins or spare ribs. Snack from the soup and salad bar. Or go all out on prime rib or filet mignon. The full menu is available in the downstairs pub.

(603) 383-4344. www.redparkapub.com. Entrées, $12.95 to $23.50. Dinner nightly, 3:30 to 10.

Red Fox Bar & Grille, Route 16, Jackson.

Where the long-established Red Parka Pub is intimate and convivial, the Red Fox is all-new and, well, huge. It moved in 2003 from a not exactly small building beside the golf course in Jackson Village to a contemporary lodge-style facility across Route 16 from Jackson's covered bridge. "People sometimes come in asking for a room," advised the woman at the hostess station, who was keeping an eye on dining rooms seating more than 250 on all sides.

Besides size, "woodfire grilling" is the hallmark of the Red Fox. Seasoned woods fire the brick oven beside the main entry, from which come handmade pizzas in countless varieties.

Other specialties are pasta dishes, at least eight kinds. Also featured are "woodfire grill specialties," from grilled salmon to baby back ribs to filet mignon. There are sandwiches and burgers, too, as well as all-American appetizers such as chicken wings and nachos.

Prices are pleasantly down to earth, and the atmosphere is casual (booths in a front dining room, an enormous bar in another). A toy-filled kids' waiting room keeps youngsters occupied.

The Sunday jazz breakfast buffet is a bargain $5.95.

(603) 383-4949. Entrées, $11.95 to $15.50. Dinner, Monday-Friday from 4, Saturday from noon. Open Sunday from 7:30.

Diversions

Downhill Skiing. Wildcat, looming across Pinkham Notch from Mount Washington, is a big mountain with plenty of challenge, a 2,112-foot vertical drop from its 4,100-foot summit, top-to-bottom snowmaking, five chairlifts and a gondola. **Black Mountain** is half its height and far smaller in scope, but its sunny southerly exposure and low-key, self-contained nature make it particularly good for families. Nearby are **Attitash** in Bartlett and **Mount Cranmore** in North Conway. **Tuckerman Ravine** on Mount Washington is where the hardy ski when the snows elsewhere have long since melted, if they're up to the climb (a 1,500-foot vertical rise for a half-mile run down).

Hikes and Drives. For more than a century, visitors have been "strolling the mile," a mile-long village loop around Jackson. The "Village Mile" is one of nine walks and hikes outlined in a handy guide published by the Jackson Resort Association. A good overview is offered by the Five-Mile Circuit Drive up Route 16B into the mountains east of Jackson, a loop worth driving both directions for different perspectives. Look for spectacular glimpses of Mount Washington, and stop for a picnic, a swim or a stroll through the picturesque cascades called Jackson Falls, part of the Wildcat River just above the village.

Shopping. It's no surprise that Jackson's biggest store remains the **Jack Frost Shop,** a landmark that's a serious ski shop as well as a fine apparel store with a few gift items. Espresso, cappuccino and deli items are among the offerings at **As You Like It** and the **Village Bistro & Grocer.** Other than a couple of small galleries and antiques shops, "downtown" Jackson consists of a post office, a town hall, the Jackson Community Church and the tiny red 1901 Jackson Library, designed by famed architect Stanford White, open Tuesdays from 10 to 4 and Thursdays from 10 to 4 and 7 to 9. For a more rigorous shopping foray, head down the valley to North Conway and its ever-expanding factory outlet centers.

Other Attractions. Heritage-New Hampshire and **Storyland** are side-by-side destinations, of interest particularly to families. The former lets visitors walk through stage sets in which dioramas, costumed guides and talking figures depict 30 events in state history. Storyland is a fairytale village with buildings, themed rides and performances for children. Nearby is the **Grand Manor,** a museum of antique automobiles. Children and non-skiers also enjoy riding the **Wildcat Gondola,** a 25-minute round trip to the summit looking across to Mount Washington.

Extra-Special

Jackson Ski Touring Foundation, Route 16A, Jackson.

Jackson is considered the best place in the East and one of the four best places in the world for cross-country skiing. That's due in large part to the efforts of the non-profit Jackson Ski Touring Foundation, founded in 1972 and now offering 100 miles of well-groomed and marked trails starting in the village of Jackson and heading across public and private lands into the White Mountain National Forest. They interlace the village and link restaurants and inns, as well as connecting with 40 miles of Appalachian Mountain Club trails in Pinkham Notch. It's possible for cross-country skiers to take the gondola to the summit of Wildcat and tour downhill via a twelve-mile trail to the village of Jackson 3,200 feet below.

(603) 383-9355 or (800) 927-6697. www.jacksonxc.org. Open daily in winter, 8 to 4:30.

Historic structures are among visitor attractions at Strawbery Banke.

Portsmouth, N.H.

A Lively Past and Present

Settled in 1623, the Portsmouth area ranks as the third oldest in the country after Jamestown and Plymouth. In many ways it looks it. The early Colonial houses hugging the narrow streets and the busy riverfront concede little to modernity.

This is no Jamestown or Plymouth, nor is it a Newport, a similarly sized and situated community with which it occasionally is compared. The city has only one large hotel, its thriving downtown blessedly few chain stores or trendy boutiques, its residents little sense of elitism. What it does have is a patina of living and working history, a pride in its past and present, and a noticeable joie de vivre.

The sense of history is everywhere, from the famed restoration called Strawbery Banke to the ancient structures dating back to the 17th century tucked here and there all across town. Named for the profusion of wild berries found on the shores by the English settlers, Strawbery Banke is a living museum of more than 45 historic buildings at the edge of downtown.

Portsmouth's pride in past and present evidences itself in the six museum homes of the Historic Portsmouth Trail and the creative reuse of old buildings around Market Square and on The Hill.

You can sense Portsmouth's joie de vivre in its flourishing restaurants (good new ones pop up every year). Their number and scope are far beyond the resources of most cities of 26,000 and give it claim to the title, "Restaurant Capital of New England." You can see it in its lively Seacoast Repertory Theater and new Music Hall. You can feel it in its Prescott Park Arts Festival, the Ceres Street Crafts Fair, the Seacoast Jazz Festival. The Seacoast is now the E-Coast in local lingo. All this helped place it on Cosmopolitan magazine's list of "Ten Hot Cities to Consider" for young professionals.

Happily, Portsmouth retains its historic sense of scale. It is an enclave of antiquity along the tidal Piscataqua River, four miles inland from the Atlantic. The Portsmouth Navy Yard is across the river in Kittery, Me. The Pease Air Force Base is west toward Dover. The shopping centers and fast-food strips are out in Newington. The beach action is down in Rye and Hampton. Many tourists stay at motels near the Portsmouth Circle.

While travelers pass by on the New Hampshire Turnpike, Air Force jets stream overhead, and tugboats and ocean vessels ply the river to and from the sea, Portsmouth goes its merry, historic and vibrant way.

Inn Spots

Martin Hill Inn, 404 Islington St., Portsmouth 03801.

The first B&B in Portsmouth (1978), the Martin Hill was acquired in 1983 by Jane and Paul Harnden, who with another couple were visiting their favorite town from Nashua, where they lived. "We had hardly heard of bed and breakfast," says Jane, "but during breakfast at the inn the owners said they would like to sell in about three years and, I thought, this is me."

It turned out that medical problems forced the owners to sell that summer, and since then the Harndens have been the friendly innkeepers who dispense gobs of information about the many restaurants in town, historic attractions and whatnot, as well as cooking delicious breakfasts and dispatching every innkeeping task themselves, without staff. "We still air-dry our sheets and iron the pillowcases while watching the TV news," says Jane. As innkeepers go, the Harndens are among the most dedicated we know.

Their handsome yellow house, built in 1820, comes with a deep and nicely landscaped back yard where 400 plants thrive and where afternoon tea is served in season. The yard was featured one year in the Unitarian Church's annual pocket garden tour. The Harndens since have installed cedar fencing around the property and converted a courtyard into an illuminated water garden.

Although the inn lacks a common room inside, guests have plenty of room to spread out in the three spacious guest rooms in the main inn, plus a room and three suites in the adjacent Guest House.

The downstairs front room, called the Library, is in shades of rose and holds two pineapple poster beds, a queen and a twin. Upstairs, the Master Bedroom, in white and Wedgwood blue, has a queensize canopy bed and oriental rugs on the wide-board floors. The Greenhouse Suite in the spiffy side guest house contains a small solarium furnished in wicker looking onto the water garden, rattan furniture in an inside sitting room and a queensize bedroom with full bath. Balloon curtains frame the windows in the Green Room, which has a small sitting room, an antique tub with a hand-held shower, and a queensize iron and brass bed that's so frilly it reminds Jane of a big crib. All rooms have modern baths, loveseats or comfortable chairs, good reading lamps, writing tables, armoires, and nice touches like potpourri in china teacups and the inn's own wildflower glycerin soaps.

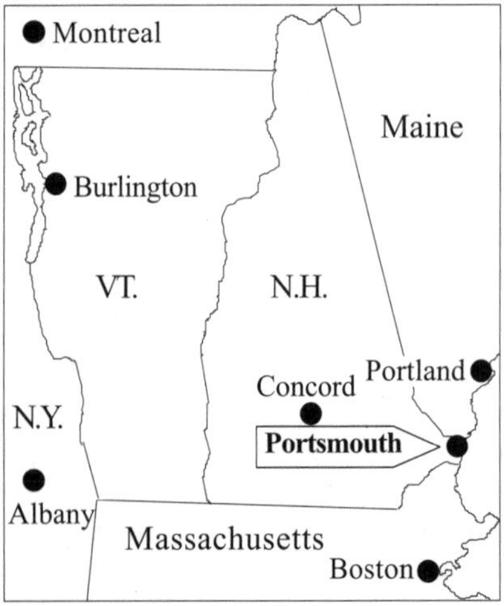

Breakfast is served on a gleaming mahogany table in the antiques-filled dining room, whose walls display three coordinated English wallpapers and paints. Orange juice might be followed

Martin Hill Inn occupies handsome 1820 house.

by Jane's scrumptious baked apple, the core filled with brown sugar. Paul makes dynamite french toast with Italian sourdough bread, slathered with almonds and accompanied by Canadian bacon and homemade cranberry relish. Our scrambled eggs with cheese and chervil were served with cranberry bread, and the coffee pot was bottomless. It's a great time for guests to compare notes on the restaurants they visited the night before and to plan the day with the help of Paul, who can even plot you out a trip up to Canada and back. Clearly, the Harndens still relish their role as innkeepers and go out of their way to be helpful and accommodating.

(603) 436-2287. www.martinhillinn.com. Four rooms and three suites with private baths. July-October, doubles $125 to $145. Rest of year: $98 to $110. Children over 12.

The Governor's House, 32 Miller Ave., Portsmouth 03801.

There is artistry here, from the framed doilies made by the current owner's grandmother displayed suavely on the living room walls to the murals hand-painted on the tiles of the guest bathrooms. And there are contemporary amenities: Bose radios and TV/DVD players in the guest bedrooms for playing selections from the innkeepers' vast CD and DVD library, the finest bedding, evening wine and cheese, personalized breakfasts and an outdoor hot tub. There's even a lighted backyard tennis court.

This stately 1917 white Georgian Colonial was the home from 1930 to 1964 of former Gov. Charles Dale, a mayor and state senator who loved Portsmouth so much that he commuted to Concord during his term as governor. It's now the home of Bob Chaffee and Barbara Trimble, Portsmouth residents who reopened the B&B in 2002 after its initial reign in the mid-1990s. "We spent the winter shopping," Bob said after they purchased and had to furnish what had served as a private residence in the interim. They targeted "the upper-end market" and furnished accordingly,

Stately white Georgian Colonial is now the Governor's House B&B.

even bringing back the former owner-innkeeper, local artist Nancy Grossman, to hand-paint a carpet on the floor of the front section of the side sun porch.

The stage is set in the elegant living room, which the new innkeepers painted dark blue with white trim. One entire wall and another large area above the fireplace are adorned with the intricate lace doilies crocheted by Barbara's grandmother years ago in Czechoslovakia. The front end of the living room holds a dining table for eight and the back section contains the governor's grand piano as it has for 70 years – about the only item that came with the house. Comfortable seating is available in the rest of the room and on the adjacent sun porch.

More artistic touches unfold, primarily in the bathrooms. A mural of the Lady and the Peacock graces the walls of the dual-head shower for two in the front-corner Peacock Room, decorated in Art Nouveau style. A life-size mermaid on the shower wall carries out the nautical theme in the Captain's Room, where a lace tablecloth made by aforementioned grandmother – chosen because of its resemblance to a fishnet – is unfurled above the unusual solid cherry and Italian leather bed. Around the double whirlpool tub in the Prescott Room are lovebirds that the artist called distelfinks, the Pennsylvania Dutch double-headed symbol of love, with phrases for affection written in French.

The Prescott is the largest and fanciest of the four guest rooms, each with an antique queensize bed dressed in Frette linens and down comforter. It has a high canopied poster bed and an antique fainting couch. More masculine is the rear Governor's Room, with deep mauve walls, a leather loveseat, handsome armoire and a quarter canopy ingeniously masking the radiator behind the mahogany sleigh bed. A butler painted on the wall of the shower is "at the governor's service."

At all guests' service in the upstairs foyer is an unusually well-stocked "Did You Forget?" closet. Opposite is an alcove with a guest refrigerator for complimentary beverages and hot and cold spring water for 24-hour coffee and tea service. Off the foyer is a cozy library holding a guest computer and, among others, the owners' extensive DVD collection of Academy Award-winning movies of the last 50 years.

Breakfast is delivered at the time and place of the guests' choosing from a check-off menu placed in each guest room. It offers a selection of fruit, baked goods, cereal and perhaps broccoli quiche.

In season, the breakfast setting of choice is the leafy patio, enveloped by rhododendrons overlooking the tennis court in the hidden back yard.

(603) 431-6546 or (866) 427-5140. Fax (603) 427-5145. www.governors-house.com. Doubles, $195 to $235 May-October, $145 to $205 rest of year. Children over 14.

Sise Inn, 40 Court St., Portsmouth 03801.

The first United States branch of a Canadian-based group called Someplace(s) Different Ltd., this is a fine operation. The company took the original Queen Anne home built in 1881 for the John E. Sise family, remodeled it with great taste and put on a large rear addition that blends in very well. Walk in the front door past the stained-glass windows on either side, gaze at the rich and abundant butternut and oak throughout, marvel at the graceful staircase and three-story-high foyer, peek into the sumptuous living room and you're apt to say, as its marketing director did upon first seeing it, "this is the real Portsmouth."

Rooms and suites on three floors and in a carriage house vary in bed configuration, size and decor. All are elegantly furnished in antiques and period reproductions with striking window treatments and vivid wallpapers. Geared to the business traveler, they have queen or twin beds, vanities outside the bathrooms (the larger of which contain whirlpool baths), writing desks, clock radios, telephones, and remote-control television and VCRs, often hidden in armoires. Some have sitting areas. Businessmen must like to watch TV in bed, for in many of the rooms we saw the TV wasn't visible from the chairs or, as is so often the case, the single chair. Windows that open, English herbal toiletries and mints on the pillow may compensate for the occasional lack of places to sit.

Or you can sit in the stylish main-floor living room, very much like an English library with several conversation areas and fresh flowers all around.

A help-yourself breakfast of fruits, juices, yogurt, cheese, cereals, granola, bagels, toasting breads and all kinds of preserves and honey is available amidst much ornate wood in the dining room.

The lower floor, notable for an antique English phone booth in the hallway, contains function rooms. A modern elevator shuttles guests between floors.

(603) 433-1200 or (877) 747-3466. Twenty-five rooms and nine suites with private baths. Mid-May through October: doubles $189, suites $229 to $269. Rest of year: doubles $125, suites $159 to $199.

The Inn at Strawbery Banke, 314 Court St., Portsmouth 03801.

You can't stay much closer to Strawbery Banke than this 1800 ship captain's house situated right up against the street, as so many in Portsmouth are. It also shows its age, but it's gradually getting improvements over the years.

All seven air-conditioned guest rooms come with private baths, although one is in the hall (and one in the attic suite is open to the room). Two rooms on the main floor share a common room. Strawberry stenciling, strawberry comforters and strawberry candies on the pillows accent the prevailing green and white color scheme here. More rooms go off an upstairs common room. One, done up in blues, has inside Indian shutters, two rattan chairs and pineapple stenciling. Another with windows on three sides contains a double and a single bed and three ice-cream-parlor chairs around a glass table. The aforementioned attic suite, with the open w.c. and shower added in the corner, must be for young, short people. It's up steep stairs and we had to duck to avoid the roof as we entered the sleeping alcove.

Innkeeper Sally Glover O'Donnell, who grew up in the family that formerly ran the Colby Hill Inn in Henniker, serves a full breakfast in a skylit breakfast room with an abundance of hanging plants. The main course at our visit was sourdough blueberry pancakes with sausages, supplemented by oatmeal, cold cereals and homemade pastries. The room looks onto a strawberry patch, bird feeders and the trellised rose garden of the historic Governor Langdon House just behind. Sally keeps cookie jars stocked for afternoon or evening snacks in the two cozy common rooms, both outfitted with television sets.

(603) 436-7242 or (800) 428-3933. www.innatstrawberybanke.com. Seven rooms with private baths. Doubles, $145 to $150 mid-May through October, $100 to $115 rest of year.

The Inn at Christian Shore, 335 Maplewood Ave., Portsmouth 03801.

An abundance of antiques, an inviting dining room with a fireplace, and rather lavishly decorated, air-conditioned guest rooms with television are attractions in this 1800 Federal house, located in the historic Christian Shore area.

Across from the Jackson House, Portsmouth's oldest, this structure was renovated and redecorated in 1978 by three antiques dealers, who sold recently to Mariaelena Koopman.

Breakfast table at Inn at Christian Shore.

In the main entry hall is a desk with baskets of candies and nuts, a grandfather clock and an etched-glass light.

The first and second floors contain five guest rooms, three with queensize beds. The other two rooms have double beds. Two rooms have fireplaces. All contain handsome furnishings, antiques, crocheted afghans and TVs.

A harvest table dominates the rough-hewn dining room, the heart of the house with its low beamed ceiling and large brick fireplace. Three smaller dining tables with upholstered wing chairs are beside windows on the sides. Accessories here include textiles from around the world, Argentine silver, pre-Columbian ceramics, contemporary paintings and African art.

A full breakfast is served by the European-born innkeeper. Omelets, a Spanish tortilla, caramelized french toast, bagels and lox, and even porridge with "a tot of whiskey" could be the fare. "Excellent breakfast – gracious hostess" was the latest entry in the guest book at a recent visit.

Brick structure housing Portsmouth Harbor Inn & Spa faces city waterfront.

(603) 431-6770. Fax (603) 431-7743. www.portsmouthnh.com/christianshore. Five rooms with private baths. Doubles, $100 to $120 mid-May through October, $95 to $100 rest of year. No children.

Portsmouth Harbor Inn & Spa, 6 Water St., Kittery, Me. 03904.

Just across the Piscataqua River in Kittery is this small establishment with a glimpse of the Portsmouth waterfront, which is within walking distance across the Memorial Bridge.

The 1889 Italianate New England structure has been gradually transformed from a two-family house. New Englanders Paula and Tim Miller returned in 2002 from a decade in separate restaurant and hospitality ventures in Charleston, S.C., to take over the B&B section earlier known as the Gundalow Inn. They quickly added a day spa in the former innkeepers' quarters in the attached barn.

The spa is clearly the Millers' priority. They offer numerous spa services and packages as their principal business and, secondarily, to fill the B&B rooms. While Paula oversees the spa, Tim handles the B&B.

Four of the five guest rooms offer views of the waterfront. All are named after gundalows (a corruption of the word gondolas), the 250-year-old flat-bottom boats with sails that plied the Piscataqua and are believed to have transported the bricks for the house downriver from Dover.

Ten-foot-high ceilings and Victorian period antiques are the rule in the second-floor rooms, one of which has windows on three sides. The bathroom in the Minx room is big enough to include both a chair and a closet. The corner Valora room, done up in bold red and black toile, boasts an antique writing desk. A curved stairway beneath a skylight leads past a plant-filled shelf to the third floor, where two guest rooms with deep clawfoot soaking tubs afford the best views of the river and of Portsmouth. We like the Royal George, which has a kingsize sleigh bed, two wicker chairs and a table beneath a skylight, an armoire, gray carpeting and cheery yellow walls. Stained-glass interior windows enhance those bathrooms without outside windows. Room amenities include TV/VCRs, hair dryers and bottled water.

Guests enjoy homemade cookies or dessert bars in a large, comfortable parlor, where breakfast is served at a table for ten. Port and sherry are put out here in the evening. A small front porch furnished in wicker catches a view of the river, as does a courtyard terrace with a gurgling fountain between the B&B and the spa.

Tim handles the breakfast chores with aplomb. The meal might begin with a fruit and granola parfait and honey-nut buns with mascarpone cheese. Baked orange-cardamom french toast was the main course the day of our visit.

(207) 439-4040. Fax (207) 438-9286. www.innatportsmouth.com. Five rooms with private baths. Doubles, $145 to $210 May-October, $110 to $145 rest of year.

The Bow Street Inn, 121 Bow St., Portsmouth 03801.

A succession of owners continues to improve this downtown riverfront establishment, which really is a cross between a motel and a small hotel. It occupies the second floor of a restored four-story brick brewery warehouse that also houses condominiums, the Seacoast Repertory Theatre and a café.

Access to the inn is by buzzer and then up an elevator. Guest rooms go off either side of a center hallway. The views are of rooftops or the street, because the condominium blocks the view of the river except from Room 6. Rather small, the rooms are furnished simply but attractively in light pastel colors with queensize brass beds (except for one with a king/twins), thick carpeting, cable TV, telephones and a single chair. One room, billed as a mini-suite for extended stays, contains a sofa and small dining table

Juice, cereal, yogurt, muffins, bagels and breads for toasting are put out in a pleasant brick dining room with three tables and a small refrigerator for guests' use. The owner "tries to make people feel at home," said one of the assistants on duty at our visit. Guest get free parking in the municipal garage on Hanover Street.

(603) 431-7760. Fax (603) 433-1680. www.bowstreetinn.com. Ten rooms with private baths. Doubles, $135 to $175 May-October, $120 to $155 rest of year.

Wentworth by the Sea, 588 Wentworth Road, New Castle 03854.

Perhaps no grand oceanfront hotel in New England was better known than the storied Wentworth, poised on a rise at the tip of the island of New Castle and host to the rich and famous for more than a century.

Closed in 1982 and its future clouded by a series of owners, the forlorn looking wooden structure with the million-dollar location was the first hotel placed on the National Trust for Historical Preservation's list of America's Eleven Most Endangered Places in 1996. It was saved from the wreckers' ball in 1997 by local investors, led by the developer who held the franchise for three Marriott properties in the Portsmouth area.

Six years and many millions of dollars later, the reconstructed hotel reopened in 2003 as a Marriott resort and spa. Care was taken to preserve the Wentworth's exterior look and heritage, but the interior reflects typical Marriott motifs and amenities rather than those of the individualized, family-owned hotel it once was.

Returning guests hardly recognize the property, now fronted by residential development where open lawns had been. The sparkling-white hotel with red roof appears squeezed between new front and back access roads, with showy landscaping and a gazebo providing lush pastoral relief.

Wentworth by the Sea hotel looms behind Little Harbor Marina at water's edge.

The elongated, four-story hotel contains 143 guest rooms, some with french doors onto miniscule balconies facing the harbor and ocean in front and the meandering Piscataqua River in back – those on the third floor are most in demand. Rooms generally are on the small side, but are equipped with marble baths and the usual Marriott attributes.

The best rooms (and views) were to be in eighteen bi-level suites at water's edge in the Little Harbor Marina. Formerly called the "Ship Building" for its vague resemblance to early ocean liners, the four-story building is a short hike downhill from the hotel. Its suites with one or two bedrooms, full kitchens, sitting/dining areas and private balconies were "destined to be *the* place to stay at the Wentworth," according to pre-opening publicity.

Three meals a day are served in two side-by-side dining rooms, one with pillars and a restored domed ceiling. Chef Daniel Dumont's contemporary, seafood-oriented menu offered fifteen entrées ($19 to $32) from tournedos of yellowfin tuna and smoky bacon-crusted "filet mignon" of lobster to beef two ways (ginger-braised short ribs and grilled sirloin) and grilled rack of pine nut-crusted lamb. Across the street in the marina, **Latitudes** offers informal waterfront dining for lunch and dinner.

Resort activities include a full-service spa, tennis and guest access to the Wentworth by the Sea Country Club and Marina.

(603) 422-7322 or (866) 240-6313. Fax (603) 422-7329. www.wentworth.com. One hundred forty-three rooms and eighteen suites. Doubles, $200 to $400. Suites, $500 up.

Dining Spots

Anthony Alberto's, 59 Penhallow St., Portsmouth.

A local institution hidden in the Custom House Cellar, this is generally considered the finest restaurant in a city of many. Tod Alberto and Massimo Morgia, who had been associated with the late Ponte Vecchio in nearby New Castle, renovated the space and named it after Tod's father.

It's elegant, dark and grotto-like with stone and brick walls, arches, exposed beams on the ceiling and oriental rugs on the slate floors. Aqua upholstered chairs, fanned napkins and yellow-over-beige tablecloths add an earthy Mediterranean look. The service and attention to detail are said to be the best in town.

The menu is high Italian, as in pan-seared spicy sea bass with tomato coulis, seared sea scallops with saffron beurre blanc, grilled veal chop with braised grape and balsamic sauce, grilled breast of duck in a port wine and ginger reduction, and grilled filet mignon with mushroom demi-glace over a gorgonzola crostini. Typical starters are tuna tartare, steamed mussels in a smoked gouda broth, potato blini with smoked salmon and caviar, and pan-roasted quail stuffed with figs and prosciutto and served with black truffle risotto. Desserts include bananas flambé, tiramisu and crème caramel.

(603) 436-4000. www.anthonyalbertos.com. Entrées, $17.95 to $29.95. Dinner, Monday-Saturday 5 to 9:30 or 10:30.

Pesce Blue, 103 Congress St., Portsmouth.

Two sometime-Californians with New England aspirations fortuitously got together to launch Portsmouth's hottest restaurant in 2002.

Joachim Sandbichler, an Austrian who spent many years in Italy, vacationed in the area while managing restaurants in California and found a potential restaurant site in the former Little Professor bookstore. He found a chef in Mark Segal, who had grown up in his family's restaurant on the grounds of the Oakdale Theater in Wallingford, Conn., before heading to California to work with top Los Angeles chefs.

Mark missed New England, learned of the Portsmouth project on the Internet, and flew east to cook an audition dinner. He got the job, and together the partners created an Italian seafood grill with a California twist – so successfully that shortly after opening, they were invited to prepare dinner at the James Beard House in New York.

Pesce Blue's 70-seat space is ultra-dramatic: long, narrow and mod, a palette of blacks, taupes and beiges. Falling curtains partially screen cinder-block walls. Pots of angular flowers and plants soar skyward in window alcoves and atop the bar. Varied lamp spheres dangle from the high ceiling.

It's a contemporary look that "puts the emphasis on the food," says chef Mark. And the food draws accolades from Boston reviewers, one of whom declared it to be "the best reason to drive 65 miles for a plate of fish."

Make that perhaps ten plates of fish, the choices changing daily. You might find sautéed Icelandic char with lemon-caper emulsion, sautéed Eastern skate with orange-ginger sauce or grilled bluefin tuna with balsamic essence. Some go for the house specialty, mixed grill – an assortment of five of the day's freshest with grilled vegetables. Others go for "the whole thing" – another specialty of crispy whole local mackerel, perhaps, or Mediterranean branzino (sea bass), salt-crusted and grilled or oven roasted.

The treats begin with such appetizers as bluefin tuna tartare, swordfish carpaccio, a salad of grilled octopus and a special of grilled Greek sardines with charred rapini and herb-tomato relish. Eight seafood pastas and risottos are available as small plates or large.

The night's menu holds only two items called "landfood," usually pan-roasted "flattened" chicken and grilled ribeye steak alla fiorentina.

Desserts include a selection of sorbets, Italian crêpes and crème brûlée served with fresh berries.

(603) 430-7766. www.pesceblue.com. Entrées, $18.50 to $26.50. Lunch, Monday-Friday 11:45 to 2. Dinner nightly, 5 to 9:30 or 10.

Contemporary seafood fare is featured in dramatic dining room at Pesce Blue.

Victory 96 State Street, 96 State St., Portsmouth.

Their wives' local connections lured two more restaurateurs to Portsmouth for this ambitious start-up in 2003.

Chef Duncan Boyd and manager George Frangos worked together in Washington, D.C., restaurants before restoring the three-story brick Federal townhouse known for more than 50 years as the home of Victory Spa Diner and later as the Victory Antiques shop.

Their restaurant on two floors is a beauty, with brick walls and tables spaced well apart from which to enjoy the glow from six fireplaces. There's a casual setting near the bar on the main floor and a more formal setting upstairs. The tables were made with planks from the wide-board floors found in the building's attic during the restoration.

A Greek immigrant chose the name for the diner in the waning days of World War II to support his new American countrymen. The name was a natural for chef Duncan to reflect New England seasonal cuisine, some of it influenced by immigrant groups that settled in the area.

A typical menu might begin with seared foie gras with poached quince, steamed mussels with chorizo sausage and sweet peppers, and a salad of seared duck breast and frisée with brandied peach vinaigrette.

Main courses range from seared dayboat scallops with sage brown butter and pan-roasted cod in native shrimp broth to hunter-style rabbit and grilled loin of beef with pinot noir sauce. The "Victory mac n' cheese" teams lobster with Vermont cheddar, aged gruyère, crimini mushrooms and roasted red peppers.

Dessert could be a selection of farmstead cheeses, peach upside-down cake with buttermilk ice cream or warm chocolate soufflé cake with caramel anglaise.

(603) 766-0960. www.96statestreet.com. Entrées, $18 to $26. Dinner, Tuesday-Sunday 5:30 to 10.

43° North, 75 Pleasant St., Portsmouth.

A chef who made Anthony Alberto's one of the best restaurants in Portsmouth left to open his own restaurant in the space formerly known as The Grotto. Geno Gulotta christened it a kitchen and wine bar and quickly showed his stuff as one of the best chefs in town.

His wife, whose father is a senior government official in Budapest, provided some of the elegant Hungarian antique sideboards and paintings that lend a distinctly continental feel to the handsome dining room.

The contemporary international menu is categorized by small plates and bowls, greens, and large plates and bowls. Among the former are crisp duck spring rolls and a pan-seared Maine crab cake with slivered endive and watercress salad, both of which come with the highest recommendation. Bigger options include pumpkin seed-crusted haddock with tomato-balsamic syrup, chile-spiced ahi tuna steak with sweet and sour plum sauce, pan-seared medallions of veal and stilton-glazed filet mignon, each with its novel presentation and accompaniments. A mixed grill of elk chop and ostrich was a hit at a recent visit.

The changing desserts are as interesting as the rest of the fare.

(603) 430-0225. www.fortythreenorth.com. Entrées, $19 to $28. Dinner, Monday-Saturday from 5.

Lindbergh's Crossing, 29 Ceres St., Portsmouth.

This bistro and raw bar with obscure references to Charles Lindbergh is across the street from the harbor in a space long occupied by the famed Blue Strawbery, Portsmouth's first gourmet restaurant. A propeller hangs on one wall of the brick and beamed downstairs bistro, site of widely acclaimed meals under its previous incarnation. A representation of Lindbergh's flight across the Atlantic flanks the stairway to the casual upstairs wine bar, where dinner also is available and no reservations are taken.

Jeffrey Tenner, the California-trained chef and co-owner, receives high marks for his contemporary Mediterranean fare, which is rooted in country French but ranges from Greece to North Africa. Expect eclectic variety in such main courses as paella, roasted cornish hen with cinnamon couscous and a chunky green olive sauce, pork roulade of cranberries, spinach and goat cheese with a pomegranate demi-glace, and pan-seared monkfish with a black olive, rock shrimp and red potato ragoût. How about a pumpkin and fig risotto with goat cheese and cashew baked stuffed apple?

The popular bistro steak sandwich comes with aged brie, red potatoes and a roasted shallot relish.

Typical starters are mussels marinière, escargots with raclette, seared foie gras on cornbread, and a plate of cheeses served with pistachio-dusted dates. Desserts are a signature "medium rare chocolate cake" (whose center is described as the consistency of chocolate pudding), almond-crusted cheesecake and crème brûlée. Espresso and cappuccino are finishing touches.

(603) 431-0887. www.lindberghscrossing.com. Entrées, $16 to $27. Dinner nightly, from 5:30. Wine bar from 4.

Jumpin' Jay's Fish Café, 150 Congress St., Portsmouth.

Fresh seafood from around the country is featured at this mod place that started small in 2000 and quickly quadrupled in size. Jay McSharry, the 30-something co-owner with chef John Harrington, named it to convey a lively and unpretentious atmosphere.

"Fish with an attitude" is how Jay describes the fare. One day's catch was yellowfin tuna from Florida, halibut from Washington, rainbow trout from Idaho and mahi mahi from Florida. Each came with a choice of sauces, among them olive tapenade, lobster velouté and spicy poblano- chipotle coulis. Lobster risotto is a signature dish. Others are haddock piccata and jonah crab and vegetable lasagna. Each night, you can order chicken, mussels, scallops or shrimp served scampi or provençal style over linguini.

Appetizers run a wide range from smoked bluefish pâté to a puff pastry poor boy and Maine crab cake with house aioli. Salads could be sashimi tuna with avocado and caesar with grilled fish.

Well spaced white tables with black chairs are situated beneath string lights in a mod red and white, high-tech setting. A circular, stainless steel bar is in the center.

Since opening his seafood place, Jay has opened three more downtown restaurants, each with a working chef as partner and serving different audiences: Radicci, almost next door, for northern Italian; Dos Amigos, and the Red Door.

(603) 766-3474. www.jumpinjays.com. Entrées, $13.95 to $22.95. Dinner, Monday-Thursday 5:30 to 9 (to 9:30 in summer), Friday and Saturday 5 to 10, Sunday 5 to 9.

The Wellington Room, 67 Bow St., Portsmouth.

A waterfront setting is enjoyed by diners in this small restaurant backing up to the river. Also enjoyed is some of the best food in town – and, an added fillip, a British-style afternoon tea.

New Zealand-born chef-owner David Robinson apprenticed in restaurants in Australia, Europe, Cincinnati and Boston before taking over the intimate space formerly occupied by the Italian-themed Porto Bello in 2002. Its 38-seat dining room, hidden from view above and behind a downtown storefront, is the right size for his one-man show.

Thanks to his global travels, his creative American cuisine bears Asian, Italian and French accents. Expect entrées such as grilled Chilean sea bass on Russian fingerling potatoes with port wine-mushroom sauce, oven-roasted haddock with chardonnay-tomato broth, roasted duck breast with a watercress and Australian shiraz reduction, and, of course, New Zealand rack of lamb, with minted blackberry-honey drizzle.

Starters include a mushroom and cheese crêpe, pan-seared foie gras and szechuan peppercorn-crusted tuna with a sesame-seaweed salad.

Afternoon tea service is the chef's tribute to his late British grandmother, for whom a proper British tea was a ritual. The à-la-carte menu offers nine loose-leaf teas from around the world as well as scones with Devonshire cream, fruit tarts, and a choice among six elegant tea sandwiches.

The most romantic tables in the house are a pair of deuces in an alcove, with windows onto the harbor.

(603) 431- 2989. www.thewellingtonroom.com. Entrées, $17 to $26. Tea, Wednesday-Sunday 3:30 to 5. Dinner, Wednesday-Sunday 5 to 9:30.

Café Mirabelle, 64 Bridge St., Portsmouth.

French chef Stephan Mayeux and his wife Chris opened this casual gourmet restaurant in the former Fish Shanty. Now very un-shantyish, it's crisp and contemporary on two floors. There are a few tables for dining downstairs in a café near the bar.

Upstairs is a cathedral-ceilinged room with beams and interesting angles, mission-style chairs at burgundy-linened tables up against tall windows, shelves of country artifacts along sand-colored walls and twinkling lights on ficus trees.

Stephan offers pure country French cuisine, unsullied by contemporary conceits. Bouillabaisse and chicken mirabelle (with prosciutto, lobster and asparagus) are menu fixtures. Also look for things like salmon épernay with scallops in a champagne and shallot-basil cream sauce, roasted pork tenderloin, magret of duck roasted in a tangy orange-cider-vinegar sauce and beef alexander roasted with shrimp and goat cheese in a zinfandel demi- glace.

Start with baked brie with walnuts and thyme in puff pastry, a mushroom crepe or coquilles St. Jacques. Finish with a profiterole, chocolate charlotte with raspberry coulis, homemade sorbet or a pear-almond tart with crème anglaise.

(603) 430-9301. Entrées, $16.95 to $27.95. Dinner, Wednesday-Sunday from 5:15.

Blue Mermaid World Grill, 409 The Hill, Portsmouth.

Two restaurateurs from Boston took over the old Codfish restaurant here and found Portsmouth receptive to their idea of new world grill cuisine. They installed the town's first wood grill, gave the restaurant an arty and whimsical decor, and dispensed spicy foods of the Caribbean, South America, California and the Southwest.

Partners Jim Smith and Scott Logan removed some walls for a more open feeling on two floors, added embellishments like a fascinating abstract mural of the Portsmouth Farmers' Market and iron animals atop some chandeliers, and identified the rest rooms with mermaids and mermen.

Our lunch testified to their success. As we sat down, tortilla strips with fire-roasted vegetables and salsa arrived in what otherwise might be a candleholder. These piqued the taste buds for a cup of tasty black bean soup, a sandwich of grilled Jamaican jerk chicken with sunsplash salsa and a sandwich of grilled vegetables with jarlsberg cheese on walnut bread. These came with sweet-potato chips and the house sambal. We also sampled a side order of thick grilled vidalia onion rings with mango ketchup. A generous portion of ginger cheesecake, garnished with the hard candy-like topping of crème brûlée, was a sensational ending.

The signature dinner dish is grilled lobster with mango butter, served with grilled vegetables and cornbread. Other treats include Caribbean pan-seared cod with coconut cream sauce, lobster and shrimp pad thai, calypso-seasoned hanger steak with papaya-pineapple salsa, bimini chicken in bourbon-coconut sauce, Jamaican jerked pork kabobs and a skewer of Moroccan lamb with couscous. Bottles of incendiary sauces are on the tables to add fuel to the fire. Cool off with desserts like homemade caramel ice cream, tia maria flan or chocolate-banana bread pudding.

(603) 427-2583. Entrées, $15.95 to $20.95. Lunch daily, 11:30 to 5. Dinner, 5 to 10 or 11.

Diversions

Portsmouth offers much for anyone with an interest in history. The Greater Portsmouth Chamber of Commerce publishes a "Walking Tour of Downtown Portsmouth's Waterfront," which also can be driven (although directions get confusing because of one-way streets). The 2.3-mile tour takes in most of the city's attractions, including some we had passed for years unknowingly. Such is the charm of an area crammed with discoveries at every turn. A newer way to tour is by horse and carriage with **Portsmouth Livery.** The talkative guide, in beard and top hat, adds dimension to the city's history as he gives sightseeing tours for $20 to $40, leaving from the Market Square carriage stand from noon into the evening, daily May-October.

Strawbery Banke Museum, Marcy Street, Portsmouth.

Billed as "an American original," this walk-through museum is the careful restoration of one of the nation's oldest neighborhoods. Its more than 45 structures across ten acres dating from 1695 to 1955 are in various stages of restoration and adaptation, depicting four centuries of cultural and architectural change. Some have simply been preserved. Some are used by working artisans (independent of the museum, they are earning their living as well as re-enacting history). Others are used for educational exhibits including archaeology, architectural styles and construction techniques and, on the outside, historic gardens. Strawbery Banke's collection of local arts and furniture is shown in ten historic houses. Significantly, these are not all homes of the rich or famous, but rather of ordinary people. As the museum's 35th anniversary program noted, "This is the real story of history – the dreams and aspirations, the disappointments and frustrations of common people." That is the glory of Strawbery Banke, and of much of Portsmouth.

(603) 433-1100. www.strawberybanke.org. Open Monday-Saturday 10 to 5, Sunday noon to 5, May-October. Rest of year except January: open for 90-minute guided walking tours offered hourly Thursday-Saturday 10 to 2 and Sunday noon to 2. Adults, $12.

Portsmouth Harbor Trail. Six of Portsmouth's finest house museums are open individually and linked by a walking tour. Considered the one not to miss is the 1763 **Moffatt-Ladd House,** a replica of an English manor house located just above Ceres Street restaurants and shops. The yellow 1758 **John Paul Jones House,** the imposing **Governor John Langdon House** (1784) and the Georgian-style **Wentworth-Gardner House** (1760) are others. Most are open six or seven days a week from June to mid-October and charge $5 or $6 each.

The Isles of Shoals. This group of nine rocky islands located about ten miles off shore are reached by the Isles of Shoals Steamship Co. cruises from Barker Wharf at 315 Market St. Charted by Capt. John Smith when he sailed past in 1614, the islands originally drew European fishermen for their "shoals" or schools of fish. The two largest islands, Appledore and Star, became summer resorts in the 1800s. Since early in the 1900s, Star Island has been operated as a religious conference center by the Congregational and Unitarian churches. Visitors hear the legends of these barren islands during cruises daily. The one at 9:25 a.m. includes a Star Island stopover that allows passengers to spend an hour exploring the island (highly recommended), There are dining and dancing excursions in the evening, and a lobster and clambake cruise.

(603) 431-5500 or (800) 441-4620. www.islesofshoals.com. Variety of cruises daily, mid-June through October. Adults, $17.50 to $26.50.

Shopping. Most of the traditional tourist shopping attractions have passed Portsmouth by, heading for the outlet strip along Route 1 north of Kittery or the shopping malls of Newington. But downtown Portsmouth has plenty of interesting local shops concentrated around Market Square.

In one of its four stores, **Macro Polo Inc.** carries inventive children's toys; we were transported back to our childhood while gazing at the assortment of marbles in the window. **Wholly Macro!** stocks handmade Texas boots among its wares. **Macroscopic** struck us as rather New Agey. The colorful glass shown in the prominent windows draws us into **Not Just Mud! Craft Gallery,** which stocks fabulous hand-blown art glass, kaleidoscopes, pottery, jewelry and titanium clocks among its contemporary crafts. **Salamandra Glass Studio** is another favorite of glass lovers. The **Paper Patch** is the shop for funny cards. **Worldly Goods** purveys birdhouses, oil lamps, interesting baskets and adorable cat pins.

Upscale shops are moving out Congress Street. Look for the block containing **Magnifico** (hand-crafted imports), **Celtic Crossing, Runner's Alley, Chaise Lounge** ("distinctive furnishings") and **Nahcotta** ("cool goods").

Among its treasures, **Les Cadeaux** stocks exotic bath salts, fancy stationery, boxes of decorated sugar cubes from Kentucky, chocolate spoons to dip in hot chocolate, lovely china casseroles with different fruits on top for handles, and preserves and mustards from Le Cordon Bleu in France. You'd have to see them to believe the high-heeled shoes made of papier-mâché and trimmed with jewelry at **Gallery 33;** we also liked the hand-carved whimsical animals here. Wearing a T-shirt urging "squeeze me, crush me, make me wine," jovial proprietor David Campbell brings a sense of fun along with expertise to his wines, specialty foods and gift baskets at the **Ceres Street Wine Merchants.** More good art and gift destinations are **Lovell Designs, Pierce Gallery, The Blue Frog** and **City & Country** home accessories. We did some Christmas shopping at the **N.W. Barrett Gallery**, which has some of Sabra Field's woodcuts and fantastic jewelry. **Artichokes** offers cookware and specialty foods. **Strawbery Banke's** working crafts shops offer the wares of potters, a cabinetmaker, a weaver, and dories made in the boat shed.

The Music Hall, an historic 900-seat theater at 28 Chestnut St., presents a year-round series of dance, music, theater and movies on the big screen.

Extra-Special

New Castle. Drive or bicycle out Newcastle Avenue (Route 1B) through the quaint islands of New Castle, the original settlement in 1623, dotted with prosperous homes. The meandering roads and treed residential properties, many with water views, mix contemporary-style houses with those of days gone by. You can view Fort Constitution with one of several towers built during the War of 1812 and visit the seacoast park at **Great Island Common,** where there are a playground, waterfront picnic tables and views of the Isles of Shoals. The old Wentworth by the Sea, a majestic resort hotel if ever there was one, reopened in 2003 as a Marriott hotel and spa. Part of its golf course was sold to make way for expensive houses. Another rewarding drive is out Maine Route 103 past the Naval Yards in Kittery to Kittery Point, where attractive houses large and small seem to be surrounded by water on all sides.

Harbor at Cape Porpoise is on view through rose trellis at The Inn at Harbor Head.

Kennebunkport, Me.

The Most and Best of Everything

For many, the small coastal area known as the Kennebunk Region has the most and best of everything in Maine: the best beaches, the most inns, the best shops, the most eating places, the best scenery, the most tourist attractions, the best galleries, the most diverse appeal.

It also plays a starring role as the summer home of former president George H.W. Bush, a visible figure around town.

All combine to create a Kennebunk mystique that has strong appeal for tourists. Actually, there are at least three Kennebunks. One is the town of Kennebunk and its inland commercial center, historic Kennebunk. The second is Kennebunkport, the coastal resort community that was one of Maine's earliest summer havens for the wealthy, and adjacent Kennebunk Beach. A third represents Cape Arundel, Cape Porpoise and Goose Rocks Beach, whose rugged coastal aspects remain largely unchanged by development in recent years.

Even before the first George Bush's election as president, Kennebunkport and its Dock Square and Lower Village shopping areas had become so congested that tourists were shuttled by bus from parking areas on the edge of town. Although some of the luster faded during the Clinton years, visitors were still drawn much as they are by the Kennedy name to Hyannis Port – and of course all the more so after George W. Bush became president in 2001.

While the downtown area can get congested, you can escape. Walk along the ocean on Parson's Way. Drive out Ocean Avenue past Spouting Rock and the Bush estate at Walker Point and around Cape Arundel to Cape Porpoise, a working fishing village. Bicycle out Beach Avenue to Lord's Point or Strawberry Island. Visit the Rachel Carson Wildlife Preserve. Savor times gone by among the historic homes of Summer Street in Kennebunk or along the beach at Goose Rocks.

One of the charms of the Kennebunks is that the crowded restaurants and galleries co-exist with events like the annual Unitarian Church blueberry festival and the Rotary chicken barbecue, and the solitude of Parson's Way.

Watercolorist Edgar Whitney proclaimed the Kennebunks "the best ten square miles of painting areas in the nation." Explore a bit and you'll see why.

Inn Spots

The White Barn Inn, 37 Beach Ave., Kennebunkport 04046.

Long known as one of the area's premier restaurants (see Dining Spots), the White Barn has become a top-rate inn under Australian owner Laurie Bongiorno. Indeed, shortly after he took over, refurbished the facility and added deluxe suites, the inn became only the second in New England to be accepted into Relais & Châteaux, the international group of prestige hotels.

The inn's 25 rooms and suites vary, as their prices indicate. A renovated cottage beside the elegant, stone-rimmed pool area is the ultimate in plush privacy with a living room, porch, kingsize bedroom, double-sided fireplace and two-person jacuzzi. Almost its equal is a cathedral-ceilinged loft suite, adjacent to the main inn with a king bed, fireplace, private deck and oversize marble bath with double whirlpool and separate steam shower.

Six in the refurbished May's Annex are the height of luxury with library-style sitting areas, dressing rooms, spacious marble bathrooms with jacuzzis and separate showers, Queen Anne kingsize four-poster beds and secretary desks, chintz-covered furniture and plush carpeting. The desk in the Blue Suite here contains a detailed book on everything about the inn and the area except how to fill the ice bucket (just phone, we were informed after walking across the way to the bar area). The only other drawback was that the armoire containing the TV was positioned so that it was not comfortably visible from the sitting area in front of the fireplace. The fireplace was laid with real wood and we were wrapped in total luxury with a personal note of welcome from the innkeeper, a bowl of fresh fruit, Poland Spring water, no fewer than four three-way reading lights (plus a portable book light delivered at turndown), much closet and drawer space in the bathroom, terry robes, Gilchrist & Soames toiletries and a couple of cookies when the bed was turned down.

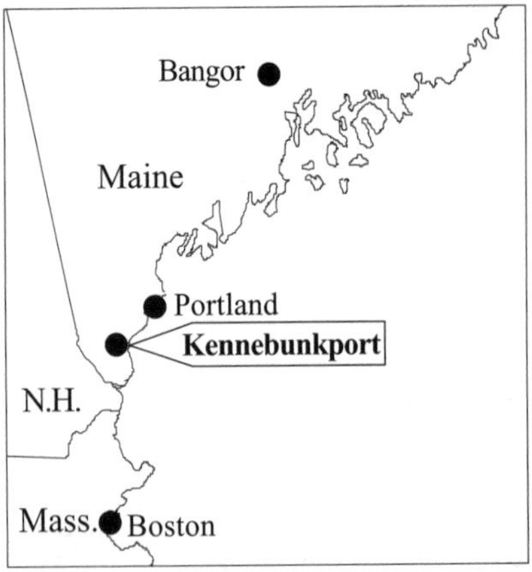

Four large rooms with cathedral ceilings in the Garden House also claim fireplaces and jacuzzis, as well as queensize sleigh beds, sitting areas with wing chairs and fine art on the walls.

Less regal are the smaller rooms upstairs in the inn, all refurbished with modernized bathrooms and whimsical artistic touches to enhance what the owner calls their "basically quaint, country-style" nature. A local artist did

Fireplace warms Lincoln Bedroom at Captain Lord Mansion.

the delightful trompe-l'oeil accents in each room – robin's eggs on a desk, car keys on a night stand, a shell book on a side table, a crane on an armoire, even a beach scene at the end of one bed and a lighthouse on the bureau.

The inn's handsome main floor contains a reception area, sitting rooms with comfortable furniture and an inviting sun porch. An elaborate tea spread is set out in one room. Guests enjoy a substantial continental buffet breakfast in a quietly elegant Colonial dining room. Fresh orange juice and slices of cut-up fruits are brought to your table by a tuxedoed waiter. You help yourself to assorted cereals, yogurts, and an array of muffins and pastries like we've seldom seen before – including at our visit a wonderful strawberry-bran muffin with a top the size of a grapefruit and a cool crème d'amandes with a sliced peach inside.

In 2003, the inn added the **Wharf Cottages and Marina,** four riverside cottage units fashioned from fish shanties on nearby Doane's Wharf Road. Each renovated with a snug queen bedroom, kitchenette, living room with fireplace and TV/VCR, they are furnished more like cabins in Arts & Crafts style. All have flagstone patios. A breakfast basket from the inn is delivered to the door.

(207) 967-2321. Fax (207) 967-1100. www.whitebarninn.com. Sixteen rooms, eight suites and one cottage with private baths. May-December: doubles $320 to $495, suites and cottage, $520 to $725. January-April: doubles $270 to $390, suites and cottage $520 to $625. Two-night minimum weekends. Wharf cottages, $525 to $545.

The Captain Lord Mansion, Pleasant Street, Box 800, Kennebunkport 04046

For starters, consider the architectural features of this beautifully restored 1812 mansion: an octagonal cupola, a suspended elliptical staircase, blown-glass windows, trompe-l'oeil hand-painted doors, an eighteen-foot bay window, a hand-pulled working elevator.

The inn is so full of historic interest that public tours are given in summer. You'd never guess that it was converted in 1978 from a boarding house for senior citizens.

Guests can savor all the heritage that makes this a National Historic Register listing by staying overnight in any of the sumptuous guest quarters and enjoying hot cider or iced tea in the parlor or games beside the fire in the large and formal Gathering Room. Rooms on three floors have been carefully decorated by Bev Davis and her husband Rick Litchfield, whose innkeeping energy and flair are considered models by their peers.

Every room has a fireplace, much in demand in the autumn and winter. All have updated baths (though some created from closets are rather small), and the corner rooms are especially spacious. Extra touches like sewing kits, Poland Spring water, and trays with wine glasses and corkscrews abound. Bev makes needlecraft "Do Not Disturb" signs for the rooms and oversees a small gift shop on the main floor.

The prime quarters seem to change with every upgrade, of which these peerless innkeepers never seem to tire. They first opened an annex called Phoebe's Fantasy with four more guest rooms, all with king or queen beds and fireplaces. Guests here take breakfast at a seven-foot harvest table in a gathering room with a chintz sofa, fireplace and television.

Lately they have made remarkable enhancements in the main building, particularly in terms of bath facilities. The first-floor Merchant Room was expanded into a deluxe suite with king canopy bed, two fireplaces, and two extravagant bath areas with heated marble floors, a ten-jet hydro-massage waterfall shower, double jacuzzi beside a fireplace, a bidet and three vanities. The Mary Lord and Excelsior rooms on the second floor gained renovated baths with heated Italian tiled floors and double whirlpool tubs. The Champion became a two-room suite with a mini-bar and a clawfoot soaking tub. The Lincoln gained a king bed and a bath with heated marble floor, marble shower and oversize antique vanity. The third-floor Mousam became a two-room suite with queen canopy bed and a new bath with a heated black granite floor and double-headed shower for two.

The mansion's basement summer kitchen with big fireplace is now a second common room that doubles as a conference area and contains the inn's TV.

Breakfast is served family-style at large tables in the country kitchen, with overflow seated in the Gathering Room at a centennial Chippendale table and chairs that belonged to the original Lord family. It includes fruit, yogurt, whole-grain muesli, a changing entrée (perhaps cheese strata, quiche or apple-cinnamon pancakes), freshly-ground coffee with a flavor of the day, hot muffins and sticky buns. Bev's zucchini bread is renowned, as are some of the hors d'oeuvres she prepares for wine gatherings for guests at Halloween and New Year's.

(207) 967-3141 or (800) 522-3141. Fax (207) 967-3172. www.captainlord.com. Eighteen rooms and two suites with private baths. June-December: doubles $239 to $399 weekends, $214 to $364 midweek; suites $269 to $449 weekends, $254 to $384 midweek. Rest of year: doubles, $249 to $329 weekends, $149 to $289 midweek; suites $249 to $375 weekends, $175 to $299 midweek. Two-night minimum weekends. Children over 6.

Bufflehead Cove Inn, Gornitz Lane, Box 499, Kennebunkport 04046.

Down a long dirt road and past a lily pond is this hidden treasure: a gray shingled, Dutch Colonial manse right on six acres beside a scenic bend of the Kennebunk

Tables are set for breakfast beside water at Bufflehead Cove Inn.

River, the kind of summer home you've always dreamed of. Owners Harriet and Jim Gott hardly advertise and don't need to. Their B&B is filled by word of mouth.

The public rooms and the setting are special here. A wide porch faces the tidal river and downtown Kennbunkport in the distance; there are porches along the side and a huge wraparound deck in back. A large and comfy living room contains window seats with views of the water, and the dining room, which is shaped like the back of a ship, has a dark beamed ceiling, paneling, stenciling and a carpet painted on the floor. There are a dock with boats and five acres of tranquility with which to surround oneself.

All bedrooms are bright and cheerful. The Balcony Room is perhaps the most appealing of those in the main house. It has a fabulous, wicker-filled screened balcony overlooking the river, a sitting area with a window seat and a chaise lounge, and a kingsize bed topped with a plump yellow floral comforter. Its spacious bathroom has a shower, refrigerator/wet bar and a corner jacuzzi for two, positioned dramatically beneath hand-painted pots of apple blossoms stretching overhead. Reflections of sun on the river shimmer on the ceiling of the River Room, which has a queen bed and a waterside balcony. The walls and ceilings are hand-painted with vines in the Cove Suite, two rooms with lots of wicker and a gas fireplace. The Garden Room in back has its own entrance and patio, a wicker sitting area, gas fireplace, a handcrafted queensize bed and grapevine stenciling that echoes the real vines outside the entry.

The crowning glory is the luxurious new River Cottage across the lawn, furnished in Harriet's usual impeccable taste and "designed with romance in mind." It has a huge cathedral-ceilinged living room with a fireplace and a soaring palladian window, a kingsize sleigh bed and a fainting couch in the window of the bedroom, an enormous bath with a double jacuzzi and a nifty bird mural, an adorable kitchen, a loft with a library and entertainment center, and a deck with a view of the river through the trees.

Our favorite is the secluded Hideaway, refashioned from the Gotts' former quarters in a cottage next to the river. Mostly windows, it holds a kingsize bed, a tiled fireplace open to both the bedroom and the living room, rattan chairs, and an enormous bathroom with a double jacuzzi surrounded by a tiled border of fish. Pears seem to be a decorative theme, showing up on the fireplace tiles and at the base of a huge twig wreath over the mantel. Outside is a private deck where early-morning coffee was provided and we would gladly have spent the day, had we not been working.

Breakfast on the inn's front porch began, in our case, with fresh orange juice and an elaborate dish of melon bearing mixed fruit and homemade pineapple sorbet. The main event was a delicious zucchini crescent pie, teamed with an English muffin topped with cheddar, tomato and bacon, and roasted potatoes with onions and salsa. Soufflés, asparagus strata, green-apple stuffed french toast, waffles and popovers are other specialties.

Wine and cheese are served in the afternoon, and there are decanters of sherry plus bottles of Bufflehead Cove sparkling water in each room. Chocolate truffles show up at nightly turndown.

Jim is a lobster fisherman. Guests may not see much of him unless they get up to join his fishing expedition at 4:30 a.m., but they know he's around by the lobster in the quiche and omelets.

(207) 967-3879. www.buffleheadcove.com. Three rooms, one suite and two cottages with private baths. June-October: doubles $155 to $295, suite and cottages $235 to $350. Rest of year: doubles $115 to $225, suites $175 to $275. Two-night minimum weekends.

Old Fort Inn, Old Fort Avenue, Box M, Kennebunkport 04046

The main lodge in a converted barn is the heart of the Old Fort Inn. You enter through the reception area and Sheila Aldrich's antiques shop. Beyond is a large rustic room with enormous beams, weathered pine walls and a massive brick fireplace, the perfect setting for some of Sheila's antiques.

That's where she and husband David, transplanted Californians, set out a buffet breakfast each morning. Guests pick up wicker trays with calico linings, help themselves to bowls of gorgeous fresh fruits and platters of pastries, and sit around the lodge, on the enclosed porch or outside on the sun-dappled deck beside the large swimming pool. Sheila bakes the sweet breads (blueberry, zucchini, banana, oatmeal and pumpkin are some); the croissants are David's forte and there are sticky buns on Sundays. They added granola and yogurt to the spread, and quickly found they were going through twenty pounds of granola a week.

The main lodge and brick carriage houses contain fourteen large and luxurious guest rooms and two suites. The elegant, antiques-appointed rooms feature canopied or four poster beds with down comforters, fine fabrics and handsome wall coverings. All rooms are air conditioned with baths outfitted with Aveda amenities and heated tile floors (some baths feature jacuzzis), private-line phones, hidden television and deluxe wet bars. Several rooms have gas fireplaces. In the hall, Sheila's artfully framed shadow boxes containing Victorian outfits are conversation pieces.

The inn is a quiet retreat on fifteen acres of immaculately maintained grounds and woodlands, away from the tourist hubbub, but within walking distance of the ocean. At night, David says, the silence is deafening. The inn offers a tennis court as well as the pool. Many guests are repeat, long-term customers, and it's easy to see why.

(207) 967-5353 or (800) 828-3678. Fax (207) 967-4547. www.oldfortinn.com. Fourteen

Wicker-filled veranda at Cape Arundel Inn overlooks ocean and Walker Point (center).

rooms and two suites with private baths. Doubles, $160 to $375, mid-June to late October; $99 to $295 rest of year. Two-night minimum stay in summer, fall foliage and all weekends; three nights on holiday weekends. Closed mid-December to mid-April.

Cape Arundel Inn, 208 Ocean Ave., Box 530A, Kennebunkport 04046.

A choice location facing the open Atlantic, comfortable accommodations and an excellent dining room commend this turreted Maine-style oceanfront inn with wraparound veranda.

Veteran restaurateur Jack Nahil, who formerly owned the White Barn Inn and the Salt Marsh Tavern, acquired the Cape Arundel in 1997 and started upgrading. He added queen and kingsize beds and in-room telephones, created more windows for what he rightly bills as "bold ocean views" and completely refurnished the adjacent 1950s motel building in a country inn motif. He also refurbished the main inn's living room and added oriental rugs.

An artist and avid gardener, he has given free rein to his talents inside and out. Throughout, his emphasis was on enhancing this "great Shingle-style structure, which is a wonderful property. It just needed some attention."

He succeeded handsomely in maintaining the appropriately simple grandeur without adding the glitz so common today. Rooms on the inn's second floor are spacious and pleasantly traditional in circa 1890s style. Rooms 2 and 3 are most coveted. The former has a queen poster bed and a private balcony overlooking the ocean, and Room 3 has a king poster bed with bow window facing the ocean. We enjoyed Room 4 on the far-front corner, which is attractively decorated in blue and white, but the view was all: two chairs in the corner from which to take in the bird's-eye panorama of the ocean and the George H.W. Bush compound at Walker Point. Room 1 at the opposite corner has a queen bed under a stained-glass window and is an expanse of yellow with a moss green carpet.

Also in demand are the rooms in the adjacent building, now called Rockbound.

Each has a full bath and TV, and a balcony with a front-on view of the ocean beyond the garden. Our end room had a queen bed with a sturdy white wood headboard crafted by a local artisan, angled from the corner to take in that bold ocean view.

A rear carriage house has a second-floor suite called Ocean Bluff, with a queen bed, a gas fireplace, TV/VCR, a deck and panoramic views over the main house.

The inn's expansive, wicker-filled veranda facing the ocean is a super place to curl up with a good book, enjoy a cocktail or a nightcap, or the morning newspaper before breakfast. Breakfast is a hearty continental buffet. Ours began with fresh orange juice, cereal, muesli, fruit and yogurt, and superior scones and croissants. The highlight was the day's extra: toasted basil-parmesan bread and a small spanakopita, prepared by the chef's wife and "presented" in the dinner style on an oversize plate.

Dinner here is better than ever, thanks to the assured Jack Nahil touch (see Dining Spots). He enhanced the dining situation and extended the inn's season.

(207) 967-2125. Fax (207) 967-1199. www.capearundelinn.com. Thirteen rooms and one suite with private baths. Mid-June to mid-October, doubles $235 to $335. Rest of year: doubles $145 to $285. Two-night minimum weekends. Closed January and February. Children over 12.

The Inn at Harbor Head, 41 Pier Road, Cape Porpoise, RR 2, Box 1180, Kennebunkport 04046.

The location of this rambling shingled home on a rocky knoll right above the picturesque Cape Porpoise harbor just outside Kennebunkport is one of the attractions at this small B&B. Out front are gorgeous gardens with a sundial. A rear terrace and lawns lead down to the shore for swimming from the dock or just relaxing in one of the oversize rope hammocks, watching the lobster boats go by.

Artistry inside the house is another attraction. The four guest quarters, two up and two down, are decorated to the nth degree with exquisite hand-painted murals. All have king or queensize canopy beds.

The entrance to the Garden Room is paved with stones and a little fountain, and original drawings of peach and plum blossoms float on the wall. French doors open onto a private, trellised deck overlooking the harbor. The downstairs Greenery, where we stayed, has a mural of fir trees by the shore, a bathroom with hand-painted tile and jacuzzi tub, and a view of the front gardens. Next time we'd opt for the upstairs Summer Suite, with the best view of the harbor from its balcony. It's painted with clouds drifting across the ceiling and comes with a kingsize wicker bed, gas fireplace and a cathedral-ceilinged bathroom with skylight, bidet and jacuzzi

The Ocean Room is different from the rest – bold and masculine with a library of books about sailing, the sea and shipwrecks, plus a trompe-l'oeil window scene painted in its skylit bathroom to simulate a window.

Rooms are outfitted with thick towels, terrycloth robes, hair dryers, irons and boards, books and magazines, good reading lights, CD players, clock radios, a decanter of port and fresh flowers from the backyard cutting garden.

Still another attraction at this appealing B&B is breakfast. From the country kitchen of innkeepers Eve and Dick Roesler come such dishes as bananas foster, pears poached with lemon and vanilla and topped with raspberry sauce, or broiled grapefruit with kirsch and brown sugar. The "Maine" course could be zucchini frittata, honey-pecan french toast, crabmeat and bacon quiche, or wild Maine blueberry pancakes with warm maple syrup. Homemade lemon-poppyseed or cranberry muffins might accompany. The meal is served at 9 a.m. in the dining room at a long table where there is much camaraderie. Coffee for early risers is available at 7:30.

Eve serves afternoon wine and cheese on the back deck overlooking the harbor. After guests leave for dinner, the Roeslers turn down their beds, light soft lights and leave seashell dishes of chocolates on the pillows.

It's little wonder that some guests stay for a week or more, and that many are honeymooners.

(207) 967-5564. Fax (207) 967-1294. www.harborhead.com. Three rooms and one suite with private baths. Doubles, $190 to $265 Memorial Day through October, early season $155 to $205. Suite, $305, early season $235. Two-night minimum weekends. Children over 12. Closed November-April.

The Captain Fairfield Inn, Pleasant and Green Streets, Box 2690, Kennebunkport 04046.

This circa-1813 Federal sea captain's mansion, listed on the National Register and overlooking the Town Green, has been greatly improved by Janet and Rick Wolf, who acquired the inn in 1999. One of the most notable changes was the conversion of a library/TV room into a music room with an ebony grand piano that guests are encouraged to play – an impromptu concert or singalong often ensues, says Rich. They also hung a copy of the long-lost portrait of Capt. James Fairfield over a fireplace to add to the collection of nautical memorabilia and paintings.

Sunny breakfast room at Captain Fairfield Inn.

The nine guest rooms have new full baths, queensize beds dressed with pretty linens and lots of pillows, and comfortable sitting areas for two. Four have fireplaces and all have telephones with data ports. The guest room on the main floor opposite the living room is a beauty. Called the Library Suite, it has a fishnet canopy queen bed, two armchairs, a fireplace and its own porch with two rocking chairs. Its bathroom recently has been enlarged and contains a double whirlpool tub and separate glass shower.

Each room is outfitted with fluffy towels, English soaps and toiletries, bottled water, hair dryers and night lights.

Beautiful woodwork and molding and fresh flowers are evident throughout. The formal living room is elegant yet comfortable. French doors open from the music room onto the garden and a large side lawn.

Breakfast, a highlight here, is served in the original open hearth kitchen, the sunny breakfast room or in summer, outside under majestic elms and surrounded by lawns and gardens. Jan bakes the muffins (mixed berry at our visit) and orange-cranberry scones. Rick does the cooking. He offers a choice of two entrées, perhaps omelet Fairfield (incorporating sweet Italian sausage, two cheeses and spinach) or pumpkin pancakes with the inn's own maple sausage. Every Sunday features blueberry crêpes and eggs benedict with Rick's special hollandaise sauce. Tea and homemade treats are offered in the afternoon, and a decanter of port awaits in the living room.

(207) 967-4454 or (800) 322-1928. Fax (207) 967-8537. www.captainfairfieldinn.com. Nine rooms with private baths. Doubles, $150 to $295 late June to late October, $110 to $250 rest of year. Two-night minimum most weekends.

1802 House, 15 Locke St., Kennebunkport 04046.

An historic setting on a quiet, out-of-the-way residential street is offered by Edric and Mary Ellen Mason in their attractive B&B, some of whose accommodations have been lately upgraded with luxury amenities. Relaxing on the side deck or broad lawns open to the fairways of the Cape Arundel golf course, you'd think you were out in the country. Inside the restored farmhouse, all is comfortable and thoroughly up-to-date, despite the structure's heritage.

All six guest quarters on the first and second floors are tastefully furnished in a Colonial motif that suits the house. Guests in each are greeted by chocolates, fresh flowers and classical music playing on the radio. We enjoyed our stay in the Camden Room in the downstairs lower front corner, which came with a gas fireplace and a queensize poster bed topped by a handmade quilt. Across the hall is the larger Arundel, beamed and historic looking, with a queen poster bed dressed in embroidered linens, two wing chairs, the original working fireplace and a double jacuzzi tub in the bath. Above it on the second floor is the Windsor, with a fishnet canopy queen bed and similar amenities. Across the hall, a new gas fireplace warms the cozy Berwick Room, while the cheery York Room offers a bath with double jacuzzi and heated tile floor.

In a separate wing of the house is the luxurious Sebago Suite, a three-room affair. Its cozy living room comes with a fireplace, wet bar, refrigerator and TV/VCR. The bedroom has a queen canopy bed draped in white organza and an adjoining marble bathroom with a dual-head shower and heated tile floor. The "Roman Garden tub room," appointed with Italian tiles, contains a two-person whirlpool tub. French doors open to a private deck overlooking the golf course.

Guests gather in an open common room, where a fire in a cast-iron potbelly stove on a brick platform warms the air on chilly days. Adjacent is the cheerful breakfast room, where intimate tables for two flank a large and convivial family table favored by most. The succulent blueberry pancakes served the morning we were there lingered long in the memory. Mary Ellen is known also for her lemon-ricotta pancakes, vegetable frittata and stuffed croissants. Cookies and lemonade are offered in the afternoon.

(207) 967-5632 or (800) 932-5632. Fax (207) 967-5632. www.1802inn.com. Five rooms and one suite with private baths. Doubles, $159 to $279, suite $299 to $379. Off-season, doubles $129 to $239, suite $259 to $299. Children over 12.

The Yachtsman Lodge & Marina, Ocean Avenue, Box 2609, Kennebunkport 04046.

When does a seasonal motel become worthy of an inn book? When it's taken over by Laurence Bongiorno of the luxurious White Barn Inn.

He gutted the interior of the old Yachtsman Motel but retained the footprint to offer the most deluxe "motel" quarters you're ever likely to see. Call it a lodge, or call

Waterfront accommodations are sumptuous at The Yachtsman Lodge.

it an inn. Laurie calls it an effort to serve families and pets in "that great netherland between casual motel and elegant inn, with a location on the water being most important."

It's exactly the kind of place in which we like to stay – a cross between motel privacy and inn amenities, with a water view. Each spacious room with vaulted ceiling is the same, done in understated style to resemble a yacht with cream-colored, bead-board walls accented with sailing prints and mahogany trim. The kingsize bed is dressed in a fluffy white goose-down duvet covered in Egyptian cotton, the TV is hidden in an armoire, and furnishings include two cushioned rattan chairs, a round table and a writing desk. The closet lights automatically to reveal terrycloth robes, a mini-refrigerator chills bottled water, and the bathroom's granite vanity bears all kinds of toiletries. The front of the room is screened from the road by lush landscaping. The back opens through french doors onto private patios with lounge furniture facing a swath of lawn about fifteen feet from river's edge. Quacking ducks that paraded by made more noise than the sleek yachts moored in the marina at our visit.

A common terrace between the two lodge buildings has plenty of lounge furniture for enjoying the afternoon spread of beverages and pastries. A huge, push-button coffee machine produces cappuccino and espresso. The sunny breakfast room holds a complimentary array of fruit, cereals and baked goods including a savory quiche prepared by the award-winning kitchen at the White Barn Inn. Also complimentary are touring bicycles and canoes. Owner Bongiorno's new 44-foot yacht is moored outside and available for charter.

(207) 967-2511. Fax (207) 967-5056. www.yachstmanlodge.com. Thirty rooms with private baths. Doubles, $299, June-August and weekends to mid-October; rest of season, $179 to $219 weekends, $149 to $219 midweek. Two-night minimum most weekends. Closed early December through March.

The Schooners Inn, 127 Ocean Ave., Box 560C, Kennebunkport 04046.

Built as an inn in 1986, this is the latest Kennebunkport hostelry to be acquired by Laurence Bongiorno of the White Barn. He undertook a major makeover, added the amenities of his other inns and turned it into one of the more luxurious waterfront inns around.

Facing the Kennebunk River near its mouth, rooms are named for schooners and are oriented to the water – some more than others, especially a couple of rooms with outdoor decks. All are crisply decorated in a high-tech look amid prevailing colors of creams and taupes. Beds are king or queensize, crafted by furniture maker Thomas Moser, who also did the cupboards that hold the TVs. White satin robes and Molton Brown toiletries from London are among the amenities.

The prime accommodation is the Savannah Suite, with a kingsize bed enveloped in a sheer white canopy beneath a raised sitting area in a large bay window opening onto an idyllic deck. Its bathroom is larger than the others and contains a jetted tub.

The curving main-floor lounge is the setting for afternoon tea and cookies. The baked goods for tea and the continental-plus breakfast are prepared by the award-winning kitchen at the White Barn Inn, as is the case with the other inns in the Bongiorno group. In a separate building in back is **Stripers Fish Shack,** serving lunch and dinner in season.

(207) 967-5333. Fax (207) 967-2040. www.schoonersinn.com. Sixteen rooms and one suite with private baths. Late June to Labor Day: doubles $330 to $345, suite $550 to $570. Spring and fall: doubles $245 to $295, suite $500 to $525. November-April: doubles $145 to $235, suite $285 to $475.

Dining Spots

The White Barn Inn, Beach Street, Kennebunkport.

Soaring up to three stories, with a breathtaking backdrop of flowers rising on tiers outside its twenty-foot-high rear picture window and illuminated at night, the elegant White Barn is almost too atmospheric for words. A local florist designs the dramatic backdrops that change with the seasons (lush impatiens in summer, assorted mums in fall, and a Christmas scene that begins with potted red cabbage and escalates to full spruce trees dressed with velvet bows, golden bells and tiny white lights). Talented executive chef Jonathan Cartwright oversees the kitchen, which seems to get better every year. And owner Laurie Bongiorno, a personable but perfectionist Australian of Italian descent, is the omnipresent host who ensures that the dining room runs flawlessly.

Little wonder that the White Barn became the AAA's first five-diamond dining establishment in all New England, or that lately it topped the ranking of any restaurant in a resort worldwide in Condé Nast Traveler's Best of the Best awards. It's *that* good.

The food is in the vanguard of contemporary American regional cuisine. Dinner is prix-fixe in four courses, with eight to ten choices for most courses. It's prepared by a kitchen staff of sixteen and served with precision by a young wait staff who meet with the chef beforehand for 45 minutes each night. Guests at each table are served simultaneously, one waiter per plate.

Up to 120 diners can be seated on new leather chairs from Italy at tables spaced well apart in the main barn and in an adjoining barn. The rooms are filled with understated antiques and oil paintings dating to the 18th century, and the loft holds quite a collection of fanciful wildlife wood carvings, including chickens, sheep and cows. The tables are set with silver, Schottsweizel crystal and Villeroy & Boch china, white linens and white tapers in crystal candlesticks. At one visit, a Russian pianist, here on a scholarship, played seemingly by ear in the entry near the gleaming copper-topped bar.

Our latest dinner, the highlight of several over the years, began with a glass of Perrier-Jouët extra brut (complimentary for house guests) and the chef's "welcome amenity," an herbed goat cheese rosette, an onion tart and a tapenade of eggplant and kalamata olives. Really interesting olive bread and plain white and poppyseed rolls followed. We'd gladly have tried any of the appetizers, but settled on a lobster spring roll with daikon radish, savoy cabbage and hot and sweet glaze, and the seared Hudson Valley foie gras on an apple and celeriac tart with a calvados sauce. Both were sensational.

Champagne sorbet in a pool of Piper Heidsieck extra-dry cleared the palate with a flourish for the main courses. One was a duo of Maine rabbit: a grilled loin with roasted rosemary and pommery mustard and a braised leg in cabernet sauvignon, accompanied by wild mushrooms and pesto-accented risotto. The other was pan-seared tenderloin of beef topped with a horseradish gratin and port-glazed shallots on a pool of potato and Vermont cheddar cheese, with a fancy little side of asparagus. A bottle of Firestone cabernet accompanied from an excellent wine list especially strong on American chardonnays and cabernets.

Dessert was anything but anti-climactic: a classic coeur à la crème with tropical fruits and sugared shortbread and a trio of pear, raspberry and mango sorbets, served artistically on a black plate with colored swirls matching the sorbets and decorated with squiggles of white and powdered sugar. A tray of petit-fours gilded the lily. After an after-dinner brandy in the inn's living room, the little raisin cookies we found on the bed back in our room sent us happily into dreamland.

(207) 967-2321. Prix-fixe, $85. Dinner nightly, 6 to 9:30, Friday-Sunday from 5:30. Closed two weeks in January. Jackets required.

Grissini Italian Bistro, 27 Western Ave., Kennebunkport.

This Italian bistro is run by Laurie Bongiorno of the White Barn Inn, who took over the old Café Topher property in 1996. He opened it up into a perfectly stunning space, with vaulted beamed ceilings three stories high and a tall fieldstone fireplace. Sponged pale yellow walls, large tables spaced well apart, comfortable lacquered wicker armchairs, white tablecloths covered with paper, pinpoint lighting, and fancy bottles and sculptures backlit in the windows add up to a thoroughly sophisticated feeling. The talented chef and some of the staff are direct from Italy.

Opera music was playing in the background as a plate of tasty little crostini, some with pesto and black olives and some with gorgonzola cheese and tomato, arrived to start our dinner. The bread, prepared in the in-house bakery, is served in slabs smack onto the table, with the server pouring an exorbitant amount of olive oil into a bowl for dipping. Everything else came on enormous white plates, except for the wine (in beautiful stemmed glasses) and the ice water (in pilsener glasses).

The exciting, oversize menu is made for grazing. Among antipasti, we loved the wood-grilled local venison sausage on a warm caramelized onion salad and the house-cured Maine salmon carpaccio with olive oil, herbs and lemon juice and topped with pasta salad. Pastas come in small and large sizes, as do pizzas.

Secondi are dishes like osso buco, wood-grilled salmon served over porcini risotto and grilled lobster served with a lemony garlic butter over fresh pasta. We split the wood-grilled leg of lamb steak with Tuscan white beans, pancetta, garlic and rosemary. The "insalata mista della casa" was a nice mixture of field greens,

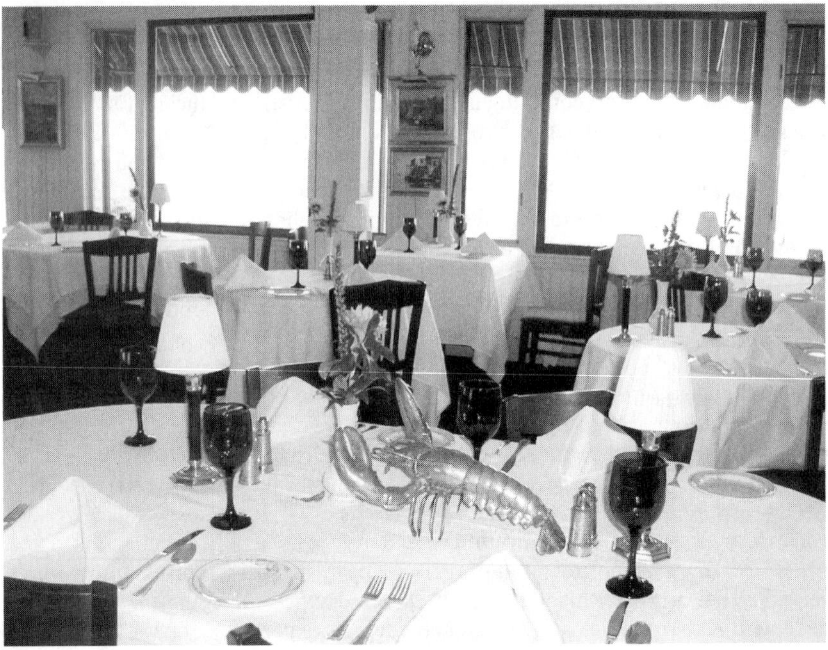

Lobster sculpture is arty centerpiece for table at Cape Arundel Inn.

kalamata olives, tomato, gorgonzola and pine nuts. Accompanying the meal was a fine reserve chianti from an affordable, all-Italian wine list.

A sampler plate of tiramisu, a chocolate delicacy and strawberries in balsamic vinegar with mascarpone cheese ended a memorable dinner.

The overflow crowds spill on warm nights onto a tiered outdoor courtyard that looks rather like a grotto.

(207) 967-2211. Entrées, $20.95 to $26.95. Dinner nightly, 5:30 to 9 or 9:30.

Cape Arundel Inn, Ocean Avenue, Kennebunkport.

What could be more romantic than dining at a window table at the Cape Arundel, watching wispy clouds turn to mauve and violet as the sun sets, followed by a full golden moon rising over the darkened ocean? That the food is so good is a bonus.

Dinner here is better than ever, thanks to the assured touch of artist/owner Jack Nahil, former owner of the White Barn Inn and later the Salt Marsh Tavern. Executive chef Rich Lemoine, who has been with him since White Barn days, presents exotic contemporary fare.

The 60-seat, two-level dining room itself is a study in white and cobalt blue. An arty display of cobalt glass is on a shelf above a painting of cobalt glass.

Our latest dinner began with remarkably good crusty basil-parmesan-rosemary bread. Appetizers were a composed spinach salad with prosciutto and oyster mushrooms and an exemplary chilled sampler of ginger poached shrimp, a Maine crab-filled spring roll and tea-smoked sirloin with wasabi citrus rémoulade, each artfully presented and interspersed with colorful slaw.

Oversize dinner plates speckled with herbs yielded a superior sliced leg of lamb teamed with cavatelli pasta and wilted arugula, and a mixed grill of duck sausage, veal london broil and lamb loin chop. Other choices ranged from pan-fried halibut with a russet and sweet potato crust with lime-cilantro tartar sauce over baby spinach to grilled duck breast and confit marinated in grand marnier with raspberry-orange demi-glace.

The dessert of cinnamon ice cream with strawberries over lady fingers was enough for two to share.

(207) 967-2125. Entrées, $24 to $36. Dinner, Monday-Saturday 5:30 to 8:30 or 9. Closed January and February.

On the Marsh Restaurant, 46 Western Ave. (Route 9), Lower Village, Kennebunkport.

The soaring, barn-like interior of the former Salt Marsh Tavern is chicly elegant, thanks to new owner Denise Rubin, an interior designer who lives in York Beach. Here she offers diners "a feast for the eyes as well as the palate."

The handsome facade is painted raspberry, the owner's favorite color. Thousands of tiny white lights in the surrounding pine and cedar trees turn the property into a twinkling wonderland at night.

Inside, the decor changes with the seasons. All the artworks on the walls, most of the antiques adorning the lofts and even the chairs and the silverware are for sale. Tables are flanked by fancy padded chairs that the owner designed and are draped to the floor in white-over-emerald cloths. Large rear windows look onto a salt marsh stretching toward Kennebunk Beach.

With an eye for the dramatic, executive chef W. Scott Lee categorizes his changing menu by "prologue" and "performance." Warm up with such preliminaries as nori-wrapped crispy crab cakes, fricassee of wild mushrooms and Maine lobster on a garlic crouton, or the house shrimp cocktail with four dipping sauces. Typical main courses are seared halibut with citrus-basil beurre blanc, marinated pork tenderloin with peppercorn-maple glaze and rack of New Zealand lamb. The "sesame grilled Atlantic salmon with personality" fairly explodes with Asian pear-mango salsa, caramelized chile paste, Maine blueberry wasabi, seaweed salad and kaffir lime jelly. Desserts include a trio of crème brûlées, dark chocolate pâté with rum crème anglaise and, the owner's favorite, blueberry-raspberry sorbet with Belgian chocolate spears.

For a different experience, there's an "chef's table" for four in the kitchen. Participants sample an eight-course tasting menu while watching the goings-on in what Scott calls the heat of battle.

A sushi bar was added upstairs in 2003.

(207) 967-2299. www.onthemarsh.com. Entrées, $19 to $30. Dinner nightly, from 5:30. Closed Monday and Tuesday in off-season and month of January.

Hurricane Restaurant, 29 Dock Square, Kennebunkport.

Ogunquit restaurateurs Brooks and Luanne MacDonald took over the old family-style Riverview Restaurant that had inspired him to get into the restaurant business. They commissioned a waitress to paint a huge mural of the river on the wall lacking a water view and, voila: Hurricane No. 2, an offshoot of the Ogunquit trend-setter. In place of the soda fountain where Brooks hung out as a teenager is a hand-crafted mahogany bar serving 60 wines by the glass to patrons in a 90-seat restaurant with views of the Kennebunk River.

The contemporary American menu features Hurricane's signature dishes and a few items unique to Dock Square. Seafood and lobster are the specialties on a roster ranging from pan-roasted arctic char served over black quinoa to the signature lobster cioppino. Fire-roasted Chilean sea bass served over a crispy duck confit and fingerling potato hash, oven-roasted Alaskan halibut with grilled apples and papaya coulis, and fennel-crusted rack of lamb finished with preserved lingonberry sauce are typical. A bento box of shrimp, scallop and salmon lumpia, Maine lobster rangoon, vegetable nori rolls and marinated beef is a specialty appetizer to be shared. The pastry chef's desserts could be warm rum raisin bread pudding with orange sabayon or chocolate-grand marnier crème brûlée.

In 2003, the Hurricane group took over the Port Bakery & Café, open daily from 6 to 6 in Kennebunk's Lower Village.

(207) 967-9111. www.hurricanerestaurant.com. Entrées, $18 to $39. Lunch daily, 11:30 to 3. Dinner nightly, 5:30 to 10:30, to 9:30 in winter.

Stripers Fish Shack, 127 Ocean Ave, Kennebunkport.

Only in Kennebunkport and White Barn Inn terms would this be called a "fish shack." Opened in 2002, this is ubiquitous owner Laurence Bongiorno's shrine to seafood, a small and casual yet chic eatery beside the Kennebunk River. Ceramic fish sculptures comprise most of the beachy decor, a dining counter looks onto the open kitchen and seafood is the attraction, of course. That and the array of window tables beside the water, and a deck for outdoor dining until the end of October.

The menu is short and deceptively straightforward, given the kitchen's creativity, and eons removed in delivery from the clam shack and fish fry idiom. Look for the day's catch (swordfish, Atlantic salmon), available charbroiled or pan seared and served – as are most entrées – with fries and what the menu calls "mushy" peas, a mix of mashed and whole peas in a rich buttery and creamy mash. Also look for lobster, bouillabaisse and blackboard specials, perhaps pan-seared scallops with lobster-cognac sauce or yellowfin tuna with provençal sauce. Perhaps the best fish and chips you ate ever comes in the form of ale-battered haddock with fries, garnished with wedges of lemon and lime.

Other favorites are the seafood platter – an array of oysters, shrimp, clams, mussels and cracked lobster – and the bento box. One night's box yielded seared scallops, gravlax, shrimp and panko-fried oysters with seaweed salad.

Soups, stews and salads are offered to begin. The only other "fishless options" are grilled chicken and broiled filet mignon. Desserts include peanut butter pie, cappuccino silk pie and crème brûlée cheesecake.

The wine list is short and select, at not exactly fish shack prices.

(207) 967-3625. Entrées, $17.95 to $30. Lunch daily in summer, noon to 3. Dinner nightly, 5 to 8:30. Closed November-April.

Arundel Wharf Restaurant, 43 Ocean Ave., Kennebunkport.

This riverfront landmark has been given a facelift, a new chef, a new menu and an extended season. The locals responded in droves, joining tourists to pack the place at all hours.

Although the waterside location has much to do with it, the food earns accolades for its quality as well as its breadth. The lobster club sandwich and the avocado stuffed with crabmeat made a fine lunch one day. The JAT (avocado-jack cheese-tomato) sandwich and a meaty lobster stew with the house salad of mixed greens and roasted yellow peppers, pecans and tomatoes were good choices another time.

We'd happily return for dinner, when the extensive menu ranges from charbroiled swordfish and roasted fillet of sole stuffed with crab and brie to the Passamaquoddy clambake – a pottery crock filled with steamers and mussels and topped with a lobster. Lobster comes seven ways. "Other interests" are served by chicken diablo, prime rib au jus, sirloin steak or venison sauté. Or you can settle for fried seafood or a basic hamburger.

Save room for dessert, perhaps bread pudding with whiskey sauce, mixed four-berry pie or blueberry-apple crisp.

(207) 967-3444. www.arundelwharf.com. Entrées, $15.50 to $34.95. Lunch daily, 11:30 to 2:30. Dinner nightly, 5 to 9 or 9:30. Closed late October to mid-April.

Diversions

The picturesque coast, which varies here in a relatively short stretch from sandy beach to rugged and rockbound, offers a variety of leisure pursuits.

Beaches. Gooch's, a curving half-mile crescent, and **Kennebunk** are two beaches with surf west of town (parking by permit, often provided by innkeepers). The fine silvery sand at Goose Rocks Beach looks almost tropical and the waters are protected. Beachcombers find starfish and sand-dollar shells here in early morning. More secluded is **Parson's Beach,** a natural sandy strand set among the tall grasses and undeveloped area next to the Rachel Carson Wildlife Refuge. The beaches are at their uncrowded best at non-peak periods and early or late in the day.

Parson's Way. A marker opposite the landmark Colony Hotel notes the land given to the people of Kennebunkport so that "everyone may enjoy its natural beauty." Sit on the benches, spread a blanket on a rock beside the ocean, or walk out to the serene little chapel of St. Ann's Episcopal Church by the sea.

Ocean Avenue. Continue past Parson's Way to Spouting Rock, where the incoming tide creates a spurting fountain as waves crash between two ragged cliffs, and Blowing Cave, another roaring phenomenon within view of Walker Point and the George Bush summer compound. Go on to Cape Porpoise, the closest thing to a fishing village hereabouts, with a working lobster pier and a picturesque harbor full of islands.

History. The Kennebunkport Historical Society has its attractions: the 1853 Greek Revival **Nott House** nicknamed White Columns, the **Pasco Exhibit Center** with changing historical exhibits and the 1899 one-room **Town House School** with exhibits of local and maritime heritage. But inland Kennebunk is more obviously historic: There's a treasure behind every door on the block at the 1825 **Brick Store Museum,** which has an excellent collection of decorative and fine arts, Federal period furniture, artifacts and textiles. It mounts a couple of major exhibits each year (photos of the great fire of 1947 were on at one visit) and offers architectural walking tours of Kennebunk's National Register historic district. Summer Street (Route 35) running south of downtown toward Kennebunkport is considered one of the architecturally outstanding residential streets in the nation; the 1803 **Taylor-Barry House** is open for tours, and the aptly named yellow-with-white-frosting Wedding Cake House (1826) is a sight to behold.

Arts and Crafts. Its scenery has turned Kennebunkport into a mecca for artisans. The Art Guild of the Kennebunks numbers more than 50 resident professionals as members and claims the Kennebunks are the largest collective community of fine art on the East Coast. Art and galleries are everywhere, but are concentrated around Kennebunkport's Dock Square and the wharves to the southeast. The **Ebb Tide Gallery** shows more than twenty artists in a stylish setting overlooking the Kennebunkport River basin, just across the bridge from Dock Square. Local, regional and national artists are represented across the street at the **Gallery on Chase Hill.** More than 105 artists show at **Mast Cove Galleries,** a lovely Greek Revival home and barn next to the library on Route 9. Spectacular contemporary American glass is shown at **Silica,** a knockout gallery in Cape Porpoise. Also in Cape Porpoise is **The Wright Gallery,** where 31 artists display on two floors of a 19th century post and beam house.

For a change of pace, visit the grounds of the **Franciscan Monastery** (where, as some savvy travelers know, spare and inexpensive bedrooms are available) and St. Anthony's Shrine. The shrines and sculpture include the towering piece that adorned the facade of the Vatican pavilion at the 1964 New York World's Fair.

Shopping. Dock Square and, increasingly, Kennebunk's Lower Village across the river are full of interesting stores, everything from the **Lavender Creek Trading Co.** for Provence-inspired gifts and home accessories to the **Port Canvas Co.,** with all kinds of handsome canvas products. Crowning the main corner of Dock Square is the decidedly upscale **Compliments,** "the gallery for your special lifestyle." It features lots of glass, including lamps and egg cups, trickling fountains and cute ceramic gulls, each with its own personality. We liked the contemporary crafts at **Kennebunkport Arts** and **Plum Dandy,** the nature-inspired jewelry and tableware at **Lovell Designs,** and the Asian ceramics at **East and Design.** Check out the birdhouses made of hats along with clothing and whimsical gifts at **Carrots & Co.,** whose theme is "because life's too short for boring stuff." **Digs, Divots and Dogs** is a gift shop catering to those interests. **Alano Ltd.** and **Carla's Corner** have super clothes. Lilly Pulitzer designs are featured at **Snappy Turtle.** The splendid **Kennebunk Book Port, Abacus,** the **Good Earth Pottery, The Whimsy Shop, Maison et Jardin** and the shops at Union Square and Village Marketplace are other favorites.

Extra-Special

Rachel Carson National Wildlife Refuge, Route 9, Kennebunkport.

A mile-long interpretive trail through saltwater marshes and adjacent grasslands leads one through an area rich in migratory and resident wildlife. The 5,000-acre reserve is named for the environmental pioneer who summered in Maine and conducted research in the area for several of her books. The trail, "paved" with small gravel, and boardwalks lead through tranquil woods until – just when you begin to wonder what all the fuss is about – the vista opens up at the sixth marker and a boardwalk takes you out over wetlands and marsh. Cormorants, herons and more are sighted here regularly, and benches allow you to relax as you take in the scene. An even better view of the ocean in the distance is at Marker 7, the Little River overlook. The widest, best view of all is near the end of the loop at Marker 11. If you don't have time for the entire trail, ignore the directional signs and go counter-clockwise. You'll get the best view first, though you may not see much wildlife.

(207) 646-9226. Open daily, dawn to dusk. Donation.

Fine view of Camden Harbor is offered from porch behind Smiling Cow Gift Shop.

Camden, Me.

Where Mountains Meet Sea

From where she stood in 1910, all that native poet Edna St. Vincent Millay could see were "three long mountains and a wood" in one direction and "three islands in a bay" the other way. Her poem, written at age 18 and first recited publicly at Camden's venerable Whitehall Inn, captures the physical beauty of this coastal area known as the place where the mountains meet the sea.

Today, the late poet might not recognize her beloved Camden, so changed is the town that now teems with tourists in summer. The scenery remains as gorgeous as ever, and perhaps no street in Maine is more majestic than High Street, its leafy properties lined with the sparkling white homes that one associates with the Maine coast of a generation ago. Back then, when you finally reached Camden after the slow, tortuous drive up Route 1, you unofficially had arrived Down East.

Those were the days, and visitors in ever-increasing numbers still try to recapture them in a town undergoing a bed-and-breakfast inn boom and a proliferation of smart, distinctive shops. A sign in the window of Mariner's Restaurant, proclaiming itself "the last local luncheonette," caught our eye: "Down Home, Down East; no ferns, no quiche."

A small-scale cultural life attract some; others like the outdoors activities of Camden Hills State Park. But the focus for most is Camden Harbor, with its famed fleet of windjammers typically setting forth under full sail each Monday morning and returning to port each Saturday morning.

Camden has an almost mystical appeal that draws people back time and again. Sometimes, amid all those people, you just wish that appeal weren't quite so universal.

Inn Spots

Norumbega, 63 High St., Camden 04843.

Imagine having the run of a grand Victorian castle overlooking Penobscot Bay – a "castle to call home," in the words of owner Kent Keatinge.

One of the great late-19th-century villas along the Maine coast, the 1886 cobblestone and slate-roofed mansion was built for Joseph B. Stearns, inventor of the duplex system of telegraphy, and for a few years was the summer home of journalist Hodding Carter. It has eight sumptuous guest quarters on the second and third floors, four more in the walkout basement, a penthouse suite to end all suites and a main floor with public rooms like those in the finest estates.

Indeed, this is a mini-Newport-style mansion, from its graceful entry with oriental carpets and ornate staircase (complete with a cozy retreat for two beside a fireplace on the landing) to the smallest of guest rooms on the garden level, which has a queen bed, TV and an ocean view from its own little deck. The room that was once the smallest has now become a sitting room for the Library Suite, a two-story affair with windows on three sides and a wraparound mezzanine to get at all the books.

The other rooms, all high-ceilinged and airy, are decorated in a fresh California style with lots of pastels and plush rugs. Each includes a kingsize bed and sitting area. The Sandringham has one of Norumbega's five in-room fireplaces in the corner and a sofa and two chairs beneath balloon curtains in the turret window. The Canaervon, full of wicker, has its own little rear porch with deck chairs. A bay window with a window seat and a private deck afford full bay views for guests in the Warwick Room, also with fireplace. Even the basement rooms, with windows and private decks onto the garden, are cheery, and the Arundel comes with a jacuzzi tub and TV.

The ultimate is the penthouse suite, up a spiral staircase from the third floor. It harbors a kingsize bedroom beneath a skylight, a regal bath with pillows around a circular whirlpool tub for two, a wet bar, a living room in pink and green, and a see-through, three-sided fireplace, plus a porch with two deck chairs and a fabulous ocean view.

The parlors, the conservatory, the downstairs lounge with pool table and TV, the flower-laden rear porches on all three floors and the expansive lawns are all available for guests' relaxation. Manager JoAnne Reuillard and staff pour tea or wine in the afternoon.

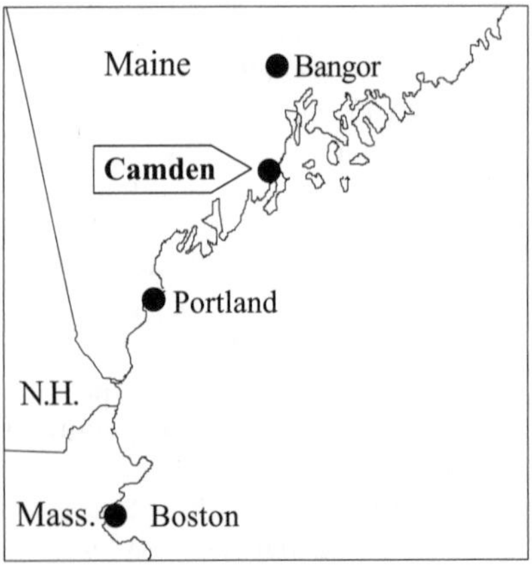

In the morning, guests gather at the large table in the formal dining room, in the sunny conservatory or outside on the deck for a breakfast feast. It includes platters of fresh fruits, homemade muffins and breads, breakfast meats and, the pièce de résistance, the main course – perhaps featherbed eggs with shrimp and hash-browns, lemon pancakes with blueberry sauce, raspberry crêpes or, in our case, french toast topped with a dollop of pink sherbet and sliced peaches, which all eight at our table agreed was about the best we'd ever had.

Norumbega is a grand Victorian mansion overlooking Penobscot Bay.

(207) 236-4646 or (877) 363-4646. www.norumbegainn.com. Eleven rooms and two suites with private baths. July to mid-October: doubles $160 to $340, suites $365 to $475. Rest of year: doubles $95 to $275, suites $250 to $375. Children over 7.

Hartstone Inn, 41 Elm St., Camden 04843.

Built in 1835 by a local merchant, this house at the edge of Camden's business district is now an expanded inn with a destination restaurant.

After operating gourmet restaurants for luxury hotel chains around the world, Mary Jo and Michael Salmon wanted to pamper guests on a smaller scale in an historic setting. They looked for a location for fifteen years. "Once we found Camden we stopped looking and started saving," said Mary Jo. "It was our dream come true."

They have markedly upgraded the guest rooms in the main house and added deluxe suites in outbuildings.

In the main house they offer eight bedrooms, two with fireplaces and all with queen beds covered with feather duvets. They perked up the decor, shunning the former country style for a more traditionally elegant look. All rooms have CD players, tiled-floor baths and triple-paned windows to muffle street noise.

Rooms vary from the cozy Tally-Ho, which looks like an English den with equestrian prints and accents and a red brick fireplace to the spacious third-floor Mansard Room, which yields a glimpse of the harbor. Hand-tied French lace curtains and a high, step-up lace-canopied bed, plump chair and loveseat convey a French look here, as do the Quimper china and accessories. TV and a jacuzzi tub are up-to-date amenities. Antique teacups from around the world are displayed on a shelf near the fireplace in the Teacup Room, whose bed beneath the skylight is dressed with a Victorian Ralph Lauren duvet and plump pillows. A collection of blue Jasperware Wedgwood is displayed in the Wedgwood Room, sedate in blue and white.

A restored carriage house in the rear offers two bi-level suites. Done in contemporary barn style, they have dark beams tempered with light walls and skylights. Their fireplaced living rooms have sofabeds for an extra guest and TVs

Hartstone Inn contains upgraded rooms and a destination restaurant.

hidden in armoires. The loft in one has a kingsize bed. Private entrances overlook the gardens in which the Salmons grow herbs and vegetables for their dining room.

Tucked away in a flower garden are two new suites with sitting rooms created in 2003 when the Salmons vacated their quarters and moved to an adjoining property they now call the Manor House on Free Street. The Cottage Suite has a queen poster bed, fireplace and bath with whirlpool tub. The Manor House contains two more large guest rooms, one the summery, cathedral-ceilinged Arbor with kingsize mahogany sleigh bed, gas fireplace and TV/VCR.

Back in the main inn, a formal parlor harbors a fireplace and a rear library is stylish in leather. There's a small game room on the third floor.

An extravagant breakfast is served in the dining room or the adjacent enclosed porch that the Salmons added. The morning of our visit began with a poached pear and pound cake with blueberry-walnut sauce. A baked egg with prosciutto and spinach tortilla followed. Michael's recipe for lobster and asparagus quiche was requested by Gourmet magazine.

(207) 236-4259 or (800) 788-4823. Fax (207) 236-9575. www.hartstoneinn.com. Ten rooms and four suites with private baths. Late June through October: doubles $115 to $185, suites $235. Rest of year: doubles $95 to $165, suites $165 to $195. Children over 12.

Inn at Ocean's Edge, U.S. Route 1, Lincolnville (Box 704, Camden 04843).

On a slope just 150 feet from the ocean, this newish hostelry has all the bells and whistles required for a four-diamond AAA rating as well as the presence of hands-on, resident owners who know that true hospitality is more than a roster of show amenities.

Ex-New Yorkers Ray and Marie Donner tiptoed, as it were, into the business when they converted a Victorian house into a six-room B&B in 1993. Five years later, they bought seven acres of vacant oceanfront property nearby and proceeded to build the inn of their dreams, with 27 deluxe rooms plus a small conference center.

Ray used his building experience on Long Island to serve as general contractor. Marie, the decorator, went through 400 rolls of wallpaper. The result was a contemporary gray structure in the Maine Shingle style – two stories and considerable roof in front and three stories and instant lawn and landscaping in back sloping down to 250 feet of ocean frontage. They added more rooms in a second "Hilltop" building in 2001.

All but one of the guest rooms face the ocean (the exception is an enormous handicapped-accessible suite that's twice the size of the rest). The others are no slouches at 400 square feet each. They are virtually the same, but with different wallpapers and linens. Each has a kingsize four-poster bed, wing chairs facing a corner fireplace, a TV/VCR, an oversize jacuzzi flanked by pillars and open to the bedroom, and a separate bathroom with the inn's own toiletries. The twelve newest come with private balconies that take full advantage of the ocean view.

When not in their quarters, guests gather in a couple of large common areas. One is a Great Room with vaulted ceiling and two levels of atrium of windows onto the oceanfront. It was being converted in 2004 into a dining area for the inn's new restaurant, to be run by local chef-caterer Scott Marquis, who closed his Marquis restaurant in Rockport.

Another common area is the front pub, where Ray's father tends a full bar. It is here that Marie puts out fancy desserts in the late afternoon, including cookies and, at our visit, a sensational blueberry pie that we persuaded her to save until after we returned from dinner. The treats continued the next morning on the large oceanfront deck, beginning with a choice of exotic juices, poached pears, homemade granola, Ray's applesauce-raisin muffins and cranberry-orange zest pancakes with bacon. Apple crêpes, cream cheese french toast and belgian waffles might be served.

In 2004, the Donners also were adding a swimming pool on their back lawn beneath the deck.

(207) 236-0945. Fax (207) 236-0609. www.innatoceansedge.com. Twenty-six rooms and one suite with private baths. Doubles, $239 to $265 early June through mid-October, $189 rest of year. Children over 14. Closed early December to April.

The Inn at Sunrise Point, U.S. Route 1, Lincolnville (Box 1344, Camden 04843).

The waterside inn of former inn reviewer Jerry Levitin's dreams has changed hands, but is continuing its travel theme. Stephen Tallon from Ireland and his wife Deanna from Australia acquired the inn in 2002 and kept it open year-round. He had managed a large travel company in Europe and she had run an inn in Alaska before settling into journalism careers with the Los Angeles Times. Tiring of life in California and later in New York, they searched for an inn of their own and found it here. "This was the last inn we looked at," said Stephen. "We knew it was right."

The inn was opened in 1992 by Jerry, a California travel writer, who took over Norman Simpson's late *Country Inns & Back Roads* guidebooks briefly. He offered three rooms in the restored 1920s shingle-style main house plus four cottages on four forested acres at the foot of a private road leading from Route 1 to Penobscot Bay in Lincolnville.

During their first full season as hands-on innkeepers, the Tallons readied another cottage, the former owner's quarters with queen bedroom, living/dining room, kitchen and deck. They named it for Jerry and Louise Levitin and decorated in a travel theme, from shelves packed with travel books to a Vermont Castings stove.

The inn is contemporary and Californian in style, but a bit cramped and pricey for some Yankee tastes. The Winslow Homer Cottage that we occupied right beside the water featured a kingsize bed, a fireplace, TV/VCR and an enormous bathroom with a jacuzzi for two and a separate shower. It was luxurious indeed, but there was nowhere to stash luggage other than in the bathroom, and the waterfront deck was so narrow as to be useless (the front porch of the main house compensated).

Also close to the water and with the same attributes is the Fitz Hugh Lane Cottage. Two smaller cottages possess queen beds and double whirlpool tubs. Although rather tight in the California style, the three inn rooms have fireplaces and music systems, queensize beds, swivel upholstered or wicker chairs in front of the window, built-in desks and armoires holding TVs and VCRs.

Guests are welcomed in the main inn with afternoon beverages. The Tallons offer a choice wine list – one of the "plush upgrades" they were adding to the inn. The main floor harbors a wonderful living/dining room that's mostly windows onto the water, an English hunting-style library with a fireplace and a small conservatory for tête-à-tête breakfasts. Deanna serves treats like grand marnier French toast, stratas, scrambles and Irish soda bread. We feasted on a terrific frittata with basil, bay shrimp and jack cheese, potatoes dusted with cayenne, crisp bacon and hazelnut coffee.

Upon departure, we found a card under our windshield: "Our porter has cleaned your windscreen to allow you to get a clear picture of our Penobscot Bay."

(207) 236-7716. Fax (207) 236-0820. www.sunrisepoint.com. Three rooms and five cottages with private baths. May-October: doubles $260 to $295, cottages $350 to $470. Rest of year: doubles $185 to $220, cottages $205 to $340. Two-night minimum in summer.

A Little Dream, 60 High St., Camden 04843.

This lacy valentine of a B&B – decorated with great flair by doting innkeeper Joanne Ball – just keeps getting better and better. Joanne and her sculptor husband Bill Fontana (much of his time is spent in remodeling these days) bought the white Victorian turreted house in 1989 and turned it into a little dream world.

From the pretty wicker and chintz furnished parlor to the elaborately decorated dining room to the conservatory they added off the dining room, everything is accessorized to perfection. Lace pillows on a chaise, tea sets, old playing cards, tiny sentimental books tucked here and there – you know that Joanne, who says "I have the nicest guests in the whole world," loves to pamper them.

The choicest lodging in the main house is the Castleview, the former master bedroom on the second floor. Done in pale green and rose, it has its own balcony, a kingsize iron canopy bed, a TV with a VCR and video library, gas fireplace and a chaise lounge in a reading nook. When the leaves are off the trees, this room has a great view of Norumbega across the street and Penobscot Bay beyond. The new Songbird Suite to the rear has a queen bed, sitting room with a window seat in the turret, and a large deck overlooking the back garden. On the main floor are two queen-bedded rooms, the soft peach-colored Garden Patio with an oversize soaking tub and the Blue Turret with gas fireplace and wicker seating in the turret.

Every room has TV and telephone, private bath, designer linens and down duvets, spa-style robes, a basket of hand towels, Crabtree & Evelyn amenities and imported chocolates. Everything is tied with ribbons. About eight pillows are on each bed and Victorian clothing is displayed everywhere.

Trellis and turret enhance Victorian B&B known as A Little Dream.

More lodging with wet bars and small refrigerators is available in the rear, three-level Carriage House, which houses Bill's studio on the lowest floor. The upstairs Treetops Suite is almost an apartment, with a skylit sitting room, a queen brass bed and the best water view from its deck. The queen-bedded Loft has a balcony with a garden view. Always perfecting, the Fontanas recently transformed the middle floor into the huge Islewatch Suite with kingsize canopy bed, a chintz sofa and wing chair, and a window seat looking onto a glorious private porch with a view of Penobscot Bay. The bath contains a double soaking tub and separate shower. The TV's whereabouts is a pleasant surprise – one of several "surprises" with which Joanne likes to entice her guests.

Breakfasts are gala happenings at A Little Dream. On lace cloths topped with flowered mats and heavy silver, you might find fresh orange juice in champagne flutes, Kentucky butter cake with crème fraîche and local blueberries, a fruit platter with honeydew melon, black raspberries, kiwis, strawberries and grapefruit, and heart-shaped banana-pecan waffles with country sausage. Smoked salmon or apple-brie omelets, fruit crêpes, lemon-ricotta soufflé pancakes or baked featherbed eggs with pears, smoked ham and a raspberry puree sauce are other specialties.

At check-in, the Fontanas will serve strawberry or peach herbal iced tea, with fresh mint from the garden, and at cocktail time, perhaps a tray of pâtés, including smoked trout, and olives.

(207) 236-8742 or (800) 217-0109. www.littledream.com. Four rooms and three suites with private baths. Mid-May through October: doubles $159 to $215, suites $205 to $285. Rest of year: doubles $115 to $135, suites $125 to $195. No children. Two-night minimum in July and August and holiday weekends. Closed in March.

Blackberry Inn, 82 Elm St., Camden 04843.

Known locally as Maine's only "Victorian Painted Lady," this B&B has been considerably upgraded and expanded under the aegis of caring innkeepers Cyndi and Jim Ostrowski. Moving here from Wilmington, Del., the couple inherited a so-so hostelry with six rooms and soon fulfilled their vision for something better. They added premium rooms with contemporary amenities and, in 2003, acquired **The Elms B&B** next door, operating the two establishments as **The Inns at Blackberry Common.**

The heart of the operation is the Blackberry, a rambling structure with many bay windows, seemingly endless public areas and an acre of gardens. Seven guest rooms are in the main house and four in the attached carriage house in the rear. The showy pressed-tin ceilings in the front parlors are repeated in the Library Room, a pleasant main-floor accommodation with a queen poster bed, gas fireplace and, like many rooms, a hand-painted sink from the Sheepscot Pottery. Upstairs, the house winds and wanders back to the rear Victorian Room with queensize poster bed, two wing chairs in front of the fireplace and a clawfoot tub in the bath.

The premium rooms are in the Carriage House. Victorian decor made no sense here, said Cyndi, so she furnished a two-bedroom suite like a Maine fishing cabin. It's a spacious affair with birch log trim, queen and twin beds, and a kitchenette. Jim's grandfather's skis from Norway are stashed in a corner next to the bed, and Cyndi's father's fishing rod and gear decorate a wall.

Two garden rooms with kingsize beds, fireplaces and jacuzzi tubs open onto the rear gardens. So does the luxurious Tree Tops, a large second-floor room that's twice the size and spans the back of the carriage house.

Guests gather in the gardens, a quiet refuge away from the Route 1 traffic, as well as in the two parlors and a living room. The center of attention may be the showy Scrabble set with 24-carat gold pieces, a souvenir of Jim's career at the Franklin Mint. Beyond is a dining room seating eighteen, with room for ten more in the garden. These are the breakfast sites for an elaborate repast – baked spiced pears with yogurt sauce and the signature cinnamon french toast with blackberry-sage sauce the day of our visit, and a tomato frittata the next morning. Tea and blackberry lemonade (the berries from the inn's own garden) are offered in the afternoon.

Seven more guest rooms are offered seasonally next door in the Elms, an 1806 Federal-style Colonial (doubles, $90 to $159). The Ostrowskis redecorated, and added a guest room and a couple of jacuzzi tubs. Guests here join the others for breakfast at the Blackberry Inn.

(207) 236-6060 or (800) 388-6000. www.blackberryinn.com. Ten rooms and one suite with private baths. Doubles, $119 to $235 May-October, $99 to $160 rest of year. Suite, $189 May-October, $155 rest of year.

The Camden Windward House, 6 High St., Camden 04843.

This handsome 1854 Greek Revival house originally was home to a prominent local shipwright and retains decorative reminders of the region's maritime history, while affording B&B guests the comforts and conveniences of today amid quite a variety of room configurations. All is overseen by Phil and Lee Brookes, who returned to their native Northeast from Kansas City in 2003 for a new career as innkeepers.

The couple continued the gourmet breakfast traditions of their predecessors, while adding amenities to enhance the guest experience. Amid period architectural elements, all bedrooms now offer king or queen hypoallergenic featherbeds, telephones with data ports, TVs, and CD-playing clock radios. Some add fireplaces, jacuzzi tubs and private decks.

Camden WIndward House is decked out in Christmas finery.

The morning meal remains a highlight of the day. Served by candlelight at individual or shared tables in the dining room, it might begin, as ours did, with a compote of roasted peaches and plums with vanilla yogurt or escalloped baked apples with mixed fruit. The day's main courses were blueberry pancakes, peaches and cream french toast, and a creamy egg casserole with white sauce and a baked tomato, offered with sausage or bacon and multi-grain toast.

The treats continue in the afternoon, when sweets and beverages appear in the library, which also contains a guest refrigerator and icemaker. Tea and popovers may be served in the garden in season.

The common rooms also include a comfortable living room, where the unusual soapstone fireplace warms chilly mornings and evenings. An adjacent deck overlooks a long back yard replete with flower gardens.

Main-floor guest accommodations include the new Chartroom Suite, whose paneled sitting room in front comes with well-stocked bookshelves, TV/VCR and a gas fireplace. The rear room has a mahogany queen arched canopy bed and french doors onto a private deck next to the gardens. The bath includes a deep jacuzzi tub.

Upstairs on the second floor are two guest rooms, each with queensize bed and sitting area, plus the Windrose Suite, a private hideaway with queen bed, sitting room, gas fireplace and clawfoot soaking tub. Nestled in the eaves of the third floor is the Crow's Nest, a cozy, two-bedroom suite with two baths and a shared sitting area.

In the rear main-floor Coastal Garden Room, a favorite of honeymooners, light pours through a skylit cathedral ceiling to reveal walls papered in a Laura Ashley floral pattern, an off-white pencil-post canopy queen bed, a wicker loveseat and a gas fireplace.

The rear loft of the restored barn has been recreated as the Quarterdeck, a large and airy space with cathedral ceiling, palladian windows and skylights, kingsize bed, fireplace, TV/VCR and jacuzzi tub with separate shower. Sliding glass doors open off the sitting area onto a deck overlooking the gardens and Mount Battie.

We were happily ensconced in the Harbor Carriage Room, an elegant, blue and white space on the main floor in the front of the restored barn. A crocheted canopy bed, two wing chairs in front of the fireplace, a TV/VCR and a clock radio with compact disc player enhanced the room. The oversize bathroom added a clawfoot soaking tub and a corner shower. Extras like a small sewing dish, a hair dryer and three-way reading lamps were typical of innkeepers who care.

(207) 236-9656 or (877) 492-9656. Fax (207) 230-0433. www.windwardhouse.com. Five rooms and three suites with private baths. Late June through October: doubles, $190 to $280. Spring and fall: $140 to $240. January-March: $120 to $200. Children over 12.

The Hawthorn, 9 High St., Camden 04843.

Elegance and comfort are the hallmarks of this 1894 Queen Anne-style beauty, one of the few in town with glimpses of the Camden harbor. Well-traveled owner Maryanne Shanahan offers ten guest quarters and a nicely landscaped back yard sloping down toward Camden Harbor and a gate opening onto the town amphitheater.

Six guest quarters are in the main inn and four in the rear carriage house, painted in barn red with a pale yellow trim that matches the house. All have queensize beds (except one with twins). Appointed in upscale cabin style, the Cloud Nine Suite covers much of the top floor with a large bedroom with TV/VCR and cozy reading area, a sitting room with gas log fireplace and a bath with clawfoot soaking tub. The regal Regency Room, second floor rear, boasts a fireplace and an extra-large bathroom with a great water view from the washstand – if you turn sideways. Framed botanical prints enhance Jillian's Suite, formed by dividing a large room into a fireplaced sitting room separated by french doors from the bedroom. The Turret room has a wicker chaise and a rocker in the turret, while everything from wallpaper to china accessories comes up roses in the twin-bedded Rose Room on the lower garden level.

The four prime accommodations, all with double jacuzzis and gas fireplaces, are in the carriage house. All have private decks or patio, aqua blue upholstered rocker or swivel chairs, and TV/VCRs. Maryanne renovated the downstairs Watney into "a sensuous and serene retreat," installing a double jacuzzi and two-person shower in its large bath. A collection of birdhouses is hung as art on the walls of the Cabriolet, prized for its garden patio. The best view is from the upstairs Norfolk, a huge room with white iron queen bed, extra day bed, gas stove and private deck overlooking shady lawn and harbor. The adjacent Broughman Room offers a mahogany poster bed, stenciling around the jacuzzi and another great water view.

Back in the main house are a double parlor with not one but two turrets. Healthful breakfasts are served at individual tables in a formal dining room or on a spacious rear deck. The fare the day we visited included a fresh fruit plate, homemade hazelnut granola and a raspberry blintz soufflé. Limeade and iced tea are offered summer afternoons on the deck.

(207) 236-8842 or (866) 381-3647. Fax (207) 236-6181. www.camdeninn.com. Eight rooms and two suites with private baths. Memorial Day through October: doubles $125 to $285, suites $175 to $240. Rest of year: doubles $90 to $185, suites $125 to $175.

Camden Maine Stay, 22 High St., Camden 04843.

Started rather simply by doting innkeepers whose skills were the envy of their colleagues, the Maine Stay expanded, upgraded and lured a repeat clientele to the point where it was the one B&B in Camden that always seemed to be fully booked when others hung out "vacancy" signs.

So retired business executive Bob Topper and his wife Juanita inherited a going concern when they took over in 2003 following the retirement of the founding innkeepers. During their fifteen-year tenure, the original 1802 farmhouse with nine

Upgraded Maine Stay Inn houses guests in comfort and style.

bedrooms sharing three baths gave way to eight bedrooms and suites, all with updated baths (some with Corian tiled showers), and a wide reputation for value and personal service.

The former Room 3, upstairs front, is typical of the accommodations as they have evolved. Formerly two small rooms with a shared bath, it is now the Christina Topper Suite with a sofabed and gas fireplace in the front sitting room, a queen brass bed in back and a private deck. The rest of the bedrooms vary in size and décor, but all live up to the term charming. The Stitchery Suite embraces what had been three bedrooms on the third floor. Several needlepoint pieces stitched by the former innkeepers adorn the walls, and end tables fashioned from old sewing machine bases are employed in the front sitting room with a gas fireplace. The rear bedroom has a high brass and iron queen bed, and a connecting room adds a twin bed. The skylit bath has a tiled shower.

The Toppers redecorated the rear Badagastein Room with keepsakes and photographs of the Austrian village where Juanita was born. They also hung photos of the former owners in a cozy front room they renamed the Smith-Robson to honor the "near legendary stature" of the former innkeepers.

The attached carriage house harbors a delightful downstairs guest room, cheery in white with blue trim and yellow accents, with queen bed, gas stove and private stone patio. You'd never guess it had been transformed from a root cellar with no windows and a dirt floor. Another favorite is the large Common Ground Room decorated with agricultural fair posters. It has a vaulted ceiling, tall windows, queen bed, Maine cottage furniture and a Vermont Castings stove, plus an outside deck.

Guests are welcome to light the fireplaces in two parlors and a library/TV room, or come into the expansive country kitchen for cookies and cheer. They're also invited to use the rear sun porch or to enjoy the seats and paths in the two-acre back yard, which backs up to Camden Hills State Park.

Breakfast is a convivial gathering, served amidst fine Aynsley china and Simon Pearce crystal at a harvest table in the dining room or at tables for two on the sun porch overlooking the garden. Juanita, who does the cooking, prepared quiche the morning of our latest visit and was planning peach french toast the next day.

(207) 236-9636. Fax (207) 236-0621. www.camdenmainestay.com. Six rooms and two suites with private baths. June-October: doubles $135 to $205 weekends, $125 to $195 midweek. Rest of year: doubles $110 to $160 weekends, $100 to $150 midweek. Children over 12.

Blue Harbor House, 67 Elm St., Camden 04843.

Ex-Californians Dennis Hayden and Jody Schmoll run this old-timer, built in 1768 and home to Camden's first settler. They offer ten guest accommodations, ranging in size from tiny front Room 4, formerly occupied by a lady who lived in the house for 96 years, to two large suites converted from a rear apartment called the carriage house. All have telephones and TV/VCRs.

The rooms are notable for attractive and varied stenciling, done by the former innkeeper who returned as Jody added more rooms. It turns up in the most interesting motifs and places. Seagulls, tulips, pineapples – you name it, you may find it stenciled somewhere. Colorful quilts, period furnishings and treasured pieces from the couple's past abound. Several of the larger rooms have gas fireplaces and clawfoot soaking tubs.

For privacy and comfort, we'd spring for one of three more deluxe rooms with separate entrances in the rear carriage house. Two have kingsize beds; the Captain's Quarters adds a circular whirlpool tub and the Bali H'ai has a gas fireplace.

Guests in this convivial establishment share a side porch, a small parlor, a sun porch/common room with TV where breakfast is served, and a second dining room for overflow. Dennis does the cooking. His favorite is blueberry pancakes, light and fluffy. He also does soufflés, rum-raisin french toast with rum-raisin ice cream, dutch babies filled with fruit, shirred eggs and lobster quiche. "I try to make every day a Sunday brunch," he says. Iced tea, cookies and sometimes homemade ice cream are served in the afternoon.

Candlelight dinners at 7 o'clock are available for house guests Thursday-Saturday by reservation. The $38.50 tab might bring lobster stew, a green salad with basil vinaigrette, rack of lamb stuffed with spinach and hazelnuts, and chocolate brownie soufflé or blueberry pie. Steamed lobster was on the docket at our latest visit. Dennis says he enjoys cooking better than his former executive job with the Korbel champagne company.

(207) 236-3196 or (800) 248-3196. Fax (207) 236-6523. www.blueharborhouse.com. Ten rooms and one suite with private baths. Doubles, $125 to $175, off-season $115 to $145. Suite, $205, off-season $175. Two-night minimum weekends. Children over 12.

Swan House, 49 Mountain St., Camden 04843.

"Birds and gulls – not traffic – wake you up here in the morning," says Ken Kohl, formerly of Chicago, who with wife Lynn took over the Swan House from a consortium of local innkeepers and imbued it with the renovations and TLC that energetic, on-site owners provide. Their location on a wooded double lot on a residential street

away from busy Route 1 is an asset. So are the comfortable, quiet guest rooms in the main 1874 Victorian house built by the Swan family, on which the Kohls built an addition for their living quarters, and in the rear carriage house nestled in the trees.

Two guest parlors are full of interesting touches. Among them are a sleigh transformed into a coffee table, covered with old Life magazines, and a game table made by Amish woodworkers. The latter has an astonishingly realistic Monopoly board made of needlepoint inlaid inside. Breakfast is served on butcher-block and glass tables in a front sun porch with a view of a hillside gazebo. Juice, strawberries in a pineapple half, homemade granola and pastries like almond coffeecake and apple crisp started the repast when we visited. Main dishes vary from pancakes to baked french toast to egg casserole.

Two bedrooms on the first floor of the main house and four more in the carriage house called the Cygnet Annex are named for swans. All but one come with canopied queensize beds. Especially popular are the upstairs Swan Lake loft with skylights, two queen beds and a day bed, a wicker loveseat and knotty pine walls hung with baskets, wreaths and artifacts. Also in demand are the quiet and cool Lohengren Suite with queensize bed and a sofabed in the sitting room, and, our choice, the queen-bedded Trumpeter Room in back with a vaulted ceiling and a private deck in the trees. From it, you can see the start of the Mount Battie hiking trail.

(207) 236-8275 or (800) 207-8275. Fax (207) 236-0906. www.swanhouse.com. Five rooms and one suite with private baths. May-October: doubles $100 to $165, suite $140. Rest of year: doubles $85 to $150, suite $125. Children over 14.

Dining Spots

Hartstone Inn, 41 Elm St., Camden.

Their work in gourmet restaurants for Hyatt and Sonesta hotels paid off for Michael and Mary Jo Salmon, who took over the small Hartstone Inn in 1998. They prettied up the dining room in beige and white, added an enclosed porch along the side and seat twenty people for prix-fixe dinners of distinction.

Michael, named the Caribbean's top chef in 1996 when he was at a Sonesta Beach resort on Aruba, buys his food fresh daily for his changing five-course menus and teaches occasional cooking classes at the inn in winter. His cuisine is contemporary and his presentations artistic – enough to attract the attention of Bon Appetit magazine, which featured the Hartstone in 2003 as one of five inns for holiday destinations across the country.

One night's dinner began with a mosaic of Maine seafood, followed by chilled gazpacho with herbed cream. Peach sorbet refreshed the palate for potato-crusted filet mignon with portobello-merlot butter. Dessert was raspberry-praline crème brûlée.

Individual warm soufflés are usually the dessert, variously featuring blueberry-hazelnut, chocolate, chambord and macadamia nut flavors. Typical main courses are Maine lobster with angel-hair pasta and asparagus, veal saltimbocca with mushroom-thyme couscous, and pistachio-crusted rack and loin of lamb with anna potatoes.

The feast can be accompanied by a selection from Michael's choice and growing wine cellar.

(207) 236-4259 or (800) 788-4823. Prix-fixe, $42.50. Dinner by reservation, Wednesday-Sunday at 7, June-October; Thursday-Sunday, rest of year.

Atlantica, 1 Bayview Landing, Camden.

The food is innovative, the surroundings convivial and the contemporary ambiance nautical at this restaurant on the Camden waterfront. Dining is on two floors, including a much-coveted upstairs turret with a single table for five, as well as outdoors on an upper deck beside the harbor and a covered terrace beneath.

It's wildly popular, so much so that we couldn't even get in at our first summer visit but did manage to snag a table near a window on a subsequent visit in the off-season, although the night was so foggy we were unable to see much of anything.

Chef-owner Ken Paquin's seafood-oriented menu might feature pan-seared yellowfin tuna with black bean-cumin vinaigrette, sautéed scallops with ginger and plum wine sauce and warm lobster-pineapple salsa, herb-rubbed hanger steak with English Stilton pan sauce, and honey-herbed lamb rack with sweet garlic lamb jus.

One of us made a most satisfying dinner of two appetizers: spicy Maine mahogany clams steamed with oriental black beans and cilantro, and crispy spring rolls filled with Maine shrimp and served with a zippy sweet Thai chile dipping sauce. The other enjoyed the caesar salad that came with the seafood pasta entrée. One of the best pasta dishes we've had, it was brimming with lobster, scallops, whitefish and shrimp in a pineapple-ginger sauce with basil and roasted macadamia nuts.

Typical desserts are orange crème brûlée and decadent chocolate cake with a hollow center filled with ganache.

(207) 236-6011 or (888) 507-8514. www.atlanticarestaurant.com. Entrées, $18 to $28. Lunch seasonally, Tuesday-Sunday 11:30 to 2:30. Dinner, Tuesday-Sunday 5:30 to 9:30, Thursday-Monday 5 to 8 in winter. Closed in November.

Cork Restaurant, 51 Bayview St., Camden.

This colorful establishment started as a small wine bar upstairs above a gourmet food and wine store known as Lily, Lupine & Fern. Chef-owner Aimee J. Ricca and partner Brian Krebs, the sous/pastry chef, relocated to a former antiques shop a few doors away. They now feature fine dining on two floors of a restored house across from the harbor.

Cork still has a wine bar, where more than 100 wines are available by the bottle, taste or glass, but the emphasis is on serious dining. The intimate interior is painted purple, an indication that this is an eclectic place. Comfortable upholstered chairs flank tables covered with floral cloths. Brian's artworks are displayed on the walls throughout.

Aimee offers three table-d'hôte meals ($47 to $54) and varies the à-la-carte menu nightly. Dinner begins with warm, yeasty rolls and good salads of baby greens dressed in a garlic-herb vinaigrette. Great appetizers are the chef's signature lobster cake (from a secret recipe), succulent and loaded with lobster meat, and a sampler of three types of local oysters on the half shell.

Entrées range from oven-roasted salmon with lime-ginger glaze to pistachio-crusted rack of lamb with bordelaise sauce. We sampled the lobster ravioli, which came in a nice broth, and lobster hibachi with wild rice and steamed spinach. Others in our party made a meal of two appetizers, beef satay with a spicy peanut sauce and crab legs, plus a trio of crab cakes served with caper sauce over wilted spinach.

Finishing touches were peach and nectarine crêpes, an individual chocolate molten cake and a trio of sorbets.

(207) 230-0533. www.corkrestaurant.com. Entrées, $20 to $29. Dinner, Tuesday-Saturday 5:30 to 9 or 9:30; Thursday-Saturday in winter.

Billowing canopy shades dining deck at Waterfront Restaurant.

The Waterfront Restaurant, Harborside Square off Bay View Street, Camden.

Rebuilt following a damaging 1995 fire, this popular restaurant is notable for its large outdoor deck shaded by a striking white canopy resembling a boat's sails, right beside the windjammers on picturesque Camden Harbor, and for its affordable, seafood-oriented international menu. Some say the location surpasses the food, though we've been well satisfied each time we've eaten here.

It's a great spot for lunch, when seven delectable salads in glass bowls are dressed with outstanding dressings, among them sweet-and-sour bacon, lemon-parmesan, dijon vinaigrette and blue cheese.

The dinner offerings turn more eclectic, although the luncheon salads are still available. Among appetizers are calamari and shrimp, mussels marinière, clam fritters and soups, perhaps chilled raspberry accented with grand marnier. The superlative smoked seafood sampler was our choice for sharing. We've enjoyed the Maine crab cakes with creamy mustard sauce, an assertive linguini with salmon and sundried tomatoes, shrimp with oriental black beans over angel-hair pasta and a special of swordfish grilled over applewood with rosemary, which was juicy and succulent. Chef Charles Butler, named "Maine Lobster Chef of the Year" in 2002, has added four lobster entrées to the menu, including the unusual lazy man's lobster and mussel thermidor. Lemon and chive-glazed chicken, grilled "baseball cut" sirloin steak and prosciutto-wrapped rack of lamb were the only meat offerings at a recent visit. All sorts of shellfish and light fare from burgers to lobster rolls are available at the oyster bar and outdoor grill.

(207) 236-3747. www.waterfrontcamden.com. Entrées, $14.95 to $24.95. Lunch daily, 11:30 to 2:30. Dinner, 5 to 10. Raw bar, 2 to 11.

Frogwater Café, 31 Elm St., Camden.

Innovative, healthful cuisine at modest prices is offered by Erin and Joseph Zdanowicz, young New England Culinary Institute graduates who moved across the country from Tacoma, Wash., to open this homey little storefront cafe in the former Galloway's, a family diner. They named it for Frogwater Lane on their favorite Bainbridge Island and stress Oregon and Washington wines on a select wine list.

Joseph's menu ranges widely, from vegetarian shepherd's pie to beef medallions served with roasted shallot-mustard sauce. Among the choices are "halibut in a bag" (baked in parchment with yellow rice and veggies and finished with a citrus beurre blanc) and braised game hen with green olive polenta. Start with some of the signature Spanish onion rings, sweet potato cakes topped with shrimp or potato-cheddar pierogies. Finish with Erin's caramel shortcake with peaches and strawberries, peach bread pudding with butterscotch sauce, chocolate-hazelnut layer cake or a creamy summer breeze tart of lemon-lime splashed with gin.

For lunch, we enjoyed a hearty bacon-leek-potato soup, an open-faced grilled baguette with feta cheese, tomato, cucumber, black olives and sundried tomato pesto, and a "BLT and Then Some Club" sandwich adding onions, cucumber and cheddar cheese on Texas toast. Sides of nippy macaroni and vegetable salads came with each, and the meal indicated the style that the couple added to the Camden dining scene. The locals return the favor by packing the place at night.

(207) 236-8998. www.frogwatercafe.com. Entrées, $15 to $24. Lunch daily, 11 to 3. Dinner nightly, 5 to 9.

Cappy's Chowder House, 1 Main St., Camden.

"The Maine you hope to meet" is one of the catchy slogans surrounding Cappy's, and local color is its strong point. The scene is barroom nautical: lobster traps hang above the bar, and green billiards-room lamps light the bare wood tables. The upstairs Crow's Nest, dark and very pubby, offers a glimpse of the harbor. The something-for-everyone menu is Down East cutesy: Maine pigskins, burgers on the bounty, Camden curly fries, mussel beach pasta and deserted islands.

The place packs in the crowds for clam chowder, a lobster salad croissant, crab cakes topped with salsa on a bed of spinach, seafood stir-fry, chicken cappenesca "and all the latest gossip." Main courses come with French bread from Cappy's Bakery & Coffee House below, rice pilaf and salad with a good house dressing. Burgers, sandwiches, salads and lighter fare are available day and night. Oysters and shrimp by the bucket are served from the raw bar during happy hour in the Crow's Nest. Cappy's souvenirs – from chowder to enameled lobster tin cups to a Cappy's miniature made by Cat's Meow – are available at its Company Store.

(207) 236-2254. www.cappyschowder.com. Entrées, $9.95 to $15.95. Open daily, 11 a.m. to midnight; winter hours vary.

Diversions

Water pursuits. Any number of boat cruises on Penobscot Bay leave from the Camden landing, where there are benches for viewing the passing boat parade. The famed windjammers are a class apart, and lately some have been giving morning and afternoon cruises, lunch and dinner cruises and even overnight trips in addition to their longer excursions. For more cruises or ferry rides to the islands, go to Rockland or Lincolnville Beach (a favorite excursion is the ferry trip to Islesboro). The Lincolnville Beach is popular for swimming. A more secluded, picturesque setting is the little-known Laite Memorial Beach with treed lawns sloping down to the water, a small beach, picnic tables and fireplaces off Bay View Street.

Inland pursuits. Some of the East Coast's most scenic hiking is available on trails in Camden Hills State Park. Mount Megunticook is the highest of the three mountains that make up the park and the second highest point on the Eastern Seaboard. If you're not up to hiking, be sure to drive the toll road up Mount Battie, an easy one-mile ride. The view is worth the $1-per-person toll. More rugged hiking is available on the trails of Camden Snow Bowl overlooking Hosmer Pond. A scenic drive is out Route 52 to Megunticook Lake, an island-studded lake that emerged eerily from the clouds the first foggy afternoon we saw it. A walking tour of Camden and a bicycle or car tour of Camden and adjacent Rockport are available through the Camden-Rockport Historical Society. A favorite drive or bicycle tour heads southeast out of Camden on Bay View Street out to Beauchamp Point and curves along Mechanic Street into Rockport. It returns to Camden via Chestnut Street. Some of the area's estates may be seen, along with belted Galloway cows grazing at Aldermere Farm.

Cultural pursuits. Summer entertainment, from band concerts to vaudeville, is provided periodically in the outdoor Bok Amphitheater next to the town library, just a few hundred feet from the harbor. The **Camden Civic Theatre** presents plays in the restored brick Camden Opera House. Classical and chamber music concerts are offered year-round at the Rockport Opera House by **Bay Chamber Concerts.** The **Conway Homestead and Cramer Museum,** a mile south of town along Route 1, includes a restored 18th-century farmhouse, a barn displaying antique carriages and sleighs, a blacksmith shop and an 1820 maple sugar house. The complex, run by the **Camden-Rockport Historical Society**, is open Tuesday-Friday 10 to 4 in July and August.

Shopping pursuits. Camden is a mecca for sophisticated shopping, and all kinds of interesting specialty stores and boutiques pop up every year, particularly along Bay View Street. On Main Street, **Planet** is a world marketplace with a trendy selection of gifts, housewares, accessories, medicinal herbals, toys, children's things and more, many with a nature or planetary theme. Planet's former location across the street is now **Emporium,** featuring contemporary women's apparel with a worldly theme. A traditional favorite for men's and women's clothing is the **House of Logan.** Gourmet foods and wines augment the traditional flowers at **Lily, Lupine & Fern.** **Surroundings** offers "durable goods" for home and garden. **The Smiling Cow,** a venerable gift shop with a myriad of Maine items, has a great view from its rear porch over the Megunticook River, which ripples down the rocks toward the harbor; you can take in the picturesque scene while sipping complimentary coffee or tea between shopping forays. **The Right Stuff** speaks for itself with home accessories and women's wear.

Along Bay View Street, **The Owl and the Turtle** is an excellent, many-roomed bookstore on two floors. **Wild Birds Unlimited** has an amazing collection of bird feeders, carved birds, birdsong tapes and the like. Custom-dyed cotton clothing is featured at **Cotton Garden.** Bed and bath accessories and lingerie are the forte of **Theo B. Camisole & Co. The Admiral's Buttons** has preppy clothing and sailing attire. We bought a handcrafted Maine wooden bucket for use as a planter from **Once a Tree,** which also has great clocks, toys, bracelets and everything else made from wood. **Unique One** stocks a great selection of sweaters done by local knitters.

Vesper Hill Chapel, Calderwood Lane, Rockport. Built of pine and resembling a Swiss chalet, this non-denominational outdoor chapel atop a rock ledge affords a great view of Penobscot Bay. It's the legacy of Helene Bok, who fulfilled a dream of building a chapel that would open out onto the world on the site of a summer estate-turned-hotel that was destroyed by fire in 1954. Mrs. Bok, friends and children created a garden showplace and a chapel sanctuary for the ages. Up to 50 people can be seated for informal meditation on Sunday mornings. Not wishing to intrude on the Quaker Meeting we came upon, we bided our time in the wonderful formal perennial and Biblical herb gardens below. More than 60 wedding ceremonies take place here annually, but the casual visitor can stop by to enjoy peace, quiet and beauty any other time from mid-April through October.

Kelmscott Farm, 12 Vancycle Road off Route 252, Lincolnville.

Eighteen rare livestock breeds are raised on this unique working farm dedicated to the preservation of endangered species. Cotswold and Shetland sheep, Gloucestershire Old Spots pigs, Kerry cattle, Toulouse geese, Aylesbury ducks, Ancona chickens and Nigerian dwarf goats are housed in barns, arks and even a piggery. Most of the animals that visitors see there or in pastures lost their commercial value years ago because they are not as productive as modern farm animals. Executive director Robyn Shotwell Metcalfe, whose family moved from California to launch the farm in 1996, says they are trying both to preserve rare breeds and to re-establish their commercial value by making products from sheep's wool and, through conservation efforts, helping farmers solve genetic problems with their animals. The old Wool Shed in the center courtyard is the farm's compass rose, a visitor center with exhibits and a farm shop. Weekend events include wool festivals, border collie trials, cooking demonstrations and even a pig's birthday celebration.

(207) 763-4088. www.kelmscott.org. Open daily except Monday, 10 to 5, May-October; 10 to 3, rest of year. Adults $5, children $3.

Extra-Special

Farnsworth Art Museum and the Wyeth Center, 356 Main St., Rockland.

What began as a modest art museum and library in 1948 has blossomed into one of the nation's leading regional art museums. With the Andrew Wyeth family deciding to make it the repository for their Maine-related works, the Farnsworth doubled its size in 1998 and again in 2000. It has sprawled across five new or restored buildings into a "campus" covering two and one-half city blocks. The heart of the complex remains the original Georgian-style brick museum and library funded by the estate of Lucy Copeland Farnsworth, which grew to the point where it now holds one of the best collections of Maine art in the world. The opening of the Wyeth Center in 1998 in the former Pratt Memorial Methodist Church put Rockland on the art map nationally. The Jamien Morehouse Wing in 2000 was the icing on the cake. Occupying the site of a former five-and-dime store, it offers more gallery space for the growing collection (now 9,000 works) as well as an excellent museum shop fronting on Main Street, which has inspired the opening of more galleries, shops and restaurants nearby. Despite rapid growth, the Farnsworth retains a sense of the personal. It is reflected in the exhibit descriptions and catalogs and is obvious in the tours of the museum's Olson House on the nearby Cushing peninsula, made famous by the Wyeth painting *Christina's World.* Dudley Rockwell, longtime Olson neighbor and Andrew's brother-in-law, gives tours and lectures there.

(207) 596-6457. www.farnsworthmuseum.org. Open daily 9 to 5, Memorial Day to Columbus Day; closed Sunday morning and Monday rest of year. Adults, $9.

Rowantrees Pottery inspired others and put Blue Hill on the map.

Blue Hill/Deer Isle, Me.

Treasure of Tranquility

Between the chic of Camden and the bustle of Bar Harbor lies a picturesque, largely unspoiled peninsula jutting into East Penobscot Bay. The area stretches across Eggemoggin Reach onto Deer Isle and Stonington. Its focal point is the tranquil treasure known as Blue Hill.

So small that the unknowing tourist could miss it, the village lies between the 940-foot-high hill from which it takes its name and an inlet of Blue Hill Bay. A few roads and streets converge from different directions and, suddenly, here it is: Blue Hill, Maine, population 1,941.

This is the center of an area long known for fine handicrafts, especially pottery. Indeed, Rowantrees Pottery owner Sheila Varnum said it was the pottery that "put Blue Hill on the map." Founded more than 50 years ago, Rowantrees has inspired a number of smaller ventures by craftspeople who cherish the simplicity of the area. Another draw in summer is the Kneisel Hall Chamber Music Festival. Blue Hill also supports a volunteer FM radio station, WERU (We Are You), with a down-home cultural programming mix.

Not for water nor resort pursuits do most visitors come to Blue Hill or Deer Isle. It's the kind of place where the sign at the outdoor phone booth warned, "This phone doesn't work the way you're used to. Dial your number, wait for the loud tone and after your party answers, deposit twenty cents." We managed to get through the second time around.

Blue Hill has no town beaches or marinas, no large shopping emporiums and only one motel. What the area has, instead, are world-famous potteries and crafts cooperatives, art studios and galleries, a handful of exceptional inns and restaurants, rural byways that remain much the way they were a generation ago and invite

Blue Hill Inn has been a local landmark since 1840.

aimless exploration, and a sense of serenity that draws the knowing few back time after time for the utter peace and quiet of it all.

Inn Spots

Blue Hill Inn, Union Street, Box 403, Blue Hill 04614.

This trim white Colonial inn with dark green shutters – a landmark in the heart of Blue Hill for more than 160 years – has been considerably spiffed up by Mary and Don Hartley.

The energetic Hartleys have enhanced the twelve guest accommodations with plush carpeting, new wallpaper and modernized bathrooms. Four have fireplaces. Some have sitting areas converted from small bedrooms. Our rear bedroom – occupied the previous night by Peter of Peter, Paul and Mary fame following a concert for Paul Stookey's hometown fans at the Blue Hill Fair Grounds – was comfortable with a kingsize bed, two wing chairs, colorful bed linens, plump towels and windows on three sides to circulate cool air, which was welcome after a heat wave. The other rooms we saw also were nicely furnished with 19th-century antiques and traditional pieces.

A luxurious efficiency suite next door is available year-round. The cathedral-ceilinged Cape House has a kingsize canopy bed plus an antique "bed in a box," a fireplace, living room with telephone and TV, kitchen and a rear deck for enjoying the back yard.

Back in the main inn, a small library-game room is furnished in antiques. The larger main parlor, where classical music plays in the background, has a fireplace and a ten-candle Persian chandelier. This is where the Hartleys serve hors d'oeuvres (perhaps smoked bluefish or local goat cheese) during a nightly innkeepers' reception for guests.

Breakfast is a culinary event. Ours started with the usual juices, a plate of cut-up fresh fruit and a wedge of apple-custard pie that one of us thought was dessert. The main course involved a choice of eggs scrambled with garden chives in puff pastry, an omelet with avocado and smoked salmon, belgian waffles with fresh strawberries or blueberry pancakes. Excellent french-roast coffee accompanied.

Outside, guests enjoy the Hartleys' perennial garden with lawn furniture, a hammock and in season a profusion of huge yellow lilies. The innkeepers occasionally charter a schooner to take guests out on East Penobscot Bay for day trips. They also sponsor seasonal concert weekends, and themed wine-tasting dinners in the off-season.

(207) 374-2844 or (800) 826-7415. Fax (207) 374-2829. www.bluehillinn.com. Ten rooms and two suites with private baths. Mid-June to mid-October: doubles $158 to $185, suites $195 and $285. Off-season: doubles $138 to $175, suites $165 and $235. Two-night minimum weekends. Children over 10. Closed November to mid-May.

Blue Hill Farm, Route 15, Box 437, Blue Hill 04614.

Located out in the country north of Blue Hill, this B&B really has a farm feeling – from the rambling farmhouse and the barn exterior of a newer addition to the goats grazing outside to the garden, stone wall, trout pond and 48 acres of woods and brooks out back.

The barn, full of fanciful touches and furnishings, includes a spacious and lofty main floor where meals are served and where there are all kinds of sitting areas – perfect for the occasional summer jazz concerts to which the inn plays host. Upstairs are seven modern, smallish guest rooms with private baths and double beds. Seven more guest rooms with double or twin beds and shared baths are in the original farmhouse to which the barn is attached. It offers a cozy, old-fashioned parlor for those who prefer more seclusion.

From an ample kitchen, innkeepers Marcia and Jim Schatz serve what they call a Maine continental breakfast: fresh orange juice, a plate of fruit and cheese, homemade granola, yogurt, cereals and, every third or fourth day, a treat of lox and bagels.

The table settings are charming: woven cloths and napkins, white china and dried flowers in baskets. Dinners are served by advance request in what the Schatzes call their "Barn Appetit" dining room. A typical meal might be poussin with Sicilian barbecue sauce, seafood wellington or peasant bouillabaisse plus salad and a dessert of homemade ice cream for $25, BYOB.

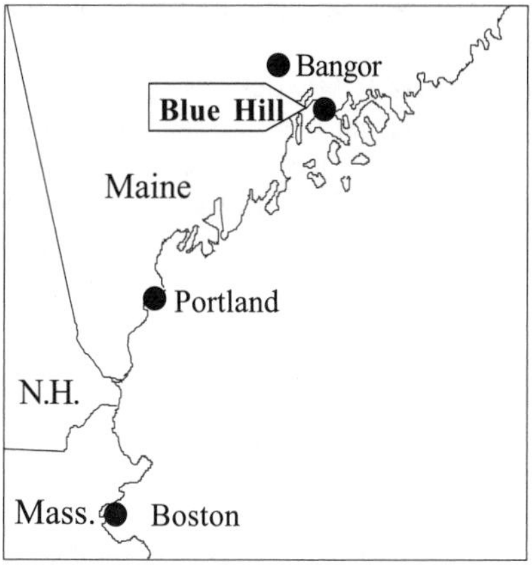

Jim, who has served as a town selectman, ran for the state legislature in 1996. "I came in second," he recalls, "and did pretty well for a Democrat around here."

Blue Hill Farm gives off good vibes. It's the kind of simple, homey place that many inn-goers look for.

(207) 374-5126. www.bluehillfarminn.com. Seven rooms with private baths and seven rooms with shared baths. Doubles, $85 to $99, June-October; $75 to $85 rest of year. Children over 12.

First Light Bed & Breakfast, 821 East Blue Hill Road, Blue Hill 04614.

How about an overnight in a former lighthouse? Book the Lighthouse Suite at this waterfront B&B. It's part of a house connected to a lighthouse tower descending to the rocks and pebbly beach beside McHeard Cove, and you can't get much closer to the water.

Owner Beverly Bartlett's most popular offering is the round bedroom on the main floor of the lighthouse tower. It has a private bath, dressing area and queen bed from which you can see the cove, and side windows yield a view of tidal waters flowing in and out of a saltwater pond.

The Seaside Garden Room and Maine Room, located on the second floor of the main part of the house, share a bath. The former has a queen bed and views of the water as well as the innkeeper's gardens. The Maine Room, which also overlooks the gardens, has a double bed and a twin.

The foyer leads into a great room with a sofa in front of sliding doors facing the cove. Guests borrow books from the library, play the grand piano or simply relax and enjoy the water view.

In the early morning, many like to climb the spiral stairs to the top of the tower to experience dawn's "first light." The wraparound view awakens guests with a "sense of awe and wonder," says Beverly. Linger over coffee, and then descend to the dining room or waterside patio for breakfast. House specialties are blueberry-stuffed french toast and Finnish oven pancakes.

(207) 374-5879. wwwfirstlightbandb.com. One room with private bath and two rooms with shared bath. Doubles, $105 to $175. Two-night minimum stay.

Eggemoggin Reach Bed & Breakfast, 92 Winneganek Way, Off Herrick Road, Brooksville 04617.

This prize of a waterside lodging establishment is situated at the end of a long driveway on 70 forested acres along a particularly picturesque section of the waterway known as Eggemoggin Reach.

Susie and Mike Canon built a main house, two duplex cottage units and a farmhouse annex with six apartment suites. They ran it as a B&B in the traditional sense for seven years, before taking back the house for family use and converting accommodations in the outlying buildings into short-term rentals. "We wanted to slow down and encourage longer stays," said Susie, ever the effervescent hostess. Her accommodations are now available by the week, or Thursday-Saturday or Sunday-Wednesday, with check-ins on Sunday or Thursday.

Our idea of a few days in paradise is a stay in one of the rustic-looking but ever-so-plush Port and Starboard duplex cottages beside the main house atop a hill facing Deadman's Cove. Paneled in pickled pine, each has a cathedral ceiling, king bed, an efficiency kitchen and a sitting area with sofabed and franklin stove. The screened porch overlooking the water was perfect for enjoying a takeout lobster dinner by candlelight.

Up a hill in a clearing is the new Bay Lodge, with six studio apartments on three levels. Patterned after the cottage units but larger, each offers a king bed, sitting area with queen sofabed, kitchenette and a substantial screened porch or deck facing Deadman's Cove head-on. Stylish furnishings, arty touches, shell mirrors and cedar showers are the rule in accommodations like the huge, lower-level Vinalhaven in which we spent a few nights and would gladly stay the summer.

Eggemoggin's newest accommodation is also their largest, The Roost, a converted

Rocking chairs take in water view from front porch of Eggemoggin Reach B&B.

apartment above a garage. It has a kingsize bed, sitting area with fireplace and a large covered porch. The Canons also rent out by the week a neighbor's carriage house as Tuckaway, with a huge great room, rear bedroom, Stickley mission-style furnishings, full kitchen and water-view decks up and down.

Though no longer a B&B, the Canons provide a continental breakfast basket upon arrival for the first morning's stay. Otherwise, guests are on their own – enjoying a tranquil quarter mile of Maine shoreline with most of the comforts of home.

(207) 359-5073 or (888) 625-8866. Fax (207) 359-5074. www.eggreachbb.com. Six suites and three cottages with private baths. Suites, Sunday-Wednesday $728 to $752, Thursday-Saturday $546 to $564, weekly $1,204 to $1,246. Cottages, $696 to $840 Sunday-Wednesday, $522 to $630 Thursday-Saturday, $1,148 to $1,400 weekly. Tuckaway, $1,792 weekly. Children over 16. Closed Columbus Day to Memorial Day.

The Inn at Ferry Landing, 77 Old Ferry Road, Deer Isle 04627.

An 1850s farmhouse at a point along Eggemoggin Reach where the ferry from Sargentville once landed has been converted into a charming waterside B&B.

Jean and Gerald Wheeler bought the property in 1996 when he left after 31 years as music director for Christ Church Cathedral in Montreal to take a similar position at St. Francis By the Sea Episcopal Church in Blue Hill. They have furnished the place with family antiques. Jean gets to exercise her passion for cooking, serving up exotic breakfasts at a mahogany table for six in the dining room. French toast made with oatmeal bread and orange slices, omelets or pain au chocolat might be the fare, leavened with organic fruit and a healthful, vegetarian orientation.

The huge living room, white with mauve trim, is airy and open with large windows on three sides. It harbors lots of seating and – given its owner's music propensity – not one but two grand pianos covered with framed family photos

Four guest quarters, two up and two down, have water views. One at the rear of the main floor has twin beds, a clawfoot tub and french doors that make a private entrance from the yard. We're partial to the second-floor suite with a brass queensize bed, a huge tub and walk-in shower, a pullout sofa and chair, a wood stove and skylights in the pitched ceiling.

Families go for the Moorings, an attached cottage in the rear annex. It's rented by the week and offers a living room with a queen sofabed, a full kitchen, a sunroom, two upstairs bedrooms and a waterfront deck.

(207) 348-7760. Fax (207) 348-5276. www.ferrylanding.com. Three rooms, one suite and a two-bedroom apartment with private baths. Doubles, $110 to $120. Suite, $165. Cottage, $1,300 per week, EP. Two-night minimum encouraged. Children over 10.

Pilgrim's Inn, 20 Main St., Box 69, Deer Isle 04627.

A welcoming, tasteful Colonial inn run with flair by Dan and Michelle Brown beckons visitors south from Blue Hill to Deer Isle. The striking, dark red 1793 house is on a spit of land with a harbor in front and a mill pond in back.

Listed on the National Register of Historic Places, the inn exudes an aura of history. The main-floor library contains an exceptional collection of books, while another parlor is a showroom for local artists.

The Browns, who owned a B&B in Maryland, took over in 2001 and quickly launched upgrades. Among them were the elimination of shared baths and the transformation of a former gift shop into the premier Rugosa Rose Cottage, a two-level affair with kitchenette, dining/sitting area and deck on the main floor and a queen bedroom with gas fireplace on the upper level.

Guest rooms in the main house are furnished in sprightly Laura Ashley style, although the sense of history is pervasive. The deluxe rooms in the rear are large with sitting areas and water views. All have wood stoves and are furnished with antiques, oriental rugs, quilts and artworks, and most now have king or queen beds. Two bedrooms on the recently renovated third floor have bathroom vanities topped with Deer Isle granite.

A vintage house next door contains two housekeeping suites. Each has a living room with sofabed and cable TV, cast-iron gas stove, queen bedroom with full bath, an efficiency kitchen and dining area, plus a large deck overlooking the water.

Besides the main-floor library and parlor, inn guests enjoy a cozy common room on the lower floor with a bay window overlooking the Mill Pond, and a small taproom.

At night the paneled taproom offers drinks to guests who gather at 6 o'clock in the downstairs common room with its eight-foot-wide fireplace and beehive oven for hors d'oeuvres before dinner in the charming dining room (see Dining Spots).

Homemade granola, ginger scones, fresh melon and omelets are featured at breakfast the next morning.

207) 348-6615 or (888) 778-7505. www.pilgrimsinn.com. Twelve rooms and three efficiency suites with private baths. Doubles, $130 to $200 in summer, $95 to $180 off-season. Cottages, $220 to $230 in summer, $165 to $210 off-season. Closed mid-October to mid-May. Cottages open all year.

Inn on the Harbor, Main Street, Box 69, Stonington 04681.

Four 19th-century buildings joined by a flower-covered common deck overlooking the harbor have been transformed into comfortable guest quarters named after schooners that sail into Stonington harbor. Christina Shipps, an international jeweler based in New York, bought the old Captain's Quarters Inn & Motel in 1995 and

Waterside decks for picnicking and lounging are featured at The Inn on the Harbor.

spent two winters renovating and refurbishing. "This place had so much potential it was just screaming for this," she said as she showed the results.

The original seventeen rooms and efficiency apartments in the complex became thirteen. The result is larger rooms with sitting areas, many queen or kingsize beds, updated bathrooms and new overstuffed furnishings good for "putting up your feet and vegetating" as you study the harbor scene through binoculars thoughtfully provided in every ocean-view room. That is, if you can tear yourself away from the lounge chairs on the enormous flower-laden deck open to all guests.

All different, rooms vary from small and cozy to suites that are rather substantial. Three on the village side compensate for lack of harbor views with extra space. In those facing the water, you're lulled to sleep by the sounds of gulls and foghorns. We especially liked the second-floor Heritage room with kingsize bed, a fireplace of Deer Isle granite and a chaise and plump club chair for taking in the scene. Another view room with granite fireplace is the main-floor Victory Chimes, also with king bed and two loveseats placed together as a sectional facing the deck garden and harbor. The innkeeper's pride and joy is the American Eagle, rebuilt in 2003 into a two-bedroom apartment with an all-glass front facing the harbor. Besides a queen bed and two twins, it has a full kitchen, dining area, living room, full bath, wood stove and a private deck. "You could happily live here," says Christina, and well we could.

A former barbershop became the adjacent Stephen Tabor cottage with high cream-colored tin ceiling and walls, queen bed, full bath, a sectional and a private deck. A two-bedroom seaview suite with sitting room is available in the Shipps House, the owner's residence out West Main Street.

A continental breakfast buffet is put out in the reception room, which also operates as an espresso bar open to the public from 11 to 6.

(207) 367-2420 or (800) 942-2420. Fax (207) 367-5165. www.innontheharbor.com. Eleven rooms, two suites and a cottage with private baths. May to mid-October: doubles $110 to $135, suites and cottage $130 and $175. Rest of year: doubles $60 to $95, suites and cottage, $95 to $130.

Goose Cove Lodge, Goose Cove Road, Box 40, Sunset 04683.

A variety of accommodations, distinguished meals and a distinct sense of place are offered at this old-timer, lately upgraded by innkeepers Joanne and Dom Parisi.

Their 1.5-mile-long dirt access road leads to the End of Beyond – the loveliest sight in the world, according to the lodge brochure. The 70-acre preserve marked by trails, wide sandy beaches and tree-lined shores is a paradise for nature lovers. At low tide, you can walk across a sand bar to Barred Island, a nature conservancy full of birds and wildlife. At night, Dom, an astronomy buff, lets guests peer through his telescope.

The Parisis have updated many of the formerly rustic accommodations and now house up to 90 guests in cottages, rooms and suites. Two suites are upstairs in the main lodge (the Lookout Suite with expansive ocean view is essentially a two-bedroom apartment). Eight more suites and rooms with woodland views are in the nearby East and North annexes. Most in demand are the nine secluded cottages and four duplex cabins, each with ocean view, sun deck, kitchenette or refrigerator and fireplace. Two new cottages, each with a beamed living room with a massive stone fireplace and a curtained queen bed alcove, have two bedrooms with twin beds and french doors onto front decks.

The lodge is the epitome of a Maine lodge: a lobby with an enormous fieldstone fireplace and stylish sofas, chairs, benches and bookcases, and the wraparound Point Dining Room (see Dining Spots) with a drop-dead ocean view across an outdoor dining deck. Guests gather for cocktails and complimentary hors d'oeuvres in the bar or on the deck before dinner, while counselors entertain children, who have their own dinner beforehand. String quartets, folk singers, a lobster fisherman or a local writer may entertain after dinner. During the day, activities include guided nature walks, sea kayaking, bicycling and bird watching. Local crafts and natural gifts are featured in the lodge's adjacent Waldron Trail Gift Shop.

Breakfast is a buffet, included in the rates.

(207) 348-2508 or (800) 728-1963. Fax (207) 348-2624. www.goosecovelodge.com. Twenty-two rooms, suites and cottages with private baths. Rates, B&B. Doubles, $170 to $550 late June to early September, $145 to $350 off-season. Two-night minimum in rooms and suites; week-long minimum in cottages July and August. Closed mid-October to mid-May.

Dining Spots

Arborvine, Main Street, Blue Hill.

John Hidake, who launched Blue Hill's acclaimed Fire Pond restaurant in 1977 and led it through its glory years, converted a rambling, 200-year-old Maine house on Tenney Hill into this fine-dining restaurant. The house also is headquarters for his Moveable Feasts catering service and the Vinery, a piano bar and bistro, open daily for lunch and light fare in what had been a deli/takeout shop at the rear of the property.

The main restaurant seats about 50 in two small front dining rooms and a larger, L-shaped room that doubles as a reception area and bar. Mismatched tables and chairs in the Shaker, Heppelwhite and Windsor styles are set with antique linens, flowers and votive candles. Oriental rugs dot the floors. Each dining area has a working fireplace and is furnished with antiques. John made some of the furniture himself.

Owner Jean-Paul Lecomte greets customers at entrance to Jean-Paul's Bistro.

Chef John and his wife Beth restored some of Fire Pond's signature dishes, but aim for eclectic cuisine. The short dinner menu features local seafood as well as heartier fare. Seasonal dishes might be broiled halibut with mushrooms and scallions in a green curry sauce, grilled yellowfin tuna with mango-red onion chutney, pork roulade with caramelized pineapple and spinach on couscous, crispy roast duckling with amaretto glaze, toasted almonds and apple-ginger chutney, and rack of lamb with porcini mushrooms, truffles and a cognac-reduction sauce.

Typical appetizers are a medley of smoked salmon, trout and mussels with horseradish cream, brie in puff pastry with figs and toasted almonds, and a salad of shrimp, grapefruit and avocado with baby spinach and toasted hazelnuts. Desserts could be grand marnier chocolate mousse, white chocolate cheesecake with berries and lemon curd tartlets.

The Vinery, a brick-floored conservatory, offers appetizers, pizzettes and light fare such as baby back ribs or a medley of sausages ($5.50 to $9.75).

(207) 374-2119. www.arborvine.com. Entrées, $18 to $24.50. Dinner, Tuesday-Sunday 5 to 9:30, Friday-Sunday in winter. Vinery, lunch in season, noon to 2; dinner, Tuesday-Sunday 5 to 11.

Jean-Paul's Bistro, Main Street, Blue Hill.

Gaelic charm and a great view of Blue Hill Bay emanate from this compelling bistro run by Jean-Paul Lecomte, a former waiter at prestigious New York City restaurants, including the 21 Club. He moved into a classic white Maine house with green shutters and started serving lunch and tea with the best water view in town. Jean-Paul takes care of the front of the house and several members of his family help out.

You can come in anytime after 11 a.m. for a cup of cappuccino and one of the delectable pastries from the patisserie. You may decide to stay for lunch. The French menu yields things like salade niçoise, croque monsieur, cobb salad, a smoked seafood platter, mussels marnière or grilled chicken with roasted red pepper on focaccia. One of us thoroughly enjoyed a spicy gazpacho and the sausage tart de provence, while the other liked the grilled chicken caesar salad, layered rather than tossed and served with a baguette. The side terrace with its custom-made square wooden tables topped with canvas umbrellas proved such a salubrious setting that we lingered over a strawberry tart and a slice of midnight chocolate cake that Jean-Paul insisted we taste, calling it a French-Japanese cake (why, we don't know).

You might even decide to stay on for tea and a snack, served amid prolific flowers and some stunning Jud Hartmann sculptures on that great terrace or at side-by-side Adirondack chairs for two on the lawn sloping toward the water.

All the atmosphere is not outside. Jean-Paul seats 80 inside in a couple of stylish dining rooms. The photogenic main room comes with cathedral ceilings, local art, white tablecloths, and blue and white spattered Bennington pottery for a simple and fresh yet sophisticated look. Wines and beers are available.

(207) 374-5852. Entrées, $8.50 to $12.95. Coffee, lunch and tea Monday-Saturday 11 to 3, July and August.

Jean-Paul at the Fire Pond, Main Street, Blue Hill.

Finally, our beloved Fire Pond is back after several false steps resulted in its (and its successor's) closing. Who better to resume its operation than Jean-Paul Lecomte, the Frenchman from New York who always dreamed of adding dinner service to his bistro across the street but lacked the time and space?

He reopened the former mill building for dinner in 2002, imparting a country French look to the upper-level dining rooms, with beamed ceilings, colorful wallpaper and blue Italian cane chairs at white-clothed tables. A dining room on the lower level adds an idyllic porch overlooking the mill stream.

Jean-Paul's loyal clientele enjoyed such entrées as Maine seafood mélange over linguini, grilled sea scallops with garlic and spinach-cream sauce, pork tenderloin flambéed with calvados and garnished with glazed apples, and three kinds of steaks with choice of sauces.

A light fare menu offers a couple of pizzas, a grilled chicken quesadilla and three hearty salads.

Starters include smoked salmon rolls filled with shrimp mousse, country pâté, portobello napoleon, and crab and lobster cakes. Dessert could be "berrymisu," blueberry crisp, apple strudel or a creamy white chocolate cheese brûlée with lime.

(207) 374-5851. Entrées, $14.95 to $17.95. Dinner, Monday-Saturday 6 to 9, July-September.

Blue Moose, 50 Main St., Blue Hill.

The building that long held Jonathan's, one of the area's better restaurants, morphed in 2003 into what was billed as a "fine family restaurant" serving three meals a day.

That translates to a casual atmosphere, particularly in the intimate front room where video games are on the wall at each booth (and were getting quite a workout at our midday visit), and an extensive, affordable menu offering something for everyone.

The larger rear dining room with rough wood walls, pitched ceiling, bow windows and a prominent bar is quieter and helps fulfill the word "fine." The dinner menu varies widely, from macaroni and cheese and chicken parmesan to bacon-wrapped trout stuffed with shrimp and grilled ribeye steak with dijon butter.

(207) 374-3274. Entrées, $6.95 to $18.95. Breakfast, lunch and dinner year-round.

Colonial structure dating to 1793 houses Pilgrim's Inn.

Pilgrim's Inn, Deer Isle.

Inn guests as well as knowing outsiders feast on some of the island's best meals, prepared by well-known Maine chef Jonathan Chase, who sold his namesake Blue Hill restaurant and took over the Pilgrim Inn's kitchen in 2002. His sous chef of fourteen years and some of his clientele came with him.

Following cocktails in the common room or outside on the deck beside the barbecue, diners adjourn to the former goat barn, where they're surrounded by candlelit tables set with flowers, farm utensils and quilts on the walls, big windows and ten outside doors that open to let in the breeze.

The four-course, prix-fixe menu changes every two weeks. Start with a soup such as Portuguese caldo verde or vegetable black bean with crème fraîche. A seasonal salad of local greens and summer vegetables follows.

The six main-course selections might include pan-seared arctic char with roasted poblano-pepper sauce, crisp roasted duckling glazed with orange and ginger, and sautéed medallions of venison with shiitake-wine sauce.

Typical desserts are chocolate- and almond-glazed amaretto cake, blueberry-rhubarb crisp with lemon ice cream, and dried fruit compote with vanilla gelato.

We'll never forget a Sunday night dinner: salad with goat cheese, homemade peasant bread, a heavenly paella topped with nasturtiums (such a pretty dish it should have been photographed for Gourmet magazine) and sensational raspberry chocolate pie on a shortbread crust.

(207) 348-6615 or (888) 778-7505. Prix-fixe, $34.50 for the public, $29.50 for inn guests. Dinner by reservation, seatings from 6:30 to 7:30.

Goose Cove Lodge, Goose Cove Road, Sunset.

The food here is some of the area's most inspired as owners Joan and Dom Parisi continue to turn what had been a charming but rustic family resort into a more upscale lodging facility and a destination restaurant. Their **Point Dining Room,** paneled in pine with wraparound windows onto the water, is augmented by a large and glorious dining deck almost at water's edge.

Guests gather for cocktails and complimentary appetizers in the bar or on the deck before dinner.

The menu changes weekly. Typical starters might be marinated tuna tartare with wasabi cream, shrimp and scallop sauté with watercress and curried garlic sauce, and chile-glazed chicken wings with sweet Thai dipping sauce. Recent main courses included Mediterranean seafood stew, twin peeky-toe crab cakes with roasted tomato-vodka sauce, pan-seared duck breast with raspberry demi-glace, New York strip steak with green peppercorn sauce and grilled butterflied lamb with rosemary demi-glace.

Desserts might be a sweet chocolate terrine with macadamia mousse and saffron-mango ice cream, and blueberry cake with blueberry ice cream.

(207) 348-2508 or (800) 728-1963. Entrées, $15 to $27. Dinner by reservation, Tuesday-Sunday 5:30 to 8:30. Closed mid-October to mid-May.

Lily's Café, Route 15, Stonington.

Deer Isle and Stonington folks head for this inauspicious looking little house across the cove from South Deer Isle for what they consider consistently the best food around. Chef-owner Kyra Alex opened in 1998 and attracted a steady following for eclectic fare that ranges from lentil salad to cold Chinese noodles to crispy baked haddock sandwich to albacore tuna melt to veggie sandwich and Lily's nutburger. That's a sampling of the all-day fare.

At night, Kyra adds a couple of specials that she decides on at about 3 p.m. and are "ready at 5." One night's choices were baked salmon and polenta with chicken sausage and tomato sauce. The previous night saw white lasagna and baked pork with roasted potatoes and gravy. The main floor of the house holds six tables, most topped with glass and dolls or shells. Nine more tables in two upstairs rooms are pressed into service on busy nights.

The restaurant hews to limited hours, never on weekends and closing at 8 p.m. We know, because we were running late and nearly didn't make it. But our innkeeper guests pulled rank and got us in for a convivial meal of delectable lamb chops, topped off with bread pudding.

Upstairs is the **Chef's Attic,** a shop featuring cottage wares and occasional art shows. There also are tables scattered around the back lawn and an organic produce stand in this establishment that's the essence of Down East Maine.

(207) 367-5936. Entrées, $5.95 to $10.95. Open Monday. Tuesday and Friday, 7 to 4, Wednesday and Thursday 7 to 8, Memorial Day through Labor Day. Closes one hour earlier rest of year.

Diversions

Culture and crafts vie with picturesque coastal scenery for the visitor's attention. Pottery and handcrafts abound in Blue Hill and, indeed, all across the East Penobscot Bay peninsula and onto Deer Isle and Stonington.

The world-famous **Haystack Mountain School of Crafts** at Sunshine on Deer Isle, which sometimes has shows, is worth the drive simply for the breathtaking view from its unsurpassed setting on a steep, forested slope with stairs down to East Penobscot Bay. Public tours are offered daily at 1 p.m. in summer.

Rowantrees Pottery, the institution inspired in 1934 by Adelaide Pearson through her friend Mahatma Gandhi, is still going strong in a rambling house and barn reached by a pretty brick path through gardens at the edge of Blue Hill. Inside, you may be able to see potters at work; veteran employees in the upstairs shop might recall for you the days when as children they joined the story hours and pottery classes run by Miss Pearson and her protégé, Laura Paddock. Sheila Varnum, who was associated with the founders since she was 3, has owned the pottery since 1976 and has continued its tradition. Named for the mountain ash trees above its green gate along Union Street, Rowantrees is especially known for its jam jar with a flat white lid covered with blueberries, as well as for unique glazes. Items are attractively displayed for sale.

Rackliffe Pottery at the other end of town is an offshoot of Rowantrees, Phil Rackliffe having worked there for twenty years. He and his family make all kinds of handsome and useful kitchenware in a work area next to their small shop on Route 172. The soup tureens with blueberry, strawberry or cranberry covers are especially nice.

Kneisel Hall Chamber Music Festival, Pleasant Street, Blue Hill, (207) 374-2203. Concerts by well-known faculty members are given Friday evenings and Sunday afternoons from late June to mid-August in a rustic concert hall off upper Pleasant Street. The series is part of the summer session of the Kneisel Hall School of Music, founded by Dr. Franz Kneisel and called "the cradle of chamber music teaching in America." Innkeepers say a summer tradition for many of their guests is to arrive on Thursday and stay through Sunday, taking in two concerts, visiting the potteries and dining well at local restaurants. Concert tickets, $19; veranda seats, $14.

Blue Hill Farmer's Market, Route 172 at the Blue Hill Fairgrounds. Each Saturday in July and August from 9 to 11:30 a.m., local farmers and artisans gather here for a real down-home event. Horse-drawn wagons give the youngsters hayrides, while residents and visitors browse through a small but interesting display of everything from local produce to goat cheese, jellies, handmade gifts, lamb's wool and patterned ski sweaters. The Blue Hill Fair, incidentally, has been going strong since 1891.

Shopping. Along Blue Hill's Main Street, big spenders are drawn to the famed **Jud Hartmann Gallery.** Here, sculptor Hartmann shows quite spectacular paintings by artist-friends along with the exceptional bronze sculptures he crafts at his studio in nearby Brooklin (he also has a gallery in foliage season in Grafton, Vt.). Everything is artfully arranged at **The Handworks Gallery,** which shows super contemporary crafts. Artist Judith Leighton's **Leighton Gallery** off Parker Point Road is considered one of the best in Maine. Other favorites include **Liros Gallery** and **Mark Bell Pottery.** Birdhouses, carved birds, hooked fish hangings, tables with driftwood bases and Victorian twig furniture appeal at **Belcher's Country Store,** an offshoot of the main store in Deer Isle. **North Country Textiles** has moved its main store here from South Penobscot, offering wonderful throws, rugs, table linens, wicker and wooden furniture, pottery and more. **The Blue Hill Wine Shop** claims the largest selection in Down East Maine, along with teas and tobaccos. **SaraSara's** offers fun and funky apparel for women. Blue Hill also supports two fine bookstores, **Blue Hill Books** and **North Light Books**.

Beside the causeway on Little Deer Isle is **Harbor Farm,** a store and showroom in an 1850 schoolhouse and a wreath-production building moved there by barge. Starting by making wreaths of wicker, Dick McWilliams and company have expanded into an impressive mail-order and retail operation of fine crafts, down-home knickknacks, practical gadgets and Christmas items. Something of a cross between, say, Tiffany's and Brookstone, it features unique, made-to-order items from birch twig swan baskets, woven coverlets, and gold and silver jewelry to wooden hooks, folding stools, English bathracks and garden shears. Behind the country store is a Christmas shop with ornaments from around the world.

In Deer Isle, the **Maine Crafts Association** shows contemporary works by members. The **Blue Heron Gallery** exhibits contemporary American crafts, featuring works by the Haystack faculty. **The Turtle Gallery** has changing exhibits of watercolors, oils, drawings, photographs, ceramics and wood carvings by area artists. **The Periwinkle** stocks books, cards, knit goods, stuffed animals and local crafts. **Dockside Quilt Gallery** is known for colorful island-made quilts. Personal favorites include famed metalsmith Ronald Hayes Pearson's stunning gold and silver jewelry at Pearson and the one-of-a-kind rugs at **William Mor Oriental Rugs.**

Stonington's long slumbering downtown is awakening. **The Clown,** which also has stores in Blue Hill and Portland, is a remarkable venture, combining English antiques, contemporary art and Italian ceramics with Italian specialty foods and wines. The fine olive oil is produced on the owners' farm in Tuscany. The **Grasshopper Shop** and the **Dry Dock** offer gifts and miscellany. Three galleries caught our eye, **West Main Street Gallery, Firebird Gallery** and the **Hoy Gallery,** displaying Jill Hoy's vibrant paintings of coastal Maine. The charming **Dockside Bookstore,** right beside the water with chairs for reading on a small deck, specializes in Maine and marine books and nautical gifts.

Visit the Fish Shop at the new **Stonington Sea Products** facility on Route 15 outside Stonington. Its hickory-smoked salmon, smoked slowly and naturally in a kiln imported from Glasgow, has been rated the finest Scottish-style smoked salmon outside Scotland.

Extra-Special

Nervous Nellie's Jams and Jellies, 598 Sunshine Road, Deer Isle.

The jam business that Peter Beerits started because he could not find employment as an artist has enabled him to work full-time producing sculptures. Still employing table-top steam kettles, his jelly business puts up small batches totaling 40,000 jars each year in a little house on the road to the Haystack Mountain School of Crafts. So many people were stopping in that Peter decided to serve refreshments as well. His **Mountainville Café** offers morning coffee and afternoon tea with homemade scones and breads (with plenty of jams – we especially like the wild Maine blueberry-ginger conserve and the hot tomato jelly). Included is a frozen drink that Peter calls a Batido, a refreshing but caloric mix of cream cheese, freezer jam and crushed ice cubes. Besides his culinary talents, Peter produces fantastic sculptures from found objects – he calls it other people's junk, obtained from the Deer Isle dump. Peter's quirky sculptures on the grounds outside the jam kitchen make this worth a visit. We were intrigued by a sculpture of a lobsterman with huge red wooden claws for arms. Lately, Peter cleared the surrounding woods to be peopled with sculptures from his studio fashioned from an abandoned store he moved to the site. Look for witches, woodsmen and owls among the trees.

(207) 348-6182 or (800) 777-6845. www.nervousnellies.com. Open daily 9 to 5, mid-May through Christmas; rest of year, by chance.

Boats in Northeast Harbor are on view from rear deck at Asticou Inn

Mount Desert Island, Me.

The Other Harbors

Mount Desert Island has long held a special appeal, first as a summer resort for society and later as the site of a national park beloved by campers and naturalists.

Its focus for us, as well as for increasing numbers of others, has always been Bar Harbor and the eastern part of Acadia National Park. Since our first vacation there some 40 years ago, we've witnessed the changes – for better and worse – as tourism impacted relentlessly. And still Bar Harbor remains dear to our hearts.

Be advised, however, that there are other harbors and another side to Mount Desert Island. The other side is the quieter side, one that its devotees call "the right side" of this fabulously varied island. This side of the island celebrates its own identity in its annual Quietside Festival, three days of activities the last weekend in June.

Even the quiet side is wonderfully diverse. Northeast Harbor and Southwest Harbor are barely two miles across Somes Sound from each other, but far apart in spirit and character.

Northeast Harbor is the yachting harbor, a haven for Rockefellers and some of the world's great boats, a moneyed place where sailing is the seasonal preoccupation. Southwest Harbor is the working harbor, where fishing and boat-building are the year-round occupation. Here and in Bass Harbor, the old-time flavor of coastal Maine remains.

Some of the choice portions of Acadia National Park are close at hand: Seawall, Wonderland, Beech Mountain, Echo Lake and Eagle Cliff. Thuya and Asticou gardens are special treats, and we know of few more beguiling water views than those up and down Somes Sound, the only natural fjord in North America.

For a different perspective than most visitors get of Mount Desert, try the other harbors on the "right side" of the island.

Sea captain's house has been stylishly refurbished as Lindenwood Inn.

Inn Spots

Lindenwood Inn, 118 Clark Point Road, Box 1328, Southwest Harbor 04679

Towering linden trees shade this turn-of-the-century sea captain's home, now grandly refurbished by ex-Australian Jim King. Jim, who had opened the Kingsleigh Inn here, returned from traveling around the world in 1993 to purchase the Lindenwood, which had fallen on lean times.

With a decorator's eye, international tastes and an assortment of cosmopolitan possessions, he redid the entire place. You'll find palm trees on the front veranda, Italian chairs and glass tables in a dining area he dubs "tropical primitive – I got tired of the country look," a collection of shells and stones in each bedroom, sleek black modern lights, potted cactus plants on the tables, pottery from Mexico and Indonesia here, a contemporary mission bed there. He splashed around lots of color, from walls to down comforters to carpets. Call it different, call it eclectic, call it international. Jim calls it "a blend of old and new" and wants the Lindenwood to be "in the vanguard of the new look."

The two parlors are contemporary, accented with green and white striped upholstered chairs. Potted plants throughout the main floor bring the outdoors inside. Upstairs are eight guest quarters of varying sizes, several with fireplaces. Check out Room 6 with its six-foot-long clawfoot tub. It's one of six with private decks or balconies affording views of the harbor. The ultimate is the penthouse suite with a curved sofa and gas fireplace, opening onto an enormous rooftop deck holding an oversize spa.

We were smitten by the poolside bungalow, with cable TV in the cathedral-ceilinged living room, an efficiency kitchen and a queensize bedroom. Just outside was the inn's heated gunite pool and a separate spa topped by a sculptured mask spraying a stream of water.

In the morning, seated in one of the small dining rooms, we helped ourselves to fresh fruit and raspberry-banana muffins from the buffet and were served a main dish of fruit crêpes. We understood well why fun-loving Jim has such a devoted repeat clientele.

(207) 244-5335 or (800) 307-5335. Fax (207) 244-3643. www.lindenwoodinn.com. Five rooms, three suites and one bungalow with private baths. Mid-June to mid-October: doubles $105 to $185, suites $245 to $275, bungalow $195. Rest of year: doubles $95 to $155, suites $195 to $225, bungalow $165. Closed mid-December to mid-March.

The Kingsleigh Inn 1904, 373 Main St., Box 1426, Southwest Harbor 04679.

A wraparound veranda full of wicker, colorful pillows and flowers distinguishes this B&B with an unusual pebbledash stucco-stone exterior. Guests enter through the country kitchen, which seems to be the heart of the house, where refreshments are available throughout the day.

Ken and Cyd Champagne Collins from Newburyport, Mass., added their own antiques and artworks to the eight bedrooms, some with harbor views and all with private baths. One has a new balcony with chairs overlooking the water. The Turret Suite on the third floor offers television and a great view from a telescope placed between two cozy wicker chairs; the bedroom comes with a kingsize bed and fireplace. The other rooms are lavishly furnished with queensize beds, Waverly wall coverings and fabrics, plush carpeting, lace window treatments, country accents and woven baskets filled with thick towels.

Afternoon tea and homemade cookies or lemon bars are served on the porch or in cool weather by the fireplace.

Bountiful breakfasts are taken by candlelight at tables for two in a dining room with gleaming hardwood floors, dark green tablecloths, and pink and green china. Juices, fresh fruit, homemade granola and muffins preceded baked German eggs at a recent visit. Other treats include crab soufflé, lemon french toast with warm Maine blueberry sauce, eggs florentine and belgian waffles with fruit topping.

(207) 244-5302. Fax (207) 244-7691. Seven rooms and one suite with private baths. June through mid-October: doubles $110 to $145, suite $240. Rest of season: doubles $75 to $115, suite $155. Closed November-April.

Asticou Inn, Route 3, Northeast Harbor 04662.

Majestically situated at the head of Northeast Harbor on a hillside where the mountains slope to the sea, the Asticou has been a bastion of elegance since 1883.

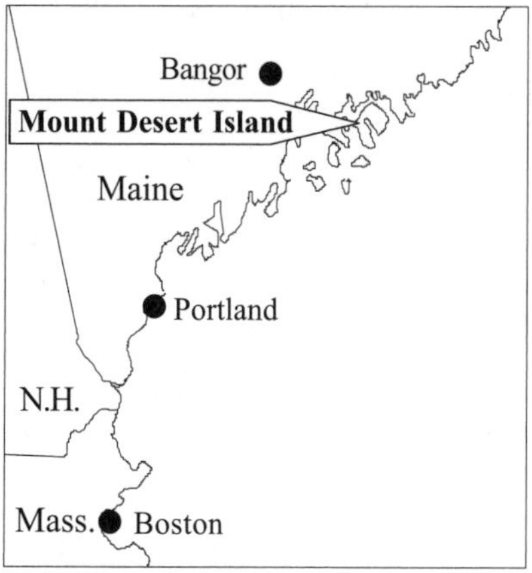

The fireplace in the lobby is always ablaze – "to take the chill off foggy mornings or late afternoons," our friendly guide informed. The lobby with its huge oriental rug and wing chairs gives way to a comfortable parlor. Beyond is a bright and breezy cocktail lounge with sliding doors onto the outdoor deck. Amid white furniture, yellow umbrellas and petunias in planters, it's a great place from which to view the goings-on in the harbor below. The enclosed east porch is used for games and television viewing. The spacious dining room (see Dining Spots)

serves three meals a day and a Thursday evening buffet that draws people from all over the island.

A carpeted staircase and a turn-of-the-century elevator lead to 30 guest rooms and suites on the second, third and fourth floors, many of them recently renovated but still with simple furnishings in the traditional Maine cottage style. Rooms vary from one with a double bed "in a less quiet spot" to a suite with a sofa, two peach chintz chairs and a desk in a sitting room, plus two twins in the bedroom. One newly renovated suite with a queen bed, sink in the bedroom and clawfoot tub in the bath has a view of the loading dock, but that is an exception. The new norm is king or queen beds or combinations and ocean views, and some of the smaller rooms have given way to form suites. Eleven more rooms and suites are available in the popular Bird Bank and Blue Spruce guest houses and Cranberry Lodge.

Most striking are the three contemporary, circular Topsider Cottages, each with two identical suites. Their interiors painted yellow with mauve accents, they come with decks, full-length windows, king beds except for one with twins, attractive sitting areas with floral chintz fabric and wicker, and efficiency kitchenettes with refrigerators, wet bars and microwaves.

All the common areas and the Topsider rooms have been redone. Rooms in the inn and Cranberry Lodge were being refurbished in phases – a total of sixteen in one year alone.

The perfectly landscaped grounds offer a swimming pool, tennis, gardens and, all the while, changing vistas of the harbor. Guests have privileges at the Northeast Harbor Golf Club. The inn also has a massage therapy center.

The MAP meal plan is no longer required – nor are jackets and ties in the dining room – as the inn continues to evolve with the times (see Dining Spots). The rates include a deluxe continental breakfast.

(207) 276-3344 or (800) 258-3373. www.asticou.com. Forty-seven rooms and suites, most with private baths. July and August: doubles $225 to $285, suites $220 to $325. Spring and fall: doubles $180 to $215, suites $200 to $230. Two-night minimum in season. Children over 6. Closed mid-October to mid-May.

The Claremont, Clark Point Road, Box 137, Southwest Harbor 04679.

The other grand dowager of Mount Desert, the Claremont was founded in 1884, a year later than the Asticou. It's the island's oldest continuously operating inn, with only three owners in its first century. It also boasts a tranquil, six-acre site near the mouth of Somes Sound.

Entered in the National Register of Historic Places as a reminder of the "prosperous, relaxed and seasonal way of life" of Maine's early summer-resort era, the original light yellow wood structure has been spiffed up of late and the name has been shortened from the Claremont Hotel and Cottages. But the inn's wraparound veranda and the heavy white Adirondack chairs lined up side by side on the rear lawn still provide a relaxing view of Somes Sound, and croquet remains the sport of choice. The annual Claremont Croquet Classic is known as the home of nine-wicket croquet.

The main building contains a lobby and living rooms full of wicker chairs and sofas, a handsome dining room and 24 guest rooms on the second and third floors, all with private baths. Twenty have been renovated to include heat and telephones. Furnishings remain simple yet comfortable, with queen or two twin beds. More rooms and suites are offered in outlying guesthouses. The Phillips House has five large rooms, a suite and a massive fieldstone fireplace in the parlor. Also available

Lawn chairs are lined up for visitors to take in view at The Claremont.

for longer stays are fourteen housekeeping cottages with living rooms, franklin stoves or stone fireplaces and decks. Cottages vary in occupancy from two in the Wentworth studios to seven in the Rowse House and in location from shorefront to wooded setting.

Besides croquet, boating and tennis are offered, and the hardy can swim from the dock in chilly Somes Sound. The Boat House and its decks are favorite spots for a light lunch or cocktails in summer.

Dinner is available for guests and the public in a candlelit dining room with windows onto the water. The short menu includes such dishes as soy-seared darne of salmon, seafood paella and grilled lamb loin chops with lamb demi-glace.

(207) 244-5036 or (800) 244-5036. Fax (207) 244-3512. www.theclaremonthotel.com. Thirty rooms, two suites and fourteen cottages with private baths. Hotel, guest houses and Cole Cottage: doubles, $220 to $240 MAP, $170 B&B, mid-July to Labor Day; rest of season, $220 to $240 MAP, $125 to $165 B&B. Cottages, $170 to $250 EP, mid-June to Labor Day; $120 to $180 rest of season. Closed late October to Memorial Day. No credit cards.

Entrées, $19 to $23. Lunch at the Boathouse, noon to 2, July and August. Dinner nightly, 6 to 9, late June through Labor Day. No credit cards.

Harbourside Inn, Harbourside Road (Route 198), Box 178, Northeast Harbor 04662.

Built in 1888 in the style of the Seal Harbor Club, this shingled hilltop inn is fresh and pleasant and unusually comfortable. "We're old-fashioned and intend to keep it that way," Geraldine Sweet explains. She and her husband, who formerly managed the Jordan Pond House, acquired the 22-room, Shingle-style mansion in 1977 from a woman who would sell only to Maine residents who would maintain the heritage.

The heritage indeed remains, from the nasturtiums nurtured from the original seeds still brightening the entry circle and the blueberry plants along the entry path to the original carpets from China, repaired when they became worn because they were too prized to be discarded. Guests gather in a pleasant parlor with wing chairs in shades of blue or on the front sun porch, all done up with bright cushions and curtains in appropriate Northeast Harbor colors, preppy pink and green.

All but one of the ten guest accommodations on the first and second floors have working fireplaces, and three have their own sun porches. Four more bedrooms on the third floor raise the total to fourteen. All have private baths and are furnished in 19th-century style. "We had great fun with the wallpapers," Geraldine said. One bathroom's paper has small red bears with big hearts on the borders, and one bedroom is papered with irises and another with fuchsias. Room 1 with a wallpapered ceiling has a Wallace Nutting bed, a collector's item. The floral-papered honeymoon suite includes a kingsize bed, fireplace and an enclosed porch with cathedral ceiling, wicker rockers, a glider and a teak deck chair from the liner Queen Elizabeth. A first-floor suite offers a sitting room with comfortable chairs grouped in front of the fireplace and a kitchenette in an alcove, a bedroom with a kingsize four-poster and a chaise lounge, and an old-fashioned tub in the bathroom. White organdy curtains in the windows frame the dark fir trees outside.

Outside are perennial gardens and a path for hiking up Norumbega Mountain and around Haddock Pond.

A continental breakfast with homemade blueberry muffins is served on the sun porch.

Lest the inn's name mislead, the Sweets stress that the once-sweeping view of the harbor from their hilltop is now obstructed by a century's growth of trees. "We're only the third owners of this wonderful property," said Geraldine. "Hopefully, our children will take it over."

(207) 276-3272. www.harboursideinn.com. Eleven rooms and three suites with private baths. Doubles, $125 to $170. Suites, $170 to $225. Open mid-June to mid-September.

Grey Rock Inn, Harbourside Road, Northeast Harbor 04662.

Remarkable gardens and a prolific hanging begonia on the porch at the front door greet visitors to this inn, said to have been a gathering place for Northeast Harbor socialites after it was built in 1910 as a private residence.

Inside the inviting large fieldstone and shingled mansion with yellow trim is a veritable showcase for British owner Janet Millet's decorating tastes: an array of wicker like you've never seen, fans and paintings from the Orient, fringed lamps, masses of exotic flowers – rather overwhelming, some find.

People who stay at Grey Rock must like eclectic elegance, for that's what they get. The two fireplaces in the living room and parlor are kept aglow, even in mid-summer, because the innkeeper finds her guests want it that way. Wicker serves as furniture and art, from table lamps to loveseats, from desk to plant stand.

Guest rooms are equally exotic. The huge main-floor corner room with canopied four-poster bed, oriental screen and private balcony could not be more romantic. The upstairs rooms are lacy, frilly and flowery, with much pale pink and green, all kinds of embroidered towels, and porches all around. Some have fireplaces, and all have views of the trees or gardens atop this wooded hilltop high above and back from the road.

Assisted by her sons Adam and Karl, Janet serves an exemplary continental-plus breakfast, including a fruit compote with eight to ten kinds of fresh fruit, assorted baked goods and bacon, occasionally eggs, and what she states is "a good cup of coffee for a British lady."

(207) 276-9360 (winter: 207) 244-4437. Fax (207) 276-9894. www.greyrockinn.com. Seven rooms and one suite with private baths. Doubles, $185 to $375 July-October, $110 to $275 mid-May through June. Children over 7. Closed November to mid-May.

Prolific plantings and hanging begonia grace entry to Grey Rock Inn.

The Maison Suisse Inn, Main Street, Box 1090, Northeast Harbor 04662.

Pick a couple of blueberries along the entry path as you arrive at this inn, surrounded by gardens designed by a previous owner who trained as a landscape architect in Switzerland. Beth and David White did a total renovation to produce six comfortable bedrooms and four suites.

Canopy beds, silk-screened wallpaper, feather pillows, down comforters, dust ruffles, antiques and Bar Harbor wicker comprise the decor. In-room telephones have been added lately. Rooms come in a variety of configurations, and suites range from one to two and one-half bedrooms. We're partial to an upstairs suite, which has a small balcony with a wicker loveseat, and the Garden Room with a separate entrance and a charming little garden ringed by cedars to make it private. Two main-floor rooms open onto outdoor porches. The suites with two bedrooms, one with eight sides, have fireplaces.

Three downstairs common rooms with fireplaces are handsomely furnished. Beach stones form an unusual inset in the mantel of the brick fireplace in the main hall of the circa-1890 summer mansion, designed in the shingle style. There are more seating areas in the gardens outside, and the Whites recently purchased an abutting acre for more outside seating and to clear some trees to provide "more water glimpses from our rooms," in Beth's words.

Recently, they erected an English Tudor stucco and Shingle-style Guest Cottage in back to add five more rooms with balconies or terraces, four with kingsize beds and three with fireplaces.

Room rates include a full breakfast with the inn's compliments at Colonel's Restaurant across the street.

(207) 276-5223 or (800) 624-7668. www.maisonsuisse.com. Eleven rooms and four suites with private baths. Early July to mid-October; doubles $135 to $225, suites $225 to $265. Off-season: doubles $75 to $195, suites $165 to $235. Closed mid-October to mid-May.

The Inn at Southwest, 371 Main St., Box 593, Southwest Harbor 04679.

This inn has been taking in guests since 1884, first as a rooming house and lately as an attractive Victorian B&B, acquired in 2001 by Sandy Johnson and Andrea Potapovs. They spent their first winter remodeling the living room, installing gas-log stoves in a couple of second-floor guest rooms and reconfiguring two rooms into suites.

Guest accommodations are named after historic Maine lighthouses and decorated accordingly. They are furnished with designer linens, down comforters, antique wicker or rattan tables and desks, ceiling fans, potpourri, plants and the like. The Cape Elizabeth, second-floor front, is the most spacious room, with a kingsize wrought-iron bed, a sitting area with a sofabed and an antique writing desk, a bay window and new gas stove. Its neighbor, the new Winter Harbor Suite, has a gas stove and sleeper sofa in the sitting room and a four-poster canopy queen bed and a bay window in the bedroom.

On the third floor is the Pemaquid Point Suite, newly fashioned from two bedrooms. One room has twin beds and a gas stove. The main bedroom comes with a queensize bed and a large window seat beneath the unusual chapel window, a feature also available in the Owl's Head Room nearby.

Guests gather in a comfortable living room with a big sofa, TV and stereo, a game table and an ornate fireplace mantel. Waverly and Schumacher wallpapers, stenciling and old pictures are included in the main-floor decor.

Elaborate breakfasts are served in the dining room or on the wraparound porch lined with geraniums and overlooking Victorian gardens. You might start with sautéed nectarines or poached pears in wine sauce and rhubarb crunch or raspberry-blueberry crisp. Eggs picante, blueberry-stuffed french toast or belgian waffles with raspberry sauce could be the main course. Other possibilities include a specialty crab-potato bake.

In the afternoon, the innkeepers offer homemade cookies in the living room.

(207) 244-3835. Fax (207) 244-9879. www.innatsouthwest.com. Five rooms and two suites with private baths. Mid-June to mid-October: doubles $110 to $165, suites $165 to $185. Rest of season: doubles $75 to $125, suites $125 to $135. Closed November-April. Children over 8.

Harbour Cottage Inn, 9 Dirigo Road, Box 258, Southwest Harbor 04679.

The Harbour Cottage has been around a while, dating to 1852 when it was built as part of the Island House, a 250-room facility that was the first summer hotel on Mount Desert Island. Subsequent B&B owners have come and gone, leaving Don Jalbert and Javier Montesinos with a nicely renovated B&B when they acquired the place in 2002. "We only had to add our own flair," said Don, who moved from Baltimore after summering in Maine for years. His French heritage teams with Javier's Spanish background to imbue the inn with a cosmopolitan style. Lady Mae, a mannikin who was seated at one side of the spacious living room at our visit, adds her own presence as she is moved around the inn.

Perched atop Dirigo Hill with a view of the harbor in the distance, the inn offers seven queensize or kingsize bedrooms and a pair of two-bedroom suites. All are bright and airy, stylishly decorated in generally bold colors. All except one have jacuzzi tubs or steam showers. Typical is the Dory, with a kingsize iron bed and a loveseat. TVs, telephones and data ports are standard.

Adjacent to the inn is the Southwester, a three-bedroom house with a great

Harbour Cottage Inn reflects heritage of first summer hotel on Mount Desert Island.

sundeck and full facilities. Another deck enhances the Carriage House, a fireplaced cottage with kitchen.

The partners also operate four rental units known as Pier One on the harbor.

Guests are partial to the breakfast pizzas, served in the dining room at tables for sixteen or on the porch. Other morning eye-openers prepared by Javiar include a smoked salmon scramble served on an English muffin and blueberry stuffed toast with Canadian bacon.

(207) 244-5738 or (888) 843-3022. Fax (207) 244-5731. www.harbourcottageinn.com. Seven rooms, two suites and two cottages with private baths. Doubles, $145 to $155 in summer, $95 to $105 off-season. Suites and cottages $235 to $250 in summer, $125 to $150 off-season. Closed November-March.

Central House Inn, 51 Clark Point Road, Southwest Harbor.

The dining area is in the kitchen of this new three-room B&B, which is as it should be. The owner/innkeeper is chef Terry Preble, longtime Bar Harbor restaurateur who closed his Preble Grill here in 2003 to open the B&B. Terry spent a year and a half painstakingly restoring the three-story structure built as a rooming house in 1887, remodeling and updating to create an early Craftsman residence.

The exterior is painted celadon green with yellow and brick red trim, and profusely landscaped. The main floor holds a snug living room as well as the kitchen open to the dining area.

One guest room occupies one side of the main floor, with two more upstairs. All are simply furnished in Mission/Craftsman style, each with hardwood flooring,, queen bed, gas stove, TV/DVD hidden in a closet or shelves and a writing desk with data port in an alcove between bedroom and bath. The baths are something else, of should we say showers? They're walk-in, enveloped in circular, tiled enclosures and bearing three shower heads. The downstairs room adds a whirlpool tub. Chairs at our early visit were at a minimum – the downstairs room lacking any place to sit and the upstairs room having one armchair each. The upstairs hall opens onto a shared rear balcony, and downstairs is a wicker front porch.

From his commercially equipped kitchen, Terry prepares a lavish breakfast. Favorites include a crabmeat and feta cheese omelet and pecan-orange belgian waffles.

(207) 244-0100 or (877) 205-0289. www.centralhouseinn.com. Three rooms with private baths. Doubles, $145 to $175, Memorial Day to mid-October; $95 to $145 rest of year. Two-night minimum.

The Moorings, Shore Road, Box 744, Southwest Harbor 04679.

Genial Downeasters Leslie and Betty King and their son Storey have run this delightfully informal, old-fashioned place since 1960 in a location they call the "Little Norway of America," and one we find the most scenic on the island, smack on the shore at the start of Somes Sound in Manset.

The rambling white house with dark shutters in the Maine style contains ten guest rooms, two of them small singles and all with private baths. There also are three motel-style efficiency units (one with two exposures billed as having "probably the finest view on the coast") and four units in three trim white cottages with wicker porches. The Kings have upgraded their rooms with cheery new wallpapers and furnishings, and the five now sport decks or balconies to take advantage of the view. Most rooms have one double or twin beds.

We dubbed our front-corner bedroom the Agatha Christie Room because several of her paperbacks were on the bureau (Betty made the rounds of all the lawn sales to pick up the books, Storey volunteered). It's the only one without a water view but, as with the other rooms, the towels were large and fluffy, the bed had colorfully patterned sheets, and a candle was in a ceramic holder beside the bed. The Pilot House cottage with living room, fireplace, screened porch and television provided more expansive accommodations at a later visit.

The fireplace glows on cool mornings in the living room, which has a television set in a windowed alcove and enough books and magazines to start a library. The coffee pot is kept filled all day in the adjacent office, where complimentary orange juice and donuts are put out every morning.

Outside, two rowboats filled with geraniums brighten the path to the front door. In back are canoes, bicycles, a pier and a stony shoreline for swimming (if you can stand the icy water), beachcombing, clamming and musseling. The Kings provide charcoal for the grills beside the shore, a memorable spot to barbecue a steak for dinner as you watch the sunset.

We're obviously fond of the Moorings. It's most unpretentious and the prices are, too.

(207) 244-5523 or (800) 596-5523. www.mooringsinn.com. Thirteen rooms and four cottage units with private baths. July to mid-September: doubles $85 to $110, cottages $105 to $150. Rest of year: doubles $75 to $100, cottages $95 to $135.

Island Watch, 73 Freeman Ridge Road, Box 1359, Southwest Harbor 04679.

Little known but aptly named, this B&B in a contemporary ranch house occupies the top of a high ridge west of town. Floor-to-ceiling windows in the living room/dining room stretching across the rear of the house and an expansive deck take full advantage of the panoramic view of islands and water.

Maxine Clark, who says she's the only native-born hostess in the B&B business locally, grew up in the Bass Harbor Lighthouse as the daughter of the lighthouse keeper. Here, in a rather spectacular house, she offers six homey guest rooms (one a single) and an efficiency suite in a separate building. All have private baths, and three afford water views. One room with a private entrance on the ground floor has a double and single bed and built-in pine counters. An adjacent room offers a similar bed configuration plus a wood stove and a large bathroom with a clawfoot tub. Everything except the red carpet is white in Room 1 upstairs, a simple room with a kingsize bed and a glorious view. The efficiency in the outbuilding contains a queensize bed in back and a small living room with a TV and half a kitchen in front, plus a small private deck.

The living room in the main house has a huge stone fireplace and TV, VCR and stereo for guests' use. We settled down on the rear deck in the early evening and found it hard to leave for dinner (there's also a front deck that catches the late afternoon sun).

The next morning we were back on that great rear deck, but managed to arise long enough to enjoy Maxine's festive breakfast at a big round table in a dining room open to the country kitchen. Her french toast with ricotta stuffing and strawberry-raspberry sauce was the main event. Fresh fruit and cereal preceded. Belgian waffles and a ham and spinach quiche are other favorites.

Maxine since has added a greenhouse at the end of the dining room so folks can now enjoy breakfast amid the plants and with an island view.

(207) 244-7229. www.islandwatch.info. Five rooms and one efficiency suite with private baths. Doubles, $85. Efficiency, $95. Two-night minimum. No credit cards. Closed late October to late May.

Dining Spots

Red Sky, 14 Clark Point Road, Southwest Harbor.

Red sky at night, sailor's delight. Red sky in morning…"we don't serve breakfast,."

So says James Lindquist, owner of this new restaurant that shines at night with delightful dinners. He summered as a child at nearby Seal Harbor and returned after working for restaurants in Mystic, New York City and Aspen to help open the Havana restaurant in Bar Harbor. In 2003, he took over the former Preble Grill here with his wife and niece as partners. They gutted the interior to produce a warm dining room in yellow and deep burgundy. The handsome new bar of white pine and mahogany was made by his brother-in-law from a tree in Camden. The bar is as deep as a table so it serves as a supper bar as well.

Folks sit at the bar as well as at white-clothed tables to enjoy a panoply of changing contemporary treats. You might start with an appetizer like Maine sea scallops sautéed with tequila and lime juice, served with an avocado puree; Maine shrimp dumplings with tamari ginger sauce, or lollipop lamb chops dusted with bitter chocolate and sweet mint.,

Typical main courses run from pan-seared tuna with a tamari glaze and sweet orange-ginger salsa to dry-aged New York strip steak with a tamarind and roasted jalapeño steak sauce. Lobster risotto with green and white asparagus and chanterelles was an early favorite.

Finish with a cheese course, four types served with fruit. Or sample innovative desserts such as belgian bittersweet chocolate pudding, sour lemon tart with strawberry sauce and raspberries, or the Red Sky's ice cream sandwich with belgian chocolate and madagascar vanilla bean ice cream.

(207) 244-0476. Entrées, $18 to $26. Dinner, Monday-Saturday 5:30 to 10.

Seaweed Café, 146 Seawall Road, Manset.

"Natural seacoast cuisine" is the billing for this diminutive newcomer, tucked away in a sweet little Cape Cod-style house in the Manset section of Southwest Harbor. Chef-owner Bill Morrison, whose fare we enjoyed at the nearby Lindenwood Inn before he launched his own venture, specializes in the fare of "Asian islands – Japan, Hawaii, Thailand" – as well as China. That gives assertive twists to New England seafood and reflects his personal inclination for organic and natural foods.

From his open kitchen on one side of the house comes a changing array of flavorful fare. Sleek black chairs are at custom-made tables amidst a decor of pale yellow and rich mahogany.

Bill's signature Japanese maki sushi rolls are a carryover from the Lindenwood, where one of us made a meal of his crab with cilantro and lobster with avocado mako sushi rolls as well as Thai mussels steamed in sake with basil, cilantro, ginger and hot pepper.

Here, the entrées might be tuna steak au poivre with wasabi béarnaise and mushrooms braised in lobster broth or five-spiced duck with grand marnier and green peppercorn demi-glace. Many make a meal of the dinner chowder or seafood stew – prepared, Bill says, with "whatever's fresh from the ocean that day."

He and his waitress make the desserts, perhaps genoise, fruit tarts and chocolate truffle cake. We found his bourbon ice cream with chocolate biscotti and a strawberry tart with mascarpone to be refreshing counterpoints to such assertive dinner flavors.

(207) 244-5072. Entrées, $18 to $24. Dinner nightly in summer, 6 to 9; Tuesday-Saturday in off-season. Closed mid-February to spring. BYOB. No credit cards.

Fiddlers' Green, 411 Main St., Southwest Harbor.

Chef Derek Wilber, son of a local boat builder, and his bride-to-be Sarah O'Neil opened this stylish restaurant to rave reviews in 1999. They gutted the old Spinnakers family restaurant and created two simple but sophisticated dining areas. One, all in yellow, has windows onto the ocean and a side deck.

Derek's short dinner menu itemizes changing choices in the contemporary regional idiom with Asian influences. Expect starters like lobster timbale with sake-infused melon, seaweeds and tobiko roe, crab cakes with a three-chile honey-mango sauce, and a treat called "the gravlax effect," smoked salmon wrapped in gravlax with sweet horseradish chèvre. Main courses could be pan-seared yellowfin tuna with tamari-mirin sauce, pan-fried spiced salmon and crab in nori with a citrus-peanut sauce, roasted duck breast with calvados-apple-maple chutney, and grilled lamb tenderloin with mint glaze. Pheasant, elk and rabbit might be featured in game season.

Typical desserts are lemon mousse napoleon, honey-mango crème brûlée, cream puffs and chocolate truffle tart.

(207) 244-9416. Entrées, $18 to $26. Dinner from 5:30, Tuesday-Sunday in summer and Thursday-Sunday in off-season, 5:30 to 9. Closed November-April.

XYZ Restaurant & Gallery, Shore Road, Manset.

The letters stand for Xalapa, Yucatan and Zacatecas, and the food represents the Mexican interior and coastal Maine. Owner Janet Strong had the West Side Gallery here for a year before opening this enterprise with cook Robert Hoyt, who's traveled in Mexico for years and describes himself as "a nut for the food there for a long, long time."

We could easily become nuts for his food, too, after a couple of dinners here. Everything is, as Robert says, "real," from the smoked jalapeño and tomatillo sauces served with the opening tortillas to the fine tequila he offered with dessert as a chaser. Busy hostess Janet recommended we try her partner's sampler plate ($14 each): two chiles rellenos and a chicken dish with mashed potato and pickled cucumber. Thoroughly smitten, we returned the next year to enjoy the pollo deshebrada (shredded chicken in a rustic sauce of chiles with cilantro and onions) and tatemado (pork loin baked in a sauce of guajillo and ancho chiles). Dessert was the sensational XYZ pie, layered ice cream and chocolate covered in warm kahlua chocolate sauce.

Part of the main floor of the Dockside Motel, the L-shaped dining room is colorful in white, red and green, the colors of the Mexican flag. The front windows look out onto Somes Sound across the road.

(207) 244-5221. www.acadia.net/dockside/xyz. Entrées, $16 to $18. Dinner nightly in summer, from 5:30. Closed mid-October to mid-May.

Café 2, 326 Main St., Southwest Harbor.

This is the new night-time operation of the wildly popular enterprise called Eat-a-Pita by day. Starting as a little lunch place in 1997 after a few years in Bar Harbor, it grew like topsy and now serves three meals a day. It's at its best at night when ex-Florida country club chef Kevin Dunn goes all out with an extensive menu of "creative gourmet fare."

The appetizers, salads and pastas are ambitious and first-rate, but it is with signature dishes like sesame-seed-crusted yellowfin tuna with a vanilla and pink peppercorn beurre blanc that the chef excels. Look for entrées like pot au feu, sea bass amandine, roasted duckling with raspberry coulis, filet of beef royale (stuffed with lobster and blue cheese) and herb-encrusted lamb loin with a pinot noir demi-glace.

Desserts, like everything else, are prepared from scratch: blueberry bread pudding with maple whisky sauce, frozen chocolate mousse in a chocolate cup with whipped cream and raspberry coulis, fruit pies, cheesecake and crisps.

The deli case and takeout area are closed off at night to create a candlelight dining area in which artifacts line the shelves and dried flowers hang from the ceiling. There's a plant-filled sidewalk patio as well for dining, day or night. Wines, exotic coffees and teas are available.

(207) 244-4344. Entrées, $18.50 to $22.50. Dinner, Tuesday-Sunday 5 to 9, Memorial Day to mid-October.

151 Main St., 151 Main St., Northeast Harbor.

With the closing of the trendy Redfield's restaurant, Northeast Harbor was left with a big niche that this newcomer helped to fill. Occupying a site that has seen many a restaurant, this venture's setting is as simple as its name. Dining is dark and intimate at small bistro tables with a bar in back.

The extensive, Mediterranean-inspired menu offers thin-crust pizzas, house-made pastas and quite a selection of small plates and large plates in the contemporary idiom. You might start with peekytoe crab cakes with citrus aioli, mussels roasted in the brick oven or the trio of house-smoked salmon, scallops and mussels, served with three sauces. The stuffed quahog is a favorite of the chef's from Rhode Island.

Large plates range from pork and beef meatloaf and chicken piccata to bouillabaisse and rack of lamb. The chef's catfish roulade was featured at the National Women Chefs & Restaurateurs Association national conference in 2002. It is stuffed with a crab cake and served over mixed greens with jasmine rice and seasonal vegetables.

(207) 276-9898. Entrées, $14 to $22. Dinner, Tuesday-Sunday from 5.

Asticou Inn, Route 3, Northeast Harbor.

A wonderful old resort hotel, this dates to 1883 but is kept belatedly up to date and elegant. A comfy bar and lounge leads into a serene, pillared dining room notable for oriental rugs and hand-painted murals of trees and flowers on the buttercup yellow walls. Most coveted seating (and generally reserved for regulars) is in the adjacent enclosed porch, with views onto the harbor beyond. The water-view terrace is also open for lunch and dinner al fresco.

On a recent sunny day, we lunched on the terrace high above the sparkling harbor. The kitchen produced a crabmeat club sandwich with potato salad, garnished with colorful specks of bell peppers and nasturtiums, and a superior seafood salad of lobster, shrimp and crabmeat tossed with vegetables and field greens.

Lobster is featured on the dinner menu. It turns up in starters of lobster chowder and lobster cake over braised greens with a roasted red pepper sauce. It's offered steamed or baked stuffed as main dishes.

Other starters range from roasted beet carpaccio to pan-seared diver scallops atop a shaved fennel salad. Typical entrées include grilled tuna steak on a fondue of scallions with beets and corn, pan-seared duck breast with a cranberry-port sauce and grilled veal chop with wild mushroom sauce.

The Sunday jazz brunch is popular with the summer people.

(207) 276-3344 or (800) 258-3373. Entrées, $24 to $32. Lunch, Monday-Saturday in July and August, 11:30 to 2. Dinner nightly, 6 to 9:30 or 10, mid-June to mid-September. Sunday jazz brunch, 11:30 to 2:30.

Jordan Pond House, Park Loop Road, Acadia National Park.

Rebuilt following a disastrous fire, the Jordan Pond House is a large, strikingly contemporary complex with cathedral ceilings, two levels, outdoor porches and decks, huge windows and one of the good Acadia Gift Shops. The setting is majestic, with lawns sloping down to Jordan Pond and the landmark Bubbles mountains rising beyond.

Lobster stew or soup and a Jordan Pond popover served with strawberry preserves and butter are popular luncheon items. At one visit we enjoyed a fine seafood pasta and a curried chicken salad, garnished with red grapes and orange slices, and shared one of the famous popovers – good but a bit pricey at $3.50, considering it was mostly air.

The all-day menu includes a variety of sandwiches and salads, appetizers and entrées from crab and havarti quiche to grilled chicken and steamed lobster. Nighttime brings a few more substantial dishes like prime rib and surf and turf. The fresh fruit ice creams are made here from original recipes dating to the late 19th century.

Even if you don't eat here, stop for tea on the lawn, an island tradition – updated lately with the addition of espresso, cappuccino and Oregon chai. You sit on old-fashioned chairs and sip your beverage along with popovers and strawberry jam.

(207) 276-3316. www.jordanpond.com. Entrées, $13 to $18. Lunch daily, 11:30 to 2:30. Tea on the lawn, 11:30 to 5:30. Dinner, 5:30 to 8 or 9. Closed mid-October to mid-May.

Lobsters and harbor view draw visitors to Thurston's Lobster Pound in Bernard.

Thurston's Lobster Pound, Steamboat Wharf Road, Bernard.

From the canopied upstairs deck, you can look below and see where the lobstermen keep their traps. Thurston's is a real working lobster wharf. If you couldn't tell from all the pickup trucks parked along the road, one taste of the lobster will convince you.

We enjoyed our lobster dinner here ($9.75 to $10.75 a pound, plus $4.75 for extras like corn on the cob, coleslaw, a roll and blueberry cake). We also sampled the chock-full lobster stew, a really good potato salad, steamers and mussels and, at our latest visit, a fabulous crab cake and a not so fabulous scallop chowder.

You place your order at the counter, wait for one of the tables on the covered deck above or on the open deck below, and settle down with a bottle of beer or wine (from a choice selection). Little wonder that the island lobster cognoscenti consider this place the best around.

(207) 244-7600. Open daily, 11 to 8:30. Closed October to Memorial Day.

The Deck House Restaurant & Cabaret Theater, 11 Apple Lane, Southwest Harbor.

An island tradition since 1970 at Bass Harbor, this moved to grand new quarters upstairs in the loft of an old canning factory in the Hinckley Great Harbor Marina complex. It's a much larger and more substantial venue for cabaret theater presented, as always, by the singing wait staff.

The dining room opens at 6:30 for dinner. The menu is as extensive as any in the area, and all the entrées are priced the same, from Maine lobster to prime rib and from pecan-crusted halibut to tenderloin steak chasseur. At 8:15, the servers become players, singing solos, duets, quartets and ensemble numbers in the round. No customer is more than four tables from the action. The emphasis is on Broadway show tunes, but barbershop quartet, mime numbers and dance also have been featured. Some attendees consider the event the highlight of their visit to Down East Maine.

(207) 244-5044. Entrées, $22.95. Dinner nightly, from 6:30; show at 8:15. Sunday brunch, 10:30 to 1. Closed mid-September to mid-June.

Diversions

Acadia National Park. The most famous sites are along Ocean Drive and the Park Loop Road out of Bar Harbor, but don't miss the park's other attractions on this side of the island. The Beech Mountain area offers Echo Lake with a fine beach, changing rooms and fresh water far warmer than the ocean. Hike up Beech Cliff for a great view of Echo Lake below (yes, you may hear your echo). Past Southwest Harbor and Manset are Seawall, created naturally by the sea, and the Wonderland and Ship's Harbor nature trails, both well worth taking.

Somes Sound and Somesville. Follow Sargent Drive out of Northeast Harbor along the fjord-like Somes Sound for some of the island's most spectacular views (it's the closest thing we know of to the more remote areas around California's Lake Tahoe). At the head of the sound is Somesville, a classic New England village and a joy to behold: the whites of the houses brightened patriotically by red geraniums, white petunias and morning glories in flowerboxes that line the street. Converted from a general store, the excellent **Port in the Storm Bookstore** stocks two floors with books and recordings. On the mezzanine, books are displayed the way they ought to be on slanted shelves around the atrium. Two resident cats and a pair of binoculars occupy a reading area in back beside Somes Sound, and you could not wish for a more beautiful spot for a bookstore. Also check out the old library with its new-fangled, wired-for-sound lounge chairs, and maybe an arts and crafts show outside. The entire town is listed on the National Register of Historic Places, and the **Mount Desert Historical Society** buildings chronicle the history of the island's earliest settlement. The Somesville Village Improvement Society conducts a bi-annual historical walking tour. The Masonic Hall in Somesville is home of the **Acadia Repertory Theater,** which has been staging five plays in two-week cycles each summer since 1973.

Museums. Southwest Harbor is widely known for its variety of birds (many consider it the warbler capital of the country), so fittingly this is the home of the **Wendell Gilley Museum of Bird Carving,** a monument to the memory of one of the nation's outstanding bird carvers. Occupying a solar-heated building, it shows more than 200 of the late local wood carver's birds and decoys, ranging in size from a two-inch woodcock to a life-size bald eagle. The museum also has special exhibitions, and films and programs on woodcarving and natural history (admission, $3.25).

Also in Southwest Harbor is the main **Mount Desert Oceanarium,** a building full of sea life and lobster lore, with a touch tank, whale exhibit, fishing boats and more (adults, $6.25). Lately, the institution has branched out with a lobster museum and a lobster hatchery, both in Bar Harbor.

Boat cruises. Untold numbers of cruises – public, private and park-sponsored – leave from Northeast Harbor, Southwest Harbor and Bass Harbor. You can take a naturalist tour to Baker Island, a lobster boat or a ferry ride to Swans Island or the Cranberry Islands, and the park's cruises are particularly informative. If you'd rather observe than ride, poke around one of the ten or more boat-building yards in Southwest Harbor.

Shopping. The area's best shopping is in Northeast Harbor, although Southwest Harbor is catching up. In Northeast Harbor, **The Kimball Shop and Boutique** are two of the snazziest shops we've seen. The shop is a pageant of bright colors and room after room of pretty china, furniture, kitchenware and almost anything else that's in. A couple of doors away is the newer Boutique, filled with zippy clothes. **Mrs. Pervear's Shop** is a nice hodgepodge of painted furniture (we loved the table with lupines painted on), handknit sweaters, yarn and more. Behind a wild awning, Margaret Hammond at **Local Color** offers hand-painted woven clothing, soft and elegant in jewel-like colors and like nothing we've seen anywhere else. Her fabulous rugs start at $975 for a tiny one. **The Romantic Room** stocks a range from wicker and straw hats to brass beds. Try **Animal Crackers** for adorable clothes for children, **Sherman's** and **McGrath's** for books, **Fourteen Carrots** for jewelry, and **Provisions** for suave groceries. Check out **Smart Studio and Art Gallery,** with Wini Smart's wonderfully evocative paintings of Maine, and her newer **Wini Smart's Garden Gallery** around the corner. **Souleiado** features fabrics from the South of France. Classic sportswear is the hallmark of **The Holmes Store.**

In Southwest Harbor, check out **Hot Flash Anny's,** the hip showroom for Ann Seavey's stained-glass pieces. Almost everything is made of glass and is one of a kind; you could spend from $4 to $4,000 here. Great sweaters and skirts are for sale at **Common Threads,** where we fell for the lupine earrings and pins. **The Sand Castle Ocean & Nature Store** features the works of more than 60 Maine artisans. **MDI Sportswear** has clothing and accessories for men and women.

Little Notch Bakery, based in The Shops at Hinckley Great Harbor Marina, is a great bakery producing more than 4,500 loaves of bread weekly for a knowing clientele, some of Down East Maine's finest inns and restaurants. Specialties include Italian breads, focaccia, olive rolls and onion rolls. Owners Art and Kate Jacobs also run the year-round **Little Notch Cafe** and retail outlet at 340 Main St. in the center of town. Art said the bittersweet belgian chocolate brownie he urged us to sample tasted like fudge, and it sure did. Had it been lunch time, we'd have gone for the grilled flank steak sandwich with roasted peppers and onions on a baguette.

Extra-Special

Asticou Terrace and Thuya Gardens, Route 3, Northeast Harbor.

You can drive up, but we recommend the ten-minute hike nearly straight up a scenic, well-maintained switchback path and stairs to the prized gardens above Northeast Harbor. A plaque relates that landscape architect Joseph H. Curtis left this "for the quiet recreation of the people of this town and their summer guests." It is easy to enjoy the showy hilltop spread combining English flower beds with informal natural Japanese effects, some common and uncommon annuals plus hardy rhododendron and laurel that appear as a surprise so far north. As you might find on a private estate, which this once was, there are a gazebo, a free-form freshwater pond, and a shelter with pillowed seats and deck chairs for relaxing in the shade. Thuya Lodge, the former Curtis summer cottage, houses a rare botanical book library. Nearby are the **Asticou Azalea Gardens,** where twenty varieties of azaleas compete for attention with a Japanese sand garden and amazed us with their Southern-style lushness in late June.

(207) 276-3344. Open daily in July and August, 7 to 7. Free.

Campobello Island lies across Passmaquoddy Bay from Eastport Chowder House pier.

Eastport/Lubec, Me./St. Andrews, N.B.

The Quoddy Loop: An International Wonderland

Franklin Delano Roosevelt chose to build his summer home on Campobello, his beloved island. The titans of Canadian industry turned St. Andrews-by-the-Sea into eastern Canada's most posh summer resort. And sea captains, fishermen and sardine packers fished for a living around Lubec and Eastport, the smallest "city" in the United States.

The two-nation wonderland where easternmost Maine meets southwestern New Brunswick is undeniably remote – a mixed blessing – and incredibly picturesque. Naturalists call it the last coastal frontier on America's East Coast.

Although linked geographically and by water, each section of the Quoddy Region has its own distinctive aura.

Eastport, on a hilly peninsula called Moose Island overlooking Passamaquoddy Bay, is America's easternmost city (population, 2,000). It was considered a sister port to Boston by seagoing travelers during the 19th century and, along with Lubec across the bay, boomed as a fishing and sardine-packing town in its heyday. After decades of decline, both now are making a comeback of sorts with port and marina facilities and a growing aquaculture industry.

Two miles across the bay but 38 miles away by road, Lubec (accent second syllable, as in Quebec), is perched European-style on a hilltop, standing out like a beacon for miles around. Lubec is the closest American point to Campobello Island, famed for the Roosevelt summer home and 2,600 acres of nature preserves in the unique Roosevelt Campobello International Park. Although part of New Brunswick, its proximity and American ties ally Campobello in spirit more with Lubec, just a short bridge's length across the Lubec Narrows, than either Eastport – to which FDR and Eleanor used to go by boat to shop – or St. Andrews.

Ah, St. Andrews. The Canadian among us will forever cherish the summer days (and nights) she spent as a teenager with a friend whose family owned a house in

St. Andrews, long a low-key watering hole for old-money Canadians and knowing Americans. Indeed, she so loves the town that she acquired a water-view townhouse there in which to relive summer memories and prepare for retirement. The town, settled in 1783 by British Loyalists fleeing the American Revolution, still looks and feels much as it did in her youth. But change is well under way with the opening of deluxe inns, fine restaurants and the world-class Kingsbrae Garden, along with a much-heralded upgrading of the championship Algonquin golf course.

Granted, this area is way Down East. But the trip is worth it and, once here, you'll want to stay. So allow time to complete the Quoddy Loop. Tour the Roosevelt home at Campobello. Eat lobster on the Eastport wharf. Luxuriate in a sumptuous inn in St. Andrews. Explore the craggy coastline. Savor an area of earthy (and watery) pleasures. Watch the monumental tides rising and falling up to 26 feet a day, ebbing and flowing with life in a quieter time and place.

Inn Spots

Accommodations are grouped here according to location. Prices quoted are in local currency. American dollars stretch farther in Canada, where a $200 room might translate to $150 U.S., with a refund available on the harmonized sales tax. This part of Canada is in the Atlantic time zone, one hour ahead of Eastern time.

St. Andrews, N.B.

Kingsbrae Arms, 219 King St., St. Andrews E5B 1Y1.

It was sheer serendipity, according to the owners of Canada's first five-star inn. Long Island innkeepers Harry Chancey Jr. and David Oxford were returning from a Maritimes vacation in 1995 when they detoured on a whim to St. Andrews.

"We thought we'd arrived in the magic kingdom," recalled Harry. The owners of the deluxe Centennial House in East Hampton extended their vacation, started house hunting and within a week took possession of an abandoned mansion in which to run a second inn.

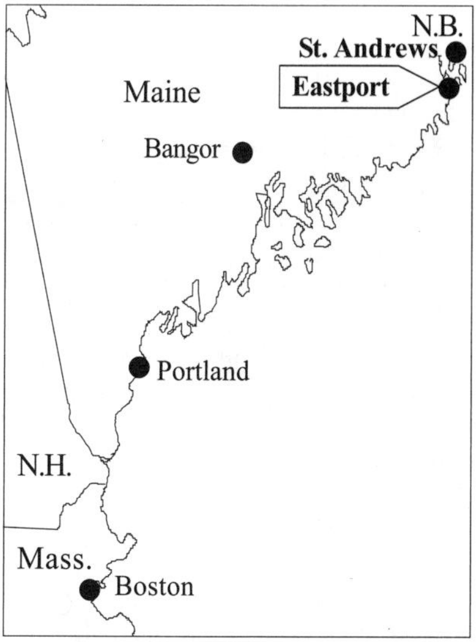

The rambling 1897 cedar-shingled house and its neighbors on a ridge at the top of King Street were among the finest in one of Canada's ritziest summer colonies. With the blessing of town officials and neighbors Lucinda and John Flemer, who funded the adjacent Kingsbrae Garden, they undertook 24 months of renovations. Now they welcome guests to a full-service inn with five luxurious rooms, three suites and a carriage house, plus all the amenities required for a designation by Canada Select as Canada's first five-star inn, membership in Relais & Châteaux and selection as a hideaway of the year in the Harper Report.

"This is the realization of a vision,"

Harry said as he led a tour before settling us like old friends into the King Suite. Kingsbrae Arms is five stars with a difference – the warmth and hospitality of its owners.

A crystal Austrian-style chandelier hangs in the entry foyer, a gift of Mrs. Flemer, with whom the owners worked closely so the world-class inn and the world-class garden would complement each other. The entry foyer leads into a plush, paneled and beamed library. Off the side of the foyer is a drawing room elegant in cream and peach colors, with a grand piano on a platform for recitals at one end, fireplaces on either side and two comfortable seating areas in between. Across the foyer are the dining room with a handsome table for twelve and a professional kitchen. A conference facility in the side carriage house includes a dining porch beneath a veranda, with the largest suite complete with kitchen and balcony above.

The rest of the luxurious guest quarters ramble across the inn's second and third floors. Harry designed the Canadian birdseye and maple four-poster beds and the patterned mahogany armoires that were built by local craftsmen. Except for antiques from their own collection, all the furnishings, fabrics and accessories were obtained locally. Along with instant gas fireplaces, each room has sumptuous seating, TV, telephone with data port, a writing desk, three-way reading lamps, porcelain doorknobs and original art on the walls. There are double whirlpool tubs, glass-enclosed showers and five-foot marble vanities in the six bathrooms that could accommodate them. Neutrogena toiletries, thick towels and embroidered waffle-weave sauna robes come with. Chocolate truffles are at bedside, complimentary beverages and snacks are in a little guest kitchen down the hall, and room service offers mini-meals. Rates include breakfast and dinner in the dining room or on the terrace, overlooking a deep back lawn leading to a secluded swimming pool.

Whimsy and surprises abound. The Queen Room has not one but two queensize rice-carved poster beds, a sitting area beside the fireplace and a deep window seat with a chandelier – a great place for reading poetry, advises Harry, who has slept in every room in the house, as good innkeepers do. An antique matrimonial bed from Shanghai, original to the house that was built by a merchant involved in the China trade, plays a decorative role beneath an elliptical window in a third-floor hallway. The Pinnacle Suite occupies an entire wing of the third floor. It comes with fireplaces ornamented with English garden tiles in both the kingsize bedroom and its mirror-image sitting room, a stocked wet bar/pantry, his and her bathrooms, and an oversize balcony. Also with a new balcony overlooking Kingsbrae Garden is the Garden Suite. It also has two fireplaces, a kingsize canopy bed draped in green, and a bath with oversize soaking tub and corner shower clad in marble. The Earl is a triple-gabled junior suite with a sitting area in one gable, a queen sleigh bed in another (with the window enveloped in a crown canopy), and the bathroom with whirlpool tub in a third gable. The King Suite has a kingsize four-poster with a draped canopy to keep out the morning light, fireplaces in bedroom and sitting room, and a wide balcony overlooking showy gardens in the rolling back yard that ends at a swimming pool. The marble in the bathroom extends to the vanity, walk-in shower, whirlpool tub and floor. These are the designs of decorator magazine editors' dreams.

The food here is equal to the rest of the experience. Our dinner lived up to its billing as like a "dinner party with friends in a private home." Following cocktails with nibbles on the terrace, guests gathered in the dining room for a leisurely, four-course repast served with aplomb. The appetizer was steamed Prince Edward Island mussels in a creamy pernod sauce, which chief chef and server Harry insisted

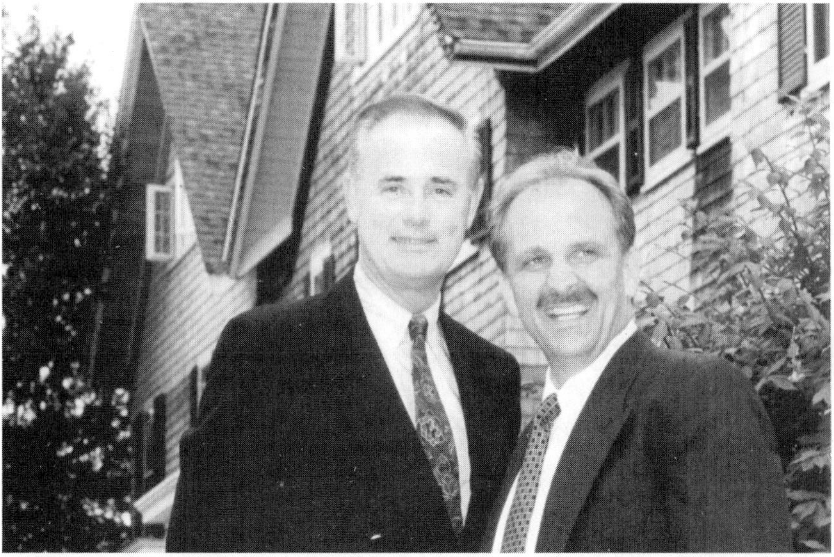
Kingsbrae Arms reflects the vision of owners David Oxford (left) and Harry Chancey Jr.

everyone soak up with extra bread. The main course was delicate pistachio-crusted Atlantic salmon with fresh peas and tarragon sauce and apple-cranberry couscous. Next came a plate of three French cheeses with Corinthian grapes, pickled gooseberries and fennel. Dessert was an almond-raspberry torte with baked maple cream. Coffee and cookies were served in the living room.

Breakfast the next day included dainty cut-up fruit with yogurt sauce, a first-rate eggs benedict and hazelnut coffee.

In 2004, the inn was adding two more suites in a newly acquired house next door. The owners renovated the former 1860 house, once a B&B known as Pippincott, for their personal quarters following the sale of their Centennial House inn in East Hampton. They also changed the pricing structure to make the daily rates all-inclusive in the manner of Twin Farms in Vermont and the Point in upstate New York. Rates are quoted in U.S. funds.

(506) 529-1897 or (877) 529-1897. Fax (506) 529-1197. www.kingsbrae.com. Two rooms, seven suites and a carriage house with private baths. Rates in American funds, full AP. Doubles, $690. Suites, $925 to $1,175. Two-night minimum; three-night minimum on summer weekends. Closed November-April.

Inn on the Hiram Walker Estate, 109 Reed Ave., St. Andrews E5B 2J6.

The former summer home of the Hiram Walker Distillery family occupies eleven sylvan acres bordering the renowned Algonquin golf course at the edge of town. Deer often browse in the back meadow morning and evening, and there's a distinct sense of tranquility and privacy.

Elizabeth Cooney, who was born in St. Andrews and later summered at the Algonquin resort with her family, returned from Toronto when her late husband Roger retired. Starting with five double rooms in 1994, she upgraded and added seven more that she touts as the grandest in New Brunswick. Hers became the second five-star inn in St. Andrews in 1997 after she started offering dinner to guests and installed the requisite swimming pool, an octagonal affair surrounded

Rear of Inn on the Hiram Walker Estate opens onto new deck and pool.

by decking, along with a hot tub topped by a pagoda. New additions are a small "Linkside Distillery Bar" with a golf motif and a tented deck area for functions.

Restored to its 1912 grandeur, the house has a somewhat stark English Norman facade in front and an inviting French chateau facade in back. The elegant interior speaks of romance. "Love" is embroidered on throw pillows, a "honeymoon table" occupies a prime position beside the window in the dining room, and a crib holds lacy pillows in the upstairs hall. Fine Canadian art collected over the years enhances the walls. Decorative magnums of Canadian Club convey the Hiram Walker heritage.

Silk damask-covered sofas, an 1851 square grand piano, oriental carpets, crystal chandeliers, antique mahogany furniture and wood-burning fireplaces accent the inn's drawing room, library and music room, and a chandeliered dining room for private parties. The main dining area is a sun porch formed by enclosing part of the huge wraparound deck at the rear.

Upstairs on the second and third floors are nine rooms and suites with four-poster beds, gas fireplaces, marble baths and TV/VCRs. Seven with kingsize beds have double whirlpool tubs. Each comes with select Canadian art on the walls, monogrammed towels, fine linens and duvets, floral fabrics, Gilchrist & Soames toiletries, chocolate truffles and the inn's own bottled water. Attractive in mauve florals, the premier Edward Walker Room has a step-up canopied four-poster king bed, a sitting area overlooking the pool and a marbleized tile bath with jacuzzi beneath the skylight. The opulent Hiram Walker Room is notable for a Waterford crystal chandelier, armoire, wood-burning fireplace, two wing chairs in celadon green, a walk-in cedar closet, and a double vanity and jacuzzi in the bathroom. The Albert Kahn Room has a jacuzzi in one corner of the bedroom and a fireplace in another corner. The newest Meadow Room, third floor rear, offers big dormer windows with the best water view.

Two kingsize rooms with private patios and a two-bedroom housekeeping suite in a carriage house overlook the fifth fairway of the golf course.

Amid much silver and crystal, Elizabeth offers breakfast ($14.95 each) at individual tables in the new, restful green dining room or on the deck overlooking the heated pool and hot tub. Fresh fruit with lemon yogurt in a brandy snifter precedes the main dish, perhaps gourmet french toast that was described as "a picture on a plate" or scrambled eggs made with whipping cream, ham glazed in maple syrup and whole wheat toast spread "with my mummy's jams and jellies."

She also offers afternoon tea for $11.95 and dinner for houseguests by reservation, $59.95 prix-fixe for four courses. Atlantic salmon poached with white wine and beef tenderloin with peppercorn sauce are house favorites. Elizabeth does the cooking, and was proud that one reviewer said she had raised dining locally to an art form.

(506) 529-4210 or (800) 470-4088. Fax (506) 529-4311. www.walkerestateinn.com. Eleven rooms and one two-bedroom suite with private baths. Rates, EP. Doubles, $225 to $450. Suite, $500.

The Windsor House of St. Andrews, 132 Water St., St. Andrews E0G 2X0.

Two Americans who summered in St. Andrews have turned a 1798 Loyalist house in the center of town into an inn and restaurant of great distinction.

Jay Remer, who restored historic properties in his native Delaware, and Greg Cohane, a graphic designer for Ski magazine, planned to move here to start an antiques shop or art gallery when friends badgered them into considering the rundown property. "We looked at it and put a down payment on it an hour later," Greg recalled. "We both came away thinking the same thing, 'This should be an inn.'"

After two years of a painstaking and historically accurate restoration that became the subject of a book, *Lady with a Past: The Restoration of a Georgian House,* the inn opened on Victoria Day 1999. Any pretension was leavened with a nationwide Queen Victoria look-alike contest. Surely the queen would have approved of the new inn: six grand guest rooms, two formal dining rooms, a charming Victorian bar, a basement billiards room, a rear garden dining courtyard and front verandas on two levels facing the main street and the harbor beyond.

The total tab: more than $2 million, including significant antiques and art collections, which make it a veritable museum and art gallery. "It's kind of a live-in museum," said Jay, who worked as an appraiser for Sotheby's fresh out of college. "Most people might have one piece like this in their house and you're not allowed to touch it," he said of the first antique table he bought at Sotheby's in 1973, now just one of countless treasures that turn up in front Room 3. "Here you can."

Two large rooms with cathedral ceilings and generous bathrooms on the third floor dwarf the four corner rooms on the second floor, each with a different mantel over the original fireplace. Yet all are spacious and furnished with queen beds (except for one double and one room with two three-quarter beds). Imposing French Empire armoires serve in lieu of closets, holding a TV and terrycloth robes. Linens and towels are of the finest quality, and the mattresses are so comfortable that guests ask about purchasing them. Marble-floor bathrooms, new old-fashioned pull-chain toilets, wide-plank floors, rich fabric window treatments and working fireplaces are hallmarks.

The third-floor corridor is lined with 62 watercolors and pen-and-ink sketches by English-born New Brunswick artist Anthony Flower – almost the entire extant collection, obtained from the artist's aging great-grandson. North America's largest collection of Sir Edwin Landseer prints are among more than 150 original 19th century art works throughout the inn. Antique cabinetry by master New Brunswick cabinetmakers Thomas Nisbet and Alexander Lawrence predominates. Almost every piece in the house has a pedigree. Surely, this is the largest and finest collection of 19th century antiques and artworks at an inn in Canada? "I know of no inn with more anywhere in North America," says Jay.

The cozy front-corner Parlour Bar with a pressed-tin gilt ceiling draws townspeople as well as inn guests. The basement with 40-inch-thick walls of local granite holds a billiards room with an antique pool table from a Newport mansion. Two small, elegant dining rooms offer refined French and Canadian cuisine for lunch and dinner (see Dining Spots).

A leisurely breakfast in the garden courtyard, amid statuary and trickling fountain, is as good as it gets. Fresh orange juice, a fruit plate and the pastry chef's muffins or scones precede the main course, perhaps the signature eggs Windsor (like benedict, except with smoked salmon on a crumpet) or cinnamon and oat-encrusted french toast.

(506) 529-3330 or (888) 890-9463. Fax (506) 529-4063. www.windsorhouseinn.com. Six rooms with private baths. Doubles, $225 to $300 June-September, $125 to $200 off-season. Closed January-March.

Treadwell Inn, 129 Water St., St. Andrews E0G 2X0.

Erected in 1820 by ship's chandler John Treadwell, this handsome house backing up to the harbor once served as the town's customs house, as noted in a stained-glass window over an entrance. Annette Lacey and Jerry Mercer, who live nearby, carefully restored it into a B&B, winning a preservation award from the St. Andrews Civic Trust for their effort.

They offer a kingsize bedroom with sitting area opening onto the harbor and the inn's largest private deck on the main floor. Four more bedrooms with queen or two double beds and sitting areas are on the second floor. Two in the rear open onto a common second-floor balcony with Adirondack chairs overlooking the harbor. The third-floor holds two efficiency suites, each with beamed and vaulted ceiling, sitting area and french doors onto a private balcony high above the water. One suite has a kingsize bed and a large whirlpool tub. The other has a queen bed and a smaller jacuzzi. Duvet comforters, TVs and telephones are standard.

Guests gather in a small main-floor common room when they're not out on the waterside decks or enjoying the gardens and lawn sloping to the harbor. A continental breakfast of homemade muffins and breads is offered in the common room, the adjoining eat-in country kitchen with panoramic view of the harbor or on an outside deck.

(506) 529-1011 or (888) 529-1011. Fax (506) 529-4826. www.townsearch.com/treadwell. Five rooms and two suites with private baths. Doubles, $145 to $185, Suites, $225 and $250.

The Pansy Patch, 59 Carleton St., St. Andrews E0G 2X0.

Claiming to be the most photographed house in New Brunswick, this fairy-tale white stucco house, with small-paned windows, towers and turrets and a roof that looks as if it should be thatched, stands across the street from the Algonquin Hotel.

Built in 1912 by the superintendent of Canadian Pacific Hotels, it was fashioned after the Normandy summer home of Jacques Cartier in St. Malo, France. Michael and Marilyn O'Connor from Massachusetts made numerous changes in the public areas. They opened up a stylish rear sun porch and veranda full of wicker for guests

The Pansy Patch offers lodging and dining in a fairy-tale white stucco cottage.

to enjoy the distant water views, and converted a small room nearby into the Gallery New Brunswick showing fine art and crafts. They converted the living room, with its beamed ceiling and huge fireplace, into a public dining room. Lunch and dinner service was added there and outside on the landscaped terraces, where the restored gardens put on quite a show.

The upstairs has five renovated guest rooms. One with a queen bed has a fireplace and bath with clawfoot tub. Another with a king bed has a window seat with a bay view. An attic suite with double bed and sofabed includes a kitchenette. The adjacent Cory Cottage offers four more guest quarters. One upstairs room here has a double bed and a clawfoot tub beneath a window in the gable. Another with a queen bed adjoins a common room opening onto a balcony with a water view; the sofabed in the common room can turn this into a two-bedroom suite, but the private bath is in the hall. A downstairs room with a hunt theme offers a queen bed and oriental rugs.

The staff serves breakfast for guests at individual tables set with pansy-rimmed china and pansy napkin rings. The fare might be eggs benedict, mushroom quiche or egg bake, accompanied by homemade granola, muffins and croissants.

The evening menu is continental, with a hint of a German accent. The dozen entrées range from seafood paella or scallops in cream sauce to wiener schnitzel, roast chicken with orange sauce and grilled lamb chops with mint jelly.

(506) 529-3834 or (888) 726-7972. Fax (506) 529-9042. www.pansypatch.com. Eight rooms and one suite with private baths. Doubles, $225 to $325. Closed October-May. Lunch, Friday-Sunday noon to 3. Dinner nightly, 6 to 10. Entrées, $21 to $28.50.

Tara Manor Inn, 559 Mowat Drive (Highway 127), St. Andrews E5B 2P2.

A former private estate built in 1869 by one of the fathers of Canadian Confederation, Tara occupies twenty secluded acres crisscrossed by sculptured, century-old hedgerows on a slope overlooking Passamaquoddy Bay in the distance.

Innkeepers Norman and Sharon Ryall started with two rooms in their residence in 1971, opened a dining room in 1980, and then added what Norman called twelve "ultra suites, the best in the Maritimes." (They are suites in size, if not in reality, son Lonny Ryall clarifies, since each consists of one large room.) The ones we saw have kingsize brass beds or two queen beds screened by spindle partitions from sitting areas containing a sofa, two chairs and a TV. Six secluded "ultra rooms," one with a whirlpool tub, share a large deck overlooking the gardens. They are extra-large and command top-dollar, but we like better the panoramic view of the bay from the ultra rooms off the third-floor balcony. Three accommodations are two-bedroom suites.

We booked one of the thirteen rooms located in the old carriage house, boathouse and servant's quarters, all with full baths and cable TV and comfortable indeed. Decor varies from early American to French provincial, much of it exceedingly fancy. All rooms are different but have striking draperies and Tara's signature collections of plates displayed in bays on the walls. Some have private balconies. The park-like grounds include a swimming pool, a whirlpool spa and a tennis court.

The inn's restaurant, the **Tupper Grill,** has downscaled its previously fancy decor, added a dining patio and expanded its dinner menu for what Lonny calls casual fine dining. Cedar-planked salmon, lobster and scallop thermidor, baked chicken and rack of lamb are offered alongside a daily three-course special and a children's menu. Prime rib is featured Saturday nights in summer.

(506) 529-3304 or (800) 691-8272. Fax (506) 529-4755. www.taramanor.com. Thirteen rooms, twelve "ultra" rooms and three two-bedroom suites. July to mid-September: doubles $144, ultra rooms $189, suites $179. Off-season: doubles $89 to $149, suites, $120 to $149. Closed November-April.

Dinner, nightly except Monday, 5:30 to 9, late May to mid-October. Entrées, $19 to $29.

The Fairmont Algonquin, 184 Aldolphus St., St. Andrews E5B 1T7.

First of the grand old Canadian Pacific hotels that spanned the country, the 238-room Algonquin preserves a tradition of gracious resort life that has nearly vanished.

One look at the red-turreted, Tudoresque hotel surrounded by lavish flower beds atop a knoll overlooking St. Andrews and Passamaquoddy Bay indicates that here is a special place. Add bellhops in kilts of the New Brunswick tartan (with incongruous-looking intercom beepers on their belts), the long lobby with comfortable peach chairs, the enormous 275-seat Passamaquoddy Dining Room with windows onto the grounds, the book-lined Library Bistro and Bar with nightly piano music, the Right Whale Pub for light fare, a large outdoor pool, tennis courts, a health club, an upgraded eighteen-hole signature golf course and the best conference facilities in Atlantic Canada. The result is a resort of world renown.

The historic hotel, started by Boston businessmen in 1889 as a private club, was acquired in 2000 by the Fairmont chain. The Algonquin completed a five-year refurbishing program for all rooms and added 54 efficiency mini-suites designed for families in a new wing. Those we saw have two queensize beds, two pillowed wicker chairs, a dining ell with refrigerator and microwave, a large bathroom loaded with amenities and a closet that lights automatically when the door is opened. Three deluxe suites here have jetted tubs, fireplaces, kitchenettes and two bathrooms.

The new Prince of Wales Wing repeats some of the architectural traits of the older section, which is wonderfully quirky in decor and layout. As one guest volunteered, "I like to walk through the old part and stay in the new." Because the hotel was rebuilt with concrete walls, ceilings and floors after a 1914 fire,rooms are unusually quiet.

The Fairmont Algonquin is a landmark for visitors to St. Andrews.

Water views enhance rooms on the third and fourth floors. The best view of all is claimed by the roof garden, which frames Passamaquoddy Bay through flower-bedecked trellises and a turreted gazebo. When not reserved for private functions, it provides a sylvan retreat for reading, sunbathing and sunset-watching.

Three meals a day are available in the resort's restaurants.

(506) 529-8823 or (800) 441-1414. Fax (506) 529-7162. Two hundred twenty-two rooms and sixteen suites. Rates, EP. Late June to early September: doubles $249 to $389, suites $419 to $519. Off-season: doubles $129 to $189, suites $299 to $399.

Rossmount Inn, 4599 Route 127, St. Andrews E5B 2Z3.

Long reigning as the St. Andrews area's best-known inn, the Rossmount declined under successors to the original owners. It's been on the upswing since its acquisition in 2001 by Swiss-born hoteliers Chris and Graziella Aerni, who had served for 25 years in the restaurant and hotel business in Toronto and Australia.

Chris, the chef, has elevated the dining room into the ranks of best in New Brunswick (see Dining Spots). His wife handles the front of the house and the accommodations, which are undergoing gradual redecoration and refurbishing.

An odd-looking box of a structure astride a hill on an 87-acre estate east of town, the new Rossmount is immediately evident to the returning visitor. A lineup of fledgling trees flanks the long front drive, and the exterior has been given a pale yellow paint job and a new peaked roof. Off the main foyer is a refurbished "lounge bar" that lives up to its name.

The second and third floors hold nine guest rooms each, opening hotel-style off a wide center hall. The most choice are two queensize and two kingsize rooms facing Passamaquoddy Bay, one of each on each floor. Other rooms have queen, double or two double beds, some with updated baths and others with original fixtures. Decor is simple but serviceable with solid hardwood furniture, leather chairs and oriental rugs. Most of the furnishings, original to the inn when it was rebuilt in the 1960s, came from an old hotel in Saint John and were crafted in northern New Brunswick.

Chef Chris burns the candle at both ends, handling breakfast duties as well as dinner. Continental breakfast ($4.95) features his homemade Swiss muesli. Full breakfast ($7.95) adds a choice of egg dishes or french toast.

Outside are a swimming pool and trails through the woods up Chamcook Mountain.

(506) 529-3351. Fax (506) 529-1920. www.rossmountinn.com. Eighteen rooms with private baths. Rates, EP. Doubles, $105 to $130 in summer, $89 to $114 in September, $69 to $87 rest of year. Closed January-March.

Harris Hatch Inn, 142 Queen St., St. Andrews E5B 1E2.

Huge rooms with working fireplaces are available in this handsome red brick house with white shutters, one of the most historic in St. Andrews. It's named after one of the town's early leading lights, and was beautifully restored in the 1960s as a private home before a dentist partitioned the ground floor into small rooms for his dental practice. "We only had to take out the partitions," said Jura Everett, innkeeper with her husband, Texas native Bob Estes, who once owned the Rossmount Inn east of town.

Here they offer three bedrooms, two each taking up one side of the second floor and a third in the attic on the third floor. Queen or kingsize iron beds, TVs, in-room coffeemakers, bottles of Perrier water, irons and sitting areas are standard. Large bathrooms include oversize garden tubs and separate showers.

The main floor holds a large guest parlor, where the dental office used to be. It opens through arched pocket doors into a rear dining room. Here is where a full breakfast – blueberry-stuffed french toast or eggs benedict with smoked salmon – is served in the morning. "I cook and Bob serves," says Jura.

They offer guests a discount off dinner at their waterfront Lighthouse Restaurant.

(506) 529-4713. Fax (506) 529-4448. Three rooms with private baths. Doubles, $85 to $125. Closed November-April.

Eastport/Lubec, Me.

Peacock House, 27 Summer St., Lubec 04652.

Once the sardine packing capital of the world, Lubec is home to the R.J. Peacock Canning Co., which now packs farmed salmon from pens in Passamaquoddy Bay and is still run by the Peacock family. Hence the name for this early Victorian beauty built in 1860 by a sea captain from England for his bride. Located on a residential side street, it passed by marriage into the Peacock family twenty years later. Four generations of Peacocks lived here, including Carroll B. Peacock, a state senator, who entertained prominent guests – from Dwight Eisenhower to Edmund Muskie to Margaret Chase Smith – here over the years.

Today, owners Dennis and Sue Baker entertain overnight guests in a nicely eclectic B&B. The Bakers moved in 2002 from Reading, Pa., after vacationing for fifteen years on remote Isle au Haut and taking to the Down East Maine lifestyle.

The main floor is handsomely appointed with the Bakers' furnishings as well as pieces from the previous owners' travels around the world. Sue brought her baby grand piano for the front living room – an addition that proves popular with guests here for the SummerKeys music school. Beyond a library with a video collection is a large sunroom, where guests pour BYOB drinks from a handsome antique wooden bar looking onto a rear patio.

The Bakers offer three comfortable bedrooms and four larger "suites" with sitting areas and TV/VCRs. The front-corner Margaret Chase Smith Suite, in which the Maine senator frequently stayed, has a queensize brass bed and a spacious bath. The most luxurious is the rear Peacock Suite, with queensize poster bed angled from the corner, a plush loveseat in front of the gas fireplace and a wet bar. Also pleasant is the Summer Room, furnished in wicker with a queen bed and white sheer curtains framing a water view.

Breakfast is served family style in the dining room at two seatings, 7:30 and 8:30. Fruit cup and the day's homemade muffins precede the main course, blueberry french toast the day of our visit and puff pancakes the next. Dennis cooks and Sue serves – 'I'm the meeter and greeter," says she. From a repertoire of eighteen choices you might have an egg dish called cactus flowers, chocolate belgian waffles with raspberries and cream or strawberry-banana french toast. English tea is served in the afternoon on the side deck.

(207) 733-2403 or (888) 305-0036. www.peacockhouse.com. Three rooms and four suites with private baths. Doubles, $85. Suites, $90 to $125. Closed November-April. Children over 7.

The Home Port Inn, 45 Main St., Box 50, Lubec 04652.

This area's longest-running inn, the Home Port opened in 1982 as something of a port in an isolated town, a tree-shaded refuge atop the Lubec hill – a location shared by a pair of churches. Built in 1880 in the Maine farmhouse style, it offers homey accommodations and the town's only fine-dining restaurant (see Dining Spots).

It's an inn in the old sense, from the restaurant to the oversize front living room, full of gathering areas where groups of guests get together near the fireplace.

Innkeeper David Gale, who took over with his wife Suzannah in 2002, grew up in his family's hospitality trade in Augusta, Ga., but "ran away from it for 40 years." After his contracting business took him to all types of lodgings all over the country, he found he was better prepared to know what the traveler wants.

The Gales are gradually redecorating the inn's seven guest rooms, which sprawl across three areas of the house. Two on the main floor are identified by their former uses: the cozy Library with a queensize bed and fireplace amidst shelves of books, and the Dining Room with two double beds. Upstairs in front are two rooms with queen beds, one the master bedroom with a four-poster and a large sofa and chair. Along the side is the inn's only kingsize bedroom, with a private bath down the hall. The rear bedroom with a double bed and a twin futon boasts a great view of Cobscook Bay.

Breakfast is continental-plus, put out in the inn's restaurant. It features homemade granola plus cereals and pastries.

(207) 733-2077 or (800) 457-2077. www.homeportinn.com. Seven rooms with private baths. Doubles, $85 to $99. Closed November-April.

Weston House, 26 Boynton St., Eastport 04631.

You don't expect to find fig trees and cactus plants in the bedrooms of a B&B in Eastport. Nor do you expect to find transplanted Californians as the innkeepers.

Jett and John Peterson made the transition with ease after their arrival from the West Coast in 1985. "We love this area," says energetic Jett, who became president of the Eastport Chamber of Commerce. "It's a very special world and we're very content in it."

Weston House occupies handsome Federal-style structure overlooking Eastport.

She has furnished the majestic yellow, Federal-style house with flair and exotic plants, among them a potted fig tree in a corner of the Audubon Room, much greenery and the odd cactus plant here and there.

The house, built in 1910 by Eastport lawyer-politician Jonathan Weston, commands a broad lawn atop a hill with a view of Cobscook Bay and Campobello Island in the distance.

Four upstairs bedrooms share two baths. The bayview Audubon Room, in which John James Audubon stayed as the guest of the owner while awaiting passage to Labrador in 1833, has a queensize four-poster bed with eyelet-edged sheets, a couple of Audubon prints on the walls and lovely scatter rugs on polished floors. The front Weston Room offers a bay view, a kingsize poster bed, fireplace, TV and telephone. "You can sit up in bed and watch the freighters in the bay," Jett advises. Terrycloth robes are provided for guests to reach the full bath in the hall.

The rear of the house harbors two smaller guest rooms, sharing a bathroom with shower and a lavatory. The side Rose Room, named for its wallpaper, has a queen bed. The rear Abbot Room contains a double bed.

The public rooms are impressive. There's a library with books and TV. In a formal front parlor with a pressed-tin ceiling, afternoon tea and sherry or port are poured in front of the fireplace beside a century-old melodeon.

Meals are served beneath baskets hung from the ceiling in a more casual kitchen-dining area.

The front porch yields a view of the gardens with a glimpse of the distant water.

Jett Peterson wants guests to "enjoy all of our house." They certainly enjoy her breakfasts of fresh orange juice, melon balls with mint and silver-dollar pancakes doused with lingonberry or hot apricot syrup one day, peach-yogurt muffins and smoked salmon-scrambled eggs the next. "I believe eating is half visual," says Jett, explaining the garnishes she adds to the presentation.

Jett will dish up five-course gourmet dinners by reservation, the price determined by the menu. A $35 meal includes hot broccoli or chilled cucumber soup, an appetizer of smoked salmon, poached salmon with cumin mayonnaise and fresh salsa, a red lettuce salad with goat cheese and red grapes, and tiramisu or a rhubarb tart based on an original recipe from her grandmother. Complimentary wine accompanies, and coffee and mints follow.

(207) 853-2907 or (800) 853-2907. Fax (207) 853-0981. www.westonhouse-maine.com. Four rooms with shared baths. Doubles, $70 to $85.

Kilby House Inn, 122 Water St., Eastport 04631.

Built in 1887, this Victorian house overlooks Passamaquoddy Bay and Campobello Island. Gregory Noyes, a high school teacher who has an unbelievable commute to school at Steuben at the western end of Washington County, opened his house as a B&B "to survive," he concedes.

His ancestors lived here and family heirlooms abound. He has decorated the property as "an English house of the period" and resisted an oppressive look in favor of an airy feeling with light painted walls and lace curtains on the windows.

The main floor holds a double parlor with pocket doors between, a dining room with a formal table and cane-seat chairs, and a welcoming kitchen with a wood-burning stove.

Upstairs are five bedrooms, three with private baths. All but one have double or twin beds. The exception is an Eastlake queensize bed with a marble-top dresser and commode and a shared bath. The front master bedroom with a canopied Sheraton poster bed enjoys a bay view, as does a side room. A rear room with private bath is considered the nicest.

Gregory prepares a full breakfast in summer, perhaps strata with coffeecake or blueberry pancakes. Weekday guests in the off-season are on their own, since Greg leaves early for his long commute.

(207) 853-0989 or (800) 435-4557. www.kilbyhouseinn.com. Three rooms with private baths and two with shared bath. Doubles, $50 to $80. No children.

Dining Spots

St. Andrews

The Windsor House of St. Andrews, 132 Water St.

A four-diamond AAA rating – only the second awarded in New Brunswick – was accorded the sophisticated restaurant at the Windsor House shortly after opening. Contemporary Canadian and French cuisine, some with appropriately English Loyalist influences, is served in two formal and elegant twenty-seat dining rooms and a tented rear garden courtyard.

We'd heard nothing but raves for the specialty eggs Windsor with smoked salmon on crumpets and the spinach and wild mushroom crêpes for Sunday brunch, and ours proved equally rewarding. What the waiter called the best-in-the-world seafood chowder lived up to its billing, laden with lobster, shrimp, scallops, haddock and salmon. One of us sampled the courtyard salad, with poached seafood served on mixed greens, and another a classic spinach salad. Others enjoyed the specialty meat pies, lamb with pearl onions in one case and beef and mushrooms in the other, both served with exquisite garden salads. Desserts were a knockout, intense lemon tart with berries; a smooth cappuccino mousse garnished with mint, a raspberry and a johnny jump-up, and a rich chocolate cream cheese brownie.

The fare prepared by chef Peter Woodworth is even more refined at night. A

Elegant parlor bar with pressed-tin gilt ceiling is attraction at The Windsor House.

recent dinner at well-spaced tables beside a gurgling fountain in the glamorous courtyard began with a complimentary amuse-gueule, baby shrimp salsa on fried leeks with cider and carrot emulsion. Appetizers included Malpeque oysters on the half shell and house-made gravlax with dijon aioli. Entrées were an assertive bouillabaisse and Quebec "duck in two acts." The latter was one of the best duck dishes we've had: pan-seared breast with cilantro butter and orange-chile-braised leg, served with wild cherry rice pilaf, snow peas and cherry tomatoes. The pastry chef, who had proved her mettle with great sourdough bread, followed up with an ethereal maple sugar crème brûlée and a double chocolate terrine with brandy crème anglaise to finish a superior meal.

Wine tasting dinners, and even scotch and champagne tasting dinners, are scheduled in the off-season.

(506) 529-3330 or (888) 890-9463. Entrées, $24 to $38. Dinner nightly, 5:30 to 9:30. Sunday brunch, 11 to 2. Fewer days in off-season. Closed January-March.

Rossmount Inn, 4599 Route 127.

Fine dining was the hallmark of the original Rossmount, and the tradition has been enhanced under new chef-owner Chris Aerni. The Swiss native, who had 25 years' experience working for others in Toronto and Australia, found his niche here. He changes his contemporary menu daily to feature seafood he hand-picks from the fishmonger in Saint John and seasonal produce from local purveyors, along with chanterelles he forages from the inn's property beneath Chamcook Mountain.

Dinner might begin with his signature cappuccino of lobster bisque with brandy, cayenne peppers and chives, smoked salmon with potato blinis and horseradish mousseline, or a fabulous salmon and avocado tartare flavored with chives and coriander.

Among main courses, the sautéed chicken breast with a two-mushroom sauce was one of the best poultry dishes we have had. Also superior was the fillet of haddock on old-fashioned potatoes with wilted greens and pickled fiddleheads. Other favorites are white wine risotto with bay scallops and chanterelles, prosciutto-wrapped pork tenderloin with polenta, and a stellar rack of lamb, the presentation changing nightly.

The chef returns to his roots for desserts such as Swiss chocolate truffle cake with strawberry coulis, mixed berry crêpe and a traditional meringue glacé with chocolate sauce. We go for the walnut butter cake with homemade maple ice cream and Chamcook Mountain maple brandy syrup.

All this is served up in a pleasant, understated dining room with well-spaced tables and changing art on the walls.

(506) 529-3351. Entrées, $15.50 to $24.80. Dinner nightly, 6 to 9:30, Wednesday-Sunday in off-season.

L'Europe, 48 King St.

Showy flowers and hanging baskets grace the alpine-looking facade of this rustic low white and brown structure one of us remembers fondly as the local dance hall in her teen years.

It's been a restaurant since 1984, but never better than under young owner Markus Ritter, a master chef from Bavaria. Markus, who had trained for fourteen years in Germany and on cruise ships, came upon St. Andrews in the usual serendipitous manner, arriving one Canada Day and putting down a deposit on the empty L'Europe building. Meanwhile, he met his bride-to-be when their paths crossed in the night while both worked in different departments in a German hotel. He and Simone moved to St. Andrews, renovated the restaurant and were married on the St. Andrews Wharf as L'Europe reopened in 2000.

They lightened up the interior, giving it a more modern look in white and pale blue. Starched white napkins stand in cylinders at each table setting and halogen lights cast a soft glow in two small dining rooms and a bar seating up to 60.

Markus offers superb contemporary continental menu from his renovated kitchen. The escargots bourguignonne and scallops mornay are good appetizers, and the composed salad is fresh as can be. Haddock fillets with tiger shrimp in a creamy champagne sauce, scallops provençal and mixed seafood are menu standbys, supplemented by nightly specials. But the emphasis is on meat dishes: chicken oriental, wiener schnitzel, and venison with red currant sauce and homemade spaetzle. The rack of lamb and filet mignon with béarnaise sauce are terrific.

Most desserts feature ice creams and fresh fruits. We usually opt for the "dessert variation à L'Europe, an excursion of our specialties" – a decadent finale to a superior meal.

Upstairs in the European style are four queensize bedrooms and three efficiency suites for overnight guests, renting for $75 to $145 nightly.

(506) 529-3818. www.leurope.ca. Entrées, $17.90 to $29.70, Dinner nightly, 5:30 to 11. Closed midweek in off-season and month of November.

The Garden Café, Kingsbrae Garden, 220 King St.

If we could have only one lunch in St. Andrews, it would be here. Actually, we've had many, and they've always turned out to be exceptional. On a crystal-clear day, there's no more idyllic setting than the leafy terrace outside the gallery dining room. You relax under a "weeping" apple tree canopy, with a postcard view of sloping lawns, floral borders, a couple of sculptures, an enormous Adirondack chair art piece that people keep climbing onto for photo ops, and a panoramic view of Passamaquoddy Bay beyond.

The kitchen produces an interesting menu ranging from sandwiches to light entrées and pasta dishes. The elegant seafood chowder is among the best we've had, and the ploughman's lunch is a satisfying platter of breads, cheese, pickles and pâtés. The day's cheese and mushroom quiche is light and ethereal, teamed with a mesclun salad. The dessert tray harbors about eight delectable-looking goodies (all different sizes, all the same price – $4.95). The cheesecake with blackberry topping, light as a soufflé, was a triumph.

(506) 529-4016. Prices, $3.50 to $12.95. Open daily, 10 to 6, mid-May to mid-October.

Niger Reef Tea House, 1 Joe's Point Road.

Overlooking Niger Reef and the blockhouse, this picturesque log house with quite a history is our favorite waterside dining spot in town. Leased from the St. Andrews Civic Trust, the simple interior holds oriental wall murals painted by artist Lucille Douglas and a corner gift shop with tea accessories. We favor the rustic waterside deck with a tranquil view of the harbor and an outdoor grill where the freshest fish and meats are barbecued for dinner.

Expanded from its former tea-house status by chef Lysa Huggins and host/partner Tim Currie, an accomplished restaurateur, it's a pure place favored by sophisticates and caters to locals well beyond the tourist season. The contemporary, healthful fare features produce and vegetables from the couple's farm garden.

Maple-glazed Atlantic salmon, grilled scallops in an orange-ginger-curry sauce and steak kabobs are worthy dinner standbys, supplemented by nightly specials – perhaps arctic char, tuna and swordfish. Grilled vegetables accompany.

The lunch menu runs from a potato tart and quiche of the day to a lobster salad sandwich. We were well satisfied with a superior ploughman's lunch and a caesar salad topped with grilled salmon, accompanied by a couple of dark ales and a marvelous strawberry tart.

Tea and scones are offered in the afternoon.

(506) 529-8007. Entrées, $16 to $18. Open daily in summer, 11:30 to 9, Sunday 10 to 9. Closed after Christmas to May.

Elaine's Chowder House Café, 24 King St.

A recent adjunct to the Tin Fish gift shop, this little winner offers a limited menu and inspired fare in tight, convivial surroundings – so convivial that the slow-as-molasses service can be forgiven. The talkative server likely will talk you into foregoing the basic lunch and dinner menu of seafood sandwiches, sushi rolls, curries and our favorite steamed mussels. Instead he'll tout the blackboard specials, one night's choice including crab cakes with salad, salmon fillet, rack of lamb and filet mignon. We were impressed with the curried chicken and vegetables and the chicken in puff pastry as well as the beer and wine selection. Homemade pies are the desserts of choice.

The artistry in the kitchen extends to the decor of the tiny enclosed porch seating sixteen diners amid white lights twinkling in the windows. Elaine Wilson's artworks share top billing with those of her husband, artist Ted Michener.

Next door for casual food is Mitch's Takeout, run by Ted, who also owns the popular Gables waterfront restaurant.

(506) 529-4496. Entrées, $14.95 to $28.95. Open daily except Tuesday, noon to 9.

Eastport/Lubec

Schooner Dining Room, 47 Water St., Eastport.

The **Wa-Co Diner** in front has been an institution at Bank Square since 1924, but recently gained a waterfront deck at the rear and a handsome dining room in between. Returning to her hometown after 35 years away, chef-owner Nancy Bishop reopened the diner, which had closed in 1997. She upgraded the fare, and her husband built the expansive, two-level deck beside the rocky shore. The nautical dining room, with vinyl cloths and oil lamps on the tables, has big windows onto the water on two sides.

The Schooner menu is an extensive collection of Maine seafood and old continental favorites. Typical are charbroiled salmon with dill-cream sauce, baked stuffed haddock with lobster sauce, chicken marsala, rack of lamb and filet mignon oscar. Coconut popcorn shrimp, bacon-wrapped scallops and broccoli cheese bites are among the appetizers. Blackboard desserts could be raspberry-cheese pie, chocolate decadence or fried apples with butterscotch sauce.

For lunch recently on the breezy waterside deck, we enjoyed a fine lobster club sandwich and one of the best crab rolls ever.

(207) 853-4046. Entrées, $6.95 to $12.95. Open daily in summer, 5:30 a.m. to 9 p.m.; winter, 6 a.m. to 8 p.m.

Eastport Chowder House, 167 Water St., Eastport.

Fish and sardine canning started in this country in the 1870s in Eastport on the wharf upon which this large restaurant stands today. For twenty years the site of the Cannery restaurant, it stood idle until the late 1990s when a succession of lessees operated it under a variety of names. In 2003 after one season as a tenant, the restaurant was purchased by Robert Delpapa, who curiously named it a chowder house (it's far more than that) and also prepared to reopen an abandoned restaurant in downtown Eastport as The Happy Crab, a year-round sports bar.

There are two large dining rooms on the upper floor, with windows onto the water. The lower level, former home to the Cannery, is now a bar and banquet facility opening onto a wharf with picnic tables (where lunch occasionally is available).

The extensive, something-for-everyone menu includes a section on chowders and stews (the clam is most popular, the waitress advised), although the lobster dinners are the best sellers. Otherwise expect the predictable baked stuffed haddock, poached salmon, baked scallops, seafood combo platter, delmonico steak and three chicken dishes. Seafood pasta is billed as the house specialty.

Desserts include blueberry pie and assorted ice creams.

(207) 853-4700. Entrées, $10.95 to $15.95. Lunch daily, 11 to 4. Dinner nightly, 4 to 9. Closed mid-October to mid-May.

La Sardina Loca, 28 Water St., Eastport.

Housed in the former A&P store where Eleanor Roosevelt shopped for groceries while summering on Campobello, this is billed as the easternmost Mexican restaurant in the United States. "The crazy sardine" name was chosen to give the sardine back to the community after many packing plants had closed, according to owner Chuck Maggiani. His son Lenny, the former chef, married a woman from Mexico, which accounts for the theme.

Wait until you see the place – a double storefront with big round tables, plastic patio chairs, a Christmas tree hanging upside down from the ceiling, posters, sign boards and a dark cantina bar hidden in back. It's crazy and colorful, to say the least.

The food isn't authentic Mexican, though people this far north probably don't care (at one busy Fourth of July visit, the blackboard specials at the entry proclaimed lobster and steak dinners for $11.95). The regular menu might offer rancho grande bifstek with salad, baked potato and corn on the cob and a Rosarita beach lobster dinner, Mexican style, with salad, rice, beans and tortillas. Of course, you can order chicken fajitas, burritos, enchiladas, tostadas, nachos and even omelets. Start, if you dare, with La Sardina Loca, billed as spicy herring steaks with hot chiles on a bed of lettuce with crackers, onions and sour cream. Dessert could be strawberry delight, kahlua parfait or caffe loca with tequila and kahlua.

(207) 853-2739. Entrées, $6.75 to $13.25. Dinner, Wednesday-Sunday from 4.

The Home Port Inn, 45 Main St., Lubec.

Food is the strong suit of this inn housed in a pale blue 1880 house run by Dave and Susannah Gale. The cheery sunken rear dining room draws discerning diners from far and wide, and the 28 seats are apt to turn twice on busy evenings.

The Gales take turns in the kitchen assisting their longtime chef. The menu shows more reach than most, from Louisiana shrimp or bouillabaisse to chicken cordon bleu and steak au poivre. Coquilles St. Jacques, mixed seafood casserole, and baked salmon with dill and shallots are house specialties.

Starters are few but choice: smoked salmon or trout, seafood chowder or crab cake on mesclun greens. Desserts include berry pies and shortcakes, walnut pie and cheesecake with fresh berries. Wine prices start in the mid teens and top off in the high thirties.

(207) 733-2077. Entrées, $13 to $19. Dinner nightly, 5 to 8, Memorial Day to Columbus Day.

Diversions

Life is simple and oriented to the water in these parts, although St. Andrews adds sophistication for those who wish. Because of the enormous range of the tides, a wide variety of marine life can be found along the shore between high and low tides. Walk the rocky beaches or explore the coastline to find shells, mussels, sea urchins, starfish, sand dollars and such. Traditionally the area's biggest tourist attraction has been the Roosevelt summer home on Campobello Island. The new Kingsbrae Garden and the upgraded Algonquin championship golf course in St. Andrews are other major draws.

Roosevelt Campobello International Park, Campobello Island.

From 1883 when he was a newborn until 1921 when he was stricken by polio here, Franklin D. Roosevelt spent most of his summers on Campobello. Here are the cottage and the grounds where the Roosevelts vacationed, the waters where they sailed, and the beaches, bogs and woods where they hiked and relaxed. The park reception center provides a touching introduction both to the Roosevelts' tenure here and to the island. Movies like "Beloved Island" are shown on the hour; "Campobello, the Outer Island" was particularly helpful in understanding the unusual nature of this area.

The Roosevelt Cottage, a 34-room red house high above Passamaquoddy Bay, is one of the most pleasant we've seen. The house still looks lived in, almost as if the Roosevelts had simply left for a quick boat ride to Eastport to pick up groceries. You can walk right into some of the rooms, which are human-size rather than grand. Unobtrusive hostesses answer questions or leave you on your own. Most of the furnishings were left by the family. You'll see the megaphone used for hailing latecomers to meals, a collection of canes, the large chair used to carry the handicapped President, the family telescope, and eighteen simple but inviting bedrooms. Outside are lovely gardens and paths to the shore. Next door is the **Hubbard Cottage,** the last Victorian summer residence in the park, now used as a conference center. Its rather luxurious main floor is open for tours except when conferences are in session.

(506) 752-2922. www.fdr.net. Cottages open daily 10 to 6 (Atlantic Time), Memorial Day to mid-October. Park open year-round. Free.

Nearly sixteen miles of scenic drives and nine miles of walking trails allow Campobello visitors to see coves, duck ponds, bogs and fog forests that typify the area. The bays still contain fishing weirs, used for catching herring. The wildflowers – especially the aroma of wild roses and the brilliant splashes of lupine all along the roads in late June and early July – are out of this world. The observation deck at Friar's Head – the best vantage point to see the entire area – is a good place to get your bearings. **East Quoddy Head Lighthouse** is a most scenic and isolated spot, seemingly at the end of the world. You can walk across to the craggy headland at low tide, but at high tide when we first were there the barrier was ten feet under a fierce current flowing two ways. We had to console ourselves with the sight of whales cavorting a quarter-mile offshore.

Lubec. The one-time sardine capital of the world is down to one remaining sardine packing plant. Other canneries now process and pack salmon harvested from pens in Cobscook Bay. Ex-Long Islander Vinny Gartmayer and his wife Holly took over an old smoked salmon business along Route 189 in 2002 and renamed it the **Bold Coast Smokehouse,** featuring "wicked good smoked salmon." In his retail showroom near the smokehouse he offers samples of lox, kabobs, pâtés and gravlax that can be shipped across the country.

Curiously, the easternmost point of land in the United States is at West Quoddy Head in South Lubec. The **West Quoddy Light,** an 1809 landmark with red and white candy stripes, stands atop a jagged cliff pounded by the open ocean. The 483-acre **Quoddy Head State Park** offers trails to the lighthouse, an island and a bog. A raised boardwalk goes through the coastal plateau peat bog, which has been declared a National Natural Landmark. Its dense moss and heath vegetation typical of the Arctic tundra are unusual. The **Downeast Interpretive Center** relocated from Lubec to the newly renovated West Quoddy Light Keepers Visitor Center.

Summer is enlivened by the ten free Wednesday evening concerts offered by the faculty of the **SummerKeys** music school. Up to 200 concert-goers gather in Lubec's Congregational Church, some of them arriving via a boat chartered from Eastport for the purpose.

Eastport. America's smallest city is evolving ever so slowly from an isolated Down East fishing village into something of a tourist destination. After the great fire of 1886 destroyed the downtown and much of the surrounding area, Eastporters rebuilt within one year with impressive – and fire-resistant – brick and granite structures. Many are listed on the National Historic Register, and sixteen landmarks are outlined in an Eastport walking tour guide – a good thing, because most are not readily apparent.

The waterfront is the scene of port and acquaculture development. The annual Old Home Week over the Fourth of July draws thousands of returnees from across the country for five days of activity, culminating in a parade featuring the governor and congressmen and an evening fireworks display. **Stage East**, corner of Dana and Water streets, presents five productions a season from April through November. More than 100 plant species and nearly 30 bird species have been observed at **Shackford Head,** a park with three miles of craggy shoreline jutting into Cobscook Bay.

Shopping. On the outskirts of Eastport at 85 Washington St., **Raye's Mustard Mill** is a must stop. The country's last remaining stone-ground mustard mill produces the mustards in which the area's sardines used to be packed. Various mustards, other Maine-made foods and crafts are on sale in the Pantry Store. We generally buy enough mustard to last for a year. The mill offers guided tours of the operation on weekdays, and recently opened the Mustard Shed lunchroom for sandwiches. Downtown Eastport appears to be mostly ramshackle or vacant stores. Exceptions include **Quoddy Crafts** and **Dog Island Pottery. The Eastport Gallery,** 69 Water St., shows the works of local artists and craftsmen. Don Sutherland produces monumental pots and vases, some with amazing blue glaze, at **Earth Forms,** a most unusual pottery at 5 Dana St. If you can find the **Harborfront Artist at Work,** look up itinerant Pittsburgh artist Jim Levendosky, who has spent five prolific summers in Eastport – most recently in a convenience store whose use he bartered for a local oil painting until he could get his trademark yellow truck back on the road.

Near Lubec, **Cottage Garden** out North Lubec Road is a fascinating enterprise where we could spend hours. Gretchen and Alan Mead share their many talents with visitors to their showy perennial gardens and an informative Shoreline Nature Center museum. The Maine Reflections and Art in the Garden shops are full of dried flower wreaths, birdhouses, twig frames, framed bird and botanical prints, hanging potpourri and even painted garden benches, all made by the owners. Their artistry extends to seven gardens on two wooded acres around their charming Greek Revival Cape house. With only an occasional assistant, they create and maintain an idiosyncratic showplace full of handmade wooden walkways and bridges, some leading to a new Asian garden that Gretchen vowed would be the last.

Three artist/entrepreneurs lately set up shop along Lubec's Water Street to showcase their own creations. One spins her own wool for the **Water Street Fiberarts Studio.** Another serves ice cream, waffles and crêpes at **Peter's Not-So-Famous Homemade Ice Cream.** Monica Elliott and Eugene Greenlaw create spectacular bonbons, clusters and truffles at **Seaside Chocolates.** The unpretentious candy kitchen and showroom are upstairs in an old R.D. Peacock sardine cannery, marked by a lobster sign out front. The treats, based on recipes from her father's chocolate business in her native Peru, cost $1.35 each (colorfully wrapped bags of twelve for $15) and are as delicious as they are caloric.

St. Andrews. Settled in 1783 following the American Revolution by United Empire Loyalists, some of whom floated their dismantled homes here from Castine, Me. (they were rebuilt and several are still standing), St. Andrews is said to have more examples of fine New England Colonial architecture than any other Canadian town. Everything from Cape Cod cottages to saltboxes to large Georgian houses with Federal detailing can be seen scattered across a grid of neatly squared lots, laid out by town planners two centuries ago and now designated a national historic district. More than 250 structures, many of them legacies of the prosperous era when St. Andrews was a port of call on the West Indies trade route and some of them quite odd-looking, are over a century old. Many are marked with descriptive plaques. The 1824 **Greenock Presbyterian Church** looks like any white Colonial New England church, except for the unique bright green oak tree carved on the exterior beneath its spire. Other St. Andrews churches, particularly those along King Street, are architecturally interesting.

Other attractions are as diverse as the famed **Algonquin Signature Golf Course** (which recently completed a $7 million upgrading for championship golf at its most picturesque), the **Aquarium at the Huntsman Marine Science Center,** the informative **Atlantic Salmon Interpretive Center,** and the landmark **St. Andrews Blockhouse,** a two-story National Historic Site built of hand-hewn timbers in 1813 to protect St. Andrews from American privateers across the harbor in Maine. Costumed guides provide tours of the **Sheriff Andrews House,** an 1820 Neo-Classic historic site. Check out the trompe-l'oeil carvings decorating the facade of the old **County Court House and Gaol,** another National Historic Site.

Whale watch, nature and sightseeing cruises are offered by six outfits from colorful ticket offices and gift shops in the jaunty **Day Adventure Center** at the entrance to the long, deep St. Andrews wharf. The area is great for whale watching as some of the best feeding grounds are found between Campobello and the Wolf Islands and out toward Grand Manan.

The bar to **Ministers Island** is under seventeen feet of water at high tide, so you don't want to get stranded out there. Visitors on guided tours to the 500-acre island get an inside look at **Covenhoven,** the 55-room estate of CP railroad magnate Sir William Van Horne, which is slowly undergoing restoration as a museum, and at the unusual bathhouse for a tidal swimming pool. Two-hour tours are scheduled twice daily in summer, timed according to the tides. They elicit fascinating insights on how one of the world's richest men lived early in the 20th century.

Ross Memorial Museum, an imposing red brick Neo-Classic house built in 1824 at 188 Montague St., is a true house museum. It was acquired and given to the town by Henry Phipps Ross and his wife Sarah as a means to display their extensive collections of decorative arts and furniture. Ross, a onetime Episcopal minister in Providence, R.I., and his wife, the daughter of the Bradstreet of Dun & Bradstreet in New York, summered here from 1902 to 1945. Guided tours are offered Monday-Saturday 10 to 4:30, mid-June to early October; closed Monday after Labor Day. Donation.

Shopping. Cottage Craft, on the waterfront at Market Square, with brightly colored skeins of wool draped around its cork fence in front, shows knit goods in lovely colors, knitting bags (one shaped like a house in which the door opens), and the neatest collection of mittens for kids you ever saw. **Boutique La Baleine** stocks cute things like stuffed animals, books by local authors, cards, apparel and a large toy section. Truly unusual is **Jarea Art Studio & Gallery,** whose principals spearheaded the painting of scenic murals on the town water tower and a downtown storefront in 2003. Jantje-Blokhuis-Multer and her daughter and son-in-law produce wondrous oils, floor cloths and folk art with found objects (three of the latter now make a triptych in our living room). We also were struck by the $195 sweaters bearing images of a whale and a covered bridge at **Serendipin' Art,** which shows local handicrafts and has a jewelry and metalsmithing studio on site. Don't miss the **Tom Smith Pottery** behind the Windsor House on Edward Street. Tom's wife Ellen, who manages the studio, makes the drawstring bags for Tom's handsome raku teabowls. The dramatic **Seacoast Gallery** at 174 Water St. features fine works by New Brunswick artists and craftspeople. Another favorite gallery is **The Crocker Hill Store,** where soothing music draws passersby in to see and buy Steven Smith's remarkable bird watercolors. A gardener of note, Steve also is known to open his back-yard garden for guided tours. Don't miss the outstanding, one-of-a-kind textile art at the **Bertha Day Studio,** 275 Water St. Bertha's hand-painted and embroidered wall hangings, vests, T-shirts (some with lupines or fiddlehead ferns), landscape cushions, small purses, tea cozies and more are truly unique. We cherish the wall hanging of a St. Andrews landscape we bought for a big anniversary.

Extra-Special

Kingsbrae Garden, 220 King St., St. Andrews.

Lucinda and John Flemer, who sold the house that became the Kingsbrae Arms inn, donated an adjacent 27-acre property and funds to operate this world-class horticultural garden, which quickly was recognized as one of the ten best in Canada. On a hilltop overlooking Passamaquoddy Bay, it is a wonderland of 28 theme gardens. They vary from a pristine white garden along the entryway and a cool blue garden to sections for heath and heather, fruits, ornamental shrubs, birds and butterflies, wildflowers, scents and sensitivity, and edibles. There are a cedar maze and a thyme labyrinth, sand and gravel gardens, and a Harry Potter secret garden. The highlight for most is the perennial garden, where classical music wafts from in-ground speakers and a fascinating Japanese "deer clapper" works by water power to scare the roaming deer from the adjacent rose garden. We've been here at all stages of the growing season, never ceasing to marvel at the embankment of splashy rhododendrons, the showy oriental lilies, the peacock gladiolus, the dwarf cosmos, the late strawberries in bloom at Labor Day, and the prolific arugula in a vegetable garden in which the corn and tomatoes failed to mature. Still young, the gardens are not as drop-dead spectacular as, say, Butchart Gardens in British Columbia. But they are subtle, and represent about 2,000 varieties. There are surprises at every turn, from a cedar hedgerow so thick you could stay dry underneath in a thunderstorm to an 1894 children's playhouse in which old-timers remember playing. Others are a working Dutch windmill circulating water to and from a duck pond, a therapy garden with raised beds accessible to patients in a nursing home adjacent, two life-size scarecrow figures made of flower pots and, for good measure, a fenced enclosure that shelters three friendly goats. A half-mile nature trail leads through a marked Acadian Forest, home to 32 species of trees beside the bay. One of four manor houses originally on the property is the site of the Garden Café (see Dining Spots), a small but exceptional gift shop and an art gallery with changing exhibits of regional art.

(506) 529-3335 or (866) 566-8687. www.kingsbraegarden.com. Open daily, 9 to 6, mid-May to early October. Adults, $8.

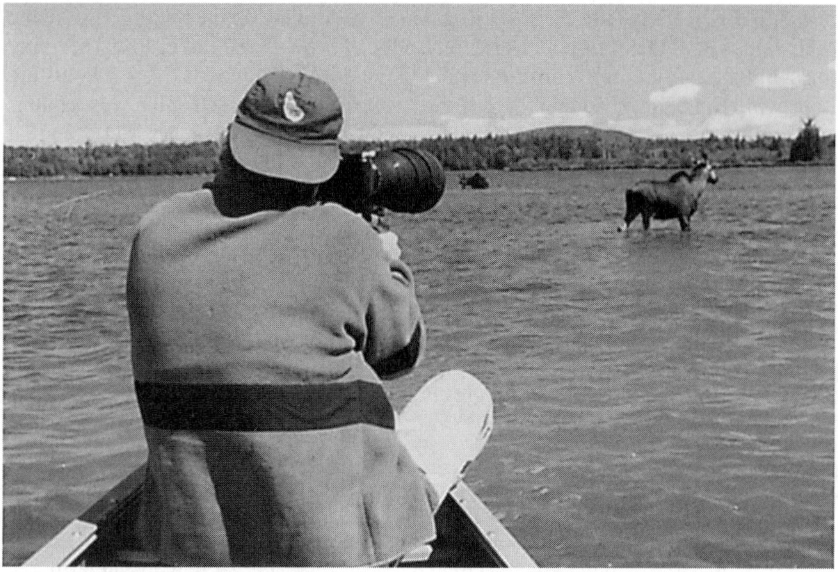

Peter Thibodeau Photo

Moose-watching is a major pastime in Moosehead Lake region.

Moosehead Lake, Me.

The Maine You Remember

The drive through interior Maine on Route 6 and 15, the only road into the Moosehead Lake region, seems endless. But the intrepid traveler need not despair. Suddenly, the road crests atop a hill and now, before you in all its glory, unfolds the majesty of Moosehead, the Northeast's largest lake.

At the near end lies Greenville (population 2,200), the region's only town of note. On all sides are mountains – small ones, to be sure, but enough to alter the landscape of what to the south had been essentially rolling flatlands. The sky-blue glacier lake spreads its tentacles like the antlers of a moose head around islands and into coves. Think of an inland sea stretching into a forest of green, rather like a freshwater version of Penobscot Bay.

The pristine lake, shaped vaguely like a moose head, is 40 miles long and 20 miles across at its widest. It's up to 300 feet deep at the base of the landmark Mount Kineo cliffs. Most of the 400 miles of shoreline, owned by paper companies more interested in raw lumber than in vacation condominiums, is undeveloped. Forestry and recreation are the area's industries.

Moosehead's mystique has always been that of a sportsman's paradise in the North Woods wilderness. The area has long been a mecca for hunters and fishermen. Increasingly, its lure is broadening to embrace nature and wildlife lovers, hikers, rafters and canoeists in summer, and cross-country skiers, downhill skiers and snowmobilers in winter.

The area is poised for what one proponent calls "eco-travel, the tourism of the future," for those who like to pursue sports year-round in the great outdoors. Already the rough co-exists with the refined. National publicity was accorded the late Road Kill Cafe, the original in a small restaurant chain poking fun at the pretensions of some of its peers, and the Lodge at Moosehead Lake, an inn revising the standards for creature comforts and style in the Maine woods. New owners are improving Big Squaw Mountain, a promising ski area. True, much of the area remains raw and primeval. But its virgin veneer is leavened by a gentleness that the great lake imparts to the mountains, by a subtle sophistication that escapes other north woods destinations.

Moose-watching is a mania, and few visitors leave without spotting at least a few – front and center during a moose cruise or safari or unexpectedly, simply feeding beside the road. The region has launched the annual Moosemania, a month of moose-related activities in late spring. Several shops convey a moose theme.

This is the natural state of "the Maine you remember," as the Moosehead Lake Region Chamber of Commerce touts it. Just you and the moose, and a few others who like to get away from the crowds.

Inn Spots

The Blair Hill Inn, Lily Bay road, Greenville 04441.

Blessed with the most majestic lake views around, this hillside house was built in 1891 by Chicago socialite Lyman Blair at the heart of a 2,000-acre working farm that became the largest in Maine. Its Chicago ties spoke to Ruth and Dan McLaughlin from suburban Oak Park. They shucked budding careers in the computer software industry in 1998 to restore and open the refined Blair estate as an upscale inn.

Like their socialite predecessor, the couple love to entertain – because of their cooking skills and hospitality, friends had christened their previous home Café McLaughlin. Here they have continued the tradition, offering lavish breakfasts and weekend dinners (see Dining Spots) in the elegant 43-seat dining room and summery enclosed side porch.

Besides the dining room, the main floor holds an elegant formal living room with a fireplace and a baby grand piano as well as a cozy library/game room. Other attributes are a spacious center foyer featuring a circular staircase and large stone fireplace, and a side sun porch with an exercise facility leading to an outdoor hot tub. Across the entire front of the inn is a glorious, 90-foot-long front veranda with wicker chairs looking down the hill to Moosehead Lake. The inn's annual summer concert series is held on the side lawn or, in event of inclement weather, in a century-old carriage barn behind the house.

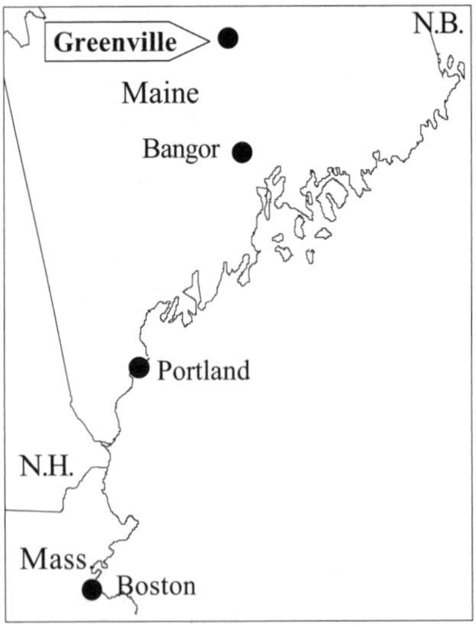

The second and third floors of the main house contain eight stylish guest quarters. Four have wood-burning fireplaces and all but one enjoy lake views. Beds are king or queensize, are topped with feather mattress pads and pillows, and are dressed with 312-count sheets

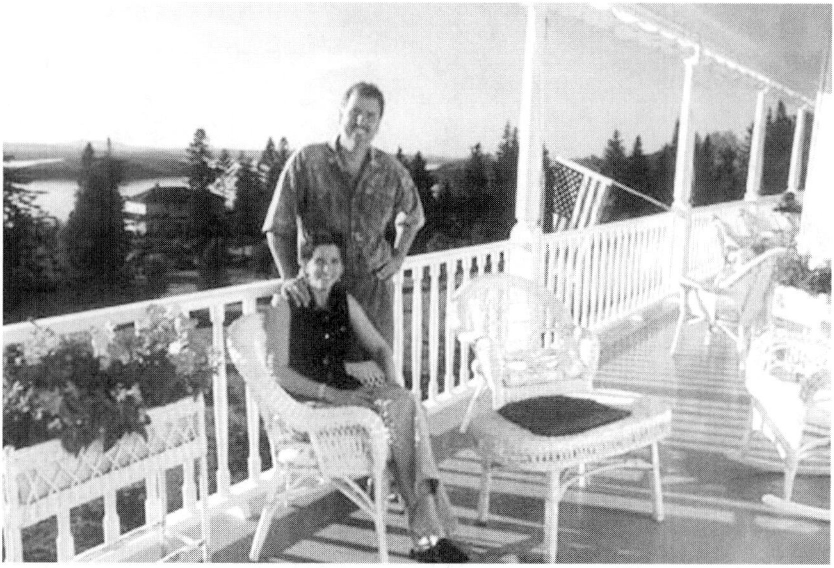

Innkeepers Ruth and Dan McLaughlin welcome guests on veranda of Blair Hill Inn.

and down comforters. Terrycloth robes and soaps and bath products from the local Maine Mountain Soap and Candle Co. are standard.

The biggest is Room 1, the original master suite with a high kingsize poster bed, overstuffed wing chairs, massive fireplace, large bay windows, and a walk-through cedar closet and dressing room. Two of the lodgings are two-bedroom suites.

Breakfast begins with broiled grapefruit or peach crisp and fruit smoothies. Lobster benedict with fresh fiddleheads or waffles with bananas and toasted pecan sauce might follow. Edible flowers garnish the plates. "People take pictures of our breakfasts," says Ruth.

(207) 695-0224. Fax (207) 695-4324. www.blairhill.com. Eight rooms with private baths. June-October: doubles, $275 to $425. Rest of year: $250 to $350. Two-night minimum weekends. Children over 10.

The Lodge at Moosehead Lake, Lily Bay Road, Box 1167, Greenville 04441.

High up Blair Hill overlooking Squaw Mountain and Moosehead Lake, this small hostelry raised the standard for low-key luxury in the wilds. As fashioned by previous owners, the 1917 Shingle-style Cape Cod Colonial is a light and airy refuge of rustic elegance and decorative flair. Sonda and Bruce Hamilton maintained the tradition upon acquiring the lodge in 2001 after owning the Evergreen Lodge south of town for six years.

As you enter the foyer with its artful arrangement of fishing creels and other piscatorial accessories, you know this is no ordinary inn. The foyer with its original gleaming silver maple hardwood floors leads to a broad living room. Here, windows open onto a full-length deck where you can look down on the lake activity in the distance and watch a sunset that's apt to be spectacular. Here and elsewhere, the high-style lodge decor is striking for flair employed with restraint. Adjoining the comfortable living room, filled with books and magazines, is a smaller parlor/library called the Keeping Room. Beyond is a summery dining room where breakfast and,

Elegant woodsy decor enhances living room at The Lodge at Moosehead Lake.

at certain times, dinner are served to houseguests. Opening onto a patio on the lower level is the Moosehead Room, a large game room with English darts and a billiards table, puzzle table and large-screen TV.

A neat little "Gone Fishing" sign, complete with a miniature rod and two tiny wooden fish, hangs gracefully on the door of each of the five bedrooms and three suites. The lodge's version of a "Do Not Disturb" sign, it flips over to say "In Camp." Utter comfort with a wildlife theme prevails within. Each room has a TV/VCR in a cabinet above a gas-lit fireplace outlined in stone, a bath with jacuzzi for two, hand-carved four-poster queensize beds with fine linens, plush sitting areas and such amenities as toiletries, hair dryers, ironing boards, terrycloth robes and little Coleman ice chests.

Our quarters in the Bear Room came with plush carpeting, an assortment of loveseats and wing chairs richly upholstered in woodsy fabrics, and a private deck. Small black climbing bears were carved upon each bedpost. The mirror in the bathroom, with a bear head on top, was carved to match. Whimsical bear accents (such as small needlepoint rugs depicting black bears, one on either side of the bed) enhanced the room at every turn.

The sophisticated decorative scheme adopts different wildlife motifs in other rooms. There are loon books and a loon-patterned table in the Loon Room, pillows in the shape of fish in the Trout Room, and antlers holding the valances in the Moose Room. Expect to find such decorative accents as a twig birdhouse in a corner, twig branches and pine cones outlining the hall windows, and full-length curtains draped smartly like an upside-down L in the bedrooms. The latest handiwork is twig stenciling – twigs running around the tops of walls in intricate patterns. These are the designs of which decorator magazines are made.

The ultimate accommodations are three fireplaced "retreat suites" in the adjacent structure, a converted boathouse. On two levels, they have sunken living rooms with lake views through sliding glass doors that open onto a deck and, below, a landscaped patio set into rocks and gardens along the hillside. Our recent stay in the Katahdin included a step-up bed with a moose antler canopy and a large, mirrored bathroom with double vanity, double jacuzzi, fireplace and crystal chandelier. Birch branches formed decorative molding around the vaulted ceiling. The other two suites are notable for unique queensize beds hung on boom chains from the ceiling and swaying lengthwise to rock occupants to sleep. "It rocks like a cradle and you sleep like a baby," one guest told Bruce.

A deer bounded across the back lawn as we prepared for breakfast the next morning. We were served a "wake-up cocktail," which turned out to be a small mixed berry milkshake in a wine glass, and soufléed eggs garnished with cantaloupe, pineapple and wild blueberries. A choice of juices and toasting breads awaited on a side table. Other entrées include apple-walnut pancakes, breakfast pizza and stuffed french toast with cream cheese and fruits.

Dinner is available to houseguests at 7 o'clock Sunday and Wednesday nights in season and Saturday night in winter. The night's menu is recited, and the five-course meal is prix-fixe ($50).

The innkeepers have kept the lodge small so guests can be pampered in style. And style this lodge has in spades.

(207) 695-4400. Fax (207) 695-2281. www.lodgeatmooseheadlake.com. Five rooms and three suites with private baths. Early June to mid-October: doubles $250 to $350, suites $425. Rest of year: doubles $205 to $275, suites $350 to $375. Two-night minimum stay. Children over 14.

Greenville Inn, Norris Street, Box 1194, Greenville 04441.

Solid furnishings and an aura of old money prevail in this established inn, built as a summer home in 1895 by a wealthy lumber baron. Embossed Lincrusta walls and gas lights convey an air of antiquity in the halls, as does the old telephone fixture on the wall. A large spruce tree painted on a leaded glass window adorns the stairway landing. Carved mantels, and mosaic and English tiles surround the fireplaces.

Foremost a restaurant of distinction (see Dining Spots), the inn added to its lodging business with six deluxe cottages clustered off to the side on a slope above the inn. Each has a sitting area, TV and front porch. Four have queensize beds and two have a full and a twin bed.

Four more bedrooms with king or queen beds and private baths and two suites are available in the main inn. Here, the best glimpses of the water are obtained from the Master Suite in front. It has a sitting room with fireplace and TV, a queen bedroom, and a spacious tiled bath with a deep tub and a separate needle-spray marble shower. Another prime accommodation is a two-bedroom suite in the attached Carriage House, which offers a queen bed and a sitting area with a wood stove and TV, a second bedroom with double bed, and a private deck with mountain views.

The rooms are nicely furnished in uncluttered Victorian style and beds are covered with colorful quilts. Ours had one of the inn's two kingsize beds and one of its two fireplaces, but had only one chair and a clawfoot tub without a shower. Our stay in the inn proved somewhat confining, what with the only common room doubling as a pre-dinner gathering place and bar for restaurant-goers and the few chairs on the side porch being in full view and earshot of people eating in the dining rooms. We don't know who was more disconcerted – we, blocking their views, or they, spoiling our quiet reading time. (Next time we would avoid the problem by booking one of the cottages.)

At breakfast the next morning, classical music muffled conversations in the three small dining rooms. New innkeepers Jeff and Terry Johannemann from the New Jersey shore, who acquired the inn from longtime owners in 2003, expanded the breakfast offerings. They supplement the traditional continental offerings with the likes of quiche lorraine or cheese blintz soufflé. They also planned to extend the season, operating the dining room weekends in winter.

(207) 695-2206 or (888) 695-6000. Fax (207) 695-0335. www.greenvilleinn.com. Four rooms, two suites and six cottages with private baths. Mid-June to mid-October, doubles $160 to $180, suites $275 to $350, cottages $180 to $195. Rest of year: doubles, $135 to $150, suites $235 to $300, cottages $160. Children over 7.

The Lakeview House, 358 Lily Bay Road, Box 1102, Greenville 04441.

Ruth Fyles and her late husband, Jim Devlin, built this large contemporary ranch on Blair Hill specifically to run as a B&B. They'd become enamored with the setting during their tenure running the acclaimed Lakeview Manor restaurant next door in the building that is now the Lodge at Moosehead Lake.

"Isn't this peaceful, quiet and gentle?" Ruth asked rhetorically as we took in the stunning lake vista through the sliding doors and windows of her living room, while a hummingbird hovered outside at a feeder. "The view still takes my breath away."

Now remarried, she changed the name from the Devlin House and upgraded the furnishings and decor.

Upstairs are two large guest rooms with kingsize beds, full baths, thick carpeting, TVs and comfortable sitting areas for reading or taking in the view. Downstairs in the walkout lower level is a suite with a queen bed and two twins, a huge bath and a family room with two sturdy couches, three lounge rockers and a big TV.

Ruth serves a hearty breakfast between 6 and 9. "We'll feed people at 6 if they're going rafting," Ruth says cheerily. Her repertoire includes cereal, muffins, bacon and eggs, raspberry pancakes and french toast.

(207) 695-2229. www.lakeviewhouse.com. Two rooms and one suite with private baths. July-October: doubles $125, suite $160. Rest of year: doubles $95 to $110, suite $125 to $150.

Pleasant Street Inn, 26 Pleasant St., Box 1261, Greenville 04441.

A rather unusual spired turret on the fourth floor tops this rambling 1889 Victorian house on a residential side street. Now called "The Tower," it offers windows on four sides and chairs around a small games table in the center, and is the venue of choice for watching the sun go down over the lake and mountains in the distance.

The Tower is one of several common areas spruced up by new owners Tim Shelep, John Cusick and Dan Turek, who lightened up the haute Victorian look favored by the previous owner. The pump organ at one end of the front dining room, the photo-realistic oil paintings done by Tim, the eclectic décor, and the cooking of John and Dan belie the inn's website visuals that this might be run by a trio of lumberjacks.

A masculine motif of plush leather prevails in the large main-floor living room. A second sitting room at the head of the stairs on the second floor is for TV-watching. More sitting areas are available on the 150-foot-long porch that wraps around the front and side.

Guest rooms vary in size and style. A white duvet covers the queen bed in the front Room 1, which comes with an English soaking tub and the original bath fixtures. Room 2 with twin beds has a hall bath with marble shower, vintage soaking tub and the original pedestal sink. Dan made the draperies by hand for a two-

Turret tower is feature of 1889 structure housing Pleasant Street Inn.

bedroom suite, each room with a queen bed. Room 6 on the third floor has a queen bed, TV and an enormous bathroom with a curved wall, marble shower and a plush wing chair. A guest favorite is front Room 8, where the new owners painted the bubble-gum pink walls a pale celery color for a more restful ambiance. It has windows on three sides and a queen bed.

In the morning, guests gather for juice and coffee in a butler's pantry as large as most kitchens. "I can't get guests out of here," says Dan, so convivial is the conversation. Out they must go, however, to tables in the dining room for the main course of perhaps three-cheese omelets or buttermilk pancakes with blueberries.

John prepares the breakfasts but turns over cooking duties at night to Dan, who offers prix-fixe dinners for guests by reservation.

(207) 695-3400. Fax (207) 695-2004. www.pleasantstreetinn.com. Five rooms and one two-bedroom suite with private baths. Doubles, $110 to $150. Two-bedroom suite, $260. Children over 14.

Evergreen Lodge, Route 15, HCR 76, Box 58, Greenville 04441.

Five miles south of town is this attractive, all-cedar structure, built as a physician's home and set back from the road amid evergreens and birches and showy flower gardens on 30 acres.

Hank and Janice Dyer took over from Bruce and Sonda Hamilton after the latter acquired the Lodge at Moosehead Lake. They offer six comfortable guest rooms, each strikingly paneled in varieties of cedar. Colorful quilts and lots of pillows enhance the contemporary lodge-style decor. Gas-log stoves have been added to the first-floor Bear and Loon rooms, each with kingsize bed. The Moose Room is done with a moose theme, incorporating blue quilts with a moose design on the queen bed and on an extra twin bed in an alcove.

Greenville Inn occupies restored 1895 lumber baron's mansion.

Guests gather in two cheery sitting rooms with TVs and fireplaces. Breakfast is served in a sunroom with a greenhouse section overlooking the perennial gardens. The fare includes fresh fruit, pastries, breakfast meats, pancakes, eggs or puffed french toast. Moose and deer are sighted occasionally on the property.

(207) 695-3241 or (888) 624-3993. www.evergreenlodgemoosehead.com. Six rooms with private baths. Doubles, $110 to $150. Children over 12.

Dining Spots

Greenville Inn, Norris Street, Greenville.

Among Greenville folk, this restaurant is "the toast of the town," in one innkeeper's words. Since 1988, it has been known for some of northern Maine's fanciest fare, served in manorial surroundings. Three small dining rooms are clad in white linens amid rich wood paneling, ornate fireplaces, embossed Lincrusta walls and distant views of Moosehead Lake's East Cove Harbor.

With a change in ownership in 2003, Austrian-born chef-innkeeper Elfie Schnetzer and daughter Susie turned over kitchen duties to Michelle Merchant, who trained with them. While maintaining their style, she lightened up the menu and varied the accompaniments.

Dining is taken seriously here, as is the solicitous service. Our leisurely midsummer meal began with a shared appetizer, a silken pâté of duck liver, truffles and port wine, served with the appropriate garnishes and a homemade roll rather than the traditional melba toast. Next came a salad of organic greens with balsamic vinaigrette on glass shell-shaped dishes and huge, piping-hot popovers, with butter presented in a silver shell.

Among main courses, we liked the breast of chicken in a very spicy peanut sauce and a trio of lamb chops with rosemary butter. Chocolate-coffee ice cream cake and plum strudel were refreshing endings among such exotic treats as profiteroles, chocolate truffle tart with pecan crust, plum strudel and citrus cheesecake with mango coulis.

Recent favorites included Chilean sea bass with mussels in a saffron broth on risotto, halibut fillet with beurre blanc and a mushroom-leek ragout, and bacon-wrapped beef filet with green peppercorn sauce.

A wood stove warms the inn's lounge/living room in which many diners choose to have cocktails or after-dinner drinks. The impressive wine list features Maine Bartlett wines as well as numerous California cabernets and a mix of French, Australian, Spanish, German and Chilean labels.

(207) 695-2206 or (888) 695-6000. Entrées, $20 to $24. Dinner by reservation, nightly 6 to 9, May-October; Friday and Saturday in winter.

The Blair Hill Inn, Lily Bay Road, Greenville.

A spectacular view of lake and mountains draws the public to this hilltop inn's seasonal restaurant, named one of the top ten in Maine in 2003 by Down East magazine. Diners take in the sunset as they enjoy cocktails and a complimentary amuse-bouche on the 90-foot-wide front veranda before adjourning to the big-windowed dining room, a picture of understated elegance, or the summery enclosed side porch.

Executive chef Jack Neal, a Culinary Institute of America graduate, takes a break from his landscaping business, to prepare exceptional contemporary international fare on weekends. The meal is prix-fixe, $50, with a modest choice among five courses that change weekly.

A typical dinner opens with a choice of crispy smoked shrimp roll over a tatsoi salad with chile-lime dressing or a golden pineapple and lobster salad tossed in miso-honey vinaigrette. A chilled red pepper and tomato soup and a green salad follow.

Main courses could be crab-stuffed salmon roulade with a scallion risotto cake over Sicilian tomato ragu, wood-grilled duck breast with cherries and merlot on a mulled sweet potato mash, and Asian barbecued hanger steak with a spicy red onion-mango chow-chow. Desserts at our visit involved a choice of crème brûlée with fruit or lemon-coconut tart over almond chocolate sauce.

(207) 695-0224. Prix-fixe, $50. Dinner by reservation, Thursday-Saturday 6 to 8:30, mid-June through mid-October.

The Black Frog, Pritham Ave., Greenville.

For casual dining with a water view, there's no better place in downtown Greenville than this. It's a sprawl of a place oriented toward the water, with tables around a bar, in a solarium and outside on a pier with a tiki bar. The setting is such, some say, that the inconsistency of the food does not really matter.

Local restaurateur Leigh Turner took over the prime location of Rod's Lakeside restaurant after the closing of the innovative Road Kill Café chain he started in Greenville Junction to lampoon what he called "the pretensions of fine dining." His current version of "North Woods Cuisine" is detailed on an irreverent menu that opens with "Canadian nachaux: Not bad for being 3,000 miles from Tiajuana." Soups, salads, burgers and "sammiches" continue the theme. Entrées are strips, fips, ribs and balls: "chish and fips, faddock hilet with satyr toss," seafood platter, froggy's famous fried chicken, barbecued ribs, steaks and mooseballs, "unquestionably the tenderest cut of the moose. Requires 48-hour advance notice and 25% deposit, $1,495."

The menu makes for fun reading, if not the most appetizing eating.

Upstairs, the Black Frog offers two lakefront housekeeping suites for $110 to $150 a night.

(207) 695-1100. www.theblackfrog.com. Entrées, $9.95 to $19.95. Open daily, 11:30 to 11:30.

Flatlander's, 36 Pritham Ave., Greenville.

Billed as "a country place for food and drink," this small downtown emporium is a cut above, thanks to its specialty of broasted chicken. You can order a three-piece chicken dinner ($6.95), including french fries and coleslaw, to eat here or take out to a picnic table in the pocket-size town park facing the harbor across the street.

If broasted chicken is not your thing, Flatlander's offers other options, from appetizers to burgers, soups to salads. Among main courses, expect a few basics like a spaghetti dinner, baked haddock, shrimp scampi with linguini, fish and chips, country ribs and ribeye steak.

Decor in the long, narrow room with a bar at the back and a shiny wood counter down the center is minimal. The handsome bare wood tables are made of Maine pine – "you can hardly find trees like this any more," their maker advised.

(207) 695-3373. Entrées, $5.95 to $12.95. Lunch and dinner daily in summer, 11 to 8 or 9; reduced hours in off-season.

Diversions

Outdoor Sports. Fishing and hunting have traditionally been the leading activities here, although neither is quite as good in terms of take as in days gone by. "Overkill," explained a Maine Guide of our acquaintance. To compensate, some of the old sporting camps have altered their focus to appeal to nature lovers, wildlife watchers and photographers. White-water rafting is popular on the nearby Kennebec and Penobscot rivers. Hikers like the 75-minute hike up the 700-foot-high landmark Mount Kineo to a renovated fire tower, which yields a panoramic view of Moosehead Lake and environs. One of the prime waterfront spots is occupied by Lily Bay State Park, an uncrowded favorite of swimmers, picnickers and campers.

Moose Watching. Everyone looks for moose, and local promoters say more moose reside in the Moosehead area than anywhere in the East. You'll likely spot them feeding in ponds and rivers shortly after dawn and before dusk. They're said to be at their most numerous around the roads and waterways near Rockwood and Kokadjo. A brochure outlines "moose safari" packages by land, sea and air.

One of the best ways to see moose and understand their habitat is to take the two-hour moose cruise offered by the Birches Resort in Rockwood. Unexpectedly plush seats accommodate up to sixteen passengers on a 24-foot-long pontoon boat. Moose were spotted on 96 of 100 excursions in the previous summer, resort co-owner Bill Willard advised. We thought we were going to be among the four percent failure rate until, at the end of our two-hour cruise up and down a jungle-like river, a lone moose suddenly obliged up close. "Every trip is different," our laconic boat pilot-guide said. Two more moose were spotted from a distance on the return trip to the resort. We also encountered two moose along Route 15 on the drive back to Greenville after dinner. Next morning, the pilot pointed out one feeding in an inlet during a half-hour sightseeing flight. That was it for moose of the live variety on our first four-day visit. As we were leaving town on Route 15 south, however, a highway sign warned: "High rate of moose crashes next three miles."

Airplane Adventures. Almost as much as moose, seaplanes define the Moosehead area, and their sheer numbers convey a different look and feel to this lake. Indeed, the lake is so favored by backwoods pilots that they converge every September on Greenville for the International Seaplane Fly-In, the largest of its kind in the Northeast. Since much of the Moosehead Lake shoreline and many sporting camps are not accessible by road, seaplanes get quickly where motor vehicles and boats cannot.

Two commercial air services offer sightseeing excursions. We found a half-hour flight around the lower half of the lake with **Folsom's Flying Service** ($30) the best way to appreciate the vastness of both lake and wilderness.

Other airplane sites may be of interest. Folsom's bases the last operating DC-3 seaplane, an ark of an Army Air Force plane fitted with pontoons, at Greenville's tiny municipal airport. The curious also may view remnants of the wreckage of a B-52, which crashed due to air turbulence against Elephant Mountain during the Cuban missile crisis in January 1963, killing seven crewmen. Access is via a logging road maintained by Scott Paper Co.

Boat Excursions. Another good way to see this area is by boat, and a variety of craft seems to be everywhere for rent or hire around Moosehead and its tributaries. Experience a bygone era with a cruise on the **Katahdin,** the last of 50 steamboats that plied the lake, ferrying cargo and people to resorts and sporting camps before cars and trucks reached the area. Now the star floating exhibit of the tiny **Moosehead Marine Museum** beside the lake at the municipal parking lot, the diesel-powered Katahdin gives three-hour cruises of the lower third of the lake on a varying schedule five days a week (adults, $21). A six-hour cruise up the lake to Mount Kineo, with a stop at the old hotel site, departs Wednesday at 10 for $27.

Shopping. Greenville's compact downtown is of interest to browsers. Moose are the pervasive theme at **Moosehead Traders,** a general store on Main Street. A moose motif also prevails, from banners to tea towels, at **Moosin' Around Maine.** At **Mud Puddle Mercantile,** a small country store and gift shop, proprietor Helen Schacht touted a tapestry shopping bag on wheels for $7.99 as "my best-seller." In addition to its namesake items, **Maine Mountain Soap and Candle Co.** carries baskets, pottery and home accessories. Look for jams and jellies, cards, baskets, books, Hummel figurines, Christmas villages and more at **The Corner Shop.** Across the street, former chef Claudine Dallam, who closed her prized Blue Moose Café nearby, now runs **Claudine's Gourmet Kitchen Shop.** A canoe hangs overhead in the **Great Eastern Clothing Co**. Mike Boutin stocks everything the sportsman needs at **Northwoods Outfitters,** where his partner serves up fancy coffees, baked goods and Internet services in the **Hard Drive Café.** Rustic lamps with carved bears for the base, carved birds, prints and moose are available at **The Woodcarver's Place.**

South of town, the **Indian Hill Trading Post** is the local version of a mall. If you can't find what you're looking for here, locals say, you don't need it.

Extra-Special

Kineo Island. You want to get away from the "crowd?" A nostalgic place to visit on a sunny day is this island, actually a peninsula and site of the late Kineo House resort. For $10, you can play golf on a scenic nine-hole course (the midway point is almost at the foot of the sheer Kineo cliffs). Rent a golf cart to poke along three miles of bumpy roads on this island attached to the mainland by a 500-foot stone causeway on the far side of the lake. Swim at the secluded and picturesque Pebble Beach beside the causeway, where knowing boaters often tie up for the afternoon. Observe moose, deer, loons and eagles in the wildlife sanctuary. Hike up Mount Kineo or scale the rocky cliffs. Take a peak at the abandoned yacht club building known as the Breakers on the point, and dream of turning it into a restaurant or a B&B. The island is reached by pontoon boat (Kineo Shuttle, hourly from 9 a.m. to 5 p.m. from the state boat ramp in Rockwood, 534-8812, $8 round trip).

White Mountains provide backdrop for boating on Kezar Lake.

Oxford Hills and Lakes, Me.

Not Where It's At – Yet

The famous – some locals call it infamous – milepost sign out in the middle of nowhere giving distances to nearby places like Norway, Denmark, Mexico, Poland, Paris, Naples, China and Peru would deceive no one.

This is anything but the center of the universe. It's more like the name on the school bus we passed, "State of Maine, Unorganized Territory."

The Oxford Hills region is an unspoiled land of hills that back up to the mighty White Mountains, sparkling lakes and tiny hamlets with English-sounding names like Center Lovell and Lower Waterford. It's an area of great beauty. National Geographic called Kezar Lake one of the nation's ten most beautiful – its other claim to fame is that Bridgton native Stephen King has a summer home along its forested shore. There's a fortuitous concentration of small country inns that epitomize the genre.

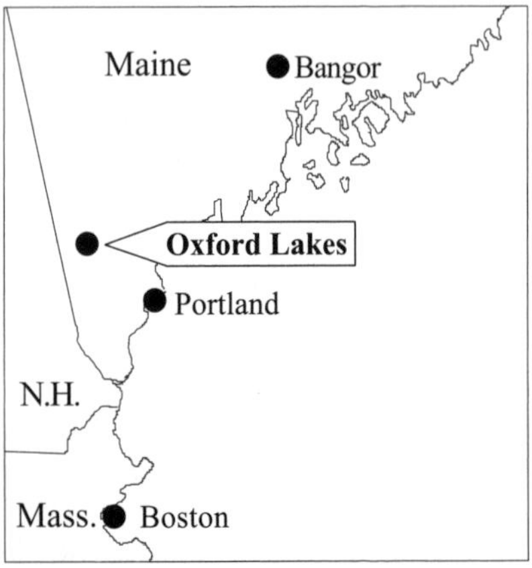

Unusual as a time capsule from the past, the area offers little in the way of formal activity or tourist trappings. "You are on your own," one inn brochure advises.

More and more people seek the serenity of western Maine. "We're really out in the country," concedes Barbara Vanderzanden of the Waterford Inne. "But we have a central location not far from North Conway or the Maine coast."

The charms of this rural retreat have yet to be discovered by the crowds. But that may be only a matter of time. Says restaurateur Michael Myers of the Lake House: "Western Maine is where it's going to be at."

It's not there yet. That remains its special joy.

Inn Spots

Admiral Peary House, 9 Elm St., Fryeburg 04037.

Splendid gardens, a clay tennis court, an outdoor hot tub and deluxe guest rooms commend this B&B in a sprawling white clapboard house that once was the home of Arctic explorer Robert Edwin Peary. Not to mention a great rear porch, screened on three sides and full of wicker rockers and loungers, from which to view the back yard. Plus a side patio with an outdoor spa.

New owner Hilary Jones, an Englishwoman, worked around the world in the hospitality industry before buying the B&B in 2003 with Derrek Schlottmann, an American chef. They had just taken over at our September visit and were learning the ropes of caring for guests in an extra-large house and property – the travails of which they posted weekly in a chatty journal on their website.

Each of the air-conditioned guest rooms in the restored 1860s farmhouse contains a queen or kingsize bed, a sitting area and a spacious bathroom (shower only) with dressing table. All are spiffily decorated with an eye to flair. Slanted roof lines and odd nooks and crannies lend an air of coziness to the Jo, a kingbedded room named for Peary's wife. It's the premier room, along with a spacious attic retreat called the North Pole. The latter is decorated in shades of peach with a kingsize brass bed, two wing chairs, and an antique bureau and writing desk. The Admiral's Quarters, dressed in creams and crimsons, features a step-up antique four-poster queen bed. A private staircase leads to the new Inuit, a large room with queensize bed topped by a quilt, lace curtains on the windows and a dressing area under the eaves.

The public rooms may be the best part. Just inside the rear entrance is a billiards table on a raised floor, separated by a railing from a large rear living room. The latter has a barnwood wall behind the fireplace, a TV/VCR in an armoire, wing chairs and two couches. Ten people can sit around the table in the open kitchen, all brick and barnwood and notable for stained glass and a chevron floor. Several smaller, more formal sitting rooms are available in the front of the house.

Derrek does the cooking for breakfast. Huevos rancheros is his specialty, but he also might create french toast stuffed with blue and cream cheeses, asparagus crêpes and pancakes with berries obtained on the property.

The inn's original owners installed the tennis court, planted the gardens and cut snowshoe trails for guests on eight acres behind the house.

(207) 935-3365 or (877) 423-6779. Fax (207) 935-7765. www.admiralpearyhouse.com. Seven rooms with private baths. Doubles, $120 to $155 summer and winter, $120 to $195 foliage, $105 to $135 rest of year.

The Waterford Inne, 258 Chadbourne Road, Box 149, Waterford 04088.

This handsome inn and antiques shop really is out in the country – half a mile up a rural lane in East Waterford. The pale yellow and mustard structure commands a hilltop view and contains eight well-furnished guest rooms, a comfortable and charming living room full of folk art, a more formal parlor and a semi-public dining room of note.

Former New Jersey school teachers Rosalie and Barbara Vanderzanden, a mother

The Waterford Inne occupies hiltop setting way out in the country.

and daughter team, carefully restored and furnished the 1825 farmhouse in 1978, eventually augmenting the original five bedrooms with more in the old woodshed leading to the red barn out back.

The common rooms and porch are unusually nice and ever so tasteful. Special touches abound in each bedroom. Duck pillows, duck wallpaper and a duck lamp grace the deluxe Chesapeake Room, once the master bedroom. It has a kingsize bed, a franklin wood stove and a super second-story porch overlooking a farm pond and mountains. A quilted whale hangs behind the bed in the Nantucket Room, complete with a map of the island and a bathroom almost as large as the bedroom itself. The Safari Room reflects Barbara's whimsy, with African wall coverings that tempt you to touch.

Fresh flowers decorate each room in summer. Electric blankets are provided in winter. And "you should see this place at Christmas," says Barbara. "Every nook and cranny is decorated and red bows are put on even the smallest folk-art lambs." In summer, the principal activity is watching the bullfrogs and birds, including a great blue heron, around the farm pond.

Full breakfasts, included in the rates, are served in the beamed dining room or in good weather on the porch. "We'll cook whatever you want," says Barbara.

Dinners for $33 are available for guests and, by reservation, for the public in the dining room filled with her pewter collection. Up to twenty can be served when the front parlor and porch are used as well. Although there is no choice, Barbara will work around special diets and asks large parties for their preference.

A typical dinner might start with cream of broccoli soup, go on to dilled scallops over angel-hair pasta with vegetables and salad not long out of the garden, and end with a fresh berry pie. Chilled cucumber soup and veal marsala might make up another dinner. Leg of lamb often appears, as do shrimp with pernod, game hens, duckling, sole, and pork or beef tenderloin. Grand marnier soufflé and pumpkin ice cream cake are frequent desserts. Guests may bring their own wine.

(207) 583-4037. www.waterfordinne.com. Six rooms with private baths, two with shared bath. Doubles, $90 to $150. Closed in April.

The Noble House, 37 Highland Road, Bridgton 04009.

Once a senator's home on three acres in a residential section overlooking Highland

Lake, The Noble House is now a comfortable B&B with six bedrooms and three suites. Rick and Julie Whelchel left the corporate world of Shaker Heights, Ohio, in 2003 to take over a turnkey operation that had slipped a bit following the departure of the original owners. "We both grew up cooking and found we were spending all our spare time in the kitchen, cooking and entertaining," said Rick. "We're thrilled," he said, to be doing it now for a change in lifestyle.

The architecturally interesting main house, built as a summer home, is a Victorian landmark. Its wraparound porches studded with white columns and an arched second-floor porch beneath a sloping roof catch the eye of the passerby.

Although they share a Victorian-antique theme, seven rooms in the rear carriage house seem more modern – some with jacuzzi baths, large windows overlooking the grounds, a window seat and perhaps a private porch. They're decorated primarily in whites and mauves, furnished in wicker and have wall-to-wall carpeting, period antiques, floral quilts with matching draperies, and frilly touches like eyelet curtains and pillows, one in the shape of a heart. Two suites are upstairs in the main house.

Guests gather in the fireplaced parlor, which harbors lots of books and a grand piano outfitted with sheet music, or in the pine-paneled family room/lounge in back, with its huge mushroom-colored sectional and a grand fireplace.

Breakfast is served on a new and spacious enclosed sun porch with a gas stove or in a Victorian dining room with a glowing fireplace. Homemade granola, yogurt and cranberry scones were preliminaries to a choice of crustless quiche or blueberry pancakes with sausage at our visit. Baked french toast was on the docket the next day. Fruit crêpes are the specialty every Sunday.

Guests can swim, canoe or use the paddleboat from the inn's lakefront property across the road, where a hammock, barbecue grill and picnic table are available.

(207) 647-3733 or (888) 237-4880. www.noblehousebb.com. Six rooms and three suites with private baths. Doubles, $125 to $155 May-October, $99 to $130 rest of year. Two-night minimum in July and August and holiday weekends. Children welcome.

Center Lovell Inn, Route 5, Center Lovell 04016.

Best known for its restaurant, this 1805 homestead offers a view of Kezar Lake with the White Mountains beyond. It's also known for its essay contests in which entrants get a chance to win an inn for a bargain. That's how Maryland restaurateurs Richard and Janice Cox acquired the inn in 1993 as winners among some 5,000 entrants who paid $100 each for the chance.

One good turn seems to lead to another, for in 2003 the Coxes ran another essay contest to turn over the inn to the winner – this time the entry fee was $125, and the Coxes were hoping for 10,000 entries. Alas, the contest failed to produce enough entries, the couple separated and Janice was left holding the bag. "I'm through with contests," she declared at our recent visit.

The three-story inn has something of a Mississippi steamboat appearance, thanks to the Floridian who added a mansard roof topped by a cupola in the 1860s. The 1835 Harmon House, a former barber shop, was moved to the site from Lovell to become a side annex.

Most of the guest quarters have been renovated. The Coxes stripped the floors, put in new baths and added queensize beds in some rooms. Two rooms and a three-room suite (two bedrooms, a den and a bath) are upstairs in the main inn. Three more rooms with private baths and two with shared bath are in the annex. The inn's main-floor parlor has patterned rugs, a fireplace and an upright piano.

Breakfast, available to the public by reservation, is extra ($7.50) from a set menu. The choices "depend on what I feel like cooking in the morning," said Janice.

(207) 925-1575 or (800) 777-2698. www.centerlovellinn.com. Five rooms and one two-bedroom suite with private baths and two rooms with shared baths. Doubles, $79 to $109, EP. Closed in November-December and mid-March to mid-April. Children welcome.

Bear Mountain Inn, 364 Waterford Road (Routes 35 and 37), Waterford 04081.

Lorraine Blais likes to consider her B&B a mini-resort. The 52 acres at the foot of Bear Mountain come with a private beach on Bear Pond, canoes and kayaks, hiking and nature trails, cross-country skiing and snowmobiling. Not to mention eighteen acres of mowed fields – "I know, because I mow them and it takes two days."

An interior designer, she returned in 1996 to her native Maine from Boca Raton, Fla. "I promised my mother I'd come home someday and I'm glad to be back," she said. She's in her element, catering to guests like the Disney Channel crew who stayed here while filming "Bug Juice" at nearby Camp Waziyatah.

The 1820 farmhouse rambles hither and yon, through a paneled living room and into a large dining room with a paneled ceiling and a fieldstone fireplace in the center. Beyond are a crafts shop that doubles as a snowmobile headquarters in the winter, featuring custom-designed sweatshirts, and a 170-year-old barn "that's my favorite part of the house." Here Lorraine came across the old wood that she had made into one of the beds in a guest room.

The front of the main floor houses aforementioned bed in one of four guest rooms that share baths. Upstairs are two large deluxe rooms Lorraine bills as suites. The Great Grizzly has all the bells and whistles: queen bed, fireplace, stocked wet bar, TV/VCR, telephone, jacuzzi for two, and a leather sofa facing wide windows onto the mountains. The Bear Paw with a Southwestern theme has a queensize Santa Fe bed, bath with double jacuzzi and a tiled shower for two, TV/VCR, private entrance and an outdoor deck.

The rear Fuzzy Bear Room has a queen bed, gas fireplace, jacuzzi tub and a view of the pond. The queen-bedded Black Bear Room has a private hall bath. A couple of two-bedroom family suites have their own baths.

The innkeeper's favorite is now the Sugar Bear Cottage, a separate space with a handmade log queensize bed, brick fireplace, TV/VCR, clawfoot tub, kitchenette and porch. It stands in opulent contrast to her new rustic cabin, which she likens to luxury camping (battery-operated lights, gas stove and grill, but no electricity or running water).

In the main inn, a guest refrigerator and "convenience center" are stocked with complimentary wines, beverages and snacks.

The hearty breakfast typically includes a fresh fruit cup, banana bread or muffins, and a main dish ranging from eggs benedict to an herbed cheese soufflé casserole. Everything served is organic and without preservatives. In season you may enjoy it on a rear deck overlooking the wildflower field.

(207) 583-4404. Fax (207) 583-2437. www.bearmtninn.com. Four rooms, two family suites and one cottage with private baths and four rooms with shared baths. Doubles, $110 to $200. Cottage $225. Luxury rooms, $275. Rustic cabin, $75. Children over 8.

Kedarburn Inn, Valley Road (Route 35), Box 61, Waterford 04088.

Built in 1858, this handsome white Colonial house with dark green shutters and broad lawns brightened with flower beds has been upgraded since its acquisition by Margaret and Derek Gibson, who had run a B&B in their native Bournemouth, England.

They added three guest rooms for a total of seven, plus a third-floor suite with a sitting room, and installed private baths in all but two. Beds come in a variety of configurations from kingsize to twins. A couple of beds are full-size, including the one in the suite. The Balcony Room is a double-deck affair with stairs up to twins in a loft, with a queen bed and a private bath below. The bedrooms are enhanced by pleasant country touches, including antiques, quilts, arrangements of dried flowers and hand-sewn linens. Margaret sewed the curtains bearing ducks and learned upholstering "to redo the furniture myself." Mints, thick colorful towels and stuffed Paddington bears are extra touches.

The front guest parlor invites with a television set, comfortable sofas and books. An outdoor patio is within earshot of Kedar Brook.

Margaret's prime interest has turned to making quilts, wreaths, baskets and dolls, which she sells in the Kedar Craft Shop that first took over the walkout basement and expanded to the main floor. "The quilts in gold frames sell as fast as I make them," Margaret advises. She now offers quilting weekends and retreats.

Her full breakfast offers a choice of eggs, omelets, pancakes or french toast in a sunny front breakfast room.

Four versions of English tea are served by reservation most afternoons from 3 to 4 o'clock.

(207) 583-6182 or (866) 583-6182. Fax (207) 583-6424. www.kedarburn.com. Four rooms and one suite with private baths and two rooms with shared bath. Doubles, $85 to $125 with private bath, $71 to $95 shared bath. Children welcome.

Pleasant Point Inn, Pleasant Point Road, Box 218, Center Lovell 04016.

Tucked in a pine forest with a sandy beach and marina on Kezar Lake is this lodging establishment and restaurant of the old school.

Taking over in 1992, Sue and Alan Perry from Plympton, Mass., redid the entire main building, reducing the number of guest rooms from 22 to 10, including two family suites that sleep up to six. The inn's highly regarded restaurant reopened in 2003 after being closed for a few years because of the press of wedding functions.

The renovated guest rooms on the second and third floors have one or two queensize beds, sprightly decor, swivel recliners or wing chairs and updated bathrooms. Most look out onto the lakeshore, where guests enjoy a great beach and dark green wooden beach chairs and benches beneath the pines.

The fourteen-acre property along Kezar Lake also includes five rustic lakefront cabins and two cottages, one with three bedrooms and the other with four. Most have fireplaces and porches and some have kitchens and living rooms. The cottages can be rented in whole or in part, as six individual one-bedroom units with private baths.

A continental breakfast is put out for guests in a lodge-style dining room with a fieldstone fireplace or on a wraparound porch.

In 2003, management of the inn was turned over to Jeff and Nancy Lamarche of New Hampshire, who had the property under contract for purchase and kept the inn open year-round.

(207) 925-3008 or (877) 698-4667. Fax (207) 925-3328. www.pleasantpointinn.com. Eight rooms and two suites with private baths. Doubles, $129 to $179 in summer and foliage, $89 to $119 off-season. Two-night minimum in summer.

Lake House, Routes 35 & 37, Box 82, Waterford 04088.

A mix of accommodations and a well-regarded restaurant are housed in this landmark structure, built in the 1790s and operating as Waterford's first tavern and inn until the 1940s.

Chef Michael Myers reopened the inn in 1984 and gradually restored the original structure fronting on an ornate, two-story, columned veranda. He installed eleven bathrooms, painted countless walls and trim, and in 1999, performed a major renovation of the rear carriage house to add three more guest rooms.

The restaurant (see Dining Spots) takes top billing on the main floor, where a small parlor with a fireplace traces in pictures how the Lake House evolved through the 1800s and 1900s. Most of the guest quarters are on the second floor, and Michael and his wife Doreen live on the third floor.

The Waterford Flat Suite had more than enough space in which we could spread out during a record hot spell, in spacious sleeping quarters with a ruffly queen bed and an adjoining reading room with a sofa, shelves lined with books and a coffeemaker. Two nearby rooms were smaller, but like ours had a homey, lived-in feeling. Not at all home-like is the air-conditioned Grand Ballroom Suite, one vast room that lives up to its name with a huge curved ceiling, a kingsize bed, seven windows, a sitting area and a free-standing clawfoot tub and shower, with a sink on a raised stage at the far end of the room.

Three rooms with queensize beds operate seasonally in the renovated carriage house behind the inn. The Pine Room, converted from the inn's 19th-century office, is named for its red southern pine walls and ceiling and its yellow pine floor. A french door in the main-floor Tally Ho opens onto a private deck.

A bottle of sparkling water is put out in each guest room, and a bowl of peanuts in the parlor staves off hunger before dinner. Breakfast, taken at 9 o'clock in the rear dining room or on the front porch, could be scrambled eggs, pancakes or waffles, accompanied by juice and a fresh fruit salad – in our case, bananas and blueberries with cream.

(207) 583-4182 or (800) 223-4182. Fax (207) 583-6078. www.lakehousemaine.com. Six rooms and one suite with private baths. May-October: doubles $120 (ballroom $170), suites $150. Rest of year: doubles $90 (ballroom $140), suite $120. Children over 6. Two-night minimum summer weekends.

The Oxford House Inn, 105 Main St., Fryeburg 04037.

Known primarily for its outstanding food, this inn run by John and Phyllis Morris also offers four guest rooms with private baths. They're located upstairs in an attractive, pale yellow and green country house fronted with a wraparound piazza.

One front corner room has a bow window and a queen and a double bed. The large Porch suite has a kingsize bed, an extra futon and an enclosed porch for a sitting area. Another with a comfy sitting area is large enough for a kingsize bed and an extra twin. The rear Sewing Room features an antique sewing table and sewing notions along with a queen bed. All rooms are furnished with period furniture and antiques and come with TV and air conditioning..

Guests share a parlor with waiting dinner patrons, but can retire as well to the large Granite Room Lounge downstairs pub with four small tables and a sitting area with a wood stove and a large TV. The wicker-filled wraparound porch is great for relaxing, and the back yard opens onto a super view of the Presidential Range.

The Morrises serve a complete breakfast. Eggs benedict, grand marnier french

The Oxford House Inn is known for good food and lodging.

toast, berry pancakes and french toast with cream cheese and marmalade or raspberry jam are among the possibilities.

(207) 935-3442 or (800) 261-7206. www.oxfordhouseinn.com. Four rooms with private baths. Doubles, $95 to $135.

Dining Spots

The Oxford House Inn, 105 Main St., Fryeburg.

Opened in 1985, this 1913 in-town country inn is run quite personally by John and Phyllis Morris, formerly of North Conway, whose dinner fare commands a wide reputation.

Seventy-five people can be seated on white chairs (their tops hand-stenciled by Phyllis) on the rear porch with a stunning view of Mount Kearsarge North, in the former living room called the Parlor, and along the screened front piazza. Tables are set with delicate pink crystal, heavy silver and Sango Mystique peach china, with candles in clay pots and napkins tied like neckties. Green floral wallpaper, Phyllis's handmade curtains and draperies, and handsome paneling enhance the parlor.

The menu, which changes seasonally, comes inside sheet music from the 1920s. Dinner begins with complimentary homemade crackers and a cream cheese spread, a salad of fresh greens and fruits (blueberries and watermelon), perhaps with a tomato-tarragon dressing or a cranberry vinaigrette, and fresh nut and fruit breads. Starters might be escargots, hot buttered brie, a house pâté and Maine crab crêpes. Crayfish bisque, cream of asparagus and chilled peach were among summer soups when we visited.

The eight entrées include champagne-poached salmon, scallops à l'orange in puff pastry, grilled pork tenderloin with plum-cinnamon port sauce, veal madeira, rack of lamb with mint-apple chutney, and pan-fried venison flamed with sherry and

Lake House offers accommodations and fine dining in landmark structure.

port and finished with currant and guava jelly, dried cherries, cloves and cinnamon. John does most of the cooking, but the desserts are Phyllis's: fruit trifles, cheesecake terrine, praline truffle, chocolate mousse, spumoni and frozen peach yogurt at one visit. Her bread pudding with peaches and blueberries is highly acclaimed.

(207) 935-3442 or (800) 261-7206. Entrées, $25 to $29. Dinner by reservation, 6 to 9, nightly in summer and fall, Thursday-Sunday rest of year.

Lake House, Routes 35 & 37, Waterford.

Almost since it reopened in 1984, the restaurant at Waterford's first inn has been making culinary waves in western Maine. A changing menu of creative regional cuisine, flaming desserts and an award-winning wine list are offered by chef-owner Michael Myers. Periodic wine-tasting dinners attract gourmands from near and far.

Each dining room is pretty as a picture. The small front room has burgundy patterned wallpaper above pale green woodwork, burgundy carpeting, shelves of glass and china, a collection of bird paintings and a picture of puffins over the fireplace. The larger rear pine-paneled dining room has a remarkable corkscrew collection, linen-clad tables set with two large wine glasses at each setting and oriental rugs on the floor. Patrons enjoy the antics of birds at window feeders behind a couple of one-way mirrors.

On a mild summer night, we chose to eat outside on the screened front porch. The Rhode Island squid sautéed with spinach ravioli and garlic sauce and the signature duck liver pâté seasoned with apples and grand marnier were excellent starters.

A dollop of kiwi sorbet preceded the entrées, a generous portion of sliced lamb sauced with curry and vodka and Michael's signature roast duckling in a sauce of peppered blackberries and red wine. Sliced potatoes, cucumbers, tomatoes and pickled corn accompanied. Lobster madagascar in puff pastry, feta-stuffed chicken with Mediterranean sauce, osso buco of pork, filet mignon and fresh salmon filleted on site and served with tequila-lime butter were other choices.

For dessert, we succumbed to a parfait pie and a light chocolate-espresso mousse served on a grand marnier sauce. Bananas foster and cherries jubilee are flamed tableside for two.

(207) 583-4182 or (800) 223-4182. Entrées, $19 to $26. Dinner nightly, 5:30 to 9, fewer days in off-season, weekends in winter. Closed April and November.

Pleasant Point Inn, Pleasant Point Road, Box 218, Center Lovell 04016.

New management reopened the restaurant at this lakefront inn to popular acclaim in 2003 after it had been closed for several years in favor of weddings and functions.

Jeff and Nancy Lamarche won plaudits for dinners, now served in the inn's former lodge-style living room with a fieldstone fireplace and a pine-paneled banquet room used for overflow.

Their chef prepares a continental/American menu ranging from lobster and scallop newburg to steak au poivre. Baked stuffed haddock, seafood fra diavolo, chicken marsala and filet mignon oscar typify the choices.

Starters are as traditional as fruit cup and shrimp cocktail and as contemporary as a lobster-stuffed portobello mushroom, and asparagus, provolone and prosciutto in puff pastry.

(207) 925-3008 or (877) 698-4667. Entrées, $18 to $24. Dinner, Tuesday-Saturday 5 to 9 Memorial Day to Columbus Day, Saturday in winter.

Center Lovell Inn, Route 5, Center Lovell.

Maryland restaurateurs Richard and Janice Cox won this venerable farmhouse-turned-inn in a much-publicized essay contest. The kitchen is overseen by Janice, who had been manager at the well-known Busch's Chesapeake Inn in Annapolis. She hired a chef and a sous chef to implement a new dinner menu.

The 40-seat Victorian dining rooms are decorated in muted peach and pink colors. Colorful quilts and print cloths were added to the wraparound screened dining porch overlooking Kezar Lake and the Presidential Range.

The new menu adds Maryland specialties such as appetizers of spicy crab balls and lump crab mousse served in a cucumber wheel, and an entrée of seafood norfolk sautéed with garlic and brandy. Other main courses could be grilled Idaho rainbow trout, cashew-encrusted salmon topped with an herbed pesto, crispy muscovy duck breast with a sour cherry-zinfandel glaze and herb-crusted rack of lamb with port wine-orange sauce.

Janice does the baking. House favorites include strawberry-rhubarb and blueberry cream pies, strawberry shortcake and key lime pie.

(207) 925-1575 or (800) 777-22698. Entrées, $22.95 to $26.95. Dinner nightly, 5:30 to 9. Closed mid-March to mid-April and November-December.

Ebenezer's Restaurant & Pub, 44 Allen Road, Lovell.

Good food is offered at this casual establishment beside the second hole of the Kezar Lake Golf Course.

Daily blackboard specials supplement a fairly extensive menu heavy on burgers, sandwiches, appetizers and salads. Expect anything from a hot dog to a lobster roll, from nachos to quesadillas, from chef's to lobster caesar salad. The Lovell sampler yields buffalo wings, chicken fingers, jalapeño poppers, crab rangoons and fries.

The printed menu lists entrées like a seafood platter, charbroiled chicken breast and sirloin tips. Specials at our latest visit were shrimp and scallop scampi, herb-roasted duck and New York sirloin. Desserts run to berry pies and hot fudge sundaes.

Dining is on an enclosed porch or a covered, trellised outdoor patio. Six beers are on tap in the bar.

(207) 925-3200. www.ebenezerspub.com. Entrées, $7.95 to $13.95. Lunch and dinner from 11:30 in summer, weekends in off-season.

The Black Horse Tavern, 8 Portland St. (Route 302), Bridgton.

A big hit in the Bridgton area is this restaurant in a barn behind a gray house whose front porch looks as if it were straight out of Louisiana. The two structures are joined by a large bar. Most of the dining is in the rear portion, where all kinds of horsey artifacts hang from the walls and stalls have been converted into booths.

The Louisiana farmhouse look is appropriate. The chef, a Maine native, acquired a cajun flair while cooking in Texas and Louisiana.

The chicken and smoked sausage gumbo and the crab-stuffed mushrooms are must starters at lunch or dinner. The huge menu lists steaks, prime rib, rack of ribs, pan-blackened sirloin, bourbon-mushroom chicken, haddock au gratin, bayou-style shrimp diane and seafood scampi over pasta. We liked the scallop pie and the night's special of mahi-mahi with shrimp and basil sauce. Hot rolls and good salads with pepper parmesan and vinaigrette dressings were served immediately upon ordering. The wine list was quite good and affordable.

Homemade desserts include Kentucky derby pie, Mississippi mud pie and carrot cake with cream cheese frosting.

(207) 647-5300. Entrées, $12.95 to $18.95. Lunch daily, 11 to 4. Dinner nightly, 4 to 10 or 11. Sunday brunch, 9 to 3.

Melby's Market & Eatery, Route 35, North Waterford.

A general store of the old school, this is also a bakery, ice cream parlor and a basic restaurant. The food operation tends to overshadow the groceries and convenience items. In an area where lunch service is infrequent to non-existent, we were famished enough to order a couple of hot dogs and a buffalo burger ($4.29), made with locally raised bison (they also feature an elk burger). There are all kinds of sandwiches, subs and pizzas at distinctly non-urban prices. An extensive array of breakfast items is available morning, noon and night. Dinner items include fish and chips, fried shrimp or scallops, and charbroiled chicken breast. Finish with an oatmeal-raisin cookie or a pie from the bakery. Wash it down with an old-fashioned frappe.

There are assorted tables and a counter for enjoying it all at this old-fashioned place full of local color.

(207) 583-4447 or (800) 281-4437. Entrées, $6.49 to $8.29. Open daily, 6 a.m. to 9 or 10 p.m.

Diversions

The area has many attributes, but they tend to be quiet and personal. One inn brochure states: "Whether you prefer browsing through local antique shops, visiting the country fairs, watching the sun rise over the misty lake as you fish from your canoe at dawn or spending a quiet evening around the fieldstone fireplace, you are on your own." Some ideas:

The Villages. General stores and the odd antiques or crafts shop are about the only merchandising in places like Waterford, North Waterford, Center Lovell and Lovell. But do not underestimate the villages' charms. As humorist Artemus Ward wrote of Waterford: "The village from which I write to you is small. It does not contain over forty houses, all told; but they are milk white, with the greenest of blinds, and for the most part are shaded with beautiful elms and willows. To the right of us is a mountain – to the left a lake. The village nestles between. Of course it does. I never read a novel in my life in which the villages didn't nestle. It is a kind of way they have." Waterford hasn't changed much since, nor have its surrounding towns. For action, you have to go north to Bethel, east to Bridgton or southwest to North Conway.

The Lakes. Kezar, peaceful and quiet and somewhat inaccessible, lies beneath the mighty Presidential Range, its clear waters reflecting the changing seasons and spectacular sunsets. The lake is relatively undeveloped and private, with access only from the marina at the Narrows, the beach at the end of Pleasant Point Road and a point in North Lovell. The rest of the time you can rarely even see it (much to our dismay, for we got lost trying). Keoka Lake, at Waterford, has a small, pleasant and secluded beach just east of the village and a sometimes crowded village beach just to the south. Hidden lakes and ponds abound, and not far distant are more accessible Long Lake and Sebago Lake.

Shopping. The hand-painted gifts, crafts and furnishings of the talented Quisisana music resort's staff are featured at the seasonal **QuisiWorks** shop along the main highway at Center Lovell. **Yankee Ingenuity** across from the Center Lovell Inn intrigues. The pottery, jewelry, carved birds and the kitchen corner with themed cookbooks appeals at the nearby **Kezar Lake Handcrafts**. More crafts are shown in **The Loft** at the Center Lovell Market. The hand-thrown porcelain feeders for hummingbirds caught our eye at **Wiltjer Pottery,** Route 37, South Waterford. At **Craftworks,** ensconced in a refurbished church in Bridgton, we browsed through the baskets, rugs, candles, Maine wines and foods, and some interesting clothing. We also liked the gifts and handicrafts at **The Cool Moose** in Bridgton.

Sports. Canoeing and kayaking are big business on the Saco River in the area around Fryeberg. Saco River Canoe & Kayak offers rentals in Fryeberg. There's golf at Kezar Lake Golf Course and hiking in the White Mountain National Forest. Skiing is available at Pleasant Mountain, Mount Abrams and Sunday River.

Extra-Special

The area is a low-key center for handicrafts, if you know where to look.

Bonnema Potters on lower Main Street in Bethel is a studio and showroom where Garret and Melody Bonnema craft and display their pottery in a barn beside their house. Seldom have we seen such appealing colors. According to the Bonnemas, their glazing is influenced by the colors in the mountains and valleys in the surrounding area. Tankards, tiles, candelabras, casseroles, teapots and much more are their wares. We especially like their lamps and a couple of them help light up our home. Open daily except Wednesday, 10 to 5.

Also worth a side trip is **Perham's,** a jewelry store and museum at the junction of Routes 26 and 219 in West Paris. The specialty here is Maine tourmaline, a dazzling array of the gem procured locally. You learn that surrounding Oxford County is one of the world's richest sources of minerals and gems. Both the museum-type displays and the jewelry showrooms are fascinating. Open daily, 9 to 5.

If it's open, the **Jones Museum of Glass & Ceramics** off Route 107 on Douglas Mountain in Sebago Center is well worth visiting (it was shuttered in 2002 and 2003 during an acrimonious dispute between owner-founder Dorothy-Lee Jones and recalcitrant trustees who sought to move to a more accessible site in South Portland – the court ruled in her favor in late 2003). Displayed here are more than 3,000 works of art, everything from Chinese porcelain and Egyptian glass to Wedgwood teapots and Sandwich lamps displayed in brilliant profusion.

Great seats for ocean-watching await on veranda of Emerson Inn By the Sea.

Rockport, Mass.

Values by the Sea

They certainly don't need more crowds, these habitués of Bearskin Neck, Pigeon Cove and Marmion Way. Nor do those who cater to them.

But bargain-conscious travelers seldom do better than in Rockport, the seaside Cape Ann resort town from yesteryear, where the costs of food and lodging consistently remain behind the times – and only lately have started to catch up.

Why such bargains? Because Rockport was developed earlier, when costs were lower, than many such coastal resorts. "We were bed and breakfast long before the craze started," notes Dwight MacCormack of Seacrest Manor. Inns here traditionally could keep their prices down because they didn't carry hefty mortgages, although recent turnover in ownership has upped the ante. Rockport's century-old ban on the sale of liquor has influenced prices, if only in lowering restaurant tabs when patrons BYOB. And no national chain stores or motels have sullied Rockport's center to drive up market values.

Its old-fashioned attributes help swell Rockport's year-round population of 7,500 to 35,000 in summer. Most folks, it seems, are on the streets near Dock Square and Bearskin Neck, the rocky fishing and commercial promontory that juts into the harbor. Parking is usually a problem. Arrive early or expect to park on distant side streets and walk. Or better yet, take the Cape Ann Trolley.

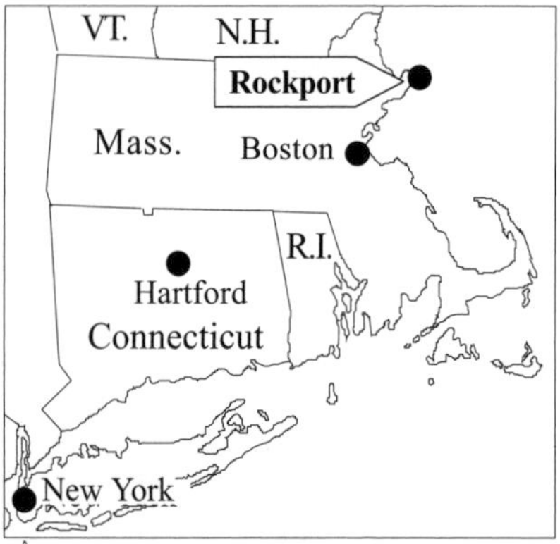

Visitors are drawn by the rocky coast more typical of Maine, the atmosphere of an old fishing village crammed with shops, the quaintness of a "dry" town in which Sunday evening band concerts are the major entertainment, and the lively arts colony inspired by a harbor listed by Walt Disney Productions as one of the nation's most scenic. In fact, Motif No. 1, a fishing shack on the wharf, is outranked as an artist's image only by the Mona Lisa. When it collapsed in the Blizzard of 1978, villagers quickly rebuilt it – such is the place of art (and tourism) in Rockport.

All around Rockport are the varied assets of the rest of Cape Ann. They range from the English look of quiet Annisquam, which is New England at its quaintest, to the commercial fishing flavor of busy Gloucester.

The allure of Rockport is so strong that its devotées return time and again.

Inn Spots

Eden Pines Inn, 48 Eden Road, Rockport 01966.

You can't get much closer to the ocean than on the rear brick patio that hovers over the rocks – or, for that matter, in most of the upstairs guest rooms – at this delightfully secluded B&B by the sea.

The setting in what was formerly a summer home could not be more attractive. The lodge-like front living room with stone fireplace, the California-style side breakfast porch with white wicker furniture and picture windows, the open rear porch full of wicker lounge chairs and flowers with a neat brick patio below, even a couple of bathroom windows take full advantage of the water view across to Thatchers Island and its twin lighthouses. Although the shore here is rocky, the inn is within walking distance of two beaches.

Innkeepers Nicky and Michael Kern inherited the furnishings and decor of longtime owner Inge Sullivan when they acquired the B&B in 2002. Their predecessor's preference for breezy California decor, Laura Ashley and Bill Blass fabrics, and marble baths remains evident. The Kerns made some infrastructure changes to extend the season through December as they planned to live here with their young children year-round.

The six guest rooms are unusually spacious and face the ocean. All come with idyllic private balconies for taking in the view. Three have king or queen beds and the rest have two double beds.

Although fairly different, each attracts. We find most appealing premier Room 4, all blue and white in decorator fabrics with two double beds linked by a dark blue curtain canopy. It has thick carpeting, a comfortable sitting area with Queen Anne chairs and an enormous bathroom done in Italian marble with a deep bathtub, a separate shower and a large window onto the ocean next to the marble vanity. Room 6 with a queen poster bed is cool in shades of mint green and has the other bathroom with an ocean view.

The Kerns put out a self-serve continental breakfast that includes fruit salad, cereals, yogurt, English muffins, toasting bread and homemade coffeecake, as well as mid-afternoon tea, lemonade and setups for drinks, along with cookies, wine and cheese. We know of few more picturesque places for enjoying them than the wicker lounge chairs on the rear patio smack beside the ocean.

(978) 546-2505. Fax (978) 546-9381. Six rooms with private baths. Doubles, $200 to $210; $140 in April, November and December. Two-night minimum weekends. Closed January-March.

Seacrest Manor, 99 Marmion Way, Rockport 01966.

Lawns and gardens, personality and a breakfast to remember – these are the hallmarks of Seacrest Manor. So is the sweeping view of the ocean beyond the trees from the second-story deck above the inn's spacious living room.

Century-old red oak shades front of Seacrest Manor.

For 30 years – one of the longest tenures of any innkeepers in New England – the B&B was run ever-so-personally by Leighton Saville, the front man, and Dwight B. MacCormack Jr., who stayed behind the scenes. Following Leighton's untimely death in 2002, Dwight kept the venture going with the assistance of Kay Henderson, their longtime assistant.

Their personal touch is so pervasive that many of the repeat guests – about 70 percent of the clientele – have left gifts. They include their own watercolors of the inn, crocheted pillows and countless knickknacks, including a collection of rabbits "which just keep multiplying, as rabbits are prone to do," according to Dwight.

The main-floor library displays so many British magazines that "our English guests tell us it feels like home," he adds. The elegant living room, where afternoon tea is served, has a masculine feel with leather chairs, dark colors and fine paintings, as well as exquisite stained glass and tiny bottles in the bow windows.

The formal dining room is decked out in fancy linens, Wedgwood china and crystal glasses at five tables for a breakfast that Town & Country magazine called one of the 50 best in America. It begins with fresh fruit cup and fresh orange juice, continues with spiced Irish oatmeal and bacon and eggs, and ends with a specialty like blueberry or apple pancakes, french toast or corn fritters.

Guests have the run of the two-acre property, which includes a remarkable, century-old red oak shading the entire front yard, prolific gardens, a couple of statues and a rope hammock strung between trees in a rear corner. The flower beds supply the small bouquets scattered through the inn. Flowers even turn up in stand-up frames, unusual English vases that the partners discovered in Bermuda. They purchased one for every room and stocked them for guests to purchase.

Six guest rooms have private baths and two that share are generally rented as a suite. Three have full ocean views and the rest have partial ocean views. Two premier second-floor rooms have direct access to the ocean-view deck. All have twin/king or queen beds, television, a clock radio, a couple of chairs and a desk. The suite has a double bed in each room.

Amenities include mints on the bedside table at nightly turndown service, fine soaps and shampoos, and overnight shoe shines. That's right, leave your shoes outside the door upon retiring and they'll be glistening beside a complimentary Boston Globe at the door in the morning.

Such is Seacrest Manor, a special place that measures up to its motto, "decidedly small, intentionally quiet."

(978) 546-2211. www.seacrestmanor.com. Six rooms and a two-bedroom suite with private baths. Doubles, $185 to $215. Suite, $185, or $98 individually with shared bath. Two-night minimum, mid-May through October. No credit cards. Closed December to March.

Yankee Clipper Inn, 127 Granite St., Box 2399, Rockport 01966.

One of Rockport's older and grander inns, the Yankee Clipper takes full advantage of its remarkable setting on a bluff, with beautifully landscaped lawns on a bit of a point jutting into the ocean.

New owners Randy and Cathy Marks took over the main inn in 2001 as Barbara and Bob Ellis, daughter and son-in-law of its founders, retired and sold off the property in various parcels. Randy, a former New York chiropractor, and Cathy, a marketing executive for a high-end health club in Boston, scaled the original 26 rooms back to eight in the 1929 art deco Georgian mansion in which the Yankee Clipper got its start. Six of the inn's rooms, all named after clipper ships, yield full ocean views – some bordering on the spectacular from sun porches or decks. Everyone shares a beauty of a deck off the third floor.

Later they added more contemporary rooms in the Quarterdeck, built in 1960 beside the water and featuring even more dramatic views. It has a knockout penthouse on the third floor with two double beds, a sofabed and velvet chairs facing floor-to-ceiling windows onto the ocean. Two ground-floor oceanfront lodgings look across gardens to the open sea.

The main floor holds a grandly furnished living room. The Markses, who reside in the inn, serve afternoon tea and coffee. They closed the former restaurant on the porch, The Veranda, to concentrate on functions. The porch setting was retained for overnight guests, who enjoy a full breakfast in summer and a continental breakfast in the off-season.

A heated saltwater pool is hidden from public view beneath the road on the landscaped, terraced grounds between the main inn and the Quarterdeck.

(978) 546-3407 or (800) 545-3699. Fax (978) 546-9730. www.yankeeclipperinn.com. Thirteen rooms and three suites with private baths. Doubles, $199 to $359 mid-June to mid-October, $129 to $259 rest of year. Two-night minimum weekends. Closed December-February.

Emerson Inn By the Sea, 1 Cathedral Ave., Rockport 01966.

White pillars grace the front entrance and rockers are lined up facing the ocean on the back porch of this recently renovated and renamed Federal-style inn, formerly the Ralph Waldo Emerson and long owned by the Wemys family of Yankee Clipper Inn fame. Bruce and Michele Coates, who were part owners of restaurants in Florida, bought the faded inn in 1999, refurbished the rooms and kept the place open year-round.

The inn is typical of a number of old-fashioned establishments in Rockport, but this one has been infused with a new energy and spirit – though the upgrading process was daunting and unending. The rooms are in two sections on several levels, none of which seem to connect with the others, and reflect their 160-year-old heritage. One corner ocean-view room we saw had a king bed, two arm chairs, a desk, a bureau and rather drab decor. More cheerful in rose colors and florals was a front room with a double and a twin poster bed. Furnishings are 19th-century antiques and reproductions.

The prime accommodations are eleven deluxe ocean-view rooms, decorated to the period. All have kingsize beds and spa tubs. Two have small electric fireplaces and two have balconies – the one with both is "the best room in the house," says Bruce.

The spacious "grand salon" lobby holds a grand piano and a buffet table with a platter of cookies and coffee and lemonade in thermos jugs. Breakfast and dinner are served in **The Grand Café** (see Dining Spots). A full breakfast is included in the rates in season; breakfast is continental in the off-season.

The broad rear lawn leads to a small saltwater swimming pool at the edge of the ocean bluff.

(978) 546-6321 or (800) 964-5550. Fax (978) 546-7043. www.emersoninnbythesea.com. Thirty-six rooms with private baths. May-October: doubles, $145 to $349. Rest of year: $95 to $279. Two-night minimum weekends in season.

Addison Choate Inn, 49 Broadway, Rockport 01966.

An in-town location draws guests to this attractive, flower-bedecked Greek Revival house built in 1851 and boasting Rockport's first bathtub – in the kitchen, no less.

That bathtub has been replaced, of course, but all five air-conditioned guest rooms and a two-room suite come with large and modern hand-tiled bathrooms with reproduction fixtures. Innkeepers Cynthia Francis and Ed Cambron run a B&B that had been renovated and redecorated from top to bottom, and repainted salmon with dark green trim. The main-floor Captain's Room, dressed in subtle period green wallpaper above the wainscoting, focuses on a fishnet-canopied, queensize mahogany poster bed. The second-floor Hearth Room (named for the chimney rising through the room) is done in blue and white accents and has a lace queen canopy bed. The third-floor Penthouse Suite, furnished in white wicker with a queen canopy bed draped in lace, has television, refrigerator and a view of the ocean across the rooftops. All rooms come with irons, robes and hair dryers.

The comfortable living room with its restored antique mantel over the fireplace, a small rear library with TV and a dining room with a beehive oven are cheery. Each contains antiques and original art. A continental-plus breakfast buffet includes fresh fruit, cereal, homemade granola, yogurt, baked goods and house-blend coffee. It's taken in the dining room or at intimate tables for two on the narrow side porch facing showy perennial gardens across the driveway.

The rear Carriage House contains two cathedral-ceilinged townhouse suites with kitchenettes, TV and loft bedrooms available by the day or week. The Choate with a spiral staircase and skylights in the bathroom and bedroom has particular flair.

(978) 546-7543 or (800) 245-7543. Fax (978) 546-7638. www.addisonchoateinn.com. Five rooms, one suite and two townhouse suites with private baths. Doubles $135 to $165 Memorial Day through October, $110 to $135 rest of year. Housekeeping suites (available May-October, three-night minimum), $175 nightly, $1,050 weekly. Two-night minimum summer weekends. Children over 12.

Flowers brighten entry and porch at Addison Choate Inn.

Linden Tree Inn, 26 King St., Rockport 01966.

Flowery and fragrant and about two centuries old, an enormous linden tree spreads its limbs beside this Victorian-style house dating to about 1850. Tobey and John Shepherd offer stylish common rooms and eighteen bedrooms, all with private baths.

Guests enter through a pleasant side sun porch into a dining room and a formal living room with elegant Victorian furnishings and oriental rugs. Twelve bedrooms in the main inn are nicely appointed with period furniture, carpeting, fresh flowers and a mix of twin, double, queen and king beds. The least expensive room in the house, the third-floor Room 34 with a double bed and a sitting area with a loveseat and chair, has devotees because of its windows on two sides onto the distant ocean and the nearby Mill Pond, where the locals ice skate in the winter. For an even better view, John leads guests up to the cupola, lit by Christmas lights in the windows and visible from all around town. An annex to the main house holds two connecting bedrooms rented as a suite.

The premium rooms are in a carriage house behind the inn. Here you'll find four modern, year-round rooms, each with a queen and twin bed, TV, kitchenette and private rear deck.

Tobey, who had worked for a large inn in New Hampshire, is an accomplished baker. Some of her treats are served with afternoon tea and lemonade, and the aroma of blueberry cake emanating from the kitchen nearly did us in upon arrival (it tasted delectable, too). The main event is breakfast around a large table or at smaller individual tables in the dining room. Expect all kinds of fresh fruits, juice and homemade coffeecakes, melt-in-your-mouth scones and breads, from mango to apple-walnut. Rhubarb cake, fig-pineapple coffeecake and banana/chocolate-chip bread are other favorites.

John, a professor at Bentley College in Waltham, helps keep the inn running year-round.

(978) 546-2494 or (800) 865-2122. Fax (978) 546-3297. www.lindentreeinn.com. Twelve rooms, one suite and four efficiency units with private baths. Mid-May through November, doubles $100 to $128, efficiencies $136, suite $165. Rest of year: doubles $90 to $100, efficiencies $110, suite $115.

Sally Webster Inn, 34 Mount Pleasant St., Rockport 01966.

A good-looking gray house with red shutters and a lovely fan door, this 1832 structure contains eight guest rooms, each named for one of its former occupants. The house has six fireplaces, original wide-plank pine floors, period door moldings, brick terraces and herb gardens.

The front parlor is known as "Sally's Share," because that is the part of the house that Sally Choate Webster inherited from her father, the local "housewright" who built it. Bearing a rather grim-faced portrait of her, the room contains family artifacts given to the inn by Sally's great-great-granddaughter, who has stayed here. Across the hall is Sally's Room, a bedroom with twin beds joined as a kingsize.

Canopy, pencil-post four-poster and Jenny Lind beds are in the guest rooms. Beds range from twin to kingsize. Two rooms with a double and twin bed accommodate three guests. A mini-suite on the second-floor has a queen bed and separate sitting area. Each room is attractively furnished to the period and outfitted with the inn's own toiletries.

Innkeepers John and Kathy Fitzgerald offer a hearty continental buffet breakfast. It's served with silver coffee pots and antique china in the dining room or, beyond through french doors, at two umbrella-topped tables on a side brick patio.

(978) 546-9251 or (877) 546-9251. www.sallywebster.com. Eight rooms with private baths. Doubles, $100 to $135, mid-June to mid-October; off-season $80 to $115. Two-night minimum weekends in season.

The Inn on Cove Hill, 37 Mount Pleasant St., Rockport 01966.

Close to the heart of town and with a super view of Motif No. 1 and the harbor from its rear third-floor deck is this Georgian-style mansion, surrounded by a white picket fence and lovingly tended gardens. It was built in 1771 and recently identified as the Caleb Norwood Jr. House, for its original owner, whose family occupied it until the mid-20th century.

Innkeeper Betsy Eck was on a visit from Shrewsbury, Mass., when she walked into the house "and felt like I was home." She made a purchase offer that afternoon for the property to longtime innkeepers who had undertaken a lengthy restoration and redecoration of the former guest house. "After 23 years, they passed the baton," said Betsy, who launched gradual improvements in the "restoration rather than renovation" mode. She eliminated two guest rooms for her live-in quarters as well as for a second-floor den with TV. She also added a dining room to stay open nearly year-round.

Five of the eight bedrooms are on the third floor. Two on the third floor share a newly updated bath that's the best in the house. Each is nicely decorated in Laura Ashley fabrics and wallpapers, and all rooms have TV sets. Most rooms sport handmade quilts and afghans and crocheted coverlets as well as oriental-style rugs. The most expensive is a third-floor room with queen canopy bed, tiled shower and a view of the harbor.

Betsy likes to point out the structure's architectural features – such as the spiral staircase with thirteen steps in the entry hall – and the antique furnishings in the living room. In removing the aluminum siding, workmen found the original clapboarding and advised the new owner that the structure was twenty years older than she had thought.

An expanded continental breakfast is served in the dining room or at outdoor tables topped by umbrellas in the side garden. Cereal, yogurt and bagels have been added to the fare. Recipes for some of the establishment's popular muffins (oatmeal, orange-buttermilk and pumpkin, among them) have been printed for guests.

(978) 546-2701 or (888) 546-2701. Fax (978) 546-1095. www.innoncovehill.com. Six rooms with private baths and two rooms with shared baths. Doubles, $95 to $145 private bath, $85 shared, Memorial Day through October; $85 to $125 private, $75 shared, rest of year. Two-night minimum weekends in season. Closed in January.

Seaward Inn, 44 Marmion Way, Rockport 01966.

The Cameron family is back at this inn of the old school, lovingly run by Anne and Roger Cameron for 50 years. After a few years under another owner, three Cameron daughters took the inn back in 2000, hired a manager and launched modest upgrades to a low-key, rustic place that has lured repeat guests year after year. They closed it after the 2001 season and, reopened in 2003, with Nancy Cameron-Gilsey as owner-innkeeper.

Facing the ocean on attractive grounds full of gardens, lawn chairs, boulders and stone fences, the complex includes the weathered main inn, a couple of outbuildings and six cottages rented by the week. (Although refurbished, the last are likened to "the cottage you remember as a child.")

The main inn offers nine old-fashioned rooms furnished with period pieces, vintage maple bureaus and desks, and the TVs and telephones common to all the accommodations. Adjacent is the Carriage House and Gull's Nest complex with five rooms, a pair of two-room suites with ocean vistas from new decks, and an oceanfront cottage. Other accommodations are in six single or multi-unit, pine-paneled cottages with granite terraces. Billed as "quaint and cozy," one has a kitchenette and several have fireplaces.

The **Seagarden Restaurant** in the main inn serves breakfast (included in the rates) and dinner to the public (see Dining Spots).

(978) 546-3471 or (877) 473-2927. Fax (978) 546-7661. www.seawardinn.com. Fourteen rooms, two suites and six cottages with private baths. Doubles, $179 to $259. Cottages, $179 to $495. Closed November to mid-April.

Dining Spots

Rockport is dry, but most restaurants invite patrons to BYOB. Some of the more prominent restaurants and biggest advertisers are considered tourist traps; innkeepers and locals rarely recommend them. Good restaurants with liquor licenses are located nearby in Gloucester and Essex.

My Place By the Sea, 68 Bearskin Neck, Rockport.

You can't get much closer to the ocean than at this restaurant at the very end of Bearskin Neck. In fact, it's so close to the ocean that twice in recent years it has been damaged in storms. The structure has been rebuilt with a crisp summery look. A two-level outdoor porch wraps around the tiny interior, with an open lower level resting right above the rocky shore and a smaller side level covered by an awning and enclosed in roll-down plastic "windows" for use in inclement weather. Floral cloths cover the tables and the atmosphere is romantic in rose and aqua.

Called My Place because a former owner couldn't think of anything else, the name has stuck. It is now owned by its chef of some years, Kathy Milbury, sister of Mike Milbury, the former Boston Bruins hockey star. Partner Barbara Stavropoulos runs the front of the house. Chef Kathy has upgraded the menu and enhanced its reputation for the best food in town. Indeed, a recent entry in one innkeeper's restaurant diary was by Californians who proclaimed My Place "the best over-all restaurant on our thirteen-state foliage tour. Excellent service, food and ambiance."

Starters could be grilled shrimp with avocado butter in a warm flour tortilla, grilled black mission figs with shaved pecorino, and lobster quesadilla with sundried tomato cream cheese and spicy salsa. Can't decide? Order the chef's seafood tasting.

For entrées, consider the signature baked swordfish with a tangy béarnaise sauce and pecan butter, pan-seared szechuan salmon on an Asian noodle pancake and Portuguese fisherman's stew in a fiery brodo. The grilled chicken might arrive with a ricotta-tomato sauce over pasta.

Dessert favorites include a warm chocolate cake with homemade maple walnut ice cream, coffee panna cotta with vanilla rum anglaise and warm apple crunch with cinnamon ice cream.

(978) 546-9667. www.myplacebythesea.com. Entrées, $22 to $29. Lunch daily, 11:30 to 4. Dinner, 4 to 9:30 or 10. Fewer days in the off-season and closed November to mid-April. BYOB.

The Grand Café, 1 Cathedral Ave., Rockport.

Emerson Inn owner Bruce Coates went to the Cornell Hotel School and with his wife Michele was involved in ownership of three restaurants in Florida for twenty years. So they know the restaurant business, and followed their dream of finding a New England inn. He and Michelle renovated the inn's dining room, adding french doors at the ocean end to open onto a screened porch for outside dining.

The spacious, hotel-style room remains patriotically old-fashioned with burgundy banquet chairs at tables set with white cloths and blue napkins. A pianist plays on weekends, and the oceanside setting is most pleasing.

The chef has updated the fare to provide contemporary as well as classic cuisine. Starters might be crab cakes with mango-basil mayonnaise, crispy sweet and sour calamari with Thai chile paste and – billed as the "ultimate lobster cocktail" – a chilled lobster martini with sundried tomato rémoulade.

Entrées range from grilled swordfish with corn salsa to porcini-dusted lamb loin finished with goat cheese and balsamic vinegar. Options include tagliatelle pasta with Ipswich clams and pancetta, citrus-ginger glazed chicken and beef tenderloin with chasseur sauce.

Dessert mainstays are chocolate lava cake and crème brûlée.

(978) 546-9500. Entrées, $22 to $28. Dinner by reservation, Wednesday-Monday 6 to 9. BYOB.

Seagarden Restaurant, 44 Marmion Way, Rockport.

In an effort to draw the public, the old Seaward Inn has a new look and a new cuisine.

Gone are the nightly choice of two traditional entrées and the wall strung with clothespins that held guests' napkins with their names over the years. Now the

Wraparound deck on the rocks yields ocean view at My Place By the Sea.

summery, wraparound dining rooms seat 75 people for fine dining, according to owner Nancy Cameron-Gilsey.

Tables are set with white linens and the Cameron family's bone china. The emphasis is what's on the plate, as well as on the watery scenery outside the windows.

The menu starts with items like seared diver scallops and Asian slaw with wasabi oil, lobster salad with sweet potato chips, and a wild mushroom ragoût.

The six entrées range from grilled salmon with white soy vinaigrette over purple sticky rice to grilled strip steak with veal demi-glace. Lamb sirloin with wild mushrooms and a port wine reduction is a house favorite.

(978) 546-3471 or (877) 473-2927. Entrées, $18 to $27. Dinner, Tuesday-Sunday 6 to 9:30, Wednesday-Sunday in off-season. Closed November to mid-April. BYOB.

The Greenery, 15 Dock Square, Rockport.

The name bespeaks the theme of this casual and creative place, but hardly prepares one for the view of Motif No. 1 across the harbor from the butcher-block tables at the rear of the L-shaped dining room. And the view from the upstairs dining room is even better.

Seafood and salads are featured, as is a salad bar and an ice cream and pastry bar out front. Otherwise the fare runs from what owner Amy Hale calls gourmet sandwiches to dinner entrées like grilled catfish with homemade tartar sauce, poached salmon with mustard-dill sauce, "bouillabaisse linguini" and roasted raspberry-glazed duck with mango chutney.

For lunch, we savored the crab quiche with a side caesar salad and the homemade chicken soup with a sproutwich. The last was muenster and cheddar cheeses, mushrooms and sunflower seeds, crammed with sprouts and served with choice of dressing. We liked the sound of the crab and avocado sandwich, now a menu fixture, and overheard diners at other tables raving about the lobster and crab rolls.

Apple-cheddar and chocolate-bourbon pecan pies, linzer torte and banana cheesecake are listed in the dessert repertoire, most of which is available to go.

(978) 546-9593. www.thegreeneryrestaurant.com. Entrées, $14.95 to $20.95. Open daily, 8 to 9:30, 8 to 7 in winter. BYOB.

Brackett's Ocean View, 25 Main St., Rockport.

This locally popular family restaurant is simple as can be, except for the sweeping view of the water on two sides of the main dining room tucked around to the rear and not visible from the entry. Windsor chairs are at bare tables topped by paper mats.

The all-day menu is priced right and contains some interesting fare, including grilled portobello salad and a cajun chicken rollup. More substantial fare includes broiled sea scallops, fried seafood platters, baked scrod au gratin, codfish cakes, chicken parmigiana and grilled liver and onions. Prime rib is offered on weekends.

Start with the crispy thin fried onion rings – the best anywhere, according to a local innkeeper. Desserts of the day could be grape nut custard pudding, strawberry-rhubarb pie and french silk pie.

(978) 546-2797. www.bracketts.com. Entrées, $9.95 to $25.95. Lunch daily except Thursday from 11:30. Dinner nightly except Thursday from 4:30. Closed November-March. BYOB.

The Lobster Pool at Folly Cove, 329 Granite St. (Route 127), Rockport.

For casual seafood with no frills beyond a view, head out of town to the north, just past Halibut Point. Sit at one of the picnic tables on the lawn overlooking Ipswich Bay and, on a clear day, you can see the coast of New Hampshire and Maine. You can order lobster, clam or crab rolls, fried seafood plates bearing fries and coleslaw, burgers, salads, homemade desserts and pies. The lobster roll, seemingly brimming with lobster meat until you find it puffed up with considerable lettuce underneath, comes on a toasted hot dog bun. There are tables inside but, as at most lobster pounds, the experience is best when you can eat outside.

(978) 546-7808. Entrees, $8.95 to $15.95. Open daily, 11:30 to 8:30, mid-May to mid-October. BYOB.

Helmut's Strudel, 69 Bearskin Neck, Rockport.

This is not a restaurant as such, but you may share a small rear deck with a seagull or two on a few weathered captain's chairs, put your coffee on a rail and savor the view of the harbor. The small bakery makes a good stop for heavenly strudels (apple, cherry, cheese, almond and apricot), blueberry croissants, bagels, cinnamon buns, croissant sandwiches, coffee, tea and "the best hot chocolate in town." The strudel is real Austrian style with 81 layers of puff pastry. Helmut's is a good break from Bearskin Neck's prevailing seafood and ice cream.

(978) 546-2824. Open daily in season, from 8 a.m.

Diversions

The Seashore. Rockport is aptly named – its harbor and shoreline have the rocky look of the Maine coast, in contrast with the sand dunes associated with most of the Massachusetts shore. Country lanes lined with wild flowers interspersed between interesting homes hug the coast and crisscross the headlands in the area south of town known as Land's End. We like the California look of Cape Hedge Beach from the heights at the end of South Street, the twin lighthouses on Thatchers Island as viewed from Marmion Way, and the glimpses of yachts from the narrow streets along the water in quaint Annisquam.

Swimming is fine at Front and Back beaches in the center of town, the expansive

Good Harbor Beach near the Gloucester line, the relatively unknown Cape Hedge and Pebble beaches at Land's End, and the Lanesville beach north of town. Parking can be a problem, but we've always lucked out.

Halibut Point State Park, Gott Avenue (off Route 27), Pigeon Cove. On a clear day, you can see Crane's Beach in Ipswich, the Isles of Shoals off the coast of New Hampshire and Mount Agamenticus in Maine from this 54-acre park along the rocky coast. In the middle of the park is an abandoned, water-filled quarry from which tons of granite made their way to some of the more notable buildings across the Northeast. The granite ledges left behind are stunning. Guided tours and demonstrations about the quarry are given weekends in season. A restored World War II fire-control tower – the only one of its kind open to the public along the New England Coast – houses the park's visitor center. The park is popular with picnickers, hikers and sunbathers. Open daily 8 to 8, Memorial Day to Labor Day; parking, $2. Open sunrise to sunset, rest of year.

Bearskin Neck. The rocky peninsula that juts into the harbor was the original fishing and commercial center of the town. Today, most of the weather-beaten shacks have been converted into shops and eateries of every description. Glimpses of Sandy Bay and the Inner Harbor pop up like a changing slide show between buildings and through shop doors and windows; arty photo opportunities abound. The point at the end of the neck provides a panoramic view, or you can rest on a couple of benches off T-Wharf and admire Motif No. 1 – the Rockport Rotary Club sign beckons, "This little park is just for you, come sit a while and enjoy the view."

Shopping. Most of Bearskin Neck's enterprises cater more to tourists than residents, and T-shirt and souvenir shops abound, although **Joan's Rainbow Legend** and **James Russell Goldsmiths** appeal to those looking for jewelry, and a great garden draws passerby to **Earth's Treasures.** Main Street and the Dock Square area generally have useful stores, including the town's first "chain store," the resorty apparel shop **Mark Fore & Strike.** Colorful fused glass plates in the window drew us into **Square Circle,** where we marveled at incredible porcelain depictions of antipasto platters, fruit salad and the like, done by a woman from Virginia. We also liked the wares at **Too Fortunate Pottery.** The **Madras Shop, Enchanted Lady** and **Sand Castles** are known for clothing. Proceeds from the well-stocked **Toad Hall Bookstore** in the old Granite Savings Bank building further environmental causes. Interesting casual clothing and jewelry are offered at **Willoughby's**, which has a cozy café in back.

Hannah Wingate House, two shops across the street from each other, and **Woodbine Antiques** are among the better antiques shops. The **Granite Shore Gallery** specializes in maritime art, decoys and fishing collectibles. Other good galleries include **An Artful Touch** and **Mosher Gallery. New England Goods** also caught our eye.

The Art Galleries. For many, art is Rockport's compelling attraction, and by 1900 the town had become *the* place for artists to spend the summer painting. More than 200 artists make the town their home, and 29 galleries are listed in the Rockport Fine Arts Gallery Guide. The 80-year-old **Rockport Art Association,** with exhibitions and demonstrations in its large headquarters at 12 Main St., is a leader in its field. You could wander for hours through places like Paul Strisik's slick gallery next to the art association or Geraci Galleries in a 1725 complex of buildings at 6 South St.

Concerts. The summer Sunday evening concerts presented at 7:30 by the Rockport Legion Band at the outdoor bandstand near Back Beach have been a Cape Ann summer tradition since 1932. A few of the original members remain active today, providing stirring concert marches, overtures and selections from Broadway musicals under the stars. The annual Rockport Chamber Music Festival presents performances Thursday-Sunday in June in the Rockport Art Association's main gallery. Other than these, the best entertainment in town may well be, as guests at Eden Pines Inn put it, "sitting on Dock Square and watching the world go by."

Museums. The Sandy Bay Historical Society and Museum shows early furnishings and exhibits on shipping, fishing, the local granite industry and Rockport history in the 1832 Sewall-Scripture House built of granite at 40 King St., a new wing and in the Old Castle, a 1715 saltbox on Granite Street (open Monday-Saturday 2 to 5 in summer, $3). The **James Babson Cooperage Shop** (1658) on Route 127 just across the Gloucester line, a small one-story brick structure with early tools and furniture, may be the oldest building on Cape Ann (Tuesday-Sunday 2 to 5 in summer, free). In Pigeon Cove at 52 Pigeon Hill St. is the **Paper House,** built 50 years ago of 215 thicknesses of specially treated newspapers; chairs, desks, tables, lamps and other furnishings also are made of paper (daily 10 to 5, April to mid-October, $1.50).

Extra-Special

Like the rest of Rockport, its museums are low-key. But you only have to go next door to Gloucester to see two of New England's stellar showplaces.

Beauport, 75 Eastern Point Blvd., Gloucester.

Interior designer Henry David Sleeper started building his summer home in 1907 to house his collection of decorative arts and furnishings. Most of the 40 rooms are small, but each is decorated in a different style or period with a priceless collection of objects. Twenty-six are open to the public. Sleeper designed several rooms to house specific treasures: the round, two-story Tower Library was built to accommodate a set of carved wooden draperies from a hearse; the Octagon Room was built to match an eight-sided table. One of the breakfast tables in the Golden Step Room is right against a window that overlooks Gloucester Harbor.

(978) 283-0800. Guided tours 10 to 4, Monday-Friday mid-May to mid-September, daily mid-September to mid-October. Adults, $10.

Hammond Castle Museum, 80 Hesperus Ave., Gloucester.

Cross the drawbridge and be serenaded by pre-recorded organ music in this replica of a medieval castle, built in the late 1920s by inventor John Hays Hammond Jr. to house his collection of Roman, medieval and Renaissance art and objects. Visitors view the largest organ ever built in a private home. Its 8,200 pipes rise eight stories above the cathedral-like Great Hall. Also on view are the unusual Renaissance dining room, Gothic and early American bedrooms, and an exhibit showing some of the inventions and patent models of a man reputed to be America's greatest inventor after Thomas Edison. Marbled columns and lush plantings watered by the castle's own rain system are on view in the Courtyard.

(978) 283-7673. www.hammondscastle.org. Open daily 10 to 5, Memorial Day to Labor Day; Saturday-Sunday 10 to 3, rest of year. Adults, $8.

Winding residential street is typical of Old Town in Marblehead.

Marblehead, Mass.

Jewel of the North Shore

It's not difficult to understand why some call this beautiful town with so much cachet the jewel of the North Shore.

Poised on a rocky headland jutting into the Atlantic, Marblehead has a lot going for it. It is seventeen roundabout miles northeast of Boston, whose skyline can be seen on clear days across the water, much as San Francisco's can be seen from suburban Tiburon. Yet it's a world removed – from big-city Boston, and even from tourist-jammed Salem, its better-known neighbor on the mainland.

Founded in 1629 and apparently named for all the rocky (not marble) ledges upon which it grew without regard for 20th-century traffic needs, Marblehead was one of the earliest and richest settlements in America. Sea captains, merchant traders and cod fishermen erected houses and public buildings grand and small. Their edifices remain in use today, posted with discreet markers saying "Built for Ambrose Gale, Fisherman, 1663" and "Joseph Morse, Baker, 1715." The more than 300 pre-Revolutionary structures in the half-mile-square historic district have changed little since. A walking tour takes one past (and occasionally inside) the one-of-a-kind Jeremiah Lee Mansion, the art galleries in the King Hooper Mansion, the 1727 Old Town House that predates Boston's Faneuil Hall, the brick-towered Abbot Hall landmark (permanent home of the famous painting "The Spirit of '76"), the Lafayette House (whose corner was removed, legend has it, to let General Lafayette's carriage pass), the Fort Sewall harbor fortification and the second oldest Episcopal church still standing in this country.

As opposed to restored Colonial Williamsburg or relentlessly perfect Nantucket,

Marblehead is a "real" historic town, lived in year-round and bearing well any foibles or blemishes. Its original character endures – and townspeople fight fiercely to keep it that way. Small treasures abound: glimpses of the harbor through vest-pocket side yards, lush impatiens in window boxes and cosmos blooms waving beside doorways, oversize benches in the many small parks, antique signs, friendly townspeople, winding and impossibly narrow streets whose one-way directional signs thwart unknowing motorists at every turn.

The fact that Marblehead is rather isolated and so difficult for visitors to navigate is both its bane and its charm. There are none of the tourist trappings that coax visitors to Salem, Gloucester or Portsmouth. It's at the end of the road, so you do not pass through town on your way to somewhere else. The tourist in a hurry may come here for a quick visit and leave perplexed as to what the fuss is about. The sophisticated traveler will be smitten and stay awhile.

Until recently, Marblehead – a bedroom suburb that seems far smaller than its official population of 20,000 suggests – offered few overnight accommodations. The first inn of note emerged in 1986, and there was a proliferation of small B&Bs only in the 1990s. Lately, trendy restaurants and tony shops have emerged, catering as much to the resident gentry on Marblehead Neck as to visitors in Old Town.

Sailors have long been lured to Marblehead, which claims to be the birthplace of the American Navy and now the yachting capital of the nation. Some 2,500 pleasure craft bob at their moorings in Marblehead's harbor. Members and guests assemble at six yacht clubs, where cannons are fired in a sonic ritual at sunrise and sundown. The town is at its busiest in late July during its century-old Race Week.

Otherwise, as the world becomes homogenized, Marblehead retains a singular sense of place. As a local newspaper put it, "There is plenty of room for hollyhocks in 18th-century dooryards, but only grudging space made for automobiles. The arts flourish, public debate is often spirited, and Santa arrives by lobster boat."

Inn Spots

Harbor Light Inn, 58 Washington St., Marblehead 01945.

Born and raised in Marblehead, Peter Conway had long wanted to operate an inn here but, like others, was stymied by the town's strict zoning regulations. Instead, he opened the Carlisle House in Nantucket, became immersed in the innkeeping business and bided his time. That time arrived in 1986, when he purchased a grand Federal mansion along the town's principal through street. He was able to win approvals from neighbors and four regulatory agencies, and opened a twelve-room B&B – "without a sign and without advertising."

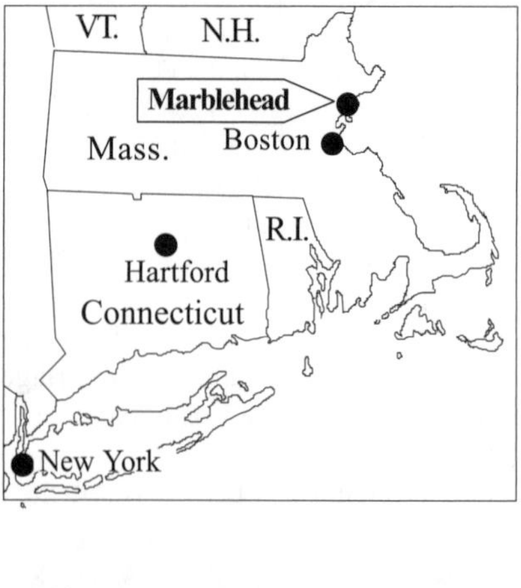

Success was immediate, thanks to receptive townspeople (old-line residents were happy finally to have a quality place in town in which to put up relatives and friends) and a ready market (all the daytrippers who heretofore had had no place in which to stay overnight). The fact that Peter was catering to the

Federal mansion in Old Town houses Harbor Light Inn.

upscale market – "I wanted to have the best rooms on the North Shore" – didn't hurt. His rooms, constantly being upgraded, are handsomely furnished to the period, generally spacious and outfitted with TVs and telephones, fine antiques, oriental rugs, Crabtree & Evelyn toiletries, private-label sparkling water and local chocolates from Stowaway or Harbor Sweets – many of the modern-day comforts and amenities generally missing in Nantucket and other historic-house accommodations are found here.

Never content, Peter bought the Federal mansion next door in 1993, connected it to his existing building and added eight more elegant guest rooms with modern baths. Five bedrooms have whirlpool tubs, eleven have working fireplaces, most have sitting areas and several have private balconies and decks. A big (for Marblehead) back yard contains lounge chairs and a heated swimming pool. Here, on a sloping lawn with a screen of thick trees, we almost thought we were in the woods, except for the sounds of the harbor in the distance (a sight now visible only from the rooftop deck when the leaves are off the trees).

Peter and wife Suzanne, who has an eye for creative decor, continue to improve their inn. Lately, they installed a gas fireplace to warm the new formal dining room and added 300-count sheets in the deluxe bedrooms. Especially in demand are the front-corner Room 22, with hand-carved mahogany queensize bed, two wing chairs, a double vanity and a double jacuzzi beneath a skylight, with a mirrored wall beside, and Room 5, with deep-red walls above the wainscoting, built-in settees beside the fireplace, two wing chairs, a hand-carved four-poster queen bed and a double jacuzzi with glass brick wall. Smaller rooms have charms as well: the third-floor Room 34 has its own sun deck, Room 36 a beamed and vaulted ceiling, and Room 4, a summery-looking ground-floor room with a pine-poster bed, has a double jacuzzi and a private screened deck near the pool. There are no curtains in the inn, Peter points out – "just inside window shutters that are easily opened and closed."

Elegant touches include fancy wallpapers, fine paintings and prints, brass or porcelain doorknobs, silver ice buckets and candy dishes, and votive candles beside the jacuzzis. The inn maintains a video library for the VCRs in the deluxe rooms.

An elaborate continental breakfast spread is put out in the dining room, which holds a table for eight and a tea table for two. Or the meal can be taken on trays to four tables beside the pool, or to one of the two elegant but cozy front parlors, where the day's newspapers await. The fare when we were there included orange juice, cut-up melon, lemon bread and especially good blueberry and cranberry-walnut muffins. Choices range from blueberry scones to Suzanne's no-fat bundt cake incorporating applesauce and yogurt. Tea is offered in the afternoon.

On Saturdays in the off-season, the Conways serve hot hors d'oeuvres by candlelight for BYOB social gatherings.

(781) 631-2186. Fax (781) 631-2216. www.harborlightinn.com. Nineteen rooms and two suites with private baths. Doubles, $125 to $195. Suites, $195 to $295. Children over 8. Two-night minimum weekends.

Pheasant Hill B&B, 71 Bubier Road, Marblehead 01945.

Expansive guest rooms and substantial common areas are hallmarks of this B&B opened by Nancy and Bill Coolidge atop a hill on which pheasants like to sit in an oak tree.

They bought the century-old house in 1992 and spent three years readying it for guest occupancy. Their renovations and decorating talents paid off in three guest suites spread out across the house for privacy. The house is furnished with antiques, hand-painted furniture and collectibles. Rich woodwork, wall sconces and pedestal sinks give a feeling of antiquity; in-room telephones, TVs and air conditioners convey a sense of creature comforts.

The Garden Suite occupies a private wing on the ground floor. It offers a king bed with a floral comforter and rag-rolled green walls in the bedroom, a sitting room with fireplace, a bath with a walk-in shower complete with a seat and a green plant, and a private deck from which you might spot the neighborhood pheasants. Upstairs is the Treetops Suite, with a front sitting room and a rear room with a king bed or two twins. Nancy, who does decorative painting on the side, painted ivy and pillars on the walls of the bathroom. She painted marbleized wainscoting along the staircase leading to the Bird's Nest, a secluded suite with sitting room and queen bed.

Much of the main floor is given over to common areas. Besides the large living room with fireplace, there's a library with a fireplace and a glimpse of the water at the foot of the hill. The sunny dining room with a table for six is the setting for an expanded continental breakfast of fruit, cereal, muffins, scones and toasted waffles.

A sun porch opens onto a rear deck, with a small, flower-ringed pond and fountain beyond.

(781) 639-4799 or (888) 202-1705. www.pheasanthill.com. Three suites with private baths. Suites, $125 to $175; off-season, $95 to $135. Two-night minimum weekends. Children over 12.

The Seagull Inn B&B, 106 Harbor Ave., Marblehead 01945.

When Skip Sigler suddenly found himself "redundant in corporate America" at age 58, he opened his family home of 25 years as a B&B. It's about the only one on posh Marblehead Neck – and thus viewed skeptically by some of his neighbors,

The Seagull Inn B&B occupies choice hilltop property on Marblehead Neck.

says Skip, although the property had been the site of a hotel, which burned down in 1940. He and his wife Ruth offer a bedroom and two suites, each with private bath and cable television. Bright and airy, their home up a hill from Marblehead Harbor is distinctly lived-in and laid-back.

Skip is a hands-on innkeeper (his wife works for an insurance company), from preparing breakfast to socializing with guests to housecleaning ("six years of college for this, but I love it"). His sideline is woodworking, and he made most of the furniture in the house.

The gathering spot is the spacious living room, with its cherry floor and door, homemade furniture and valances, and a remarkable carved wooden chess set on a table in the corner.

All guest quarters come with refrigerators and TV/VCRs. The smallest is the book-lined Library, paneled in barnwood, with a queensize bed, bathtub and separate shower. Skip painted the sea scenes on a bedroom wall in the two-room Seabreeze Suite with queensize bed and a sitting room with a sofa and daybed. The biggest accommodations are in the two-story Lighthouse Suite with its own side deck. It offers a living area with sofabed, daybed and kitchen and, upstairs, a bedroom with queensize bed.

Climb one more flight of stairs to the rooftop deck, from which the Boston skyline can be seen when the leaves are off the trees.

In his newer profession, Skip is a convivial host, chatting away the morning and pouring wine in the evening. His continental breakfast includes fresh fruit and lemon or banana-walnut breads.

(781) 631-1893. Fax (781) 631-3535. www.seagullinn.com. One room and two suites with private baths. Double, $175 weekends June-October, $125 to $150 rest of year. Suites, $200 and $250 weekends June-October, $150 to $225 rest of year. Children welcome.

Tuscanino B&B, 117 Lafayette St. (Route 114), Marblehead 01945.

Tuscanino, or "little Tuscany" in Marblehead, is a B&B in transition. It's also an enigma, and no one in Marblehead seemed to know quite what to make of it. Upon opening in 2003, it was a B&B, a dance studio, a gallery and a health spa.

It's the creation of Martha and Greg Coles, young artists who met doing African dances (he's an African drummer and singer). After she studied in Florence and he got his MBA from Harvard, they bought a split-level house near her parents' home in Marblehead. The house burned down and they rebuilt a Tuscan Revival villa like those Martha loved in Tuscany. Then they tried to figure out what to do with a house this size – "to get a return on investment," in the words of Greg, the promoter and front man. Someone at the Chamber of Commerce suggested a B&B.

Theirs is no ordinary B&B. On a narrow property, the "villa" is turned sideways to the busy street so the passerby scarcely notices it. The guest enters into a wide-open kitchen/dining area leading to a sunken living room/garden room used for massage therapy. The entire space holds not much furniture beyond a dining table, a few stools at the kitchen island, a bench and a theatrical 58-inch TV/DVD. The multi-purpose basement level contains a mirrored dance studio with a fireplace, a sauna and steam room.

Accommodations are on the second floor. Two smallish rooms off the main hallway, one with twins and one with a double bed, share a hall bath. The larger rooms are billed as suites. The premier Maestro has a fireplace at the foot of the queensize brass bed, a built-in satellite sound system and big-screen TV/DVD, and french doors opening onto a rear balcony overlooking a peastone terrace and garden in the making. The master bath contains a double jetted tub, a glass-enclosed shower with a bench and massaging showerheads for two, double vanity, bidet and a flat-screen TV. The walk-in closet is ample enough to bed down a small child and contains laundry facilities. The Vittoriana in front was designed with an Old World feel, with a queen bed angled from a corner, a queensize sofabed, TV/entertainment center, fireplace and a skylit bath with clawfoot tub. Off the hall outside the room is an arched cutaway balcony for two beneath a skylight for sunset viewing, perhaps with a bottle of chianti.

A healthful breakfast consists of fruit, cereals, yogurt, waffles or muffins.

(781) 631-2865. Fax (781) 631-0992. www.tuscanino.com. Two rooms with private baths and two rooms with shared bath. Doubles, $125 shared, $175 to $210 private.

Herreshoff Castle, 2 Crocker Park, Marblehead 01945.

You can stay in a replica of a Viking castle – or at least in the carriage house of one. Well-connected Marblehead natives Chris and Michael Rubino, who occupy the three-story stone castle formerly owned by yacht designer Francis Herreshoff, offer the adjacent carriage house overlooking a shared garden courtyard.

The hideaway is a beauty. A sofa/daybed, bathroom with shower and a galley kitchen bearing framed photographs of the designer of America's Cup yachts are on the first floor. Upstairs is a wow of a bedroom with a 25-foot high ceiling, its four wood-planked sides tapering inward and upward as in a boat. The stone walls, gothic doors, stained-glass windows, antique double bed and massive armoire impart a look of antiquity. The telephone and TV set give access to the outside world. A stairway leads down to the walled courtyard/dining area surrounded by perennial gardens, gargoyles and griffins. Guests think they're in Europe next to a castle with parapets, turrets and gothic windows. And just outside are Crocker Park and the waterfront, where Michael swims daily in summer when he gets home from work.

Guests in carriage house (right) of Herreshoff Castle may think they're in Europe.

Chris puts out pastries and the makings for an expanded continental breakfast in the galley kitchen.

(781) 631-1950. Fax (781) 631-2178. www.herreshoffcastle.com. One suite with private bath. Double, $185. Two-night minimum. Closed early December to mid-April.

Darci's Parkside Inn, 4 Wyman Road, Marblehead 01945.

Joe and Moe Darci raised four children in this 1910 Victorian-style residence that was his family home. When their kids left the nest, they extensively renovated the place, added five tiled bathrooms and opened a nicely equipped B&B that backs up to the playing fields of Seaside Park. They cater to business guests, families and extended stays.

All five accommodations have queensize beds (except for one king and one double) with "pillow-top" mattresses, TV/VCRs, private-line phones and oriental rugs on hardwood floors. Two guest rooms are rather modest, but the angled-ceilinged Skylight Room on the third floor is quite spacious with a kingsize sleigh bed and a writing desk beneath the skylights, a couple of wing chairs on either side of the exposed brick chimney, and a bath with skylit shower that Moe finds "really cool."

Two suites add sitting rooms and kitchenette/wet bars. One called the front suite has a queen wicker bed and a sofabed. The back "big suite" has a double jacuzzi tub with a marble surround beneath big windows in a corner of the spacious sitting room, a leather sofabed, a queensize brass bed in the loft and a private balcony overlooking the park.

Continental breakfast is offered at a table for eight in the chandeliered dining room.

(781) 631-5733 or (888) 273-7704. www.dpinn.com. Three rooms and two suites with private baths. Doubles, $99 to $150. Suites, $150 to $220.

The Bishops Bed & Breakfast, 10 Harding Lane, Marblehead 01945.

Commercial fisherman Hugh Bishop, member of an old Marblehead family, was raised in this waterfront house that his grandparents purchased in 1920. It was strictly a family home until his wife Judy entered the picture. They were married after meeting again at their 40th high school class reunion. She renovated the house and opened it as a B&B in 1997.

The setting is most attractive. It's at the edge of town on a secluded point of land looking across Doliber's Cove to Brown's Island, Peaches Point and Little Harbor. The lawn is set up for croquet and golf-ball nests. Hugh, who's full of wonderful tales of Marblehead (his father started the frostbite sailing derby here), may be persuaded to take guests out on his boat.

The Bishops share their home with guests in two suites, named after family boats. The Landfall is a main-floor retreat at the side of the house with a kingsize bed, full bath, large dressing room and sitting area with TV. It has two private entrances; one through the side greenhouse and the other from the back yard.

Upstairs is the Mistress Suite, two ocean-view rooms, one with a queen bed and the other a sitting room with a club chair facing the window – "the best seat in the house," says Judy. Then she retracts, when showing the bathroom facilities. "That," she points out, "is the best seat in Marblehead."

Guests relax in a front living room with TV but tend to gather in the rear breakfast area open to the kitchen. Its walls are a veritable gallery of historic sailing pictures. With a view of the water, it's the convivial setting for a continental breakfast of fresh fruits, granola, yogurt and homemade pastries.

(781) 631-4954. Fax (781) 631-2102. www.bishopsbb.com. Two suites with private baths. Suites, $160 and $170. Two-night minimum weekends. Children over 12.

Brimblecomb Hill B&B, 33 Mechanic St., Marblehead 01945.

Built in 1721 by one of the first summer visitors to Marblehead, this house in the heart of Old Marblehead is run as a B&B by Gene Arnould, art gallery owner, organizer of jazz concerts and ex-Congregational minister who's considered one of the more interesting people in town. He lives on the second floor, and turns over the first floor to guests.

Everything here is properly historic. "Ben Franklin stopped by to visit," the B&B advertises. "You can spend the night."

The Isaac Mansfield Room (named for the original owner) is the largest, an end room with its own bath, queensize maple poster bed, cottage pine chest, shelves of books and wide pumpkin pine flooring. Two small rooms in the rear, reached by a separate entrance, share a full bath. One has a queen bed and one a double bed. Each has basic furnishings, carpeting and a rocking chair.

Guests enjoy a small common room with fireplace, games table and a grand piano. A buffet breakfast of fruit, cereal, muffins and croissants is put out in the morning.

(781) 631-3172 or 631-6366. www.brimblecomb.com. One room with private bath and two rooms with shared bath. Doubles, $110 with private bath, $85 shared.

Stillpoint, 27 Gregory St., Marblehead 01945.

Blessed with a fine location that catches a glimpse of Marblehead's harbor, this fine old house also is blessed with an innkeeper who cares. Sarah Lincoln-Harrison, who founded the local bed-and-breakfast association, is devoted to wholesome living, environmental innkeeping, healthful food and eco-tourism. She's an innkeeper with a mission, you might say.

"This B&B is a good teaching tool to show by experience how people can live more wholesome lives," says Sarah as she warms to her subject. If asked, she'll tell

Chef-owner Frank Pellino displays bottle from wine rack at Pellino's.

about the energy-saving compact fluorescent lights in the front parlor and the new water purification system "so even the showers are healthier now." Over breakfast, she apologizes that this B&B isn't completely chemical-free. "We'd have to get rid of the gas stove," she explains, even though she does not use it for breakfast.

This serene lady, a widow who was remarried to a widower and moved into his home, is particularly proud of her "edible landscape" – the former side lawn now transformed into raised beds with a medley of organic herbs, vegetables, flowers and medicinals.

The accommodations are comfortable as well as comforting, simple yet refined. There are two bedrooms (one with a double bed and one with twins and windows on three sides). They share a full hall bath, and the first taker may get a private bath. There are lots of local magazines and environmental literature, but no television "because that's not what we're about," says Sarah. She prefers a wholesome, restful atmosphere – which includes a side deck beneath a flowering crabapple tree, with a good view of the harbor below.

Breakfast includes an assortment of juices, fruits and organic cereals, homemade applesauce, muffins (perhaps morning glory) and no-fat bread for toasting, along with local preserves – "all as organic as possible, even the butter," notes Sarah.

Guest-room diaries are full of praise and uplifting messages written by sensitive or sensitized guests. Wrote one couple who stayed three weeks: "Sarah's serenity and sense of connectedness to the earth and people is a calming force in this retreat from the mainstream hubbub. Her edible landscape is both beautiful and delicious."

(617) 631-1667. www.stillpointbedandbreakfast.com. Two rooms with shared bath. Doubles, $80 shared, $100 private. Children over 10.

Dining Spots

Pellino's, 261 Washington St., Marblehead.

This diminutive downtown hideaway is generally first on locals' lists of favorite restaurants. Naples-born chef-owner Francesco (Frank) Pellino's white-clothed tables as well as five booths ensconced behind arches and fitted out with old church pews are much in demand. Twinkling white lights outline the front windows above a colorful vest-pocket garden.

Whole roasted garlic cloves are served with olive oil for spreading on the crusty Italian bread that begins each meal. The signature veal pellino is sauced with port wine, shiitake mushrooms, sundried tomatoes and herbs, and the garlic-crusted rack of lamb comes with chianti-rosemary jus. Other main-course treats vary from jumbo prawns in a potato crust with ginger and orange soy sauce to roasted duck breast glazed with balsamic vinegar and chambord, served fanned and laced with cranberries.

Pasta dishes here are the best in town, from shrimp diavolo tossed with linguini to lobster ravioli. Favorite starters are grilled calamari on a bed of mesclun greens, beef carpaccio and grilled portobello mushroom with mozzarella and tomatoes.

The area newspaper called Frank's warm "volcano" chocolate cake, garnished with a strawberry and a scoop of gelato, arguably the world's best dessert. Tiramisu, chocolate mousse cake and cappuccino gelato are other favorites.

The wine list has been cited by Wine Spectator. Wine-tasting dinners and cooking classes are offered here in the winter.

(781) 631-3344. www.pellinos.com. Entrées, $17.95 to $32.95. Dinner nightly, 5 to 10.

The Landing, 81 Front St., Marblehead.

This off-again, on-again waterfront restaurant is very much on again. New owners gutted the interior in 2000 to produce a pub in front and a nautical look in the rear dining area overlooking the harbor. Walls of mirrors bear colorful sails and a two-level deck is beside the water. The deck is warmed with propane heat for use in winter.

Executive chef Stephen James's fare received good reviews. At a recent visit, main dishes included three versions of scrod (from provençal to fish and chips), sole veronique, Caribbean grilled chicken and shrimp, veal oscar and steak au poivre. A perennial favorite is lobster basilica, tossed with mushrooms and tomatoes in a pesto cream sauce over fettuccine. Typical starters were tempura tuna skewers, scallops wrapped in smoked bacon, crab cakes with capers and armagnac sauce, and grilled portobello mushrooms. Desserts include crème brûlée, double chocolate parfait cake and white chocolate mousse.

Weekend brunch is deservedly popular, and there's no better place for enjoying it than the waterfront deck.

(781) 639-1266. www.thelandingrestaurant.com. Entrées, $17.95 to $26.95. Lunch, Monday-Friday 11:30 to 2:30. Dinner nightly, 5 to 9 or 9:30. Weekend brunch, 11:30 to 3.

Maddie's Sail Loft, 15 State St., Marblehead.

This kind of local hangout (a fixture since 1946) is not our cup of tea, but we're obviously in the minority because it's generally packed at all hours and the bar is a favorite watering hole, known for wickedly potent drinks. Except for the mural of Marblehead and the harbor at the foot of the stairs, the scene and the setting could be anywhere, which is probably why we don't find it particularly alluring.

Nevertheless, for lunch you won't go wrong with the prize-winning clam chowder, a basic burger, grilled cheese or roast beef sandwich in the $2 to $5 range. You might be stunned to find a clam roll for $10.50 or Boston scrod for $13.95. The latter are also available at dinner, when the fare ranges from fish and chips to excellent fried scallops, a combination seafood platter, baked stuffed jumbo shrimp or Marblehead seafood pie. Hearty portions and a convivial seafarer's atmosphere draw the throngs.

(781) 631-9824. Entrées, $8.95 to $15.95. Lunch, Monday-Saturday 11:45 to 2, Sunday 11:45 to 4. Dinner, 5 to 10. Pub serves continuously from 11:45 to 11:30. No credit cards.

The Barnacle, 141 Front St., Marblehead.

Considered on a par with Maddie's Sail Loft, this crowded, no-nonsense restaurant at least has a water view – one of the best in town. In fact, you can sit at a narrow counter running the width of the restaurant smack dab against the windows at the rear and feast on the panorama as you eat, or on a narrow, wraparound outdoor deck during the summer.

The short menu stresses New England seafood basics, from lobster roll to fillet of haddock. Featured at dinner are such standards as haddock au gratin, broiled scallops, "jumbo shrimp scampi," broiled sirloin, and surf and turf. All entrées are served with salad, potatoes, rolls and butter — "no substitutions." The tables are almost on top of each other and the nondescript decor is vaguely nautical. Patrons at the small, crowded bar in front also get a good view.

(781) 631-4236. Entrées, $10.95 to $18.95. Lunch daily, 11 to 4:30. Dinner, 5 to 9 or 10. Closed Tuesday in winter. No credit cards.

Flynnie's on the Avenue, 28 Atlantic Ave., Marblehead.

Colorful fish painted in the windows lure patrons into this up-and-down establishment that formerly housed Jacob Marley's and later the Sandbar. It's been up since it was taken over by Jeff Flynn, who also runs a seasonal family restaurant called Flynnie's at the Beach at Devereux Beach.

Here, dining is taken more seriously at polished, close-together tables amid antique mirrors and hand-painted glass in a convivial, homey setting with a curved bar in back. One of the best chefs in town, Louise Moore, a vegetarian, prepares an extensive menu at affordable prices. Her exotic salads are first-rate. Ditto for the grilled vegetarian rollup, the garden burger, the California chicken BLT and the blue cheese and turkey baguette.

You can get things like those for lunch or dinner. The latter menu also adds quite a variety from scrod florentine to Southern fried chicken to grilled club steak au poivre. The surf and turf here combines steak tips and lobster pie. How about a novel vegetarian dish? The "farmer's market barbecue" brings grilled potato, corn on the cob, a vegetable skewer, a spinach and grape tomato salad and watermelon, with a Jack Daniel's barbecue sauce for dipping. We were impressed with the poppyseed-seared halibut with mango-yogurt drizzle and the "beach bowl" – with mussels, clams, scallops and shrimp sautéed with snap peas and grape tomatoes in a lemon-garlic-wine sauce over linguini.

As Jeff says, with a meat-and-potatoes owner and vegetarians for a chef and manager, "crazy things have been known to happen."

(781) 639-2100. www.flynnies.com. Entrées, $12 to $16. Lunch daily, 11:30 to 4:30. Dinner nightly, from 4:30.

Diversions

On a presidential visit more than 150 years after it was founded, George Washington remarked that Marblehead had the look of antiquity. It still does (even more so, no doubt), particularly in the Old Town historic district near the harbor. It has so many ledges and glacial outcroppings that early settlers simply built where they could. Streets are winding and narrow, many seem to be one-way the wrong way, parking is limited and directional signs are few. A map of town from the seasonal Chamber of Commerce information booth at Pleasant and Essex streets is a must. Even then, it takes most visitors several days to get their bearings.

Driving Tour. With said map and a willingness for trial and error, orient yourself by driving along Pleasant Street (Route 114), the main drag from Salem through the uptown commercial center. It eventually intersects with **Washington Street,** the historic main street winding from uptown through Old Town, where the most notable landmarks are located. Get to the start of one-way **Front Street** to drive along the harbor and out to the views from **Fort Sewall,** the 1742 fortification at the mouth of the harbor, where during the War of 1812 the frigate Constitution found shelter from the pursuing British. Another good view is from **Old Burial Hill** off Orne Street, one of the oldest graveyards (1638) in New England; a plaque notes that 600 Revolutionary heroes and several early pastors are interred at the top of the hill, the highest point in town. Return to Pleasant Street and head west to **Ocean Avenue,** the access route to Marblehead Neck. At the causeway is **Devereux Beach,** a sandy strand for sunning and swimming. The other side of the causeway overlooks Marblehead Harbor with all its moored pleasure craft and affords vistas of Old Town and **Marblehead Neck.** Turn left on Harbor Avenue and then Foster Avenue and pass the posh Eastern and Corinthian yacht clubs and lovely homes beside the harbor. At the tip of the neck is **Chandler Hovey Park,** where protected benches on the rocks are good vantage points to see Marblehead Light and the passing boats. Continue around to Ocean Avenue with a stop at the alley leading to **Castle Rock** (one of the many public access points to the water throughout Marblehead). The rock may be of less interest than the multi-million-dollar castle residence beside. More palatial homes face the ocean on the way to the **Audubon Bird Sanctuary,** unmarked but reached off Risley Road. Head back to the causeway and where Ocean Avenue intersects with Harbor Avenue you'll be greeted by a stunning view of the Boston skyline across the water.

Walking Tour. Thus oriented, get out and walk – the best way to see and sense Marblehead. A Chamber of Commerce map outlines rewarding walking tours of one or two miles. We did ours just after daybreak, when all was still and many Marbleheaders were out walking their dogs and taking their morning constitutional. Go slowly, so as to savor (and not miss) all the little treasures and to make your own discoveries. Here are some highlights, in addition to those itemized below. Colorful houses and gardens enliven winding **Lee Street,** including a residence marked by one of Marblehead's ubiquitous plaques, this one saying "Built in 1735 for Thomas Roads, innholder." (Others to be encountered were built for merchants, bakers, boat builders, blacksmiths, shoremen, fishermen and countless others, giving a fascinating who's who of early Marblehead.) Off Gregory Street, climb the steps of **Prospect Alley** to reach Boden's Lookout, a hilltop aerie above the harbor, next to a gray house built in 1710 for John Boden, shoreman. Pass the **Lafayette House,** with its cutout corner beside Union Street, and head down Water Street to the imposing **Boston Yacht Club,** one of the nation's first, where rockers are lined up on the long waterfront porch. Beyond is **Crocker Park,** a stony outcrop harbor blessed with long benches for viewing the harbor goings-on. A plaque, dedicated to George

Washington's Navy, tells of "the first American vessels to engage in naval operations against an enemy...the forerunners of the U.S. Navy." They were manned by Marblehead sailors. Stop at the **Town Landing** at the foot of State Street to see working fishing boats. From the 1727 **Old Town House** area in the center of Old Town, take brief side trips to see Old North Church, the Unitarian-Universalist Church and St. Michael's Episcopal Church. None is quite as imposing as **Abbot Hall,** the 1877 town hall whose red brick tower is Marblehead's most visible landmark. The creaky main floor displays much Marblehead memorabilia; foremost is Archibald Willard's famed "Spirit of '76" painting, a larger-than-life piece made famous during the nation's centenary celebration and now framed permanently against a red velvet backdrop in the selectmen's meeting room here.

Jeremiah Lee Mansion, 161 Washington St., Marblehead.

Step through the door of this impressive house and you're back in 1768. Almost every feature of this house, built by one of the richest traders in the local "codfish aristocracy," is original. Lee's residence was described by a Boston newspaper at the time as "the most elegant and costly home in the Bay State Colony." You're told that Lee emulated the houses of the British aristocracy, from the simulated cut-stone blocks of the Georgian wooden facade to the original rococo carving and architectural features inside. Guides point out the intricate carved spindles and newel posts (bearing spirals within spirals) of the unsupported Santo Domingan mahogany staircase with its free-standing landing, a focal point of the massive entry foyer. On either side of the landing are copies of portraits of Jeremiah and Martha Lee, among the few full-length portraits by John Singleton Copley. Most unusual is the exotic, hand-painted wallpaper created in England to exact specifications for the hallway and several grand chambers; the Lee is the only public house this old where you can see the original wallpaper on the same walls. The house is full of unique attributes and furnishings, from original fire backs and fireplace tiles to Colonial Revival gold draperies and "important" North Shore furniture – all gifts to the sponsoring Marblehead Historical Society from local families and Louise du Pont Crowninshield, an honorary director who summered in Marblehead and contributed much toward saving the house. The bedchambers and servants' quarters on the third floor have been turned into museum rooms to display local artifacts, including dolls, children's furniture, shoes, a wonderful sea captain's crib and a room of paintings by local folk artist J.O.J. Frost. This mansion, billed as the most beautiful Colonial mansion in the country, is not to be missed.

(781) 631-1768. Open Tuesday-Saturday 10 to 4, Sunday 1 to 4, June to mid-October. Adults, $5

King Hooper Mansion, 8 Hooper St., Marblehead.

Less awesome than the Jeremiah Lee Mansion around the corner, this is a much-used building that's headquarters of the Marblehead Arts Association. It's actually two structures joined together: the original built in 1728 and a Georgian front added in 1745. There are fourteen fireplaces, original Delft tiles, pumpkin pine floors, double dentil moldings and formal British gardens in the rear, but the home of the wealthy merchant trader who was respectfully nicknamed King by his sailors is not overly daunting – except perhaps for the arched brick wine cellar off the basement kitchen or the enormous third-floor ballroom, now a handsome display space for changing art exhibitions. The oldest piece in the house is a blanket chest from the

1600s. Here you learn that the powder room was originally used by men to powder their wigs, and that the good-night bidding to "sleep tight" derived from the need to tighten the ropes beneath the mattress on the canopy bed.

(781) 631-2608. Open Tuesday-Saturday 10 to 4, Sunday 1 to 5. Donation.

Shopping. Especially good specialty stores are concentrated around Washington Street in Old Town. They're also scattered along School Street, Atlantic Avenue and Pleasant Street in the uptown area.

In the heart of Old Town is **Uncommon Stock,** with an uncommonly choice selection of kitchenware, cookbooks, pottery and accessories that lure us inside at every visit. Across the street is **The Flag Hanger,** with decorative flags and gifts.. Most unusual is Joan Wheeler's **Russian Gallery,** a trove of things Russian, including dozens of matrioshka nesting dolls, lacquered boxes, shawls, small colorful pens and eggs, even T-shirts. Downstairs are Russian watercolors and prints. **The Marblehead Kite Co.** carries everything that says Marblehead – T-shirts, coffee mugs, sweatshirts of sailboats on the harbor titled Marblehead Rush Hour and, yes, kites. Some of the cards here made us laugh out loud. Also specializing in Marblehead items is **Arnould Gallery,** with many local prints and some carved swans clad in straw hats. Nearby, **Much Ado** is crammed with rare books and **O'Rama's,** which started selling antique lingerie and linens, expanded into a line of jewelry, frames, soaps, teapots and boxes, all very dainty and feminine. The **Hilliard-Sanford Gallery** shows fine American crafts. **Jambu** has exotic jewelry and gifts. At the **Garden Collection,** proprietor Rebecca Ellis stocks all kinds of flowery gifts, botanical note cards, floral aprons and pottery with a floral or garden theme. We liked her T-shirts with cats or bird feeders.

Uptown are **C'est la Vie** with imaginative gifts of the kind found in decorator show houses, as well as unusual picture frames, china and glass, and exquisite baby things; **Accessories by Blass**, with unusual pins, pocketbooks and umbrellas, and the excellent **Spirit of '76 Bookstore. Lavender Home & Table** takes its inspiration from Provence.

Extra Special

Hestia Products, 13 Hawkes St., Marblehead.

Generally unknown by residents as well as visitors, the little showroom here displays fine miniatures produced in the rear "factory" and sold to collectors across the country. Linda Macdonald, a Marblehead mother of four, turned her hobby of designing unique products in clays and porcelains into a lucrative business. Her original designs, which range from Christmas ornaments and miniature buildings to figurines and garden statues, are first sculpted in clay. Latex molds are made for mass-producing air-dried plaster units, which then are individually hand-painted and sealed by about fifteen women, many of whom work at home. We were struck by the AmeriScape ornaments devoted to different places, from Charleston to Cape May to Breckenridge to Natchez – not to mention Marblehead, for which a different design is produced each year. There are garden statues of cats, rabbits and dogs, as well as nativity scenes (to which collectors add characters over the years). We picked up a few finely sculpted and detailed woodland animals for Christmas gifts.

(781) 639-2727 or (800) 365-1262. www.hestiaproducts.com. Open Monday-Saturday, 9 to 5.

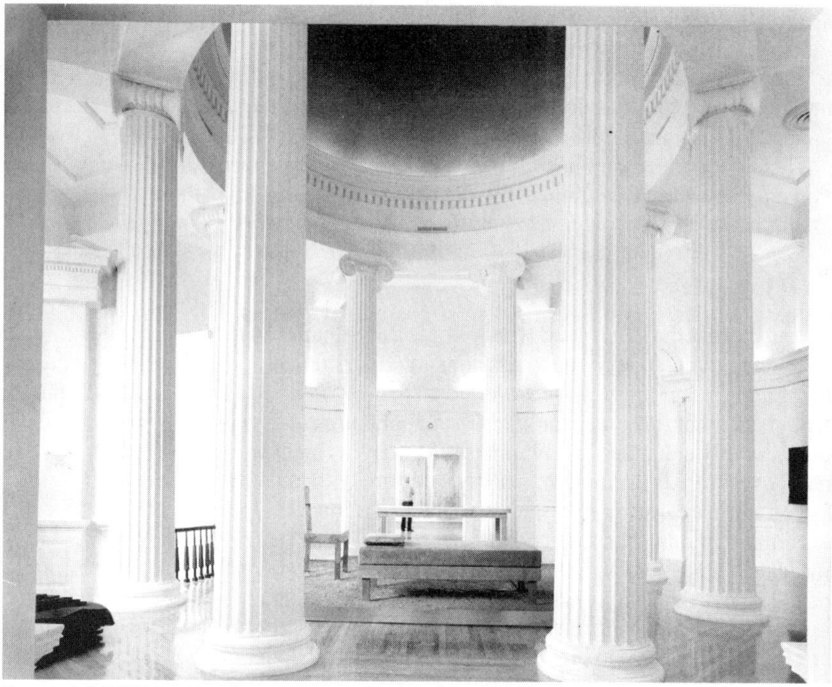

Renovated 1846 octagonal rotunda is a focal point of Williams College Museum of Art.

Williamstown, Mass.

Arts Town of the East

Blessed with an uncommonly scenic setting and the riches that prestigious Williams College attracts and returns, this small college town in the northern Berkshires is an arts center of national significance.

Newsweek called the annual Williamstown Theatre Festival "the best of all American summer theaters." Connoisseur magazine said its three leading museums make it "an unlikely but powerful little art capital." U.S. News and World Report revealed that educators consider Williams College tops among academic institutions in the country.

Local promotion pieces note that Williamstown has been cited as "the most culture-saturated rural spot in the nation." That status has broadened lately with the opening of the long-awaited MASS MoCA – billed as the largest contemporary art center in the world – in the old textile mills of neighboring North Adams, five miles to the east.

Williams, its associates and benefactors have inspired these superlatives. But they have geography and nature to thank for what some call "The Village Beautiful." Somewhat isolated in a verdant bowl, Williamstown dwells at the foot of Mount Greylock, the highest peak in Massachusetts, surrounded by Vermont's Green and New York's Taconic mountains. Not only do these provide great outdoor activities (in particular, golf, hiking and skiing). They also help Williamstown retain a charmed rural flavor that seems far more village-like than its population of 8,200 might suggest.

Williamstown is a sophisticated little town of great appeal, one that unfolds as you delve. The youthful dynamic of 2,000 college students is not always apparent in the broader community – at least in summer, during tourist season. Besides natural and cultural attractions, there are good restaurants, selective shops and a handful of inns and B&Bs.

This is one place that has long been special. If you simply drive around town, you may not sense the subtle blend of sophistication and small town that is the real Williamstown. Here you must stop, stay awhile and explore.

Inn Spots

The Orchards, 222 Adams Road (Route 2), Williamstown 01267.

Opened to the tune of many millions of dollars in 1985, this three-story country hotel and restaurant meanders around a small, landscaped courtyard containing a free-form, rock-bordered pond with a fountain. It has aged well and has been considerably enhanced following its rescue from foreclosure by Sayed M. Saleh, a hotel executive from Boston, who moved here with his wife and daughter.

The inn's interior layout separates the restaurant and lounge from the 48 guest accommodations. Winding corridors expand into a gracious drawing room, where intricate chandeliers hang from the cathedral ceiling and polished antique furniture of the Queen Anne style warms the space. Complimentary scones and English tea are served on fine china in the afternoon and, perhaps, dessert and coffee or liqueurs after dinner. Coffee and breakfast pastries are served there (gratis) before the dining room opens in the morning.

Check out the inn's collection of antique silver teapots and the Victorian-era tin soldiers and guardsmen on display. You can also catch up with the latest magazines in the spacious library.

The guest rooms are large, comfortable and redecorated in what our informant called less of a Laura Ashley and more of a Pierre Deux look.

The Orchards' original pink and green motif (for the location's heritage as an orchard) has been muted in favor of a more sumptuous look – or, as the owner put it, "tastefully decorated in the style of a graceful English country estate, with antique furniture and artwork."

Amenities include telephones in bathrooms as well as bedrooms and TV/VCRs secreted in armoires. Each room is different within the prevailing theme: marble bathrooms with terrycloth robes and Lord & Mayfair bath oils and soaps, separate dressing area with a second vanity and a small refrigerator. Cookies are left when the beds are turned down at night.

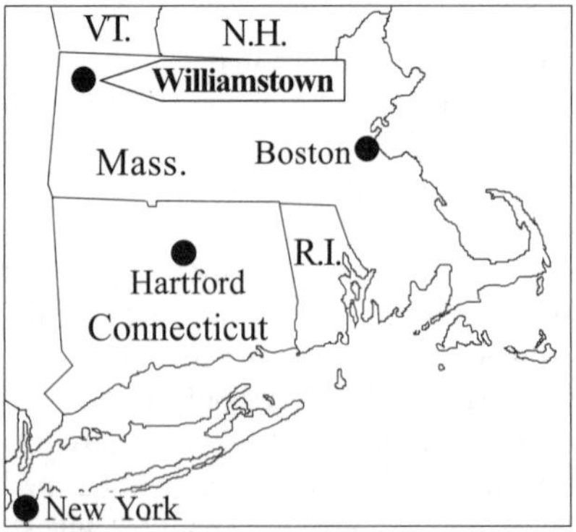

The premier room we saw had a king bed with a wood and curtained canopy headboard and a fainting couch at its foot, three plush chairs plus a window seat in the bay, a corner fireplace and a writing desk.

Twelve rooms have working fireplaces, including a third-floor suite with king bed and a spa shower and jacuzzi tub.

The inn has a sauna and jacuzzi,

American Modern-style Field Farm Guest House backs up toward pond.

exercise room, four function rooms, an antiques shop, a plush cocktail lounge with a fireplace and a small outdoor pool flanked by a sundeck.

Three meals a day are available in the elegant dining room, recently redecorated with gold brocade walls, blue carpeting and a wall mural of a Berkshires scene. Now called **Yasmin's** (for the owner's daughter), it offers a short menu of contemporary cuisine. Dinner choices at our latest visit ranged from seared Maine scallops on truffled risotto to yogurt-marinated lamb loin skewers on saffron couscous. Although the dining room strikes some as pretentious, the inn merits its ranking as the only Mobil four-star, AAA four-diamond hotel in Massachusetts west of Boston.

(413) 458-9611 or (800) 225-1517. Fax (413) 458-3273. www.orchardshotel.com. Forty-seven rooms and one suite with private baths. Memorial Day to early November: doubles $175 to $305, suite $375. Rest of year: doubles $150 to $250, suite $325. Two-night minimum weekends in season.

Entrées, $26 to $31. Lunch daily, noon to 2. Dinner, 5:30 to 9. Sunday brunch, 10 to 2.

Field Farm Guest House, 554 Sloan Road, Williamstown 01267.

When the 1948 American Modern-style home of arts patron Lawrence H. Boedel became available following the death of his widow in 1984, The Trustees of Reservations didn't quite know what to do with it. Restorationists David and Judy Loomis of River Bend Farm B&B (see below) proposed running it as a B&B and, true to their word, they ended up doing just that. They got it up and running, turning over operations in 1996 to the Trustees and resident innkeepers.

A stay in one of the five guest rooms in this rural hilltop home surrounded by 316 acres of conservation land is intriguing, given the home's history. The word "home" is used advisedly, for that's exactly what it is – looking much as the Bloedels left it, with the exception of some of the fabulous collection of paintings they donated to the Williams College Museum of Art and the Whitney Museum of Art in New York City. At a recent visit, eight of the original pieces were back on indefinite loan from the Williams Museum.

Guests have the run of a spacious living room, dining room, galley kitchen and grounds, which are striking for their sculptures, views and trails. Throughout the 5,000 square-foot house, much of the furniture was made by Bloedel, a 1923 Williams graduate and onetime college librarian.

All five guest rooms retain their original baths and vary in size. The huge main-floor Gallery Room, which the original owner used as a studio, has a kingsize bed, a black walnut floor and a separate entrance.

Upstairs in this house that might be described as a mixture of art nouveau and Danish modern are four more guest rooms, recently updated with king or queensize beds.

In the North Room, tiles of butterflies flank the fireplace (fascinating tiles surround all the fireplaces). It has its own balcony, a dressing table with mirrored surface and a walk-in closet with sliding drawers. The newly renovated, sleekly modern master bedroom features a kingsize platform bed with handmade mattress and designer furnishings, a fireplace with tiles of trees and birds, and an enormous private deck. The East and West rooms also are comfortable but considerably smaller.

A full breakfast is served in the dining room, which opens onto a small porch. Fresh fruit, yogurt, homemade granola and banana bread precede the main course, perhaps a cheese omelet, blueberry pancakes or tomato-basil frittata (the ingredients for the last picked from the garden).

The architecturally interesting house, built of Western cedar and fronted by a mass of yellow creeping hydrangeas, was designed by architect Edward Goodell.

Outside are the original swimming pool fed by an underground spring, a tennis court, picnic tables, woodlands, pastures, a pond, and four miles of trails for wildlife-watching or cross-country skiing. The property has been a working farm since Williamstown was incorporated in 1765. It's now leased to a farmer who raises corn and cows.

Don't be misled by the name. Field Farm Guest House is not a farm in the usual sense, but rather a home lived in by a wealthy and interesting man. You'll be charmed staying here among the stylish furnishings of the period and enjoying the tranquil grounds.

But book early. Field Farm enjoys one of the highest occupancy rates of any New England B&B – so much so that the rates have been raised substantially in an effort to reduce occupancy and subsequent wear and tear. "The B&B is here to preserve the house," we were told. "Not to hurt it."

(413) 458-3135. Fax (413) 458-3144. www.guesthouseatfieldfarm.org. Five rooms with private baths. Doubles, $150 to $250.

The Williamstown Bed and Breakfast, 30 Cold Spring Road, Williamstown 01267.

An attractive white Victorian house built in 1880 with room to spare; this was turned into a sparkling B&B in 1989 by Kim Rozell and Lucinda Edmonds. "I cook and Lucinda cleans," quipped Kim at our first visit. Both perform their functions to perfection, although now they share the duties and sometimes switch roles.

Kim's breakfasts are feasts, taken at a table for eight in the dining room. Start with fruit, cereals and homemade baked goods, but save room for the main course – perhaps blueberry pancakes, waffles, baked eggs or cheese blintzes. Spinach pie and oatmeal scones were treats when we last were here.

Lucinda's "cleaning" is evident throughout the house. Besides the comfy living room outfitted in a crisp, almost contemporary style, there are four spiffy guest

The Williamstown Bed and Breakfast occupies Victorian-era house on broad lawn.

rooms with updated baths and comfortable wing chairs on the second floor. Two rooms have queensize poster beds, a third has a double bed and one has two twins. White cotton comforters top each bed.

Appointments are a blend of antique and modern, with an emphasis on oak furniture, mini-print wallpapers with vivid borders and a refreshing absence of clutter often associated with Victoriana. Typical of the caring touches are the bottles of Poland Spring water in each room.

The personable hosts, who do all the work themselves, seem to know everything there is to know about the area and share their enthusiasm with guests.

(413) 458-9202. www.williamstownbandb.com. Four rooms with private baths. Doubles, $110 to $130. Children over 12. Two-night minimum summer and fall weekends. No credit cards.

River Bend Farm, 643 Simonds Road (Route 7 North), Williamstown 01267.

This handsome Georgian Colonial was built in 1770 by Col. Benjamin Simonds, one of Williamstown's thirteen founders, and the house exudes 18th-century authenticity.

Preservationists David and Judy Loomis acquired the house in 1977, spent years restoring it with great care and attention to detail, and started sharing its treasures with B&B guests.

Guests enter the rear keeping room, where black kettles hang from the huge hearth, one of five fireplaces off the central stone chimney. The room is full of hooked rugs, antiques, dried flowers and grapevine wreaths. Here's where the hosts serve what they call a healthful continental breakfast of fresh fruit, homemade granola, honey from their own beehives, muffins and breads.

All the lighting here and in the adjacent parlor comes from small bulbs in tin chandeliers and period lighting fixtures. The Loomises removed layers of flooring atop the original 1770 boards in the parlor. "Just to think that Ethan Allen stood here on the same floor is exciting," says Dave. The house contains what authorities

River Bend Farm provides Colonial experience in house built in 1770.

consider to be the best examples of period woodwork in town, as well as notable corner cupboards, paneling and iron work.

Four bedrooms share two baths, one upstairs with a tub and the other downstairs in the old pantry and harboring an ingenious corner shower with tiles that Dave fashioned from roof slate. Three rooms are upstairs off a hall containing a giant spinning wheel. The front corner room has a crocheted coverlet over the four-poster double bed and plenty of room for two wing chairs in a sitting area. Two other upstairs rooms, each containing a double and a twin bed, are good for families. A downstairs bedroom in a former parlor is lovely, decorated in blues and whites with well-worn oriental rugs.

Dave says the B&B proceeds help finance the ongoing restoration of this old home and tavern, which is listed on the National Register of Historic Places. Spending a night or two here is to immerse oneself in history. Or, as Judy tells it, "guests say it's like staying in a museum but you can touch the stuff."

(413) 458-3121. Four rooms with two shared baths. Doubles, $100. Closed November to mid-April.

The Williams Inn, Junction of Routes 7 and 2, Williamstown 01267.

After the old Williams Inn was taken over by Williams College, the Treadway built a replacement (supposedly "on-the-green at Williams College," though not by our definition). Not a typical country inn, this is a Colonial-modern hotel/motel, now independently owned by Carl and Marilyn Faulkner.

The 103 rooms on three floors come with two double beds (a few kingsize), color TVs and early American furnishings. A new North Wing in 2003 added 22 "premier king-bedded rooms" and a two-room suite, furnished in hotel style.

Three meals a day are available in the large and formal dining room with ten big brass chandeliers. The dinner menu features such traditional choices as yankee pot roast and liver and onions along with chicken dijonnaise, roast duck bigarade, veal piccata and, standing out at our latest visit, scallops and lobster in bourbon cream sauce with fennel and scallions.

(413) 458-9371 or (800) 828-0133. Fax (413) 458-2767. www.williamsinn.com. One hundred twenty-four rooms and one suite with private baths. Mid-April to mid-November: doubles $150 to $290, suite $450 to $500. Rest of year: doubles $135 to $250, suite $375 to $425.

Entrées, $17.25 to $25.50. Lunch, Monday-Saturday 11:30 to 2:30. Dinner nightly, 5:30 to 9:30 or 10. Sunday, brunch 11:30 to 2, dinner 5 to 9.

Jae's Inn, 1111 South State St. (Route 8), North Adams 01247.

Opened with little fanfare in 2003, this is one of the more distinctive small, full-service country inns to appear in New England in years. Boston restaurateur Jae Chung returned to his home area to purchase the little-known Twin Sisters Inn two miles south of North Adams and transform it into an upscale inn, restaurant and spa with a contemporary Asian accent.

He artfully renovated and expanded the century-old building from four bedrooms and two shared bathrooms to eleven guest rooms with marble baths and jacuzzi tubs, gas fireplaces and flat-screen TVs with DVD players. Much of the furniture is pine, as are the flooring and the occasional wainscoting. All but two beds are queensize, covered with quilts. Each room has a desk (some of them rather old-fashioned and child-like), a rocking chair and, usually, a single armchair. Three on the walk-out lower level beneath the dining porch open onto private patios at the side. A less-compact room on the main floor harbors the inn's only kingsize bed. Each is different, notable for wood floors dotted with oriental rugs and light-colored painted walls dominated by colorful art.

Not only the rooms but also the walls of corridors and dining areas are hung with gilt-framed artworks, many of them oriental from Jae's collection. You can't go anywhere without finding art – even in the public restrooms. (No paper towels or blow driers here. Real wash towels are stacked on the granite counters.)

Sections of the main floor and lower level hold a variety of fitness and spa facilities, from treadmills and universal weight system to two massage rooms, a sauna and a beauty parlor.

In back are a porch and a flagstone patio with lounge furniture and an ornamental kiva stove beside a small, angular swimming pool. Beyond the pool are a tennis court and a basketball hoop.

Continental breakfast is included in the rates.

Lunch and dinner are available in the main-floor restaurant and lounge (see Dining Spots). A plaque beside the gleaming pine bar says it is dedicated to the Class of 1982 of Drury High School in North Adams. Jae arrived from Korea at age 13, grew up above the store his parents ran in neighboring Clarksburg, and captained the Drury basketball team. He studied fine arts in college before opening the first of a highly successful chain of Asian cafés bearing his name in Boston in 1990. He closed all but two to concentrate on his new local endeavors, which include his acquisition and renovation of the old Le Jardin inn and restaurant in Williamstown.

(413) 664-0100. Fax (413) 664-0105. www.jaesinn.com. Eleven rooms with private baths. Doubles, $160 weekends, $125 midweek.

The Porches Inn at MASS MoCA, 231 River St., North Adams 01247.

A 1961 Williams College graduate spearheaded the development of this 47-room

Heated stone patio surrounds pool behind The Porches Inn complex.

inn that emerged phoenix-like from six Victorian row houses across the street from MASS MoCA.

Museum director Joseph Thompson persuaded John Wadsworth Jr., retired chairman of Morgan Stanley/Asia, to develop the project and turn management over to the Fitzpatrick family of the Red Lion Inn in Stockbridge. The structures originally had individual porches, so two broad front porches – reminiscent of that at the Red Lion Inn – were built to link the structures.

Like the lobby of the Red Lion, the focal point here is one building that holds the reception area, a couple of breakfast rooms and two living rooms. The one in the front has a blazing fireplace on the side and four vivid red leather chairs around a circular coffee table in the center.

The interior design is rather eclectic and not at all the antique look of the Red Lion Inn or that of the buildings' late 1800s period. Innkeeper Olivier Glattfelder calls it ''retro-edgy, industrial granny chic,'' a style that harmonizes well with the museum's combination of nostalgia and high tech. It prompted the British edition of Condé Nast Traveler to rate it one of the 32 "coolest new hotels" in the world in 2002.

Roughly eight to ten guest rooms are in each of six connected houses. They vary in size but generally are quite spacious. Eight on the second floor have private porches to supplement the broad front porches that give the inn its name. Dressed with Frette linens and topped with feather duvets and hand-sewn coverlets, beds are king or queensize and in some cases there are two queens or an extra sofabed. TV/DVDs are hidden in armoires, and telephones are cordless. A mix of mid-19th century and contemporary furnishings, along with light beadboard walls and wooden floors painted in bold colors, convey the "less is more" look of today's urban inn. The vintage 1950s lamps in each room were purchased off eBay, as were accessories and artworks in a quirky art collection dominated by paint-by-number pictures. Mirrors have been ingeniously fashioned from recycled window frames. Many of the slate-floor bathrooms have jetted or clawfoot tubs and separate "deluge showers." Shaker-style wall pegs serve as towel and bathrobe holders. Some quarters are loft suites on two levels, connected by spiral staircases. Three are extended-stay suites in a new seventh building.

Out back is a heated swimming pool with an adjacent hot tub, part of a nicely landscaped back lawn and heated stone patio against a wooded slope. A pavilion beside holds an indoor recreation room and sauna.

A complimentary European-style buffet breakfast features fruit, yogurt, cereals, a signature coffeecake and sticky buns, bread and cheese. It's available in a cheery breakfast room, in guest rooms or on the porch. For breakfast in bed, the meal is delivered in a stainless-steel workman's lunchbox, with a vase of flowers on the side.

(413) 664-0400. www.porches.com. Twenty-nine rooms and 21 suites with private baths. Memorial Day to Veterans Day: doubles $160 to $295, suites $225 to $325. Rest of year: doubles $135 to $259, suites $185 to $269.

Dining Spots

The Mill on the Floss, 342 Route 7, New Ashford.

Genial Maurice Champagne, originally from Montreal, is the chef-owner at this established and well-regarded restaurant, tops on everyone's list locally for special-occasion dining. He loves to socialize, and one reason he designed the open, blue and white tiled kitchen was so that patrons could come up and talk with him as he cooked.

The dark brown wood building, pleasantly landscaped, was once a mill. Inside it is cozy, with beamed ceilings, paneled walls, a hutch filled with Quimper pottery, white linens and many hanging copper pots.

Assisted by his daughter Suzanne, Maurice presents classic French fare. Among starters are chicken liver pâté, escargots in garlic butter, prosciutto and melon, and soups like cold cucumber or black bean. Entrées range from crab cakes dijonnaise to rack of lamb. Sweetbreads in black butter, coq au vin and tournedos with béarnaise sauce are some. The fish of the day could be herb-encrusted cod beurre blanc, halibut meunière or poached salmon hollandaise.

For dessert, you might find crème caramel, deep-dish pie and frozen grand marnier soufflé, or you might prefer café diablo for two. Wines are quite reasonably priced.

(413) 458-9123. www.millonthefloss.com. Entrées, $23.50 to $29.50. Dinner, Tuesday-Sunday from 5.

Mezze, 16 Water St., Williamstown.

Contemporary restaurants come and go in Williamstown, but this has endured. It opened in hip quarters in the former Potter's Wheel craft gallery down the street but was destroyed by fire. Owner Nancy Thomas got sidetracked briefly with her new Eleven restaurant at MASS MoCA, but reopened in 2002 in the quarters occupied by the short-lived Main Street Café.

The space is perfect for her sophisticated bistro concept. Interesting uses of wood convey a mountain décor, from upright slabs of lumber serving as a divider in the foyer to a birch tree trunk serving as one of the columns in the skylit dining room. White-clothed tables are spaced well apart in the black and white room with polished wood floors. The other side of the foyer leads to a spacious bar/lounge, mod and spare with wide-board floors and banquette seating. A tavern menu is available here, and it's *the* place to see and be seen.

Nancy initially gave the food a Mediterranean and Moroccan twist, thanks to her mother from Morocco. But chef James Tracey's contemporary American fare dominates the menu now. Typical starters are scallop seviche with avocado, pickled red onions and cilantro, and variations on salad, as in duck confit and poached egg with frisée and house-smoked bacon vinaigrette.

Main courses range from roasted wild coho salmon in a porcini mushroom broth to rack of lamb with thyme. Roasted free-range chicken, seared duck breast and braised beef short ribs were recommended at our autumn visit.

Desserts included chocolate-peanut tart with caramel ice cream, coconut macaroons with concord grape sorbet and maple pot de crème with a gingersnap cookie.

A Mezze plate of antipasti plus beef stroganoff and grilled hanger steak with bordelaise sauce were featured on the bar menu.

(413) 458-0123. Entrées, $22 to $26. Dinner nightly, from 5:30.

Hobson's Choice, 159 Water St., Williamstown.

This country-rustic place with paneled walls and beamed ceilings is a favorite of locals. Old tools hang on the walls, Tiffany-type lamps top tables and booths, and there are a few stools at the bar in back. Around the front door are wonderful panes of stained glass with flowers and birds therein. A rear addition was opened in 2001 to provide more dining space and an open lobster tank.

Chef-owner Dan Campbell moved from Montana to lend a Western accent to the extensive steak and seafood menu. Hand-cut steaks, prime rib, five versions of chicken, cajun shrimp and grilled or blackened Norwegian salmon, scallops and fish of the day are featured for dinner. You can create your own surf and turf combo, perhaps Alaskan king crab and buffalo steak. Or you can make a meal out of pasta marinara or the salad bar, which is known for its organic produce.

Start with shrimp wontons, sautéed mushrooms, tuna carpaccio or fried calamari. Finish with mud pie, grand marnier fudge parfait, apple strudel or death by chocolate.

(413) 458-9101. Entrées, $15 to $21. Dinner nightly, 5 to 9:30.

Thai Garden, 27 Spring St., Williamstown.

An offshoot of a gourmet Thai restaurant of the same name in Keene, N.H., this opened in the downtown storefront formerly occupied by Sandy Smith's highly rated Cobble Café, which closed when he joined a parade of local restaurateurs to North Adams.

Now one of seven Thai Gardens extending from Saratoga Springs to Boston, the food is exotic and equally highly rated. The setting here is serene in beige and green.

The extensive menu is designated as to spiciness, with up to three chiles (for drunken squid stir-fried with bell peppers, baby corn, mushrooms, broccoli and more). Seafood gra prow, seafood curry and spicy fish fillet are two-chile dishes. But the menu notes that the chiles and spices are toned down by other ingredients on the principle that "there must always be a harmony in a dish." Those preferring less incendiary tastes can opt for steamed ginger salmon, tamarind duck or a combo called "three buddies" – chicken, beef and pork loin sautéed with pineapple, corn, snow peas and mushrooms.

Desserts include homemade Thai custard, coconut and ginger ice creams, and chilled lychees.

(413) 458-0004. Entrées, $7.95 to $15.95. Lunch daily, 11:30 to 3. Dinner nightly, 5 to 10.

Asian cuisine is served in cheery porch dining room at Jae's Inn.

Spice Root, 23 Spring St., Williamstown.

Modern Indian cuisine is served up in a modern Indian setting in this, the fifth in a series of highly rated Indian restaurants run by the Chola Group in New York and Connecticut.

The décor is anything but traditional Indian. It's spare in rich reds, with a few beaded wall hangings, iridescent colored light spheres suspended from the ceiling and gleaming silver steel-backed chairs at close-together tables. The weighty copper menu reveals the usual Indian fare, from "hot! hot!" shrimp vindaloo to lamb cooked with mint and mango in a masala sauce. Tandoori specialties include various kabobs. The menu lists ten vegetarian specialties and seven "popular dishes" from Bombay.

Appetizer platters include a sampling of vegetable or meat treats, including samosas. The naan, paratha and poori breads are popular as well. There's an $8.95 lunch buffet daily, and lunch boxes are available to go.

(413) 458-5200. www.fineindiandining.com. Entrées, $12 to $19. Lunch daily, 11:30 to 2:30, Sunday noon to 3. Dinner nightly, 5 to 10 or 11..

Jae's Inn, 1111 South Main St., North Adams.

The Asian cuisine that captivated Boston fans has been transplanted to an unlikely outpost south of gritty North Adams. Jae Chung returned to his home area to open a sleek, Asian fusion restaurant in a country New England setting.

The 50-seat restaurant and bar with a living-room-like lounge and fireplace occupies the front portion of the main floor of his new inn and spa. Dining is in a small and elegant room behind the reception desk and a larger, more casual enclosed dining porch paneled in pine, even on the ceiling, with windows on three sides. Oriental artworks enhance the olive green walls, and small colored lights dangle from the ceiling. Angular blue cobalt wall sconces and cobalt glassware accent the pine tables. Colorful leaves were artfully nested in the potted palms at our autumn visit.

More artistry is evident in the cuisine, which Jae calls a fusion of Korean, Japanese and Thai. The fare is about the same as in his Boston area restaurants, which we've enjoyed over the years, and includes extensive sushi selections and designer rolls.

A couple of "lunch boxes" ($7.95 to $8.95) produced a fine midday repast of extra-good hot and sour soup with shrimp tempura in one case, the signature "tidbits" (chicken satay, grilled shrimp and a sea scallop) in the other. Each came in a box with two sauces, rice, salad, broccoli, a California roll and a couple of shrimp dumplings called shumai.

At night, the kitchen turns out all kinds of decorative (and tasty) morsels, from a seafood pajon pancake and tuna tartare to ginger custard, dark chocolate mousse and lemon framboise for dessert. In between are all kinds of noodle, pad thai, rice and curry dishes, We would have liked to have tried the hosomaki in seaweed rolls, the hot and spicy kimchi stew, the famous Korean bibim bab (marinated chicken or beef with vegetables cooked in a hot stone pot), the ribeye bulgoki, the spicy Korean pork, the grilled tuna steak with wasabi dipping sauce – in fact, almost everything on the menu. That, however, would take a number of return visits, something area residents are better able than we to do. They already have made it a local favorite.

(413) 664-0100. Entrées, $11.95 to $16.95. Lunch daily, 11:30 to 4. Dinner nightly, 5 to 9 or 10.

Eleven, Building 11, MASS MoCA, North Adams.

The fine-dining restaurant at MASS MoCA is not unlike the museum itself: cool and contemporary, and an artistic as well as a culinary treat. Some find the modernist look with sculpted multi-level white ceiling, cream-colored walls, mod gray upholstered chairs at bare tables and gray-tinted glass windows onto the outdoor courtyard stark to the point of being austere. But the bud vases with different flowers on each table are artistic, and the recessed colored fluorescent lighting turns the space into a work of art, especially at night.

''People interested in contemporary art are also interested in contemporary food,'' says chef-owner Nancy Thomas, who opened here shortly after fire temporarily interrupted her trendy Mezze restaurant venture in Williamstown.

Lunch-goers find a short, affordable menu of soups, salads (perhaps cobb or tuna niçoise) and sandwiches, plus extras like pad thai, a Mezze cheese and Berkshire Mountain bread plate or spicy lump crab summer rolls

The dinner menu adds starters like crispy calamari with chipotle aioli and pulled pork quesadilla. Nighttime entrées range from tuna au poivre on braised french lentils to spice-seasoned duck breast with couscous and plum chutney. More basic fare might be black pepper tagliatelle with creamy walnut sauce and pecorino, and a hamburger with fries.

Carrot cake with walnut ginger icing is a typical dessert.

(413) 663-2004. Entrées, $15 to $20. Lunch daily, 11 to 3. Dinner 5 to 9 or 10. Closed Monday-Thursday, November to Memorial Day.

Diversions

Williamstown's scenic beauty is apparent on all sides, but less known is the composite of its art and history collections. You get a hint of both on arrival simply by traversing Main Street east from the green at Route 7. The hilly street with broad lawns leading to wide-apart historic homes, imposing college buildings and churches – totally lacking in commercialism – is more scenic and tranquil than the main street of any college town we know.

Art and history are best appreciated when viewed close up, away from the crowded settings of the huge museums. As Connoisseur magazine reported, this intimacy is "the great gift" of Williamstown.

Sterling and Francine Clark Art Institute, 225 South St.

The most widely known of the town's museums chanced upon its Williamstown location through an old family connection with Williams College and the fact that eccentric collector Sterling Clark, heir to the Singer sewing machine fortune, wanted his treasures housed far from a potential site of nuclear attack. Clark's neoclassical white marble temple opened in 1955 (he and his wife are buried under its front steps) and was expanded in 1973 by a red granite addition housing more galleries and one of the nation's outstanding art research libraries. A 1996 addition opened still more galleries. Lately mounting major exhibitions that draw more than 100,000 visitors a summer, the Clark has particularly strong holdings of French 19th-century paintings (36 Renoirs), English silver, prints and drawings. The Clark was the single largest source for the Renoir exhibition at Boston's Museum of Fine Arts. Shown mostly in small galleries the size of the rooms in which they once hung, the highly personalized collection of Monets, Turners and Winslow Homers quietly vies for attention with sculptures, porcelain and three centuries worth of silver (Sterling Clark liked good food and the silverware to go with it). All this is amid an austere yet intimate setting of potted plants and vases of dried flowers, furniture and benches for relaxation.

(413) 458-2303. www.clarkart.edu. Open daily late June to Labor Day, 10 to 5; rest of year, Tuesday-Sunday, 10 to 5. Adults $10, June-October; free, rest of year.

Williams College Museum of Art, Main Street.

A $4.5 million extension to its original octagonal building in Lawrence Hall makes this museum a sleeper in art circles. Itself a work of art, it contains an 1846 neoclassical rotunda with "ironic" columns that are decorative rather than functional. The eight sides of the rotunda are repeated in soaring newer galleries with skylights, some of their walls hung with spectacular wall art. Once headed by Guggenheim director Thomas Krens, the museum houses fourteen galleries and a staggering 12,000 works spanning the history of art, from 3,000-year-old Assyrian stone reliefs to the last self-portrait by Andy Warhol. In an effort to complement the better-known Sterling and Francine Clark Art Institute's strengths in the 19th century, this museum stresses contemporary, 17th- and 18th-century American art and rare Asian art. It features special exhibitions rivaling those of many a metropolitan museum.

(413) 597-2429. www.williams.edu/WCMA. Open Tuesday-Saturday 10 to 5, Sunday 1 to 5. Free.

Nearby is the **Hopkins Observatory,** the oldest working observatory in the United States (1836), offering exhibits on the history of astronomy plus planetarium shows and viewings through college telescopes.

Chapin Library, Stetson Hall, Williams College.

Nowhere else are the founding documents of the country – original printings of the Declaration of Independence, the Articles of Confederation, the Bill of Rights and drafts of the Constitution – displayed together in a simple glass case on the second floor of a college hall. This remarkable library contains more than 30,000 rare books, first editions and manuscripts. You might ask to see James Madison's copy of Thomas Paine's *Common Sense.* One floor below is the Williamsiana Collection of town and gown, while the lowest level of Stetson contains the archives of band leader Paul Whiteman, with 3,500 original scores and a complete library of music of the 1920s.

(413) 597-2462. Open Monday-Friday, 9 to noon and 1 to 5. Free.

Williamstown Theatre Festival, Adams Memorial Theater, Williams College. Founded in 1955, the professional summer festival presents "some of the most ambitious theatre the U.S. has to offer," in the words of the Christian Science Monitor. It won the 2002 Regional Theatre Tony Award for outstanding achievement and contribution. Such luminaries as Dick Cavett, Edward Herrmann and Marsha Mason return summer after summer to the festival they call home for productions of everything from Chekhov and Ibsen to Tennessee Williams and Broadway tryouts, all the while mingling with the townspeople. The festival offers more than 200 productions a summer on its 520-set Main and adjacent 96-seat Nikos stages, outdoor Free Theatre and weekend Cabaret in Goodrich Hall.

(413) 597-3400. www.wtfestival.org. Festival performances Tuesday-Saturday, mid-June through August. Tickets prices vary, from $20 to $53.

Williams College. Besides the aforementioned highlights, the campus as a whole is worth exploring. Its buildings (more than 50 and counting), predominantly in red brick and gray granite, range through almost every period of American architecture. The lawns and plantings and sense of nature all around contribute to a pleasant walking tour.

Nature. The prime spot – as well as the area's dominant feature – is the **Mount Greylock State Reservation,** a series of seven peaks with a 3,491-foot summit that is the highest in Massachusetts. You can drive, hike or bike to the summit for a spectacular five-state view. Other memorable views are obtained by driving the Taconic Trail through Petersburg Pass and the Mohawk Trail above North Adams. The 2,430-acre **Hopkins Memorial Forest** northwest of the campus is an experimental forest operated by the Williams College Center for Environmental Studies, with fifteen miles of nature and cross-country trails, plus the Moon Barn museum showing old photographs, farm machinery, implements and tools, and the Buxton Garden, a one-acre farm garden designed to have certain flowers in bloom at all seasons. Williams College also recently acquired **Mount Hope Park,** a former estate with extensive gardens and grounds.

Recreation. Golf is the seasonal pastime at the semi-private Taconic Golf Club, on the south edge of town and ranked as one of the tops in New England, and at the public Waubeeka Golf Links in the valley at South Williamstown. In summer, you can swim in the 74-degree waters of Sand Springs Pool & Spa, founded in 1813 and the oldest springs resort still in operation in the country. In winter, there's skiing nearby at Jiminy Peak.

Shopping. The college-community stores are generally along Spring Street, which runs south off Main Street opposite the main campus and between such campus appendages as museum, science center and sports complex. **Zanna** and **Jackie's**

carry apparel of appeal to college women. Try the **Clarksburg Bread Co.** for chunky cheddar cheese bread or an oatmeal-cranberry scone. More than 40 varieties of coffees and 25 of loose teas are available at **Cold Spring Coffee Roasters. Library Antiques** shows dhurrie rugs, English country pine furniture, Turkish pillows, china, gifts and more, as well as Asian art at the related **LiAsia Gallery** across the street. More good art is available at **Harrison Gallery.** The **George M. Hopkins Store** offers wood furniture and collectibles.

Water Street, a parallel street that blossomed later, has distinctive shops including the **Cottage** for classy gifts and clothing, **The Mountain Goat** for outdoors equipment, the **Plum Gallery** and **Room,** for home accessories.

For foodies, the most interesting shopping of all may be at **The Store at Five Corners,** an 18th-century general store gone upscale, just south of Williamstown at the junction of Routes 7 and 43. Expect to find Epicurean spices, Mendocino pastas, interesting wines, gifts, Italian biscotti and homemade fudge along with an espresso bar, baked goods from the store's bakery, and an assortment of breakfast and lunch items from the deli. There are tables upon which to enjoy, inside or out.

Extra-Special

MASS MoCA, 87 Marshall St., North Adams.

The country's largest contemporary art center features an ambitious array of exhibitions and performances on a 19th-century factory campus that quickly transformed gritty North Adams into an up-and-coming cultural and entertainment hub. Short for Massachusetts Museum of Contemporary Art, this is the remarkable result of a dozen years of ups and downs for a host of players from the director of the Williams College of Art and visionary architects to three different governors and the state. Spearheaded by museum director Joseph C. Thompson, an art historian trained at Williams College, they transformed the thirteen-acre site into a 21st-century facility for art and technology while preserving the fabric of the old textile mills. The 27 red-brick buildings, listed on the National Historic Register and abandoned following the 1985 closing of the once-mighty Sprague Electric Co., are linked by an elaborate system of interlocking courtyards, viaducts and elevated walkways. Galleries, sculpture parks and performance arenas co-exist with e-commerce start-ups dubbed Silicon Village.

Nineteen high-ceilinged galleries – one as long as a football field – total more than 100,000 square feet of exhibit space. MASS MoCA focuses on the work of artists charting new territory; works that blur the lines between visual and performing arts and works that have never been exhibited because of their size or materials (including a Chinese dragon boat at our latest visit). A lack of good signage and edifying descriptions suggests the uninitiated are better off on guided tours (offered several times a day in summer and fall and weekends year-round).

The museum opened in 1999 after being given up for dead at least four times. Now it is a national model of not only how to re-use old buildings but how to experience art and architecture today. "I have seen the future," wrote a Wall Street Journal reporter, "and it is MASS MoCA." Even if you don't like modern art, you'll likely be impressed by this.

(413) 662-2111. Open daily 10 to 6, June-October; Wednesday-Monday 11 to 5, rest of year. Adults, $9.

Lenox, Mass.

The Good (and Cultured) Life

The gentle beauty of the Berkshires has attracted generations of artists, authors and musicians – as well as their patrons who appreciate the good life. At the center of the Berkshires in both location and spirit is Lenox, a small village whose cultural influence far exceeds its size.

In the 19th century, Lenox was home for Nathaniel Hawthorne, Edith Wharton, Henry Ward Beecher and Fannie Kemble. Herman Melville, Henry Adams, Oliver Wendell Holmes, Henry Wadsworth Longfellow, William Cullen Bryant, Daniel Chester French and (later) Norman Rockwell lived and worked nearby.

Such was the allure of this tranquil mountain and lake country that many prominent Americans built palatial "cottages" here. Lenox became "the inland Newport" for such families as Westinghouse, Carnegie, Procter, Morgan and Vanderbilt. Indeed, some of America's 400 summered in Newport and spent the early autumn in the Berkshires.

The artists and the affluent helped make Lenox in the 20th century a center for the arts. Tanglewood, across from Hawthorne's home, is the summer home of the Boston Symphony Orchestra. Shakespeare & Company moved to the campus of the late National Music Center from The Mount, allowing author Edith Wharton's estate and gardens to come into their own as a house museum and cultural center. Ventfort Hall is being restored into another cultural stage and a museum of the Gilded Age. The Frelinghuysen Morris House & Studio has been opened to the public as a showcase of abstract art. Nearby are the Lenox Arts Center, the Berkshire Theater Festival, Jacob's Pillow Dance Festival and the Aston Magna Festival concerts.

The Lenox area's cultural attractions are well known. Less so are some of its other treats: the picturesque Stockbridge Bowl (a lake), the Walker sculpture garden, the Pleasant Valley wildlife sanctuary, the trails at the John Drummond Kennedy Park, the landmark Church on the Hill, the mansions along Kemble and Cliffwood streets, and the scenic weekend rail excursions offered from Lenox to Stockbridge by the Berkshire Scenic Railway Museum.

Attractions of a more specialized nature are offered at the Kripalu Center for Yoga and Health and at Canyon Ranch in the Berkshires.

Staying in some of Lenox's inns is like being a houseguest in a country mansion. Besides lodging in style, visitors may dine at some of New England's fanciest restaurants and enjoy $90 orchestra seats in the Shed at Tanglewood. The budget-conscious can find more reasonable places in which to stay and eat, and, while picnicking on the Tanglewood lawn, can hear the BSO almost as well as those in the Shed.

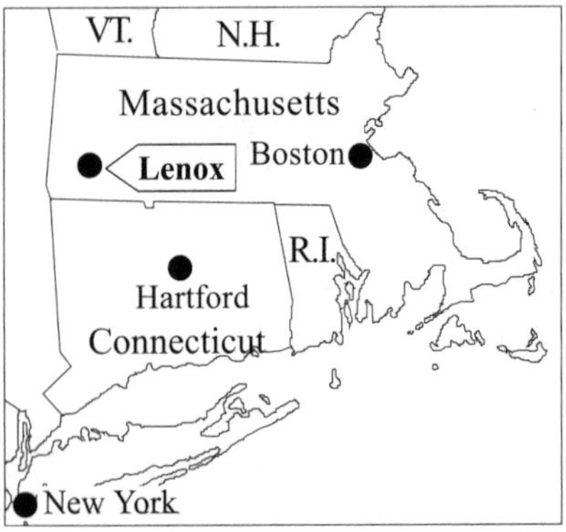

Inn Spots

Most Lenox inns require a minimum stay of three nights on summer weekends,

Blantyre is a Tudor-style replica of a castle in Scotland.

and weekend prices usually extend from Thursday through Sunday. Peak season is generally considered late June to Labor Day and late September to mid-October.

Blantyre, 16 Blantyre Road, Box 995, Lenox 01240.

This rambling, Tudor-style brick manor off by itself on 85 private acres was built in 1902 as a summer retreat for a millionaire in the turpentine business. A replica of the Hall of Blantyre in Scotland, it used to be called Blantyre Castle, and was a memorable place for dining in the baronial style. Today, "castle" has been dropped from the name, but the regal feeling remains in lodging as well as in dining (see Dining Spots).

In 1981, the structure was carefully restored even to the insides of the huge closets by owner Jane Fitzpatrick, whose Red Lion Inn in adjacent Stockbridge has welcomed guests in the New England tradition for so many years. The result is worthy of a castle, or at the very least an English-style country-house hotel: a majestic foyer with staircase of black oak, public rooms with high beamed ceilings, rich and intricate carved paneling, crystal chandeliers and fireplaces with hand-carved mantels, and eight elegant suites and guest rooms, five with fireplaces.

The ultra-deluxe Paterson Suite ($800 a night) contains a fireplaced living room with a crystal chandelier, a large bedroom with kingsize bed and two full bathrooms. Victorian-style sofas and chairs make comfortable sitting areas at the foot of the ornate queensize four-poster beds in the Laurel and Cranwell suites. Even the smallest Bouquet and Ribbon rooms are fit for would-be barons and baronesses, if only for a night or two. And the two-room Ashley suite is considered a steal at $400 a night.

A typical bathroom has terrycloth robes and piles of towels, a scale, a wooden valet, heated towel racks, embroidered curtains and at least ten kinds of soaps and assorted toiletries.

Twelve rooms in more contemporary style, several of them split-level loft suites, are available in the carriage house near the pool. They have been totally renovated, down to the hand-painted tiles and marble floors of their sparkling bathrooms. All have decks or balconies and wet bars.

There also are four cottages. The newest, an expansion of the original Ice House, is now considered the prime accommodation. The main floor resembles that of a sumptuous country cottage, complete with full kitchen, for $950. A wall of stone embraces the raised hearth in the manorial living room, which opens onto a screened porch. A balcony goes off the bedroom, where the kingsize canopy bed is draped in fabric that matches the chaise. The bathroom, bigger than most people's bedrooms, harbors a whirlpool tub and a walk-in rainforest shower. Downstairs and available jointly ($1,300) or separately ($400) is a kingsize bedroom opening onto a private patio.

Fees include the use of four tennis courts (whites required), a swimming pool, jacuzzi, sauna and competition bent-grass croquet lawns on the property.

Fruit, cheese and mineral water await guests on arrival. Cocktails and after-dinner coffee and cordials are offered in the main foyer and the crystal-chandeliered music room. "Proper evening dress" is required in the house after 6 p.m.

A complimentary continental breakfast is served in the conservatory or on the terrace. More substantial items are available for a surcharge.

Guests are pampered to within an inch of their lives. Blantyre was the first American hotel to win the coveted International Welcome Award from the prestigious Relais & Châteaux association. It also was the top-rated inn and resort in New England in the Zagat hotel survey. Guests don't mince words in the oversize guest book in the entry hall. Many write simply: "Heaven" or "Perfection."

(413) 637-3556. Fax (413) 637-4282. www.blantyre.com. Twelve rooms, eight suites and four cottages with private baths. Doubles $350 to $600, suites $410 to $800, cottages $600 to $1,300. Two-night minimum weekends and foliage. Children over 12. Closed early November to early May.

Wheatleigh, Hawthorne Road, Lenox, Mass. 01240.

Understated European-style opulence and luxury are the hallmarks of this exotic Italian palazzo built in 1893 as a wedding gift for the Countess de Heredia and lately refurbished and embellished to the tune of many millions of dollars by owners Susan and Linwood Simon and their general manager, French-trained hotelier François Thomas from Paris.

The setting on 22 sylvan acres is grand, even palatial, but as refashioned in 2002 by a New York design team the interior decor is unexpectedly minimalist, producing what the New York Times Magazine called the most European small hotel in America. "The most sophisticated country house hotel in America" is how Andrew Harper described it in his Hideaway Report.

The imposing entrance of the beige brick building framed in wrought iron leads into a soaring Great Room with modern and traditional sitting areas, a majestic staircase rising to the second floor, parquet floors and fine art all around.

To enhance the classical Renaissance architecture, the guest room style is a light European look in muted beige and taupe colors with a mix of English and French antiques and European-modern furnishings. Bedrooms have French-designed bedspreads of imported silk, and more comfortable seating than in the past. Bathrooms were redone in imported English limestone or Italian marble, with silver-

Wheatleigh occupies exotic Italian palazzo on 22 acres near Tanglewood.

plated fixtures from England and Bulgari toiletries from Italy. Each room now has a TV/VCR and a portable telephone for those who want to be in touch wherever they are. Here and there on the walls are large and splashy canvases by painter Daniel Cohen.

Of the nineteen guest accommodations, eight are spacious, seven medium-size and four small (one with a built-in double bed is, frankly, tiny – ten-by-twelve feet to be precise). Nine of the best have fireplaces and six add private terraces or balconies.

The most exotic is the Aviary Suite, an unusual two-story affair joined by an outside spiral staircase enclosed in glass. Its upstairs has a kingsize bedroom with large windows onto a garden, dark chestnut ceiling and pale brick walls. Adjoining is an expansive "wet room" with an open shower, one of Wheatleigh's original deep soaking tubs and a separate water closet. The sitting room on the main floor is surrounded by glass and opens onto a terrace.

We preferred the main-floor Terrace Suite, formed by enclosing part of a portico that matches the dining portico. One snug section has a kingsize bed with fabric headboard. It opens onto the portico, where two curved loveseats and a massive coffee table face each other in an enclosure of glass, bronze and brick. A pot of hot spiced cider, served by one of the staff clad in black, warmed our arrival on a chilly November afternoon.

That evening we enjoyed one of the best meals of our lives in Wheatleigh's main-floor restaurant (see Dining Spots). Breakfast the next morning was another extravagance and began – a first in our experience – with an amuse-bouche. This one was a caramelized apricot topped with crème fraîche, so good that we asked the chef for the particulars. The main courses were poached eggs Wheatleigh (rather like eggs benedict, but with wild mushrooms in the hollandaise sauce) and a souffléd omelet of smoked salmon and cheese. Each was accompanied by asparagus spears and roesti potatoes – more "vegetables" at breakfast than we'd experienced at dinner the night before.

Wheatleigh offers extras beyond extravagant food and lodging. A section of the basement holds a state-of-the-art fitness room with computerized equipment that tallies how you're doing as you watch the overhead TV. Adjacent is a massage room with a masseuse on call. Outside are a tennis court, a heated swimming pool hidden in a glade and tranquil grounds within walking distance of Tanglewood.

All these indulgences exact a price, of course. Those with the wherewithal find the sybaritic experience as good as it gets.

(413) 637-0610. Fax (413) 637-4507. www.wheatleigh.com. Seventeen rooms and two suites with private baths. Rates, EP: doubles $545 to $955, suites $1,150 and $1,350. Tanglewood and foliage weekends: doubles $695 to $1,155, suites $1,350 and $1,550.

Stonover Farm Bed & Breakfast, 169 Undermountain Road, Lenox 01240.

Their first guest was vocalist Linda Ronstadt in 2002, and since then "we've never looked back." So says Tom Werman, who switched to innkeeping after a 23-year career as a leading record producer in Los Angeles. He and his wife Suky returned to their East Coast roots to restore a 110-year-old "cottage" that served as the farmhouse to the Stonover Estate. It's now a luxurious B&B offering both convenience and charm – a combination they found missing in most of their travels.

By convenience Tom means creature comforts, which this with-it establishment offers in spades. Guest suites are spacious and come with high-end amenities. And the stylish common areas are many and varied.

The charm is in the details of the restored stone house and stable plus the setting on eight rural acres of sylvan tranquility not far from Tanglewood. Stones are evident in the facade of the handsome brown house with blue trim, the stone walls outlining the property and the stone fireplace that melds into a wall of stone in the plush living room, with a plant-filled greenhouse opposite. The unusual walls of the dining room are tan-tinted brick.

Although the foundation is solid New England, the Wermans reconfigured the interior of the house and joined it to the stable, wrapping around an idyllic courtyard terrace looking onto a duck pond. A California decorator friend furnished the place in a light and airy, uncluttered style. All is embellished by an eye-popping collection of contemporary art gathered by four artisans whom Suky, a former museum educator, represents.

Guests are comfortably housed in three second-floor suites and the outlying Rock Cottage. Beds are king or queensize, with fourteen-inch thick mattresses dressed in Frette linens and fabric duvets. The typical sitting room has a Shaker desk with a Bose radio, telephone, a sofabed and a rocker. It opens into a bedroom with an entertainment center concealing a 27-inch flat-screen TV and DVD player. One suite has a gas fireplace and a bath with jacuzzi tub and separate shower. Other bathrooms, all full of slate, tile and marble, contain walk-in showers for two and one has a soaking tub.

A stone fireplace warms an enormous living/dining room in the four-room cottage, which has a kingsize bedroom on the main floor, twin beds upstairs in an aerie called the sleeping turret, and a full kitchen.

"I'm a media man so I make sure guests have all the media here they need," Tom explained as he showed his cassette collection and a guest computer with high-speed internet access in a media room off the plush library.

Forested hillside envelops Stonover Farm Bed & Breakfast.

The hospitable host also makes sure guests are well fed. He serves wine and imported cheeses in the afternoon, by the fire in the living room or library, or outside on the courtyard terrace. A lavish breakfast is served at a table for eight in the former creamery with windows on three sides and vaulted ceiling rising to a cupola. Tom does the cooking for both healthy and hearty options, serving up guests' choice of omelets, eggs any style, french toast or pancakes, with thick sliced bacon cooked on his AGA stove. His goat cheese omelet with sautéed mushrooms quickly became a favorite.

"It's just heaven here," says Tom, who refers to the Stonover property as "the greatest place on earth." His enthusiasm is contagious. Initial guests already had the rooms half booked for the next summer the September day we were there. The Wermans had plans to add two more extra-large suites on two floors of a barn close by.

(413) 637-9100. www.stonoverfarm.com. July-August and October: doubles $350, cottage $475. Rest of year: doubles $250, cottage $350.

Cliffwood Inn, 25 Cliffwood St., Lenox 01240.

A magnificent classic Colonial built in Stanford White style about 1890 by the then-ambassador to France, this is almost a stage set for the furnishings of innkeepers Joy and Scottie Farrelly, acquired during their periods of residence in Paris, Brussels, Italy and Montreal when he was with Ralston Purina Co. Among them are 24 pieces of fine Eldred Wheeler antique reproduction furniture, which are scattered through the house and available for purchase.

The three-story mansion has ten working fireplaces, one of them in the bathroom off a third-floor guest room.

A large foyer gives access to all three main-floor public rooms, each of which has French doors opening to the full-length back porch overlooking a swimming pool and a gazebo. Underneath the porch is a cedar-walled enclosure housing a counter-current pool and spa for guests to enjoy year-round.

At one end of the house is a living room with twelve-foot-high mirrors and a white marble fireplace. The music room in the center leads to the formal dining room, which has a dark green marble fireplace.

Upstairs are seven air-conditioned guest rooms, all with private baths and six with working fireplaces. Each is named for one of the Farrellys' ancestors (a scrapbook describing the particular one is at the foot of each bed, and it turns out they were an illustrious lot). The Walker-Linton Suite, with a sitting room fashioned from a former bedroom, has a step-up four-poster bed. A Victorian loveseat faces the fireplace in the Helen Walker Room, pretty in pink, white and rose. The Nathaniel Foote Room on the third floor comes with a canopied queensize Sheraton field bed and side tables, two wing chairs in front of the fireplace, a plush armchair in the window corner and no fewer than four oriental rugs, one from Saudi Arabia. A gaily painted lunch pail is a decorative accent in one room, and Joy has crafted folk-art boxes for Kleenex in the others. You'll be intrigued by her many ingenious decorating touches.

In the early evening, the Farrellys put out wine and hors d'oeuvres, perhaps salmon mousse, marinated olives and hot artichoke dip.

Tiring of the routine that burns out some of their colleagues, they no longer serve the "copious continental breakfast" for which they traditionally were known. Guests still gather over morning coffee on the porch in season.

(413) 637-3330 or (800) 789-3331. Fax (413) 637-0221. www.cliffwood.com. Seven rooms with private baths. Late June through Labor Day: doubles $159 to $254. Late spring and early fall: $136 to $200. November to mid-May: $114 to $173. Three- or four-night minimum stay Tanglewood weekends. Three-night minimum some other weekends. Two-night minimum foliage weekends. Children over 11. No credit cards.

The Gables Inn, 103 Walker St., Lenox 01240.

Edith Wharton made this her home at the turn of the century while she was building her permanent edifice, the Mount. Her upstairs room is one of the most attractive in the original Berkshire "cottage" built in the Queen Anne style. Ask innkeeper Frank Newton to show you the famous eight-sided library where she once wrote some of her short stories.

The seventeen guest rooms and suites are full of verve and Victorian warmth. The Jockey Club Suite offers a brass bed in a niche, an ample sitting area with two sofas facing a large-screen TV, and a private entrance from the back-yard pool area. Also in demand are two large second-floor suites built out over a former roof. Both have cathedral ceilings, high windows, swagged draperies, working fireplaces and TVs. One, the Teddy Wharton, is masculine in hunter green and mauve. It contains a leather sofa, two wing chairs and a carved bas-relief of Shakespeare in the bedstead. More feminine in pink and teal floral prints is the Edith Wharton Suite with a four-poster bed and Gibson Girl prints on the walls.

The Tanglewood Suite, downstairs in back, has a private garden patio. Fashioned from two former guest rooms, the bedroom with a queen canopy bed opens onto the secluded patio and the walls of the sitting room are hung with framed Boston Symphony Orchestra programs from 1899 and 1900.

We like the Show Business Room, full of signed photos of old stars and a library of showbiz volumes, with which to curl up on the chintz loveseat in front of the fireplace. The Presidents' Room is aptly named, with lots of memorabilia and memoirs, including a long handwritten letter from Michael Dukakis thanking the Newtons for their hospitality after he was stranded here when his car broke down following a Tanglewood concert.

Lenox inns are known for sumptuous dining facilities, like this breakfast room at The Gables.

Frank, a former banker and sometime pianist, writes and produces summertime shows featuring name entertainers at the Lenox Town Hall Theater. His wife Mary conducts quilting seminars and takes in guests down the street in the home they restored in 1992, built by a cousin of Edith Wharton and called **The Summer White House.** Here (at 17 Main St., 637-4489), Mary "really fusses" as she pampers overnight guests in six spacious bedrooms with private baths and prepares fancy continental breakfasts. "This is our home," she says, "and we treat everyone here as our house guests."

The Newtons first operated the Gables as a restaurant before converting their banquet hall into lodging and making theirs "a special inn." That explains the spectacular breakfast room, with one long table in the center and, along the sides, six round tables for two skirted in pink, green and white. Full breakfasts are served. French toast, pancakes, waffles or eggs are typical fare, supplemented by sour-cream cake, bran muffins and pumpkin, lemon-almond and banana breads.

In the back yard are a tennis court and an enclosed, solar-heated swimming pool with a jacuzzi.

"We like to be hosts and to enjoy our guests," says Frank. That they do very well.

(413) 637-3416 or (800) 382-9401. Fax (413) 637-3416. www.gableslenox.com. Thirteen rooms and four suites with private baths. Mid-May through October: doubles $190 to $210, suites $250. Rest of year: doubles $99 to $130, suites $160. Three-night minimum stay during Tanglewood and some holidays. Two-night minimum in October and holiday weekends. Children over 12.

Six rooms with private baths at Summer White House, doubles $210, July and August only.

The Birchwood Inn, 7 Hubbard St., Lenox 01240.

Former fashion and travel editor Ellen Gutman Chenaux has upgraded this lovely Colonial Revival house, listed on the National Register and dating to 1767 when it was the site of Lenox's first town meeting. She provided the finishing touches in interior décor for the hilltop property across from Lenox's Church on the Hill.

The bedrooms are generally large, particularly three deluxe rooms that have fireplaces, featherbeds and sitting areas with TVs. The Dana in the front corner is romantic in rose, ecru and sage green with a four-poster canopy queen bed and spacious sitting area with loveseat and fainting couch. The Dewey with a kingsize poster bed and sofabed is elegant in plum, moss green and cream. The Egleston is notable for its clawfoot tub and a garden view. Seven other rooms on the second and third floors come with queen or king/twin beds. One on the third floor is a mini-suite with queensize bedroom and an adjoining sitting room with daybed, gas fireplace and TV.

Two first-floor rooms share a front porch in the adjacent 125-year-old carriage house. Also rated deluxe, each has a queensize featherbed, TV and fireplace, and the Post Room has a mini-refrigerator.

Ellen welcomes guests with tea and brownies or chocolate-chip cookies on the wide front porch or in the enormous sunken living room, where wraparound walls of books are available for the borrowing and a piano has been added for playing. There are two separate seating arrangements here, one in front of the fireplace, as well as window seats along an outside wall. Another cozy parlor with a fireplace and TV set leads into the large dining room, where five tables are available for two seatings for breakfast. The menu is posted daily. At our autumn visit it listed cider-baked apples, cranberry-orange nut bread and blueberry buttermilk pancakes. Ellen does the baking, while assistant innkeeper Jeff Steinberg handles most of the cooking. Their favorite recipes are offered in the inn's cookbook, *Breakfast at Birchwood.*

(413) 637-2600 or (800) 524-1646. Fax (413) 637-4604. www. birchwood-inn.com. Twelve rooms with private baths. Late June to Labor Day: doubles, $180 to $275 weekends, $160 to $235 midweek. Rest of year: doubles, $120 to $230 weekends, $110 to $200 midweek. Three-night minimum summer weekends, two nights weekends rest of year. Children over 12.

The Cornell Inn, 203 Main St., Lenox 01240.

When Vermont innkeepers Billie and Doug McLaughlin sold the I.B. Munson House they had restored in Wallingford to be near their daughter and grandchild in Pittsfield, Billie never expected to own another inn. Not many months passed, however, before Doug urged the purchase of the aging Cornell Inn in Lenox.

"It was bad enough restoring one house," recalled Billie. "Now we had to do three." Taking over what both called "a dump" in 1998, the couple closed the inn's restaurant and set about renovating and redecorating all 31 guest rooms in the inn's three-building complex, which turns out to be bigger than it looks from the outside.

Doing much of the work themselves (Billie hung new wallpaper in every room), they produced a variety of comfortable accommodations in several styles. The thirteen rooms in the main 1888 house are done in the Victorian manner with antique appointments. Five here have fireplaces, and the premier Alexandra also has a king bed, whirlpool tub and private deck.

Ten deluxe rooms in the 1777 MacDonald House across the showy garden area are Colonial, all with whirlpool tubs and all but one with fireplaces and sitting areas on private porches or decks.

The eight-room carriage house in the rear has what Billie calls a country primitive feeling. Four have whirlpool tubs and decks overlooking Kennedy Park, and four others have fireplaces. Two are loft suites with efficiency kitchens.

Most beds throughout the complex are queensize. Nineteen rooms have fireplaces and sixteen have whirlpool tubs.

The main house offers two homey common areas, an intimate pub and a country dining room where an ample buffet breakfast includes a hot entrée of the day. The dining room opens onto a spacious deck beside a Japanese-style rock garden and koi ponds separated by a waterfall.

(413) 637-0562 or (800) 637-0562. Fax (413) 637-0927. www.cornellinn.com. Summer: $200 to $400 weekends, $120 to $275 midweek. Rest of year: $110 to $300 weekends, $80 to $150 midweek. Three-night minimum weekends in summer, two-night minimum weekends rest of year. Children over 13.

Applegate Bed & Breakfast, 279 West Park St., Lee 01238.

Just across the Lenox town line is this sparkling white Georgian Colonial with a pillared porte cochere. It was built by a New York surgeon in the 1920s as a weekend retreat and now is one of the area's more inviting B&Bs.

Applegate is set nicely back from the road on six tranquil acres bearing venerable apple trees, towering pines, flower gardens and a beckoning swimming pool. Inside are elegant common rooms, six guest rooms and an effervescent welcome by Gloria and Len Friedman, she a retired educator and psychotherapist and he a retired computer executive. The Friedmans purchased Applegate in 1999, moving from their home in New York City.

Off a lovely entry foyer are a fireplaced dining room, where three tables are each set for breakfast for four, and a large living room equipped with a grand piano. To the side of the living room is a sun porch, newly enclosed for use as a reading and TV room. Off the dining room is a screened back porch facing the pool and gardens.

A carved staircase leads to the four main guest rooms. The master suite has a kingsize poster bed, family photos on the mantel above the working fireplace, a sitting area with a sofabed and two chairs, and a great steam shower. The other rooms are slightly less grand in scale, holding queensize beds. One has Shaker-style pine furniture, another a walnut sleigh bed and a third an antique white iron bed and white and blue wicker furnishings. Two newer rooms are situated in a far wing of the house. One is a sunny corner space swathed in pale lavenders and greens with a tiger-maple four-poster, a sitting area and the best view of the grounds. The other is a smaller room done up in Victorian style with an antique bed.

The premier accommodations are now four luxury rooms, each with kingsize bed, fireplace, double whirlpool tub or soaking tub, wet bar, sofa and TV/VCR. Two of these with private balconies are on the third floor of the main building and two with private patios are located on the ground floor of the former garage and carriage house. The carriage house also had a second-floor apartment for the chauffeur. It has been converted lately into a cottage apartment with two queensize bedrooms, living room with TV/VCR, kitchen facilities and bath with whirlpool tub.

Chocolates and decanters of brandy are in each room. The Friedmans offer wine and cheese around 5 p.m. The continental-plus breakfast, including cereal and yogurt, is served amid stemware and Wedgwood china.

(413) 243-4451 or (800) 691-9012. Fax (413) 243-9832. www.applegateinn.com. Ten rooms and a two-bedroom cottage with private baths. June-October: doubles, $160 to $310 weekends, $125 to $260 midweek. Rest of year: $110 to $245 weekends, $95 to $220 midweek. Three-night minimum summer and holiday weekends, two-night weekend minimum in June, September and October. Children over 12.

The Rookwood Inn, 11 Old Stockbridge Road, Lenox 01240.

This majestic Victorian in the heart of Lenox is a favorite of families and people seeking heart-healthy food. Amy Lindner-Lesser, assisted by her two teen-aged daughters, continued the theme following the untimely death of her husband Stephen in 1999. Avid travelers and partial to antiques and old houses, the couple had been working toward buying and operating their own inn since their first B&B experience in 1981 in Cape May, N.J. Steve quit his job to enroll in The Restaurant School in Philadelphia, graduated first in his class and moved his family to Lenox to the former Quincy Lodge, a onetime tavern that had been Victorianized.

The Rookwood is a frilly, large and rambling house with the requisite gables and turrets in front and back. Recently repainted, it's a true "painted lady" in three shades of mauve with khaki and plum accents.

The twenty guest rooms vary, and two on the third floor have been enlarged. All have telephones and baths with luxurious robes, plush towels and hair dryers. Some have fireplaces, clawfoot tubs and poster or canopy beds. Fancy wallpapers and bed covers or quilts are the norm. There's plenty of space for guests to spread out in fireplaced common rooms or on the wicker-furnished front veranda.

Guests gather for breakfast at six tables in the side dining room. Amy employs many of Steve's recipes, which she was getting together to complete his planned Rookwood cookbook. "Low fat and high taste is our priority," she says. That translated the weekend of our visit to broiled grapefruit and challah french toast with blueberries one day, and granola-yogurt parfait and a spinach-roasted red pepper strata the next. Baked apples and blintz soufflé were on tap the following day.

(413) 637-9750 or (800) 223-9750. Fax (413) 637-1352. www.rookwoodinn.com. Twenty rooms with private baths. Late June to Labor Day: doubles, $180 to $375 weekends, $140 to $300 midweek. June and September-October: $140 to $350 weekends, $115 to $275 midweek. Rest of year: $125 to $250 weekends, $100 to $225 midweek. Three-night minimum summer weekends, two-night minimum other weekends. Children welcome.

Dining Spots

Wheatleigh, Hawthorne Road, Lenox.

Like the European country-house hotels with which it has been likened, the pride of Wheatleigh is its renowned main-floor restaurant – long a destination for gourmands.

It includes a handsome chandeliered dining room and a large and glamorous, truly cool glass-enclosed portico, pristine in white and with floor-to-ceiling windows on three sides. Their round tables are set with white linens, service plates in three patterns, delicate wine glasses, flickering oil lamps and vases of fresh flowers.

Off the dining room is the intimate Library lounge, a sleek misnomer (shelves of china rather than books) that offers a lighter menu for lunch and supper and is favored by regulars who don't care to eat grandly every night.

Executive chef J. Bryce Whittlesey heads a kitchen brigade of fifteen that prepares three prix-fixe tasting menus each evening – three-course regular and four-course vegetarian (both $88) and six-course fish menu ($115).

Wheatleigh's kitchen uses exotic ingredients and is said to be labor-intensive. You know why when you see the night's regular offerings. You might start as we did with the golden ossetra caviar and oyster "progression," the first of several that evening and yielding three choice oysters in various dress. Other starters, these from the fish tasting menu, were truly exceptional bay scallops served with apple

Wheatleigh dining portico overlooks grounds.

relish and blood orange vinaigrette in large scallop shells and Maine sea urchins with Dungeness crab salad and pearl tapioca froth. Next came a whole roasted lobster with cardamom and star anise butter, followed by line-caught dover sole roasted on the bone and served with sautéed chicken oysters and poultry jus. Our other main course from the regular menu was described simply as "local young lamb with variation on butternut squash." That turned out to be two simultaneous "progressions" – lamb shoulder, confit and rack, each of the three with a different version of squash, about the only vegetables we saw all evening.

Desserts were an ethereal lemon soufflé with lemoncillo sauce and apple tart normande, two small apple custard tarts flanking crème fraîche and calvados-cider sorbet.

(413) 637-0610. www.wheatleigh.com. Prix-fixe, $88 and $115. Dinner nightly by reservation, 6 to 8:30; closed Monday-Wednesday in winter. Library, lunch daily in season, noon to 2; dinner, 5 to 9:30. Sunday brunch, 9:30 to 1.

Church Street Café, 65 Church St., Lenox.

This is the casual, creative kind of place of which we never tire, the one we keep returning to for a quick but interesting meal whenever we're in Lenox.

Owners Linda Forman and Clayton Hambrick have furnished three small dining rooms and an outdoor deck simply but tastefully. On one visit we admired all the amusing paintings of zebras on the walls, part of the changing art exhibits and all for sale. We also liked the bar stools painted like black and white cows, udders hanging below, as well as the ficus trees lit with tiny white lights, the white pottery with colorful pink and blue flowers, the artworks lit by track lights in the gallery room, the flute music playing in the background, and the jaunty outside dining deck.

Once Ethel Kennedy's chef, Clayton also worked in a creole restaurant in Washington and that background shows. Blackened redfish might be a dinner special. Louisiana shrimp and andouille filé gumbo is apt to be a dinner appetizer and a luncheon entrée. Lately, the fare has acquired some Asian accents, as in an appetizer of tuna taki with sesame-soy dressing or a main dish of grilled lemongrass chicken with nuoc clam sauce. These join such traditional favorites as sautéed Maine crab cakes with dilled tartar sauce and grilled lamb loin with red wine sauce.

Our latest lunch included a super black bean tostada with three salsas and the Church Street salad, a colorful array of goat cheese, chick peas, sprouts, eggs and red pepper, with a zippy dijon vinaigrette dressing on the side and whole wheat sunflower seed rolls, so good that we accepted seconds.

Among desserts, the chilled cranberry soufflé topped with whipped cream, the apple walnut crisp and the chocolate macadamia nut torte are superior.

(413) 637-2745. www.churchstreetcafe.biz. Entrées, $22.50 to $29.50. Lunch, Monday-Saturday 11 to 2. Dinner nightly, 5:30 to 9. Sunday brunch in summer and fall. Closed Sunday and Monday in off-season.

Spigalina, 80 Main St., Lenox.

After serving as garde-mange at Wheatleigh, Culinary Institute of America grad Lina Aliberti opened her own restaurant in a small house in the center of Lenox. The main floor was transformed into a Mediterranean-style bistro and bar focusing on a large center fireplace with a Count Rumford oven. Forty-two diners can be seated at well-spaced tables inside, with an equal number on the front. The tables are covered with cloths portraying colorful blue and yellow provençal-style plates.

The restaurant is a play on the chef's name (she originally called it Semolina, but had to drop it for trademark purposes). The new name means wheat stalk in Italian and Spanish.

The innovative menu is Mediterranean in spirit: entrées perhaps of grilled salmon niçoise, free-range chicken marinated in Moroccan preserved lemon and herbs, and grilled veal loin chop with polenta. Expect such starters as seafood paella salad, wild mushroom baklava, mixed grill kabob over couscous salad and crispy kataifi-wrapped goat cheese on field greens.

Desserts vary from a frozen coffee and amaretto parfait with chocolate ganache glaze to a duo of coffee and caramel pots de crème. The desserts are prepared by the Swiss baker and maitre d'hotel, Serge Pacaud, whom Lina recently married.

(413) 637-4455. www.spigalina.com . Dinner nightly, 5 to 9, Thursday-Monday in off-season. Closed mid-February through March.

Bistro Zinc, 56 Church St., Lenox.

French authenticity and nuances are everywhere evident in this newish bistro and bar opened by young Lenox native Jason Macioge in partnership with Charles Schultz. The gracefully curving bar in the rear cocktail lounge is topped with polished zinc, the restroom doors are made of lettered wood wine crates and the tables in the mirrored front dining room are as close together as any in Paris.

The menu is so authentic as to appear a bit ho-hum, as real French bistro menus tend to be. The food, though rather minimal in portion, is not at all ho-hum. We lunched in the bar on a superb French onion soup gruyère, a salad of goat cheese, arugula and roasted tomato, and a special entrée of cumin-crusted lamb, fanned around couscous that never before tasted so delectable. A not-so-classic tarte tatin was nonetheless delicious, paired with vanilla ice cream drizzled with caramel sauce. The bill was presented in a Zinc folder with a postcard.

The abbreviated menu sampled at lunch is similar but much expanded at night. Expect appetizers like mussels marinière, Vietnamese vegetable spring roll, crispy grilled quail stuffed with prosciutto and salads, perhaps one of frisée with pancetta and a poached egg. Typical entrées are leek-crusted halibut with lemon beurre blanc, bacon-wrapped pork loin with balsamic glaze, wood-roasted organic chicken with tarragon jus, steak frites and steak au poivre. Desserts at our visit were vanilla crème brûlée, profiteroles with mocha ice cream, something called "birthday cake" and a platter of petits fours, lemon tart and cookies.

The all-French wine list is priced in the twenties (a house carafe goes for $18), although there's a large selection from the reserve cellar. The bar book touts American single-barrel bourbons and single-malt scotches from Scotland.

(413) 637-8800. Entrées, $21 to $28. Lunch, Wednesday-Monday 11:30 to 3. Dinner, Wednesday-Monday 5:30 to 10.

Blantyre, 16 Blantyre Road, Lenox.

An English country-house hotel setting is the backdrop for the contemporary cuisine offered by British-born executive chef Christopher Brooks. The dining experience starts with champagne and canapés in the baronial living room or on the terrace, where orders are taken before diners adjourn to the formal dining room or two smaller rooms. The tables are set with different themes, the linens, china and crystal changing daily as the Fitzpatrick family adds to the collection.

A typical dinner starts with a "surprise," perhaps foie gras or veal sweetbreads with sauternes and carrot sauce. Just a couple of bites to whet the appetite for what's to come – maybe seared scallops and a trio of roasted parsnips with a truffle dressing, loin of rabbit with a carrot-ginger puree and watercress salad, or seared foie gras with caramelized pickled pears and toasted brioche. Main courses could include arctic char with a crab cake and red wine-thyme sauce, pan-roasted pheasant breast with foie gras-chestnut jus, and roasted loin of antelope with sage gnocchi, braised rutabaga, stuffed cabbage leaves and huckleberry sauce.

For dessert, how about bitter Swiss chocolate cake with sour orange compote and blackberry sorbet, white chocolate mousse and plum roulade with ginger-lime sauce, or lemon meringue tart with blueberry compote and passion-fruit coulis?

Most guests take coffee and cordials in the Music Room, where a harpist and pianist play on weekends.

(413) 637-3556. www.blantyre.com. Prix-fixe, $80. Lunch in July and August, Tuesday-Sunday 12:30 to 1:45. Dinner by reservation, nightly in summer and foliage season, 6 to 8:45; otherwise, Tuesday-Sunday. Jackets and ties required. Closed early November to early May.

Café Lucia, 90 Church St., Lenox.

Jim Lucie transformed an art gallery cum cafe into an expanded cafe with art as a sideline. "We're a restaurant that shows and sells art," explains Jim, who opened up the kitchen so patrons can glimpse the goings-on.

Jim's Italian cuisine is favored by locals, who praise his pasta creations, baked polenta with homemade sausage and Italian codfish stew. The osso buco with diced vegetables and risotto is so good that it draws New Yorkers back annually, and Jim reports he almost had a riot on his hands when he took the linguini and shrimp alla medici off the menu (it was promptly restored, even though he had offered it on specials). Lamb stew served over white Tuscan beans with celery, carrots, shallots and escarole appealed at one visit. Another time we were tempted by the grilled tuna niçoise.

Start with carpaccio with arugula and shaved reggiano or a ragu of rabbit and wild mushrooms over soft polenta. End with a fruit tart, flourless chocolate torte or one of the gelatos. Those desserts, a fine port or brandy and cappuccino can be taken on a spacious awning-covered deck or at tables spilling onto a gravel patio and lawn on summer evenings.

(413) 637-2640. Entrées, $20 to $30. Dinner nightly in summer, from 5:30. Closed Sunday and Monday in winter.

Firefly, 71 Church St., Lenox.

Chef Laura Shack, a former New York caterer and student of James Beard, converted her former Roseborough Grill in 2003 into a fusion restaurant and tapas bar in 2003. She dropped her former lunch service to concentrate on dinner and a lively bar, drawing a receptive crowd of late-night diners.

There's seating for a total of 140 in the bar-lounge, in two dining rooms and outside on porches. The former antiquey, country-style theme has given way to an urbane decor with a fiery yellow and red motif.

"Eat, Drink, Laugh," urges her new menu. It features entrées ranging from miso-grilled salmon with fennel salad to Asian barbecued ribs with wasabi mashed potatoes and braised baby bok choy. Typical appetizers are tempura ahi nori rolls, mussels steeped in local hard cider and a quesadilla of Moroccan lamb, Merguez sausage and manchego cheese.

(413) 637-2700. Entrées, $18 to $27. Dinner nightly, 5 to 10. Tapas, Friday and Saturday to 11. Bar open to 1.

Dish, 37 Church St., Lenox.

Shortly after opening in September 2003, this tiny place was recommended by several locals for its breakfast and lunch. It turned out, however, that chef Nicholas Caplan had his sights on a higher calling: bistro dinners.

Taking over the old Church Street Deli, Nick and his wife Devon spruced up the 25 seats, put cloths and candles on the table and applied for a beer and wine license. Nick, who cooked for seventeen years in San Francisco and Boston, was a partner in Once Upon a Table in Stockbridge before opening his own place.

Egg and tofu plates are featured at breakfast in the $5.50 to $6.50 range. Creative salads and sandwiches in the $7 range are offered at lunch. The short dinner menu ranges from grilled mahi mahi to braised lamb shanks.

(413) 637-1800. Entrées, $13 to $18. Breakfast, lunch and dinner daily in season. Open year-round.

Diversions

Tanglewood, West Street, Lenox.

The name is synonymous with music and Lenox. The summer home of the Boston Symphony Orchestra since 1936, the 210-acre estate above the waters of Stockbridge Bowl in the distance is an idyllic spot for concerts and socializing at picnics. The 6,000 seats in the open-air Shed are reserved far in advance for Friday and Saturday evening and Sunday afternoon concerts. Up to 10,000 fans can be accommodated at $14 to $18 each on the lawn (bring your own chairs, blankets, picnics and wine, or pick something up from the cafeteria). Free open rehearsals for the Sunday concerts are scheduled Saturday mornings at 10:30. The acoustically spectacular Seiji Ozawa Hall seats 1,200 inside and another 200 on sloping lawns so situated that you can see right onto the stage. It's used for chamber music concerts and student recitals most weeknights in summer and for community events in spring and fall.

(413) 637-1940 or (800) 274-8499. Concerts, Friday and Saturday at 8:30, Sunday at 2:30, last weekend of June through August. Tickets, $14 to $90.

Frelinghuysen Morris House & Studio, 92 Hawthorne St., Lenox.

Set back down a ten-minute walk on 46 acres next to Tanglewood is this relatively new cultural prize. It was the summer home of opera singer Suzy Frelinghuysen and painter George L.K. Morris, both key members of the American Abstract Artists Group, who championed Cubism long after it went out of style. Morris designed the striking, Bauhaus-inspired structure. Preserved as it was in the early 1940s, the tiered white house harbors paintings, murals and sculptures by Picasso, Braque, Léger and Gris as well as the late owners' own works and those of American Cubist friends. Guides lead hourly tours to help immerse the visitor into the artists' pre-World War II world, when championing abstract art was highly controversial. Walking trails in the woodlands surrounding the house museum lead past a monumental sculpture, "The Mountain," a reclining woman on a raised platform that Morris commissioned from his friend Gaston Lachaise.

(413) 637-0166. www.frelinghuysen.org. Hourly tours Thursday-Sunday 10 to 4, July 4 to Labor Day, Thursday-Saturday through October. Adults, $9.

Ventford Hall/Museum of the Gilded Age, 104 Walker St., Lenox.

A new museum is emerging in Ventfort Hall, the imposing Elizabethan-style mansion built in 1893 for Sarah Morgan, the sister of J.P. Morgan. Partially restored and open for tours, it is reflective of the 75 so-called "Berkshire Cottages" built in Lenox around the turn of the last century when the village became a Gilded Age resort. Through lectures, exhibits, theatrical performances and special events, the museum interprets the great changes that occurred in American life, industry and society during the late Nineteenth Century.

(413) 637-3206. www.gildedage.org. Guided tours daily on the hour from 10 to 2, Memorial Day through October. Adults, $8.

Pleasant Valley Wildlife Sanctuary, 472 West Mouintain Road, Lenox. The Massachusetts Audubon Society maintains a 1,500-acre nature preserve high up Lenox Mountain next to Yokum Brook. A museum of live and stuffed animals and seven miles of nature trails through forests, meadows and marshes are a pleasant refuge for a few hours. Open daily, July-October, Tuesday-Sunday rest of year. except Monday year-round.

Close by, the town-owned **John Drummond Kennedy Park** offers nearly fifteen miles of old carriage roads and groomed trails for hiking and cross-country skiing.

The restored 1902 Lenox station, a National Register landmark east of town, is the home of the **Berkshire Scenic Railway Museum,** 10 Willow Creek Road. Besides model railroads and antique rail equipment, it offers a permanent exhibit, "Gateway to the Gilded Age," featuring the Berkshire Cottages. In 2003, it also started twenty-mile round trip rail excursions in 1920s vintage coaches along the Housatonic River from Lenox to Stockbridge, weekends Memorial Day through October; adults, $12.

Shopping. Lenox offers some of the most exclusive shops in the Berkshires. Along Church Street, Italian ceramics and other contemporary art is featured at **Cose D'Argilla,** one of the many new galleries popping up in town. **Mary Stuart Collections** has wonderful needlework, potpourris and fragrances, children's clothes fit for royalty, heavenly lingerie and fine glass, china and antiques. Neat casual, natural-fiber clothes are at **Glad Rags,** children's clothing and accessories at **Gifted Child,** and fine American crafts, jewelry and wearable art at the **Hoadley Gallery. Weaver's Fancy** displays lovely weavings, from placemats to pillows to coats. Huge crinkled glass sculptures caught our eye at the **Wit Gallery**, as did the colorful metal art and ceramics at **Hotchkiss Mobiles Gallery.**

On Walker Street you'll find **Talbots** for classic clothes and **Evviva!** for contemporary by designers with a background in the arts. **Tanglewool** sells English cashmeres and other hand knits, Italian bags, Arche shoes from France, creative jewelry, and imported yarns and knitting patterns; everything here has flair. The works of more than 400 artisans are shown at the **Hand of Man** crafts gallery.

For an ice cream fix, head to **Bev's Homemade Ice Cream,** 38 Housatonic St., where Beverly Mazursky and sons make all the wonderful flavors in two machines behind the counter. They're known for their raspberry-chocolate chip, served in a sugar cone. You can order gelatos, frappes, smoothies, sherbet coolers and even a banana split, as well as espresso and their ever-popular Jamaican patties (different kinds of Caribbean breads with such fillings as beef, mixed veggies and broccoli-cheese).

Next door at 26 Housatonic is **Betty's Pizza Shack,** the third effort of young restaurateur Jason Macioge (of Bistro Zinc and Pearl's in Great Barrington). A potted palm tree at the entry sets the stage for a "shack" like you thought you'd never see: A riot of blues, reds, purples and orange. Walls and ceiling of corrugated silver. A decor of surfboard and sharks and different colored lights. A curving counter with seats of cushion-topped garbage cans. Oh, yes. The food is a hip collection of pizzas, salads, "samiches" and "bevvies" for the hip young crowd that frequents the place.

The lately reinvented Lenox Shops north of town along Route 7 is home to several new shops and **Chocolate Springs,** a chocolate and pastry café. Chef-owner Joshua Needleman returned to his home area after training at pastry boutiques in New York and Paris. Here he produces exotic chocolates and delectable dessert pastries, served with coffee or tea in a sleek retail showroom and salon-style dining area. One taste of his champagne-cognac bonbon and we were hooked.

Extra-Special

The Mount Estate & Gardens, 2 Plunkett St., Lenox.

Like Jefferson's Monticello, novelist Edith Wharton's Mount is an "autobiographical house." It was designed by its owner – a Renaissance woman whose graces in the art of living made her the Martha Stewart of her day – as a compelling reflection of her storied life and work. Restored to the tune of $9 million so far, one of the icons of American architecture is on display as never before. For its centennial in 2002, seven top designers furnished the stunning public rooms "in the style of Edith Wharton," as if she were their client today. In 2003, the bedroom suite – the private sanctum where the first woman to win the Pulitzer Prize for literature wrote each morning – was opened to public view. She designed and built the 42-room Georgian Revival mansion based on the principles outlined in her best-selling 1897 book *The Decoration of Houses,* which is still in print today. The 50-acre estate combines English, French and Italian elements in a classic New England setting above Laurel Lake. It includes three acres of formal gardens in the Italian style, a stable, a bookstore and the Terrace Café, which is open seasonally for light lunch and refreshments on the same terrace where Wharton entertained the likes of Henry James and the Vanderbilts. "It is an exquisite and marvelous place," James wrote, a precursor to what visitors find today.

(413) 637-1899. www.edithwharton.org. Open May-October, daily 9 to 5. Adults, $16.

Two churches and Dunbar House lie beyond Shawme Pond in center of Sandwich.

Sandwich, Mass.

Cape Cod's First Town

If you've never detoured off the highway on your way out Cape Cod, it's time you did.

Hidden off main Route 6 and even out of reach of meandering Route 6A is a little enclave – very different from the prevailing norm – representing Cape Cod's oldest town and a different way of life.

Established in 1638 by settlers from the Plymouth colony, the center of Sandwich is a quiet village untouched by creeping commercialism. "People bypass us on the way out to Hyannis or Provincetown," said the docent at the Sandwich Glass Museum. "They don't realize the treasures they are missing."

The Old Boston & Sandwich Glass Co., founded in 1825, grew to be the largest industry on the Cape for half of the 19th century. It transformed a rural farm town into a thriving mill center known worldwide for blown and pressed glass. But the glass company's fortunes faded in the late 1800s, and with it ended the growth of Sandwich. It's now a museum center and, actually, a living museum.

Sandwich's museums and its aura of history attract knowing visitors who like to combine their beach expeditions with a dose of culture. As the first town on the Cape – in terms of geography as well as history – Sandwich also attracts daytrippers, weekenders and people who prefer the personality of B&Bs to the anonymity of chain motels.

The renowned Dan'l Webster Inn dates to 1692, but only lately has really come of age. Also relative latecomers are a cluster of smaller inns and B&Bs in historic structures in the heart of the village. The structures were there, but the B&Bs emerged only in the last decade or so as Sandwich quietly became a destination.

From any inn it's a leisurely stroll through the village center around Town Hall Square along Water Street and Main Street and onto Jarves Street. You'll pass the Town Hall, the library, the Christopher Wren-inspired spire of the First Church of Christ, three museums, an English tearoom, a working gristmill and an artesian well. You'll likely see swans and ducks paddling on Shawme Pond, which glistens beside the Thornton W. Burgess Museum and, beyond, one of Cape Cod's oldest houses. Dozens more houses, part of a National Register historic district, catch the eye.

Spend a few hours at Heritage Museums & Gardens, famed for showy rhododendrons among its 100 acres of gardens. It also houses a military museum, an art museum and a renowned collection of antique and classic cars.

Cross the picturesque salt marshes on the citizen-built Sandwich boardwalk to view Cape Cod Bay from the sand dunes. Bicycle along the Cape Cod Canal and the scenic Old King's Highway (Route 6A).

You may decide to save Hyannis and Provincetown for another time.

Inn Spots

The Dan'l Webster Inn, 149 Main St., Sandwich 02563.

This village inn likens itself to a boutique hotel and looks and feels far newer than its heritage dating to 1692. That's because the old parsonage-turned-Fessenden Tavern, a Patriot headquarters during the Revolution, and subsequent inn was destroyed by fire in 1971. It was rebuilt to look old. The Daniel Webster connection results from the lengthy stays of the famous orator here and the personal legacies found in some of its rooms.

The Catania family – restaurateur Vincent of the regional Hearth 'n Kettle chain and his five sons and a daughter – purchased the establishment in 1980 and began turning it into a small hotel. They retained the old Jarves Wing, where traditional rooms come with poster beds, TVs enclosed in armoires, pleasant sitting areas and all the inn's considerable amenities, from hair dryers to nightly turndown service. They built the Fessenden Wing, with deluxe rooms including a corner room with side balcony, queen canopy bed, a sofa and a wing chair. They purchased and gutted the Fessenden House in front, turning its apartments into four deluxe suites with fireplaces and jacuzzi tubs. They created a luxury penthouse suite in the main inn with a canopy king bed, skylit jacuzzi encased in Italian marble and a handsome living room. They turned the 1832 Quince Tree House down the street into five more suites with jacuzzis and fireplaces. One even has a grand piano in the living room. Lately, they added a second floor to the Jarves Wing and produced eight sumptuous rooms with kingsize canopy or poster beds, gas fireplaces, private balconies overlooking manicured gardens and luxurious baths with two-person showers. In a corner of each room is a two-person jacuzzi enclosed in columns and surrounded by a heated tile floor. The Catanias liken them to Roman baths.

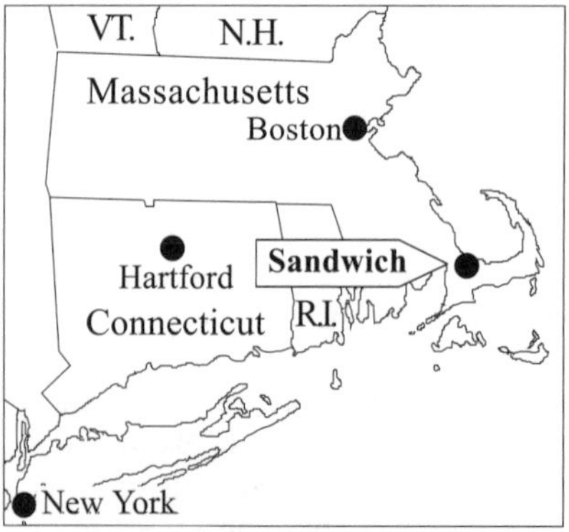

Our quarters in the Fessenden House's Ezra Nye suite, named for the

Quince Tree suite is ready for guests at The Dan'l Webster Inn.

Sandwich sea captain who built the house in 1826 for his bride, were most comfortable. The sizable living room with a marble fireplace had a plush sofa, coffee table, two wing chairs, a writing desk and a low reproduction chest that opened to reveal a TV. The bedroom contained a step-up queen canopy bed. The bathroom had a jacuzzi tub and another sink in the dressing area, which had a substantial vanity containing aloe shampoos and toiletries, a Saks Fifth Avenue soap, a handy little sewing kit and a leather bucket filled with ice.

The inn operates a well-regarded restaurant and tavern (see Dining Spots) at the rear of the main building, plus a gift shop where some of the stock appeals to doting grandmothers. There's a "gathering room" for reading or card playing off the lobby. In season, a pool, almost hidden by flowers and shrubs, beckons in the rear gardens beside a gazebo and the salt marsh. The flowers and seasonal displays in front of the inn's porte-cochere attest to the caring touches offered by the Catania family and their staff.

(508) 888-3622 or (800) 444-3566. Fax (508) 833-3220. www.danlwebsterinn.com. Forty-five rooms and nine suites with private baths. Memorial Day to mid-October: doubles, $169 to $379. Rest of year: $109 to $319. Two-night minimum weekends.

The Belfry Inne & Bistro, 8 Jarves St., Sandwich. 02563.

Stylish – some would say rather novel – accommodations and a well-regarded restaurant and bar (see Dining Spots) are the hallmarks of this ever-expanding inn. It began in a former rectory and soon took over the old Catholic church next door, where the decorator's imagination ran wild. In 2003 it acquired the adjacent Village Inn and a former Congregational meetinghouse for more accommodations.

Local banker Christopher Wilson started with nine rooms in the 1879 residence of a prosperous clothing merchant named Drew. Each is spiffily decorated and enhanced by good art, some of it done by Christopher's mother, an artist in Jaffrey, N.H.

Ingenious decorative touches such as an arch above a jacuzzi, Laura Ashley accents and whimsical colors are employed throughout.

There's a clawfoot soaking tub near the queensize hand-turned walnut spool bed in the front Martha Southworth Room, with a shower in the bathroom for those who prefer. An English griffin-footed brass soaking tub occupies a raised platform by a window in the front queensize George Drew Room, which also has a separate shower as well as a gas fireplace. The premier John Drew Room with mahogany queen poster bed has a double jacuzzi tub in the bathroom and a gas fireplace in the sitting area. On the third floor, the skylit Sara Drew Room with kingsize antique iron bed and corner fireplace is delightful in mint green and white, while the companion Ida Drew Room with kingsize spool bed and double skylights is stunning in black and white with an English rose trellis theme. Hand-painted murals of Alice in Wonderland characters brighten the hallway and stairs leading to the belfry tower. Here three pillowed seats face more wonderland scenes, a view across the treetops (the bay is on view after the leaves fall) and a handwritten poem from the book on the ceiling, "...up above the world you fly, like a tea tray in the sky."

None of this truly prepares the guest, however, for the six rooms upstairs in the former church, now called the Abbey. Named for a day of the week to represent God's creation from the Book of Genesis, each has a vaulted ceiling with skylights, gas fireplace, Ultra massage whirlpool tub for two, television and balcony.

Enter Tuesday, see the queen bed with the back of a pew for a headboard against a showy compass window of stained glass and you'll think you'll be sleeping beneath an altar. Clad in woven Belgian blue and gold tapestry, the bed faces an enormous recessed fireplace and the outdoor balcony is walled four feet high so you can't see out if you're seated – the better to feel penitent? Enter Saturday and find deep purple striped walls, a kingsize pew bed dressed in blue tapestry and a stained-glass window of Michael the Archangel. The jacuzzi is in the bedroom, and the shower in the bathroom.

Five simpler rooms and a two-bedroom suite came on line in 2003 when the Belfry acquired the old Village Inn, an 1860 Federal-style building. It came with a separate building that housed the Sandwich Artworks studio, used for painting workshops. Chris planned to expand the art enterprise in his new First Church Meetinghouse.

Four more rooms and a bridal suite – spacious affairs with fireplaces and whirlpool tubs in the Abbey style – were due to open in the Meetinghouse in spring 2004. Chris designed them for longer stays and added a conference and gallery area, music room, dining room and chef's kitchen, plus a spiral staircase from the old choir loft to the bell tower for "a pretty dramatic view."

Meanwhile, back at the inn – the main inn that started it all – a swimming pool with cabana was added in the courtyard area between the Drew House and Abbey.

Inn guests relax around the pool, in the belfry tower, a Victorian sitting room and bar in the Drew House or a dining room recently turned into something of a café for desserts, tea and wine.

Breakfast begins with a buffet of fruit, cereal and pastries. The main course could be individual omelets, tarragon eggs with diced ham and béarnaise sauce, asparagus-mushroom quiche or peach french toast. You'll leave well-fed, much-indulged and, perchance, uplifted.

(508) 888-8550 or (800) 844-4542. Fax (508) 888-3922. www.belfryinn.com. Sixteen rooms with private baths. June to mid-October: doubles, $135 to $215. Rest of year: $110 to $165. Meetinghouse, doubles $350. Two-night minimum weekends.

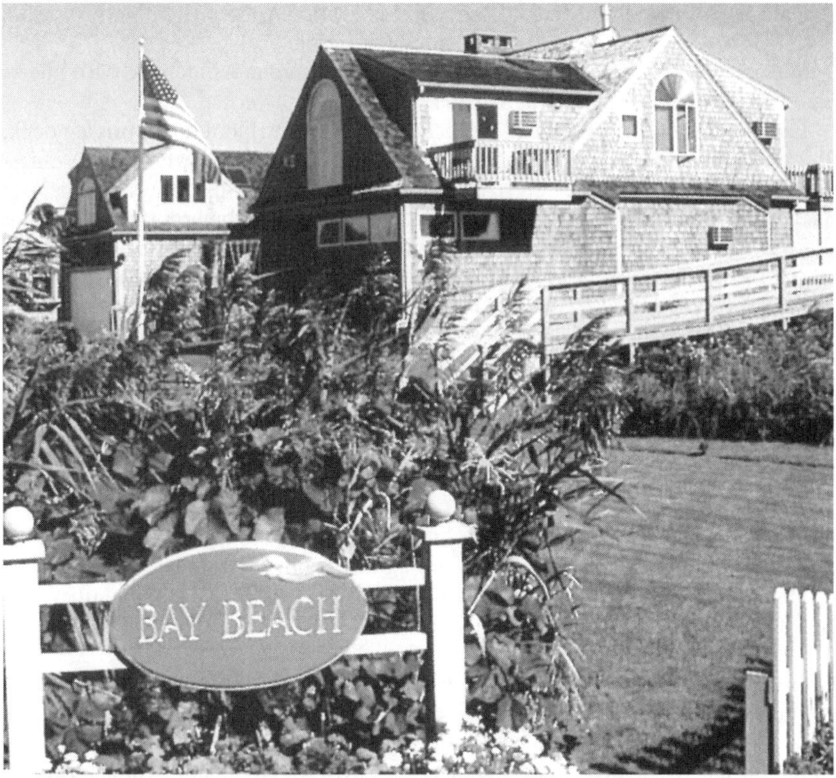

Bay Beach offers guest rooms with decks and views of Cape Cod Bay.

Bay Beach, 3 Bay Beach Lane, Box 151, Sandwich 02563.

If you love the luminous light of the Cape as we do, you'll love Bay Beach, which has an abundance of it. Facing Cape Cod Bay, almost beside the wide-open marshes over which the Sandwich boardwalk is built and with colorful gardens in front, this is a perfect place for those who crave an oceanfront location with all the comforts of home – and then some.

Real and Emily Lemieux sold their nearby motel in 1988, built a glamorous home on the beach, bought the land next door, erected a B&B addition and added suites in their home as their children vacated.

The result: several of the most amenity-laden accommodations and one of the top locations on Cape Cod. Yet this showy but low-profile B&B remains relatively unknown among its peers in Sandwich.

"We're a well-kept secret," Real said as he led a tour. Even so, they have been happily filled ever since they were awarded an AAA four-diamond rating.

Arrangements of flowers from the gardens abound. On the main floor, huge windows frame a view of the ocean and marshes in the large California contemporary style living-dining area, off which is a spacious deck. From here you can see the entrance to the Cape Cod Canal and, on a clear day, Provincetown. The raised hearth fireplace is welcome on stormy days. From the modern open kitchen come lemonade or cider and cookies in the afternoon (fancy teas on cooler days). Breakfast is put out buffet style from 8 to 10:30, and guests may take it on trays to their rooms, private decks or common decks, or socialize in the dining area. There's always a hot dish like belgian waffles, fruit crêpes or egg casserole.

Wine, cheese and crackers in their own mini-refrigerators are ready for guests upon arrival. Chocolates are at bedside.

Each bedroom comes with a king bed, fireplace, whirlpool tub, a private deck, thick carpeting, TV/VCR, private phone line and mostly rattan-type furnishings. One on the first floor has a kingsize bed dressed in florals and an enormous jacuzzi in the center of the room, plus a double shower in the skylit bathroom. Upstairs is a suite with a better view and a merely ordinary-size double jacuzzi.

(508) 888-8813 or (800) 475-6398. Fax (508) 888-5416. www.baybeach.com. Three rooms with private baths. Doubles, $245 to $345. Three-night minimum weekends, two-night minimum midweek. Children over 16. Closed November-April.

Isaiah Jones Homestead, 165 Main St., Sandwich 02563.

This 1849 Italianate B&B is elegantly furnished with prized antiques and oriental carpets in high Victorian style. It's been that way since it was launched in 1987 by Cathy Catania of the Dan'l Webster Inn family and maintained thus by subsequent owners.

Doug and Jan Klapper, corporate dropouts from Connecticut, maintained the tradition, although they added two new guest rooms in a rear carriage house overlooking gardens and a fish pond. Both rooms have whirlpool tubs and fireplaces and are decorated in what Doug calls light Victorian cottage style. The queen beds are triple-sheeted, as in the rest of the establishment.

The Deming Jarves Room in the front of the house is the largest of the five original guest rooms. Its Victorian half canopy queen bed facing out from the corner is part of an antique set with an armoire and matching cheval mirror. The floral draperies match the bedspread and pillows. There's a large bath with jacuzzi and separate shower.

Downstairs beneath the Jarves in what once was the parlor is the Dr. Jonathan Leonard Room, with fishnet canopy queen poster bed, two wing chairs and a massive armoire. Two side closets have been converted into a two-part bathroom. A jacuzzi tub and fireplace are features of the Lombard Jones Room, while the Samuel Beale Room offers a fireplace, step-up mahogany queen bed and an alcove sitting area. The rear Thomas Dexter Room comes with an Eastlake queen bed, an Eastlake dresser and two Victorian parlor chairs. Hatboxes and old christening dresses are among the decorative accents.

Beyond a small reception room is a long side parlor with a dining area at one end and a Victorian sitting area at the other. An enormous Victorian breakfront of carved mahogany is a focal point and showcases prized dining pieces.

The Klappers serve a full breakfast by candlelight. Eggs florentine and lattice yeast coffeecake were featured the day of our visit. Broccoli quiche, sausage and sticky buns were the fare the day before. Afternoon tea is available upon request.

(508) 888-9115 or (800) 526-1625. Fax (508) 888-9648. www.isaiahjones.com. Seven rooms with private baths. Late May through October: doubles, $125 to $165. Rest of year: $110 to $155. Two-night minimum in season and all weekends. Children over 12.

Capt. Ezra Nye House, 152 Main St., Sandwich 02563.

The most celebrated shipmaster Sandwich ever produced built this house because he felt his earlier residence – now the Fessenden House at the Dan'l Webster Inn –

Capt. Ezra Nye House was built in Federal style by famous shipmaster in 1829.

too confining after days at sea with the sky as his ceiling. A painting of his packet ship, The Independence, hangs over the fireplace in the parlor today.

Becky and Mike Hanson moved from Duxbury, Mass., in 2002 to become only the seventh owners of the Federal-style house built in 1829. The original B&B in Sandwich offers pleasant common rooms and six overnight accommodations.

Beyond the parlor, which has a sofa and not one but two Victorian-style settees, are a stenciled dining room and a small den with a TV.

The Hansons consider their grandest accommodation to be the Blue Room, upstairs in the front corner of the rambling house. It has a queensize carved mahogany four-poster bed and a loveseat beside the working fireplace. Decor in three other rooms with queensize canopy or poster beds varies from mahogany to wicker to country pine. The Calico Room is named for the calico cat on the pillow and the calico spread on the bed. At the rear of the second floor is the Peach Suite with a white wicker kingsize bed and an electric fireplace, plus a small room with a TV.

Out back on the ground level is the Lilac Suite, with a private entrance, a queen bed and a small sitting room with TV.

The dining room is the setting for a gourmet breakfast. Apple compote and baked blueberry pancakes with sausage were served the morning of our latest visit. Baked pear and crème brûlée french toast were planned the next day.

(508) 888-6142 or (800) 388-2278. Fax (508) 833-2897. www.captainezranyehouse.com. Four rooms and two suites with private baths. June-October: doubles $130 to $145, suites $155. Rest of year: doubles $105 to $125, suites $125. Two-night minimum in summer and weekends. Children over 10.

The Inn at Sandwich Center, 118 Tupper Road, Sandwich 02563.

Facing the village square, this beautifully restored 18th-century saltbox commands an expansive hillside across from the Sandwich Glass Museum. From the bedside chocolates to the coordinated sheets and fabric patterns to the matching terrycloth robes and herbal bath products in each room, owners Jan and Charlie Preus do things right.

The Lottie Chipman Room sets the stage. Decorated in mauve and porcelain white, it has a queensize bed with an antique lace coverlet. It is one of three guest rooms with working fireplaces. The Hallstead Room has an antique reproduction queen bed, sitting area and a view of the rose garden. The Robert Morse Room has a queen iron bed and opens onto a deck. From a display closet next to its fireplace you can see the bricks of the original chimney. Each of the other rooms bears interesting architectural and decorative nuances as well. The bathtub in one is beside a window overlooking Town Hall Square.

The heart of the house – literally – is the elegant keeping room with its original 1750 beehive oven and fireplace. The rest of the structure was built around it in 1829. The dining table was made of old wood by the "Barnstable Table Maker" and seats ten. Here, seasonal fruits and homemade muffins and breads get summer breakfasts off to a good start. The main course could be french toast or pancakes. Breakfast is continental in the off-season.

Antiques and artworks are shown to good advantage in the elegant front parlor, where guests relax with a glass of sherry or brandy beside the fireplace.

Hybrid tea roses, perennials and more than 700 bulbs brighten the gardens

(508) 888-6958 or (800) 249-6949. Fax (508) 888-2746. www.innatsandwich.com. Five rooms with private baths. May-October: doubles, $130 to $170. Rest of year: $110 to $150. Two-night minimum certain weekends. Children over 12.

Burbank's Windfall House, 108 Main St. (Route 130), Sandwich 02563.

An 1818 Colonial up against the street, this good-looking B&B is full of history. Innkeeper Ted Diggle, who acquired the house in 1998 to turn it into a B&B, keeps an album of photographs and postcards that detail its transition from inn to rooming house to private home.

The sense of history is palpable in the dining room, which contains the original beamed ceiling, wide-plank floor, beehive oven and a table for eight set with mismatched antique chairs and a parson's bench. More contemporary in feeling is the living room, its beams and wide-board flooring upstaged by the appurtenances of today: television, stereo, current magazines and such. A dutch door opens onto a small porch overlooking the yard and gardens.

The house has six guest rooms, one with an efficiency kitchenette tucked behind louver doors. Rooms have queen or double beds, and are furnished with antiques and period pieces. The upstairs Samuel Burbank master bedroom, named after the second owner of the house, has a step-up queensize cherry poster bed angled from the corner and a fireplace. A hand-stenciled rug on the floor leads to the bathroom. Across the hall, the two smallest rooms, each with a double bed, share a bath.

Only a strip of herb garden separates the front of the house from the roadway. It is here that Ted grows the many garnishes that accompany his breakfasts. He also lavishes attention on his wide side yard, a colorful retreat of plantings, statuary, a gazebo and a Japanese koi pond.

When not gardening, he becomes a short-order cook for breakfast by candlelight. Guests make their choices the night before from a varied menu starting with juices, fruits and pastries. The main-course options are eggs any style, create-your-own omelet and fruit-flavored pancakes. Tea is offered in the afternoon.

(508) 888-3650 or (877) 594-6325. Fax (508) 833-9819. www.windfallhouse.com. Four rooms with private baths and two with shared bath. Memorial Day through October: doubles, $85 to $135. Rest of year: $75 to $110.

Dining Spots

The Dan'l Webster Inn, 149 Main St., Sandwich.

Upwards of 350 dinners a night are served in the three dining rooms and tavern at this popular inn. The wonder is that they do it so successfully, offering excellent food, deftly served, with piano entertainment and an impressive wine list.

The Catania family's ownership of the Cape Cod-based Hearth 'n Kettle restaurant chain stood them in good stead for this adventure in fine dining. Rob Catania, the Culinary Institute-trained executive chef here, oversees the kitchen, markets his lobster chowder and founded the family's pioneering aquafarm in nearby Barnstable to raise striped bass and hydroponic produce. Brother Richard Catania put together the award-winning wine list that's notable for only nominal markup on select French vintages. The entire family was behind the $500,000 worth of 1997 renovations that enlarged the atmospheric tavern into a tavern dining room, and opened up the Music Room and adjacent Heritage Room.

The inn now can offer all things to all people, supplementing its traditional fine-dining fare with an extensive tavern menu featuring thin crust gourmet pizzas and offering a selection of main courses in half portions at lower prices.

Many of the dining areas were fairly crowded starting at 4:30 the weeknight we stopped in to make a reservation. Returning at 8:15, we found a glamorous crowd of inn guests and locals enjoying sophisticated fare in the stunning, high-ceilinged Conservatory that brings the outdoors in. The extensive menu is made for grazing, which is what we did. The daily sampler of the signature lobster chowder and two soups served with crostini (chicken-vegetable and an assertive roasted garlic with shrimp that was a standout) was more than enough for two to share. One of us noshed on the scallops casino appetizer and a huge salad of aquafarm greens with gorgonzola cheese, white raisins and pistachios. The other sampled a half entrée of lobster, shrimp and scallops with julienned vegetables over cappelletti from a choice of five. They represented about one-third of the menu that ranged from roasted horseradish-encrusted scrod to prime rib, veal oscar and rack of lamb with cabernet sauce. Kiwi sorbet was a refreshing ending to a satisfying meal.

The thin-crust pizzas are said to be great in the dark and atmospheric tavern, which offers a substantial menu and folk singing on weekends.

(508) 888-3623 or (800) 444-3566. Entrées, $16.95 to $28.95; light entrées, $11.95 to $16.95. Lunch and dinner daily, 11:30 to 9 or 10.

Aqua Grille, 14 Gallo Road, Sandwich.

The folks from the highly regarded Paddock Restaurant in Hyannis knew a good thing when they saw it. When the owner of the old Captain's Table retired, they snapped up the building overlooking the Sandwich Marina and the Cape Cod Canal. They gutted the structure to redo it in style and added some flair to the fare.

An inner dining room with a three-sided fireplace is surrounded by an enclosed, wraparound porch looking onto the marina and canal. An outdoor terrace is used for both specialty cocktails and dining.

Co-owner Gert Rausch, the German-born chef, adds global touches to predictable Cape Cod offerings. The menu ranges widely from fried seafood to pastas, but the best treats emanate from the wood grill. Look for items like a pecan-crusted pork chop served with a beer sauce and a pepper-mustard filet of beef sauced with

Dining is in church, and lodging there and in rectory at The Belfry.

cabernet wine. Nut-crusted halibut with a citrus beurre blanc, New Orleans-style crab cakes, and veal scaloppine with house-made German noodles and a wild mushroom ragoût are staples on the menu. Among specials the night of our visit, we were tempted by the Bock beer-marinated ribeye steak with creamy six-peppercorn and cognac sauce, the recipe for which was requested by Bon Appétit magazine.

Appetizers run the gamut from a trio of Southwestern dips served with blue corn tortilla chips to bay shrimp quesadillas stuffed with cilantro and goat cheese and served with ancho chile crème fraîche.

(508) 888-8889. www.aquagrille.com. Entrées, $14.95 to $19.95. Lunch daily, 11:30 to 2:30, Sunday from noon. Dinner nightly from 5. Closed November-March.

The Belfry Inne & Bistro, 8 Jarves St., Sandwich. 02563.

The main floor of the former Catholic church has been transformed into the inn's bistro and it's an awesome space. It's half open to the soaring curved ceiling, with tables draped and skirted in heavenly white. Guest rooms are ensconced on lofts on three sides.

The contemporary international fare is as elegant as the setting, enhanced lately by chef George Willette, fresh from the lofty Bay Tower restaurant in Boston. A recent autumn menu opened with appetizers like pastrami-cured salmon rolled in a celery root and potato cake with a honey-mustard vinaigrette, a jonah crab cake with tomato-chipotle mayo and smoked duck sausage ravioli with maple glaze.

Main courses ranged from pan-seared scallops and lobster with saffron sauce over creamy white truffle and vegetable risotto to bacon-wrapped veal tenderloin with sherry-mustard sauce. The halibut was crusted with hazelnuts and served in a brown butter pumpkin sauce. Roasted Vermont quails were stuffed with mushrooms, pecans and apricots and sauced with apricot brandy.

Apple pudding cake, crème brûlée and anjou pear strudel typify the changing selection of desserts. They are so highly regarded that some people stop in late in the evening for a sweet and a drink.

(508) 888-8550 or (800) 844-4542. Entrées, $21 to $29. Dinner, Tuesday-Saturday from 5. Closed three weeks in January.

Amari's Ristorante & Bar, 674 Route 6A, East Sandwich.

Contemporary Italian cuisine is the theme at this newcomer along the shore road.

The extensive menu offers wood-oven pizzas and pastas as well as a selection of entrées at affordable prices. The "Italian classics" (scampi piccata, marsala and bonserra) are available with a choice of fish, chicken or meat over pasta. From the grill come salmon with roasted garlic sauce, chicken Tuscany and grilled steak with red wine demi-glace.

Among appetizers, the Cal-Amari (fried squid, with or without a spicy cherry pepper sauce) is the house favorite. The best value is the antipasto misto, which changes daily. The Tuscan-style mussels and the twin crab cakes with a salad of baby spinach and mandarin oranges also are recommended. Big hitters go for the surf and turf caesar salad, embellished with shrimp and grilled steak.

(508) 375-0011. Entrées, $13.95 to $18.95. Lunch, Saturday and Sunday, noon to 4. Dinner nightly, 4 to 9 or 10.

The Dunbar Tea Shop, 1 Water St., Sandwich.

This charming shop – a haven for anglophiles – offers Cape Cod's only British tea room. It was opened in 1991 by a family from England, who sold to Paula and David Hegarty.

They maintained the tea room and outside tea garden, but added British beers and European wines. British treats are featured for lunch and afternoon tea ($9.75). Spicy pumpkin soup, crab tart, cheshire lamb crumble and blueberry sour cream cheesecake were blackboard specials at our visit. They supplement such standbys as crumpets, pâté, a smoked salmon platter, a stilton and fruit platter, Welsh tarts, shepherd's pie, ploughman's lunch and shortbread squares.

The tea shop in front is a trove of loose and bagged teas and tea-related accessories, from kettles to cozies. A book shop annex advertises British topics and first editions.

(508) 833-2485. www.dunbarteashop.com. Entrées, $6.75 to $10.95. Gift shop open daily, 10 to 5. Tea room, 8 to 6 in summer and fall, 11 to 4:30 in winter and spring.

Diversions

Sandwich Glass Museum, 129 Main St., Sandwich.

The transformation of Cape Cod's oldest town from small farming community into one of the world's leading manufacturers of glass objects is traced chronologically in this colorful museum operated by the Sandwich Historical Society. The Boston & Sandwich Glass Co. thrived here starting in 1825, its more than 500 employees refining the art of pressing glass in molds and creating exquisite blown pieces. Competition and lower prices took their toll, however, and a prolonged strike closed the factory permanently in 1888. The museum underwent a major makeover for 2003, yielding a multi-media theater that shows the story of glassmaking in Sandwich, a new furnace for glassblowing demonstrations and a contemporary glass gallery. More than 5,000 pieces of Sandwich glass are on permanent display in thirteen galleries, with occasional video areas for explanation. The pieces, from 800 cup plates to rare banquet lanterns and iridescent Trevaise art glass, are of particular interest to collectors. The Historical Society adds some idiosyncratic finds, including an old rocking cradle on wheels and a Quaker marriage certificate above a display of glass remnants. The remarkable map-like rendition of Cape Cod, made of Sandwich glass fragments, fascinates on the way out from the gift shop.

(508) 888-0251. www.sandwichglassmuseum.org. Open daily 9:30 to 5, April-December; Wednesday-Sunday 9:30 to 4, February and March. Closed in January. Adults, $3.75.

Heritage Museums & Gardens, 67 Grove St., Sandwich.

The incredible display of rhododendrons are the primary attraction for most at the former estate of Charles O. Dexter, but there's much more at this museum of Americana founded by the Lilly pharmaceutical family. Dexter's renowned rhodies – more than 125 varieties – are at their best in late May and early June. We were surprised to find some late-bloomers still a brilliant red in mid-October. The remains of the day lily, heather, herb and hosta gardens and the holly dell appealed around the 76 tranquil acres as well. Also impressive were the Lilly collections of firearms and hand-painted miniature soldiers, a working 1912 carousel (well visited by school groups) and wonderful folk art exhibits at the Art Museum. The collections of duck decoys and shore birds, the scrimshaw and Nantucket lightship baskets, the children's chocolate mug collection are stunning. So is the American flag fashioned from plastic objects found on local beaches. Some people spend hours ogling the 37 shiny antique and classic cars in the Shaker Round Barn, a perfect display space with two circular floors showing Gary Cooper's 1930 Duesenberg and William Howard Taft's White Steamer, the first official White House auto. A free shuttle bus makes stops every twenty minutes around the far-flung property. The Carousel Café offers light breakfast, lunch and afternoon snacks. The Old Barn Garden Shop sells plants and garden supplies, and there are all kinds of neat things in the main gift shop by the parking area.

(508) 888-3300. www.heritagemuseumsandgardens.org. Open daily 9 to 6 (Wednesday to 8), May-October; Wednesday-Sunday 10 to 4, rest of year. Adults, $12.

Thornton W. Burgess Museum, 4 Water St., Sandwich.

The works and spirit of the renowned children's author and naturalist, the best-known Sandwich native in this century, are preserved in this restored 1776 Cape Cod house beside Shawme Pond. His animal characters are in evidence in the pint-size museum with nature exhibits on one side of the house and a shop on the other. A couple of herb gardens are out back.

Two miles east off Route 6A in East Sandwich are the **Green Briar Nature Center and Jam Kitchen,** operated by the Thornton W. Burgess Society and featuring the 57-acre Briar Patch conservation area, nature trails, an award-winning wildflower garden and a fascinating, 100-year-old jam kitchen producing and selling jams, chutneys and relishes in the style of a century ago.

(508) 888-6870. www.thorntonburgess.org. Open Monday-Saturday 10 to 4, Sunday 1 to 4, April-October; weekends in December; adults, $2. Green Briar open same hours, April-December, also Tuesday-Saturday 10 to 4 January-March. Donation.

Hoxie House, 18 Water St., Sandwich.

The oldest house in Cape Cod's oldest town, a restored 1675 saltbox overlooking

Shawme Pond, looks its age. One hardly knows what to make of its fortress-like front façade or its curving room in back. Inside is a two-story wonder of primitive antiquity – all the more so when you learn that people lived here until 1953 without running water, plumbing or electricity. Our guide called it "the best, most inexpensive tour on the Cape." A combination ticket gives admission to **Dexter's Gristmill,** built in 1640 and still in operation at the foot of Shawme Pond in Sandwich Center. Corn is ground daily here, and you can usually see ducks and swans on the pond.

(508) 888-1173. Open Monday-Saturday 10 to 5, Sunday 1 to 5, mid-June to mid-October. Adults, $1.50 each property. Combination ticket, $2.50.

SHOPPING. Most of Sandwich's treasures are in its museums, as you might deduce when you note the signs at the principal Main and Jarves street intersection identifying the likes of the Boston Organ & Piano Co. and Sandwich Chiropractic. No Gap or Benetton here. Old houses harbor treats like **The Weather Store,** with everything from tiny compasses to big weather vanes and CDs about the weather, and **Madden & Co.** with gourmet foods, antiques and "gatherings for the country home." Handmade stoneware, porcelain bowls, plates, watercolors, oil paintings and more are displayed at **Shawme Pond Pottery,** 1690 home and studio of artist Margaret Tew Ellsworth. **The Nodding Violet** offers antiques, collectibles and vintage home furnishings.

The **Sandwich Antiques Center** shows the wares of more than 100 dealers, with glass a principal commodity. The Old King's Highway (Route 6-A east of Sandwich) offers unexpected discoveries of the antiques and gift variety, plus the **Glass Studio,** where you can see a glass blower at work.

Extra-Special

Giving Tree Gallery & Sculpture Garden, 550 Route 6A, East Sandwich.

"Where Art and Nature Meet" is the theme of Judith Smith's nifty indoor-outdoor collection of American crafts, all with a peg to nature. Doing basically everything herself, this Renaissance woman has transformed a dilapidated summer cottage and grounds into two floors of exhibit space, sculpture gardens, a nature preserve and even a coffeehouse. Enter the little cottage in front and view the stylish crafts, including some great jewelry and pottery, of some of the 200 artists represented. Go downstairs to the art gallery to view some mighty good Cape landscapes. Classical music plays as you head out to the mysterious and mystical sculpture garden in a 200-year-old bamboo grove. Here sculptures on pedestals, in trees and on the ground interplay randomly with nature. Follow a path decorated with crushed glass through an open iron pyramid where you might want to sit on a bench and meditate for an hour or so. A rickety, makeshift boardwalk winds through the bamboo forest to the edge of a wide-open marsh and wildlife sanctuary, two more revolving sculptures and a changing landscape that is the essence of beauty. Continue on across the 50-foot rope suspension bridge that Judith and a friend built – open to "one person at a time" and not for the fearful, although it isn't very far off the ground. Look back and see a little Stonehenge in a clearing. You return into another space full of sculptures: fish hanging on trees, a girl on a swing, reptiles on the grass. Coffee, soup, light lunches, biscotti and cookies are for sale in the coffeehouse with tables outside for taking in the whole experience.

(508) 888-5446 or (888) 246-3551. www.givingtreegallery.com. Open daily, 10 to 5.

Chatham, Mass.

Serenity Beside the Sea

Of all Cape Cod's towns, we are fondest of Chatham, a sophisticated, sedate and serene enclave of affluence beside the sea. This is the elbow of the Cape, where the hubbub of much of the Cape's south shore yields to treed tranquility before the land veers north to face the open Atlantic and form the dunes of the National Seashore.

Known originally as "The First Stop of the East Wind," Chatham is one of the Cape's oldest towns (settled in 1656) and one of its most residential. Hidden in the trees and along the meandering waterfront are large homes and estates.

Explore a bit and you may see the gorgeous hydrangea walk leading up to a Shore Road mansion. Across from a windmill in a field of yellow wildflowers sparkling against a backdrop of blue ocean, it's the essence of Cape Cod. Or you may follow Mooncusser's Lane and find that the road ends abruptly at the water. Admire the view from the drawbridge on Bridge Street as well as the classic views of the Chatham Light.

Because it's so residential, Chatham has escaped the overt commercialism and tourism of much of the Cape. It does not cater to transients; some inns and motels encourage long stays, and many of its accommodations are in cottages or rented houses.

The summer social scene revolves around private clubs and parties. But almost everyone turns out for the Friday evening band concerts in Kate Gould Park.

Although Main Street, which winds through the center of town, seems filled with pedestrians and shoppers, chances are they're residents or regulars. Perhaps its air of stability and tradition is what makes Chatham so special.

Inn Spots

Wequassett Inn, Pleasant Bay, Chatham 02633.

Blessed with a fine location above its private beach and peninsula separating Round Cove from Pleasant Bay, this inn reflects its Indian name for "crescent on the water." The new blends quite nicely with the old in a resort compound with structures dating back more than 200 years. Eighteen Cape Cod-style cottages, motel buildings and condo-type facilities totaling 104 rooms are distributed across 22 rolling, beautifully landscaped acres amid colorful flowers of the season and huge old pines.

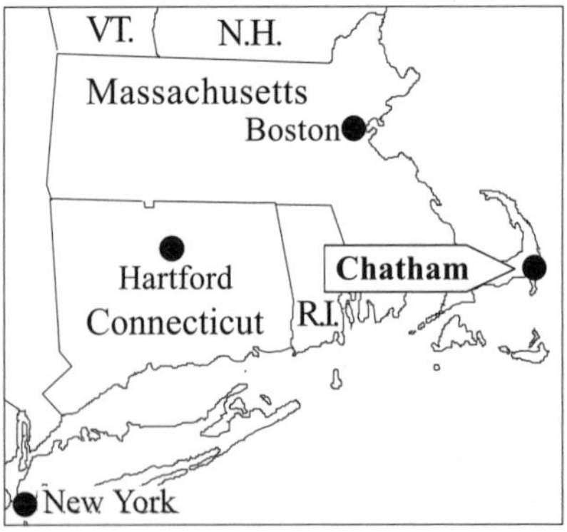

Large guest rooms and suites are furnished traditionally with cheery colors, patterned fabrics, pine furniture, quilted bedspreads, duck-print wall hangings and needlepoint rugs. We like best the 37 water-view rooms, with windows onto the bay and decks for outdoor lounging. Others are partial to the tennis villas, many with cathedral ceilings and private balconies

Historic Eben Ryder House is centerpiece of Wequassett Inn.

overlooking the woods or courts. Rooms have cable TV, clock radios, mini-refrigerators, phones, air-conditioning and Crabtree & Evelyn toiletries.

At the disposal of guests are five tennis courts with a resident pro, sailboats and canoes, a large swimming pool, a half-mile-long beach and a small health and fitness center, newly ensconced in what had been a game room. A boat shuttles swimmers to the barrier beach that protects Pleasant Bay.

The dining facility underwent a $2 million renovation in 2002 and reopened under a new name, **Twenty-Eight Atlantic.** Floor-to-ceiling windows on three sides yield bay views in a large room that became more formalized, with rich wood paneling, subtle maritime paintings and candles in huge glass hurricane lamp chandeliers. A two-tiered garden terrace off the lounge overlooking Pleasant Bay is a pleasant place for cocktails. Behind the dining room is **Thoreau's,** a club-like bar with leather and suede furnishings, fireplace and mahogany bar. Also new is the beachy **Outer Bar & Grille.** Beside the bay with a canopied deck above the water and large tropical-style rattan chairs at glass tables, it offers lunch and dinner daily in summer.

These are the varied settings for superior food created by executive chef Bill Brodsky, most recently from the Charleston Grill in the Charleston Place hotel in South Carolina, who brought his culinary team with him.

Menus come in weighty double covers that contain gel resembling sea water, sand and shells. The food descriptions cannot do justice to the complexities of their innovative, sometimes overwrought combinations of ingredients nor their architectural presentations.

Dinner might start with chipotle-spiced yellowfin tuna tartare with ossetra caviar and Maine crab, tempura soft-shell crab with sesame-coconut vinaigrette, and Wellfleet oysters four ways. The evening's soups – game bird consommé with shaved truffle, lobster-corn bisque and chilled heirloom tomato soup with crab and avocado mousse – are available individually or as a sampling of three. One of the composed salads yields macerated clams and kalamata olives with a smoked tomato vinaigrette.

Main courses range from skillet-seared bluefish paired with an assertive saffron-smoked mussel risotto to a fricassee of Cape shellfish bathed in a sambuca-scented fumet. We liked the herb-roasted lamb loin with a maple-balsamic reduction and a mushroom-potato cake, and the beef tenderloin tournedos with grand marnier mole and a coriander-mango-corn salad.

Desserts could include crème brûlées, cranberry mousse in an almond tuile with a red and white sauce underneath looking as lacy as a doily, and a frozen chambord mousse in a parfait glass. With candles lit and reflecting in the windows, it's a romantic atmosphere in which to linger over cappuccino and cordials.

(508) 432-5400 or (800) 225-7125. Fax (508) 432-5032. www.wequassett.com. Ninety-three rooms and eleven suites with private baths. Rates EP. Late June to Labor Day: doubles $340 to $535, suites $590 to $1,100. Off-season: doubles $125 to $470, suites $230 to $775. Closed December-March.

Entrées, $20 to $38; light fare in tavern and grill, $11 to $26. Lunch daily, 11:30 to 2. Dinner, 6 to 10. Closed December-March.

The Captain's House Inn of Chatham, 369-377 Old Harbor Road (Route 28), Chatham 02633.

There's more than a touch of England amid all the Americana of this supremely elegant and comfortable inn that originated two decades ago in Captain Hiram Harding's restored 1839 home, set on shaded lawns screened by high hedges in a sedate residential section north of the village.

Jan and David McMaster took over one of the few small AAA four-diamond inns in New England and have taken it to a higher level. Dave, former CEO of a computer company he founded in California, expanded the dining porch, added a few whirlpool tubs and built four deluxe rooms with fireplaces. He also developed English perennial gardens with a three-tiered fountain pond in a rear corner of the two-acre property. His latest additions were a heated outdoor swimming pool and an exercise facility.

Jan, a proper Brit from Bournemouth, injected her heritage into an inn whose staff already imparted an English accent. For some years, the Captain's House had hired hotel students from the University of Bournemouth in Jan's hometown, a striking coincidence, and the McMasters continued the tradition, as well as adding staff from Jamaica. Jan serves an elaborate and true English tea in the afternoon. She also has expanded the breakfast offerings to include smoked salmon corncakes with broiled tomatoes and cheese, waffles with strawberries or blueberries, quiches and apple crêpes to supplement the traditional fresh fruit, breads and muffins, all served at individual tables in the sunny breakfast porch.

Said breakfast area is a beauty in white and dusky rose. An addition projects eight feet out into the gardens with floor-to-ceiling windows. The floor is tiled and trailing wisteria is stenciled on the walls. Two fancy serving areas along the sides simplify breakfast service at individual linen-covered tables set with sterling silver and china.

The entrance hall and living room retain the original pumpkin pine floors and are furnished with antiques, fine rugs and period wallpapers.

Thirteen of the sixteen guest accommodations have fireplaces and all have king or queen beds, TV/VCRs and telephones with data ports. Some have whirlpool tubs, mini-refrigerators and coffeemakers. Fine antiques are evident throughout.

The original nine bedrooms in the main Greek Revival house have been reconfigured lately into three rooms and two suites.

Rooms with beamed and peaked ceilings are among the more deluxe in a rear carriage house. Also coveted is the Captain's Cottage, where the sumptuous Hiram Harding room looks like a library with dark walnut paneling and beamed ceiling, fine oriental rugs on the wide-plank floor, large fireplace, plush sofa and side chairs, and lace-canopied kingsize four-poster bed. A jacuzzi tub has been added here, as well as in the recently enlarged Lady Mariah room adjacent. In the latter, an old kitchen

The Captain's House Inn of Chatham occupies residential site north of village.

was converted into what Jan calls a "fantasy bathroom," a smashing space with a double whirlpool flanked by four pillars and two wicker chairs facing a corner fireplace. The fireplace is also on view from the extra-high, step-up kingsize bed.

Top of the line are three jacuzzi accommodations in the Stables, a new building behind the cottage. The upstairs Lydia Harding suite has fireplaces in both living room and bedroom, a kingsize bed and french doors leading to a full-length balcony. Each of the two downstairs rooms has a queen canopy bed, fireplace and a private deck, and a TV/VCR is hidden in an 1875 chest or the armoire.

Bottled water is in each guest room. Turndown service is available, and guests find an evening snack.

(508) 945-0127 or (800) 315-0728. Fax (508) 315-0728. www.captainshouseinn.com. Twelve rooms and four suites with private baths. Mid-May through October: doubles $235 to $350, suites $250 to $425. Rest of year: doubles $185 to $250, suites $185 to $295. Three-night minimum, July-September; two-night minimum other peak periods. Children over 12.

Chatham Bars Inn, Shore Road, Chatham 02633.

The colorful landscaping with luxuriant flowers, gas lanterns and brick steps tiered up the hillside toward the main entrance of this venerable inn/resort "make a statement," in the words of its management. So do the beautifully refurbished Victorian foyer and South Parlor, the front veranda awash in wicker, and the redecorated dining room and tavern.

Such statements signal the changes since Carl Lindner, the Ohio big-business entrepreneur who's lately into hotels, acquired the property in 1993. His vision was to restore the hotel to its original grandeur, circa 1914.

The Chatham Bars complex of an imposing inn and charming oceanfront houses and cottages existed virtually as a private club from its beginnings as a hunting lodge in 1914. One of the last great oceanfront resorts, it's perched on a bluff with half a mile of shoreline overlooking Pleasant Bay and the barrier beach separating it from the Atlantic.

Rooms run the gamut from 40 of the traditional type in the main inn to sumptuous suites in 25 cottages, many of them houses containing two to eight guest rooms and common living rooms with fireplaces. We enjoyed watching the surf pummeling the now-famous breach in the barrier beach from the balcony off the plush sitting room of our cottage suite, which was suavely decorated in shades of mauve and rose.

Thirty-three more rooms in three buildings were added in 1999. Newly renovated cottages – variously outfitted with tiled fireplaces, built-in TVs, lighted closets, hand-painted cabinets, window seats, oversize beds and even a grandfather's clock – are the ultimate in taste, comfort and low-key luxury. At the north end of the main hotel are two master suites. One of 1,300 square feet on the second floor has two bedrooms, a parlor and a living room with decks on all sides.

For meals, the resort has a stately **Main Dining Room** in which award-winning executive chef Hide Yamamoto offers cutting-edge cuisine, jackets are required for dinner and dinner dances have been launched on summer Saturday nights. Formerly head chef at the Ritz-Carlton in Washington, D.C., the Japanese chef combines French cuisine with pan-Asian influences in such signature dishes as tuna tartare with wasabi roe and lime vinaigrette, sautéed foie gras with banana tempura, and Chatham lobster paella with mango, avocado, beets and a cilantro-ginger sauternes sauce. There's a more casual **North Beach Tavern** in space formerly known as the Inner Bar. Lunch, continental breakfast with an omelet bar and special events take place at the inviting **Beach House Grill** at water's edge, where the pool area has been enlarged and croquet lawns added. Guests enjoy an adjacent nine-hole golf course, five tennis courts and a sandy beach.

Although the theme throughout is understated luxury, the Chatham Bars is distinguished by its service-oriented staff and its mix of accommodations. You can mingle and make merry in the main inn, or get away from it all in a house by the sea.

(508) 945-0096 or (800) 527-4884. Fax (508) 945-4978. www.chathambarsinn.com. One hundred sixty-three rooms and 42 suites with private baths. Rates, EP. Mid-June to mid-September: doubles $320 to $450, suites $460 to $1,600. Spring and fall: doubles $200 to $330, suites $350 to $1,210. December-March: doubles $150 to $200, suites, $210 to $590.

Entrées, $28 to $38. Dinner nightly in Main Dining Room, 6 to 10, May-November; jackets required. Lunch at Beach House Grill, daily in summer, 11:30 to 3.

Chatham Wayside Inn, 512 Main St., Box 685, Chatham 02633.

When we first vacationed in Chatham three decades ago, the Wayside seemed the quintessential New England inn – located in the heart of town and containing a lively tavern that was perfect for an after-dinner drink. If the food was mediocre and the accommodations somewhat threadbare, no matter. It had a captive audience then.

But tradition carries an inn only so far. Upscale newcomers lured away its business, and the Wayside fell upon hard times. The 1860 landmark was rescued from foreclosure by a pair of local businessmen, who closed for a total rehab and reopened with a new look, a new layout and 24 upstairs guest rooms. The next year, 32 more guest rooms opened in a new three-story annex out back, occupying the site of four razed cottages. These parkside units have patios and balconies for front-row seats for the Friday night band concerts in Kate Gould Park.

Today, this inn is thoroughly up-to-date, and has regained its role as the archtypical in-town New England inn, 21st century style.

Rooms in the main inn are nicely furnished with an abundance of chintz, vivid fabrics and Waverly prints. They come in three styles: Colonial, European traditional

Crowd gathers in front of The Cranberry Inn at Chatham for town's annual parade.

and country pine. All have king or queensize beds and thick carpeting, five have private balconies or terraces and two claim jacuzzis. TVs are ensconced in highboys or on chests facing the beds, and Lord & Mayfair toiletries await in the bathrooms. A writing desk is tucked into one of the nooks and crannies of a dormered third-floor room. "Everything looks and feels old," said our guide as she showed us around, "but you can be assured it's new."

Three meals a day are served in the inn's spacious restaurant and tavern (see Dining Spots).

(508) 945-5550 or (800) 391-5734. www.waysideinn.com. Fifty-six rooms with private baths. Rates, EP. Doubles, $185 to $375 mid-June through Labor Day, $105 to $295 rest of year. Two-night minimum in summer and peak weekends.

The Cranberry Inn at Chatham, 359 Main St., Chatham 02633.

Once named the Traveler's Home and later the Monomoy House, this pale yellow frame inn dating from the 1830s is Chatham's oldest inn. It was grandly renovated and expanded by two sets of owners before it was acquired in 1999 by Kay and Bill DeFord of Concord. Their son Will, a Johnson and Wales-trained chef, is their stand-in at the inn and cooks breakfast for guests.

The entry/reception room is enhanced by oriental carpets, fine art, a baby grand piano and rare tables with board games. The handsome tavern/lounge has been glamorized with beamed ceiling, fireplace, oriental art and old hotel registers found in the attic from a century ago. The redecorated dining room is a picture of elegance in showy navy and cranberry, with fabric-covered wood chairs. The landscaping includes English gardens and a nature trail leading to a cranberry bog, the old Mill Pond and out to the ocean.

In the rooms, the beds are triple-sheeted, the pillows are down feathers, the towels are 100 percent cotton Dundee, and the windows are outfitted with vinyl blackout shades. Most beds are queensize four-posters. Crystal cranberry glasses are in each room, and the ice buckets are vinyl-coated in cranberry color. Previous owners had doubled the fourteen original guest rooms in size, thanks to an addition on the east end. All have new baths, telephones and television. They also added four fireplaced "suites," each with comfortable sitting areas and a couple with private balconies.

Breakfast is chef Will's choice, perhaps omelets, eggs benedict or waffles. Complimentary hors d'oeuvres are served during cocktail hour in the tavern.

(508) 945-9232 or (800) 332-4667. Fax (508) 945-3769. www.cranberryinn.com. Eighteen rooms with private baths. Mid-June through Labor Day: doubles $195 to $260. Late spring and early fall: $150 to $225. November to April : $110 to $180. Children over 12.

The Bradford of Chatham, 26 Cross St., Chatham 02633.

This venerable establishment, nicely situated in a residential section just off Chatham's Main Street, has been expanded and upgraded by the owners of the Chatham Wayside Inn. They razed the original motel in which the rambling inn complex got its start, gutted the interior of every other building but one, and built three new structures.

The result is a nicely landscaped, two-acre compound of nine white houses in the Cape Cod style, each with four or five guest rooms. Where the Wayside aims to be the quintisesential "village inn," the management likens this to "a village within a village." The houses are spread around the property, with the landmark 1860 Captain Elijah Smith House continuing to serve as guest registration area. Its main floor holds a lounge and game room set up for checkers and backgammon, plus a fireplaced breakfast room overlooking an expanded swimming pool area. Here is where a complimentary continental-plus breakfast is served. Upstairs are four large guest rooms done in the Colonial hotel style employed throughout.

Each room and each building is different. All are virtually new, except for the Jonathan Gray building which was merely redecorated. Rooms have one kingsize, one queensize or two queen beds. Cherry reproduction furniture and muted colors are the norm. Twelve rooms have gas fireplaces and sixteen have whirlpool tubs. All come with TVs, telephones and the comforts of an upscale hotel. Room 233 in the Jonathan Gray has a small balcony, while Room 122 in the Mulberry house has a private front porch. Upstairs in the Mulberry is a suite with a kingsize poster bed, a lounge chair and ottoman facing the fireplace, and a living room with a sofabed.

(508) 945-1030 or (800) 562-4667. Fax (508) 945-9652. www.bradfordinn.com. Twenty-seven rooms and eleven suites with private baths. Late June to Labor Day: doubles, $185 to $425. Late spring and early fall: $155 to $350. November to April: $105 to $295. Children over 12.

The Cyrus Kent House Inn, 63 Cross St., Chatham 02633.

Restored into one of Chatham's first B&B's in 1985, this 1877 sea captain's home was acquired in 1999 by Sandra and Steven Goldman, she a former flight attendant and he a TV executive who lived in California but summered in Chatham until his retirement.

Fine antiques and original art from their California home dignify the common areas and guest rooms, all brightened lately by fresh flowers from Steve's expanded gardens. "He says there are seven," Sandra said as she pointed out a few during a spring tour. Where one ends and another begins may not be immediately obvious, but even the untrained eye could tell they were special. A gazebo was being installed in the midst of the rear gardens for guests to enjoy the scene.

The main house and subsequent additions hold six guest rooms, a junior suite

Cyrus Kent House Inn occupies 1877 sea captain's home.

and a two-bedroom suite. Queensize four-poster beds, wing chairs, TV/VCRs, clock-radios and telephones are the norm. Some add fireplaces and decks. A favorite is the original Cyrus Kent master bedroom, elegantly decorated in ecru with a chandeliered entry foyer and a new gas fireplace in the corner. We like the recently remodeled and enlarged Hydrangea Room, which has two wing-back reclining chairs in a cozy nook in front of the fireplace. A kingsize canopy bed and a wood-burning fireplace grace the Edwin Reed room in the back of the house. The General's Quarters is a suite with a kingsize bedroom in the back and a bedroom with two twins and a fireplace in front, sharing a bath with a whirlpool tub.

The rear carriage house harbors a couple of deluxe junior suites. One on the main floor with a beamed ceiling and a fireplace in the center is furnished in Shaker country style with a four-poster queen bed. The upstairs Aerie suite is larger and more formal with a skylit vaulted ceiling. A palladian window is the focal point of its elegant living room.

An elaborate breakfast of fresh fruit compote, granola, yogurt and homemade muffins culminates in a hot baked entrée, perhaps waffles or a soufflé. It's taken on the back patio or in the wainscoted dining room at individual tables with lace runners, silver and china. Afternoon tea is offered in the off-season in the elegant living room, where decanters of sherry and port are available.

Elaborate crystal chandeliers grace the dining room, living room and main hall. You'd never guess that Steve obtained them off eBay.

(508) 945-9104 or (800) 338-5368. www.cyruskent.com. Seven rooms and three suites with private baths. Doubles, $155 to $245 June to mid-October, $120 to $180 in spring; $105 to $165 rest of year.

Moses Nickerson House, 364 Old Harbor Road, Chatham 02633.

Located across the street from the Captain's House Inn of Chatham, this elongated, 1839 whaling captain's house is remarkable for its narrow width and extreme depth. The main house is one room wide so rooms have windows on both sides. A newer section adds a lovely solarium breakfast room, outfitted with white wrought-iron furniture on a brick floor, and two large guest rooms.

The house is decorated with flair, and the delicate, hand-painted designs on the doors are a trademark. The English parlor is pretty in rose and cream with a collection of Sandwich glass. Afternoon tea and cookies are served here in front of the fire.

Off the parlor is the front Emily Dickinson Room, which has a hand-painted queen poster bed and a painted armoire amid tons of lace; some of the author's works are on the fireplace mantel. Six more spacious rooms with queensize beds and sitting areas are in one section above the living room, up steep ship's stairs from the dining room or in the newer rear section. The door to each is stenciled in keeping with the theme of the room, which is decorated according to its name: Country, Simple Victorian, Romantic, Cape Cottage, Old-Fashioned and such.

Climb those ship's stairs if you can to see a room with a great window seat full of pillows, a fishnet canopy four-poster bed and a stenciled bathroom. Once here, you may have difficulty leaving – one lanky fellow had to back down the stairs.

A collection of pewter lines a high shelf in the skylit breakfast solarium, which looks onto an arbor and a fishpond outside. Here is where Linda Watts, innkeeper with her husband George, serves a full breakfast. The main event could be a Canadian bacon soufflé one day and stuffed french toast the next.

The grounds attract with nice touches like statues, bird feeders and a wooden seagull perched in the crook of an old tree. The manicured lawn and the well trimmed hedges are the purview of George, who met his wife-to-be at the Moses Nickerson House in 1995. She was the new innkeeper from Philadelphia and he, a vacationing Canadian government worker, happened to be one of her early guests. They were married six months later and have run the inn with TLC ever since.

(508) 945-5859 or (800) 628-6972. Fax (508) 945-7087. www.mosesnickersonhouse.com. Seven rooms with private baths. Memorial Day through October: doubles $149 to $209. Rest of year: $95 to $149. Two- or three-night minimum in season. Children over 12.

Carriage House Inn, 407 Old Harbor Road, Chatham 02633.

High-school sweethearts Jill and James Meyer from New Jersey fell in love with Chatham during family vacations. They finally settled here in 2003, taking over a six-room B&B where he put into practice his degree in hospitality management from Boston University.

The young couple offer six guest rooms in their Cape Cod-style house and carriage house at the corner of Old Harbor and Shore roads. All have oversize showers in the updated bathrooms and queensize beds, dressed in chintz and floral fabrics. TV/DVDs, coffeemakers and hair dryers are standard. Three are on the second floor of the main house. The charm of the large side room appeals here, as does a rear room done in pink and green chintz and wicker.

The choicest accommodations are in the renovated rear carriage house, away from the road. Each has an arched window beneath a vaulted ceiling, a corner fireplace and, a boon in summer, a private flower-bedecked sitting area outside.

Guests gather by the fireplace in the main house. Breakfast is served at a table for six in the chandeliered dining room, or at three tables for two on a sun porch.

James is the chef, cooking up such treats as seafood strata, pumpkin pancakes, upside-down apple french toast or gingerbread waffles. Fruit, cereal, yogurt and homemade biscuits or scones accompany.

(508) 945-4688 or (800) 355-8868. Fax (508) 945-8909. www.thecarriagehouseinn.com. Six rooms with private baths. Late June to Labor Day: doubles, $170 to $195. Late spring and early fall: $140 to $165. January to late April: $105 to $130.

The Old Harbor Inn, 22 Old Harbor Road, Chatham 02633.

For a change of pace, consider this newer home built for a physician who delivered half the babies in Chatham. Judy and Ray Braz from nearby Brockton saw its for-sale ad in the Boston Globe and, although they had rarely traveled to the Cape, bought the B&B in 1996. Built in a very different style than the Cape Cod norm, it had just been expanded to retain the residential flavor. Now it's nicely decorated and furnished in a more contemporary kind of way.

The stage is set in the fireplaced living room, all cream and green with comfortable seating. To the rear is a skylit breakfast sunroom with wicker furniture, leading onto a large and attractive deck with spiffy lounge furniture. The back yard has a new fish pond and won a garden-club award for its landscaping.

The eight guest rooms, all with full baths and TV/VCRs, have king or queen beds with designer linens. Appointed in a country look, they bear the different names the town was called before it became Chatham. Largest of three upstairs in the main house is a secluded hideaway called Port Fortune with kingsize bed, Laura Ashley linens, a loveseat and upholstered chair.

The prime accommodation is the main-floor Stage Harbor Suite. Its living room has a large TV/VCR and the stately bedroom a kingsize rice cherry four-poster with matching bureau and a chaise lounge. The bath contains a walk-in glass shower and a new double jacuzzi.

Two more guest rooms occupy the first floor of a rear wing. They are equally light, bright and airy, and contain the thick rugs, designer fabrics, candy and assorted amenities featured in the rest of the house. A second floor was added atop this wing to produce two deluxe rooms, each with gas fireplace and skylit, vaulted ceiling. The North Beach is decorated in pinks with a king bed and a rattan couch. The South Beach is more masculine with a queen sleigh bed, pocket doors and built-in cabinets.

A continental-plus buffet breakfast of fruits, cereals, and homemade breads and muffins is served in the morning.

(508) 945-4434 or (800) 942-4434. Fax (508) 945-7665. www.chathamoldharborinn.com. Eight rooms with private baths. Summer: doubles $179 to $259. Fall and spring: $159 to $239. Winter: $129 to $199. Children over 12.

Port Fortune Inn, 201 Main St., Chatham 02633.

Formerly the Inn Among Friends with a restaurant in front, this ocean-view establishment was renovated in 1997 by Mike and Renée Kahl. They converted the restaurant building into three guest rooms, a reception room and a breakfast room for house guests as well as enlarging and refurbishing rooms in the main Cape Cod house in the rear.

All rooms now have updated bathrooms, telephones and queensize poster beds. Some rooms have two beds. Five have TVs and refrigerators in pine cabinets. A main-floor suite has a high rice-carved mahogany poster bed in the bedroom and an elegant sitting room with a sofabed. The rooms are appointed with antiques and reproductions and are color-coordinated from window treatments to wastebaskets – the rims of which Renée wrapped in curtain fabric. She also planted the colorful gardens that flank the hillside in front of the main inn.

Two large bedrooms upstairs in the front building over the former restaurant yield water views. So do a couple upstairs in the main house, where guests have access to a large sitting room and a brick patio amid the terraced perennial gardens.

Renée bakes the pastries for the continental-plus breakfast buffet in the refurbished restaurant.

(508) 945-0792 or (800) 750-0792. www.portfortuneinn.com. Eleven rooms and one suite with private baths. Mid-June to Labor Day: doubles $150 to $210, suite $260. Spring and fall: doubles $135 to $165, suite $205. April: doubles $100 to $130, suite $165. Two-night minimum weekends in season. Children over 12. Closed November-March.

Dining Spots

The Impudent Oyster, 15 Chatham Bars Ave., Chatham.

With a name like that and an innovative menu, how could this place miss? Always jammed and noisy, patrons crowd together at small glass-covered tables under a cathedral ceiling, with plants in straw baskets balanced overhead on the beams. A huge mirror on the side wall makes the place seem bigger.

Benches accommodate waiting diners at Impudent Oyster.

Owner Peter Barnard's international menu, based on local seafood, is an intriguing blend of regional, Chinese, Mexican, Indian, Greek and Italian cuisines, among others. For dinner, we couldn't resist starting with the drunken mussels, shelled and served chilled in an intense marinade of tamari, fresh ginger, Szechuan peppercorns and sake, with a side portion of snow peas and red peppers. The Mexican chicken, chile and lime soup, one of the best we've tasted, was spicy and full of interesting flavors. Also delicious were the spinach and mushroom salads with either creamy mustard or anchovy dressings.

Main dishes range from the specialty barbecued yellowfin tuna marinated in orange juice and soy sauce to seafood fra diablo. We liked the feta and fennel scrod, a Greek dish touched with ouzo, and the swordfish with sundried tomato and basil sauce. A plate of several ice creams made with fresh fruit was a cooling finale.

The menu changes frequently, and is supplemented by nightly specials. It's the kind of cuisine of which we never tire, although we might prefer to have it in a quieter setting.

(508) 945-3545. Entrées, $19.95 to $24.95. Lunch daily, 11;30 to 3, Sunday noon to 3. Tavern menu 3 to 5. Dinner nightly, from 5.

Pisces, 2653 Main St. (Route 28), South Chatham.

"Coastal cooking" is the theme of this summery charmer, ensconced in a sweet yellow house up against the road. Chef-owner Susan L. Connors named it for a favorite Barbados eatery on the water, adding it's "a good name for a mostly seafood restaurant."

Sue, who became executive chef at the Inn at Harvard in Cambridge at age 25, is a veteran of top Boston area restaurants. For her first solo venture, she gutted the former Andiamo restaurant and created a stylish 50-seater that's nicely nautical in white and royal blue. Booths and white-clothed tables are set against a backdrop of white walls hung with seashore artworks. A couple of brass fish sculptures are focal points.

The menu is rolled up in a blue ribbon. Untie it to reveal a panoply of culinary treats. Look for appetizers such as seared rare tuna drizzled with wasabi-lime mustard and soy glaze, served with a gingered vegetable salad, and mussels sautéed with white wine, lemon and herbs and served with grilled garlic crostini. Sue's risotto of the day is always a good choice, as are her pasta dishes, perhaps lobster and asparagus ravioli in a sweet corn and leek broth with a touch of cream.

Typical main courses are a Mediterranean-style fisherman's stew in a spicy tomato-lime-cilantro broth with a grilled white corn tortilla for dipping, seared rare spice-rubbed tuna with sweet and spicy soy glaze, and cornmeal-crusted local cod with tomato-lemon-caper aioli. Meat-eaters are well served by the likes of veal T-bone chop with portobello mushroom and balsamic demi-glace and grilled garlic-rubbed ribeye steak topped with gorgonzola butter.

Sweet endings could be a signature oreo cookie cheesecake, bananas foster and white chocolate biscuit with mangos.

(508) 432-4600. Entrées, $18 to $24. Dinner nightly in summer, from 5; Wednesday-Sunday in off-season. Closed December-March.

Vining's Bistro, 595 Main St., Chatham.

We've had lobster in myriad forms, but never before wrapped in a flour tortilla with spinach and jalapeño jack cheese, and here called a warm lobster taco. With lime crème fraîche and homemade two-tomato salsa sparked with cilantro, it is an appetizer fixture on the multi-ethnic menu. That and the warm roasted scallop salad with grilled eggplant and yogurt dressing served on wilted bok choy that we tried at our first visit prompted us to return.

The bistro is owned by Steve Vining, who used to have La Grand Rue in Harwichport. It's upstairs in a retail complex called the Galleria, with beamed cathedral ceilings and big windows onto Main Street. Vining's is a casual and friendly place where a large stuffed bear was seated at the bar at a recent visit. Many of executive chef Myles Huntington's multi-ethnic dishes are done on the open grill, using woods like cherry, apple and hickory.

For an autumn dinner, we were tempted by the grilled bouillabaisse as well as the grilled salmon with stir-fried watercress, ginger and sesame and the Malaysian seafood clay pot with all kinds of seafood in a spicy coconut-curry broth. One of us enjoyed the clam and mussel stew, served with arugula, tomatoes and sausage over fettuccine. The other made a meal of a couple of appetizers, the warm lobster taco (again) and Thai chicken satay, plus a bistro salad with feta cheese and kalamata olives. Portions were huge and the food assertive, prompting a faint-hearted couple of our acquaintance to shun the place as "too spicy." They wouldn't even think of trying the fiery rasta pasta, made with Scotch bonnet peppers and incorporating Jamaican jerked chicken, hot sausage and banana-guava ketchup.

There's a small and sophisticated wine list, plus a long list of beers (some imported from Kenya, China and Thailand) to go with. End your meal with maple-pecan bread pudding, cappuccino cheesecake or chocolate pudding cake.

(508) 945-5033. www.viningsbistro.com. Entrées, $17.50 to $24. Dinner nightly, 5:30 to 10, Wednesday-Saturday in off-season. Closed in winter.

Sosumi, 14 Chatham Bars Ave., Chatham.

Chef-owner David Olearcek and a sushi chef run this Asian bistro in a sleek, Japanese-looking space across from the Impudent Oyster. It's quite a sight with chartreuse and brick walls beneath an exposed raftered ceiling. And the food represents quite a change for the land of clams and cod.

The menu is exotic and "untraditional," according to David. Starters could be grilled peppered shrimp with jalapeño-mango sorbet, barbecued octopus with crispy fried onions, lobster and shiitake gyoza with ponzu sauce and seafood egg rolls with mandarin orange duck sauce. Salads vary from seaweed salad with sosumi vinaigrette to salmon skin salad with shiso leaves and enoki mushrooms.

Typical entrées are sea scallops tempura with ginger ketchup, wok lobster with ginger and garlic on shiitake rice cakes, roast duck in red curry sauce and barbecued beef short ribs with cold spicy soba noodles. The "jambalasia" mixes grilled scallops, shrimp and Thai chicken sausage with fire-roasted red peppers on sweet and spicy cilantro rice. There also are selections from the sushi bar.

Dessert could be a banana spring roll with chocolate-cardamom mousse, grilled pineapple with kiwi sauce or coconut crème brûlée.

(508) 945-0300. Entrées, $16 to $24. Lunch daily except Tuesday, noon to 2:30. Dinner nightly except Tuesday, 5:30 to 10. Closed in off-season.

Chatham Wayside Inn, 512 Main St., Chatham.

The Wayside has been restored to its early status as a village inn, smack dab in the middle of the main shopping district. And nowhere is that more evident than in its expanded restaurant and tavern. The former canopied side deck has been enclosed into a sun porch for year-round dining. The vintage-look bar and dining room have been enhanced by handsome murals of Chatham painted recently by artist Hans de Castellane.

The shady front courtyard facing the passing Chatham street scene remains the place to see and be seen in season. We faced a considerable wait at 2 o'clock on a July weekday to snag an outside table for lunch. The wait was worth it for the setting and for a superior grilled chicken salad on mixed greens, loaded with raisins and sundried cranberries.

The extensive dinner menu covers all the bases, from fish and chips to filet mignon. Starters could be crab cakes with jalapeño tartar sauce, Portuguese stuffed quahogs, calamari salad or Asian-style beef carpaccio.

Look for entrées like grilled ahi tuna with a cilantro-sambal vinaigrette, seared Chilean sea bass with fumé blanc sauce, chicken française and rosemary-roasted rack of lamb with two mustard sauces, creole chicken and grilled pork tenderloin glazed with apple cider and rum-raisin sauce. The signature "short stack" pairs grilled medallions of swordfish and filet mignon with spinach and grilled onions, layered on a bed of mashed potatoes.

Crab cake benedict and Mediterranean frittata are featured at Sunday brunch.

(508) 945-5550 or (800) 391-5734. Entrées, $18 to $30. Breakfast daily, 8 to 11. Lunch, 11:30 to 4. Dinner, 5 to 9 or 10.

Restored Chatham Wayside Inn attracts diners as well as overnight guests.

Christian's, 443 Main St., Chatham.

This long-popular restaurant suffered with the departure of founding chef Christian Schwartz, who left to pursue his sweet potato-chip business. The new owners from the Wayside Inn retained the same concept, menu and staff, but the implementaton faltered.

Originally, Christian's offered fine dining in two formal downstairs dining rooms and casual dining upstairs. Lately the fare has expanded into one basic menu serving all. It follows the cinema theme of the upstairs, with every item named for a movie. The garlicky prawns with veggies on angel hair we remember from earlier days was called "The Green Mile," and the medallions of veal sautéed with shrimp, garlic, lemon and white wine, a memorable presentation at the time, was "Two for the Road." Grilled salmon over farfalle with shredded parmesan is "A Fish Called Wanda." The highest priced item, New Zealand rack of lamb with a rosemary demi-glace, is called "The Color of Money." You can order basic ("Little Big Man:" calves liver and onions) or exotic ("Sea of Love:" lobster, shrimp and scallops tossed with scallions, garlic, artichoke hearts, mushrooms and sundried tomatoes over penne).

Clams casino, crab cakes on a pool of roasted red pepper aioli, and fiery snow crab and corn fritters are among the appetizers. House-made pizzas with a salad make a light meal.

Artist Hans de Castellane painted a terrific mural of Broadway in the '20s for the enclosed deck upstairs.

(508) 945-3362. Entrées, $14 to $26. Dinner in season nightly, 5 to 10, upstairs and down. Downstairs closed Columbus Day to mid-April. Upstairs closed a couple of days a week in winter.

The Chatham Squire Restaurant, 483 Main St., Chatham.

Once little more than a bar and still a hangout for summering collegians, the Squire has soared lately with its food, to the point where on recent visits everyone was mentioning it as one of the best bets in town. The atmosphere is perky, the decor old Cape Cod, with murals of local scenes and the bar decked out with old license plates and sailing flags. Regulars like to sit at the bar, which faces Main Street, and watch the passing parade as they slurp hearty fish chowder or peel their own shrimp from the raw bar.

At lunch, burgers are served with those yummy Cape Cod potato chips. We enjoyed a thick and clammy clam chowder with a blue cheeseburger, and the day's blue-plate special, a platter of fish cakes and beans, served with coleslaw and brown bread for $7.50. The grasshopper mousse torte was great for dessert.

Dinner entrées range from baked codfish to grilled beef tenderloin with madeira sauce and mushrooms. Nightly specials might include scallops miso, grilled ocean perch with a cilantro and smoked tomato cream sauce, codfish cheeks jambalaya, gulf shrimp sautéed with artichoke hearts and leeks, and roast Long Island duckling with grapefruit and dark rum sauce. At our latest visit, the three-course dinner du jour for $11.95 was the best bargain in town.

Start with the whistling oysters or Cape Codder pâté with sundried cranberries, walnuts and bartlett pears. Finish with Boston cream cake or pumpkin-cranberry mousse pie.

(508) 945-0945. www.thesquire.com. Entrées, $14.95 to $22.95. Lunch daily, 11:30 to 5. Dinner nightly, 5 to 11; shorter hours in winter.

Diversions

From Chatham's choice location at the elbow of Cape Cod, all the attractions of the Cape are at your beck and call. People who appreciate Chatham tend not to head west toward Hyannis but rather north to Orleans, Wellfleet and the Truros, if they leave Chatham at all.

Beaches. Although Chatham has more beach area and shoreline than any other Cape Cod town, much of it is privately owned or not easily accessible. Those with boats like the seclusion of the offshore sandbar at the southern tip of the Cape Cod National Seashore, a barrier beach that sheltered Chatham from the open Atlantic until it was breached in an infamous 1987 winter storm. Swimming is available by permit at such town beaches as Harding Beach on Nantucket Sound or the sheltered "Children's Beach" at Oyster Pond. Those who want surf and open ocean head for Orleans and the state beaches to the north.

Monomoy National Wildlife Refuge. Accessible by a short boat trip from the visitor center (reached by car) on Morris Island, the wilderness North and South Monomoy Islands stretching south into the Atlantic are a haven for birds – 285 species, at latest count. The nearly 3,000-acre refuge encompasses barrier beaches, dunes, salt marsh, tidal flats, freshwater ponds and seaside thickets that are a natural habitat for nesting gulls, terns, herons and other shore birds. The only national wilderness area in Southern New England is a major stopping point for migratory waterfowl along what ornithologists call the Atlantic Flyway.

Chatham Fish Pier. The fish pier down the slope off Shore Road is popular with sightseers who want to see the real thing. Boats make their run to the fishing grounds ten to one hundred miles into the Atlantic and return with their catch to the pier starting in the early afternoon, depending on tides. Visitors may watch from an observation balcony. Harbor tours also are available here.

Museums. The **Old Atwood House Museum** at 347 Stage Harbor Road, owned and maintained by the Chatham Historical Society, is one of the town's oldest houses (1752). Upwards of 2,000 antiques are shown in its fourteen display rooms. Among its offerings are seashells, Sandwich glass and the nationally known murals of Alice Stallknecht Wight, "Portrait of a New England Town." Changing exhibits illustrate Chatham life through photos, paintings and artifacts. The complex also includes the Stallknecht Mural Barn and the Nickerson Camp. The museum is open Tuesday-Friday from 1 to 4 and Saturday from 10 to 1, early June through September; adults, $3. Also open Tuesday-Saturday 10 to 4 in summer is the 38-year-old **Chatham Railroad Museum,** the former town depot now filled with more than 8,000 models, relics and photos, plus a new diorama of the Chatham rail yards. A 1910 New York Central caboose is available for boarding. Other historic sites are the **Mayo House** on Main Street, the old **Chatham Grist Mill** and the **Chatham Light.**

Shopping. Some of Cape Cod's finest shops are located along tree-lined Main Street, and more seem to open every year, spreading down alleys and encroaching on the residential section to the east. A MacKenzie-Childs table caught our eye at **Lion's Paw** at 403 Main, a branch of the outstanding Nantucket gift shop. Across the street, **Epiphany** offers home and tabletop accessories with a European flair. Wooden mermaids line the entry walk at **Mermaids on Main,** and inside are the most colorful items with mermaid and fish themes. **Tale of the Cod** at 450 Main is a ramble of rooms filled with gifts and furniture. The jewelry appeals at the **Dolli Llama** and **Forest Beach Design.** The **Regatta Shop** has accessories with a nautical accent. **Mark, Fore & Strike** has classic apparel for men and women. **Chapman** carries original resort wear and women's accessories. Specialty clothing, unusual jewelry, gallery items and home accessories are featured at **Pentimento. Monomoy Coffee Co.** at 447 Main is the place for espresso and pastries. **Chatham Presence** offers gifts and its companion **Chatham Accents** specializes in Cape-style furnishings.

The **Wayside Gallery** is a joy to pop into. Owner Helene Wilson, wife of the Wayside Inn's co-owner, seeks fun and frivolous things. "I'm from New York and look for something different," says she. "If it doesn't make me smile, I don't buy it." The stock in her large shop made us smile from start to finish. Especially intriguing was the life-size man made of dryer lint with a pocket watch on a chain and a sign saying "please don't touch the grandfather clock – it makes him cranky!" The clock quickly sold for a cool $1,200. Less esoteric but still fun were a table hand-painted with bunnies and a rug shaped like a cow. The new **Wayside Gallery II** specializes in home furnishings, accessories and gourmet food items.

Extra-Special

Town Band Concerts. It's hard to fathom in sophisticated Chatham, but upwards of 6,000 people turn out for the Friday evening band concerts, a town tradition every July and August, in Kate Gould Park. Brightly colored balloons bob festively around the Whit Tileston Band Stand, named for the man who conducted the event for 45 years. His successor, George Goodspeed, waves his baton and the band plays on. The 40 instrumentalists, most of them townspeople who rehearse weekly during winter, are joined by the multitudes for rousing singalongs. The natural amphitheater is good both for listening and for watching the children (and often their elders) dance to the music. Before the concerts' 8 p.m. start, St. Christopher's Episcopal Church offers chowder suppers, First United Methodist Church serves lobster roll suppers and the Lions Club runs a hot dog stand in front of the Wayside Inn.

Nantucket, Mass.

Island of History and Romance

Stepping onto Steamboat Wharf after a ferry ride twenty miles into the Atlantic is a bit like stepping onto another land in another time.

"This is the island that time forgot," announces one of Nantucket's visitor guides. "Steeped in tradition, romance, legend and history, she is a refuge from modernity."

Flanked by brick sidewalks, towering shade trees and gas lamps, the cobblestone streets lead you past more fine old sea captains' homes still standing from Nantucket's days as the nation's leading whaling port than most people see in a lifetime. The 400-plus structures from the late 1700s and early 1800s that make up the historic district represent the greatest concentration in America, evoking the town's description as "an architectural jewel."

So much for the island that time forgot. The island's romance draws thousands of well-heeled visitors to a sophisticated side of Nantucket that is uniquely chic and contemporary. More distant than other islands from the mainland and yet readily accessible to the affluent, Nantucket is all the more exclusive.

That's the way island businessman-benefactor Walter Beinecke Jr. planned it when he created the Nantucket Historical Trust in 1957 and later co-founded the Nantucket Conservation Trust. His efforts led to the preservation of 11,800 acres of open space – more than one third of the island's land total. Through his historic and real estate interests, the village has been transformed into what magazines call "a perfect oasis – neat, tidy and relentlessly quaint – for upscale vacationers."

It's a bit precious and pricey for some tastes, this town in which whaling fortunes were amassed and which now is predicated on tourism for the elite. Once you get away from Nantucket village and Siasconset, you'll find the folks on the south beaches and the west side of the island let their hair down. The week our family roughed it, so to speak, in a friend's cottage near the beach at Surfside was far different from the fall weekends starting a decade later when we returned, as so many couples do, for getaways in Nantucket village, 'Sconset or Wauwinet.

Nantucket is perfect for an escape – away from the mainland and into a dream combining Yankee history and the *Preppy Handbook.* You don't have to wear Nantucket red trousers or dine at the famed Le Chantecleer, although many do. Simply explore the village's treasures, participate in its activities, or relax and watch a select world go by.

Inn Spots

The inn and B&B phenomenon started later on Nantucket and is changing faster than in most areas. The town's traditional boarding and guesthouses are being upgraded, and more and more are staying open longer each year. Many B&Bs require two- or three-night minimum stays in season, although there seems to be some flexibility. Some that have minimums do not mention them in their brochures.

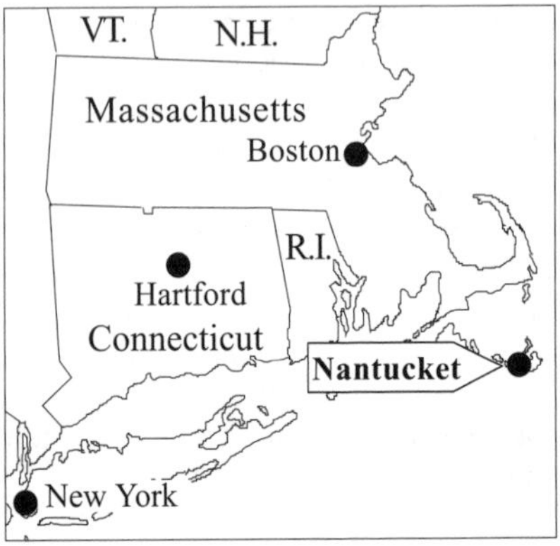

Wicker-furnished back porch looks onto harbor at The Wauwinet.

The Wauwinet, 120 Wauwinet Road, Box 2580, Nantucket 02554.

Grandly restored in 1988, this understated "country inn by the sea" is the most elegant on Nantucket and among the most deluxe in New England. Newton (Mass.) developers Stephen and Jill Karp, longtime Nantucket summer homeowners, spared no expense in turning the weathered old Wauwinet House into the ultimate in taste and comfort.

Its waterside location is unmatched – a private, parkland/residential area on a spit of land with the Atlantic surf beyond the dunes across the road in front, the waters at the head of Nantucket Harbor lapping at the lawns in back.

Twenty-five rooms are available in the inn. Our bay view room in the inn was not large but was nicely located on a third-floor corner facing the harbor so that we were able to watch spectacular sunsets every night. Fresh and pretty, it had a queensize bed with a striped dust ruffle and lace-trimmed pillows, wicker and upholstered armchairs, and a painted armoire topped with a wooden swan and two hatboxes (one of the inn's decorating signatures). The modern bathroom contained a multitude of thick white towels and a Nantucket lightship basket of Crabtree & Evelyn amenities. During turndown service, the towels were replenished and mints placed by the bed.

All the rooms we saw had different, striking stenciled borders (some turning up in the most ingenious places), interesting artworks and sculptures, ceiling fans and such fillips as clouds painted on the ceiling. The deluxe rooms with kingsize or two queen beds included bigger sitting areas, but many did not seem to be as well located as ours was. Every room holds a TV/VCR, tapes for which may be ordered from a selection of 500, along with a bowl of gourmet popcorn.

Five courtyard cottages across the road contain more rooms and suites. One is a four-bedroom cottage with kitchenette and fireplace.

The inn's main floor harbors a lovely living room and library done in floral chintz, a back veranda full of wicker that you sink into, a restaurant and a small, classy lounge. Outside, chairs are lined up strategically on the back lawn, a croquet game is set up, drinks and snacks are available at a small beachside grill, and a resident pro gives lessons on two tennis courts tucked away in the woods. You can swim from a dock or a not particularly inspiring beach along the harbor, or walk a couple of minutes from the hotel through the dunes to the most gorgeous, unoccupied and seemingly endless strand we've seen on the Atlantic coast.

Friendly service is provided by a staff of 110, an unusually high ratio for the maximum of 80 guests. A van transports guests back and forth to town for shopping or to catch the ferryboat. Sherry, port and cheese are served houseguests every afternoon in the library.

Three meals a day are available in the spacious Topper's (see Dining Spots) and an adjacent patio facing the harbor. A full breakfast is included in the room rate. Guests may order any item from strawberry and rhubarb pancakes to egg white omelet with spa cheese and fresh vegetables.

(508) 228-0145 or (800) 426-8718. Fax (508) 325-0657. www.wauwinet.com. Thirty-three rooms and two cottage suites with private baths. Mid-June to mid-September: doubles $600 to $1,150, cottage suites $1,025 to $2,300. Off-season, $200 to $850, cottages, $580 to $1,500. Four-night minimum in summer. Closed late October to early May.

The White Elephant, 50 Easton St., Nantucket 02554.

The White Elephant is no longer the "white elephant" of Nantucket. Hardly.

The image was acquired years ago based on the size and quality of the old-timer's rooms relative to their lofty prices. In 2000, it was upgraded and expanded by the owners of the Wauwinet, who earlier had taken one of the island's oldest hotels and transformed it into a Relais & Chateaux property.

A superb harborfront location offers lush lawns, fancy walkways lined with hedges, and plantings that focus on a white elephant statue in the middle, two nine-hole putting greens and a pleasant pool to the side of the outdoor terrace and restaurant. The hotel includes a new fitness center and offers spa treatments.

The newest lodgings in the renovated hotel have kingsize beds. Many have working fireplaces and some have harbor views. The interior design was overseen by the same New York firm that refurbished the Wauwinet. Rooms vary widely in terms of size and view, although are often priced the same. We're partial to the corner rooms with windows onto Children's Beach, although others find them too public and cherish the privacy of the interior.

Eleven rose-covered cottages scattered about the harborfront property have been redecorated. They offer one to three bedrooms and the living rooms of some have bay windows overlooking the water. A few have kitchenettes.

The Breakers annex, located on the White Elephant's grounds, is like a small inn. It offers 25 spacious guest rooms, all with private patios or balconies. Breakfast may be enjoyed there or in the new harborside lounge.

Newest are accommodations at Fifty-Seven Easton St., a newly built four-bedroom home near the hotel.

A complimentary buffet breakfast is served in the **Brant Point Grill,** which offers three meals daily. The grill is billed as Nantucket's premier steak and seafood house, but locals report the harborfront setting is better than the food.

(508) 228-2500 or (800) 445-6574. Fax (508) 325-1195. www.nantucketislandresorts.com. Fifty-two rooms and eleven cottages with private baths. Late June to September: doubles $500 to $700, cottages $500 to $1,400. Spring and fall: doubles $270 to $600, cottages $400 to $1,200. Closed late October to mid-April.

Architecturally rich Nantucket holds treasures like The Jared Coffin House.

The Jared Coffin House, 29 Broad St., Box 1580, Nantucket 02554.

One of New England's grand old inns, the famed Jared Coffin House is handsomely furnished with museum-quality pieces. It's also active and busy – like a train station 24 hours a day, islanders say, in something of an exaggeration.

The public rooms, restaurant, taproom with entertainment and outdoor patio are busy, that is. For this is a center for Nantucket life and a must visit for tourists, if only for a drink or to sample one of the restaurant's brunches or buffets.

The island's earliest three-story house was the largest in town when it was built in 1845. Its restoration was accomplished by Walter Beinecke Jr. and the Nantucket Historical Trust, which acquired it in 1961 for $10,000, renovated and furnished it, and finally sold it in 1975 to longtime innkeeper/owners Phil and Peg Read for more than $750,000 – an early example of the gentrification of Nantucket.

The 60 guest rooms are scattered in six buildings, two of which are connected to the main 1845 Jared Coffin House. Three are in houses 30 feet on either side of the main complex. All have private baths and telephones and most have television. Thirty rooms have a queen-size canopy bed. Singles, twins, and doubles are also available. Rates include a full breakfast.

Some guests prefer the seven twin and double rooms upstairs in Jared's former home, each furnished with period antiques, artworks and island-woven fabrics. Others covet one of the three large rooms with queensize canopy beds and sitting areas in the 1700s Swain House attached to the main building or, across the street, one of the eighteen queensize canopy rooms in the 1821 Henry Coffin House and the Greek Revival Harrison Gray House.

The public areas are a sight to behold, the living room and library furnished in priceless Chippendale and Sheraton antiques.

Breakfast, included in the rates, offers such choices as eggs florentine, grand marnier french toast and belgian waffles.

Jared's, the inn's large, hotel-style main dining room, features a mix of creative and classic American cuisine. Less formal dinners and a "light bite" menu are available in the beamed, pine-paneled **Tap Room** downstairs. Lunch here or on the patio might be the "Pride of New England," a choice of jumbo frankfurter or deep-fried codfish cake with baked beans, brown bread and coleslaw.

(508) 228-2400 or (800) 248-2405. Fax (508) 228-8549. www.jaredcoffinhouse.com. Sixty rooms with private baths. Early May through October: doubles, $150 to $375. Rest of year: doubles, $125 to $170.

Union Street Inn, 7 Union St., Nantucket 02554.

Former hotel manager Ken Withrow and his wife Deborah have given this restored 1770 house – converted earlier from a guest house into a luxury B&B – the professional, in-residence care it needed, as well as a complete room redecoration and upgrade in amenities. Its twelve spacious guest quarters come with private baths (all but one with shower only), antique furnishings, air conditioning and cable TV. Six have wood-burning fireplaces with their original mantelpieces. Many have canopy or four-poster beds (three kingsize and the rest queens), dressed in Frette linens and pique-woven duvets. Scatter rugs dot the original wide-plank pine floors.

A second-floor suite offers a sitting room with a loveseat and telephone and a bedroom with queen canopy bed, fireplace, VCR, refrigerator and wet bar. The popular main-floor Captain's Room also comes with a fireplace, a kingsize poster bed and two arm chairs.

Because of its location (and zoning), the Union Street can offer more than Nantucket's highly regulated continental breakfasts. The Withrows serve things like scrambled eggs and bacon, blueberry pancakes, french toast and, every fourth day, eggs benedict. These are in addition to a cold buffet that includes a fruit platter, cereals and muffins. The repast is taken in a large dining room or at three handsome garden tables on the side patio beneath an ivy-covered hillside.

"Debbie cooks and I'm the bus boy," says Ken, who had been manager of the Hyatt UN Plaza Hotel in New York and the Ambassador East Hotel in Chicago. They wanted their own business and a family life for their son, and found both here.

(508) 228-9222 or (800) 225-5116. Fax (508) 325-0848. www.union-street-inn.com. Eleven rooms and one suite with private baths. Mid-June through mid-September: doubles $195 to $380, suite $410. Spring and fall: doubles $100 to $210, suite $235. Two-night minimum in season. Children over 6. Closed January-March.

The Pineapple Inn, 10 Hussey St., Nantucket 02554.

Local restaurateurs Caroline and Bob Taylor spent nearly $1 million in 1997 to transform an 1838 whaling ship captain's house into one of Nantucket's more comfortable B&Bs.

Taking the name from the Colonial symbol of hospitality, the Taylors offer twelve air-conditioned guest rooms with private white marble baths. Each has a king or queen bed topped with goose down comforters, cable television and a telephone with modem. Handmade Eldred Wheeler four-poster canopy beds are featured, along with oriental carpets, reproduction furniture and 19th-century antiques and artworks.

"We set out to create the highest lodging standard for the island's historic inns," Bob said. The Taylors were known for their breakfasts during the fifteen years they

Breakfast is a highlight for guests at The Pineapple Inn.

owned and operated the Quaker House Inn and Restaurant here before they turned their attention to the Pineapple.

They had to scale down breakfasts to continental-plus, but claim some of the best homemade pastries in town. The pastries – accompanied by fresh orange juice, a fruit plate, pastries and cappuccino – get the day off to a good start. We got to sample a savory tart of spinach, cheese, basil and sundried tomatoes, teamed with a slice of the day's nectarine and blueberry tart, a delicious and custardy affair. The meal is served at a table for ten in the chandeliered dining room or outside beneath umbrella-covered tables beside a fountain on a bricked garden courtyard.

Two tapestry sofas face each other in front of the fireplace in the side parlor, painted burnished yellow with mauve accents.

(508) 228-9992. Fax (508) 325-6051. www.pineappleinn.com. Twelve rooms with private baths. Mid-June to late September, peak weekends and special events: doubles, $195 to $325. Off-season: doubles, $125 to $250. Closed late October to late April.

Cliff Lodge, 9 Cliff Road, Nantucket 02554.

In a residential neighborhood overlooking town and harbor, the eleven guest rooms in this 1771 sea captain's house are more comfortable and have more flair than many in Nantucket. And there are all kinds of neat places to sit, inside and out.

John and Debby Bennett bought the establishment in 1996 and quickly enhanced the gardens, a talent he learned from his father, a professional landscaper. A Nantucket native, he met his wife-to-be at the local hospital, where both were employed.

Debby serves a buffet breakfast in one of the main-floor sitting rooms, each with a fireplace. Guests can eat here or adjourn to the patio, where the hostess matches the tablecloths with the flowers that are in bloom. Fresh fruit, cereal, muffins and Portuguese toasting bread are typical fare. In the afternoon, Debby offers hot or iced tea and snacks.

Bedrooms are notable for spatter-painted floors, Laura Ashley wallpapers, frilly bedding, fresh flowers and antiques. Many boast kingsize beds and fireplaces, and all have private baths, telephones and TVs nicely built into the walls or concealed in armoires. Room 6 on the third floor yields a view of the ocean, and two others offer harbor views. A second-floor apartment comes with a fireplaced sitting room, kingsize bedroom, kitchen and private deck.

Few B&Bs have so many neat places to sit and relax, inside or out. There are five sitting rooms on three floors, a rooftop deck with a view of the harbor, reading porches and a couple of brick patios beside the lovely gardens.

(508) 228-9480. www.clifflodgenantucket.com. Twelve rooms with private baths. Mid-June through September: doubles, $175 to $265. Spring and fall: $135 to $175. November-March: $105 to $135. Children over 12.

The Sherburne Inn, 10 Gay St., Nantucket 02554.

The first time Pittsburgh corporate types Dale Hamilton III and Susan Gasparich traveled to Nantucket, they took their bicycles off the ferry, pedaled a couple of blocks and decided, "this was the place," in Dale's words. Thirty days later, they were back on the island negotiating the purchase of the Sherburne (née The House at 10 Gay) Inn.

Balcony view from The Sherburne Inn.

Within the year, Dale had sold his construction companies in Pennsylvania and the pair were in residence in this structure, which was built as the Atlantic Silk Factory, but has served as a lodging establishment for most of its 160 years.

Dale and Susan continued the renovating and redecorating launched by the previous owner. They offer eight guest rooms, all with king or queen beds. Four are on the main floor and four on the second; a beautiful winding staircase connects the two. Interestingly, there's a fireplaced parlor with television on each floor.

The bedrooms, bright and cheery, are decorated to the Federal period. They contain canopy and poster beds, oriental rugs and fine artworks. We liked No. 8 upstairs in the rear with a king bed, clawfoot tub with shower and a private balcony overlooking the side and rear yards. Another room holds a small library and a mini-refrigerator.

Susan bakes blueberry or rhubarb muffins to supplement the natural breads, bagels and English muffins served for continental breakfast. The meal is taken in the main-floor parlor, on a deck on one side of the house or in the yard surrounded by gardens and a privet hedge on the other side. Tea and cookies or wine and cheese may be served in the afternoon.

(508) 228-4425 or (888) 557-4425. Fax (508) 228-8114. www.sherburneinn.com. Eight rooms with private baths. Mid-June to mid-October: doubles, $185 to $310. Rest of year: doubles, $85 to $250. Children over 6. Two- or three-night minimum most periods.

Ships Inn, 13 Fair St., Nantucket 02554.

Built in 1831 by whaling captain Obed Starbuck, this house occupies the site where Martha Coffin Mott, the first woman abolitionist, was born in 1793. Nicely restored in 1991 by chef-owner Mark Gottwald and his wife Ellie, it now claims some of Nantucket's most comfortable accommodations as well as a small restaurant of distinction.

Named after ships that Starbuck commanded, the ten guest rooms contain many of the original furnishings and most have queen beds, although bed configurations vary. They have been refurbished with new wallpapers and tiled baths and come with interesting window treatments, Neutrogena toiletries and mini-refrigerators in cabinets beneath the TV sets. Most have reading chairs and half have desks. All but two tiny single rooms are more spacious than most Nantucket bedrooms.

Guests enjoy mid-afternoon tea with coffeecake and cookies in the large living room. A continental-plus breakfast of fruit, cereal, scones and muffins is set out in the morning.

Chef Mark, who trained at Le Cirque in New York and at Spago in Los Angeles, oversees the restaurant on the lower level (see Dining Spots). The Gottwalds winter with their children in Vero Beach, Fla., where they operate Ellie's, an acclaimed restaurant on the Intra-Coastal Waterway. They and much of their staff go back and forth between Vero Beach and Nantucket.

(508) 228-0040. www.nantucket.net/lodging.shipsinn. Ten rooms with private baths. Doubles, $210 to $235. Three-night minimum in season. Children over 10. Closed late October to Memorial Day.

Centerboard Guest House, 8 Chester St., Box 456, Nantucket 02554.

One of the more elegant and romantic of Nantucket's B&Bs is this winner of a restoration at the edge of the historic district. It was established and stylized by a Long Island artist and interior designer, who sold in 1998 to Debbie Wassil from Cape Cod.

There's a big window seat here in the living room, outfitted with a TV and stereo, and the floors bear a pickled finish. Adjacent is a casually formal dining room, with cane chairs around a handful of tables, where "the largest continental breakfast you could imagine is served," according to the innkeeper. A big bowl of fruit (from kiwi to blueberries), granola and cereals, assorted muffins (blueberry-cranberry and mandarin orange-chocolate chip, at a recent visit) and Portuguese breads are the fare.

A two-room suite on the first floor was inspired by a masculine sitting room in an English manor house. It has a library-style living room in dark woods and hunter green, a bedroom with a queensize canopy feather bed with down comforters, and a glamorous bathroom in deep green marble, with a jacuzzi in one section, a large marble-tiled shower in another, and the sink and w.c. in still another. The suite has two TVs and plush furnishings, and no fewer than six bouquets of fresh and dried flowers were scattered about when we stayed.

Upstairs, the theme is romantic – one of Victorian elegance and charm, in the owner's words. All with telephones, TVs and refrigerators stocked with soft drinks, the four guest rooms here are bright, airy and decorated in soft pastels. Three have queen beds and one has two double beds. They come with ceiling fans, iron and brass bedsteads, lacy pillows, bathrooms with baskets of Gilchrist & Soames toiletries, and even a couple of murals painted by Martha's Vineyard artist Richard

Immarrino. A studio apartment in the basement, which Debbie likens to a houseboat, has built-in double beds and a kitchenette. It sleeps two to five.

(508) 228-9696. www.centerboardguesthouse.com. Five rooms, one studio and one suite with private baths. Summer and special events, doubles $210 to $285, suite $335 to $425. Spring and fall: doubles $135 to $195, suite $265 to $335. Late fall through early spring: doubles, $110 to $135, suite, $225 to $255.

Anchor Inn, 66 Centre St., Nantucket 02554.

Built by a whaling ship captain, this B&B in the heart of the historic district was the home in the 1950s of the Gilbreths of "Cheaper by the Dozen" fame, who wrote of their experience in the book *Innside Nantucket.* Today it's run very personally by Charles and Ann Balas, active Nantucket promoters who have been resident owners and outgoing hosts since 1983. Retired from their former Nantucket Fine Chocolates store, they have been known to put out chocolates at night in the inn's front parlor.

The interior retains its original random-width floorboards and antique paneling. Eleven guest rooms, named after whaling ships, have tiled baths with hair dryers, queen or twin beds, and period furnishings. TVs and telephones have been added lately. There's the usual Nantucket parlor with fireplace, a rust-colored corduroy sofa and wing chairs.

To the accompaniment of classical music, Charles's homemade muffins are served for continental breakfast on the enclosed wraparound side porch, its windows covered with café curtains.

Guests relax on a pleasant patio with lounge furniture in the side pocket-garden.

(508) 228-0072. www.anchor-inn.net. Eleven rooms with private baths. June to mid-September and most weekends: doubles $165 to $275. Rest of year: $65 to $135. No children.

Seven Sea Street, 7 Sea St., Nantucket 02554.

This guest house of post and beam construction was built in 1987 on the last vacant lot in town by the Parker family, who also run the Tuckernuck Inn. Matthew Parker and his wife Mary offer rooms with queensize fishnet canopy beds, built-in oak desks, rocking chairs, TV/VCRs in armoires, phones and painted furniture that Matthew assembled himself. All contain small refrigerators and modern baths with a vanity outside, and suites have gas-stove fireplaces. Deluxe mattresses, 310-thread count sheets, robes, hair dryers and a box of Nantucket chocolate-covered cranberries are in each room in the main house as well as in an adjacent guest house.

Also available are two suites. One has a fireplaced sitting room with extra queen futon and the other is billed as a deluxe suite/apartment with fireplaced great room and kitchen.

Guests have use of a couple of small common rooms on the second floor, the widow's walk deck with a view of the harbor, an indoor whirlpool tub and a pleasant brick patio edged by gardens and hedges.

Matthew or an assistant innkeeper bake blueberry and cranberry muffins for continental breakfast, which they serve with coffee cake and fresh fruit on fine china in the dining room.

(508) 228-3577. Fax (508) 228-3578. www.sevenseastreetinn.com. Nine rooms and two suites with private baths. Late June to Labor Day: doubles $245, suites $295 to $325. Spring and fall: doubles $135 to $195, suites $195 to $275. January to mid-April: doubles, $95, suites $155 to $195. Children over 5.

Dining rooms are decorated in Williamsburg style at 21 Federal.

Dining Spots

21 Federal, 21 Federal St., Nantucket.

One of Nantucket's larger and higher-profile restaurants, 21 Federal is on two floors of a sand-colored house with white trim, designated by a brass plaque and elegantly decorated in Williamsburg style. There are six dining rooms of museum-quality, Federal period decor, some with their white-linened tables rather too close together for privacy.

Our latest lunch in a small room next to the convivial bar produced a smashing pasta – spaghettini with two sauces, one thyme-saffron and one smoked tomato, topped with crabmeat-stuffed shrimp – and a grilled shrimp salad with Greek olives, feta cheese, pine nuts and spinach. Three varieties of breads came with, and a tropical fruit sorbet was a refreshing ending.

Even more memorable was a summer lunch in the courtyard, where white-linened tables create an elegant setting. The pheasant and wild rice soup of the day and a linguini salad with shrimp and pine nuts were out of this world. The five-salad sampler proved less interesting.

Chef Russell Jaehnig chef changes the short dinner menu weekly. Expect main courses like grilled swordfish with mole and avocado salsa, sautéed halibut with lobster risotto and foie gras butter, seared pork chop with rosemary-apple chutney and, from the grill, aged sirloin steak or veal loin chop with a creamy gratin of potatoes and leeks.

For starters, how about tuna, crab and avocado napoleon with cilantro vinaigrette or a slow-roasted portobello mushroom with parmesan pudding? Finish with warm chocolate lava cake with kahlua caramel or one of the great homemade ice creams and sorbets.

This is Nantucket dining at its best, not as pretentious or as pricey as some and more exciting than many.

(508) 228-2121. www.21federal.net. Entrées, $23 to $33. Lunch, Monday-Saturday in summer, 11:30 to 2:30. Dinner, Monday-Saturday 6 to 9:30 or 10. Closed January-March.

Topper's at the Wauwinet, Wauwinet Road, Nantucket

Named for their owners' dog, whose portrait is in one of the dining rooms, this restaurant is a favorite of the Nantucket gentry, who book its tables days – even weeks – in advance. Dining is leisurely in two elegantly appointed, side-by-side rooms with large windows. Upholstered chairs in blue and white are comfortable, tables are well spaced (or screened from their neighbors), and masses of flowers are all around.

Chef Christopher Freeman joined the Wauwinet in 1997 from the Mayflower Inn in Connecticut, where he was known for high-caliber regional cuisine, a style he has refined here. Among appetizers, we were impressed with the signature lobster crab cakes with smoked corn, jalapeño olives and a divine mustard sauce, and the coriander-seared yellowfin tuna sashimi with soba noodles and pickled vegetables, served on handmade sushi boards of purple heart wood.

Every main course we've had here has been superior. Included were roast rack of lamb with potato-fennel brandade and grilled veal chop with wild grape compote, both accompanied by baby vegetables (tiny pattypan squash and carrots about a big as a fingernail) and a wedge of potatoes. The hearty Nantucket lobster stew – incorporating nearly three pounds of lobster, salsify, leeks, island tomatoes and tomalley croutons – is a perennial hit. So are the caramelized sea scallops with french green lentils and seared foie gras vinaigrette.

Desserts include a signature chocolate marquise with raspberries and grand marnier and an "ABC tart" comprised of almonds, rum-soaked bananas and chocolate that's to die for.

The sparkling Wauwinet Water pours freely from antique cobalt blue bottles, the breadsticks and French baguettes are crusty, salt and pepper are served only on request, and the Wine Spectator grand award wine list is strong in American and French vintages from a selection of more than 900.

The Wauwinet Lady, a 26-passenger water launch, offers complimentary round-trip excursions from town to Topper's for lunch or dinner in season.

(508) 228-8768 or (800) 426-8718. Entrées, $32 to $42. Lunch, Monday-Saturday noon to 2. Dinner nightly, 6 to 9:30, jackets requested. Sunday brunch, noon to 2. Closed November to mid-May.

The Boarding House and The Pearl, 12 Federal St., Nantucket.

The Boarding House provided our first great meal on Nantucket during its inaugural summer of 1973. It since has moved around the corner to considerably larger quarters, and several owners (and chefs) have come and gone. Taken over by Seth and Angela Raynor (he a former sous chef at 21 Federal and both veterans of the famed Chanticleer in Siasconset), it's better than ever.

A cathedral-ceilinged Victorian lounge with small faux-marble tables on a flagstone floor opens into a sunken dining room. The latter is striking as can be in rich cream and pink, with a curved banquette at the far end in front of a mural of Vernazzia. Villeroy & Boch china of the Florida pattern graces the nicely spaced tables, which allow for one of Nantucket's more pleasant dining situations.

Upstairs is their crowning fillip, a showy, aquatic-look, designer restaurant called **The Pearl,** specializing in high-style coastal cuisine. It's serene in white and blue, with an aquarium at the entrance and a scrim curtain giving the illusion of floating at sea. Billed as a separate restaurant for more leisurely dining, "it's like two siblings in a family," said Angela.

Equal to the dramatic settings is the cooking of Seth, one of 30 chefs chosen to appear on the "Great Chefs of the East" public television series. We were impressed with our latest dinner here: mellow sautéed crab cakes with scallion crème fraîche and grilled quail with crisp fried onion rings and baby mixed greens, for starters, and main courses of pan-roasted salmon with Thai curried cream and crispy rice noodles and a spicy Asian seafood stew with lobster, shrimp and scallops. Coffee ice cream with chocolate sauce and a dense chocolate-kahlua terrine were worthy endings.

Chef de cuisine David Buchman oversees the Boarding House, while Seth directs the larger Pearl, a spectacular showcase for leisurely, seafood-oriented dinners. Typical starters here are an island-style seafood platter featuring Nantucket oysters, sashimi of striped bass, a martini of yellowfin tuna and steamed ginger shrimp dumplings. Main courses might marry sautéed local flounder with seared New York State foie gras or dish up wok-seared lobster with vegetable lo mein and grilled lime. The outdoor terrace appeals for cocktails and a bistro lunch or supper.

Boarding House, (508) 228-9622. www.boardinghouse-pearl.com. Entrées $25 to $34. Patio lunch in summer, Wednesday-Sunday noon to 2; dinner nightly, 6 to 10, fewer nights in winter.

The Pearl, (508) 228-9701. Entrées, $29 to $45. Dinner nightly, 6 to 10, late-night menu to midnight. Closed January-March.

American Seasons, 80 Centre St., Nantucket. (508) 228-7111.

Eclectic American food and more rational prices make this one of Nantucket's restaurant hits. Whimsical décor characterizes the simple square dining room, in which a local artist hand-painted the table tops to resemble game boards and added a stunning wall mural of a vine-covered Willamette Valley hillside in Oregon. An outdoor patio is pleasant in summer.

Chef-owner Michael Getter and his executive chef, Michael LaScola, categorize the menu by regions – Pacific Coast, Wild West, New England and Down South – each with two or three appetizers and entrées. You're supposed to mix and match, pairing, say, a Florida rock shrimp gumbo with andouille sausage, okra and biscuits with a lobster and corn enchilada in a blue cornmeal crêpe from the West. Those and a lentil salad with goat cheese, frisée and grilled leeks made a memorable meal. Or you could start with a Pacific foie gras crème brûlée with rhubarb and fuji apple compote and move on to a "New England" main course of grilled leg of lamb with a goat cheese bread pudding, roasted eggplant and tomato chutney in a candied garlic sauce.

The all-American wine list has been honored by Wine Spectator.

(508) 228-7111. www.americanseasons.com. Entrées, $24 to $30. Dinner nightly in summer, 6 to 10, fewer nights in off-season. Closed January to April.

Le Languedoc, 24 Broad St., Nantucket.

Although the Grennan family offer guest rooms in four buildings, their attractive white building with blue shutters across from the Jared Coffin House complex is noted most for its dining, as it has been since 1975.

Downstairs is an intimate café with checkered cloths. Upstairs are four small dining rooms with peach walls and white trim, windows covered with peach draperies and valances, and changing art from a local gallery. Nicely spaced tables bear hurricane chimneys with thick candles and vases, each containing one lovely salmon-hued rose.

Among appetizers, smoked Nantucket pheasant with cranberry relish was very good and very colorful with red cabbage and slices of apples and oranges on a bed of lettuce. One of us sampled chef Neal Grennan's noisettes of lamb with artichokes in a rosemary sauce. The other had sautéed sweetbreads and lobster in puff pastry, in a sauce that included shiitake mushrooms, cognac and shallots. Nicely presented on piping hot oval white plates, they were accompanied by snow peas, broccoli, pureed turnips, yellow peppers, sweet potato and peach slices. Other interesting choices include cedar-planked salmon with lobster mashed potatoes, grilled rare tuna with seaweed salad and truffled loin of rabbit with sundried cherries.

For dessert, we passed up strawberry pie and pears poached in a reduction of port to share a dense chocolate hazelnut torte spiked with grand marnier.

You can dine less expensively but quite well in the café. Lunch is available here and on a canopied sidewalk terrace.

(508) 228-2552. www.lelanguedoc.com. Entrées, $21 to $38. Lunch seasonally, Tuesday-Saturday noon to 2. Dinner nightly, 6 to 9:30. Closed January to mid-April.

Straight Wharf Restaurant, Straight Wharf, Nantucket.

Seafood is showcased in this summery restaurant that is the height of chic on the waterfront. The interior is a pristine palette of shiny floors and soaring, shingled walls topped by billowing banners and hung with striking paintings by an island artist. Beyond is a canopied, rib-lit deck overhanging the harbor. The "in" place is the noisy side bar and lounge, with crowds usually spilling outside onto a terrace in front. The same kitchen serves both, with a sophisticated seafood menu in the dining room and deck and more rustic, casual grill fare in the bar.

Starters are standouts, among them the signature smoked bluefish pâté with focaccia melba toasts, a rich lobster bisque heavily laced with sherry, seared beef carpaccio with shards of parmigiano-reggiano, white truffle oil and mesclun, and local black bass with a vegetable mignonette. A sauté of halibut with lobster and morels and grilled rare tuna with white beans, escarole and roasted garlic were excellent main courses. Choices range from pan-roasted local cod with clams and smoked sausage to rosemary-grilled rack of lamb with eggplant and lamb cassoulet. The dessert specialty is warm Valrhona chocolate tart with orange cardamom gelato, but we usually go for the trio of refreshing fruit sorbets.

(508) 228-4499. Entrées, $32 to $42. Dinner by reservation, nightly except Monday 6 to 10. Open Memorial Day to late September. Grill, $15 to $22, no reservations.

Cioppino's, 20 Broad St., Nantucket.

Considered the "friendliest" restaurant in Nantucket, this relaxed restaurant is run by welcoming owner Tracy Root, the former maître-d' at Chanticleer, and his wife Susan, who was a bartender at the Summer House, both in Siasconset.

Dining is in a couple of small rooms on the main floor, pretty in white, black and mauve. Upstairs are larger rooms, one with a skylit peaked ceiling and a stunning mural of what looks to be Monet's garden by a Nantucket artist. In season you can dine at umbrellaed tables on the rear patio.

The dinner menu ranges widely from grilled sea bass with smoked mango relish to rack of lamb provençal. San Francisco cioppino is a house specialty.

At an autumn lunch, we enjoyed the special fried oysters with béarnaise sauce, a nouvelle presentation with rice, broccoli, strained zucchini and swirled yellow squash. Also excellent was the caribbean shrimp and avocado salad. Good sourdough rolls came first; a mellow key lime pie was the finale. On our way out, we paused to look at the wine labels inlaid in the bar, representing a few of the owner's collection of more than 12,000 labels.

(508) 228-4622. Entrées, $19.75 to $31. Lunch daily, 11:30 to 2:30. Dinner nightly from 5:30. Sunday brunch.

Ships Inn, 13 Fair St., Nantucket.

Dinners here have received considerable attention since chef-owner Mark Gottwald and his wife Ellie took over. Mark, who trained at Le Cirque in New York and at Spago in Los Angeles, oversees the cooking duties with a sizable kitchen staff, some of whom accompany the couple in the winter to Florida, where they run the acclaimed Ellie's in Vero Beach.

Ship's Inn offers dining and lodging.

The dining room on the ground level here is attractive with apricot walls over white wainscoting, exposed beams, a white fireplace in the center of the room, candles in the many-paned windows, and white-linened tables dressed with candles and fresh flowers. There also are tables for eating in the adjacent Dory Bar.

The California-French cuisine is bold and flavorful. Among entrées, you might find grilled halibut with tomato vinaigrette, grilled shrimp with Asian greens and lime-soy broth, crispy salmon with cabernet sauce and niçoise vegetables, roast duck with plum wine jus and steak au poivre. Or consider a pasta, perhaps rigatoni with duck confit with port-wine glace. Start with fried calamari with ponzu sauce or a smoked sirloin salad with white truffle vinaigrette. Finish with raspberry sorbet or chocolate-soufflé cake.

(508) 228-0040. Entrées. $22 to $34. Dinner, Thursday-Monday 5:30 to 9. Closed November-April.

Black-Eyed Susan's, 10 India St., Nantucket.

This small and funky storefront – for years merely a breakfast diner – is lovingly tended by Susan Handy and Jeff Worster, both with long backgrounds in local restaurants. They still serve breakfast, featuring things like sourdough french toast with orange Jack Daniels butter and pecans and a spicy Thai curry scramble with broccoli and new potatoes. Most dishes come with a choice of hash browns or black-eyed peas.

Jeff, a chef-taught chef, obtained a lot of his cross-cultural culinary ideas while cooking in Beverly Hills. From his open kitchen behind the dining counter come such pasta dishes as wild-mushroom ravioli on carrot-ginger puree with organic greens and romano cheese. Moroccan lamb stew on minted couscous, grilled halibut with salsa verde and oyster gumbo were a few of the intriguing dishes on his fall dinner menu. Lighter eaters could order a huge hearts of romaine salad with caesar dressing for $8. There's one dessert a night, perhaps a cobbler or bread pudding.

The atmosphere is social as in a European café at dinner, and singles love to eat at the long counter. Summer diners usually face long waits for a table.

(508) 325-0308. Entrées, $17 to $26. Breakfast daily, 7 to 1. Dinner, Tuesday-Saturday 6 to 9. BYOB. No credit cards. Closed six weeks in winter.

Fifty-Six Union, 56 Union St., Nantucket.

Chef-owner Peter Jannelle and his wife Wendy offer light, healthful global fare in this casually elegant eatery located in a former diner called the Elegant Dump on the outskirts of downtown.

Tourists rarely find the welcoming place, which seats about 100 in a pair of dining rooms set with nicely spaced white-clothed tables flanked by black windsor chairs. Those in the know go for such starters as curried mussels in a Thai yellow curry broth over scallion and ginger rice, grilled shrimp with lemongrass and ginger, and sweetbread strudel with walnuts, chèvre and prosciutto in a brandy demi-glace.

Everyone raves about the Javanese spicy fried rice, a year-round menu mainstay in which shrimp and chicken are tossed with sambal, ginger and Asian vegetables. Other favorite main dishes include pan-seared ahi tuna rubbed in Japanese seven-spice powder and served with sesame-garlic vinaigrette, grilled Jamaican jerked chicken with spicy caribbean fruit salsa and jicama slaw, and grilled sirloin steak with a red wine and caramelized onion demi-glace. The mixed grill might combine lamb, smoked chicken sausage and pork tenderloin with creamy mascarpone polenta.

The most extravagant dessert is the chocolate mousse tower bearing chocolate rum mousse, hazelnut praline ganache and a chocolate shortbread crust.

(508) 228-6135. Entrées, $24 to $33. Dinner nightly in summer, 6 to 10, Wednesday-Sunday 6 to 9 in off-season. Sunday brunch, 10 to 1.

Diversions

Nantucket's attractions run the gamut from beaches to history to architecture to art and antiques. Except for the beaches, almost everything the visitor needs or wants to do is right in Nantucket village, and easily reached on foot or by bicycle or moped. A number of pamphlets detail interesting walking tours.

Twenty-five buildings and sites of special interest are maintained by the Nantucket Historical Association, which offers a combination pass to twelve for $15. Among them:

The Whaling Museum, the largest complex and one most visitors pass just after they leave the ferry, is considered the nation's best after the New Bedford Whaling Museum. Originally a candle factory, it contains an original beam press still poised to render whale spermaceti into candles and oil. Rooms are devoted to scrimshaw, whaling equipment and objects brought home by seamen from the South Seas. A whale jaw with teeth, the skeleton of a 43-foot whale and whalecraft shops – a sail loft, cooperage, shipsmith and such – are among the attractions.

Fair Street Museum and Quaker Meeting House. Nantucket's art museum records the lives of early citizens in portraits. An upstairs gallery houses more recent works and special exhibitions. The adjoining Meeting House was built in 1838.

Farther from the center of town are the **Oldest House** (1686), the **Old Mill** (1746) and the **Old Gaol** (1805). Numerous other structures are under Historical Association auspices, but if you simply walk any of the streets fanning out from the center you'll stumble onto your own finds. Don't miss central Main Street, particularly the three handsome Georgian mansions known as **The Three Bricks.**

Tours. The best of several is the 90-minute walking tour led by Dirk Gardiner Roggeveen, (508) 221-0075, a twelfth-generation Nantucketer and island historian. He goes "where the buses don't," through hidden alleys and byways, all the while spinning tales of Nantucket lore. Robert Pitman Grimes, (508) 228-9382, also a Nantucket native, entertains visitors with interesting tidbits about island history on a nearly two-hour tour of the island in a suburban van.

Art Galleries and Antiques Shops. Besides beaches and good food, it's said that visitors are attracted to Nantucket by all the galleries and antiques shops. They certainly have a wide choice: one brochure is devoted to antiquing on Nantucket, and one of summer's big events is the annual antiques show in early August. Such Nantucket scenes as cobblestoned streets, deserted moors and rose-covered cottages in Siasconset appeal to artists, whose works hang in galleries all along the wharves.

Shopping. Nantucket is a shopper's paradise and, were it not for the cobblestoned streets and salt air, you could as easily picture yourself in Newburyport or New Canaan. Specialty stores with names like **Nobby Clothes, Beautiful People** and **The Cashmere Shop** compete with the more traditional like **Murray's Toggery Shop** and **Mitchell's Book Corner,** all across the several square blocks of "downtown" Nantucket. We love the **Lion's Paw,** an exceptional gift shop full of cheerful pottery; check out the animal's tea party. Other standouts are **Zero Main** for suave women's clothing, **Rosa Rugosa** for painted furniture and household decorative items, the **Forager House Collection** of folk art and accessories and **Nantucket Looms** with beautiful, whimsical woven items and a sweater in the window for "only $750."

Majolica offers colorful hand-painted Italian ceramics. **The Spectrum** is good for arts and crafts. **The Complete Kitchen** is one of the better kitchenware stores we've seen. **Claire Murray** has fabulous hand-hooked rugs, and **Lilly Pulitzer** offers her trademark apparel.

Extra-Special

Nantucket Lightship Baskets. The lightships that protected boats from the treacherous shoal waters off the south and east end of the island in the mid-18th century spawned a cottage industry indigenous to Nantucket. The crews of the South Shoal Lightship turned to basket-weaving to while away their hours on duty. Their duty ended, the seamen continued to make baskets ashore – first primitive and heavy-duty types for carrying laundry or groceries, later more beautiful handbags appealing to visitors. The latter were inspired by the Sayle family, who continue the tradition at their shop at 112 Washington St. Today, Nantucket's famed baskets come in all shapes and sizes (including 14-karat gold miniatures) and seem to be ubiquitous in the shops and on tanned arms. The handbags have ivory carvings on top and carry hefty price tags.

Edgartown, Mass.

Fall for the Vineyard

One of the best things about visiting an island is the ferry ride over from the mainland. The ringing of ships' bells, the deep blast as you depart, the hustle and bustle of getting cars on and off – they all add to the anticipation of what is to come.

Even though the trip to Martha's Vineyard from Wood's Hole takes less than an hour, that's time enough to listen to the buoys clanking, and to watch one shore fade in the distance and another grow closer.

It's time enough also for a transition – to leave mainland cares behind, before arriving at Vineyard Haven or Oak Bluffs and stepping into a different milieu.

The Vineyard is nothing if not varied. There is bustling Vineyard Haven, the island's principal commercial center and not all tht different from the mainland you left behind.

Oak Bluffs, where the many-splendored gingerbread cottages around the tabernacle display a rainbow of hues, was founded as a Methodist campground. It's also a Victorian beach resort and summer home to many upper class African Americans.

At the other end of the island are Aquinnah and the Native American-owned restaurants and shops atop windswept Aquinnah, its Gay Head cliffs a mosaic of colors and an Eastern mini-version of the Big Sur.

In the interior of West Tisbury and Chilmark, the landscape is such that you might not even think you were on an island.

Then there's Edgartown, as up-to-date as a resort town can be while still reflecting a heritage back to 1642. It's a prosperous seaport village, which boomed during the whaling days of the 19th century and became a yachting center in the 20th century. It's been in the news the last few years during summer visits by former President Clinton and entourage.

Long a retreat for the rich and famous as well as the rich and not-so-famous, Edgartown is best appreciated in the off-season. The crowds are gone, but the charm remains as benign autumn weather lingers at least through Thanksgiving. The beaches are deserted except for strollers. The waters are left for the fishermen and a few hardy sailors and wind-surfers. Cottages and condos are battened down for the winter.

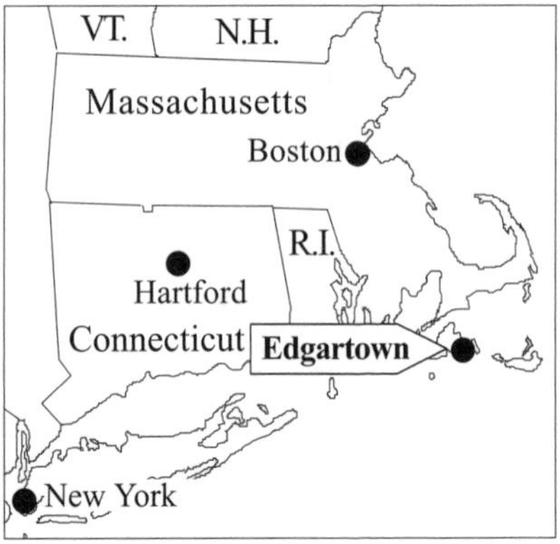

Autumn is the season that islanders and knowing visitors look forward to, particularly in Edgartown, a year-round haven for retirees and escapees from the mainland. Many inns and restaurants remain open most of the year, but prices are reduced. You can be near the ocean in a moderate clime, and immerse yourself in a delightful community.

"Fall for Martha's Vineyard," the magazine ads entice in trying to boost autumn trade. It's hard to imagine how anyone wouldn't.

Inn Spots

The Charlotte Inn, 27 South Summer St., Edgartown 02539.

You register at a front desk so ornate that it is pictured in the centerfold of an Architectural Digest inn book. Behind is a small, deluxe restaurant in which you dine romantically in an indoor-outdoor garden reminiscent of New Orleans or Europe. You relax beforehand on the side porch running the depth of the Summer House, rejoicing in the fountains and flowers and a scent resembling eucalyptus. The ice for your drinks comes in a silver engraved thermal bucket custom-made in England. And later you retire to one of 25 guest accommodations that are so lavishly and tastefully furnished as to defy expectation.

Coach House Suite at The Charlotte Inn.

The Charlotte Inn compound, which Gery and Paula Conover have developed from a private home he acquired in 1971, is nothing short of a masterpiece. It carries the aura of moneyed elegance that's the hallmark of Relais & Châteaux properties. But it's also a very personal place, a reflection of Gery's desire to have an art gallery and of Paula's flair with flowers, decorating and stitchery. She made many of the needlepoint pillows that enhance each guest room.

The compound is a landscaper's dream, full of exotic greenery, vivid flowers, trickling fountains and trellised arbors. Gery laid the spacious courtyard in front of the Coach House Suite brick by brick, and tends to the flowers with old watering cans from one of his many and diverse collections.

Rooms are in the main two-story 1860 house, a rear carriage house that Gery built without blueprints in 1980, the 1705 Garden House (so called because of its lovely English garden in back) across the street, the 1840 Summer House next door, and the Coach House Suite.

The much-photographed deluxe suite upstairs in the Carriage House has an English hunting feel to it: a queensize four-poster bed, a mahogany sleigh bed redecorated as a sofa, a working marble fireplace, a beamed cathedral ceiling, thick beige carpeting, walls covered in hunter green or red and green stripes, a TV and stereo hidden away in a chest, and a treasury of bric-a-brac that includes a gentleman's riding boots. Even more to our liking is the Coach House Suite, bigger and less masculine, outfitted like a well-planned house. The bed is covered with Frette linens, there's a tiny balcony and the living room, with its easy chairs and hassocks, is exquisite. The walk-in dressing room/closet is a fantasy of hats, fans and hat boxes. Downstairs is what general manager Carol Read calls the garage; it would be a museum anywhere else. Here – amid so many museum-quality treasures – it goes relatively unnoticed by all but the Coach House occupants, who have their own museum for the duration upstairs. The suites command top dollar, and Gery says they're booked nearly every night.

The other accommodations vary in size and style (the prevailing decorating motif is English country), but all have queensize or twin beds triple-sheeted in Frette linens, are luxuriously appointed and supremely comfortable. Some have fireplaces, and most have small TVs, Bose radios and antique rotary-dial telephones. The service is first-rate. Upon returning from dinner in the inn's restaurant, L'Etoile (see Dining Spots), we found the hand towels had been replaced, the bottled water replenished and the silver ice bucket refilled.

The Conovers were much in evidence the next morning. Gery watered the last of the season's flowers and Paula greeted guests and poured coffee for breakfast in the ever-so-elegant Green Room, richly paneled in 200-year-old mahogany imported from England. Fresh orange juice, toast and omelets cooked to order got the day off to an auspicious start after a memorable stay in an inn that makes you feel you're a special guest in the finest of homes.

(508) 627-4751. Fax (508) 627-4652. Twenty-three rooms and two suites with private baths. June-October and weekends in May: doubles $295 to $550, suites $695 and $795. November-April weekends and May midweek: doubles $295 to $475, suites $550 to $595. November-April midweek: doubles $295 to $425, suites $450 to $495. Two-night minimum weekends. Children over 14.

Hob Knob Inn, 128 Main St., Box 239, Edgartown 02539.

Refashioned as one of the most deluxe places to stay in Edgartown, this summery, sophisticated B&B reflects the tastes of owner Margaret White. A Colorado commercial property manager, she was looking for a new life on the Vineyard where she had summered with her parents. Her realtor pointed out the Governor Bradford Inn and asked if she'd ever thought of running an inn. "I said, 'show me the numbers' – and here I am."

Maggie White took over the comfortable but rather charmless Gothic Revival structure she called "kind of a vanilla box" in 1996. She closed it and redecorated every room with taste and flair, added guest services and hired a fulltime breakfast chef. She reopened the inn as the Hob Knob, named for the bygone country estate in Ohio of her sporty grandparents from Cleveland. "All it takes is attention to detail and guest services," says she.

The door to each guest room is hand-painted with a mock porcelain plaque bearing the room number and a cow, with a miniature outline of the island hidden somewhere in its spots. The cow motif represents the live herd that Maggie raises on her farm in West Tisbury

The sixteen rooms on three floors come with kingsize beds (except for two with twins), updated private baths, chintz fabrics, TVs and telephones. The rooms we

Gothic Revival house has been transformed into Hob Knob Inn.

saw were nicely appointed in crisp English country style. Down pillows and comforters, all-cotton sheets, and Caswell-Massey toiletries are the rule. Pastel-colored walls in each room are dotted with lineups of antique plates. The plates are the signature of Maggie's cousin, an interior designer, who acquired them at estate sales in Cleveland.

Common rooms include a library with fireplace, a dining room overlooking Main Street, a conference room and a compact health center and mini-spa in the basement. The Hob Knob's 27-foot Boston Whaler is available for charter, skipper included. Maggie will prepare a gourmet picnic basket for $20 each.

Fresh-squeezed lemonade and afternoon tea with hot scones and finger sandwiches greet arrivals on the side porch. Breakfast, cooked to order offers a choice of omelets, eggs benedict, frittatas, waffles, pancakes and such. Maggie's specialty is the mag-a-muffin, two poached eggs atop tomatoes and Canadian bacon on an English muffin.

(508) 627-9510 or (800) 696-2723. Fax (508) 627-4560. www.hobknob.com. Sixteen rooms with private baths. Memorial Day through October: doubles, $200 to $525. Rest of year: $125 to $300. Children over 7.

The Victorian Inn, 24 South Water St., Edgartown 02539.

Masses of impatiens brighten the striking facade of this inn, nicely located across from the famous Pagoda Tree in an area of ship's captain's homes. It's as Victorian as can be, well deserving of its listing in the National Register. It's also generally as luxurious as can be, from its elegantly furnished rooms to the gourmet breakfasts served in the English garden backing up to the Charlotte Inn compound in the rear.

Innkeepers Stephen and Karyn Caliri from Plymouth happened to be staying here when they learned the inn was being sold at auction. They put in the winning bid and set about a five-year upgrading plan, promising the inn would be "pretty spiffy when we're done." To start, they restored the fireplaces in the parlor and breakfast room to working order and redecorated the dining room in shades of rich reds and pink. They since have enhanced all fourteen guest rooms, all with updated bathrooms (only two with tubs) and some with inviting sitting areas. Karyn's favorite is the large and elegant Room 9 with king poster bed, Empire chest and sofa in the bay window. It and another deluxe room at the rear have porches with deck chairs and loungers overlooking the English garden and the carriage house of the Charlotte Inn. Stephen is partial to the third-floor Room 10, with queen canopy bed, dusty rose carpeting and two balconies, one facing the harbor. He also likes Room 14 with kingsize plantation bed and trundle beneath, white sofa and green armchairs and a deck beyond. Rooms vary considerably in size and appeal, as the range in rates suggests. Deep, rich shades of rose, green and blue are the prevailing colors, and some of the sheets and shower curtains are patterned with roses. Decanters of sherry and bowls of apples are put out in the Victorian parlor, where tea or lemonade are offered in the afternoon.

Karyn and a chef share the cooking chores for the four-course breakfast, which also is available to the public by reservation from 8 to 10 a.m. Fresh fruits, five kinds of juices and a pastry basket filled with assorted muffins (from orange to banana) and croissants start the repast. Main courses could be pumpkin pancakes, eggs benedict, fish cakes topped with poached eggs and creamed spinach, or Mexican eggs with cheese, corn and chiles. In summer, breakfast is served outside at white tables on a delightful brick patio amid the greenery and flowers of the English garden.

(508) 627-4784. Fourteen rooms with private baths. Memorial Day to Columbus Day: doubles, $185 to $385. Rest of year: $100 to $195. Children over 8.

Point Way Inn, Main Street at Pease's Point Way, Box 5255, Edgartown 02539.

Remodeled from a 150-year-old whaling captain's house, this recently renovated and redecorated B&B offers a variety of comfortable accommodations and hospitality galore.

Each of the guest rooms, grouped off various stairways in separate sections of the house, has its own bath and seven contain fireplaces. Under owners John Glendon and Claudia Miller from Connecticut, what had been a loveable mishmash now is eclectic and stylish, and a couple of smaller rooms have been reconfigured for more space. Three large rooms have balconies overlooking the garden. One room has a private patio and another has a private entrance that opens onto the main patio in the garden.

Three small rooms on the first and second floors with four-poster double beds are painted a cheerful yellow or pale blue and accented with florals. Light yellow ochre rag-rolled walls enhance the second-floor honeymoon Room 6 with queen poster bed and an updated bathroom. Room 7 on the second floor, handsome with sponged walls in beige and sage, has a living room with a sofabed and a balcony off the queensize bedroom. Room 12 is a third-floor beauty with queen poster bed, a sofabed and armchairs flanking the antique working fireplace. Its balcony has a retractable awning.

Separate from the other rooms and accessible from the garden is the main-floor Garden Room with a wrought-iron daybed and a queen bed decked out in red Ralph Lauren linens and duvet.

Reconfigured in 2001 was the large Deck Suite, opened up from two rooms with a kingsize bed in one section and two twins in another. It has a kitchenette and dining area, separate sun room, its own deck and private entrance.

Sea grasses and sculpture gardens are featured outside Point Way Inn.

The living room comes with a fireplace, games, complimentary wine and a well-stocked honor bar. In the breakfast room, the staff puts out a buffet of fresh orange juice, cereals, homemade granola, popovers, coffeecake, muffins, breads and waffles.

Tea, espresso or lemonade and cookies (oatmeal, just like our mothers used to make, at one visit) are an afternoon highlight. In season they're served in the sculpture garden, full of interesting sea grasses and bearing the works of Claudia, an artist from Bavaria.

And, typical of these hospitable innkeepers, they offer to loan guests the inn car.

(508) 627-8633 or (888) 711-6633. Fax (508) 627-3338. www.pointway.com. Twelve rooms and one suite with private baths. Mid-June to Labor Day: doubles $250 to $425, suite $700. Interim season: doubles $150 to $300, suite $400. November-April: doubles $100 to $200, suite $300.

The Shiverick Inn, Pent Lane at Pease's Point Way, Box 640, Edgartown 02539.

Built in 1840 for the town physician, this mansion was restored in 1984 by Philadelphia descendants of the Shiverick line and opened as the Dr. Shiverick House, a fancy if somewhat austere-feeling inn. Subsequent owners warmed up an antiques-filled masterpiece that some had found intimidating.

New owners Paul Weiss and Bryan Freehling take pride in what their brochure calls the meticulous preservation of "the graceful formalities of this distinctive period." They call it "grand elegance."

Inside the oak double-door entry is a high-ceilinged entrance hall with the original mahogany staircase and a remarkable showpiece spool cabinet, exemplary of the American, English and French antiques from the 18th and 19th centuries.

Ahead is a formal parlor/dining room, notable for gorgeous rugs over random-width floorboards restored from a barn in Vermont. A crystal chandelier hangs over

Rear cottage adds to lodging accommodations at Jonathan Munroe House.

the dining table, and porcelain figures line the mantel. Balloon draperies frame the parlor's windows onto a spacious garden room, which has a long sofa along one wall, wrought-iron furniture with ivy-patterned seats, and a long tiled counter (painted with ivy) for breakfast or cocktail service. Beyond is a delightful patio and garden colorful with pink and white flowers, which are also on view from an upstairs porch. A sunny library is made for relaxing.

The inn has ten guest rooms and suites on the first and second floors. Each has a full bath and six have working fireplaces. They are sumptuously furnished with four-poster or canopy beds and plush down comforters, Frette linens, a variety of art objects and antiques, oriental rugs, and rich wallpapers and fabrics.

A full breakfast starts with fresh fruit, cereal, yogurt and granola. The afternoon brings tea or lemonade, depending on season.

(508) 627-3797 or (800) 723-4292. Fax (508) 627-8441. www.shiverickinn.com. Eight rooms and two suites with private baths. June through mid-October: doubles $295 to $345, suites $385. Rest of year: doubles $145 to $220, suites $165 to $245. Children over 12.

The Jonathan Munroe House, 100 Main St., Box 5084, Edgartown 02539.

His family used to run the Darien Inn in Vermont's Northeast Kingdom, so Chip Yerkes comes by his sideline naturally. A building contractor on the Vineyard, he applied his carpentry talents in 1994 to his unassuming house built in 1840 and created a comfortable B&B.

Guests check in at a corner cabinet in the small front parlor, usually in time for the wine and cheese hour. Beyond are a larger, fireplaced parlor and a rear dining porch, where personable Chip and his assistants serve a gourmet breakfast of fresh fruits, baked goods, cereals and a choice among four entrées. The meal also may be taken in season on the rear patio.

The house contains six guest rooms, furnished simply but comfortably with king or queen beds and floral comforters with matching curtains. Four with marble fireplaces come with jacuzzi tubs. Bose radios and complimentary sherry are among the amenities. There are no televisions on the premises.

We were among Chip's first paying guests in his rear garden cottage. Snug and modern, it has a living room with a plush sofa and a wicker chair facing a brick fireplace, an old wood chest for a coffee table, an antique wood desk bearing a diary in which the previous guests waxed ecstatic, and a kitchenette with a ceramic sink, microwave, pottery dishes and an antique side-by-side dining table set for two. Paneling enhances the staircase and second-floor landing, where the whirlpool tub is ensconced beside votive candles and sconces for lighting. The queensize bed is situated beneath a vaulted ceiling in the bedroom. The cottage's screened porch may well be the best place in town to enjoy the carillon hymns played nightly from the St. Andrew's Episcopal Church nearby.

(508) 627-5536 or (877) 468-6763. www.jonathanmunroe.com. Six rooms and one cottage with private baths. May-October: doubles $190 to $250, cottage $350. Rest of year: doubles $99 to $170, cottage $250. Children over 12.

The Edgartown Inn, 56 North Water St., Box 1211, Edgartown 02539.

The plaque on the side of this weathered 1798 whaling captain's residence notes that Daniel Webster, Charles Sumner and Nathaniel Hawthorne once were guests here. The place fairly oozes history and character, so we did not expect to find such comfortable, nicely furnished rooms at prices that represent good value.

Rooms in the main inn, the rear garden house and "Le Barn" vary from three simple rooms with sinks in the room and a shared bath to the spacious King's Room with double beds at either end and a fabric loveseat in the center, facing the bow window and the harbor. The large Nathaniel Hawthorne Room, pretty in Williamsburg blue-green trim and floral wallpapers, comes with kingsize bed and two wicker chairs. Quite idyllic with its own balcony is the skylit Dogwood Room, one of two large and quiet rooms in the rear Garden House, each with private balcony overlooking the garden courtyard. It has a kingsize wicker bed, pretty floral wallpaper and draperies, and television. Most rooms are carpeted and nicely refurbished by longtime owner Earle Radford, a Kansas City artist who moved to Chappaquiddick and whose paintings adorn the inn's hallways and small front TV/common room.

The inn claims "the best breakfast on the island." The meal is served on the rear garden courtyard or in a small, convivial dining room where every inch of wall and shelf space is covered with bric-a-brac. The focal point is Henry King, for six decades the inn's handyman and man Friday, who was outfitted in a bright red uniform with matching bow tie at our visit (he changes his colors daily, we're told, and donned a tuxedo for a formal state dinner honoring his dedication and commitment to the hospitality industry in 1996). He served us juice, coffee and a plate of carrot cake before taking orders for poached eggs on the inn's famous cheese toast and scrambled eggs with oatmeal toast. The eggs, nothing out of the ordinary, came with three slices of crisp bacon and only one of toast, but the character of the place more than compensated.

(508) 627-4794. Fax (508) 627-9420. www.edgartowninn.com. Sixteen rooms with private baths and four rooms with shared bath. Rates, EP. Memorial Day through September: doubles, $110 to $250; $90 to $195 midweek in June and September. April to Memorial Day and October: $85 to $180. Closed November-March. No credit cards.

Breakfast, open to the public: $5.50 continental, $8.50 full.

The Daggett House, 59 North Water St., Edgartown 02539.

For a waterfront location, this bed-and-breakfast inn with 31 guest rooms and suites in three houses and a cottage is unsurpassed in Edgartown. The long, narrow rear lawn with flowers, benches and umbrellaed tables slopes down to the water and a private pier next to the Chappaquiddick Ferry landing. Chappaquiddick Island is on view across the harbor.

Guest rooms, all with private baths, are in the main 1750 Daggett House with its Colonial tavern downstairs, the newer (early 1800s Greek Revival) and larger Captain Warren House across Water Street, and the seaside Garden Cottage, which has three double rooms. The newest acquisition is the Thomas House up a lane across the street. Six junior suites each offer a queen bedroom, living room with sofabed and a kitchenette.

Generally quite spacious, most rooms are furnished with oversize canopy and four-poster beds, artworks and antiques.

Until the Thomas House came along, those of most recent vintage were two suites. The Chappaquiddick in the main house offers a bedroom and bath with whirlpool tub downstairs, an enclosed patio with jacuzzi and a spiral staircase leading up to a living room, kitchen area and private deck overlooking the harbor. Television and telephones are offered here and in the Widow's Walk Suite, formerly the owner's quarters atop the Captain Warren House. It has two bedrooms, two baths, a living room with sofabed and a private jacuzzi atop the widow's walk with a panoramic view of the harbor.

After the inn's location, the next best thing is the historic tavern room, which dates from the 1660s and above which the house was later built. The island's first tavern, it looks the way an early tavern should look, with its unusual beehive fireplace chimney, dark beams, wide pine hardwood flooring, old tools and bare wood communal tables for six, where conviviality is the norm. A local artist who illustrates resident Carly Simon's books painted the stunning Daggett House mural that now graces one wall.

Breakfast, featuring wonderful toast made from bread from the recipe of the late Lucille Chirgwin, who with her husband Fred owned the inn for 40 years, costs \$7.50 to \$11.75 (for crab cakes supreme – two poached eggs atop crab cakes with hollandaise sauce and home fries). It's available to the public as well, and the ambiance and menu are such that people gladly wait for a table while sipping coffee on the rear terrace, lately equipped for outdoor dining.

Hidden near the fireplace in the tavern room is a secret staircase that provides steep, low-ceilinged access to an upstairs guest room with kingsize bed, gold wallpaper and a view of the harbor.

Off the entrance to the main inn is a small living room with sofas, wing chairs and a television set. Tea, lemonade and cookies are served here in the late afternoon.

Among the fourteen rooms in the Warren House are several efficiencies good for families.

The two sons of the Chirgwins have turned over innkeeping duties to a manager.

(508) 627-4600 or (800) 946-3400. Fax (508) 627-4611. www.thedaggetthouse.com. Twenty-three rooms and eight suites with private baths. Rates EP. Mid-May to mid-October: doubles \$155 to \$295, suites \$250 to \$595. Rest of year: doubles \$115 to \$135, suites \$120 to \$185. Two-night minimum in season, weekends in off-season. Children accepted. Main house and Thomas House open all year; Captain Warren House and Garden Cottage open April to November.

Summery dining room at Charlotte Inn houses L'Etoile restaurant.

Dining Spots

L'Étoile, South Summer Street, Edgartown.

Ensconced at the rear of the Charlotte Inn, this bow-windowed conservatory/ dining room is chic and utterly charming. It's a picture of pristine elegance in white and green, with brick walls, skylights, spotlit paintings, lush ferns, a blooming hibiscus tree and a trickling fountain. Well-spaced tables seat 45 inside, and another twenty can be accommodated seasonally on a garden patio.

The food prepared by French-trained chef-owner Michael Brisson, who formerly cooked at the much-acclaimed L'Espalier in Boston, is superlative. Dinner is prix-fixe, averaging $78 for three courses with about five choices for each, or $120 for the chef's tasting menu.

A single, long-stemmed pink rose was on each table as we savored a recent autumn meal to remember, from exceptionally good sesame-sourdough and honey-whole wheat cranberry rolls to the shortbread and chocolate truffles accompanying the bill. Appetizers of local scallops and foie gras bore complex, understated sauces, as did the main courses, pheasant and rack of lamb. Most impressive was the amount of meat on both the pheasant, deboned and served sliced with pumpkin raviolis, and on the lamb, rare and juicy and – hard to believe – too much to finish.

Desserts were a fabulous warm tarte tatin with cinnamon stick ice cream and a coconut parfait with berry coulis. The latter was almost as refreshing as the mulled pear sorbet with pomegranate seeds that was the "intermezzo" between appetizer and entrée. Every course, every taste testified to the artistry in the kitchen.

(508) 627-5187. Prix-fixe, $75. Dinner by reservation, 6:30 to 9:45 nightly in summer; Tuesday-Sunday in late spring and early fall, Thursday-Saturday rest of year. Closed January to mid-February.

Alchemy, 71 Main St., Edgartown

Chef-owner Scott Caskey closed Savoir Fare, a fifteen-year seasonal favorite here, to concentrate on this new and larger enterprise. He and wife Charlotte took over the space once occupied by Martha's restaurant and produced a lively bistro and bar serving lunch and dinner year-round. They seat 140 in two Parisian-style dining rooms on two floors, two bars and a billiards room.

Alchemy is defined as "transforming something," said Charlotte, "and we're making something new out of this restaurant."

Indeed, their bistro is as popular as ever and Scott's cooking is as creative as ever, even if the menu strikes some as quirky. At a fall visit, we didn't see anything that compelled for lunch, especially at prices starting in the low teens for a cheeseburger with fries, and including a salad called "red, white and greens" with oregano vinaigrette, artichoke croutons and chèvre. Said salad was on the dinner menu as well, along with braised veal cheeks on a celery-root latke and "pumpkin patch" raviolis for appetizers.

Recent dinner entrées included fennel-pollen-dusted halibut in an artichoke bisque with fried potato gnocchi, brined cornish hen saltimbocca over a fricassee of cannelloni beans and smoked ham hocks, pork chop Milanese, and grilled beef tenderloin with a sauternes beurre blanc and shaved foie gras.

The Caskeys and crew have fun "mixing potions" (another definition of alchemy), and the results, while sometimes uneven, are widely applauded.

(508) 627-9999. Entrées, $26 to $32. Lunch, Monday-Saturday noon to 2:30, Wednesday-Saturday in off-season. Dinner nightly, from 5:30, Thursday-Monday in winter.

Atria, 137 Main St., Edgartown.

The Brick Cellar Bar is Edgartown's hottest night spot, and the upstairs dining room in an elegant white sea captain's house occupies a lofty culinary realm as well. The restaurant is named for the brightest of the three stars forming the Southern Triangle constellation, whose position in the night sky guided 19th century whalers sailing from Martha's Vineyard.

Chef Christian Thornton imparts Mediterranean and Asian accents to contemporary New England fare featuring local, organic products. Expect such starters as crab and artichoke pot pie, rare ahi tuna tempura with miso vinaigrette and wasabi caviar, oven-roasted foie gras with vanilla french toast and vintage balsamic vinegar, and crispy ginger-spiked quail with sweet chile glaze. Main courses range from sake-marinated cod with miso broth to braised Indian beef curry with basmati rice. Seared Atlantic halibut with lobster-saffron broth and roasted duck with spicy plum sauce and duck confit spring rolls are favorites.

Desserts could be molten chocolate cake with cappuccino ice cream, Indian rice pudding with candied pistachios or vanilla crème brûlée.

Dine in understated elegance on the enclosed wraparound porch or the inner dining room, or outside on the romantic rose garden terrace. Afterward, join the night crowd downstairs in the brick-walled bar. Watch the tropical fish in the lighted aquariums and enjoy live music in cushy leather club chairs or at the brass bar.

(508) 627-5850. www.atriamv.com. Entrées, $22 to $36. Dinner nightly, 5 to 10.

Opus, 31 Dunes Road, Edgartown

Here is one glamorous restaurant, upstairs in the new Winnetu Inn & Resort main building with tall windows onto an equally glamorous outdoor deck and a view of the ocean across the dunes at South Beach. The setting is sleek in understated gray with elegantly set tables spaced well apart.

Executive chef Roy Breiman from California's Napa Valley orchestrates the precious menu in terms of overtures, compositions and finale.

Dinner might open with a "chilled bowl of hand-picked lettuces" with toasted walnuts and sour-cherry vinaigrette for a cool $8 or a roasted red beet "tower" with herbed goat cheese, micro greens, shallot chutney and 25-year balsamic vinegar for $12. Compose yourself with grilled turbot "au laurier" in a bay-leaf emulsion, herb-marinated chicken breast with a ruby port-vanilla reduction or roast pepper-crusted tenderloin of angus beef with a huckleberry reduction. Finales include a caramelized banana charlotte and black currant soufflé.

A harpist serenades diners on weekend evenings, and a jazz quartet entertains during Sunday brunch.

(508) 627-3663. Entrées, $24 to $37. Lunch seasonally, 11 to 2. Dinner nightly, 5:30 to 9 or 10, weekends in off-season. Sunday brunch in off-season, 11 to 2. Closed December to Memorial Day.

Lattanzi's, Old Post Office Square, Edgartown.

Lattanzi's is the Italian showplace for chef-owner Albert Lattanzi, who had been chef for years up the street at the former Andrea's. Taking over our old-favorite Warriner's Restaurant, he lightened up the paneled walls of the elegant library room to produce a Mediterranean look, and topped the white linened tables with butcher paper for an Italian bistro feeling.

The atmosphere is refined and the food so abundant that some complain the portions are much too big. The manager advises that almost everyone takes the leftovers home in a Lattanzi basket, and many phone to say how much they enjoyed them the next day. Chef Al makes his pastas by hand, cooks his meats on a hardwood grill and buys his seafood from fishermen who come to his back door as soon as they get off the boat.

The pasta dishes are highly rated, especially the arrabbiata with spicy pork sausage and tomato and the fettuccine picante with anchovies, hot cherry peppers and garlic. One skeptic said he never knew a lasagna dish could be so good. Main courses range from calamari fra diavolo to Canadian hardwood-grilled porterhouse steak alla florentina and a stellar veal chop with porcini-mushroom cream. The mixed grill with lamb, hot Italian sausage, pork and spicy peach chutney and the grilled pork loin with apricots and pine nuts appealed the night we were there.

Appetizers here are good but superfluous. Save room instead for a stellar tiramisu, the chocolate-hazelnut cake, the fresh fruit tarts, one of the sorbettos or, at the very least, a cheese plate. The wine list focuses on Italian vintages.

(508) 627-8854. Entrées, $22 to $38. Dinner nightly from 6, June-September; rest of year, Wednesday-Sunday from 5.

The Seafood Shanty, 31 Dock St., Edgartown.

This contemporary, three-level spot is anything but a shanty. Edgartown's best harbor view for dining is from the recently expanded upstairs deck with a raw bar above a glass-enclosed porch with water on three sides. Plastic chairs with deep blue mesh frames, bare tables with blue and white mats and bare wood walls add up to an attractive nautical setting.

You pay for the location, right next to Edgartown's Memorial Wharf. Our lunch for two a few years ago came to $30 for a cup of clam chowder and a spinach salad, plus a pasta salad loaded with seafood. The sunny Indian summer setting was such, we admit, that we lingered over a second beer.

The seafood dinner entrées are fairly traditional and simple, from baked scrod to New York strip steak, from three grilled seafood items to prime rib. Lobster is offered in five versions: risotto, royale and lobster cakes, as well as steamed and baked stuffed (plus a lobster quesadilla for an appetizer). The most innovative item on a recent menu was mojo shrimp: a stack of Louisiana johnnycakes topped with tangy shrimp.

Dessert could be amaretto cheesecake, chocolate-hazelnut mousse or key lime pie.

Light fare is served upstairs in the Shanty Lounge and Deck.

(508) 627-8622. www.theseafoodshanty.com. Entrées, $17.95 to $32.95. Lunch daily, 11 to 3. Dinner, 5 to 10. Open May-October.

Mad Martha's, 7 North Water St., Edgartown.

One of a group of ice-cream parlors around the island, this offers an amazing variety of flavors (we loved the Bailey's Irish cream overflowing from its crackly cone, $2.25) and concoctions, from walkaway waffle sundae to oreo cookie nookie. The most outrageous is the pig's delight ($18): a dozen scoops of ice cream topped with the usual banana-split trimmings. "Order by saying `oink,'" advises the sign at the door, and some do.

Diversions

Edgartown is an eminently walkable town and everything (except some of the beaches) is within walking distance. That's fortunate, for in summer the place tends to be wall-to-walk people, bicycles and cars. The shops, restaurants and inns are compressed into a maze of narrow streets leading from or paralleling the harbor. Interspersed with them and along side streets that live up to the description "quaint" are stately large white whaling captain's homes, neatly separated from the brick sidewalks by picket fences and colorful gardens. Here you see and sense the history of a seaport village preserved from the 19th century.

Walk around. Don't miss the churches: The Old Whaling Church, the tall-columned Greek Revival structure that doubles as the Performing Arts Center, the little St. Andrew's Episcopal Church with its beautiful stained-glass windows, a cheery interior and a carillon that tolls quite a concert across town in the late afternoon; the imposing First Federated Church with old box pews and a steeple visible far at sea. Other highlights are the newspaper offices of the revered Vineyard Gazette in a 1764 house across from the Charlotte Inn, the towering Pagoda Tree brought from China as a seedling in a flower pot early in the 19th century and now spreading over South Water Street to shade the Victorian and Harborside inns, the Old Sculpin Art Gallery showing works of various artists, and all the august sea captain's homes of diverse architectural eras along Water and Summer streets in particular.

Martha's Vineyard Historical Society/Vineyard Museum, 59 School St., Edgartown.

Here is a block-size museum complex worth a visit. The eleven rooms of the 1765

Thomas Cooke House are filled with early island memorabilia. You're apt to see historians at work in the Gale Huntington Library of History, through which you pass to get to the Francis Foster Museum, which has a small maritime and island collection. Outside is a boat shed containing a whaleboat, fire engine and old wagon, plus the original Fresnel lens from the old Gay Head Lighthouse, mounted in a replica of the lighthouse lantern and watch room, and still lighted at night.

(508) 627-4441. Open Tuesday-Saturday 10 to 5, June to mid-October; Wednesday-Friday 1 to 4 and Saturday 10 to 4, spring and fall; by appointment late December to mid-March. Adults, $7.

The Vincent House Museum, 99 Main St., Edgartown.

The Vineyard's oldest house (1672) contains most of its original woodwork, glass and hardware. During recent restoration, some of the walls of the unfurnished house were left exposed to demonstrate the types of construction used. The museum offers tours of the nearby Dr. Daniel Fisher House (1840), an imposing Federal presence on Main Street, and the Old Whaling Church (1843), where summer resident André Previn and Friends were about to give a benefit concert at our latest visit.

(508) 627-8619. Open Monday-Saturday noon to 3, May to Columbus Day. Admission $4, museum and tour $6.

Felix Neck Wildlife Sanctuary, off Edgartown-Vineyard Haven Road, Edgartown.

With blinds on Sengekontacket Pond, this is a favorite spot for birders, but we know locals who try to walk portions of the six miles of marked nature trails every day. The sanctuary embraces 350 acres of beach, marsh, fields and woodlands. The executive director has been instrumental in bringing back the endangered osprey to the island. Naturalists offer bird walks, canoeing, stargazing and snorkeling, among special activities. A visitor center in a renovated barn has freshwater and saltwater tanks containing local species.

(508) 627-4850. Visitor center open daily, 8 to 4 in summer; Tuesday-Sunday 9 to 4, rest of year. Grounds open daily, 8 to 7. Adults, $3.

Beaches. Katama Beach, the public part of the seemingly endless South Beach along the open shore three miles south of Edgartown, has excellent surf swimming, a tricky undertow, shifting dunes and a protected salt pond inhabited by crabs and scallops. A shuttle bus runs from Edgartown in summer. Non-surf swimming is available at the picturesque Joseph A. Sylvia State Beach, a narrow, two-mile-long strip between Edgartown and Oak Bluffs. Back toward Edgartown is Bend-of-the-Road Beach; its shallow waters are good for children. In town is Lighthouse Beach at Starbuck's Neck, on the harbor at the end of Fuller Street and seldom crowded.

Chappaquiddick Island. Reached by a five-minute ride on the On Time ferry from Edgartown, it has a public beach facing the Edgartown Harbor at Chappy Point, plus the Cape Pogue Wildlife Refuge and Wasque Reservation beaches. These are remote and secluded, three miles from the ferry – best reached by car as bicyclists may find it difficult negotiating some of the sandy roads (but parking is limited). On the way you'll pass the forested My Toi Preserve, a surprising Zen-like oasis of Japanese gardens, and the Chappaquiddick General Store and gasoline station, surrounded by abandoned cars and the only commercial enterprise of size on the island. The sponsoring Trustees of Reservations, which continues to buy up open land here, offers countless hiking trails as well as a variety of activities on

Chappaquiddick, from fishing trips to natural history tours – three-hour guided expeditions over ten miles of remote barrier beaches (reservations, 627-3599).

Shopping. Main Street and adjacent streets are crammed with interesting stores. **The Fligors'** (billed as the Vineyard's most delightful store for 41 years) is an intriguing maze of rooms and levels that make it almost a department store. Suave gifts, Claire Murray rugs, dolls, resort clothing (fabulous handknit sweaters for every holiday imaginable), toys, Christmas shop, a basement sale room – you name it, Carol and Richard Fligor probably have it. They also offer The Fligor Apartments at 69 North Summer St., (508) 627-4745, four newly renovated and furnished one-room efficiency cottages done in a colorful grape motif for $295 a night.

We enjoy popping into the **Vermont Shop,** the idea for which was thought up in one snow-less winter by Robin Burke, who has a ski house there. It has expanded to the point that 40 percent of the merchandise mix comes from elsewhere, but you'll find Woody Jackson cows, Vermont pottery and foods like common crackers and cheeses. We liked the ceramic steamers and came out with an interesting pair of titanium earrings. Nevin Square is a conglomeration of nice shops behind the Colonial Inn. Also of interest are the fine arts at **Christina Gallery** and **Willoughby's,** the hand-painted furniture and accessories at **Once in a Blue Moon,** the colorful ceramics at **Designs Gallery,** the clothing and folk art at **Chica,** the antiques and gifts at **Past and Presents,** and the jewelry at **The Golden Basket** and **Sine Qua Non, Ltd.** All manner of unusual wooden things from spoons to birdhouses to a $1,200 rocking horse intrigue at the unique **In the Woods.**

Women's clothing is shown at **Saffron** and sweaters from Australia are featured at **Island Pursuit.** Pick up your foul-weather gear at **Sundog,** which has the correct kind of Vineyard apparel – as does **Very Vineyard,** even more so.

If you get bushed from all this shopping and walking, rest awhile on the benches atop the Memorial Wharf pavilion off Dock Street, a salubrious vantage point for contemplating the harbor.

Extra-Special

Chicama Vineyards, Stoney Hill Road, West Tisbury.

The wild grapes that gave Martha's Vineyard its name have been cultivated since 1971 by ex-Californians George and Catherine Matheisen and daughter Lynn Hoeft, who make "the kinds of wines we like to drink," Catherine says. They specialize in dry viniferas, among them a robust shiraz, a Summer Island red that's meant to be drunk young, and the first Martha's Vineyard-appellation merlot. Much of the winemaking operation is outside and rather primitive, as you might expect after negotiating Stoney Hill Road, a long mile of bumps and dirt that we'd rename Stoney Hole. Several hundred people make the trek on a busy summer day and relish the shop's choice of wine or herbal vinegars, dressings and jams, all neatly displayed in gift baskets and glass cases lit from behind so the herbs show through. In the fall, the Christmas shop also offers festive foods, wreaths and hot mulled wine.

(508) 693-0309 or (888) 244-2262. www.chicamavineyards.com. Open Monday-Saturday 11 to 5, Sunday 1 to 5, Memorial Day to Columbus Day, to 4, mid-November through December; reduced hours, rest of year.

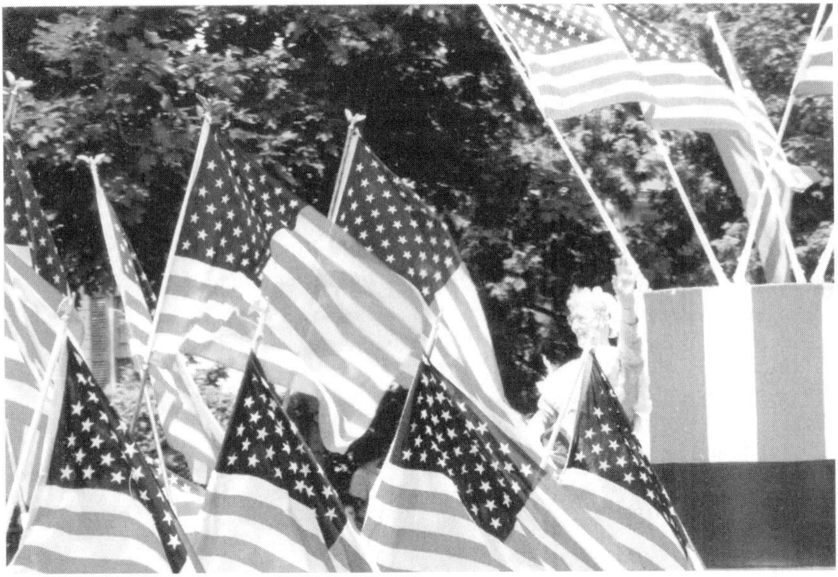

Bristol is decked out in flags for oldest Fourth of July parade in the nation.

Bristol, R.I.

The Perfect Seaside Town

Visitors fall in love with the picturesque town of Bristol.

They tell docents at the Blithewold mansion that they dream of living there. They often stop at local real estate offices to check out the listings. They tell shopkeepers, restaurateurs, innkeepers – almost anybody they encounter – what a wonderful town they inhabit.

Although off the beaten tourist path, Bristol has a way of drawing people.

Is it the salubrious location along Narragansett's East Bay, with an uncommon amount of public access to the water? Is it the town's aura of history and a distinct sense of place? Or is it the community's manageable size (population 22,500), small enough to know and care about people yet big enough to offer urban amenities? Perhaps it's a certain quality of life that manifests itself in any number of ways, depending upon the eye of the beholder.

"If we could live anywhere, it would be in Bristol," says Trish Hafer, a Southern belle turned local innkeeper. She and her husband have five houses and can afford to live anywhere. They settled in a waterfront Bristol mansion in 2000 to open one of the more sumptuous B&Bs in the land.

Inns and B&Bs came lately to Bristol, although history did not. With a street plan laid out in 1680, Bristol has outstanding examples of architecture spanning three centuries from Federal and Greek Revival homes to 19th-century country garden estates to modern showplaces outside the historic district. Some of the most imposing are schools and museums.

With a harbor on Narragansett Bay, the town became an early shipbuilding and maritime center. The fruits of its prosperity are evident throughout the stately historic district and along the waterfront, here and along the posh Poppasquash peninsula reached by a causeway.

Bristol proper has no fewer than 35 parks and designated public access points along the water. The best is Colt State Park, the former Colt family farm and estate on the peninsula. A three-mile drive and four miles of bicycle trails pass along the bay and through 464 acres of orchards, lawns, picnic groves and playfields. Nearby, the Coggeshall Farm Museum off Poppasquash Road quietly depicts life on a 1790s marsh farm.

Other local attractions include the Blithewold Mansion and Gardens, Brown University's Haffenreffer Museum of Anthropology and Linden Place, a majestic 1810 Federal mansion.

The red, white and blue center stripes down the middle of Hope Street, the main thoroughfare, mark the route of the nation's oldest Fourth of July parade. Townspeople and their historic houses and stores are dressed perfectly in patriotic regalia for the occasion. It's a colorful phenomenon equaled only by the Grand Illumination – perfectly pristine tiny white lights twinkling everywhere as if by local edict for the Christmas season.

Flag-waving Bristol people, it seems, like to show off their perfect place.

Inn Spots

Point Pleasant Inn, 333 Poppasquash Road, Bristol 02809.

"The best place in the world is Bristol," says Trish Hafer, a recent arrival and co-owner with her husband Gunter of this luxurious waterfront B&B in a semi-private residential enclave on Poppasquash Neck. The Hafers have the means to live anywhere – he commutes between five residences across the country – but this is the grandest, "and meant to be shared," in Trish's words.

To fulfill her wish to run a luxurious inn, the Hafers undertook a year of renovations to the 17,000-square-foot, 33-room English country manor house built in 1940 for industrialist Commodore Charles B. Rockwell and known variously as Rockwell Manor and Point Pleasant Farm. They reconfigured a number of bedrooms into six deluxe B&B rooms and suites, the maximum that zoning in this prime waterfront peninsula jutting into Narragansett Bay would allow.

Our quarters in the Narragansett master suite were sumptuous indeed: a living-room-size space with a kingsize poster bed dressed in Italian linens, TV in a built-in cabinet, two leather chairs and a desk in an alcove facing the harbor through the rear window, and not one but two bathrooms at opposite corners of the room – his with a walk-in shower, hers with a dressing room, shower with multiple heads and whirlpool tub. Trish, a real Southern belle whose background was in culinary and hotel management, pays attention to detail. She had thought of everything and then some, stocking the room with terry robes, a Bose radio, luxurious toiletries, chocolates and the latest magazines.

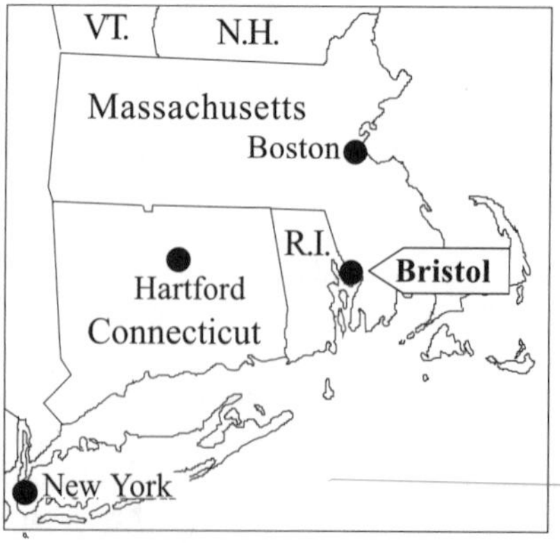

Stone mansion known as Point Pleasant Inn is centerpiece of 25 waterfront acres.

Other rooms are smaller but similarly equipped. The Admiral's suite with king bed and jacuzzi occupies a far corner of the house. Its sitting room contains a twin day bed. One of three second-floor bedrooms opens through french doors onto a large rear balcony, overlooking the pool area and the water. This one, with a massive kingsize carved poster bed and armoire, is the Bristol Harbor room, "to my mind the most beautiful of all," says the Hafers' housekeeper. A smaller bedroom, opened recently in the butler's quarters on the ground floor, is known as the Captain's Quarters and reflects the Hafers' sailing interests. All rooms have tubs and separate showers, telephones and TVs.

A TV room/den on the second floor is whimsically decorated with oars on the walls and an airplane propeller between art works. Coffee, juice and banana bread are put out here for guests in the morning. Breakfast is served in the formal dining room, a two-section beauty bearing original murals of famous Bristol mansions in one section and wraparound windows onto the water in the other. The main course in our case was french toast stuffed with cream cheese and marmalade, accompanied by bacon and a fruit smoothie.

The Hafers greet guests with cocktails and hors d'oeuvres in the huge living room, and maintain an open bar off the dining room. Gunter, one of the largest contractors in Colorado, may show some of his construction handiwork here in the music room, the wine cellar, the downstairs billiards and game room, the sauna and gymnasium, and his handyman's dream of a workshop at the back of the five-car garage. Outside on their 25 acres of waterfront paradise are a canopied patio, terraces, gardens, a swimming pool, a hot tub and a quarter-mile of harbor frontage facing Bristol across the way.

(401) 253-0627. www.pointpleasantinn.com. Four rooms and two suites with private baths. Doubles, $300 to $625. Closed November to mid-April.

Rockwell House Inn, 610 Hope St., Bristol 02809.

Built in the Federal style in 1809 by the first marshal of Bristol's famous Fourth of July parade, this imposing house now exhibits Georgian, Greek Revival, Italianate and Victorian attributes – so much so that it was featured in the Smithsonian magazine for its eclectic architecture and decorative pieces.

Rockwell House Inn occupies architecturally varied 1809 mansion.

It was a private residence until 1991, when Debra and Steve Krohn purchased it for Bristol's first B&B. They share their home with guests in four bedrooms and several common areas furnished with antiques in traditional style. Two large front-corner bedrooms, one the former library on the ground floor and the other upstairs, come with kingsize beds, gas fireplaces and comfortable seating. Another large corner bedroom on the second floor has a king bed and an in-room vanity set in an antique mission oak desk. A smaller room in back has a carved queen bed and an unusual armoire/dresser converted from an antique ice chest. Terrycloth robes, hair dryers, lighted makeup mirrors and irons are among the guest room amenities.

The high-ceilinged main floor is notable for inlaid hardwood floors, eight-foot pocket doors and hand stenciling on the walls. The front and back parlors open to each other. Here, guests enjoy a TV/VCR and an extensive video collection, including the latest movies from Steve's mother, who is in the entertainment business and nominates for the Academy Awards. A wall of framed celebrity photos testifies to her connections and Steve's hobby of collecting autographs.

A decanter of sherry awaits guests on the bar in the "courting corner" of the rear parlor, and a guest refrigerator upstairs is stocked with beverages.

Debra is known for her breakfasts, which start with a "Victoria sundae" of fresh fruit topped with homemade granola and vanilla yogurt and may culminate in walnut-raisin bread french toast stuffed with cream cheese and strawberry preserves. Dutch puffed pancakes with cranberries, walnuts and apples was the fare at our latest visit. The meal is taken in the candlelit dining room, on a spacious enclosed back porch or on a patio beside a trickling waterfall and fishpond, overlooking an unexpectedly deep back yard. Debra calls it "our secret garden."

(401) 253-0040 or (800) 815-0040. www.rockwellhouseinn.com. Four rooms with private baths. Doubles, $175 to $199. Children over 12. Two-night minimum weekends.

Bradford-Dimond-Norris House, 474 Hope St., Bristol 02809.

This majestic white house with an Ionic-columned veranda topped by an ornate Chinese Chippendale balustrade stands at the town's main intersection, across from the imposing Linden Place, now a house museum.

Dating to 1792, the house gained a third floor and enough embellishments following the Civil War to warrant its nickname, "The Wedding Cake House." Suzanne and Lloyd Adams opened it as a B&B in 1995 after a year's renovations. They furnished it with four-poster beds, antiques and paintings in elegant Colonial style.

A guest room at the rear of the main floor has a fishnet canopy bed, fainting couch and Victorian sofa, opening to a second room with a twin bed. The other bedrooms are on the second floor, including a prized front corner room with fishnet canopy bed and wide-board floor. All rooms have queensize beds and TVs.

The formal front parlor features a baby grand piano. An expanded continental breakfast of fruit, yogurt, cereals and homemade pastries is taken at a table for eight in the chandeliered dining room or on the rear veranda.

(401) 253-6338 or (888) 329-6338. Fax (401) 253-4023. www.bdnhouse.com. Four rooms with private baths. Doubles, $110 to $140.

Hearth House, 736 Hope St., Bristol 02809.

The ten fireplaces in this 1798 Colonial house make the new name a natural for the former Parker Borden House B&B, as orchestrated by Angie and Tony Margiotta. Former New York City teachers, they happened to visit Bristol, fell in love with the town and found it the perfect spot for realizing Angie's dream of operating a B&B. They imparted something of a theatrical flair, thanks to Angie's background as a high school drama teacher who had her own cabaret act.

Facing the waterfront across a busy intersection, the dark red house smack up against the sidewalk has three guest accommodations, each with kingsize bed and a fireplace or wood stove. They manifest a flair for dramatic colors, especially fiery reds.

Roses are the theme on the comforter and the rose-colored walls in Victorian Rose Room, whose lace-curtained windows yield a glimpse of the harbor. The Skylight Garden Room, colorful in vivid green, has a skylight above the bed and an enclosed sitting porch looking onto the rear garden. The Harbor View Suite comes with two fireplaces and a bath/sitting room with a tiled jacuzzi tub.

A second-floor common room contains a fireplace and satellite TV/VCR, plus refreshments in a guest refrigerator. Both Margiottas are into cooking, and the fruits of their labors are served for breakfast at a table for six in the dining room. Guests relax two at a time in the glider swing in the back yard.

(401) 253-1404. www.hearthhouse.com. Two rooms and one suite with private bath. Doubles, $130 and $140. Suite $160. Two-night minimum weekends. Children over 12.

1808 William's Grant Inn, 154 High St., Bristol 02809.

A mural of Bristol harbor in the front hall welcomes guests to this five-bay Colonial/Federal house first granted by Deputy Governor William Bradford to his grandson in 1808. The mural is one of several plus countless cupboard-door designs hand-painted by the mother of a former innkeeper and retained by former Army officer Warren Poehler and his wife Diane, who added collections from their own travels to the B&B they acquired in 1998.

"This was the first time we could unpack everything," their son Matthew said, and the family wasted no opportunity. Bric-a-brac is displayed in the dining area open to the kitchen. Stuffed rabbits line the mantel above the fireplace in the Blithewold guest room. More teddybears than most ever hope to see are underfoot in the upstairs hallway.

The collections generally do not take away space from what are actually five fairly ample guest rooms, each with queensize bed and gas fireplace. Each is themed in decor according to its name. Three are on the main floor, and two on the second, where the owners reside. The front-corner Sturbridge Room on the ground floor is properly historic, with bath facilities in former closets on either side of the brick chimney. The premier room is on the side toward the rear, off the dining area with understated antique nautical decor and a whirlpool tub. Antique equestrian décor graces the front-corner Middleburg Room upstairs.

The other front-corner upstairs room has been turned into a guest parlor, with TV set, piano and a tray of complimentary liqueurs in a corner. The Poehlers put out chocolate-chip cookies along with coffee and tea service in every bedroom.

Two tables in the dining area open to the kitchen are the setting for a substantial breakfast, from Portuguese french toast to New Zealand egg and bacon pie. Guests are especially fond of Diane's portobello benedict.

In season, guests enjoy a back porch and a leafy backyard with a koi pond whose occupants not only thrive but also multiply each winter.

(401) 253-4222 or (800) 596-4222. Fax (401) 254-0987. www.wmgrantinn.com. Five rooms with private baths. Doubles, $100 to $115 April-October, $95 to $105 rest of year. Two-night minimum weekends. Children over 12.

Bristol Harbor Inn, 259 Thames St., Bristol 02809.

Almost by happenstance, three historic buildings have been restored into a 40-room boutique hotel along the waterfront.

Local innkeeper Lloyd Adams and two Syracuse University classmates had no idea that would happen when they decided to buy the old Historic Bank of Bristol (1797), the DeWolf Rum Distillery (1800) and the Wardwell Coal & Lumber buildings stretching from Thames Street to the wharf. They had reunited at the Phillippines home of one of them after an initial gathering at the Bradford-Dimond-Norris Inn here and decided to do a business venture together. One partner, a lumber man from upstate New York, remembered having seen the old lumber yard for sale, so they decided to buy the prime waterfront property and figure out what to do with it later. They asked half a dozen firms for feasibility studies, and one suggested an inn as the centerpiece of a multi-use retail, restaurant and apartment complex to be called Thames Street Landing.

The inn opened in 2001, really more a hotel than an inn with a two-story lobby and rooms off central corridors on three floors. Eight snug "historic" rooms in the former 1797 bank building closest to the street come with queen beds, gas fireplaces and reproduction Federal mahogany furniture and brass chandeliers. Their red and brown decor gives way to beachy light browns and tans as rooms with more contemporary furnishings proceed toward the water. Water-view suites with ample sitting rooms and queensize bedrooms offer more space. Some rooms have kingsize or two double beds. About half have water views through windows that open, although none have balconies. TVs, telephones and hair dryers are standard amenities.

A complimentary continental breakfast is offered in the main-floor Counting Room.

Sun sets over Poppasquash Neck across from Bristol Harbor Inn.

In 2004, the owners planned to open a full-service, fine-dining restaurant in the lumber company's adjacent stone warehouse in partnership with well-known Providence restaurateur Jaime D'Oliveira. A main-floor lounge, a second-floor dining room and a wraparound dining deck beside the harbor were in the works for a restaurant in the style of the co-owner's Mill's Tavern in downtown Providence.

(401) 254-1444 or (866) 254-1444. Fax (401) 254-1333. www.bristolharborinn.com. Twenty-eight rooms and twelve suites with private baths. May-October: doubles $119 to $209, suites $169 to $209. November-April: doubles $89 to $109, suites $119 to $129.

Dining Spots

Hotpoint, 31 State St., Bristol.

The antique neon sign outside the entrance has been around longer than this stylish bistro. Chef-owner Jim Reardon thought it represented a cool name for the restaurant he established in a former appliance store. So Hotpoint it is, a reference to the cutting-edge cuisine that's both the most innovative and the most consistent in town.

White-clothed tables covered with strips of butcher paper are dressed with flowers in the beige and taupe bistro dining room with a couple of tables beside the front window and a three-stool bar with an espresso machine in back. Votive candles flicker as you savor treats from shrimp scampi and lobster cardinale to chicken marsala and steak au poivre. There's a special menu of comfort foods available early on weeknights. Among the more creative possibilities are a salmon burrito with mango barbecue sauce, sea scallops around blue cheese polenta, and molasses-marinated pork tenderloin glazed with bourbon and maple syrup. Kangaroo salad, ostrich au poivre and venison tenderloin with juniper berry demi-glace might be specials during game season, which extends from October into January.

Start with the superior saffron-scented seafood chowder or a lobster bisque redolent with basil and brandy. How about a sesame shrimp salad, margarita-cured gravlax or Maine crab cake topped with smoked jalapeño mayonnaise? Finish with banana cheesecake, mocha crème brûlée or flourless chocolate cake.

Creative omelets and four versions of eggs benedict are available at Sunday brunch.

(401) 254-7474. www.hotpointbistro.com. Entrées, $17.99 to $27.99. Dinner nightly, 5 to 9 or 10. Sunday brunch, 10:30 to 2:30.

Roberto's, 301 Hope St., Bristol.

Creative Italian cuisine is the hallmark of this cozy restaurant. It was opened in 2001 by chef Robert Myers, who cooked earlier at Puerini's in Newport, and manager Robert Vanderhoof. The pair tweaked their first names for the venture to reflect the Italian-oriented menu.

There are a handful of starters that change daily, such as black angus beef barley soup, escargots tossed with fettuccine, portobello mushrooms sautéed with plum tomatoes and shallots in dry madeira wine and homemade polenta. But almost everyone starts with the fabulous Tuscan bread salad, a medley of vegetables sautéed with shallots, cannellini beans, Italian bread and rosemary.

Among pasta dishes, the shrimp piccata over fettuccine and the mixed seafood possillipo over linguini come highly recommended. Chicken and veal dishes may be prepared in five styles, from san remo to marsala. Tournedos with a roasted garlic demi-glace is a favorite among beef dishes.

All these treats and more are served in a cozy front room, where tables seating 28 are appointed with white linens, candles and fresh flowers. A second dining room with four tables and a small bar area is in back.

(401) 254-9732. Entrées, $14 to $20. Lunch, Monday-Friday 11:30 to 2:30. Dinner nightly, 5 to 9 or 9:30.

Redlefsen's, 444 Thames St., Bristol.

European visitors come here for "a taste of home," in the words of proprietor Walter Guertler. He and his wife Sally took over a popular rotisserie and grill from its Swedish founders, keeping the name but relocating to expanded quarters on the waterfront. Walter knew exactly what he wanted after 27 years as owner of a Dutch manufacturing firm who traveled all over Europe, noticing that the restaurateurs in the small towns he visited always seemed to be having more fun than the board chairmen with whom he was dining. "I wanted his job," he said of the prototypical restaurateur.

He's been having fun ever since, presiding over a small-town restaurant he converted from an old truck garage. A large, high-ceilinged, skylit dining room with yellow walls and well-spaced, sturdy wood tables is separated from a convivial bar/lounge by a large fireplace open to both sides. A cuckoo clock and trompe-l'oeil paintings of European villages lend a cosmopolitan air. A small front patio with a harbor view is popular in summer.

The chef's menu reflects some of the European favorites the Guertlers brought with them, although these have been updated lately to appease American tastes. That may be fortunate, because the specialty wiener schnitzel that two in our party ordered was so like cardboard as to be nearly inedible. The baked scallops and the roasted chicken were much better. The options, which rarely change, ranged from baked scrod and grilled rainbow trout with mustard-dill sauce to lobster pot pie, pecan-encrusted pork tenderloin and grilled lamb chops with a maple-brandy sauce. Regulars praise the grilled bauerwurst and bratwurst, served with sauerkraut. Lightly grilled gravlax, Maryland crab cakes and fried dim sum are among the appetizers. A "daisy crêpe" containing vanilla ice cream and topped with chocolate sauce and nuts is the signature dessert.

Walter encourages diners to adjourn to a plush sitting area by the fire in the lounge for coffee and after-dinner drinks.

(401) 254-1188. Entrées, $15 to $23. Lunch, Tuesday-Friday 11:30 to 2:30. Dinner, Tuesday-Sunday, from 5. Brunch, Saturday 11 to 3, Sunday noon to 3.

The Lobster Pot, 119 Hope St., Bristol.

Although it's been around since 1929, the Lobster Pot has never been better than since Jeff Hirsh took over and upgraded both decor and cuisine. A vast place with equally vast windows onto the harbor, it has one of the better water views of any restaurant – you almost feel as if you're on a boat. A tiled fireplace, photos from Mystic Seaport, and white linens and china on the tables complete the setting.

Dinner is by candlelight with traditional Yankee fare – lobster, of course, but also all kinds of seafood, steaks, poultry and veal, including veal oscar. Lobster comes in bisque, stew, ravioli, newburg, sauté, salad, fried and in clambake, as well as in sizes up to three pounds. There's little unusual, although in this area bouillabaisse and welsh rarebit, served with caesar salad, might qualify. More of the same is available at lunch, as are seven salads and lunchy things from lobster club sandwich to eggs oscar.

Desserts tend to be liqueur parfaits, ice cream puffs and Indian pudding.

(401) 253-9100. Entrées, $15.50 to $25.95. Lunch, Tuesday-Saturday 11:30 to 3:30. Dinner, Tuesday-Saturday 3:30 to 10, Sunday noon to 9.

S.S. Dion, 520 Thames St., Bristol.

"Seafood and sunsets" are the specialties of Sue and Steve Dion, who combined the initials of their names for their twenty-year-old restaurant with a clamshell logo, a nautical setting and a water view across the street. Tropical fish entertain in a large aquarium as classical music plays and candles flicker in hurricane chimneys at well-spaced tables. There's outside dining under an awning overlooking the harbor across the street in summer.

Steve is the host and Sue the head chef, preparing stylish seafood and pasta fare – an extensive assortment of things like scrod classico, crab cakes with horseradish mayonnaise, baked stuffed shrimp, seafood casserole, littlenecks on capellini and seafood fra diavolo. Grilled fish choices are available with any of five sauces. There are the usual suspects among chicken, veal and beef entrées. Lately, Sue has added Asian twists as in poached scrod with ginger and soy, oriental linguini and chicken teriyaki.

A spread of dill and cream cheese with crackers awaits diners at each table. Brownie pie and strawberry shortcake are favorite desserts.

(401) 253-2884. Entrées, $13.95 to $19.95. Dinner, Monday-Saturday from 5.

Aidan's Pub & Grub, 5 John St., Bristol.

They cover the outdoor deck for St. Patrick's Day festivities at this popular Irish pub known locally as an adult hangout for authentic food and ale. The formula proved successful for Irish-born owner Aidan Graham, a sometime drummer who hails from County Westmeath in the midlands of Ireland. He opened a second, more formal Aidan's in Newport and, more recently, added the Judge Roy Bean Saloon at the foot of State Street.

Locals consider his original the real thing, a lively space with a noisy bar at one end and low round tables elsewhere. At the far end, attractively on view from the street, is a large and appealing dining deck with a glimpse of the harbor.

Regulars rave about the awesome burgers and the traditional fish and chips that are the best around. They also go for the Irish specialties, among them bangers and mash, Dublin pot pie, the Irish mixed grill (limerick bacon, Irish sausage and pork chops), and shepherd's pie topped with mashed potatoes worth eating just on their own. Order the sirloin steak rare, for it's sautéed in Irish whisky and arrives sizzling on a platter so hot it keeps on cooking at the table. Accompany with a pint of ale or two. And finish with the Bailey's Irish cream pie.

(401) 254-1940. Entrées, $7.50 to $15.95. Open daily, 11:30 to 10 or 11.

Quito's, 411 Thames St., Bristol.

There's a small seafood store in front, so you know the fish is fresh as can be in Al Quito's no-nonsense restaurant next to a park at water's edge. The emphasis is family casual at booths and tables inside. In season, the tables of choice are outside on a canopied patio.

Fried seafood is featured, served with coleslaw and fries ("no substitutes") and available for takeout. Rather unexpected, from the looks of the place, is the variety of other dishes, from scrod oregano and scallops florentine to grilled swordfish or tuna and pan-seared scallops, served with potato and vegetables. There are seafood chowders and stews, pastas, caesar salads (with lobster or sirloin) and seafood casseroles.

The variety extends to the sandwich menu, with options from an "all-natural, low-fat garden burger" to a crab cake sandwich on a homemade roll.

(401) 253-4500. Entrées, $13.95 to $22.95. Open daily except Tuesday, 11:30 to 9, Sunday to 8. Closed Monday and Tuesday in March-April and October-December. Closed January and February.

J.F. Goff's Pub, 251 Thames St., Bristol.

If you really want food with a view, consider this casual newcomer at the foot of the Thames Street Landing complex. The spacious outdoor deck is on the wharf, right at water's edge, with waves lapping almost underfoot. The rooftop deck, employed at busy times as a bar or for private parties, affords a panoramic view.

An extensive all-day menu of burgers, sandwiches, wraps and salads at rather hefty prices is offered inside and out, around the bar and in a casual dining area. A blackboard posts more substantial specials, changing weekly but typified by crab claws, pork chops, turkey dinner, mixed grill and a game platter. They were out of the caesar salad with jonah crab when we stopped for lunch, but the clam chowder was good, the burger was burnt and hard as a rock, and the clam cakes were at least filling if bland. The folks at the next table ordered a platter of nachos so big that most of it went home in a styrofoam container. The setting remains etched in our memories, while the food was best forgotten.

(401) 253-4523. Entrées, $8 to $16. Lunch and dinner daily, 11:30 to 9 or 10.

Blithewold Mansion is flanked by broad lawns, showy gardens and arboretum.

Diversions

Bristol is the southern terminus of the new East Bay Bicycle Path, a cyclist's dream that extends fourteen miles along Narragansett Bay from Colt State Park north to Providence.

Blithewold Mansion, Gardens & Arboretum, 101 Ferry Road, Bristol.

Built of stone in 1908 as a summer residence by Pennsylvania coal magnate Augustus Van Wickle, this 45-room English-style manor house is surrounded by 33 acres of landscaped grounds, gardens and exotic plants beside Narragansett Bay. His wife Bessie, a horticulturalist, and their daughter Marjorie developed an arboretum and extensive gardens that were left to the citizens of Bristol following Marjorie's death on the estate in 1976 at age 93. A 100-foot giant sequoia (the biggest east of the Rockies and so tall that it wears a lightning rod for protection) is a highlight of the arboretum. A bamboo grove the size of a tennis court, a rose garden, showy display gardens, water and rock gardens, and more than 250 species of trees and shrubs (especially Asian) are viewed along self-guiding trails. One leads across a stone bridge over a pond to a century-old rock garden with salt-tolerant plants nestled beneath trees beside the shore. More than 50,000 daffodils burst into bloom in the Bosquet woodland in April.

The mansion, listed on the National Register, is furnished much as it was early in the last century, with most of the original wallpaper and prized possessions still intact. Twelve rooms on two floors are open for self-guided tours. Included are a daughter's bedroom with Stickley furniture and the cozy maid's room. The master bedroom, with twin canopy Dutch marquetry beds and hand-painted wallpaper depicting a Dutch village scene, opens onto a sun porch bigger than most bedrooms. Visitors remark favorably that the house looks more lived-in and livable than the Newport mansions.

(413) 253-2707. www.blithewold.org. Self-guided tours of mansion and grounds, Wednesday-Sunday 10 to 4, mid-April to Columbus Day, adults $10. Grounds open year-round, daily 10 to 5, adults $5.

1810 columned mansion known as Linden Place is landmark in center of town.

Linden Place, 500 Hope St., Bristol.

The most prominent landmark in the heart of town is the columned 1810 Federal mansion built for Gen. George DeWolf of the seafaring Rhode Island family, a merchant who made his fortune in the slave-trading business and fled the town in 1825 when forced into bankruptcy following the failure of his Cuban sugar crop. The grand house was occupied by four generations of descendants, including his grandson Samuel Pomeroy Colt (founder of U.S. Rubber Co., now Uniroyal, and director of 26 leading corporations). The mansion hosted four American presidents, served as a summer home for actress Ethel Barrymore and was featured in the movie, "The Great Gatsby." The interior holds a dramatic Honduras mahogany spiral staircase as well as artworks and furnishings from five generations who occupied the house until 1989, when it was saved from possible demolition by a friends group. The two-acre property features a ballroom, summer house, a carriage house, 19th century sculptures, gazebos and rose gardens.

(401) 253-0390. www.lindenplace.org. Open Thursday-Saturday 10 to 4, Sunday and holidays noon to 4, May-October and December. Adults, $5.

Herreshoff Marine Museum, 1 Burnside St., Bristol.

This museum bordering Narragansett Bay is considered Rhode Island's most important maritime site. From 1863 to 1945, the Herreshoff Manufacturing Co. produced the world's finest yachts here with cutting-edge design and engineering. The first U.S. Navy torpedo boats and mammoth schooners were among its output, along with a record eight consecutive successful defenders of the America's Cup from 1893 to 1934. The museum displays more than 60 classic sailing and power yachts, some of which can be boarded. Also shown is a unique collection of 535 study models used to create the designs and now works of art in themselves. In addition, it showcases hundreds of artifacts and memorabilia from the Herreshoff legacy, including steam engines, photos, correspondence, silver and china, tools and even the notes and spectacles of the famed naval architect, Capt. Nathaniel Herreshoff. The museum operates the America's Cup Hall of Fame here. The property encompasses the old family homestead, seven former company buildings and a large portion of the company waterfront.

(401) 253-5000. www.herreshoff.org. Open May-October, daily 10 to 5. Adults, $8.

SHOPPING. The most interesting boutiques and shops are spread out along Hope Street, in the vicinity of State Street. Antiques is a common denominator of many, including **Alfred's, Da Vinci's Ltd.** and **Jesse-James Antiques. Paper, Packaging and Panache** is one of the best card and stationery shops we've seen. **Kate & Company** has specialty foods, gifts, clothing and home accents, while **European Kitchen** mixes cookware from France and Italy. **Good Books** speaks for itself. **The Potted Garden** is a small plant store with colorful ideas displayed on its side deck.

Food is a big deal in the area, from **Café La France,** the local hangout for coffee and sandwiches, to **Tivoli** for ice cream, coffee and pastry desserts to the **Basically British Tea Room.** There's even **Woof,** a bakery for dogs.

The new Thames Street Landing offers a variety of boutiques, including **The Claddagh Connection, Old China Trader** and **Chatelaine** for women's clothing and shoes. Our favorite **Gray's Ice Cream of Tiverton** has a branch here.

Extra-Special

Colt State Park, Colt Drive, Route 114, Bristol.

Every state should be so lucky as to have a park like this. And Bristol is the fortunate benefactor of local industrialist Samuel Pomeroy Colt's largesse, a 464-acre recreational paradise on the former Colt farm along Narragansett Bay. It's considered the "gem" of the state parks system – and that could apply nationally, rather than just to little Rhody. A three-mile loop drive is Bristol's condensed answer to the Seventeen-Mile Drive on California's Monterey Peninsula. It hugs the Narragansett Bay shoreline and weaves around pastures, tidal ponds, ornamental statues, groomed fruit trees, manicured lawns and thick woods. Along the way you pass open bay vistas, hiking trails and bicycle paths, a saltwater fishing pier, boat launch, picnic groves (more than 400 picnic tables at 45 scattered sites), ten large playfields, the open-air Chapel-By-the-Sea and the huge stone barn that housed Colt's herd of prized Jersey cows. Colt, the nephew of Hartford's Samuel Colt of revolver fame, bought and combined three farms on Poppasquash Neck in the early 1900s to breed what he hoped would be the world's best Jersey herd. He designed a system of roads that linked them together and built the fanciful stone bridge over the Mill Gut salt marsh that is part of the elaborate trail network. On a brilliant Columbus Day afternoon, we encountered countless strollers and picnickers, kite flyers, a man with a walking stick exercising his pet goats, and a family outing of Hassidic Jews playing baseball. All were enjoying the legacy left by Samuel Colt on marble gates at the entrance, inscribed "Private Property, Samuel P. Colt, Open to the Public."

(401) 253-7482. Open daily year-round, sunrise to sunset. Free.

Newport, R.I.

A Many-Splendored Place

For the visitor, there are perhaps five Newports.

One is the harborfront, the busy commercial and entertainment area along the wharves and Thames Street. This is the heart of Newport, the place from which the Tall Ships and America's Cup winners sailed, the area to which the tourists gravitate.

Another Newport is a world apart. It's up on fabled Bellevue Avenue among the mansions from the Gilded Age. Here the Astors, Vanderbilts, Morgans and others of America's 400 built their summer "cottages," palatial showplaces designed by the nation's leading architects. Here near the Casino at the turn of the century was a society summer resort unrivaled for glitter and opulence.

A third Newport is its quaint Point and Historic Hill sections, which date back to the 17th and 18th centuries when Newport was an early maritime center. Here are located more Colonial houses than any other place in the country, and some of the oldest public and religious edifices as well.

A fourth Newport is the windswept, open land around Ocean Drive, where the surf crashes against the rocky shore amid latter-day mansions and contemporary showplaces. This is the New England version of California's Pebble Beach and Seventeen-Mile Drive.

And then there's the rest of Newport, a bustling, Navy-dominated city that sprawls south along Aquidneck Island, away from the ocean and the other Newports.

Join these diverse Newports as history and geography have. The result is New England's international resort, a wondrous mix of water and wealth, of architecture and history, of romance and entertainment.

You can concentrate on one Newport and have more than enough to see and do, or try to savor a bit of them all. But likely as not, you won't get your fill. Newport will merely whet your appetite, its powerful allure beckoning you back.

Inn Spots

Newport has at least 200 inns and B&Bs, more than any other place in the country, according to local officials. They vary widely, and many of the more advertised ones lack the personal touch conveyed by owners who are also in residence as innkeepers. Of recent vintage are some excellent inns whose owners lavish TLC on their guests as well as their properties.

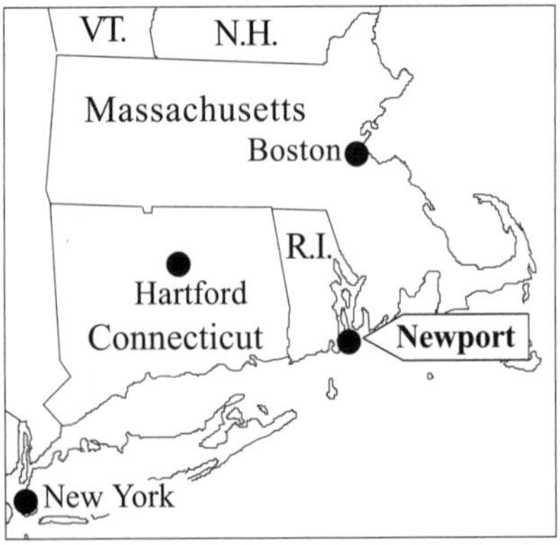

Cliffside Inn, 2 Seaview Ave., Newport 02840.

Newport's most luxurious large B&B is based in a summer villa built in 1880 by a Maryland governor. It was meticulously yet extravagantly upgraded by the late Winthrop Baker of Wilton, Conn., who lavished big bucks and great taste on

Self-portrait of artist Beatrice Turner overlooks breakfast table at Cliffside Inn.

turning his first East Coast inn into one of the nation's best.

Cliffside has up to three working fireplaces in each of its sixteen accommodations. Its bathroom "salons" – fourteen with whirlpool tubs and the others with steam baths – are some of America's most glamorous. All blend rich Victoriana and stately king or queen beds with airy Laura Ashley freshness, telephones and TV sets. Some "digital video" rooms feature media centers and flat-screen TVs with an alphabet soup of LCD, DVD, CD and CVR).

Low-key Victoriana prevails in the main house, from the half-tester bed and Victorian loveseat in the elaborate Turner Suite to a two-story Tower Suite with six sides, topped by a cupola. The tower's entire lower floor is devoted to a wood-paneled bathroom, including whirlpool tub, marble shower and bidet. Upstairs is a bed-sitting room beneath an octagonal cathedral ceiling, with Eastlake queen bed, fireplace and bay window.

The main-floor Victorian Room has a new whirlpool bath plus a dresser and a queensize four-poster bed bearing a shell headboard that was acquired at a Woolworth estate auction in Connecticut. The enlarged Garden Suite is a great summer space with a bay window off the front porch and a 28-foot-long "habitat bathroom" beneath, so-called "because you can live in it," what with a Victorian book nook at one end and french doors at the other opening onto a private courtyard.

The newest and, some think, the nicest accommodations are in the Cliffside Cottage, a onetime ranch house near the Cliff Walk at the foot of the property. It's been transformed into three suites, each with three fireplaces and sound-system bathrooms. The Seaview on the lower floor is a stone-walled hideaway with a wood-burning fireplace and an antique French kingsize bed. Its plush sitting room shares a see-through gas fireplace with the marble bathroom, which has an Allure bath, shower and sound system tub to end all systems. Upstairs, the Atlantic has a queen plantation bed, stone fireplace and sitting room with a media center. The kingsize Cliff has not one but two sitting rooms – a living room and a study.

There are fine gathering places as well. The large fireplaced parlor is cheerfully decorated in shades of orange-coral and moss green; the faille draperies are a sight to behold. Classical music and opera play in the afternoon as guests enjoy hot apple cider, lemonade or tea, hot or iced, depending on the season, with treats like duck liver pâté, shrimp in puff pastry and brie with crackers. They help themselves to juices, sodas and the like stocked in a cabinet. They relax on the wide front veranda, which yields glimpses of the ocean down the street.

The guest's every need is fulfilled by a pampering staff headed by innkeeper Stephen Nicolas and Win Baker Jr., the owner's son. They serve not only the afternoon canapés but also a memorable breakfast. In our case it began with orange juice, two kinds of muffins and a remarkable (for winter) array of raspberries, blackberries and strawberries to lather upon homemade granola or mix with yogurt. The pièce de résistance was eggs benedict with a subtle hollandaise sauce.

There's food for the soul, too, in Cliffside's hundred or so paintings by reclusive artist Beatrice Turner, onetime owner of the house, whose life story and background are full of mystery. More than 100 images of her art, including a haunting self-portrait above the breakfast credenza, remain on permanent display. They add still another dimension to a luxurious inn of distinction.

(401) 847-1811 or (800) 845-1811. Fax (401) 848-5850. www.cliffsideinn.com. Eight rooms and eight suites with private baths. Doubles, $245 to $425. Suites, $375 to $575. Add $50 weekends, May-October. Children over 13.

The Francis Malbone House, 392 Thames St., Newport 02840.

Elegant decor, an abundance of flowering plants and a rear courtyard retreat make this a favorite with those who like to be in the thick of things along Lower Thames Street. Five local partners acquired the imposing residence in 1990 and converted it into one beautiful inn.

The downstairs common rooms are uncommonly inviting, the burgundy, pale pink and blue striped upholstery on some of the sofas and chairs in two high-ceilinged parlors matching the handsome draperies. In the rear library, the colors are also coordinated with the oriental carpet. All three rooms have fireplaces, and there's a TV/VCR in the library. At a spring visit, the rooms abounded with a profusion of colorful houseplants, from African violets to hydrangeas to an hibiscus that had burst into bloom in a sunny window that morning.

Upstairs off a center hall are eight corner rooms on two floors, all with updated bathrooms (two with tubs) and six with fireplaces. The front rooms are bigger and afford harbor views. Each is exquisitely furnished with antique queensize beds covered by monogrammed duvet covers in white. Baskets of Gilchrist & Soames toiletries are in each bathroom and interesting magazines are displayed in the bedrooms. Queen Anne furnishings, TVs and telephones with data ports are the norm here and throughout the B&B.

On the main floor, a side hallway with a shelf of cobalt blue glass leads past the library to the sunken Counting House Suite (built as an office by the physician who once owned the house) with a private entry, a kingsize canopy bed facing the TV, a sitting area with a sofabed and two wing chairs, fireplace, dining table and a large bath with an oversize marble shower and a corner jacuzzi for two.

Although still the premium accommodation, the suite has competition from the

Extravagant breakfast is served in rear courtyard at Francis Malbone House.

nine new courtyard rooms in the rear, all with kingsize poster beds and jacuzzi tubs, writing desks, fireplaces and TVs hidden in recessed bookshelves. Bigger, more private and quiet because they're away from the street traffic, they encompass all the amenities that "we couldn't have in the original house and wanted here," in the words of innkeeper Will Dewey. A couple open onto private courtyards with wrought-iron furniture. The courtyard suite adds a wet bar and a sitting area.

Two luxurious accommodations were opened lately in the 1710 Mason House at the rear of the property. The downstairs holds a living room, dining room, kitchen and sunroom with a courtyard. These are common areas for two spacious upstairs lodgings, each with king or queen bed, fireplace, and jacuzzi tub and TV in the bathroom.

Breakfast is served in the inn's spectacular 40-seat dining room off a corridor walled with glass and Portuguese tiles leading to the courtyard wing. It's a beauty in pale yellow and gray with a candle chandelier hanging from a fifteen-foot-high domed ceiling and tall shelves displaying Will's collection of blue and white English china.

Will, a culinary graduate of Johnson & Wales University in Providence, and his staff prepare a full breakfast, starting with fresh fruits, breads, muffins and perhaps raspberry croissants or cinnamon-raisin strudels. The main course possibilities range from eggs benedict or a variety of quiches to belgian waffles. Homemade cookies and beverages are offered in the afternoon.

(401) 846-0392 or (800) 846-0392. Fax (401) 848-5956. www.malbone.com. Sixteen rooms and four suites with private baths. Mid-April to mid-November: doubles $245 to $340, suites $395 to $475. Rest of year: doubles $99 to $260, suites $200 to $345. Three-night minimum weekends Memorial Day through October, two-night minimum weekends rest of year. Children over 12.

Castle Hill Inn & Resort, 590 Ocean Drive, Newport 02840.

Gnarled trees on a hillside, reminding us of the olive groves in Portugal, make the approach to this reborn inn on 40 seaside acres a bit mysterious as well as picturesque. When you reach the brown shingle-style Victorian landmark at the crest of the hill, the view of Narragansett Bay and the Atlantic is breathtaking. Equally stunning are the refurbished accommodations, as orchestrated by the father-and-son ownership team of Tim and Paul O'Reilly of the Newport Harbor Corp., who reassumed control and started fulfilling the oceanside mansion's potential.

The mansion was built in 1874 as a summer retreat for Alexander Agassiz, the Harvard marine biologist and explorer. It holds eight Victorian guest rooms and two suites, most with king or queen beds, double whirlpool marble baths, fireplaces and original antiques. The original master bedroom is large enough for two queensize sleigh beds. The main level of the new Turret Suite, beneath a reconstructed 30-foot-high turreted roof, has a kingsize canopy bed, a gleaming soaking tub in the window, and a bath with oversize marble shower. A spiral mahogany staircase leads to its loft sitting area and a 360-degree view.

Beside the mansion, the Swiss-style Chalet, the scientist's former laboratory, was converted into a function facility and two grand guest rooms. Kingsize canopy beds, double whirlpool baths and fireplaces were provided for its upstairs bedroom and a bridal suite.

Six outlying Harbor House units perched on a cliff were winterized and given kingsize beds, whirlpool baths, televisions, fireplaces and french doors onto semi-private decks overlooking the bay.

The first eight rustic cottages to be enlarged, refurbished and called beach houses – elegant with vaulted ceilings, oak hardwood floors, bead-board paneling and beachy decor – rank with the best in southern New England. Each has a kingsize bed, TV and a distressed leather couch that converts into a queen bed in the sitting area, fireplace, granite-counter galley kitchen, double whirlpool tub and separate shower, and an outdoor deck facing the ocean.

A complimentary breakfast with a choice of juices, fruits and entrées is served to overnight guests in the Sunset Room. The fare includes lobster omelets, eggs benedict, french toast made with raisin challah and smoked salmon with breakfast garnishes.

(401) 849-3800 or (888) 466-1355. Fax (401) 849-3838. www.innatcastlehill.com. Twenty-two rooms, three suites and eight cottages with private baths. Mid-June to mid-October: doubles, $450 to $725 weekends, $295 to $650 midweek; suites, $725 to $1,450 weekends, $650 to $1,200 midweek; cottages, $5,075 weekly. Rest of year: doubles $285 to $625 weekends, $145 to $350 midweek; suites $395 to $1,250 weekends, $225 to $800 midweek; cottages $485 to $695 weekends, $250 to $450 midweek.

The Chanler at Cliff Walk, 117 Memorial Blvd., Newport 02840.

Here is the ultimate mansion hotel – in Newport, the city of fabled mansions, no less. The $10 million renovation of the old Cliff Walk Manor took two years longer and more expense than anticipated, but even skeptics agreed it was worth the wait. The extravagant French Empire-style showplace, enveloped in lush landscaping, reopened in 2003 with considerable fanfare.

The well-known Newport landmark was built in 1873 as the summer home of Congressman John Winthrop Chanler of New York, whose wife was an Astor. John and Jean E. Shufelt purchased the four-and-one-half-acre property in 2000 and

Grandly restored Chanler at Cliff Walk overlooks Atlantic Ocean.

launched a major renovation and upgrade for reopening as "a small, elegant European hotel."

John had undertaken a similar renovation earlier at the Mission Point Resort on Michigan's Mackinac Island. Given his wife's associations with Newport and their experience opening the five-room La Farge Perry House, a B&B at 24 Kay St. here, he saw an upside potential for the derelict three-story building at the terminus of the Cliff Walk.

The original 25 guest rooms were reconfigured into 20, each with a different theme. All have king or queensize beds and jacuzzi baths and all but two have gas fireplaces. Most come with crystal chandeliers and the up-to-date furnishings typical of latter-day Newport mansion. Plump beds, fine paintings, flat-screen TVs, DVD players, wet bars and heated tile bathroom floors are the norm.

Rooms are truly sumptuous and not at all kooky, as one might expect given their Disneyesque themes. The idea was to provide a "uniquely different lodging experience" in each room, in John Schufelt's words. The idea was fulfilled brilliantly.

Some rooms are defined and decorated by era – Greek Revival, English Tudor, Louis XIV, Colonial, Federal, French Provincial, Victorian and Mediterranean, among them. Those, in the main house, range in price from the Gothic and Williamsburg at the low end to the Neo-Classical at the high end. Others in the old east wing have ocean-facing decks with hot tubs and a more casual New England island theme. Martha's Vineyard, the largest, is considered the bridal suite. Three garden villas in front with floral names and themes have both baths with jacuzzis and private garden courtyards with hot tubs under pergolas and two sitting areas to compensate for their smaller size and lack of ocean views.

Three meals a day are served in the inn's luxurious Spiced Pear restaurant (see Dining Spots). The mahogany paneled lounge and the adjoining outdoor terraces overlooking the ocean also provide food and drink.

(401) 847-1300. Fax (401) 847-3620. www.thechanler.com. Twenty rooms with private baths. July-August: doubles, $895 to $1,095. Spring and fall: $445 to $1,095 weekends, $345 to $895 midweek. Winter: $395 to $695 weekends, $295 to $595 midweek.

Whirlpool tub and fireplace are among amenities in Victoria Suite at Abigail Stoneman Inn.

Abigail Stoneman Inn, 102 Touro St., Newport 02840.

"Menus" for pillows, bathing and tea, and a "water bar." These are four one-of-a-kind luxury amenities that set Newport's most deluxe small B&B apart.

Opened in 2002 by Winthrop Baker of the Cliffside Inn and his expanding Legendary Inns of Newport group, it occupies the classic Renaissance-style Victorian built in 1866 by renowned Newport architect George Champlin Mason. Inside is the group's most lavish establishment yet. Not so much for the five accommodations, sumptuous as they are, what with their predictable art theme (here 75 artworks of Newport women, in honor of Abigail Stoneman, Newport's first female innkeeper), high-style Victorian antique furnishings, kingsize beds, fireplaces, marble baths with two-person whirlpool tubs, steam baths and extravagant media centers concealed behind mirrors or in armoires. But rather for the complimentary "amenities menus" that take personalized room service to a higher level.

Even guests who have – and expect – everything probably don't have some of these.

The pillow menu offers guests twenty styles of pillows from a collection worth more than $10,000. There are wool, anti-snoring, maternity, magnetic therapy buckwheat hull and who-knows-what-all pillows. We tried the mediflow water pillow and the head cradle, but quickly reverted to the four perfectly adequate pillows already on the bed.

For bathing in some of the most glamorous whirlpool-tub settings you'll ever find, the British Penhaligon amenities would suffice anywhere else. Here you can supplement them with a choice of 30 imported soaps, bath salts, foams and oils from halfway around the world. The leftovers go home in a soap "doggy bag."

The inn's J.B. Finch Pub is a water bar, offering 25 of the world's best bottled waters – a selection of which you'll also find in the entry hall and in your room. The inn went through 120 cases of the trendy Voss artesian water from Norway in its first five months.

And then there are the teas, an exceptional offering of 35 kinds, available around the clock and sometimes taken in a cozy Tea for Two Room off the entry hall. The afternoon tea service was cited as one of nineteen best in America in the 2002 book, *The Great Tea Rooms of America.* It's served daily at 4:30 in the parlor, accompanied by a changing feast of savories and sweets equal to those of the finest restaurants.

The amenities upstage even the inn's third-floor suite named – appropriately – Above and Beyond. A soaring spiral staircase opens into an opulent oak-paneled library with two reading areas, fireplace and media center. Off the library are two kingsize bedrooms, a kitchen/dining area and a marble bath with shower. A secret compartment hidden behind framed faux books in the library leads to the ultimate "bathing salon." Ensconced in a dormer window is a wood-paneled whirlpool tub for two amidst an array of plants, a chandelier and a wall-sconce lighting system with sixteen individual lights on dimmers.

Breakfast is a gourmet event, taken at individual tables in the parlor or, by most guests, in their rooms. Ours culminated in an asparagus, ham and tomato omelet, expertly prepared and served by the charming William, known across Newport as Billy Rose, an ex-shoeshine boy who danced professionally with Martha Graham and the Alvin Ailey troupe. He "came with the house," having worked at the former James B. Finch House before the B&B ascended to a higher level.

How high? An early entry in the inn's guestbook extolled: "Nothing can compare, only dreams."

(401) 847-1811 or (800) 845-1811. www.abigailstonemaninn.com. Two rooms and three suites with private baths. Doubles, $425. Suites, $525 and $625. Add $50 weekends May-October.

The Old Beach Inn, 19 Old Beach Road, Newport 02840.

Unusual touches prevail in this romantic, intimate B&B run by Luke and Cyndi Murray. One is the old anchor embedded in the third-story turret of the home built as the Anchorage in 1879. Another is the ornate wedding bed with lace draped in the center in the Forget-Me-Not bedroom. How about the palladian arch leading into the jacuzzi bathroom off the Ivy Room, handsome in dark green and burgundy with a faux book case along one wall and an antique wood-burning fireplace?

The Murrays offer seven guest rooms with private baths. Cyndi says she likes "a lot of different styles." They are reflected in the English country decor in the rooms, named after flowers and full of whimsical touches. In the Rose Room, carved roses dress the kingsize bed. Done up in sage, rosemary and cream, the room has a fireplace, a hand-painted dresser with hand-carved rose drawer pulls and even the white commode cover is sculpted like a rose. Check out the bishop-sleeve draperies with valances in the first-floor Wisteria Room, and the wicker loveseat and chair in the Forget-Me-Not Room. Cyndi decorates for the season, especially at Christmas, but the front hall's original stained-glass window representing the four seasons shines at all times.

Ever upgrading, the Murrays added two rooms with separate entrances in the rear carriage house, part of which they converted into meeting space for small groups. These have TVs and a more contemporary air. The Sunflower, lovely in pale yellow and burgundy, is furnished in wicker. It's done in a sunflower motif, from the lamps on a nightstand to a hand-painted shelf.

Guests gather in a front parlor or a larger Victorian living room. Here, two plush chairs and a couch face a glass cocktail table resting on four bunnies. The room holds a rabbit fashioned from moss, a tiled fireplace and a copper bar in the corner.

The Murrays serve breakfast at four tables in the dining room or outside on the porch or a brick patio overlooking a pleasant back yard with a gazebo and fish pond. It usually involves juice, fruit, homemade granola and pastries, plus a main dish such as egg casserole, quiche or, perhaps on Sundays, blueberry-stuffed french toast.

(401) 849-3479 or (888) 303-5033. Fax (401) 847-1236. www.oldbeachinn.com. Seven rooms with private baths. May-October: doubles, $135 to $350. Rest of year: $85 to $275. Two-night minimum weekends in season. Children over 12.

Adele Turner Inn, 93 Pelham St., Newport 02840.

The folks from the Cliffside Inn acquired the Admiral Benbow Inn, upscaled and refurbished it with the predictable amenities in 2001. They named it for the mother of artist Beatrice Turner, whose summer home eventually became the Cliffside.

This 1855 structure, notable for 27 tall arched windows and listed on the National Register, is along a prime residential street descending to the waterfront.

Gas fireplaces were installed in all of the three-story inn's thirteen guest quarters. King and queensize beds, elegant quilts and window treatments, new rugs and carpeting, TV/VCRs and telephones are common to all.

The kingsize Tycoon Suite on the third floor with a 43-foot-stretch along the front of the house offers a water view, one of three new double whirlpool tubs and a digital media center. It's decorated with antique money, and stock and bond certificates from the Robber Baron Era. The rear Harbor View Spa Room with an ornate French queen bed and nautical decor has a rooftop deck with a private hot tub.

The pampering service and luxuries for which Cliffside is known are duplicated here – in some cases, literally. Breakfast and full afternoon tea service are prepared by the chef from Cliffside, and homemade dessert treats accompany nightly turndown service.

The building's largest single space, previously devoted to an innkeeper's apartment, was converted into a stunning Victorian parlor with not one but two fireplaces. It's furnished with period antiques, rich fabrics and four large portraits of Adele Haas Turner, painted by her daughter. The new innkeeper from the Cliffside resides in a room on the third floor.

(401) 847-1811 or (800) 845-1811. Fax (401) 848-5850. www.adeleturnerinn.com. Ten rooms and three suites with private baths. Doubles, $185 to $450. Suites, $395 to $475. Add $50 weekends May-October.

Ivy Lodge, 12 Clay St., Newport 02840.

A striking, three-story entry hall, 33 feet high and paneled in carved oak, awaits visitors to this attractive B&B, tucked away at the end of a residential street behind Bellevue Avenue.

New owners Daryl and Darlene McKenzie, former mortgage bankers from Dayton, Ohio, have upgraded the accommodations in a house that had been described by an 1886 newspaper as "one of the prettiest cottages in Newport."

They offer eight guest rooms and suites, a particularly appealing one fashioned from the former library on the main floor with red silk wallpaper, a red felt settee at the foot of the queensize mahogany bed, a Delft-tiled fireplace and a double jacuzzi and a separate shower.

Upstairs, all the baths, some of which had been in the hall, now connect with the

Oak-paneled entry hall three stories high greets visitors to Ivy Lodge.

bedrooms through ingenious architectural reconfigurations. The McKenzies added six gas fireplaces and three jacuzzi tubs. Each room now has TV and telephone, a small refrigerator in the closet, steam iron and hair dryer. The most-requested room, the stately yet cheery yellow Turret with kingsize bed, comes with a flat-screen TV with VCR/DVD, two-person jacuzzi and double vanity. Although decor is Victorian, Darlene shunned the "froufrou look for something more eclectic."

The paneling in the common areas is awesome and there's "no plaster in any part of the hall," as the 1886 newspaper article put it. Upstairs bedrooms go off galleries, supported by fluted and carved columns, around the hall.

A small reception parlor is pretty in pink, wicker and chintz. It is enhanced by a fireplace and floral prints. Beyond is a large and elegant living room.

The twenty-one-foot-long table in the chandeliered dining room is set for sixteen, with room to spare. Here, the McKenzies serve fruit salad and yogurt, baked goods and homemade granola. These are preliminaries to the main course, a choice of sweet or savory – perhaps gingerbread pancakes with lemon sauce or tomato-basil-cream cheese frittata.

In the afternoon, candles are lit on the fireplace mantels and tea and snacks are put out to welcome guests. A wraparound veranda is fine for lounging beside the tranquil grounds. The McKenzies added a goldfish pond and lawn games.

(401) 849-6865 or (800) 834-6865. Fax (401) 849-2919. www.ivylodge.com. Eight rooms with private baths. May-October: doubles, $259 to $399 weekends, $139 to $259 midweek. Rest of year: doubles $209 to $299 weekends, $129 to $209 midweek. Three-night minimum weekends in season, two-night weekends rest of year.

The Victorian Ladies, 63 Memorial Blvd., Newport 02840.

All is light and airy in these two Victorian beauties, one behind the other and separated by a lovely brick courtyard with a gazebo, birdbath, wicker furniture and tempered-glass tables, surrounded by colorful flower boxes. Innkeepers Helene and Donald O'Neill gutted and renovated the houses, opening the first of Newport's more comfortable and inviting B&Bs in 1987.

Eleven guest rooms are decorated in a Victorian theme with a light touch. One of the nicest has a queensize bed and sitting area; it is fresh and feminine with dhurrie rugs and rose carpeting, puffy curtains, down comforters, eyelet ruffles, thick pink and blue towels, potpourri and vials of dried flowers on the doors.

Although Helene had never decorated before, she did a gorgeous job throughout. The small pink and blue parlor has a crystal chandelier and crystal sconces on the mantel; the fireplace was ablaze the chilly October morning we first visited. Balloon curtains adorn the parlor and the adjacent dining room, where an enormous 1740 hutch-sideboard of English pine displays plates and country knickknacks.

The O'Neills added two deluxe suites upstairs above their quarters in the rear caretaker's cottage. Both contain lavender carpeting with which Helene paired a pale yellow color scheme in one suite and red and dark green in the other. One has a wicker loveseat and a corner writing desk. Both have telephones in addition to the television sets common to all rooms.

Don, a contractor, built the gazebo and the courtyard, and his green thumb shows in a profusion of flowers in the surrounding gardens. Lately he installed a Japanese koi pond and garden.

Helene serves up a marvelous breakfast, from all kinds of muffins to grand marnier french toast, eggs benedict, or an egg and spinach casserole. "She loves to cook and keeps expanding her repertoire," says Don. "I'm the dishwasher."

(401) 849-9960. www.victorianladies.com. Eleven rooms with private baths. May to early November: doubles, $175 to $225. Rest of year: $125 to $155. Two-night minimum weekends. Children over 10.

Hydrangea House Inn, 16 Bellevue Ave., Newport 02840.

Two antiques dealers launched this B&B in former office space above a Bellevue Avenue storefront, now transformed into a Victorian townhouse with a colorful, deep purple facade. So you expect it to be decorated to the hilt, and it is. Dennis Blair and Grant Edmondson turned their former antiques shop and art gallery into public rooms, decorated accordingly, and some of their antiques and artworks moved into guest rooms upstairs.

A section of the gallery became an elegant living room with a fireplace and stenciled moldings, where guests await the opening of the doors to the formal dining room for breakfast. "They meet and talk and by the time they sit down they're all friends," says Dennis. That makes for a convivial breakfast at a mahogany table set for fourteen, with a fireplace and tapestry wall hangings beside and a crystal chandelier overhead.

It's an elegant backdrop for the morning repasts cooked up by Grant, from his relocated and remodeled kitchen with a new AGA stove.. He offers fresh orange juice, granola, homemade breads and perhaps raspberry pancakes or seasoned scrambled eggs. In summer, the venue moves to a remarkable second-story veranda, a 16-by-30-foot deck filled with plants, where afternoon tea is offered. It lends a far more residential, verdant feeling than you'd suspect from the building's front.

The inn expanded into an adjacent building and renovated in 2004 to produce nine reconfigured rooms, some enlarged into split-level affairs and all now with fireplaces and jacuzzi tubs. The 50-foot-long Hydrangea room on the third floor is furnished with Edwardian antiques. It has a kingsize canopy bed, a fireplace, a skylit double whirlpool tub encased in Italian marble in the room, a steam bath in the bathroom, and a TV/VCR and stereo system. Similar attributes characterize the main-floor King Edward Room, decorated in royal blue and gold and also with a king bed.

Four second-floor guest rooms go off a wide second-floor hallway with stippled gold walls painted with a pastry brush to look like marble. Each is decorated with splashy draperies and wallpapers that match; the fabrics may be repeated on the bed headboards or, in one case, a valance over the shower.

The rear of the second floor opens onto the spacious veranda, overlooking a showplace garden, complete with a spreading bamboo tree. The third floor opens onto a sundeck formed by the roof for the veranda below.

The latest renovation also produced a basement spa with a massage table, steam bath and sauna.

(401) 846-4435 or (800) 945-4667. Fax (401) 846-6602. www.hydrangeahouse.com. Eight rooms with private baths. Doubles, $175 to $310 Memorial Day through October, $145 to $280 rest of year. Three-night minimum weekends Memorial Day through October, two-night minimum weekends rest of year. Children over 13.

Architects Inn, 31 Old Beach Road, Newport 02840.

The 1873 Woodbine Cottage in which local architect George Champlin Mason resided has been turned into one of Newport's nicest B&Bs. Harlan and Sheila Tyler chucked their corporate careers locally and spent a year renovating the house a few blocks from where Sheila was raised.

Beige with white gingerbread trim, the vaguely Swiss-style house was perfect for their B&B purpose. It had been custom-made by the town's leading architect, who designed some of Newport's finest homes in the late 19th century and was joined in his practice by his son.

That accounts for the name change in 2003 from the former George Champlin Mason House.

The Tylers offer three elegant guest rooms, each spacious with queensize bed, working fireplace, sitting area and TV/VCR. The most popular is the Redwood Room with majestic canopy bed and a clawfoot soaking tub. Two suites with king or queensize beds have sitting rooms with new fireplaces. The premier Perry Suite also has a jacuzzi tub.

Guests enjoy the large main-floor living room and library, each with fireplace and eleven-foot-high ceiling.

A fireplace also enhances the dining room, where breakfast begins with a buffet of cereal, muffins, yogurt, fresh fruit and juices. A plated seasonal fruit, perhaps warm apple compote or bananas foster, follows. The main event could be eggs benedict, breakfast casserole or french toast made with Portuguese bread. Harlan does the baking, Sheila the cooking and both serve.

The side porch is employed for breakfast and afternoon refreshments in season.

(401) 847-7081 or (888) 834-7081. Fax (401) 847-5545. www.architectsinn.com. Three rooms and two suites with private baths. Doubles, $175 to $275 May-October, $99 to $185 rest of year. Children over 12.

Dining Spots

The Black Pearl, Bannister's Wharf, Newport.

Our favorite all-around restaurant in Newport – and that of many others, judging from the crowds day and night – is the informal tavern, the fancy Commodore's Room and the deck with umbrella-topped tables that comprise the Black Pearl.

Up to 1,500 meals a day are served in summer, the more remarkable considering it has what the manager calls "the world's smallest kitchen." Waitresses vie with patrons for space in the narrow hall that runs the length of the building; white-hatted chefs and busboys run across the wharf, even in winter, to fetch fresh produce and fish – sometimes champagne – from the refrigerators in an outbuilding.

It's all quite colorful, congenial in spirit and creative in cuisine. And – unusual for a resort area – the chef and all the key managers are starting their third decade with the establishment.

You can sit outside under the Cinzano umbrellas on Bannister's Wharf and watch the world go by while you enjoy some of the best clam chowder ever, thick and dill-laced. You also can enjoy a pearlburger, served with mint salad in pita bread and good fries, plus a variety of other sandwiches, salads and desserts. Inside, the tavern is cozy, dark and noisy, usually with a line of people waiting for seats, and the fare is basically the same as outside, with a few heartier entrées available at lunch or dinner. Desserts are delectable, especially the Black Pearl cheesecake followed, perhaps, by cappuccino laced with kahlua and courvoisier.

Candlelight dinners in the dressy Commodore Room are lovely, the lights of the waterfront twinkling through small paned windows. The beamed sloped ceilings, dark walls and tables set with white linen topped with vases of freesia make an attractive dining room.

Chef J. Daniel Knerr uses light sauces and stresses vegetables and side dishes in his contemporary fare. Expect entrées like sautéed soft-shell crabs, gray sole meunière, salmon fillet with mustard-dill hollandaise, roast duckling with green peppercorn sauce, rack of lamb and dry-aged T-bone steaks.

(401) 846-5264. Entrées, $19.50 to $35; tavern, $14.50 to $27. Dinner in Commodore Room, 6 to 11; jackets required. Tavern and outdoor cafe open daily from 11. Closed six weeks in winter.

Restaurant Bouchard, 505 Thames St., Newport.

After training in France and sixteen years as executive chef at the famed Le Chateau in New York's Westchester County, Albert J. Bouchard III decided in 1995 it was time to be on his own. He and his wife sought out a small establishment where he could exercise "total artistic control," which turned out to be the former tea room in a 1785 Georgian-style house.

The restaurant is a beauty in celadon and cream, with well spaced tables dressed in floor-length cloths. Four shelves of demi-tasse cups and saucers, part of his father's collection, separate the front section from the back. A small bar in the front room looks to be straight out of Provence.

The food is classic French with contemporary nuances in the style of his former domain. Typical entrées run from seafood gratin in a gruyère and boursin cheese sauce to crispy veal sweetbreads in a tarragon sauce. Dover sole, salmon persille, coffee-crusted magret of duck sauced with balsamic and brandy, medallions of lamb with a curried herb-red wine sauce, and pheasant with truffle sauce are possibilities.

Starters like asparagus and lobster in puff pastry, house-smoked salmon wrapped around goat cheese and confit of duck with oriental sauce earn acclaim. So do the chocolate crêpes and individual soufflés for dessert.

(401) 846-0123. www.restaurantbouchard.com. Entrées, $23.50 to $28. Dinner nightly except Tuesday, 6 to 9:30 or 10. Sunday brunch, 11 to 2.

White Horse Tavern, Marlborough and Farewell Streets, Newport.

This imposing burgundy structure is the oldest operating tavern in the country, built as a residence in 1673 and serving as a tavern since 1687. Inside is a warren of small rooms with wide-board floors, exposed beams, small-paned windows and big fireplaces on two floors.

Window table at White Horse Tavern.

Now a fancy restaurant, its elegant Colonial atmosphere symbolizes Newport for some. We find its historic charms particularly appealing in the off-season, when the fireplaces are lit. They made a pleasant backdrop for a lunch that included an interesting yogurt-cucumber-walnut soup, baked marinated montrachet cheese, halibut in a brandy-grapefruit sauce and a somewhat bland chicken salad resting in half an avocado.

At night, the tuxedoed staff offers a fancy menu and prices to match. Expect main courses like bouillabaisse, poached fillet of lemon sole with a sherried shrimp sauce, orange-cognac glazed duck breast, individual beef wellington or châteaubriand for two. Starters could be ragoût of wild mushrooms in puff pastry, baked oysters topped with spicy ratatouille or confit of duck and chèvre raviolis. For most, this is special-occasion dining, topped off by such masterful desserts as a three-cherry tart on a chocolate crust in a pool of vanilla cream sauce or triple silk torte on a bed of raspberry melba.

(401) 846-3600. www.whitehorsetavern.com. Entrées, $28 to $36. Lunch, Wednesday-Saturday 11:30 to 2:30. Dinner nightly, 5:30 to 9:30 or 10, jackets required. Sunday brunch, 11 to 2.

Castle Hill Inn & Resort, 590 Ocean Drive, Newport.

The dining experience at this refurbished Oceanside inn has been elevated by New Mexico-born chef Casey Riley, who transferred here after opening Agora at the Westin Hotel in Providence and serving as sous-chef at Boston's famed L'Espalier. The inn closed in the winter of 2003 for renovations that produced a new kitchen and stage for modern American cuisine accented by global flavors.

A recent autumn dinner menu opened with a robust, two-flavor soup of spinach-yukon potato and celery root-white truffle with candied yams and spiced pecans. Another complex starter was foie gras of duck with quince, grand marnier and cheddar upside-down cake. Main courses ranged from skillet-roasted yellowfin tuna and more foie gras to grilled Texas antelope with a venison cassoulet. The chef's Carolina brook trout was stuffed with lobster and served with a crawfish étouffée. The beef filet was crusted with roquefort, glazed with chanterelles and garnished with butter-poached crabmeat.

The pastry chef's desserts are equally extravagant. Typical are caramel-apple tarte tatin with crème fraîche ice cream and a trio of soufflés: toasted filbert, frozen caramel and fallen chocolate with Tahitian crème anglaise.

Meals are served in the oval Sunset Room, a large windowed porch jutting out toward the bay, just across from the romantic mahogany bar and lounge. Redecorated with a billowing cream-colored taffeta canopy on the ceiling, this is also the setting for Castle Hill's long-popular Sunday brunch – that is, when it's not taken to the accompaniment of live jazz on the inn's lawn sloping toward the sea.

(401) 849-3800 or (888) 466-1355. Entrées, $23 to $39. Lunch, noon to 3 daily in summer, Friday-Saturday in off-season. Dinner nightly, 6 to 9; jackets requested. Sunday brunch, 11:30 to 3.

The Spiced Pear, 117 Memorial Blvd., Newport.

The glamour of the newly restored Chanler at Cliff Walk boutique hotel is evident in the mahogany-paneled, fireplaced lounge, the chic Spiced Pear restaurant and the idyllic side garden terrace overlooking the Atlantic.

Executive chef Richard Hamilton, a Le Cordon Bleu graduate who was executive chef and co-owner at the acclaimed Magnolias in Nashville, Tenn., executes a contemporary regional menu for "high-end dining." His custom-designed show kitchen is at the heart of the restaurant, partly visible on the left as you enter from the lounge.

The serene main dining room at the far end yields ocean views from floor-to-ceiling windows on two sides.

The chef has been widely honored for his culinary expertise and his playful, innovative style. We sampled his Spiced Pear fare twice – at the opening party as well as at a pre-opening James Beard Foundation dinner in New York – and found it lived up to advance billing. Especially good were his appetizers of peeky toe crab on green papaya puree, the diver scallop with ossetra caviar, smoked salmon and champagne, and the foie gras with grape jelly.

The signature lamb loin with tomato-mint relish and the venison with mushrooms and garlic proved excellent main dishes. But the real hit of the evening was the buttery poached lobster paired with "macaroni and cheese," actually a creamy orzo rice laced with shallots, mascarpone cheese and truffle oil.

The pastry chef's desserts included a tarte tatin prepared with mango rather than apple, a delicate chocolate cake surrounding a smooth mousse and cherry filling, and a trio of chocolate, vanilla and hazelnut ice creams.

Our experience, admittedly not the norm, differed from the local reports of pretension and flawed service in the early going. Pretension may come with the territory, but the service lapses presumably will be fixed with time.

As the chef fiddled with formats, the original à-la-carte dinner menu was changed in the off-season to a variety of prix-fixe tasting menus. The standard was $45 for three courses, but there was a five-course vegetarian menu, a six-course tasting menu paired with wines, and a twelve-course chef's table menu for $125.

(401) 847-2244. Prix-fixe, $45. Entrées, $26 to $58. Lunch daily in season, 11:30 to 2:30, weekends in off-season. Dinner nightly in season, 5:30 to 10, Wednesday-Sunday in off-season.

The Place, 28 Washington Square, Newport.

The Place, a wine bar and grill, is the au-courant adjunct of Yesterday's, a pubby Washington Square institution. It's the place for what many consider the most exciting food in Newport.

Yesterday's owners Maria and Richard Korn built the room as a showcase for their chef of sixteen years, Alex Daglis. Alex moved to a separate kitchen, put together a different staff and devised a contemporary American menu with a European flair that, Richard says, "expands and challenges your tastes."

We'd gladly order anything on his dinner menu. Folks rave about the changing entrées, from the fennel-encrusted tuna with mandarin-ginger vinaigrette to the mustard-crusted rack of lamb with apple-honey demi-glace. But we never got beyond the appetizers, so tempting that we shared and made a meal of five. The shrimp and corn tamales, the exquisite scallops with cranberries and ginger, the gratin of wild mushrooms, and raviolis of smoked chicken and goat cheese were mere warmups for a salad of smoked pheasant with poached pears and hazelnuts. Each was gorgeously presented on black octagonal plates. An apple crêpe with apple sorbet was a crowning finale

To accompany, many wines are served by the glass. You also can get "flights" of wine (four samples of reds or whites) or "schooners" of microbrews (four seven-ounce pilsner glasses ensconced in a handmade wooden schooner).

The long, narrow dining room on two levels is elegant with white linens, brass rails, oil lamps, Victorian lights and sconces. An incredible vaudeville curtain from New Bedford, framed and back lit on one wall, provides quite a conversation piece.

More casual fare is served day and night in Yesterday's, rechristened an Ale House to differentiate it from the wine bar and grill.

(401) 847-0116. www.yesterdaysandtheplace.com. Entrées, $20.95 to $28.95. Dinner nightly, 5:30 to 10 or 11, fewer nights in off-season..

Asterix & Obelix, 599 Lower Thames St.

One of Newport's more trendy and eclectic restaurants is run by the scion of a family of Danish restaurateurs. John Bach-Sorenson alighted from Copenhagen in Newport – "it reminded me of home" – and looked for a restaurant site. He found it in a working auto-repair garage.

He transformed it into an airy, high-ceilinged and colorful space with a part-open rear kitchen, a remarkable handcrafted bar along one side and mismatched chairs at white-linened tables dressed with votive candles and vases of flowers. Two front garage doors open to the street for a European sidewalk cafe atmosphere in summer.

John calls the fare Mediterranean-Asian and when he's cooking – which has become infrequent lately with his subsequent ventures – the food is first-rate. The menu ranges widely from lobster fricassee and sole meunière to free-range chicken Peking style and steak au poivre. You might find roasted baby snapper Cantonese style or filet mignon à la milanaise. You can opt for mussels marnière with frites or "le petite obelix:" one-half lobster, ten oysters, three shrimp and six clams ($32).

Key lime pie, crème brûlée and profiteroles are favorite desserts.

The place is named for John's two favorite French comic-strip characters, known for fighting the bureaucracy, which he had to do to win a wine and beer license.

He also runs Boulangerie Obelix, a bakery and sandwich shop at 382 Spring St. In 2003 he took on La Petite Auberge, a classic French restaurant at 19 Charles St.

(401) 841-8833. Entrées, $19 to $32. Dinner nightly, from 5.

The Mooring, Sayer's Wharf, Newport.

The Mooring has about the best waterfront location downtown, thanks to its former incarnation as the New York Yacht Club station. The inside is all blue and nautical, with a fireplace ablaze in the off-season. The original upstairs deck has been enclosed to increase the interior dining space by 50 percent. Happily, there's still plenty of outside dining on the downstairs brick patio, brightened by colorful geraniums and hailed by its owners for the best al fresco dining east of the Mississippi.

The lines for meals can get long (a very spicy bloody mary served in a pilsner glass may help). Or you could stop in during off-hours for a gin and tonic, a bowl of prize-winning clam chowder, or coffee and a piece of orange ambrosia pie. Our party of four had to wait only ten minutes for a table for lunch on the breezy patio as we eyed the "glacial" salads and hefty sandwiches passing by. We sampled the warm salmon salad, the seafood quiche with coleslaw, steamed mussels with garlic bread and a terrific scallop chowder we deemed even better than the Mooring's award-winning clam chowder.

A recent winter lunch produced aforementioned clam chowder, better than ever, as well as an open-faced, knife-and-fork concoction that lived up to its billing as the ultimate grilled cheese sandwich. We also enjoyed the day's blue-plate special ($12.95): a cup of chowder, succulent grilled salmon with tomato-basil sauce, french fries and coleslaw.

Dinner choices are as elevated as grilled yellowfin tuna topped with shrimp and vegetable salsa, baked stuffed lobster, seafood scampi, garlicky loin lamb chops and black angus sirloin. They're also as basic as crab-crusted cod, crab and artichoke casserole, meatloaf and a steak sandwich, all priced in the low teens.

The Mooring's more casual annex, the seasonal **Smokehouse Café,** is known for its smoked foods, chowders and barbecued ribs and wings that, the manager said, are out of this world.

(401) 846-2260. www.mooringrestaurant.com. Entrées, $12.95 to $27.95. Lunch and dinner daily, noon to 9 or 10.

Tucker's Bistro, 150 Broadway.

For romance, there's no more idyllic place in Newport than this newish French bistro in the heart of the out-of-the-way restaurant row beloved by locals along Broadway. Co-owners Tucker Harris and Ellen Coleman have fashioned a 1920s deco bistro in a double storefront. The bar is in a small room with a library look. Most of the dining takes place in couple of larger rooms with white-clothed tables holding antique shaded lamps amidst red lacquered walls hung with impressionist paintings and a ceiling draped in vine branches, rhinestone strands and twinkling white lights. Tucker likens the decor to a cross between art gallery and bordello.

The fare is primarily Mediterranean. The partners tweak the regular printed menu with a trio of daily specials, including soft-shell crab tempura and baked striped bass fillet with gorgonzola sauce at our visit. Otherwise, expect about a dozen entrées, from lobster and scallop stew or chipotle-glazed Atlantic salmon fillet to five-spiced duck, pork shanks braised in bourbon and molasses, and veal pot-au-feu.

Appetizers go international, as in Thai shrimp nachos, sautéed pierogis, escargots crostini, grilled pizzas and beef carpaccio. Desserts are Tucker's forte. His specialty is a signature banana pudding, but he may offer chocolate cheesecake and a pecan bread pudding with white chocolate and dried cranberries as well.

(401) 846-3449. www.tuckersbistro.com. Entrées, $17.95 to $26.95. Dinner nightly, from 6.

Diversions

The Mansions. Nowhere else can you see such a concentration of palatial mansions, and nine are open to the public under individual or the collective auspices of the Preservation Society of Newport County. If you can see only one, make it Cornelius Vanderbilt's opulent 72-room **The Breakers,** although romantic **Rosecliff** of "The Great Gatsby" fame and the museum-like **Elms** would be other choices. After you've seen them all, as we have, you may find refreshing the Victorian **Kingscote,** which looks lived-in and eminently livable. Schedules and prices vary, but all are open daily at least from May through October; in winter, Rosecliff is open daily and The Breakers and The Elms are open weekends..

Historic Sites. Newport has more than 400 structures dating from the Colonial era. **Touro Synagogue** (1768), the oldest place of Jewish worship in the country, offers fascinating though limited guided tours. **Trinity Church** (1726) at the head of Queen Anne Square has the only remaining central pulpit and the second oldest organ in the country. The **Quaker Meeting House** (1699) is the oldest public building in Newport. **St. Mary's Church** (1848), where Jacqueline Bouvier was married to John F. Kennedy, is the oldest Catholic parish in Rhode Island. The **Redwood Library** (1748) is the nation's oldest library building in continuous service. The **Old Colony House** (1739) is the nation's third oldest capitol building and is still used for public ceremonies. The **Hunter House** (1748) is considered one of the ten finest Colonial homes in America, while the **Wanton-Lyman-Hazard House** (1690) is the oldest house still on its original site. The **Samuel Whitehorne House** (1811) is a Federal showplace. The **Old Stone Mill** may have been built as early as 1100 by the Vikings. The military is represented in the Revolutionary fortification at **Fort Adams State Park** and the **Artillery Company of Newport** museum, as well as the **Naval War College** museum.

Water Sites. Ocean Drive winds along Newport's spectacular rocky shoreline, between Bailey's Beach where the 400 swam (and still do) and Brenton Point State Park, past weathered clapboard estates and contemporary homes. The Cliff Walk is a must for a more intimate look at the crashing surf and the backs of the mansions. Narragansett Bay is visible along the nine-mile trip run by the Old Colony & Newport Railway to Portsmouth. King Park along Wellington Avenue has a sheltered beach with a view of the Newport waterfront; the ocean surf rolls in at Easton's Beach.

Sports Sites. Yachting reigns across the Newport waterfront. The **Museum of Yachting** and the wharves off Thames Street and America's Cup Avenue appeal to sailing interests. In the landmark Newport Casino is the **International Tennis Hall of Fame,** housing the world's largest collection of tennis memorabilia and the Davis

Cup Theater, where old tennis films are shown. Outside are thirteen grass courts for tournaments and public use.

Shopping. Innumerable and oft-changing shops line Thames Street, the Brick Market Place, Bannister's and Bowen's Wharves, Spring Street and, uptown, fashionable Bellevue Avenue. If the past is an indication, there will be more when you're there.

The fun begins outside the Gateway Information Center, where a store called **Kelly & Gillis,** a.k.a. Signs of Intelligent Life.com, advertises ridiculous gifts, accessories and home furnishings. Occupying a corner location at the entrance to Bowen's Wharf is the **Museum Store** of the Preservation Society of Newport County; here you'll find everything from cards to throws, from china dogs to nautical memorabilia. Of special interest along Lower Thames Street are places like **Tea & Herb Essence,** which offers a little of everything from passion fruit teas to herbal remedies and handmade soaps. At **Thames Glass,** you can watch owner Matthew Buechner and his fellow glass blowers at work in their fascinating studio. For sale in his adjacent shop are some of his creations, including fabulous fish, flowers, vases and ornaments. Potter-in-residence Bridget Butlin shapes wonderful stoneware at **Thames Street Pottery.** We were particularly taken by all the fish-shaped clocks and dinner plates. On Spring Street, check out **Edna Mae's Millinery Store,** which carries unique hats made exclusively for the owner. Sweet pillows, quilts and prints are among the offerings at **Sarah Elizabeth's.**

Other downtown favorites are **Knits & Pieces** for handknit sweaters, **Collage** for jewelry and gifts, **Primavera** for unusual gifts and garden accents, and **Rue de France** for French country decor and accessories. **Mark, Fore and Strike** features yachting attire. **Irish Imports** carries gorgeous wool things, and **Michael Hayes** carries designer men's and women's fashions. Up on Bellevue Avenue, check out more Michael Hayes stores (including one for children) and **Cabbages & Kings** for gifts and accessories that appeal to those who still live in Newport's "cottages." **Runcible Spoon,** an outstanding kitchen shop, displays gaily colored pottery amid the lobster platters and garlic salsas. **Cadeaux du Monde** bills itself as a museum where all the exhibits (art and handicrafts) are for sale.

Extra-Special

Green Animals, 380 Cory's Lane off Route 114, Portsmouth.

It's worth the drive north of town to see the incredible topiary gardens that live up to their name, Green Animals. Run by the Preservation Society of Newport County, the property displays 80 trees and shrubs sculpted into shapes of a camel, giraffe, lion and elephant at the corners of the original garden, plus a donkey, ostrich, bear, horse and rider, dogs, birds and more. The animals are formed of California privet, while the geometric figures and ornamental designs are of golden and American boxwoods. Willed to the society in 1972 by Alice Brayton, one of its stalwart members, the delightful small country estate sloping toward Narragansett Bay also has espaliered fruit trees, a grape arbor, dahlia and vegetable gardens, and a gift and garden shop where you can buy forms to make your own topiary. Ten rooms in the Brayton House contain original furnishings and Victorian toy collections.

(401) 847-1000. Open daily 10 to 6, late May to early October. Adults, $10.

Old Lighthouse Museum is landmark in Stonington.

Watch Hill and Stonington

Vestiges of the 19th Century

They face each other across Little Narragansett Bay from different states, these two venerable communities so different from one another.

Watch Hill, a moneyed seaside resort of the old school and something of a mini-version of Newport, occupies a point at the southwesternmost tip of Rhode Island. "Still echoing with the elegance of past years," in the words of one inn's brochure, Watch Hill is strikingly seasonal, battening down the hatches after Labor Day. The resort has enjoyed better days, although the large brown shingled "cottages" remain lived in, the shops generally fashionable and the atmosphere clubby. It is here that sheltered Long Island Sound gives way to Block Island Sound and the Atlantic, opening up the surf beaches for which Rhode Island's South County is known.

Stonington, on the other hand, is a peninsula cut off from the rest of southeastern Connecticut. Quietly billing itself as "a place apart," it's an historic fishing village and an arts colony. It is obviously very much lived in, year-round. Old houses hug the streets and each other. The Portuguese fishing fleet adds an earthy flavor to an increasingly tony and sophisticated community. Better than any other town along the Connecticut shore, the Borough of Stonington and its rural township of North Stonington let you sense times gone by.

These two choice vestiges of the 19th century are linked – in terms of geography – by the small Rhode Island city of Westerly, through which you drive from one to the other, unless you go by boat.

In recent times, Watch Hill and Stonington have been upstaged by Newport and Mystic and, more recently, by the Mashantucket Pequot Indians' wildly successful Foxwoods Resort Casino complex in Ledyard. They have been bypassed by many of the trappings of tourism, particularly in terms of overnight accommodations. Neither town wants – nor can handle – crowds. Each in its own way clings to its past, and is the better for it.

Inn Spots

The Inn at Stonington, 60 Water St., Stonington, Conn. 06378.

The old Harborview Restaurant was destroyed by fire, and from its ashes in 2001 rose this luxury B&B facing the waterfront, the first real place to stay in the borough. Owner Bill Griffin spared little expense in producing a handsome gray and white-trimmed, three-story inn up against the sidewalk in front, with docks and water behind.

The twelve guest rooms in the main building, four on the first floor and eight on the second, come with fireplaces and ten have jacuzzi tubs. Beds are queensize or kingsize. Furnishings are "very high-end," Bill said, with English-style fruitwood furniture and rich fabrics. "No two rooms are even remotely the same in terms of decor." Upholstered club chairs, some with ottomans, are the norm, as are built-in shelves around the fireplaces. Half the rooms have water views and french doors leading onto private balconies. The best view may be from the cheery yellow third-floor sitting room with a balcony outfitted with all-weather, Parisian-style bistro chairs.

On the main floor are an intimate bar and a living room/dining area where a substantial continental breakfast is served. Complimentary wine and cheese are offered in the afternoon.

Six larger guest rooms with high ceilings were added in 2003 in a brick annex next door. All have jacuzzi tubs and five have kingsize beds and fireplaces. One village-side room has two double beds. The smallest room is cheery in neon celery green. The two seaside rooms contain small sitting areas and refrigerators. One is a deluxe room offering a large balcony with a view of the harbor.

The Inn at Stonington fronts on Cannon Square in historic borough.

The main inn includes a basement exercise area and has kayaks and bicycles for guests.

(860) 535-2000. Fax (860) 535-8193. www.innatstonington.com. Eighteen rooms with private baths. Memorial Day to Labor Day: doubles, $195 to $395 weekends, $175 to $295 midweek. Spring and Fall: doubles, $195 to $395 weekends, $149 to $265 midweek. Winter: doubles, $155 to $295 weekends, $135 to $195 midweek.

Stonecroft, 515 Pumpkin Hill Road, Ledyard, Conn. 06339.

Ten deluxe guest accommodations and an acclaimed restaurant (see Dining Spots) are attributes of this inn created by a much-traveled Chase Manhattan international banker, his counselor wife and his son, a chef. Lyn and Joan Egy started their inn in phases, first renovating the handsome yellow 1807 Georgian Colonial residence that had stood empty for five years. In 1998 they finished off a rear three-story barn with a fieldstone tavern and dining room on the ground floor and six deluxe guest rooms upstairs.

Country French furnishings lend a comfortable, elegant look to the four downstairs common rooms of the main house – from the Snuggery library that once was a "borning" room to a luxurious rear great room with nine-foot-wide fireplace to the fireplaced dining room in which breakfast is served by candlelight on Villeroy & Boch china. To the rear of the great room is the Buttery, smallest of the guest rooms with a beamed ceiling, queen bed, full bath and its own terrace.

A young artist-friend of the Egys painted the mural of a hot-air balloon scene along the front staircase to be "cheerful and uplifting, as in the inn-going experience," said Joan, whose counseling background and interest in psychosynthesis as a way of life seemed attuned to innkeeping. The stairway leads to two front corner bedrooms, one with a queen bed and one with a king. All are equipped with top-of-the-line mattresses and bath amenities that include inflatable tub pillows and aromatherapy bath salts for relaxation.

Up a steep rear stairway reached through an unusual cut-out door is the premier Stonecroft Room with kingsize four-poster bed, loveseat and 22-inch-wide chestnut floorboards ("the 24-inch boards were reserved for the king," Joan advised). The walls above the wainscoting bear the young artist's wraparound mural depicting a day in the life of Stonecroft about 1820.

The six new rooms and suites in the barn are more upscale. Each has a sitting area, a gas fireplace with a built-in TV overhead, and a large bath with double whirlpool tub and separate shower. They're elegantly furnished in country French or English styles, plus one in Colonial decor for Yankee purists. All open to private or shared wraparound balconies. Our room was named for Orlando Smith, discoverer of Westerly granite, whose portrait and granite samples were framed above the bureau. That distinguishing bit of trivia seemed not of great interest to previous occupants, whose guestbook entries detailed romance in words and sketches.

Terrycloth robes, bath sheets rather than towels, Crabtree & Evelyn toiletries and soft music throughout the common areas help provide a serene, therapeutic stay.

Breakfast is a four-course event. Juice and Lynn's baked bananas, pineapples and mangos in a lemon-rum sauce might precede buttermilk waffles with strawberries and whipped cream, herbed scrambled eggs with turkey bacon or a cloud (so-called because it's four inches high) omelet layered with smoked salmon or cheese. The final course might be ginger scones or strawberry-rhubarb crisp.

The six-acre rural property is surrounded by 300 acres of Nature Conservancy woodlands and stone walls.

860) 572-0771. Fax (860) 572-9161. www.stonecroft.com. Eight rooms and two suites with private baths. Weekends: doubles $200 to $245, suites $300. Midweek: doubles $150 to $195, suites $250.

Shelter Harbor Inn, 10 Wagner Road, Westerly, R.I. 02891.

The Watch Hill area's best choice for both lodging and dining is this expanded farmhouse dating to the early 1800s, set back from Route 1 and off by itself not far from the edge of Quonochontaug Pond.

The original three-story main house contains a fine restaurant (see Dining Spots), a sun porch with a bar, a small library with the original fireplace and ten guest rooms, plus a rooftop deck with a hot tub and a water view that you must see to believe. Suffice to say that it's a scene straight out of California. The barn next door has been renovated with ten more guest rooms, plus a large central living room on the upper level opening onto a spacious redwood deck. Newest accommodations are in the front Coach House, which has four deluxe rooms with fireplaces, upholstered chairs and telephones.

Most rooms have queensize beds, seven have working fireplaces and about half have TV. As innkeeper Jim Dey continues to upgrade and expand with a contemporary flair, his most select rooms may be those renovated or added upstairs in the main house. Three on the second floor offer fireplaces and decks with a view of Block Island Sound in the distance. One particularly nice room comes with a brick fireplace, brass screen, rose carpet and a terrace.

Out front are two paddle tennis courts and a professionally maintained croquet court that's also used for bocci. In summer, the inn's van transports guests to and from a private beach that Jim calls the finest along the Rhode Island shore.

A full breakfast, including perhaps banana-bread french toast or ginger-blueberry pancakes, is included in the rates and is available to the public.

(401) 322-8883 or (800) 468-8883. Fax (401) 322-7907. www.shelterharborinn.com. Twenty-three rooms with private baths. Doubles, $126 to $198. Two-night minimum weekends. Children accepted.

Weekapaug Inn occupies peninsula jutting into saltwater pond, with ocean beyond.

Weekapaug Inn, 25 Spray Rock Road, Weekapaug, R.I. 02891.

Dating to 1899, this grand seaside resort of the old school is venerable, refined and ever-so-Yankee. It has been run like a club all these years by four generations of one family.

The guests tend to be repeat and long-term. Many of the friendly young staff came here as children with their families. Longtime owners Bob and Sydney Buffum, whose winters are spent running the Manasota Beach Club in Englewood, Fla., got to know most of their guests – a trait being continued by their son Jim and his wife Dee Dee, the current owners and innkeepers.

The inn's chatty weekly newsletter, Innsights, details the events of the week ahead, reports the winners of tournaments past, and lists the week's "arrivals."

The rambling, weathered-gray, three-story hotel doesn't look quite as you'd expect, perhaps because its reincarnation is a product of the late 1930s when it was rebuilt after the original was destroyed by a hurricane. But there are few waterfront inn sites to rival it on the East Coast: on its own peninsula, with a saltwater pond in back, the ocean to the distant front and starboard, and lawns, a yachting basin, tennis courts and a mile and a half of private beach in between.

The guest rooms and suites, most with twin beds (some placed together to form kingsize) and old-fashioned baths, are simple but immaculate. Eleven rooms have queensize beds. A few small rooms have been joined to make larger rooms, and two are suites with a sitting area and two baths. One guest's room is painted just the way she likes it; after all, she stays the whole season. She and her neighbors occupy the nicest wing, which the staff calls "The Gold Coast."

The common areas are larger and more distinctive than in most similar resorts. On the ground floor, a summery dining room has floor-to-ceiling windows onto the wildflowers outside. Above it on the second floor are the front desk and a lobby full of games and books. Off it is the large and comfy Sea Room, a living room also used for games, bingo and movies. In front is a card room, which is all windows on three sides. Then there's the paneled and beamed Pond Room in which guests pour their own drinks from bottles they have stashed in their cubbyholes, and warm their tootsies by the fire on cool evenings.

A full breakfast is served, and a nicely presented buffet lunch is served daily. Lobster is often among the eight or so choices on the updated dinner menu, which, to the public, is $38 prix-fixe for six courses.

(401) 322-0301. Fax (401) 322-1016. www.weekapauginn.com. Forty-five rooms, two suites and one cottage with private baths; eight rooms with shared baths. Rates AP: Doubles, $425. Single, $295; child, $125. Three-night minimum. No credit cards. Open mid-June through Labor Day.

Buffet lunch ($16) by reservation, daily 12:30 to 1:30. Prix-fixe ($35) dinner nightly by reservation, 6:30 to 8; jackets required. BYOB.

Antiques & Accommodations, 32 Main St., North Stonington, Conn. 06359.

The name of this attractive yellow house, built in 1861 with the gingerbread trim of its era, is appropriate. For owners Ann and Thomas Gray are antiques dealers who sell many of the furnishings in their showplace B&B near the center of the quaint hamlet of North Stonington.

Memories of traveling in England inspired the Grays to furnish their home in the Georgian manner with formal antique furniture and accessories. Six rooms and suites, all with private baths and canopied beds, are named after English towns where their favorite B&Bs are, among them Broadway and Tetbury. All have fresh flowers and evening sherry.

Besides a parlor with TV, the main house offers an elegant downstairs bedroom with yellow painted walls glazed with gold, a queen bed, working fireplace and a stereo system. Upstairs are another guest room with wing and side chairs, and a bridal room filled with photographs of honeymooners who have stayed there.

Families and couples traveling together go for suites in the 1820 Garden Cottage, a two-story affair beyond landscaped gardens in back. Rooms here contain some remarkable stenciling, sponge-painted furniture, marbleized dressers and floral curtains, along with the antiques that characterize the rest of the establishment, most of them early American and country and all available for purchase. "You can sleep in a canopy bed and then take it home," advises Ann.

Each floor of the cottage contains a sitting room and a kitchen. Geared for families, the lower floor offers three queensize bedrooms, one with a fireplace, and a bath. Upstairs is a more self-contained two-bedroom suite, each bedroom with Eldred Wheeler lace canopy queen bed, private bath and gas fireplace. The common room here comes with a wet bar and a fireplace.

In 2001, the Grays purchased a house next door and added three more guest rooms. One with a working fireplace contains a small library reflecting the couple's love of antiques, travel, cooking and gardening.

The Grays serve a four-course breakfast by candlelight in the formal dining room or on the flower-bedecked front porch. It always includes fresh fruit in an antique crystal bowl, perhaps melon with a yogurt, honey and mint sauce or hot plum applesauce. Main courses could be eggs benedict, quiche, strata or an apple-rum puff garnished with strawberries.

"Breakfast goes on for hours," says Ann. "One Sunday, the last people got up from the table at 12:30." These hospitable hosts also have been known to dispense wine late into the evening while everyone lingers on the front patio.

(860) 535-1736 or (800) 554-7829. Fax (860) 535-2613. www.antiquesandaccommodations.com. Seven rooms and two suites with private baths. May-November: doubles $189 to $269 weekends, $99 to $189 midweek; suites $249 to $349. December-April, doubles $99 to $189, suites $189 to $289.

Antiques & Accommodations is based in attractive house dating to 1861.

Randall's Ordinary, Route 2, North Stonington, Conn. 06359.

A dirt road lined with stone walls leads to this remote ordinary (British definition: a tavern or eating house serving regular meals). It's anything but ordinary, from its hearth-cooked meals (see Dining Spots) to its overnight accommodations in a rural farmhouse dating to 1685 or in a restored barn that, in comparison, seems rather contemporary. Not to mention the fact that the current owner is the Mashantucket Pequot Tribal Nation of Foxwoods casino fame.

First the accommodations. Anyone cherishing the past would enjoy the three rooms upstairs in the main house with queensize beds and hand-loomed coverlets, decorative fireplaces and baths with whirlpool tubs. They are spacious and, except for modern comforts, look much as they would have in the 18th century.

Twelve newer-feeling rooms and suites are located at the rear in a restored 1819 barn, which was dismantled and moved from Richmondville, N.Y. It's attached to a milking shed and a silo, which has been converted into the enormous Silo Suite, complete with domed jacuzzi loft above a circular silo bedroom, a skylit loft living room and a master bedroom with rustic Adirondack queen bed. Designed in what might be called a rustic contemporary style, all the rooms here retain original beams, barn siding and bare floors. Most have queensize canopy beds, baths with whirlpool tubs and heat lamps, TVs and telephones. Four have loft bedrooms with skylights and spiral staircases from the sitting rooms. Formerly rather spartan, the rooms have been refurbished with art works and new period furniture for a warmer ambiance.

Guests are served a continental breakfast of fresh fruit and muffins in the barn. More substantial breakfasts, including such period treats as maple toast with fried apples and Shaker apple salad, venison sausage, codfish cakes with baked beans and biscuits, and chipped beef on biscuits are available for an extra charge in the main house.

(860) 599-4540 or (877) 599-4540. Fax (860) 599-3308. www.randallsordinary.com. Ten rooms and five suites with private baths. Weekends: doubles $169, suites $195 and $350. Midweek: doubles $149, suites $165 and $300. Two-night minimum weekends in season.

House of 1833, 72 North Stonington Road, Mystic, Conn. 06355.

Carol and Matt Nolan spent two years and toured 36 states to find the perfect place to run a B&B before settling on this pillared, Greek Revival mansion on three hillside acres in Old Mystic. Built by banker Elias Brown in 1833, it must have been the most imposing house in town. Or so it's depicted by an artist in a stunning mural that wraps around the curving staircase to the second floor and shows the way the hamlet looked at the time.

The Nolans moved East from San Francisco, purchased the private residence and undertook renovations to create a luxurious B&B. They gutted the bathrooms, which had been modernized, and redid them to the period. They installed a Har-Tru tennis court next to the swimming pool, bought six eighteen-speed bicycles and produced an assistant innkeeper, bright-eyed son Alexander, a year after opening in 1994.

Theirs is one gorgeous house, from the formal dining room that dwarfs a long breakfast table set for ten, to the five large guest bedrooms, all with queen beds, fireplaces and private baths, some of them quite spacious and unusual. The front part of the double parlor, outfitted in Greek Revival, opens into a Victorian section notable for a crystal chandelier, a grand piano and an antique pump organ. A heavy door off the front parlor leads to the Peach Room, the former library. Here's a guest room with a mahogany canopy bed draped in peach fabric, a plush settee with matching chair on an oriental rug, a private wicker porch facing the pool, and a bathroom with a walk-in shower through which one passes to get to the double whirlpool tub.

The second floor has three more guest rooms with thick carpeting and fine fabrics. Carol calls one room in the middle the Oak Room because of its furniture rather than for its prevailing rose color because "every B&B has a Rose Room." Its bathroom across the hall contains a luxurious soaking tub. The Ivy Room in front, named for its Waverly wallpaper and fabrics, has a bathroom fashioned from two closets, with a vanity in the room.

Although Carol oversaw most of the decorating, she and Matt each picked one room to bear a personal imprint. She did the rear Verandah Room in cream and celadon green with a light pine queen bed enclosed in wispy sheer curtains, a ladyslipper clawfoot tub on a platform beside the fireplace and a little wicker balcony. Matt designed the secluded third-floor Cupola Room, masculine in plum and gold with a four-poster bed draped from the ceiling, a potbelly stove and a double whirlpool tub. Stairs rise to a cupola, with two seats from which to observe the sunset.

Breakfast begins with Matt's decorative fresh fruit plates ("he gets very creative," says Carol). His artistry continues as he plays light contemporary music on the grand piano during the main course, perhaps baked custard french toast, eggs florentine in puff pastry with honey-mustard sauce or a specialty quiche with eggs, cottage cheese and corn chips.

Chocolate-chip cookies and tea or lemonade greet guests upon arrival.

(860) 536-6325 or (800) 367-1833. www.houseof1833.com. Five rooms with private baths. Memorial Day to mid-November: doubles, $179 to $249 weekends, $129 to $179 midweek. Rest of year: doubles, $129 to $179 weekends, $99 to $149 midweek. Two-night minimum on weekends.

Another Second Penny Inn, 870 Pequot Trail, Stonington, Conn. 06378.

Guests at this atmospheric, 1710 Colonial home on five rural acres enjoy large

Another Second Penny Inn conveys ambiance of a 1710 Colonial home.

accommodations with updated amenities, gourmet breakfasts and a distinct feeling of times gone by. The B&B takes its name from a parable cited by the president of Mills College when colleague Jim Wright had second thoughts about having splurged to buy an old wooden yacht: "If you have two pennies, with the first buy bread for your stomach, and with the second buy hyacinths for your soul." Jim named the boat "Second Penny," and with his wife Sandra began referring to soul-nourishing events as "second pennies." When he retired from Mills College and moved east from California to open a B&B, its name was a natural.

The house had been a tavern at one time and retains a big old kitchen the Wrights use for hearthside cooking as well as an upstairs suite with a swinging partition in the middle that could be raised to open enough space for a dance hall. The hooks that held up the partition are still evident in the ceiling, but otherwise the wall is now stationary. On one side is a queensize poster bed, gas fireplace and a bath with jetted clawfoot tub. On the other is a sitting room with a day bed.

The Denison Room has a queensize poster bed, gas fireplace and a bathroom so big it holds not only a jetted clawfoot tub but also a small refrigerator, a dressing table and a yellow slipper chair in the middle. The front Noyes Room comes with two twin beds that can be joined as a king, an electric fireplace and a full bath. All rooms are decorated in Colonial style with oriental rugs and handmade quilts employed as wall hangings. Each comes with private telephone, TV/VCR, clock radio, small fridge, fluffy robes and hair dryer.

Guests gather in a cozy front library and in the dining room for a breakfast to remember. The morning of our visit brought vanilla poached pears, maple-oatmeal-walnut muffins, a garden vegetable quiche and the usual "dessert," a selection of Jim's homemade sorbets, including apple, kiwi, peach and mulled cider. An apple-cranberry compote with yogurt and an omelet of cream cheese, crabmeat and chives was on tap the next day.

(860) 535-1710. Fax (860) 535-1709. www.secondpenny.com. Two rooms and one suite with private baths. Doubles, $155 to $185 weekends, $115 to $139 midweek. Children over 8.

The Villa, 190 Shore Road, Westerly, R.I. 02891.

A romantic, Mediterranean-style complex flanking a garden courtyard with swimming pool, hot tub and poolside service is unexpected in this area. The house, built in the 1920s by an Italian family who was talked into hosting visitors from Italy, has been a rather mysterious, seductive retreat since its founding as a B&B in 1974 by a bachelor owner. It was mainstreamed in 2003 by new innkeepers Barbara and Michael Cardiff, who had run the largest day spa resort and retreat center in Southern California.

They cater to couples in the "Land of Amore," offering plush accommodations with the amenities of a well-endowed Mediterranean villa. Gourmet breakfasts are offered in the dining room of the main building, but most guests prefer to have it delivered to their rooms. The Cardiffs also fulfill poolside service from a well-stocked guest refrigerator and wet bar beside the courtyard. For this is a place for self-indulgence.

The main house has a small and fancy parlor/dining area that seldom is used and four distinctive guest rooms with queensize beds, thick carpeting, TV/VCRs, mini-refrigerators and microwaves. At one end of the ground floor is the Rosa Maiorano Room, a wood-paneled hideaway with a queen bed and a two-person jacuzzi facing the gas fireplace. On the second floor are the Venezia, a two-room tribute to Venice with a cozy sitting room and a small bathroom with shower, and the Roma, which features a black and white tiled Roman bath with a mirrored jacuzzi for two. A steep, watch-out-you-don't-bump-your-head stairway leads to the third-floor Cielo, a skylit aerie with a large sitting area with dining table, full bath and a glimpse of the ocean through the front window.

The prime accommodations are across the courtyard in a rear carriage house. The ground floor holds the Blue Grotto with original stone walls and other walls painted an iridescent green as on the Isle of Capri. A kingsize bed angled from one corner faces a double jacuzzi in another. A fireplace warms a sitting area, and an armoire conceals the TV. Upstairs is the even larger Verona, appointed in bright blue and white with vaulted ceiling, kingsize bed, sitting/dining area, and bath with bidet and shower. A double jacuzzi beneath the skylight is "for wishing on stars." Overlooking the courtyard is a tight little Romeo and Juliet balcony.

All the guest quarters are self-contained with the prerequisites for romance. Guests who leave their cocoons indulge in the heated pool, the adjacent hot tub and gardens embellished with exotic flowers in many pots and containers.

Breakfast is hearty continental on weekdays. On weekends Michael cooks pancakes, waffles or his signature scrambled eggs. Signature? "Yes, with cheese and herbs."

(401) 596-1054 or (800) 722-9240. Fax (401) 596-6268. www.thevillaatwesterly.com. Six rooms with private baths. Doubles, $140 to $255 Memorial Day to Columbus Day, $95 to $195 rest of year.

Woody Hill B&B, 149 South Woody Hill Road, Westerly, R.I. 02891.

The sign at the door says "Martha Stewart doesn't live here." And first-time guests may have second thoughts on the approach road through a transitional neighborhood. But fear not. Near the end of the road is a secluded, charming home that high school English teacher Ellen L. Madison shares with guests. They enjoy comfortable accommodations amid historic ambiance, plus lovely grounds with perennial gardens, a large swimming pool and twenty acres of woods and fields.

Enter the living room of this rambling reproduction Colonial and sense the past with wide-plank floors, tiny windowpanes, antique furnishings and hooked rugs. Beyond is a paneled rear keeping room that's atmospheric as can be. Here, beside a walk-in fireplace, is where guests enjoy hearty breakfasts of fruit cups followed by pancakes, waffles or bacon and eggs. Ellen also does hearthside cooking here for optional dinners in the winter.

Three large guest rooms are offered in one end of the house. Off the keeping room is the Garden Room with a double bed and a private entrance from the garden.

Upstairs is the Family Room with two queen beds, one enveloped in privacy curtains. It opens onto a sundeck shared with the owner's quarters. Nearby is the Queen Anne Room with cherry and mahogany furniture, a queen canopy bed (without the curtains) and TV. It has a private hall bath.

Ellen is quite the conversationalist at breakfast, and most guests hate to leave. Her hospitality was honored in 2000 when Rhode Island's South County Tourism Council gave her its annual B&B Award for 25 years of "sharing a tastefully appointed, antique-filled home providing a high quality bed and breakfast experience."

(401) 322-0452. www.woodyhill.com. Three rooms with private baths. Doubles, $135, off-season $105.

Orchard Street Inn, 41 Orchard St., Stonington, Conn. 06378.

The use of the old Lasbury Guest House was grandfathered, which explains how this seaside B&B emerged in 2003 in a tightly zoned town where such uses are not encouraged. New York building contractor Richard Satler and Regina Shields gutted the interior of the old guest house to produce three plush accommodations in a bright yellow cottage along the ocean marsh.

Each section of the cottage has its own entrance off a private patio, a queensize bed, all-new bath, TV, refrigerator and loveseat. The spiffy, summery decor is best in the rear Delphinium Room, with vaulted ceiling, high queensize poster bed, wicker loveseat and a larger patio facing the wetlands.

Their cottage completed, the couple were planning some changes in the main house, where they live. In the reception area, they have bistro tables where Regina serves a full breakfast – fruits, muffins, croissants and perhaps an omelet.

(860) 535-2681. Three rooms with private baths. Doubles, $160 to $175 April-December, $130 to $145 in winter.

Watch Hill Inn, 38 Bay St., Watch Hill, R.I. 02891.

This large, unassuming white wood structure with waterfront terrace and dining room has been renovated and upgraded under new ownership.

Four guest rooms were eliminated to make space for private baths for all sixteen rooms on the second and third floors. Two of the sixteen rooms are "junior suites," with a sofabed that accommodates an extra guest.

Formerly advertised as rustic and quaint, the inn dating to 1845 is now billed as "charming," with rooms "decorated in the warm New England seacoast style." Although only a few in front have water views, all are carpeted and have queen or two twin beds with frilly spreads and pillows, lacy curtains, telephones, fans, and clawfoot tubs or showers. They look a lot more comfortable than they used to.

That said, it's still much less an inn than a hotel-motel – complete with a makeshift front office/porch with about as much personality as a 1950s motel counter. There are no welcoming common rooms. Instead there may be lots of coming and going the 200-seat Sunset Room, a banquet facility that caters to functions, and the casual **Seaside Grille,** which serves lunch and dinner daily in season.

A continental breakfast is offered in the bar-lounge.

(401) 348-6300 or (800) 356-9314. Fax (401) 348-6301. www.watchhillinn.com. Fourteen rooms and two suites with private baths. Mid-June to early September: doubles, $245 to $265 weekends, $175 to $200 midweek. Rest of year: doubles, $150 to $175 weekends, $100 to $125 midweek. Two-night minimum weekends.

Dining Spots

The Up River Café, 37 Main St., Westerly, R.I.

This stylish bistro in a restored woolen mill along the Pawcatuck River at the edge of downtown Westerly ranks among the area's best.

Taking over the former Three Fish restaurant, Daniel and Jennifer King from California added a fireplace in the casual, brick-walled River Pub as well as a second fireplace in one of four white-clothed dining rooms with large windows overlooking the water. They also added a large and perfectly idyllic dining patio beside the river on a peninsula with water on two sides.

The regional American menu is so enticing that choosing is a quandary. Typical main courses are Atlantic salmon marinated in miso and sake, seared Stonington sea scallops bearing a white truffle sauce on lobster-mushroom risotto, fire-roasted lamb chops with aged goat cheese and medallions of beef tenderloin with green peppercorn sauce. A burger on a baguette with house-made pickles and fries is among the offerings. So are such appetizers as a jonah crabmeat, spinach and artichoke gratin with house-made pita chips, Asian fried calamari with wasabi aioli, lobster nachos and a grilled pizza that changes daily.

The lobster nachos with spicy homemade guacamole were sensational but more than one of us could finish for lunch. The other reveled in the signature crab cake sandwich on a house-made burger roll, a hefty, spilling-over-the-sides affair that leaves competitors in the dust. Served with chipotle rémoulade, veggie slaw and fries, it was an unbelievable value for $8.

Neither of us had room for such desserts as guava crêpes with hot passion fruit sauce, warm chocolate and banana bread pudding with Dan's drunken bourbon sauce, the Chickie's root-beer float or even the assorted cookie plate.

(401) 348-9700. Entrées, $18 to $28. Lunch daily, 11:30 to 5. Dinner nightly, 5 to 10.

The Grange at Stonecroft Inn, 515 Pumpkin Hill Road, Ledyard, Conn.

The widely acclaimed new restaurant in the renovated barn is Stonecroft's crowning glory.

The expansive, granite-walled dining room on the ground level is furnished like that of an English country manor, with a lounge area of high-back couches facing a fireplace and well-spaced tables set with cream-colored linens and Villeroy & Boch china. Floor-to-ceiling, multi-paned windows yield a grand view of a landscaped stone terrace for outdoor dining, a grapevine-covered pergola and a water garden. It is a pastoral, thoroughly delightful setting for sensational fare prepared by European-trained chef de cuisine Drew Egy, the innkeepers' son.

Dinner begins with an amuse-bouche, usually a couple of morsels – perhaps a spring roll with apricot-fennel filling, a shumai dumpling and a mushroom tart – that hint of the heavenly tastes to come. Herbed focaccia with caramelized onion butter accompanies. We were smitten by a couple of sensational starters, baja-style scallop

Granite-walled dining room at The Grange at Stonecroft Inn is attractive for dining.

ceviche with cucumber and a grilled tortilla and the trio of exotic shrimp: curry-coconut with spiced banana chutney, spicy rangoon with ginger-hoisin sauce, and chile-cilantro grilled over cucumber.

Asian grilled tuna is a signature main course, sliced and fanned on the plate around a dollop of pungent wasabi, sliced maki rolls, sticky rice and julienned vegetables. Another signature is rack of New Zealand lamb marinated in cabernet and rosemary, the loin grilled, sliced and served over the braised ribs with plum tomato relish. Neither was available the autumn night we dined, but we were well satisfied with the paupiette of veal paillard stuffed with artichokes and bel paese cheese and wrapped in prosciutto, and the pan-roasted duck breast and confit with bing cherry glaze and a fabulous brie and wild rice risotto.

Desserts are knockouts. The house specialty is the night's chocolate trio, at our visit a little pot of intense chocolate mousse, three homemade truffles and a chocolate fudge brownie, plus a bonus, chocolate ice cream with a stick of white chocolate. An equal triumph was the banana and Bailey's Irish cream cheesecake with bruléed bananas and chocolate sauce.

(860) 572-0771 or (800) 772-0774. Entrées, $20 to $36. Dinner by reservation, nightly except Tuesday 5 to 9.

Shelter Harbor Inn, 10 Wagner Road, Westerly, R.I.

The restaurant at the Shelter Harbor Inn has long been one of the area's more appealing. The original dining room with stone fireplace has bare floors, country curtains and bentwood chairs at white-linened tables topped with hurricane lamps. Beyond is a newer two-level dining room, which has rough wood beams and posts, brick walls and comfortable chairs with curved backs. It overlooks a flagstone terrace with white tables and chairs.

The food is worthy of the setting. At Sunday brunch, we liked two of the day's specials, baked oysters and lamb shanks with rice pilaf. Although the former was

…h and the latter too large, we managed by sharing the two as well as feasting on the "surprise salad" of greens, radicchio, orange slices, cantaloupe, kiwi and strawberries with a creamy poppyseed dressing.

At dinner, be sure to try the Rhode Island johnnycakes with maple butter and, among appetizers, the crab and salmon cakes or the duck confit with cannellini beans. Entrées run from sautéed calves liver to hazelnut chicken to grilled angus sirloin. Choices are as diverse as horseradish-crusted scrod, cedar-grilled salmon, finnan haddie, veal osso buco and blackened tenderloin tips.

Desserts include an award-winning sour cream apple pie, chocolate mousse cake, Indian pudding and chocolate-peanut butter torte.

(401) 322-8883 or (800) 468-8883. Entrées, $15.95 to $21.95. Breakfast daily, 7:30 to 10:30. Lunch, 11:30 to 3. Dinner, 5 to 10.

Water Street Café, 143 Water St., Stonington, Conn.

This acclaimed café and its related market and deli traded spaces in 2003. Former New York hotel chef Walter Hoolihan and his wife Stephanie moved their café into the former market and adjacent Mothers café across the street. The market moved to the vacated café space and morphed into a deli.

The café was clearly the winner in the exchange, as were its legion of fans. They gained a considerably larger space, with close-together tables in an arty and funky, bright red and black dining area on one side and more tables in front of a curving solid Honduras mahogany bar in the old Mothers space. It's still convivial and, for some, too colorful and noisy. And no reservations are taken. But hey, most find the food more than compensates.

From his somewhat larger new kitchen, Walter fulfills a with-it, contemporary, all-day menu, supplemented by specials that change nightly. Typical starters are lobster spring rolls with soy sauce, crab fritters, tuna tartare, escargot pot pie, a prosciutto quesadilla and a warm duck salad with asparagus and sesame-orange dressing. London broil and sweet and sour spareribs conclude the all-day menu. Evening yields about fifteen blackboard specials, perhaps pepper-seared halibut with roast corn-shiitake salsa, herb-crusted salmon with fennel-beet risotto, duck and scallops with oyster mushrooms, and pan-roasted veal porterhouse with littleneck clams and arrabiata sauce.

Desserts vary from pear-mango bread pudding and coconut-walnut-chocolate cake to crème caramel and poached pears with ginger ice cream.

The Sunday brunch is arguably the best deal around.

(860) 535-2122. Entrées, $15.95 to $18.95.Lunch, Thursday-Monday 11:30 to 2:30. Dinner nightly, 5 to 10 or 11. Sunday brunch, 10 to 2:30.

Noah's, 113 Water St., Stonington, Conn.

This endearing restaurant – known for good food, casual atmosphere and affordable prices – has been gussied up. The once-funky double storefront now has fine art on the walls of the main dining room and a front room that contains a handsome mahogany bar and offers a bar menu.

Owners Dorothy and John Papp post contemporary international specials daily to complement traditional dinners on the order of broiled flounder, cod Portuguese and grilled chicken. The night's numerous specials have been upscaled lately and are a tad pricier, as you'd expect for dishes like prosciutto-wrapped monkfish with chianti sauce, spice-rubbed mako shark, grilled bluefish with mango-lime relish, grilled rare salmon with wasabi and pickled ginger, and lobster and monkfish sauté. Seafood is featured, but you might find grilled brace of quail with chardonnay cream sauce or veal flank steak with pinot noir sauce.

The fare is mighty interesting, from the house chicken liver pâté with sherry and pistachios to the mushroom strudel and the Korean bean and onion pancakes at lunch (many of the same items are offered on the bar menu). A bowl of clam chowder with half a BLT and a bacon-gouda quiche with side salad made a fine lunch for two.

Save room for the scrumptious homemade desserts, perhaps chocolate-yogurt cake, bourbon bread pudding, or what one local gentleman volunteered was the best dessert he'd ever had: fresh strawberries with Italian cream made from cream cheese, eggs and kirsch.

(860) 535-3925. www.noahsfinefood.com. Entrées, $12.25 to $23.95. Breakfast, 7 to 11, Sunday to noon. Lunch, 11:15 to 2:30. Dinner, 6 to 9 or 9:30. Closed Monday.

Randall's Ordinary, Route 2, North Stonington, Conn.

Colonial-style food, cooked as of 200 years ago and served by waitresses in period garb. That's the formula for success created by this unusual restaurant's founder and continued by the same kitchen team under the ownership of the Mashantucket Pequot Indians, best known for their nearby Foxwoods Resort Casino.

Up to 75 dinner patrons gather at 7 o'clock in a small taproom where they pick up a drink, popcorn, crackers and cheese before they tour the farmhouse dating to 1685. Then they watch cooks preparing their meals in antique iron pots and reflector ovens in an immense open hearth in the old keeping room.

Dinner is served prix-fixe in three atmospheric but spartan dining rooms. There's a choice of four or five entrées, perhaps roast capon with wild rice stuffing, roast ribeye beef, roast pork loin, hearth-grilled salmon and Nantucket scallops with scallions and butter – a signature dish that is truly exceptional. The meal includes soup (often onion or Shaker herb), anadama or spider corn bread, squash or corn pudding, a conserve of red cabbage and apples, and desserts like apple crisp, Thomas Jefferson's bread pudding or pumpkin cake.

Lunch, with similar food but less fanfare, is à la carte and considered great value by local innkeepers.

(860) 599-4540. Prix-fixe, $39. Breakfast daily, 7 to 11. Lunch, noon to 2, weekends to 3. Dinner nightly, 5:30 to 9.

Skipper's Dock, 66 Water St., Stonington, Conn.

Jerry and Ainslie Turner, who made the Harborview into one of the great restaurants in Connecticut, are back at its last remaining adjunct, the Skipper's Dock on the water at pier's end in Stonington harbor.

A total makeover turned Skipper's into a cheery, year-round restaurant and tavern with fireplaces ablaze in cool weather and lots of nautical memorabilia and nostalgia. The result is a happy cross between the haute Harborview (destroyed by fire and rebuilt as the Inn at Stonington) and the casual Skipper's Dock of old.

Much of the food reflects the Harborview's creativity, although consistency and service at busy times has been a problem lately. You can still get a mug of creamy clam chowder and a baker's dozen cherrystone clams or Connecticut blue point oysters. You also can get stuffed quahogs Portuguese and oysters Ainslie, toasted with garlic aioli and panko crumbs. These are just for starters. Main dishes include borview's classic Marseilles-style bouillabaisse and an intriguing newcomer, and wild mushroom pie crusted with cheddar duchess potato. Others could be ahi sesame tuna, coquilles St. Jacques, pan-seared duck breast bigarade and blackjack ribeye steak with whisky sauce. The dessert list features the Harborview's signature grasshopper pie, a Vermont maple-pecan pie and crème brûlée with fruit.

The food and service seem to be best at lunch, when some of the aforementioned treats are offered along with eggs benedict, an oyster po-boy, and a grilled scallops and warm spinach salad. They're also offered day and night in the Harbar, a high-style pub with framed magazine covers on the walls and boating gear hanging overhead. The best place to eat is, of course, on the expansive deck right out over the water.

(860) 535-0111. Entrées, $14.95 to $23.95. Lunch daily, 11 to 4. Dinner nightly, 4 to 9 or 10.

Custy's International, 138 Norwich-Westerly Road (Route 2), North Stonington, Conn.

Custy's, "the world's most famous buffet," is back – in the developing Route 2 corridor in North Stonington, of all places. It turned up in late 2003 in a spanking new but weathered gray and lobster red building along the road to the Foxwoods Resort Casino after having disappeared from view – and memory – at its original stomping ground next to the Quonset Point Naval Air Station in North Kingston, R.I.

The new Custy's has a lounge with live music and free hors d'oeuvres and a nautical dining rooms with a central lobster pot and steak barbecue pit. It builds on the tradition of the original: a 60-foot-long buffet line with mountains of baked stuffed clams and scallops, salads, broiled seafood, the signature orange duck and tropical ham, baked stuffed chicken, a cold seafood bar and 30 desserts. But true gluttons don't fill up on all this. The draw is all the lobster, steak and cocktail shrimp that you can eat (two-hour limit, no doggie bags) for $62.50. If the buffet is too much, you can order à la carte. The entire table must choose one or the other for obvious reasons. And, says proprietor James Yemma, no one leaves hungry.

(860) 599-1551. Buffet, $62.50. Entrées, $14.95 to $25. Dinner, Wednesday-Thursday 5 to 9, Friday 5 to 10, Saturday 2 to 10, Sunday 1 to 8. Major holidays, buffet only from noon.

The Olympia Tea Room, 74 Bay St., Watch Hill, R.I.

This mélange of booths and tables on a checkered black and white floor looks much as it did when it opened in 1916. Waitresses in black and white tea-room outfits à la Schrafft's scurry around serving iced tea and desserts like Hartford cream pie.

Upscaled recently, the menu offers something for everyone, and everyone always seems to be partaking, inside the atmospheric room with a soda fountain at one end and out front at tables on the sidewalk. You can snack on smoked bluefish pâté, nachos with homemade guacamole, hummus, steamed mussels or pizza, or order a fried fish sandwich or a turkey waldorf plate. More substantial offerings range from fish and chips to seafood casserole and Kansas City sirloin steak. Specials at a recent visit were chicken marsala and osso buco.

Between meals, stop at this local institution for Darjeeling tea, cappuccino, a glass of beer or wine, a frappe or an ice-cream sundae.

(401) 348-8211. Entrées, $10.95 to $21.95. Open daily, 8 a.m. to 10 p.m., May-October.

Diversions

Watch Hill and Stonington are small, choice and relatively private places off the beaten path. The crowds head east to Rhode Island's South County beaches, particularly the vast Misquamicut State Beach where the surf thunders in, or west to Mystic, where Mystic Seaport and the Mystic Aquarium combine with the Foxwoods Resort Casino and the newer Mohegan Sun Casino to make the area Connecticut's busiest tourist destination.

Stonington Borough. Who wouldn't fall for the historic charms of this once-thriving seaport, founded in 1649 and not all that changed since the 19th century? The last commercial fishing fleet in Connecticut is manned by the resident Portuguese, who stage a colorful Blessing of the Fleet ceremony every July. To savor fully the flavor, walk the two narrow streets through the borough. They and their cross streets are lined with historic homes, many of them marked by the Stonington Historical Society and some once occupied by the likes of John Updike, Eve Merriam, Peter Benchley and L. Patrick Gray. The house where artist James McNeill Whistler painted Whistler's Mother later was home for Stephen Vincent Benet. Edgar Allen Poe and Capt. Nathaniel Brown, who discovered Antarctica, also lived here.

Palmer House, 40 Palmer St., Stonington.

The majestic, sixteen-room Victorian mansion that Capt. Nathanial Palmer and his seafaring brother Alexander built in 1852 was saved by the historical society from demolition in 1994 and opened to the public as a fine example of a prosperous sea captain's home. Several rooms contain memorabilia from the brothers' adventures, family portraits and local artifacts. The piano in the parlor is the only original piece remaining in the house, but rooms are furnished with period pieces. The craftsmanship completed by local shipwrights is evident in the sweeping staircases and built-in cabinetry. The cupola yields a view of the surrounding countryside and sea.

(860) 535-8445. Open Tuesday-Sunday 10 to 4, May-October. Adults $4.

Old Lighthouse Museum, 7 Water St., Stonington.

The first lighthouse in Connecticut is perched on a rise above Stonington Point, where the villagers turned back the British. Opened by the historical society in 1927, this museum is a tiny storehouse of Stonington memorabilia. Whaling and fishing gear, portraits of the town's founding fathers, a bench dating back to 1674, articles from the Orient trade and an exquisite dollhouse are included in the six small rooms. You can climb up circular iron stairs of the tower to obtain a view in all directions.

(860) 535-1440. Open Tuesday-Sunday 10 to 5, May-October; daily in July and August, by appointment rest of year. Adults $4.

Watch Hill. This staid, storied resort community protects its privacy (parking is limited and prices are high), but things get busy on summer weekends. The lineups of low, weathered shingled shops and storefronts here could only be in Watch Hill. Youngsters line up at the entrance to the Watch Hill Beach for rides on the **Flying Horse Carousel** (1867), thought to be the oldest merry-go-round in the country.

…ses on this National Historic Landmark, suspended from a center frame, swing out when in motion. Each horse is hand-carved from a single piece of wood and they bear real tails and manes, leather saddles and agate eyes.

Napatree Point. If you can find a place to park, hike out to Napatree Point, a privately owned conservation area extending half a mile beyond the Watch Hill parking lot. The walk on the sandy spit to the ruins of a Spanish-American War fort at the far end opposite Stonington can take an hour or a day, depending on one's beachcombing and bird-watching interests.

Shopping. Water Street in Stonington is home to several special shops, with more opening every year. Fine antiques are the specialty at such places as **Grand & Water, Orkney & Yost** and **Devon House Antiques.** At the **Hungry Palette,** silk-screened and hand-printed fabrics can be purchased by the yard or already made up into long skirts, wrap skirts, sundresses and colorful accessories like Bermuda bags. **Findings** offers fine home furnishings and accessories. **Cumulus** stocks handcrafted jewelry and gifts. The expanding **Fun! Company** went from one to three Water Street outlets before consolidating at 71 Cutler St. with room after room of closeouts of clothing, home accessories and toys.

In Watch Hill, stores are seasonal and tend to come and go. Unique American crafts and gifts are featured at **Puffins,** where we admired the handcrafted jewelry, aluminum sand-cast pieces and pottery birdhouses from Tennessee. **Comina** offers exceedingly colorful international furnishings, gifts and accessories at its seasonal shop. The Feather Bed & Breakfast birdhouse appealed among the gifty things at the **Country Store of Watch Hill. Seaport Studio** offers "port wear" and art. **The Lily Pad,** a good art gallery, also offers antiques.

Between expeditions, stop in Stonington at **Stonington Vineyards,** 523 Taugwonk Road, where Nick and Happy Smith run a growing winery operation. Among their premium vinifera wines are a fine chardonnay and a cabernet franc. The first crop of local grapes was scheduled to be harvested in 2004 at the new, state-of-the-art **Jonathan Edwards Winery,** successor to the Crosswoods Vineyards at 74 Chester Maine Road in North Stonington.

Extra-Special

Quimper Faience, 141 Water St., Stonington.

Bet you didn't know that the world headquarters of the famed hand-painted French dinnerware and decorative pottery is located along the main street of downtown Stonington. It seems that Paul and Sarah Janssens, Stonington residents who had imported and distributed the ware through their Quimper retail store here since 1979, helped save the 300-year-old Quimper factory from bankruptcy in 1984. They and several investors purchased the faiencerie (the second oldest company in France), continued its operations and turned their storefront and an upstairs apartment here into the retail and mail-order headquarters. This is the flagship store, and Quimper/Stonington now has three company stores (one in Paris) and wholesales to others. Quimperware, best known for its colorful Breton peasant motifs and always hand-painted and signed by the artist, is still produced at the factory in Brittany. Fifty-eight artists paint the patterns on the pieces, no two of which are the same.

(860) 535-1712. www.quimperfaience.com. Open Monday-Saturday 10 to 5.

Stone wall borders attractive campus of Pomfret preparatory school.

Northeast Connecticut

The Quiet, Gilded Corner

Few people realize that Connecticut's oft-overlooked "Quiet Corner" of hill towns and mill villages once was a fashionable summer resort of the Lenox-Newport ilk.

Starting in the late 1870s, it was known as "Newport without the water." During its gilded days, wealthy New Yorkers and Bostonians summered in Pomfret and Woodstock on vast country estates with dreamlike names like Gwyn Careg, Courtlands and Glen Elsinore.

John Addison Porter, a Hartford newspaper editor and Pomfret resident, wrote in 1896 that his town was "one of the natural garden spots of the state – the ideal peaceful New England landscape. It bears on its face the unmistakable signs of being the abode of people of culture. No town of its size in Connecticut represents more wealth, but this is used unostentatiously and is in perfectly good taste."

The Depression and post-war priorities took their toll on the wealth, as did the move to the South of the textile mills upon which the local economy had been based. The quiet corner became the neglected corner.

But not for long. Area officials and the National Park Service turned their efforts toward forming a National Heritage Corridor to preserve a region called "the last green valley" in the crowded megalopolis between Boston and Washington, D.C.

Meanwhile, sleepy Putnam, once the area's leading mill town, rapidly turned into the antiques center of New England. The change stimulated both the locale's economy and its psyche.

More than 30 B&Bs have opened in the last two decades. As restaurateur Jimmie Booth, who moved many years ago from New York to her husband's family farm and launched the renowned Golden Lamb Buttery restaurant: "Everything's changing out here. We're not the quiet corner any more. The developers are building in all the woods around."

Developers indeed are at work, but the change everyone talks about locally is relative. Northeast Connecticut remains the state's least-developed area – "classic New England without traffic or kitsch," as the New York Times described it. "The Street" in Pomfret carries much of the grace of a century ago. A low-key sophistication is lent by Pomfret, the Rectory, Hyde and Marianapolis preparatory schools and the headquarters of firms like Crabtree & Evelyn, one of the area's largest employers.

The visitor has a rare opportunity to share in the good life here. You can stay in restored inns that once were the homes of the rich and famous. You can have bed and breakfast with the aristocracy in houses filled with family treasures. Your host may be an artist, a furniture maker, a music lover, an architect, a marketing consultant or a carpenter. In no other area have we found the innkeepers and their facilities as a group so understated and so fascinating.

You'll feel as if you're a character in a Currier & Ives etching in this area of rambling stone walls, rolling hills and fertile farmlands, languishing mill towns and tranquil villages. But get yourself going. As the antiquers have discovered, the Quiet Corner won't be quiet forever.

Inn Spots

Friendship Valley, 60 Pomfret Road (Route 169), Box 845, Brooklyn 06234.

Classical music soothes and Southern hospitality is dispensed at this delightful B&B, once a stop on the Underground Railroad. Prudence Crandall, the Canterbury educator who was hounded out of town for teaching young women of color in her academy in the 1830s, named this 18th-century, Georgian-style country house when it was occupied by one of her benefactors. Abolitionist William Lloyd Garrison, who was married here in the 1830s, wrote of Friendship Valley: "this place that I love more than anywhere."

The name fits, for Beverly and Charles (Rusty) Yates run a very friendly B&B in a bucolic valley of twelve wooded acres and wetlands near what passes for the center of tiny Brooklyn. Transplanted Texans, Rusty, an architect, and Beverly, a former high school counselor in Houston, are the perfect hosts. She helped spearhead the area's B&B association, serves on the board of the area's visitor district and extols the area's virtues to one and all.

The couple took over what had been a two-room B&B, added more bathrooms and now offer five guest rooms, named for the five previous owners of the house, which is listed on the National Register. The prime accommodation is the Prince Suite, transformed from a wood shed at the rear of the main floor, with a beamed and vaulted ceiling, queen mahogany rice poster bed, a jacuzzi tub and a private entrance. Upstairs in the main house are four more bedrooms, one combinable into a two-bedroom suite. All have private baths and three have fireplaces. They convey a decidedly historic but comfortable air, from the step-up queensize four-poster in the Benson Room to the antique twin beds from France in the Wendel.

The entire house is handsomely

B&B in 18th-century house lives up to its historic name, Friendship Valley.

appointed with period furnishings, prized antiques and well-worn oriental rugs. Guests enjoy two small front parlors, one a library and the other a fireplaced living room with cable TV hidden in a cabinet. Beyond are a formal dining room (in which the fireplace mantel came from the home of the founder of Cleveland, Ohio) and a lovely breakfast porch overlooking the gardens. These are the settings for a hearty breakfast of juice, fruit plate and main course, served with fine china, silver and linens. Quiche, pancakes and baked french toast could be the fare. "I cook," advises Beverly, "but Rusty says he's the juice and fruit chef."

She also offers tea and dessert in the afternoon or evening.

(860) 779-9696. Fax (860) 779-9844. www.friendshipvalleyinn.com. Four rooms and one suite with private baths. Doubles, $140 to $170. Children over 7.

Celebrations, 330 Pomfret St., Pomfret 06259.

From Miss Vinton's School for Girls to the Pomfret Inn to a private residence to apartments. This 1885 Queen Anne Victorian house has had a checkered history, but you should see it now.

Jean and Bill Barton from West Hartford took over the grand B&B that had been known as Karinn and painted the exterior a festive rose. They offer comfortable common areas and five themed guest rooms.

From the wraparound porch, enter the grand foyer with antique furnishings along the sides and a large buffet at one end. On the right is a library with books and board games. On the left is a large parlor/TV room with a fireplace. The Bartons turned what had been the adjacent music room into the dining room, which opens past a sunny, plant-filled area onto a side deck overlooking restored gardens.

There's more: past the skylit kitchen is a paneled barroom used by the original inn, with two benches from the old tavern in the corner. Here is where groups sometimes gather for BYO beverages.

The main floor with five working fireplaces offers more public space than many an inn with twenty guest accommodations. But here there are only five, with plans for three more.

Climb the grand staircase to the front northeastern corner of the second floor. Here is the Far East Suite with pale green floral wallpaper, a queensize iron bed with a swagged canopy headboard, a fireplace and a few Asian treasures. Its bathroom with a shower adjoins a small sitting room. The front corner Sweet Celebrations "is our romance room," says Jean. The former master bedroom and the biggest in the house, it has an ornate canopied kingsize iron bed enveloped in white, a fireplace and the polished wood floors and colorful Thibault wallpapers characteristic of the house. The Lady Slipper Suite down its own side hallway offers a carved mahogany queen bed, a collection of whimsical footwear and a bath with clawfoot tub and hand-held shower. Beyond is a large sitting room with an antique day bed and windows on three sides. Toward the rear of the second floor are two more bedrooms, Miss Vinton's with a queensize mahogany bed, and Enchanted Garden, with a queensize oak bed. Both of their baths have clawfoot tubs.

Jean has fun decorating the house seasonally – the first time we caught up with her she was changing the theme from Valentine's to St. Patrick's Day. She also likes to welcome guests with afternoon tea and sweets and, in the evening, her homemade herbal cordials. Her husband wanted a sambuca so she complied with a concoction called "licorice lovers." Others are blueberry-lemon verbena and ginger-pear brandy, all made from scratch.

In the morning, she puts out coffee, muffins and coffeecake for early-risers. Then the fireplaced dining room is the setting for an elaborate fruit course; perhaps triple ginger-baked pears, sautéed bananas, spiced oranges or grilled pineapple. The main event might be pepperoni breakfast pie or irish cream french toast.

Why the name for the B&B? Both Bartons were in corporate management and consulting (Bill still is) and knew how people needed to "step back from the crazed corporate life," in Jean's words. "We provide a respite so they can celebrate the everyday pleasures."

(860) 928-5492 or (877) 928-5492. Fax (860) 928-3306. www.celebrationsinn.com. Three rooms and two suites with private baths. Doubles, $125 to $175. Suites, $150. Children over 8.

The Inn at Woodstock Hill, 94 Plaine Hill Road, Box 98, Woodstock 06267.

The 1816 Christopher Wren-style home of Henry Bowen, whose landmark shocking-pink summer cottage is up the road, was willed in 1981 to the University of Connecticut, which had no use for it. Enter a group of investors who restored the house with great taste and opened in 1987 with more ambition than the locale could immediately afford. The inn has stabilized nicely since the arrival in 1989 of chef-partner Richard Naumann.

The atmosphere of an English manor house pervades the inn's spacious and attractive common rooms, restaurant and 22 guest rooms. The main living room, a library, the morning/TV room and a small dining room in particular are a kaleidoscope of chintz fabrics, fine paintings, plush oriental rugs and tiled fireplaces.

More Waverly floral chintz accents the prevailing peach, pink and blue color scheme in the guest rooms. All are sleek and comfortable with reproduction antiques and wicker furniture, chairs and loveseats, thick carpeting and modern baths, some with double marble sinks. Television, telephones and air-conditioning come with. Six rooms have fireplaces and six have four-poster beds. Quiet rooms with rear

Former summer cottage for Bowen family is now The Mansion at Bald Hill.

views look across the valley. The premier Room 209 has a beamed cathedral ceiling, and a large cedar closet off another room on the third floor has been converted into a bathroom.

An outside entrance leads to a cozy lounge, where colorful wine labels under glass top the bar. Here in a wing connected to a barn are two dining rooms that form the heart of the inn's elegant restaurant (see Dining Spots).

Back in the main inn, a continental-plus breakfast is served in the morning room or the dining room. An assortment of fresh fruits, juices and cereals accompany muffins, croissants, coffeecake, and sometimes brioches and sticky buns. Warm mulled cider or lemonade and a decanter of sherry await arriving guests in the afternoon.

(860) 928-0528. Fax (860) 928-3236. www.woodstockhill.com. Twenty-two rooms with private baths. Doubles, $130 to $200.

The Mansion at Bald Hill, 29 Plaine Hill Road, Box 333, South Woodstock 06267.

The 1892 shingled and stucco mansion that served as a summer cottage for the Bowen family was opened to B&B guests in 2003 by Peter and Sharon Cooper. They own the Harvest Restaurant in Pomfret, successor to their original restaurant known as Harvest at Bald Hill nearby.

Hidden off by itself on Bald Hill amid several acres of gardens, terraces and grounds, the 21-room mansion is a throw-back to the Gilded Era. The main floor with its ten-foot-high ceilings, plaster cornices and crown molding is a treasure trove of grand public areas: foyers and a music room paneled in hazelwood, a library of olive wood and a formal dining room of stained oak with floor-to-ceiling cabinets stocked with Bowen family china, silver and glassware. A parlor with one of the mansion's thirteen fireplaces opens onto both library and dining room as well as a wide stone terrace along the back of the house.

While the public areas remain much as they have for more than a century, the Coopers have refurbished and updated the guest quarters on the second and third floors. They offer eight bedrooms and suites with private baths, and five smaller rooms with shared baths in the former servants' wing.

One of the largest is Mrs. Bowen's Suite, restored to its early grandeur with a majestic kingsize poster bed, a huge window seat in the bay window, writing desk, TV hidden in the armoire, and a couple of wing chairs beside the fireplace. The bath has a clawfoot tub as well as a baby's bathtub, a bidet and marble sinks. A tad smaller is Mr. Bowen's Room, with a kingsize sleigh bed, two wing chairs by the window and a new bath with glass shower. Beside the fireplace is a plump white chair and a half with ottoman, which Sharon calls "a sweetheart chair" for two. At the other end of the second floor is Roxanna's Suite, named after the couple's daughter. It has a queensize iron bed in a window alcove overlooking the garden, another window seat, a sitting area and a bathroom with an enormous walk-in shower. Other rooms vary from the kingsize Wentworth – hard to believe it served as Mrs. Bowen's dressing room – to the smallest Garden Room, cheerful in coral tones with a queen bed and a modern bathroom.

As the Coopers neared the end of their renovation stage, they planned to create a bridal suite from a third-floor common room recently used as a conference area by the corporate owner. It was to have a jacuzzi tub for two in the sun room and a balcony over the garden.

The Coopers share cooking duties at breakfast, preparing the likes of omelets, eggs benedict, Swedish pancakes and crème brûlée french toast. Before or after, guests enjoy the formal gardens and grounds in a tranquil wooded setting.

(860) 974-3456. www.mansionatbaldhill.com. Four rooms and four suites with private baths and five rooms with shared baths. Doubles, $120 to $165, ($95 shared). Suites, $150 to $250.

B&B at Taylor's Corner, 880 Route 171, Woodstock 06281.

The inside of this restored 18th-century center-chimney Colonial is ever so historic, but the five acres outside are positively awesome. Walk out the rear of what once was the front of the house and you're greeted by stunning perennial gardens – more plots that one person can take care of – and even a pet cow.

"I never gardened in my life," says Peggy Tracy, innkeeper with her husband Doug, both Northeast Corner natives. She learned fast after the couple purchased the residence in 1996 and converted it into a B&B. "These perennials popped out of the ground that first spring" and she and a helper have been gardening ever since. The gardens were started by a former owner who ran an herbary. The Tracys added Jessie Brown, a Scotch Highland cow, for guests to pet as she grazes in the back yard.

Inside the house, which is listed on the National Register of Historic Places, are eight working fireplaces and two beehive ovens. One of the latter is the first sight guests see as they enter the front keeping room. Beyond is a formal parlor with TV; on a wall the Tracys have framed a mysterious confession found hidden between bricks in the chimney and written by someone seeking forgiveness in 1795. Across the hall is a large, fireplaced dining room with hooked rugs on the floors and Hitchcock chairs at a table for six. Here Peggy serves breakfast on her collection of fine Danish porcelain – continental on weekdays, supplemented by entrées like oven omelets, french toast or Finnish pancakes on weekends.

Up creaky stairs are two spacious rear bedrooms with queensize beds angled from the corners. A front bedroom has a queen and a twin bed, and all have fireplaces

Eighteenth-century center-chimney Colonial is home for B&B at Taylor's Corner.

and telephones. Stuffed animals are on each bed, and colorful comforters, antique chairs, bedside candies and fresh flowers are the norm. Downstairs off the keeping room is a single bedroom, the original borning room, with a twin bed.

(860) 974-0490 or (888) 503-9057. Fax (860) 974-0498. www.bnbattaylorscorner.com. Three rooms with private baths. Children over 12. Doubles, $125 to $140 weekends, $95 midweek.

Cobbscroft, 349 Pomfret St., Pomfret 06258.

This rambling white house almost up against the road is home to artists Janet and Tom McCobb as well as a furniture and art gallery for the works of watercolorist Tom, who has a studio in the rear barn, and those of artist-friends.

Guests are received in a library with a gorgeous needlepoint rug and deep shelves full of books and a TV. Beyond is a large gallery/living room hung with a variety of art, all for sale and all very enticing. Some is by Janet, who paints furniture, decorative objects and frames in a faux style. Off the library are a double and single guest room joined by a bathroom, rented as a family suite. Upstairs are three more guest rooms with baths. One with twin beds has lacy white spreads and curtains, a sofa and knickknacks including little dolls. A front corner room has charming stenciling done by Janet, a four-poster bed, chaise lounge and oriental rug. Its bathroom has gold-plated fixtures and an oval, clawfoot tub like none we've seen; Janet said it's a birthday tub and was able to hold her four granddaughters at once when they were small. Over the living room is what the McCobbs call the bridal suite, a wondrous affair with windows on three sides, a working fireplace, a loveseat, dressing table and a bed covered in frilly white linens.

Breakfast is served at a long table in the bright yellow dining room, full of country touches like a collection of lambs. The table is flanked by Queen Anne chairs and topped by two wooden chickens and eggs as a centerpiece. In her extra B&B kitchen (away from the family quarters), Janet prepares hot apple crisp or melon in season, croissants, scrambled eggs, quiche or strata. In the afternoon, she serves tea with cinnamon toast or fruit bread. Guests may help themselves to brandy in the living room after dinner.

(860) 928-5560. www.cobbscroft.com. Three rooms and a two-room family suite with private baths. Doubles, $90. Suite, $125. Children over 12.

Daniel Trowbridge House offers guests historic ambiance on a working farm.

Daniel Trowbridge House, 193 Hampton Road (Route 97 North), Pomfret Center 06259.

More than most, this distinctive B&B lives up to the cliché, "a step back in time." The house is truly historic: a mix of original features and painstaking renovation in a 1730s Colonial house. It's set on an 80-acre working farm that has been cultivated by the owner's family and their predecessors for 300 years.

Chickens are apt to join owner Tom Campbell as he emerges from the barn to lead guests into the antiques-filled house that he and his wife, Cris Cadiz, share with overnight guests in three atmospheric guest quarters.

Barely out of college, the couple restored the house themselves over a period of several years. Tom is a carpenter and furniture maker by trade, crafting custom furniture and flooring from antique wood he obtains from demolished structures. His talents are everywhere evident in the house they turned into a home. The dining room holds his fabulous chestnut farm table for eight, a side table and a corner cupboard. The bedrooms harbor his handmade beds. And the country kitchen with its floor of antique chestnut is a showplace – "this took the most time," Cris recalls.

Although Tom made much of the furniture, the couple had help with the decorating, particularly in the bedrooms. A friend painted a primitive yet realistic mural of the rural scene outside the window in the front-corner Colonial Room, which has a queensize turned-post bed and the original pumpkin pine floor. A local artist painted an antique mural that wraps around the entire front-corner Rufus Porter Room. It bears all the original elements of the 19th-century itinerant artist and looks as if it has been there for 150 years. The room has a queensize poster bed and, as with the others, it's for sale. "Guests can buy the beds they sleep on," advises Cris.

The entire back of the second floor is given over to the spacious North Suite, where a new bath with shower goes off the queen bedroom and a sitting room across the foyer has a murphy-style bed.

The couple plan to add two guest rooms in the attic. Efficiency cottages are planned eventually outside.

Guests hang out in a charming living room with a woodstove. The back yard descends to a farm pond, and Tom has cut walking paths so guests can explore the rolling countryside.

The couple's chickens furnish fresh eggs for breakfast. Cris employs the bounty from her gardens to prepare omelets with fresh herbs, fruit crêpes and blueberry pancakes. She offers complimentary beverages and local wines in the evening.

(860) 974-3622. www.danieltrowbridgehouse.com. Two rooms and one suite with private baths. Doubles, $135. Suite, $155. Two-night minimum required. Children over 10.

Chickadee Cottage, 70 Averill Road (Route 44), Pomfret Center 06259.

The chickadees that descend on the bird feeders outside her rural house inspired the name for this charming B&B. Moving here from the Philadelphia area, Sandra Betner got the idea for a B&B from neighbors, who operated the Golden Hill Farm for a spell.

She shares the stylish yellow Cape Cod house with guests in two large, sunny rooms furnished with family heirlooms and antiques. The "cottage" above a detached three-bay garage is a spacious hideaway with a separate entrance and plant-laden sundeck, a canopied double bed, corner kitchen, a big farm table, sitting area with a sofabed and a gas-log woodstove. Upstairs in the main house is the Countryside Room with windows on three sides. It has a plump queensize bed, sitting area with a dhurrie rug and a refurbished bath. Each accommodation has TV, telephone and air conditioning. Guests enjoy use of the stylish living room.

Occupants of the cottage may have breakfast there or in the dining room of the main house. The meal also can be taken on the full-length deck behind the house.

"People always are amazed how peaceful this setting is," says Sandy. The house is on four rural acres, with open public lands on three sides. The 30-mile Air Line State Park Trail, part of an abandoned railroad bed, passes on the hill behind the house and connects with five miles of walking trails in the Connecticut Audubon Society's little-known, 667-acre Bafflin Audubon Society nature sanctuary nearby.

(860) 963-0587. Fax (860) 963-0594. www.chickadeecottage.com. One room and one cottage with private baths. Double, $135. Cottage, $210. Two-night minimum most weekends. Children accepted in cottage.

Clark Cottage at Wintergreen, 354 Pomfret St., Pomfret 06258.

An eighteen-room gray Victorian house at the end of a long driveway turns out to have been built for the superintendent of the old Clark estate. It's now a B&B, and innkeeper Doris Geary points out other structures still on the vast property, which affords a view across the valley.

Doris and her husband Stan, retired business manager at the Rectory School, offer four light and airy guest rooms (two with private baths and the other two adjoining as a family suite). Most coveted is the front corner room, which has striking green painted Italian furniture, including an incredible kingsize bedstead with an oval mirror in the headboard. The furnishings, nicely set off against peach walls, can be admired from a mushroom velvet loveseat. Plush beige carpeting enhances a rear room with a sofa, twin beds and a porch for taking in the valley view. It forms a suite with an adjoining room with a brass bed and a wood stove in the fireplace. A fourth room has a queensize bed with a quilted headboard and stuffed dolls amid the pillows.

On the main floor is a colorful entry hall with window seats and turn-of-the-century spool banisters framing the stairway. Guests enjoy a formal, fireplaced parlor and a dining room with another fireplace and a long polished table.

The Gearys serve a full breakfast of fresh fruit and a main dish like pancakes or french toast stuffed with cream cheese and nuts.

(860) 928-5741. Fax (860) 928-1591. Two rooms with private bath and a two-room family suite. Doubles, $65 to $110. Children welcome.

Dining Spots

The Golden Lamb Buttery, Hillandale Farm, 499 Wolf Den Road, Brooklyn.

For more years than we care to remember, Golden Lamb Buttery has been our most cherished restaurant. We love it for summer lunches, when the surrounding fields and hills look like a Constable painting. We love it for summer evenings, when we have cocktails on a hay wagon driven by a tractor through the fields and listen to a talented folksinger's pure voice as she sings and plays guitar. We love the picnic suppers followed by, perhaps, dancing to an eighteen-piece band playing songs from the '40s and '50s, or maybe a musical done by a local theater company on occasional Wednesday and Thursday nights in summer. And we love fall lunches and dinners ensconced beside the glowing fireplace. We especially love the Elizabethan madrigal dinners served in December, when a group of renaissance singers carol through the rooms and pork tenderloin is a festive main course. And everyone loves Jimmie and Bob Booth, the remarkable owners of the farm on which the restaurant stands – she the wonderful chef and he the affable host.

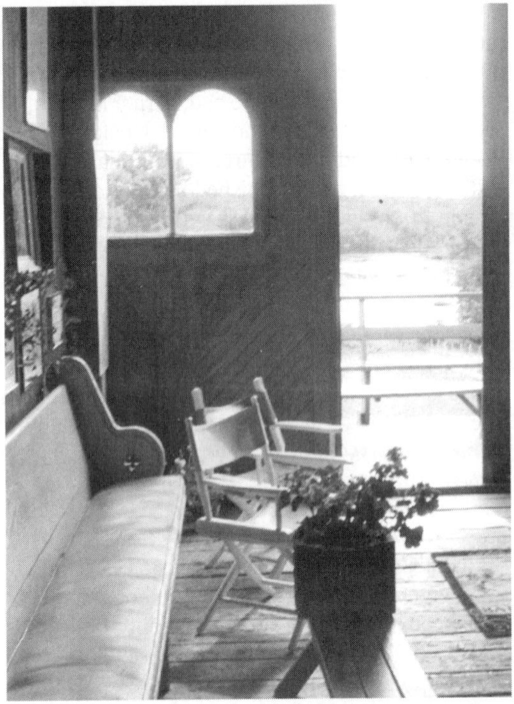

Pond is on view from Golden Lamb Buttery's barn.

You can tell as you enter through the barn, where a 1953 Jaguar convertible is displayed among such eclectic items as a totem pole and a telephone booth, that you are in for an unusual treat. Step out on the back deck and gaze over the picturesque scene as waitresses in long pink gingham skirts show the blackboard menu ($65 prix fixe) and take your order. After you are seated following the hayride, the table is yours for the evening.

Appetizers consist mostly of soups, and Jimmie makes some knockouts. Using herbs from her garden – especially lovage, her favorite – she might concoct country cottage, minestrone mother earth, cabbage soup made with duck stock or, in summer, a cold soup like raspberry puree or cucumber.

There is usually a choice of four entrées, always duck and often salmon, châteaubriand and lamb. These are accompanied by six to eight vegetables, served family style and to us almost the best part of the meal. Marinated mushrooms are always among them and, depending on the season and what's in the garden, you might find celery braised with fennel, carrots with orange rind and raisins, tomatoes with basil and lime juice or a casserole of zucchini and summer squash with mornay sauce. Jimmie cooks without preservatives or salt, and believes strongly in fresh and healthful food. Desserts might include a chocolate roll made with Belgian chocolate, coffee or grand marnier mousse, or butter cake with fresh berries.

This unfoldment takes place in dining rooms in the barn or the attached building with a loft that was once a studio used by writers. The old wood of the walls and raftered ceilings glows with the patina of age, as do the polished wood tables in the flickering candlelight. Colored glass bottles shine in the windows, and the whole place is filled with barny things like decoys, deacons' benches, pillows, bowls of apples and rag rugs. Add classical music and a bottle from Bob's well-chosen wine list, and you will likely find yourself in the middle of a midsummer night's dream.

For lunch, entrées in the $13 to $18 range could include pasta parmesan, seafood crêpes, salmon quiche, the delicious Hillandale hash and Londonderry pork stew.

(860) 774-4423. Prix-fixe, $65. Lunch, Tuesday-Saturday noon to 2:30. Dinner, Friday and Saturday, one seating at 7:30. Dinner reservations required far in advance. Closed January-March. No credit cards.

The Harvest, 37 Putnam Road, Pomfret.

A longtime local favorite, The Harvest at Bald Hill, reopened in large and stylish new quarters at a prime Pomfret location and turned out to be better than ever. Peter Cooper, a former chef at the Brown University faculty club in Providence, took over the Lemuel Grosvenor House (circa 1765) and built a substantial addition.

The establishment focuses on an open lounge with a cherry wood bar and several dining tables in the center, a semi-open kitchen and a floor-to-ceiling wall of wines showcasing the Harvest's award-winning wine cellar at the entry. Around the periphery are a grill room with a fireplace, a couple of handsome fireplaced dining rooms, two dining porches, a cocktail terrace and a banquet facility. The place seats 250, and at our latest visit Peter was preparing to serve 800 diners for Thanksgiving. Decor is elegant country in burgundy and green, with local artworks on the walls and the oil lamps in hurricane chimneys illuminated even at noon

The menus change seasonally to reflect the harvest. The traditional lunch service was discontinued recently, but not before three of us enjoyed good french bread, a shared appetizer of gyoza (tasty Japanese dumplings), sautéed scrod with winter vegetables and two excellent – and abundant – salads, caesar with Thai chicken and grilled salmon with citrus wasabi vinaigrette. These were so filling we couldn't begin to think of such delectable desserts as mascarpone cheesecake, a classic marjolaine, peach bourbon upside-down cake or cardamom crème brûlée. Not even the signature raspberry sorbet and vanilla ice cream with raspberry coulis in a white chocolate truffle shell broke our resolve.

The extensive dinner menu appeals as well. Appetizers intrigue: escargots bruschetta, a French-style tapas sampler, Indian vegetarian samosas, gyoza, and a grilled scallop martini with pineapple salsa and crispy wontons. Main courses vary widely from cedar-planked roast salmon with ginger butter and seared sesame tuna with teriyaki glaze to roast duckling with orange-raspberry sauce, tenderloin of pork au poivre, the signature grilled lamb with rosemary and garlic, and seven steak-house versions of steaks and chops. The emphasis on the harvest shows up spectacularly in the vegetable and bean sauté, the Pacific Rim vegetable grill and the roasted vegetable roulade Santa Fe.

An extensive menu of Japanese cuisine, including sushi by a Japanese chef, is offered with the regular menu except on weekends.

(860) 928-0008. www.harvestrestaurant.com. Entrées. $14.95 to $25.95. Tuesday-Saturday 5:30 to 8 or 9, Sunday, brunch 11 to 1:45, dinner 3 to 8.

The Vine Bistro, 85 Main St., Putnam.

The antiques district in up-and-coming downtown Putnam is enlivened by a good little contemporary American bistro. Lisa Cassettari operates a stark white space accented with blond tables (dressed with white linens at night) and large, colorful paintings done by a local artist. The name reflects her aim to serve fresh fare, as in the vineyard proverb: "The grape is most delightful when first picked from the vine."

At lunch, things get off to a good start when the ice water is poured with a slice of lemon into an oversize brandy glass. Plates puddled with olive oil, garlic and rosemary arrive for soaking up the good, crusty bread. There is quite a selection of soups, sandwiches and salads, including an unusual caesar salad served with Maryland crab cakes. A specialty is vodka rigatoni, which one of us tried and pronounced successful. Others in our party sampled an appetizer of portobello mushrooms sautéed with spinach, roasted peppers, tomatoes, garlic and olive oil, and a generous sandwich of turkey, swiss and whole berry cranberry sauce. A sensational finale was tangerine sorbet, served in a frozen tangerine on a big white plate squiggled with raspberry puree. Pumpkin cheesecake laced with cognac was another winner.

Much the same fare is available at dinner, minus the sandwiches and plus half a dozen specials. Expect treats like vodka rigatoni with jumbo shrimp, sautéed salmon with a velvety dill sauce, "chicken d'vine" with artichoke hearts, veal marsala and locally raised duckling. The beef tenderloin is finished with a chive demi-glace and served with baked macaroni of three cheeses and peas.

(860) 928-1660. Entrées, $17.95 to $27.95. Lunch, Tuesday-Sunday 11 to 4. Dinner, Tuesday-Saturday 5 to 9, Sunday 5 to 7.

The Inn at Woodstock Hill, 94 Plaine Hill Road, Woodstock.

This glamorous restaurant spreads across three rooms of an equally glamorous inn. It has earned its spurs over the years under German chef Richard Naumann.

The setting is elegant, whether in the main inn, a small dining room with banquettes draped in chintz in the carriage house or, beyond, the long, narrow main dining room with windows onto fields and forest. Blue armchairs are at tables set with Villeroy & Boch china and pink napkins stashed in big wine glasses.

For a springtime lunch, we were seated in the small, pretty peach and blue dining room in the carriage house, the armchairs a bit too low (the banquettes are the right height) and the atmosphere a bit too hushed until some more lunchers trickled in. Most of the menu struck us as more appropriate for dinner, with main courses ranging from seafood newburg vol au vent to filet mignon Madagascar, a staple on the evening menu. The menu listed three tempting sandwiches (chicken dijon and beef tip wraps and croque monsieur), appetizers of the dinner variety, a couple of

Former Bowen home and carriage house are now The Inn at Woodstock Hill.

soups and two salads, one of mixed greens and the other the house version of a chef's salad. Chosen to follow an excellent baked french onion soup, it turned out to be a rather strange concoction lacking the advertised boiled egg and topped with salami, turkey and cheese. It did come with a super mint-apple dressing, however. One of us ordered the day's pasta off the appetizer list, a fine dish of ravioli stuffed with mushrooms and a sundried tomato sauce that was almost a salsa. Another sampled the chicken dijon wrap topped with bacon and melted swiss cheese, served with potato chips and chunks of fruit, too much to finish.

Based on our almost-dinner lunch, we would expect dinner here to be fine. The extensive continental/American menu features dishes like blackened tuna steak with spicy creole sauce, mustard-glazed salmon with slivered ginger, grilled duck breast with a cognac-bordelaise sauce, roast pork tenderloin with cranberry-peach chutney, and baked rack of lamb dijon. Most of the desserts at our visit were chocolate-based.

(860) 928-0528. Entrées, $17.50 to $27. Lunch, Tuesday-Saturday 11 to 2, April-December. Dinner Monday-Saturday 5 to 9. Sunday, brunch 11 to 2, dinner 3:30 to 7:30.

Sharpe Hill Vineyard, 108 Wade Road, Pomfret.

Once they find this out-of-the-way prize, visitors sample wines in a tasting room that looks like a taproom of the 1700s. The serious adjourn by reservation to eat in a twelve-table fireside tavern attached to the winery or outside in a perfectly idyllic, umbrella-tabled wine garden amid espalier-style greenery, beside vineyards climbing 700 feet up Sharpe Hill. Catherine Vollweiler, co-owner and the executive chef, is known for definitive cuisine served properly and personally in what she is fond of calling "my house." Her house in this case is a building attached to the winery with a cooking hearth and kitchen downstairs, two fireplaces in a soaring white center chimney, and dining space for 40 amid antiques, glittering silver and a fresco of coastal Connecticut in a raftered loft upstairs.

Lunch is offered her way – that is to say, the big meal of the day – at two seatings, noon and 3. It's the way she likes to partake when vacationing in Europe with her husband, whose parents live in Monte Carlo. "You can't get a sandwich but rather a beautiful meal to experience what wine is really for," says Catherine. If you want something light, she might suggest grilled sea bass with a boiled white potato drizzled with virgin olive oil, paired with a glass of chardonnay and followed by a green salad. Want something heartier? How about smoked trout, followed by Jamaican-jerked chicken with mango chutney or wood-grilled lamb chops, and perhaps a fruit and cheese platter or one of the desserts delivered fresh from a New York bakery.

The choice of eight entrées on the à la carte menu changes weekly. On Friday nights in summer, the winery offers weekly theme dinners. Dinner is served weekends the rest of the year.

Day or night, the experience is a delicious, sensual taste of the French countryside in northeastern Connecticut.

(860) 974-3549. www.sharpehill.com. Lunch by reservation, Friday-Sunday in summer, Sunday in winter, seatings at noon and 3. Entrées, $16.95 to $24.95.

Dinner by reservation, Friday at 6:30 or 7, second Friday of the month in summer, every Friday and Saturday in winter. Entrées, $24 to $30.

The Vanilla Bean Café, 450 Deerfield Road (Junction of Routes 169, 44 and 97), Pomfret.

This popular little café in a 150-year-old barn is run by Barry Jessurun and siblings Eileen (Bean) and Brian, with occasional appearances by the rest of the family.

Here is a true place, where the turkey sandwich is "not that awful turkey roll," says the blackboard menu, but "the real thing, roasted here at the Bean." Ditto for the albacore tuna sandwich, the house-smoked meats, the spicy lentil or falafel burgers, the award-winning chili, Brian's signature fish cakes and the hearty soups (ham and bean, fish chowder, chicken gumbo). The dinner menu might include a large bean burrito, chicken teriyaki with vegetables, smoked mozzarella and basil ravioli, plus blackboard specials.

Diners partake at tables beneath an eighteen-foot-high ceiling in one room containing the food counter and an aquarium or in a larger side room with a piano for musical entertainment on weekends. The entertainment proved so popular that the Bean added a third room beyond with sofas and overstuffed chairs. Beer and wine, espresso and cappuccino are featured.

(860) 928-1562. www.vanillabeancafe.com. Entrées, $11 to $16. Open Monday and Tuesday 7 to 3, Wednesday-Friday 7 to 8, weekends 8 to 8, to 9 on music nights and in summer.

Diversions

Heritage Corridor. Much of the Quiet Corner was designated a National Heritage Corridor in 1994. The area's 25 hill and mill towns are cooperating with the National Park Service to promote regional greenways and preserve the rural quality of life from encroaching development. On the annual Walking Weekend each Columbus Day Weekend, experts in their fields guide upwards of 3,000 people on a total of 45 walks, visiting towns, farms, forests, parks and more.

A booklet called **"Hill Towns and Mill Villages,"** prepared by the Association of Northeastern Connecticut Historical Societies, is a helpful adjunct for touring rural Woodstock, Pomfret, Brooklyn and Canterbury as well as the nearby mill villages of Thompson, Putnam, Killingly and Plainfield. We particularly enjoy "The Street" lined with academic buildings, churches and gracious homes in Pomfret, the

Woodstock Hill green with a three-state view available behind Woodstock Academy, and the stunning Thompson Hill common.

Other little treasures are the spireless **Old Trinity Church** in Brooklyn, the oldest Episcopal church now standing in the oldest diocese in the country (open some summer afternoons but used only once a year on All Saints Day); the one-room law office of Daniel Putnam Tyler in Brooklyn, and the brick one-room **Quassett School** in Woodstock. The Brooklyn and Woodstock fairs are among the nation's oldest.

A favorite driving tour follows Scenic Route 169 which slices north-south through the heart of this region. Buildings and land along both sides have been placed on the National Register. The 32-mile stretch is the longest officially designated scenic road in Connecticut and one of the nation's ten most scenic as designated by Scenic America.

Roseland Cottage, 556 Route 169, Woodstock.

Roses and the Fourth of July were the twin passions of Woodstock native Henry C. Bowen, a New York merchant and publisher who planted a rose garden outside his summer house, upholstered much of its furniture in pink and named it Roseland Cottage. To his wild pink Gothic Revival mansion trimmed in gingerbread for his famous Independence Day celebrations came the day's luminaries, among them Ulysses S. Grant, Benjamin Harrison, Rutherford B. Hayes and William McKinley. The house, its furnishings and pink parterre garden remain much as they were in the 19th century. In the rear barn is the oldest extant bowling alley in a private residence; balls of varying sizes line the chute.

(860) 928-4074. Open Wednesday-Sunday 11 to 5, June to mid-October. Adults, $4.

The Prudence Crandall Museum, Routes 14 and 169, Canterbury.

The site of New England's first black female academy has a fascinating history to reveal. Asked to educate their children, Prudence Crandall ran afoul of townspeople when she admitted a black girl in 1833. They withdrew their children, so she ran a boarding school for "young ladies and misses of color" until she was hounded out of town. Now a museum, the house is interesting for its architecture and exhibits on 19th-century Canterbury, blacks and Miss Crandall. It was closed for part of 2003 because of state fiscal problems, but reopened on a reduced schedule.

(860) 546-9916. Open Wednesday-Sunday 10 to 4:30, February to mid-December. Adults, $2.

Sharpe Hill Vineyard, 108 Wade Road, Pomfret.

The first grapes were planted in 1992, and already the wines produced by winemaker Howard Bursen have won their share of world-class medals. Steven Vollweiler, a New York business owner of German and French parentage, scoured the Northeast to find a microclimate perfect for the growing of wine grapes. He found it in the back of beyond on a 100-acre hill in an unlikely corner of Connecticut and planted what his wife Catherine calls "noble grapes to achieve grand cru status." They built a big rust-colored barn to hold winemaking equipment and an 18th-century-style taproom furnished with antiques for tastings. Next came an outdoor wine garden for lunch and an attached tavern to serve gourmet meals (see Dining Spots) to fulfill their passion for antiques, wine and food.

The Vollweilers' 25 acres of chardonnay, pinot blanc, vignoles, St. Croix and cabernet franc grapes gave their winemaker plenty to work with. Bursen, a Cornell-trained viticulturalist who earlier was involved in Pomfret's pioneering but short-lived Hamlet Hill Winery, masterminds production of wines that have upstaged California's in blind tastings. Sharpe Hill's honeyed vignoles and its crisp reserve chardonnay were rated two of the Northeast's best wines by Wine Spectator in 2002. Seven wines sell at the winery from $9.99 for the crisp semi-dry Ballet of Angels to $19.99 for the late-harvest vignoles. After finally reaching the place, we couldn't leave without acquiring at least one bottle of the chardonnay.

(860) 974-3549. www.sharpehill.com. Wine tastings, Friday-Sunday 11 to 5.

Shopping. Until the Putnam Antiques District emerged, shopping was centered in South Woodstock. **Scranton's Shops,** a ramble of rooms in an 1878 blacksmith shop, is full of country wares from more than 90 local artisans. The array is mind-boggling, and we defy anyone to get out without a purchase. Nearby, **The Livery Shops** and **Garden Gate Florist** offer more small rooms given over to floral arrangements and local artisans who show their wares on consignment. At one visit, the impressive, one-of-a-kind items included an amusing picnic dish set with flies and ants painted on, the striking dishes of Majilly Designs, and the watercolors of innkeeper Tom McCobb, one of which inspired a surprised "hey, that's my house" from our tour guide. Other shoppers like **Coco's Cottage** for clothing and gifts, the **Flying Carpet Studio** for handcrafted rugs and canvases, and **Resourceful Judith** for garden ornaments. The **Gathering Basket** is a fresh food market and deli, and **Java Jive** offers lunch as well as coffee and music.

In the center of Pomfret is **Martha's Herbary,** featuring herbal gifts and garden accessories.

Extra Special

The Putnam Antiques District. A major antiques district, with more than 500 dealers and twenty shops, has emerged in downtown Putnam. It started in 1991 when Jere Cohen restored an old department store at Main and Front streets into the **Antiques Marketplace,** renting space to 250 dealers on three floors and producing the largest group showroom in Connecticut. More than a dozen antiques stores quickly followed. Word spread that here was the antiques capital of New England, if not the entire Northeast, stocking an incredible array of goods from tag-sale trinkets to fine furniture. The entire scene draws noted collectors and designers as well as dealers and common folk. On one floor of the 22,000-square-foot marketplace, Jere Cohen shows the largest selection of antique Stickley furniture in New England at his **Mission Oak Shop.** Down the street, the 30,000-square-foot **G.A. Renshaw Architecturals** features architectural antiques, furniture, salvage items and other major pieces in a variety of period rooms. **The Great Atlantic Auction Company** offers bars, fountains and statues for restaurant interiors. A former drug store has been turned into **Jeremiah's,** a large multi-dealer shop, now full of odds and ends. A former bank building has been transformed into the suave **Antiques Unlimited,** purveyor of quality furniture, accessories and silver, some at rather substantial prices. A camera shop became **The Little Museum Company.** A former A&P supermarket is now **Pink House Antiques,** crammed to the rafters with tag-sale schlock. British antiques and books, along with such hard-to-find foods as haggis, bridies and salad cream, turn up at **Mrs. Bridges' Pantry,** which operates a tearoom daily except Monday. Poke around town and you'll find your own discoveries.

Oliver Cromwell warship was launched in Essex from what is now Steamboat Dock.

Essex and Old Lyme, Conn.

River Towns, Arts and Charm

Nearing the sea after lazing 400 miles through four states, the Connecticut River wends and weaves between forested hillsides and sandy shores. Finally it pauses, almost delta-like, in the sheltered coves and harbors of Essex and Old Lyme before emptying into Long Island Sound.

A sand bar blocked the kind of development that has urbanized other rivers where they meet the ocean. Indeed, the Connecticut is the nation's biggest waterway without a major city at its mouth.

It is in this tranquil setting that Essex was settled in 1635, its harbor a haven for shipbuilding in the past and for yachting in modern times. From Essex the first American warship, the Oliver Cromwell, was launched in time for the Revolution. From Essex, leading yachtsmen sail the Atlantic today.

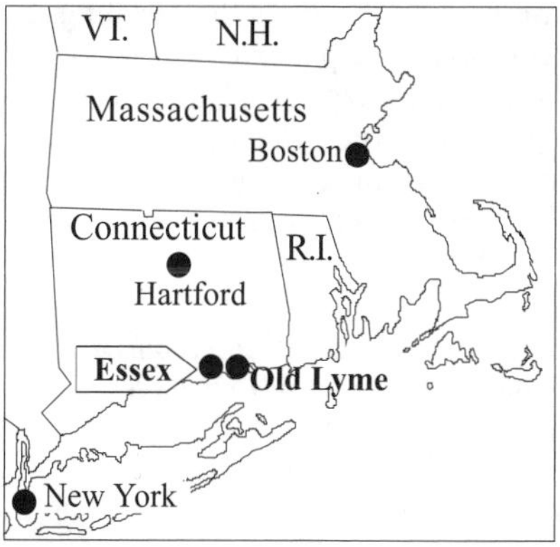

Touted by the New Yorker magazine as "a mint-condition 18th century town," Essex relives its past in the Connecticut River Museum at Steamboat Dock, in the boatworks and yacht clubs along its harbor, in the lively Tap Room at the Griswold Inn, and in the lovely old homes along Main Street and River Road.

Across the river from Essex and its shoreline neighbor Old Saybrook is Old

Lyme, which has less of a river feel but exudes a charm of its own. In a pastoral area that is now part of an historic district, artists gathered at the turn of the century in the mansion of Florence Griswold, daughter of a boat captain. The American Impressionist movement was the result, and the arts are celebrated and flourish here to this day.

Just inland from historic Essex along the Falls River are Centerbrook and Ivoryton. They and Old Lyme provide a setting in which fine inns and restaurants thrive. Up river are Deep River, Chester, Hadlyme and East Haddam, unspoiled towns steeped in history.

You still have to drive the long way around to get from one side of the river to the other, unless you take the tiny ferry that has been plying between Chester and Hadlyme for more than 200 years. The Valley Railroad's steam train and riverboat link the towns as in the past, offering visitors scenic ways to see both river and shore.

Inn Spots

Copper Beech Inn, 46 Main Street, Ivoryton 06442.

This imposing mansion, shaded by the oldest copper beech tree in Connecticut, has been enhanced by new owners Ian and Barbara Phillips, who formerly owned the historic Bradley Inn at Pemaquid Point in Maine. After luring a chef from Nantucket and extensively refurbishing of the dining facilities (see Dining Spots), they started upgrading the accommodations.

Upstairs in the main inn are three period guest rooms and a new suite. The most deluxe is the elegant master bedroom, big enough to include a kingsize carved mahogany poster bed, a couple of sitting areas and a new gas fireplace. Its renovated bath has been tiled in marble and boasts an Ultra Bath hydro-massage tub – the first of many planned for the inn – and a heated floor. Billed as the honeymoon suite, it's the only room without television. Another room here with queensize poster bed and antique soaking tub has a new gas fireplace, while a third room has a queensize sleigh bed with a clawfoot tub and new rainforest shower. A new suite has a king bedroom and a sitting room.

Nine deluxe guest rooms are located in the carriage house behind the inn. Each has a jacuzzi tub and french doors onto an outdoor deck or balcony overlooking the gardens. Second-floor rooms have cathedral ceilings with exposed beams. Mahogany queensize beds, club chairs, TVs and telephones are the norm. The first three newly renovated rooms here have marble baths with radiant floor heating and hydro-massage tubs, which the innkeeper considers a step above the old jacuzzi tubs (and charges accordingly). Two rooms have kingsize beds. The furnishings here, as opposed to other large inns in the area, can be described as sumptuous.

Guests relax in an elegant, wraparound solarium in the front of the inn. A continental-plus breakfast buffet of fresh fruit, cereals, croissants and pastries is set out here, augmented lately with a couple of prepared egg dishes such as coddled eggs or quiche.

(860) 767-0330 or (888) 809-2056. www.copperbeechinn.com. Twelve rooms and one suite with private baths. Doubles, $175 to $335 weekends, $155 to $315 midweek.

The Inn & Vineyard at Chester, 318 West Main St., Chester 06412.

The Inn at Chester, a hostelry built in 1983 around the historic 1776 John B.

Century-old maple tree shades expansive new deck at The Inn & Vineyard at Chester.

Parmelee House on twenty rural acres west of town, has a new name and a new look. The official name now is amended by a small vineyard, but the more significant name is that of owner Edward Safdie – as in "Edward Safdie is back." That's how the initial press release announced the reopening of the renovated inn in 2003, as if that would tell it all.

It tells a lot. Ed Safdie is the nationally known restaurateur, hotelier, spa innovator and cookbook author who in 1995 sold the nearby Norwich Inn & Spa he had created in the image of his famed Sonoma Mission Inn & Spa in California. A resident of Old Lyme, he came out of retirement in 2003 to purchase the fading Inn at Chester and remake it in his own image and that of his wife Carlene, an Old Lyme antiques dealer.

He closed the inn for three months to renovate every bathroom and refurbish every guest room. The restaurant was reborn (see Dining Spots), the tavern redecorated, an enormous outdoor terrace added and the White Barn function room retooled for a planned Connecticut wine tasting center. The last is typical of the activities and promotions he envisioned to make the inn a destination for visitors.

And, yes, he planted a small vineyard of vidal blanc grapes – "the first organic vineyard in New England," he said – behind and to the side of the inn for harvesting in 2007, estimating 500 bottles for on-premises consumption.

The inn has 44 guest rooms and suites in two wings of 1980s construction. Carlene Safdie and fellow antiques dealer Tom Vanderbeck of Hadlyme decorated in a minimalist, country elegant look with pencil-post beds, Eldred Wheeler furniture, French toile and Schumacher fabrics, and Berber carpeting. Most rooms contain a wing chair and a windsor chair. Two rooms come with twin beds and five with kingsize; the rest are queensize, a few with canopies. Each room is different within the prevailing theme. Walls are generally painted in light colors, although some beneath mansard roofs on the third floors are wallpapered, even on the ceilings.

One room and a suite have fireplaces. French doors were added to sixteen rooms on the main floor, opening onto private decks and patios. Each room has a flat-screen TV, data port and cordless telephone (the last can follow you to the bathroom, the lounge, the outdoor terrace or wherever, Ed Safdie points out). The newly tiled baths have pedestal sinks and massage showerheads. Clear plastic makeup kits hold quite an array of spa-quality toiletries from Gilchrist & Soames.

Besides the various restaurant and function venues, the main floor holds Carlene Safdie's small antiques shop and some very public sitting areas furnished with priceless antiques. One is in the lobby and a second is set up in a row along the main corridor. Another is beside a soaring fireplace in what Ed calls the "grand reception area" leading to the dining room and tavern. On the lower level is a library/game room with a billiards table and two stone fireplaces.

A continental breakfast of fruit, granola, cereal and house-baked pastries is served in the tavern. The dining room offers a spa menu, as popularized in Safdie's bestsellers: *Spa Food* and *New Spa Food.*

"I didn't want to do another spa," says the man called the father of the American spa movement. "Spas are everywhere these days." Instead, he planned facilities for the wellness-minded individual, including exercise trails for walking or jogging and hiking, a new tennis court and wellness treatment rooms for relaxation or deep tissue massage services.

Ed Safdie, who has sold all his other hotel and restaurant properties from California to Monte Carlo, was on hand here seven days a week to ensure the success of his latest venture.

(860) 526-9541. Fax (860) 526-1607. www.innatchester.com. Thirty-nine rooms and five suites with private baths. Doubles, $145 to $295. Suites, $250 to $595.

Bee and Thistle Inn, 100 Lyme St., Old Lyme 06371.

Stately trees, gardens all around and a flower-bedecked entrance welcome visitors to this cheery yellow inn, set on five acres bordering the Lieutenant River in the historic district of Old Lyme. Built in 1756 with subsequent additions and remodeling, the structure is a delightful ramble of parlors and porches, dining rooms and guest rooms.

With sofas to sink into and fireplaces ablaze, the parlors on either side of the entry hall are inviting. On sunny days, the enclosed porches beyond are great for lingering over breakfast or lunch. The restaurant (see Dining Spots) is often cited as the most romantic in Connecticut in a country-inn kind of way.

New innkeepers Philip and Marie Abraham offer eleven upstairs guest rooms with period country furnishings. They vary in size from small with double beds to large with queensize canopy beds and loveseats. Room 2 with a queen bed has a new gas fireplace and Room 3 has a new kingsize bed. Four-poster, fishnet canopy and spool beds are covered with quilts or afghans. Some rooms have wing chairs and ruffled curtains, and one even has a washstand full of flowers. Nooks are full of games and old books are all around.

Breakfast, previously available for an extra charge, is now complimentary for inn guests. It's served on the sunny dining porches, a great place to start the day. There's a choice of two entrees, perhaps eggs benedict and almond-encrusted French toast or shirred eggs with spinach and Maine blueberry pancakes.

(860) 434-1667 or (800) 622-4946. Fax (860) 434-3402. www.beeandthistleinn.com. Eleven rooms with private baths. Doubles, $110 to $219.

Addition blends into original structure and enhances lodging at Old Lyme Inn.

Old Lyme Inn, 85 Lyme St., Box 787 B, Old Lyme 06371.

New owners have upgraded the venerable Old Lyme Inn and added sumptuous B&B accommodations in their historic home down the street. Keith and Candy Green, who moved from New York to Old Lyme in 1986, bought the elegant 1850s mansion in 2001 and revamped the restaurant operation (see Dining Spots).

Eight guest rooms in the inn's north wing are decorated in Empire or Victorian style. Marblehead mints are perched atop the oversize pillows on the canopy and four-poster beds, comfortable sofas or chairs are grouped around marble-top tables, and gleaming white bathrooms are outfitted with herbal shampoos and Dickenson's Witch Hazel made in nearby Essex. Five rooms in the older part of the inn are similarly equipped but smaller. All rooms have televisions and telephones. Most beds are cannonball or canopy queensize, two with an extra sofabed. Continental breakfast is included in the rates.

The Greens also offer four B&B rooms in their 1895 landmark home at 2 Lyme St. Called **Rooster Hall** and elegant as can be, it comes with 2,000 square feet of porches and terraces overlooking parterre gardens, a dining room set for sixteen and a third-floor recreation center with fitness equipment, billiards table and ping-pong table. A rear suite is equipped with a kitchenette and a whirlpool tub. The enormous master suite has two stunning baths – hers white and frilly with a whirlpool tub and his, dark and clubby with a central shower enclosed in glass.

(860) 434-2600 or (800) 434-5352. Fax (860) 434-5352. www.oldlymeinn.com. Thirteen rooms with private baths. Doubles, $165 to $185 weekends, $135 to $165 midweek. B&B, four rooms with private baths, doubles $175 to $235. Two-night minimum, May-Labor Day.

Riverwind, 209 Main St., Deep River 06417.

A sense of history pervades this charming, atmospheric B&B, and new owners Roger and Nicky Plante seek to capitalize on it. Taking over in 2002 from the longtime owner who had infused it with an eclectic Southern air reflecting her Virginia background, the Plantes redecorated Riverwind more in keeping with their Massachusetts roots. Instead of the wooden and stuffed animals, knickknacks and memorabilia of earlier days, "we wanted a more simple, country, Shaker look," said Nicky.

The house feels older than its 1850 date because a rear addition was built to look 100 years older than the existing 1850 inn. The result is a seamless blend of old and new.

Riverwind is unusual in that it offers eight guest rooms and an equal number of common areas that afford space for mingling or privacy. The heart of the house is the beamed keeping room and dining room with a huge fireplace in the new/old section at the rear. In front, the Plantes brightened up the formerly dark living room and rejuvenated the library and game room, as well as an upstairs sitting room with a fireplace and herbs hanging from the beams. The enclosed front porch has been opened up and made cheerier with a lineup of white rocking chairs.

Bedrooms on two floors vary in configuration and style. Six have queen beds and two have one or two double beds. All are air-conditioned and appointed with period antiques and stenciling. The blue and white Hearts and Flowers Room comes with flowers on the bedroom wallpaper, hearts on the bathroom wallpaper and a specially made, heart-filled, stained-glass window. Zelda's is a two-room suite that's delightfully Gatsby. Every room is charming, but the ultimate is the rear Champagne and Roses Room with a private balcony, a bathroom with a shower and a Japanese steeping tub, a queensize half tester bed canopied in pink and blue floral fabrics, and a sofa that converts into an extra bed. Others might prefer the new, third-floor Moonlit Suite. It comes with a mission-style queen bed and a fullsize sleigh bed, a brick fireplace, double jacuzzi tub and satellite TV.

From a twelve-foot stone cooking fireplace in the keeping room comes a variety of breakfast treats. Puffed french toast stuffed with cream cheese and blueberries, belgian waffles or egg casserole might follow fresh fruit in the form of soup, salad or parfait and homemade breads or coffee cake. Guests are welcomed with sherry and baked snacks in the afternoon. In cool weather, mulled apple cider awaits by the crackling fireplaces at this hospitable B&B.

(860) 526-2014. Fax (860) 526-0875. www.riverwindinn.com. Six rooms and two suites with private baths. Doubles, $110 to $210. Suites, $160 to $210. Children over 12. Two-night minimum weekends.

Griswold Inn, 36 Main St., Essex 06426.

The Griswold Inn has historic appeal matched by few inns in this country. There's the requisite taproom containing a steamboat-Gothic bar, potbelly stove and antique popcorn machine – Lucius Beebe called it probably the most handsome barroom in America. Copious meals and a celebrated hunt breakfast are served in four dining rooms that are a kaleidoscope of Americana. And the floors in some of the guest rooms list to port or starboard, as you might expect of an inn dating to 1776, when it was built as Connecticut's first four-story structure.

Commandeered by the British during the War of 1812, the inn was found to be long on charm but short on facilities – an observation that some think holds true to this day. All 31 guest accommodations in the main inn, the annex and in houses across the street come with private baths, air conditioning and telephones, and all but nine in the annex have been enhanced cosmetically of late. That means updated

Griswold Square complex in Essex faces historic Griswold Inn across the street.

bath fixtures, fabric window treatments and wide-plank hardwood floors with oriental rugs.

Two rooms we saw upstairs in the inn covered a range from standard facing the street (twin beds and a small bathroom with glass-door shower) to a suite with queen bed, sitting alcove with a convertible loveseat lit by a lamp so dim as to be useless for anything but romance, and again a bath with glass-door shower.

Six suites with fireplaces across the street in a retail complex known as Griswold Square are the most deluxe, in a comfortable and historic way. Two above the Red Pepper shop each have a bedroom and a sitting room with gas fireplace. The Garden Suite is a two-story house involving a large room upstairs with two double beds and, downstairs, a living room with sofabed, wet bar, dining table and a bathroom. It served as the honeymoon suite until the Fenwick Suite opened next door. The Fenwick's main room is equipped with a kingsize bed, a brick fireplace and two wing chairs in opposite corners. An intimate sitting room with sofa and club chair leads to a large bath with clawfoot tub and separate shower.

A complimentary continental breakfast buffet of juice, coffee and danish pastry is put out in the Steamboat Room section of the restaurant.

The "Gris," as it's known to neighbors and travelers from near and far, serves hundreds of meals a day (see Dining Spots), and the Sunday hunt breakfast is an institution. Before and after dinner, the Tap Room is a happy hubbub of banjo players, a singalong pianist and sea chantey singers, depending on the night. You can snack from the raw bar, sample popcorn from the old red machine, hoist a few brews and readily imagine you've been transported 200 years into the past.

(860) 767-1776. Fax (860) 767-0481. www.griswoldinn.com. Fifteen rooms and sixteen suites with private baths. June-October: doubles $105 to $140, suites $165 to $225. Rest of year: doubles $95 to $125, suites $150 to $200.

Deacon Timothy Pratt House B&B, 325 Main St., Old Saybrook 06475.

Listed on the National Register, this 1746 center-chimney Colonial once was the home of the deacon at the pillared Congregational meetinghouse across the street.

It served five generations of Pratts and now houses an expanding B&B. Former electrical engineer Shelley Nobile opened with four guest quarters and in 2003 added three more rooms in the former James Pharmacy building she acquired next door.

The main house holds four spacious rooms, each with canopied queensize bed and jacuzzi tub and all but one with a working fireplace. All have TVs and stereo/CD players. A fishnet canopy bed is angled from the corner in the Sunrise Room, which has two Queen Anne wingback recliners and an oversize jacuzzi. The premier accommodation here is a suite with a carved four-poster rice queen bed, working fireplace, french doors opening onto a TV room with a day bed and an extra-large bathroom with a double jacuzzi.

Similar facilities and amenities went into the three newest rooms next door, where Shelley was continuing to operate the James Gallery, a gift shop and an old-fashioned ice cream parlor and soda fountain dating to 1896. Two on the second floor have vaulted ceilings and working fireplaces.

A pleasant living room is furnished with period pieces and decorative accents characteristic of the rest of the house.

A full breakfast is served by candlelight on weekends in a formal dining room with an extra-long table for twelve. The fare might be pancakes or waffles one day and a special egg dish the next. A continental breakfast buffet is offered on weekdays. A sideboard holds afternoon beverages, cookies and decanters of port.

(860) 395-1229. Fax (860) 395-4748. www.connecticut-bed-and-breakfast.com. Eight rooms and one suite with private baths. July-October: doubles, $180 to $220 weekends, $120 to $150 midweek. Rest of year: doubles, $160 to $200 weekends, $100 to $130 midweek. Children over 6 accepted midweek. Two-night minimum weekends.

Bishopsgate Inn, Goodspeed Landing, Box 290, East Haddam 06423.

Situated down a long driveway a block from the Goodspeed Opera House, this 1818 Colonial house was built by an Essex shipbuilder and once occupied by a Goodspeed.

Now it's lovingly run by energetic Colin and Jane Kagel, who first became acquainted with Connecticut while he was with the U.S. Submarine Service in Groton, and their son Colin, wife Lisa and young daughter.

"Ours is a real family enterprise," says Jane. And a winning one, at that. The house is full of books, artworks and family collections. Among them are Jane's silver urns in an open cupboard above the huge fireplace in the living room and Colin's prized canvas-backed working decoys on a shelf in the upstairs sitting room.

The six guest rooms with featherbeds and antique furnishings are decorated with character. Four have working fireplaces. The most dramatic is the Director's Suite, with a beamed cathedral ceiling, a kingsize brass and iron bed, its own balcony and a dressing area off a theatrical bathroom with lights around the mirror of the double vanity and its own sauna.

Lisa cooks full breakfasts in the 1860 kitchen, which has a small fireplace and baking oven. Her crustless spinach quiche is a favorite, as are her waffles and eggs benedict. All are served by candlelight at a long table in a beamed dining room where there's a lot to look at.

(860) 873-1677. www.bishopsgateinn.com. Six rooms with private baths. Doubles, $105 to $135. Suite, $165.

Dining Spots

Gabrielle's, 78 Main St., Centerbrook.

This Victorian-era house with a gazebo-like front porch has been a culinary landmark in the area since 1979, first as Fine Bouche, a French restaurant and patisserie, and later as Steve's Centerbrook Café. Gabrielle's emerged in 2003 when master chef Steve Wilkinson sold the property he had occupied for nearly a quarter century to concentrate on his newest culinary endeavor, Esteva in Guilford.

A trio of new owners tore down walls and turned what had been a sun porch, several small rooms and alcoves into more open areas nicely separated by dividers. They painted the walls ecru with white trim, and added stunning art works and green plants for color. They named it for the daughter of one of the owners.

Gabrielle's is a chic and stylish setting for food that follows suit. Co-owner Michael Achille, the chef who studied culinary arts at the Rhode Island School of Design, offers a diverse menu of contemporary and artistic American fare.

Meals begin with the arrival of a wire container of crusty breads, to dip into olive oil laced with tarragon and poured from a mini-carafe. The breads, great on their own, were perfect later for sopping up the sensational buttery wine and garlic broth in which the "moules and frites" arrived at lunch. The array of P.E.I. mussels was so abundant that the bowl provided for shells had to be emptied and resupplied twice. The frites were unusual strands of fries, so remarkably thin they were difficult to handle but addictive when paired with the tarragon aioli dip. The broth turned out to be more distinctive than the day's hearty chicken, butternut and lentil soup. The cornmeal-crusted fried oysters with chipotle aioli was a good follow-up.

These and other mainstays on the lunch menu turn up as appetizers and small plates at night. The fairly extensive dinner menu also offers salads, thin-crust pizzas and fifteen entrées from pan-seared sea scallops with sake-mirin glaze and Asian vegetables to grilled New York strip steak with roasted walnut and gorgonzola butter. Thai-style seafood stew, frenched chicken breast stuffed with goat cheese, and penne with a veal and pork ragu indicate the kitchen's range.

Dessert choices proved less interesting at our visit. Among them were white and dark chocolate mousse, crème brûlée, linzer torte and apple-almond tart with french vanilla ice cream. The wine list is affordably priced and holds good values.

(860) 767-2440. www.gabrielles.net. Entrées, $21 to $25. Lunch, Tuesday-Friday and Sunday 11:30 to 3. Dinner, Tuesday-Sunday from 5 to 9 or 9:30.

Restaurant du Village, 59 Main St., Chester.

Here's as provincial French a restaurant as you will find in this country, from its canopied blue facade with ivy geraniums spilling out of flower boxes to the sheer white-curtained windows and french doors opening onto the side brick entryway. The 40-seat dining room is charming in its simplicity: a few French oil paintings, white linens, carafes of wild flowers and a votive candle on each table.

Alsatian chef Michel Keller and his Culinary Institute-trained American wife Cynthia run the highly rated establishment with T.L.C. A third-generation pastry chef, Michel bakes perhaps the best French bread in this country. Among his appetizers, standouts are the cassoulet, a small copper casserole filled with sautéed shrimp in a light curry sauce; the croustade with grilled vegetables, and escargots with shiitake mushrooms in puff pastry. We also like the baked French goat cheese on herbed salad greens with garlic croutons.

Main courses could be pan-seared tuna steak topped with tapenade, rabbit flamande, roast duck with kumquats, tournedos of beef with a cognac and green peppercorn sauce, and Cynthia's specialty, a stew of veal, lamb and pork with leeks and potatoes. Typical among the changing desserts are an open fruit tart with blueberries and peaches in almond cream, a gratin of passion fruit, paris-brest and soufflé glacé.

(860) 526-5301. Entrées, $27 to $31. Dinner, Tuesday-Saturday 5 to 9, Sunday 5 to 8:15. Closed Tuesday in winter.

Copper Beech Inn, 46 Main Street, Ivoryton.

Surrounded by gardens and shaded by the largest copper beech tree in Connecticut, this venerable inn has four elegant, newly refurbished dining rooms. The chandeliered main Ivoryton Room, formerly rather stiff and austere, has been warmed up in a rich and sumptuous Victorian motif. The paneled Comstock Room with a beamed ceiling retains the look of the billiards parlor that it once was. Between the two is a pretty garden porch with a handful of romantic tables for two. Windows in the clubby blue Copper Beech Room with its cozy bar afford views of the great tree outside. Tables in each dining room are set with crisp white cloths and dressed with lavish flowers.

This is a place to be pampered. Expect dinner to take a couple of hours, and pick a choice selection from the Wine Spectator award-winning cellar that gets better all the time.

The formal, contemporary French fare has been refreshed by executive chef William Von Ahnen, who moved to the Copper Beach after sixteen years at the famed Chantecleer in Nantucket, where he last served as sous chef. He is joined in the kitchen by his wife Jacqueline, who also worked at the Chantecleer and is the inn's pastry chef.

Written as always in French with English translations, the menu ranges widely from fillet of grey sole stuffed with a scallop mousse and served with a lobster claw and a lobster-ginger sauce to roasted rack of Colorado lamb with a rich red wine sauce. Indeed, all the food seems to be rich here, at least as served during a special holiday dinner following the new chef's arrival.

Ultra-rich starters were the charcuterie platter of assorted house-made pâtés and terrines, smooth and tasty when spread on Jacqueline's wonderful crusty rolls, and a puff pastry stuffed with juicy duck in wine sauce. The sautéed foie gras with a caramelized blackberry-chardonnay sauce was garnished with plump blackberries. Main courses include a fabulous lobster française, a house specialty deglazed with madeira, brandy and cream and garnished with black truffle risotto, and tasty grilled shrimp and mussels served with a pinot noir sauce and a fricassée of wild mushrooms. We barely had room left to sample the sautéed rabbit (rich), the magret and confit of duck with armagnac-laced dried plums (rich) and the veal osso buco teamed with sweetbreads (again, rich).

Not to mention Jacqueline's spectacular desserts, a chocolate ganache cake, chocolate mousse enrobed in a chocolate shell, a creamy, mixed-fruit tart and – finally – a light and ethereal tarte tatin with calvados ice cream. An after-dinner sip of single-batch bourbon sent us happily on our way with memories of a superior meal.

(860) 767-0330 or (888) 809-2056. Entrées, $23 to $39. Dinner, Tuesday-Sunday 5:30 to 9:30.

Bee and Thistle Inn welcomes guests for dining as well as lodging.

Bee and Thistle Inn, 100 Lyme St., Old Lyme.

This cheery yellow inn's highly regarded restaurant consistently wins statewide awards for romantic dining and desserts. Owner Philip Abraham, a Culinary Institute of America-trained chef, found he could not do justice to both cooking and innkeeping duties. In 2003 he brought on another CIA chef, Christopher Rydell, formerly of the Copper Beech and the Tavern at Old Sturbridge Village, to continue the culinary tradition.

Dining on the enclosed side porches overlooking the lawns is a country-style treat. Ladderback chairs are at tables with blue and white cloths or mats. Windows open to let in the breeze. Baskets hang from the ceiling in one, and hanging plants thrive in the other.

Luncheon choices are generally of the brunch and dinner variety. Instead of soups and sandwiches expect substantial salads and entrées from mushroom strudel and seafood stew to fillet of sole and grilled tournedos of beef.

Candlelight dinners are served on the porches or in a small rear dining room, where a jazz duo entertains on Friday nights and a harpist plays on Saturdays.

Regulars like to start with cocktails in the living room as they peruse the menu. Entrées range from ale-steamed haddock garnished with clam fritters to roast loin of lamb with thyme glaze and mushroom ragoût. The crab cakes with saffron aioli and the filet mignon here were sensational, their simple names failing to do justice to the complexities of their preparation or that of their accompaniments. We also enjoyed the thin-sliced, rare breast of duck served on a passion fruit puree with a spiced pear beggar's purse.

Start with the house-cured gravlax with an English cucumber salad or the escargots in puff pastry. Finish with the ginger-scented pear dumpling, a triple-nut bourbon tartlet, chocolate truffle torte or one of the homemade ice creams and sorbets.

(860) 434-1667 or (800) 622-4946. www.beeandthistleinn.com. Entrées, $23 to $30. Lunch, Wednesday-Saturday 11:30 to 2. Dinner, Wednesday-Sunday from 5:30. Sunday brunch, 11 to 2.

The Inn & Vineyard at Chester, 318 West Main St., Chester.

New owner Edward Safdie has run twenty celebrity restaurants from California to Monaco, so he knows good food – and demands it. That's why he devoted much of his early effort here to expanding and enhancing the restaurant operation.

The 50-seat tavern was totally refashioned in a modern, drop-dead red motif, with leather banquettes, windsor chairs and upholstered chairs at a polished wood bar. The main post and beam dining room in the 200-year-old barn retains its rough-hewn walls, fieldstone fireplace, wrought-iron chandeliers and soaring windows. Up to 150 diners can be seated here, in the new loft or in the adjacent Hunt and John D. Parmelee rooms. Outside beneath a century-old maple tree is a new, three-tiered deck seating 150 diners overlooking a pond and a fountain.

Safdie installed a new $200,000 kitchen and gave free rein to executive chef Michael Fichtel, formerly sous chef at Miche Mache in Stamford and the Steelhead Grill Restaurant in Pittsburgh. They seek the best ingredients available, flying in greens from Ohio, lamb from Colorado and tuna from Hawaii.

The basil-crusted rack of lamb and the herb-seared ahi tuna in a spicy Thai vegetable broth, in fact, quickly became signature dinner dishes. Other entrées could be grilled Hawaiin opah with mango puree, rosemary-scented Pennsylvania free-range chicken roasted on the rotisserie and seared venison medallions with lingonberry sauce.

Featured dessert at our visit was a fall apple sampler: a mini-apple pie, caramelized apple bread pudding, apple crisp and a dollop of vanilla bean ice cream. Bailey's Irish crème brûlée and homemade ice creams were others.

Meat loaf with truffled mashed potatoes and vegetables was the hit of the season in Jack's Tavern. You can get anything from a grilled chicken sandwich with arugula, prosciutto and brie to grilled Atlantic salmon with herbed beurre blanc here for lunch or dinner. Both the dining room and tavern menus are available seasonally on the Maple Terrace, which also has a barbecue menu.

(860) 526-9541. Entrées, $16.95 to $32, tavern $12.50 to $21.95. Lunch, Tuesday-Saturday 11:30 to 2:30. Dinner, Tuesday-Sunday 5:30 to 9:30. Sunday brunch, 11 to 2.

Old Lyme Inn, 85 Lyme St., Old Lyme.

Thrice given three-star ratings by the New York Times and its desserts featured in successive issues of Bon Appétit magazine, the Old Lyme Inn has been a mecca for traveling gourmands since 1976. Under new owners Keith and Candace Green, expectations were high but results inconsistent. A general manager and a new chef came aboard in 2003 following a scathing review in the New York Times.

The traditional Victoriana has been eliminated in favor of a stylish Federal decor the Greens felt more appropriate for Old Lyme. They produced The Grill, casual but smart, white-tablecloth dining areas that are open daily, and turned the vast and formerly austere restaurant into the smaller and warmer Winslow Dining Room and Lounge, open weekends for dinner and live piano music. The grill is actually three dining venues seating a total of 75: the original tap room graced with Old Lyme Impressionist paintings, a parlor with four corner tables and a fireplace, and the center hall (formerly the lobby), now divided by partitions into cozy dining areas.

The Greens created the new menus for what Keith calls "hearty American food," from a prime steak burger (yes, a burger on the dinner menu at the Old Lyme Inn) to a classic beef wellington. The signature poussin, a whole baby chicken roasted with garlic and rosemary, arrives with all the trimmings of a mini-Thanksgiving dinner. Grilled red snapper, lobster pot pie and grilled pheasant breast and leg confit are among the possibilities. Appetizers are more exotic, from venison soup and oyster stew to steak tartare, pan-seared foie gras and caviar three ways. In addition to the regular menu, which is available in both grill and dining room, the inn offers a prime steak menu, with sides in the steakhouse idiom.

Desserts include crème caramel, chocolate mousse and mocha butter crunch pie.

(860) 434-2600 or (800) 434-5352. Entrées, $17.50 to $36.50. Lunch, Monday-Saturday noon to 2. Dinner nightly, 6 to 9 or 10. Sunday, brunch 11 to 3, dinner from 11.

Griswold Inn, 36 Main St., Essex.

Even when its kitchen was closed for nearly a year as a new one was built, the famed "Gris" kept going with an abbreviated menu. You'd expect no less from an institution that since its founding in 1776 had served "precisely 3.1416 times the number of meals which had been cumulatively prepared in all the steamships of the Cunard Line, the dirigibles Graf Zeppelin and Hindenburg, and the Orient Express," as a statement to customers noted.

A meal at the Gris, whether prepared in old kitchen or new, is an experience in Americana. There's much to see in a variety of dining rooms: the important collection of Antonio Jacobsen marine oils in the dark paneled Library, the Currier and Ives steamboat prints in the Covered Bridge Room (actually fashioned from a New Hampshire covered bridge), the riverboat memorabilia in the Steamboat Room, the musket-filled Gun Room with 55 pieces dating to the 15th century. Together, they rank as one of the outstanding marine art collections in America.

The menu is a mixed bag of seafood, meat and game, ranging from pesto-crusted sea bass and sea scallops and lobster in puff pastry to chicken pot pie, prime rib and New York strip steak with house-made worcestershire sauce. Three versions of the inn's patented 1776 sausages are served as a mixed grill with sauerkraut and German potato salad at dinner. They're in even more demand for lunch, when you also can get eggs benedict or Welsh rarebit, a goat cheese and arugula salad or yankee pot roast.

At our latest lunch, a wicker swan full of packaged crackers helped sustain us as we waited (and waited) for our orders of crostini and shepherd's pie. The oil lamps were lit at noon, the place was hopping and the atmosphere was cheery on a dank autumn day. That we remember, more than the food.

The ever-popular Sunday hunt breakfast ($16.95) is an enormous buffet of dishes ranging from potato-encrusted cod, hunter's stew and corned beef hash to scrambled eggs and a soufflé of grits and cheddar cheese.

(860) 767-1776. Entrées, $18.50 to $27. Lunch, Monday-Saturday 11:45 to 3. Dinner, 5:30 to 9 or 10. Sunday, hunt breakfast 11 to 2:30, dinner 4:30 to 9.

Sherlock's 221, 9 Halls Road, Old Lyme Marketplace, Hall's Road, Old Lyme.

This wine bar and grill in the Old Lyme Marketplace strip plaza occupies the storefront space formerly known as Anne's Bistro. It took its new name in 2003 following a contest among customers who linked the name of owner Lynne Sherlock with the address of detective Sherlock Holmes.

Customers praise the variety of Mediterranean-inspired offerings, from caramelized scallops drizzled with white truffle oil on roasted beet risotto to rack of lamb with mango mint slaw. Favorite appetizers are the crab cake with rémoulade sauce and grilled corn relish and the lobster and scallop sausage simmered in a lobster sauce.

The signature pasta choice is sautéed lobster and crab with shiitake mushrooms on fresh rolled fettuccine. About half the entrées and most of the pastas also are available at lunch, which offers interesting salads and sandwiches. Specialty cakes and desserts come from the grill's bakery adjunct.

There's a wine bar at the back of the dining room, which bears a stylish Mediterranean bistro look in earth colors. A few tables are outside for sidewalk dining in season.

(860) 434-9837. Entrées, $17 to $24. Lunch, Tuesday-Saturday 11:30 to 2:30. Dinner Tuesday-Saturday 5 to 9 or 10, Sunday 4 to 8.

The Black Seal, 15 Main St., Essex.

This appealingly nautical place is good for casual dining and local color. All the decorative items hanging along the walls and from the ceilings of the front tavern and the rear dining room could distract one from the food, of which there's something for everyone day and night.

Basically the same fare is offered at lunch and dinner, though lunch brings more sandwiches and dinner more entrées. Graze on things like chile nachos, fire-pot chili, stuffed potato skins, cajun shrimp, Rhode Island clam chowder, California burgers, and cobb and caesar salads anytime.

At night, entrées run from wok of the day to steak au poivre. Grilled tuna with caper-shallot sauce and whitefish baked in parchment paper with wine, cream and chives were specials at a recent visit. Desserts could be chocolate mousse terrine, pumpkin-praline torte and chocolate-raspberry cake.

(860) 767-0233. Entrées, $13.95 to $17.95. Lunch, daily 11:30 to 3:30, weekends to 4. Dinner, 5 to 9:30 or 10. Sunday brunch, 11:30 to 2.

La Vita Gustosa, 9 Main St., East Haddam.

Moving in 2003 from Chester into larger quarters across from the Goodspeed Musicals Opera House, this lively restaurant and bakery provided a welcome, we-try-harder alternative to the traditional Gelston House for captive theater audiences.

Chef-owner Lorenzo Cacace and his father renovated the casual main dining room with a homey Italian look and built a shiny oak bar for a new lounge and dining addition with dark wood tables they restored. Lorenzo's wife Jacqueline is the hostess, overseeing orders in the front bakery/deli and seating patrons in the dining room or on an outdoor patio.

The all-day menu is traditional Italian, offering pastas, seafood, and chicken or veal dishes by the dozen. Jacqueline recommends the fried eggplant rollatini topped with marinara, the penne alla vodka, the veal saltimbocca and the zuppa di pesce (seafood stew). Shrimp comes in six variations, from florentine to fra diavolo. All items are available in lunch or dinner portions, as are pizzas with house salad. The bakery provides breads and desserts.

(860) 873-8999. Entrées, $14.95 to $25.95. Lunch, Tuesday-Sunday 11:30 to 4. Dinner, Tuesday-Sunday 4 to 9 or 10.

Gelston House River Grill, 8 Main St., East Haddam.

The Carbone family of Hartford restaurant fame took over the white Victorian confection long known as the Gelston House and succeeded where others have failed.

The elegant main dining room is a huge enclosed porch with big windows on all sides overlooking the Connecticut River. The setting is all-important, so the mixed reviews of food and service are predictable for a busy place subject to the demands of theater-goers.

The contemporary menu is severely limited at dinner, which should mean better quality and service than the consensus indicates. Recent starters were two salads, a wild mushroom risotto, salmon cake with spicy rémoulade and mussels provençal. The six entrées ranged from salmon fillet with tomato aioli to New York strip steak with compound butter. One was a vegetarian penne dish.

The lunch menu is twice as extensive and better received. In season, the outdoor Beer Garden is popular for lunch and casual suppers.

(860) 873-1411. Entrées, $18 to $24. Lunch, Wednesday-Saturday 11:30 to 2:30. Dinner, Wednesday-Saturday, 5:30 to 9. Sunday, brunch 11 to 2:15, dinner 4 to 8.

Diversions

The Essex Waterfront. As a living and working yachting and shipbuilding town, the Essex waterfront is a center of activity. For yachtsmen, it holds some of the same cachet as Marblehead, Mass., or Oxford, Md.

Connecticut River Museum, 67 Main St., Essex.

Restored in 1975 from an 1878 steamboat warehouse, this interesting structure at Steamboat Dock is a living memorial to the Connecticut River Valley in an area from which the first American warship was launched. The main floor has changing exhibits. Upstairs, where windows on three sides afford sweeping views of the river, the permanent shipbuilding exhibit shows a full-size replica of David Bushnell's first submarine, the strange-looking American Turtle, plus a model of a Dutch explorer ship that sailed up the river in 1614.

(860) 767-8269. www.ctrivermuseum.org. Open Tuesday-Sunday, 10 to 5. Adults, $5.

The museum property also includes a small waterfront park with benches and the 1813 Hayden Chandlery, now the Thomas A. Stevens maritime research library. Just to the south off Novelty Lane are the historic Dauntless Club, the Essex Corinthian Yacht Club and the Essex Yacht Club. The historic structures here and elsewhere in town are detailed in an informative walking map, available at the Connecticut River Museum.

Uptown Essex. Besides the waterfront area, Methodist Hill at the other end of Main Street has a cluster of historic structures. Facing tiny Champlin Square is the imposing white **Pratt House** (circa 1648), restored and operated by the Essex Historical Society to show Essex as it was in yesteryear (open June-Labor Day, weekends 1 to 4, $2). The period gardens in the rear are planted with herbs and flowers typical of the 18th century. The society also operates the adjacent **Hill's Academy Museum** (1833), an early boarding school that now displays historical collections of old Essex. Next door in the academy's former dormitory is the Catholic Church and, next to it, the Baptist Church, one of only two Egyptian Revival structures in this country.

Old Lyme. One of Connecticut's prettiest towns has a long main street lined with gracious homes from the 18th and 19th centuries, including one we think is particularly handsome called Lyme Regis, the English summer resort after which the

Florence Griswold Museum was once the retreat of the Old Lyme artists.

town was named. Lyme Street, over the years the home of governors and chief justices, is a National Historic District.

Florence Griswold Museum, 96 Lyme St., Old Lyme.

This is the pillared 1817 landmark in which the daughter of a boat captain ran a finishing school for girls and later an artists' retreat, with most of the rooms converted into bedrooms and studios in the barns by the river.

Now run as a museum interpreting its early status as a boarding house for artists and the home of American Impressionism, it has unique painted panels in every room. Especially prized is the dining room with panels on all sides given over to the work of the Old Lyme artists, who included Childe Hassam. Across the mantel the artists painted a delightful caricature of themselves for posterity. The arts colony thrived for twenty years and its works are on permanent display in the second-floor galleries. They include major works by Childe Hassam and John Henry Twachtman, and the largest collection of Willard Metcalf paintings in the world. Also on view are selections from the priceless Hartford Steam Boiler Collection of American Art, recently donated to the museum by the insurance company.

Changing exhibitions are produced in the striking new Krieble Gallery, a modernist, white and silvery series of barn-like buildings backing up to the Lieutenant River. Three soaring, skylit galleries were showing variations of a world-class exhibit called "The American River" at our latest visit. Both the building and its contents elicited a pertinent comment in the guest book: "Wonderful views, inside and out."

(860) 434-5542. www.flogris.org. Open Tuesday-Saturday 10 to 5 and Sunday 1 to 5. Adults, $7.

The **Lyme Art G**allery, next door to the Florence Griswold Museum, is headquarters of the Lyme Art Association, founded in 1902 and the oldest summer art group in the nation. It exhibits six major shows each season (Tuesday-Saturday 10 to 4:30 and Sunday 1 to 4:30, closed Christmas week and between shows). Nearby at 84 Lyme St. is the handsome, Federal-style **Lyme Academy of Fine Arts,** with changing exhibits and workshops (Monday-Saturday 10 to 4). The works of Lyme's American Impressionists are hung in the Town Hall, and the public library often has exhibits.

Deep River, just above Essex and reached most rewardingly via the River Road, is a sleepy river town best known for its annual ancient muster of fife and drum corps. Up river are the delightful town of **Chester,** an up-and-coming area of restaurants and shops; the restored **Goodspeed Opera House** at East Haddam, where lively musicals are staged in a Victorian structure beside the river, and actor William Gillette's eccentric stone **Gillette Castle** on a hilltop above the river at Hadlyme. All are well worth a visit.

Shopping. The choicest shopping opportunities for visitors are in Essex. The **Talbots** store confronting visitors head-on as they enter the downtown section of Essex sets the tone. Also fashionable in different ways are **Silkworm, J. Alden Clothier, Stonewear Clothing, J. McLaughlin** and a colorful place called **Equator. A Pocketful of Posies,** billed as a shabby chic boutique, opened in 2004 in the former quarters of the famed Clipper Ship Bookstore. Pillows and tableware are featured among home accessories at **Portabella. Fenwick Cottage** stocks unusual gifts and decorative accessories. Another concentration of stores is farther down Main Street at Griswold and Essex squares. **Red Balloon** offers precious clothes for precious children. Lilly Pulitzer is featured at **The Yankee Palm.** At **Red Pepper,** we saw items we had never seen anywhere else, among them interesting glasses and goblets in all kinds of colors made in Upstate New York, and cat pins by a woman who lives on a farm with seven cats. The shop carries clothing from small designers, almost all made in this country – which is unusual these days. **Hattitudes** stocks more kinds of hats than we ever expected to see. The **Essex Coffee & Tea Company** dispenses fancy beverages. Behind it is **Sweet P's,** a candy and ice cream shop. Nearby is **Olive Oyl's** for carry-out cuisine and specialty foods.

Extra-Special

Essex Steam Train and Riverboat, 1 Railroad Ave., Essex.

Its whistle tooting and smokestack spewing, the Valley Railroad's marvelous old steam train runs from the old depot in the Centerbrook section of Essex through woods and meadows to the Connecticut River landing at Deep River. There it connects with a riverboat for a 90-minute cruise past Gillette Castle to the Goodspeed Opera House and back. The two-and-one-half-hour trip into the past is rewarding for young and old alike. Themed excursions, including the Santa Special and Polar Express, run some weekends in the off-season. Railroad buffs enjoy the working railroad yard, vintage rail cars and exhibits gathered around the National Register landmark depot. The Essex Clipper dinner train runs two-hour excursions on weekends in a vintage luxury dining car, Friday at 7:30, Saturday at 7 and Sunday at 4, June-October. The fare with dinner is $60.

(860) 767-0103 or (800) 377-3987. www.essexsteamtrain.com. Train and Riverboat trips run five times daily in summer, Wednesday-Sunday in late spring and early fall. Adults, $24 train and riverboat; $16 train only.

Farmington Valley, Conn.

The Best of Both Worlds

A long mountain range separates the Hartford area from its outlying western suburbs. The Talcott Mountain range – "the mountain," as it's called locally – shields the Farmington River valley from the capital city and creates a place apart.

It is a special place of bucolic landscapes, meandering streams, venerable structures and lingering history. It's the place where their founders established no fewer than five private preparatory schools, where a pioneering woman architect gave her home as a prized museum, and where many executives of corporate Hartford today make their homes.

The "valley," as it's known locally, expands or contracts, depending on who is doing the defining. It always includes historic Farmington, home of the exclusive Miss Porter's School and some of the area's finest estates as well as office parks and corporate headquarters. Here you find a country club occupying one of the prime four corners in the center of town.

It includes Avon, a forested expanse of newer houses that command the region's highest prices. It includes Simsbury, a suburb that has lost more of its obvious 17th-century heritage than has Farmington but has retained more sense of community than Avon. For these purposes, the valley does not include Canton, Granby or, for that matter, our hometown of West Hartford, which originally was the largest town in the Farmington Valley Visitors Association but does not consider itself part of the valley at all.

The valley is a place more for seeing and doing than for contemplation. Hot-air ballooning, hang-gliding, horseback riding, river tubing and kayaking are the activities of note after tennis and golf. The International Skating Center of Connecticut in Simsbury adds another dynamic. There are museums to explore, countless shops (from boutiques to art galleries), interesting restaurants, rural byways and, recently, a handful of inns and B&Bs that qualify the valley as an inn spot as well as a special place.

Although this is suburbia, don't expect to see tract houses or many commercial strips. Most of the houses are tucked away on large wooded lots off winding roads. Except along the busy main Route 44, the shops are in old houses and new clusters.

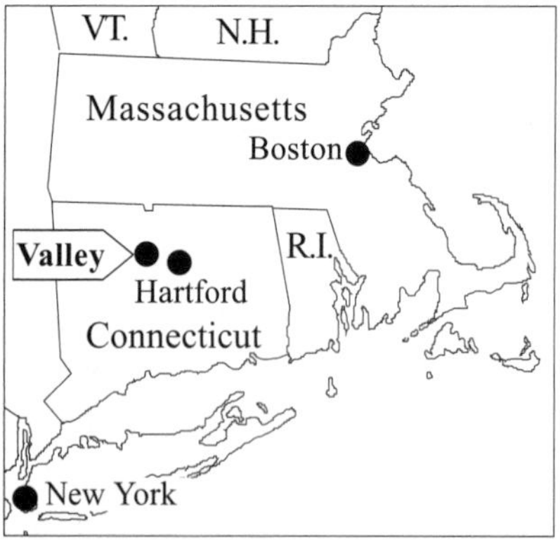

Stray from the mainstream, which is easy to do in the valley. You won't believe that a "suburb" is just around the corner, or that a city is just over the looming mountain range. Partake of suburban and rural pleasures, but know that the diverse offerings of Hartford are only a dozen miles away.

"We have the best of both worlds," say leaders of the Farmington Valley Visitors Association. They have much to promote and increasingly receptive takers.

Colonial Revival mansion is now Merrywood Bed & Breakfast.

Inn Spots

Merrywood Bed & Breakfast, 100 Hartford Road (Route 185), Simsbury. 06070.

Michael Marti, a retired Pratt & Whitney manager, and his German-born wife Gerlinde had traveled the world, so they knew exactly what they wanted when they decided to open the valley's first professional, fulltime B&B. They found it in the old Glover estate, a 1939 Colonial Revival brick mansion hidden in five acres of an evergreen forest on the side of Avon Mountain.

They offer common areas unusual in both decor and number on the main floor, plus a second floor with two air-conditioned bedrooms and a suite. All have the creature comforts typical of a deluxe hotel, from sitting areas with TV/VCRs and a collection of old black and white movies to mini-refrigerators stocked with complimentary beverages.

Enter the impressive foyer and find a living room that is, well, unique. The furnishing are all antiques from the Continent, but most startling is the large display on the wall of spread-out Indian robes, hats from the Far East and, on the floor beneath, a lineup of at least twenty pairs of children's wooden shoes, mostly Dutch. Gerlinde collects textiles and was a dealer in antiques, and both are displayed liberally throughout the house. Off the living room is a large enclosed sun porch. Behind the living room is a sunny, well-stocked library of particular interest to travelers. Breakfast may be served here or in a formal, somewhat formidable dining room outfitted in ornate Jacobean carved furniture that originated, Michael thinks, in a church in Germany or Italy. From a butler's pantry and adjacent kitchen comes the morning's meal, a wide selection from belgian waffles to german pancakes to eggs hussard, the choices checked off by the guest the night before.

Upstairs are the rear Empire Room (all American Empire antiques) with kingsize poster bed and the front Victorian Room, frilly and feminine with a queen bed draped from head to ceiling to foot in twenty feet of an antique lace tablecloth. The

Four-story-high turret is focal point of restored facade of The Linden House.

Continental Suite harbors a small queensize bedroom, an exotic bathroom with a sauna in a closet, and an enormous living room with two sitting areas, a Louis XV writing desk and, in one section, a full kitchenette used by long-term business guests who stay here.

Light opera or new-age music plays on a sound system throughout the house. Outside are walking paths and gardens.

The Martis bill theirs as "a bed and breakfast adventure." Responsive guests would agree.

(860) 651-1785 or (866) 637-7993. Fax (860) 651-8273. www.merrywoodinn.com. Two rooms and one suite with private baths. Doubles, $150. Suite, $175.

The Linden House, 288 Hopmeadow St., Simsbury 06070.

A circular stairway suspended in the four-story-high turret is one of the remarkable architectural details in this new Victorian B&B.

The stairway was installed once and then removed and rebuilt farther back from the windows. It was part of a lengthy and total renovation of the 1860 structure that formerly held railroad apartments and only got plumbing and heating in the 1950s. Julia and Myles McCabe from New York's Westchester County bought it as a retirement project. The renovation turned out to be much more extensive than they anticipated. "We could have built three houses for what this is costing," Julia rued in her Irish accent as she and her husband readied the finishing touches for opening. Only an old staircase to the couple's private quarters and the seven fireplace mantels were left from the original structure.

Beige with green trim, the structure is striking and ornate on the outside with the landmark turret and a deep side porch. The interior has spacious rooms, but normal-height ceilings as opposed to the high ceilings of most Victorian houses.

The couple created five bedrooms, all with working fireplaces. Beds are king or queensize, except for one with two twins. Telephones and TVs are standard. A main-floor guest room in front of the side living room has a tiled bathroom with a jacuzzi tub. The upstairs bedrooms have clawfoot tubs, and the two largest on the third floor have chaise lounges. Julie furnished with oriental rugs and plush down comforters and duvets. "We had a house full of beautiful furniture and accessories collected over the years," she said.

The dining room is large enough to hold a round table in one part and a long table in the middle. Here, Julia serves a hearty breakfast, offering french toast on Saturday and quiche on Sunday. "We offer a different dish every day of the week," she said. Arriving guests are greeted with refreshments in the afternoon.

The B&B takes its name from a spreading linden tree in the front yard. The property stretches well back from Route 10 to the Farmington River, and the McCabes exercised their love for gardening once they got the interior finished. The back yard includes a new gazebo.

(860) 408-1321. Fax (860) 408-9072. www.lindenhousebb.com. Five rooms with private baths. Doubles, $130 to $150. Two-night minimum weekends. Children over 12.

Simsbury 1820 House, 731 Hopmeadow St., Simsbury 06070.

Listed on the National Register of Historic Places, this country manor on a gentle rise above Simsbury's main street was restored by some of Hartford's movers and shakers, among them a corporate leader, a decorator and a restaurateur.

A veranda full of wicker, luncheon tables and baskets of hanging flowers greets guests at the entrance of the imposing gray building, reopened as an inn in 1986 and since taken over by the local group known as Classic Hotels of Connecticut. The entry and the public rooms retain the remarkable wainscoting, carved molding and leaded-glass windows of the original structure; all the gilt-framed oil paintings are reproductions. The living room, sunroom and dining room are furnished in the manner of a country estate, although they appear quite business-like when used by day for meetings and functions.

Reproduction and English antiques grace the 21 guest rooms on the inn's three floors. King and queensize four-poster beds, wing chairs, chintz curtains, and shades of mauves and blues predominate. Most of the baths have windows and have been tucked ingeniously into the nooks and crannies with which the house fascinates (one bathroom goes around a corner and is almost bigger than its bedroom). Most rooms have comfortable sitting areas for reading but not for watching television – the TVs are entrenched in front of the beds.

Across the side lawn designed by Frederick Law Olmsted, the Carriage House offers eleven more rooms and a suite, some of them on two or three levels and decorated in dark and masculine tones, a couple with an equine theme. Particularly interesting is the "executive suite" with its own garden terrace, a sitting room like a men's club and, up a couple of stairs, a room with a kingsize four-poster bed and an armoire. Beyond is a bathroom with a jacuzzi tub big enough for two, a separate shower, and his and her sinks. "European romance in Southern New England" is how one guest described a stay here.

A continental breakfast of fruits, juices, granola, cereal, homemade muffins and breads is taken in the inn's hearth room on the lower level. The inn's downstairs restaurant now caters to functions. An abbreviated dinner menu (entrées, $15.95 to $24.95) is available Monday-Thursday nights from 5 to 8 in the Eaglewood Café.

(860) 658-7658 or (800) 879-1820. Fax (860) 651-0724. www.simsbury1820house.com. Thirty-two rooms and one suite with private baths. Doubles, $119 to $175. Suite $229.

Gazebo frames front view of The Simsbury Inn.

The Simsbury Inn, 397 Hopmeadow St., Simsbury 06089.

Built in 1988 and stylish as can be, this is really a sleek, gracious hotel with 98 rooms and suites. A fireplace warms the soaring lobby with its parquet floors that lead to the Nutmeg Cafe and the reception desk. Upstairs past a stunning antique chandelier is Twigs, a fireside lounge with a semi-circular bar. Guests pass a wine cellar along the hallway to Evergreens, the inn's restaurant. An indoor pool opens to the outside in summer and adjoins an exercise room with whirlpool and sauna.

Up the elevators are curving hallways leading to the light and pleasant guest rooms on three floors. Pineapples top the headboards of the beds, each covered with custom-designed pastel spreads. Lace curtains or draperies, antique clocks, remote-control TVs, work desks, closets with removable coat hangers and two double beds or one kingsize are standard. Bathrooms have superior lighting, solid brass fixtures, mini-refrigerators, built-in hair dryers and a basket of the inn's own amenities, including a small sewing kit. Beds are turned down on request and fresh towels are added to the ample supply on hand.

Four mini-suites have sitting areas, some with fireplaces. Two larger suites each have a living room attractive in Colonial Williamsburg style with a chintz sofa, an oriental rug over deep blue carpeting, a round table circled by four Queen Anne chairs and a TV with VCR hidden in an armoire. Another TV and a kingsize four-poster on a raised platform are in the adjoining bedroom. Extra touches like electric shoe polishers set the inn apart.

Breakfast is available in the Nutmeg Café, and lunch and dinner in Evergreens Restaurant and Twigs Lounge. The menu of contemporary American/continental fare ranges from pastas and pan-seared spiced salmon to grilled venison loin and rack of lamb with a pesto glaze. Pub food is offered in Twigs Lounge.

(860) 651-5700 or (800) 634-2719. Fax (860) 651-8024. www.simsburyinn.com. Ninety-two rooms, four mini-suites and two suites with private baths. Doubles, $169 to $199. Suites, $219 to $400.

Entrées, $21 to $28. Lunch, Tuesday-Friday 11:30 to 2. Dinner, Tuesday-Saturday 5:30 to 9 or 10. Sunday brunch, 11 to 1:30.

Avon Old Farms Hotel, 279 Avon Mountain Road (Junction of Routes 10 and 44), Avon 06001.

What started long ago as an ordinary motel has grown like topsy up and around a hill through two major additions and many levels into first an inn and now a hotel. The enterprising Brighenti family have parlayed it into something of a local lodging empire, acquiring the financially troubled Simsbury Inn, then the Farmington Inn and lately the Simsbury 1820 House. The group is now called Classic Hotels of Connecticut.

The original 24-room Avon motel with exterior doorways remains opposite the main entrance and the large, homey lobby where coffee is put out all day near the fireplace. Above the lobby, a second floor curves uphill to become the main floor. Eventually the visitor enters the grand newer wing, a soaring spectacle of three marble floors with an open lobby, curving staircases and an elevator.

The 160 rooms and suites have kingsize or two double beds or a queensize bed with pullout sofa. They are distinguished by handsome watercolors of Farmington Valley scenes – more than 400 originals in all – and Currier & Ives etchings framed on the walls. Each has two telephones, Gilchrist & Soames toiletries, thick Irish towels and Egyptian cotton sheets,

Rooms increase in size and price as they wind up the hill. Those in the newer Georgian-style wing adopt a luxury-hotel style with kingsize pencil-post beds, stenciled borders matching the fabrics, and bathroom scales. Many yield woodland views. Two mini-suites have sofas and three Queen Anne chairs.

There are exercise rooms and a sauna, and the twenty acres of grounds include a stream and a pool.

Three meals a day are served in the hotel's **Seasons Restaurant** (see Dining Spots), a glass-enclosed dining room overlooking woods and stream, with a handsome new pub beside. A light continental breakfast is included in the rates.

(860) 677-1651 or (800) 836-4000. Fax (860) 677-0364. www.avonoldfarmshotel.com. One hundred fifty-eight rooms and two mini-suites with private baths. Doubles, $149 to $199. Mini-suites, $250.

The Farmington Inn, 827 Farmington Ave., Farmington 06032.

Totally gutted and refurbished, the old Farmington Motor Inn has been transformed into an inn of taste and value in the historic center of Farmington.

More than most refurbished motels, this seems like an inn, from its lovely reception area with a fireplace, a couple of comfortable seating groupings, and a basket of shiny red apples and a platter of cookies, to the jaunty second-floor Victoria's Café. A continental-plus breakfast with cereals and pastries is served here.

Seventeen artists were commissioned to paint 150 local landmarks and landscapes to complement the inn's country decor as well as pique guests' interest in the Farmington Valley, according to Michael Brighenti, spokesman for the family owners.

Seventy-two rooms and "junior suites" go off interior hallways. Each has a recessed door beneath an overhead spotlight and bears a brass nameplate – "like entering your own home or apartment," as the manager put it. Rooms have king, queen or two double beds and are decorated in country or traditional style. The country involves light pine furniture and overstuffed club chairs. The traditional means dark cherry furniture, teal carpeting and mauve Queen Anne wing chairs. Bathrooms in white Italian marble have lucite fixtures, separate vanities and baskets of toiletries.

The TV/VCRs are hidden in armoires in the junior suites, far from the bed and at an awkward angle from the sofas in the oversize rooms. With swagged draperies and substantial furnishings in teal and pink decor, the suites represent good value.

(860) 677-2821 or (800) 648-9804. Fax (860) 677-8332. www.farmingtoninn.com. Fifty-nine rooms and thirteen junior suites with private baths. Doubles, $109 to $129. Suites, $149 to $159.

Dining Spots

Métro Bis, 928 Hopmeadow St., Simsbury.

The name is French, but this is a classic contemporary American bistro, thanks to young chef-dynamo Christopher Prosperi and his wife, Courtney Febbroriello. They took over a French winner in 1998 and made it into an even bigger winner with modern Franco-American cuisine and Asian accents.

The long, narrow dining room is stylish in cream, dark wood and sage green, with a small bar up front, a partially open kitchen in back and lineups of white-clothed tables in between. Chris grew up in a New York family of foodies – his mother managed a restaurant, his father was the senior pastry instructor at the Culinary Institute of America, and he and his two brothers are Culinary Institute of America graduates. His wife got into the act and more, shedding fascinating insights in her new book, *Wife of the Chef, The True Story of a Restaurant & Romance.*

Chris's food enthusiasm is contagious, from the complimentary amuse-bouche that begins dinner to the sweets that end it. Start with yellowfin tuna carpaccio with wakame seaweed, a torchon of Sonoma foie gras, house-smoked salmon with tomato-dill cream cheese and ossetra caviar, or a crispy goat cheese and potato tart. Entrées range from chile-seared catfish in a roasted red pepper broth to grilled tandoori marinated leg of lamb. Grilled gorgonzola-crusted New York strip steak with a rosemary-scented demi-glace is a signature dish. Desserts are terrific, from a mocha panna cotta with port wine sorbet to an intense chocolate ganache and a chocolate velvet torte with raspberry coulis.

Robust flavors prevailed in a recent lunch memorable both for the tastes and the reasonable prices. The taste parade began with superior breads, accompanied by both a hummus spread and extra-virgin olive oil. One of us relished the crispy Thai spring rolls filled with chicken, mixed vegetables and clear noodles, all enlivened by the accompanying sweet and sour dipping sauce. The other was smitten by the lamb gyro on a Greek pita with shredded lettuce, shaved onion, tomato and tzatziki sauce. The crowning flourish was a warm apple tart with cinnamon ice cream, beautifully presented on an oversize plate.

With a glass of house wine and tip, the bill came to $35. You don't often eat so well for so reasonable a tab.

(860) 651-1908. www.metrobis.com. Entrées, $17.95 to $21.95. Lunch, Monday-Saturday 11:30 to 2:30. Dinner, Monday-Saturday 5 to 9:30.

Apricots, 1593 Farmington Ave., Farmington.

Outside on a jolly terrace beside the Farmington River. Inside on an enclosed upstairs porch, its windows taking full advantage of the view, its white walls painted whimsically with branches of apricots. Beyond in a more formal dining room of brick and oak. Or downstairs in a cozy pub with exposed pipes painted with more apricots. These are the varied settings offered by one of the Farmington Valley's more popular and enduring restaurants.

The food is usually equal to the setting, thanks to the inspiration of Ann Howard, a Farmington resident first known for her cooking lessons and later the Ann Howard Cookery, from which she and her staff catered some of the best parties in town. In 1982 she reopened an abandoned French restaurant in an old trolley barn sandwiched between Route 4 and the river, calling it Apricots, "a juicy pub." The upper porch and dining rooms were expanded in 1998.

We know folks who eat dinner at least once a week in the cozy, convivial pub, which offers items like grilled swordfish, shrimp and andouille sausage étouffée, and venison stew. We prefer the upstairs porch with its view of the passing river. For lunch, we've enjoyed the spinach and strawberry as well as the cobb salads, the specialty chicken potpie, a vegetarian focaccia pie with romaine and radish salad, a creamy fettuccine with crabmeat and mushrooms, grilled lime chicken and wonderful mussels.

At night, when the dining room turns serene, entrées run from sautéed sea scallops and spinach tossed in pesto cream to cashew-crusted rack of New Zealand lamb with bordelaise sauce. Seasonal favorites are grilled swordfish with lemon-dill aioli, pan-seared breast and confit of duck with a tart dry cherry sauce, and pan-seared venison loin with roasted garlic demi-glace. Start with lobster wontons with a sweet-hot chili sauce, escargots with boursin cheese in puff pastry, or warm lamb and wilted spinach salad with portobello mushrooms, feta cheese and pancetta vinaigrette. Finish with apricot gelato, vanilla bean crème brûlée, lemon torte or one of the heavenly cakes. Or indulge in the Ann Howard ice cream sandwich: chocolate biscuits with almonds and white chocolate chunks held together with praline ice cream and set atop strawberry sauce with white chocolate lace.

The staff, some of whom have been at Apricots for years, treats customers like the old friends that many of them are.

(860) 673-5405. Entrées, $20 to $28; pub, $8.95 to $13.50. Lunch, Monday-Saturday 11:30 to 2:30. Dinner nightly, 6 to 10; pub from 2:30. Sunday, brunch 11:30 to 2:30, dinner 5:30 to 9.

Max-A-Mia, 70 East Main St., Avon.

A fabulously successful offshoot of Hartford's inspired Max Downtown, this suburban hot spot is hot. Hot as in trendy, hot in value and hot in popularity. And why not, when you can dine well and happily on a variety of thin-crusted pizzas called stone pies, assertive pastas (some baked al forno in the wood-fired oven) and a few grills at wallet-pleasing prices. The formula works, for the place expanded and relocated the bar into an adjacent storefront.

A birthday lunch became quite festive here when four of us sampled the sautéed chicken livers (served elaborately with white beans, roasted shallots, arugula, plum tomatoes, porcini mushrooms and fresh herbs), the sautéed catfish topped with a cucumber salad and served over a roasted plum tomato and lavender coulis, the PLT (prosciutto, arugula, roma tomatoes and fresh mozzarella served on focaccia), and a di Bella Luna stone pie with white clams, sweet roasted peppers, pancetta and parmigiana. An order of bruschetta and a bottle of pinot grigio from the all-Italian wine list accompanied. Tiramisu, ricotta cheesecake with amarone cherries, chocolate polenta cake with cappuccino sauce and chocolate-hazelnut gelato were better than any birthday cake.

At night, the fare varies from antipasto misto and beef carpaccio to sautéed lemon sole, brick-roasted half chicken and oak-grilled strip steak. As if the wide-ranging menu weren't enough to draw regulars back, the daily specials here are really special. The food takes precedence over the decor, which is sleek but simple in yellow and brown with wood trim, track lighting and a mix of tables and booths. A bottle of olive oil is the centerpiece on each. The lively crowd provides the rest of the color.

(860) 677-6299. www.maxrestaurantgroup.com. Entrées, $14.95 to $24.95. Open daily, 11:30 to 10 or 11. Sunday, brunch 11 to 2:30, dinner 4 to 9.

Piccolo Arancio, 819 Farmington Ave., Farmington.

Of all the contemporary Italian restaurants sprouting like topsy, this is one of the more warm and inviting. Brothers Salvatore and Dino Cialfi, owners of Hartford's acclaimed Peppercorns Grill, branched out with "as authentic-looking a trattoria as you'll ever see in Connecticut," in Dino's words, "because it's like the ones where we lived in Italy."

They converted the ground floor of a former office building next to the Farmington Inn into a couple of dining rooms done up in Mediterranean earth tones, with rich mahogany trim and a ceiling of light blue to give the impression of being outside. They lately expanded into an adjacent space, relocating the bar and some plump club chairs to a new lounge and gaining another dining room. Tapes of Italian music provide background music.

From a wood oven, wood grill and rotisserie in the semi-open kitchen, chef Sal serves what he calls rustic, simple fare. That translates to robust pizzas, quite a selection of homemade pastas and basic grills. More complex are such entrées as grilled peppered yellowfin tuna with sweet and sour carrot sauce, grilled coriander-crusted pork tenderloin with a caramelized onion sauce, osso buco and grilled veal chop with a truffled porcini mushroom sauce. Tuscan-style pot roast hits the spot on a winter night.

Start with a classic carpaccio, baked escargots with crispy gnocchi and mesclun greens or a choice of bruschettas. Crème catalana with fresh berries, chocolate soufflé cake, warm chocolate bread pudding and a trio of homemade gelati are typical desserts.

(860) 674-1224. www.piccoloarancio.com. Entrées, $17 to $24. Lunch, Monday-Friday 11:30 to 2:30. Dinner, Monday-Saturday 5 to 10 or 11.

Avon Old Farms Inn, 1 Nod Road, Avon.

The sign inside the old entry identifies this as one of the twenty oldest restaurants in the country. The sign serves a purpose, for the huge new banquet and conference facility, a focal point in back, conveys quite another impression.

Established in 1757, this is strictly a restaurant and function house (a hotel of similar name but separate ownership is across the busy intersection of Route 44 and Route 10). The restaurant inexplicably was closed to the public in 2002 to concentrate on functions, but was reopened in 2003 by popular demand.

The heart of this endearing place has always been the seven dining rooms that sprawl through a series of additions hugging the old Albany Turnpike in front. The choicest is the Forge Room, far at the end of the old building. A splendid tavern atmosphere is this, with rough dark stone walls, flagstone floors, cozy booths made from old horse stalls, and lots of equestrian accessories hanging from dark beams. Bright red tablecloths and red leather chairs add color to the room, which is one of the most atmospheric around.

The Sunday champagne brunch has been voted the state's best for years by Connecticut magazine readers. Set up in the main dining room, the spread is dished out by twenty servers at two long banquet tables, then taken to one of the six other rooms, which have enough nooks and crannies to offer privacy. Up to 700 people may be served at three seatings.

New American cuisine in a quintessential Yankee setting is featured at lunch and dinner, when service is personal and each dining room functions almost as its own restaurant.

Ex-Manhattan chef Charles Simmons oversees an extensive menu. The dinner version opens with treats like lobster bisque, portobello tempura, Thai shrimp sizzled tableside for two, and banana-coated oysters fried crisp and served over plantain chips with a roasted jalapeño aioli.

Traditional favorites like baked stuffed shrimp and prime rib with a popover have been augmented lately by cutting-edge fare: pan-seared sea bass with a spicy citrus sauce, lemon pepper-coated broiled swordfish with a tequila-lime glaze, veal osso buco and filet mignon with gorgonzola butter and port wine demi-glace. The English trifle is still a masterpiece among desserts.

(860) 677-2818. www.avonoldfarmsinn.com. Entrées, $18 to $25. Pub menu, $7 to $9. Lunch, Monday-Saturday noon to 2:30. Dinner, Monday-Saturday 5:30 to 9:30 or 10:30. Sunday brunch, 10 to 2:30.

Pettibone's Tavern, 4 Hartford Road (Route 185), Simsbury.

For history and ambiance, few restaurants can match Pettibone's, which was built in 1780 as the first stagecoach stop beyond Hartford on the Boston-to-Albany Turnpike. It has offered respite to the traveler for more than two centuries, most recently as part of the Chart House chain. In 2003, a former Chart House chef and manager bought the place and took it back to its origin. The Chart House was here "only 30 years – a mere interloper," in the words of co-owner Erich Kronschnabel, the manager.

The mustard-colored inn has tables in a ramble of properly historic rooms as well as two pretty sun porches, summery all year long in green and white wicker. Even the enormous upstairs lounge is comforting with a wraparound bar and salon-style tables and chairs in a couple of open rooms.

Ask one of the waiters to tell you about the ghost of the house, who can be seen in a portrait in the front foyer (ours was a believer after he'd heard her call his name). She's been known to drop dishes, make glassware move and the like. But she only operates at quiet times, which are rare when Pettibone's is open, such is its popularity.

Matt Tofil, officially the proprietor, is back in the kitchen as chef. His menu is typically steak and seafood but with twists, as in spiced ahi tuna with ginger-soy butter and herb-crusted rack of lamb. Yes, you can still get baked stuffed shrimp, prime rib au jus and teriyaki sirloin and the usual steakhouse sides. But you also can order macadamia-crusted mahi mahi with frangelico-peanut sauce and mango coulis, or the Dr. Atkins cowboy steak special, an eighteen-ounce delmonico steak with broccoli and cauliflower au gratin.

Start with the raw bar sampler, coconut-rum shrimp or lobster spring rolls. Finish with the specialty hot chocolate lava cake spiked with Godiva liqueur.

The Pettibone's tavern menu is broader than most and considered excellent value.

(860) 658-1118. Entrées, $16.95 to $26.50. Tavern menu, $7.25 to $13.95. Lunch, Monday-Friday 11:30 to 2. Dinner nightly, 5 to 9 or 9:30. Sunday brunch, 10 to 1.

Seasons Restaurant, 279 Avon Mountain Road , Routes 10 and 44, Avon.

Off an atrium in a wing of the Avon Old Farms Hotel is a glass-enclosed restaurant, upgraded from a café and known for fine regional American cuisine.

The semi-circular back Garden Room looks out onto the woods, Talcott Mountain Stream and the changing seasons. It is colorful in pink, green and white with balloon curtains framing the view and green beams on the ceiling. Piano music and monthly art shows provide entertainment. There's a stylish pub with a casual menu at the side.

Chef Charles Williams carried on the tradition launched by founding chef Glenn Thomas, changing the fare with the seasons. At a recent visit, we were tempted by entrées like oatmeal-crusted salmon with maple cream, crispy pan-seared halibut with tomato jam, cassoulet, crispy Long Island duck with rhubarb and cherry chutney, and prosciutto-wrapped veal chop. Lobster and corn chowder, tangy crab fritters, brie en croûte and sweet potato pierogi with basil cream sauce make good starters. Among desserts are chocolate mousse cake, raspberry linzer torte and homemade sorbets.

(860) 677-6352. Entrées, $22 to $29. Lunch, Monday-Friday 11:30 to 2. Dinner, Monday-Saturday 5 to 9 or 9:30. Sunday brunch, 10 to 1.

Diversions

Stanley-Whitman House, 37 High St., Farmington.

The most painstakingly accurate restoration said to have been undertaken in a New England house preceded the reopening of this 1660 structure that houses the Farmington Museum, one of the best examples of a 17th-century frame overhang house in New England. With rare diamond-paned windows, it is furnished with early American pieces, many the gifts of local residents. It offers a fascinating glimpse into the life and conditions enjoyed – or endured – by the early colonists. The grounds reflect the utilitarian uses of a Colonial dooryard garden with culinary, medicinal and herbal plantings.

(860) 677-9222. www.stanleywhitman.org. Open May-October, Wednesday-Sunday noon to 4; rest of year, Saturday and Sunday noon to 4. Adults, $5.

The Phelps Tavern Museum and Homestead, 800 Hopmeadow St., Simsbury.

Three centuries of Simsbury history are recreated in this evolving two-acre complex. The focal point is the Phelps Tavern Museum, where period rooms and interactive exhibition galleries interpret its use as an inn from 1786 to 1849. Included are the tavern, card room, kitchen, guest rooms, ballroom and meeting room. Three generations of the Phelps tavern keepers are chronicled along with the social history of taverns in New England. The low-key complex also has a one-room schoolhouse, a probate court building, sheds full of Victorian carriages and a museum store. Visitors enjoy award-winning period gardens and the reproduction of a 1683 meeting house, nicely hedged and screened from a nondescript shopping plaza.

(860) 658-2500. www.phelpstavernmuseum.com. Open Tuesday-Saturday, noon to 4. Adults, $6.

Heublein Tower, Talcott Mountain State Park, Route 185, Simsbury.

A national historic site, the landmark, 165-foot-high tower built in 1914 as part of a summer home by the Gilbert Heublein family (of Heublein liquor fame) atop Talcott Mountain is open to the public as an observation tower and small museum. The four-state view from the top is smashing during fall foliage, but worth the 1.2-mile climb from the parking lot at any time. Along the ridge you may see members of the Connecticut Hang Gliding Association soaring from the cliffside trail that's considered one of the best gliding spots anywhere.

(860) 677-0662. Open April 15 to Labor Day, Monday-Friday 10 to 5; Labor Day to early November, daily 10 to 5. Free.

Arts and Crafts. Of special interest is the **Farmington Valley Arts Center,** 25 Arts Center Lane, Avon, (860) 678-1867. A park-like setting of century-old factory buildings in Avon Park North off Route 44 contains a complex of studios for more than 20 artists, who open at their whim but often can be seen at work on weekends. The Fisher Gallery Shop is open all year, Wednesday-Saturday 10 to 5, Sunday noon to 4; extended hours in November-December. The Center's annual Christmas show and sale is a great place to pick up holiday gifts.

Outdoor Activities. The **Farmington River** is popular with canoeists and bird-watchers. Hikers can walk along sections of its banks in Farmington, Avon and Simsbury. Water-skiers may be seen jumping in the Collinsville section of Canton. A popular activity is **tubing.** Young and old alike enjoy riding double-inflatable tubes down the river from Satan's Kingdom State Recreation Area in New Hartford to Canton. Tubes may be rented at Satan's Kingdom. The newest activity is **kayaking.** Rentals are available from Collinsville Canoe & Kayak along Route 179 in Collinsville, which claims to be New England's biggest such outfitter.

For reasons best known to those involved, the same mountain and valley that are so good for hang-gliding are also favorable for **hot-air ballooning.** Three outfits float over the area in season, presenting a colorful spectacle at dawn and sometimes at dusk. The hour's ride is quite an event, which explains the price ($175 to $200 per person). Rides are available in Farmington through KAT Balloons, (860) 678-7921, or A Windriders Balloon, (860) 677-0647, and in Simsbury through Livingston Balloon Co., (860) 651-1110.

International Skating Center of Connecticut, 1375 Hopmeadow St., Simsbury, (860) 651-5400. Olympic champions Oksana Baiul, Viktor Petrenko and Ekaterina Gordeeva were among those in early residence at this eye-popping center, which emerged quickly from concept to reality in 1994. Up-and-coming skaters from across the world make Simsbury their temporary home as they work their way into the international spotlight. Two side-by-side indoor rinks are busy day and night with Olympic training sessions, hockey games, skating lessons and public skating hours (mostly on weekends). Also here are a pro shop, the Skater's Café and even a video arcade featuring hockey games.

Shopping. This sophisticated suburban area provides a variety of shopping opportunities, from the upscale stores (Lord & Taylor, Nordstrom, Restoration Hardware, Harry and David, Brooks Brothers, Williams-Sonoma and Abercrombie's) at **Westfarms** mall on the Farmington-West Hartford border to freestanding shops throughout the valley.

Historic atmosphere pervades the site and shops of Old Avon Village along Route 44. Browsers like the setting and such stores as the **Little Silver Shop,** the **Village Goldsmith and Galway Stallard** (for home accessories). The shops get tonier as Old Avon Village melds into the Shops at River Park. You'll find every with-it children's outfit at **Kids & Co.** A branch of **The Secret Garden of Martha's Vineyard** carries gifts, paper goods and toiletries. **The Pampered Bath** and **Sports**

Fine Colonial Revival country house is home of prized Hill-Stead Museum.

Buff speak for themselves. For distinctive paper goods and stationery, there's no better place than **Lettres.**

Nearby is Avon's Riverdale Farms, which advertises "today's shopping amid yesterday's charms." Some buildings have been converted from barns from a 19th-century dairy farm, while others are newly built (the latest looks barn-like from the outside but plants cascade down a two-story atrium inside its handsome interior). The tenant mix changes frequently.

The Simsburytown Shops are the most interesting in Simsbury. **The Work Shoppe** offers gifts and accessories of timeless tradition (though their neat bird "lunch stations" were hardly traditional). **Finula's** stocks women's sportswear and **Say Cheese/La Grande Pantrie,** cheeses, specialty foods and kitchen accessories.

Extra-Special

Hill-Stead Museum, 35 Mountain Road, Farmington.

This exceptional cultural treasure is important on three fronts: art, architecture and furnishings. The 36-room white clapboard house with rambling wings and a Mount Vernon facade is considered one of the finest Colonial Revival country houses in America. Willed as a museum by its designer and last occupant, architect Theodate Pope Riddle, it's a pleasantly personal masterpiece of a mansion that remains as she left it. Hung on its walls is the matchless collection of one of the earliest American collectors of Impressionist paintings before they became fashionable – what Henry James in 1907 called "wondrous examples of Manet, of Degas, of Claude Monet, of Whistler." The furnishings include remarkable mementos of an early 20th-century family, from Corinthian pottery and Chinese porcelain to a first edition of Samuel Johnson's *Dictionary* and a handwritten letter from Franklin D. Roosevelt. As you are guided on a 50-minute-long tour through nineteen intact period rooms, it is "as if the owners, having to be away for the afternoon, nevertheless invited you to stop for a time to delight in their house and collection," as a museum guide puts it. The 152-acre property's elaborate sunken gardens, designed by landscape architect Beatrix Farrand, have been reconstructed to their pre-1925 state. A renowned poetry festival is held in the sunken garden every summer.

(860) 677-4787. Open Tuesday-Sunday, May-October 10 to 5, April-November 11 to 4. Adults, $9.

Litchfield/Lake Waramaug

Connecticut's Colonial Country

Nestled in the hills of Northwest Connecticut, picturesque Lake Waramaug boasts an alpine setting that appeals enough to an Austria-born innkeeper to call it home. Nearby is Litchfield, the quintessential Colonial Connecticut town preserved not as a restoration in the tradition of Williamsburg, with which it has been compared, but as a living museum community.

The lake and the town, ten miles apart, represent the heart of the Litchfield Hills, a chic yet sedate area of prep schools and foxhunts, of church spires and town greens. The landed gentry who call this never-never land home are joined by celebrity New Yorkers who savor its low-key lifestyle.

Hills rise sharply above the boomerang-shaped Lake Waramaug. Its sylvan shoreline is flanked by a state park, substantial summer homes and three country inns. With little commercialism, it's enveloped in a country feeling, away from it all.

Litchfield, a small county seat whose importance long has transcended its borders, is perched atop the crest of a ridge. Its beautiful North and South streets are lined with gracious homes and exude history (George Washington slept here, Harriet Beecher Stowe was born here, Ethan Allen lived here, the nation's first law school and its first academy for girls were founded here). The village is so preserved and prized that only in recent years has it attracted the inns, restaurants and the kind of shops that affluence demands.

The area between Lake Waramaug and Litchfield also encompasses the quaint hamlet of New Preston, the sedate hilltop village of Washington and the bustling little retail center of Washington Depot.

Between the hills and lakes are fine natural and low-key attractions – Connecticut's largest nature sanctuary, a world-famous garden center, two farm wineries, state parks and forests. Connecticut's entire Northwest Corner has much to commend it, but there's no more choice a slice than Litchfield and Lake Waramaug.

Inn Spots

Mayflower Inn, Route 47, Washington 06793.

Head up a winding driveway past a scenic pond and through a forest of rhododendron to the hilltop site of the penultimate country-house hotel in America. A $15-million makeover vaulted into the national limelight the once-sleepy inn hidden away on a wooded site above the campus of The Gunnery, the private school that used to own and operate it.

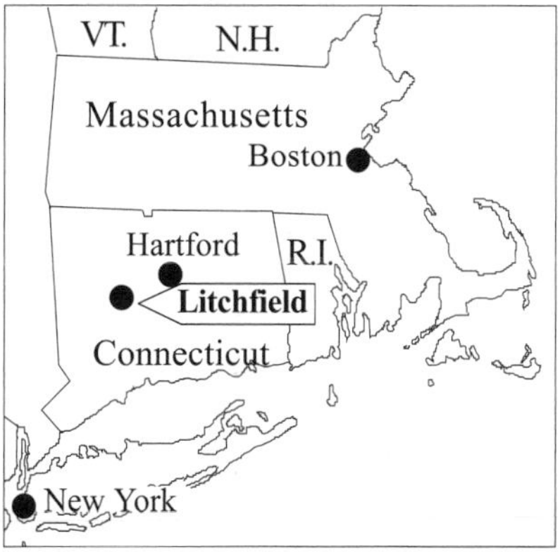

"Stately" is the word to describe the entire place as styled in 1992 by New York owners Robert and Adriana Mnuchin and steered since by general manager John Trevenen. The Mnuchins – he a Goldman Sachs whiz for 30 years and she a retailer and born-to-shop collector – have a weekend home here and, with an obsession for detail, created a posh country retreat that others can only hope to emulate.

The Mayflower was the first Connecticut property to become associated with the Relais & Châteaux hotel group and the first in New England to win both Mobil five-star and AAA five-diamond awards. It also recorded a stunning 80-plus percent annual occupancy rate. Said manager Trevenen, with a trace of Australian accent: "We've reached the niche where we want to be."

The Mnuchins spared no expense in producing 25 guest rooms and suites that are the ultimate in comfort and good taste. A staff of 85 adds to the feeling of pampered luxury. Fifteen rooms are upstairs on the second and third floors of the main inn. Ten more are in two guesthouses astride a hill beside a magnificent tiered rose garden leading up to a heated swimming pool and a tennis court. More rooms were planned for the Mayflower's destination garden spa, scheduled to open in 2005 on a fifteen-acre property adjacent to the inn.

Fine British, French and American antiques and accessories, prized artworks and elegant touches of whimsy – like four old trunks stashed in a corner of the second-floor hallway – dignify public and private rooms alike.

Opening off the lobby, an intimate parlor with a plush leather sofa and chairs leads into the ever-so-British gentleman's library. It possesses one of the largest collections of mystery novels in Connecticut, Playbills from the 1930s, and the complete works of Wharton and James, plus a curved bay window looking across the side veranda to manicured lawns.

Across the back of the inn are three dining rooms (see Dining Spots), and along one side is an English-style bar. Downstairs is a state-of-the-art fitness center that would do many a private club proud. The outlying Teahouse is a tranquil, Adirondack-style lodge favored for corporate board retreats. Opposite the front desk is a gift shop offering small antiques, Italian leather goods, cashmere sweaters, jewelry and such of appeal to Adriana's New York set (the first guests to book a suite were Mike Nichols and Diane Sawyer, who were at the inn for Stephen Sondheim's birthday party).

Suite or no, each guest room is a sight to behold and some are almost unbelievably glamorous. Room 24 offers a kingsize canopy four-poster feather bed awash in pillows, embroidered Frette linens, a feather duvet and a chenille throw. An angled loveseat faces the fireplace, and oversize wicker rockers await on the balcony. Books and magazines are spread out on the coffee table, the armoire contains a TV and there's a walk-in closet. Wainscoted in mahogany, the paneled bathroom, bigger than most bedrooms, has marble floors, a double vanity opposite a glistening soaking tub, a separate w.c. area and a walk-in shower big enough for an army. Even all that didn't prepare us for a second-floor corner suite with a large living room straight out of Country Life magazine, a dining-conference room, a lavatory, a bedroom with a kingsize canopied four-poster and a second bathroom, plus a porch overlooking the sylvan scene. And so it goes, room after room of great comfort and élan – each full of surprises and "everything with a story behind it," according to our guide. An extravagant collection of 18th and 19th century art adorns the walls. Fancy toiletries and fresh orchids and nosegays of roses (Adriana's favorite flowers) are much in evidence. The rear balconies and decks off the rooms in the guesthouses face the woods and are particularly private.

The outside is equally magnificent, from the acres of lawns shimmering in emerald green to the exotic specimen trees strategically placed all around. The 28 acres of

Library at Mayflower Inn is dressed in finest British country-house style.

horticultural Eden include terraced Shakespeare, rose and cutting gardens. The Mnuchins had a hiking trail blazed to the top of the big hill they renamed Mayflower Mountain, where a ring of stones is now "Meditation Circle."

Breakfast, available from a full menu, is an extravagance that's likely to add $30 to $40 more to an overnight bill for two. The oversize Limoges breakfast cups were custom-designed for the Mayflower based on what the Mnuchins enjoyed during whirlwind travels to Europe as they planned their inn.

From the beguiling botanical and canine prints in the hallways to the weeping Alaskan blue atlas cedar and boxwood gardens outside, the place is a treasure for those who want the finest.

(860) 868-9466. Fax (860) 868-1497. www.mayflowerinn.com. Seventeen rooms and eight suites with private baths. Rates, EP. Doubles, $400 to $650. Suites, $700 to $1,300. Two-night minimum weekends. Children over 12.

The Boulders Inn, East Shore Road (Route 45), New Preston 06777.

This venerable inn across the road from Lake Waramaug has been grandly refurbished with an eye to attracting a more moneyed clientele. Innkeeper Martin O'Brien handles the day-to-day management for owner Steven F. Goldstone, retired chairman and chief executive officer of RJR Nabisco Inc., who quickly but quietly put the inn in an upscaling mode in 2002.

The new look is evident in the public rooms, all redecorated in plush Adirondack style, and in four new rooms and suites fashioned from the former innkeepers' quarters in the rear carriage house.

Boulders remain integral to the decor of the main inn, jutting out from the walls of the intimate inner dining room as well as comprising the massive fireplace chimney. They contribute to an elegant, lodgey feeling that's enhanced by the handsome, dark-paneled living room that sprawls across the front of the substantial residence built in 1895. Six stunning, oversize lodge chairs face the lake, while a leather sofa and chairs flank the stone fireplace. A cozy library is furnished in contemporary American country style.

The beige, chocolate and taupe colors employed throughout the public areas lend an urban chic look to the lodgings as well.

Five accommodations with king or queen beds are upstairs in the main inn. Three rooms facing the lake offer large, cushioned window seats to take in the view. The Northwest "junior suite" has a king poster bed dressed in the white linens and down comforters common to all, a loveseat and plump chair in the sitting area, a TV/DVD player hidden in the armoire and Molton Brown toiletries from London in the bathroom.

The most luxurious are seven rooms (four of which may be joined to become a pair of suites) in a rear carriage house with plush chintz seating in front of stone fireplaces. Typical is the newly opened New Preston Room appointed with queen bed, antiques, imported wool carpeting, luxury fabrics, turn-of-the-last-century artworks and a tiled bathroom with granite vanity. It incorporates the latest media/telephone systems and has a private garden patio.

Eight more contemporary rooms in four outlying duplex cottages along the rear hillside are most in demand. Renovated and upgraded with king or queen four-poster beds, air conditioning and fireplaces, the guest houses have decks in front and back facing lake and woods. Four have double whirlpool tubs. More guest cottages were in the planning stage.

New on the lower level of the main lodge is a state-of-the-art fitness room. A former guest room on the second floor has become a massage room.

Meals are served in the airy, six-sided Lake Dining Room with windows onto Lake Waramaug and seasonally on three tiered patios outside (see Dining Spots). Breakfast and afternoon tea are included in the rates.

(860) 868-0541 or (800) 455-1565. Fax (860) 868-1925. www.bouldersinn.com. Seven rooms, three suites and eight cottages with private baths. Doubles, $350 to $595. Suites, $395 to $875. Two-night minimum weekends

The Huckleberry Inn, 219 Kent Road, Warren 06754.

One of New England's more sumptuous, charming and personality-driven B&Bs opened in 2002, just as Andrea DiMauro planned it. A personal chef for affluent families in suburban New York for twelve years, the perky, 33-year-old blonde had married well (a building contractor who could restore their newly acquired 1779 farmhouse for the purpose). She traveled to innkeeping seminars to learn from "the professionals," crunched the numbers and set about filling a niche in the Litchfield Hills: the wide gap between the small, makeshift B&B in someone's house and the larger, high-end inn staffed for the purpose.

With husband Sam doing the heavy work, the newlyweds spent two years restoring, enhancing and readying the handsome yellow house for guests in three plush bedrooms and three distinctive common areas. They also gutted a former blacksmith shop/garage into an idyllic, two-level cottage in which celebrities have chosen to hide out.

The house came with the patina of age: hand-hewn beams, wide-plank chestnut floors, intricate woodwork and warming fireplaces. The couple created bathrooms where there hadn't been any – luxurious baths with whirlpool tubs, tumbled marble showers and heated marble floors. They furnished with plump, oversize beds, pressed linens and goose down comforters, TV/VCRs, exotic toiletries and showy art.

Latest creature comforts reside in restored 1799 farmhouse called The Huckleberry Inn.

Andrea "had so much fun decorating," a talent manifested particularly in the bedrooms. The kingsize bed in the elegant Honeybee Room is dressed in a pristine white linen canopy, with a plump chair and ottoman beside the fireplace. The smaller Ladybird Room is "country traditional." Its tight, windowless bathroom has a remarkable painting of a local farm scene encased in a frame that resembles a window, beside two old washboards hung artfully on the wall. The mid-size Dragonfly Room is eclectic with walls painted claret and olive. The oriental rug is arranged at an angle at the foot of the queen sleigh bed. An enormous gilt frame hung against the claret wall literally frames assorted gilt mirrors inside. Two brass and crystal wall sconces match the chandelier in the bathroom. That bath has a curving, extra-deep whirlpool tub with a brass hand-held shower shaped like a telephone and a matching antique chandelier overhead.

Guests enjoy watching Andrea cook organic breakfasts, while sipping espresso and cappuccino made with the special Huckleberry blend from her shiny Capresso "coffee center" machine on a sideboard in the dining room. They view the proceedings when the pocket shutters open to reveal a wide pass-through window in her showplace country kitchen. The blackboard menu posts the morning's offerings: at our visit, citrus fruits with cardamom glaze and pomegranate seeds, cranberry-pumpkin bread, baby bella and fontina omelets with sausage links, and the grand finale – a smidgen of ginger crème brûlée. The four-course repast is taken at tables in the dining room or the adjacent stone-floored sun porch, both as country chic as the rest of the house.

The breakfast dessert is "a little extra the guests don't expect," says Andrea. Others are the complimentary Hopkins Vineyard wine in the rooms and the array of liqueurs stashed in a remarkable mahogany liquor cabinet (made during Prohibition to look like a radio) in the cozy, fireplaced living room. The personal touches and over-all welcome account for an usually large repeat clientele.

(860) 868-1947 or (866) 868-1947. Fax (860) 868-6014. www.thehuckleberryinn.com. Three rooms and one cottage with private baths. Doubles, $185 to $285. Cottage, $365.

The Birches Inn, 233 West Shore Road, New Preston 06777.

A trucker from nearby Middlebury poured big bucks into a total renovation of this venerable inn on Lake Waramaug. After he found innkeeping was not his forte, he leased the property to Nancy Conant of West Hartford, owner of the late Inn on Lake Waramaug across the lake. Formerly known for its restaurant (see Dining Spots), the lodging has come to the forefront under her tenure.

The inn's second floor offers five handsome guest rooms. The lakeview Room 7, the largest, has a king bed, two armchairs, an impressive armoire, TV, telephone and hand-painted bureau. Its bathroom with a double vanity comes with the terry robes, hair dryer and Caswell-Massey toiletries common to all. Four more accommodations with TV and telephone were added in 2001 in the Birch House behind. Two rooms on the second floor have king beds and whirlpool tubs. The first floor contains a suite plus a fourth bedroom, both with queen beds.

Most coveted are three rooms in the Lake House across the road. They're smaller but share an extended deck beside the water, and the views are spectacular. "You can almost fish from the porch," one chef said wistfully as he led a tour. One has a king bed with a brass headboard, a loveseat, a wicker rocker and a whirlpool tub.

Guests enjoy continental breakfast in the main inn in a sunny room overlooking the front deck. Wine and cheese are put out in the afternoon in a small parlor with a fireplace.

(860) 868-1735 or (800) 525-3466. Fax (860) 868-1815. www.thebirchesinn.com. Eleven rooms and one suite with private baths. May to mid-November: doubles, $200 to $375 weekends, $150 to $325 midweek. Rest of year: doubles $150 to $325 weekends, $125 to $200 midweek.

Toll Gate Hill, 571 Torrington Road (Route 202), Litchfield 06759.

The rural 1745 landmark home near the Torrington town line in which Captain William Bull once took in travelers on the Hartford-Albany stage route has been restored and reopened as a small inn and a restaurant. After having been closed for several years, the establishment was revived in 2003 by the John Pecora family of Farmington. Their daughter Alicia, who trained in hospitality at the Schiller International University in Florida, London and Madrid, took up residence as innkeeper.

Inviting it is, this historic structure listed on the National Register of Historic Places. It's situated back from the road in a stand of trees, its red frame exterior dimly illuminated at night and appearing to the traveler much as it must have more than two centuries ago.

The restaurant (see Dining Spots) is based in the old tavern, where the six original guest rooms are located. The previous owner opened four more guest rooms and suites in the adjacent "school house." A new Captain William Bull House with ten more rooms and suites and a lobby/reception area was added toward the rear of the property.

The most choice guest rooms are those in the outbuildings. They're furnished in Hunt Country pine with comfort in mind, and an emphasis on coordinated Hinson and Schumacher fabrics, bright colors, queensize canopy beds, upholstered chairs and loveseats, and TVs. Fireplaces are attractions in three rooms and five suites; the latter also have mini-refrigerators and VCRs. In the soaring two-story lobby, the paisley print on the walls is repeated in the chairs and curtains. Balconies off rooms in the new building overlook the woods.

Landmark 19th-century hilltop structure above Lake Waramaug houses Hopkins Inn.

The nicest rooms in the main inn are three larger ones on the second floor, each with a working fireplace. A small parlor for house guests is located on the second-floor landing next to the ballroom.

A continental breakfast is available in the downstairs banquet room of the new Captain William Bull House or may be delivered on trays to guests' rooms. Alicia bakes assorted muffins and her mother Jolanta bakes pecan-cinnamon bread. Sometimes they produce quiche on weekends.

(860) 567-1233 or (866) 567-1233. Fax (860) 567-1230. www.tollgatehill.com. Fifteen rooms and five suites with private baths. Doubles $115 to $170, suites $195, mid-April to January and all weekends. Midweek, January to mid-April: doubles, $95 to $135, suites $160. Two-night minimum holiday weekends. Children and pets welcome.

The Hopkins Inn, 22 Hopkins Road, New Preston 06777.

This landmark yellow inn astride a hill above Lake Waramaug is known far and wide for its European cuisine (see Dining Spots), and we often recommend it when asked where to take visitors for lunch in the country. Its reputation was built by Swiss-born innkeepers and has been continued since the late 1970s by Austrian Franz Schober and his wife Beth, joined lately by their son, Toby Fossland.

Built in 1847 as a summer guest house, the Federal structure with several additions was converted from a boarding house into an inn in 1945, and the guest rooms have been considerably enhanced by the Schobers. Warmed only by small heating units (thus used only from late March through December), the eleven guest rooms and an apartment on the second and third floors have been sparingly but comfortably furnished with brass or wood bedsteads, thick carpeting, floral wallpapers, chests of drawers and the odd loveseat or rocker. Nine rooms have private baths. A new two-bedroom apartment has been added in an annex.

Guests share a couple of small main-floor parlors with restaurant patrons, and may use the inn's private beach on the lake. There's no better vantage point for lake-watching than the expansive outdoor dining terrace, shaded by a giant horse chestnut tree and distinguished by striking copper and wrought-iron chandeliers and lanterns. Breakfast is available for house guests.

(860) 868-7295. Fax (860) 868-7464. www.thehopkinsinn.com. Nine rooms with private baths, two rooms with shared bath and two apartments. Doubles, $85 to $110 EP. Apartments, $160 EP. Two-night minimum weekends.

Dining Spots

West Street Grill, 43 West St., Litchfield.

The food here is the subject of raves from food reviewers and the perfect foil for the trendoids who make this their own at lunch and dinner seven days a week. The two rooms were full the winter Saturday we first lunched here, and the host rattled off the names of half a dozen celebrities who had reserved for that evening.

The grill is the kind of place weekending New Yorkers love. It's sleek in black and white, with a row of low booths up the middle, tables and mirrors on either side, and a back room with stunning trompe-l'oeil curtains on the walls. The only color comes from the changing fine art on a side brick wall and from the power clientele.

The kitchen has maintained its culinary high through a succession of talented chefs, thanks to co-owner James O'Shea's magic touch. Our first lunch here began with a rich butternut squash and pumpkin bisque and the signature grilled peasant bread with parmesan aioli. Main dishes were an appetizer of grilled country bread with a brandade of white beans and marinated artichokes and a special of grilled smoked pork tenderloin with spicy Christmas limas. Among the highly touted desserts, we succumbed to an ethereal crème brûlée and an intense key lime tart that was really tart. With two generous glasses of wine, the total lunch bill for two came to a rather New Yorkish $50.

Memorable as it was, lunch was nothing compared with a special tasting dinner showcasing the summer menu. That extravaganza began with beet-green soup, grilled peasant bread with roasted tomato and goat cheese, corn cakes with crème fraîche and chives, roasted-beet and goat-cheese napoleons with a composed salad, and nori-wrapped salmon with marinated daikon, cucumbers and seaweed. A passion fruit sorbet followed. By then we felt that we had already dined well, but no, on came the entrées: tasting portions – which we shared back and forth – of pan-seared halibut with a beet pappardelle, spicy shrimp cake with ragoût of black beans and corn, grilled ginger chicken with polenta and ginger chips, and grilled leg of lamb with a ragoût of lentils, spicy curried vegetables and fried greens, including flat-leaf spinach. A little bit here, a little there, and next we knew emerged a parade of desserts: a plum tart in a pastry so tender as not to be believed, a frozen passion fruit soufflé, a hazelnut torte with caramel ice cream and a sampling of sorbets (raspberry, white peach and blackberry).

Both meals testified amply to West Street's culinary prowess.

(860) 567-3885. Entrées, $22 to $37. Lunch daily, 11:30 to 3, weekends to 4. Dinner, 5:30 to 9:30 or 10:30.

Thomas Moran's Petite Syrah, 223 Litchfield Turnpike (Route 202), New Preston.

Chef Thomas Moran worked around the world for the Four Seasons hotel chain and then cooked for six years for the demanding Relais & Chateaux clientele at the Mayflower Inn. Although not exactly a household word, his name carried weight locally when he and his wife embarked in 2003 on their first solo venture, an intimate

Chef-owner welcomes guests at copper bar in Thomas Moran's Petite Syrah.

bistro in a small white dormered house that long housed the French restaurant Le Bon Coin in the Woodville section of New Preston.

His theme is "California Meets New England," a reference to the light, creative California style with Asian accents he imparts to local ingredients. Appetizers like Maine jonah crab spring roll and a duck confit quesadilla with spicy Chinese sambal are examples.

The short menu changes nightly. At our December visit, you could start with saku tuna tartar with pickled ginger or seared foie gras with pear compote and baby greens. Main courses ranged from Maine diver scallops with steamed cockles, shrimp wontons, Thai noodles and ponzu soy broth to venison medallions with sautéed potato cake and cranberry-chestnut essence. The Florida tilapia fillet was sauced with rice wine-garlic-chile vinaigrette and served with mashed potatoes and baby vegetables. Desserts included a classic crème brûlée and chocolate decadence cake with praline ice cream.

The chef claims "a love affair with the California wine country," which accounts for naming his restaurant for a wine indigenous to California. His small lounge with a copper-topped bar is painted a wine red. He renovated the entry so the lounge is partly open to the beamed dining room appointed in white and brown. The open feeling extends to the guest experience. The exuberant chef tries to meet and greet diners upon arrival "and then do what I like best – cook for fun."

(860) 868-7763. Entrées, $22 to $29. Lunch, Saturday and Sunday 11:30 to 3. Dinner, Thursday-Monday 6 to 11.

Mayflower Inn, 118 Woodbury Road (Route 47), Washington.

The three serene dining rooms along the back of the house are as stately as the rest of this grandly refurbished inn. They're appointed in English country-house style with upholstered high-back chairs at tables covered with white linens over patterned salmon skirts that match the draperies. Tapestries and wrought-iron furniture decorate the garden room.

New chef Jamie West from California's San Ysidro Ranch changes the menu frequently. A recent autumn visit produced the likes of crab-stuffed halibut in pernod beurre blanc, roasted free-range chicken with cranberry chutney, and herb-marinated veal chop with wild mushroom sauce. Starters included duck liver pâté, house-smoked salmon with crisp lavasch and tomato-caper relish, and togarashi-seared ahi tuna sashimi with Chinese mustard sauce.

Desserts are extravagant, from maple crème brûlée to the "chocolate symphony" – a chocolate mousse pyramid, chocolate-caramel tart, chocolate truffle and white chocolate ice cream. Some happily settle for the signature plate of Mayflower cookies.

Some of the dinner appetizers and pastas turn up on the lunch menu. The outdoor terrace with its view of manicured lawns and imported specimen trees is an idyllic setting in season.

(860) 868-9466. Entrées, $18 to $32. Lunch daily, noon to 2. Dinner nightly, 6 to 8.

The Boulders Inn, Route 45, New Preston.

Boulders form a good part of the decor at this inn's redecorated restaurant, jutting out from the walls of an intimate inner dining room and bar as well as in part of the smashing six-sided Lake Dining Room where, through large wraparound windows, almost every diner has a view of Lake Waramaug across the road. The latter is au courant in cream and chocolate brown, with upholstered chairs covered in gray-beige fabric. Interestingly, the best "view" tables are those for two placed neatly around the perimeter – their positions dictated by individual pinpoint spotlights overhead. Three tiered patios add seats for outdoor dining in season.

The contemporary American fare, long a Boulders strong point, changes with the chefs. The latest gave it an international flavor with main courses like grilled swordfish chop with Israeli couscous, jasmine tea-smoked duck breast with an Asian pan-fried noodle and vegetable omelet, and grilled kobe beef ribeye steak with ponzu and wasabi cream. One of the five entrées on the winter menu was falafel and curried vegetables with raita. Featured appetizers were a wild mushroom and bûcheron cheese bruschetta and a scallop and blue crab terrine with coconut emulsion and Thai-spiced lobster oil.

Desserts included caramelized apple crêpes, pumpkin flan, maple crème brûlée, and assorted gelatos and sorbets. An artisan cheese board also was offered.

(860) 868-0541 or (800) 455-1565. Entrées, $28 to $39. Dinner nightly except Tuesday, 6 to 9; weekends only, November-April.

The Birches Inn, 233 West Shore Road, New Preston.

Big windows in this inn's spacious dining room look out onto a patio and down the lawn toward Lake Waramaug. Painted coral with eucalyptus green trim, the room seats 70 at well-spaced tables draped in white over floral undercloths.

The formerly cutting-edge cuisine has been toned down a bit and made more affordable lately through a succession of chefs. A recent autumn menu featured such entrées as seared halibut with a creamy truffle broth, pan-roasted duck breast with cured foie gras and a black fig glaze, and tandoori-marinated grilled leg of lamb. Typical appetizers are yellowfin tuna tartare with wasabi oil and crispy pappadam, Maryland crab cakes with lemon-chive crème fraîche, and a crispy wonton and duck confit napoleon with blood orange sauce.

Dessert could be marsala panna cotta with berries, chocolate-kahlua mousse cake with strawberry coulis, or apple tart with caramel and spiced rum hard sauce.

(860) 868-1735 or (800) 525-3466. Entrées, $20 to $25. Dinner, Wednesday-Monday 5:30 to 9, May-October; Thursday-Monday, rest of year.

The Hopkins Inn, 22 Hopkins Road, New Preston.

On a warm summer day or evening, few dining spots are more inviting than the large outdoor terrace under the giant horse chestnut tree at the entrance to the Hopkins Inn. With the waters of Lake Waramaug shimmering below and a bottle of wine from the Hopkins Vineyard next door, you could imagine yourself in the Alps. No wonder Austrian chef-owner Franz Schober feels right at home.

Dining inside this 1847 Federal structure is rewarding as well. Two dining rooms stretch around the lake view side of the inn; the overflow goes to a paneled Colonial-style taproom up a few stairs. One dining room is Victorian, while the other is rustic with barn siding and ships' figureheads on the walls.

The menu reflects the Austrian and Swiss dishes of the chef's heritage. You might start with pâté maison, eggs à la russe, escargots or bundnerteller. Dinner entrées still include specialties like wiener schnitzel and sweetbreads Viennese that we remember fondly from years past. Trout meunière, chicken cordon bleu, loin lamb chops and filet mignon with béarnaise sauce appeal to traditional palates. In spring, you can get shad roe; Beth Schrober says her husband's roast pheasant with red cabbage and spaetzle is especially popular in fall. Vegetables are special, especially unusual things like braised romaine lettuce.

Regulars cherish the frozen grand marnier soufflé glacé and strawberries romanoff. The varied wine list offers half a dozen from Switzerland as well as several from Hopkins Vineyard. Finish with a flourish with cappuccino or liqueured coffees.

The luncheon menu offers many of the same specialties at lower prices. Entrées like lamb curry, veal à la Suisse and sirloin steak are in the $10 to $15 range. Little wonder the place is so popular.

(860) 868-7295. Entrées, $18.75 to $24.75. Lunch, Tuesday-Saturday noon to 2, Saturday only in April, November and December. Dinner 6 to 9 or 10. Sunday 12:30 to 8:30. Closed January-March.

Toll Gate Hill, 571 Torrington Road (Route 202), Litchfield.

Good food and historic ambiance are the hallmarks of the restaurant in the restored 1745 house and tavern in which Captain William Bull fed stagecoach passengers along the old Hartford-Albany stage route.

Carlton Rodgers, former executive chef at the Hartford Club, showed up in 2003 to help the Pecora family reopen the inn and restaurant, which had been closed for several years. He restored the Toll Gate's signature shellfish pie in puff pastry, which turned out to have been a takeoff on the famed lobster pot pie that he had developed at the Hartford Club. Working in a newly renovated kitchen here, he offers an ambitious menu far more in keeping with the 21st century than the 18th.

Consider his appetizers of flounder carpaccio, tea-smoked duck summer rolls with a lychee salsa, the barbecued pork crostini with crawfish aioli on polenta tea cakes, and an updated escargots bourguignonne "lightly tossed in a zinfandel bosnian herb butter veloute."

Main courses range from cedar-planked salmon tournedos glazed with mangos and honey to dried fruit-crusted rack of lamb with madras curry sauce. Steamed fillet of red snapper, quail escabèche and maple-lacquered pork porterhouse are among the possibilities.

Desserts might be caramelized apple crêpe, pineapple-white chocolate bread pudding or chocolate ravioli with hazelnut gelato.

Meals are served in two small, charming dining areas on the old tavern's main floor and upstairs in a ballroom complete with a fiddler's loft for piano and other musical entertainment. Tall booths are featured in the old tavern with its dark wood and wide-plank floors. The more formal room, dressed with peach linens and Villeroy & Boch china, is enhanced by wall murals of 18th-century Litchfield painted by a local artist.

(860) 567-1233 or (866) 567-1233. Entrées, $18 to $24. Lunch daily, noon to 3. Dinner, 5:30 to 9:30 or 10:30. Sunday brunch, 11:30 to 3:30. Closed Tuesday and Wednesday in off-season.

3W & the Blue Bar, 3 West St., Litchfield.

Traditionalists don't know quite what to make of this new establishment with the odd name (for its address and the color of its bar in back) and its specialty of sushi. Some dismiss it as a funky, Soho-style sushi bar and a singles hangout.

But chef Erly Gallo and his partner, Jennifer Hallock – locals, both – knew what they were doing when they took over what was the County Seat coffeehouse and café.

They transformed its prime corner space facing the Litchfield green into an urbane, salon-style setting for dining at blond pine tables amid brick walls, hardwood floors and a pressed-tin ceiling. There's a small sushi bar in front. In back, screened from the two-level dining area by a wide curtain/partition of bamboo, is the blue bar with stone counter tops. Call it a vaguely Asian look, Litchfield style.

Chef Erly rolls the sushi – the usual selection, plus one of tempura-style lobster, a New England roll of tuna with avocado, sesame and tobiko, and an Alaskan roll substituting salmon for tuna. A Philadelphia roll combines smoked salmon, cream cheese and scallions.

But the Asian-inspired fare goes far beyond sushi. For dinner, look for such starters as pan-seared crab cakes with roasted garlic-tomato aioli, Chinese sausage and rock shrimp shumai, tuna carpaccio, a crunchy Thai salad and a dim sum trio for two.

Main courses range from sesame-encrusted tuna loin with wasabi crème fraîche to scotch-marinated sirloin with a brown sugar and soy demi-glace. Less adventurous palates are appeased with lemon-chervil fillet of sole, chicken breast in wild mushroom sauce, or caramelized apple pork loin. The winter menu even offers a "traditional" beef stew.

Desserts come from the in-house bakery around the corner.

(860) 567-1742. Entrées, $17 to $28. Lunch, Monday-Friday 11 to 3. Dinner nightly, 5:30 to 9:30 or 10:30.

G.W. Tavern, 20 Bee Brook Road, Washington Depot.

This restaurant of many changing names has seen several big-bucks renovations over the years. But none more so than the one that transformed the late Bee Brook, a highly rated fine-dining establishment, into a downscaled pub and tavern.

Open the latch on what must be the oldest barn door around to enter the main tavern dining room with an upscale Colonial look, oriental carpets on the floors and wonderful murals of surrounding towns on the walls. The rear porch beside the stream has been enclosed for year-round casual dining. The outdoor terraces are popular in summer.

Chef-owner Robert Margolis features "good, simple pub food." At a recent autumn visit, the changing menu started with stuffed potato skins and Buffalo-style chicken wings as well as fried oysters with homemade tartar sauce and salmon cakes with curried mango chutney. The hefty salads held more interest.

Main courses are equally varied. Go basic with burgers, meat loaf, chicken pot pie, and fish and chips. Or splurge on Maryland crab cakes, braised lamb shank bordelaise or filet mignon with brandied cream sauce. Desserts include pumpkin pie," blueberry cobbler and triple chocolate cake.

The initials on the name stand for George Washington, whose hatchet is carved in the sign out front. This is, after all, another of those towns named for the first president.

(860) 868-6633. Entrées, $12.50 to $30. Lunch daily, 11:30 to 5:30. Dinner nightly, 5:30 to 10 or 11. Saturday and Sunday brunch, 11:30 to 2:30.

Diversions

Lakes and Parks. Lake Waramaug State Park at the west end of the lake is a wonderfully scenic site, its picnic tables scattered well apart along the tree-lined shore, right beside the water. The lake's Indian name means "good fishing place." It's also good for swimming and boating, and is blessedly uncrowded. On the north and east sides of the lake are the forested Above All and Mount Bushnell state parks. Not far from Lake Waramaug on the road to Litchfield (Route 202) is **Mount Tom State Park.** It has a 60-acre spring-fed pond for swimming and again picnic tables are poised at shore's edge. A mile-long trail rises to a tower atop Mount Tom.

White Memorial Conservation Center and Nature Museum, 80 Whitehall Road, Litchfield.

Off Route 202 just west of Litchfield are 4,000 acres of nature sanctuary bordering Bantam Lake. Thirty-five miles of woodland and marsh trails are popular with hikers, horseback riders and cross-country skiers. This is a great place for observing wildlife, birds and plants in a variety of habitats. The recently expanded nature museum has good collections of Indian artifacts, butterflies, live and stuffed animals, interactive exhibits, and an excellent nature library and gift shop. Spectacular dioramas and giant photo murals depict the wetlands, fields, old-growth forest and upland hardwood forest that make up Connecticut's largest nature sanctuary.

(860) 567-0857. www.whitememorialcc.org. Museum open, Monday-Saturday 9 to 5, Sunday noon to 5; adults $4. Grounds open free year-round.

White Flower Farm, Route 63, Litchfield.

This institution three miles south of Litchfield is a don't-miss spot for anyone with a green thumb. People come from across the country to see the place made famous by its catalog, wittily written by the owner under the pen name of Amos Pettingill. Ten acres of exotic display gardens are at peak bloom in late spring; twenty acres of growing fields reach their height in late summer. Greenhouses with indoor plants, including spectacular giant tuberous begonias, are pretty all the time.

(860) 567-8789. www.whiteflowerfarm.com. Shop and grounds open daily 9 to 5:30, April-Christmas.

Litchfield Historic Sites. The Litchfield Historic District is clustered along the long, wide green and out North and South streets (Route 63). The seasonal information center on the green has maps for walking tours, which are the best way to experience Litchfield. Note the bank and the jail with a common wall at North and West streets. Along North Street are Sheldon's Tavern, where George Washington slept, plus the birthplace of Harriet Beecher Stowe and the Pierce Academy, the first academy for girls. South Street is a broad, half-mile-long avenue where two U.S. senators, six Congressmen, three governors and five chief justices have lived. Here too is the **Tapping Reeve House & Law School** (1773), the first law school in the country. The house with its handsome furnishings and the tiny school with handwritten ledgers of students long gone are open Tuesday-Saturday 11 to 5 and Sunday 1 to 5, mid-April through November, $5. The fee also includes admission to the **Litchfield History Museum,** which has seven galleries of early American paintings, decorative arts, furniture, textiles and local history exhibits.

Litchfield Congregational Church faces green.

Wineries. Two of New England's premier wineries occupy hilltop sites overlooking the beauty of Litchfield and Lake Waramaug. **Haight Vineyard,** Connecticut's first farm winery just east of Litchfield, occupies an English Tudor-style building with a large tasting room and gift shop at 29 Chestnut Hill Road. Guided winery tours on the hour and a fifteen-minute vineyard walk are among the attractions. You can pick up a bottle of award-winning covertside white or chardonnay plus a pink T-shirt ("Never bite the foot that stomps your grapes"), wine accessories and such. Open Monday-Saturday 10:30 to 5, Sunday noon to 5.

Hopkins Vineyard, 25 Hopkins Road, New Preston. A hillside location with a good view of Lake Waramaug marks this family operation personally run by Bill and Judy Hopkins, dairy farmers turned winemakers, and their offspring. The rustic red barn provides a quick, self-guided tour from an upstairs vantage point, an attractive showroom and tasting area, and the country-sophisticated Hayloft Wine Bar upstairs, where on weekends you can order a cheese and pâté board and wines by the glass and savor a view of the lake. The gift shop sells wine-related items like baskets, grapevine wreaths and stemware, even handmade linen towels. The winery's cat may be snoozing near the wood stove, upon which a pot of mulled wine simmers on chilly days. On nice days, sip a hearty cabernet franc or an estate chardonnay in a small picnic area overlooking the lake. Open Monday-Saturday 10 to 5, Sunday 11 to 5, May-December; Wednesday-Sunday in March and April, Friday-Sunday in January and February.

Shopping. Good shops have sprung up in the center of Litchfield. In an historic carriage house in a quaint courtyard behind the village green is **Cobble Court** with "a new breed" of home furnishings on two floors. Also in Cobble Court is Troy Brook Visions, furniture maker. On the green is **Workshop Inc.,** a boutique with updated women's apparel and accessories; downstairs is a gallery of home furnishings, from wicker furniture to pillows and dhurries to unusual placemats. **Barnidge & McEnroe,** a good bookstore, has an espresso bar up front. **Hayseed** stocks a great selection of cards along with jewelry, sweaters and clothing for the country lifestyle. **Kitchenworks** has expanded its kitchenware and gourmet shop on West Street, near the new **Talbots** store. Others of appeal to specific interests are **Jeffrey Tillou Antiques,** the **Thomas McKnight Gallery, Bella Cosa** for Italian ceramics and **R. Derwin Clothiers.**

New Preston, a mountain hamlet down the hillside from Lake Waramaug, has interesting shops. Just the ticket for weekenders looking to outfit themselves and their country homes is the expanded **J. Seitz & Co.** Now occupying two floors of a converted auto garage overlooking a waterfall, Joanna Seitz features spirited clothing, accessories, gifts and furniture. Antiques, accessories and interior design are the focus of a changing lineup of shops with names like **Betsey & Duane, Déjà vu Antiques, City House-Country House** and **The Village Barn and Gallery.** Interspersed amid them all you'll find select cookware at **New Preston Kitchen Goods**. Across the street, check out the New York-based **Lou Marotta & Friends** for antiques plus new furniture, jewelry, baby clothes, men's wear, bath products and what have you.

Extra-Special

The Pantry, Titus Road, Washington Depot.

One of our favorite places for lunch and shopping is this upscale gourmet shop lovingly run by Michael and Nancy Ackerman. A counter displays and a blackboard lists the day's offerings from an extensive repertoire, and you can get anything to take out as well. The fare is innovative, with especially good soups, salads, sandwiches and desserts. A spring visit brought forth soups like celery-leek and curried cauliflower. Among entrées were fresh tuna and swordfish niçoise with tarragon carrots, torta rustica, salmon cakes with mixed green salad and a vegetarian chili with watercress cabbage slaw. Continental breakfast is served from 10 to 11:30; a huge sticky bun and cappuccino would make a good break from nipping around Washington Depot's shops. In summer, poached salmon is a favorite, more salads are offered, and soups like gazpacho teem with fresh vegetables. For dessert, chocolate indulgence, mayan torte and pecan tart with ginger ice cream are worth the calories. Tables, decorated perhaps with lilies in flat bowls, are set amidst high-tech shelves on which are just about every exotic chutney, mustard, vinegar, extra-virgin olive oil and the like that you could imagine, as well as kitchenware and tableware, baskets and pottery.

(860) 868-0258. Entrées, $6.50 to $8.95. Open Tuesday-Saturday 10 to 6. Lunch from 11:30 to 3:30. Tea 3:30 to 5.

Index

A

B

C

D

I

J

K

L

M

S

T

Also by the Authors

Inn Spots & Special Places / Mid-Atlantic. The second volume in the series, this book by Nancy and Richard Woodworth covers 34 favorite destinations from western New York through the Mid-Atlantic region to southeastern Virginia. First published in 1992; revised and expanded fifth edition in 2003. 536 pages of timely ideas. $18.95.

Inn Spots & Special Places in the Southeast. The newest in the series, this book by Nancy and Richard Woodworth covers 26 special areas from North Carolina to Florida. With its emphasis on fine inns and good restaurants, the series now covers the entire East Coast, from Eastport, Me., to Key West, Fla. Published in 1999. 376 pages of fresh ideas. $16.95.

Getaways for Gourmets in the Northeast. The first book by Nancy and Richard Woodworth appeals to the gourmet in all of us. It guides you to the best dining, lodging, specialty food shops and culinary attractions in 24 areas from the Brandywine Valley to Montreal, Cape May to Cape Cod, the Finger Lakes to Boston. First published in 1984; updated seventh edition in 2003. 602 pages to savor. $19.95.

New England's Best. This new book by Nancy and Richard Woodworth is a comprehensive guide to the best lodging, dining and attractions around New England. It's the culmination of 30 years of living and traveling in New England by journalists who have seen them all and can recommend the best. Published in 2002. 602 pages of valuable information. $18.95.

Best Restaurants of New England. This new edition by Nancy and Richard Woodworth is the most comprehensive guide to great restaurants throughout New England. The authors detail the dining ambiance, menu offerings, hours and prices for more than 1,000 restaurants. First published in 1990; revised third edition in 2002. 520 pages of delicious information. $16.95.

Waterside Escapes in the Northeast. This new edition by Nancy and Richard Woodworth relates the best lodging, dining, attractions and activities in 36 great waterside vacation spots from the Chesapeake Bay to Cape Breton Island and from Niagara-on-the-Lake to Martha's Vineyard. First published in 1987; revised and expanded fourth edition in 2001. 490 pages to discover and enjoy. $16.95.

The Originals in Their Fields

These books may be ordered from your local bookstore, on line or direct from the publisher, pre-paid, plus $2 shipping for each book. Connecticut residents add sales tax.

Wood Pond Press
365 Ridgewood Road
West Hartford, Conn. 06107
Tel: (860) 521-0389
Fax: (860) 313-0185
E-Mail: woodpond@ntplx.net
Web Site: www.getawayguides.com.

"Easy, miss," the captain said. "If you'll just put down that gun, we can talk."

"You go ahead and talk. I can hear just fine," Shannon snapped.

One of the soldiers laughed. "I bet you can do more than that, sister."

For the first time Shannon realized how she must look. Her wrapper hung about her loosely, revealing her thin nightgown. Her red hair was flying about her face in even more confusion than usual, defying the pins she had used in an attempt to tame it while she slept. She would have liked to smooth it down and pull her wrapper tight, but she didn't intend to move. She leveled the gun at the lead man and hoped the moonlight didn't reveal too much.

The officer turned to his company and spoke sharply. "The next man who speaks out of turn will answer to me." His voice brought instant silence.

"I beg your pardon, miss," he began. "I'm Captain Randal Hunt with the 7th Ohio Regiment now in Lexington. We're on the trail of a band of guerillas."

"They've been here and gone," she answered, and for a moment the gun she held wavered. "They've shot my father . . ."

A Heart Divided

Ann Gabhart

WARNER BOOKS

A Warner Communications Company

WARNER BOOKS EDITION

Cover art by Elaine Duille

Warner Books, Inc., 75 Rockefeller Plaza, New York, N.Y. 10019

A Warner Communications Company

Printed in the United States of America

First Printing: December, 1980

10 9 8 7 6 5 4 3 2 1

To Darrell

A Heart Divided

CHAPTER 1

Shannon Marsh sat up in bed. The bit of moonlight sifting through the windows assured her that no one was in the room with her. Yet something had pulled her from sleep as surely as if a hand had reached out and shaken her shoulder.

She yanked on her wrapper as she went out into the hall. Only then did she hear the sounds of horses outside. At this time of the night, that could mean nothing but trouble. Without making a sound, Shannon hurried down the stairs. She needed no light to guide her feet, although it was almost totally dark here in the middle of the house. This wasn't the first time she'd slipped down the stairs during the deep hours of night. The darkness had often been a friend to Shannon, hiding her from those who might try to stop her midnight rides on Satin.

Now she eased the draperies back from the front

window just enough to peek out. Guerrillas! There was no mistaking the tight band of men approaching the house. The neighborhood had been full of the talk of these raiders who had no allegiance to any cause but their own enrichment. Shannon peered out at the men, searching furtively for a face she might recognize, but they were cast in shadow, a part of the night.

Then she saw her father. The white of the nightshirt he'd tucked into his pants flashed through the dark as he moved out away from the house to stand in front of the men. Her eyes caught the glint of metal in the hand he held close to his side. At least he had his pistol.

While Shannon watched the men stop their horses and wait for her father, something cold gripped her heart, almost stilling it in her breast. Her father moved slowly, but without hesitation, to meet them. Shannon told herself that it was going to be all right. Her father knew how to handle trouble.

But then the growl of a low voice came from among the men. Shannon couldn't hear what he said, but she saw her father jerk back from the words.

"Never!" he shouted. He'd never backed down from anything, and he wouldn't start now with a bunch of outlaws from the war. "You thieving renegades! I'll shoot the lot of you before I let you take that horse."

Shannon whirled away from the window and ran for her father's study. It took only seconds to reach up over the door and pull down the shotgun, but it was already too late. The sound of her father's pistol sang through the night and was followed an instant later by a half-dozen shots.

Shannon burst through the front door, firing wildly while the blast of another gun came from the slaves' quarters. The mounted men spun their horses around and galloped away, but her father didn't lift himself up from the ground. Shannon ran to him and was kneeling beside him, raising his head into her arms before the impact of fear hit her.

"Papa, are you all right?"

"They were after horses." His voice was weak, only an echo of the defiant tone of minutes ago. "The leader asked for Marsh Queen." He coughed and clutched at Shannon.

"Shh, Papa. Don't try to talk," Shannon said. Her hand had found warm blood soaking through his shirt just below his heart.

He shook his head impatiently. "But Queenie's foal by Lexington will be the best that's ever come off Marshland."

"I know, Papa."

"It's up to you now, Shannon, to take care of her. To take care of everything." His voice was getting fainter, so she had to lean close to hear him.

"No, Papa!" Tears pushed at her eyes, and a scream gathered in her throat, but she strained to keep her voice gentle and calm. "Aunt Mamie will fix you up as good as new."

"Not this time, Shannon." His eyes met hers clearly in the moonlight. "My dear Shannon, if only you'd been the boy."

His body shook with his last struggle for breath while life left him. Then he was still. Shannon held her father a minute longer as her faint hopes evaporated away into nothingness; then she gently laid him down on the ground. She could feel everything inside her whirling about madly, shifting, rearranging, and she knew that nothing would ever be the same again. The girl who had knelt by her father had known one kind of life; the one who stood up now would know another.

She wanted to fight against the change, to deny it. She wanted to wipe away the night and go back to the hours of sunlight. She wanted to be in the kitchen, with

Aunt Mamie fussing over her, urging her to eat more supper. Just the thought of Aunt Mamie made Shannon long to run to the safety of those warm black arms, to hide somehow from the horror of what had just happened. But time couldn't be moved backward, and even now the minutes were ticking past while her father lay on the ground, the warmth of life leaving his body.

"Miss Shannon? Is you all right?" Tom broke into her reverie.

The Negro stood beside her with a lantern and a rifle. Almost absent-mindedly she wondered where he'd found the gun. Slaves weren't supposed to have guns, but it didn't matter. She opened her mouth and was surprised to hear her voice come out so strongly. "I'm all right, Tom, but I think Papa's dead." The words left a cold place inside her.

Tom bent over her father. "Not the master." The old black man moaned. "You oughta let them outlaws have the horses when they come, Master Marsh. Weren't no use a fighting."

Shannon stared into the dark and listened to Tom talking to her father as though he could still hear. Rage flooded through her. There was no reason to the world. All her father had wanted was to keep Marshland away from the war and to protect his land and horses from both the North and the South.

But the war wouldn't stay away. It was like a creeping vine, each day growing over another foot of the world she had known and choking out the lives of people. Uncle Simon lay dead in some nameless grave at a place called Shiloh. Colin and Jett were somewhere in the South riding behind General Morgan. And now her father had been senselessly murdered while trying to save a horse.

"Miss Shannon!" The sound of panic in Tom's voice interrupted her thoughts. "There's horses coming."

"Quick, go tell Adam to hide Queenie out in the

woods in the east pasture till it's safe." Her father had died to keep that horse here.

"I can't leave you here alone, Miss Shannon."

"Do as I say, Tom!" Her voice was harsh. When he still hesitated, she said more softly, "You'll be more help hiding out with that gun than here. Where'd you get it anyway, Tom?"

"The master hisself give it to me when Mr. Simon and then Mr. Colin rode off to the war. Said he might need some help if looters come around, but I didn't hear them till it was too late."

Shannon could hear the horses clearly now. "Run, Tom!" she insisted.

He went without another word. Shannon saw the barn door open, and in the next moment Adam led Queenie away through the night. They had just disappeared into the blackness of the trees behind the house when the horsemen came into sight.

Shannon raised her gun to her shoulder. The men riding up had no way of knowing it was empty. She took a few steps forward to meet them, concentrating on showing no fear, though she couldn't keep from thinking how like her father she must look and how she'd surely have no more chance than he had had against the raiders.

But the men coming toward her now were not the guerrilla band, and the relief that passed through Shannon made her arms feel weak. She took a deep breath and steadied her grip on the gun as she waited for the small party of Union soldiers to pull up in front of her. She wouldn't lower the gun. Not yet. There were some who said the soldiers were as bad as the outlaws, and in truth the outlaws who were deserters often wore their Army uniforms. Yet this group looked to be riding in regular military order. When they stopped in front of her, Shannon spoke to the man who appeared to be in charge. "What do you want?"

"Easy, miss," the man said. "If you'll just put down that gun, we can talk."

"You go ahead and talk. I can hear just fine," Shannon snapped back.

One of the soldiers laughed. "I bet you can do more than that, sister."

For the first time, Shannon realized how she must look. Her robe hung about her loosely, revealing her thin nightgown. Her red hair was flying about her face in even more confusion than usual, defying the pins she used in an attempt to tame it while she slept. She would have liked to smooth it down and pull her wrapper tight, but she didn't intend to move now. She leveled the gun at the lead man and prayed that the moonlight wasn't revealing too much. Even with Tom's help she couldn't fight ten men.

The officer turned to his company and spoke sharply. "The next man who speaks out of turn will answer to me." His voice brought instant silence. He turned back to Shannon. "I beg your pardon, miss. I'm Captain Randal Hunt with the 7th Ohio Regiment now in Lexington. We're on the trail of a band of guerrillas reported to be in the area."

"They've been here and gone."

"I hope they didn't harm you in any way," he said, and again there was a half-suppressed laugh from one of the soldiers.

Shannon was glad this Captain Hunt was between her and the men behind him. He sat straight on his horse with the proud posture of a man who is always in charge no matter what happens. That's the way her father had been until tonight. The thought of her father made her hands shake on the gun, and for a second it wavered. She pulled it back up steady and said, "They shot my father."

In one quick movement, Captain Hunt was off his

horse and beside her father's body. "Couldn't have been more than a half hour," he said almost to himself. He looked up at Shannon. "Which way did they ride out?"

Shannon shook her head a bit. "I don't know." Once she'd come out the door, she'd had no thought except to get to her father.

He turned to his men and barked out quick orders. The group divided and rode out to pick up the trail. He watched them for a moment before coming back to Shannon.

She was still holding the gun, but it was anything but threatening. He took hold of the barrel and lifted it out of her hands. Then he put his hand on her arm. "I'm sorry about your father."

They were very close, and she could see his face clearly. There was no doubting his sincerity. His eyes held nothing but kindness. Yet his very touch set off the rage inside her, and she pummeled him with her fists. He was part of this awful war, and she struck out at him blindly, unreasoningly.

He was startled, but there was no answering anger in his face, only understanding. He could have slapped her to bring her away from her hysteria or turned and left her there alone in the dark. Instead, he gently pulled her to him and held her tightly against him until all her fight was gone.

For a moment they stood like that. Shannon, quiet in his arms, drew comfort from the rough feel of his coat against her cheek and his manly smell. She couldn't move time back, but just for that moment it seemed to stand still and she didn't have to face the truth, not while the captain had his arms around her.

"It's all right, miss," he said softly into her hair.

The words meant to calm her only brought the reality of the present back to her. Things couldn't be all right. Her father was dead, and fresh anger surged back through her. What gave this stranger the right to tell her that anything was all right? She yanked away from him and said, "Get off my land! Just go away and leave us alone!"

He didn't try to reach out to her again. Her anger held him away from her as surely as if she had thrown up a stone fence between them. Finally, without another word, he turned and mounted his horse.

Shannon watched him ride away and hated herself for wanting to stay in the captain's arms. She brushed impatiently at the hot, bitter tears biting into her cheeks. She had no time for any of that, even if her grief was tearing at her soul. Her father had given her a job to do before he died. She must take care of Marshland and all those on it. The horses, the family, the blacks. She was responsible for everything.

She looked around to see Tom coming from the barn and her mother and Clay peeking out the front door of the house. No, she had no time for tears. She might never again. She took a deep breath and pushed all the wild grief inside her into a big chunk that sat heavy on her chest.

Then she yelled at Clay, "Come here and help Tom carry Papa into the house."

Clay moved out on the porch and called back, "I can't. I don't have on my shoes."

Shannon was very tired suddenly. "Neither do I, Clay." In a softer voice that he couldn't hear, she added, "Our father is dead. What difference do shoes make?"

Shannon kept vigil by her father's body throughout the rest of the night. Aunt Mamie had wanted to stay with her, but Shannon had sent her off to bed. She'd wanted to be alone.

Just before dawn, Shannon took out the family Bible. She opened it and ran her finger down the family record page. The older entries were in her Grandfather Clay's hand, but all the newer ones were her mother's tiny perfect letters. It didn't seem right for her father to be reduced to such a small line in the Bible. Shannon found a pen and wrote, "Emmett Marsh shot to death this sixth day of June, 1863 at the age of 55."

Her writing looked out of place, almost blasphemous next to the other entries, and her father's death filled only one line. His whole existence was reduced to a few lines: the date of his birth, his marriage to Olivia Clay, and now his death. Shannon pushed the Bible back up on the shelf and left the house.

The barn was quiet when she went in. The slaves wouldn't be about their work for another half-hour or so. Shannon led a small black horse out of one of the stalls and quickly saddled him.

She rode Satin out to the back pasture slowly, drinking in the sight of the land awakening to the sun. She watched the dew lifting from the grass and heard the birds stirring in the trees. Her father should be there beside her to share it, but his eyes were shut now to the beauty of the land forever. The sadness billowed up inside her, almost choking her.

When at last they reached the back pasture, she let Satin have his head, and he reveled in the freedom to run. Shannon's long hair pulled loose from its pins and flew out behind her, and she thought of nothing but the wind in her face and the power of the horse beneath her. Only here, alone in the pasture with her horse, could she let her spirit go free. Here she could melt into Satin, and together they became something wild and free.

Satin began to slow, and Shannon spoke softly into his ear. She let him unwind in a slow gallop and then turned back to the barn. It wasn't until then that she saw the man who was watching her from the edge of the field. Satin nickered nervously, and Shannon soothed him with a touch.

She knew at once that it was the Union captain, by the way he sat his horse. She pulled Satin up and waited for him to come up to her.

CHAPTER 2

While she waited, Shannon smoothed down her skirt, making sure her ankles were covered, as if by doing that she could pull a ladylike composure over herself. She touched her hair, but there was no way to straighten the thick curls of red spilling about her shoulders and down her back.

With a shrug she turned her attention to the man coming toward her. He was slim but with a full, generous look about him. His light brown hair hung almost to his collar and his moustache was sprinkled with blond. Tiny wrinkles framed eyes that were the color of a clear summer sky. He looked so warm and friendly that it didn't matter that he wasn't really handsome. Shannon kept her eyes on his face and tried not to think about the feel of his strong arms around her the night before.

He stopped his horse in front of her and took off his

hat. "I'm sorry to bother you, Miss Marsh, but your man at the barn said I might find you here."

Shannon repressed the smile that wanted to come to her lips in response to his. "He should have told you to wait at the barn."

"He did, but I'm afraid I insisted on seeing you at once."

"I guess it doesn't matter now, since you're already here," she said. "What can I do for you, Captain?"

Instead of answering her question, he said, "Where did you learn to ride a horse like that?"

Shannon touched Satin's neck lightly. "You don't *learn* to ride like that, Captain Hunt. You either can or you can't."

The captain nodded. "I've watched some jockeys ride who seem to have a special touch. Can you ride any horse with that kind of control or only this one, Miss Marsh?"

For the first time, Shannon smiled. She couldn't keep from it. "I really don't know about *any* horse, Captain—just the ones I've ridden." She looked at him boldly. "I guess I don't ride in exactly a ladylike way. Are you shocked?"

"Shocked?" He smiled and nodded. "Well, I'll admit it is a little surprising to ride out to a pasture, expecting to see you gently strolling the field, and see you flashing by instead."

"I assure you, I am very much the proper lady—except in the early morning privacy of my own field. Not many people are so determined to see me."

"I should think the young men would be determined to see you no matter where you are."

"You're very kind, sir. But even if that were so, the war seems to keep the young men otherwise occupied."

"Yes, the war. You can almost forget about it in this meadow," he answered, surveying the grassy expanse before he reluctantly started his horse back toward the barn.

Shannon paced Satin to walk beside his horse. "But the war never is very far away, is it?" she said.

He shook his head. "I've seen meadows just as calm and beautiful as this echo with the sounds of cannon." His smile disappeared as he remembered things he wished he could forget.

For a few minutes they rode without speaking. Finally he said, "With which side are your sympathies, Miss Marsh?"

"Are you making a survey for the provost marshal?" Shannon's voice was cold.

"I guess that wasn't exactly a fair question. But believe me, I don't report to the provost marshal. I was just curious."

After a moment Shannon said thoughtfully, "I tried not to take sides, but I've found that is the most difficult thing of all to do. It makes you everybody's enemy." Shannon looked around her. They could see the house and barns laid out in front of them now, bathed in the full morning sun. Something inside her tightened together at the sight. "Papa tried so hard to keep the war away from all this. He loved Marshland as though he'd been born here instead of in Ireland. He'd never had any land before he married my mother, and to him the land was the most important thing of all."

"I think I can understand how he felt," the captain said. "I was born in Woodford County on a small farm. Nothing like this, but it was ours. When I was eight, Pa had to give up and go into town to find a job. I guess he still grieves over that plot of land." He looked at her. "Is the land important to you, Miss Marsh?"

"Not the way it was to my father, because I never knew his hunger for it. I've always been able to walk out on it and know in my heart that I belong here. I think that every morning when Papa woke up, he was freshly surprised and proud. That's the reason he couldn't stand to see any of it taken from him."

The captain nodded. "Then I suppose he could have done no less than he did last night."

Shannon knew what he said was true, but she still couldn't accept it. Maybe she'd never be able to.

Tom came out to meet them when they reached the barn, and the captain slid off his horse quickly to help Shannon dismount. Shannon let him lift her down. "Thank you, Captain. It seems your mother was more successful in teaching you the gentleman's role than mine was in teaching me the lady's."

Tom was frowning. "The master done told me not to let you take Satin out to the back pasture less'n somebody went with you, Miss Shannon."

"It's all right, Tom. Papa wouldn't have cared this time." Satin pricked up his ears as Tom took the reins, and Shannon said, "Do you want me to rub him down, Tom?"

"Now don't you go baby coddling me, Miss Shannon. I ain't so old that I can't handle this devil, but you might ask him not to bite me again. It's got so hackles raise on my neck everytime he turns his head."

Shannon smiled. "All right, Tom, if you think it'll help."

"That horse knows what you say the rest of the time, don't he?"

Shannon went to Satin's head. "You go along with Tom, and behave yourself now, Satin." The horse nuzzled her hair. Shannon stroked his neck and said, "Be a good horse."

When Shannon turned back to the captain, he was watching her with a look on his face that she couldn't read. "Is something wrong?" she asked.

He shook his head. "No, just different. Would you really have rubbed down that horse yourself?"

"Sure, why not? Tom's getting old, and now that so much of the help has gone, we all have to help out. Besides, Satin can be mean when he wants to be, and I just don't know what we'd do if anything happened to Tom."

The captain shook his head again, and Shannon smiled. "I've shocked you again, haven't I?" Then she sighed. "I guess I shock everyone except myself. But tell me, Captain, you surely didn't ride all the way out here just to watch my remarkable behavior. What is it you want?"

With a sigh he pulled his mind back to business. "I need to fill out a report about last night." He saw the frown fly across her face. "But if you'd rather not right now, I can come back another time."

"Really, Captain Hunt. You chase me out to my back pasture, and then you say you can wait. Either it is, or it isn't, important."

"I would like to make sure that I have the correct names, and I thought you might have remembered something about the guerrillas."

"You didn't catch them then."

He shook his head. "They knew the country too well. It would help if you could say what color they were wearing."

"You mean, if they were Union or Confederate? Is the Union Army actually acknowledging that there are outlaws wearing blue?"

"You sound more and more like you're on the side of the South, Miss Marsh."

"I certainly didn't mean to, Captain," Shannon said with a touch of bitterness. "We can't afford too many more fines from the Union government."

"All that has nothing to do with me."

"Perhaps, Captain. But you are here on Army business, aren't you? And you do wear the blue." She took a deep breath and pulled her feelings under control. When she spoke again, her voice was cool. All traces of friendliness were gone. "If you'll come inside, Captain, I'll give you whatever information you need."

"Certainly, Miss Marsh," he said, trying to match her businesslike manner.

They met her mother in the front hall. "Shannon, you didn't go riding in that dress, did you?" she said, frowning. "Well, at least you had to use the sidesaddle. And your hair, Shannon, go fix it at once."

"Not now, Mother. We have a visitor." Shannon turned to the captain. "This is Captain Hunt, Mother. Captain, my mother, Olivia Clay Marsh." She spotted Clay hovering in the doorway behind her mother. "And this is my brother Clay."

"It's a pleasure to meet you, Mrs. Marsh, and you, Clay." He made a stiff little bow toward her and then nodded to Clay. "Are there other family members here, Miss Marsh?"

"I don't see why that would be any of your business, Captain, but no, there aren't. My other brother, Colin, is with General Morgan."

Her mother gasped. "How dare you call him your brother!"

Shannon turned to her. "He is my brother, Mother, and Clay's too." Their eyes met, and a battle raged between them for a brief moment before her mother looked away.

"Half-brother," her mother said weakly. She looked at the captain. "I'm not feeling good. If you'll excuse me . . ." At once Clay was by her side, helping her upstairs.

Shannon watched them go up the stairs and wished

she hadn't upset her mother. But Colin was her brother, and Shannon would never deny that.

"I hope this won't take long," she said as she led the captain into her father's study. "I have to see to the arrangements for my father's funeral."

"I just need a few minutes of your time." He took a piece of paper out of his pocket and jotted down the information Shannon gave him in answer to his questions. Finally he folded the paper and put it away. "Now can you remember anything about the men last night that might help us track them down?" he asked.

Shannon shook her head slowly. "I only saw them riding away. But there is one thing."

Captain Hunt leaned toward her. "What?"

"Before he died, Papa said they asked for Marsh Queen by name."

"Marsh Queen?"

"She's one of our best. Papa just had her bred to Lexington."

"I saw Lexington run. He's one of the greatest stallions in the country."

"If not the greatest," Shannon said. "Are you a horseman, Captain Hunt?"

"I worked for a stable in New Orleans before the war."

"I always wanted to see the racing at New Orleans, but Papa never let me go with him to tracks out of state. It wasn't considered quite the thing to do, you know, to take horses out of Kentucky to race. Raising horses around here is very much a gentleman's sport, but Papa went into it to make money. He said he couldn't sit around waiting for buyers to come to him. He wanted to show them what he had and that Kentucky was the best place in the world for breeding fine racehorses."

"A few people were beginning to agree with him about that before the war." Captain Hunt waited a moment before asking, "But who would have heard about this special horse?"

"I don't know." Shannon went over to her father's desk and touched the papers her father had been working on the night before. The grief she'd kept pushed back suddenly welled up inside her as she looked down at his bold handwriting, but she wouldn't let herself lose control in front of this man again. She stilled her emotions and turned back to the captain. "I suppose everybody would. Papa liked to talk about his horses."

He stood up, and for a minute Shannon thought he might touch her again, but he didn't move. Only his eyes reached out and captured hers with a gentle look. In that moment he seemed to be offering her something that Shannon didn't know how to accept. With effort she turned her eyes away from his.

Only then did he speak. "I won't take up any more of your time."

She followed him out to the porch. He hesitated for an instant before he said, "I'm sorry we had to meet under such sad circumstances. I'd like to come back some time, Miss Marsh, when I'm not representing the Army."

"If you'd like, Captain. Perhaps we could go riding."

"I'm not at all sure my Blackie could keep up with your horse."

"I wasn't challenging you to a race, Captain. Just a ride."

His laugh reached deep inside her and warmed her. He said, "I'm not sure a ride wouldn't be a race with you." He mounted his horse and raised his hat. "Till we meet again, Miss Marsh."

She watched him go, feeling the warmth slipping away as he rode out of sight until there was nothing but a cold emptiness left inside her.

To the left she could see two of the blacks digging in the family graveyard, and just coming into sight on the lane was a dark heavy wagon. The undertaker she'd sent for had arrived. She wanted to run back to the barn and take another horse out, letting the wind blow away the truth. But she couldn't. The truth wouldn't go away... her father was dead. He'd never again stand between her and the world. Now it was her time to deal with the world and to make sure Marshland survived the war.

Shannon's body stiffened, and the determined look that had settled in her eyes almost hid the grief. She stood still in front of the great house and waited for the undertaker to make his slow progress up to her.

CHAPTER 3

The house was full of people who'd come to Emmett Marsh's funeral. The funeral was over, but still the people stayed. As Shannon circulated among the guests, making sure they were fed and had seats, she thought the gathering had gradually become more like a party than a funeral. She didn't think her father would have minded though. It was the type of gathering he would have enjoyed and one that was out of his reach while he was alive. Despite his marriage into a respected family, the people of the region never would accept a common Irish horse-trader into their social circle. Only a few of the neighbors had even been inside Clay Manor since Shannon's grandfather had died.

Shannon avoided most of the people who were so formally offering their condolences, but when she saw Becky Noble coming toward her, she didn't turn away.

Becky's father was one of the few who had allowed Shannon and Clay Marsh to play with his children. Becky was fair and delicately pretty with a childish innocence, and Shannon had always liked her even though they were nothing alike.

"I'm so sorry, Shannon," Becky said, and Shannon didn't doubt the sincerity of the tears streaming down her face. Becky could cry over a ripped petticoat.

"Thank you for coming, Becky," Shannon said, embracing her friend.

"I just don't see how you can be so strong, Shannon. If it were me, I just wouldn't be able to do a thing but cry."

"Truth is, I am a little tired. Let's find a place to sit down for a few minutes."

They found a seat, and Becky reached over and took Shannon's hand. "I don't know how you stood it, seeing your daddy shot like that. It must have been awful."

Shannon allowed herself to say, "Yes, it was," but she wouldn't let herself think about that now. Changing the subject abruptly, she asked, "How are things at Woodlawn?"

Becky switched back easily to her own troubles. "Oh, everything is just awful. Two more of our blacks just took off yesterday, and General Ashe sent a message out to Daddy telling him that he'd have to pay another fine. And we don't have any more money."

"I wish I could help, Becky."

"Oh, I know. No one has any money—at least no one who isn't owned by the Union Army." Becky touched her nose with a lace handkerchief. "But that's not the worst of it. Daddy says he's going to Virginia to join Lee's army."

"He's too old to join the Army," Shannon said as her eyes sought out Becky's father, Mr. William Noble, who was across the room talking with her mother. Because he'd always been kind to her, she felt a deep affection for him.

"That's what Mama says, but he just won't listen. Says he has to go and do his part."

"Then there's nothing you can do?"

"Mama says maybe Jett will talk him out of it when he comes home."

"What makes you think Jett's coming home soon?"

Becky put her hand over her mouth. "Oh, I wasn't supposed to tell that. Mama would be cross if she knew I'd let it slip. But I can't see how it could hurt for you to know, because Jett's sure to come and see you anyway. I never could figure why you two just didn't go on and get married before Jett rode off with Morgan."

"There wasn't time," Shannon said, but she knew that wasn't completely true.

There had been time, and everyone in the neighborhood had been expecting them to marry for over a year. People said they were a perfect match. Jett was dark and handsome, and sole heir to the large estate of his father, and though Shannon wouldn't inherit Marshland, the farms would nevertheless be joined by family ties. Still, when Jett asked her to marry him the summer of '61, Shannon had put him off. It wasn't that Shannon wasn't fond of Jett; it just hadn't seemed to be the proper time to get married, especially with the war separating them.

"Maybe not, but I certainly would have married Colin if he'd asked me."

"Oh, Becky! You know your mother would never let you marry Colin. I'm not sure she even approves of Jett marrying me."

"You're not exactly the type of girl a mother would dream of for a daughter-in-law," Becky agreed.

Shannon smiled. "I'm not even the type of girl a mother wants for a daughter."

"Why, Shannon! What a thing to say."

"Never mind, Becky. You know me. I'm always saying things I shouldn't. But when is Jett supposed to come home?"

"I don't know." Becky was whispering now. In a crowd like this there were bound to be some Union people. "But we've heard that Morgan is getting ready for another raid up this way."

"Then Colin will be coming too."

"I know. Isn't it exciting?"

"Becky, you really should forget about Colin. He's never shown any interest in you, and you just upset your parents, going on like this."

"But I've grown up since Colin left. He'll look at me now."

"Even if he did, it would still be hopeless. Your parents could never accept my father's illegitimate child into their family."

"Then we can run away together."

Shannon knew that Becky wasn't serious, still she said, "I don't think you'd care for life away from the comforts of home. If you're so determined to marry a Marsh, maybe you should cast your eye on Clay."

Becky laughed. "Clay? Why, he's just a boy!"

"He's the same age you are. Seventeen."

"Oh, Shannon, really. Clay? That's ridiculous."

"I suppose you're right." Shannon sighed and looked around. "I really should get up and make sure everything is going all right. I wish everyone would just go home."

"Your mother seems to appreciate her friends offering their condolences," Becky said.

Shannon looked into the next room where she could see her mother seated in the middle of a tight group of sympathizers. She was the proper picture of a mourning widow, and even Shannon couldn't tell if her grief was real or feigned. She would have said, however, that her mother cared nothing at all for her father. Shannon had known it was a marriage arranged entirely by her grandfather, but she didn't know why. It seemed a cruel thing to force a daughter to marry a man she couldn't stand.

Aunt Mamie had told Shannon that it had changed her mother, turning her inward until she seemed sometimes to be slipping away from life itself. Then after Shannon was born, Olivia had been bedridden for a year. It wasn't until several years later, when Clay was born, that Olivia came back into the real life, enough to make sure that Clay grew up to be a Clay and not a Marsh. She wouldn't let Emmett near the boy.

Yet her father had never protested. He cared for Olivia as though she were a rare treasure, and he put her comfort above all else. Once, when Shannon was feeling resentful toward her mother, she had chanced her father's anger by asking him why he never got mad at her mother.

He had frowned at his daughter, and for a few minutes she'd thought he wasn't going to answer. Finally he'd said, "I doubt that you could ever understand, Shannon. Your mother is a special woman. She's intelligent, refined, and beautiful in her way, with a pure soul that's never known the sinful ways of the poorer man, and on top of it all, she's rich with land. She should've married an English lord instead of a poor Irish horse-trader." He'd looked toward the house and then around at the barns. "Ah yes, child, I'd crawl to her on my hands and knees every day if she asked me just to thank her for giving me Marshland and a son and a daughter as well."

Shannon hadn't understood anything then, but as the years passed, she began to know what her father meant, and she could no longer resent her mother. In time she hadn't even minded the love her mother showered on Clay and Clay alone.

Now, as she looked at her mother, she could read the expression on her face. Mixed in with the sadness was relief.

Suddenly there was a stir in the room and voices rang from the hall. Then silence fell while they watched Colonel Price Robards enter and walk directly toward Shannon's mother.

"What's he doing here?" Becky said with hate in her voice.

The same hate was plain on many of the faces in the room. Colonel Robards had few friends among those present. He had used his position in the home guard to rule ruthlessly over much of Fayette County. Shannon saw her mother shrink back from him as he hung over her. Mrs. Marsh didn't know who this man was, but she found him exceedingly unattractive with his red face, small eyes, and loud voice.

A shiver ran down Shannon's back as she remembered a conversation she'd overheard between the colonel and her father only a few months ago. Robards had hinted that he would forget her father's Southern sympathies if he would encourage his daughter to show some interest in him. Shannon hadn't been too worried then. Her father stood between them, protecting her. But now her father was gone.

Shannon took a deep breath and stood up. She wouldn't let him upset her mother. "Colonel Robards," she said. Her voice sliced across the room, carrying a bite of warning. He turned and looked at her so boldly that Shannon wanted to fold her arms across her breasts to protect herself from his eyes. Defiantly, she stood perfectly still and waited for him to speak.

"My dear Shannon," he said, coming across to take her hand. His tone was much too familiar. "I had to come tell you how sorry I am."

"I find that difficult to believe, Colonel." She had

determined to be polite to him, but his touch made her recoil. She pulled her hand away.

His face changed, grew harder, but still there was the assurance in his eyes that this time he would win. "Would you rather that I'd come to search the house for traitors?" He looked at the silent people around him.

"That sounds more like the truth, Colonel." Shannon heard a few sharp intakes of breath around her. She gestured toward the piano. "Feel free to search through our music. I don't think you'll find any copies of 'Dixie,' but there might be one of 'Rally round the Flag, Boys.' "

Colonel Robards would not be put down. His eyes ravished her more boldly than before as he said, "Perhaps I should search milady's bedchamber for hidden weapons."

Shannon didn't let her eyes waver from his. She would not let him get the upper hand. Not this time. "If you so desire. I'll have one of the servants show you the way."

"You show the way." The challenge was obvious in his eyes and voice.

"I'm afraid that wouldn't be possible, Colonel. Now if you'll excuse me, I have guests." His smile was so offensive that Shannon had to clasp her hands together to keep from striking out at him.

"Perhaps another time," he said and bowed slightly to her. "Until we meet again, Shannon. I can assure you, we will meet again."

After he left the people around her slowly began talking again. William Noble came up to her and said, "Do you think that show of defiance was wise, Shannon?"

Shannon sighed. "Probably not."

His kind eyes were filled with concern. "Have you and Olivia considered going to Canada until this is all over?"

"I can't leave Marshland, Mr. Noble."

"I understand how you feel, Shannon, but you have your mother to consider."

"She wouldn't want to leave Clay Manor. You know that. And things aren't that bad yet."

"I hope you're right." His voice was weary. He touched her arm and said, "I can't be much help to you against Robards. He's been trying to have me arrested for months now. But if there's ever anything I can do, let me know."

"Thank you, Mr. Noble. It makes me feel better to hear you say that."

He leaned over and kissed her on the cheek. "Jett would never forgive me if I let something happen to you, Shannon. Nor would I forgive myself. I'm looking forward to having you for a daughter."

Darkness fell before all the people finally left. Shannon stood at the door for a long time after the noise of the last team of horses had died away. When at last she came back inside, her mother still sat in the same chair, a faraway look on her face.

"Mother, are you all right?"

Her mother came away from her thoughts slowly. "There were people here today who hadn't been in Clay Manor since Father died. It makes me wonder what kind of friends they are."

"They wouldn't have come today if they hadn't cared for you, Mother. It was Papa they couldn't accept."

"I know." She sighed, and her whole body slumped lower in the chair. "Emmett never tried to be accepted."

"He didn't know how to, Mother. And even if he had, I doubt that it would have made any difference."

"I could never accept him either. He was so different from Father. I never told anyone this before, Shannon, but I never planned to marry at all. It wasn't as if Father needed a heir. There was Simon." A frown creased her face. "Of course, now even Simon is gone. So maybe Father was right to insist that I marry Emmett."

"Why did you if you didn't love him?"

"Because I loved Father." Her eyes went to her father's portrait on the wall. "He was so strong I could never go against him. Yet strangely enough, he was sensitive too. Emmett had strength, but it wasn't the same. I'd like you to understand, Shannon, but it's hard to explain when I don't really understand myself."

"It doesn't really matter anymore, Mother," Shannon said.

"I think it does." She looked down at her hands and was quiet for so long that Shannon didn't think she was going to say any more. But then she said, "I should have tried to care for Emmett."

"He never blamed you, Mother."

"I know. He treated me like a queen. But he never really talked to me or let me have a say in any of the business."

"Did you want to, Mother?"

"No, I suppose not, but even if I had, I'd have been afraid to go against him. He and Father had terrible arguments before Father died."

"About the slaves?" Shannon had heard bits of the stories from Aunt Mamie.

Her mother nodded. "Father never believed in separating families or even selling a black off the land unless he'd done something bad. But Emmett said the only way we could keep the farm rich was to deal in slaves." A strange look came over her face as she remembered. "I thought Father would kill him the night he found out that Emmett had sold Mamie's husband down the river."

"But he didn't."

Her mother covered her face with her hands. "No, Father died instead. He'd had a bad heart for years."

"I'm sorry." It seemed a strange thing to say after so many years, but Shannon could see that her mother still grieved as though her own father's death were a fresh wound.

"Emmett was sorry too. He stayed out in the barn for a week without coming to the house. I was never sure if he was grieving over Father or because the farm passed on to Simon, even though Simon was only sixteen at the time."

Shannon didn't know what to say because she could imagine her father regretting the loss of the farm more than anyone's death.

Her mother dropped her hands back to her lap. "After a while Simon went to Emmett. All Simon ever wanted was to go to school and become a lawyer. He had no interest in the farm, so he and Emmett worked out an agreement. Emmett could have a free hand managing the farm, but there would be no more slaves sold."

"That's when Father began to work with the horses?"

"Yes. And he was so kind to me and contrite that I thought I might learn to live with being his wife . . . especially after Clay was born." Olivia frowned again. "Then he let that boy stay on just because some hillbilly farmer came to the door saying the child was Emmett's son. If he had cared anything for my feelings, he would have sent the boy away."

Shannon kept her voice gentle. "He couldn't do that, Mother. He knew Colin was his child. You only have to look at Colin to see that."

Olivia's mouth straightened into a thin line. "Even so, he should have sent the child away for your sake and for Clay's. To have you associated all your life with a boy like that . . . it's unseemly."

"I love Colin, Mother. You must know that."

She nodded. "You love him more than Clay, your real brother."

"No, Mother. Just in a different way. Colin and I are more alike than Clay and I will ever be." Shannon saw the look on her mother's face. "I don't say that to hurt you, Mother, but only because it's true."

"You've always been too honest, Shannon. Sometimes a lady has to pick and choose her words to avoid hurting others."

"I'll try to be kinder," Shannon promised.

"I do wish you wouldn't introduce him as your brother."

"Very well, Mother. But wherever I live, Colin will have to be welcome too."

"I wonder if your young man, Jett, will agree to that."

"Jett and I aren't married yet."

"But you will be as soon as this horrible war is over."

"I suppose," Shannon said.

Her mother didn't say any more about Jett. She reached out her hand then and let it hover over Shannon's arm for one brief moment before she withdrew it. "I know we've had our differences, Shannon. I wanted you to grow up one way, but your father gave you the freedom to grow up another." She shook her head to keep Shannon from saying anything. "That doesn't matter now. What matters is that we have to go on from here together. We'll both miss your father in our different ways. He protected us."

"And he loved us, Mother."

Suddenly there was a tightening of fear around her mother's eyes. "That man tonight . . . the coarse one. He never should have been allowed in the house."

"Colonel Robards?" When her mother nodded,

Shannon went on. "Don't worry, Mother, I won't let him bother you again."

"Thank you, Shannon," her mother said. She looked at her a long moment. "Perhaps we could still learn to care for each other . . . even now."

Shannon leaned over and touched her lips to her mother's forehead. She couldn't remember kissing her ever before. "Yes, Mother, I think we could. . . . Now you'd best go up to bed."

When her mother stood up, she swayed slightly on her feet, and Shannon said, "Do you want me to help you up the stairs?"

"I can make it, but you might send Mamie up to help me get ready for bed. I'm so tired."

"All right, Mother." Shannon followed her to the steps and watched her begin to climb them. For the first time, she thought her mother looked old.

Out in the kitchen Aunt Mamie looked up from the dishes she was washing to comment, "You look tired Shannon."

Shannon nodded. "And so do you." Suddenly everyone looked terribly old to her. "Forget about the rest of this till morning, Aunt Mamie. Then I'll see that you have some help."

"Whatever you say, Miss Shannon."

Shannon looked at Aunt Mamie and longed for the days when being mistress and slave hadn't mattered and they had been more like mother and daughter. She touched Aunt Mamie's arm. "Please don't call me miss, Aunt Mamie."

Aunt Mamie's arms went around her. "Aw, child, I do love you."

Shannon rested a moment in the safety of those arms before she stepped back. "I don't know what I'd do without you, Aunt Mamie."

"Me neither, child. I 'spect you'd be nigh on lost."

Aunt Mamie smiled. "Is there anything else I can do for you before I go to bed?"

"Mother wants you to help her get ready for bed."

Aunt Mamie nodded. "Today has been hard on Miss Olivia. She's just not as strong as you," she said as she left the room.

Shannon didn't follow her. Instead, she stepped out the back door and walked through the night to the graveyard. All day she'd had to think about others and push away her own feelings, but now it was time for her to face her grief.

The night air was pleasant after the hot stuffiness of the house. The call of a distant whippoorwill blended in gently with the other night sounds. In the graveyard the air of tranquillity was disturbed by the raw gash of the new grave in the earth.

Shannon stood above the grave for a long time, thinking of nothing at all. Then as pictures of her father passed through her mind, she felt the tears wet on her cheeks and sank to her knees.

"Shay," a soft voice whispered behind her, and warm hands rested on her shoulders.

Shannon looked up at Sally. Without saying any more, Sally knelt beside her. Shannon was glad Sally was with her. They'd always been close, reaching out to each other in friendship and love. When they were children, strangers visiting Clay Manor often mistook them for sisters. With her light skin and finely drawn features Sally could have been Shannon's real sister. A long time ago Aunt Mamie, Sally's mother, had explained to Shannon that Sally's grandfather had been a plantation owner in old Virginia.

Finally Shannon said, "I don't think I can do it, Sally—take care of all this. Not without Papa."

"Of course you can, Shay," Sally's voice was soft as the night. "Tonight there are doubts. There are always doubts at night . . . and fears. But tomorrow will be different. You'll know what to do, just as you always have. You remember the time you helped John run away. There were doubts that night too."

"I had to do that. Papa never understood, but I had to help John."

"I know, Shay. And tomorrow you'll do what you have to do again. Nothing will ever defeat you, Shannon Marsh."

They stood up and started back to the house together. "I wish I could be sure of that," Shannon said when they reached the spot where their paths parted.

"Tomorrow you'll be sure." Sally reached over and kissed Shannon's cheek. "Good night, Shay."

Shannon watched Sally walk away toward the cabin she shared with Adam. She stood still for a long time after Sally disappeared through the cabin door, letting the dark gather around her. If she could only believe that Sally was right.

CHAPTER 4

July brought fresh rumors that Morgan's raiders were approaching central Kentucky, and soon the entire country was either running scared or unfurling the stars and bars of the Confederate flag. The Union troops were reinforced around Lexington until Shannon was sure the Confederates wouldn't dare to approach the town. Still, every time Shannon saw her, Becky insisted that Jett would come home.

The weeks since her father's death had passed slowly as Shannon handled the days one at a time and worked to keep everything going. It wasn't as hard as she had feared.

Of course, there was Colonel Robards. He'd stopped in at the house once, and another time had stopped her in town, but she managed to keep him at a distance. He'd looked at her in that vulgar way of his, and Shannon felt that he was only biding his time. He worried her, but since there was nothing she could do about him, she covered over the worry with work. Sometimes she helped Aunt Mamie and Sally in the kitchen, but most of the time she worked at the barn with Adam and Tom. They were the only slaves left. The others had slipped away after her father's funeral.

One day early in July, when Shannon slowed Satin down after their early morning ride, she looked up to see Captain Hunt at the edge of the field. Even though she hadn't seen him since the day after her father died, she wasn't surprised. In fact she'd been expecting him to come for over a week, and now a strange light feeling settled around her head as she rode over to him.

He took off his hat and smiled.

"Good morning, Captain. Did you come for that ride or are you on business?"

"I told you the last time we met, Miss Marsh, that Blackie and I would be a poor match for you and your Satin."

Shannon laughed. "Perhaps you'd feel more comfortable riding with me if I went to the barn and put a sidesaddle on one of the old mares."

"You're an outrageous woman, Shannon Marsh."

Her eyes didn't waver from his. "I'm aware of that, Captain."

He laughed, and suddenly the sun seemed brighter to Shannon. It felt good to be here in the meadow with this man whose clear blue eyes appraised her in such a frank approving way.

But then he looked away from her to the trees on the far side of the field. "I see Tom is still allowing you to ride out here alone."

"I'm afraid he has little choice."

His eyes came away from the trees back to her. "But it might be dangerous for you."

"Sometimes I think it might be dangerous anywhere, and perhaps this place is safest of all." Shannon paused, then went on. "At least Robards has never followed me out here."

"But I have." He suddenly looked very serious.

"Is that a threat, Captain?" she said lightly.

"You have nothing to fear from me, Miss Marsh." He reached over and touched her hand.

She turned her hand over under his—so hard and strong—and the warmth traveled from him to make every inch of her tingle.

"Do you think it would be all right if I called you Shannon?" he asked.

Satin stepped sideways in a skittish movement, and Shannon pulled her hand away to calm him. She longed to reach back to the captain and let him capture her hand once again, but she didn't. She simply said, "If you so desire, Captain Hunt."

She began walking Satin back toward the barn. She needed to slow down the way her blood was racing everytime she looked at the man next to her. After all he was practically a stranger.

"Shannon," he said. "That has a lovely sound."

"It's a name my father brought from Ireland. He said something about a river by that name."

Although Shannon could feel him gazing at her, he didn't speak again until they had reached the barn. She let him help her dismount before she said, "I'll have to see to Satin now."

"What about Tom?"

"Tom has enough to do. He and Adam are the only men left." Shannon hesitated a moment, then said, "If you have the time, I could show you around the barn."

"Aren't you afraid that's a little like showing the pirate where the treasure's hidden?"

"Have you need of a horse, Captain?"

"Not today, but there might come a day when I would."

"If that day comes, I think you could find the horses with or without my help, Captain."

His laugh was free and open. "Which horse would you rather I take?"

"You can be sure that I'll do my best to leave you the poorest of choices."

Shannon began unsaddling Satin, talking gently to the horse while she worked.

Captain Hunt stepped closer and said, "Let me do that for you."

Satin whipped his head around with a warning nicker. Shannon laughed. "I don't think you'd better. I'm afraid I've spoiled Satin the last few weeks so that now he'll hardly let anyone but me touch him."

He took the saddle from Shannon and put it away in the tack room. When he came back, he walked to Satin's head, holding a hand up to still Shannon's warnings. Satin minced backward away from him. Then suddenly he reached out and nipped the captain's arm. But Captain Hunt acted as though he hadn't felt a thing. He spoke to the horse and confidently touched his nose. Satin quivered and shook his head, but the man's hand was still there when once more the horse was still and relaxed.

"It seems that you have a way with horses, Captain," Shannon said. "I guess I can't call Satin a one-man horse anymore."

"I wouldn't say that. Your horse and I have just reached a truce. It would take a long time to win his real trust."

Shannon rubbed the horse down and put him in his stall while the captain brought his feed. She came out of the stall and pushed her hair back. The barn was hot even though the morning was still young.

Captain Hunt watched her. "You shouldn't be doing this kind of work, Shannon."

She stood as tall as she could and challenged him with her eyes. "And why not, Captain?"

"If I'm going to call you Shannon, don't you think you could call me Randal?"

"Perhaps . . . but you didn't answer my question. Do you think it's improper for a young lady to be in the barn?" She didn't wait for him to answer. "But of course you do. You've already called me outrageous."

Shannon looked around her. Ever since she'd first stepped into the barn as a small child following after her father, it had been a place of wonder and excitement to her. While she was growing up, the barn had always been in a flurry of activity, with men tending the horses and every stall occupied by a horse that held out the promise of a perfect blood line. She had shared her father's dream that someday one of their mares would have a colt that would make those who saw him run catch their breath in wonder. Now, even with more than half the stalls empty and the tackroom deserted, she still felt the privilege of being able to work with the beautiful animals.

"And I suppose you're right," Shannon went on to say. "My problem started twenty years ago, the day I was born."

"What do you mean?"

"As you can see, I was born the wrong sex. Papa always said I should have been the boy."

"I'm very glad you aren't," he said softly.

Shannon thought that he might reach out at that moment and touch her, but he didn't. Instead, he caught her eyes with his and held them until finally Shannon, afraid of what she was feeling, pulled them away to look down the center of the barn.

"Would you like to see Marsh Queen, Captain?"

Without waiting for an answer, she moved away from him, leading the way through the barn. Shannon began clucking at the mare when she got near her stall. "Morning there, Queenie."

The mare stamped her feet and shook her head. Shannon said, "I know, girl. It's hot as blue blazes in here. I'll see that you get outside in a little bit."

"Do you talk to all your horses, Shannon?" Randal asked with a smile. "You sound almost as though you think they understand you."

"Are you so sure they don't? Besides, you must realize, Captain, that talking to the horses isn't so bad when you consider that I have a worse problem. Sometimes I think they're talking back to me."

"Do they say nice things?"

"Mostly. Or maybe I just don't listen when they don't."

Randal laughed, and Shannon couldn't keep from laughing with him. Everything was lighter and looser when he laughed. Even the sun seemed to stream more brightly through the windows, and all the shadows melted away back into the corners.

"Let's see this horse you're so proud of," he said.

Shannon led Queenie out of her stall. "She's a perfect brood mare. See her lines. She comes down from Grecian. Put that together with Lexington . . ."

" . . . and you should have a winner," he said.

Suddenly Shannon was serious. "*If* I can keep her long enough. She won't foal until spring."

"That's not so long."

"There could be a dozen raids before then." Shannon put Queenie back into the stall. The shadows had returned.

"Shannon," Randal said, "if it comes to it, you'd have to give up the horse. You can't fight these guerrillas."

"I guess I've found that out already, Captain."

She looked away from him, staring out at nothing, and he knew she was thinking of her father. "But if I let them take Queenie now," she said, "it will all have been such a waste."

"There will always be another horse. It's people who are important," he said and touched her shoulder. He wanted to bring her away from her sad thoughts and back to the laughing girl of moments ago.

"The war doesn't allow people to be important," she said. "In a war a hill can be more important than hundreds of soldiers and a horse more important than any man."

"They wouldn't have shot your father if he'd given them the horse," Randal said gently.

"Can you be sure of that? War makes killing easy."

"No, Shannon, killing is never easy."

Shannon looked at him and saw the regret on his face. She'd brought back painful memories and pointed up the hard future ahead of them. She put her hand on top of his. "Do you think it will all be over soon?"

"The war?" When she nodded, he went on. "It's funny, but when I joined up, they said it wouldn't last but a few months. Both sides would see the foolishness of it, and the differences would be settled. Either that or the Union would put down the rebellion quickly and easily. Trouble was, nobody gave the rebels credit for their courage and dedication to their cause. We were going to go out and teach them all a lesson, and then it would be over."

"But it wasn't that way, was it?"

He shook his head. "They came at us stronger and more determined than we'd ever expected, and our side wasn't ready. Things went their way for a while."

"But now?"

"Now? That is the question, isn't it?" He was quiet

for a while before he said, "The North is too strong. The South will lose. But they won't give up until they're beaten, and that's going to take a long time."

"And a lot of lives," Shannon said.

"I wish it had never started."

"I wonder how things will be even after it's settled. I've seen so many families torn apart with brothers and friends going off to different sides."

"I have a brother with the South."

"I'm sorry, Randal. I hope you never meet him on the battlefield."

Randal shook away the cloud of family worries her questions had recalled. He'd come to warn Shannon to be careful, not to talk about his personal problems. "There's something I need to talk to you about, Shannon."

"So this *is* an Army visit after all, Captain Hunt." Shannon moved away from his hand.

"In a way, but I came as a friend. Will you let me be a friend?"

Shannon kept her eyes away from his. "What do you need to talk about, Captain?"

"This war is going to get worse. We both know that, Shannon. We can't pretend that we're just a young man and his girl out for a pleasure stroll on a Sunday morning."

"It's not Sunday, and I wasn't pretending anything of the sort. If nothing else, your blue uniform would make it more than a little difficult to forget the war." Still, Shannon felt a sadness settling inside her. It had been nice talking about the horses and laughing together, but the war was between them now. She might as well let him have his say.

"You said something about Colonel Robards out in the field," Randal said.

"Yes." Shannon's voice was guarded.

"How well do you know him?" Randal asked.

"I've met him a few times. He's been around this area for a long time, but he wasn't exactly in our social circle." Shannon tried not to let Randal hear her aversion to the man. "Why do you ask?"

"He was never an important man before the war, but the war has brought him a certain amount of power—a power he enjoys using."

"You don't sound very respectful of a superior officer, Captain."

"Shannon, would you try to forget that I'm a captain in the Union Army, for just a few minutes?" He took hold of her shoulders and made her look at him. "Believe me, I want to be a friend."

She couldn't doubt the truth in his eyes. "All right, Randal. I know Colonel Robards, and I detest the man. But that doesn't change anything. He's still in favor with the Union men in control around here, and we have to live with that fact and try to avoid trouble with him."

"He hates men who are as independent as your father was, and he's using his position to take revenge on as many of them as he can. I've heard that the military is planning to make some new rules against suspected Secessionists soon, and I know Robards plans some arrests."

"Do you know who is on his list?"

Randal shook his head. "I don't know whether anyone knows except Robards. Why?"

"William Noble, who owns the farm bordering Marshland, is a dear friend of mine. I wouldn't want to see him have to go to jail."

"He won't have to worry for a few days. Right now the troops are busy getting ready for Morgan. . . . you know that he has entered Kentucky, don't you?"

"I've heard rumors, but I can't see what that has to do with me."

"Don't play games with me, Shannon. You told me yourself you had a brother riding with Morgan."

"What are you trying to say?"

"I'm trying to warn you, Shannon. If you're caught helping the rebels, things will be hard for you and your family."

"Yes, I've heard that the Union is arresting women now and even building prisons for them." Shannon's face showed her contempt. "But believe me, Captain, I have no reason to expect Colin to visit home."

"I'm not sure I can believe that. Morgan's men have a reputation for trying to go home whenever they pass through Kentucky."

"And if that happens, are you planning to arrest me, Captain?"

"You're making this hard for me, Shannon. I just wanted to warn you. I've already told you that I'd never do anything to harm you. But I'm not the only Union officer in Fayette County."

"What are you suggesting I do, Captain? Bar the door if my brother dares to come see me?"

"I'm only asking you to be careful, Shannon."

"Perhaps if Morgan's men are coming in the force as I've been hearing, then it's you who should be careful, Captain."

"Would that matter to you, Shannon?" His eyes burned into hers.

Shannon looked away from him. "If you can be a friend, then so can I," she said softly.

"Then please promise me you'll be careful, Shannon. And if your brother comes, that you'll keep watch so he'll have time to get away if a Union patrol comes by."

"You sound as though you're giving aid to the enemy," Shannon said, trying to keep her voice light. But she couldn't hide the worry his words caused her.

"I can't think of you as the enemy." His hands tightened on her shoulders. "You haven't promised yet."

"All right, Randal, I promise that I will be very careful. Now, does that make you feel better?"

"You can't know how much better."

Shannon thought he might kiss her then, but he dropped his hands to his sides and looked away from her. When he spoke again, his voice was low. "Things are going to get worse. I see it in the officers I talk to. The election's coming up next month, and the Union people are determined that no person with any hint of Southern sympathy even be represented. And now the guerrilla raids are stirring up feeling against the Confederates. If Morgan comes through here, I can't say what might happen when he leaves."

While he talked, Shannon felt the shadows coming out of the corners and spreading until they threatened to block out the sunshine and plunge everything into darkness. It was almost a shock to her to feel the hot warmth of the sun hit her face when they stepped out of the barn.

After Randal left, she walked to the house slowly, going over in her mind the things he'd said. It was true. Things were going to get worse. Yet, when she looked around, everything seemed so peaceful. The sun glinted off the weather vane on the barn roof, and the huge oak trees offered their shade to the house just as they always had. And there was the house looking as though it would stand forever, with its four great columns holding up the porch roof.

Her eyes followed the lattice railing around the top of the roof. She remembered the times as a child she had watched from there for her father to come home and how she'd run down from the roof to be lifted up in his strong arms. He'd swung her high in the air, but she'd never been afraid. She knew her father would take care of her. Now she longed for that feeling of security again. Without realizing it, her eyes turned back to the road where the dust raised by Randal's horse had just settled.

Her mother called out from the sitting room as Shannon came in the door. "Who was that?" she asked.

"Do you remember the Captain Hunt who was here the day after Papa was killed?"

Her mother nodded. "Oh yes, Captain Hunt. Is he a Kentuckian?"

"I think he said he was born in Woodford County."

Her mother was thoughtful for a moment before she said, "Seems as though I remember some Hunts there who used to work on my cousin's farm. A large family and poor as church mice as well as I remember."

"He seems to be doing well enough for himself now. He worked at one of the stables in New Orleans before the war."

"I've tried to tell you, Shannon, anybody can be a stable boy. It takes much more than that for one to be a lady or a gentleman."

Shannon tried not to let her mother's words upset her. It had never helped to get angry with her mother anyway. "I sometimes wonder, Mother, who made up the rules about being a lady or gentleman."

"Why, Shannon, I believe you're taking up for this Captain Hunt." Her mother looked at her closely. "Surely you aren't allowing yourself to get interested in someone like him." Then her mother waved her hand in the air, dismissing the idea. "But of course, you couldn't be. You're betrothed to Jett Noble."

Shannon sighed. "That's right, Mother." Why did that make her feel so weary, she wondered.

"Shannon, I don't think you realize how fortunate you are that a man like Jett is interested in marrying you and that his family is willing to accept you."

"Yes, I know, Mother." Shannon laughed, but the

sound was empty. "Especially since I can't even get my own mother to do that, can I?"

As Shannon turned and walked quickly to the kitchen, the image of Jett's face came to her mind. He was handsome with strong features and black hair that curled down his neck, but his startling gray-green eyes surrounded by dark lashes held none of the kindness that shone in his father's eyes. Shannon thought back to the year before the war, when she and Jett were together so much. When Jett was happy, he laughed easily and often, with a contagious charm, but there were other times—times when there was no laughter, only anger. She wondered if the war had changed him.

If he came home, as Becky was so sure he would, then she would judge for herself. Randal had said that Morgan's men were already in Kentucky. Shannon thought of Jett and Colin and all the others riding through the state, setting fires, capturing trains, shooting at any person who resisted their advance—and being shot at.

She shook her head in an attempt to clear it of the pictures in her mind. She went out into the garden and began picking beans frantically. If only she could block out the feeling that the war was out there waiting to swallow them all up.

Two nights later Shannon heard horses coming as she prepared for bed. Shouldering her father's gun, she went to the front door to wait, but even before they got close enough for her to see their faces, she knew. She dropped the gun, threw open the door, and ran out to meet Morgan's men . . . her men.

CHAPTER 5

"Colin!" Shannon cried.

The rider in the lead slid off his horse and lifted her up in a bear hug. "Ah, it's my beautiful sister now, for sure."

Shannon laughed and cried at the same time. Until that moment she hadn't realized just how worried she'd been about Colin. She'd been trying to cover over the fear that she might never see him again, but now that he was here, the relief washing over her made her weak.

"Hey, girl, where's my welcome?" Jett said.

Colin turned her loose, and she let Jett pull her close. "It's good to see you, too, Jett."

He laughed. "So I'm just a nice added attraction. I tell you, Colin, I may have to get jealous."

"Don't be silly, Jett," Shannon said. Jett's arms were strong and tight around her, and when he kissed her full and long, she responded as she always had. But it wasn't quite the same. Something had changed. Shannon stepped back, hoping Jett hadn't noticed.

He hadn't. "It's been a long time between kisses, girl," he said, pulling her to him again.

Something moved in the darkness behind them. Shannon spun away from Jett and said, "Is that you, Tom?"

In the moment before there was an answer, Colin and Jett both pulled out their guns.

"It's me, Miss Shannon," Adam said. "I thought you might need some help." He stepped closer.

"It's all right, Adam. This is my brother, Colin, and Jett Noble."

They could see his shape but not his face. Colin said, "I don't remember an Adam. Is he new?"

"Papa brought him to the farm a little after you left." Shannon spoke carefully. Ever since the first day she'd met him in the barn, she had respected Adam and his pride. Being a slave ate at his soul. "Adam's almost as good as you are with the horses, Colin."

"Is he a slave?" Jett's voice cut through the air.

Shannon hesitated. She didn't want to answer that.

Adam spoke up in a high voice. "Yessir. I's been bought and paid for, masser."

"Then what's he doing with a gun?" Jett demanded.

"Haven't you heard, masser?" Adam's voice lowered. "President Lincoln done gone and set us niggers free."

"I'll have you horsewhipped for that." Jett lunged at Adam.

Adam stepped neatly out of the way, and Shannon moved in front of Jett. "I'll have none of that, Jett Noble. If Adam is a slave, then he's my slave, and you'll do nothing to any of my people."

Jett turned with a jerk and walked away from them. Colin looked toward Shannon, and then followed Jett.

"I don't like being treated like a child, Miss Shannon."

"Or a slave. I know, Adam, but he might have killed you. If you won't think of yourself, then think of Sally."

"I do everyday. Why do you think I'm still here?"

"I don't know, Adam. Sometimes I think it might be better if you'd just go on and leave, if that's what you want."

"I don't want to leave Sally here."

"Then take her with you."

"That's where you've got me beaten, Miss Shannon. She won't go, and you know it—even if you set her free, which you won't."

"Adam, in my eyes Sally has always been free. The only thing that ties her to me is friendship."

"She'd go if I asked her to. She loves me more than she loves you, you know."

Shannon said quietly, "Tom and Mamie will stay with us. You needn't feel bad for leaving."

"You take the cake, Miss Shannon." Adam laughed softly. "I never met a white woman like you."

"Nor a black one either, I dare say," Shannon said with relief. He wasn't going to leave.

"That's God's own truth."

"Then you'll stay?"

"You know that already, don't you, miss? But it won't be for long. Just till Morgan's bunch get through here. You might need some help."

"I need some help now, Adam. Not from Morgan's men, although you might. You'd best stay out of Jett's sight. It's no telling what he might do."

"He's devil mean."

"I'm engaged to marry him, Adam."

"I hope for your sake, Miss Shannon, that some soldier in blue finds him first."

"Adam!" Shannon spoke sharply, but then sighed. "It's no use talking about this. But I need to make sure no Union soldiers find him—or Colin—while they're here."

"I'll keep watch for you, Miss Shannon," he replied soberly, then melted away into the night.

Shannon turned and went back to the two men at the door. Jett was no longer pacing, but his anger was still alive and pushing out of him. "I intend to talk to your father about this. We can't tolerate that kind of behavior in our slaves."

"I don't think Adam is going to be a slave much longer," Shannon said. "He and Tom are the only men we have left now. I can't very well chase them away, too."

"What happened to the others?" Colin asked.

"They just left."

"Didn't Emmett do anything about it?" Colin asked.

Shannon waited for the tears. She'd often thought of the comfort of crying in Colin's arms when she told him about their father. But now there were no tears, only a weary heaviness on her heart. The words came out flat and cold. "Papa isn't going to do anything about anything ever again, Colin. Papa is dead."

"What happened?" Colin's voice was tight and strained, and the hand he put out to touch her was shaking.

"Strange," Shannon said. "I never thought you would care."

"Whatever else he was, he was still my father, Shannon."

"And he was Clay's, too, but Clay didn't care." Shannon let her shoulders droop, but then she shook off her sadness. "Come on in, and I'll tell you about it while I fix you something to eat." Shannon sliced bread and ham while she told them. It didn't take long. There wasn't much to tell, especially since she carefully omitted any mention of Randal Hunt.

"Could you tell which side they were from?" Jett asked.

"I don't believe they were soldiers at all. Just outlaws," Shannon said.

"Well, at least you're all right," Jett said, looking her over in the light of the lamp. "They didn't bother you, did they?" Suddenly there was a worried question in his eyes.

"They didn't rape me, if that's what you mean. They didn't even touch me." Shannon's voice was hard.

"I'd hate to be the man to try," Colin said with a small smile. "If I know you, sister dear, you came out that door loaded for bear."

Shannon smiled, feeling the irritation that Jett's question had brought seep away. Jett had always been able to get her back up, without even trying, and Colin had always been able to smooth her feathers back down.

She put the sandwiches and mugs of coffee in front of them before she sat down across the table. Her gaze was drawn to Colin first. It felt so good to have him there, close enough to be able to reach across and touch. She remembered the first time she saw Colin. He was ten years old and about twice as big as she was. She'd come down the stairs, and he was standing in the hall, pretending not to notice the angry words flying between the man and woman in front of him.

Shannon had heard her father say, "He's my son, and he stays." His voice had a tone that Shannon had long ago learned to obey instantly.

When her mother passed her on the steps, Shannon had shrunk away from the cold fury on her face because she was afraid her mother might be angry at her. But she'd swept on past without even seeing her.

Then her father had called to her. "Come here, Shannon. I want you to meet your new brother."

Shannon had gone to stand in front of the boy dressed in funny clothes. She was five, and only two years before they'd brought a baby to her and told her it was her new brother, Clay. Because she didn't know what else to do, she'd tried to kiss him, but when the baby began crying, they'd yanked him away. She hadn't known what to do with this new boy her father called a brother either. But she had looked up at his face, and it was so sad and lonely that she couldn't keep from grabbing his hand and kissing its rough skin. The boy had smiled at her, and in that moment a bond had been forged between them.

Her father had laughed. Shannon could still hear that laugh and how it had echoed in the long hall, but there had been a bitter edge to it and to his voice when he said, "Well, boy, you've found one friend in this house anyway." Her father had stared at Colin with narrowed eyes. "Make sure you never give the child any reason to regret her love."

And he hadn't. Over the years, he'd watched over her, protecting her as best he could and helping her do all the things that no one else thought she could do. The only time he'd not taken her side was when he told her she'd have to grow up and start acting like a lady.

Now she looked into his greenish brown eyes and smiled. He was so like their father except for those eyes. She wondered if maybe her father's eyes hadn't been like that once, long before she was born, with the yearning and seeking just below a surface calm.

He met her eyes, and she asked, "Is it bad?"

The question took him off guard, but he knew what she meant. He looked at her without answering in words, but she could see the answer in his eyes. When he spoke, he didn't tell the truth. "Not so bad."

"What's that?" Jett asked. He'd been sitting back, letting Shannon and Colin talk about Emmett Marsh's death, but he didn't like being on the outside of their tight, close circle. He wanted to be inside with them. He reached over and took Shannon's hand.

Shannon looked at Jett, and in the lamplight she was struck, as she was each time she saw him, by how handsome he was. But there were changes she wondered about—in the tight lines around his mouth, in the new long beard, and in the hair down on his collar. She let his eyes draw hers. There was power in his eyes, and assurance. He'd always been able to make her feel that she should be grateful for his attention.

Still, she couldn't keep from warming to him when he smiled as he was smiling now. They sat there gazing at each other, and it was almost as if he'd come for a Sunday evening visit.

But Colin's answer to Jett's question quickly gave lie to that. "The war," he said.

Jett reached over with his other hand and softly stroked her cheek. "You shouldn't worry your pretty little head about such things, Shannon."

Shannon moved her face away from his touch, but she didn't pull her hand away from his. "It's a little hard to ignore the war, Jett," she said, "especially when it keeps coming to visit."

"You should go to Canada, Shannon." Jett was serious now. "That's what I've told Mother and Becky to do."

"Have you been to Woodlawn already?"

"We just came from there," Colin said.

"I've been worried about Mr. Noble," Shannon said. "I've heard that Robards plans to have him arrested."

"Robards will have a long way to go then. Father is leaving for Virginia tomorrow morning."

"I'm sorry to hear that," Shannon said.

Jett's eyes flashed. "You should be proud. The time has come for all loyal men of the South to stand together."

"But your father is too old to go to war."

"You're never too old to fight for what you believe in," Jett said.

"Maybe not," Shannon said. "But I'd hate for anything to happen to Mr. Noble."

"Mr. Noble can take care of himself," Colin said gently. "And it couldn't be much worse than being locked up in some military prison."

"Robards would enjoy putting your father in prison. He hates Mr. Noble," Shannon said.

"Robards, that—" Jett swore. "He could barely keep food on the table for his family before the war, and now look at him. He thinks he's the most important man in Fayette County just because a bunch of cowardly home guards ride behind him." Jett made a sound of disgust. "The Union has to go to the bottom of the heap to get its officers. All the good men are with the South."

Colin was watching her closely. He said, "Has Robards been bothering you, Sis?"

Shannon wouldn't worry him. There was nothing he could do anyway. "Nothing I can't handle."

But she could never hide anything from Colin's eyes. "Maybe you should pack up and go to Canada with Becky and Mrs. Noble," he said. "Your mother would be safe, and Aunt Mamie could go with you."

"It's not that bad yet, Colin. Really it isn't. And you know I can't just go off and leave the farm. What would I do with the horses?"

"You can't worry about horses at a time like this," Colin said. "This is a war, Shannon."

"But Queenie—you remember Queenie—she's going to have a foal by Lexington."

"She'll have the foal whether you're here or in Canada," Colin said.

Jett said, "Morgan could always use some good horses."

"You can't have my horses." Shannon's mouth straightened to a grim line.

Colin smiled. "It's no use talking to Shannon about the war. All she thinks about are the horses and this farm. Emmett taught her that."

Jett's face darkened for a moment, but then he smiled too. "I guess you can't expect a woman to understand." He came around the table and sat close to her. "But I can expect her to care some about me too. When all this is over, I still plan to come back and tame you, Shannon Marsh."

"And what's that supposed to mean?" Shannon tried to say it flippantly, but some of the irritation got through in her voice. Everything Jett said to her tonight seemed to set her on edge.

"I can show you better than tell you, girl." His mouth on hers then was warm and alive, demanding a response.

She'd never had trouble responding to his kisses before. They'd had plenty of arguments over the years, but when they made up and kissed, it had always settled everything. Now she couldn't quite let herself relax.

He stroked the back of her neck and then caught her thick loose hair in his hands. "That red hair of yours haunts me in my dreams. I want to see it on the pillow next to mine."

"Jett, we're not alone."

Jett laughed. "You can't be worrying about Colin. He knows more about both of us than we'd ever want told."

"Maybe he should tell me some of the things he knows about you, Jett. I hear the girls down south are real beauties." Shannon pulled away from Jett enough to look around at Colin. "Tell me, brother. How many girls has he left pining for him down south?"

"Leave me out of this, Sis. I just stopped by for a bite to eat and a sight of home. Jett's the one who came courting."

Jett took her face in both his hands. He smiled. "Don't you worry. There's plenty of girls down there who admire my smile, but none of them needs taming like you." He kissed her again, tightening his hold on her hair.

The back door creaked open, and Jett jerked away from her to grab his gun.

"Who is it?" Shannon said sharply.

"It's me," Sally said. She walked quickly into the light of the lamp.

Both men took in sharp breaths at the sight of her. Sally was even more beautiful than usual with her hair tumbling about her shoulders, her eyes wide with excitement, and her full breasts pushing against the thin fabric of the dress she'd pulled over her nightgown.

Jett made a whistling sound under his breath. "She's worth a fortune," he said.

Sally's eyes flicked toward him for a second before coming back to Shannon. "Adam says there's men coming."

"How much time have we got?" Colin asked, standing.

"None," Sally said crisply. "I brought your horses around. You must leave at once."

"Go," Shannon said, kissing them both quickly. "I'll keep them from following for as long as I can."

Colin caught her hand. "Be careful, Sis."

"I should be telling *you* that."

"I'm not so sure," he said, and then they were disappearing out the back door.

Shannon smoothed down her hair as she ran toward the front of the house. "Let them get away," she prayed. And then because Aunt Mamie always said it wasn't right to demand things from God, she added, "Please."

CHAPTER 6

Clay met Shannon in the hall. "What's going on?" he asked, rubbing his eyes.

"Trouble. You'd better go on back up to bed," she said.

"You shouldn't say things like that to me."

Even without being able to see him clearly, Shannon knew that his mouth was twisted in a pout.

"After all," he went on, "I am head of the house now. Mother told me so. All this is mine now, you know."

"Really, Clay, I haven't time to argue with you. There are men coming for heaven only knows what reason." Shannon hurried on to the door. Half to herself she said, "I hope Adam got Queenie away."

Clay followed her. "Do you think the guerrillas who

killed Father have come back again?" There was fear in his voice.

"I don't know," Shannon said, touching the gun that still leaned against the door. "I don't think so. It's more likely a troop of Union soldiers."

"What would they be doing here this time of night?"

"They're not here for a social call. That's for sure." Shannon decided she'd wait until later to tell Clay about Colin and Jett. The less he knew when the soldiers came, the better.

"You're hiding something from me. You've always treated me like a baby, Shannon. You and Colin were always taking sides against me." The pout was back in his voice.

"That's enough, Clay!" She spoke more sharply than she'd intended, but she had no time to appease him now. She could hear the horses coming down the lane. "Just stay out of the way, and let me handle this."

Clay swore under his breath, but Shannon pretended not to hear. "Light a lamp," she said.

The riders were in army formation, and Shannon felt a bit of relief. She hadn't known how she would fight guerrilla raiders, but perhaps she could delay the Army. She tried to decide how much time had gone by since Jett and Colin had slipped out the back door. It hadn't been long enough.

She touched the gun, but she didn't want to appear hostile. She wished there was time to put it away. She put her hand on the doorknob and whispered. "Remember, Clay, let me do the talking."

"I wish you'd tell me what's going on."

"Later." She combed her hair with her fingers again and rubbed the spot on her chin that still burned where Jett's beard had scratched her. Then she took a deep breath and stepped out on the porch. Clay hovered in the hall behind her.

Enough light pierced out through the night for her to recognize Robards at once. She forced calmness into her voice. "Colonel Robards . . . to what do we owe this midnight visit?" Her eyes went to the man to the left of him. It was Randal, but she brought her eyes back to Robards without a flicker of recognition.

"I have reason to believe you are hiding enemy soldiers here," Colonel Robards said.

"That would be a foolish thing for me to do, now wouldn't it, Colonel?"

"Very. There'd be extreme consequences to pay for such a traitorous action."

"Well, I can assure you, Colonel, there are no Confederate soldiers here. Now if you would please be on your way and stop disturbing us with your witch hunts."

He laughed. "I'm afraid it won't be that easy to get rid of us." He turned away from her. "Captain, take some men and search the barn and slaves' quarters. Lieutenant, cover the back of the house." He turned back to Shannon. "I'll search the house myself."

Shannon felt the pull of Randal's eyes on her, but she refused to look toward him. With a sudden movement he wheeled his horse away toward the barn.

Shannon pushed open the doors for Robards and the men following him. "You're wasting your time, Colonel," she said.

The soldiers spread through the front rooms while she and Clay and the Colonel waited in the hall. After their search the men came back shaking their heads and then started for the stairs.

Shannon ran and stood in front of them at the bottom of the stairs. "There's no one up there but my mother." She stared straight at Robards. "You'll not disturb my mother."

One of the soldiers looked toward Colonel Robards. "You want us to go up?" he asked and put a hand on

Shannon's arm. Robards nodded, and the soldier pushed Shannon out of his path.

Shannon clenched her hands together to keep from striking out at him. "Clay, go with them," she said. "See that they don't bother Mother."

Clay bounded up the steps ahead of the soldiers, leaving Shannon and Robards alone. Clay had taken his lamp with him, and the hall was dark with shadows. Shannon lit another lamp. There was only the slightest tremble to her hand as she put the chimney back in place.

But it was a tremble that Robards caught. "Ah, Shannon, you could save yourself all this, if only you would."

Shannon took a quick breath and turned to face him. She'd let him see no more fear. "I don't know what you mean, Colonel," she lied. She met his stare squarely.

He smiled, sure of himself. "I think you do, my dear."

His eyes glittered with ill-concealed greed, and she felt exposed in front of him. But she didn't clasp her arms across her breasts as she longed to or drop her eyes from his.

He took a step toward her, but at that moment his men came back down the stairs. "No one up there but the old lady just like she said," one of them reported.

"If there are rebels in the area, Colonel, don't you think you're wasting valuable time here?" Shannon said. She thought Jett and Colin had had enough time to get away by now, and she wanted these men out of her house.

"We haven't searched the kitchen yet," Robards said.

The kitchen. Shannon thought suddenly of the plates and cups on the table, but she couldn't keep him from his search. "All right," she said. "Let's get this over with."

When she pushed open the kitchen door, she saw with relief that Sally had cleared everything away but one cup still half full of coffee. Sally was gone. Shannon hoped she'd had time to get back to her cabin without any of the soldiers seeing her.

Robards's eyes went around the room and then back to Shannon. "There's coffee still warm on the stove."

"Yes, would you like a cup?" Shannon said.

A look of irritation crossed his face. "Who was here drinking that coffee before we came?"

"I don't suppose there's anything wrong with having a cup of coffee in my own kitchen, is there?"

"In the middle of the night? That's a little late to have your coffee." Robards raised his eyebrows. He didn't believe her, but he couldn't prove she lied.

"I can't see how that's any of your business, Colonel. But if you must know, I've been having trouble sleeping since my father was killed."

"I know a cure for insomnia." The lust in his eyes flamed out at her again. A shiver of disgust ran through Shannon, and she hid her hate only with difficulty.

Just then Randal came into the kitchen. He peered first at Shannon and then at Robards. When his gaze returned to Shannon, he could see the fear that she was trying so hard to hide. A sudden rush of feeling welled up inside him. He stepped between her and Robards.

"There was no one in the barn, Colonel," he said.

"Very good, Captain," Robards said impatiently. "Now step out of the way. The lady and I are talking."

There was nothing Randal could do. He stepped out of the way and looked at Shannon again, willing her to look at him, but she didn't even seem to know he was there.

"We've said all that needs to be said, Colonel. You've searched my house and grounds and have found nothing. Now I must ask you to leave."

"You haven't fooled me, Shannon. I know they've been here, and we'll catch up with them yet." He laughed shortly. "Let's see, I believe you have a fiancé with the rebels, and then there's that bastard who claims to be your brother."

This time Shannon couldn't control her anger. She struck out at him, and the noise of the slap filled the too quiet room. During the moments it took the red mark to form on his cheek, she thought he might strike her in return, but then he just laughed. The sound carried more menace than a blow.

"You'll be sorry for that, my dear," Robards said. "Perhaps you'd like to apologize now." He came close to her, almost touching her body.

"Leave my house at once!" she said.

His face was close to hers, and his every word was a threat. "I'll leave for now . . . but I'll be back, and we'll share some of your late-night coffee."

"Get out!"

"We should be pursuing the enemies, sir," Randal said in a tight voice. His fingers were twitching on the handle of his saber. If Robards didn't back away from Shannon, he wasn't sure he could keep from drawing it.

Robards stepped back. "Don't just stand there," he said to his men. "Go mount up." He gave Shannon one last look before turning to the door.

Randal's eyes never left Shannon. When the tremble passed over her as soon as Robards turned away, Randal longed to go to her and hold her, and somehow protect her. He took a step toward her, and finally she looked at him. But the hatred she'd felt for Robards was still there, and some of it spilled over on to Randal. Her eyes refused to accept the look of caring in his, and when he came near enough to reach out and touch her hand, she jerked back away from him.

His eyes on her softened with understanding. "I'm

sorry," he whispered before he quickly followed the other men out of the house.

She stood rigid, staring after them. She couldn't pretend to herself that everything was all right anymore. Robards's face, with its open threat, would linger too clearly in her mind. And Randal was with him.

Clay touched her shoulder, and she jumped. "Shannon, are you all right?"

"Yes, of course," she said. "Follow them out and make sure they all leave. Then lock the doors before you go back to bed, Clay."

"You promised to tell me what was going on here tonight," Clay said. "I'm not a little boy who can't be trusted anymore."

Shannon looked at Clay. He was just a little taller than she, with a slim body that had yet to fill out with a man's strength. A frown spoiled the classic perfection of his features, but a new look of growing maturity tempered the youth in his eyes. Maybe, Shannon thought, she hadn't been fair to Clay. Maybe he could shoulder his share of the load on the farm. Perhaps now was the time to begin drawing closer to him. There had never before been a time when they so urgently needed to work together.

"All right, Clay. We'll talk, but first make sure they leave." She had to be sure Robards had left.

"Then you'll tell me everything?"

Shannon nodded, and Clay went off like a child who'd been promised a special reward for doing a chore. Shannon's knees began to tremble uncontrollably, and she sank down at the table. She wanted to cry or scream, or leap on to Satin's back for a wild ride through the night. But she couldn't do any of that. She could only let the worry wind itself into a hard knot inside her while she waited for Clay to come back.

She was so tense that it was a few minutes before

she realized that Clay had returned and was sitting across the table from her.

"Shannon," he said with concern. He'd never seen her so lacking in control before.

She came away from her worries slowly. "Did they go?" When he nodded, she said, "All of them? Are you sure?"

"I'm sure, Shannon. I watched them mount up and ride out of sight."

"They didn't go back to the barn first, did they?"

"No. Why should they?"

"No reason. I was just thinking about the horses." She let out a long breath. "Well, Clay, what do you want to know?"

"Everything," he said eagerly. Shannon had never treated him like an adult. She'd always been too busy to pay him much mind at all.

"Everything," Shannon said with a resigned smile. "I don't even know everything myself. I don't even know what Robards wants from me." She dropped her face in her hands and knew that wasn't true. She knew exactly what he wanted, and the thought of it made her sick inside.

"Don't worry about him, Shannon. I won't let him hurt you," Clay said.

Shannon looked up at him. He was sincere, anxious to prove himself to her. She touched his hand. "It'll be all right, Clay. I can take care of myself," she said quietly. "I just hope Jett and Colin get away back to their camp."

"Then they *were* here tonight. Why didn't you wake me?"

"There wasn't time."

His face lit up with excitement. "Was Jett all right? Did they tell you about their raids with Morgan?"

"They didn't say much about the war. They weren't

here long, but they were both all right—tired looking and thinner than when they went away, but all right." Shannon paused in thought, then said, "You like Jett a lot, don't you, Clay?"

"Of course. Everybody does. He always used to talk to me when you and Colin didn't even know I was around. I'm glad you're going to marry Jett." Clay caught her small sigh and asked anxiously, "You are, aren't you?"

"I suppose we will when the war is over. But Clay, I never meant to leave you out of things. You just always seemed so little, and then you were afraid of the horses. And Mother didn't want us to be around you. You know that, Clay."

Clay nodded. "I know. But I'm not little anymore, and I'm not afraid either." There was a new set to his chin that worried Shannon.

"What do you mean, Clay?"

"You won't like it, Shannon, but if I'd known Jett was here tonight, I'd have gone with him when he left."

"You can't mean that," Shannon said. What would her mother do if Clay went to war?

"And why can't I? There are plenty of soldiers in the Army younger than I am. I'm almost eighteen, and I should be doing my part."

"But we need you here, Clay."

"You don't act like it."

"Maybe not, but you know how Mother needs you."

"Oh, Mother would understand."

"I don't think she would, Clay—especially if you go to the South. Mother's family has always supported the Union."

"A man has to do what he feels is right."

"Is it what you feel, or do you just want to ride with Jett?" Shannon said, watching him closely.

Clay's face darkened, and he stood up. "You're still treating me like a child. But you'll see. Jett will come back, and next time I'll ride south with him."

"All right, Clay," Shannon said quietly. "But you have to think of Mother. You know how it hurt her when Uncle Simon went away. I don't think she's ever really accepted the fact that he's dead. If you go away, she might take to her bed."

"I don't want to make Mother unhappy, but I've got to be a man." He turned and started out of the room.

"Clay—" she said, and he stopped without turning around. She went on. "Promise me you won't go without telling me first."

He turned slowly, and their eyes met. "You'll know, Shannon. Nothing happens around here that you don't know."

Shannon looked at him for a long moment before saying, "Good night, Clay."

She watched her young brother walk out of the kitchen and heard him bounding up the stairs to his room. Then she reached over and put out the lamp, and let the darkness gather around her like the worries gathering in her mind, shutting out any hope. She'd always thought she could fight almost anything, but there was no way to hold back the war.

CHAPTER 7

All through July reports and rumors flew from person to person like bees from flower to flower. Shannon knew that Morgan and his men had passed over the Ohio River into Indiana at Brandenburg, with the Union Army only a few hours behind them. Since then she'd heard nothing she could be sure was fact, except that Morgan's band was still moving through town after town, advancing on into Ohio, with the Union forces following them relentlessly.

Not long after Jett and Colin visited Marshland, Shannon and Clay went to Woodlawn to help Becky and Mrs. Noble pack for their move north to Canada. Mr. Noble had already left for Virginia to join General Lee.

When it was time to go home, Shannon kissed Becky goodbye. "We'll miss you, Becky."

Becky's eyes filled with tears. "You could come with

us, Shannon. That's what you and your mother should do."

"I can't do that, Becky."

"You should. Robards isn't going to let up on us until he sees us all ruined. He'll use any means to get his way."

Shannon soothed her. "Don't worry about us. We'll be all right."

"But two women alone. What chance do you have?"

"Surely Colonel Robards hasn't sunk so low as to threaten women," Shannon said in a light voice. "And Clay is still here to help us."

Becky looked at Clay. "If he were old enough to help, he'd be with General Morgan instead of hiding behind his mother's skirts."

Clay's face turned bright red. "I'm not hiding behind anyone, Becky Noble. And when Jett comes back, I'll be riding south with him."

Becky's face changed. She went over to Clay and said, "That's wonderful, Clay. I'll be praying for you." She pulled his face down and kissed him full on the lips. Clay's face turned an even deeper shade of red.

Mrs. Noble came up to them and said with a tolerant smile, "Becky! You're embarrassing Clay." It had been evident for a long time that she looked with far more approval on a possible match between Clay and Becky than between Shannon and Jett.

"I think he's enjoying being embarrassed, Mrs. Noble," Shannon said. Mrs. Noble was a small woman, but she had a commanding presence. New worry lines around her eyes and neat mouth gave an unusually stern look to her face. Shannon had never been able to like her, but she did wish her well. Now as she touched her lips to the woman's cool cheek, she told her, "I hope things go smoothly for you on your trip."

"Thank you for your help, Shannon. Perhaps you

really should consider going with us," Mrs. Noble suggested again.

Shannon shook her head. "Mother's not really been well since Uncle Simon was killed. I don't think she would want to leave Clay Manor even if she were able."

"Do you think I want to leave Woodlawn?" Mrs. Noble said, looking at the beautiful mansion behind them. The place already had a deserted air about it. She sighed. "But I have very little choice."

Shannon felt a moment of sympathy and reached out to touch her but then drew her hand back. "I know. Mother and I may have to leave in time, but for now we'll try to stay."

Mrs. Noble nodded. "It's different for you anyway. Olivia and her family always were Unionists. That may help her in the days to come." She turned back to Shannon. "And then she has you, Shannon. I have never admired your strong will or the way you try to do things only a man should do. And I don't admire it now, but it may help you to survive this war."

Shannon was quiet for a moment, letting Mrs. Noble's critical words slide around her. Then she said, "You'll be back at Woodlawn soon, and the house will be open and your family will be together again, Mrs. Noble."

"I wish I could believe that, Shannon, but it's not likely that we'll all be together ever again. This war will leave its mark on every family, and I'm afraid that when I return home, there'll be empty places at the table."

Their eyes met, and Shannon could not deny the truth of those words. The war had already taken her father and Simon. The unspoken question that charged the air between them was who would be next.

In the days that followed Shannon heard Mrs. Noble's words echo in her mind often, as the news concerning Morgan and his raiders came to her ears. More and more Union soldiers were being sent against him. Twice they had him boxed in, but each time, Morgan managed to slip away with most of his troops, although his losses were reported to be heavy. Shannon worked even harder to keep from thinking about Colin and Jett.

One afternoon when she was in the barn feeding the horses, she heard Adam call out. "I hear a rider coming, Miss Shannon."

She went to the barn door and looked out.

"You want me to fetch the gun, Miss Shannon?" Adam asked.

Shannon shook her head. "It's all right, Adam. It's Captain Hunt." Her heart skipped a beat as she said his name. She'd blocked out any thought of Randal since the night he'd come with Robards. It was too painful to think of their being on the same side, because if he was with Robards, he was against her. But now she remembered the clear sincerity of his blue eyes, and suddenly nothing else mattered.

Adam walked up behind her. "You're right there, Miss Shannon. We don't have nothing to worry about from the captain."

"How can you be sure, Adam?"

"That night the Union soldiers came, the captain saw Sally before she got back to our cabin, but he didn't give her no trouble. Just made sure she got inside safe before the other men saw her. He's a good man."

A warm feeling spread through Shannon while she watched Randal riding closer. "Good morning, Captain Hunt," she said when he drew up in front of them.

Adam stepped to the horse's head. "Looks like your horse could use some feed and water, Captain."

"That he could, Adam," Randal agreed, dismounting. He still hadn't looked at Shannon, and she was suddenly afraid of the news he might be bringing.

After Adam had taken the horse away, Shannon couldn't stand the silence building between them. She said, "Perhaps you'd like some refreshments as well, Captain. Aunt Mamie will be glad to fix you something." He certainly looked as though he could use some food. There were hollows around his eyes and lines of fatigue tracing his lips.

He shook his head, and finally he brought his eyes to meet hers. "Is there someplace we can sit down to talk, out of this sun?"

Shannon led him to a bench under an arbor of vines where it was cool and pleasant. She waited until he had sat down beside her before she asked, "What is it, Captain?"

"Morgan has been captured in Ohio. My company just returned from there."

Shannon had to summon up her courage to ask the next question. "And Colin?" She sat stiffly, barely breathing while she waited for his answer.

"He was taken prisoner. And so was Jett Noble." A frown crossed Randal's face.

"Thank God. At least they're alive." She didn't like to think about Colin being locked up in a prison, but as long as he was there, no one would be shooting at him.

Randal was quiet for a long moment before he said, "I just wanted to tell you so you wouldn't worry too much when you heard the news. I guess I'll be getting on back."

When he moved to rise again, Shannon touched his arm. "Is something wrong, Randal? You weren't hurt in the battle, were you?"

"Would you care?" he said, staring at her intently.

She didn't know what to say. This was a side of Randal she hadn't seen before. She watched while the gentle blueness of his eyes changed to a wintry blue.

He went on. "I mean, what difference does it make

to you what happens to a man in a blue uniform?" He looked away from her at the leaves above him.

"I told you, Captain Hunt, that I tried not to take sides in this war."

"You have to take sides, Shannon. When you hide Confederates in your house, you're taking sides."

"And when I entertain Union soldiers, I'm taking sides too." He looked so tired and unhappy that instead of his unreasonableness making her angry, she longed to reach out and stroke his face, and smooth away the lines. Most of all she wanted the smile to come back to his eyes. She smiled and said, "I do believe you're trying to start an argument, Captain?"

He turned back to her, but he didn't return her smile. "Why didn't you tell me that you were engaged?" he asked suddenly.

The question surprised her, and it took Shannon a minute to answer. "You didn't ask me. Just as I have no idea if you have a wife and five children waiting for you down in New Orleans."

He couldn't keep from smiling as he said, "Five?"

"You mean you have more?" Shannon said, feeling the tenseness vanish between them and the easy feeling come back.

"I guess it was silly to think that a beautiful girl like you wouldn't be taken."

Shannon didn't like the way that sounded. She didn't want to be taken—not if it meant that Randal would get that closed faraway look in his eyes. She said carefully, "My family has always assumed that Jett and I would get married. Papa thought it might join not only us but also our farms sometime in the future. We could have married the summer before Jett left with Morgan."

Some of the tired lines faded from Randal's face. "But you didn't."

Shannon shook her head, looking down at her

hands. "I didn't feel that the time was right." She knew that Randal was gazing intently at her, but she wouldn't look up. "And now it seems best to wait till the war is over."

"Then you are going to marry him?"

"Perhaps when the time comes I will," Shannon said slowly.

"And maybe you won't?"

She didn't answer, but her eyes came up to meet his. He put his arms around her and gently pulled her to him. Then his lips were on hers, softly at first and then with more insistence.

Shannon felt tingles rush through her as her lips responded to his. At that moment there seemed to be nothing in the world but the two of them touching.

"Shannon." Clay's call brought Shannon back to earth.

She pulled back from Randal, but she couldn't pull away from his eyes. They seemed to want something from her that she couldn't give. "We shouldn't have done that," she said.

"Why not?" he said. He could scarcely keep himself from pulling her close again, but he knew the moment had passed. He had loved Shannon ever since the day he first saw her. She'd looked so brave and yet so very vulnerable as she stood guard in front of her father's body. But now, despite the kiss, he was sure that she didn't feel the same way.

After all, he thought as he drank in the sight of her, she was the most astonishingly beautiful woman he'd ever seen. There was nothing neat and tidy or anxious to please about her, like the other girls he'd known. He had only to shut his eyes to see her and her black horse racing wild and free across the meadow like a dream just beyond reach. And what was he? Just a poor sharecropper's son who was wearing a uniform that was the wrong color. He felt a rush of hate for Jett Noble who had the promise of her love.

"Shannon!" Clay called again, this time louder and closer to them.

Shannon stood up and immediately missed the touch of Randal's leg against hers. "I'm here, Clay," she called.

Clay said, "What are you doing hiding out here, Shannon?" Only then did he see Randal. "What's he doing here?" His voice was cold.

"You remember Captain Hunt, don't you, Clay?" Shannon said evenly.

Clay's eyes narrowed as they flicked from her to Randal and then back to her. He said, "What are you doing out here with him?"

She didn't like the sound of Clay's voice. "I think you should apologize to our visitor for your rudeness, Clay."

Clay stepped closer to Randal. "You were with Robards the other night, weren't you?" He didn't wait for an answer. "Maybe I couldn't make you leave my property then, but I can now. Get off!"

Shannon clutched Clay's arm. "That will be enough, Clay. You will return to the house and wait for me there." Clay spun around to face her. For a moment his will battled against hers, but he had no chance of winning.

A flush spread across his cheeks as he said, "If you want to entertain the Union Army one by one, I can't stop you, Shannon, but you'd better remember that they are the enemy. This one's the same as Robards." He turned on his heel and stalked away.

Her anger drained away as she watched Clay walk through the garden back to the house. Now she was only sad because there seemed no way for them to become closer to each other. They were always backing away into separate corners.

"I'm sorry, Shannon," Randal said behind her. "I don't want to cause trouble between you and your brother."

Shannon shook her head. "Clay and I are so different that sometimes it's hard to remember that we have the same parents, and right now he's having a rough time. He's trying so hard to become a man, and Mother doesn't know how to let him." Shannon was silent for a moment. "And I suppose I don't either. It scares me to think about his going off to war."

"He's right about one thing though, you know." Randal's voice deepened with concern. "Even if he was wrong about me, Robards is your enemy."

The thought of Robards made Shannon feel heavy and tired. She wanted to shut him out of her mind entirely. Then she said, "Was Clay wrong about you, Captain Hunt?"

He put his hands on her shoulders and turned her back to face him. "I've already told you that I want to be your friend, if you'll let me."

"Friends," Shannon said. "Everybody wants to be friends. Even the colonel tells me I should be friendlier to him."

A hard look came into Randal's eyes, and his hands on her shoulders tightened. "Stay away from him, Shannon."

Shannon laughed shortly. "I'm afraid that isn't the problem, Captain. Perhaps you could tell *him* to stay away from me."

"If he so much as touches you . . ." Randal began. His face was completely transformed, and all traces of the man who'd just gently held her were gone.

"Randal," Shannon said quietly, "it's all right. Robards won't bother me."

Randal wanted to believe that because he knew there was no way he could protect her from Robards.

Though he wanted to stay with her and to keep her safe, he had to return to the business of war. He said, "I have to get back to town before they miss me. Don't worry about Colin. They treat the prisoners fairly well up in Ohio."

"Thank you for coming and telling me, Randal." There was a long silence between them while his eyes searched hers before he turned away. She stopped him. "Perhaps you'd like to come for dinner some night."

He looked back at her and thought he could see eagerness in her eyes. "What about Clay?" he said.

"I'll talk to Clay. He won't care, really. He's angry because of the other night. That's all. But if you'd rather not come . . ." Shannon let her voice trail away.

"Friday night?" he asked, and she nodded. "I'll see you then." His eyes touched hers once more before he turned and walked swiftly back toward the barn to get his horse.

Shannon wanted to sink back down on the bench and try to straighten out the way she felt, but she'd told Clay to wait for her, and she might as well talk to him and get it over with.

He was in the hall, pacing back and forth. Before she could say a word, he said, "I don't want that man setting foot on my property again."

"Captain Hunt came out of kindness to tell us that Morgan has been captured."

"And to gloat about a Union victory no doubt."

"No, Clay. So that I would know that Jett and Colin have been captured but that they are both still alive."

"You mean Jett's in a prison camp?"

"I'm afraid so."

"Well, he won't be there long. He'll escape and come back through here. Then I'll be going with him." Clay stopped pacing long enough to stare at Shannon while he said, "And he won't like what's been going on around here."

"The captain is a friend, Clay, and right now we need friends."

"Like Robards?" Clay spit out.

Shannon kept her voice calm. "Robards is definitely not a friend."

"Whatever. I don't want that Captain Hunt here again."

Clay looked so ridiculous trying to give her orders that Shannon had to smile. "Maybe I should tell you that the captain is coming for dinner on Friday."

"I won't allow an enemy at my table or in my house."

"He's not my enemy, Clay, and though it may be your house through whatever trick of nature made *you* a boy instead of me, I still live here. As long as that's so, I'll entertain whomever I want." Shannon's voice was firm. "Unless you want me to pack up and leave."

Clay's face changed. "You know I don't want that, Shannon."

Shannon looked at him without saying anything more, and Clay went on. "But Jett's not going to like it when I tell him about you and this Captain Hunt."

"Then perhaps you shouldn't tell him," Shannon said and walked away before he could say any more.

CHAPTER 8

The weather turned hot and sultry with a bank of clouds gathering almost every evening to threaten a storm that boomed and flashed in the distance but never came any closer. Nearly all the horses were out to pasture because of the heat trapped in the barn by midmorning.

Now when Shannon and Satin went for their morning ride, she made the rounds to check on the horses. She always counted the mares, and then went over to the yearling pasture to watch the young colts and fillies. Even the hot weather couldn't keep the colts from running sleek and shiny across the green field.

There were several that looked promising. Adam and Tom had begun working with a few of them already, but they didn't have enough help to do the proper job. Shannon had thought about selling some of the horses. Other horsemen around the area were selling their animals up north. Some said they might as well before the Yankees or rebels got them for free.

Shannon watched the yearlings' legs flashing in the early morning sunshine, and despite her worries she smiled as she looked around her. At least Marshland was secluded several miles off the main roads. Yet the guerrilla raiders had found them once, and her smile disappeared as Shannon thought about the likelihood of their returning.

But she couldn't keep from smiling long on this day, especially out in the fields with the rich land spreading out around her. She'd never been off the farm for more than a day, except for a single short trip north with her father. All she'd ever needed was here at Marshland. The land was so much a part of her that she could almost feel the connecting tendrils reaching out from her feet into the ground.

She guessed that Grandfather Clay must have felt the same way when he first staked out as his own this stretch of land in the Bluegrass. Owners of the smooth rolling land with its giant stands of trees must have realized as they looked out over it that they belonged to the land as much as it belonged to them.

Yet there had been Clays who didn't feel the same as she did. Shannon was sure that her grandfather had at one time, before the death of his wife and four of his children in the cholera epidemic had destroyed a part of him. Though he clung to the land, the pleasure had gone out of it. Maybe that was why her Uncle Simon had never seemed to care about the land. All he wanted was to go north to school and become a lawyer. He'd left all the running of the farm up to his brother-in-law Emmett, insisting only that he not deal in slaves. Simon wanted to free the slaves, but he'd never been able to convince Shannon's father that slavery was wrong, and he couldn't fight Emmett. Finally he'd died trying to change the South.

Shannon had never been close to Simon. He'd never had time for anything but his books. Often he and her mother would read aloud to each other for the pure joy of hearing the words spoken. It was Simon who'd encouraged Olivia to send some of her poems to the newspapers. Only a few had ever been published, but those few brought a secret happiness to Olivia that she could share only with Simon.

Shannon remembered the day Simon left for the war. He'd looked around at the farm as though he were seeing it for the first time. Shannon knew he suddenly didn't want to leave. She'd gone over to him and said, "You'll be back, Uncle Simon."

He'd looked at her with a sad smile, and again she'd wondered why he'd never taken a wife. He was certainly handsome enough in his dignified way. "Ah, Shannon, if we could all have your optimism," he had said. "But now that I must leave, I'm beginning to think your father is right and that we should leave the fighting of this war to the madmen. I'm going to miss all of this . . . much more than I ever supposed." Then he did something that he'd never done before. He leaned over and kissed her softly on the cheek.

"You don't have to go," Shannon had told him.

"Ah, but there you're wrong," he'd said. "Despite the way I feel this minute, there are more important things than the land. Someday, when it comes your time to leave, you'll understand, Shannon."

Baffled, she'd watched him ride away, and even now she could not imagine a reason for leaving Marshland. She breathed deeply, pulling the strength of the land inside her. She didn't like to think of leaving Marshland to go to Woodlawn to live, even though the farms lay side by side. Perhaps that more than anything else had been the reason she'd hesitated when it came time to marry Jett.

When the war ended, she wouldn't be able to hesitate any longer. It would be time to marry. She was already twenty. But how would she be able to leave Marshland? She looked up at the sun and was surprised to see it already high in the sky. She turned Satin toward the barn and let him run. It was Friday, and she had a lot to do before nightfall. Then she thought of Randal, and she smiled into the wind.

By the time she had finished all her outside work, it was late afternoon, and when she went into the kitchen, Aunt Mamie put her hands on her broad hips and said, "Look at the mess you are, Miss Shannon. You ought to leave such work as that to the men folks. It just ain't right for a lady to get so dirty and smelly. You'd think you'd been out there cleaning stalls."

Shannon smiled. "You might think that, Aunt Mamie." She sniffed the fragrant air of the hot steaming kitchen. "Something smells delicious."

"I told you I'd fix you a fine table for that young man you've asked over, but I don't know as how even my good cooking will get him to stay when he gets a look at you. Or maybe I should say a whiff."

Shannon laughed. "I'm going to take a bath. Don't worry about that."

"I'm not. Sally's done fixing it for you up in your room." Aunt Mamie turned back to the stove to lift a top off a pot and stir.

Shannon, sensing that Aunt Mamie still had something she wanted to say, asked, "What's the matter, Aunt Mamie?"

Aunt Mamie turned back around and wiped the sweat off her face with a corner of her apron. "Your mama says she won't be coming down to eat, that she and Master Clay will be wanting their dinner in her room."

"Don't let it worry you, Aunt Mamie."

"There ain't no reason for it to worry me none, but I

sorta thought it might put a bother on you." The black woman eyed her carefully.

Shannon sighed and shook her head. "It's just Clay. He's got this crazy idea that I'm interested in this Captain Hunt and that I shouldn't be because of Jett. And he just can't see straight mostly because Randal's wearing that blue uniform."

Aunt Mamie's eyes searched hers before she said, "Are you sure it's so crazy, sugar child?"

Shannon couldn't keep from smiling. It was the first time Aunt Mamie had called her that since her father had died. She went to her and kissed her cheek.

"That wasn't no answer," Aunt Mamie said. "You used to come running to tell me when a boy no more'n looked cross-eyed at you. Why, I remember that time you and Mr. Jett first took up with each other and that terrible race you had where you almost broke your neck, riding like a heathen right out on the main road."

Shannon laughed. "I thought you and Mother would both faint when I rode up that day. And Papa wouldn't let me ride for a week, but I won, you know."

Aunt Mamie shook her head. "You'd never known how not to win. Trouble was, neither had Mr. Jett. I never seen a madder young gentleman in all my days." A little smile began to play around her mouth.

"It was funny, wasn't it, Aunt Mamie?"

Finally Aunt Mamie laughed, throwing back her head and filling the kitchen with the sound. But then she hushed and looked sharply at Shannon again. "But it's when you stop talking about something that I know it's really important. Is that the way it is with this Yankee captain?"

"Captain Hunt has tried to be kind to us. I thought the least I could do was invite him to dinner. That's all, Aunt Mamie."

Aunt Mamie nodded, but there was doubt in her

eyes. "Whatever you say, Shannon. I'll see that you have a fine meal to thank him with. Now run on along and let Sally help you get all fixed up. The captain ain't never seen you in your company clothes. He'll be in for a big surprise."

"You know it's only proper that I wear my black dress. It's not been much over a month since Papa was killed."

Aunt Mamie put her arms around her. "You think your Papa would have been happy seeing you in black? Wear that dark green dress he brought you back from his last trip north. That's the way your Papa liked to see you, all dressed up and showing off that hair. I never seen a man so proud of a head of hair as he was of yours."

"He told me once that his mother's hair was red."

"I reckon that was it." Aunt Mamie reached out and stroked Shannon's hair. "You let Sally put it up for you. That girl has a way with hair."

"I thought I might just let it hang loose."

Aunt Mamie clucked her tongue. "Now you know, child, that a lady just don't entertain without putting her hair up."

"The captain's seen me with my hair down."

"He's seen you in your nightgown too, but I didn't figure you was gonna wear it to dinner."

Shannon laughed. "All right, Aunt Mamie, you win. I'd better get started if I'm going to have to dress up like a princess."

"You is a princess, sugar child, and don't you ever forget it. I'll set the little table in the dining room for two."

"You could just set it here in the kitchen, and then we could all eat together."

"Land of Goshen, child! Won't you never learn what's proper? It's a good thing you've got your old Aunt Mamie to teach you. Now scat on upstairs."

Shannon ran up the stairs, still laughing.

"What's so funny?" Sally asked when Shannon came into the room. She looked up from pouring a bucket of steaming water into the big tub she'd pulled out into the middle of the room. "Or maybe you just can't keep from laughing because a certain captain is coming to call."

"Oh, Sally, you're as bad as your mother. It's just as I told her. I feel that I owe the captain a little hospitality after all the kindness he's shown us."

Sally looked at Shannon knowingly and smiled. "Whatever you say, Shay. You'd better get in this tub before the water cools off."

Shannon stripped off her clothes and sank into the tub with a sigh. "It feels good. I didn't know I was so tired till now."

"You're working too hard. Adam says you try to do everything. What you've got to remember, Shay, is that you're not a man, no matter what you might wish."

Shannon looked down at the full curves of her body. "That would be a little hard to forget. But there's just so much to do."

"And if there wasn't, you'd be out there looking for something till you found it. I never seen anybody so attached to a bunch of four-legged critters."

Shannon laughed. "You're beginning to sound like Aunt Mamie again."

Sally wet Shannon's hair and then soaped it. "That don't bother me none. Mama's got more sense than the lot of us put together."

"I can't argue with that." Shannon pushed Sally's hands away and worked the lather on her hair herself. "Look, I can do this. I don't need you to wait on me, Sally."

Sally began pouring water over Shannon's head to rinse away the soap. "I ain't got nothing else to do. Sometime I'll let you help wash my hair."

"You wouldn't let me get close to your hair."

Sally laughed. "You remember what happened the last time I did. You gave me the awfullest haircut."

"Well, I was going to let you do mine next, but Aunt Mamie caught us first."

Sally shook her head. "I thought she was going to cry."

"I thought she was going to wear me out. I never was so surprised as when she started laughing."

"What would we do without Mama?"

"I don't know," Shannon said. "Or what I'd do without you either, Sally."

Sally was suddenly too quiet. Shannon looked around at her and said, "I'm sorry I said that, Sally. I know what a spot that puts you in."

"Adam wants to leave. You know that, don't you, Shay?" Sally sank down on a chair as her large brown eyes filled with tears.

"And what do *you* want, Sally?"

"I don't know, Shay. Everybody I love is here, except for John, and we knew the night he left that we'd probably never see him again. But Adam thinks I'm afraid to leave just because I'm not free. He doesn't understand about a home because he never had one." Sally looked off through the window, but she wasn't seeing anything. "He never even knew his father, and he was sold away from his mother when he was just a boy. Since then nothing's been good for him." Sally shuddered before she said, "He has plenty of reason for hating the whites."

Shannon stood up and began drying off. "But *you* don't." When Sally didn't answer, Shannon looked at her and caught a guarded look on her face. Shannon frowned. "Has anyone bothered you, Sally?"

Sally shook her head. "You and Mama have always protected me, but I'm scared the day will come when this light skin of mine is going to bring me trouble. You heard what Mr. Jett said the other night."

"You don't have to worry about that. You know I'd never sell you. If it will make you feel better, I'll draw up papers to make you and Adam legally free. Of course, I'll have to get Clay and Mother to sign them."

"Are you so sure they will?"

"Of course," Shannon said.

"I don't know. I've heard Master Clay talk of going to join the rebels."

"But that's not because he believes in slavery. He just thinks anything Jett does is naturally the right thing."

"And do you think if it were Mr. Jett's decision that he would set me free?"

"That's not Jett's decision," Shannon said shortly. She sat down and began tugging at the tangles in her wet hair.

Sally took the comb from Shannon's hand and began working it gently through her hair. Shannon watched her in the mirror, then finally said, "You're free now, Sally. You and Adam can leave whenever you want. I'll give you two horses and fix you a paper so you'll be safe till you get north."

Sally's eyes met hers in the mirror. Suddenly her eyes brimmed with tears that overflowed onto her cheeks. "I don't want to leave, Shay, but if Adam goes, I'll have to go with him. I love him."

"I know," Shannon said. They were quiet with their thoughts a few moments before Shannon asked, "How does it feel to really be in love?"

"There's all kinds of love, Shay, but what I feel for Adam is different. There couldn't ever be anything more important to me than Adam. No matter what happens in the days to come, I'll always love Adam."

"But how did you know?"

"It sort of crept up on me, and one day I just knew.

It was as though a beautiful flower had sprung up in my heart overnight and made the whole world good."

Shannon didn't say anything. Instead, she watched the rapt expression in Sally's eyes that explained better than her words.

Sally shook herself a little. "That must have been how Mama felt about her first husband. I can tell she's never felt that way about Daddy." Sally was quiet a moment before she went on. "She told me once that love was for those free enough to hunt for it."

"No wonder she looks so sad sometimes."

"Oh, don't go feeling sorry for Mama," Sally said, concentrating on fixing Shannon's hair again. She wound a few locks into a knot at the back of her head. "You don't feel that way about Mr. Jett, do you, Shay?"

"I once thought I could learn to, but now I'm not sure. There's always something getting between us."

"Maybe that something is a certain Yankee captain." Sally smiled.

Shannon shook her head, but the image of Randal's face was there before her with his smile and pure blue eyes. Still, despite the fact that her heart speeded up and a flush eased across her cheeks, she said, "Don't be silly. What do I know about this Captain Hunt?"

"It's not what you know that's important, Shay . . . it's what you feel."

CHAPTER 9

Shannon had been ready and waiting for an hour. She sat in the library office with a book open in her lap, but when the shadows began to fall about her, she didn't move to light a lamp. It had never occurred to her while she was dressing that Randal might not come. Now the idea gnawed at her, making her feel very alone.

Aunt Mamie had taken Clay and her mother their dinner up on trays long ago. Now she could hear her coming down with the empty trays. Aunt Mamie's steps paused momentarily at the bottom of the stairs before she went on toward the kitchen.

Shannon stood up, telling herself there was no reason to sit and wait all night. She'd get out of her stiff tiresome dress and then eat her dinner. Just before she reached the stairs, she heard the sound of a rider outside.

Carefully she pulled the draperies back from the

front window to peek out. It was Randal. She recognized his shape even though she couldn't see his face in the dark. She waited until he had knocked lightly on the door before she pulled it open. "Come in," she said, then stepped back to where the light in the entrance hall fell full upon her.

"Shannon?" Randal said, and then the sight of her left him speechless. Golden highlights glistened in the intricate pattern of curls piled on top of her head, and her eyes reflected the dark emerald of her gown. Her neckline plunged low, revealing the delicate skin of her bosom. Everything about her looked so inviting he almost reached out to fold her into his arms, but her eyes stopped him with a mischievous look.

"Why, Captain! You seem surprised. Don't you recognize me?" Shannon smiled and stepped a bit closer to him.

He swept her a deep bow. "Good evening, my lady. Could you possibly be the same young lady I found racing across the pasture just a few weeks ago?"

"Perhaps," Shannon said, feeling the laughter bubbling up inside her like a joyous brook. "Only time will tell."

"I hope I'll be around to see," he said and then apologized. "I'm sorry I'm so late, Shannon. I had to wait until I had finished all my duties for the day."

"Did Robards know you were coming?" Shannon asked, her smile slipping away.

Randal frowned and shook his head. "I saw no reason for him to know."

Robard's name brought a worrisome shadow over them. Shannon shook herself a bit and said, "I'm not going to worry about him tonight."

"What are you going to do?"

Shannon flashed him another mischievous smile.

"First I think we'd better eat before Aunt Mamie throws all that food out to the dogs."

She leaned over the lamp nearest them in the hallway to blow it out. The light touched her face, highlighting the scattering of freckles across her nose. Randal felt something inside him soften and spread as he watched her.

She looked up at him and asked, "Is something wrong?"

"No, not a thing," he said and followed her in to the dining room.

Aunt Mamie had set the small table in the corner of the dining room with their best dishes and candles.

Randal picked up a fork. "You must have taken these out of hiding."

Shannon laughed. "I dug them up out of the garden just this afternoon. I didn't think you'd be slipping them off the table into your pockets, but if I was wrong, we might find some pewter in the kitchen."

Randal laughed too. "I guess you wouldn't care if the Army took your forks as long as they left your horses alone."

Aunt Mamie pushed the serving cart through the door. "Are you ready to eat, Miss Shannon?"

Shannon jumped up. "Here, let me do that, and you can go and get supper ready for Tom."

Aunt Mamie pulled up to her full height and looked Shannon in the eye. "You just go and sit back down, Miss Shannon. Tonight you is going to act like a lady even if you pretend you don't know how."

"Yes, ma'am," Shannon said with a smile.

Aunt Mamie served their food and then said, "Now I'll leave you alone. When you get ready for your dessert, you just ring this little bell, Miss Shannon."

Shannon took the silver bell that Aunt Mamie must

have spent an hour polishing just for this dinner. "Oh, Aunt Mamie, when I get ready for dessert, I'll come to the kitchen and get it."

"If you knows what's good for you, missy, you'll ring the little bell," Aunt Mamie said before she went back into the kitchen.

Shannon looked from the bell to Randal, who was trying hard to keep from laughing. "I guess I'll have to act the proper lady tonight and ring the bell," Shannon said. "When Aunt Mamie takes that tone of voice there's no arguing with her."

Randal finally laughed. "You told me once that you could act the lady if you had to. I guess now we'll see."

"Well, I suppose. But I'd much rather just be me."

"That suits me," Randal said. He reached over and touched her hand. "When I first saw you tonight, I thought I'd never seen but one woman more beautiful."

"Really, Captain Hunt? And who might that be, if I may be so bold to ask?"

"She was a wild young thing riding a horse across a meadow as though she knew the secret of the wind."

His eyes captured hers, and they looked at each other for a long time without speaking. Then Shannon said, "You know, I'm not really beautiful. Not like Sally is. My mouth is too wide, and I've got these horrid freckles across my nose, not to mention this impossible hair."

Randal ran his finger lightly over the freckles on her nose. "That's what makes you better than beautiful. It makes you real."

A strange feeling pushed its way through Shannon, making her feel so weak that she was almost frightened. She wanted to pull her gaze away from his and retreat to a safer level, but his eyes clung to hers, refusing to turn her loose.

The loud clang of a dropped pan echoed through the

kitchen doors, and suddenly their moment of rapture was gone. Shannon said, "We really should eat. Aunt Mamie worked all day fixing this."

As they began eating, Shannon worried that perhaps Randal had not felt the intenseness that had overtaken her in that moment between them. He'd told her that she was beautiful, but many men had said that to her, although not in the same way. She sneaked a look up from her food, and his clear untroubled eyes were waiting for her with a smile that started in their depths long before it reached his lips. She looked quickly away before his eyes captured hers again. Perhaps she was misreading the look, and he was being nothing more than friendly.

Shannon never had had many friends, not real friends. There were Sally and Colin, but they had family ties to hold them close. She liked Becky, but she wasn't someone Shannon could lean on or confide in. It had always been that way. Shannon never had known how to make friends. Even when she had attended the girls' academy in town, she'd been a loner, obviously different from the other young girls there. Some of the girls had tried to make friends with her despite the social stigma attached to Shannon's family because of her father's acceptance of Colin, but Shannon had told flat meaningless secrets and held her private thoughts tightly to herself for fear that she might lose some important part of herself.

That's the way she felt now with Randal. It would be safer to keep their friendship light and simple, but she wasn't sure that she could.

"Would you like some more ham?" Shannon asked when he'd cleaned his plate for the second time.

He shook his head. "I've never tasted food so good."

"Aunt Mamie is one of the best cooks in the country. She'd say the best."

"I'd believe her."

"Wait till you taste her pie."

“I’m not sure I can eat any more.”

Shannon laughed. “You’ll have to, or you’ll hurt her feelings. She’s probably watching through the crack in the door now.”

“Bring it on then,” Randal said.

Shannon started to stand up but then quickly sat back down. “I guess if I don’t want her to take a switch to me, I’d best ring the bell.” She shook the silver dinner bell. “I feel ashamed, sitting here letting Aunt Mamie wait on me after she’s worked so hard all day.”

“You’re making her happy,” Randal said.

Aunt Mamie came through the doors with a tray. When she saw the empty bowls on the cart, her smile spread across her face.

“Mamie, the dinner was delicious,” Randal said. “You don’t suppose you could come down and cook for the Army.”

Aunt Mamie laughed, pleased with the praise. “Now don’t you go giving them officers of yours any ideas.”

“I’ll go along with that,” Shannon said. “I don’t know what I’d do without Aunt Mamie.”

“You’d get along, child,” Aunt Mamie said. “But not near so good, I reckon.” She cut them each a huge piece of cherry pie and then ladled on heaps of sweet whipped cream.

Shannon held up a hand to stop her. “That’s enough, Aunt Mamie. You’ll make me so fat I’ll have to loosen my stays.”

Aunt Mamie clucked her tongue. “What a way to talk, Miss Shannon! And in front of the captain. I thought I’d taught you better than that. Besides, if I know you, you don’t even have on any stays to loosen.”

A blush ran across Shannon’s cheeks. “Now, Aunt Mamie, don’t go telling all my secrets.”

Randal was smiling at them both, feeling very comfortable sitting at the elegant little table in the large dining room. He felt the same easy affection there as he used to feel in his mother's small hot kitchen, where the food had always tasted good too. When Aunt Mamie had gone back to the kitchen, this time promising to go on to her own cabin and her own supper, Randal said, "You and Mamie are very close, aren't you?"

Shannon looked up from the bite of pie over which she was lingering. "She's been my mother for years, maybe since the day I was born. My own mother was too sick to care for me after I was born, and when she did get better, she wasn't pleased with the way I turned out."

"But you must have been an adorable little girl."

Shannon shook her head. "No, not at all. I was always long legged and awkward while I was growing up, and my freckles seemed to grow together on my face, Then there was my red hair. Mother never liked red hair, said it just didn't seem to belong in a refined family."

"That must have been hard on you."

Shannon looked up, surprised. "Hard on me? Maybe it would have been if it hadn't been for Aunt Mamie. Aunt Mamie wouldn't have cared if I'd sprouted two horns." Shannon smiled. "In fact, sometimes I think she's tempted to search through my hair to see if I have."

"Has Mamie always belonged to your family?"

"Sometimes I'm not sure who belongs to whom," Shannon said. "But she's always been part of my mother's family."

"That must make her very loyal to you."

Shannon studied her pie a moment before answering. "I suppose she feels loyal to me, Clay, and Mother, but she hated my father." She hesitated before she went on. "I guess it's not too unusual for a slave to hate a master, but Aunt Mamie had her reasons. Papa sold her first husband down the river. That happened before I was born, but it's had its effect even on my life. When my mother more or less turned me over to Aunt Mamie to raise, it was she who made sure that I grew up knowing how wrong it is for people to own other people in any way."

"Did you learn the lesson well?" Randal asked. He watched Shannon struggle with herself. It would always be hard for her to speak ill of her father.

Shannon nodded. "Do you know how it is to love two people and know the hate one feels for the other and that there's nothing you can do about it?" She didn't wait for him to answer. It seemed that once she'd begun, she couldn't stop until she'd told him everything. "Aunt Mamie never spoke against my father to me. She knew that my mother was disappointed with me, and so was Papa at first. He desperately had wanted a boy, but I guess my red hair and freckles reminded him of his family back in Ireland, and he grew to love me in his own way. Aunt Mamie didn't want to spoil that love, but at the same time she built up a conscience in me that is worlds different from Papa's, even Mother's. Sometimes, while I was growing up and I was out playing with other little white girls, I'd realize how different I was from them. Their slaves were their servants, while my slaves are my family."

"Did you mind being different?"

"Sometimes. Of course, when Papa took in Colin, it put us off the local social list. Not that I cared, but it was hard on Mother." Shannon pushed the rest of her pie away. Her appetite disappeared with the memory of the taunts that her schoolmates had thrown at her and Colin. "But I never felt bad when I was with Aunt Mamie and Sally and John. They let me belong without any rules made up beforehand."

Shannon paused in thought before she said, "I guess all this sounds strange to you, Randal. Most people don't think about slaves having pride."

"Not me. There was a time when the slaves would

pass me and my father with their heads held high because they thought we were below their notice," he said, but there was no bitterness in his voice. "I guess other folks thought we were poor white trash, but we never thought so. We were just poor."

"But happy," Shannon said.

"How can you tell?"

"Oh, by the way you talk and the way you can smile without a lot of reason to smile."

Randal nodded. "We were happy. Mama always made sure of that. She still does for Pa." He waited a minute before going on. "Weren't you happy, Shannon?"

"Happy? You know you never really think about being happy when you're growing up. You're just whatever you are. But I guess I was happy . . . in most ways." Shannon fell silent while she remembered. When she spoke again, it was almost as if she were talking to herself. "Except the year I was fifteen. If I could only wipe away that year."

"What happened, Shannon?" Randal wasn't sure he should ask, but he couldn't keep from wanting to know everything about her.

"I guess when you get to be fifteen, it's time to grow up," she answered. "At least, that's what everybody else thought, so they began pushing fine clothes on me, telling me that I was a young lady now and that I couldn't follow Papa to the barn anymore and that it wasn't proper for young ladies to play with the boys. Unless, of course, it was a big game of romance, and they made sure I had plenty of opportunity for that. I don't know how Mother ever got me invited to so many parties. They might have tried to send me off to a boarding school if Papa hadn't already spent all our money on horses."

Shannon shook her head and went on. "Even Colin sided against me. Always before he'd taken my side, no matter if I was right or wrong. But then, all of a sudden he wouldn't even let me go riding with him. They tried to keep me from riding at all, but they couldn't."

Randal laughed. "I can imagine. So instead of becoming the perfect lady they had in mind, you rebelled."

"Not really. I learned to be smart. I went along with them on some things, but I held on to that part of me they were trying to destroy. They thought it was something I'd grow out of naturally. And who knows? Maybe I would have if they hadn't tried to force me to."

"I doubt it, don't you, Shannon?"

Shannon shrugged. "I don't know. Anyway, I kept on riding horses without a sidesaddle and speaking my mind, and I refused to bat my eyes at men. It nearly killed Mother." Shannon looked up at Randal. "Do I frighten you?"

He shook his head. "Not too much, anyway."

"I scared the boys at those parties—all of them except Jett. I think I presented a challenge to him. He wants to tame me."

The mention of Jett made Randal frown, but Shannon didn't notice. She was too involved in remembering. "But as awful as all that was, it was John who put the scar on that year that will always be there."

"Who was John?" Randal asked, relieved that she didn't want to talk about Jett anymore.

He wasn't sure at first that she was going to answer. Then she said, "I don't know why I'm telling you all this. I've never told anyone else. Only Sally knows the whole story, and that's because she was part of it. It's strange how something that happened five years ago can still hurt so much."

He waited without speaking, knowing that Shannon needed to talk it out.

"John was Aunt Mamie's son, and he and I were the same age. I guess when we were babies, she used to bounce him on one knee and me on the other. Sally was a couple of years younger than we were, and until I was five, they were my only playmates. We were a group." Shannon smiled. "Me with my freckles and red hair, Sally with her light skin and dark hair, and John, black as the night."

Shannon was quiet for a long moment before she went on. "John had to go to work in the barns as soon as he was big enough to carry a bucket of feed. He didn't mind the work, but he hated being a slave. Aunt Mamie made sure of that the same way she'd made sure I didn't accept slavery as a white man's right." Her voice grew quieter. "John ran away when he was fourteen. He didn't get far, and when they brought him back, Papa had him whipped. I hated Papa that day. I was sick all night, and the next morning I knew that when John tried again, he'd make it . . . because I would help him."

"Did he try again?"

Shannon nodded. "But only after I'd made plans for him. For months I kept my eyes and ears open, and then I began to see things that I'd never noticed before. I knew who would help and who wouldn't. When John was ready to go, I wrote him a road pass and told him where to go." Shannon paused for a moment. "And then I gave him a horse."

Randal waited for her to go on, but when she didn't, he asked, "Did he make it that time?"

"Yes." Shannon couldn't tell Randal the rest of it—how her father had raged, cursing and slapping her across the room when he found out what she'd done. She'd never told even Sally that.

Randal watched her go away from him into herself, remembering things she couldn't bear to bring out in the open. Then she lifted her chin, and the green of her eyes flashed with determination as she pulled up strengths from deep inside her. When she spoke, her voice was quiet but firm. "I was never sorry."

He longed to go around the table and take her in his

arms to protect her even from her memories, but something about her held him away, as if she were afraid to let anyone get too close. So he just watched as the determined look slowly faded away, until she was once more relaxed and smiling.

"I'm afraid I've been a terrible bore," she said. "I ask you to dinner and then weep on your shoulder."

"You didn't, but I want you to know that if you ever need a shoulder to weep on, mine's available."

Shannon resisted the pull of his eyes. Quickly she turned the conversation to lighter things, asking him about his family. He accepted the change and told her stories about the mischief he and his brother had found to get into while they were growing up. It was easy now for the two of them to laugh together and keep the mood light.

Late into the evening, after Randal had ridden away, Shannon sat in the quiet shadows of her bedroom and faced the fact that her life had been altered by the smiling young Yankee captain. Before she'd met him, she'd expected without a doubt that eventually she would marry Jett and that they'd build their farms into an empire of sorts. She'd never been sure that she loved Jett, but she'd been sure that love wasn't really necessary. Now she wasn't sure of anything, except that when she closed her eyes, Randal's smiling eyes were there waiting for her.

She shook herself and got up to get ready for bed, while telling herself that maybe she had been reading things into Randal's smile that truly weren't there. After all, each time he'd come, it had been on business—except for tonight, when she'd invited him. And even then he hadn't tried to kiss her good night. She reminded herself then that from now on it would be best for her to remember that she was committed to Jett and that she'd made him a promise before the war, a promise that would be hard to break. She pushed the thoughts of Randal away.

But before she slipped off to sleep, the thoughts sneaked back, and her promise to Jett seemed a faint echo from a distant past.

CHAPTER 10

August began with a new term of martial law in Kentucky. General Ashe handed down the order from his Louisville headquarters on the last day of July, just in time for the August elections.

But the election was far from Shannon's mind as she went about her chores. No one at Marshland could vote, and even when her father was still alive, his interest in politics had been limited to an occasional wager on the outcome. He said that politics were a lot like horse races but that he didn't have time to study men as he did horses.

So while the troops stationed at the polls in Lexington and around the state refused the vote to supporters of the opposing party, things went on at Marshland the same as any other day.

A week later General Ashe came to Lexington to be

welcomed by a series of parties. Shannon received an invitation to one of them from Robards, but though she knew Robards expected her to come, she sent him a letter of regret anyway. She doubted that refusing him was a smart thing to do. He wouldn't soon forget her slight.

Even Aunt Mamie said, "Maybe you should go, sugar child. There's just so far you can push that no good son of a devil. And much as I hates to admit it, child, he's got the upper hand right now."

"I can't do it, Aunt Mamie. I never was any good at pretending."

Aunt Mamie nodded. "That's for sure. You can't even tell half-truths. Maybe I ought to have taught you how."

"Maybe you were the one who taught me to tell only the truth," Shannon said. She paused for a moment. "But the Colonel wants more than a flattering game of flirtation. I don't like to think about what he wants." Shannon held the shudder close to her, but Aunt Mamie noticed anyway.

She laid a hand on Shannon's shoulder. "Now don't you fret, child. It won't come to that, even if we have to go to Canada."

"I couldn't leave the farm," Shannon said.

Aunt Mamie shook her head. "It's just a piece of land. It'll still be here whether you are or not. There's some things you just can't do, Shannon, even if it means saving the whole of Kentucky."

Shannon looked at Aunt Mamie's solemn face and laughed. "Don't look so worried, Aunt Mamie. Robards can't do anything I don't let him do."

"I hope you're right, child, but things has been awful strange round abouts here lately. Soldiers coming out and arresting folks if they so much as whistle the wrong tune. I reckon that half the men in this Bluegrass country is locked up in some prison somewhere or other, if they ain't in one of the armies." Aunt Mamie shook her head and turned back to her cooking. "Strange times is on us, and there ain't no way of knowing when it'll all end."

"Or how," Shannon said. She went out of the kitchen, trying to push away the feeling that the war's shadow was about to fall over them again with new hardships.

A few days later Clay went into town and returned with the mail. There were letters from Becky, Colin, and Jett. Shannon read Becky's letter first, sharing parts of it with Clay. The Nobles were settled in a comfortable house, but Becky was lonesome and her mother was depressed. Still, they were making the best of it. They belonged to a group of Southern sympathizers who got together to sew for the soldiers, to share news, and sometimes even to have a party. Shannon skimmed over the part about Colin, not reading any of it aloud to Clay.

Jett's letter was short, almost businesslike. He was a man of action, and the prison confinement was wearing on him so that even through the words of his letter, Shannon could feel his restlessness. Despite the few lines of endearments, Shannon handed the letter to Clay to read when she had finished. Clay grabbed it, eating up Jett's words.

Shannon saved Colin's letter until last.

"Dear Sis," he wrote. *"I hope this letter finds you well and gives you some reassurance about our own state. I guess you know by now that General Morgan's raid into Ohio wasn't a complete success. With a little more luck and if the river hadn't flooded, we would have been safely across the river and on into Virginia before they ever brought up enough men to trap us. But we had just too many hours in the saddle. Toward the end men were*

falling from their horses, not because the enemy had shot them but because they were so tired. We left them sleeping where they fell.

"Jett said we had too many men . . . made it hard for us to maneuver like we used to. Be that as it may, they finally cornered us. We're at Camp Douglas in Chicago, but they took Morgan, and most of his officers, to the Ohio Penitentiary, just like he was an ordinary criminal.

"If we'd known that was going to happen, you can bet we'd still be fighting or dead. Jett says we shouldn't have surrendered anyway. Prison's harder on him than me. One thing about it, it makes a man miss home more. Jett talks about you all the time. I don't think you'll be able to put him off any longer if this war ever ends."

Shannon turned the letter over and read on.

"They're trying to work up a prisoner exchange, so we may be free before you know it. Anyway, don't worry about us. Not much is happening in here. But I do want you to promise me that you won't do anything foolhardy. I've been worried about you ever since we last met. There are lots of things more important than horses. Try to remember that, Shannon. For me.

"We're giving our letters to a doctor who's been in to look after the wounded. He seems a decent enough sort, and he's promised to post them for us. With love, Colin."

Shannon put the letter on the table. Clay grabbed it up and read it almost as eagerly as he had Jett's. When he'd finished, he said, "I wish I'd been with them."

"Then you'd be there in prison too . . . or perhaps dead."

"But I'd have been doing my part, and I'd rather be with them than sitting here nursemaiding a bunch of women."

Shannon shook her head. "The more you talk, Clay, the more I know you aren't ready to go off to war."

"It doesn't matter what you think," Clay said, standing as tall as he could with a fierce determination darkening his eyes. "You can't keep me from going."

"Then I guess it's just as well that Jett's in prison."

"I'll go by myself if I have to. I know which way the South lies."

Shannon knew she'd said too much. She didn't want to push Clay into proving his courage by leaving. She chose her words carefully. "I'm sorry, Clay. I know that you could go right now if you wanted to, but why don't you wait? You saw what Colin wrote, that they were trying to work out a prisoner exchange. And if you have to go, you know Mother would feel better about it if you were with Jett."

Clay relaxed a bit. "I won't leave right away," he said. "But I *am* going. You understand that, don't you, Shannon?"

"I know, Clay, but I still don't want you to go. Do *you* understand that?"

For a moment the anger between them melted away, revealing what could almost be a bond of love between them that a brother and sister should share.

Clay said, "You will tell me the next time Jett comes?"

Shannon hesitated a moment, then nodded. "If he comes again, you'll know."

So the days passed with the uneasy fear of the future hanging over them. August became September, and at Marshland they prepared for winter as best they could. Randal rode out several times, but his visits were brief stolen times between his hours of duty.

During these times he helped with the chores and watched Shannon for some sign that might encourage him, but he saw none. She seemed determined to hold him away, accepting him as a friend but refusing to allow anything more. He didn't push her, for he felt he should be happy to have her friendship. After all, what did he have to offer her? The only things he owned were his horse and the clothes on his back. All the money he'd made in New Orleans had gone to helping his parents buy a place in Ohio. Not that he regretted it, but that left him with nothing to give a girl like Shannon who already had so much.

So he had decided to be patient. He wouldn't give up, but he thought time was on his side. Then, late in September, his regiment finally got orders to move out to battle. They'd been expecting them for months. At one time he'd been anxious for them, but now he wished they'd never come, because it would mean having to leave Shannon.

The day Randal had to say goodbye he came early, knowing he would find Shannon racing Satin in the back pasture. He wanted to make sure the picture of her as a wild free spirit was clear in his mind to take along with him when he left.

As he watched her, he felt his heart pounding so hard he thought it might burst with the love she'd won from him without even trying. The other girls he'd known had flirted and played games with him while trying to win his affections. Shannon had done nothing. She'd stormed into his heart, taking complete control just by being what she was.

He marvelled at her skill as she took a fence effortlessly, and he wanted her to belong to him. But he knew that no one could ever own Shannon. She'd have to come to him freely, and if she did, she'd bring more love than any one man could ever deserve.

She slowed down, looked up, and saw him. A smile lit up her face, and his heart jumped with hope. But he forced it back down. When he came back from the war, he would fight for her if he had to, but it wouldn't be fair to ask for commitments from her now. Not when he didn't know what the next few months might bring on the battlefields in Virginia.

"Randal," she said when she got close enough, "what are you doing here so early? And looking so dour. Don't tell me. You've come to arrest me for giving aid and comfort to the enemy."

Randal smiled. "Have you been?"

"Not lately. Unless, of course, you're the enemy."

Shannon laughed. It had been a good month, for she'd been able to push the shadows of the war away from her. She knew they were still there though, threatening to cover her, but for now Jett and Colin were away from the battlefield, Clay was safe at home, and Sally had said no more about leaving with Adam. But mostly she knew it was because of Randal. Randal, with his gentle smile and open acceptance of her the way she was.

"I guess in some people's eyes I am. Like your brother's," he said.

"Oh, you can't pay too much mind to Clay. He's young and anxious to prove himself."

"He could try proving himself around here by helping you out a little," Randal said.

"I don't think Clay was meant to be a horseman. He plans to take up law as a profession, and I guess he's right when he says cleaning out horse's stalls will do nothing to help train him for that."

"It might teach him a little kindness and humility. They're always good things to know."

"You didn't come out here at the break of dawn to talk about Clay's shortcomings," Shannon said. She slipped off her horse and led Satin around. The morning was crisp and cool with the smell of fall in the air. Already a few of the leaves in the woods were touched with color.

Randal dismounted and walked beside her. For a while they didn't talk but together soaked in the early morning wonder of the land. Finally Randal said, "You really love this place, don't you, Shannon?"

His question surprised her, and she let a few minutes pass before she answered. "Marshland is all I've ever known or wanted. I can feel my roots going back and tying me to everyone in my family who ever loved this land."

"But I thought you said that you were nothing like your mother's people, the Clays." The deep feeling she'd revealed in her answer bothered him.

"I'm not, in looks or in most other ways, but I guess a beautiful piece of land like this can get its hold on anyone. It did my father, and he never was a Clay."

Randal looked at the trees touching the sky beyond them. "Is this all Marshland, as far as you can see?"

Shannon turned, then pointed to the east. "There, just beyond that clump of trees, that's Jett's farm."

"Jett's farm," he echoed. What he didn't say hung in the air between them—that the Noble land lay next to the Marsh land, just begging to be joined. Finally he turned back to look at Shannon. He caught the rapt look on her face and felt a spear of hopelessness pierce him. "You'll never leave it, will you?"

"What? What did you say, Randal?" Shannon asked, turning away from the land back to him.

"Nothing," he said quietly, and the smile was completely gone from his blue eyes, making them darken like the sky before a storm.

"Is something wrong?"

He looked at her for a long moment with a question in his eyes, but he didn't say anything.

His sudden change in mood puzzled Shannon. She asked, "Have I said something to upset you?"

His smile came back, but it was a sadder smile. "No, Shannon. I just wanted to tell you how nice these past few weeks have been. I'll always carry a memory of you with me."

Something close to panic shot through Shannon. She tried to keep her voice light. "You sound as though you're leaving and never coming back."

He turned away from her, afraid that his eyes would reveal too much of his feeling for her. "We got orders to move out of Lexington and get back into the action."

"Oh no," Shannon said. Then she was quiet, trying desperately to pull back under control the wild feelings coursing through her.

"I wanted to come and say goodbye before I left."

"When will you go?" Her words were slow and measured.

"Tomorrow."

"Where to?"

"We're to join the Army of the Potomac unless our orders are changed again. My company will be sent where we're needed the most."

"But won't you be back?"

He turned back to her then, and his eyes burned into hers. "Who can know what the future holds, Shannon? But God willing, I will return." He added silently, God willing, I won't be too late and your bright flame will still burn free.

Randal couldn't leave without kissing Shannon one more time. Her lips softened under his, yielding sweetly at first, then responding eagerly. He pulled away while he still could and cupped her chin in his hand. He kissed the freckles on her nose and thought he saw the beginnings of tears in her eyes. He almost told her then that he loved her, but he stopped himself. It wouldn't be right—not until he returned.

"Goodbye, Shannon. Please be careful."

Shannon watched him mount his horse. "God be with you, Captain Hunt."

He looked down at her. "Perhaps you'll pray for me."

"If you wish, but I'm afraid I've never given God much reason to listen to my prayers."

"Then just think of me in the mornings when you bring Satin out to run," he said.

"And will you think of me?"

His voice was hoarse when he answered her. "Every morning when the sun comes up and every night when it goes down." What he didn't tell her was that she'd be in his mind all the minutes in between as well.

He turned his horse away from her without another word. She watched him ride away, slowly at first and then faster, as though he were anxious to get away from her and be done with the leave-taking.

"Goodbye, Randal," she said softly just before he disappeared over a rise. "I will see you again. I know I will."

CHAPTER 11

October brought perfect autumn weather with clear, warm days and crisp frosty nights that painted the leaves until the entire area around Marshland was a breathtaking spectacle of beauty. But Shannon could take no delight in the beauty spread before her eyes. To her the first leaves drifting down pointed up only the nearness of winter.

Yet there was more to her gray mood than just the threat of winter. It was the bleakness that had fallen over her the day Randal rode away. She'd often touched her lips, remembering his kiss, before she would dive back into her work in an attempt to block out the feelings that memory would awaken. But no matter what she did, there was a lonely ache inside her that refused to go away. It poked and probed at her, sometimes keeping her awake till dawn.

One night when Randal had been gone a little over two weeks and Shannon lay in bed, rubbing yet more of Aunt Mamie's special cream on her work-roughened hands, she heard a noise outside her window. She kept perfectly still and listened as a soft whistle floated up to her. She'd recognize that signal anywhere. She and Colin had used it as children whenever they would sneak out for midnight rides.

She leaned out the window and saw a figure silhouetted in the moonlight. It wasn't Colin. It was Jett, and he was alone. "Come quickly, Shannon," he called, "Colin's hurt, and he needs you."

Without a word she turned away from the window and began pulling on the workclothes she'd just taken off. Within minutes she was ready. She hesitated outside her door, remembering her promise to Clay. But before she had time to make up her mind, his bedroom door opened, and he was there beside her.

"What's going on?" he asked.

She hesitated again, wanting to say that she was just going out to check the horses, but her very silence told him.

"Jett's here," he said, "and you weren't going to tell me."

"You didn't give me time to decide what to do," Shannon whispered. "I don't want you to go. We need you here, Clay."

He'd already turned back to his room. "I'm going."

"What will I tell Mother?"

"You'll think of something. You can handle anything, can't you, sister?" He looked back over his shoulder at her. "You were very good at entertaining Yankees while Jett was in prison. Maybe you should worry about what you're going to tell Jett."

"Why should I? There's nothing to tell," Shannon

said coldly. "If you're not ready in three minutes, we'll leave without you."

"And are you joining the Confederates as well, sister? That will be a shock to Mother."

"Not so much as your leaving will be," Shannon said wryly. "But we have no time for games, Clay. Colin has been hurt. I have to go help him."

"Ah, Colin," Clay began, but Shannon didn't wait to hear whatever else he was about to say. She was already going down the stairs.

Jett met her at the door. "Are you ready?" he said.

Shannon shook her head. "I have to go to Aunt Mamie's cabin to get some medicines. While I get them, Tom can get the horses."

"I'll need a fresh mount, and so will Colin if he is to go on."

"If? You sound as though there's some doubt." Panic rose in her. "Is he hurt that bad?"

Jett put his arms around her. "Now take it easy, Shannon. Colin's going to be all right, but he's got a leg wound. I'm just not sure he'll be able to ride." He tipped her face up. "Sometimes I think you set more store by that almost brother of yours than you do me."

Shannon fought down the anger that flared up in her at the word *almost*. She said, "He needs me more than you right now."

"I'm not so sure," Jett answered. His voice was low and husky as he pulled her close. "Kiss me."

She thought it would only delay matters if she didn't, so she lifted her mouth obediently. But the kiss was only lips against lips without any response coming from inside her as it once had when Jett held her.

He raised his head a little. "What's the matter, Shannon?"

"Nothing. It's just that I'm worried about Colin. Don't we need to hurry?"

He let her go then, but when they entered Aunt Mamie's cabin, she could still see the question in his eyes.

"Mercy, child," Aunt Mamie said. "What's wrong? And Mr. Jett, we thought you was in prison up in Ohio."

"I was, Aunt Mamie, but we decided that a prison was no place to win this war for the South. We've been digging at night while the guards slept, ever since they took us there, and a few nights ago we finally came up outside the fence."

"Is that how Colin got shot?" Shannon asked.

Jett shook his head. "We got clear away or else we wouldn't have gotten away at all. Colin was hurt before they captured us. The wound was healing, but all that movement when we were running to get away opened it up again, and now he's feverish. He wanted me to leave him and go on alone, but I couldn't."

"I never thought you liked Colin," Shannon said.

"He's a good soldier," Jett said with a small shrug. "Colin and I have been riding together for over two years. More than once he's stood between me and death, or I've been there to help him. I'd be hard put to say which of us owed the other now."

Shannon's heart softened toward Jett, and she wished she could kiss him again, this time making more of an effort to satisfy him. But there wasn't time, so she said, "Tom, get Satin and Reida, and two of the other horses. Good strong horses that can move fast and stay on the move."

"Why four hourses?" Jett asked. "Don't tell me you're going to contribute a horse to the Confederate cause after you practically threatened to shoot me last time if I went toward the barn."

"I'm giving you more than another horse," Shannon said. "I'm letting you take away another brother."

Just then Clay came in with his pack. "She's not *letting* me. I'm just going."

"So you finally decided to be a man," Jett said.

Shannon wanted to cry out that he was still a boy, but she bit her lip and remained silent. Clay would be a man soon enough now, if he lived long enough. But she wouldn't think of that. He was with Jett, and Jett knew how to survive.

Jett looked little the worse for his months in prison, except for an unusual pallor, and his hair was trimmed shorter than she'd ever seen it. His eyes still burned with the same fire and confidence they had when he left to ride with Morgan.

Aunt Mamie handed Shannon a pack of medicines and clean rags to use as bandages. "I don't like you going out like this, child," she said. "What if that Colonel Robards and his home guard catches you with Mr. Jett?"

"They won't," Jett said. "They're just a bunch of hayseeds who hasn't got nerve enough to join the real army. They won't catch us."

"Maybe I should go instead, Miss Shannon. You don't know nothing about doctoring."

"No, Aunt Mamie. I'll be all right."

"Come on, Shannon," Jett said. "Tom has the horses ready."

"Here," Aunt Mamie said, stuffing Tom's cap on Shannon's head. "At least cover your hair."

"It's dark, Aunt Mamie. No one will see me."

"Do as she says," Jett said. "It might be morning before you get back. It wouldn't be good if anybody recognized you out; there's not another girl for miles around with hair like yours, Shannon."

"They can be thankful for that," she said as she

pushed her hair up into a knot and pulled Tom's hat down tight over it. "You got some blacking for my face now, Aunt Mamie?"

"Go on with you, child," she said, pushing Shannon toward the door. "You is practically as brown as any little darkie now, what with staying out in the sun all the time without a hat."

"I'll explain everything to Mother when I get back, but maybe you should spend the rest of the night at the house in case she wakes before then."

"Now don't you worry. I'll see to Miss Olivia. You just make sure you take care of yourself." A frown crossed her face. "I don't like this, child. I wish the young captain was still in Lexington. I'd feel easier if I knew it was his men on patrol that might see you."

Shannon touched Aunt Mamie's face and smiled before she went outside, where Tom was waiting for her. He was rubbing his arm as he gave her Satin's reins, and she said, "He didn't bite you again, did he, Tom?"

"Just a little, Miss Shannon. He is a devil."

"But he can run, Tom. How he can run."

They followed Jett's lead, letting their horses gallop when he did and going slow and quietly when he motioned them to. During one of the slower paces, Jett came back to ride alongside Shannon. "Who is this captain Aunt Mamie was talking about?" he asked.

Clay, who was just ahead of them, turned a bit on his horse and said, "Yes, sister, why don't you tell Jett all about Captain Hunt?"

Shannon kept her voice calm, trying to keep out the irritation of having to explain about Randal now. "He was the captain of a company that was at Lexington for a while. He tried to be kind to us after Papa got killed, that's all."

Clay made a sound of disgust. "*If* you can call

rousting up the whole household in the middle of night to search through all the rooms kind."

"Oh hush, Clay!" Shannon spoke sharply. "That wasn't Randal at all. That was Robards, and you know it. Randal had to follow orders."

"Randal?" Jett's voice took on an edge. "It seems that you two must have gotten very friendly."

"It never hurts to have friends, Jett, especially during times like these." Shannon wished Aunt Mamie hadn't mentioned Randal.

"And where is this Randal now?"

"He's gone to join the Army in Virginia."

"Then perhaps I'll meet him on the battlefield someday. I might enjoy that."

The hate in Jett's voice silenced Shannon. She could only hope that meeting never happened.

"Why so quiet?" Jett asked, touching Shannon's arm. Suddenly he reached out and stopped her horse.

Shannon couldn't see his face, but she could feel the tension in the darkness between them. She would have liked to put off this moment, but there was no avoiding it now.

He curled his fingers around the back of her neck and pressed hard against her skin. "You belong to me, Shannon. You've always been my girl, and you always will be."

Shannon bit back a sharp retort. He made her feel like something he'd bought and paid for. But she couldn't fight with him, not now—not with Colin out there somewhere, waiting for them. She took a deep breath and said, "You have no reason to be jealous, Jett."

"I'm not." He began caressing her neck. "I want you so much. If only there were time tonight . . ."

"Jett, please. Clay can hear."

"I don't care," he said. "I just want you to remember one thing, Shannon . . . as soon as this war is over, we're going to be married without any more delays."

"Are you asking or telling?"

"I don't have to ask. You're mine, Shannon, and don't you forget it." His voice softened a bit. "Do you remember the night you promised you'd be waiting when I came home from the war? You had tears in your eyes. You can't have forgotten that."

Shannon shook her head. "No, I haven't forgotten." She thought back to that night. He'd been on fire with the war fever and his impatience to be in the thick of the action. His kisses had burned with excitement not entirely for her but for what lay ahead, and she had returned those kisses with a passion that matched his, wondering why she'd refused to marry him during the summer. While he was with her, he'd made a place for himself in her mind and heart, but after he rode away, her own life billowed out and left no empty place aching for his return. Still, she had promised.

"It'll be good, Shannon. You'll see. Together we'll make Woodlawn and Marshland into an estate that the whole world will know about and admire."

Suddenly he rode on ahead, and they moved swiftly through the night with renewed urgency. It seemed forever before Jett began to slow up once more. The shape of a barn loomed up out of the darkness in front of them. Shannon looked quickly around her. There were no other buildings in sight.

Jett whistled, and from inside the barn a faint whistle sounded in answer.

Shannon was off her horse and almost to the barn door before Jett's voice stopped her. "Take your horse inside with you. Clay and I will keep watch. Try to fix him up good enough to ride, and hurry up about it. This isn't the best spot for a couple of rebels to hide out . . . or to get caught."

Shannon caught Satin's reins and led him through the door. "Colin?" she whispered. "Where are you?"

The barn was a box of total blackness.

"Here, Shannon," Colin said.

Shannon pulled a candle out of her pack and lit it. The light flickered up, throwing ghostly shadows all around her. She followed the sound of Colin's voice. He was lying on a small heap of hay, and for a moment Shannon was struck speechless by the sight of his gaunt face.

"It's just the candle, Sis," Colin said. "I'm not really so bad off that you need to faint."

"I've never fainted in my life," Shannon said indignantly, kneeling beside him. "And you know it, Colin Marsh."

Colin's laugh ended in a sort of choked cough. "It's good to see you," he said when he could talk again. He reached a trembling hand out and touched Shannon's cheek. "It's hard to have a sister like you. Every girl I ever met I had to put up against you, and there was just no way they could ever come out on top. Plenty of times I've wished we weren't brother and sister."

"Colin, you must be delirious," Shannon chided him. "You're not making sense."

Colin smiled a bit. "That could be," he said. "I thought I might die here, that Jett would go on to the South as I told him to. This seemed a funny place to die."

"You're not going to die," Shannon promised. She brushed away all the loose hay and made a bare place on the dirt floor to set the candle. Then she gently cut away the cloth from around his wound. It looked bad, much worse than she'd imagined, and she wished Aunt Mamie were there to tell her what to do.

"It's not very pretty, is it, little sister?" Colin said. "They talked about cutting my leg off there for a while up in Ohio, but I told them I didn't see much sense in that. A one-legged man doesn't make much of a horseman, and if I had to die, I'd just as soon die on two feet."

There was little Shannon could do other than apply the medicine Aunt Mamie had sent and wrap a clean bandage around his leg. Then she put a light cool hand on Colin's forehead. "You're sick, Colin. You can't go anywhere."

"Just what do you suggest, Sis, that I stay in this little barn forever?"

"No, of course not. I'll go home, get the buggy, and come back for you. You can stay at home until you're better."

Colin smiled. "You know better than that, Shannon. We're on enemy ground. They put people like me in prisons or hang them."

Shannon shivered. "Don't say things like that."

"That's why you've got to help me up on a horse. Once I get south, then I can find a safe place to get well."

"You'll never make it, Colin." There was panic in Shannon's voice.

"Sure I will, Sis. Jett has stuck by me this far. He'll help me."

"Clay's with him now."

"Clay?"

"He's going to join the Army."

"The South?" Colin said. "Your mother will never survive it."

"She'll have to. There was no way I could stop him. He's almost eighteen now."

"Then I've got another reason to make myself go on south. I'll have to watch over Clay and see that he lives through this mess. And that'll take a lot of watching." Colin pulled himself to a sitting position and couldn't manage to stifle a groan when the pain stabbed at him.

Shannon said nothing. It was a waste of time to argue with Colin when he had his mind made up.

"Here, help me up, and then call Jett. We need to get out of here before daylight." His voice was different, all business, and his main business at the moment was survival.

He drew himself up using Shannon as support, and then leaned against a post while she went to the door. Jett was there before Shannon could open it, and he looked past her to Colin. "They're coming."

"Do you have his horse?" Shannon said, and within seconds the animal was in the barn and they were helping Colin mount.

Colin said, "Go on, Jett. I'll catch up with you if I can, and if I can't, there's no use in the two of us getting caught."

There was silence between them for a moment before Jett said, "Take care, Colin. We'll try to lead them away." Swiftly he pulled Shannon to him and kissed her hard. "Go home as fast as that wicked black horse will take you, and don't stop for anybody. There's no way you can explain being out here in the middle of the night."

Then Jett and Clay were out the door, and she mounted Satin to the sound of their horses galloping away.

"Go, Shannon!" Colin said. "And don't look back."

Without another word, Colin slapped Satin's rear, and the horse exploded out of the barn taking Shannon back home again.

CHAPTER 12

Shannon had almost reached the stand of trees before she looked back. The sky had begun to lighten the east, and she could see Colin riding slowly away from the barn in the opposite direction. He'd never get away if he didn't go faster.

Shannon pulled Satin to a stop inside the shelter of the trees. Why didn't Colin go on? Then she knew. He was trying to make sure she got away, even if it meant being captured himself.

He disappeared from sight just moments before the soldiers rode out into the open with their guns ready. With a shiver, Shannon recognized Robards in the front line. If he caught her, he could do with her what he wanted. She melted back into the shadows of the trees, suddenly aware of every crackle of the leaves and brush.

Then, despite the fear pushing through her, making

her heart pound, she waited to see if Colin would get away. A few of the men ran into the barn. In minutes they were back, making their report to Robards. Robards moved his arm in a sweeping motion, and his men fanned out to search for tracks. They would find Satin's trail in the morning frost in seconds. There was nothing she could do now but try to get away herself.

She touched Satin's neck, and they began slipping away through the trees. She could only hope the shadows were hiding her movements. Then she was out of the trees facing yet another wide meadow. There was no one behind her yet. If she could make it through the clearing without being seen, she'd be home free.

Shannon leaned low over Satin's neck and clucked her tongue. Under her the horse responded, and they skimmed across the field. But just before they reached the next stand of trees, there was a shout and then a shot behind her. She didn't look back. She let Satin have his head going into the trees, and a low branch stung her face, almost knocking her off. Shannon wished she knew the country better. She might have avoided the trees entirely, but it was too late to worry about that. She could only crouch low on Satin's back and strain her eyes ahead to see if the soldiers had circled around on her. She needed to find a road. There wasn't a horse anywhere that could best Satin on a good level stretch.

Shannon came out of the trees into the dawning light cautiously. Then she pulled Satin to a stop for a precious moment while she took her bearings. It would do her little good to elude the soldiers if she was only making a circle that led into their midst.

There to the east was the road she had taken earlier. It would take her back toward Marshland. But first she had to get through the high stone fence between her and the road. She could see no gaps.

Suddenly she heard voices behind her again. The soldiers would spot her in minutes. Satin pranced nervously as a shiver of fear swept through Shannon.

She took a deep breath. "I know you're tired, boy, but it's our only chance. And it's not much of a fence."

Shannon closed her mind to all doubt that they might not make a clean jump and started Satin toward the fence. She leaned low and whispered encouragements to Satin while the fence loomed up closer and closer. At just the right second, Satin went into the air, flew clear of the fence, and landed softly on the other side. Wisps of hair escaped from Shannon's hat and streamed out behind her in the wind.

"Good boy," Shannon whispered. But there was no time for congratulations as another shot rang out behind her. Shannon chanced a quick look over her shoulder.

Three soldiers were milling about on the far side of the fence. Suddenly one of the men raised his gun and leveled it at her again. "Stop!" he shouted.

But she'd rather take her chances with her horse than with Robards. Shannon crouched low and asked Satin for yet one more rush to carry her out of danger. One bullet and then another whistled by her before all was quiet behind her. The only sounds were the rush of the air against her face and Satin's hoofs racing toward safety.

By the time Shannon thought she'd left them far enough behind she found herself passing familiar farms, and she took to the fields again. She didn't want to meet anyone on the road who might recognize her. She let Satin slow to a walk.

The sun was full up when she topped the rise and saw Marshland spread out in front of her. She waited for the peace to wash over her as she soaked in the scene. But it didn't. She was grateful to be home, but there was no peace. Only holes of emptiness torturing her with thoughts of those who were no longer there.

Suddenly she wished she could look across the field as she had before and see Randal on his black horse, waiting for her to finish her morning ride. She needed to see him smile and to let his eyes sink deep into hers.

But she shook her head at such foolish dependency. She didn't need anyone or anything. Not as long as she had all that lay there in front of her. If she could keep the land and the horses safe, then everything would be okay. Jett would come home, and they would marry. Then she'd have the land. Clay was like Simon. He would never care about running the farm. It would be as though Marshland belonged to her.

Yet, as Satin moved on toward the safety of the barn, a heavy empty place remained in Shannon's heart that even the beauty of the land couldn't fill.

Adam and Tom were waiting for her at the barn door.

"Are you all right, Miss Shannon?" Tom said, coming up to take her horse. "Me and Mamie been beside ourselves with worry."

Shannon realized suddenly how tired she was when her feet hit the ground. For a moment she thought her legs might not hold her up. But she said, "Here, I'll do that."

"Now, Miss Shannon," Tom said, "you look too tired to clean your own self up much less this horse." Tom rubbed Satin's foam flecked neck. "Besides, he's too tuckered to be mean to me this morning."

"What happened, miss?" Adam's eyes were intent on her. "You ran that horse near to death."

Shannon stroked Satin. "If it hadn't been for Satin, I'd be keeping company with Robards right now."

"What about Mr. Jett and your brothers?" Tom asked.

Shannon frowned. "I don't know. I think Jett and Clay probably got away. They left before I did."

"They left you there to face the soldiers alone?" Adam's voice showed his scorn.

"They were going to try to lead them away."

"What about Mr. Colin?" Tom said.

Shannon couldn't keep the worry away then. "I wish I knew. I don't think he could've made it away. His leg was in an awful shape, and he could barely sit his horse."

"Mr. Colin always was a strong one, Miss Shannon," Tom said, trying to reassure her. "I wouldn't worry too much about him. If he had any lead at all, he probably outrode them."

"I wish I could believe that, Tom, but I feel that something awful has happened."

Adam spoke then, and his voice was almost gentle. "Why don't you go on in and let Mamie fix you up something to eat? Then you just go on to bed. Me and Tom will see that all the work down here gets done without you today."

Shannon walked toward the house, every step heavier and harder to take. She'd have to tell her mother about Clay's going. She wished she could turn back to the barn and bury herself in work rather than bear such news to her mother. But there was no one else to tell her just as there'd been no one else when the man brought the letter about Simon.

First she let Aunt Mamie feed her while she answered all her questions, avoiding any mention of her own narrow escape, but Aunt Mamie saw past her words.

"You ain't going nowhere in the middle of the night no more, missy. I shouldn't have let you go last night. Lawsy, when I think of what might have happened." Aunt Mamie put her hands to her head.

Shannon swallowed her coffee. "It's over now, Aunt Mamie. I'm home." She stared over her cup at the wall.

"But the others ain't," Aunt Mamie said, finishing her thought. "Now child, don't go worrying yourself silly till you know you've got reason to worry."

"If you'd seen Colin's leg, you'd know I have reason now. He said they tried to amputate it up in that prison camp."

Aunt Mamie put her hands on Shannon's shoulders. "But they didn't."

"Colin said he wouldn't let them." Shannon sank her face into her hands and fought back tears. "Oh, Aunt Mamie, he was hot with fever, and his eyes had a funny glassy look. I just don't think he could've made it very far on that horse."

"Now, now, child. If they did catch him, they'll just take him off to prison. Then he won't be no worse off than he was, and they'll probably have a doctor around to see to him."

"I guess you're right," Shannon said, raising up. She pushed her half-eaten breakfast away. "I can't put it off any longer. I have to tell Mother. What did you tell her?"

"Nothing," Aunt Mamie said. "I don't reckon she knows Mr. Clay's gone."

Shannon stood up. "Maybe I'd better clean up a little first. Mother might faint at the sight of me before I even get around to telling her about Clay."

"Miss Olivia's stronger than you think, child. She'll bear up under this new trouble."

"I don't know, Aunt Mamie. You know what Clay means to her."

"Well, it ain't like he's dead. He'll be back. She's stood up to lots worse. You younguns think there ain't no trouble like the kind we're having right now, and Lord knows it's grievous. But me and your mother lived through '33, when death took hold of this house and shook it, nigh on wiping us all out. And it was a kind of dying a body couldn't fight, that cholera was." Aunt Mamie shivered at the memory.

"I know, Aunt Mamie," Shannon said gently. When Shannon was six, there'd been another outbreak of cholera in Fayette County. Their house had escaped, but Shannon would never forget the terror in her mother's eyes that year. "But do you think we can fight what's happening to us now? Seeing our men go off to war to shoot at one another, while we just have to sit here and wait."

Aunt Mamie shook her head. "I reckon that's why it's so hard on you, child . . . because you can't fight it."

Shannon washed quickly and pulled on a clean dress. She sat down to comb her hair, already missing the ease and freedom of the riding pants she'd grown accustomed to wearing while working with the horses. When she'd finally combed out all the tangles, she tied her hair back at the nape of her neck. Leaning close to the mirror, she ran her finger over the light scratches that stood out angrily on her cheeks where the branches had stung her.

She stared into the mirror, remembering her nightmare ride through the woods and the bullets that whistled past her. It seemed almost as though she had dreamed it all, but it wasn't a dream. Clay had gone, and Colin was probably in Robards's hands right now. She couldn't push it away as she wanted to. She had to face it.

With a sigh she stood up and went to her mother's bedroom. Shannon knocked and waited for permission to enter. Her mother's mornings had always been sacred to her. She dabbled in her poetry, writing a few chance lines or reading her favorite books, and worked on her fine embroidery.

"Mother, I need to talk to you," Shannon said through the door.

She heard her mother sigh, and then there was a rustle of papers and petticoats as she quickly straightened her desk. She had never shared any of her work with Shannon, except the time she'd tried to teach her embroidery. But her mother's patience had been too short, and Shannon's fingers too clumsy even if she'd wanted to learn.

Her mother opened the door to her. Nowhere in the whole of Clay Manor was the personality of Olivia mirrored as it was in her bedroom. Everything in the room was tidy and neat and treasured for its intricate design, from the secretary desk with its small chair to the elaborately embroidered pillows lining the back of the settee in the far corner. Her narrow white ruffled bed was in another corner, looking like a young girl's bed. And yet her mother had given birth to two children in that very bed. Shannon wondered if she'd really belonged in this room even then. She knew she didn't now.

"I'm sorry to disturb your morning, Mother."

Her mother's eyes were searching her for clues to the reason for Shannon's visit. "You look very tired, Shannon. Didn't you sleep well?"

Shannon hesitated. Surely there was a gentle way to tell her mother.

A funny look came across her mother's face. When she spoke, her voice was faint. "The last time you came like this it was with Emmett to tell me you'd heard news of Simon. Emmett couldn't find the words to tell me, but you did."

"I had to, Mother."

"I know," her mother said, running a finger lightly across a book on her desk. "It seems such an injustice . . . to live through the cholera only to be shot and forgotten on some nameless field. Poor Simon. He had such promise. I've no doubt that he could have been a senator in time, perhaps even governor."

"Yes."

"I've never known you so at loss for words, Shannon. Whatever it is, tell me and get it over with. What could it be anyway? I daresay you're all right, since I can see you standing there. And Clay is safe under our roof. Has something happened to that other one?"

"I don't know. Colin's been wounded, but I don't know where he is now. It's not Colin. Didn't Clay talk to you?"

"Clay? Of course. He talks to me all the time."

Shannon searched for the right words. Before she could speak, her mother's face paled, and she said, "You mean, about joining the Confederates? He wasn't serious though. That was just a childish whim."

"No, Mother, Clay refused to be a child any longer. He rode off with Jett last night."

"No! He wouldn't have gone without telling me goodbye." Her mother stood up, paced around the room, and then sank down in her chair again. "I wish I could believe you were lying to me, but you're not, are you?"

"I'm sorry, Mother," Shannon said softly.

"Are you really?" her mother said, suddenly bitter. "All his life Clay has been trying to prove himself to you. To prove he's as strong as you. Now you've forced him into joining the war."

"That's not true, Mother. I didn't want Clay to go."

But her mother went on as though she hadn't heard her. "So you have what you wanted. Clay has gone off just as Simon did, and he may find the same fate. Then you'll be happy, won't you, Shannon?"

"How can you say such a thing, Mother?" Shannon cried.

"Then the farm will be yours. You're just like your father. When he couldn't get control of the farm through me, he acted so outrageously that poor Father's heart failed under the strain of fighting against him. Emmett hadn't counted on Simon, but this horrid war solved that problem for him. Just as you hope it will solve yours."

"You really believe all that?" Shannon whispered. Her mother's words cut through Shannon. She loved the land, and she felt it was more hers than Clay's, but she hadn't forced Clay to ride off to the war. Or had she? Maybe there was a grain of truth in what her mother said about Clay proving himself to her.

"I don't know what happened between Papa and Grandfather," Shannon protested. "It doesn't matter now anyway, they're both gone beyond the land. But Clay is my brother. . . . I would never wish him dead."

"Then why did you let him go? You could have kept him here." Her mother's voice was pathetic.

"I tried, but Clay had made up his mind. He wouldn't listen to anything I said."

Her mother bent her head and began crying. Shannon thought she ought to try to comfort her, but her mother's words stood between them, making a fence Shannon wasn't sure she'd ever be able to climb.

Still she couldn't keep from feeling pity for her mother when she whispered, "He was all I had left."

"He'll be back, Mother. He's with Jett, and Jett will take care of him."

Shannon left the room, quietly shutting the door behind her. She touched her fingers to her dry eyes and wished for the relief of tears. But she had no time to dwell on her feelings. Sally was running up the stairs two at a time.

"Shannon!" she called.

Shannon ran to meet her. "What is it?"

Sally's dark eyes were wide with a touch of fear. "Colonel Robards and his men are coming."

CHAPTER 13

For a moment Shannon couldn't move. She felt as though everything were crashing down around her while she struggled to hold up just one last piece of roof over her head. But she wouldn't give up yet. She looked at Sally, who was watching Shannon anxiously, and said, "Run to my room, and do something with my clothes just in case he has another search party in mind. And then get Aunt Mamie to come sit with Mother." As Sally started off, Shannon reached out and stopped her with a touch. "And stay out of sight, Sally. There's no telling what Robards's men might do."

"Try not to make him mad, Shay, and maybe he'll go away without making any trouble."

Shannon frowned. "I'll try. . . . but I think he came to make trouble this morning."

Shannon smoothed down her hair as she went down

the steps, trying at the same time to smooth down her nerves. She forced her hands to stop shaking and tried to blank out the panic from her mind. Then she heard the horses. She wanted to run back upstairs and hide, but there was no one but her to meet this threat. She clamped down hard on her fear and held her head high as she went on to the door.

By the time Robards pulled his horse up in front of the house, she had herself completely under control. She stepped out on the porch and waited for him to speak. Perhaps he wouldn't even dismount but would continue on his way.

That was a vain hope. He watched her for a moment with a smile before saying, "Good morning, Miss Marsh."

The words were simple enough, but there was no mistaking the undercurrent of threat in his voice. His arrogance as he got off his horse and came up to her showed he was sure that he had the upper hand.

"Colonel," Shannon said. Her voice gave no hint of the uneasy fear in her stomach. "What brings you to Marshland so early?"

He laughed and turned to his men. "You hear that, men. The little lady wants to know why we're here." The men following his lead laughed too.

Shannon looked at him coolly while her panic grew just under the surface.

"You look peaked this morning, Miss Marsh. Didn't you sleep well last night?"

"Very well, thank you." He knew all about last night. That was easy enough to tell. But she would never admit it, and there was little way he could prove it. Still, perhaps he didn't need proof.

Robards motioned to one of his men, and the man turned his horse toward the barn.

"What do you think you're doing?" Shannon asked.

"We just want to check something out," he said.

"Some of my men reported to me that a woman on a black horse gave them the slip early this morning while we were rounding up some guerrillas."

"You're surely not accusing me of being a guerilla, Colonel Robards?" Shannon's voice was incredulous.

He reached out and touched a strand of her hair. Shannon clasped her hands in front of her to keep from striking out at him.

"They said she had red hair."

"I've never supposed that I am the only person in Kentucky to have red hair. Unless you have some further proof of misconduct on my part, I suggest you leave."

"We'll wait till my man gets back from the barn."

Robards looked around. "Where's your brother?"

"Clay has gone to be with some friends."

"And just where are those friends?"

Shannon didn't know how much longer she could stand this edging about. He was like a wolf circling his prey, waiting to catch her at a weak moment. He must have Colin. What else would explain his smug attitude? But he'd said he'd been rounding up guerrillas. Dear God, please, Shannon thought. He surely hadn't accused Colin of being a guerrilla. The very thought struck new terror in her heart. She clamped down a tight control on it and said, "I can't see how that's any of your concern."

"You're playing games with me, Miss Marsh," Robards said, and then seeing his man returning from the barn, he added, "But your time has just about run out."

"There's a black horse there all right," the man said. "Been run hard this morning."

"How do you explain that, Miss Marsh?" Robards said.

"I don't have to explain anything to you, Colonel, but it so happens that I ride Satin every morning at daylight."

"At daylight? Come now, Miss Marsh. We know

better, don't we? But it doesn't matter. I didn't come here to arrest you."

"Then why are you here?"

"To bring you some news."

He waited, but Shannon wouldn't beg him to tell her. She'd hold onto her composure no matter what.

Finally he said, "We have your bastard brother. Caught him trying to get away from his hideout in an old barn. Somebody had just brought him a fresh horse, but we got him anyway. I took him in as a guerrilla." He paused and smiled before he said, "He'll probably hang."

She wanted to shut out his last words, but she couldn't. They relentlessly pushed inside her. It was a long time before she could speak. Then she said, "Colin is a member of the Confederate Army and as such is entitled to treatment accorded to any prisoner of war."

"He didn't look like a soldier when I found him."

Finally there was no way to hold back her hatred. "You're disgusting."

"I never claimed I wasn't." He smiled, stepped nearer to her, and lowered his voice. "You people always treated me like I was dirt. Even your father looked down on me when he was no better than me. He just horse-traded himself into a good thing with old man Clay. Then he took on airs like he couldn't be seen with those he used to do business with. Well, now the shoe's on the other foot."

"I'll go over your head to General Ashe in Louisville."

He laughed, and the sound went all through her. "The good General Ashe recommends that all sisters, mothers, and wives of Johnny Rebs be sent out of the country. We both think a lot like General Butler down in New Orleans, if you know what I mean."

Shannon stood rigidly still. She would not slap him

because that was what he wanted her to do. In New Orleans Butler had given his soldiers permission to treat hostile women as harlots. "I know exactly what you mean." Her words were clipped and sharp. "But that has nothing at all to do with my brother."

"Maybe it does," he said softly. "Your brother's fate could rest in my hands. If I say he's a soldier, he's a soldier. But if I were to say that he's a guerrilla, then who knows what might happen." He paused and let his eyes travel down over her body slowly. "You're a very beautiful woman, Shannon Marsh. It might be that you could influence my decision."

Shannon felt a sickness spreading all through her. She wanted to get this man out of her sight, but she couldn't. Not yet. She still needed to find out one more thing. "Where's Colin?" she asked as if she hadn't even heard his proposition.

His eyes played with her for a moment before he said, "He's on his way to Louisville and to jail. But you won't be able to see him. Some prisoners don't get visitors."

"I find that difficult to accept."

"I think you might find a lot of things difficult in the next few months, Miss Marsh." He laid his hand on her cheek. "But you'll do them, my dear, because that's the only way you can save your brother. So think about it, but don't take too long. You might not have much time."

Shannon jerked away from his touch. "There's no way I'll ever make any kind of deal with you."

"We'll see." He turned and got back on his horse. He looked down at her. "There'll come a day when you'll come to me on your hands and knees, begging."

If she'd had a gun then, she would have killed him as easily as she'd pinched the head off a horsefly. She didn't move until he and his men rode out of sight. Then she walked stiffly into the house and into the library office, where she let her knees give way under her. She sat very still while the sickness inside her subsided and tried not to think at all. But Colin's face was before her with the special smile he always saved for her. Then Robards was there too, with his small greedy eyes and rough hot hands, and she felt the illness in her again. If going to Robards was the only way to save Colin, could she do it?

The silence fell about her. This small room in the very heart of the house was always quiet, but now it seemed as though she were the only person left in the place even though she knew that wasn't so. Still she was the one who was responsible for the farm, her mother, the slaves, and now maybe even Colin's life. It all rested squarely on her shoulders.

If only Randal were still in Lexington. He would help her. But he was gone, perhaps forever. The news from the battlefields carried the numbers of casualties listed impersonally as if the entire war were just a game of numbers, and at the end they would tally up the number of dead like a score.

The possibility that she might never see Randal again left her feeling even more alone, with fear closing in on her and choking out all hope.

Shannon stood up suddenly. She could do anything she had to do except sit and dwell on her fears. She'd go out and work with the horses. If she were busy, then she wouldn't have so much time to think. And as soon as she could, she'd go to Louisville and make sure that Colin was all right. Never mind what Robards said about visitors. They couldn't keep her from seeing her brother.

But for now she'd work, and as long as she could let her eyes follow a colt during a workout, maybe she wouldn't see the shadows edging in from the sides.

Two days later Shannon boarded a train for Louisville. The trip was long and tiring, and when Shannon finally stepped off the train onto the crowded platform, she looked around with an edge of doubt creeping up on her. Then she straightened her hat and cape and found a cab.

When she told the driver where she wanted to go, he shook his head and said, "Maybe you'd be better off just to sit right here and wait for the next train back to wherever you come from. That place just ain't no place for a lady." He was a short, wiry black man with deep creases on his face to show his age.

Shannon stepped up into the carriage. "I'm going to see my brother." And then because his eyes were kind and concerned, she went on. "They will let me see him, won't they?"

"I couldn't rightly say, miss. Mostly they do let the prisoners have visitors, but it's sometimes according to who's on duty at the time. It surely would've been better for one of your menfolk to come."

"My menfolk are all gone," Shannon said.

"I'm sorry to hear that," the man said, looking at her more closely. "I used to know a little girl who had hair like yours. You wouldn't happen to be Emmett Marsh's little gal, now would you?"

Shannon smiled and nodded, trying to reach back and pull out a name to match the old man's face.

He shook his head. "Now don't go worrying yourself trying to remember me. I was just a rider who was about over the hill when your pa give me a few more mounts before I had to face the truth and find me another line of work."

"Captain Ned," Shannon cried. "Of course I remember you. You used to put me up on the horses when Papa wasn't looking."

The old man laughed. "I reckon I shouldn't have, but even then you could ride better than me."

Shannon shook her head. "You were the best."

"Were is right. It just got so I couldn't do it no more; so I got this job here hauling people around and trying to see that my horse gets enough to eat. Poor old thing. We're both about ready for the glue factory."

"I wish you would come work for me at Marshland."

He shook his head. "Those days are over for me, miss, and I reckon your pa might have something to say about that anyway."

"Papa's dead."

"I'm sorry to hear that." He paused for a respectful moment before he went on. "Tell me, Miss Shannon, are you still crazy after the horses?"

"I guess next to my family, those horses mean more to me than anything in the world."

"Now don't you be going and making the mistake I made, missy, always thinking about nothing but horses." Captain Ned shook his head. "Never had time to look for a good woman or have the babies I used to think about sometimes. And now I ain't got nothing but memories of the wind in my face and the power under me racing for the finish line."

"But they're good memories, aren't they, Captain Ned?"

"Memories like that can't warm your heart when you get old and lonely." He turned away from her and climbed up to the driver's seat. He flicked his reins, and they began moving.

Shannon's mind filled with worries about Colin. She couldn't go home without seeing him.

At the prison, Captain Ned started to help her down but then stopped. "You sure you won't change your mind, Miss Shannon. I hate to let you go in there by yourself." He thought for a moment. "Why don't you stay right here while I go in and see how the land lies?"

"Would you, Captain Ned? I'll pay you for your time."

"Now just don't you worry about that." He disappeared inside the large gray building.

Union soldiers were scattered around the building. A few sent her curious glances, but most of the men didn't even notice she was there.

Captain Ned wasn't gone long. "It's all right, Miss Shannon. The man on duty now is a nice enough feller. A Lieutenant Adams. He said he'd do what he could for you."

"Thank you, Captain Ned. I can't tell you how much I appreciate your help." She handed him some money. "Do you think you could come back here in an hour or so and take me back to the station?"

He nodded. "I'll be right here waiting, Miss Shannon. Don't you worry none about that."

Lieutenant Adams was a stout, balding man who looked up at Shannon sympathetically when she was shown to his office. "Please take a seat, Miss Marsh."

"Thank you, sir."

"Captain Ned tells me you're wanting to see your brother. His name?"

"Colin Marsh."

He searched through the papers scattered about his desk. "With all the prisoners they're bringing in now, it's hard to keep things organized, and there's talk of converting even more buildings into prisons." Finally he pulled out a paper. "Here we have it. Colin Marsh taken prisoner day before yesterday as a suspected guerrilla." The Lieutenant sent her a sharp look. "Captain Ned didn't tell me your brother was a guerrilla."

"He's not, Lieutenant. He's a soldier, and he was captured while riding with Morgan. He's been at Camp

Douglas up in Ohio. I'm sure you got word of the escape from that prison camp."

He leaned back and stroked his chin. "Seems I did hear something about a few men tunneling out. You say your brother was one of them. Then why does this report show him as a guerrilla?"

Shannon chose her next words carefully. "Maybe the arresting officer made a mistake," she said. "Believe me, my brother is admittedly a rebel, but not a guerrilla."

The Lieutenant picked up a pen. "I'll make a note of what you say here on his record and look into it. It could mean a lot to your brother." He scribbled on the paper for a moment. Then he looked at her again. "Where are you from, Miss Marsh?"

"My mother has an estate over in Fayette County."

"Horses?"

"Some."

"I used to go to the races a lot before the war. Still do when I can. I saw Lexington run a couple of times. Now there's a horse."

Shannon nodded, but she didn't want to talk about horses. "May I see my brother now?"

He studied the paper and then her. "I suppose it would be all right. You know, of course, that your brother has been wounded." He looked down at the paper again. "It says here that he's not in very good shape." He looked up at her doubtfully.

"I must see him, Lieutenant," Shannon pleaded.

"Very well." The Lieutenant stood up. "I'll have one of my men show you to his cell." He called to one of the men outside his office. When the man came in, he gave him a paper. "Parker, escort this lady to see her brother, and stay with her until she leaves."

Shannon stood up. "Thank you, Lieutenant Adams. You've been most kind."

He nodded. "I'll have to ask you to make your visit brief."

"Whatever you say, sir," she said and followed the soldier named Parker out into the yard and across to another building.

When they stepped through the doorway, Shannon hesitated while her eyes adjusted to the dim light. The smell of too many men in too small a space wafted out to her. There was a heaviness to the air, and she could feel the depression of the men locked in the building.

She waited while Parker spoke to a guard. Then the doors were unlocked in front of them, and they were moving through the halls between rooms full of prisoners.

Occasionally a man would see her passing and call out, or there would be a groan. But still Shannon said, "It seems awfully quiet in here."

The soldier said, "Most of the men in here are sick. They ain't feeling much like making noise."

Shannon didn't say any more. Finally Parker stopped and pointed to the room to his right. He said, "I'll wait here for you, miss. Don't be long."

Colin was stretched out on a narrow cot. Shannon knelt beside him and put her hand on his forehead. He was even sicker than he'd been the night he was captured.

Slowly his eyes flickered open. "I must be dreaming," he said. He shut his eyes and then opened them again. "Is that really you, Sis?"

"It's really me."

"What in the world are you doing here? Don't tell me they've thrown you in jail, too?"

Shannon smiled. "Not yet, but there are those who think it might be a good idea."

"You shouldn't have come, Shannon." His voice was heavy with worry.

"I had to, Colin. You were here."

He reached up and pushed her hand away from his forehead. "Well, now that you've seen me, get out of here and don't come back. This is no place for ladies."

"I can see that, but then I never did claim to be much of a lady."

"You've been a lady since the day you were born, Shannon. Anybody with any sense can see that." A flicker of pain crossed his face.

"Your leg's worse, Colin. Has a doctor been to see you?"

"There was one in here sometime. Talked about cutting my leg off again, but I told him it was too late for that anyway. If I'm going to die, I'd just as soon do it all in one piece."

"Don't say things like that, Colin. If only I could take you home."

"There's not much chance of me going home for a while. Maybe not till the war's over."

"There might be a way," Shannon said.

Colin looked at her sharply. "You're talking about Robards, aren't you?"

"What makes you think that?"

"I heard him talking the night he caught me. He said I was just what he needed, and that now a certain young lady would have to get down off her high horse and deal with him."

Shannon turned her eyes away from him. "He was just talking."

Colin grabbed her arm. "Look at me, Shannon, and don't try to lie to me. I've known you too long for you to fool me."

Shannon reluctantly met his eyes. "He wants me. It's simple enough."

"You can't have anything to do with the likes of

him." Colin's eyes were on fire. "I'll kill him for even suggesting such a thing to you."

"Take it easy, Colin. I didn't make any deals." Shannon soothed him back down. She waited a minute for him to calm down before she said, "He turned you in as a guerrilla."

"It doesn't make any difference. We're all prisoners."

"He said they'd hang you," Shannon said. "I won't let them kill you, Colin, no matter what I have to do."

Colin was quiet for a long time. Finally he said, "It could be they're going to get tough on guerrillas. But I'm not one of them, and the men in charge will know that. Robards hasn't got that much power here in Louisville." Suddenly Colin's hands were gripping her arms tightly. "But you've got to make me a promise, Shannon. . . . no matter what, even if they hang me, you've got to promise not to have anything to do with Robards."

"I can't promise that, Colin."

His eyes burned into hers for a long minute. "Shannon, I'm not worth that kind of sacrifice."

"You're my brother."

He let go of her and fell back on the cot. He closed his eyes. When he spoke, his voice was low but firm. "If you don't promise me, Shannon, I'll find a way to kill myself as soon as you go home. Then you won't need to make any deals."

"You mean that, don't you?" Shannon said softly.

He opened his eyes and looked at her. "More than anything I've ever said in all my life. You don't hold the monopoly on sibling love. Don't you remember what Emmett told me the first time we met?" Shannon nodded with the beginnings of tears in her eyes, and Colin went on. "That I should never betray the love you offered so freely. You were special even then, Shannon, and so beautiful, even with your wild hair that looked as though it had never seen a comb and your freckles. I won't let you give yourself away for me."

Shannon smoothed Colin's hair back from his face. She knew he was dead serious. "All right, Colin, I promise, but only if you'll promise to get better. And I'll be back next week to see how well you're keeping your promise."

"I don't want you to come back, Shannon," Colin said, and then a ghost of a smile slipped across his face. "But I guess one promise a day is all I can expect to get out of you."

"Goodbye, Colin." Shannon kissed him lightly on the cheek and then quickly left the room before he could see her tears. She followed Parker out, not seeing anything but Colin's gray face. She'd made him a promise, but sometimes promises were made to be broken.

CHAPTER 14

Colin was better the next time Shannon went to see him, still not well but with the fever gone from him. At each visit, he had improved until he was up and around, although he moved slowly and dragged his foot. Shannon doubted that he would ever regain full use of his leg, but at least he could walk, and eventually he'd be able to ride again.

On her visit in early December, Colin was full of the news that Morgan had escaped from the Ohio Penitentiary. Colin sat on his cot and looked out the window. "It makes me wish I were out of here and with him."

"You wouldn't be able to fight even if you were," Shannon said.

"You don't know General Morgan as I do, Shannon." Colin's eyes glazed over with admiration. "The General can make men do things they never thought they could. He'll be in Tennessee rounding himself up another command before the Yanks do much more than miss him. And you can bet that Jett and Clay will be with him."

"I'd just as soon not think about Clay being in the war at all."

Colin touched Shannon's arm. "Maybe Clay was always tougher than we gave him credit for."

"He's not tough at all, and you know it, Colin."

"Well, then maybe the war will help him get that way. It's time he grow up."

"If he's lucky enough to live that long," Shannon muttered.

"You worry about us too much, little sister. There are some things you just have to let happen."

"Why shouldn't I change things if I can?"

"But you can't, Shannon . . . especially now. You can't stop the war."

"Maybe not, but I can keep hoping that it will be over soon and my brothers will be home."

Colin smiled. "And your fiancé, right? Maybe it's Jett you're worried about instead of Clay."

Shannon shook her head. "Jett can take care of himself. He wouldn't want me to worry about him."

"When I think of the children you and Jett will have," Colin said and laughed, "I'm not sure I want to be around to try to head them away from mischief. You two are so hardheadedly stubborn."

Shannon tried to imagine a child that she and Jett might have, but she couldn't. Lately she'd had a hard time bringing Jett to mind at all. There was always those gentle blue eyes waiting for her just a thought away. But Colin knew nothing of Randal. Shannon said, "I'm not hardheaded or stubborn either . . . maybe a little willful, as Aunt Mamie would say."

"A little? That's calling a tornado a pleasant breeze."

"Oh, Colin."

"Okay, let's see how stubborn you really are. Since my leg's better, I figure they're going to move me over to another prison soon. Maybe even out of Louisville. I hear Grant has been sending trainloads of prisoners up here from the South. They're going to need more room here."

"What are you trying to tell me, Colin?"

"That I don't want you to come back to see me after I'm moved. The other prisons are too crowded. I don't want you anywhere near them. Will you promise?"

"I've already made you too many promises." It was the first time either of them had mentioned the promise she'd made on her first visit to him.

His eyes darkened, and his hands hardened into fists. "You're keeping your promise, aren't you?"

"What do you think?"

Colin looked at her sharply. "I think you'd better be. I meant what I said."

Shannon sighed. "I haven't even seen Robards since then. I think he's waiting for me to come to him."

"But you won't. You've promised."

"Yes, I promised, but I'm not sure I should have. And I won't promise not to come and see you anymore."

"What if I ask them not to let you in?"

"They won't listen to you. You're just a prisoner. I'm a loyal citizen who will quite willingly assent to taking the oath of allegiance if I'm asked to."

Colin gave her a strange look. "What does that prove?"

"Would you take the oath?"

"Of course not."

"Then it proves that even as much as we are alike, we are still different."

"If you were a man, you'd be fighting for the North, wouldn't you, Shannon?"

"I don't know. Maybe I would just pay the bounty and not fight at all, but I couldn't fight for the South."

Colin was quiet for so long that Shannon said, "Does that bother you?"

He shook his head. "Not really. I never thought about it before, but if I had, I would have known. You've been an abolitionist in your own way all your life."

"How could I be any different with Aunt Mamie raising me? But there's more to the war than that. You were never one to hold up slavery as an honorable institution. Why did you choose the South? Was it states' rights?"

"It's funny. I've had a lot of time to think about that since I've been here, and I really don't know. I guess because of Jett and maybe because Simon went to the Yankees. I figured that whatever he picked had to be against me. Maybe I just joined to belong finally somewhere." Colin looked at her. "You know, Shannon, I was an equal in Morgan's troops right from the very first raid into Kentucky."

"You've always belonged in my heart, Colin," Shannon said softly. "I'm proud that you're my brother."

"Maybe that's why I wanted to belong everywhere else as well." Colin shook away his solemn seriousness and smiled. "And maybe I just liked the way the Johnny Rebs yelled better than the Yanks."

"Is it as bloodcurdling as they say?"

"You mean the Rebel yell? Well, I don't know. I've never been on the receiving end, but I've seen some mighty pale Yanks, and even more that just turned tail and ran when they heard us coming across the field."

"Will it be over soon, Colin?"

"I don't know, Shannon. Stuck in here it's hard to tell just what's happening out on the battlefield."

"Randal says it's just a matter of time till the North overpowers the South."

"Randal? Who's he? Some new general Lincoln's dug up?"

She shouldn't have mentioned Randal. She hadn't meant to, because how in the world would she explain him to Colin when she didn't really understand herself. She felt her face warm with the beginnings of a flush. "No . . . he's just a soldier I met during the summer."

"A Union soldier?"

Shannon nodded. Since she'd gone this far, she might as well tell him the whole thing. "Captain Randal Hunt. His company was stationed in Lexington during the summer. He was out on patrol the night Papa got shot, and since then he's tried to help me. But he's gone now, back to Virginia."

Colin was watching her closely. Finally he said, "I think there's more to this than you're telling. Does Jett know about him?"

"Why should he?" Shannon said. "I'll probably never see Randal again. We met, he was kind to me, and then he left. That's all and nothing more."

Colin's forehead crinkled with a worried frown. "I don't know what Jett would do if you weren't waiting for him when he got home."

"There's no reason why I won't be waiting. Jett and I made our plans long ago. The only thing standing in our way now is the war."

Colin said no more, but he looked at her as though her words didn't match her eyes. Their talk drifted back to the farm and the horses until it was time for Shannon to leave.

All the way back to Lexington Shannon thought about what she'd said to Colin about Jett. She would be waiting when the war ended. She'd never really doubted that, but the thought brought her no joy.

Suddenly she thought of the way Randal had looked at her the day he rode off to the fighting, and she knew there was more, much more than the war standing between Jett and her.

When she finally reached home, Shannon went out to the barn even though it was nearing dark. The day had left her tired and discouraged, and she wanted to draw hope and strength from her horses.

It was dark in the barn, but she didn't light a lantern. She could see the shapes of the horses, and that was enough. She walked slowly among the stalls, talking to each of the horses in turn. There were several mares who would be ready to foal early in the spring. Her father had always wanted a few foals to drop early on in the year, but most of the mares weren't to foal until later, when the spring weather would be more appropriate for the young foals.

Shannon stopped in front of a stall where a brown mare nickered and nuzzled at Shannon's arm. Shannon rubbed the mare's nose and said, "How you doing, Berry, old girl? I wish I could have seen you when you were winning all your races."

Berry had always been one of Shannon's favorite horses. She was small and game with an affectionate nature. Every year she produced a fine colt that was almost running when it hit the ground. But now she was getting old, and Shannon had a vague feeling of uneasiness about her.

"We ought to have given you a rest this year, old girl," she said.

The barn door creaked open behind her. "Is that you, Miss Shannon?" Adam called.

"Yes, Adam." Shannon gave Berry a last pat and moved toward the door. "I was just visiting the horses."

"You want me to light a lantern?"

"No. I'll be going on to the house in a minute."

Adam hesitated at the door. Then he turned and said, "You've been fair to me, Miss Shannon. I guess I owe it to you to tell you."

"Tell me what?" Shannon asked even though she already knew what he was going to say.

"Me and Sally will be leaving come the first of the year."

Although Shannon was expecting his words, her heart still sank. She said, "We'll miss you."

Adam was silent for a long time. "Sally said you wouldn't try to stop us."

"What are you going to do?" Shannon asked.

"I don't know. Maybe join up with the Army."

"You can't take Sally with you to the Army. She'd be better off here until you get back."

"You don't need to go worrying about Sally. I'll take care of her. Nobody will bother her as long as I'm around."

"But what if you're not around? What if you get killed or captured?"

"Maybe Sally was wrong, and you're trying to stop us." There was a sharp edge to his voice.

"I'm only thinking of Sally."

"And you think that I'm not."

"I don't know, Adam. Are you? Sally's safe here with people who love her. And you want to take her with you where there are all sorts of men and where heavens knows what will happen. You call that love?"

"Then you will try to stop us?" His voice was hard.

"No," Shannon said softly. "But I'll grieve for Sally when you go."

When she went into the house, Aunt Mamie called to her from the kitchen, but Shannon pretended not to hear. She went on into the library office and sat down at her father's desk. She lit the lamp and began writing. If Sally and Adam were going to leave, they would at least have their papers to take with them.

Ownership of slaves now in December 1863 was something of a confused affair in Kentucky. Lincoln's Emancipation Proclamation had freed the slaves in only the rebel states, leaving slavery intact in the loyal border states, so some law officials in Kentucky still tried to capture and return runaway slaves. But if the Union won the war, Shannon was sure that it would be only a matter of time until slavery came to an end in all the states.

Shannon wouldn't wait until the end of the war. Today on Marshland slavery would end. She quickly wrote out the papers and signed her name. In the morning she would get her mother to sign them too. That would be legal enough. Of course, Sally and Adam couldn't make the papers public unless they went north, because Kentucky also had a law forcing all freed negroes to leave the state.

The next day her mother looked at the papers with a tiny frown. "What's this all about, Shannon?" she asked.

"It's stated there quite clearly, Mother. Those papers give Aunt Mamie, Tom, Sally, and Adam their freedom."

Her mother's frown deepened, and she looked up at Shannon. She hadn't recovered from Clay's going. No cream could ever erase the new lines etched in the fine pale skin around her mouth and eyes. She wore a plain black dress, and she'd pulled her hair straight back in a tight knot.

Shannon had always thought her mother was a beautiful woman, with her hair softly shaped about her face and the pinks and blues of her dresses setting off the grayish blue of her eyes. But now the black gave her mother's skin a gray tint, and the severe hairstyle made her face too small and sharp. Shannon noticed the new hollows in her cheeks and was suddenly worried.

"Mother, are you ill?" she asked.

But her mother shook her head. "Not in the way you mean, Shannon. But yes, I suppose I am ill in a way. I won't be well until I see Clay here in this room again."

"I worry about Clay too."

"Do you, Shannon?" her mother said. "I thought you spent all your concern on others. That you have even more concern for those horses down there than you do for your brother."

Shannon sighed. "You know that's not true."

"It's the way your father always was—always at the barn . . . always making yet one more deal."

Shannon started to say that was only because he had no reason to come to the house, but she bit back the words. She wouldn't argue with her mother about things of the past. "Would you please sign the papers?"

Her mother looked down at the papers on her desk. "But what will we do without the blacks? We need them to take care of things."

"Sally and Adam are leaving the first of the year anyway, and I don't think Aunt Mamie and Tom will want to go."

"They are Clay's slaves now. You know that, don't you, Shannon? You don't have any claim to the farm or anything on it. It all goes to Clay, the first born son. That's the way my father's will read."

"Yes, Mother, I know. But Papa gave me some money before he died. When Clay returns home, I'll pay him a fair amount for the slaves."

"Very well. I can't argue with you anyway." She picked up a pen and quickly wrote her signature on the papers. She handed them to Shannon and then turned away from her. "Now go away, Shannon, and leave me alone."

"If that is what you want, Mother." Shannon looked at her mother's back, wishing that somehow long ago they had formed ties that would have let them comfort each other now, but it was an empty wish.

It was almost as empty as her mother's voice. "That is what I want."

Shannon went downstairs and gave the papers to Aunt Mamie and Sally who were in the kitchen.

Aunt Mamie looked at them blankly and said, "What is this, child?"

"It's your papers," Shannon said simply. "You're free now."

Tears sprung to Aunt Mamie's eyes. "I'm free?"

Sally had been quickly reading the papers. Shannon had taught her how to read as she herself learned in school. Now Sally said, "We're all free, Mama. You and me and Tom and Adam."

Aunt Mamie sat down at the table and bawled.

"What's wrong, Aunt Mamie?" Shannon asked, concerned.

"Don't worry, Shay," Sally said. "You know that Mama cries only when she's happy."

"I thought I knew how she felt," Shannon said. "But I didn't know it meant that much to her."

"No matter how you try, Shay, you can't understand how much because you've never been a slave," Sally said. There was a faraway look in Sally's eyes that shut Shannon out.

Shannon wanted to draw them to her, to keep them close, just as she'd wanted to hold Colin close when he told her not to come and see him again. No matter what she did, it seemed that her loved ones were being divided from her by some invisible barrier while she stood more and more alone.

CHAPTER 15

"Are you sure you'll be all right, Miss Shannon?" Tom asked for the tenth time.

"I'm sure," Shannon answered with a smile. "You won't be gone but a few hours, Tom."

He went on as if he hadn't heard her. "I mean, I don't have to go. I went to church only a month ago."

Shannon shook her head at Tom. It had been almost two weeks since she'd given the servants their papers, and they all went on doing the same things they'd always done. But now that they were being paid for their work, it seemed to Shannon that Tom walked a little straighter, Aunt Mamie's songs echoing through the house while she cooked were happy lilting tunes, and some of the anger was gone from Adam's eyes.

Shannon said, "Now don't you go giving me as an excuse not to go with Aunt Mamie."

Tom climbed up into the buckboard. Shannon had offered to let them use one of the carriages, but Tom had laughed. "Now what would all them folks think when they saw this old nigger drive up in a fine rig like that. Likely as not they'd take us off to the jail and whip us for stealing," he'd said.

Now Tom picked up the reins and hesitated again. "It just don't seem right leaving you here to do for yourself, Miss Shannon. Are you sure you'll be all right?"

Shannon laughed. "Everything will be fine, Tom. Marshland can make it without you for one Sunday night."

"It ain't Marshland I'm worried about," Tom said.

Adam eyed the sky. "I'm not sure any of us ought to be going. Hear that. Sounds like thunder."

They all looked to the west. December had been warm, and now a bank of black clouds was forming on the horizon while a few lighter clouds were shifting around overhead.

Sally said, "A little rain won't melt us. You just don't want to go."

Sally's mouth turned down with disappointment. She'd wanted to take Adam to church to show him off. They were having a special meeting, and there was sure to be a large congregation.

Aunt Mamie poked Tom. "Get them horses moving. I didn't get all spiffied up to stay at home and watch it rain." She looked over her shoulder and called, "Now you take care, child, and we'll be back before you know it."

As they disappeared around the bend, Shannon looked at the skies again. The clouds seemed to be hanging more heavily, and suddenly an uneasy chill shook her as the wind fluttered her skirts. Perhaps she'd been wrong to send them all off. She looked back at the road, but they were gone.

Shannon shook herself. She wouldn't let a little bad weather spook her, but still as she went into the house, she felt a sense of foreboding. Something was going to happen. Of course, she reasoned with herself, it was going to rain and that was all. She wouldn't start jumping at shadows.

The house was oppressively quiet as Shannon started up the stairs. There was no clatter or song drifting out from the kitchen, and Sally wasn't moving softly about straightening the house. Shannon's mother was there, but her presence was felt in only one small corner of the house. Since Clay had left, she rarely came out of her rooms even to go out into the gardens as she once had.

Shannon paused at the top of the stairs and looked back down at the double front doors and the hall. Suddenly it was alive with all those who had once come home through those doors. Even though they'd never come home again, they seemed to be there all around her—her father and Simon and even all those she'd never known who were yet still a part of her because they'd lived and died on Marshland.

She turned away from the ghosts of the past and went on to her room. She'd change into her work clothes and check the horses. The storm might be making some of them nervous.

Shannon jumped when her mother spoke behind her. "So you let them all go. They won't be back, you know."

Shannon turned around. "They just went to church, Mother, just as they have dozens of times before."

Her mother's face was paler than usual with dark circles under her eyes. Her frown shut away any sign of beauty. "But before, they knew they had to come back. This time they know they don't."

"They could've left anytime, and even if I wanted

to, there is nothing I could do to stop them." Shannon's voice was tired. "But they'll be back, Mother, just as always."

"You're so sure. You're always so sure about everything." Her mother pointed a finger at her. "Tell me what you'll do if they don't come back. Then who will take care of all this?" She waved her hands around.

"I will, Mother. And I'll take care of you."

"You can bring me food, Shannon, but who is there to love me now that you've sent Clay away?"

Shannon started to tell her once more that she hadn't sent Clay away, but she'd only be wasting her breath. She sighed and said, "I would love you, Mother, if you'd let me."

A strange look came over her mother's face. She stared at Shannon for a moment and finally said, "Emmett used to say that." Then she clamped her mouth together and shook her head. "But it wasn't so, and it isn't so when you say it either."

Her mother turned back to her room. Shannon said, "Aunt Mamie laid out our supper on the table. I'll bring you a tray if you wish."

"Don't bother," her mother answered without looking back, "I'm not hungry."

Shannon waited until her mother's door was shut before she moved on to her own room. As she changed clothes, she thought that surely if she tried hard enough she could find a way to reach out to her mother. Then she shook her head. It did no good to hide from the truth. Her mother had closed her out ever since she was a baby, and there was nothing Shannon could do to open those gates. Only her mother could do that.

When Shannon went outside again, the clouds were thundering closer, but it still wasn't raining. Instead, the clouds seemed to be gathering and pulling all their power together before letting any of it loose.

Shannon hurried down the lane between the big oak trees shaking their heads in the wind. In the barn some of the horses were nickering nervously in their stalls, while others munched on their feed without concern.

Shannon walked between the stalls, talking softly to the mares and colts who looked skittish and excited. Next Shannon made sure the doors and windows were secure, and then she found odd jobs to do to keep from having to return to the house. At least the barn was full of life and hope and purpose, while the house seemed to be part of the past with no future.

When the daylight began to dim, Shannon started back to the house. A pinkish gray light colored the air. Just as Shannon reached the porch, a sheet of rain swept by her. She stood close against the house and watched the rain pour. When she was a child, she had liked to run out in the rain and dance to the music of the wind and water. Then when she came in, Aunt Mamie would scold her while wrapping her in a big towel and making her drink warm milk. She'd felt so safe, as if everything would always be as warm and secure feeling as Aunt Mamie's kitchen.

Shannon shivered as the wind threw a splatter of raindrops against her. She thought of all the soldiers out in the fields with no place to get in out of the rain. She wondered if Clay was already wishing he were home, but she thought not. Not with Jett there with him. And Randal . . . where was he now? Maybe shooting at his own brother or hers.

She wrapped her arms around herself and tried to hold away the chill caused more by her thoughts than by the cold rain. She wished for the safe, warm feelings she'd had as a child wrapped in that towel with Aunt Mamie's scoldings settling softly about her. All at once she remembered the way she'd felt when Randal had wrapped his arms around her that day in the garden. It had seemed so natural and so right. She closed her eyes for a moment and let Randal come to her thoughts instead of trying to shut him out as she usually did. But then the rain was blowing in on her again, taking her from her thoughts with a cold dash of water. As she went into the house, she was lonelier than ever, wondering if she'd ever see him again.

The evening passed slowly while Shannon caught up on some paper work. There were the letters she'd dreaded writing to inform business associates of her father's death and other correspondence to answer. While she worked, she listened to the rain and alternated between wishing that Aunt Mamie and the others were already home to hoping they would stay somewhere in town till the rain was over.

Finally the rain leveled off to a steady drizzle, and Shannon began listening intently for the wagon. At midnight she decided they must have found a place to wait over till morning, and she got up to go to bed. But before she started up the stairs, she stepped out the front doors into the dark. Before, she'd blamed her uneasiness on the rain, but now the rain was almost over, and still the uneasy feeling was growing inside her.

Something was wrong. Maybe her mother had been right, and they weren't coming back. But no, Aunt Mamie wouldn't leave them. Shannon was sure of that. Then what was causing this worry? Was it just because the house seemed so empty with only her and her mother there?

She stood still a long time, letting the dark wrap its cloak around her. The air was turning cooler now, and by morning the unseasonable warmth would be gone. The weather would be more as December should be. It might even snow. Shannon shivered and turned to go in.

At that moment her ears picked up a noise, and she

waited. She heard the creak of a wagon and felt the relief wash over her. They were back.

But why were the horses moving so slowly? It was almost as if they were driving themselves. Shannon ran down the drive to meet them.

"Aunt Mamie! Sally!" she called.

A moan answered her as the wagon halted. "What's wrong?" Shannon demanded. She wished she'd brought a lantern out with her.

"Shay," Sally said and then broke down and cried.

"Let's get on to the house, out of this rain," Aunt Mamie said. Her voice was tightly controlled.

Where were Tom and Adam? Even in the dark Shannon could see that the men weren't with them, but the questions could wait until they were inside. Shannon led the horses and wagon to Aunt Mamie's cabin. She helped Aunt Mamie and Sally down out of the wagon and inside.

"You're both practically drowned. You should have stayed in town till morning," Shannon said, rushing to find them towels.

She gave a towel to Sally, but she just looked at it as though she didn't know what to do with it. Gently Shannon took the towel back and began drying Sally's hair. "You'll have to get those wet clothes off," she said.

Aunt Mamie was methodically drying herself and removing her wet clothes. Her eyes had a dull, beaten look.

"Where's Tom and Adam?" Shannon asked.

Sally began crying afresh and buried her face in the towel. Aunt Mamie stared at the wall and said, "They're gone. They took them."

"Who took them?" Shannon grabbed Aunt Mamie's shoulders and shook her. "Tell me what happened. Now!"

Aunt Mamie's eyes came around to look at Shannon. "We went to church just like we planned," she said. "We even got there before the rain came up, and there was a fine crowd of folks there too. And I got to see Josie. I reckon I hadn't seen Josie since she got sold from Mr. Evans place back two or three years ago."

"What happened?" Shannon said, trying hard to keep from shouting.

Aunt Mamie's voice went flat, and her eyes went back to staring at nothing. "They took them. That's the way it's been all my life. The white folks just come and take my men away. And there just ain't nothing I can do."

Shannon looked at her a minute and gave up. She turned to Sally who was crying softly now. She sat down beside her and took her hands. "Can you tell me what happened, Sally?"

"Oh, Shay," Sally cried and grabbed her hands tightly. She almost fell back into sobs, but she stopped herself. "It was awful. The church service was so good with everybody singing and praising the Lord and listening to Preacher Harris. When we come out, we was all talking and laughing so much that it was a minute before we noticed what was going on." Sally's face turned pale. "There were all these soldiers waiting around the church."

"You're not making any sense. What were soldiers doing around your church?"

"They took the men." Sally's voice was barely a whisper.

"They took the men?" Shannon couldn't take in what she was saying.

Sally nodded slowly, and her eyes filled with new tears.

Aunt Mamie spoke. "All of them 'cepting the ones they thought might be too old or too little."

"But why?" Shannon asked.

"You think they'd tell us niggers that? But I overheard them telling some white folks standing about to mind their own business. That the Army had asked the people around abouts to give them some of their niggers to help build the railroads back. But seeing as how nobody was volunteering, they was going to do some recruiting on they own." Aunt Mamie's eyes landed on one of Tom's working hats. "Poor old Tom . . . he won't hold up under all that heaving and towing."

"And Adam didn't even want to go to church," Sally said. "If I'd listened to him, we'd all be in bed, and none of this would've happened."

Aunt Mamie shook her head. "It would've happened, baby . . . just not to us."

"I'll go to town and get them back," Shannon said.

Aunt Mamie really looked at Shannon for the first time since she'd climbed down out of the wagon. "Don't be silly, child. You can't do that. Besides, it wouldn't do no good. They done gone with them. We'll just have to make out the best we can without them."

"But they won't keep them. They'll let them come home after they've repaired the rail line," Shannon said, hunting for something hopeful to offer them.

"Then there'll be something else to have them do," Sally said. Her tears had disappeared, and she sat quietly now.

Aunt Mamie's voice was the same as if she were talking about what she was cooking for dinner, but Shannon could see the depth of pain in her eyes. "When the white folks take them away, they don't bring them back."

"But all that's changing, Aunt Mamie. The war is changing it."

"How? By carrying away my man?" Aunt Mamie shook her head. "That's what the Army done for me."

"He'll be back, Aunt Mamie," Shannon said.

But Aunt Mamie acted as though she hadn't heard. "First it was Joe, then John, and now even old Tom." Tears welled up in her eyes.

Sally went to her mother then and put her arms around her. Without words, they shared their sorrow and comforted each other. Shannon watched them for a moment before she slipped out the door. There was nothing she could do to help them, and their grief shut her out. She'd always thought that even if she didn't really fit in with her own family, she would always belong with Aunt Mamie. But even that wasn't so. She fit nowhere. She'd thought that if she could solve all the problems, help everyone be happy, that would make her belong. Now the problems loomed larger and larger, each a new obstacle that sat squarely in her way. For the first time in her life, she had to admit that she couldn't make them disappear. She might not even be able to go around them.

Adam and Tom were gone. They were four women, totally alone and easy prey for the guerrillas or anyone else. And even if she could keep them all safe, how could she ever take care of the farm and horses by herself? Leave it all and go to Canada. She could hear Jett's words echoing in her mind.

But she couldn't. Even if she belonged to no family, she did belong to the land, and the land demanded that she stay. So she would do what had to be done, and each day would pass until finally the war was over.

She took a deep breath and moved away from Aunt Mamie's cabin. First she had to take the horses and wagon to the barn. That was easy. But what would tomorrow bring?

CHAPTER 16

As the days of December passed, a cloud of grief settled over Clay Manor. Still, somehow they kept things going. Sally tried to help Shannon at the barn, but she was afraid of the horses and was little help except for carrying the feed.

The one morning Shannon caught her being sick just outside the barn. Shannon held Sally's head until she finished heaving. When Sally straightened up and leaned against the side of the barn, Shannon asked, "What is it, Sally?"

Sally avoided Shannon's eyes. "Nothing," she said. "I'll be all right in a few minutes."

Shannon was really concerned. She couldn't remember Sally ever being sick. "Is working here in the barn too hard for you?" She put her hand on Sally's arm.

"Don't be silly," Sally said, stepping away from her. "I'm a slave, bred to work."

Shannon wanted to reach out to her again, but the bitterness in Sally's voice held her away. "Not anymore. You have your papers."

Sally shook her head sharply. "What good did papers do Adam?"

"Sally," Shannon said softly. "Why are you shutting me out like this? I want to help you."

"Then get Adam back."

"Don't you think I would if I could? You know I tried." Shannon had gone into town the next morning, but it was too late. There was nothing she could do. The Army had taken Tom and Adam. The army would decide if and when they could return.

Suddenly Sally burst into tears, and this time she let Shannon put her arms around her. After a few minutes she said, "I'm sorry, Shay. I know none of this is your fault, but I need Adam here with me so much. I don't know how Mama stood it when they sold off her Joe. And John was on the way then too."

"Too?" Shannon looked at Sally closely. Then she smiled. "You're going to have a baby?"

Sally nodded, but there was no answering smile.

"That's wonderful," Shannon said. She looked at Sally's unhappy face and added, "Isn't it?"

"I don't want to have my baby alone like Mama had to. I want Adam to be with me."

"He will be, Sally. Adam will be back long before you have your baby."

"Listening to you, Shay, I can almost believe it. But then I remember Mama, and I know that just saying something doesn't make it so."

"But this is different. Adam hasn't been sold anywhere. He'll be back as soon as the Army is through with him. Then you can take your papers and go north, where you'll be safe."

"What if something happens to Adam? What if he never comes back?"

"Nothing will happen to him," Shannon said. "But even if it did, you'd still have a part of him in your child."

Sally was thoughtful for a moment. "That's what Mama always said about John. That he was all she had left of her Joe. I think that's why it was so hard on her when John left, even though she wanted him to be away and free."

"Funny," Shannon said, "I thought Tom was John's father."

"Oh no. Mama and Tom didn't marry until I was almost a year old." Sally quickly drew in her breath and turned her eyes away from Shannon's.

There was a heavy silence between them for a moment. Finally Shannon asked, "Then who was your father, Sally?"

Slowly Sally's eyes came up to meet Shannon's again. She said, "I don't suppose that two folks have to be married to have a baby."

"Are you saying that Tom is your father?"

Sally hesitated for just an instant. "Yes, of course," she said.

Shannon knew she wasn't telling the truth, and there could be only one reason for that. "You really are my sister, aren't you, Sally?"

Suddenly Sally's face hardened. "No. I'm black, and you're white. We've been friends of sorts, but we can never be sisters." Then without another word, she turned away from Shannon and ran to the house.

"Wait, Sally," Shannon called, but she was almost glad when Sally didn't stop. Shannon needed time to get everything straight in her head. Her father and Aunt Mamie. It just didn't seem possible.

Shannon went back into the barn, sank down on a stool in the tack room and tried to make her mind go blank. She wasn't ready to face the meaning of Sally's words, but she couldn't shut it out. Too many things came back to her, like the way Aunt Mamie had avoided being around her father whenever she could. The way her father had sometimes looked at Sally. The way she'd been allowed to teach Sally to read. Sally had known all along that they were sisters.

The barn door creaked open behind her, and Aunt Mamie hesitated just inside the door. "I'm over here," Shannon called. She watched Aunt Mamie as she came through the barn. She'd never realized before what a beautiful woman she must have been. She still had a look of beauty about her as she moved.

"Shannon?" she said hesitantly. "Are you all right, child?"

"Of course, Aunt Mamie. Why shouldn't I be?"

Aunt Mamie looked at her for a long minute. Finally she said, "I didn't want you ever to know."

"Why?"

"I thought it might hurt you. I knew how much you loved your father."

"I did, Aunt Mamie, but I never thought he was all good." Shannon stood up and touched Aunt Mamie's arm. "It must have been hard for you. I know how proud you've always been."

"Too proud for a nigger. That's what they always told me, and I reckon they were right. But something in me always said that someday I'd be as free as any white man. Then when the children came along, I didn't care so much about my own self anymore. I just wanted them to be free. It was the happiest day of my life when I knew John had finally got clean away."

"How you must have hated Papa," Shannon said.

"I won't deny it. Many are the times I would have liked to kill him if only I could have found a way. But I had the children to think of . . . and you."

Shannon remembered her father the way she'd loved him. He'd had a passion and zest for life that spilled over and a tender welcoming smile for her almost any time she went to him. But then she thought of him the way Aunt Mamie must have, and it made her shiver. She said, "And why didn't you hate me?"

"I've wondered that myself more than a time or two. But that first day when I helped you into the world, I laid you up next to your mama, and she wouldn't even pull back the wrappings to look at you. You was such a pitiful little thing. She just wanted me to take you away. So I held you, and you reached out your tiny little hand and wrapped it around my finger. From that moment you was the same as my own child. You nursed at my breast and grew healthy and strong." Aunt Mamie's eyes softened with the memory. "From the very beginning I knew you was something special, child. After that it didn't matter what your father did. I loved you."

Shannon leaned over and kissed Aunt Mamie. "Thank you, Aunt Mamie. Maybe someday you'll be able to forgive Papa for what he did to you."

Aunt Mamie's face hardened. "Some things go beyond forgiveness—things that stay in your mind like a dark stain that no amount of time will fade away."

And because there was nothing Shannon could say to erase Aunt Mamie's pain, she came away from the past and said, "I'd better finish up my chores. It'll be dark soon."

The frown eased off Aunt Mamie's face, and she said, "I'll send Sally back down to help you."

Shannon shook her head. "This work's too hard for her. She can stay at the house and help you."

"But you can't do all this by yourself, child. I'd say you've lost ten pounds in the last few months."

"Now don't start worrying about me. I'm strong as a horse," Shannon said.

"But it was too much for you and Tom and Adam all put together."

"I'll just do what has to be done and let the rest go till the men come home. Anyway, I'm going to Louisville tomorrow, and while I'm there, I'll get us a new hand."

"You shouldn't ought to go to Louisville by yourself, child. It ain't safe, and you told me yourself that Mr. Colin didn't want you to come no more."

"But I'm going anyway. It's almost Christmas."

Aunt Mamie gave up. "I reckon you know how to take care of yourself by now, and I reckon as how maybe you always did, but I just wanted to think you needed me."

"I'll always need you, Aunt Mamie." Shannon brushed another kiss across her cheek. "Right now though, I think you ought to go see about Sally. She needs you the most."

"Poor baby. It was just too much for her, Adam being yanked away like that. One minute she was on top of the world and the next everything was taken from her."

"Not everything."

Aunt Mamie's eyes were old and wise as she looked at Shannon. "Yes, but the most important thing. You'd know if you'd ever really felt for a man what she feels for Adam."

After Aunt Mamie left, Shannon went on about her chores, but her steps were heavy. Her whole childhood had been rearranged and altered with a few words. Even though she tried to hold it away, she felt bitterness seeping into her memory of her father. She'd been such a fool to not have known, and now she wondered if those days had been happy only for her. How had she grown up in the midst of so much hate and misery without seeing it?

Suddenly she felt a compelling need to talk to someone who could make everything all right again. Of course, Colin would help her understand, and when she understood, then this bitter new pain would be easier to bear.

When she went to visit him the next day, Colin couldn't help her either. "I thought you knew, Shannon."

Shannon shook her head. "Why would I know? No one ever told me."

"No one ever had to tell me." Colin looked at Shannon with sympathy, but he was also puzzled. "I don't see why this bothers you so. It's not that unusual, you know."

"I just want to try to understand."

"That's easy. When your mother locked Emmett out of her bedroom, he had to go somewhere."

"But why to Aunt Mamie? Why couldn't he have gone to one of those places?"

"You're being naive, Shannon. Mamie was a beautiful negro woman, and Emmett was her master. You should know that Emmett didn't share any of your abolitionist feelings."

"I never thought he did," Shannon said. Then she asked, "Do you?"

"What? Share your abolitionist feelings?" Colin halfway smiled. "I was fighting for the South, little sister."

"That doesn't answer anything. What I'm saying, Colin, is that Sally is as much your sister as I am."

"She may be in fact, though I know very few men who claim their black offspring, and Emmett certainly never claimed Sally." Colin took Shannon's hand. "She never was my sister in feeling. Shannon, there's more between you and me than just a blood tie. We've been friends from the moment we met."

Shannon looked down at the floor. There was no use

talking about Sally anymore. No one could explain the situation away. She'd just have to accept it and go on. Now she really looked at Colin for the first time since she'd arrived. "You're thinner, Colin, and pale."

"I could say the same about you." He turned her question back on her. "Aren't things going well at Marshland?"

She hesitated. She wouldn't tell him about Tom and Adam. She said, "As well as can be expected, considering."

"Considering what? Why do I have this feeling that you're hiding something from me?"

"Oh, there are all the usual problems on a farm. I was just never in charge of all of them before. The training is getting behind because we don't have enough hands. And then there's Berry. I don't know what got into Papa breeding her so early last year. She's beginning to look ready to foal."

"Berry's a tough old mare. She'll be all right."

"She's getting old. I heard Tom say she must be close to twenty."

"Well, don't worry. If she has trouble and Tom can't handle it, you can get Old Man Thompson out from town."

When Shannon got ready to leave, Colin said, "I know you came because it's almost Christmas, so I didn't say anything this time. But I meant it, Shannon, about your not coming anymore. This is just no place for you to be."

They had moved Colin, and his new prison was dirtier and even more crowded. The guards had been insulting as they'd shown her in to see Colin, and the whole atmosphere of the building was oppressive.

"I won't promise not to come back," Shannon said, "but I will stay away for a while, if that's what you want."

Colin breathed a sigh of relief and said, "Don't look so tragic, little sister. It'll only be for a little while."

"I can't help it." Shannon felt the tears pushing at her eyelids, but she wouldn't allow herself the weakness of crying. She shook away the tears and tried to explain. "The war is tearing my life apart, snatching first this and then that from me while I just stand by doing nothing."

"Poor Shannon. You should have been a man. It's the sitting at home and waiting that's hard on you. If you could be in the thick of it, you'd be like Jett, relishing every battle."

He hadn't understood at all, and Shannon felt even worse. Always before he'd known what she was thinking without her even trying to explain, but he'd been away to the war for over two years. In that time, Shannon had grown, changing from a stubborn, willful child into an adult with duty sitting heavily upon her shoulders. She shook her head, but she didn't say anything more while yet another childhood support fell away. Always Colin had been there, and he always had understood. Always, but not anymore.

Colin touched her cheek. "Look at the bright side, Shannon. The war snatched me up and plopped me down right here where you could come visit me."

"And now you tell me I can't even do that."

"More than anything else I want you to be safe and away from all this. You tell Tom that I said not to let you go out alone anymore—not even to ride that devil horse in the back pasture."

Shannon bent down and kissed Colin's cheek. "All right, Colin, I'll tell him." There was no need for him to know how alone they were when there was absolutely nothing he could do about it.

As she left the prison, she realized that she'd been going to Louisville to lean on Colin. She'd always fancied herself strong and independent, but all her life she'd been leaning on someone, running out barking like a dog that takes courage from its master's presence. Aunt Mamie, Papa, Colin, and even Tom and Adam had supported her. Now the problems were beyond Aunt Mamie's ability to help, and the others were gone out of her reach. Would she have the courage to stand up and fight alone?

She might be able to answer that if she could only know what the coming year would bring. Last Christmas she never could have imagined the way her life would change in one short year, and three Christmases ago she still had been a child in a child's world when war was just something the men argued about after dinner.

Still it did no good to wish for the past. Life went on, and the changes each day brought would be part of her life from now on. A crisp breeze whipped her skirts, and she shivered as she walked across the yard to Captain Ned's cab.

A soldier in blue started toward her, and for just a moment her heart beat faster. Then he was close and nodding to her with a stranger's smile. Her heart sank, and the tears sprang up to push at her eyes again. She'd thought he was Randal. Suddenly Randal's face was before her, and her whole being hungered after him. She stopped in the middle of the walkway and took a quick sharp breath. She could deny the truth no longer. She carried Randal's gentle smiling eyes around with her because she loved him.

"Is anything wrong, miss?" the soldier asked, bringing her back to the present.

Shannon shook her head. "No. No, thank you." But as she began walking again, she thought that was far from true. She'd let her life get too complicated. She was going to marry one man although she loved another. She sighed and shook it all away from her. It would be best not to think about it at all. Not now anyway. There would be time enough for her to straighten all that out when the war was over. Now she needed to think about getting a hand to help with the horses.

But as she went on she let the memories she had of Randal creep back close to her heart.

CHAPTER 17

Shannon studied the boy driving the carriage. Toby wasn't exactly what she'd been looking for. He was too young, only thirteen, and small for his age, and he'd cost entirely too much now that they needed to count every penny. But when she'd told Captain Ned that she was looking for some help, he'd said, "There's a boy works back at the stable where I keep my horse. He's as close to being a son to me as I'll ever have. I been saving up for a year to try to buy him." Captain Ned had nodded his head. "You'll like Toby. He'd make a fine jockey if he had half a chance."

She had liked Toby as soon as she'd seen how his hands gentled when he touched a horse. Then it had simply been a matter of making the deal and handing over nearly four hundred dollars.

When they reached the barn, it was dark. Shannon

lit a lantern and turned to Toby. He kept his eyes to the ground. She said softly, "Toby, I know this is all strange, but it won't be so bad."

"Yes'm," Toby said, still not looking up.

Shannon caught a quiver in his voice, and she thought the boy might be crying. "Did you have family in Louisville, Toby?"

"No, ma'am. I ain't had no family that I can remember 'cepting for Captain Ned."

"Are you afraid of me, Toby?"

Toby's eyes flicked up to her face and then back to the ground. "I ain't sure, ma'am, but I reckon I might be."

Shannon put out her hand and raised his chin until she could see his face. He was so young, with an appealing childlike look to his wide eyes. "It'll be all right, Toby. When the war's over, you'll be free. That won't be so long from now, and in case something happens to me before then, I'll give you your papers so that you'll have them."

"What if I run away?"

"Have you tried to run away before?"

Toby nodded. "I used to, but I always got caught and whipped. Then Captain Ned told me just to be good and maybe he could get enough money to buy me. We were going up north together." Toby's eyes changed, and his whole body tightened up. But he didn't look away from Shannon. He said, "Maybe I'll run away, and me and Captain Ned can still go north."

Shannon shook her head. "Captain Ned's my friend."

A look of disbelief crossed Toby's face. "I ain't never met the first white I'd call a friend."

"I can see that, but maybe someday you will." Shannon turned away from him and began putting away the harness.

"Don't you want me to do that?" Toby asked.

"Tonight you watch, and then next time you'll know where everything goes." When she finished, Shannon pointed out the bed in the tack room. "You can sleep here tonight. Tomorrow I'll fix one of the cabins for you."

"Yes'm."

Shannon watched him for a moment and then said, "Toby, I need you to help me with the horses, and as long as you're here, you'll have a place to sleep and enough to eat. But if you want to run away, I won't come after you."

Shannon didn't wait for an answer. She went on to the door and just before closing it behind her she said, "Good night, Toby."

When morning came Toby was still there, and after Shannon took him to meet Aunt Mamie, she didn't think she'd have to worry much about him running away anymore. Aunt Mamie saw his lonely eyes and took him straight to her heart. "You remind me of my boy John," she said.

Shannon remembered how tall and gangly John had been, completely opposite from the boy who stood in front of Aunt Mamie now. Toby was short, economically built without even an inch to waste. Shannon disagreed, "They don't look a thing alike," she said.

"Listen to you, child. You always was one for facts. I didn't say Toby here looked like John. I said he reminded me of him." Aunt Mamie piled hot cakes on Toby's plate.

"Don't fatten him up too much, Aunt Mamie. He'll get too heavy to ride the colts." Shannon turned to Toby. "As soon as you eat, come on down to the barn, and we'll get to work."

"You'd better sit down and have some more breakfast too. You ain't hardly ate nothing at all for a month of Sundays." Aunt Mamie shook her head and clucked her tongue at Shannon. "And what with today being Christmas too."

Shannon smiled. "I was afraid you were going to forget about Christmas this year."

"Now when did I ever forget about Christmas. I'd best be rustling up some cakes for dinner," Aunt Mamie said as she began rummaging through her spice jars and humming a little tune to herself.

Shannon's smile grew wider. Tonight there'd be something special to eat, and she'd read the Christmas story from Aunt Mamie's old Bible just as she had every year since she'd learned to read. It was good that there would be something the same this Christmas, even though nearly everything else had changed so much.

In the days that followed, Toby caught on quickly to whatever Shannon wanted him to do. Together they kept the horses cared for, and her fear of having to sell them faded.

Shannon's hands roughened from the hard work, and no amount of Aunt Mamie's special cream could keep the cold from chapping her skin. But Shannon couldn't imagine not being out in the barn, carrying feed or currying the horses. She felt it had been another girl who had tried to learn needlework and the other intricate arts of ladyhood. Even then the thread and needle had always felt so dead in her hands, but the reins or a currycomb bespoke activity and life.

Still, despite her busy days, there was a heaviness in her heart that often brought the threat of tears late at night. Shannon tried to shut out all thoughts of Randal while she tried to think of Jett and remember the promise she'd made him before the war. But Jett seemed too far away to reach even in her thoughts.

Anyway, the war kept getting in the way with its

guns and hills that must be taken by one side or the other while the grass grew slippery with fallen soldiers' blood. Late at night in her most despairing moments when she could not block it out, there would come to her mind pictures of dead soldiers lying in the mud. Her mind would torture her by changing the faces to those she knew and loved. But then when sleep would finally overtake her, she could no longer hold Randal's eyes away. He'd come to her in her dreams to comfort her until once more the morning came.

The last day of 1863 was unusual weather, mild with the threat of rain by midafternoon when Shannon checked the mares. She stopped in front of Berry, who stood listless in her stall with glazed eyes. "Hey, girl, what's the matter?" Shannon stroked the mare's neck, but Berry shied away from her touch. Shannon turned to Toby. "What do you think, Toby?"

Toby's eyes narrowed as he slowly looked over the mare before answering. "I don't know, Miss Shannon. Maybe it's just that we haven't been getting her out enough for exercise. She's been restless all morning."

Shannon looked at Berry. "I can't find Papa's records, but she looks ready to foal. Have you ever helped bring a foal?"

Toby nodded and said, "A mare don't need no help if all goes right, but still there's a few that sometimes need a little doctoring."

Shannon hadn't seen very many mares drop foals. Her father had always chased her away if he caught her hanging about. Now she said, "I've got this feeling that something's not right."

Toby slipped into the stall and ran his hands all along Berry. "It's her time all right, but there's nothing we can do for her till she starts."

"I wish Tom was here. He'd know what to do."

"I'll do the best I can for you, Miss Shannon."

Shannon put her hand on his shoulder. "I know you will, Toby. Together we'll manage it somehow."

Then there was nothing to do but wait. When night came, Shannon admitted that whatever happened with Berry was going to be too much for Toby and her to handle. She remembered Colin telling her to send for Old Man Thompson if she needed him. So when Toby came back from eating his supper, Shannon had a pony all saddled and ready for him to leave. She didn't like sending Toby out into the weather. It had been raining since dusk, and now the sharp pinpricks of sleet had joined the rain. But they had to have help.

Shannon gave him a note and told him where to go. Then she said, "Old Man Thompson knows about as much about horses as any man in Fayette County. Tell him I promise to pay him well."

Toby mounted up. "What if something happens before I can get back?"

Shannon looked at the mare. She was nearly wild with the pain now. Shannon said, "If I have to, I'll put her out of her misery."

"I'll be back as soon as I can."

"Be careful, Toby, and if the storm gets worse take shelter somewhere."

Shannon watched him ride away to be swallowed up by the rain. She went to the house to get her gun. Then back at the barn she sat down to wait. For a while she tried talking to the mare to calm her, but it was useless. Berry had gone into a red hot world of pain. She had dropped to the floor and lay there writhing uncontrollably.

It was senseless to wait. Toby would never get back in time even if he did make it to town in the storm. Outside the rain had been completely replaced by stinging pellets of sleet, and the wind had picked up, pushing hard

against the sturdy barn. It would be dangerous to ride out in this. Toby would have to take shelter.

For a moment Shannon hesitated to pick up the gun, but she couldn't let Berry suffer needlessly. Once she'd made the decision, she didn't waver. Her hands were steady as she checked the load and sighted the gun.

Berry looked up at her as if she knew what was coming. Shannon whispered, "Be still, girl. It'll all be over in a second."

She pulled the trigger back smoothly and fired a clean shot into the mare's head. Berry shuddered one last time and was still. Then the barn door was blowing open behind Shannon, and two figures were pushed in on the wind.

The man took in Shannon, the gun, and the mare in an instant. He yelled, "Hurry, boy. Get the knives. We might save the colt yet."

"Randal?" For a moment Shannon thought she must be dreaming. It seemed impossible that it was Randal who had burst into the barn in front of Toby.

But it wasn't a dream. He was really there. Without looking around at her, he said, "You'll have to help, Shannon . . . if you think you can keep from fainting."

"I won't faint," Shannon said, kneeling beside him and the dead mare.

They were strong words, words she almost put a lie to as they tore Berry apart to yank out the foal.

"It's alive," Randal said, carefully wiping the foal off.

Shannon looked at the pitiful little hump of bones and wet black skin lying in front of her. It would never know its mother's nudge and care. "But for how long?" Shannon said.

Randal looked up at her then and thought she was the most beautiful thing he'd ever seen. He longed to let his eyes feast on her, but first he had to try to save the foal and take some of the defeated look out of her eyes. He turned back to the foal. "It's a filly," he said.

"Blackberry," Shannon said.

"Well, Miss Shannon," Toby said, "now the little thing has got to live 'cause you gave it a name."

Shannon almost smiled at Toby. "If she does, it'll be because of you, Toby. I shouldn't have sent you out in that storm."

"Don't you worry none about that, Miss Shannon. I wasn't gonna let a little wind scare me."

"See if you can strip some milk out of the mare's bag, Toby," Randal said. "You don't have another mare nursing, do you?"

"No," Shannon said. "It's too early in the year."

"I thought as much. I wonder what your father could have been thinking about. It's bad business to have mares foal this early."

"Papa had his own way of doing everything," Shannon said, defending her father. "Ways no one else understood. But most of the time it worked out well for him."

Shannon watched the foal. The rigors of her birth had almost been too much for her, and Shannon thought the little filly wanted nothing so much as to lay her head down on the soft straw. But everytime the foal looked about to give up, Randal would nudge her, and she'd raise her head to stare around at them with a bewildered look.

"She'll have to get up, but it'll be better if we don't help. The more she does for herself the better chance she'll have," Randal said quietly.

"How long will we wait?" Shannon asked. The little filly had won a place in her heart simply because she'd come so hard.

"A few more minutes," Randal said, gently nudging the filly again. "Did you get any milk, Toby?"

"Not much."

"It'll have to do. Find something to use to feed her."

"Even if she gets up, do you think that she'll live without her mother?" Shannon asked.

"Stranger things have happened," Randal said.

Then silence fell between them as they waited. The sleet had stopped, but the wind still pushed gusts against the barn while the air seeping between the cracks was colder every minute. Suddenly there was a loud crack and then a crash as a limb gave way to the wind and side-swiped the edge of the barn roof as it fell.

The little foal shuddered and rose up on her hind legs. She wobbled there a moment and fell back down. But once she'd tried she didn't seem to be able to give up, and after a few moments' rest she was edging up to her feet once more. Finally, while they held their breaths, the foal got all her hoofs on the ground and stood there wobbling and staring back at them. She took one shaky step and then another while it looked as though she might fall in a heap at any second.

"Get ready with the milk, Shannon," Randal said.

Toby held out the bottle he'd put the milk in, but Shannon said, "No, Toby, you do it. If this foal lives, it'll be something of a miracle and one that you brought about by finding Randal. So you feed her, and Blackberry will be yours."

Toby's face lit up. "You mean it, Miss Shannon? You'd give me this filly?"

"If you can keep her alive, she's yours," Shannon said.

"I'll keep her alive." Toby stepped slowly up to the foal. She grabbed at the bottle he held out as though it was just what she'd been expecting.

Shannon looked at Randal and found his eyes waiting for her. Her heart jumped with eagerness. More than anything in the world she wanted him to cross the room and put his arms around her, but she turned away from him before he could see the desire in her eyes.

She watched Toby carefully feeding the filly for a moment. Then she said, "I'd better go up to the house. They'll be worried about us. I'll bring some milk down for Blackberry in a little bit, Toby." She turned to Randal again, but she kept her eyes away from his. "Maybe you'd like something to eat, Randal."

"Some coffee might be good," Randal said. He gave Toby some last-minute instructions about keeping the foal warm, before he followed Shannon out of the barn.

When they opened the door, the blast of cold wind and snow hitting their faces took their breaths. Shannon felt the chill reach through her as the wind pushed her back, but then Randal's strong arm was around her, helping her along the snowy path past several fallen limbs, and the chill was gone.

She knew they were close to the house when the kitchen light filtered out to them. Suddenly, without thinking about what she was doing, she turned in his arm and fit her body close to his. She knew only that she didn't want this moment of closeness to end.

He accepted her into his arms and gently lifted up her chin, and their lips met. The snow and wind whirled about them, but Shannon didn't feel the cold.

CHAPTER 18

Then the door was open, and Aunt Mamie was calling out through the dark, "Is that you, child?"

Reluctantly Shannon pulled away from Randal to answer. "Yes, Aunt Mamie."

"Then get yourself inside this house before you catch your death of cold," Aunt Mamie fussed.

Randal pulled her close for a few seconds longer before he let her loose. He could see her in the dim light Aunt Mamie's lantern was spreading through the dark. He brushed a bit of snow off her hair and said, "We have to go in."

"Yes, I suppose," Shannon said and turned toward the kitchen door.

"Who's that with you? It sure ain't Toby," Aunt Mamie said, peering into the dark.

"It's Captain Hunt," Shannon said.

"Well, land a Goshen. What's he doing here? I thought he'd done gone off to the war."

"I don't know how, but somehow Toby found him out on the road tonight."

Randal watched Shannon move on into the light of the kitchen while his desire for her grew. She'd filled his arms like no other girl ever had or ever would. He wanted Shannon, but not unless she came to him freely with nothing between them. Not Noble, the land, her family, or the horses.

"Randal, aren't you coming?" Shannon waited for him.

When they stepped into the kitchen, Aunt Mamie gasped. "Has one of you been hurt?"

"Everything's all right, Aunt Mamie."

"Where's young Toby?" Her fears were still not answered.

"He's down at the barn with the new foal," Shannon said.

"Then old Berry came through after all," Aunt Mamie said.

Shannon shook her head wearily. "I shot Berry, but the foal may live. If Toby can get it to eat. You'll need to take the milk we've got in the house down to Toby, and then you can go on to bed."

"But what about you and the captain here? Don't you want me to fix you something to eat?"

"After I get cleaned up, I'll fix us something, but you can take Toby something as you go."

It was on the tip of Aunt Mamie's tongue to tell Shannon it wasn't proper to entertain gentlemen in the middle of the night, but Shannon's look stopped her. Shannon wasn't a child anymore. The war had changed her into a woman, and if Shannon was going to be entertaining men, Aunt Mamie had the feeling that Captain Hunt would be the very man she herself would pick for Shannon.

Aunt Mamie gathered up some food and the milk. Before she went out the door, she stopped in front of the captain who'd been standing quietly by the door. "It's good to see you, Captain, sir. There's some water out in the back room. You can wash up there."

She sent one last look Shannon's way, but Shannon had already left the kitchen to go clean up. Aunt Mamie turned back to Randal. "You won't hurt her, will you, sir? I mean she thinks she's tough, and she makes other folks think that too, but her old Aunt Mamie knows . . . she's soft underneath."

Randal took Aunt Mamie's hand in his. "You don't have to worry about me ever hurting Shannon, Mamie." If only he could protect her!

"I knew you was a good man the first time I laid eyes on you, Captain." She picked up the lantern and hurried out the door.

Later Randal and Shannon sat at the table and ate without talking. Shannon had changed to a soft worn wrapper with no frills that molded next to her body in a familiar way and looked more alluring than any amount of ruffles or ribbons could have. She'd tugged some of the tangles out of her hair, and now soft curls framed her face. Randal wore some of Colin's old clothes while his uniform dried out by the fire.

Shannon wanted to know what he'd been doing. She hungered to hear him speak and yet at the same time his just being there was enough. The homey closeness of the kitchen wrapped around them, insulating them from the outside world. Everytime Shannon looked up, his eyes were waiting for her just as they had in her dreams, except that now there seemed to be a question deep behind the smile—a question that Randal wouldn't ask, and that Shannon wasn't sure she could answer if he did.

Finally Randal said, "Where are Tom and Adam?"

"The Army took them. They'd gone into town to church, and when they came out, the soldiers were waiting. They said they needed them to repair some railroad bridges."

"I guess that's true enough. Some of the lines are in bad shape."

"Perhaps, but the Union isn't winning any friends around here now that the military has taken over. You'd think Kentucky was an enemy state that had been captured."

"In a way it is, Shannon . . . especially here in the Bluegrass. There are more Secesh people than Union."

"But the fact is Kentucky didn't secede."

"Maybe not as a state, but a lot of the people seceded in their hearts. The entire state's been torn apart by the war."

"It's going to get worse the way the army is ruling us." Bitterness crept into Shannon's voice. "All that half the people around here wanted was just to stay out of it."

"Once the war started they couldn't stay out of it. That's why most of the men joined up on one side or the other. Just like your brother."

"Brothers," Shannon corrected him. "Clay rode south in October with Jett the night Robards captured Colin." Briefly she told him about Colin's escape from the prison camp in Ohio and his recapture.

"I'm sorry about Colin," he said and frowned. "Does that mean you and your mother are here alone?"

"We have Aunt Mamie, Sally, and Toby."

He looked at her for a long time before he said,

"You should have gone north or at least moved into town. What will you do if another guerrilla band comes?"

"I don't know. I can't be playing 'what if' games, but I'm not leaving Marshland."

Determination tightened the lines of her face, but he thought he saw a touch of doubt, perhaps even fear, in her eyes. He wanted to stay with her and protect her, but he couldn't. He had to finish out the war. He reached across the table and covered her hand with his. "The Army will let Tom and Adam come back soon."

Shannon sighed. "Tom will come back, but Adam had already planned to join the Army. He won't be back except to get Sally."

He kept his hand on hers. Her hand felt so small and vulnerable under his. Just looking at her no one would ever guess at her strength . . . but would she be strong enough? There was a vague uneasiness about her that made him wonder if she'd told him everything. "You say Robards captured Colin?"

She nodded, but she didn't want to talk about Robards.

Randal wouldn't let it pass. He asked, "Has he been bothering you?"

"No," she answered carefully. "I haven't even seen him since that night. Maybe he's forgotten about me." She tried to say it lightly, but it didn't come out that way. Robards was there, waiting, with his threat hanging over her head.

"I wouldn't worry too much about him." Randal tried to reassure her. "He's not nearly so important as he thinks he is."

"But he has important friends in high places." She wished she hadn't said that. Randal needed no extra worries to carry back to the war with him. Quickly she changed the subject. "Why are you in Kentucky? Has your company been sent back to this area?"

He shook his head. "I heard that my father was sick, so I got a leave to see him. I came up from Chattanooga last week."

"You were at Chattanooga? I thought you went east when you left here."

Randal nodded. "We did, but not much has happened there since Gettysburg. Both armies are trying to gather strength enough for a new offensive, so when they formed a regiment to join General Grant in Tennessee, my company joined up with 'Fighting Joe' Hooker. We went by rail. They said we covered over a thousand miles in eight days."

"I read about that in a paper I saw. There was something about a Battle Above the Clouds."

"We were there."

Had it really been only weeks ago that they'd opened up the cracker line into Chattanooga to get food to the Union troops trapped there? They'd made a trail through the wild terrain of the mountains where guerrilla hideouts abounded. There'd been the feeling as they went through the mountain passes that one wrong step would be their last. Then came the battle. Here in this kitchen with Shannon, it was hard to believe all that had happened just weeks ago with men falling in front of him, their lives snuffed out as easily as candles. They'd marched on up the slope, closing ranks when one fell until finally they could call the mountain theirs. And then the news correspondents gave the battle some romantic name. Now Randal said quietly, "The newspapers never tell the whole story."

Shannon watched Randal's frown grow deeper as he remembered the battle. She wondered how it would have been if they'd met in a ballroom or at a dinner party without the war's shadow hanging over them. But then she knew that couldn't be. Without the war their lives never would have touched each other. While he looked away from her thinking of the past, she studied the strong line of his jaw and the wide generous mouth tightened now by his dark memories. It was all she could do to keep from reaching out to smooth away the frown lines from around his eyes.

Then his eyes came away from the war and back to her. She didn't look away. She let his eyes capture hers though she was afraid he was reading the secret she'd been trying to hide from even herself. Something was happening between them. Something Shannon wasn't ready to face. Not yet . . . not while the war still ruled their lives.

"Will it be over soon?" Shannon asked softly.

Randal didn't answer for a long time, but finally he said, "I think not. A war's just not that easy to end when neither side is ready to give up."

"Do you still think the North will win?"

"I'm sure of it now. It's just a matter of time."

"And of lives lost."

"Men go to war to fight for what they believe. Some of them never come home."

She wanted to ask him if he would come back. The question was on her tongue to be spoken, but there could be no answer. She shivered.

"Are you cold?" he asked.

She nodded, although the cold she felt had nothing to do with the temperature dropping outside.

It was late, but neither of them wanted to end the night. So instead, Randal built up the fire and pulled a deacon's bench out of the corner close up to its warmth. "Come sit over here," he said.

She fit quite naturally against him with her head resting on his shoulder. For a long time even words seemed an intrusion on their closeness, so they were quiet while they listened to the wind blow around the house and drew in the warmth of the fire and each other.

When they finally began talking again, it was as if they'd made an unspoken agreement to speak no more of the war. Instead, they talked of the horses, and then Randal carried Shannon back with him to his childhood, telling her about the hunts he'd gone on with his father and brothers and the struggles they'd sometimes faced to keep going. But mostly he told her of the happiness the family had shared. There'd been no locked bedroom doors in his family.

"I'd like to meet your parents," she said.

"They're just plain folks. Ma's never had anything fancy in all her life except a jeweled comb Pa gave her once, and he found that on the street." Suddenly he was comparing the differences in their families. Despite himself his arm stiffened a bit against her. He didn't belong here holding her. He was the poor little white boy who had to go around to the backdoor to ask for, and sometimes almost beg for, a day's work.

Shannon felt him withdrawing from her and wanted to keep him close. "They had love," she said. "That's more than some people ever have."

His arm tightened gently around her again, and with his other hand he turned her face up to his. Their kiss was long and tender, demanding nothing but revealing everything. Then a clock chimed in the house. It was near dawn. Randal stretched and rose to add wood to the fire, and Shannon fixed his breakfast.

In the cold light of morning all their troubles flooded back. The war was with them again, and Randal began worrying about leaving her there so vulnerable and open to attack.

He drank the last of his coffee, set down the cup, and asked, "Don't you have friends you could stay with in town?"

Her eyes meeting his were unyielding. "This is my home. I won't leave Marshland."

"For any reason?" Suddenly his question dealt with more than her safety.

"I can't leave the land. I belong here. No matter what else happens, I have to keep enough of the farm together so that we'll have a starting place when the war does end."

"But the land will be Clay's when he returns, won't it?"

Shannon looked beyond him to the window where the first light filtered in, and there was quiet determination in her voice. "Names in a will don't matter as much as how I feel. This land will always be mine. I'll never leave it."

She didn't seem to realize how her words pierced Randal's heart. Just a short while ago, when she'd yielded her lips to him so sweetly, he'd felt his hopes bound. The war would end, and she would go with him. They'd start out fresh with a farm of their own somewhere. But now he realized that Marshland held claim to her more than he ever could.

"Someday, when I have my own place, maybe I'll know how you feel about this land," he said quietly. "But now I can help feeling that any land would be empty without someone you care about to share it."

Shannon shook her head impatiently. No one ever understood about the land. "People come and go, and the years blend together in a jumble of seasons, but the land is always here, passed on through the Clays as a heritage. The land is my history."

Randal's gaze was intent. "Sometimes it's best to abandon the past."

It was a long time before she said, "I'm not sure I could do that, even if I wanted to."

He wanted to say more. The time seemed to be

right, but he wouldn't ask for commitments from her while he was still fighting in the war, and maybe he had another reason as well. He was afraid that she would refuse him and leave him with no hope for tomorrow. Already her words made it hard for him to hold on to the hope that someday she would be his. But with the memory of her soft against him, he'd have enough to take back to the battlefield with him. Every man needed a future to dream about as he marched against the enemy and as each moment might be his last.

"I'll be going through Louisville," Randal said. "I could take a letter to Colin for you."

"I was in Louisville only a week ago, but if you have the chance, you might tell him we're all right and that he will have his wish. I won't be coming to see him for a while."

Randal nodded, and then there was no way to postpone his leave-taking any longer. After he'd changed back to his uniform, Shannon put on a heavy wool cape to walk out with him to the barn. A thick layer of snow crunched under their feet, and the air froze the breath in their noses.

Randal and Shannon didn't speak on the way to the barn. All the words they dared to say had already been spoken. Nothing was left now but goodbye.

At the barn they found Toby and the foal cuddled together under a heavy blanket, fast asleep.

"Maybe the foal will make it after all," Randal ventured.

"If Toby has anything to say about it, she will."

After Randal saddled his horse, he looked at Shannon a long time, memorizing her face, before he leaned over to kiss her softly. "I'll be back," he promised. Then he led his horse out of the barn, and once he was mounted, didn't look back.

Shannon folded her arms around her as though she could hold his warmth there. But too quickly Randal disappeared from sight, and there was no shutting out just how alone she really was.

CHAPTER 19

Winter passed slowly, and though every day was a struggle at Marshland, Shannon never considered giving up. Somehow she kept things going in spite of the ever-increasing money problems. She had to sell a few of her horses to keep the rest of the horses in fodder and to pay one of the provost marshal's fines. Robards came to collect the money.

"There are ways you could avoid these fines, Shannon," he said when she handed him the money.

Shannon kept her voice calm with difficulty. "You have your money. Now please leave."

Robards laughed. "I won't rush you, Shannon. Not now, because I know sooner or later you'll come to me. I have something more important to you than money."

"You have nothing that could ever bring me to you." Shannon's voice was cold and crisp.

"Haven't you heard the latest orders? There's going to be retaliation for these guerrilla raids. The Governor has ordered five rebels to be arrested for each outrage, and then the military will be allowed to decide what to do with them."

He reached over to touch Shannon's arm, but she stepped deftly away from him.

Robards's face darkened as he warned, "It would be best to make friends with the military, my dear. Or maybe you don't care as much as I thought you did for your woods colt brother."

Shannon held her anger down. She could tell by the way he lazily watched her that he wanted her to strike him. It would give him an excuse to attack her. She clasped her hands tightly together and said, "I must ask you to leave. Good day, Colonel."

But he didn't move. He took a long lingering look at her before saying, "I'll leave this time, my dear, but if I were you, I'd carefully consider my suggestions." He put a familiar hand heavy on her shoulder. "After all, I could take you by force anytime I wanted. Of course, I'd prefer that you come to me freely. You'd have everything to gain and nothing to lose because one way or another I plan to have you, Shannon Marsh."

Shannon felt her face grow pale, but she stood very still, not fighting against his touch. Her words were measured and spoken carefully. "I have a servant with a gun trained on you this very moment. To shoot you he knows might mean his own death; but he's very loyal, and if I give the signal you will die first, Colonel Robards. Now get off my land."

He kept smiling, but the corners of his mouth stiffened a bit. "You're bluffing," he said.

"Would you care to call my bluff?"

Robards backed up. "I told you I'm in no hurry. I'll wait. You know where to find me when the time comes."

Shannon didn't move for a long time after he left. Suddenly she felt like abandoning the fight for Marshland. She would be safe in Canada. She never would have to feel Robards hot damp hands on her again. Then the anger surged up through her again. She wouldn't be run off her own land! But from now on she'd keep a gun close at hand, and she'd teach Toby to shoot.

With her resolution firm again, Shannon walked out to the barn. The day was one of the gifts of late winter in Kentucky—mild, with the promise of spring real in the air. Toby had put Blackberry out for exercise in a small corral on the south side of the barn. He'd worked a near miracle in keeping her alive during the worst of the winter, and now her legs were strong. As Shannon watched the little filly frisk about in the warm air, she felt new hope and determination filling her. She wouldn't give up.

Tom came back in March, looking as though he'd been gone three years instead of three months. Adam wasn't with him.

"He wouldn't come back with me," Tom said when Sally ran out to meet him. "He's joined up with the Army. He said you'd understand."

Sally didn't cry. Her tears had all been shed weeks ago, but she swallowed hard and said, "He'll be back." There was a lost pitiful sound to her voice.

Shannon put her arms around Sally. Since that day in the barn, when Shannon had found out they were really sisters, Sally had been a stranger to her, avoiding any closeness at all. Now Sally stiffened and backed away. Shannon said, "Don't shut me out, Sally. Please let me be your friend."

Sally looked at Shannon and said, "Adam will be back to get me. I know he will."

Shannon tried to answer the plea in Sally's eyes. "Of course he will, Sally. They'll all come home . . . just as soon as the war's over." It was a promise women were making to themselves all over the country, north and south. The last shot would be fired, and then the men would come home. But they couldn't quite shut away the truth that many of the men would never be home again.

Sally pulled away from Shannon. It wasn't the time to divide herself from her closest friend, but she couldn't help it. The empty place Adam's going had left inside her was so immense it set her apart from all of them, even her mother. Sally fled toward the house.

"Sally!" Shannon started after her.

Aunt Mamie put a hand on Shannon's arm to stop her. "There ain't nothing you can do for her, child, but let her be. It's just that down deep she don't really believe he'll ever be back, no matter what she says."

"But he will be back, Aunt Mamie. He loves her."

Aunt Mamie shook her head. "I ain't saying he don't. But who knows who's gonna come back from this. Poor baby," Aunt Mamie said, looking after Sally. "She was raised too gentle for a black. It was the wrong thing to do, but I always tried to protect her. You did too in your own way, Shannon."

Shannon nodded. Sally never had been as strong as she. It was just natural to try to keep her from getting hurt.

"And now we can't protect her no more," Aunt Mamie said.

There's no one to protect any of us, Shannon thought. Only her own wits and courage remained to keep them going. The load fell heavy on her shoulders, and she wanted to let it drop around her feet. Then she looked all around . . . at the house, the barns, and at the fields lying beyond with the first green touch of spring. She pulled her shoulders up straight and brushed back her hair with a quick firm motion. It was worth it. Whatever she had to do. Out of nowhere Randal's words echoed in her mind. "Some things are more important than the land."

Maybe that was true, but for now the land under her feet was the one reality in her life. Everything else was just dreams.

With Tom home, Shannon breathed a bit easier. At least he knew what to do when the spring began to warm into summer and the mares began dropping their foals. With Tom there to anticipate and treat any problems, everything went smoothly.

Even Queenie's long awaited foal came easily. He dived into the world eagerly and was scrambling to his feet almost at the moment he hit the ground.

Tom stood back and watched the colt. "There's a real winner for you, Miss Shannon," he praised. "You can see his clean straight lines. That one's gonna be a runner."

Shannon smiled. For a minute the war receded in her thoughts, and nothing seemed to matter as much as the new colt trying out his wobbly legs. "He's a beauty all right," she agreed.

Tom nodded. "The master sure enough knew what he was about when he matched Queenie up with Lexington. Pity he never got to see this little horse."

With the mention of her father, the war came back, and when Toby asked her what she was going to name the colt, she said, "Bittersweet."

Two lines of verse that she'd seen on her mother's desk came to her mind.

Where once the sweet sun of happiness shone,
Now bitter does the wind of death moan.

She hadn't asked her where the lines came from, but Shannon was sure that they were her mother's own work.

She went in to visit with her mother almost every afternoon, but though they talked, their words just hung in the air between them, never joining the two of them in any way.

Since Clay's leaving, her mother had shut everything away from Shannon. If Clay returned, Shannon thought her mother might recapture some of her spirit. And if he did not? That thought didn't even bear thinking upon.

Shannon was surprised by how much she missed Clay. The habits that had always irritated Shannon when she was near him now seemed to be reasons for affection or at least understanding. There'd been no word at all from him since he'd ridden away with Jett.

During the spring Shannon went to Louisville to visit Colin. He greeted her with a frown, refusing to show any pleasure at seeing her. "I told you not to come back, Shannon. Why don't you listen to me?"

"I did listen. I haven't been here since Christmas." She leaned over and kissed his cheek. It had been a struggle to get in to see him at all. Finally the guards showed her to this windowless room with its two chairs and a table, where she'd had to wait for more than an hour before they brought Colin in. She said, "Aren't you even going to say hello?"

"Hello," he said, still frowning.

He looked terrible. He'd lost so much weight that there were deep hollows in his cheeks, and his skin was pasty white. A noticeable scattering of gray streaked through his reddish brown hair, but it was his eyes that bothered her most. He'd closed them down to her, shutting out her questioning gaze, and Shannon felt as though she were visiting a stranger.

"That's better," she said when he replied. "Now we'll just start all over. Why don't we pretend that we're at home and none of this has ever happened?" She so wanted to see him smile and laugh and just act interested in living again. There was something so vacant about him.

But his frown only deepened. "Some things are too hard to pretend." Then he tried, reaching deep inside him to remember the things people talked about when every waking moment wasn't weighed down by the struggle to survive. "How are things at Marshland?" he asked.

Shannon appreciated the effort he made, but she wanted to know about his life in prison. Neither by word or glance would he tell her. So instead, she tried to smile and talk as though everything was all right, without searching his eyes for glimpses of the hell he was living through. "Queenie had her colt . . . a real beauty. With the right training, he'll be taking all the money in a few years."

A few years. It was hard for Colin even to think past the next day. "I'm glad you got your colt, Shannon," he said.

He was quiet then for a long time while Shannon chattered about first one horse then another. She knew he had stopped listening, but she felt she had to keep talking.

Finally he said, "I've been worried about you ever since I found out that you were alone out on the farm."

"You shouldn't have worried," Shannon said. "Besides, Tom came back, and the young boy I bought back in December works hard for me, so we're not really as alone as all that. But how did you find out?"

"Your young captain came to see me."

"Randal?" She felt the familiar lift when she thought of him.

Colin heard the lift in her voice. "Just exactly what is he to you, Shannon?" he asked.

Shannon looked down at the table. It was a few minutes before she could summon up an answer. "I don't know, Colin." Then she looked directly at him, and her words were just a whisper. "But I think I love him."

Colin nodded as though her words didn't surprise

him at all. "I sort of liked him . . . even if he is a Yank. But what about Jett?"

"What about him?"

"Come now, Shannon, you're avoiding the obvious. Jett plans to marry you the first chance he gets."

"Nothing's changed."

"Do you really believe that?" Colin shook his head. "Shannon, I'm surprised. You're better at pretending games than I thought."

"I'm not pretending anything. I promised Jett I would marry him, and I will, as soon as the war ends."

"But you just said that you love this Randal."

"I didn't say that love had anything to do with my plans to marry Jett. I'm just doing what's best, joining the two farms in the easiest possible way."

"You talk as though you're nothing more than a bridge between two divided pieces of land. Oh, Shannon! If nothing else, you should have learned the folly of that kind of matchmaking from the misery of your mother's marriage to Emmett. Their union made Marshland prosper, but look at the cost."

"It was worth it to Papa," Shannon said.

Colin met her eyes squarely then and said, "Was it, Shannon?"

"Are you saying that I shouldn't marry Jett?"

"I never could tell you what to do, even when you were just a bit of a girl, so I won't start trying now. You'll have to decide for yourself which is more important to you . . . love or the land."

"Why can't I have both?" Shannon cried. "I don't want to have to choose," she protested.

Colin reached out and touched her face. "Maybe you won't, Shannon. Maybe when Jett comes back, you'll find that there's love in your heart for him too."

Shannon didn't say anything. She knew she would never love Jett, not the way she loved Randal.

Shannon went away from the prison with a heavy heart. She had watched Colin being taken away by the guards. He'd shuffled his feet like a defeated old man, and, all at once, she'd been worried that if the war didn't end soon, he wouldn't survive his time in prison.

The things he'd said about Jett troubled her. She hadn't let herself face the problem before. Her promise of marriage to Jett was so far away, while her love for Randal was here and now. Still she wasn't ready to trust the feeling she had for Randal. It was like a star that had suddenly appeared out of nowhere in a dark sky and that might vanish just as suddenly. Marriage to Jett, on the other hand, would be much like a hill rising steadily and constantly on the horizon but never getting any closer.

The next time she went to visit Colin, she was told that the prison's rules had been changed. No visitors were allowed, and all her appeals were to no avail. The guards let her hand over a letter to him, but Shannon left feeling certain that it wouldn't ever reach him.

Everyone was out of her reach—Randal, Clay, Jett, and now Colin. And even at Clay Manor Shannon couldn't reach her mother, or Sally, though she spoke with them every day. The shadow of the war kept lengthening and growing, spreading out its dark fingers to places that had never before heard the clamor of battle.

Through May the battles raged throughout Virginia. Grant was in charge of the Army now, and he doggedly trailed after Lee, refusing to retreat despite the ever-increasing number of wounded and dead.

Shannon read the reports from the battlefields, but she couldn't determine whether the war was nearing an end. All she knew was that men had died, and the fear that one of those men might have been Randal tormented her. With each passing day she wished she'd told him that she loved him before he went away. It suddenly seemed important that he know, even though she could make no promises to go with him.

In June came the news, whispering through the towns like the wind pushing through the trees before a storm, that Morgan once again was on the move and heading into Kentucky. The Confederates needed horses.

As she went about her chores, Shannon picked out the horses that she would let Jett take when he and Clay came. She didn't doubt that they would come, wanting more than she would be willing to give.

CHAPTER 20

Shannon walked slowly on her way to the house from the barn. Dusk was settling across the fields like an old woman spreading her skirts comfortably about her before sitting down to rest. It was Shannon's favorite time of day. All the chores had been done, and not until night stole in and swallowed the last light of the day did her worries return full force.

Two riders were approaching through the fields, and she stopped to watch them. They were Clay and Jett! No one sat a horse exactly like Jett. She put her hands on her hips and waited.

Jett reached her first, jumping the pasture fence, while Clay went around to the gate. Jett slid off his horse and pulled her into his arms. His lips came down hard on hers demanding a warm response. Shannon remembered

Randal's lips touching hers, asking for nothing but making her want to give him everything.

Finally Jett lifted his head and held her back at arm's length. His eyes darkened. "You look like a boy and smell like a horse."

Shannon looked down at Clay's pants and shirt she had taken to wearing. They were so much easier to work in than even her simplest skirt. She said, "I guess I do, Jett. It's hard to stay sweet smelling after a day in the barn." She laughed. "I guess I'm not much to come home to."

"I wouldn't say that exactly." He pulled her to him again, and while he kissed her, his hands ran possessively all over her. "Let's go find a bed."

Shannon wasn't ready for that. Maybe someday, but not now. Now his touch made her want to run to her room and lock the door. Suddenly Randal's eyes were there in her mind, watching her, and she wondered if she would ever again be ready for Jett's touch.

Confused, she pushed Jett back and twisted away from him. "We're not married yet," she said.

Jett's hands tightened on her shoulders. "But we will be soon. It won't hurt to have a taste of what's to come."

"No," Shannon said and jerked away from him.

His eyes narrowed to dark slits and Shannon measured the threat building in him and dangerously matching his desire. She spoke quickly to calm him. "I can't. Not until we're married, Jett."

"Ever the lady," Jett said and laughed. "You have more of your mother in you than I thought. But surely not so much that you can't enjoy a kiss."

Shannon tried to respond by remembering how Jett had once made her body warm to his touch. But all that was too long ago. Now another man's smiling eyes came between them.

Jett stood back and looked at her. "I come home from the war, and you can't even give me a proper kiss. What's the matter with you, Shannon?"

"I kissed you," Shannon said.

"*You* might call that a kiss. I don't."

"It's the war," Shannon said, making excuses. "It keeps me tight with worry."

"Maybe that Yankee captain has been back to visit since we left," Clay said as he came up behind them.

Shannon whirled around to face him. "Clay, are you all right?" She would have hugged him, but his look stopped her. He wasn't the same unsure boy who had ridden away less than a year ago. Arrogance floated about him now as he looked down at her.

"It didn't take you long to step into my breeches," Clay said, getting off his horse.

His eyes were as hard as his voice, and for a moment Shannon was too surprised to speak. Finally she simply said, "These were a pair you'd outgrown before you left, and they fit me. A dress is unhandy when I'm working with the horses. The twirl of skirts makes some of them nervous."

"Just remember, dear sister, you fit into my clothes, but you'll never take my place. This all belongs to me. Not one inch of it is, or ever will be, yours."

Shannon's temper rose, but then her anger was gone, leaving in its place only a heavy sadness. She said softly, "That's true. But the same blood that runs through you runs through me and through our ancestors before us, and because of that, I aim to see that Marshland makes it through this war with enough left to start on when peace comes. I owe that to the first Clay to settle here and to Papa."

Clay nodded. "But don't you ever forget it's all mine now. And right now, I've come to get some of my horses to take back to the Army."

"I've been expecting you," Shannon said. "Will you be able to stay for a meal?"

Clay looked at Jett. Jett shook his head. "We're out ahead of the General, but he'll be along with the main body of soldiers before long. Lexington will be ours in a few hours."

"Will there be a fight?" Shannon asked.

"There's always a fight, but so far we haven't met much of anything but some green home guards." Jett's face showed his contempt. Then he looked to the east where Lexington lay a few miles away and smiled. "It'll be good to take the town."

"Clay, you will go up to see Mother, won't you?"

"I don't know if I'll have time," Clay replied indifferently. "How is the old girl anyway?"

"Not good. It was hard on her when you left." Shannon paused and studied Clay, sadly wondering whether the little brother she'd known was buried so deeply that he'd never be found again? Shannon spoke softly again. "It would kill Mother if she knew you'd been here and didn't see her." Then she looked away from Clay, appealing silently to Jett.

"You go on in and see Miss Olivia while Shannon and I get the horses," Jett said.

"Are you sure you won't need me?" Clay was reluctant to leave Jett's side. His newfound assurance faded when he wasn't around Jett.

"Go on, Clay. We wouldn't want to deprive Miss Olivia of the sight of her son. Besides, I want to see Shannon alone, for a few minutes anyway." His face had a smile, but his eyes hardened with authority.

"All right," Clay said, "I'll go see Mother. I want to get a couple of Papa's bottles anyway." He took a few steps away and then turned. "Don't leave without me, Jett."

Jett shook his head. "I'll need you after I get the

horses rounded up," he said and then added, "Get the bottles, Clay, but don't open them. Keep them for later." His voice carried the sound of command.

Shannon waited until Clay went into the house before she said, "Clay's not drinking that much, is he? Not at his age."

"A boy old enough to get shot at is old enough to drink, but Clay hasn't learned how to handle his whiskey yet." Jett's eyes were suddenly demanding. "I didn't send him off, though, so we could talk about *him*."

Shannon turned away from the question in his gaze. He wanted to know about Randal, and there was nothing she could say that wouldn't deepen his jealousy. She said, "The horses are penned up out this way."

Jett followed Shannon into the barn, then he grabbed her shoulders and twisted her around. His fingers dug into her skin, and his eyes burned with anger that was ready to explode. He said, "I want to know about this Yankee that Clay was talking about."

Shannon stood still and looked up at him. He'd always been quick to get angry, but then so had she. They'd had plenty of fights in the past, fights that let a lot of angry words fly between them until neither of them was very mad anymore. Those fights of long ago usually had ended with a laugh and a kiss, and sometimes with a rough-and-tumble tussle that would awaken desires in both of them. But Jett was different now. The war had changed him, changed them both, and this anger that she saw so clearly now on Jett's face and deep within his dark eyes was different. He was no longer playing games, and Shannon felt fear tighten down her back. She didn't feel revulsion as she did when Robards touched her, but the fear was sickeningly the same.

"I told you before," she said very quiety, "Captain Hunt was quartered in Lexington for a while. After Papa was killed, he came out to help on the farm a few times.

He's worked with horses in New Orleans some, but he went to Virginia to join the Army of the Potomac, almost a year ago."

Jett didn't loosen his grip on her, nor did the fire drain away from his eyes. He said, "Good. Then maybe he's dead. The damn Yanks have been dying like flies in the wilderness, trying to run down General Lee."

His words sliced through her, because she knew how true they were. None of the news from Virginia had been good. Some of the newspapers were calling Grant a butcher. She willed herself not to let Jett see any response, but she wasn't entirely successful.

"That bothers you? That he's dead?" Jett's eyes burned into hers as his anger grew.

Shannon spoke carefully. "He was a nice man. I don't like to think of anyone I know dying on the battlefield."

His hands tightened on her, and when he spoke, his voice was too calm. "I don't believe that's all."

"You can choose to accept my word or not. I can't prove it."

A tight smile touched his lips. "I think there's a way you might."

He pulled her to him roughly and mashed his mouth down on hers. Shannon pushed against him, but it was useless.

Suddenly a voice called out from somewhere in the barn. "You want me to shoot him, Miss Shannon?"

Jett twisted away from Shannon and pulled his gun, but he couldn't tell where the voice had come from. "If it's that nigger, I'll kill him."

Shannon jumped in front of Jett. "No! Put your gun away! Nobody's going to shoot anyone." Then when Jett didn't do as she said, she went on. "Stay where you are, Toby, and don't make a sound. And whatever you do, don't shoot. This is Jett Noble. He owns the farm over the hill."

If Toby shot, Jett would be dead. Shannon was almost sure of that, because she'd taught Toby and taught him well.

Shannon took a deep breath and tried to gauge Jett's anger. She waited until it began to ebb down. "Don't do anything stupid, Jett. I've got horses in this barn," she said, seeing his eyes move slowly around the walls. He still held his gun ready. "Put your gun away."

Jett didn't look at her. "That nigger deserves to die. This is twice he's stepped out of his place."

Shannon was puzzled for a moment, but then she remembered the night Jett had met Adam. "But this isn't the same one. Adam joined the Union Army months ago, and we haven't seen him since. Toby's new, just a boy, and he's only doing what I've taught him to do if he thinks I need help." Shannon paused, thinking of the orders she'd given Toby. "You're lucky you're still alive."

Jett was slowly calming down. "You were stupid to teach a nigger to shoot."

"Perhaps," Shannon agreed. "But we are awfully alone out here. We need to be prepared for anything. I don't like the thought of being helpless if someone attacks."

"A nigger with a gun won't protect you." His anger had cooled to a simmer. "You need a man for that. You need me."

"Maybe so, but in the meantime I'll have to use what I've got and that's Toby and Tom."

"Don't put too much trust in the blacks. They're running off in droves down south. They say they trail after the Yankee armies for miles sometimes." He put his gun back in his belt. "You can tell your boy to come out now."

"No, Toby! Stay where you are."

"Don't you trust me, Shannon?"

"That's a little hard to answer after what's been happening here." Shannon met his eyes squarely.

Jett put out his hand and softly stroked her cheek. "You're so beautiful, Shannon, when you get the fire in your eyes like now . . . and so different from anyone else I've ever known. That's why I have to have you. You belong to me, you know."

When Shannon didn't say anything, he went on. "I guess I did push you a little too hard a few minutes ago, but a woman like you could make any man go a little crazy. You remember the promise you made before I left with the General?"

Shannon remembered, but that seemed so long ago, in such a different time. When she recalled the goodbyes she'd exchanged with Jett, it was almost as though she were remembering a pledge between two strangers. She said slowly, "Sometimes I wonder if the war hasn't changed everything too much, Jett."

"Things are different now, Shannon, but when it's all over and we come home, it'll be the same again. We'll have a big wedding at the house. I can see you now, coming down the stairs." He touched her hair. "You'll have to get somebody to fix your hair. We wouldn't want you looking as though you'd ridden your horse to the wedding. All the best people will be there."

Shannon tried to visualize it, but she couldn't. She'd thought about their wedding many times before Jett had left, but even then the picture had never come clear. She said, "Who would we ask? All the best people or only those with sympathies toward the South?"

Jett's mouth tightened. "Those who sided with the North are the same as dead to me."

"Don't we have enough dead already?"

Suddenly Jett remembered to whom he was talking. He smiled and put his arms around her. "You don't want to worry your pretty little head about all that. Let us men take care of the war."

Shannon wished she could, but the war was not something she could push away and let anyone else take care of. It was stalking her with its hands reaching out, trying to grasp ever more of her life. But she couldn't explain any of that to Jett, even if there had been time. It was easier just to let him put his arms around her and not say anything, to let him think that she was the same girl he'd left behind three years ago. He would be gone again in less than an hour, and there would be another time for talking and for explaining that the memory of a Yankee captain made it hard for her to want to keep the promise she'd made to Jett.

Clay opened the barn door. "Come on, Jett, you've had plenty of time for all that. We've got to go if we're going to catch General Morgan."

Jett waited another minute before he turned Shannon loose. Then he said, "Remember, you promised. You'll be mine the next time I come home, and no Yanks better come messing around here unless they're ready to die."

"Come on, Jett," Clay urged again. "Let's get the horses and go. I don't want to miss my first big fight."

Shannon said, "You can take the horses out back."

"I'll take all I want," Clay said. "They're my horses. In fact I promised a friend to bring him back a high-spirited one."

"Some of those you're taking are as high-spirited as you could possibly want, Clay."

"I don't know. I'll bet they're just your rejects, Shannon. How about that black horse you used to ride? Satin, wasn't it? We'll take him," Clay said with a nod.

"You can't have Satin. He's my horse," Shannon said. "No one can ride him but me anyway."

"Come now, sister. You may be a fairly decent rider, but you can't surpass my friend."

"He's still my horse, Clay. Papa gave him to me."

"But Papa had no right to give you any of my inheritance. We'll take the horse."

Shannon clamped her mouth together. She would not beg Clay, no matter how it hurt to see Satin go. Without another word she attached a lead rope to Satin's halter and handed it to Clay. "Tell your friend to go easy with him. He's never felt the whip."

She ran her hand over Satin's back, and the horse turned his head and nickered, sensing in her touch that something was wrong. She thought of all their early morning rides and the night she'd outrun Robards' men. She turned away then and left the barn. She couldn't . . . wouldn't watch them go, and waited till the air carried no more sounds of hoofbeats.

Then she remembered Toby and went back to the barn to find him. "Toby, you can come out now. They're gone."

The boy crawled out from behind a post in one of the stalls and then stretched his legs and arms.

"I'm sorry you had to stay there so long, Toby."

"Did I do right, Miss Shannon? I mean, with the gun and all. I thought that man was trying to hurt you."

"You did just what I wanted, Toby. You had no way of knowing that Jett was a friend."

"If you ask me, Miss Shannon, he didn't act much like no friend. And then they took even your horse."

"It wasn't really my horse. The man with Jett was Clay, my brother. Everything here . . . is his. I've known that since the day he was born."

"Then why do you work so hard on it? You could

go up north somewhere, where you'd be safe, Miss Shannon."

"I know, Toby, but I can't." She looked away from him, out at nothing, and said, "Clay may own it on paper, but I own it in my heart."

CHAPTER 21

As the days passed, bits and pieces of news about Morgan's raid through central Kentucky drifted out to Marshland. Morgan had taken Lexington just before midnight. People had come out on the streets waving the stars and bars when Morgan rode in, after the Union troops retreated. But the happy celebrating soon turned to puzzled dismay when the blazing fires lighted up the skies and the night became a cover for looters as some of Morgan's men ran wild through the streets. Ten thousand dollars disappeared from the Branch Bank of Kentucky, and no horse anywhere in town was safe.

When Morgan and his men finally moved out to Georgetown, there was a sigh of relief. Then came news that Morgan was burning Cynthiana. Shannon had gone to town for supplies, and the people she talked to there were confused. Morgan had been a hero to many of them, and they couldn't understand his letting his troops despoil a part of Kentucky where the people, by and large, had held Southern sympathies since the war's beginning. They talked openly to Shannon, knowing that Jett and Clay were with Morgan.

She looked in the direction of Cynthiana and said, "Maybe the reports were exaggerated. Maybe they burned only Union stores there, as they did here."

The man carrying out her purchases shook his head. "You didn't see them the other night. We weren't sure they wouldn't burn the whole of Lexington down. We bolted the doors and hid. I tell you, the war's done something terrible to them boys."

Before she left town, she heard that a Union force under the leadership of General Burbridge had caught up with Morgan and sent the Confederates into retreat. There was no information on casualties, just that Morgan had been surprised with almost no ammunition and that Burbridge had recovered many of the stolen horses.

Shannon sent Toby to town every day afterward to see what news he could hear. When several days passed with no word of Clay or Jett, Shannon breathed more easily, certain they must have gotten away. Then her mind turned to the problem of getting her horses back. It was ten days before the Union decided they would return the horses to the rightful owners, but only if they could prove their loyalty to the Union. Shannon went to town immediately.

She went first to see the horses. She picked out only three of her horses there, but her heart lifted when she saw that one of them was Satin. She hurried to the office that was handling the claims, but when she found herself in front of Colonel Robards' desk, her heart fell with a sickening thud.

Robards insisted on seeing her in private, but it wasn't until he spoke that Shannon realized he'd gotten the wrong idea about her being there. He sat back in his chair and looked at her for a long time. With a half-smile of smug satisfaction, he said, "So, you've finally come to your senses, Shannon."

Shannon stiffened in her chair. She wanted to get up and leave, but she wanted her horses more. She kept her voice brisk. "I've come about my horses. There are at least three of Marshland's stock in that bunch outside."

Robards looked at her blankly as her words sank in. "Your horses?"

"Yes. They were taken from my farm by Morgan's men." She held his stare boldly and wouldn't let him see her fear of him. It would give him too much advantage over her.

A smile worked across his face like a snake across a rock. "Horses! I should have known. It would have been better for you to come for the reason I mistakenly presumed. I'm getting tired of waiting, my dear."

Shannon pretended not to know what he meant and said, "I'm prepared to take the loyalty oath if necessary to get my horses."

Robards made a sound that might be called a laugh. It brought shivers to Shannon's back. He said, "Do you truly think that if you say a few clever words, everything will be settled and you can take your horses?"

Shannon said nothing, for that was exactly what she'd been hoping.

Robards went on. "It's not going to be quite that easy for you, Miss Marsh. The order that came down said the owners would have to prove their loyalty to the Union."

"I thought that taking the oath was sufficient proof," Shannon said, surprised to hear her voice coming out so clean and strong, as though Robards' leer wasn't making her sick inside.

"For some perhaps, but not for you." Robards

shuffled some things on his desk and picked up a pen before leaning back to stare at her again. "I believe that your brother, Clay Marsh, is with Morgan. Is that correct?"

"The horses were taken from my farm against my will," Shannon said.

"That's what all the people hereabouts would say but of course, we know better, now don't we, my dear? We know about the people who came out cheering when they heard Morgan was coming. You may have been one of them."

"The horses were taken against my will," Shannon repeated.

"Perhaps. But with your brother—who, as I understand, is the legal owner of Marshland—fighting with Morgan, it's hard to see any loyalty to the Union coming from his farm. We can't very well go giving Confederates their horses back, now can we?" Robards smiled and held up his hands in a helpless gesture. "I'd help if I could."

She didn't say a word, but she knew he wasn't finished.

He looked at her and then down at the pen he held in his hands. "Of course, there might be a way."

Shannon's eyes focused on the pen that he was twirling between his short, flat fingers. At the thought of those hands touching her, Shannon felt nausea rise in her. She stood up. "You may keep the horses."

She turned to go, but his next question stopped her. "How is your other brother? The one in the federal prison in Louisville." His voice was soft, but the threat was plain.

She turned back to face him, but he didn't wait for her reply. "I've heard things are getting worse down there," he said. "I might be able to help him. . . . but only as a favor to you, of course."

Shannon still could not speak; she stared unseeing at the pen in his hands as he methodically turned it.

He went on in a slow, measured voice. "I've heard that sometimes terrible things happen to men in prison." He paused then to punctuate the horror of that thought. "Of course, I could bring him here, where I could keep a closer watch on him. You know, I'm not an *un*important man in Lexington now, and . . . if I suggested it, they might even release him. But, if I said not . . ." Suddenly the pen snapped in two between his fingers.

Shannon jumped, and Robards smiled. He was enjoying every bit of the hold he had over her now.

"It all depends on you, my dear," he said. "I told you once before that I am a patient man, but there are . . . limits to my patience." His eyes swept over her. "I remember seeing women like you, before the war. So high and fine that they wouldn't even speak to the likes of me on the street. But you won't be so fine the day you finally come to me, Shannon. And you will come."

"Never," Shannon whispered.

He raised up his hand with the two pieces of pen still in it. "It's an awful thing to hold a man's life in your hands." Then casually he dropped the broken pen to the floor. "I'll be waiting for you, Shannon."

Shannon fled from the room and out into the summer sunshine as though the building were choking the very breath from her. She didn't know how long she'd been standing on the steps gulping in the air and trying to rid her mind of the picture of the pen rolling off Robards's hand before Toby found her.

"Miss Shannon, are you all right?" he asked.

It took a while for Shannon to clear her mind of Robards and respond to Toby. "I'm all right, but I didn't get the horses."

"That's what I came to tell you. They got a man

down there, trying to catch Satin. The poor horse has about gone wild."

It was a relief for her to have something else to think about as she followed Toby through the streets to the pen. A short, slim man was circling Satin with a rope. The blood seeping through his shirt sleeve was no redder than the color of his face.

The men standing about were baiting the man who held the rope, egging him on. "Come on, Sammy," one of them prodded. "Thought there hadn't never been a horse you couldn't handle. And this one's little to boot."

The man named Sammy glanced around at them. "I ain't through with this devil yet. I'll teach him a thing or two."

Satin stood still—as though he didn't even see the man until he'd almost got the lead rope on the horse, and then in a lightning-quick movement the horse put his teeth into the man's arm again, then trotted to the other side of the pen.

The other men laughed, and Sammy swore. "If I can't catch him with a rope, I will with a bullet," he said, going to get his gun.

"No," Shannon shouted. She hitched up her skirt and scrambled over the fence into the pen. "That's my horse. You leave him alone."

For a moment the laughter stopped as the men stared at her. Then Sammy said, "Now miss, I just reckon you'd better get on out of here and leave this up to me. Even if the horse is yours, I don't reckon he'd ever do you any good the way he is . . . wild and all."

"Give me the rope, and I'll catch him for you if you promise not to shoot him." Shannon held out her hand.

The men began laughing again, and one of them said, "What the heck, Sammy, give her the rope. It might be fun."

Sammy hesitated for a minute, and another voice called out, "You afraid the little woman might show you up?"

His face turned even redder as he handed her the rope. "If you're fool enough to try, I don't care. But don't expect no help from me."

Shannon looked at Satin. His sides were heaving in his panic. He could very well be too frightened to know her. Then she whistled, and his ears came up. She whistled again and held out her hand. Satin came over to her with a whinny as if to ask why she'd let all this happen to him.

She fastened the rope to his halter and spoke quietly into his ear. Satin nuzzled her neck. The men on the side began laughing again. One of them said, "Well, Sammy, I guess you don't know as much about horses as you thought. Go on out there and get him, now that the little lady has caught him for you."

Sammy began walking toward them, but Shannon said, "Stay away from him! You've done enough harm to him for one day." She led Satin over to the fence, knowing that she'd planned to do this all along. She wouldn't let them have Satin. Not a bunch of foot soldiers who knew nothing about handling a high-spirited animal.

She looked down at her long full skirts with impatience, but she'd ridden in skirts before, although never without a saddle and bridle. Still Satin would do whatever she wanted.

"Let's go home, boy," Shannon said. In one swift movement she hiked up her skirts and, grabbing the horse's neck, pulled herself up.

The men stood staring at her, not sure what they should do next.

"Open the gate," Shannon ordered.

Toby quickly slid open the gate and then melted

back into the crowd before anyone could be certain who had done it. That was all Satin needed—the open path in front of him and Shannon's order to go.

Outside town Shannon waited for Toby hidden in some trees, in case some of the men followed her, but they didn't. When Toby finally came in the carriage, she tied Satin to the back and climbed up in the seat beside him.

Toby's words poured out. "You shoulda seen the looks on those white folks when you up and got on that horse's back, Miss Shannon."

Shannon sighed. "It's something a lot of them will never forget." They'd hold it in their minds forever, another mark to hold against that Shannon Marsh, another proof to them that blood always shows through in the end. Then they'd shake their heads and wonder why Edward Clay had ever let his daughter marry that Irishman.

Suddenly Shannon laughed. "It doesn't really matter anymore that I don't act the lady I should." All at once the laugh died because she was remembering Robards letting the broken pen slide off his hand. Before it was all over, she might be even less a lady than she thought.

After putting up Satin, Shannon went into the house through the kitchen. The kitchen was empty, and the stove was cold. Shannon looked around, thinking how she'd always depended on Aunt Mamie to be there and how totally empty the room seemed without her.

"Aunt Mamie," she called out, eager for the reassurance just the sight of the old black woman gave her. Aunt Mamie was always the same. She was there to lean on, to depend on, and most of all to love Shannon just because she was and not because she did anything special. She stepped outside and called again. "Aunt Mamie!"

When Aunt Mamie came running out of her cabin,

Shannon knew immediately that this time Mamie needed her. "Child, where have you been?"

"What's wrong, Aunt Mamie?"

There were tears in Aunt Mamie's eyes. "It's Sally. My poor baby. She done been trying to have that baby of hers ever since morning, and the pain just keeps getting worse, but ain't nothing happening."

"But you know about babies, Aunt Mamie. Can't you do something?"

"I tried, Lord knows I've tried . . . everything I know." Aunt Mamie moaned. "I'm feared the baby's dead, and Sally will be soon. She's suffering awful."

"Did you send for the doctor?" Shannon demanded.

"I didn't rightly know what to do. Miss Olivia said to wait till you got back, but then I made Tom go on. But he ain't come back. He said the doctor might want a piece of paper, that he wouldn't come on his say so."

Shannon called for Toby, her voice ringing in the stillness of the late afternoon. Then she ran back to the kitchen to scribble out a note on a scrap of paper. Toby raced off, and Shannon followed Aunt Mamie into the cabin.

Sally lay on the bed, pale and limp. Aunt Mamie went over and pulled the cover away from Sally's abdomen and put her ear to the skin. A contraction seized Sally's body. It was so strong that it heaved her up and almost off the bed.

Shannon hesitated just inside the door, not knowing what to do. Then she looked across the room at the girl who'd shared her childhood and who'd always pretended she was her sister until the day she found out that she really was. Whatever had happened, they'd shared friendship and love, and now Shannon wanted somehow to share the pain that was tearing Sally apart.

She went to the bed and bathed Sally's face with a damp cloth.

Sally looked up as the pain eased for the moment. "Oh Shay, it's so awful. I don't think I can bear it."

Shannon gently stroked her forehead. "Just hang on, Sally. It'll be over soon."

Another pain grabbed Sally, and she bit her lips to keep from screaming. "I can see the head," Aunt Mamie shouted. "Just a little bit more, Sally. One more time."

But it was several more times, and each time she grimly and silently fought a new pain, Shannon thought Sally would faint away completely. But though her breath grew shallow and quick, Sally kept a hold on consciousness, while Shannon willed her strength to flow from her hands to Sally.

Then the baby was out, free from Sally's body. Shannon looked at the little brown body limp in Aunt Mamie's hands. It was a boy, perfect in every way but with no flush of life spreading through his body. Aunt Mamie worked over the baby, desperately trying to force a cry of life from him, but it was hopeless. The baby was stillborn. Sally pushed herself up on her elbows, looked at the baby, and then at Aunt Mamie. Aunt Mamie slowly shook her head.

Then the screams came spiraling up from deep inside Sally as she fought against the truth of that small still body. Shannon held her down to keep her from harming herself until finally a merciful darkness slipped over her.

It was a full minute after silence fell over the cabin before Shannon could move. She looked over at Aunt Mamie and the tears dripping unnoticed off her chin as she held the baby. "Poor little child," Aunt Mamie whispered, and Shannon wasn't sure if she'd meant the baby or the mother.

Shannon gently took the baby from her. "Take care of Sally now, Aunt Mamie."

Shannon washed the baby and wrapped him in a soft

white blanket and laid him in a box. There seemed to be no reason for him to be so still. Then Shannon looked back at Sally's face as she moaned in her sleep, and she wondered if there was ever any reason to suffering. It was something that just was.

CHAPTER 22

As June ended and July began with its hot, dry weather, Sally hovered between life and death. The doctor, who had finally arrived after the baby was born, didn't hold out much hope for Sally.

He'd looked into Sally's eyes. They had closed as she fought the truth and when they opened again held a curious blank look. He shook his head as Shannon followed him out to his buggy and put his bag on the seat before turning to her. "That's just the way it is with these people sometimes. I suppose they just decide there's no reason for them to get well," he said.

"You mean Sally might die?" She spoke the words painfully and from the need to hear them denied.

But the doctor said, "There's no reason why she should die except that maybe she wants to. Anyway, there's nothing I can do for her." He climbed into his buggy, looked at Shannon, and shook his head again. "A shame. A few years ago a light-skinned woman like her would have been worth a fortune, but now, well, it's a shame."

Shannon let him go on his way without a word. Then she went back into the cabin to sit by Sally. She wouldn't let Sally die. She'd make her want to live. She'd make her want to live for the future when people wouldn't look at her and calculate how much she was worth.

Shannon never left Sally's bed except to get a few hours of sleep and only when Aunt Mamie took her place. Aunt Mamie sat by Sally and grieved for her. Each day Shannon would say, "She won't die. We won't let her."

Aunt Mamie would look at Sally's wan face and shake her head with a resigned sadness before she left to go back to her chores.

The days passed dry and hot. There'd been no rain for over a month, and the pastures had begun to brown in the heat. Shannon paid little heed to the drought or anything else. Even when she heard there had been a great fire in Louisville, she didn't leave Sally to seek out news of Colin.

Then the news sought her out in a special message from Robards. He informed her that he'd arranged for Colin to be transferred to a prison in Lexington. That was all, but Shannon read the true meaning between the neatly written words of the message.

A few days earlier President Lincoln had ordered Kentucky into complete martial law, and the Army's power had grown overnight into a multi-armed monster that controlled people's lives. Shannon crumpled Robards's letter in her hand and turned to the man who'd brought the message.

"Will there be a reply?" the man asked, and Shannon was sure by his bold look that he knew exactly what Robards expected the reply to be.

She shook her head. "Just tell Colonel Robards that I received his message."

Then she went back in to Sally. Colin could take care of himself a little longer. He always had.

One day Sally's fever was finally gone. Her skin was cool to the touch, and she let Shannon feed her the soup Aunt Mamie brought. After she'd eaten, Shannon plumped her pillows, and Sally lay back down.

She kept her eyes on Shannon and said, "Why didn't you leave me alone, Shay?" Her voice was weak but clear.

"I just want to take care of you, Sally," Shannon said. "I love you."

Sally turned her head away then. She shut her eyes, and Shannon thought she'd gone back to sleep. But after a few minutes, Sally spoke again. "Do you really love me, Shay? Or is it that you need to prove something to yourself? Maybe to prove how noble you are to love a nigger."

"Sally!" Sally's words had hurt her, and Shannon started to deny it instantly, but then she couldn't. There was a tiny grain of truth in what Sally said. "I never thought of you as a nigger," Shannon said finally.

Sally raised up off her pillow and stared at Shannon. "But I am, Shay. I am. My skin's white . . . almost as white as yours, and I've been raised gentle, with you even teaching me to read. But don't let that fool you. I've got black blood, the black blood of my mother."

"You also have the blood of your father. The same blood as I have."

Sally lay back down. "You may be proud of that, but I am not. I've wished for years that Tom was really my father."

Shannon shut her eyes, and suddenly it was hard even to remember what her father had looked like. His face was sliding away into the forgotten and even forbidding past. "I can't hate him," she said.

"That is as it should be," Sally said quietly. "He loved you, but I was only a product of his passions."

"I still love you, Sally," Shannon said.

Sally smiled weakly, but her eyes were sad. "I suppose you do, Shay, but you don't love me enough to set me free."

"But I have already. I gave you your papers."

"There are different ways of being free. I mean really free."

"I don't understand, Sally."

"You wouldn't let me die, Shay," Sally said. "I wanted to die, but you wouldn't go away. Every day you were here demanding that I eat, demanding that I breathe. You wouldn't leave me alone."

"But why, Sally? Why did you want to die?"

Sally stared away at nothing, and it was a long time before she spoke. "If the baby had lived, I could have stood it. For him I would have lived, just like Mama lived for John. But without the baby I have nothing."

"We've had no word that Adam is dead. He'll be back."

"Do you truly think there'll be word of the blacks who die? No, they'll be nameless niggers thrown into a common grave." Sally's voice was bitter. She shook herself a bit before saying, "But it doesn't matter. Even if he lived through the war, Adam would never come back for me. I knew that the day he didn't come home with Tom. I guess . . . in a way I always knew he'd leave me."

"But of course he'll come back. He loves you."

Sally lifted her hands and let them fall limply back to the bed. "I suppose in his way he did. And if he'd known about the baby, he might have come back, but he didn't." She shut her eyes and went on in a flat voice. "Yes, he loved me, but my skin next to his was always white, always reminding him of the hatred he had for all whites. Even in moments of our deepest pleasure in each other, he hated the whiteness of my skin. He couldn't live with that forever."

Shannon knew nothing to say as she watched the sadness settle deep into Sally's eyes. She finally whispered, "And Aunt Mamie needs you."

"No . . . Mama loves me, has always loved me, and always will. Much the same as she loves you. But she didn't try to make me live. That very first night I heard her praying for me even though it was as though I were somewhere far away. Then she kissed me and said I was in God's hands. She knew, and she understood because she loves me."

"Knew what?"

"She knew that in my heart I had already died. Don't you see, Shay? You kept my body alive, but the best part of me has already died . . . died and been buried in that little box where you put my baby."

"But life is worth fighting for," Shannon insisted. "Any life."

Sally turned her face toward the wall. "I'm tired, Shannon. Go away and let me sleep." When Shannon hesitated, Sally went on. "You needn't worry. I won't die. The time for that is past."

So Shannon left her alone and went back out among her horses to work with Tom and Toby once more. It was good to be out in the air, away from the sickroom. Here in the barn things were simpler, just a matter of how much grain to feed and whether there was time for training. When she was working with a horse, she could almost forget to worry about the future.

Then she heard about the first retaliatory shooting. A man was shot in Henderson County by guerrillas, in the same way her father had been killed. But now there were new orders and new ways of dealing with guerrilla outrages. Two men were taken from the military prison in Louisville to Henderson, and then shot. The Army showed no mercy.

She went at once to see Colin to reassure herself that he was still all right. She hadn't been at this prison before. Since the day she'd ridden Satin away, she hadn't been to town at all. She was reluctant to take the chance of meeting Robards.

At first she didn't think she was going to be allowed to see Colin. The guards refused to let her enter, until one of them consulted a superior officer. Suddenly the path was opened to her.

For a moment after she stood facing Colin, she didn't want to believe that the man in front of her was her brother. He'd lost so much weight that his eyes had sunk back in his head, and his every movement seemed to take painful effort. "You look awful," she said.

He smiled, and some of the old Colin came to his face. "The food's not the best around here, but I'm making it. You look good, Shannon, but maybe a little tired. Have you been working too hard?"

Shannon shook her head. "I've been worrying though."

"What about, Sis? Surely not about me. I'm a tough old nut to crack, and when this war gets over, I'm going to walk out into the sunshine and begin like I ought to have years ago."

"Begin what?"

"My own life. I've lived too long in the shadow of Marshland. I've had a lot of time to think, and I'm going west. Maybe all the way to California. Nobody out there will care who my mother was." Colin reached over and touched her hand. "But how did you get in to see me? Most of the men's people are being turned away."

"I don't know. The last time I came to Louisville they wouldn't let me in."

"So that's why you didn't come. And I thought it was because you'd finally decided to listen to me."

"I always listen to you, Colin."

Colin half laughed. "And then do whatever you want. Is that right, Shannon?"

"I would have come sooner. I knew you were here in Lexington, but Sally was sick. She lost her baby."

"Is she all right now?"

"She's up and about, but she's not better. I don't know if she'll ever be better. When her baby died, she lost the will to live."

Colin was looking at her with sympathy. "In time she may get better, Shannon. They say time can heal anything, but you can't make her well any more than you can turn back to a happier day."

"I know." Shannon looked down the hall to the guard who was beginning to sway impatiently. "They said I couldn't stay long, but I had to see you and find out if you were all right."

"And do you see?"

"I see," Shannon said. She saw that he was not all right but that at least he was alive, and as long as he was alive there was hope.

Colin caught her frown. "You've heard about the shootings. Is that what's bothering you?"

Shannon hesitated and then nodded her head. "It made me afraid for you."

"They don't have anything to do with me." Then when he saw the doubt that still remained in her eyes, he went on. "I'm not a guerrilla. I'm a Confederate soldier. They won't shoot soldiers."

"Of course not," Shannon agreed, but she was remembering her interview with Robards.

Almost as if Colin read her mind, he said, "Remember the promise you made to me when I was first captured last year?"

Shannon shook her head. "I made no promises."

"Shannon," Colin said. His voice was soft and insistent.

Shannon shook her head again. "You asked me to promise, but I didn't."

"But you did, Shannon, and I'm holding you to that promise. It was a trust between us. You are to make no deals with anyone on my behalf."

When Shannon didn't say anything, he said with a touch of panic in his voice, "You haven't already, have you, Sis? I know Robards was the one who saw to it that I was sent here, but it wasn't because of anything you've done. Was it?"

"No, Colin," Shannon said quietly. "I've made no deals with Robards."

"Keep it that way." It wasn't a request. It was an order. His face softened then, and he said, "I'm the one who's supposed to see that *you* never get hurt. Remember?"

"I remember," Shannon whispered. "But all that seems so far away now. Something out of another time. Maybe even out of another life."

"No. It was part of us. You and me, brother and sister." Colin smiled and closed his eyes. "I remember the first time I saw you, with your big green eyes set in that baby face and all that fiery red hair sticking out every which way. I don't know exactly how to describe those eyes. They were so alive with life and yet so innocent. I remember how the feeling swelled up in me that I wanted to protect that innocence. It was so beautiful and fragile, like a tiny wildflower blooming in the woods that you step around carefully to leave undisturbed."

He opened his eyes and stared at her intently. Suddenly the smile was gone, and he said, "Your eyes still are that way, Shannon. Somehow you've hung on to that innocence, despite all that's happened. I won't let it be crushed because of me."

It was a minute before Shannon could speak, and then her voice was barely loud enough for him to hear. "I can't let you die."

"You know, Sis, there have been times I wished I could die just to get out of this place. There are things worse than dying," Colin said without feeling. Then there was a charge of feeling in his voice as he continued, "Knowing you'd let that depraved coward put a finger on you would be a thousand times worse than dying, Shannon. I couldn't live knowing you did that for me."

"Don't talk like that, Colin."

"I'm sorry, Sis. Like I said, this is all just talk. I'm a soldier. They won't bother me. They'll just keep me here until the war's over." He patted her hand. "Don't come back to see me again. Maybe Robards will forget about me if he doesn't see you."

Shannon nodded, and then aware that the guard was approaching, she whispered, "I don't know what else to say."

Colin smiled a little. "Say I love you, brother, and I promise to do what you say."

"I love you, brother," Shannon repeated and then hesitated for only a second before she went on. "And I promise to do what you say."

"See . . . it's not so hard to let me have my way sometimes," Colin said as he stood up, resignation returning to his face when he turned to follow the guard. As Shannon watched, she thought that he no longer even looked like her brother. Then he glanced back at her and winked. She winked back despite the tears that threatened to spill over.

She had moved only a few steps down the hallway toward the door when she felt someone watching her. She looked over her shoulder, and there at the end of the hall was Robards. He didn't speak to her or beckon. He was there just watching and waiting, and his very stillness was more threatening than if he'd come after her.

Shannon could scarcely keep from running as she hurried outside. Standing in the heat of the sun, Shannon felt cold, as though a deep shadow hid the brightness of the sun and would never allow it to penetrate and shine upon her again.

CHAPTER 23

August came and brought rain to relieve the drought, but it brought no relief for Shannon's fears. She tried to shut herself away from it by staying at Marshland, but the horror sought her out. Nearly every time Toby went to town for supplies, he'd carry a message back to the farm. Sometimes it was a newspaper clipping and other times a copy of a military report stuffed into an envelope. Nothing more, but Shannon knew who sent them.

She read the report of yet another retaliatory killing by the Army before she carefully burned the paper until nothing but light wisps of black ashes were left. She felt as though, inside, she was turning into the same black ash as fear and reason fought to control her. She couldn't let Robards kill Colin—not if she could prevent it. But she'd promised Colin. Still it wasn't the promise that stopped her as much as the sickness that rose in her when she thought of Robards.

She went to bed at night with the worry settling over her mind like a black cloud and got up every morning with it still there. She took Satin out to ride in the early morning cool, but the time had passed when the wind in her hair could blow her problems away. Her only peace came from seeing the farm lying unchanged around her. Of course, there were fewer horses, and some of the fences had been torn down or fallen into disrepair; but the land was there, holding the same promise it had always.

She tried not to think about what would happen when Clay and Jett came home from the war. She tried not to wonder if there'd still be a place for her here then, because she was no longer sure she could marry Jett knowing that she loved Randal.

The thought of Randal comforted her. The memory of the last kiss they'd shared was as bright and clear in her mind as the first star each evening. But she'd heard nothing from him since then, and sometimes late at night when the dark closed in on her, the thought that he might be dead would force its way into her mind. All the stories of the battles would march through her mind—the Wilderness, Spottsylvania, and especially Cold Harbor, where so many had died so quickly.

Then she'd recall the gentle smile in Randal's eyes, and for a while she'd be reassured. The night would be night again and not a spreading darkness about to swallow her up. She'd pull the thought of Randal up over her like a blanket, and sleep would come. But morning always brought the reality that Randal was not close by but faraway on some unknown battlefield.

The sight of Sally moving about her chores like a ghost of her former self became a symbol of the gloom hanging over Clay Manor. It touched them all with hopelessness. Through Sally, Aunt Mamie seemed to be reliving all her own grief, and no more were songs hummed or sung in the kitchen. Shannon's mother stayed hidden away in her room, waiting for Clay to return and refusing anything Shannon had to offer. Shannon no longer even made the effort of a daily visit to her. There was no way she could help her mother, especially not now with her own worries tearing her apart.

Only at the barn did the routine continue in some semblance of normalcy. The horses knew nothing of man's wars, and Blackberry nuzzling Toby's pockets for a windfall apple could still bring a smile to Shannon's lips. The little filly was small and shaggy, stunted by her hard beginning, but when she ran there was a smooth beauty in her movement. Then there was Bittersweet with his promise outlined in his clean lines. Sometimes when Shannon watched him race across the pasture, she could feel some of the old eagerness return. When the time came, it would be good tc begin work with a colt that showed such natural running ability.

So the days of August drifted into September with a sameness that belied the panic growing in Shannon. If only the war would end, she prayed; but though Grant had Lee's army undei siege at Petersburg, there was no sign that the Southern army was collapsing.

September brought news of General Morgan's death in Tennessee. All the while in Kentucky, the guerrilla bands were increasing in number and strength as the Union troops futilely chased after them. Even when a band was cornered and cut down, it seemed that two new outlaw groups sprang up to take its place. In an effort to control the guerrillas rampaging across the state, the Army struck back by stepping up their own shootings and hangings as a deterrent to the outlaws.

October edged by, with the crisp pleasant days of autumn gloriously painting the trees, but no one at

Marshland took any notice. Shannon counted the passing days and tried to control her panic by remembering Colin's words. He was a soldier, not an outlaw guerrilla, and the Union would honor the prisoner of war. But these words rang hollow to Shannon. She longed to go visit him again, but the thought of Robards kept her on the farm.

Finally there was no pushing away her worries any longer. The time for facing them came in with the first brisk threat of winter weather. On the first day of November, a man in Woodford County died at the hands of a band of guerrillas. Unlike her father's death, this death would not go unnoticed by the authorities. There would be a payment in blood.

The next day the afternoon shadows were already moving across the field when Shannon received the message. The order had been given. Four men were to be taken from the prison in Lexington to a farm in the county and shot. Colin's name jumped out at Shannon from the list. Robards had grown tired of waiting.

"Where?" Shannon asked the young soldier who'd brought her the message. She glanced frantically at the sun and knew Robards hadn't meant for her to have time. "And when?"

The man's face was not without pity for Shannon. He hadn't quite gotten used to the killings yet himself even though he'd watched his share. Now he shook his head. "I don't rightly know, miss. There ain't nothing you can do about it now anyhow."

"He can't do this."

"It could be he already has," the soldier said. "I'm sorry, miss, but your brother ought not to have gotten mixed up with them guerrillas."

"But he didn't." Her voice cried out for some bit of justice.

The young soldier turned away from the pain on her face. There wasn't anything he could do, except wish the

Colonel had sent someone else as his messenger. Looking into this woman's wounded green eyes was worse than staring down a cannon. "I'm real sorry, miss," he said as he mounted his horse.

"Wait," Shannon said. "Will you show me where?"

He refused to look at her again. "I wish I could help you, miss. Really I do. But I don't rightly know the spot myself. I come from up yonder in the hills. This here settlement country is new to me. All I know is they said something about a Major Smith's farm over in Woodford."

He rode away quickly before she could stop him again. Shannon wasted no time watching him. She ran for the barn. There had to be a way she could stop this. She had Satin saddled and ready to go in minutes. Pausing only long enough to tell Toby that she might not be back until tomorrow, she was soon flying across the fields, recklessly plunging into every short cut that came to mind. She pushed Satin as she'd never pushed any horse before, and the horse, sensing her urgency, responded with all his power.

Two or three times she slowed down enough to be sure that she was still headed in the right direction. The sun was already beginning to dip below the horizon when a farmer volunteered the information that he'd seen a group of Union soldiers pass his way.

"Did they have prisoners with them?" Shannon asked.

The farmer nodded. "That mean anything to you?"

Shannon didn't answer but began to move away.

"You'd best rest your horse," the man called. "You been riding him too hard."

But Shannon had no time. She had to get to Colin before it was too late.

She came around a bend in the road, and there ahead of her was the line of blue she'd been chasing across the countryside. And even though she'd been expecting what she now saw in the pasture, the sight still shocked her. The surrounding fields were peaceful with the quiet of the evening falling across them. In the distance a few cows raised their heads from their grazing and then dropped their mouths to the ground once again. They understood nothing of the blue figures moving about slowly, setting up a moment of death.

Shannon picked out Colin immediately, but he hadn't looked up at the sound of her horse. Then she saw Robards off to one side. Shannon slid off her horse and ran to him.

"You've got to stop them," she said, the panic in her voice ringing in the still air.

His eyes swung from the men in the field to her. There was satisfaction there but no mercy. He said, "And so you've come at last, my dear. I told you all along that you would come to me."

"You've got to stop this," Shannon repeated.

"You made good time from your farm. I never expected you to make it." He looked at the field and back at her. "So. You want me to stop this."

"Yes," Shannon said. There was no more time for backing down now. She'd do whatever had to be done to save Colin's life.

Robards's eyes burned into hers, and his hand came up to her arm. "I might be able to see that your brother is returned to Lexington to prison. I suppose three deaths would do as well as four, but it would be a lot of bother. Perhaps if I could be sure that bother will be worthwhile." His hand slid from her arm to her waist. "You're still a desirable woman, even with the smell of horse about you." He started to pull her close to him.

"Shannon!" Her name shot across the field.

She turned her head, and there was Colin, standing tall and straight with no surrender about him. Even with the distance between them, she knew what his eyes were demanding from her. Inside her something screamed. She wanted to shut his demand away from her, but she couldn't ignore it. She had to obey. It was the only way to prove how much she loved him.

She jerked loose from Robards' grasp and ran to Colin. "I could've saved you," she cried. "Why wouldn't you let me save you?"

Colin shook his head, and a ghost of a smile touched his face. "It's time for me to die, Shannon," he said. "There's nothing anyone can do."

"But it's because of me that he's doing this."

"It's because of you that I don't mind dying so much." He leaned over and touched his lips to hers. "I've loved you since the moment I first saw you, but I never loved you as a brother loves a sister."

"Colin," Shannon began, but he cut her off.

"Shh. Don't say anything, Shannon. Just be happy for me, Shannon. The rest doesn't matter. Now go away from this and pretend it didn't happen."

"Get that woman out of the way!" Robards commanded.

"Colin, I won't let you die," Shannon said as though she might yet keep it from happening, but her voice already carried the pain of grief.

The two soldiers bearing down on her heard and understood her pain, and they hesitated.

"Be happy, Shannon," Colin said again before the soldiers took hold of her gently and forcibly moved her away from him.

One of the men stayed by her side with his hand wrapped tightly around her arm. "I'm sorry about this, miss, but orders are orders. Let me take you back where you won't have to watch."

Shannon didn't resist. She let him begin leading her away, but then Robards' voice cut across their path.

"Miss Marsh will stay, Corporal." Robards's eyes showed the pleasure he was getting from her pain. He said, "She needs to see the results of rebellion."

So Shannon turned back to the field and quietly waited. She was defeated. There was nothing she could do but endure the horror proceeding out in the pasture before her eyes.

For the first time she noticed the other men lined up beside her brother. Two of the others were facing death with the same stoic resignation as Colin. It was almost as if they had already been released, leaving only a shell of themselves behind to face this last bit of inhumanity. But the last man was staring about wild-eyed, as though he might still find a way to take flight.

Shannon was vaguely aware of the soft sounds of the approaching night welling up around her. Then the high-pitched scream of a screech owl made her tremble as she watched the line of blue straighten out and take form opposite the four prisoners. She looked straight at Colin then and saw that he'd sought her out in his last moment. His smile reached across the field and touched her. She must have moved forward because the soldier's hand tightened on her arm.

Then suddenly the command was shouted out to fire, followed immediately by the exploding sound of the guns. Colin's body was pushed back by the force of shots finding their target.

It was a minute before Shannon realized the unearthly screams she heard were coming from her own throat. The soldier held her in a bear hug as she struggled to get free.

"Easy, miss," he said, as though he were attempting to calm a wild animal. "He's dead. It won't do no good to go to him now."

All at once Shannon thought of the pleasure Robards must be getting out of the pain she was feeling. She forced herself to be still and refused to release her sobs though they almost strangled her. The soldier continued to hold her for another minute. He said, "I'm sorry, miss. I sure do wish I could've spared you that."

For the first time Shannon looked at him. He was a plain middle-aged man who looked as though he might have been a farmer before he'd joined the Army. He'd gone to war to save the Union, and now the Army had him shooting down unarmed men in a tragic play of vengeance. He still had his arms around her, and he was comforting her as he might his own daughter. Shannon wanted to say something to thank him for caring, but the sight of the blue he wore, the same blue as Robards, stilled the words in her before she could speak.

He said, "You'd better get away from here now before the Colonel gets back to you. There's a little house about a mile down the road. They're friends of mine. Just tell them that Billy Joe sent you, and they'll see to it that you're safe tonight."

"But my brother?" Shannon said.

"He's gone, miss . . . maybe somewhere better than this hell we're making on earth. Now go on before Colonel Robards looks around this way."

Night was falling swiftly now, and Shannon walked away from the opening into the shadow of trees close to the road. She whistled softly, and Satin came to her. It took only minutes to find the house the soldier had told her about.

At the name Billy Joe, the door swung open. There were questions on the lips of the old couple standing inside, but they went unasked when the two saw Shannon's face. Shannon followed the man to the barn to care for Satin, but Satin was too tired to fight against a stranger's touch. He stood quietly while the man rubbed him down and fed him.

At the house the woman had a plate ready for

Shannon, but when Shannon shook her head, she took the food away without comment and led her to a small room where a cot had been readied for her.

"I laid out one of my nightgowns," the woman said. "It ain't fancy, but it's clean and worn soft."

Shannon stood in the middle of the room in a confused daze. Then the sobs she'd been pushing back broke through and shook her body. The woman put her arms around Shannon and began to pat and sooth her. After a while when Shannon had quieted, she gently and patiently undressed her as if she were a helpless child and put her to bed.

Before she picked up the candle to leave, the old woman leaned over her and kissed her forehead. "Whatever it is, child, likely it won't seem so bad come morning."

Then she left the room, closing the door softly behind her. Shannon lay on the narrow cot and stared into the darkness of the room. The woman's words hung in the air, but they were no comfort. Tomorrow could never change what had already happened.

CHAPTER 24

The weeks following Colin's death took on a hazy unreality for Shannon. She went through her days doing what had to be done, but often at the end of the day, she could not remember how the hours had passed. The shadow of the war that had been stalking her had finally caught and defeated her.

When her father had been killed, Shannon had grieved for him, but she felt no guilt. Nothing she could have done would have prevented his death. That wasn't true with Colin, and that fact tormented her as the days passed. If she had gone to Robards soon enough, Colin would still be alive. Over and over she relived that horrible moment when Colin reeled back from the force of the shot, until she sometimes had to shut her mind down to all thought.

Aunt Mamie alternated between begging and scolding Shannon to bring her away from her grief.

Finally one day Shannon said, "Why don't you leave me alone, Aunt Mamie?" She looked up and her eyes fell on Sally moving silently through the hall. "Why don't you talk to Sally instead?"

Aunt Mamie turned sad eyes toward her daughter. For a minute Sally almost seemed to notice, but then she drifted on away. "Why didn't you leave Sally alone, Shannon?" Aunt Mamie said.

Shannon dropped the dress she was mending into her lap. She said, "Because I wanted her to live. I wanted her to be like she used to be."

"And I want you to live, child," Aunt Mamie said.

"But what about Sally? Don't you care about her?"

For a moment Aunt Mamie's hands fell idle on the dough she was kneading. Then she began working the dough again, slowly and thoughtfully. She said, "It's different. Sally lost so much that I'd just be tormenting her if I tried to get her to come back from wherever she's gone to get away from her sorrow. But you child, you've got your whole future ahead of you."

Shannon looked down. "There're too many dark spots in the future."

"There's always been dark spots for you, Shannon. You just never noticed them before because you was too busy making them light. You always were a fighter, ready for anything. It just ain't like you to sit around grieving like this."

Shannon picked up the dress and began making small exact stitches around the patch. Aunt Mamie just didn't understand what had defeated Shannon. She'd shot Colin just as sure as if she'd had her finger on one of the triggers.

Aunt Mamie went on. "Mr. Colin wouldn't want you to be going on like this, Shannon child. You know he wouldn't. I don't reckon I ever saw another brother dote so on his sister. If you'd asked him for the moon and stars he'd 'a' tried to fetch them for you." When Shannon didn't look up or respond, Aunt Mamie sighed. She pounded the dough and muttered to herself. "Maybe if that captain came back, he could get through to you."

But even the comfort of Randal's memory had deserted Shannon during this darkness of her spirit. Always when she pulled Randal up in her mind, there was the blue uniform, the symbol of the hated Union army, and all she could see was that line of men in blue raising their guns before her eyes.

The days passed as the routine on Marshland carried forward. Snow fell sometimes. The sun shone on other days, but to Shannon they were all the same.

Colin had been dead two months when Shannon looked up from the horse she was exercising to see the rider in blue waiting at the end of the track. She knew it was Randal at once, but the joy that bounded up inside her faded immediately.

Randal watched her walking the horse slowly toward him and knew something was wrong. There was a droop about her shoulders and a lack of interest in the way she sat her horse. When she came close enough for him to see the flatness in her eyes, a strange fear began growing inside him. For months he'd been looking forward to the moment he'd see her again. The long nights on the battleground had been easier to bear because always there was the feeling that Shannon was safe on her farm. He'd seen her going about her chores and riding the black horse like the wind across the pasture. He'd remembered the sweet response of her lips to his the last time they'd been together, and he'd been almost sure that when he returned, she'd listen eagerly as he declared his love for her. But something had happened. She hadn't been protected here. The violence of war had not spared this bit of space he'd felt was so far from the battlefields he'd left behind him.

She didn't greet him but sat on her horse watching him for a long time, almost as though she expected him to disappear. The darkness of her mind had been so complete that she'd never really expected to see Randal again. She'd expected him to be lying in some shallow grave just as Colin was. But Randal didn't disappear. He was there with his soft eyes so full of tenderness that Shannon couldn't completely deny the warming spark beginning to kindle inside her. Still she pushed it away The war had a way of taking those she loved from her, and the war was not yet over.

Finally she spoke. "Good morning, Captain. What brings you to Marshland? Not Union business, I hope." Bitterness had crept into her words.

Randal smiled. He wanted more than anything to take her into his arms, but whatever was wrong was separating her from him too much for that. So he said, "You, Shannon. You were always what brought me to Marshland."

He thought for a minute she might cry. The wounded look was deep in her eyes. He'd seen men come away from battles with the same expression of shock and exhaustion as if they could bear no more. He'd have to go easy with her. "What's wrong, Shannon?"

She turned away from him and slid off her horse. "I've got to walk Folly now, Captain." She started off to the barn.

Randal felt as though she'd dismissed him and even wanted him to go. But he wouldn't leave until he found out what had happened to her. He dismounted and followed her. "It's not captain any more," he said, searching for something to say. "I'm a major now. If you stick around long enough in the Army, they have to promote you."

Her eyes went to his uniform and then quickly away.

"Not that it matters," he said.

Again she didn't respond, but as they walked together, she seemed more accepting of his presence. He was content to match his pace to hers.

Then she said, "The war? Is it over?" She had purposely buried herself on the farm away from the news, forbidding Toby to bring back any kind of news from town.

"No, not yet. But my term of enlistment was up, so when I heard that my father had died, I went home to see about my mother. I'm on the way back to join up again now."

"Why?"

Randal thought a moment before he answered. "I can't just ride away from it. I have to see it through. I don't think it will be long now. We've heard that Lee's men are about out of supplies. They can't hold out much longer, and if Lee surrenders, it'll be the same as over."

"Then the Union will win?"

"There's not been much doubt of that for a long time," Randal said.

"But it's not over yet, is it?"

Randal shook his head. "The Johnny Rebs don't give up easy."

The talk of war made Shannon tremble. It brought too near the scenes of death she had been trying so desperately to shut out. Mechanically, she took the horse back to his stall and began rubbing him down. She knew that Randal was waiting for her to tell him what had laid this darkness upon her, but she couldn't. Not yet. Maybe never. She put the brush down and stepped out of the stall. "I'm sorry about your father," she said.

"Pa had a hard life," Randal said. "It just finally caught up with him."

"You don't sound too upset," Shannon said.

Randal's voice was gentle. "Pa was good to me, and I loved him. His dying can't change that or make the memories I have of him fade away."

Shannon turned away from Randal before he could see the tears his words brought to her eyes.

"It's different," he said. "Pa was old, and he'd been sick a long time. Not like your father's death at all."

Shannon seemed not to hear him. She said, "Would you like to see the foal you helped save last year?"

"You mean it lived?"

"With Toby mothering her, she didn't have much choice." Shannon led the way through the barn. "I think Toby has her outside right now."

They watched the boy and the young filly for a few minutes without speaking. Finally Randal said, "She's a good-looking animal . . . quick and light on her feet. You might win some races with her later on."

"I think Toby will spoil her too much ever to be able to train her properly. But he might want to race her. I don't know."

"Then you really gave the horse to him."

Shannon nodded. "The same as I gave them all their freedom." She was quiet for a long time, staring at nothing, before she said, "But I'm not sure I can give what isn't mine to give."

"You mean everything really belongs to Clay?"

Shannon nodded. "He told me that all this was his, and he's right. All except that horse and Toby. I bought Toby myself, and now he's free. It doesn't matter what the President's emancipation paper says about Kentucky. Toby's free, and somehow I aim to make sure that horse stays his."

Randal saw Shannon's eyes lift from Toby and his horse to the land lying behind him and around them. He said, "You don't need it, Shannon. It's not that important."

"But it is, Randal," she said. "It's the only thing left I can depend on."

This time Randal couldn't stop himself. He reached out and pulled her into his arms. She came willingly like a lost bird seeking shelter from the storm. "What's wrong, Shannon?" he asked again.

Suddenly she stiffened and pulled away from him. Then, as if they'd never touched, she said, "Will you come in and let Aunt Mamie fix you something to eat? I know she'd take pleasure in seeing you again."

Randal followed Shannon. He wouldn't press her. He would wait until she was ready to share her pain with him.

A big smile split Aunt Mamie's face when they went into the kitchen. "Lands of Goshen, if it ain't the captain."

"Major now," Shannon said to Aunt Mamie. "I thought maybe you could fix him something to eat while I change out of my workclothes."

Randal reached out a hand and stopped Shannon before she could leave the room. "You will come back, won't you?"

Shannon looked away from the plea in Randal's eyes and said, "Of course."

Only then did Randal let her go. He watched her disappear down the hall before he turned back to Aunt Mamie. He could see the pain etched deep in the new lines on the old black woman's face. "What's happened here, Aunt Mamie?" he asked.

Aunt Mamie shook her head. "It's been a time of grief, I'm telling you, Major. First the men being gone like they were and then Adam not coming back and my Sally having her baby the way she did. I don't reckon there's anything harder on a woman than bringing forth a dead baby. Sally woulda died if it hadn't been for Shannon. Shannon just wouldn't let her go. She sat by her every minute of the day and would have the night too, if I hadn't."

"Is Sally all right now?"

Aunt Mamie looked at him. "You met my Sally, didn't you? You was the one who saw to it that the soldiers didn't bother her." She waited for Randal to nod before she went on. "She ain't the same now. She's just shut everything away from her. I reckon maybe in time she'll come back to us."

"But there's surely more. That's not what's changed Shannon."

"I suppose it might be part of it. All that's happened way back to when her pa got shot. Maybe seeing how Sally shut her pain away, Miss Shannon thought she could do the same. But there ain't no way she can do that. She always was a fighter, and it just nigh on tears my heart out to see her giving up like this."

"You still haven't told me what happened," Randal insisted.

"It was that Robards. He's one of the devil's own." Aunt Mamie put a plate of food in front of Randal and then sank down in a chair across from him. "She should be telling you all this. Not me."

Randal reached over and grabbed Aunt Mamie's shoulders. Robards's name had opened an ugly fear inside Randal. "Tell me! I have to know."

Aunt Mamie's eyes filled with fear at the strange look on the major's face, but then she nodded with understanding. "I'll tell you what I know, which ain't the whole story, just bits and pieces I've been able to guess at."

Randal sat back and waited. Aunt Mamie took a deep breath and said, "It started way back when they captured Mr. Colin. Maybe before that. Maybe even before the war, the first time Robards set eyes on Shannon. But it got worse when he brought Mr. Colin to Lexington and put him in jail there. Miss Shannon went in to see him once, but then she wouldn't go no more. She wouldn't even talk about Mr. Colin. She just walked around with a frown growing between her eyes, and she'd nigh on jump out of her skin if you so much as said boo. I guess I oughta tried to get her to talk about it some, but what with the way Sally was we just all sorta shut ourselves away from each other."

Aunt Mamie looked down and began folding the corner of her apron over into straight creases. "Things just sorta slid on by, and that's when the army went to shooting prisoners. About the same time, Toby began bringing letters home from town when he went in after supplies. I saw Shannon burning one of them, and her hand shook so that she like to never get the paper caught."

"What were they about?"

"I don't know, but I'm sure that Robards had something to do with them." Aunt Mamie shook her head. "Then the soldier came back last fall. I reckon it was around the first of November. Soon as he left, Shannon took off, not even telling nobody where she was going. I saw her riding away, not bothering with the roads but leaping all those fence across the pastures. She didn't come back till the next day. And then all she'd say was that Mr. Colin was dead . . . that the Army had done it . . . that it wouldn't help none to cry. She said crying wouldn't change nothing. Then before she cleaned up or anything, she went and got out her daddy's guns and loaded them. I asked her what she was doing that for. She looked at me with the coldest eyes I ever saw and said she was going to kill him if he ever stepped foot on Marshland."

"Robards?"

Aunt Mamie lifted her hands and let them fall back in her lap. "She wouldn't say. I thought maybe after she'd rested she'd be all right again, but since then she ain't done nothing but grieve. She don't seem to care about nothing no more. Oh, she works with the horses and all, but it ain't the same. All the fight's gone out of her."

Randal looked away from Aunt Mamie to the hall. Shannon had had time to change by now. He said, "I don't think she's going to come back down."

"Can't you help her, sir?" Aunt Mamie begged with tears in her eyes. Suddenly she dropped out of her chair to her knees. "I just can't bear seeing both of my babies like this. Please, sir, help her."

Randal put out a hand and lifted up Aunt Mamie. "You don't have to do that, Aunt Mamie. I want to help her. If you only knew how much I love her." His eyes went back to the doorway. "But will she let me help her?"

CHAPTER 25

Randal walked quietly up the steps and down the hall. He felt awed by the house with its elegant hand-carved stair rails and the crystal chandeliers hanging from the tall ceilings. But it wasn't the rich beauty of the house that bothered him as much as the deep aura of sadness that hung over it. It was hard for him to believe this hallway had ever heard the cries of happy children at play. Rather, he imagined that Shannon as a child had slipped along the hall and stairway as silently as he moved now, running from its solemn gloom to the warmth and love of Aunt Mamie's kichen.

He stopped in front of the second door on the left, Shannon's room. Across the hall was Mrs. Marsh's room. Aunt Mamie had warned him not to disturb her. "It might frighten Miss Olivia if she was to look out and see you. Miss Olivia ain't well, you know. She always was weakly, but since Mr. Clay left, she's just nigh on wasted away." Aunt Mamie looked across the room at nothing. "Miss Olivia, she never had no fire about her. She was too gentle for the likes of the master, but I thought Shannon had enough fire in her to fight anything."

"It'll be all right," Randal had assured the old black woman, but now here in the hallway he was touched by the pervading sadness. He turned away from the mother's door. He couldn't help her, but he wouldn't let Shannon become part of the gloom. He knocked lightly on her door.

"I'm too tired to come down, Aunt Mamie," she called without coming to the door. She paused a moment before saying, "Tell the major goodbye for me."

Randal slowly pushed open the door. Shannon sat at her dressing table in her chemise. Her hair fell around her shoulders, but here and there he could see a scattering of freckles, and he wanted to touch his lips to each and every one of them. He studied the delicate line of her arm as she moved a comb through the tangles of her hair.

Her eyes met his in the mirror, and for a long moment she didn't move. Then she dropped her hands and her eyes. "You shouldn't have come up here, Randal," she said quietly.

Randal carefully closed the door behind him. He walked over behind her and took the comb from her hand. "Here. Let me help you." He began to gently work the comb through the waves of her hair. "Tell me if it pulls."

"What do you know about combing a woman's hair?" Shannon's eyes came up to meet his briefly and then skittered away again, as though she were afraid of what she saw there.

"My horses never complained when I worked on them."

She almost smiled. "They didn't have manes like mine."

"That's true," he said, fighting the urge to bury his face in her thick hair. He exchanged the comb for a brush and brushed a lock at a time, letting it slide richly off his hands.

She closed her eyes and sat quietly. After a moment the stiffness in her back began to ease away until she was leaning against him lightly.

Even after every tangle had been combed and brushed smooth, Randal continued to pull the brush gently through her hair. Sometimes when his hand touched the softness of her skin under her hair, it was all he could do to keep from letting it linger there. In the mirror he saw the delicate swell of her breasts under the thin cloth of her chemise, but he made his eyes turn back to her face. There were new lines around her eyes, and a strained tightness about her mouth. But she was still the most beautiful women he'd ever seen.

He wanted to kneel down beside her and touch his lips to her closed eyes and to the delicate hollow in her neck. He wanted her to be his in every way. He felt she would let him, that she wouldn't fight against him, but even as he thought about it, he knew it wasn't really what he wanted. He wouldn't take advantage of her in a weak moment. She was too precious to him.

So he continued brushing her hair, choking down the rush of desire that flooded through him. Owning her body for a few minutes could never compare with receiving her love for a lifetime.

Finally Shannon opened her eyes and looked at him in the mirror. "Why did you follow me up here? You should have just gone away."

"I wanted to help you, Shannon," he said.

"You mean, you're not here to rape me," she said

with a kind of detached interest. "There are others who have entertained the idea."

A touch of challenge came to her eyes, and she seemed more like the Shannon he knew. He smiled. "I'd rather you came to me willingly."

Suddenly her eyes went cold. Her voice was barely a whisper. "That's what Robards said." She dropped her eyes to stare at the table. "But I didn't go."

Randal's grip tightened on the handle of the brush. "Has Robards harmed you?"

Shannon didn't look up. "It would have been better if he had," she said.

Randal pulled her up and around to face him. "No. That could never be better." His hands tightened on her shoulders. "I'll kill him if he's so much as touched you," he said. His hatred took him away from her for a moment, but then he was back, pulling her to him and wrapping his arms around her.

Shannon felt as though she could stay in his arms forever. Suddenly the shadows casting about her seemed to grow lighter.

Randal spoke softly into her hair. "I love you, Shannon. I've loved you almost from the first moment I saw you, and no matter what happens, I'll always love you."

She wanted to tell him she felt as he did, but the darkness had lain over her mind too long, and the words caught and stuck in her throat. She held the words inside herself, as if by keeping them secret she could protect herself from hurt.

But Randal didn't need any words from her. He was content to have her listen and accept his love, for now. With her yielding so softly in his arms, it was easy for him to believe that someday she'd be ready to love him in return.

He pulled back a little from her and said, "I'm sorry about Colin, Shannon."

Then the bleak reality of Colin's death came between them again. Shannon pulled away from Randal's touch, and all the darkness of her grief fell back around her. Again in her mind the line of blue was forming across the peaceful evening pasture. Once again they were raising their guns as Colin sought out her eyes.

Randal saw the dullness slipping back over her. "What is it, Shannon?"

"They wore the same blue as you."

"Who?" Randal asked. He could feel the distance opening between them, and he feared that it might be a distance he could never bridge.

Shannon's eyes went away from him to a picture in her mind. "They tied his hands behind his back and shot him. Soldiers the same as you."

"I wasn't one of the men who shot your brother, Shannon," Randal said quietly.

"Would you have stopped it if you'd been there?" Shannon didn't wait for him to answer. She shook her head and said, "There was a good man there. He was kind to me, but he couldn't stop it. Nobody could have done that but me." Shannon shuddered, and a forlorn look slipped across her face. "I would have, but Colin wouldn't let me. He said he'd rather die than know I'd gone to Robards."

Hatred flared in Randal. He'd killed many men in the last three years, but he'd done it only to survive himself and to save the Union. He'd killed reluctantly and sometimes even sorrowfully, but he'd never felt this personal hatred before. It made him want to choke the life from Robards with his bare hands.

"Colin meant what he said, Shannon," Randal said when the first flush of his hatred had eased. It didn't go away. It would always be there in his mind, and if ever he could, he would see that Robards paid for Shannon's suffering. "Colin cared for you."

"He loved me," Shannon said simply. "But I didn't love him enough. . . . I stood by and let him die."

"It's over now and finished, Shannon. Let it go."

"But it wasn't right."

"You can't blame the whole Union Army for what Robards did."

"Robards led the group, but it was the Army that gave him the power to kill Colin—and not only Colin but many others no more guilty than he."

Shannon came away from the past then and looked at Randal, but she wouldn't meet his eyes. Her eyes stayed on his uniform. "That's the same army you fight for," she said. "They wore the same blue as you."

"I won't always wear this uniform. What happens when I take off the blue?" If she would only bring her eyes up to look at his face, he might reason with her.

"There'll always be a stain. It should be on your very soul for serving an army that shoots defenseless men."

He couldn't reach her. She'd gone too far away in her pain, but still he had to try. "We're in a war, Shannon, Wrongs are committed by both sides. Colin's dying was wrong, just as your father's death was wrong."

Shannon sank back down on the stool in front of her dressing table. She studied her hands in her lap. "Papa died defending all that he believed in. He was protecting his horses at all cost. He could have done no less, but his death wouldn't be changed even if they'd shot a dozen prisoners. Colin died for nothing."

"Did he, Shannon?" Randal gently tipped her face up with his hand. Though she didn't pull away from his touch, she still avoided his eyes. He went on speaking in a voice as gentle yet insistent as a spring breeze. "Colin died to protect you. Only you can decide if it was for nothing."

She closed herself away from his words. "Go away, Randal. You shouldn't have come," she said. "I can't stand even the sight of the blue you wear."

His hand went from her chin to caress the contours of her face. "Look at *me,* Shannon, not my uniform."

But she shook her head. "I can't."

"Someday?" he asked. He needed something, some hope to take back with him to the battlefield.

"I don't know," she whispered.

"I won't give up, Shannon. I'll be back."

Her eyes slowly came up to meet his. She wanted to accept the abundance of love that flowed from those treasured eyes, but she pulled herself up short. "What if you should die?" she cried.

His eyes stayed calm and sure. "Then I'll wait for you in eternity."

Again she turned away from him, refusing him. "Go away and leave me alone, Major."

He leaned over and very softly kissed her lips. "I love you, Shannon. Remember that. I have enough love for both of us."

Then he was gone. Shannon turned to stare at herself in the mirror, but she saw nothing. She was listening to his footsteps going out of the house and then the faint sound of his horse leaving. Even after the hoofbeats had faded away past imagining, she still listened.

Finally she saw her face in the mirror, and the deep green eyes staring back from the glass seemed not to belong to her. They accused her. Randal was gone because she'd sent him away, and now he might never return. All at once the eyes in the mirror glinted with the beginnings of tears, and she couldn't endure it. She slammed her brush into the glass.

The pieces of mirror showered about her hands. One point nicked her finger, and without moving she watched a tiny spurt of blood. It didn't matter. Nothing mattered any more. She'd made the darkness around her complete by sending Randal away.

For a long time she sat there, feeling the emptiness of her soul. Then she stood up and put the dirty clothes she'd just taken off back on. She went outside and walked away from the house and across the fields. She tried to let her love of the land fill the emptiness inside her, but this time the land failed her. Everything about her was ashes, dry, soft, and ready to blow away, leaving her with nothing.

CHAPTER 26

Winter inched its slow path toward spring, and Shannon continued to move about her chores woodenly, waiting for whatever might happen next. Guerrilla bands struck many of the neighboring farms, but they always missed Marshland. Shannon would listen for them at night and wonder what she'd do if they came, for now not even the horses seemed worth fighting for.

Many were the nights she tried to remember her father's dream of the great horses that Marshland would someday produce as she waited for the morning to dawn, and yet that dream eluded her now. Sometimes thoughts of Randal came unbidden to her mind, but she pushed them away quickly as the pain of her sending him away sliced through her.

When spring came, Shannon could not ignore the

news about the war. The long fighting in Virginia ended when Lee's army surrendered. The Confederacy was defeated, although a few soldiers were still fighting in the South. Then, not even a week later, President Lincoln was shot. Shannon remembered seeing him once, long ago in Lexington, when she was but a child. He'd been tall and ugly, but she remembered the genuine smile that had shown in his eyes when he spoke to her as they passed on the street. She wished she could feel sorrow for his death, but there was too much sorrow in her heart already.

Another month passed before General Duke, who'd taken over Morgan's forces, surrendered in Georgia. The long rebellion was truly ended when Jefferson Davis was taken into custody. The war between brothers and neighbors was over, but the hatred would continue for years.

The Confederate soldiers began drifting back into Kentucky to pick up their lives where they'd left off. At the end of May, Jett and Clay came riding in. Shannon looked up from her chores to see them and felt no welcome in her heart. This time they had come to stay, and once again her life must change, just as it had the night her father died.

She turned the young colt she'd been working with over to Toby with regret. Then she went to meet them.

Defeat had made no change in Jett. He came to her as cockily as ever, grabbed her up in his arms, and kissed her long and hard before he backed away from her a few steps. "That's one good thing about coming home," he said.

"The war is truly over?" Shannon asked.

Jett nodded. "We gave them a fight they'll never forget, and if they hadn't murdered General Morgan, we might be fighting yet."

"I don't think this war will ever be forgotten by anyone," Shannon said.

When she started to turn away from Jett, he stopped her. "I deserve a better welcome than that."

She submitted her lips to him and let him pull her body close to his, but she took no warmth from his nearness. When he was finished, she pulled away to go to Clay. He was leaning against the fence, taking a sip from a small flask he'd pulled out of his pocket.

"Clay? Are you all right?" she asked him.

He smiled a bit foolishly. A high red color spread across his cheekbones, and his eyes weren't quite able to find her. He said, "Of course, sister dear. I'm home, aren't I?"

"You're drunk," Shannon said with sudden realization.

Clay shook his head. "Not really. I can get drunker. Can't I, Jett?"

Jett laughed. "That's the truth. This morning I thought I might have to put him across the saddle to get him the rest of the way home."

"Get some coffee and sober up, Clay. You can't go up to see Mother like this." Shannon felt the disgust creep into her voice.

"Mama shouldn't be too shocked," Clay said. "Dear old father never went in to her without a bottle of good bourbon under his belt." Clay pulled out the flask and took another quick drink. When he had swallowed, he said, "How is the old girl anyway?"

"I haven't been in to see her for a while, but Aunt Mamie says she's doing fair. She hasn't left her room since you were last here."

"Not even once?" Clay asked.

Shannon shook her head. "She's been grieving for you, but seeing you like this will only make her grieve more."

Clay pushed out his mouth in a pout. "Oh very well.

I'll go drink your coffee and go see Mother. But not because you told me to. I was going to anyway."

Shannon waited until he was in the house before she turned on Jett. "How could you let him get this way?"

"You mean, Clay?" Jett said, surprised by her attack on him. "Clay's old enough to drink a little if he wants to."

"A little? He can't even walk straight." A bitter sadness swept through her. Clay had come home but not as the boy who'd left. Neither had he come home a man. He was more like someone who'd stopped growing but had never grown up.

Jett looked toward the house. He didn't want to think about Clay and Clay's problems. It wasn't his fault that the boy hadn't measured up. He said, "There's some who just can't face what war is. I guess Clay was sorry he'd ever decided to ride south with me, once they went to shooting at him. He needed to find some courage somewhere, and that somewhere for him was a bottle."

"But the war's over now. He won't need any more of that kind of courage."

Jett looked back at her and shook his head. "I think what took the most courage for him was coming back and facing you."

"That's not true." She couldn't bear the thought of yet another life ruined because of her.

Jett shrugged. "Maybe not. Anyway, I'm not going to worry about the kid's problems." Jett pulled her to him again. "I've got better things to think about right now."

After a moment he lifted his lips from hers and said, "I've waited a long time for you, Shannon. I don't intend to wait any longer."

Shannon's back stiffened, but she didn't pull away from him. She let him turn her and begin walking to the house. She'd always known that someday she would marry Jett. Now that he was home from the war, there was no longer any reason to put him off. He'd waited as long as he would.

Suddenly, in her mind, Randal stood watching her, with understanding and sadness filling his eyes. She longed to make the smile come back to his eyes and to feel his arms around her again, but she'd sent him away. The picture of him in her mind receded slowly into shadow, and confusion flooded through her.

Jett's arm was heavy around her as they went in the front doors. He was talking in her ear, but she didn't know what he was saying. Then over and above the confusion, she felt the first tinge of panic. She wasn't ready. Not yet. As they moved down the hall toward the stairs, she said, "We have to talk first."

Jett didn't stop. He nuzzled her ear. "We can talk tomorrow. I'm in the mood for something else right now."

"No," Shannon said sharply, yanking herself away from him. "We'll talk now."

For a minute their wills battled, and Shannon wasn't sure whether or not Jett's anger would take control of him. If it did she knew that struggling against him would be useless, but he pulled his temper back in check. "I've waited this long, I can wait a few minutes more."

Shannon led the way to the small library office. She searched her mind for the words to say. How could she tell him she'd marry him but that everytime she looked at him, there would be another man between them? How could she tell him that she didn't love him, had in fact *never* loved him? She looked up at him and was suddenly aware that he didn't love her either.

"You don't love me," she said.

A frown flitted across Jett's forehead. "What's the matter with you, Shannon? I'm going to marry you."

"What's that got to do with love?"

But Jett didn't answer that question. Instead, he said, "What difference does any of that make? I want you, and you want me. I never figured you to be a romantic who would have to hear a lot of flowery words."

"I'm not," Shannon said. She would be practical but not foolish. "But we'll marry first."

"I've waited long enough." Jett's voice was stormy. "I intend to have you now. Tonight." He took a step toward her.

"No." She said the word softly, but it reached out and stopped Jett with the force she felt.

He studied her. "Sometimes I don't think you want to marry me at all, Shannon Marsh." He was quiet for a moment, deep in thought. Then a dark red flush was spreading across his face, and his fists clenched. "Has that Yankee been around here again?"

Shannon met his anger head on even though she thought he might hit her. "He was here," she said, "but I sent him away."

"Good," he said, and all at once his anger began draining away. He walked quickly around the room and then dropped into one of the chairs. He looked up at her where she still stood in front of the desk. "So it has to be marriage first," he said, "Or maybe you're still playing games with me, Shannon. Maybe you just like to keep me hanging around."

Shannon shook her head. "I told you I'd marry you before you went away with Morgan. I meant it." And she had meant it then, she thought, but she wasn't the least bit sure she meant it now.

"All right then, when is it to be? I won't wait for you forever. If you keep putting me off, I won't come back. Then it'll be your turn to be sorry because, you see, you need me."

She started to say something, but he raised his hand and stopped her. "You need me in many ways. First in the way any high-blooded female needs a man. I like that touch of wild Irish blood in you, Shannon. We'll get along well in bed, and that's always been the most important thing to me."

"You talk like you're dealing in horses."

Jett laughed. "Since we have eliminated love, then we have to look at this in a business way. You're a sensible woman, Shannon. You have something I want, and if you were honest with yourself, you'd admit that you want it as much as I do. But there's something more you need from me." He waited for her to ask, but she stared at him without speaking. "Marshland."

"I don't need you for that. Marshland is already mine."

"Is it?" Jett said. "You must admit that the farm is Clay's now. You'll have to let him take over control of it now that he's back."

"Of course," Shannon said.

"You say that easily, but it won't be that easy for you. Clay doesn't know anything about running a farm. He'll keep the wrong horses and buy worse ones. Clay's a lot like Miss Olivia . . . no business head at all. It's a shame. I'd hate to see the place fall to ruin, maybe even be sold out of the family."

Shannon couldn't imagine Marshland not being a part of the Clay heritage. "That'll never happen while I'm alive."

Jett looked at her with pity, as though she were a particularly dense child. "But, you see, there won't be anything you can do about it. It'll be out of your hands."

"If that's true, what good will it do for me to marry you?"

"Clay looks up to me," Jett said. "He'll do whatever I say."

"And what will he do when we marry?"

"You know as well as I that our families have been planning our marriage and the joining of our farms for years. Together we'll have one of the largest farms in the

Bluegrass, and there's power in owning that much land. Now that the war's over, we can build an empire, Shannon."

"You could do all that without me."

Jett smiled and nodded. "Yes, I think I could, but I want the farm and you."

Shannon went over to the small window between the bookshelves. From it she could see out over the front pasture. A group of yearling colts swept across the fresh green grass. She could pick out Bittersweet from his graceful, smooth movements. The shadow of the war was gone, and she'd brought Marshland and her horses safely through. Now she thought of the new foals that had been dropped in the last few weeks and the promise they held. She thought of the years ahead, and all the horses she would see foaled, watch grow, and help train.

The farm was like a web that tied her to all that had been and to all that would be. Here was where she belonged. She couldn't leave it or see it fall into ruin under Clay's management. She turned back to Jett. "I never said I wasn't going to marry you."

"When?" The word was sharp.

"I don't know," Shannon began.

But he interupted. "Tomorrow. I'll bring a preacher out from town."

"Don't you think we should wait until your mother and father and Becky get home from Canada?"

"Father's dead. Killed last year in Virginia," Jett said.

Shannon looked down. "I'm sorry. I'll miss him."

"He always did like you," Jett said. "Said you were one of a kind." Jett rose, and paced across the room and came back again. "I guess you're right about Mother, though. She'd want us to wait until she could be at the wedding. Damn!"

Shannon didn't say anything.

"A week then," he said. "I'll go get them, and while I'm gone, you can be getting ready."

Shannon nodded, and Jett came over to her. He pulled up her chin and made her meet his eyes. "This is your last chance, Shannon. If you put me off this time, I don't really care what happens to you. But I can tell you one thing, I'll make sure you won't have a place around here."

"You don't have to threaten me," Shannon said and looked away from him. "I said I would marry you."

Jett's voice softened. "It'll be good, Shannon. You'll see. We'll make a good couple. Even Colin always said so. Where is he now?"

Shannon swallowed hard and shook her head. "Colin's dead," she said. "The Army shot him last year."

Jett was quiet for a minute. "That's too bad," he said finally, "but maybe it's just as well."

Shannon only half heard the rest he said, something about checking on his farm before heading north to get his mother and Becky, but his last words were clear. "I'll be back in a week. I expect you to be ready then."

Shannon heard the door close. Slowly she turned back to the window. The same field was there with the same promising young horses moving about it. She could look out at it with assurance now that a part of it would always be hers. That was what she wanted, she told herself. Then why wasn't the field as green as it was before? Why was this sudden sense of loss ripping through her, leaving behind a hollow pain that settled deep inside her?

Suddenly Colin's last words to her rang in her ears. "Be happy," he'd said, but he didn't know how much he was asking from her.

CHAPTER 27

It was completely dark when Sally drifted into the room to check the windows. Securing the windows was always her final chore of the day. She didn't carry a lamp because she liked the feel of the darkness about her.

When Shannon spoke, Sally jumped. "The window's shut in here, Sally," Shannon said.

Sally hesitated. For almost a year she'd been shutting herself away from the others, neither sharing her own pain nor feeling theirs. But lately she'd begun to feel the returning of life. Her baby had died, and she'd probably never have another. But she still had her mother and Shannon.

"Shay? Is that you?" she said.

Shannon said, "I'm sorry if I frightened you, Sally. I didn't realize it was so late."

"What are you doing in the dark?" Sally lit the lamp

on the desk, and the light slowly edged out into the corners of the room.

Shannon sat in a small straight chair near the window. Her eyes had been fixed on the nothingness of the dark, and now they shifted to her hands folded in her lap. "I'm going to get married next week," Shannon said.

"That's no reason to look like you lost your last friend," Sally said. "Or is it? What's wrong, Shay?"

"I don't know, Sally. Everything's different from the way I thought it would be. So much has changed. It was all so easy before the war. Papa was here, and the horses, and I could look ahead into the future and everything was all lined out in front of me with only one way to go. I wanted it that way then, but now I just don't know."

Sally sat down across from Shannon. "Things have changed, Shay. None of us is the same, and we won't ever be able to go back to the way we were."

Shannon nodded. Maybe it wasn't that the war had changed her life so much as that she'd changed inside, and now she wasn't ready to recognize that change. "Maybe I should have married Jett before he left for the war."

"And that would make things all right now?"

"I don't know. I've always planned to marry Jett. It was just something that was going to happen like the sun going down at night. It's just the sensible way to combine our farms. Almost like the marriage of the land itself."

"Land's just land, Shay. It can be bought and sold, but never married. And if marrying Mr. Jett was so right, you wouldn't be huddled here in the dark grieving about it."

"I don't know what to do." Shannon looked at Sally, wanting someone to tell her what she should do.

"Oh, Shay," Sally said gently. "You've always known what to do. You just do what has to be done the way you always have. Just think about the way you've run the farm since your father got killed. You took care of all of us, and when my baby died, you made me keep on living." Sally's voice clouded with feeling.

"But you said that was wrong. You wanted me to leave you alone."

Sally nodded. "But you couldn't, and now I know that you were right. You did what you did because you loved me. You could have done no less."

"Even if that's true, I still failed Colin. When he needed help, I did nothing."

"But don't you see, Shay? That was what had to be done."

"You don't understand, Sally. I could have saved his life. All I had to do was go to Robards."

"Do you think Mr. Colin would have wanted that? No, it was hard for you to let him die, but it was what you had to do."

Shannon didn't answer for a long time. She was thinking of the way Colin had looked at her. Finally Shannon nodded, then said, "And now I have to marry Jett."

"Do you, Shay?"

"It's the only way I can keep from losing Marshland, and Marshland is all I have left."

"Is it?"

Sally's questions tormented Shannon by pushing the truth toward her where she could no longer refuse to face it. "I'm part of Marshland. I can never leave."

"Poor Shay." Sally reached over and touched her. "You know, Adam left me, but if he ever decides to come back, there won't be anything that can hold me away from him. When you love a man enough, nothing else matters as much as being with him."

"I couldn't leave Marshland."

"You can't hide from it any longer, Shay. You've got to decide what you love the most."

"I don't know what you mean," Shannon cried.

"I think you do," Sally said gently.

"But I sent Randal away. He'll never come back." As she said the words, she clutched her arms about herself, trying to keep away the cold that crept toward her.

"Do you love him?" Sally asked.

Shannon shut her eyes and saw Randal there, waiting. She nodded. "I love him," she said simply.

"And so you finally know what true love feels like. I told you there was no denying the feeling when it comes to you." Sally leaned over and kissed her before she stood up.

Shannon caught her hand. "But I still don't know what to do."

"I think you do. I think you've known for a long time."

"I couldn't leave you and Aunt Mamie."

"Dear Shay. I was foolish to ever doubt the sincerity of your love. But our lives are changing too, more even than yours. They can't have slaves in Kentucky after they've set them all free down south, and we'll be free soon, really free. Mama's wanted that for a long time."

"What'll you do?"

"In time we may leave here. Maybe we'll try to find John. I don't guess nothing would make Mama any happier than seeing John again. Whatever happens, we'll be free, Shay, and it's time you were free too."

"But I've always been free."

"Have you, Shay? Sometimes I wonder if the chains binding you to this place aren't stronger than the ones on me." She started out of the room.

Shannon stopped her before she could go out the door. "Sally," she began, but she didn't know what to say. Sally had come back away from her grief to help her, and Shannon could find no words to thank her.

But Sally knew. "It's all right, Shay. Sometimes sisters make the best friends."

After Sally left, Shannon blew out the lamp and climbed the stairs to her room. She walked slowly trying to gather close to her the feel of the house. Her fingers lingered on the familiar carved lines of the stair rail. When she saw the line of light inching out under her mother's door, she hesitated in front of the door. She was tempted to knock and go in to her, to tell her one more time that she cared for her and to seek her mother's love in return. But then she turned away to her own door.

She lit her lamp, and its flame illuminated the dressing table with the bits of broken mirror still clinging to its frame. And the fear rose in her. What if Randal was dead? What would she do then? She shut her eyes and felt the nearness of him. He couldn't be dead. She would know if he were dead. But even if he was, Shannon knew that she couldn't stay here and lead a life of lies with Jett.

She dug out the purse she had hidden deep in her bureau, with the bit of extra money she'd saved to pay any other fines the Union might levy on Marshland. She set aside some of the money in a separate purse to give to Aunt Mamie before she left, then quickly gathered a few extra clothes before she lay down on the bed.

Sleep eluded her as her thoughts whirled from one idea to another. At times it seemed to her as though even the house were whispering to her, trying to change her mind. But she listened with a dull ache inside her, knowing that tomorrow she would truly get up and leave this room never to see it again.

At the first dim light of dawn, she rose and went out to the barn. She picked out a horse to ride, and Satin nickered at her in protest at her choosing another mount. "Don't worry, boy," she said, "you'll get enough riding before the day is through."

Out in the pastures, she watched the farm wake up to the spring morning. The mares suckled their foals, and the yearlings ran about flashing their legs in the early morning light that sifted through the trees on the horizon. She caught herself picking out the ones with the most promise and the ones that needed some special attention when their training began, and she pulled herself up short. That would be someone else's problem.

When the first touch of sun hit her back, she reined the horse in and headed back to the house reluctantly. She rode slowly. The farm was always beautiful in May. Shannon remembered the many times she'd ridden out like this with her father to look over the new crop of horses. He'd never spoken of the beauty of the land, but she'd known how he felt by the hush that fell over them sometimes. It wasn't just a feeling of appreciation for the richness of the soil, but there was love between her father and the land. That love he had passed along to Shannon, and it had almost taken possession of her life.

She pulled her horse to a stop on a little rise and looked behind her at the gently rolling land with the backdrop of trees lifting up their leaves to the early morning sun. Ahead of her the house and barns lay with the same serene lines as always. The war had come and gone, and Marshland had survived. Below her to the left was the small rock-fenced graveyard. Suddenly she seemed to hear the voices of all those who'd lived here and been reclaimed by the land, calling to her to stay, and she faced a dark moment of despair.

Then Randal's words rang in her head. "You don't need it, Shannon," he'd said. She couldn't be sure he was right, but all at once she was sure that she needed love so much more.

When she got back to the barn, Tom and Toby had already begun their morning chores. Toby came to take her horse. "You out riding without Satin? No wonder he was in such a bad humor when I took his feed to him."

Toby had grown in the year and a half since she'd brought him to Marshland. But he was still a boy, and the concern she felt in leaving Aunt Mamie and Sally spilled over on him. She said, "I'm leaving Marshland today, Toby."

His mouth dropped open in surprise. "But Miss Shannon, you can't do that. Who'll take care of everything?"

"It's Clay's farm. Now that he's home, he'll have to take care of it." And perhaps he would do better without me to rely on, she thought.

Toby was silent for a few minutes as he tried to adjust to what she'd told him. Finally he announced, "I want to go with you."

She started to say something, but he plunged on. "I belong to you, not to your brother. You bought me."

She touched his shoulder. "No, Toby. I told you a long time ago you were free. If you don't want to stay on here, you can leave. Go north and do whatever you like."

Uncertainty filled his eyes for a moment, but then he said, "I want to go with you, Miss Shannon. Please let me."

"Your life might be easier here, but if you want to you're free to come along."

Toby's eyes lit up. "Captain Ned said you was a good woman the day you bought me."

"But you didn't believe him."

"I shoulda known that Captain Ned wouldn't never lie to me."

Shannon sighed. "I doubt that I'm doing you a favor taking you with me." Before she turned away she said, "Have Blackberry and Chessie ready to go in an hour. I'll saddle Satin myself."

At the house she found Clay rummaging through the liquor cabinet. "It's early for that, isn't it?" she said softly.

Clay straightened up. "I'm just checking out the supplies. We wouldn't want to be low at the wedding."

"The wedding?"

"Jett told me before he left yesterday." Clay stretched out on the day bed. "Golly, it's good to be home. It got so there at the end I didn't care who won the war just so it was over." Clay raised up quickly and looked at her. "But don't tell Jett I said so. He wouldn't understand."

"I suppose not. There are lots of things that Jett doesn't understand." Shannon sat down across from Clay. He was still such a boy. Maybe all his life he would never be more than that, and then maybe after she left, he'd become a man because he'd have to. She asked her brother, "Will you be able to run the farm, Clay?"

"Of course," he said with a wave of his hand. "If you could do it, I surely can. And now with you and Jett getting married—well, forming a partnership of sorts—Jett will be around to help."

Shannon didn't say anything, and he sat up to look at her. "You know, for a while there I wasn't sure you'd keep your promise to Jett when that Yank kept coming around. What was his name?"

"Randal Hunt," Shannon said softly.

"Yeh. Anyway I thought you acted like maybe you'd fallen for him. I'm glad you've come to your senses."

Shannon smiled. "You're right, Clay. I've come to my senses just in time. I'll be leaving Marshland in a little while."

For a few minutes Clay stared at her blankly. Then his eyes filled with bewilderment. "What are you talking about?"

"I'm not going to marry Jett."

Clay's face turned red. "I'll cut you off with nothing. You'll never be welcome at Marshland again."

"I know, Clay," Shannon said calmly.

"But you told Jett you'd marry him next week." Clay's voice took on the sound of a little boy.

"Yesterday I thought perhaps I would, but now I know I can't."

"Is it that Yankee."

"Yes."

"Where is he?"

"I don't know."

"You mean, you haven't heard from him, and you're going to leave without knowing where he is? That's the craziest thing you've ever done, Shannon."

"Maybe so," Shannon admitted.

"What if he's dead? What will you do then?" Clay asked. "You needn't expect to come back here."

"You don't have to worry, Clay. After today you'll never have to stand in my shadow again."

Suddenly Clay covered his face, and Shannon knew he was crying. He muttered something that sounded like, "I don't want you to go."

Shannon went to him and put her arms around him while a surge of tenderness welled up in her. "It's all right, Clay. You'll do fine without me. All you need is the chance to prove yourself." He shook his head, and she went on. "Jett still will be partners with you, and if you think you need a wedding, you can always marry Becky. She'll be ready for marriage now."

"What have I got to offer a girl like Becky?"

"Everything, Clay. You're Clay Marsh, and believe me, both your names are to be proud of. Marshland is one of the oldest and finest farms in Kentucky, and there's a colt out there in the pasture that just might make you a fortune in the years to come. You can do it, Clay, if you want to."

Clay looked up at her, wanting to believe what she said. He said, "But what about Jett?"

"Jett," she said. "You know, Clay, I may be doing Jett the biggest favor of all by leaving."

"He'll be mad."

Shannon smiled and nodded her head. "But only for a little while. Tell me, Clay, how many women did he have down south?"

Clay flushed. "There were always a few girls wanting to show how much they appreciated the soldiers fighting for them," he said.

"Jett will find a new girl up here just as quickly. I wouldn't have been right for him anyway. I never really fit anywhere. I wasn't the right kind of daughter for Papa and certainly not for Mother, but then no matter how I tried I couldn't belong to Aunt Mamie's family either. And you know yourself the times I was sent home from school in disgrace. I've never fit anywhere, because I could never be the way other people expected me to be. But none of that matters with Randal."

Shannon kissed his cheek and stood up. She was almost to the door when he called to her. "I didn't really mean it, Shannon. You can come back to Marshland any time you want."

"Thank you, Clay." But as she went out of the room to say the rest of her goodbyes, she knew she'd never return. Marshland held nothing for her any longer. Her roots had been severed, and one by painful one she was clipping off the tendrils that still bound her here.

CHAPTER 28

Shannon had expected Aunt Mamie to cry, but she didn't. Instead, she smiled and hugged her. "That's my child, taking hold like I always knew she could."

"You act like you'll be glad to see me go," Shannon said, a little hurt.

"No, child, that ain't it at all. I don't rightly know how I'll stand it when you're gone, but I don't reckon it'll be no worse than seeing you like you been lately." Aunt Mamie stood back and looked at her. "You got your fight back, and I know I don't have to worry about you no more, no matter where you are."

Now as Shannon began saddling Satin, she thought of the difference between Aunt Mamie's send off and her mother's. Her mother hadn't believed she was serious at first. She sat back and looked at Shannon with disbelief until Shannon's silence made her accept the truth.

"You're really going," her mother had finally said.

"Yes, Mother. Clay's here now to take over, and I've decided I can't marry Jett. So I'm leaving."

"I can't believe it." An odd flush spread out across her mother's face.

Now Shannon smoothed Satin's neck and leaned her head into his mane, wishing she could forget parts of the scene with her mother. It would have been better if they could have parted friends, but she supposed that was foolish. They'd never been anything close to friends. She shouldn't expect things to change just because she was leaving.

It was her mother's parting shot that had cut so deeply. "You know," she said, "there's only one way a woman on her own can make her way in the world."

Shannon had been leaving the room, and she'd stopped with her hand on the doorknob and looked around. Her mother had continued. "At least the color of your hair will suit you well. Men like bright colors on their town women."

For a minute Shannon had been speechless. Then she'd said, "You carried me in your body for nine months. I'm flesh of your flesh. Why do you hate me so much?"

"Don't you know how I hated it when he came in to me and touched me with his rough clumsy hands." She shuddered and looked at Shannon. "You were the result of that."

"But so was Clay."

She shook her head. "No. Clay has no part of Emmett Marsh in him."

"He was his father."

"I made him promise to leave the baby alone, and in time Clay became totally my child, with no part of Emmett at all. But you . . . from the very beginning you were like your father. You looked like him, thought like him, and acted like him. And I hated him."

For a moment longer Shannon had watched her mother. There was no answering hate in her heart, only pity. She'd said, "Goodbye, Olivia." She would no longer mock the word by calling her mother.

She fastened the cinch on Satin just as Toby came up to her. "I'm all ready, Miss Shannon," he said.

"Let's go then," Shannon said, lifting herself up on Satin. Toby jumped up on Chessie bareback. Chessie was a soft brown brood mare that had been bred late last season. She wouldn't have her foal for at least a month, and she was gentle, easy to handle.

Shannon sat on Satin and looked back at the house. She waved at Tom, Aunt Mamie, and Sally who'd come out to watch them leave. Then, with a flick of the reins, they moved down the lane through the oak trees and out the gates. That quickly she'd left it all behind, and once she was out on the road, a peculiar lightness hit her, making her feel almost as though she might float in the air.

But Toby's question brought her down to the ground quick enough. "Where are we going, Miss Shannon?"

She'd been so involved with cutting off her past that she hadn't considered the future, except in a vague far distant way. She was going to find Randal. It had been simple in her mind, but now it wasn't so simple. "I don't know," she said. Toby waited quietly while she thought. Finally she said, "Maybe we'll go to Louisville, and you can hunt up Captain Ned."

They stayed in Franklin County the first night, where Shannon called upon a favor from an old family friend who asked a lot of questions but got very few answers. The next day they moved on to Louisville, where Shannon found a room in a run-down boarding house. Toby went to stay with Captain Ned.

When Captain Ned came to see her, he looked around at the neighborhood and then back at her before shaking his head. "It ain't right you being here, Miss Shannon. A lady like you don't belong in a place like this. You oughta stayed at Marshland."

"What's done is done and can't be undone," Shannon said. "Besides, this is only until I find something better." Or her money ran out, she thought. But she wouldn't worry about that yet. She'd just take each day, maybe even each hour, one at a time.

As the days went by and the money in her purse began shrinking away, that's just what she did. The woman who ran the boarding house let her help with the housework in exchange for her room and board, but still there were the horses to feed. Despite the odd jobs that Toby found about town, it was clear that the money would soon be gone.

Late one night she sat on her bed in the tiny room that gave off an air of grime no matter how often she cleaned it. A longing welled up in her for the clean, airy rooms back at Clay Manor. Just her heavy four-poster bed wouldn't even fit in the room she was in now, with its narrow cot and the mirror spotted with green hanging on the wall.

She thought of what they'd be doing at Marshland, and her homesickness vanished. If she were there, she would be Mrs. Jett Noble. She couldn't have stayed and not married him.

Jett hadn't come looking for her . . . she hadn't expected him to. He'd given her a choice, and although he clearly hadn't expected her to choose to leave, she had. Her memory would always be a burr of irritation prickling his hide, but he hadn't wanted her enough to swallow his pride and chase after her.

Now she looked around the small room with its privations, and in her heart she knew she'd made the right choice. Even if she never found Randal, she had tried. She had enquired about him at the Army headquarters, but his unit had been dispersed. Now she must try to question men who had come back. She blew out the lamp and lay down in the dark. For a moment the thought of Randal brought her peace. But then she recalled his words of love and her final words of refusal. The thought of all the love she'd rejected pressed down on her and made her feel like crying. But it wasn't the time to cry, not with her purse almost empty. It was a time for planning.

All night long she built up plans and then let them fall away when she realized how impossible they would be. When morning dawned, she faced the fact that she'd have to sell one of the horses to give her more time. Then, perhaps she would go to Ohio and search out Randal's mother. Shannon thought she would help her.

That day she went to the stable and got Satin. She groomed him carefully, talking softly to him all the while. Then she led him through the streets to the auction area.

As she walked, she pushed down the lump in her throat. The horse was following her so trustingly. Her steps slowed a bit, and Satin nuzzled her back. She and the horse had shared so much during the years since her father had given him to her. Satin had been a castoff from that year's crop of yearlings because of his stubborn nature, but it hadn't taken long for Shannon to earn the trust of the colt. He'd grown into a beautiful animal, a bit short in the legs, but it had never slowed him down. For Shannon he had the heart to try anything.

She'd already lost him once and gotten him back, but there would be no return this time. This time she was agreeing to let him go.

She edged her way in among the crowd. People were there with every sort of animal, and Shannon waited, stroking Satin's neck to keep him calm until she saw the man in charge beckoning to her. Suddenly she wished she'd brought Chessie, even though the new colt by her side held all the promise for the future that remained to her. She leaned her head against Satin for a moment and whispered, "I'm sorry, Satin. But I have to."

She pushed down her feelings and led the horse to the front. When she gave the rope to the man at the edge of the platform where the auctioneer stood above the crowd, Satin turned and nickered in puzzlement.

"It's all right, boy," she soothed but Satin pricked up his ears and nipped at the man holding him.

The man tightened the lead rope around his nose, and Satin turned wild eyes toward Shannon. When she didn't come forward to free him, he tried to rear, but the man's hold was too strong.

The auctioneer began talking quickly to get a bid before the horse showed his real temper. "All right now, folks. We've got us a real winner here. Well cared for and with lots of spirit. Let me hear a bid for this thoroughbred."

A short squat man on the front row yelled, "Twenty five."

"Surely my ears deceive me," the auctioneer said. "This animal could run circles around any horse I've sold today."

"But would he let you ride him while he was doing it?" a voice called back, and laughter spread through the crowd.

"The little lady handled him easy enough. Come now, surely we have some sport in the crowd who can face the challenge of a high-bred horse."

There was a silence, and Shannon felt her heart sink. It was bad enough to have to part with Satin, but then to practically give him away. She wished she had the money to buy him back, but she could do nothing but watch while the panic rose in his eyes.

Suddenly a strong clear voice called out from the back of the crowd. "One hundred dollars."

"Now there's a gentleman who knows a fine piece of horse flesh when he sees it. And he's getting a real bargain too." He waited a few minutes longer for another bid before he shouted sold.

Shannon went over to the man holding Satin. "I'll hold him until the buyer makes his way to the front."

"The man must be a fool or too far back to see good," the man said. "This horse ain't nothing but trouble."

Shannon walked to the side of the platform to wait. She eased Satin back until he was calm again, even though she felt like a traitor misleading him. "I shouldn't have brought you, boy, but there's nothing I can do now. Maybe your new owner will know how to treat you."

"I believe that's my horse, miss," a familiar voice said behind her.

As Shannon whirled to face . . . Randal, her heart floated up inside her as light as a butterfly. She stood staring at him a moment. He still wore the blue uniform, and for a minute she was haunted by the memory of Colin's death. But there were also Colin's last words to remember. He wouldn't want her to put his dying between her and her chance at happiness.

Her eyes lifted from the blue cloth and touched his face. He'd changed, somehow hardened in the months since he'd been gone, and there was no smile on his face or in his clear blue eyes. Maybe his love for her had died. If it had, it would be no one's fault but her own.

The doubts stilled the happy flutter of her heart, and when she spoke, her voice was flat and cold to her ears. "I guess you've bought yourself a horse, Major." Then her tone softened. "If I have to part with Satin, I'm glad that he's to go with you." She held out the rope.

He ignored her outstretched hand while his eyes searched her face. Then quickly he looked up and around her before his eyes came back to hers. "What are you doing here? And alone?"

She couldn't tell him that she had come in search of him. She said slowly, "I had to leave Marshland." A vivid picture of the fields sprang to her mind, and again she felt the loss.

Randal saw her pain. "I didn't think you'd ever leave your farm," he said.

"Things and people change." Shannon half smiled and pulled her eyes away from his. "I could have had everything just as I'd always wanted—the farms combined—and I think Jett even would have let me help with the horses."

"Then why didn't you stay?" Randal's voice was reaching into her, demanding the truth.

"It wasn't enough." She looked back up at him and saw the smile trickling into his eyes. She held out the rope again and said softly, "Here's your horse."

This time he reached out and put his hand over hers. "I don't want the horse without his rider."

He'd waited so long for this moment, a moment he'd felt during the long months since he'd last seen her would never come. There had been times in the final encounters of the war when he'd defied the enemy fire, not caring if he lived or died because without Shannon nothing seemed to be worth living for. Now he thanked God that he was alive.

But despite Randal's smile, doubt still lingered in Shannon's mind. "Don't feel like you have to do this, Randal. I'll get by somehow."

"Was there ever any doubt that you could?" Randal said, and his smile changed to gentle laughter. He picked her up and swung her off her feet while Satin danced back nervously. "I want you, Shannon. I need you. I love you, Shannon Marsh . . . forever and always and most of all now."

Her laughter joined his and mingled together, joining them in a way touching could not. Then their lips found each other, and he kissed her openly, not even noticing the crowd around them.

Shannon pulled back just enough to see his face. A soft light joy crept through her body until even her toes tingled with delight. She'd found her place, a place to belong at last. Randal was all the roots she'd ever need.

He was talking about his plans. "We'll go west, all the way to California. There's some land there that I know will be right for raising horses." He stopped short and looked at her. "You will go with me, won't you?" he asked.

Shannon raised up on her toes and kissed him gently. No war, no trouble, no words, not even death would ever really separate them again.

He looked at her while the tenderness welled up inside him. "We'll call the farm Shannondale. But first things first . . . let's go find a preacher."

The crowd parted in front of them, touched by the radiance of their happiness. Shannon looked up into Randal's eyes and released the past, scattering it behind her like ashes in the wind. Ahead of her was a future that she was more than ready to challenge now, with this new joy lighting up her heart.

Somewhere from deep in her mind a picture of Colin sprang up, but the soldiers were gone. There was only Colin, loving her in a way she'd never understood, and now he was smiling. Then he was disappearing, almost as if he were purposely fading from her life to give her a clear beginning.

The full strength of the summer sun touched her as

she finally stepped out of the shadow that had haunted her and into the brilliance of Randal's love.

"I love you, Randal Hunt," she said softly.

"Forever and always?" he asked.

"Forever and always and most of all now."

ROMANCE...ADVENTURE... DANGER...

THIS TOWERING PASSION
by Valerie Sherwood *(81-486, $2.50)*
500 pages of sweet romance and savage adventure set against the violent tapestry of Cromwellian England, with a magnificent heroine whose beauty and ingenuity captivates every man who sees her, from the king of the land to the dashing young rakehell whose destiny is love!

THIS LOVING TORMENT
by Valerie Sherwood *(95-745, $2.75)*
Born in poverty in the aftermath of the Great London Fire, Charity Woodstock grew up to set the men of three continents ablaze with passion! The bestselling sensation of the year, boasting 1.3 million copies in print after just one month, to make it the fastest-selling historical romance in Warner Books history!

THESE GOLDEN PLEASURES
by Valerie Sherwood *(95-744, $2.75)*
From the stately mansions of the east to the freezing hell of the Klondike, beautiful Rosanne Rossiter went after what she wanted—and got it all! By the author of the phenomenally successful THIS LOVING TORMENT.

LOVE'S TENDER FURY
by Jennifer Wilde *(81-909, $2.50)*
The turbulent story of an English beauty—sold at auction like a slave—who scandalized the New World by enslaving her masters. She would conquer them all—only if she could subdue the hot unruly passions of the heart! The 2 Million Copy Bestseller that brought fame to the author of DARE TO LOVE.

DARE TO LOVE
by Jennifer Wilde *(81-826, $2.50)*
Who dared to love Elena Lopez? She was the Queen of desire and the slave of passion, traveling the world—London, Paris, San Francisco—and taking love where she found it! Elena Lopez—the tantalizing, beautiful moth—dancing out of the shadows, warmed, lured and consumed by the heart's devouring flame.

LILIANE
by Annabel Erwin *(91-219, $2.50)*
The bestselling romantic novel of a beautiful, vulnerable woman torn between two brothers, played against the colorful background of plantation life in Colonial America.

AURIELLE
by Annabel Erwin *(91-126, $2.50)*
The tempestuous new historical romance 4 million Annabel Erwin fans have been waiting for. Join AURIELLE, the scullery maid with the pride of a Queen as she escapes to America to make her dreams of nobility come true.